STATIC AND DYNAMIC ASPECTS OF GENERAL DISEQUILIBRIUM THEORY

THEORY AND DECISION LIBRARY

General Editors: W. Leinfellner (*Vienna*) and G. Eberlein (*Munich*)

Series A: Philosophy and Methodology of the Social Sciences

Series B: Mathematical and Statistical Methods

Series C: Game Theory, Mathematical Programming and Operations Research

Series D: System Theory, Knowledge Engineering and Problem Solving

---

SERIES C: GAME THEORY, MATHEMATICAL PROGRAMMING AND OPERATIONS RESEARCH

VOLUME 13

Scope: Particular attention is paid in this series to game theory and operations research, their formal aspects and their applications to economic, political and social sciences as well as to socio-biology. It will encourage high standards in the application of game-theoretical methods to individual and social decision making.

The titles published in this series are listed at the end of this volume.

STATIC AND DYNAMIC ASPECTS OF GENERAL DISEQUILIBRIUM THEORY

P. Jean-Jacques HERINGS
Tilburg University
Tilburg, The Netherlands

KLUWER ACADEMIC PUBLISHERS
Boston/London/Dordrecht

Distributors for North America:
Kluwer Academic Publishers
101 Philip Drive
Assinippi Park
Norwell, Massachusetts 02061 USA

Distributors for all other countries:
Kluwer Academic Publishers Group
Distribution Centre
Post Office Box 322
3300 AH Dordrecht, THE NETHERLANDS

Library of Congress Cataloging-in-Publication Data

A C.I.P. Catalogue record for this book is available from
the Library of Congress.

Printed on acid-free paper.

Printed in the United States of America

CONTENTS

ACKNOWLEDGEMENTS

This monograph is the result of research carried out over a period of four years. The research was supported financially by the Cooperation Centre Tilburg and Eindhoven Universities. I would like to thank CentER at Tilburg University and CORE and IRES at the Université Catholique de Louvain for creating an exciting research environment by inviting many interesting guests.

I am very grateful to Dolf Talman for following the process of writing this monograph so closely, but also for being a good friend. His enthusiasm concerning the use of simplicial methods in economics has been a great source of inspiration to me. Jan van Geldrop introduced me into the field of differential topology. Without his critical remarks this monograph would not have existed in its present form. Further, I would like to thank Jacques Drèze, Gerard van der Laan, Heraklis Polemarchakis, and Pieter Ruys for stimulating my thinking on economic theory and for creating excellent research atmospheres at CORE, Free University Amsterdam, again CORE, and Tilburg University, respectively. I wish to thank Antoon van den Elzen, Gerard van der Laan, Dolf Talman, and Zaifu Yang for the meticulous proofreading of the entire manuscript. In particular Antoon did a great job in making sure that every single step in any proof was not only correct, but also understandable.

Furthermore, I want to thank all my colleagues who helped me to accomplish this monograph by means of stimulating and helpful discussions and remarks. In lexicographical order I want to mention especially René van den Brink, Eric van Damme, Chuangyin Dang, Pierre Dehez, Egbert Dierker, Hildegard Dierker, Hans Haller, Harold Houba, Kazuya Kamiya, Mamoru Kaneko, Alan Kirman, Sergei Kokovin, Hans Kremers, Cuong Le Van, Thijs ten Raa, Willy Spanjers, Stef Tijs, Walter Trockel, Valeri Vasil'ev, Richard Venniker, Harry Webers, Claus Weddepohl, Bas Werker, Yoshitsugu Yamamoto, and Lin Zhou. Finally, I wish to express my gratitude towards my parents, relatives, and friends for their support and encouragement. The last sentence of these acknowledgements has been reserved to thank the most important person in my life, Suzanne, for her kindness, patience, and constant support.

1

INTRODUCTION

1.1 THE AXIOMATIC ANALYSIS OF ECONOMIC EQUILIBRIUM

Mathematical economics uses mathematical tools and reasoning to describe and explain economic reality. At the core of mathematical economics is general equilibrium theory. This monograph describes and analyses various general equilibrium models, treating theory from an axiomatic point of view, which may lead to a deeper understanding of problems, may help to avoid incorrect reasoning, and may improve communication within the economic science.

Characteristic for general equilibrium theory is that the economic reality, also called the economic system, is modelled as a whole, so that all existing interdependencies are taken into account. This differs from partial equilibrium analysis which studies a single market and neglects the influence of other markets. Often it is assumed that it is possible to isolate the economic system and to leave other systems (such as the political, cultural, technological, and ecological ones) out of consideration. Certainly, in general there will be an interaction between these systems. One of the parts of this monograph takes into account the interaction between the economic system and the political system, which turns out to be important. In the axiomatic point of view, the elementary parts of the economic system, the primitive concepts, are carefully distinguished. Then assumptions are made with respect to these primitive concepts. These assumptions are comparable to axioms that are made in mathematics. The primitive concepts are considered to be exogenous variables, assumed to be given, whereas the endogenous variables are determined as the outcome of

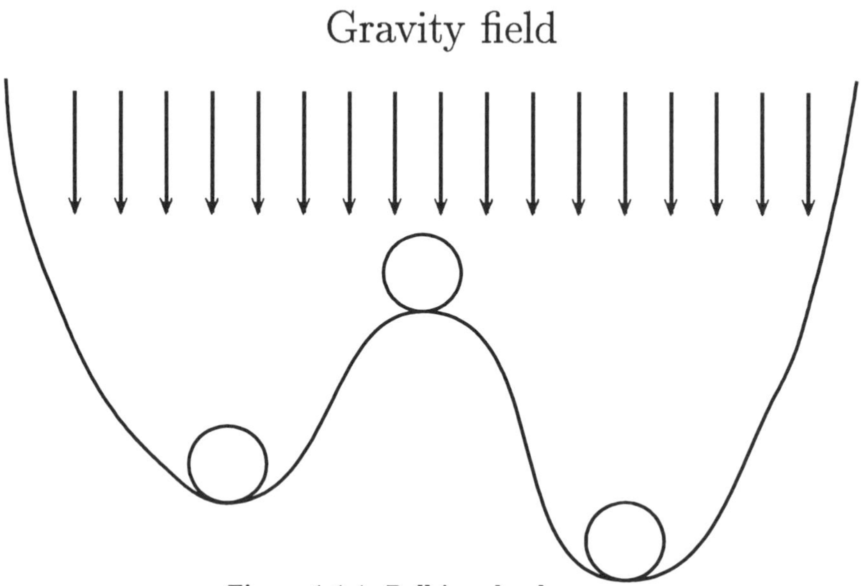

Figure 1.1.1. Ball in a landscape.

the theory. A general equilibrium model of the economic system is referred to as an economy.

An economy is described by specifying of the values of all primitive concepts. A state of an economy is described by specifying the values of all endogenous variables. General equilibrium theory provides a definition for a state to be an equilibrium state, also called equilibrium, usually meaning that when such a state is reached by the economy, no change occurs. Although it is not always possible to employ the methodology used in the physical sciences in economic science, it is difficult to resist making a comparison between the states of an economy and the states of a ball in a landscape (see Figure 1.1.1 to clarify some concepts).

The landscape and the ball are considered to be exogenously given. A state of the ball is determined by its position in the landscape and its speed. In Figure 1.1.1, assuming a gravity field as depicted and the existence of some friction, the three equilibrium states of the ball are drawn. Notice that to define an equilibrium state in this situation, no knowledge concerning the initial state of the ball is required and the amount of information needed concerning the state of the ball at each point in time is very limited. Similarly, an equilibrium state as defined in a general equilibrium model of the economic system only uses a limited amount of information concerning the development of the economic system in time, and is therefore essentially a static concept.

An important first question to be answered for a general equilibrium model of the economic system is whether an equilibrium state actually exists. In the example of the landscape, it is clear that some assumptions with respect to the shape of the landscape can guarantee the existence of an equilibrium. If the equilibrium in an economy can be guaranteed to be unique, then a theory has been obtained to predict the value of the endogenous variables. However, both in the example of Figure 1.1.1 and in general equilibrium models of the economic system, uniqueness of equilibrium is too much to be hoped for. Moreover, since the exogenous variables can only be measured subject to some error, it is important for making predictions that small changes in these variables do not lead to large changes in the equilibrium states, so a kind of continuity is required.

The example of the landscape makes clear that a complete dynamic model of the state of the ball would lead to a resolution of the problem of which of the three equilibria will result. A complete dynamic general equilibrium model of the economic system, also called an adjustment process, determines the state of the economy at each point in time. To obtain such a specification, one needs to know the initial state of the economy and the change of the state of the economy. Then the equilibrium states of the economy are exactly those states where no change of the state occurs. In the example of Figure 1.1.1 a dynamic model of the state of the ball corresponds to imposing a law of motion. If there exists an equilibrium of the economy and if a complete dynamic general equilibrium model is specified, then the question whether, given some initial state, the adjustment process will eventually reach an equilibrium becomes relevant, i.e. whether the adjustment process converges to an equilibrium. This question is called the equilibrium stability question. *A priori,* it is not clear at all *whether* for every initial state the adjustment process eventually reaches an equilibrium, even if this equilibrium is known to be unique. In the example of the ball, the existence of some friction is needed to guarantee this, unless the initial state is an equilibrium.

This monograph will consider several general equilibrium models of the economic system, several descriptions of its state, and several models of the change of the state of the economy.

1.2 OBJECTS OF THE MONOGRAPH

To carry out the ideas as described in the previous section, and hence to obtain a general equilibrium model of the economic system based on the primitive concepts of the economic system, there is a need for simplification and abstraction. Obviously, one should take care that the simplifications made and abstractions used are the appropriate ones, something which is often difficult to judge. The following paragraphs provide a simplified and abstract model of the economic system, known as the Arrow-Debreu model.

Several primitive concepts in the economic system can be distinguished. First of all there are the agents acting in the economic system. It is assumed that there are two types of agents, consumers and producers. Second, there are all kind of commodities present in the economic system. The value and the allocation of these commodities in the economic system should be regarded as the central question of the economic science. Each agent in the economic system is assumed to have a set of admissible actions available, and, guided by his objectives, each agent is assumed to choose within this set of admissible actions, an optimal action.

The action a consumer takes consists of the choice of a consumption bundle, that is a list of quantities supplied and demanded for all available commodities, thereby being restricted by exogenously given limitations of for example a physiological nature. The consumption set determines the set of admissible actions of a consumer. For a producer, the set of admissible actions is given by the production possibility set, describing all production possibilities, i.e. all technologically feasible transformations of commodity bundles into other commodity bundles. The production possibility set is exogenously given by the state of the technology.

The objectives of the consumer are determined by his exogenously given preference relation, specifying for any two commodity bundles the one that is preferred, or specifying indifference, or even impossibility of comparison. The objectives of the producer are given by profit maximization, where it is important to know the value of a commodity bundle in order to determine the profit of a specific action of the producer.

The value of a commodity bundle is assumed to be determined by the price system, specifying the value of one unit of each commodity, the price of this commodity. The price system is considered to be an endogenous variable, according to the theory. Finally, a specification of all commodities initially owned by the consumers, the initial endowments, and of the distribution of the profits generated by the producers to the consumers, the profit shares, is given. This, together with the price system, determines the income of a consumer and yields further restrictions on his set of admissible actions by requiring that the value of an admissible action of a consumer should not exceed his income. In this way the budget set of the consumer is obtained.

Trade is assumed to take place according to the market mechanism. A market is assumed to exist for every commodity. In the market for a commodity, the various agents acting in the economic system express their supply and their demand for this commodity corresponding to the optimal action chosen, while taking the price system as given. Given the price system and assuming all agents to be price takers, the total excess demand in the economic system is determined, obtained by subtracting for every commodity the total supply of the agents from the total demand of the agents. The relation associating with every price system all possible resulting total excess demands is called the total excess demand relation. This completes a very simplified and abstract description of the economic system. The state of the economy is given by the prevailing price system and the optimal actions given this price system of all the agents acting in the economy. When these optimal actions exist for every price system, the total excess demand relation is called the total excess demand correspondence. Often assumptions are made such that, given a price system, the optimal action of every agent is unique. Then the state of the economy is fully described by the price system, and the total excess demand relation is called the total excess demand function.

Given a price system, the optimal actions of all the agents together are not necessarily compatible, i.e. the total excess demand is not necessarily equal to zero in every market. A market is said to be in equilibrium if the optimal actions of the agents with respect to this market are compatible, so the total supply equals the total demand in this market. An equilibrium state or equilibrium of the economy is defined as a price system together with compatible optimal actions of the agents with respect to all markets. Such a price system is called an equilibrium price system.

The work of Adam Smith, "An Inquiry into the Nature and Causes of the Wealth of Nations," attempted first to give a theory of the economic system as a whole. Central in his work is the idea that although there are many agents in the economic system, possibly with conflicting interests, and although each agent acts in his own self-interest, the final allocation of commodities in the economic system is an efficient one. The price system is assumed to change according to Adam Smith's famous invisible hand, which leads to an equilibrium price system.

The first complete general equilibrium model should be attributed to Walras (1874). Therefore, an equilibrium state in the general equilibrium model as discussed in the previous paragraphs is often called a Walrasian equilibrium. A kind of equilibrium existence proof already appears in the work of Walras. Walras remarked that the number of equations expressing the equality of supply and demand in all markets is equal to the number of commodities and therefore to the number of prices. Assuming that it is possible to describe the state of the economy by the price system, the number of prices is equal to the number of endogenous variables. Moreover, since only the relative prices matter, Walras chose one of the commodities to be the numeraire commodity that has a price equal to one, thereby reducing the number of endogenously determined variables by one. Furthermore, Walras argued that the number of equations that express the equality between supply and demand can be reduced by one, due to the fact that equilibrium in all markets except one implies the equality of supply and demand in all markets. Finally, Walras concluded that an equilibrium should exist owing to the equality of the number of free endogenous variables and the number of independent constraints.

Walras also discussed stability issues. The adjustment process of the economic system that Walras had in mind is known as the Walrasian tatonnement process. Assuming that the state of the economy is completely determined by the price system, such a dynamic model corresponds to a description of the initial state, the starting price system, and a description of the change in the price system. Therefore, such an adjustment process is called a price adjustment process. Let some initial state of the economy be given. First, the price of one of the commodities, say commodity 1, is adjusted until the supply and the demand for this commodity become equal. To make the adjustment, the price of that commodity is raised if its demand exceeds its supply, and its price is decreased in the opposite case. The basic idea behind this adjustment of the price of a single commodity is that a positive excess demand in the market implies that the demand of some of the agents is not satisfied. Such an agent can offer a price that is slightly higher than the current price of the commodity, thereby attracting all the supply. Similarly, every supplier of the commodity can ask a price that is slightly higher than the current price of it, while still being able to sell all his supply. Notice that in this intuitive reasoning the assumption of price taking behaviour of the agents is abandoned. The same process is then successively repeated for the markets for the other commodities. It was claimed by Walras that the supply and the demand for a commodity is more affected by the change in its own price, than by the change in other prices. Therefore, Walras argued, when all prices are adjusted in the way as described, the markets are closer to an equilibrium state than they were before. Repeating this process, an equilibrium is eventually reached. This also yielded a second kind of equilibrium existence proof of Walras.

The work of Edgeworth (1881) and Pareto (1909) should also be mentioned. These authors studied efficient allocations in the economy, i.e. allocations such that it is impossible to improve the welfare of some agents without worsening the welfare of others. Moreover, they analysed the relationship between Walrasian equilibria and efficient allocations.

Obviously, both equilibrium existence proofs of Walras do not satisfy the current standards of rigor in mathematics. The first rigorous treatment of the Walrasian equilibrium existence problem and also of the problem of uniqueness of the Walrasian equilibrium was given in Wald (1936). He gave a proof of the existence and the uniqueness of the Walrasian equilibrium in some interesting cases. However, it is not possible to give reasonable assumptions with respect to the primitive concepts such that these cases result. The use of some significant advancements in mathematics, like Brouwer's fixed point theorem (Brouwer (1912)) and Kakutani's fixed point theorem (Kakutani (1941)), enabled the problem of the existence of a Walrasian equilibrium to be solved in Arrow and Debreu (1954) and McKenzie (1954). These papers made only assumptions with respect to the primitive concepts in order to show the existence of a Walrasian equilibrium.

Stability of the Walrasian equilibrium was investigated in Hicks (1939), who defines stability in an essentially static way. Samuelson (1941) defined the first explicit dynamic general equilibrium model of the economic system and a related notion of stability. Samuelson gave a mathematical formalization of the reasoning of Walras, when the prices of the commodities are simultaneously increased proportional to the total excess demand. The question whether the Walrasian equilibrium is stable turned out to be even more difficult to answer than the question of whether a Walrasian equilibrium exists. Several conditions with respect to the total excess demand function under which the Walrasian tatonnement process (as formulated by Samuelson) converges to some Walrasian equilibrium price system were given in Arrow and Hurwicz (1958) and Arrow, Block, and Hurwicz (1959). In the latter paper, the Walrasian tatonnement process was shown to be stable if the total excess demand function satisfies gross substitutability in the finite increment form. This assumption means that if the price of some commodity is raised, then the demand for all other commodities increases. This assumption reflects the idea that if the price of some commodity is raised, then the demand for all other commodities is increased due to the fact that these commodities become relatively cheaper. Unfortunately, the assumption of gross substitutability in the finite increment form does not follow from assumptions made with respect to primitive concepts. Examples given in Scarf (1960) and the lack of structure of the total excess demand function (see Debreu (1974)) make clear that the Walrasian tatonnement process does not converge to a Walrasian equilibrium price system for a large class of economies. For a discrete time version of the Walrasian tatonnement process even chaotic behaviour may be expected, see Day and Pianigiani (1991). Even if the Walrasian tatonnement process converges to a Walrasian equilibrium price system, convergence may take too much time and will not take place, a point of view considered in Blad (1978).

The lack of stability of the Walrasian tatonnement process leads to the question how the allocation of the commodities in the economic system is determined when trade has to take place at a price system that is not a Walrasian equilibrium price system. In this case the interdependence between the various markets causes a lot of problems, since the inequality of supply and demand in some markets results in some consumers not being able to obtain their desired amount of some commodities. However, as a consequence consumers will change their supply and demand in other markets, again causing other shortages or excesses. Notice that many real-world phenomena are in accordance with these observations, examples being the existence of unemployment in the labour market, tensions in the market for houses, the existence of butter mountains, wine pools, milk lakes, and dung-hills, and problems in the foreign exchange markets. Often the shortages or excesses in the examples mentioned above are the consequence of government interventions like minimum wages, the linkage between the wages of civil servants and the wages paid in industry, upper bounds on the rent for houses, minimum prices for agricultural products, or fixed exchange rates. This gives another reason for the price system not being completely flexible, but instead being subject to certain restrictions. Finally, it is often argued that prices, especially wages, are sticky in the short run.

The goal of Part II of the monograph is to give a general equilibrium model for the determination of the value and the allocation of commodities when the price system is not completely flexible, but might be restricted by all kind of constraints, and therefore price rigidities are present in the economy. The resulting set of price systems is determined by the set of admissible price systems, which is assumed to be exogenously given. Since it is possible that no Walrasian equilibrium price system is an element of the set of admissible price systems, the resulting general equilibrium models of the economic system are known as disequilibrium models. It turns out that it is no longer sufficient to describe the state of the economy by the price system and the optimal actions at this price system of the various agents. Instead, the maximal amounts the agents are allowed to supply and to demand for the various commodities, called a rationing scheme, should be included in the description of the state. Another primitive concept needed is the rationing system, specifying all admissible rationing schemes and describing how shortages or excesses are allocated in the economy. This also leads to different equilibrium concepts, that yield the so-called constrained equilibria. The analysis performed in Part II is static in nature and that part is therefore called "Static Aspects of Disequilibrium." Seminal work on this topic has been done in Bénassy (1975b), Drèze (1975) (see also Drèze (1991)) and Younès (1975). The approach taken in Part II is closely related to the one of Drèze.

It has been remarked above that government interventions are a particular source of causes for restrictions with respect to the price system and therefore for the possible exclusion of all Walrasian equilibrium price systems. Part II of the monograph considers these restrictions to be exogenously given, so they are part of the description of the economic system. Part III aims to make government behaviour, and consequently the restrictions with respect to the price system, endogenously. Therefore, that part is called "Endogenously Determined Disequilibrium." In Part III it is no longer assumed that the economic and political systems are separated. Instead these systems are considered jointly, which results in the political economic system. Next follows a definition of the political economic system, the state of the political economic system and equilibrium. This involves the introduction of another type of agent, a political candidate, his set of admissible actions being the set of admissible price regulations, and his objectives being the maximization of the expected plurality or of the probability of winning the elections. The state of the political economic system is determined by the proposals made by the political candidates. Again a different equilibrium concept is needed, called a political economic equilibrium. Also Part III is essentially static in nature. One of the basic questions to be answered is whether government intervention will typically lead to the exclusion of a Walrasian equilibrium price system in a democratic society, or in other words, whether in general, in a democracy, the political candidates will impose price regulations on the economic system.

Although the Walrasian tatonnement process is often used in the literature as a dynamic general equilibrium model of the economic system, it is not clear whether this is the correct model. Therefore, a natural question to ask is whether other dynamic general equilibrium models of the economic system are more appropriate and whether these models yield convergence to a Walrasian equilibrium price system. Similarly, the stability of the constrained equilibria studied in Part II of the monograph should be investigated. This determines the goal of Part IV of this monograph, which is to obtain adjustment processes that sustain the various equilibrium concepts and that are tools of equilibrium selection if more than one state of the economic system satisfies the definition of an equilibrium state. Therefore, Part IV is called "Dynamic Aspects of Disequilibrium Theory." Ideally, an adjustment process converges to an equilibrium under reasonable assumptions on the primitive concepts and the initial state of the economy, while the adjustment process itself should have a nice economic interpretation. In this respect, the work of Smale (1976), van der Laan and Talman (1987a, 1987b), and Kamiya (1990) concerning general equilibrium models of the economic system with a completely flexible price system should be mentioned. Smale (1976) specifies a price adjustment process that converges to a Walrasian equilibrium price system. However, the initial state of the economy has to satisfy some serious restrictions. In Kamiya (1990) the initial state is allowed to be arbitrary and the assumptions made with respect to the total excess demand function of the economy are reasonable. Nevertheless, these assumptions are not implied by ones made with respect to the primitive concepts. The price adjustment process introduced in van der Laan and Talman (1987a) makes no restrictions with respect to the starting price system. Moreover, their process has a nice economic interpretation. The analysis of the stability properties of this price adjustment process are the starting point of the analysis performed in Part IV. It should be remarked that there are some negative results in the literature with respect to the existence of adjustment processes that are stable for a large class of economies (see Saari and Simon (1978) and Saari (1985)). However, as also remarked in Saari (1985), it might be possible that the negative results can be circumvented if the adjustment process depends upon the values of the prices. Part IV carefully investigates this idea.

Over the last two decades many important and basic existence problems raised in general equilibrium theory have been successfully solved by constructive approaches. Most of the literature on this issue has been derived from the pioneering work of Scarf (1967) (see also Scarf (1973)). Scarf introduced an algorithm that generates a sequence of adjacent primitive sets in the unit simplex, every point in the unit simplex corresponding to a price system. Furthermore, the algorithm terminates in a finite number of steps with a primitive set containing an approximate Walrasian equilibrium price system. Kuhn (1968) proposes such an algorithm with simplices instead of primitive sets. Such an algorithm is therefore called a simplicial algorithm. These algorithms can be interpreted as following a path of points with certain properties (see Zangwill and Garcia (1981) and van der Laan and Talman (1983)). A serious drawback of the algorithms of both Scarf and Kuhn is that they cannot start with an arbitrary price system. Thus, if an approximate Walrasian equilibrium price system is known, then it is not possible to use this information and start the algorithm from there. Later, more efficient and sophisticated algorithms were developed, for example the homotopy method proposed in Eaves (1972), the sandwich method described in Kuhn and MacKinnon (1975), which is closely related to an algorithm given in Merrill (1972), and the variable dimension algorithm introduced in van der Laan and Talman (1979). All these methods allow for an arbitrary starting price system.

Shoven and Whalley (1973, 1992) and Kaneko and Yamamoto (1986) used simplicial algorithms to compute an approximate equilibrium in a model with taxation and in a model with indivisible commodities, respectively. Brown, DeMarzo, and Eaves (1994,1996) describe a procedure to find an equilibrium in a model with incomplete markets. By providing constructive equilibrium existence proofs, the computational approach often gives additional insight into the problems under consideration. Moreover, constructive approaches make it possible to actually compute an equilibrium or to follow an adjustment process, thereby being of importance for applied work too. This monograph investigates whether constructive approaches yield insights into the problems considered in Part II with respect to the existence of constrained equilibria and in Part IV with respect to the search for adjustment processes sustaining the various equilibrium concepts that are considered.

1.3 CONTENTS OF THE MONOGRAPH

The monograph consists of four parts, each of which is self-contained. Part I deals with the mathematical and economic preliminaries needed and consists of two chapters.

Chapter 2 provides the mathematical preliminaries. In fact, that chapter contains an essentially complete and self-contained overview of the mathematical notions to be used later on. The goal of Chapter 2 is to make the monograph as accessible as possible. Of special importance for the developments of this monograph are the sections dealing with notation, topology, relations and correspondences, fixed points, triangulations, and differential topology.

Chapter 3 deals with the economic preliminaries. The general equilibrium model of the economic system as presented in Arrow and Debreu (1954) is described (see Debreu (1959) for a complete account of this model). The chapter describes some primitive concepts of the economic system, like commodities, agents, consumption sets, production possibility sets, preference relations, initial endowments, and profit shares, and discusses all assumptions made with respect to these primitive concepts in some chapter of this monograph. Some attention is devoted to necessary and sufficient conditions needed for the representation of a preference relation by a utility function. Some well-known results of the total excess demand relation are derived as well. The chapter defines a Walrasian equilibrium and states the assumptions with respect to the primitive concepts guaranteeing the existence of a Walrasian equilibrium. Moreover, the chapter presents two results known as the first and the second fundamental welfare theorem, which make statements with respect to the efficiency of a Walrasian equilibrium and the possibility of achieving a given efficient allocation by means of a redistribution of initial endowments and profit shares. Next follows a general formulation of adjustment processes and some stability concepts. Moreover, the Walrasian tatonnement process is introduced and the result shown in Arrow, Block, and Hurwicz (1959) concerning the stability of the Walrasian tatonnement process if the total excess demand function satisfies gross substitutability in the finite increment form is stated. Then Scarf's example (see Scarf (1960)) is treated, showing that the Walrasian tatonnement process may not be stable for some economies. Finally, the result given in Debreu (1974) is presented, which implies that there is very little structure on the total excess demand function. From this it follows that there is a considerable class of economies for which the Walrasian tatonnement process is not stable.

Part II of the monograph considers the static aspects of disequilibrium theory. Part II consists of four chapters.

Chapter 4 provides a general equilibrium model of the economic system for the case that price rigidities or price regulations may be present in the economic system. Since the presence of restrictions with respect to the price system may exclude all Walrasian equilibrium price systems, it is possible that there exists a mismatch between the supply and the demand at any admissible price system. The description of the state of the economy therefore includes the maximal amounts all consumers are allowed to supply and to demand for the various commodities (i.e. a rationing scheme). Moreover, a set of admissible price systems and a rationing system are introduced as primitive concepts. The total excess demand relation now depends on both the price system and the rationing scheme. Special attention is devoted to giving necessary and sufficient conditions for the representation of the rationing system by a rationing function. The assumptions made with respect to the rationing system are shown to be very weak and allow for many possibilities. The Walrasian equilibrium concept is generalized and replaced by the constrained equilibrium concept, following the approach taken in Drèze (1975). It is shown that there exists an uncountable number of constrained equilibria. There is said to be rationing in a market if the maximal amounts the agents in the economy are allowed to supply and to demand in this market influence the behaviour of the agents. Similarly, supply rationing in a market and demand rationing in a market are defined. Well-known properties such as the existence of a trivial supply constrained equilibrium (i.e. with full rationing on supply in all markets), the existence of a trivial demand constrained equilibrium (i.e. with full rationing on demand in all markets), the existence of constrained equilibria without rationing in the market for an *a priori* specified commodity (called a Drèze equilibrium with respect to the market for this commodity), the existence of constrained equilibria without demand rationing and without rationing in the market for at least one commodity (called a supply constrained equilibrium), and the existence of constrained equilibria without supply rationing and without rationing in the market for at least one commodity (called a demand constrained equilibrium) follow as special cases from the existence theorems of that chapter. Finally, it is shown that the equilibrium relation, assigning to each specification of the initial endowments of the consumers and of the set of admissible price systems, the set of all possible constrained equilibrium allocations, is an upper hemi-continuous correspondence. To prove these results, the chapter provides a generalization of an existing continuity result of the budget relation.

Chapter 5 shows that in a general equilibrium model of the economic system allowing for price rigidities, there exists a connected set of constrained equilibria that contains both trivial constrained equilibria. The proof of this theorem combines results in the areas of mathematical programming, using simplicial algorithms with integer labelling, with those in topology. The result is proved without using differentiability assumptions and is also extended to the case with upper hemi-continuous total excess demand correspondences. All known existence results for the general equilibrium model discussed follow as easy corollaries to these results. In fact, it is shown that the connected set of constrained equilibria containing the two trivial constrained equilibria, contains an equilibrium of any type considered in Chapter 4. Although the proof of the result is constructive when the total excess demand relation is a continuous function, this is not the case for the result with respect to upper hemi-continuous total excess demand correspondences.

Chapter 6 provides a fully constructive proof of the existence of a connected set of constrained equilibria that contains both trivial constrained equilibria in a general equilibrium model of the economic system with price rigidities. To achieve this goal, the chapter proposes a simplicial algorithm with vector labelling. Using such an algorithm, it is possible to compute approximate constrained equilibria for the case when the total excess demand correspondence is upper hemi-continuous. To show the convergence of the algorithm of that chapter, specific degeneracy problems have to be solved for. The algorithm presented in Chapter 5 is not intended to be a good computational device, but is used only to show some theoretical properties of the set of constrained equilibria. This differs from the algorithm of Chapter 6, which is much more efficient. The accuracy of the approximate constrained equilibria obtained by the algorithm is also discussed.

Intersection theorems can be used to prove the existence of solutions to mathematical programming problems, game theoretic problems, and problems in general equilibrium theory. In all existing intersection theorems, conditions are given under which the intersection of certain sets in the cover of some given set is non-empty. Chapter 7 formulates conditions under which the intersection is a continuum of points that satisfy some interesting topological properties. More precisely, the intersection theorems are formulated on the unit cube and it is shown that both the vector of zeroes and the vector of ones lies in the same component of the intersection. Therefore, the intersection theorems of that chapter belong to a new class. It is shown that these intersection theorems are closely related to equilibrium existence problems in an economy with price rigidities. To prove the intersection theorems, a non-constructive proof of the existence of a connected set of constrained equilibria that contains both trivial constrained equilibria is given, using Browder's fixed point theorem. The intersection theorems of Chapter 7 generalize the well-known results on the unit simplex given in Knaster, Kuratowski, and Mazurkiewicz (1929) (KKM Lemma), in Sperner (1928) and Scarf (1967) (Scarf Lemma), in Shapley (1973) (KKMS Lemma), and in Ichiishi (1988) (Ichiishi Lemma). Moreover, the results can be used to sharpen the usual formulation of the Scarf Lemma on the unit cube.

Part III of the monograph determines price rigidities endogenously. The two chapters of that part assume that there exists a numeraire commodity and they focus the attention on Drèze equilibria with respect to the market for the numeraire commodity.

There exists an extensive literature about economies with price rigidities, in which price rigidities are exogenously given. Chapter 8 considers the interaction between the political system and the economic system. In this way it is possible to determine endogenously the price regulations that are imposed upon the economic system by the government. To describe the political economic system, some additional primitive concepts have to be specified. Another type of agent, a political candidate, is introduced. A political candidate chooses a price regulation in his set of admissible price regulations. His objectives are determined by the maximization of either the expected plurality or the probability of winning the elections. The expectations of the political candidates with respect to the voting behaviour of the consumers are described by means of voting functions. The description of the state of the political economic system is given by the price regulations and associated Drèze equilibria that are proposed by the political candidates. A definition of a political economic equilibrium is given, being a Nash equilibrium of a game played between the political candidates. Under some conditions it is shown that if the price of a commodity is sufficiently high, then no trade takes place in this market in a Drèze equilibrium of the economy irrespective of the price regulations that are imposed. This result is used to give sufficient conditions for the existence of a political economic equilibrium in mixed strategies and a political economic equilibrium in pure strategies. A standard example is presented to show the existence of a political economic equilibrium in which both political candidates propose price regulations excluding the Walrasian equilibrium price system.

Chapter 9 questions whether the example given in Chapter 8 is a degenerate case. Or, in other words, does it hold that for a considerable class of political economic systems both political candidates propose price regulations corresponding to the same Walrasian equilibrium? It is not difficult to construct examples in which both political candidates propose price regulations such that a Walrasian equilibrium results. Moreover, it is well-known that Drèze equilibria may be very inefficient. Nevertheless, it turns out that the example given in Chapter 8 corresponds to the generic case. Furthermore, another model of the political economic system is given where the political candidates are considered to choose only among local options given some status quo. The status quo is considered to be some Walrasian equilibrium. The political candidates are assumed to have the possibility to choose directions of motion away from the status quo or to stay at the status quo. Some motivation for considering only local options is given by institutional restrictions, commitments made in the past, or costs of acquiring information with respect to proposals that are not close to the status quo. The objectives of the political candidates are determined by the marginal change in the number of votes corresponding to a certain direction of motion. The description of the state of the political economic system is given by the directions of motion proposed by the political candidates. The related equilibrium concept, being a Nash equilibrium of the game played between the political candidates, is called a directional political economic equilibrium. Sufficient conditions for the existence of such an equilibrium are given. Moreover, it is shown that, generically, the political candidates choose directions of motion away from the status quo. Therefore, in the models of a political economic system considered in Part III of the monograph, Walrasian equilibria are unstable and the political candidates have incentives to impose price regulations on the economic system.

Finally, Part IV of the monograph, consisting of three chapters, deals with dynamic aspects of disequilibrium theory.

Chapter 10 shows that, generically, the price adjustment process introduced in van der Laan and Talman (1987a) converges to a Walrasian equilibrium price system. The prices are adjusted in such a way that the prices of commodities with a negative total excess demand are kept relatively minimal, i.e. the ratio of such a price with respect to the starting price is minimal, the prices of commodities with a positive total excess demand are kept relatively maximal, while the prices of commodities that are in equilibrium are allowed to vary between the relative minimum and the relative maximum. The assumptions made with respect to the consumption sets, preference relations, and initial endowments are standard. No restrictions are made with respect to the starting price system. The well-known fact that, generically, the number of Walrasian equilibria is odd, follows as a special case of the main theorem. If the demand functions satisfy gross substitutability in the finite increment form, then convergence always takes place. In this case the prices of commodities with a negative (positive) excess demand are strictly decreasing (increasing), and therefore the qualitative behaviour of the process resembles the Walrasian tatonnement process. Moreover, in every market the absolute value of the total excess demand is monotonically decreasing. This implies that a market attaining an equilibrium state at some point in time, stays in equilibrium during the remainder of the price adjustment process.

Chapter 11 assumes that the price system is completely fixed. It describes an adjustment process for an economy with a numeraire commodity, which, generically, converges to a Drèze equilibrium. Again, the attention is focused on Drèze equilibria with respect to the market for the numeraire commodity. The adjustment process proposed is an adjustment process in rationing schemes or, equivalently, in quantities and is therefore called a quantity adjustment process. The total excess demand as a function of the rationing schemes does not satisfy the assumptions under which any of the existing price adjustment processes converges to a Walrasian equilibrium. The main features of the quantity adjustment process under consideration are as follows. If there is a negative total excess demand in a market at some point in time, then the rationing schemes are adjusted in such a way that, compared to the initial state, supply rationing in this market is strengthened and demand rationing in this market is weakened. Similarly, if there is a positive total excess demand in a market at some point in time, the rationing schemes are adjusted in such a way that, compared to the initial state, supply rationing in this market is weakened and demand rationing in this market is strengthened. The assumptions made with respect to the consumption sets, preference relations, initial endowments, and the rationing function are standard. No restrictions are made with respect to the initial state of the economy, which determines the starting point of the adjustment process. Moreover, it follows from the main theorem that, generically, the number of Drèze equilibria is odd.

Chapter 12 considers also an economy with price rigidities. An adjustment process in prices and quantities is described for an economy with a numeraire commodity. In the short run the non-numeraire commodities have a flexible price level with respect to the numeraire commodity, but their relative prices are mutually fixed. In the long run, prices are assumed to be completely flexible. Markets are kept in equilibrium through rationing, and an adjustment process in prices and quantities is described, which converges from a demand constrained equilibrium with no rationing in the market for the numeraire commodity to a Walrasian equilibrium. Along the path initially all relative prices are kept fixed and the price level is increased. Rationing schemes are adjusted to keep markets in equilibrium. In so doing, the process reaches a short-run constrained equilibrium with no supply rationing and no rationing in the market for the numeraire commodity and at least one of the other commodities. The process allows for a downward price adjustment of the non-numeraire commodities in the market for which there is no rationing, and reaches a Walrasian equilibrium in the long run. In contrast with Chapters 10 and 11, markets are in equilibrium during the entire adjustment process. Another difference between those chapters and Chapter 12 is that the attention is focused on approximate equilibria.

PART I

PRELIMINARIES

2

MATHEMATICAL PRELIMINARIES

2.1 INTRODUCTION

In this chapter the mathematical concepts and results that are used in this monograph are presented. Only some elementary notions from set theory and the foundations of the real number system are taken for granted. For this the reader is referred to Sections 1.2 and 1.5, respectively, of the excellent book of Debreu, see Debreu (1959). Together with these two sections the exposition given here yields a complete and self-contained overview of the mathematical notions to be used later on.

Section 2.2 starts by introducing some notation that is used in this monograph.

Section 2.3 describes some topological notions, like compactness and connectedness, that are frequently used in the subsequent chapters. The notion of connectedness is employed in Chapters 5, 6, 7, 10, 11, and 12. It is very useful both in Part II concerning the static aspects of disequilibrium theory and in Part IV on disequilibrium dynamics. The notions of paths and loops play an important role in Chapters 10, 11, and 12. These topological concepts are used to describe the structure of certain sets of points related to adjustment processes. Moreover, they are used to give very general definitions for convergence of adjustment processes. Topological properties of sets like being dense or being residual give some indication about the size of a set. Such properties are needed in Chapters 4, 9, and 10.

In Section 2.4 some concepts related to vector spaces are introduced. Especially the notions of convexity and of dimension turn out to be important in what follows. Vector spaces are also needed when formulating Glicksberg's fixed point theorem in Section 2.6. Moreover, matrices and some of their elementary properties are introduced in that section.

In Section 2.5 the concept of a relation is presented. Relations turn out to be very useful in Chapter 3 to describe preferences of economic agents. Also a special type of relation, called a correspondence, is introduced. Definitions, characterizations, and results that concern several forms of continuity of correspondences are given. Correspondences are important in almost every chapter of this monograph.

Fixed points are an essential ingredient throughout the monograph. Part II deals with equilibrium existence problems in finite dimensions. It is well-known that such an equilibrium existence problem is related to Kakutani's fixed point theorem. In Chapter 7 it is shown that additional insight into the equilibrium existence problems of Part II can be obtained by using Browder's fixed point theorem. Part III concerns equilibrium existence problems in infinite dimensions and is related to Glicksberg's fixed point theorem. In Section 2.6 the above mentioned fixed point theorems are formulated.

Many of the results to be presented are proved by using concepts from mathematical programming. In particular simplicial algorithms turn out to be very useful. These are methods developed to solve problems related to Kakutani's fixed point theorem by computing an approximation of such a fixed point. A simplicial algorithm generates a piecewise linear path of points in a simplicial subdivision. This path yields valuable insights into the structure of the set of equilibria in the models to be presented in Chapter 4, as is shown in Chapters 5 and 6. Moreover, simplicial algorithms make it possible to actually compute an approximation of an equilibrium or of a continuum of equilibria as in Chapters 5 and 6. These algorithms can also be used to approximate a path of points generated by an adjustment process, see Chapters 10, 11, and 12. The main concepts needed to describe a simplicial algorithm, like a simplicial subdivision and a piecewise linear approximation, are gathered in Section 2.7.

In Section 2.8 some concepts from measure theory needed in Chapters 8, 9, 10, and 11 are exposed. In Chapter 8 measure theory is used to describe the strategies of economic agents. In Chapters 9, 10, and 11 some statements are made which are typically valid but not necessarily always. Measure theory is used to show that the cases where these statements are not true are very rare.

In Section 2.9 some concepts related to differential calculus are exposed and the inverse function theorem is given. Moreover, necessary and sufficient conditions are given for an element to be a maximizer of a function on a certain set. These necessary conditions are needed in Chapters 10 and 11 when describing points generated by an adjustment process, taking into consideration the optimizing behaviour of economic agents.

Section 2.10 concludes this chapter with some notions from differential topology. The definitions of a manifold, a manifold with generalized boundary, and a regular constraint set, and some results like the implicit function theorem and the transversality theorem are given. These concepts are very useful to describe the structure of the set of points followed by the adjustment processes in Chapters 10 and 11. Moreover, in Chapters 9, 10, and 11 some results from differential topology are employed when statements are made that are typically true, but not necessarily always.

All concepts and results mentioned in this chapter are fairly well-known, and therefore no proofs are given. However, references are provided for all results. A number is associated with every important definition and theorem mentioned in this chapter. Whenever such a definition or theorem is used in the remainder of the monograph, a reference is made to this number. The presentation is minimal in the sense that no results are given that are not needed in what follows. Moreover, the results are presented in a self-contained way.

2.2 SOME NOTATION

The quantifiers for every, there exists, and there does not exist are denoted by $\forall$, $\exists$, and $\nexists$, respectively. Let a *set* (*collection*) X be given, then $x \in X$ denotes that x is an *element* (*member*) of X or that x *belongs* to X, and X is said to *contain* x. Similarly, $x \notin X$ denotes that x is not an element of X. Let $\mathcal{X}$ denote a *property* that an element of X has or does not have. Then $\{x \in X \mid x \text{ has property } \mathcal{X}\}$ denotes the set of elements of X that have property $\mathcal{X}$.

Let sets X and Y be given. Then $X \subset Y$ denotes that the set X is a *subset* of Y, and Y is said to *contain* X, $X \cap Y$ denotes the *intersection* of X and Y, $X \cup Y$ denotes the *union* of X and Y, $Y \setminus X$ denotes the *complement* of X in Y, and $X \times Y$ denotes the *Cartesian product* of X and Y. The *empty set* is denoted by $\emptyset$. The sets X and Y are said to be *disjoint* if $X \cap Y = \emptyset$. The set X is called a *proper subset* of Y if $X \subset Y$ and $Y \setminus X \neq \emptyset$. Let I be a set and, for every $i \in I$, let a set X^i be given. Then $\cap_{i \in I} X^i$ denotes the intersection of the sets X^i, $\cup_{i \in I} X^i$ denotes the union of the sets X^i, and $\prod_{i \in I} X^i$ denotes the Cartesian product of the sets X^i. When the set I is empty, then no intersection, union, or Cartesian product is defined.

The *set of natural numbers* is denoted by $\mathbb{N}$, i.e. $\mathbb{N} = \{1, 2, \ldots\}$, $\mathbb{Z}$ denotes the *set of integers*, i.e. $\mathbb{Z} = \{\cdots, -1, 0, 1, \cdots\}$, $\mathbb{Z}_+$ denotes the *set of non-negative integers*, i.e. $\mathbb{Z}_+ = \{0, 1, \ldots\}$, $\mathbb{Q}$ denotes the *set of rational numbers*, i.e. every element q of $\mathbb{Q}$ is of the form $\frac{m}{n}$ with m and n integers and $n \neq 0$, and $\mathbb{R}$ denotes the *set of real numbers*. For $m \in \mathbb{Z}_+$, the set of integers $\{1, \ldots, m\}$ is denoted by I_m and the set of integers $\{0, \ldots, m\}$ is denoted by I_m^0. Notice that $I_0 = \emptyset$ and $I_0^0 = \{0\}$. The *set of signs* is denoted by $\mathbb{S}$, i.e. $\mathbb{S} = \{-1, 0, +1\}$.

Let some $m \in \mathbb{N}$ be given. Then $\mathbb{N}^m$ denotes the m-fold Cartesian product of $\mathbb{N}$, i.e. $\mathbb{N}^m = \prod_{i \in I_m} \mathbb{N}$, $\mathbb{Z}^m$ denotes the m-fold Cartesian product of $\mathbb{Z}$, i.e. $\mathbb{Z}^m = \prod_{i \in I_m} \mathbb{Z}$, $\mathbb{Z}_+^m$ denotes the m-fold Cartesian product of $\mathbb{Z}_+$, i.e. $\mathbb{Z}_+^m = \prod_{i \in I_m} \mathbb{Z}_+$, and $\mathbb{Q}^m$ denotes the m-fold Cartesian product of $\mathbb{Q}$, i.e. $\mathbb{Q}^m = \prod_{i \in I_m} \mathbb{Q}$. The *set of sign vectors*, denoted by $\mathbb{S}^m$, is defined as the m-fold Cartesian product of $\mathbb{S}$, i.e. $\mathbb{S}^m = \prod_{i \in I_m} \mathbb{S}$. For every sign vector $s \in \mathbb{S}^m$, the sets $I^-(s)$, $I^0(s)$, and $I^+(s)$ are defined by $I^-(s) = \{i \in I_m \mid s_i = -1\}$, $I^0(s) = \{i \in I_m \mid s_i = 0\}$, and $I^+(s) = \{i \in I_m \mid s_i = +1\}$. The *$m$-dimensional Euclidean space* is denoted by $\mathbb{R}^m$, and is defined as the m-fold Cartesian product of $\mathbb{R}$, i.e. $\mathbb{R}^m = \prod_{i \in I_m} \mathbb{R}$.

An element of $\mathbb{R}^m$ is also called a *point* or a *vector*. All vectors of $\mathbb{R}^m$ are assumed to be *column vectors*, unless mentioned otherwise. A vector $x \in \mathbb{R}^m$ can be written as $(x_1, \ldots, x_m)^\top$, with, for every $i \in I_m$, x_i denoting *component* i of x. The symbol $\top$ is used to denote the *transpose* of a vector, and changes a *row vector* into a column vector and vice versa. The element of $\mathbb{R}^m$ with every component equal to zero is denoted by 0^m and the element of $\mathbb{R}^m$ with every component equal to one by 1^m. For $i \in I_m$, the i-th *unit vector* of $\mathbb{R}^m$ is denoted by $e^m(i)$ and is defined by letting $e_i^m(i) = 1$ and by letting the other components of $e^m(i)$ be equal to zero.

Given two real numbers x^1 and x^2, one writes $x^1 \leq x^2$ or $x^2 \geq x^1$ if x^1 is less than or equal to x^2, and $x^1 < x^2$ or $x^2 > x^1$ if x^1 is less than x^2. A real number x is said to be *negative* if $x < 0$, *non-positive* if $x \leq 0$, *non-negative* if $x \geq 0$, and *positive* if $x > 0$. Notice that all elements of the set of non-negative integers, $\mathbb{Z}_+$, are non-negative. The *absolute value* of a real number x, denoted by $|x|$, is defined by $|x| = -x$ if $x < 0$, and $|x| = x$ if $x \geq 0$. The greatest integer less than or equal to a real number x is denoted by $\lfloor x \rfloor$.

Given two elements x^1 and x^2 of $\mathbb{R}^m$, $\leq, <$, and $\ll$ on $\mathbb{R}^m$ are defined by $x^1 \leq x^2$ if $x_i^1 \leq x_i^2$, $\forall i \in I_m$, $x^1 < x^2$ if $x^1 \leq x^2$ and $\exists i' \in I_m$ such that $x_{i'}^1 < x_{i'}^2$, and $x^1 \ll x^2$ if $x_i^1 < x_i^2$, $\forall i \in I_m$. Similarly, $\geq$, $>$, and $\gg$ are defined for elements of $\mathbb{R}^m$. The *non-negative orthant* of the m-dimensional Euclidean space, denoted by $\mathbb{R}_+^m$, is defined by $\mathbb{R}_+^m = \{x \in \mathbb{R}^m \mid x \geq 0^m\}$. The *positive orthant* of the m-dimensional Euclidean space, denoted by $\mathbb{R}_{++}^m$, is defined by $\mathbb{R}_{++}^m = \{x \in \mathbb{R}^m \mid x \gg 0^m\}$.

A subset S of $\mathbb{R}^m$ is called an *interval* if $x^1, x^2 \in S$ and $x^1 \leq x \leq x^2$ for some $x \in \mathbb{R}^m$ implies $x \in S$. For elements a, b of $\mathbb{R}^m$, it is possible to define the intervals $(\leftarrow, b) = \{x \in \mathbb{R}^m \mid x \ll b\}$, $(\leftarrow, b] = \{x \in \mathbb{R}^m \mid x \leq b\}$, $[a, b) = \{x \in \mathbb{R}^m \mid a \leq x \ll b\}$, $[a, b] = \{x \in \mathbb{R}^m \mid a \leq x \leq b\}$, $[a, \rightarrow) = \{x \in \mathbb{R}^m \mid a \leq x\}$, $(a, b) = \{x \in \mathbb{R}^m \mid a \ll x \ll b\}$, $(a, b] = \{x \in \mathbb{R}^m \mid a \ll x \leq b\}$, and $(a, \rightarrow) = \{x \in \mathbb{R}^m \mid a \ll x\}$. The sets $(\leftarrow, b)$, (a, b), and $(a, \rightarrow)$ are called *open intervals* and the sets $(\leftarrow, b]$, $[a, b]$, and $[a, \rightarrow)$ are called *closed intervals.* The sets $[0^m, 1^m)$, $[0^m, 1^m]$, $(0^m, 1^m)$, and $(0^m, 1^m]$ are called *unit intervals.* Notice that $\mathbb{R}_+^m = [0^m, \rightarrow)$ and $\mathbb{R}_{++}^m = (0^m, \rightarrow)$.

For $n \in \mathbb{N}$, for every $j \in I_n$, let $x^j \in \mathbb{R}$ be given. Then the *product* $x^1 \cdots x^n$ is denoted by $\prod_{j \in I_n} x^j$. The product $\prod_{j \in \emptyset} x^j$ is defined to be equal to one. In $\mathbb{R}^m$ *addition* and *multiplication* by an element of $\mathbb{R}$ is derived from addition and multiplication on $\mathbb{R}$ by performing addition and multiplication componentwise. For $n \in \mathbb{N}$, for every $j \in I_n$, let $x^j \in \mathbb{R}^m$ be given. Then the *sum* $x^1 + \cdots + x^n$ is denoted by $\sum_{j \in I_n} x^j$. For every $x^1, x^2 \in \mathbb{R}^m$, the *inner product* of x^1 and x^2, denoted by $x^1 \cdot x^2$, is defined by $x^1 \cdot x^2 = \sum_{i \in I_m} x_i^1 x_i^2$.

Let S^1 and S^2 be subsets of $\mathbb{R}^m$. Then the *sum* of S^1 and S^2, denoted by $S^1 + S^2$, is defined as the set $\{x \in \mathbb{R}^m \mid \exists x^1 \in S^1, \exists x^2 \in S^2, x = x^1 + x^2\}$. Let λ be an element of $\mathbb{R}$ and let S be a subset of $\mathbb{R}^m$. Then the *product* of λ and S, denoted by λS, is defined as the set $\{x \in \mathbb{R}^m \mid \exists \bar{x} \in S, x = \lambda \bar{x}\}$. For $n \in \mathbb{N}$, for every $j \in I_n$, let a subset S^j of $\mathbb{R}^m$ be given. Then the sum $S^1 + \cdots + S^n$ is denoted by $\sum_{j \in I_n} S^j$.

For every $x \in \mathbb{R}^m$, the *1-norm* of x, denoted by $\|x\|_1$, is defined by $\|x\|_1 = \sum_{i \in I_m} |x_i|$, and the *Euclidean norm* of x, denoted by $\|x\|_2$, is defined by $\|x\|_2 = \sqrt{\sum_{i \in I_m} (x_i)^2}$. For every $\bar{x} \in \mathbb{R}^m$, for every $\delta \in \mathbb{R}_{++}$, the *open m-dimensional ball* in $\mathbb{R}^m$ with *center* $\bar{x}$ and *radius* δ, denoted by $B^m(\bar{x}, \delta)$, is defined by $B^m(\bar{x}, \delta) = \{x \in \mathbb{R}^m \mid \|x - \bar{x}\|_2 < \delta\}$ and the *closed m-dimensional ball* in $\mathbb{R}^m$ with *center* $\bar{x}$ and *radius* δ, denoted by $\overline{B}^m(\bar{x}, \delta)$, is defined by $\overline{B}^m(\bar{x}, \delta) = \{x \in \mathbb{R}^m \mid \|x - \bar{x}\|_2 \leq \delta\}$. For every $\bar{x} \in \mathbb{R}^m$, for every $\delta \in \mathbb{R}_{++}$, the $(m-1)$-*dimensional sphere* in $\mathbb{R}^m$ with *center* $\bar{x}$ and *radius* δ, denoted by $\widetilde{B}^{m-1}(\bar{x}, \delta)$, is defined by $\widetilde{B}^{m-1}(\overline{x},\delta) = \{x \in \mathbb{R}^m \mid \|x-\overline{x}\|_2 = \delta\}$. The $(m-1)$-*dimensional unit simplex* in $\mathbb{R}^m$, denoted by Δ^{m-1}, is defined by $\Delta^{m-1} = \{x \in \mathbb{R}^m \mid \sum_{i\in I_m} x_i = 1$ and $x_i \geq 0,\ \forall i \in I_m\}$. For every subset I of I_m, the set $\Delta^{m-1}(I)$ is defined by $\Delta^{m-1}(I) = \{x \in \Delta^{m-1} \mid x_i = 0,\ \forall i \in I\}$. Notice that $\Delta^{m-1}(\emptyset) = \Delta^{m-1}$ and $\Delta^{m-1}(I_m) = \emptyset$. The set $\dot{\Delta}^{m-1}$ is defined by $\dot{\Delta}^{m-1} = \{x \in \mathbb{R}^m \mid \sum_{i\in I_m} x_i = 1$ and $x_i > 0,\ \forall i \in I_m\}$. The *m-dimensional unit cube* in $\mathbb{R}^m$, denoted by Q^m, is defined by $Q^m = [0^m, 1^m] = \{x \in \mathbb{R}^m \mid 0 \leq x_i \leq 1,\ \forall i \in I_m\}$. For every subset I of I_m, the set $Q^m(I)$ is defined by $Q^m(I) = \{x \in Q^m \mid x_i = 0,\ \forall i \in I\}$. Notice that $Q^m(\emptyset) = Q^m$ and $Q^m(I_m) = \{0^m\}$.

Let X and Y be two sets. If with every element x of X is associated exactly one element y of Y, then a *function* f from X into Y is defined, denoted by $f : X \to Y$. Let a function $f : X \to Y$ be given. The set X is called the *domain* of f. If x is an element of X, then $f(x)$ denotes the element y of Y associated with x and is called the *image* by f of x. If $X = \emptyset$, then a function f from X into Y is denoted by $\emptyset$. Let S be a subset of X and let T be a subset of Y. The *image* of S by f, denoted by $f(S)$, is defined by $f(S) = \{y \in Y \mid \exists x \in S,\ y = f(x)\}$ and the *inverse image* of T by f, denoted by $f^{-1}(T)$, is defined by $f^{-1}(T) = \{x \in X \mid f(x) \in T\}$. The image by f of X is called the *range* of f. The function $g : S \to Y$, defined by $g(x) = f(x),\ \forall x \in S$, is denoted by $f_{|S}$, and is called the *restriction* of f to S. If $\overline{X}$ is a set that contains X, and $g : \overline{X} \to Y$ is a function that satisfies $g(x) = f(x),\ \forall x \in X$, then g is called an *extension* of f to $\overline{X}$. The function f is said to be *injective* if $f^{-1}(\{y\})$ contains at most one element for every element y of Y, and f is said to be *surjective* if $f(X) = Y$. If the function f is injective and surjective, then the function that associates with every element y of Y the element x of X satisfying $f(x) = y$ is called the *inverse* of f and is denoted by $f^{-1} : Y \to X$.

Let X be a set. For every $i \in I_m$, let f_i be a function from X into $\mathbb{R}$, and let $f : X \to \mathbb{R}^m$ be a function such that $f(x) = (f_1(x), \ldots, f_m(x))^\top,\ \forall x \in X$. The functions $f_1, \ldots, f_m$ are called the *components* of f.

A set X is said to be *finite* if the number of its elements is a non-negative integer. A set X is said to be *countable* if there exists an injective function f from X into a subset of $\mathbb{N}$. Let I be a set and, for every $i \in I$, let a set X^i be given. The intersection $\cap_{i\in I} X^i$ is said to be *finite* if the set I is finite and is said to be *countable* if I is countable. The notions *finite union* and *countable union* are defined similarly. It is easily shown that a countable union of countable sets yields a countable set.

Let X be a finite set of elements. Then $\#X$ denotes the *cardinality* of X, i.e. the number of elements of X. For every sign vector $s \in \mathbb{S}^m$, the integers $i^-(s)$, $i^0(s)$, and $i^+(s)$ are defined by $i^-(s) = \#I^-(s)$, $i^0(s) = \#I^0(s)$, and $i^+(s) = \#I^+(s)$.

Let a set X be given. The collection of all subsets (including the empty set) of X, denoted by 2^X, is called the *power set* of X. A function $f : \mathbb{N} \to X$ is called a *sequence* in X and is denoted by $(x^n)_{n\in\mathbb{N}}$, where $x^n = f(n)$, $\forall n \in \mathbb{N}$. If $(x^n)_{n\in\mathbb{N}}$ is a sequence in X and $(n^m)_{m\in\mathbb{N}}$ is a sequence in $\mathbb{N}$ such that $n^m < n^{m+1}$, $\forall m \in \mathbb{N}$, then $(x^{n^m})_{m\in\mathbb{N}}$ is called a *subsequence* of $(x^n)_{n\in\mathbb{N}}$. For $m \in \mathbb{N}$, a function $f : I_m \to X$ is called a *finite sequence* in X and is denoted by $(x^1, \ldots, x^m)$ or by $(x^i)_{i\in I_m}$, where $x^i = f(i)$, $\forall i \in I_m$. For a finite set X with cardinality m, an injective function $\pi : I_m \to X$ is called a *permutation* of the elements of X, and is denoted by $(x^1, \ldots, x^m)$, where $x^i = \pi(i)$, $\forall i \in I_m$. Notice that $\pi(I_m) = X$ in this case. For a subset S of X, the function $\chi_S : X \to \{0, 1\}$, defined by $\chi_S(x) = 1$, $\forall x \in S$, and $\chi_S(x) = 0$, $\forall x \in X \setminus S$, is called the *characteristic function* of S.

2.3 TOPOLOGY

The material treated in this section can be found in any introductory book on topology, see for instance Dugundji (1965), Munkres (1975), or Armstrong (1983).

The definition of a topological space is given since this framework is general enough to describe many important notions used in this monograph.

Definition 2.3.1 (Topological space)
A topology *on a set X is a non-empty collection of subsets of X, called* open sets *of X, such that any union of open sets of X is an open set of X, any finite intersection of open sets of X is an open set of X, and both the empty set and X are open sets of X. A* topological space *X is the set X together with a topology on it.*

An open set of a topological space X is said to be *open* in X.

Let X be a topological space and let $\mathcal{B}$ be a collection of sets such that every open set of X is the union of the members of some subset of $\mathcal{B}$. Then the collection $\mathcal{B}$ is called a *base* for the topology on X.

For $m \in \mathbb{N}$, for every $i \in I_m$, let X^i be a topological space and let $\mathcal{B}$ denote the collection of all subsets of $\prod_{i \in I_m} X^i$ of the form $\prod_{i \in I_m} S^i$, where the set S^i is open in X^i for every $i \in I_m$. Then the collection $\mathcal{B}$ is a base for a topology on $\prod_{i \in I_m} X^i$, called the *product topology*.

A topological space X is called a *Hausdorff space* if any two different elements of X are contained in two disjoint open sets of X.

Let the m-dimensional Euclidean space $\mathbb{R}^m$ be given and consider the topology on $\mathbb{R}^m$ given by the collection of subsets S of $\mathbb{R}^m$ satisfying that for every $x \in S$ there exists $\delta \in \mathbb{R}_{++}$ such that $B^m(x, \delta) \subset S$. In the entire monograph it is assumed that this is the topology on $\mathbb{R}^m$. This topology coincides with the m-fold product topology on $\prod_{i \in I_m} \mathbb{R}$. The topological space $\mathbb{R}^m$ can be shown to be a Hausdorff space.

Let S be a subset of a topological space X. The *induced topology* on S is defined as the collection of sets obtained by the intersection of open sets of X with S. When a subset S of $\mathbb{R}^m$ is considered as a topological space, then it is assumed in the entire monograph that S has the induced topology.

Let X be a topological space. A subset S of X is called a *closed set* of X if its complement $X \setminus S$ is open in X. A closed set of X is said to be *closed* in X. Clearly, any intersection of closed sets of X and any finite union of closed sets of X is closed in X. Moreover, both the empty set and X are closed in X. Clearly, the Cartesian product of a finite number of closed sets is closed in the product topology. The *closure* in X of a subset S of X is defined as the smallest closed set of X that contains S, i.e. the intersection of all closed sets of X containing S, and is denoted by $\text{cl}(S)$.

When a subset S of $\mathbb{R}^m$ is said to be open or closed, then it is assumed in the entire monograph that it is open or closed in $\mathbb{R}^m$, unless mentioned otherwise. Notice that open intervals are open and closed intervals are closed.

Let X be a topological space and let S be a subset of X. The set S is said to be *dense* in X if $\text{cl}(S) = X$. The set S is called a *residual set* in X if S contains a countable intersection of open, dense subsets of X. Notice that a countable intersection of residual sets also is a residual set. The topological space X is called a *Baire space* if every countable intersection of open, dense subsets of X is dense in X.

The Euclidean space $\mathbb{R}^m$ can be shown to be a Baire space, see also Theorem 2.3.15. Hence, every residual set in $\mathbb{R}^m$ is dense in $\mathbb{R}^m$. There exist dense sets in $\mathbb{R}^m$ that are not residual sets in $\mathbb{R}^m$. Consider for example the set $\mathbb{Q}^m$. Clearly, $\mathbb{Q}^m$ is dense in $\mathbb{R}^m$. Suppose $\mathbb{Q}^m$ is a residual set in $\mathbb{R}^m$, then, clearly, $\mathbb{Q}^m + \{\sqrt{2}\}$ is a residual set in $\mathbb{R}^m$ too. Therefore, $\emptyset = \mathbb{Q}^m \cap (\mathbb{Q}^m + \{\sqrt{2}\})$ is a residual set in $\mathbb{R}^m$, and since $\mathbb{R}^m$ is a Baire space it holds that $\text{cl}(\emptyset) = \mathbb{R}^m$, a contradiction.

Let X be a topological space and let S be a subset of X. The *interior* in X of S is defined as the union of all open sets of X contained in S and is denoted by $\text{int}(S)$. The *boundary* in X of S is defined as the intersection of S with the closure of $X \setminus S$ and is denoted by $\text{bd}(S)$. The *frontier* in X of S is defined as the intersection of the closure of S with the closure of $X \setminus S$ and is denoted by $\text{fr}(S)$. It can be shown that $\text{cl}(S) = \text{int}(S) \cup \text{fr}(S)$, see for instance Dugundji (1965), Theorem 4.11, page 72. The element x of X is called a *limit point* in X of S if every open set of X that contains x also contains at least one element of S. The element x of X is called an *accumulation point* in X of S if every open set of X that contains x also contains at least one element of $S \setminus \{x\}$.

Theorem 2.3.2
Let X be a topological space and let S be a subset of X. Then the set S is closed in X if and only if all limit points in X of S are contained in S.
See Armstrong (1983), Theorem 2.2, page 29.

Let $(x^n)_{n\in\mathbb{N}}$ be a sequence in $\mathbb{R}$. The sequence $(x^n)_{n\in\mathbb{N}}$ is said to *diverge* to $-\infty$, denoted by $x^n \to -\infty$, if for every $\overline{n} \in \mathbb{N}$ there exists $n' \in \mathbb{N}$ such that $n > n'$ implies $x^n < -\overline{n}$. The sequence $(x^n)_{n\in\mathbb{N}}$ is said to *diverge* to $+\infty$, denoted by $x^n \to +\infty$, if for every $\overline{n} \in \mathbb{N}$ there exists $n' \in \mathbb{N}$ such that $n > n'$ implies $x^n > \overline{n}$. The sequence $(x^n)_{n\in\mathbb{N}}$ is said to *converge* to $\overline{x} \in \mathbb{R}$, denoted by $x^n \to \overline{x}$ or by $\lim_{n\to+\infty} x^n = \overline{x}$, if for every $\varepsilon \in \mathbb{R}_{++}$ there exists $n' \in \mathbb{N}$ such that $n > n'$ implies $|x^n - \overline{x}| < \varepsilon$.

Let $(x^n)_{n\in\mathbb{N}}$ be a sequence in $\mathbb{R}^m$. Then the sequence $(x^n)_{n\in\mathbb{N}}$ is said to *converge* to $\overline{x} \in \mathbb{R}^m$, denoted by $x^n \to \overline{x}$ or by $\lim_{n\to+\infty} x^n = \overline{x}$, if $x_i^n \to \overline{x}_i$, $\forall i \in I_m$. In this case the sequence is said to be *convergent*. The element $\overline{x}$ is uniquely determined and is called the *limit* of the sequence. Obviously, the notions related to convergence are well defined if there exists $n' \in \mathbb{N}$ such that the element x^n is only defined for every $n \geq n'$.

Let X be a subset of $\mathbb{R}^m$, let $\overline{x}$ be an element of X, and let S be a subset of X. Then the element $\overline{x}$ is a limit point in X of S if and only if $\overline{x}$ is the limit of some sequence in S. Therefore, it follows by Theorem 2.3.2 that the set S is closed in X if and only if for any element x of X that is the limit of a sequence in S it holds that $x \in S$.

Let topological spaces X and Y, an element $\overline{x}$ of X, and a function $f : X \to Y$ be given. The function f is said to be *continuous* at $\overline{x}$ if for every open set O' of Y containing $f(\overline{x})$ there exists an open set O of X containing $\overline{x}$ such that $f(O) \subset O'$. The function f is said to be *continuous* if it is continuous at every $x \in X$. The function f is continuous if and only if for every open set O' of Y it holds that $f^{-1}(O')$ is open in X. The set of continuous functions from X into Y is denoted by $C^0(X, Y)$. The function f is called a *homeomorphism* if it is continuous, injective, surjective, and has a continuous inverse. The topological spaces X and Y are called *homeomorphic* if there exists a homeomorphism $f : X \to Y$.

Let a subset S of $\mathbb{R}^m$, a subset T of $\mathbb{R}^n$, and an element $\overline{x}$ of S be given. It is well-known that a function $f : S \to T$ is continuous at $\overline{x}$ if and only if $(x^n)_{n \in \mathbb{N}}$ being a sequence in S, $x^n \to \overline{x}$, $y^n = f(x^n)$, $\forall n \in \mathbb{N}$, and $\overline{y} = f(\overline{x})$ implies $y^n \to \overline{y}$.

Let X be a topological space. The topological space X is called an *arc* if X and the closed unit interval $[0, 1]$ are homeomorphic, X is called a *loop* if X and the *unit circle* in $\mathbb{R}^2$, being the set $\widetilde{B}^1((0,0)^\top, 1)$, are homeomorphic. If X is an arc and $f : [0, 1] \to X$ is a homeomorphism, then $f(\{0, 1\})$ is called the *relative boundary* of X, $f(0)$ and $f(1)$ are called *boundary points* of X, and $X \setminus f(\{0, 1\})$ is called the *relative interior* of X. It can be shown that both the relative boundary and the relative interior of X are independent of the homeomorphism chosen, see Armstrong (1983), page 193, problem 36. A continuous function $f : [0, 1] \to X$ is called a *path*. The elements $f(0)$ and $f(1)$ are called the *beginning* and *end points* of the path f, respectively, and $f(0)$ and $f(1)$ are said to be *joined* by the path f. Since $\mathbb{R}^m$ and $\mathbb{R}^n$ are homeomorphic if and only if $m = n$, Theorem 2.3.3 is quite surprising.

Theorem 2.3.3
There exists a path $f : [0, 1] \to \Delta^2$ that is surjective.
See Armstrong (1983), Section 2.3, page 36-38.

Since Theorem 2.3.4 implies that an injective, surjective path $f : [0, 1] \to \Delta^2$ is a homeomorphism, and since it is well-known that $[0, 1]$ and Δ^2 are not homeomorphic, it follows that the path f in Theorem 2.3.3 is not injective.

Let a set X be given. A *cover* of X is defined as a collection of subsets of X whose union equals X. A subset of a cover of X is called a *subcover* if it covers X. Let X be a topological space and let $\overline{x}$ be an element of X. An *open cover* of X is defined as a collection of open sets of X whose union equals X. Similarly, a *closed cover* of X is defined as a collection of closed sets of X whose union equals X. The topological space X is said to be *compact* if every open cover of X has a finite subcover. A subset of a topological space is said to be *compact* if it becomes a compact topological space when given the induced topology. Clearly, the Cartesian product of a finite number of compact sets is compact in the product topology.

Theorem 2.3.4
Let X be a compact topological space, let Y be a Hausdorff space, and let $f : X \to Y$ be a continuous, injective, and surjective function. Then the function f is a homeomorphism.
See Armstrong (1983), Theorem 3.7, page 48.

Let a topological space X be given. The topological space X is said to be *connected* if there do not exist two disjoint, non-empty, open sets of X whose union equals X. Obviously, the topological space X is connected if and only if there do not exist two disjoint, non-empty, closed sets of X whose union equals X. A subset of a topological space is said to be *connected* if it becomes a connected topological space when given the induced topology. Let x be an element of X. The *component* of x in X is defined as the union of all connected subsets of X containing x. It is easily seen that each component is connected and therefore the component of x in X is the largest connected subset of X containing x.

Let a topological space X be given. The topological space X is said to be *path-connected* if every two elements of X can be joined by a path $f : [0,1] \to X$. A subset of a topological space is said to be *path-connected* if it becomes a path-connected topological space when given the induced topology. Let x be an element of X. The *path-component* of x in X is defined as the union of all path-connected subsets of X containing x. It is easily seen that each path-component is path-connected and therefore the path-component of x in X is the largest path-connected subset of X containing x.

Theorem 2.3.5
Let a topological space X and an element x of X be given. Then the path-component of x in X is contained in the component of x in X.
See Munkres (1975), Theorem 4.3, page 162.

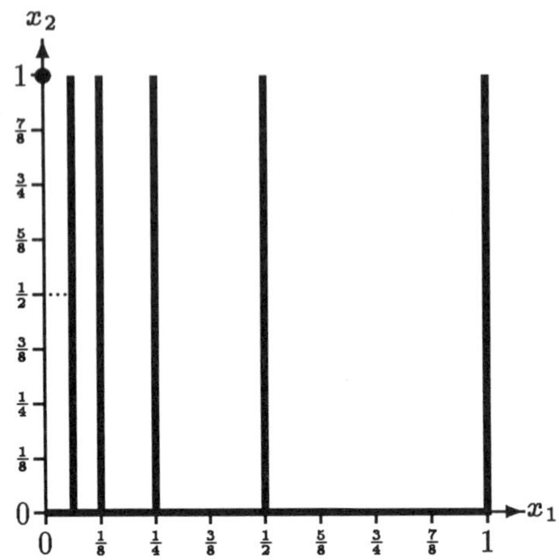

Figure 2.3.1. A set that is connected but not path-connected.

The following example shows that the converse of Theorem 2.3.5 is not true.

Example 2.3.6
Let the subset S of $\mathbb{R}^2$ be defined by

$$\begin{aligned} S = & \left\{ x \in \mathbb{R}^2 \middle| \, 0 \le x_1 \le 1 \text{ and } x_2 = 0 \right\} \\ & \cup \left\{ x \in \mathbb{R}^2 \middle| \, \exists n \in \mathbb{Z}_+, \; x_1 = 2^{-n}, \text{ and } 0 \le x_2 \le 1 \right\} \\ & \cup \left\{ (0,1)^\top \right\}. \end{aligned}$$

In Figure 2.3.1 the set S is depicted. In Munkres (1975), Example 7, page 156, it is shown that the set S is connected, but not path-connected.

Let a topological space X and an element x of X be given. The *quasi-component* of x in X is defined as the intersection of all subsets of X containing x that are both open and closed in X.

Theorem 2.3.7
Let a topological space X and an element x of X be given. Then the component of x in X is contained in the quasi-component of x in X.
See Munkres (1975), Exercise 3, page 163.

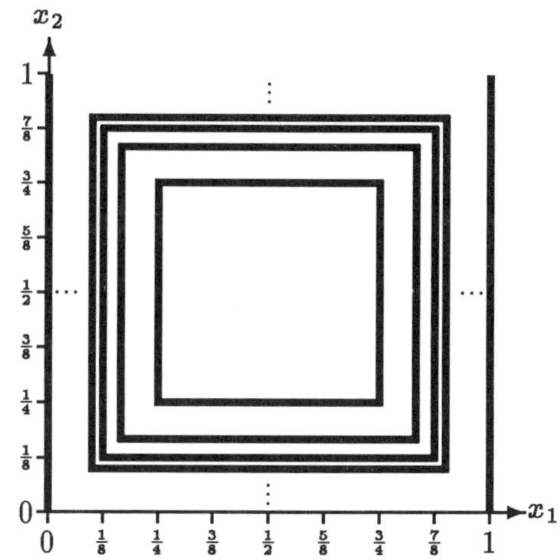

Figure 2.3.2. A set S with the component of $(0,0)^\top$ in S being a proper subset of the quasi-component of $(0,0)^\top$ in S.

The following example is a modified version of Steen and Seebach Jr. (1970), Example 115, page 137, and it shows that the component of an element might be different from its quasi-component.

Example 2.3.8
Let

$$\underline{S} = \left\{ x \in \mathbb{R}^2 \,\middle|\, x_1 = 0 \text{ and } 0 \leq x_2 \leq 1 \right\},$$
$$\overline{S} = \left\{ x \in \mathbb{R}^2 \,\middle|\, x_1 = 1 \text{ and } 0 \leq x_2 \leq 1 \right\},$$

and, for every $n \in \mathbb{N}$, let S^n be a square with center $(\frac{1}{2}, \frac{1}{2})$ and diameter $\frac{n}{n+1}$, i.e. S^n is the set of elements x of $\mathbb{R}^2$ satisfying $|x_1 - \frac{1}{2}| \leq \frac{n}{2n+2}$ and $|x_2 - \frac{1}{2}| \leq \frac{n}{2n+2}$, while $|x_1 - \frac{1}{2}| = \frac{n}{2n+2}$ or $|x_2 - \frac{1}{2}| = \frac{n}{2n+2}$. Let the set S be defined by $S = \underline{S} \cup \overline{S} \cup (\cup_{n \in \mathbb{N}} S^n)$. The set S is depicted in Figure 2.3.2. Since, for every $n \in \mathbb{N}$, the set $\cup_{j \in I_n} S^j$ is open and closed in S, it holds that the quasi-component of $(0,0)^\top$ in S is a subset of $\underline{S} \cup \overline{S}$. Clearly, the set $\underline{S}$ is the component of $(0,0)^\top$ in S. Therefore, by Theorem 2.3.7, it holds that the set $\underline{S}$ is a subset of the quasi-component of $(0,0)^\top$ in S. Since every open and closed set in S containing $\underline{S}$ also contains $\overline{S}$, it holds that the quasi-component of $(0,0)^\top$ in S is given by the set $\underline{S} \cup \overline{S}$.

Let X be a set and let $\mathcal{X}$ be a collection of subsets of X. The collection $\mathcal{X}$ is called a *partition* of X if the sets in $\mathcal{X}$ are *pairwise disjoint*, i.e. the intersection of any two different sets in $\mathcal{X}$ is empty, and the union over all sets in $\mathcal{X}$ equals X. If X is a topological space, then the collection of components, the collection of path-components, and the collection of quasi-components of X are partitions of X. A partition of a topological space X is said to be *locally finite* if for every $x \in X$ there exists an open set O of X containing x such that the collection of sets in the partition having a non-empty intersection with O is finite.

Let a subset S of $\mathbb{R}^m$ be given. The set S is said to be *bounded from below* if there exists $\overline{n} \in \mathbb{N}$ such that, for every $x \in S$, $x \geq -\overline{n}1^m$. The set S is said to be *bounded from above* if there exists $\overline{n} \in \mathbb{N}$ such that, for every $x \in S$, $x \leq \overline{n}1^m$. The set S is said to be *bounded* if it is both bounded from below and bounded from above. A function f from a set X into S is said to be *bounded* if $f(X)$ is bounded. It is well-known that a bounded sequence in $\mathbb{R}^m$ has a convergent subsequence. A partition of the set S is said to be *bounded* if every set in the partition is bounded.

Let a subset S of $\mathbb{R}^m$ be given. Then the set S is compact if and only if S is bounded and closed, see for example Armstrong (1983), Theorem 3.1, page 44. Moreover, the set S is compact if and only if every sequence $(x^n)_{n \in \mathbb{N}}$ in S has a subsequence converging to an element of S, see for instance Munkres (1975), Theorem 7.4, page 181. The following two theorems are also helpful in verifying the compactness of a set.

Theorem 2.3.9
Let S be a closed set of a compact topological space. Then the set S is compact.
See Armstrong (1983), Theorem 3.5, page 47.

Theorem 2.3.10
Let S be a compact subset of a Hausdorff space. Then the set S is closed.
See Armstrong (1983), Theorem 3.6, page 47.

The following three theorems are very helpful in showing the connectedness of a set.

Theorem 2.3.11
Let S be a connected subset of a topological space. If $S \subset T \subset \mathrm{cl}(S)$, then the set T is connected.
See Munkres (1975), Theorem 1.4, page 149.

Theorem 2.3.12
Let S be a subset of $\mathbb{R}$. Then the set S is connected if and only if S is an interval.
See Armstrong (1983), Theorem 3.19, page 57.

Theorem 2.3.13
Let X and Y be topological spaces and let $f : X \to Y$ be a continuous function. Then $f(X)$ is compact if the set X is compact, $f(X)$ is connected if X is connected, and $f(X)$ is path-connected if X is path-connected.
See Munkres (1975), Theorem 5.5, page 167, Theorem 1.5, page 149, and the remark on the top of page 156.

Let a set X, a subset S of X, and a function $f : X \to \mathbb{R}$ be given. An element $\overline{x}$ of S is said to *minimize* f on S, $\overline{x}$ is called a *minimizer* of f on S, and $f(\overline{x})$ is called the *minimum* of f on S if $f(\overline{x}) \leq f(x)$, $\forall x \in S$. An element $\overline{x}$ of S is said to *maximize* f on S, $\overline{x}$ is called a *maximizer* of f on S, and $f(\overline{x})$ is called the *maximum* of f on S if $f(\overline{x}) \geq f(x)$, $\forall x \in S$. Using Theorem 2.3.13 it is not difficult to show the following result.

Theorem 2.3.14
Let X be a non-empty, compact topological space and let $f : X \to \mathbb{R}$ be a continuous function. Then there exists a minimum and a maximum of f on X.
See Munkres (1975), Theorem 6.4, page 175.

The topological space X is said to be *locally compact* if for every $x \in X$ there exists an open set O of X such that $x \in O$ and $\mathrm{cl}(O)$ is compact. Notice that every compact subset of $\mathbb{R}^m$ is locally compact, but also that every open set of $\mathbb{R}^m$ is locally compact.

Theorem 2.3.15
Every locally compact Hausdorff space is a Baire space.
See Dugundji (1965), Theorem 10.1, page 249.

Let X and Y be locally compact topological spaces. A continuous function $f : X \to Y$ is *proper* if the inverse image of every compact subset of Y by f is a compact subset of X.

2.4 VECTOR SPACES

For any result mentioned in this section without reference, see for instance Edwards (1973) or Strang (1980).

To formulate Theorem 2.6.2, the concept of a vector space is needed.

Definition 2.4.1 (Vector space)
A set V together with a function $f : V \times V \to V$, written as $f(v^1, v^2) = v^1 + v^2$, $\forall (v^1, v^2) \in V \times V$, and a function $g : \mathbb{R} \times V \to V$, written as $g(\lambda, v) = \lambda v$, $\forall \lambda \in \mathbb{R}$, $\forall v \in V$, is a vector space *if*

$$
\begin{array}{ll}
\forall v^1, v^2, v^3 \in V, & (v^1 + v^2) + v^3 = v^1 + (v^2 + v^3), \\
\exists \underline{0} \in V,\ \forall v \in V, & v + \underline{0} = v, \\
\forall v^1 \in V,\ \exists v^2 \in V, & v^1 + v^2 = \underline{0}, \\
\forall v^1, v^2 \in V, & v^1 + v^2 = v^2 + v^1, \\
\forall v \in V,\ \forall \lambda^1, \lambda^2 \in \mathbb{R}, & (\lambda^1 \lambda^2) v = \lambda^1 (\lambda^2 v), \\
\forall v^1, v^2 \in V,\ \forall \lambda \in \mathbb{R}, & \lambda (v^1 + v^2) = \lambda v^1 + \lambda v^2, \\
\forall v \in V,\ \forall \lambda^1, \lambda^2 \in \mathbb{R}, & (\lambda^1 + \lambda^2) v = \lambda^1 v + \lambda^2 v, \\
\forall v \in V, & 1v = v.
\end{array}
$$

Let a vector space V together with the functions f and g be given. The function f defines *addition* in V and the function g defines *multiplication* in V. In subsets of $\mathbb{R}^m$ addition and multiplication is always defined as in Section 2.2. Then $\mathbb{R}^m$ is a vector space.

Let V be a vector space. The elements $v^1, \ldots, v^m$ of V are said to be *independent* if $\lambda^i \in \mathbb{R}$, $\forall i \in I_m$, and $\sum_{i \in I_m} \lambda^i v^i = \underline{0}$ implies $\lambda^i = 0$, $\forall i \in I_m$. A subset S of V is said to be *independent* if every finite number of pairwise different elements of S is independent. An independent subset S of V not being a proper subset of another independent subset of V is called a *basis* for V. If a finite set S with cardinality k is a basis for V, then it can be shown that every basis for V has k elements. In this case the integer k is called the *dimension* of V and the vector space V is said to be *k-dimensional*.

A vector space V, being a subset of the Euclidean space $\mathbb{R}^m$, is k-dimensional for some $k \in \mathbb{Z}_+$ with $k \leq m$. Notice that the m-dimensional Euclidean space $\mathbb{R}^m$ has dimension m and that the set $\{e^m(1), \ldots, e^m(m)\}$ is a basis for $\mathbb{R}^m$.

Let a vector space V and a subset S of V be given. The set S is called a *cone* if $v \in S$ implies $\lambda v \in S$, $\forall \lambda \in \mathbb{R}_+$. The set S is said to be *convex* if $v^1, v^2 \in S$

implies $\lambda v^1 + (1-\lambda)v^2 \in S$, $\forall \lambda \in [0,1]$. The element $\lambda v^1 + (1-\lambda)v^2$ is said to be a *convex combination* of v^1 and v^2 with *weights* λ and $(1-\lambda)$. Clearly, the intersection of convex sets is a convex set. The *convex hull* of S, denoted $\text{co}(S)$, is defined as the smallest convex subset of V that contains S, i.e. the intersection of all convex subsets of V containing S.

Let two vector spaces V and W be given. A function $f : V \to W$ is said to be *linear* if $f(v^1 + v^2) = f(v^1) + f(v^2)$, $\forall v^1, v^2 \in V$, and $f(\lambda v) = \lambda f(v)$, $\forall \lambda \in \mathbb{R}$, $\forall v \in V$. A function $f : V \to W$ is said to be *affine* if there exists an element $\overline{w}$ of W such that the function $g : V \to W$, defined by $g(v) = f(v) - \overline{w}$, $\forall v \in V$, is linear. Let S be a subset of V and let T be a subset of W. A function $f : S \to T$ is said to be *linear* if it is the restriction to S of a linear function from V into W and f is said to be *affine* if it is the restriction to S of an affine function from V into W. A function $f : S \to T$ is said to be *piecewise linear* if there exists a collection of sets being a locally finite partition of S such that f restricted to any set of this partition is affine.

For $m, n \in \mathbb{N}$, an $m \times n$ *matrix* M is a rectangular array of m rows and n columns of real numbers,

$$M = \begin{bmatrix} M_{11} & \cdots & M_{1n} \\ \vdots & & \vdots \\ M_{m1} & \cdots & M_{mn} \end{bmatrix}.$$

If $m = n$, then M is called a *square matrix*. Notice that a vector $x \in \mathbb{R}^m$ is an $m \times 1$ matrix. The $m \times n$ matrix M satisfying $M_{ij} = 0$, $\forall i \in I_m$, $\forall j \in I_n$, is denoted by $0^{m \times n}$.

Let an $m \times n$ matrix M be given. For every $i \in I_m$, the vector $(M_{i1}, \ldots, M_{in})$ is called the i-th *row* of M and is denoted by $M_{i\cdot}$, and, for every $j \in I_n$, the vector $(M_{1j}, \ldots, M_{mj})^\top$ is called the j-th *column* of M and is denoted by $M_{\cdot j}$. The maximal number of independent columns of the matrix M equals the maximal number of independent rows of M and is called the *rank* of M.

The *sum* of two $m \times n$ matrices M^1 and M^2, denoted by $M^1 + M^2$, is the $m \times n$ matrix M, defined by $M_{ij} = M^1_{ij} + M^2_{ij}$, $\forall i \in I_m$, $\forall j \in I_n$. The *product* of an $m^1 \times n$ matrix M^1 and an $n \times m^2$ matrix M^2, denoted by $M^1 M^2$, is the $m^1 \times m^2$ matrix M, defined by $M_{i^1 i^2} = \sum_{j \in I_n} M^1_{i^1 j} M^2_{j i^2}$, $\forall i^1 \in I_{m^1}$, $\forall i^2 \in I_{m^2}$.

The $m \times m$ matrix M, defined by $M_{ii} = 1$, $\forall i \in I_m$, and $M_{i^1 i^2} = 0$, $\forall i^1, i^2 \in I_m$ with $i^1 \neq i^2$, is called the *m-dimensional identity matrix* and is denoted by I^m. An $m \times m$ matrix M is said to be *invertible* if there exists an $m \times m$ matrix

M' such that $MM' = I^m$ and $M'M = I^m$. It is easily shown that there exists at most one such matrix M', called the *inverse* of M and denoted by M^{-1}. It is well-known that an $m \times m$ matrix M is invertible if and only if it has rank m.

The *determinant* of a square matrix M, denoted by $\det(M)$, is defined inductively as follows. The determinant of a 1×1 matrix M is the real number M. For an $m \times m$ matrix M, for $i^1, i^2 \in I_m$, let $M^{i^1 i^2}$ denote the $(m-1) \times (m-1)$ matrix obtained by deleting the i^1-th row, $M_{i^1 \cdot}$, and the i^2-th column, $M_{\cdot i^2}$, of M. Let i' be an element of I_m. Then the *determinant* of an $m \times m$ matrix M satisfies

$$\det(M) = \sum_{i \in I_m} (-1)^{i'+i} M_{i'i} \det\left(M^{i'i}\right).$$

It can be shown that the $m \times m$ matrix M is invertible if and only if $\det(M) \neq 0$.

Let M be an $m \times n$ matrix. The set $\{x \in \mathbb{R}^m \mid \exists y \in \mathbb{R}^n,\ x = My\}$ is called the *column space* of M. The set $\{y \in \mathbb{R}^n \mid My = 0^m\}$ is called the *nullspace* of M. If the matrix M has rank k, then the column space of M is a k-dimensional vector space and the nullspace of M is an $(n-k)$-dimensional vector space.

Finally, some results concerning the representation of a linear function by a matrix are presented. It can be shown that a function $f : \mathbb{R}^m \to \mathbb{R}^n$ is linear if and only if there exists an $n \times m$ matrix M such that $f(x) = Mx$, $\forall x \in \mathbb{R}^m$. It is easily shown that the matrix M is uniquely determined.

For $m \in \mathbb{N}$, let V be an m-dimensional vector space and let $\{v^1, \ldots, v^m\}$ be a basis for V. It is easily verified that for every $v \in V$ there exist unique real numbers λ^i, $\forall i \in I_m$, such that $v = \sum_{i \in I_m} \lambda^i v^i$. Therefore, every $v \in V$ can be identified with a unique vector $(\lambda^1, \ldots, \lambda^m)^\top \in \mathbb{R}^m$ and the vector space V can be identified with $\mathbb{R}^m$. For $n \in \mathbb{N}$, let W be an n-dimensional vector space and let $\{w^1, \ldots, w^n\}$ be a basis for W. As before, every element w of W can be identified with a unique vector $(\mu^1, \ldots, \mu^n) \in \mathbb{R}^n$ and W can be identified with $\mathbb{R}^n$. Let f be a function from V into W. The function f is said to be *represented* by the $n \times m$ matrix M if $v \in V$ is identified with $\lambda \in \mathbb{R}^m$ and $\mu = M\lambda$ implies that $f(v) \in W$ is identified with $\mu \in \mathbb{R}^n$. The matrix M is easily shown to be unique. It can be shown that the function f is linear if and only if there exists an $n \times m$ matrix M representing f, see Mas-Colell (1985), Section B.3, page 14.

For $m \in \mathbb{N}$, let V be an m-dimensional vector space and let $f : V \to V$ be a linear function. Let a basis for V be given and let the function f be represented by the $m \times m$ matrix M. It can be shown that the determinant of M is independent of the choice of the basis for V, see Mas-Colell (1985), Section B.4, page 15. The *determinant* of the function f is defined as the determinant of the matrix M.

2.5 RELATIONS AND CORRESPONDENCES

Let X and Y be two sets. A *relation* φ from X into Y associates with every element x of X a subset $\varphi(x)$ of Y, and is denoted by $\varphi : X \to Y$. The set X is called the *domain* of φ. If x is an element of X, then $\varphi(x)$ is called the *image* by φ of x. Let a subset S of X and a subset T of Y be given. The *image* by φ of S, denoted by $\varphi(S)$, is defined by

$$\varphi(S) = \{y \in Y \mid \exists x \in S,\ y \in \varphi(x)\}.$$

The image by φ of the domain of φ is called the *range* of φ. The *inverse image* by φ of T, denoted by $\varphi^{-1}(T)$, is defined by

$$\varphi^{-1}(T) = \{x \in X \mid \varphi(x) \cap T \neq \emptyset\}.$$

The relation $\mu : S \to Y$, defined by $\mu(x) = \varphi(x)$, $\forall x \in S$, is denoted by $\varphi_{|S}$, and is called the *restriction of φ to S*. The set

$$\{(x, y) \in X \times Y \mid y \in \varphi(x)\}$$

is called the *graph* of φ. If Y is a topological space and $\varphi(x)$ is compact for every $x \in X$, then the relation φ is said to be *compact-valued*. If Y is a topological space and $\varphi(x)$ is closed for every $x \in X$, then the relation φ is said to be *closed-valued*. If Y is a vector space and $\varphi(x)$ is convex for every $x \in X$, then the relation φ is said to be *convex-valued*.

Let sets X^1, X^2, X^3 and relations $\varphi^1 : X^1 \to X^2$ and $\varphi^2 : X^2 \to X^3$ be given. Then the *composition* of φ^1 and φ^2, denoted by $\varphi^2 \circ \varphi^1$, is the relation from X^1 into X^3 defined by $\varphi^2 \circ \varphi^1(x) = \varphi^2(\varphi^1(x))$, $\forall x \in X^1$.

A *binary relation* on a set X is defined as a relation from X into itself.

Definition 2.5.1 (Properties of binary relations)
A binary relation φ on a set X is

reflexive *if, for every* $x \in X$, $x \in \varphi(x)$,
transitive *if, for every* $x^1, x^2, x^3 \in X$, $x^2 \in \varphi(x^1)$ *and* $x^3 \in \varphi(x^2)$ *implies* $x^3 \in \varphi(x^1)$,
complete *if, for every* $x^1, x^2 \in X$, $x^2 \in \varphi(x^1)$ *or* $x^1 \in \varphi(x^2)$,
symmetric *if, for every* $x^1, x^2 \in X$, $x^2 \in \varphi(x^1)$ *implies* $x^1 \in \varphi(x^2)$,
anti-symmetric *if, for every* $x^1, x^2 \in X$, $x^2 \in \varphi(x^1)$ *and* $x^1 \in \varphi(x^2)$ *implies* $x^1 = x^2$.
a pre-ordering *if it is reflexive and transitive,*
an ordering *if it is reflexive, transitive, and anti-symmetric,*
an equivalence relation *if it is reflexive, symmetric, and transitive.*

Notice that a complete binary relation is also reflexive.

Let φ be a binary relation on a set X, let μ be a binary relation on a set Y, and let $f : X \to Y$ be a function. Let both φ and μ be a pre-ordering. The function f is said to be *decreasing* if $x^2 \in \varphi(x^1)$ and $x^1 \in \varphi(x^2)$ implies $f(x^2) \in \mu(f(x^1))$ and $f(x^1) \in \mu(f(x^2))$, and if $x^2 \in \varphi(x^1)$ and $x^1 \notin \varphi(x^2)$ implies $f(x^1) \in \mu(f(x^2))$ and $f(x^2) \notin \mu(f(x^1))$. The function f is said to be *non-increasing* if $x^2 \in \varphi(x^1)$ implies $f(x^1) \in \mu(f(x^2))$. The function f is said to be *non-decreasing* if $x^2 \in \varphi(x^1)$ implies $f(x^2) \in \mu(f(x^1))$. The function f is said to be *increasing* if $x^2 \in \varphi(x^1)$ and $x^1 \in \varphi(x^2)$ implies $f(x^2) \in \mu(f(x^1))$ and $f(x^1) \in \mu(f(x^2))$, and if $x^2 \in \varphi(x^1)$ and $x^1 \notin \varphi(x^2)$ implies $f(x^2) \in \mu(f(x^1))$ and $f(x^1) \notin \mu(f(x^2))$.

Let φ be a binary relation on a set X and let S be a subset of X. Then an element $\underline{x}$ of X is called a *lower bound* of S for φ if there exists no $x \in S$ such that $\underline{x} \in \varphi(x)$ and $x \notin \varphi(\underline{x})$. A lower bound $\underline{x}$ of S for φ is called an *infimum* of S for φ if there exists no lower bound $\widehat{x}$ of S for φ satisfying $\widehat{x} \in \varphi(\underline{x})$ and $\underline{x} \notin \varphi(\widehat{x})$. The set of infima of S for φ is denoted by $\inf(S)$. If $\underline{x} \in \inf(S) \cap S$, then the element $\underline{x}$ is called a *minimal element* or *minimum* of S for φ. The set of minima of S for φ is denoted by $\min(S)$. Similarly, $\overline{x} \in X$ is called an *upper bound* of S for φ if there exists no $x \in S$ such that $x \in \varphi(\overline{x})$ and $\overline{x} \notin \varphi(x)$. An upper bound $\overline{x}$ of S for φ is called a *supremum* if there exists no upper bound $\widehat{x}$ of S for φ satisfying $\overline{x} \in \varphi(\widehat{x})$ and $\widehat{x} \notin \varphi(\overline{x})$. The set of suprema of S for φ is denoted by $\sup(S)$. If $\overline{x} \in \sup(S) \cap S$, then the element $\overline{x}$ is called a *maximal element* or *maximum* of S for φ. The set of maxima of S for φ is denoted by $\max(S)$. The element $\overline{x}$ of S is called a *worst element* of S for φ if $x \in \varphi(\overline{x})$ for every $x \in S$. The element $\overline{x}$ of S is called a *best element* of S for φ if $\overline{x} \in \varphi(x)$ for every $x \in S$.

Notice that $\leq$ induces a binary relation φ on $\mathbb{R}^m$, defined by $\varphi(x) = [x, \rightarrow)$, $\forall x \in \mathbb{R}^m$. The binary relation φ is a pre-ordering but it is not complete unless $m = 1$. If S is a subset of $\mathbb{R}^m$, then $\inf(S)$ denotes the infimum of S for $\leq$, $\min(S)$ denotes the minimum of S for $\leq$, $\sup(S)$ denotes the supremum of S for $\leq$, and $\max(S)$ denotes the maximum of S for $\leq$ if the infimum, minimum, supremum, and maximum, respectively, exists. In this case $\inf(S)$, $\min(S)$, $\sup(S)$, and $\max(S)$, respectively, are uniquely determined and therefore are assumed to denote an element instead of a set. If S is a finite subset of $\mathbb{R}^m$, then $\inf(S)$ is obtained by taking the componentwise minimum of the elements of S, and $\sup(S)$ is obtained by taking the componentwise maximum of the elements of S. The *infinity norm* of an element x of $\mathbb{R}^m$ is defined by $\|x\|_\infty = \max(\{|x_i| \mid i \in I_m\})$.

Notice that $\subset$ induces a binary relation φ on $2^{\mathbb{R}^m}$, defined by $\varphi(S) = \{T \in 2^{\mathbb{R}^m} \mid S \subset T\}$, $\forall S \in 2^{\mathbb{R}^m}$. The binary relation φ is a pre-ordering, but it is not complete. If a member of a subset of $2^{\mathbb{R}^m}$ is said to be *minimal* or *maximal*, then it is a minimum or a maximum of this subset for φ.

A relation φ from a set X into a set Y such that $\varphi(x) \neq \emptyset$ for every $x \in X$ is called a *correspondence*. Notice that a correspondence $\varphi : X \rightarrow Y$ can be considered as a function if $\varphi(x)$ contains exactly one element for every $x \in X$.

Now upper hemi-continuity of a correspondence is defined.

Definition 2.5.2 (Upper hemi-continuity)
Let topological spaces X and Y and an element $\overline{x}$ of X be given. A correspondence $\varphi : X \rightarrow Y$ is upper hemi-continuous *at $\overline{x}$ if for every open set O' of Y that satisfies $\varphi(\overline{x}) \subset O'$ there exists an open set O of X containing $\overline{x}$ such that $\varphi(O) \subset O'$. The correspondence φ is* upper hemi-continuous *if it is upper hemi-continuous at every $x \in X$.*

Notice that a correspondence being both upper hemi-continuous and a function is a continuous function.

Theorem 2.5.3
Let topological spaces X and Y and an upper hemi-continuous correspondence $\varphi : X \rightarrow Y$ be given. If T is a closed set of Y, then $\varphi^{-1}(T)$ is a closed set of X.
See Hildenbrand (1974), Proposition 1, page 22.

Theorem 2.5.4
Let compact topological spaces X and Y and a compact-valued, upper hemi-continuous correspondence $\varphi : X \rightarrow Y$ be given. If S is a compact subset of X, then $\varphi(S)$ is a compact subset of Y.
See Hildenbrand (1974), Proposition 3, page 24.

The following theorem yields as a corollary that the composition of two continuous functions is continuous.

Theorem 2.5.5
Let X^1, X^2, and X^3 be topological spaces and let $\varphi^1 : X^1 \rightarrow X^2$ and $\varphi^2 : X^2 \rightarrow X^3$ be upper hemi-continuous correspondences. Then the correspondence $\varphi^2 \circ \varphi^1 : X^1 \rightarrow X^3$ is upper hemi-continuous.
See Hildenbrand (1974), Corollary of Proposition 1, page 22.

Often it is possible to give easy characterizations of upper hemi-continuity.

Theorem 2.5.6
Let a subset S of $\mathbb{R}^m$, a subset T of $\mathbb{R}^n$, an element $\overline{x}$ of S, and a compact-valued correspondence $\varphi : S \rightarrow T$ be given. Then the correspondence φ is upper hemi-continuous at $\overline{x}$ if and only if for every sequence $(x^n)_{n \in \mathbb{N}}$ in S converging to $\overline{x}$ and every sequence $(y^n)_{n \in \mathbb{N}}$ in T with $y^n \in \varphi(x^n)$, $\forall n \in \mathbb{N}$, there exists a subsequence of $(y^n)_{n \in \mathbb{N}}$ that converges to some element of $\varphi(\overline{x})$.
See Hildenbrand (1974), Theorem 1, page 24.

Theorem 2.5.7
Let a subset S of $\mathbb{R}^m$, a compact subset T of $\mathbb{R}^n$, an element $\overline{x}$ of S, and a compact-valued correspondence $\varphi : S \rightarrow T$ be given. Then the correspondence φ is upper hemi-continuous at $\overline{x}$ if and only if for every sequence $(x^n)_{n \in \mathbb{N}}$ in S converging to $\overline{x}$ and every sequence $(y^n)_{n \in \mathbb{N}}$ in T with $y^n \in \varphi(x^n)$, $\forall n \in \mathbb{N}$, converging to $\overline{y} \in \mathbb{R}^n$ it holds that $\overline{y} \in \varphi(\overline{x})$. The correspondence φ is upper hemi-continuous if and only if the graph of φ is closed in $S \times T$.
See Debreu (1959), 1.8.d, page 17.

The following results are also often helpful in proving the upper hemi-continuity of correspondences.

Theorem 2.5.8
Let a subset S of $\mathbb{R}^m$, a subset T of $\mathbb{R}^n$, and a compact-valued, upper hemi-continuous correspondence φ from S into T be given. Then the correspondence $\mu : S \to T$, defined by $\mu(x) = \mathrm{co}(\varphi(x))$, $\forall x \in S$, is a compact-valued, convex-valued, upper hemi-continuous correspondence.
See Hildenbrand (1974), Proposition 6, page 26.

Theorem 2.5.9
Let a subset S of $\mathbb{R}^m$, a subset T of $\mathbb{R}^n$, and closed-valued, upper hemi-continuous correspondences φ^1 and φ^2 from S into T be given such that $\varphi^1(x) \cap \varphi^2(x) \neq \emptyset$, $\forall x \in S$. Then the correspondence $\varphi : S \to T$, defined by $\varphi(x) = \varphi^1(x) \cap \varphi^2(x)$, $\forall x \in S$, is upper hemi-continuous.
See Hildenbrand (1974), Proposition 2, page 24.

Theorem 2.5.10
Let a subset S of $\mathbb{R}^m$ and, for $k \in \mathbb{N}$, for every $i \in I_k$, a subset T^i of $\mathbb{R}^n$ be given. Let $\varphi^i : S \to T^i$, $\forall i \in I_k$, be a compact-valued, upper hemi-continuous correspondence. Then the correspondence $\varphi : S \to \prod_{i \in I_k} T^i$, defined by $\varphi(x) = \prod_{i \in I_k} \varphi^i(x)$, $\forall x \in S$, is upper hemi-continuous. Moreover, the correspondence $\mu : S \to \sum_{i \in I_k} T^i$, defined by $\mu(x) = \sum_{i \in I_k} \varphi^i(x)$, $\forall x \in S$, is upper hemi-continuous.
See Hildenbrand (1974), Proposition 4, page 25, and Proposition 5, page 25.

Next, lower hemi-continuity of a correspondence is defined.

Definition 2.5.11 (Lower hemi-continuity)
Let topological spaces X and Y and an element $\overline{x}$ of X be given. A correspondence $\varphi : X \to Y$ is lower hemi-continuous *at $\overline{x}$ if for every open set O' of Y that satisfies $\varphi(\overline{x}) \cap O' \neq \emptyset$ there exists an open set O of X containing $\overline{x}$ such that $\varphi(x) \cap O' \neq \emptyset$, $\forall x \in O$. The correspondence φ is* lower hemi-continuous *if it is lower hemi-continuous at every $x \in X$.*

Theorem 2.5.12
Let X^1, X^2, and X^3 be topological spaces and let $\varphi^1 : X^1 \to X^2$ and $\varphi^2 : X^2 \to X^3$ be lower hemi-continuous correspondences. Then the correspondence $\varphi^2 \circ \varphi^1 : X^1 \to X^3$ is lower hemi-continuous.
See Hildenbrand (1974), Proposition 7, page 27, and Corollary of Proposition 1, page 22.

Often it is possible to give easy characterizations of lower hemi-continuity.

Theorem 2.5.13
Let a subset S of $\mathbb{R}^m$, a subset T of $\mathbb{R}^n$, and an element $\overline{x}$ of S be given. Then the correspondence φ is lower hemi-continuous at $\overline{x}$ if and only if for every sequence $(x^n)_{n\in\mathbb{N}}$ in S converging to $\overline{x}$ and for every element $\overline{y}$ of $\varphi(\overline{x})$ there exists a sequence $(y^n)_{n\in\mathbb{N}}$ in T such that $y^n \in \varphi(x^n)$, $\forall n \in \mathbb{N}$, and $y^n \to \overline{y}$.
See Hildenbrand (1974), Theorem 2, page 27.

The following theorem is useful for showing the lower hemi-continuity of a correspondence.

Theorem 2.5.14
Let a subset S of $\mathbb{R}^m$ and, for $k \in \mathbb{N}$, for every $i \in I_k$, a subset T^i of $\mathbb{R}^n$ be given. Let $\varphi^i : S \to T^i$, $\forall i \in I_k$, be a lower hemi-continuous correspondence. Then the correspondence $\varphi : S \to \prod_{i\in I_k} T^i$, defined by $\varphi(x) = \prod_{i\in I_k} \varphi^i(x)$, $\forall x \in S$, is lower hemi-continuous. Moreover, the correspondence $\mu : S \to \sum_{i\in I_k} T^i$, defined by $\mu(x) = \sum_{i\in I_k} \varphi^i(x)$, $\forall x \in S$, is lower hemi-continuous.
See Hildenbrand (1974), Proposition 8, page 27, and Proposition 9, page 28.

Finally, continuity of a correspondence is defined.

Definition 2.5.15 (Continuity)
Let topological spaces X and Y and an element $\overline{x}$ of X be given. A correspondence $\varphi : X \to Y$ is continuous *at $\overline{x}$ if it is both upper and lower hemi-continuous at $\overline{x}$. The correspondence φ is* continuous *if it is continuous at every $x \in X$.*

The following result shows that an upper hemi-continuous correspondence is continuous at many elements.

Theorem 2.5.16
Let a subset S of $\mathbb{R}^m$, a subset T of $\mathbb{R}^n$, and a compact-valued, upper hemi-continuous correspondence $\varphi : S \to T$ be given. Then there exists a residual set in S such that the correspondence φ is continuous at every element of that set.
See Fort (1949), Theorem 3, page 239, and Dierker (1974), Theorem 8.5, page 84.

The following theorem is known as the *maximum theorem.*

Theorem 2.5.17 (Maximum theorem)
Let a subset S of $\mathbb{R}^m$, a subset T of $\mathbb{R}^n$, and a continuous, compact-valued correspondence $\varphi : S \rightarrow T$ be given. Let $f : S \times T \rightarrow \mathbb{R}$ be a continuous function. The relation $\mu : S \rightarrow T$ is defined by $\mu(x) = \{\bar{y} \in \varphi(x) \mid f(x, \bar{y}) \geq f(x, y),\ \forall y \in \varphi(x)\}$, $\forall x \in S$, and the relation $g : S \rightarrow \mathbb{R}$ is defined by $g(x) = \{f(x, y) \mid y \in \mu(x)\}$, $\forall x \in S$. Then μ is an upper hemi-continuous, compact-valued correspondence and g is a continuous function.
See Hildenbrand (1974), Corollary of Theorem 3, page 30.

2.6 FIXED POINTS

Let φ be a relation from a set X into a set Y. The element x of X is called a *fixed point* of φ if $x \in \varphi(x)$.

Related to the concept of a fixed point is the notion of a zero point. Let φ be a relation from a set X into $\mathbb{R}^m$. The element x of X is called a *zero point* of φ if $0^m \in \varphi(x)$. As mentioned in Section 2.1 several fixed point theorems are essential for the theory developed in this monograph. The first one is known as *Kakutani's fixed point theorem.*

Theorem 2.6.1 (Kakutani's fixed point theorem)
Let S be a non-empty, compact, convex subset of $\mathbb{R}^m$ and let $\varphi : S \rightarrow S$ be a convex-valued correspondence such that the graph of φ is closed in $S \times S$. Then there exists an element x of S such that $x \in \varphi(x)$.
See Kakutani (1941), Theorem 1, page 457, and Corollary of Theorem 1, page 458.

Notice that by Theorem 2.5.7 the correspondence φ in Theorem 2.6.1 has a closed graph if and only if φ is a compact-valued, upper hemi-continuous correspondence. If the correspondence φ in Theorem 2.6.1 is a function, *Brouwer's fixed point theorem* is obtained, see Brouwer (1912).

A *linear topological space* is a Hausdorff space V with a vector space structure such that the functions $f : V \times V \rightarrow V$ and $g : \mathbb{R} \times V \rightarrow V$ given in Definition 2.4.1 are both continuous when the set $V \times V$ and the set $\mathbb{R} \times V$ is given the product topology. The following generalization of Kakutani's fixed point theorem is known as *Glicksberg's fixed point theorem.*

Theorem 2.6.2 (Glicksberg's fixed point theorem)
Let S be a non-empty, compact, convex subset of a linear topological space X and let $\varphi : S \rightarrow S$ be a convex-valued correspondence such that the graph of φ is closed in $S \times S$, where the set $S \times S$ is given the topology induced from the product topology on $X \times X$. Then there exists an element x of S such that $x \in \varphi(x)$.
See Glicksberg (1952), Theorem, page 171.

If the correspondence in Theorem 2.6.2 is a continuous function, then *Tychonoff's fixed point theorem* is obtained, see Tychonoff (1935).

Finally, an extension of *Browder's fixed point theorem* as formulated in Theorem 2 in Browder (1960) is given. Theorem 2.6.3 is a special case of Theorem 3 in Mas-Colell (1974a).

Theorem 2.6.3 (Browder's fixed point theorem)
Let S be a non-empty, compact, convex subset of $\mathbb{R}^m$ and let $\varphi : S\times[0,1] \rightarrow S$ be a convex-valued correspondence such that the graph of φ is closed in $S\times[0,1]\times S$. Then the set $F_\varphi = \{(x,\lambda) \in S \times [0,1] \mid x \in \varphi(x,\lambda)\}$ contains a connected set F^c_φ such that $(S \times \{0\}) \cap F^c_\varphi \neq \emptyset$ and $(S \times \{1\}) \cap F^c_\varphi \neq \emptyset$.
See Mas-Colell (1974a), Theorem 3, page 230.

Notice that by Theorem 2.5.7 the correspondence φ in Theorem 2.6.3 has a closed graph if and only if φ is a compact-valued, upper hemi-continuous correspondence.

2.7 TRIANGULATIONS

In this section some notions needed to describe simplicial algorithms are given. For more details concerning these notions the reader is referred to Todd (1976), Garcia and Zangwill (1981), and Doup (1988).

For $t \in \mathbb{Z}_+$, let points $x^1, \ldots, x^{t+1}$ of $\mathbb{R}^m$ be given. The element x of $\mathbb{R}^m$ is said to be an *affine combination* of these points if there exists $\lambda^i \in \mathbb{R}$, $\forall i \in I_{t+1}$, such that $x = \sum_{i\in I_{t+1}} \lambda^i x^i$ and $\sum_{i\in I_{t+1}} \lambda^i = 1$.

Let S be a convex subset of $\mathbb{R}^m$. The *affine hull* of S, denoted by aff(S), is defined as the set of all affine combinations of elements of S. It is easily shown that the set aff$(S) - S$ is a vector space. The *dimension* of S is defined as the dimension of the vector space aff$(S) - S$ and is denoted by $\dim(S)$. If $\dim(S) = k$, then the set S is said to be *k-dimensional.* Notice that $\dim(\Delta^{m-1}) = m-1$, $\dim(\dot{\Delta}^{m-1}) = m-1$, and $\dim(Q^m) = m$.

Let S be a convex subset of $\mathbb{R}^m$. The *relative boundary* of S, denoted by rb(S), is defined as the boundary of S in aff(S). Similarly, the *relative frontier* and the *relative interior* of S, denoted by rf(S) and ri(S), respectively, are defined as the frontier of S in aff(S) and the interior of S in aff(S), respectively. Notice that $\dot{\Delta}^{m-1} = \mathrm{ri}(\Delta^{m-1})$.

For $t \in \mathbb{Z}_+$, let points $x^1, \ldots, x^{t+1}$ of $\mathbb{R}^m$ be given. These points are said to be *affinely independent* if $\lambda^i \in \mathbb{R}$, $\forall i \in I_{t+1}$, $\sum_{i \in I_{t+1}} \lambda^i x^i = 0^m$, and $\sum_{i \in I_{t+1}} \lambda^i = 0$ implies $\lambda^i = 0$, $\forall i \in I_{t+1}$. A *t-simplex* in $\mathbb{R}^m$, denoted by σ, is defined as the convex hull of $t+1$ affinely independent points $x^1, \ldots, x^{t+1}$ of $\mathbb{R}^m$, so $\sigma = \mathrm{co}(\{x^1, \ldots, x^{t+1}\})$, and is also denoted by $\sigma(x^1, \ldots, x^{t+1})$. The points $x^1, \ldots, x^{t+1}$ are called the *vertices* of the t-simplex $\sigma(x^1, \ldots, x^{t+1})$. It is easily shown that the t-simplex $\sigma(x^1, \ldots, x^{t+1})$ has dimension t and is equal to the set

$$\left\{x \in \mathbb{R}^m \,\middle|\, \forall i \in I_{t+1},\ \exists \lambda^i \geq 0,\ \textstyle\sum_{i \in I_{t+1}} \lambda^i = 1 \text{ and } x = \sum_{i \in I_{t+1}} \lambda^i x^i \right\}.$$

A t-simplex is sometimes called a *simplex* if the dimension t is clear from the context.

A subset S of $\mathbb{R}^m$ is called a *polytope* if there exists $t \in \mathbb{Z}_+$ and there exist points $x^1, \ldots, x^{t+1}$ of $\mathbb{R}^m$ such that $S = \mathrm{co}(\{x^1, \ldots, x^{t+1}\})$. Obviously, a t-simplex is a polytope. A finite Cartesian product of simplices is called a *simplotope.* Clearly, also a simplotope is a polytope.

Given a t-simplex σ, its vertices $x^1, \ldots, x^{t+1}$ are uniquely determined. A $(t-1)$-simplex τ that is the convex hull of t vertices of a t-simplex $\sigma(x^1, \ldots, x^{t+1})$ is called a *facet* of σ. There is exactly one vertex of a t-simplex $\sigma(x^1, \ldots, x^{t+1})$, say x^i, for some $i \in I_{t+1}$, that is not a vertex of a facet τ of σ, and therefore τ is called the facet of σ *opposite* x^i, and, similarly, x^i is called the vertex of σ *opposite* τ. A k-simplex τ, for some $k \in I_t^0$, is called a *face* or *k-face* of a t-simplex σ if all the vertices of τ are vertices of σ. The *barycentre* of a t-simplex $\sigma(x^1, \ldots, x^{t+1})$ is given by $\sum_{i \in I_{t+1}} \frac{1}{t+1} x^i$ and is obviously an element of σ.

It is now possible to give the definition of a simplicial subdivision, also called triangulation, of a convex subset of $\mathbb{R}^m$.

Definition 2.7.1 (Simplicial subdivision or triangulation)
For $t \in \mathbb{Z}_+$, let S be a convex t-dimensional subset of $\mathbb{R}^m$. A collection Σ of t-simplices is a simplicial subdivision *or* triangulation *of S and the set S is said to be* triangulated *by Σ if*

1. $\cup_{\sigma \in \Sigma} \sigma = S$,
2. *the intersection of two t-simplices of Σ is either empty or a common face,*
3. *if a facet τ of a t-simplex $\sigma^1 \in \Sigma$ is a subset of $\mathrm{rb}(S)$, then there is no t-simplex $\sigma^2 \in \Sigma$ such that $\sigma^2 \neq \sigma^1$ and τ is a facet of σ^2, and if τ is not a subset of $\mathrm{rb}(S)$, then there is exactly one t-simplex $\sigma^2 \in \Sigma$ such that $\sigma^2 \neq \sigma^1$ and τ is also a facet of σ^2.*

Theorem 2.7.2
For $t \in \mathbb{Z}_+$, a triangulation of a compact, convex t-dimensional subset S of $\mathbb{R}^m$ contains a finite number of t-simplices.
See Todd (1976), Theorem 2.3, page 27.

Let the collection Σ be a triangulation of a compact, convex subset of $\mathbb{R}^m$. Then the *mesh size* of Σ, denoted by $\mathrm{mesh}(\Sigma)$, is defined by

$$\mathrm{mesh}(\Sigma) = \max\left(\{\|x^1 - x^2\|_\infty \,|\exists \sigma \in \Sigma,\ x^1, x^2 \in \sigma\}\right).$$

In Chapters 5 and 6 a triangulation of the set Q^m with an arbitrarily small chosen mesh size is needed. Here an example of such a triangulation is given. It is called the K-triangulation of Q^m and it is obtained by taking a subset of the K-triangulation of $\mathbb{R}^m$, introduced in Freudenthal (1942).

Definition 2.7.3 (K-triangulation of Q^m)
*Let some $n \in \mathbb{N}$ be given. The K-*triangulation *of Q^m with* grid size $\frac{1}{n}$ *is the collection of all m-simplices $\sigma_{(x^1,\pi)}$ with vertices $x^1, \ldots, x^{m+1} \in \mathbb{R}^m$ satisfying $x^1 = \sum_{i \in I_m} \frac{a^i}{n} e^m(i)$ for some $a^1, \ldots, a^m \in I^0_{n-1}$, $\pi : I_m \to I_m$ is a permutation, and $x^{i+1} = x^i + \frac{1}{n}\, e^m(\pi(i))$, $\forall i \in I_m$.*

It is easily verified that the mesh size of the K-triangulation of Q^m with grid size $\frac{1}{n}$ is equal to $\frac{1}{n}$. The K-triangulation of Q^2 with grid size $\frac{1}{6}$ is illustrated in Figure 2.7.1.

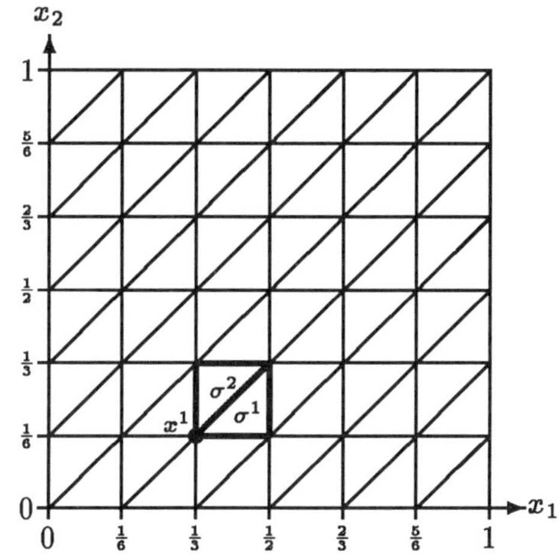

Figure 2.7.1. The K-triangulation of Q^2, $n = 6$.

Consider the point $x^1 = (\frac{1}{3}, \frac{1}{6})^\top$ in Figure 2.7.1. There are two possible permutations of the elements of I_2, $\pi^1 = (1, 2)$ and $\pi^2 = (2, 1)$. Therefore, the 2-simplex $\sigma^1 = \sigma_{(x^1, \pi^1)}$ has vertices $x^1 = (\frac{1}{3}, \frac{1}{6})^\top$, $x^2 = (\frac{1}{2}, \frac{1}{6})^\top$, and $x^3 = (\frac{1}{2}, \frac{1}{3})^\top$, and the 2-simplex $\sigma^2 = \sigma_{(x^1, \pi^2)}$ has vertices $x^1 = (\frac{1}{3}, \frac{1}{6})^\top$, $x^2 = (\frac{1}{3}, \frac{1}{3})^\top$, and $x^3 = (\frac{1}{2}, \frac{1}{3})^\top$.

In Chapter 10 a triangulation of the set Δ^{m-1}, for some $m \in \mathbb{N} \setminus \{1\}$, with an arbitrarily small chosen mesh size is needed. Here an example of such a triangulation is given. It is called the V-triangulation of Δ^{m-1} and is introduced in Doup and Talman (1987).

Let a point v of $\dot{\Delta}^{m-1}$ be given, i.e. $v \in \mathrm{ri}(\Delta^{m-1})$. The point v is considered to be fixed in the entire description of the V-triangulation of Δ^{m-1}. The *set of admissible sign vectors*, denoted by $\mathcal{S}$, is defined by

$$\mathcal{S} = \left\{ s \in \mathbb{S}^m \,\middle|\, \exists i^1 \in I_m,\ s_{i^1} = -1, \text{ and } \exists i^2 \in I_m,\ s_{i^2} = +1 \right\}.$$

Notice that there are $2^m - 2$ elements of $\mathcal{S}$ containing no zeroes. For every $s \in \mathcal{S}$, the subset $A(s)$ of Δ^{m-1} is defined by

$$A(s) = \left\{ x \in \Delta^{m-1} \,\middle|\, \begin{array}{l} \frac{x_i}{v_i} = \min\left(\left\{ \frac{x_\imath}{v_\imath} \,\middle|\, \imath \in I_m \right\}\right),\ \forall i \in I^-(s), \\ \frac{x_i}{v_i} = \max\left(\left\{ \frac{x_\imath}{v_\imath} \,\middle|\, \imath \in I_m \right\}\right),\ \forall i \in I^+(s) \end{array} \right\}.$$

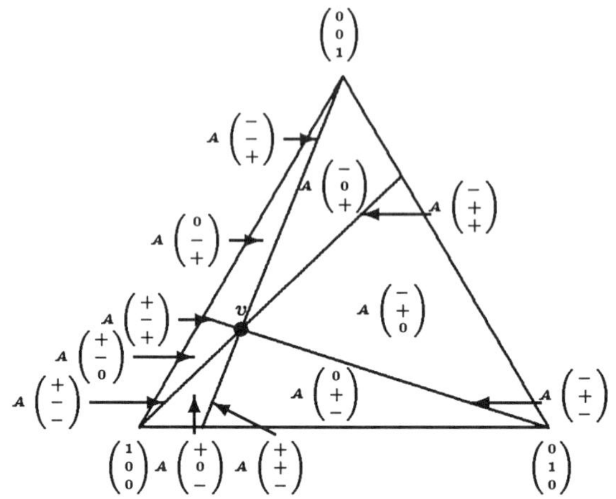

Figure 2.7.2. The sets $A(s)$, for $s \in \mathcal{S}$, $m = 3$, $v = (\frac{11}{18}, \frac{1}{9}, \frac{5}{18})^\top$.

An alternative but equivalent definition of $A(s)$, $\forall s \in \mathcal{S}$, is given by

$$A(s) = \{x \in \Delta^{m-1} |\ \exists \alpha, \beta \in \mathbb{R},\ 0 \leq \alpha \leq 1 \leq \beta, \text{ and } \\ x_i = \alpha v_i, \quad \forall i \in I^-(s), \\ \alpha v_i \leq x_i \leq \beta v_i, \forall i \in I^0(s), \\ x_i = \beta v_i, \quad \forall i \in I^+(s)\}.$$

For every $s \in \mathcal{S}$, the integer t^s is defined by $t^s = i^0(s) + 1$. It is not difficult to show that, for every $s \in \mathcal{S}$, $\dim(A(s)) = t^s$. Moreover, it holds that $\cup_{s \in \{\bar{s} \in \mathcal{S} | t^{\bar{s}} = m-1\}} A(s) = \Delta^{m-1}$. For $m = 3$ and $v = (\frac{11}{18}, \frac{1}{9}, \frac{5}{18})^\top$, the sets $A(s)$ are depicted in Figure 2.7.2 for all $s \in \mathcal{S}$. For convenience, "-1" is replaced by "$-$" and "$+1$" by "$+$" in Figure 2.7.2. The V-triangulation of Δ^{m-1} is constructed in such a way that for every $s \in \mathcal{S}$ the set $A(s)$ is triangulated by a subset of the V-triangulation of Δ^{m-1}.

For every non-empty subset I of I_m, $p(I)$ denotes the *relative projection* of v on $\Delta^{m-1}(I_m \setminus I)$, i.e.

$$p_i(I) = \frac{v_i}{\sum_{\iota \in I} v_\iota}, \forall i \in I, \\ p_i(I) = 0, \quad \forall i \in I_m \setminus I.$$

For every $s \in \mathcal{S}$, the collection Π^s is defined by

$$\Pi^s = \{\rho : I_{t^s - 1} \to I^0(s) | \rho \text{ is a permutation of the elements of } I^0(s)\}.$$

Notice that if $s \in \mathcal{S}$ is such that $t^s = 1$, then $\Pi^s = \{\emptyset\}$, and if $s \in \mathcal{S}$ is such that $t^s = 2$, then $\Pi^s = \{\overline{\rho}\}$ with $\overline{\rho} : I_1 \to I^0(s)$ the unique permutation of the elements of $I^0(s)$. In general the set Π^s contains $(t^s - 1)!$ different permutations as its elements. For every $s \in \mathcal{S}$, the set $A(s)$ is subdivided in subsets $A(s, \rho)$ with $\rho \in \Pi^s$. For every $\rho \in \Pi^s$, the set $A(s, \rho)$ is triangulated by a collection of simplices, which is a subset of a collection of simplices obtained by taking the image by a certain affine function of the K-triangulation of $\mathbb{R}^{t^s}$. The V-triangulation of Δ^{m-1} is then obtained by taking the union for all $s \in \mathcal{S}$ with $t^s = m - 1$ and for all $\rho \in \Pi^s$ of the triangulations of the sets $A(s, \rho)$. For every $s \in \mathcal{S}$, for every $\rho \in \Pi^s$, the point $q(0)$ of $\mathbb{R}^m$ is defined by

$$q(0) = p\left(I^+(s)\right) - v,$$

and, for every $i \in I_{t^s-1}$, the point $q(\rho(i))$ of $\mathbb{R}^m$ is defined by

$$q\left(\rho(i)\right) = p\left(I^+(s) \cup \rho\left(I_i\right)\right) - p\left(I^+(s) \cup \rho\left(I_{i-1}\right)\right), \ \forall i \in I_{t^s-1}.$$

For every $s \in \mathcal{S}$, for every $\rho \in \Pi^s$, $\rho(0)$ is defined to be the number 0 and the set $A(s, \rho)$ is defined by

$$A(s, \rho) = \Big\{ x \in \Delta^{m-1} \Big| \ \forall i \in I^0_{t^s-1}, \ \exists \alpha^i \in [0, 1], \ \alpha^{t^s-1} \leq \cdots \leq \alpha^0, \\ x = v + \alpha^0 q\left(\rho(0)\right) + \cdots + \alpha^{t^s-1} q\left(\rho(t^s - 1)\right) \Big\}.$$

Notice that $x = v + \sum_{i \in I^0_{t^s-1}} \alpha^i q(\rho(i))$ implies $x = \lambda^0 v + \sum_{i \in I_{t^s}} \lambda^i p(I^+(s) \cup \rho(I_{i-1}))$ with $\lambda^0 = 1 - \alpha^0$, $\lambda^i = \alpha^{i-1} - \alpha^i$, $\forall i \in I_{t^s-1}$, and $\lambda^{t^s} = \alpha^{t^s-1}$. Clearly, $\sum_{i \in I^0_{t^s}} \lambda^i = 1$ and $\lambda^i \geq 0$, $\forall i \in I^0_{t^s}$, so the point x is a convex combination of the point v and t^s relative projections of v.

Definition 2.7.4 (V-triangulation of Δ^{m-1})
Let a point v of Δ^{m-1} and some $n \in \mathbb{N}$ be given. For every $s \in \mathcal{S}$, for every $\rho \in \Pi^s$, $\Sigma(s, \rho)$ is the collection of all t^s-simplices $\sigma_{(x^1,\pi)}$ with vertices $x^1, \ldots, x^{t^s+1} \in \mathbb{R}^m$ satisfying $x^1 = v + \sum_{i \in I^0_{t^s-1}} \frac{a^i}{n} q(\rho(i))$ for some $a^0, \ldots, a^{t^s-1} \in I^0_{n-1}$ with $a^{t^s-1} \leq \cdots \leq a^0$, $\pi : I_{t^s} \to \{0\} \cup I^0(s)$ is a permutation such that $a^{i-1} = a^i$, $\rho(i - 1) = \pi(j^1)$, and $\rho(i) = \pi(j^2)$, for some $i \in I_{t^s-1}$ and some $j^1, j^2 \in I_{t^s}$, implies $j^1 < j^2$, and, finally, $x^{i+1} = x^i + \frac{1}{n} q(\pi(i))$, $\forall i \in I_{t^s}$. For every $s \in \mathcal{S}$, $\Sigma(s)$ is the collection $\cup_{\rho \in \Pi^s} \Sigma(s, \rho)$. The V-triangulation of Δ^{m-1} with respect to v and with grid size *$\frac{1}{n}$ is the collection $\Sigma = \cup_{s \in \{\bar{s} \in \mathcal{S} | t^{\bar{s}} = m-1\}} \Sigma(s)$.*

It can be shown that the collection Σ given in Definition 2.7.4 satisfies the conditions of a triangulation given in Definition 2.7.1. Moreover, the collection

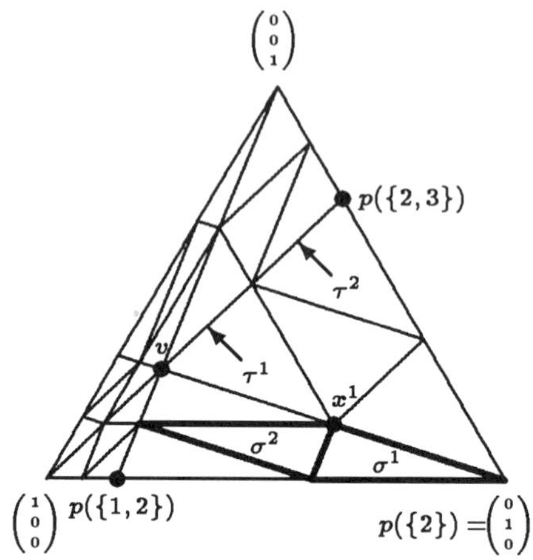

Figure 2.7.3. The V-triangulation of Δ^2, $v = (\frac{11}{18}, \frac{1}{9}, \frac{5}{18})^\top$, $n = 2$.

Σ is constructed in such a way that for every $s \in \mathcal{S}$ an appropriate collection of t^s-faces of the $(m-1)$-simplices of Σ triangulates $A(s)$.

Theorem 2.7.5
Let the collection Σ be the V-triangulation of Δ^{m-1} with respect to $v \in \dot{\Delta}^{m-1}$ and with grid size $\frac{1}{n}$ for some $n \in \mathbb{N}$. Then, for every $s \in \mathcal{S}$, for every $\rho \in \Pi^s$, the collection $\Sigma(s, \rho)$ equals the collection $\{\tau \subset A(s, \rho) \mid \exists \sigma \in \Sigma,\ \tau$ is a t^s-face of $\sigma\}$ and triangulates $A(s, \rho)$. Moreover, for every $s \in \mathcal{S}$, the set $A(s)$ is triangulated by $\Sigma(s)$.
See Doup, van der Laan, and Talman (1987), Lemma 3.3, page 247.

It is easily shown that the V-triangulation of Δ^{m-1} with respect to $v \in \dot{\Delta}^{m-1}$ and with grid size $\frac{1}{n}$, for some $n \in \mathbb{N}$, has mesh size equal to $\frac{1}{n}\max(\{1 - v_i \mid i \in I_m\})$, hence the mesh size can be made arbitrarily small. The V-triangulation of Δ^2 with respect to $v = (\frac{11}{18}, \frac{1}{9}, \frac{5}{18})^\top$ and with grid size $\frac{1}{2}$ is illustrated in Figure 2.7.3.

Consider the admissible sign vector $\bar{s} = (0, +1, -1)^\top$ of $\mathcal{S}$. Since $I^0(\bar{s}) = \{1\}$, it holds that $t^{\bar{s}} = 2$, and therefore $\Pi^{\bar{s}} = \{\bar{\rho}\}$ with $\bar{\rho} = (1)$. Since $I^+(\bar{s}) = \{2\}$, it holds that $q(\bar{\rho}(0)) = q(0) = p(\{2\}) - v = (0, 1, 0)^\top - v = (-\frac{11}{18}, \frac{8}{9}, -\frac{5}{18})^\top$, and $q(\bar{\rho}(1)) = q(1) = p(\{1, 2\}) - p(\{2\}) = (\frac{11}{13}, \frac{2}{13}, 0)^\top - (0, 1, 0)^\top = (\frac{11}{13}, -\frac{11}{13}, 0)^\top$. Hence, $A(\bar{s}) = A(\bar{s}, \bar{\rho}) = \mathrm{co}(\{v, (0, 1, 0)^\top, (\frac{11}{13}, \frac{2}{13}, 0)^\top\})$. Consider $x^1 = v + \frac{1}{2}q(0) + 0q(1) = (\frac{11}{36}, \frac{5}{9}, \frac{5}{36})^\top \in A(\bar{s})$, i.e. $a^0 = 1$ and $a^1 = 0$. There are two possible permutations of the elements of I_1^0, $\pi^1 = (0,1)$ and $\pi^2 = (1,0)$. Since $a^0 \neq a^1$, both permutations are allowed. Hence, in Figure 2.7.3, both $\sigma^1 = \sigma_{(x^1,\pi^1)}$ and $\sigma^2 = \sigma_{(x^1,\pi^2)}$ are members of $\Sigma(\bar{s}) = \Sigma(\bar{s}, \bar{p})$. To illustrate Theorem 2.7.5, notice that in Figure 2.7.3 the collection $\{\tau^1, \tau^2\}$ triangulates the 1-dimensional set $A((-1,+1,+1)^\top)$, being equal to $\text{co}(\{v, p(\{2,3\})\})$.

In Chapter 11 a triangulation of Q^m satisfying properties as in Theorem 2.7.5 is needed. Here an example of such a triangulation is given. The example is called the V-triangulation of Q^m and is closely related to the V-triangulation introduced in Doup and Talman (1987) for a Cartesian product of unit simplices.

Let a point v of Q^m be given. The point v is considered to be fixed in the entire description of the V-triangulation of Q^m. The *set of admissible sign vectors,* denoted by $\mathcal{S}$, is defined by

$$\begin{aligned} \mathcal{S} = \{ s \in \mathbb{S}^m | \ & \exists i \in I_m,\ v_i = 0 \text{ and } s_i = +1, \text{ or} \\ & \exists i \in I_m,\ 0 < v_i < 1 \text{ and } s_i \in \{-1,+1\}, \text{ or} \\ & \exists i \in I_m,\ v_i = 1 \text{ and } s_i = -1 \}. \end{aligned}$$

Notice that $s \in \mathcal{S}$ implies $I^-(s) \cup I^+(s) \neq \emptyset$. For every $s \in \mathcal{S}$, the integer t^s is defined by $t^s = i^0(s) + 1$ and the set $A(s)$ is defined by

$$\begin{aligned} A(s) = \{ x \in Q^m | \ \exists \alpha \in [0,1],\ & x_i = \alpha v_i, && \forall i \in I^-(s), \\ & \alpha v_i \le x_i \le 1 - \alpha + \alpha v_i, && \forall i \in I^0(s), \\ & x_i = 1 - \alpha + \alpha v_i, && \forall i \in I^+(s)\}. \end{aligned}$$

It is not difficult to verify that, for every $s \in \mathcal{S}$, $\dim(A(s)) = t^s$. It is also easily shown that $\cup_{s \in \{\bar{s} \in \mathcal{S} | t^{\bar{s}} = m\}} A(s) = Q^m$. For $m = 2$, for $s \in \mathcal{S}$, the sets $A(s)$ corresponding to $v = (0,0)^\top$, $v = (\frac{1}{2}, 0)^\top$, $v = (\frac{1}{2}, \frac{1}{2})^\top$, and $v = (\frac{1}{4}, \frac{3}{8})^\top$ are illustrated in Figure 2.7.4.

For every $s \in \mathcal{S}$, the set $\mathcal{R}^s$ is defined by

$$\begin{aligned} \mathcal{R}^s = \{ r \in \mathbb{S}^m | \ & r_i = -1, && \forall i \in I^0(s) \text{ with } v_i = 1, \text{ and } \forall i \in I^-(s), \\ & r_i \in \{-1,+1\}, && \forall i \in I^0(s) \text{ with } 0 < v_i < 1, \\ & r_i = +1, && \forall i \in I^0(s) \text{ with } v_i = 0, \text{ and } \forall i \in I^+(s)\}. \end{aligned}$$

For every $s \in \mathcal{S}$, the set $A(s)$ is subdivided into sets $A(s, r)$ with $r \in \mathcal{R}^s$. For every $r \in \mathcal{R}^s$, the set $A(s, r)$ is triangulated by a collection of simplices, which is a subset of a collection of simplices obtained by taking the image by a certain affine function of the K-triangulation of $\mathbb{R}^{t^s}$. The V-triangulation of Q^m is then obtained by taking the union over $s \in \mathcal{S}$ with $t^s = m$ and over all

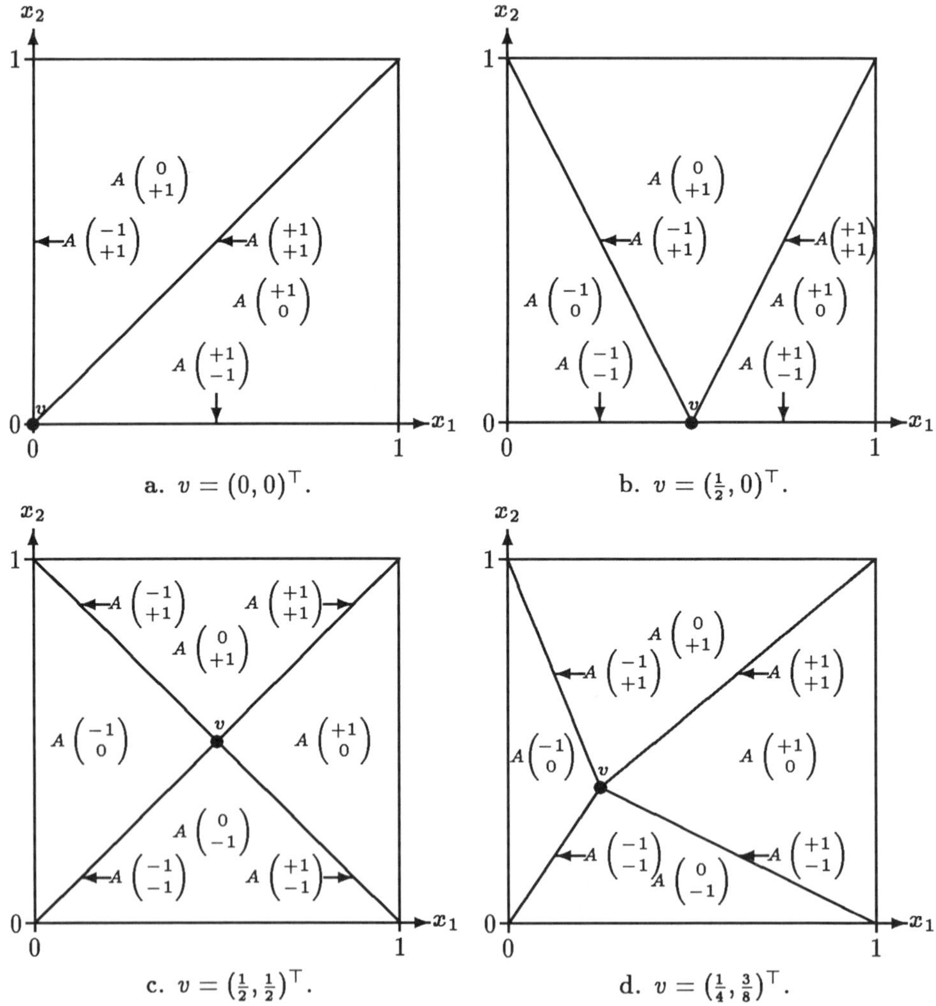

Figure 2.7.4. The sets $A(s)$, for $s \in \mathcal{S}$, $m = 2$.

$r \in \mathcal{R}^s$ of the triangulations of $A(s,r)$. For every $s \in \mathcal{S}$, for every $r \in \mathcal{R}^s$, the point $q(0) \in \mathbb{R}^m$ is defined by

$$\begin{aligned} q_i(0) &= -v_i, \quad \forall i \in I^-(r), \\ q_i(0) &= 1 - v_i, \forall i \in I^+(r). \end{aligned}$$

For every $s \in \mathcal{S}$, for every $r \in \mathcal{R}^s$, for every $i \in I^0(s)$, the point $q(i) \in \mathbb{R}^m$ is defined by

$$\begin{aligned} q(i) &= v_i e^m(i) && \text{if } i \in I^-(r), \\ q(i) &= (v_i - 1)e^m(i) && \text{if } i \in I^+(r). \end{aligned}$$

For every $s \in \mathcal{S}$, for every $r \in \mathcal{R}^s$, the set $A(s,r)$ is defined by

$$A(s,r) = \Big\{ x \in Q^m \Big| \ \forall i \in \{0\} \cup I^0(s), \exists \alpha^i \in [0,1], \alpha^i \le \alpha^0 \text{ and } x = v + \textstyle\sum_{i \in \{0\} \cup I^0(s)} \alpha^i q(i) \Big\}.$$

Notice that for every $s \in \mathcal{S}$ the set $A(s)$ is subdivided into 2^k subsets $A(s,r)$ with $r \in \mathcal{R}^s$, where $k = \#\{i \in I^0(s) \mid 0 < v_i < 1\}$.

Definition 2.7.6 (V-triangulation of Q^m)
Let a point $v \in Q^m$ and some $n \in \mathbb{N}$ be given. For every $s \in \mathcal{S}$, for every $r \in \mathcal{R}^s$, $\Sigma(s,r)$ is the collection of all t^s-simplices $\sigma(x^1,\pi)$ with vertices $x^1, \ldots, x^{t^s+1} \in \mathbb{R}^m$ satisfying $x^1 = v + \sum_{i \in \{0\} \cup I^0(s)} \frac{a^i}{n} q(i)$ for some a^0, a^i in I^0_{n-1} with $a^i \le a^0$, $\forall i \in I^0(s)$, $\pi : I_{t^s} \to \{0\} \cup I^0(s)$ is a permutation such that $a^0 = a^i$, $\pi(j^1) = 0$, and $\pi(j^2) = i$, for some $i \in I^0(s)$, for some $j^1, j^2 \in I_{t^s}$, implies $j^1 < j^2$, and, finally, $x^{i+1} = x^i + \frac{1}{n} q(\pi(i))$, $\forall i \in I_{t^s}$. For every $s \in \mathcal{S}$, $\Sigma(s)$ is the collection $\cup_{r \in \mathcal{R}^s} \Sigma(s,r)$. The V-triangulation of Q^m with respect to v and with grid size *$\frac{1}{n}$ is the collection $\Sigma = \cup_{s \in \{\bar{s} \in \mathcal{S} | t^{\bar{s}} = m\}} \Sigma(s)$.*

It can be shown that the collection Σ defined above satisfies the conditions of a triangulation given in Definition 2.7.1. Moreover, the collection Σ is constructed in such a way that for every $s \in \mathcal{S}$ an appropriate collection of t^s-faces of the m-simplices in Σ triangulates $A(s)$.

Theorem 2.7.7
Let the collection Σ be the V-triangulation of Q^m with respect to $v \in Q^m$ and with grid size $\frac{1}{n}$ for some $n \in \mathbb{N}$. Then, for every $s \in \mathcal{S}$, for every $r \in \mathcal{R}^s$, the collection $\Sigma(s,r)$ equals the collection $\{\tau \subset A(s,r) \mid \exists \sigma \in \Sigma, \tau \text{ is a } t^s\text{-face of } \sigma\}$ and triangulates $A(s,r)$. Moreover, for every $s \in \mathcal{S}$, the set $A(s)$ is triangulated by $\Sigma(s)$.
See Doup and Talman (1987), remark below Definition 3.3, page 332.

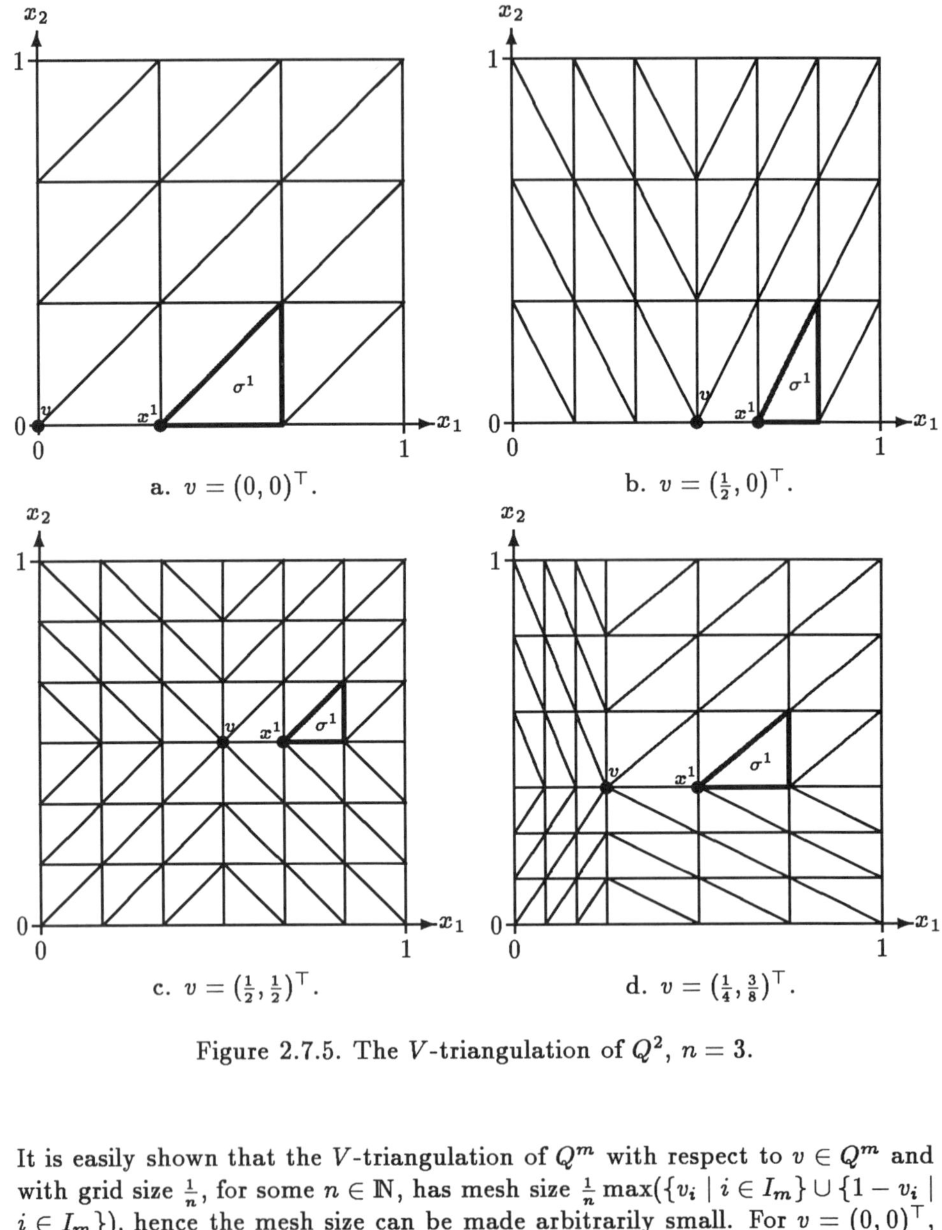

Figure 2.7.5. The V-triangulation of Q^2, $n = 3$.

It is easily shown that the V-triangulation of Q^m with respect to $v \in Q^m$ and with grid size $\frac{1}{n}$, for some $n \in \mathbb{N}$, has mesh size $\frac{1}{n} \max(\{v_i \mid i \in I_m\} \cup \{1 - v_i \mid i \in I_m\})$, hence the mesh size can be made arbitrarily small. For $v = (0,0)^\top$, $v = (\frac{1}{2}, 0)^\top$, $v = (\frac{1}{2}, \frac{1}{2})^\top$, and $v = (\frac{1}{4}, \frac{3}{8})^\top$, the V-triangulation of Q^2 with respect to v and with grid size $\frac{1}{3}$ is illustrated in Figure 2.7.5.

Consider $\bar{s} = (+1, 0)^\top$. Notice that for every point v mentioned in the previous paragraph it holds that $\bar{s} \in \mathcal{S}$. The set $A(\bar{s})$ is given by $\text{co}(\{v, (1,0)^\top, (1,1)^\top\})$. In the case where $v = (0,0)^\top$ or $v = (\frac{1}{2}, 0)^\top$ it holds that the set $\mathcal{R}^{\bar{s}}$ only contains the element r^1 given by $r^1 = (+1, +1)^\top$ since $I^0(\bar{s}) = \{2\}$. In this case $q(0) = (1 - v_1, 1)^\top$ and $q(2) = (0, -1)^\top$. In the case where $v = (\frac{1}{2}, \frac{1}{2})^\top$ or $v = (\frac{1}{4}, \frac{3}{8})^\top$ it holds that $\mathcal{R}^{\bar{s}} = \{r^1, r^2\}$ with $r^1 = (+1, +1)^\top$ and $r^2 = (+1, -1)^\top$. Now the element r^1 yields the points $q(0) = (1 - v_1, 1 - v_2)^\top$ and $q(2) = (0, v_2 - 1)^\top$ and r^2 induces the points $q(0) = (1 - v_1, -v_2)^\top$ and $q(2) = (0, v_2)^\top$. In all four cases, consider $x^1 = v + \frac{1}{3}q(0) + \frac{1}{3}q(2) \in A(\bar{s}, r^1)$, i.e. $a^0 = 1$ and $a^2 = 1$. There are two possible permutations of the elements of $\{0, 2\}$, π^1 given by $\pi^1 = (0, 2)$ and π^2 given by $\pi^2 = (2, 0)$. Since $a^0 = a^2$, it follows that only the permutation π^1 is allowed. So, $\sigma^1 = \sigma_{(x^1, \pi^1)}$ is a member of $\Sigma(\bar{s}, r^1)$.

Many more triangulations of Δ^{m-1} and Q^m are proposed in the literature. Some other triangulations of Δ^{m-1} are the Q-triangulation and a number of variants of the V-triangulation, one of these being a triangulation proposed in Tuy, Thoai, and Muu (1978), see Doup (1988), the T_1-triangulation, see Dang and Talman (1990), and some barycentric triangulations, see Scarf (1973) and Zangwill (1977). Some other triangulations of Q^m are the Q-triangulation and the V'-triangulation, see Doup (1988), the Q'-triangulation, see van der Laan and Talman (1982), and the D_1-triangulation of $\mathbb{R}^m$ restricted to Q^m, see Dang (1991a). For more details about these and other triangulations, the reader is referred to Todd (1976), Doup (1988), and Dang (1991b). The following result is valid for every triangulation.

Theorem 2.7.8
For $t \in \mathbb{N}$, let the collection Σ be a triangulation of a convex t-dimensional subset S of $\mathbb{R}^m$, and let the subset T of $\text{rb}(S)$ *be such that $T = S \cap \text{aff}(T)$ and* $\dim(T) = t - 1$. *Then the collection $\bar{\Sigma}$ given by $\bar{\Sigma} = \{\tau \subset T \mid \exists \sigma \in \Sigma,\ \tau$ is a facet of $\sigma\}$ is a triangulation of T.*
See Todd (1976), Theorem 2.3, page 27.

Finally, the notion of a piecewise linear approximation is defined.

Definition 2.7.9 (Piecewise linear approximation)
For $t \in \mathbb{Z}_+$, let a compact, convex t-dimensional subset S of $\mathbb{R}^m$, a subset T of $\mathbb{R}^n$, a triangulation Σ of S, and a correspondence $\varphi : S \to T$ be given. A function $F : S \to \mathbb{R}^n$ is a piecewise linear approximation *of φ with respect to Σ if for every vertex x of any $\sigma \in \Sigma$ it holds that $F(x) \in \varphi(x)$ and for every*

element x of S it holds that $F(x) = \sum_{i \in I_{t+1}} \lambda^i F(x^i)$, when $x \in \sigma(x^1, \ldots, x^{t+1})$ for some t-simplex $\sigma \in \Sigma$ and $x = \sum_{i \in I_{t+1}} \lambda^i x^i$ for some $\lambda^i \in \mathbb{R}_+$, $\forall i \in I_{t+1}$, with $\sum_{i \in I_{t+1}} \lambda^i = 1$.

A piecewise linear approximation F of a correspondence with respect to a triangulation Σ is uniquely determined when the images by F of all the vertices of every $\sigma \in \Sigma$ are specified. Therefore, it follows that a piecewise linear approximation of a function with respect to a triangulation is uniquely determined. Often it is important to know the accuracy of the piecewise linear approximation of a continuous function with respect to some triangulation. Then the following result is useful.

Theorem 2.7.10
Let S be a compact subset of $\mathbb{R}^m$, let T be a subset of $\mathbb{R}^n$, and let $f : S \to T$ be a continuous function. Then, for every $\varepsilon \in \mathbb{R}_{++}$, there exists $\delta \in \mathbb{R}_{++}$ such that, for every $x^1, x^2 \in S$ with $\|x^1 - x^2\|_\infty < \delta$, $\|f(x^1) - f(x^2)\|_\infty < \varepsilon$.
See Munkres (1975), Theorem 7.3, page 180.

2.8 MEASURE THEORY

This section is mainly based on Hildenbrand (1974), Taylor (1985), and Kelley and Srinivasan (1988).

The set of real numbers can be extended to the *set of extended real numbers*, denoted by $\mathbb{R}^*$. This is done by adding the elements $-\infty$ and $+\infty$ to $\mathbb{R}$. The set $\mathbb{N}^*$, defined by $\mathbb{N}^* = \mathbb{N} \cup \{+\infty\}$, is called the *set of extended natural numbers*, the set $\mathbf{Z}^*_+$, defined by $\mathbf{Z}^*_+ = \mathbf{Z} \cup \{+\infty\}$, is called the *set of extended non-negative integers*, and the set $\mathbf{Z}^*$, defined by $\mathbf{Z}^* = \{-\infty\} \cup \mathbf{Z} \cup \{+\infty\}$, is called the *set of extended integers*. The sets $\mathbb{R}^{*m}$, $\mathbb{N}^{*m}$, $\mathbf{Z}^{*m}_+$, and $\mathbf{Z}^{*m}$ are defined as the m-fold Cartesian product of the sets $\mathbb{R}^*$, $\mathbb{N}^*$, $\mathbf{Z}^*_+$, and $\mathbf{Z}^*$, respectively. An element of $\mathbb{R}^{*m}$ is assumed to be a column vector. The element of $\mathbb{R}^{*m}$ with every component equal to $-\infty$ is denoted by $-\infty^m$ and the element of $\mathbb{R}^{*m}$ with every component equal to $+\infty$ is denoted by $+\infty^m$.

The complete ordering $\leq$ on $\mathbb{R}$ is extended to a complete ordering on $\mathbb{R}^*$ as follows. It holds that $-\infty < +\infty$, $-\infty < x$, $\forall x \in \mathbb{R}$, and $x < +\infty$, $\forall x \in \mathbb{R}$. It easily follows, see Taylor (1985), page 5, that every subset of $\mathbb{R}^*$ has a uniquely determined infimum and a uniquely determined supremum that is an element of

$\mathbb{R}^*$. The ordering $\leq$ on $\mathbb{R}^{*m}$ is derived from the ordering $\leq$ on $\mathbb{R}^*$ in the same way as the ordering $\leq$ on $\mathbb{R}^m$ is derived from the ordering $\leq$ on $\mathbb{R}$. Moreover, the binary relations $\ll, <, >, \geq$, and $\gg$ on $\mathbb{R}^{*m}$ are defined in the obvious way. The sets $\mathbb{R}^{*m}_{+}$ and $\mathbb{R}^{*m}_{++}$ are defined by $\mathbb{R}^{*m}_{+} = \{x \in \mathbb{R}^{*m} \mid x \geq 0^m\}$ and $\mathbb{R}^{*m}_{++} = \{x \in \mathbb{R}^{*m} \mid x \gg 0^m\}$.

Let $(x^n)_{n\in\mathbb{N}}$ be a sequence in $\mathbb{R}^*$. The sequence $(x^n)_{n\in\mathbb{N}}$ is said to *converge* to $\overline{x} \in \mathbb{R}^*$, denoted by $x^n \to \overline{x}$ or by $\lim_{n\to+\infty} x^n = \overline{x}$, if for every element x^- of $\mathbb{R}^*$ with $x^- < \overline{x}$ there exists $n^1 \in \mathbb{N}$ such that $n > n^1$ implies $x^- < x^n$, and if for every element x^+ of $\mathbb{R}^*$ with $x^+ > \overline{x}$ there exists $n^2 \in \mathbb{N}$ such that $n > n^2$ implies $x^n < x^+$. In this case the sequence $(x^n)_{n\in\mathbb{N}}$ is said to be *convergent* and the point $\overline{x}$ is called the *limit* of $(x^n)_{n\in\mathbb{N}}$. Obviously, the notions related to convergence are well defined if there exists $n' \in \mathbb{N}$ such that the element x^n is only defined for every $n \geq n'$.

Let $(x^n)_{n\in\mathbb{N}}$ be a sequence in $\mathbb{R}^{*m}$. Then the sequence $(x^n)_{n\in\mathbb{N}}$ is said to *converge* to $\overline{x} \in \mathbb{R}^{*m}$, denoted by $x^n \to \overline{x}$ or by $\lim_{n\to+\infty} x^n = \overline{x}$, if $x^n_i \to \overline{x}_i$, $\forall i \in I_m$. Notice that this notion of convergence coincides with the one given for sequences in $\mathbb{R}^m$ in the case when x^n, $\forall n \in \mathbb{N}$, and $\overline{x}$ are elements of $\mathbb{R}^m$.

Addition in $\mathbb{R}^*$ is an extension of addition in $\mathbb{R}$ and is defined by the following rules, $(-\infty) + (-\infty) = -\infty$, $(+\infty) + (+\infty) = +\infty$, and, for every $x \in \mathbb{R}$, $x + (-\infty) = (-\infty) + x = -\infty$ and $x + (+\infty) = (+\infty) + x = +\infty$. Notice that $(-\infty) + (+\infty)$ is not defined. *Multiplication* in $\mathbb{R}^*$ is an extension of multiplication in $\mathbb{R}$ and is defined by the following rules. For $\lambda \in \mathbb{R}^*$, if $-\infty \leq \lambda < 0$, then $\lambda(-\infty) = (-\infty)\lambda = +\infty$ and $\lambda(+\infty) = (+\infty)\lambda = -\infty$, if $0 < \lambda \leq +\infty$, then $\lambda(-\infty) = (-\infty)\lambda = -\infty$ and $\lambda(+\infty) = (+\infty)\lambda = +\infty$, and $0(-\infty) = (-\infty)0 = 0(+\infty) = (+\infty)0 = 0$. In $\mathbb{R}^{*m}$ *addition* and *multiplication* by an element of $\mathbb{R}^*$ is derived from addition and multiplication in $\mathbb{R}^*$ by performing addition and multiplication componentwise.

Let S^1 and S^2 be subsets of $\mathbb{R}^{*m}$ such that $x^1 \in S^1$, $x^2 \in S^2$, and there exists $i \in I_m$ with $x^1_i = -\infty$ implies $x^2_i \neq +\infty$, whereas $x^1 \in S^1$, $x^2 \in S^2$, and there exists $i \in I_m$ with $x^1_i = +\infty$ implies $x^2_i \neq -\infty$. Then the *sum* of S^1 and S^2, denoted by $S^1 + S^2$, is defined as the set $\{x \in \mathbb{R}^{*m} \mid \exists x^1 \in S^1,\ \exists x^2 \in S^2,\ x = x^1 + x^2\}$. Let λ be an element of $\mathbb{R}^*$ and let S be a subset of $\mathbb{R}^{*m}$. Then the *product* of λ and S, denoted by λS, is defined as the set $\{x \in \mathbb{R}^{*m} \mid \exists \overline{x} \in S,\ x = \lambda\overline{x}\}$.

Let $(x^n)_{n\in\mathbb{N}}$ be a sequence in $\mathbb{R}^*$ such that, for every $n \in \mathbb{N}$, $x^n \geq 0$. For every $n \in \mathbb{N}$, the sum $x^1 + \cdots + x^n$ is well defined using the properties mentioned in the previous paragraph and is denoted by $\sum_{j\in I_n} x^j$. Let the sequence $(\overline{x}^n)_{n\in\mathbb{N}}$ in $\mathbb{R}^*$ be such that, for every $n \in \mathbb{N}$, $\overline{x}^n = \sum_{j\in I_n} x^j$. It can be shown that this sequence always converges to some element of $\mathbb{R}^*$, denoted by $\sum_{n\in\mathbb{N}} x^n$. Moreover, it can be shown that the limit is independent of the order of addition.

Consider the topology on $\mathbb{R}^*$ given by the collection of subsets S of $\mathbb{R}^*$ satisfying that for every $\overline{x} \in S$ either $\overline{x} = -\infty$ and there exists $\widehat{x} \in \mathbb{R}$ such that $\{x \in \mathbb{R}^* \mid -\infty \leq x < \widehat{x}\} \subset S$, or $\overline{x} \in \mathbb{R}$ and there exists $\delta \in \mathbb{R}_{++}$ such that $B^1(\overline{x}, \delta) \subset S$, or $\overline{x} = +\infty$ and there exists $\widehat{x} \in \mathbb{R}$ such that $\{x \in \mathbb{R}^* \mid \widehat{x} < x \leq +\infty\} \subset S$. Consider the topology on $\mathbb{R}^{*m}$ given by the product topology. In the entire monograph it is assumed that this is the topology on $\mathbb{R}^{*m}$. The topological space $\mathbb{R}^{*m}$ can be shown to be a Hausdorff space.

Let a subset S of $\mathbb{R}^{*m}$, a subset T of $\mathbb{R}^{*n}$, and an element $\overline{x}$ of S be given. It is not difficult to show that a function $f : S \rightarrow T$ is continuous at $\overline{x}$ if and only if $(x^n)_{n\in\mathbb{N}}$ being a sequence in S, $x^n \rightarrow \overline{x}$, $y^n = f(x^n)$, $\forall n \in \mathbb{N}$, and $\overline{y} = f(\overline{x})$ implies $y^n \rightarrow \overline{y}$.

A collection $\mathcal{A}$ of subsets of a non-empty set X such that $X \in \mathcal{A}$, $E^n \in \mathcal{A}$, $\forall n \in \mathbb{N}$, implies $\cup_{n\in\mathbb{N}} E^n \in \mathcal{A}$, and $E^1, E^2 \in \mathcal{A}$ implies $E^1 \setminus E^2 \in \mathcal{A}$ is called a *σ-algebra* of X. The pair $(X, \mathcal{A})$ consisting of a non-empty set X and a σ-algebra $\mathcal{A}$ of X is called a *measurable space* and the members of $\mathcal{A}$ are called *$\mathcal{A}$-measurable.*

Let $\mathcal{A}$ be a σ-algebra of a non-empty set X. Then $\emptyset \in \mathcal{A}$ since $\emptyset = X \setminus X$. Therefore, any finite union of members of $\mathcal{A}$ is contained in $\mathcal{A}$. Moreover, any countable intersection of members of $\mathcal{A}$ is contained in $\mathcal{A}$ since $\cap_{n\in\mathbb{N}} E^n = E \setminus \cup_{n\in\mathbb{N}}(E \setminus E^n)$ with $E = \cup_{n\in\mathbb{N}} E^n$. An example of a σ-algebra of X is the collection of all subsets of X.

Let $\mathcal{E}$ be a non-empty collection of subsets of a non-empty set X. The intersection of all σ-algebras $\mathcal{A}$ of X such that $\mathcal{E} \subset \mathcal{A}$ is a σ-algebra of X and is called the σ-algebra of X generated by $\mathcal{E}$.

Let a non-empty set X be a topological space and let $\mathcal{B}(X)$ be the σ-algebra generated by the collection of all open sets of X. The members of $\mathcal{B}(X)$ are called *Borel sets* of X and $\mathcal{B}(X)$ is called the *Borel σ-algebra* of X.

Let two measurable spaces $(X^1, \mathcal{A}^1)$ and $(X^2, \mathcal{A}^2)$ be given. A function $f : X^1 \rightarrow X^2$ is said to be *measurable* if for every $E \in \mathcal{A}^2$ it holds that $f^{-1}(E) \in$

$\mathcal{A}^1$. When a function $f : X^1 \to \mathbb{R}$ is considered, then it is always assumed that on $\mathbb{R}$ the Borel σ-algebra is taken.

Theorem 2.8.1
Let measurable spaces $(X^1, \mathcal{A}^1)$, $(X^2, \mathcal{A}^2)$, and a function $f : X^1 \to X^2$ be given. Let $\mathcal{E}$ be a non-empty collection of subsets of X^2 that generates the σ-algebra $\mathcal{A}^2$. If for every $E \in \mathcal{E}$ it holds that $f^{-1}(E) \in \mathcal{A}^1$, then the function f is measurable.
See Hildenbrand (1974), 3, page 41.

Let $(X, \mathcal{A})$ be a measurable space. A function $\mu : \mathcal{A} \to \mathbb{R}^*$ is called a *measure* on $\mathcal{A}$ if for every $E \in \mathcal{A}$ it holds that $\mu(E) \geq 0$, $\mu(\emptyset) = 0$, and μ is *countably additive*, i.e. when the sets E^n, $\forall n \in \mathbb{N}$, are pairwise disjoint members of $\mathcal{A}$, then $\sum_{n \in \mathbb{N}} \mu(E^n) = \mu(\cup_{n \in \mathbb{N}} E^n)$. For every $E \in \mathcal{A}$, the extended real number $\mu(E)$ is called the *measure* of E. A measure $\mu : \mathcal{A} \to [0, 1]$ satisfying that $\mu(X) = 1$ is called a *probability measure*. A triple $(X, \mathcal{A}, \mu)$ given by a non-empty set X, a σ-algebra $\mathcal{A}$ of X, and a measure μ on $\mathcal{A}$ is called a *measure space*. If X is a topological space, then a measure $\mu : \mathcal{B}(X) \to \mathbb{R}$ is called a *Borel measure*. If X is a topological space and μ is a Borel measure, then there exists a smallest closed set E of X such that $\mu(E) = \mu(X)$, called the *support* of μ.

Let a measure space $(X, \mathcal{A}, \mu)$ be given. A property $\mathcal{X}$ is said to hold for *almost every* $x \in X$ if the set $E = \{x \in X \mid x \text{ does not have property } \mathcal{X}\}$ is a member of the σ-algebra $\mathcal{A}$ with $\mu(E) = 0$. A subset S of X is said to be *negligible* if for some $E \in \mathcal{A}$ it holds that $S \subset E$ and $\mu(E) = 0$. The measure space $(X, \mathcal{A}, \mu)$ is said to be *complete* if every negligible subset of X is a member of $\mathcal{A}$.

A measure often used for $\mathbb{R}^m$ is the Lebesgue measure. It is constructed as follows. For $a, b \in \mathbb{R}^m$ with $a \ll b$, the *volume* of the open interval (a, b) of $\mathbb{R}^m$, denoted by $\text{vol}(a, b)$, is defined by $\text{vol}(a, b) = \prod_{i \in I_m} (b_i - a_i)$. For every subset S of $\mathbb{R}^m$, a *Lebesgue covering* of S is defined as a countable collection of non-empty, open intervals of $\mathbb{R}^m$, say $\{(a^i, b^i) \mid i \in I\}$ with I a countable set, satisfying $S \subset \cup_{i \in I} (a^i, b^i)$. The function $\mu^* : 2^{\mathbb{R}^m} \to \mathbb{R}^*$, called the *Lebesgue outer measure*, is obtained by defining, for every $S \subset \mathbb{R}^m$,

$$\mu^*(S) = \inf \left(\left\{ \textstyle\sum_{i \in I} \text{vol}(a^i, b^i) \middle| \, \{(a^i, b^i) | i \in I\} \text{ is a Lebesgue covering of } S \right\} \right).$$

It is easily verified that $\mu^*(\emptyset) = 0$, $\mu^*(S) \geq 0$, $\forall S \subset \mathbb{R}^m$, and $\mu^*((a, b)) = \mu^*(\text{cl}((a, b))) = \text{vol}(a, b)$ for every $a, b \in \mathbb{R}^m$ with $a \ll b$. Moreover, if S^1 and S^2 are subsets of $\mathbb{R}^m$ with $S^1 \subset S^2$, then $\mu^*(S^1) \leq \mu^*(S^2)$, and if, for every $i \in I$

with I a countable set, S^i is a subset of $\mathbb{R}^m$, then $\mu^*(\cup_{i\in I} S^i) \leq \sum_{i\in I} \mu^*(S^i)$. It should be remarked that $(\mathbb{R}^m, 2^{\mathbb{R}^m}, \mu^*)$ is not a measure space since the function μ^* fails to be countably additive. A subset E of $\mathbb{R}^m$ is said to be μ^*-*measurable* if for every $S \subset \mathbb{R}^m$ it holds that $\mu^*(S) = \mu^*(S \cap E) + \mu^*(S \setminus E)$. Let $\mathcal{A}'$ be defined as the collection of μ^*-measurable subsets of $\mathbb{R}^m$. The function $\mu' : \mathcal{A}' \rightarrow \mathbb{R}^*$ is defined by $\mu'(E) = \mu^*(E)$, $\forall E \in \mathcal{A}'$. The function μ' is called the *Lebesgue measure* for $\mathbb{R}^m$.

Theorem 2.8.2
The collection $\mathcal{A}'$ is a σ-algebra of $\mathbb{R}^m$ containing $\mathcal{B}(\mathbb{R}^m)$ as a proper subset and the triple $(\mathbb{R}^m, \mathcal{A}', \mu')$ is a complete measure space.
See Taylor (1985), Theorem 4.7.5, page 199, Theorem 4.7.6, page 200, and Theorem 4.7.7, page 200.

The σ-algebra $\mathcal{A}'$ does not contain all subsets of $\mathbb{R}^m$, see for example Taylor (1985), page 212. Since the measure space $(\mathbb{R}^m, \mathcal{A}', \mu')$ is complete, it follows immediately from the construction of the measure μ' that a subset S of $\mathbb{R}^m$ has Lebesgue measure zero if and only if for every $\varepsilon \in \mathbb{R}_{++}$ there exists a Lebesgue covering $\{(a^i, b^i) \mid i \in I\}$ of S such that $\sum_{i\in I} \text{vol}(a^i, b^i) < \varepsilon$.

Now a theory of integration can be developed. Attention is restricted to integration over a probability measure since this is all what is needed in what follows. Clearly, the approach given can easily be extended to other measures. Let a measurable space $(X, \mathcal{A})$ be given. A function $f : X \rightarrow \mathbb{R}$ is said to be *simple* if $f(X)$ is a finite set and, for every $x \in \mathbb{R}$, $f^{-1}(\{x\}) \in \mathcal{A}$. Hence, if $f : X \rightarrow \mathbb{R}$ is a simple function, then $f(X) = \{a^1, \ldots, a^m\}$, with $a^i \in \mathbb{R}$, $\forall i \in I_m$, and letting $E^i = \{x \in X \mid f(x) = a^i\}$, $\forall i \in I_m$, it holds that $f(x) = \sum_{i\in I_m} a^i \chi_{E^i}(x)$, $\forall x \in X$. Using Theorem 2.8.1 it easily follows that a simple function f is measurable.

Let a measurable space $(X, \mathcal{A})$ be given and let $f : X \rightarrow \mathbb{R}$ be a measurable function satisfying $f(x) \geq 0$, $\forall x \in X$. A sequence of simple functions $(f^n)_{n\in\mathbb{N}}$ with the property that for every $x \in X$ both $f^n(x) \rightarrow f(x)$ and $0 \leq f^n(x) \leq f^{n+1}(x)$, $\forall n \in \mathbb{N}$, is called a *regular approximating sequence* for f. In Taylor (1985), Theorem 5.1.9, page 237, it is shown that a regular approximating sequence $(f^n)_{n\in\mathbb{N}}$ for the function f exists.

Let a measure space $(X, \mathcal{A}, \mu)$ be given with μ a probability measure. Let $f : X \rightarrow \mathbb{R}$ be a simple function and let, for $m \in \mathbb{N}$, for every $i \in I_m$, $a^i \in \mathbb{R}$ and $E^i \in \mathcal{A}$ be such that $f(x) = \sum_{i\in I_m} a^i \chi_{E^i}(x)$, $\forall x \in X$. The *integral* of f is denoted by $\int_X f d\mu$ and is defined by the real number $\int_X f d\mu =$

$\sum_{i\in I_m} a^i \mu(E^i)$. Now let $f : X \to \mathbb{R}$ be a measurable function satisfying $f(x) \geq 0$, $\forall x \in X$. If $(f^n)_{n\in\mathbb{N}}$ and $(g^n)_{n\in\mathbb{N}}$ are two regular approximating sequences for f, then $\lim_{n\to+\infty} \int_X f^n d\mu = \lim_{n\to+\infty} \int_X g^n d\mu$, see Taylor, Lemma 5.4.1, page 253. The function f is said to be *summable* if $\lim_{n\to+\infty} \int_X f^n d\mu < +\infty$. In this case the *integral* of f, denoted by $\int_X f d\mu$, is defined as this limit, $\int_X f d\mu = \lim_{n\to+\infty} \int_X f^n d\mu$. Next, let $f : X \to \mathbb{R}$ be an arbitrary measurable function. The functions $f^- : X \to \mathbb{R}$ and $f^+ : X \to \mathbb{R}$ are defined by $f^-(x) = -\min(\{f(x), 0\})$, $\forall x \in X$, and $f^+(x) = \max(\{f(x), 0\})$, $\forall x \in X$. Hence, $f(x) = f^+(x) - f^-(x)$, $\forall x \in X$. Using Theorem 2.8.1 it is not difficult to show that if the function f is measurable, then the functions f^- and f^+ are also measurable. Now f is said to be *summable* if both f^- and f^+ are summable and in this case the *integral* of f, denoted by $\int_X f d\mu$, is defined by $\int_X f d\mu = \int_X f^+ d\mu - \int_X f^- d\mu$. It can be shown that every bounded measurable function is summable.

Let $(X^1, \mathcal{A}^1, \mu^1)$ and $(X^2, \mathcal{A}^2, \mu^2)$ be measure spaces with μ^1 and μ^2 probability measures. The σ-algebra of $X^1 \times X^2$ generated by the collection of sets $E^1 \times E^2$ with $E^1 \in \mathcal{A}^1$ and $E^2 \in \mathcal{A}^2$ is called the *product σ-algebra* of the σ-algebras $\mathcal{A}^1$ and $\mathcal{A}^2$ and is denoted by $\mathcal{A}^1 \otimes \mathcal{A}^2$. For every subset S of $X^1 \times X^2$, for every $x^1 \in X^1$, let the set $S(x^1)$ be defined by $S(x^1) = \{x^2 \in X^2 \mid (x^1, x^2) \in S\}$ and, for every $x^2 \in X^2$, let the set $S(x^2)$ be defined by $S(x^2) = \{x^1 \in X^1 \mid (x^1, x^2) \in S\}$. Let some $E \in \mathcal{A}^1 \otimes \mathcal{A}^2$ be given. In Taylor (1985), Theorem 7.5.1, page 339, it is shown that $E(x^1) \in \mathcal{A}^2$, $\forall x^1 \in X^1$, and $E(x^2) \in \mathcal{A}^1$, $\forall x^2 \in X^2$. So, both the function $f^1 : X^1 \to \mathbb{R}$ and the function $f^2 : X^2 \to \mathbb{R}$, defined by $f^1(x^1) = \mu^2(E(x^1))$, $\forall x^1 \in X^1$, and $f^2(x^2) = \mu^1(E(x^2))$, $\forall x^2 \in X^2$, are well defined. In Taylor (1985), Theorem 7.5.3, page 340, it is shown that the functions f^1 and f^2 are measurable and that $\int_{X^1} f^1 d\mu^1 = \int_{X^2} f^2 d\mu^2$. Notice that since μ^1 and μ^2 are probability measures it holds that the functions f^1 and f^2 are bounded, and therefore f^1 and f^2 are summable. For every $E \in \mathcal{A}^1 \otimes \mathcal{A}^2$, the real number $\mu(E)$ is defined by $\mu(E) = \int_{X^1} f^1 d\mu^1 = \int_{X^2} f^2 d\mu^2$. Then $\mu : \mathcal{A}^1 \otimes \mathcal{A}^2 \to \mathbb{R}$ is called the *product measure* of the measures μ^1 and μ^2 and is denoted by $\mu = \mu^1 \times \mu^2$. From Taylor (1985), Theorem 7.5.4, page 343, it follows that μ is indeed a probability measure.

2.9 DIFFERENTIAL CALCULUS

This section is mainly based on Rudin (1976) and Jongen, Jonker, and Twilt (1983).

Let an open set U of $\mathbb{R}^{m^1}$, an element $\overline{x}$ of U, and a function $f : U \to \mathbb{R}^{m^2}$ be given. The function f is said to be *differentiable* at $\overline{x}$ if there exists a linear function, denoted by $\partial f(\overline{x})$, from $\mathbb{R}^{m^1}$ into $\mathbb{R}^{m^2}$, called the *derivative* of f at $\overline{x}$, such that for every sequence $(h^n)_{n\in\mathbb{N}}$ in $\mathbb{R}^{m^1}$ with $h^n \neq 0^{m^1}$, $\forall n \in \mathbb{N}$, and $h^n \to 0^{m^1}$ it holds that

$$\frac{||f(\overline{x}+h^n) - f(\overline{x}) - \partial f(\overline{x})(h^n)||_2}{||h^n||_2} \to 0.$$

The function f is said to be *differentiable* if it is differentiable at every $x \in U$. Since the set U is open, it holds that there exists $n' \in \mathbb{N}$ such that, for every $n \geq n'$, $\overline{x} + h^n \in U$, so then $f(\overline{x} + h^n)$ is well defined. It is easily shown that if the function f is differentiable at $\overline{x}$, then the function $\partial f(\overline{x})$ is uniquely determined. Moreover, it is easily shown that if the function f is differentiable at $\overline{x}$, then f is continuous at $\overline{x}$.

The following result is known as the *chain rule.* Let an open set U^1 of $\mathbb{R}^{m^1}$, an element $\overline{x}$ of U^1, an open set U^2 of $\mathbb{R}^{m^2}$, a function $f^1 : U^1 \to \mathbb{R}^{m^2}$, and a function $f^2 : U^2 \to \mathbb{R}^{m^3}$ be given such that U^2 contains $f^1(U^1)$, f^1 is differentiable at $\overline{x}$, and f^2 is differentiable at $f^1(\overline{x})$. Then the function $f : U^1 \to \mathbb{R}^{m^3}$, defined by $f(x) = f^2(f^1(x))$, $\forall x \in U^1$, is differentiable at $\overline{x}$ and $\partial f(\overline{x}) = \partial f^2(f^1(\overline{x})) \circ \partial f^1(\overline{x})$, see for instance Rudin (1976), Theorem 9.15, page 214.

Let an open set U of $\mathbb{R}^{m^1}$, an element $\overline{x}$ of U, and a function $f : U \to \mathbb{R}^{m^2}$ be given. For every $i \in I_{m^1}$, the i-th *(first order) partial derivative* of f at $\overline{x}$, or the *(first order) partial derivative* of f at $\overline{x}$ with respect to x_i, denoted by $\partial_{x_i} f(\overline{x})$, is defined by $\widehat{x} \in \mathbb{R}^{m^2}$ if for every sequence $(h^n)_{n\in\mathbb{N}}$ in $\mathbb{R}$ with $h^n \neq 0$, $\forall n \in \mathbb{N}$, and $h^n \to 0$ it holds that

$$\tfrac{1}{h^n}\Big(f(\overline{x} + h^n e^{m^1}(i)) - f(\overline{x})\Big) \to \widehat{x}.$$

Since the set U is open, it holds that there exists $n' \in \mathbb{N}$ such that, for every $n \geq n'$, $\overline{x} + h^n e^{m^1}(i) \in U$, so then $f(\overline{x} + h^n e^{m^1}(i))$ is well defined.

Let an open set U of $\mathbb{R}^m$, an element $\overline{x}$ of U, and a function $f : U \to \mathbb{R}^n$ be given. For every $i \in I_m$, it is easily shown that the partial derivative $\partial_{x_i} f(\overline{x})$ exists if and only if the partial derivative $\partial_{x_i} f_j(\overline{x})$ exists for every $j \in I_n$. Moreover, it holds that $\partial_{x_i} f(\overline{x}) = (\partial_{x_i} f_1(\overline{x}), \ldots, \partial_{x_i} f_n(\overline{x}))^\top$. If the i-th partial derivative of f at $\overline{x}$ exists for every $i \in I_m$, then $\partial_x f(\overline{x})$ denotes the *matrix of partial derivatives* of f at $\bar{x}$, i.e.

$$\partial_x f(\bar{x}) = \begin{bmatrix} \partial_{x_1} f_1(\bar{x}) & \cdots & \partial_{x_m} f_1(\bar{x}) \\ \vdots & & \vdots \\ \partial_{x_1} f_n(\bar{x}) & \cdots & \partial_{x_m} f_n(\bar{x}) \end{bmatrix}.$$

Let an open set U of $\mathbb{R}^m$, an element $\bar{x}$ of U, and a function $f : U \to \mathbb{R}^n$ that is differentiable at $\bar{x}$ be given. Then it can be shown that for every $i \in I_m$ the i-th partial derivative of f at $\bar{x}$, $\partial_{x_i} f(\bar{x})$, exists and that $\partial f(\bar{x})(x) = \partial_x f(\bar{x})x$, $\forall x \in \mathbb{R}^m$, see for instance Rudin (1976), Theorem 9.17, page 215. So, the uniquely determined matrix representing the linear function $\partial f(\bar{x})$, see also Section 2.4, is given by $\partial_x f(\bar{x})$.

Let an open set U of $\mathbb{R}^m$ and a function $f : U \to \mathbb{R}^n$ be given. If the partial derivative $\partial_{x_i} f(\bar{x})$ exists for every element $\bar{x}$ of U, then $\partial_{x_i} f : U \to \mathbb{R}^n$ is a function, called the i-th *(first order)* partial derivative of f or the *(first order) partial derivative* of f with respect to x_i. The function f is said to be *continuously differentiable* if for every $i \in I_m$ the function $\partial_{x_i} f$ is continuous. It can be shown that if the function $f : U \to \mathbb{R}^n$ is continuously differentiable, then f is also differentiable, see for instance Rudin (1976), Theorem 9.21, page 219.

Let an open set U of $\mathbb{R}^m$, an element $\bar{x}$ of U, and a continuously differentiable function $f : U \to \mathbb{R}^n$ be given. For every $i^1, i^2 \in I_m$, the *second order partial derivative* of f at $\bar{x}$ with respect to x_{i^1} and x_{i^2}, denoted by $\partial^2_{x_{i^1} x_{i^2}} f(\bar{x})$, is defined by $\partial^2_{x_{i^1} x_{i^2}} f(\bar{x}) = \partial_{x_{i^1}}(\partial_{x_{i^2}} f)(\bar{x})$ if this expression is well defined. If for every $i^1, i^2 \in I_m$ the function $\partial^2_{x_{i^1} x_{i^2}} f : U \to \mathbb{R}^n$ is continuous, then the function f is called a *twice continuously differentiable function.* In a similar way, for every $r \in \mathbb{N}$, the *r-th order partial derivatives* of the function f can be defined, and f is called r *times continuously differentiable* if all partial derivatives of f up to the order r are continuous functions. If f is a function from U into $\mathbb{R}$, then $\partial^2_{xx} f(\bar{x})$ denotes the matrix having for every $i^1, i^2 \in I_m$ the element $\partial^2_{x_{i^1} x_{i^2}} f(\bar{x})$ in column i^1 and row i^2.

For a function $f : U \to T$ with U an open set of $\mathbb{R}^m$ and T a non-empty subset of $\mathbb{R}^n$, all notions mentioned above are defined in an identical way. For every $r \in \mathbb{N}$, $C^r(U, T)$ is defined as the set of r times continuously differentiable functions from U into T. The set $C^\infty(U, T)$ is defined by $C^\infty(U, T) = \cap_{r \in \mathbb{N}} C^r(U, T)$. An element of $C^\infty(U, T)$ is called a *smooth function.* It easily follows that $C^\infty(U, T) \subset \cdots \subset C^1(U, T) \subset C^0(U, T)$. For any $r \in \mathbb{N}$, the order of taking the partial derivatives to obtain an r-th order partial derivative does not matter for the resulting value of the partial derivative of an element of $C^r(U, T)$, see Rudin (1976), Corollary of Theorem 9.4.1, page 236.

The following result is easily verified, but nevertheless surprising.

Theorem 2.9.1
The function $f : \mathbb{R} \to \mathbb{R}$, *defined by* $f(x) = 0$, $\forall x \leq 0$, *and* $f(x) = \exp(-\frac{1}{x})$, $\forall x > 0$, *is an element of* $C^\infty(\mathbb{R}, \mathbb{R})$.
See Jongen, Jonker, and Twilt (1983), page 41.

A result related to Theorem 2.9.1 is given in Theorem 2.9.2.

Theorem 2.9.2
For every $\alpha, \beta \in \mathbb{R}$ *with* $0 < \alpha < \beta$, *there exists a function* $f \in C^\infty(\mathbb{R}^m, [0, 1])$ *such that, for every* $x \in \mathbb{R}^m$, $f(x) = 1$ *if* $||x||_2 \leq \alpha$, $0 < f(x) < 1$ *if* $\alpha < ||x||_2 < \beta$, *and* $f(x) = 0$ *if* $||x||_2 \geq \beta$.
See Hirsch (1976), page 41-42.

The following result is known as the *inverse function theorem.*

Theorem 2.9.3 (Inverse function theorem)
For $r \in \mathbb{N}^*$, *let an open set* U *of* $\mathbb{R}^m$, *an element* $\overline{x}$ *of* U, *and a function* $f \in C^r(U, \mathbb{R}^m)$ *be given. If* $\partial_x f(\overline{x})$ *is an invertible matrix, then there exist open sets* U^1 *and* U^2 *of* $\mathbb{R}^m$ *such that* $\overline{x} \in U^1$, *the function* $g \in C^r(U^1, U^2)$, *defined by* $g(x) = f(x)$, $\forall x \in U^1$, *is injective and surjective,* $g^{-1} \in C^r(U^2, U^1)$, *and* $\partial_x g^{-1}(g(\overline{x})) = (\partial_x g(\overline{x}))^{-1}$. *If* U^1 *and* U^2 *are open sets of* $\mathbb{R}^m$ *and* g *is a function of* $C^r(U^1, U^2)$ *such that* g *is injective, surjective, and* $g^{-1} \in C^r(U^2, U^1)$, *then* $\partial_x g(\overline{x})$ *is invertible for every* $\overline{x} \in U^1$.
See Mas-Colell (1985), Theorem C.3.1, page 20.

For $r \in \mathbb{Z}_+$, let an open set U of $\mathbb{R}^m$, a subset T of $\mathbb{R}^n$, and a function $f \in C^r(U, T)$ be given. For every $k \in \mathbb{Z}^m_+$ with $||k||_1 \leq r$, the function $\nabla^k f : U \to \mathbb{R}^n$ is defined by letting, for every $\overline{x} \in U$, $\nabla^k f(\overline{x})$ be the value of the $||k||_1$-th order partial derivative obtained by taking, for every $i \in I_m$, k_i times the partial derivative of f with respect to x_i at $\overline{x}$. Notice that $\nabla^{0^m} f = f$ and, for every $i \in I_m$, $\nabla^{e^m(i)} f = \partial_{x_i} f$.

Let some $r \in \mathbb{Z}^*_+$ and an open set U of $\mathbb{R}^m$ be given. A topology on the set $C^r(U, \mathbb{R})$ is needed in Chapter 9. The following topology, called the C^r-topology, is used. The C^r-topology is defined by giving a base for it.

Definition 2.9.4 (C^r-topology)
Let $r \in \mathbb{Z}_+$, $\bar{r} \in \mathbb{Z}_+^*$ with $r \leq \bar{r}$, and an open set U of $\mathbb{R}^m$ be given. A base for the C^r-topology on $C^{\bar{r}}(U, \mathbb{R})$ is given by the collection

$$\left\{ V_{g,\epsilon}^r \,\middle|\, g \in C^{\bar{r}}(U, \mathbb{R}) \text{ and } \epsilon \in C^0(U, \mathbb{R}_{++}) \right\},$$

where

$$V_{g,\epsilon}^r = \left\{ f \in C^{\bar{r}}(U, \mathbb{R}) \middle| \; \forall k \in \mathbb{Z}_+^m \text{ with } \|k\|_1 \leq r, \; |\nabla^k g(x) - \nabla^k f(x)| < \epsilon(x), \; \forall x \in U \right\}.$$

A subset O of $C^\infty(U, \mathbb{R})$ is open in the *C^∞-topology* on $C^\infty(U, \mathbb{R})$ if there exists $r \in \mathbb{N}$ such that O is open in the C^r-topology on $C^\infty(U, \mathbb{R})$.

Let $r \in \mathbb{N}^*$, a subset S of $\mathbb{R}^m$, and a subset T of $\mathbb{R}^n$ be given. A function $f : S \to T$ is called *r times continuously differentiable* if for every element x of S there exists an open set U of $\mathbb{R}^m$ containing x and a function $g \in C^r(U, \mathbb{R}^n)$ such that $g(x) = f(x)$, $\forall x \in S \cap U$. The set of r times continuously differentiable functions from S into T is denoted by $C^r(S, T)$. A function $f : S \to T$ is called a *C^r diffeomorphism* if f is injective, surjective, $f \in C^r(S, T)$, and $f^{-1} \in C^r(T, S)$. The sets S and T are called *C^r diffeomorphic* if there exists a C^r diffeomorphism $f : S \to T$. Although the above definitions are of a local character, the following result shows that they can be made global.

Theorem 2.9.5
For $r \in \mathbb{N}^*$, let a subset S of $\mathbb{R}^m$, a subset T of $\mathbb{R}^n$, and a function $f \in C^r(S, T)$ be given. Then there exists an open set U of $\mathbb{R}^m$ containing the set S and there exists a function $g \in C^r(U, \mathbb{R}^n)$ such that $g(x) = f(x)$, $\forall x \in S$.
See Jongen, Jonker, and Twilt (1983), Lemma 3.1.5, page 103.

Differentiability properties are often employed in optimization. Before giving necessary and sufficient conditions for an element to be a maximizer of a function on a certain set, some properties of functions are given first. Let a subset S of $\mathbb{R}^m$, an element $\bar{x}$ of S, and a function $f : S \to \mathbb{R}$ be given. The function f is said to be *quasi-convex* at $\bar{x}$ if $f(\hat{x}) \leq f(\bar{x})$ for some $\hat{x} \in S$ and $\lambda\hat{x} + (1-\lambda)\bar{x} \in S$ for some $\lambda \in [0,1]$ implies $f(\lambda\hat{x} + (1-\lambda)\bar{x}) \leq f(\bar{x})$. The function f is said to be *quasi-convex* if it is quasi-convex at every $x \in S$. The function f is said to be *quasi-concave* at $\bar{x}$ if $f(\hat{x}) \geq f(\bar{x})$ for some $\hat{x} \in S$ and $\lambda\hat{x} + (1-\lambda)\bar{x} \in S$ for some $\lambda \in [0,1]$ implies $f(\lambda\hat{x} + (1-\lambda)\bar{x}) \geq f(\bar{x})$. The function f is said to be *quasi-concave* if it is quasi-concave at every $x \in S$.

Let an open set U of $\mathbb{R}^m$, an element $\overline{x}$ of U, and a function $f : U \to \mathbb{R}$ be given. The function f is said to be *pseudo-convex* at $\overline{x}$ if f is differentiable at $\overline{x}$ and if $\partial_x f(\overline{x})(\widehat{x}-\overline{x}) \geq 0$ for some $\widehat{x} \in U$ implies $f(\widehat{x}) \geq f(\overline{x})$. The function f is said to be *pseudo-convex* if it is pseudo-convex at every $x \in U$. The function f is said to be *pseudo-concave* at $\overline{x}$ if f is differentiable at $\overline{x}$ and if $\partial_x f(\overline{x})(\widehat{x}-\overline{x}) \leq 0$ for some $\widehat{x} \in U$ implies $f(\widehat{x}) \leq f(\overline{x})$. The function f is said to be *pseudo-concave* if it is pseudo-concave at every $x \in U$.

The following result gives sufficient conditions for an element to be a maximizer of a function on a certain set.

Theorem 2.9.6
Let an open set U of $\mathbb{R}^m$, an element $\overline{x}$ of U, a function $f : U \to \mathbb{R}$, and a function $g : U \to \mathbb{R}^n$ be given. Let the function f be pseudo-concave at $\overline{x}$ and let the function g be differentiable and quasi-concave at $\overline{x}$. If there exists $\lambda \in \mathbb{R}^n$ such that

$$\begin{aligned} \partial_x f(\overline{x}) + \lambda^\top \partial_x g(\overline{x}) &= 0^{m\top}, \\ \lambda^\top g(\overline{x}) &= 0, \\ g(\overline{x}) &\geq 0^n, \\ \lambda &\geq 0^n, \end{aligned}$$

then $\overline{x}$ is a maximizer of f on the set S given by $S = \{x \in U \mid g(x) \geq 0^n\}$.
See Mangasarian (1969), Theorem 10.1.2, page 153.

The following result gives necessary conditions for an element to be a maximizer of a function on a certain set.

Theorem 2.9.7
Let an open set U of $\mathbb{R}^m$, a function $f : U \to \mathbb{R}$, and a function $g : U \to \mathbb{R}^n$ be given. Let the element $\overline{x}$ be a maximizer of f on the set S given by $S = \{x \in U \mid g(x) \geq 0^n\}$ and let the functions f and g be differentiable at $\overline{x}$. Then there exists $\lambda \in \mathbb{R}^n$ and $\mu \in \mathbb{R}$ such that

$$\begin{aligned} \mu\partial_x f(\overline{x}) + \lambda^\top \partial_x g(\overline{x}) &= 0^{m\top}, \\ \lambda^\top g(\overline{x}) &= 0, \\ g(\overline{x}) &\geq 0^n, \\ \lambda &\geq 0^n, \\ \mu &\geq 0, \end{aligned}$$

while $\lambda_j > 0$ *for some* $j \in I_n$ *such that* $g_j(\overline{x}) = 0$ *and* g_j *is not pseudo-convex at* $\overline{x}$, *or* $\mu > 0$.
See Mangasarian (1969), Theorem 10.2.2, page 154.

2.10 DIFFERENTIAL TOPOLOGY

This section is mainly based on Golubitsky and Guillemin (1973) and Jongen, Jonker, and Twilt (1983, 1986). For a nice introduction into the field the reader is referred to Milnor (1965).

Intuitively, for some $k \in \mathbb{N}$, a k-dimensional manifold is a set that is locally like $\mathbb{R}^k$. The following definitions make this statement more precise.

Definition 2.10.1 (Topological manifold)
For $k \in \mathbb{Z}_+$, *a subset* X *of* $\mathbb{R}^m$ *is a* k-dimensional topological manifold *if for every element* x *of* X *there exists an open set* U *of* X *containing* x, *an open set* V *of* $\mathbb{R}^k$, *and an injective and surjective function* $\phi : U \to V$ *such that* $\phi \in C^0(U, V)$ *and* $\phi^{-1} \in C^0(V, U)$, *i.e.* $\phi : U \to V$ *is a homeomorphism.*

Definition 2.10.2 (C^r manifold)
For $k \in \mathbb{Z}_+$, *for* $r \in \mathbb{N}^*$, *a subset* X *of* $\mathbb{R}^m$ *is a* k-dimensional C^r manifold *if for every element* x *of* X *there exists an open set* U *of* X *containing* x, *an open set* V *of* $\mathbb{R}^k$, *and an injective and surjective function* $\phi : U \to V$ *such that* $\phi \in C^r(U, V)$ *and* $\phi^{-1} \in C^r(V, U)$, *i.e.* $\phi : U \to V$ *is a* C^r *diffeomorphism.*

The pair (U, ϕ) in Definition 2.10.2 is called a *chart* of X around x and (V, ϕ^{-1}) are called *local* C^r *coordinates* for U. The function ϕ is called a C^r *coordinate system* for X around x.

Definition 2.10.3 (Piecewise C^r manifold)
For $k \in \mathbb{Z}_+$, *for* $r \in \mathbb{N}^*$, *a subset* X *of* $\mathbb{R}^m$ *is a* k-dimensional piecewise C^r manifold *if* X *is a* k*-dimensional topological manifold that is a finite union of* C^r *manifolds.*

If X is a k-dimensional topological manifold, a k-dimensional C^r manifold, or a k-dimensional piecewise C^r manifold, then the *dimension* of X is said to be k.

In Definition 2.10.3 it is allowed that the dimension of some of the C^r manifolds whose union is equal to X is less than k.

Examples of m-dimensional C^∞ manifolds are the set $\mathbb{R}^m$ and any open set of $\mathbb{R}^m$. The set $\widetilde{B}^{m-1}(0^m, 1)$ can be shown to be an $(m-1)$-dimensional C^∞ manifold. The set $\mathbb{N}$ is a 0-dimensional C^∞ manifold. The empty set is a k-dimensional C^∞ manifold for every $k \in \mathbb{Z}_+$. Clearly, for every $r, \overline{r} \in \mathbb{N}^*$ with $r < \overline{r}$, it holds that a $C^{\overline{r}}$ manifold is also a C^r manifold. For some $r \in \mathbb{N}$, let a function $f \in C^r(\mathbb{R}, \mathbb{R}) \setminus C^{r+1}(\mathbb{R}, \mathbb{R})$ be given. Then the set $\{x \in \mathbb{R}^2 \mid x_2 = f(x_1)\}$ is a C^r manifold, but not a C^{r+1} manifold, see Jongen, Jonker, and Twilt (1983), Example 3.1.1, page 91. The set Q^m is neither a C^r manifold for any $r \in \mathbb{N}^*$ nor a topological manifold. The set $S = \{x \in \mathbb{R}^2 \mid \min(\{x_1, x_2\}) = 0\}$ is a 1-dimensional topological manifold, but it is not a C^1 manifold. It is the union of the 1-dimensional C^∞ manifold $S^1 = \{x \in \mathbb{R}^2 \mid x_1 = 0 \text{ and } x_2 > 0\}$, the 0-dimensional C^∞ manifold $S^2 = \{x \in \mathbb{R}^2 \mid x = (0,0)^\top\}$, and the 1-dimensional C^∞ manifold $S^3 = \{x \in \mathbb{R}^2 \mid x_1 > 0 \text{ and } x_2 = 0\}$. Therefore, the set S is a 1-dimensional piecewise C^∞ manifold. The set Q^m is not a piecewise C^1 manifold since it is not a topological manifold.

For $k \in \mathbb{Z}_+$, for $r \in \mathbb{N}^*$, let a k-dimensional C^r manifold X, an element $\overline{x}$ of X, and a coordinate system ϕ for X around $\overline{x}$ be given. Then the set $\partial\phi^{-1}(\phi(\overline{x}))(\mathbb{R}^k)$ is called the *tangent space* of X at $\overline{x}$ and is denoted by $T_{\overline{x}}X$. It can be shown that the set $T_{\overline{x}}X$ does not depend on the choice of the coordinate system ϕ. The 1-dimensional C^∞ manifold $\widetilde{B}^1((0,0)^\top, 2)$, the tangent space of $\widetilde{B}^1((0,0)^\top, 2)$ at $x^1 = (2,0)^\top$, $T_{x^1}\widetilde{B}^1((0,0)^\top, 2)$, and at $x^2 = (\sqrt{2}, \sqrt{2})^\top$, $T_{x^2}\widetilde{B}^1((0,0)^\top, 2)$ are shown in Figure 2.10.1.

For $k \in \mathbb{Z}_+$, for $r \in \mathbb{N}^*$, a characterization of a k-dimensional C^r manifold is given in the following theorem. This characterization is also sometimes used as a definition of a k-dimensional C^r manifold, see for instance van Geldrop (1981).

Theorem 2.10.4
For $k \in \mathbb{Z}_+$, for $r \in \mathbb{N}^*$, a subset X of $\mathbb{R}^m$ is a k-dimensional C^r manifold if and only if for every element x of X there exists a C^r coordinate system $\phi : U \to V$ of $\mathbb{R}^m$ around x satisfying $\phi(x) = 0^m$ and $\phi(X \cap U) = \{y \in V \mid y_i = 0, \forall i \in I_{m-k}\}$.
See Jongen, Jonker, and Twilt (1983), Theorem 3.11, page 89.

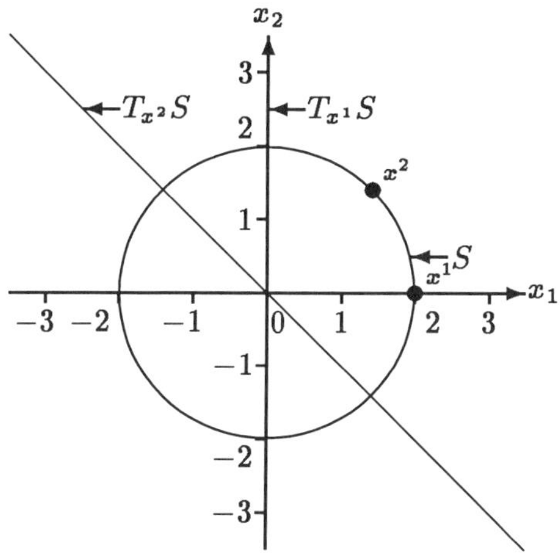

Figure 2.10.1. The set $S = \widetilde{B}^1((0,0)^\top, 2)$, the tangent space $T_{x^1}S$, and the tangent space $T_{x^2}S$, with $x^1 = (2,0)^\top$ and $x^2 = (\sqrt{2}, \sqrt{2})^\top$.

Notice that, by definition, the function $\phi : U \to V$ in Theorem 2.10.4 is a C^r coordinate system of $\mathbb{R}^m$ around x if $x \in U$, U and V are open sets of $\mathbb{R}^m$, ϕ is injective and surjective, $\phi \in C^r(U, V)$, and $\phi^{-1} \in C^r(V, U)$.

For the purposes of this monograph the concept of a manifold is too restrictive. Especially sets like the unit simplex Δ^{m-1} or the unit cube Q^m are frequently studied in Part IV of this monograph, both not being manifolds. Hence, the notion of a manifold with generalized boundary is introduced.

Definition 2.10.5 (Manifold with generalized boundary)
For $k \in \mathbb{Z}_+$, for $r \in \mathbb{N}^*$, a subset X of $\mathbb{R}^m$ is a k-dimensional C^r manifold with generalized boundary (MGB) *if for every element x of X there exists a C^r coordinate system $\phi : U \to V$ of $\mathbb{R}^m$ around x and an integer $\ell(x)$, $0 \le \ell(x) \le k$, satisfying $\phi(x) = 0^m$ and*

$$\phi(X \cap U) = \left\{ y \in V \,\middle|\, y_i = 0,\ \forall i \in I_{m-k},\ \textit{and}\ y_i \ge 0,\ \forall i \in I_{m-k+\ell(x)} \setminus I_{m-k} \right\}.$$

If X is a k-dimensional C^r manifold with generalized boundary, then the *dimension* of X is said to be k. From Jongen, Jonker, and Twilt (1983), Lemma 3.1.3, page 97, it follows that the dimension k, for every MGB X, and the integer $\ell(x)$, for every element x of X, are independent from the choice of the coordinate system. Intuitively, a k-dimensional manifold with generalized boundary is in a neighbourhood of $\bar{x} \in X$ as the set $\{x \in \mathbb{R}^k \mid x_i \geq 0, \forall i \in I_{\ell(\bar{x})}\}$.

Using Definition 2.10.5 it is easily verified that the set Q^m is an m-dimensional C^∞ MGB with $\ell(x) = \#(\{i \in I_m \mid x_i = 0\} \cup \{i \in I_m \mid x_i = 1\})$, $\forall x \in Q^m$. The unit simplex Δ^{m-1} is an $(m-1)$-dimensional C^∞ MGB with $\ell(x) = \#\{i \in I_m \mid x_i = 0\}$, $\forall x \in \Delta^{m-1}$. These results follow immediately from Theorem 2.10.11. Notice that the set $\{x \in \mathbb{R}^2_+ \mid x_1 = 0 \text{ or } x_2 = 0\}$ is not an MGB.

Theorem 2.10.6
For $k \in \mathbb{Z}_+$, for $r \in \mathbb{N}^*$, let the set X be a k-dimensional C^r MGB. Then every component in X is a path-connected k-dimensional C^r MGB.
See Jongen, Jonker, and Twilt (1983), Lemma 3.1.1, page 93, and Exercise 3.1.4, page 97.

For $k \in \mathbb{Z}_+$, for $r \in \mathbb{N}^*$, let the set X be a k-dimensional C^r MGB. The set $B^l(X)$ is defined by

$$B^l(X) = \{x \in X \mid \ell(x) = l\}, \ \forall l \in I_k^0.$$

For every $l \in I_k^0$, a path-component of $B^l(X)$ is called a *stratum* of X. Clearly, the collection of strata of X is a partition of X. The set $B^0(X)$ is called the *relative interior* of X. The set $X \setminus B^0(X)$ is called the *relative boundary* of X. These definitions of relative interior and relative boundary are consistent with the corresponding definitions in Section 2.3 for arcs and in Section 2.7 for convex sets. In the case when $X = B^0(X)$ it follows that the set X is a k-dimensional C^r manifold by Theorem 2.10.4. If $X = B^0(X) \cup B^1(X)$, then the set X is called a *manifold with boundary*. The following theorem yields that the relative boundary of a manifold with boundary is a manifold.

Theorem 2.10.7
For $k \in \mathbb{Z}_+$, for $r \in \mathbb{N}^*$, let the set X be a k-dimensional C^r MGB. For every $l \in I_k^0$, the set $B^l(X)$ is a $(k-l)$-dimensional C^r manifold.
See Jongen, Jonker, and Twilt (1983), Lemma 3.1.4, page 98.

From Theorem 2.10.6 and Theorem 2.10.7 it follows that a stratum of an MGB is a manifold. The following result is often useful in showing that a set is an MGB.

Theorem 2.10.8
For $k \in \mathbb{Z}_+$, for $r \in \mathbb{N}^*$, let the set X be a k-dimensional C^r MGB and let the

function $f : X \to Y$ be a C^r diffeomorphism, where Y is a subset of $\mathbb{R}^n$. Then the set Y is a k-dimensional C^r MGB. If the set S is a stratum of X, then the set $f(S)$ is a stratum of Y.
See Jongen, Jonker, and Twilt (1983), Corollary 3.1.3, page 103.

Compact 1-dimensional MGB's have a particular nice structure, as follows from the following theorem.

Theorem 2.10.9
For $r \in \mathbb{N}^*$, let the set X be a compact 1-dimensional C^r MGB. Then the set X has a finite number of components, each being C^r diffeomorphic to either the unit circle $\widetilde{B}^1((0,0)^\top, 1)$ or the unit interval $[0,1]$.
See Mas-Colell (1985), H.6, page 35.

An interesting class of sets are the so-called regular constraint sets. Let U be an open set of $\mathbb{R}^m$ and let, for some $n^1 \in \mathbb{Z}_+$, for some $n^2 \in \mathbb{Z}_+$, functions $\widetilde{g}_j : U \to \mathbb{R}$, $\forall j \in I_{n^1}$, and $\widetilde{h}_j : U \to \mathbb{R}$, $\forall j \in I_{n^2}$, be given. The set $M[\widetilde{g}, \widetilde{h}]$ is defined by

$$M[\widetilde{g}, \widetilde{h}] = \left\{ x \in U \,\middle|\, \widetilde{g}_j(x) = 0, \ \forall j \in I_{n^1}, \text{ and } \widetilde{h}_j(x) \geq 0, \ \forall j \in I_{n^2} \right\}.$$

For every element x of U, the set $J^0(x)$ is defined by $J^0(x) = \{j \in I_{n^2} \mid h_j(x) = 0\}$. In the above definitions n^1 and n^2 are allowed to be zero, in which case $\widetilde{g}$ and $\widetilde{h}$ are denoted by $\emptyset$, respectively.

Definition 2.10.10 (Regular constraint system and regular constraint set)
For $n^1, n^2 \in \mathbb{Z}_+$, for $r \in \mathbb{N}^*$, let U be an open set of $\mathbb{R}^m$ and let $\widetilde{g}_j : U \to \mathbb{R}$, $\forall j \in I_{n^1}$, and $\widetilde{h}_j : U \to \mathbb{R}$, $\forall j \in I_{n^2}$, be C^r functions. The pair of functions $(\widetilde{g}, \widetilde{h})$ is a C^r regular constraint system *if for every element $\bar{x}$ of $M[\widetilde{g}, \widetilde{h}]$ the set*

$$\left\{ \partial_x \widetilde{g}_j(\bar{x})^\top \,\middle|\, j \in I_{n^1} \right\} \cup \left\{ \partial_x \widetilde{h}_j(\bar{x})^\top \,\middle|\, j \in J^0(\bar{x}) \right\}$$

is an independent set. The set S is a C^r regular constraint set (RCS) *if there exists a C^r regular constraint system $(\widetilde{g}, \widetilde{h})$ such that $S = M[\widetilde{g}, \widetilde{h}]$.*

Let $\widetilde{g} = \emptyset$ and let the function $\widetilde{h} : \mathbb{R}^m \to \mathbb{R}^{2m+1}$ be defined as follows. For every $i \in I_m$, $\widetilde{h}_i(x) = x_i$, $\forall x \in \mathbb{R}^m$, $\widetilde{h}_{m+i}(x) = 1 - x_i$, $\forall x \in \mathbb{R}^m$, and $\widetilde{h}_{2m+1}(x) =$

$\sum_{i\in I_m} x_i$, $\forall x \in \mathbb{R}^m$. Then $M[\tilde{g}, \tilde{h}] = Q^m$, but the pair of functions $(\tilde{g}, \tilde{h})$ is not a C^r regular constraint system for any $r \in \mathbb{N}^*$. This follows from the fact that $J^0(0^m) = I_m \cup \{2m+1\}$ and since a subset of $\mathbb{R}^m$ containing $m+1$ elements can never be independent. Now let $\tilde{g} = \emptyset$ and let the function $\tilde{h} : \mathbb{R}^m \to \mathbb{R}^{2m}$ be defined by letting for every $i \in I_{2m}$ component $\tilde{h}_i$ of $\tilde{h}$ be as before. Then, again, it holds that $M[\tilde{g}, \tilde{h}] = Q^m$. It is easily verified that the pair of functions $(\tilde{g}, \tilde{h})$ is a C^∞ regular constraint system. Hence, the unit cube Q^m is a C^∞ RCS.

Let the function $\tilde{g} : \mathbb{R}^m \to \mathbb{R}$ be defined by $\tilde{g}(x) = \sum_{i\in I_m} x_i - 1$, $\forall x \in \mathbb{R}^m$, and, for every $i \in I_m$, let the function $\tilde{h}_i : \mathbb{R}^m \to \mathbb{R}$ be defined by $\tilde{h}_i(x) = x_i$, $\forall x \in \mathbb{R}^m$. It is easily verified that the pair of functions $(\tilde{g}, \tilde{h})$ is a C^∞ regular constraint system. Since $M[\tilde{g}, \tilde{h}] = \Delta^{m-1}$, it holds that the unit simplex Δ^{m-1} is a C^∞ RCS.

Theorem 2.10.11
For $r \in \mathbb{N}^*$, let the subset X of $\mathbb{R}^m$ be a C^r RCS and let the pair of functions $(\tilde{g}, \tilde{h})$ be a C^r regular constraint system such that $M[\tilde{g}, \tilde{h}] = X$, where $\tilde{g}$ has n^1 components. Then X is a k-dimensional C^r MGB with $k = m - n^1$. Moreover, $\ell(x) = \#J^0(x)$ for every element x of X.
See Jongen, Jonker, and Twilt (1983), Lemma 3.1.2, page 94.

Theorem 2.10.11 shows that the dimension of a non-empty RCS is well defined. In many cases Theorem 2.10.11 can be used to show that a certain set is an MGB.

Next, the tangent space and the tangent cone of a manifold with generalized boundary are defined.

Definition 2.10.12 (Tangent space and tangent cone)
For $k \in \mathbb{Z}_+$, for $r \in \mathbb{N}^*$, let the set X be a k-dimensional C^r MGB. Let $\bar{x}$ be an element of X and let the function ϕ be a C^r coordinate system for $\mathbb{R}^m$ around $\bar{x}$ with the properties given in Definition 2.10.5. The tangent space *of X at $\bar{x}$, denoted by $T_{\bar{x}}X$, is the set $\partial\phi^{-1}(0^m)(\{0^{m-k}\} \times \mathbb{R}^k)$ and the* tangent cone *of X at $\bar{x}$, denoted by $C_{\bar{x}}X$, is the set $\partial\phi^{-1}(0^m)(\{0^{m-k}\} \times \mathbb{R}_+^{\ell(\bar{x})} \times \mathbb{R}^{k-\ell(\bar{x})})$.*

It can be shown that both the tangent space $T_{\bar{x}}X$ and the tangent cone $C_{\bar{x}}X$ as defined in Definition 2.10.12 do not depend on the choice of the coordinate system. Moreover, in the case where the set $X \setminus B^0(X)$ is empty, the definition of a tangent space as given in Definition 2.10.12 coincides with the definition given before. It is also easily verified that a tangent cone is indeed a cone. Since $\partial\phi^{-1}(0^m)$ is a C^∞ diffeomorphism, it holds by Theorem 2.9.3 that $\partial_x\phi^{-1}(0^m)$ is an invertible matrix and therefore $T_{\overline{x}}X$ is a k-dimensional vector space. Moreover, it follows from Theorem 2.10.8 that $C_{\overline{x}}X$ is a k-dimensional MGB.

In the case when a set X is an RCS, the following theorem gives an easy way to determine the tangent space of X at an element of X.

Theorem 2.10.13
For $k \in \mathbb{Z}_+$, for $r \in \mathbb{N}^*$, let the subset X of $\mathbb{R}^m$ be a k-dimensional C^r RCS, let $\overline{x}$ be an element of X, and let the pair of functions $(\widetilde{g}, \widetilde{h})$ be a C^r regular constraint system such that $X = M[\widetilde{g}, \widetilde{h}]$. Then

$$T_{\overline{x}}X = \left\{x \in \mathbb{R}^m \,\middle|\, \partial\widetilde{g}(\overline{x})(x) = 0^{m-k}\right\}.$$

See Jongen, Jonker, and Twilt (1983), Example 3.2.2, page 111.

For $r \in \mathbb{N}^*$, let the subsets X of $\mathbb{R}^m$ and Y of $\mathbb{R}^n$ be C^r manifolds, let $\overline{x}$ be an element of X, and let f be a function of $C^r(X, Y)$. Let U be an open set of $\mathbb{R}^m$ such that $X \subset U$ and let the function $g \in C^r(U, \mathbb{R}^n)$ be such that $g(x) = f(x)$, $\forall x \in X$. Such a function g exists by Theorem 2.9.5. It can be shown that $\partial g(\overline{x})_{|T_{\overline{x}}X}$ is a function from $T_{\overline{x}}X$ into $T_{f(\overline{x})}Y$. Moreover, the function $\partial g(\overline{x})_{|T_{\overline{x}}X}$ does not depend on the choice of the function g. The *derivative* of f at $\overline{x}$, denoted by $\partial f(\overline{x})$, is defined by $\partial f(\overline{x}) = \partial g(\overline{x})_{|T_{\overline{x}}X}$. The element $\overline{x}$ is called a *regular point* of f if $\partial f(\overline{x})(T_{\overline{x}}X) = T_{f(\overline{x})}Y$. Otherwise $\overline{x}$ is called a *critical point* of f. Let an element $\overline{y}$ of Y be given. The element $\overline{y}$ is called a *critical value* of f if it is the image of a critical point of f. Otherwise $\overline{y}$ is called a *regular value* of f. Notice that every element y of $Y \setminus f(X)$ is a regular value of f.

For $r \in \mathbb{N}^* \setminus \{1\}$, for $m \in \mathbb{N} \setminus \{1\}$, let the subset X of $\mathbb{R}^m$ be an m-dimensional C^r manifold with boundary. Let $\overline{x}$ be an element of $B^1(X)$. With the element $\overline{x}$ is associated the vector $\widehat{g}(\overline{x})$ of $\mathbb{R}^m$ satisfying $\widehat{g}(\overline{x}) \cdot x = 0$, $\forall x \in T_{\overline{x}}B^1(X)$, $\widehat{g}(\overline{x}) \cdot x \leq 0$, $\forall x \in C_{\overline{x}}X$, and $\|\widehat{g}(\overline{x})\|_2 = 1$. It is easily verified that the vector $\widehat{g}(\overline{x})$ is uniquely determined. The function $\widehat{g} : B^1(X) \to \widetilde{B}^{m-1}(0^m, 1)$, obtained by associating with every element x of $B^1(X)$ the vector $\widehat{g}(x)$, is called the *Gauss map* of $B^1(X)$. It can be shown that the function $\widehat{g}$ is continuously differentiable and that, for every $x \in B^1(X)$, $\partial\widehat{g}(x)$ is a function from $T_xB^1(X)$ into $T_xB^1(X)$, see Mas-Colell (1985), page 39. For every $x \in B^1(X)$, the determinant of the linear function $\partial\widehat{g}(x)$, for the definition see Section 2.4, is called the *Gaussian curvature* of $B^1(X)$ at x.

Let C^1 manifolds X, Y, and Z, Z being a subset of Y, an element $\overline{x}$ of X, and a function $f \in C^1(X,Y)$ be given. The function f is said to intersect Z *transversally* at $\overline{x} \in X$, denoted by $f \pitchfork Z$ at $\overline{x}$, if

$$f(\overline{x}) \notin Z, \text{ or } f(\overline{x}) \in Z \text{ and } T_{f(\overline{x})}Z + \partial f(\overline{x})(T_{\overline{x}}X) = T_{f(\overline{x})}Y.$$

The function f is said to intersect Z *transversally* if $f \pitchfork Z$ at every $x \in X$. The following theorem follows almost immediately from the definition of transversality.

Theorem 2.10.14
For $k^1, k^2, k^3 \in \mathbb{Z}_+$, for $r \in \mathbb{N}^*$, let a k^1-dimensional C^1 manifold X, a k^2-dimensional C^1 manifold Y, and a k^3-dimensional C^1 manifold Z, Z being a subset of Y, be given, and let the function $f \in C^1(X,Y)$ be such that $f \pitchfork Z$. If $k^1 - k^2 + k^3 < 0$, then $f^{-1}(Z) = \emptyset$.
See Golubitsky and Guillemin (1973), Proposition 4.2, page 51.

The following result is complementary to Theorem 2.10.14.

Theorem 2.10.15
For $k^1, k^2, k^3 \in \mathbb{Z}_+$, for $r \in \mathbb{N}^*$, let a k^1-dimensional C^r manifold X, a k^2-dimensional C^r manifold Y, and a k^3-dimensional C^r manifold Z, Z being a subset of Y, be given, and let the function $f \in C^r(X,Y)$ be such that $f \pitchfork Z$. If $k^1 - k^2 + k^3 \geq 0$, then $f^{-1}(Z)$ is a $(k^1 - k^2 + k^3)$-dimensional C^r manifold.
See Mas-Colell (1985), I.2.1, page 43.

The following result is an easy corollary to Theorems 2.10.14 and 2.10.15.

Theorem 2.10.16
For $k^1, k^2 \in \mathbb{Z}_+$, for $r \in \mathbb{N}^*$, let a k^1-dimensional C^r manifold X, a k^2-dimensional C^r manifold Y, and a function $f \in C^r(X,Y)$ be given. Let the element $\overline{y}$ of Y be a regular value of f. If $k^1 - k^2 < 0$, then $f^{-1}(\{\overline{y}\}) = \emptyset$, and if $k^1 - k^2 \geq 0$, then $f^{-1}(\{\overline{y}\})$ is a $(k^1 - k^2)$-dimensional C^r manifold.
See Mas-Colell (1985), H.2.2, page 38.

For Theorem 2.10.18 the notion of Lebesgue measure zero in X for a subset of a manifold X needs to be defined. For $k \in \mathbb{Z}_+$, for $r \in \mathbb{N}^*$, let the subset X of $\mathbb{R}^m$ be a k-dimensional C^r manifold and let S be a subset of X. Then the set S is said to have *Lebesgue measure zero* in X if there exists a countable cover $\{U^n \mid n \in \mathbb{N}\}$ of S and charts (U^n, ϕ^n), $\forall n \in \mathbb{N}$, such that $\phi^n(U^n \cap S)$ has Lebesgue measure zero for every $n \in \mathbb{N}$. In the case where X is an m-dimensional C^r manifold, being a subset of $\mathbb{R}^m$, Theorem 2.10.17 is used to show that the notions of Lebesgue measure zero and Lebesgue measure zero in X coincide.

Theorem 2.10.17
Let a subset S of $\mathbb{R}^m$ having Lebesgue measure zero and $f \in C^1(S, \mathbb{R}^m)$ be given. Then $f(S)$ has Lebesgue measure zero.
See Golubitsky and Guillemin (1973), Proposition 1.3, page 30.

For $r \in \mathbb{N}^*$, let the subset X of $\mathbb{R}^m$ be an m-dimensional C^r manifold and let S be a subset of X. Using Theorem 2.10.17 it follows that if the set S has Lebesgue measure zero, then S has Lebesgue measure zero in X. Now assume that the set S has Lebesgue measure zero in X. Then there exists a countable cover $\{U^n \mid n \in \mathbb{N}\}$ of S and charts (U^n, ϕ^n), $\forall n \in \mathbb{N}$, such that the set $V^n = \phi^n(U^n \cap S)$ is of Lebesgue measure zero for every $n \in \mathbb{N}$. For every $n \in \mathbb{N}$, since $(\phi^n)^{-1} \in C^r(V^n, \mathbb{R}^m)$, it follows, from Theorem 2.10.17 and the fact that a subset of a set with Lebesgue measure zero has Lebesgue measure zero, that $(\phi^n)^{-1}(V^n)$ has Lebesgue measure zero. Consequently, the set $\cup_{n \in \mathbb{N}}(\phi^n)^{-1}(V^n) = S$ has Lebesgue measure zero.

Theorem 2.10.18 (Transversality theorem)
For $k^1, k^2, k^3 \in \mathbb{Z}_+$, for $r \in \mathbb{N}^*$, let a k^1-dimensional C^r manifold X^1, a C^r manifold X^2, a k^2-dimensional C^r manifold Y, a k^3-dimensional C^r manifold Z, being a subset of Y, and a function $f \in C^r(X^1 \times X^2, Y)$ be given, with $r \geq \max(\{1, k^1 - k^2 + k^3\})$. For every $x^2 \in X^2$, the function $f^{x^2} \in C^r(X^1, Y)$ is defined by $f^{x^2}(x^1) = f(x^1, x^2)$, $\forall x^1 \in X^1$. Then $f \pitchfork Z$ implies $f^{x^2} \pitchfork Z$, except for a subset of X^2 having Lebesgue measure zero in X^2.
See Mas-Colell (1985), I.2.2, page 45.

The result above concludes the presentation of the mathematical background for this monograph.

3

ECONOMIC PRELIMINARIES

3.1 INTRODUCTION

In this chapter a general equilibrium model of the economic system is developed, called the Arrow-Debreu model. This chapter is based on Debreu (1959), where a complete exposition of this model is given. In the Arrow-Debreu model both the value and the distribution of all goods and all services in the economic system is determined, the central questions of the economic science. Therefore, this model yields the fundamentals for most of modern economic theory. The Arrow-Debreu model has been the subject of extensive research during the last forty years and has led to an impressive collection of results and a solid body of knowledge. The conclusions of the investigations into this model are summarized in many nice textbooks, like Arrow and Hahn (1971), Mas-Colell (1985), and Hildenbrand and Kirman (1988), on which this chapter also relies heavily. In this monograph new results concerning the Arrow-Debreu model are given. Also, various extensions of this model are considered. The purpose of this chapter is to present the Arrow-Debreu model, to give an overview of the various assumptions made in this monograph with respect to the basic elements of this model, and to discuss the reasonability of these assumptions. Moreover, this chapter gives rise to a number of questions not solved by the Arrow-Debreu model. These questions are addressed in the various parts of this monograph.

Section 3.2 is devoted to the description of the basic ingredients of any model of the economic system, commodities, agents, and value. The value and the distribution of commodities over agents acting in the economic system is the central question in economic science. Therefore, the primitive concepts commodity, agent, and value, should be carefully defined. In this chapter there are two types of agents, producers and consumers. To model the interaction between these agents, one needs to know the set of admissible actions of each agent, the objectives of each agent, and the outcome for each one of the agents given a specification of an admissible action of every agent. The action of a producer consists of the choice of a production plan, while the action of a consumer is the choice of a consumption bundle. The set of admissible actions of a consumer is also determined by the prevailing allocation mechanism, being the market mechanism. In the market mechanism the agents of the economic system are assumed to act in a decentralized way and are guided by the price system, the only information transmitted by the model of the market mechanism given in this chapter. The price system determines the value of a commodity bundle. As a consequence of the market mechanism it is not possible for a consumer to choose a consumption bundle having a value that exceeds his wealth.

In Sections 3.3 and 3.4 some technological restrictions on the set of actions of a producer and a consumer, respectively, are described. This is done by introducing a production possibility set for a producer and a consumption set for a consumer. Various assumptions concerning these sets made in the monograph are discussed. A consumption set yields physiological and possibly legislative constraints on the set of actions of a consumer. When the wealth constraint imposed by the market mechanism is also taken into account, then the budget set of a consumer is obtained. A production possibility set specifies the set of admissible actions of a producer, while a budget set specifies the set of admissible actions of a consumer.

In Sections 3.5 and 3.6 the objectives of producers and consumers, respectively, are described. The objectives of a producer are determined by profit maximization. Hence, an optimal action of a producer consists of choosing a production plan in his set of admissible actions with the highest value. An optimal action of a consumer consists of choosing a consumption bundle in his set of admissible actions that is best according to his preferences. In Section 3.6 special attention is devoted to the various assumptions made in the monograph with respect to the preferences of consumers. Given the specification of the set of admissible actions, the objectives of each agent, and the description of the allocation mechanism, it is possible to describe the behaviour of each of the agents in the economic system.

In Section 3.7 the Arrow-Debreu model of the economic system is completed by describing the resources of the consumers in the economy, being the amounts of all commodities initially available to them, and their share in the profit generated by a producer. The wealth of a consumer is determined by the value of these resources. The economy is now obtained by a specification of the production possibility sets of all the producers and of the consumption sets, preference relations, and resources of all the consumers. The behaviour of all agents in the economy is expressed by the total excess demand relation, specifying for each price system the balances of every commodity resulting from optimal actions of the agents. This relation is introduced and some of its properties are derived.

In Section 3.8 the definition of a Walrasian equilibrium is given. A Walrasian equilibrium is a state of the economy, i.e. a specification of a price system and of optimal actions of the producers and the consumers, such that the optimal actions of the agents are compatible. It is argued why a Walrasian equilibrium is an equilibrium state of the economy. An important question to be answered in Section 3.8 is whether there exist price systems that make the optimal actions of agents compatible, i.e. whether a Walrasian equilibrium exists.

In Section 3.9 two important results, called the first and second fundamental welfare theorem, respectively, are presented. These theorems state that decentralized decision making by agents leads to an efficient allocation of resources and that every efficient allocation of resources can be obtained as the result of decentralized decision making by agents. In Section 3.10 an example is presented, which is used throughout Part II of this monograph to illustrate the theory of that part. It concerns a standard example with two commodities and two consumers having preference relations that can be represented by Cobb-Douglas utility functions.

Section 3.11 deals with some stability issues. General formulations of dynamic processes and of some stability concepts are given. Then a specific model of a price adjustment process, the Walrasian tatonnement process, is described and properties of the total excess demand function guaranteeing convergence to a Walrasian equilibrium price system of this process are given. In Section 3.12 an example is presented for which the Walrasian tatonnement process does not converge to a Walrasian equilibrium price system. This example is used throughout Part IV of this monograph to illustrate the theory presented in that part. Section 3.13 concludes with a discussion concerning the possibility of the existence of other models of price adjustment having better stability properties and with a motivation for the problems analysed in the various parts of this monograph.

3.2 AGENTS, COMMODITIES, AND VALUE

In the model of the economic system given in this chapter it is assumed that two types of *agents* are present. There is a finite number of *producers,* say L, indexed by $h \in I_L$, and a finite number of *consumers,* say $M \in \mathbb{N}$, indexed by $i \in I_M$. These concepts are abstractions of the real world for the sake of the theory, a producer being an abstraction of a firm and a consumer of a household.

Commodity is the collective noun for *goods* and *services.* A good is defined by three characteristics, its *physical characteristics,* its *location* or *place of availability,* and its *date of delivery* or *time of availability.* Services are also regarded as goods. For the development of the theory the difference between goods and services is not important and therefore the word commodity will be used. Two commodities are assumed to be different if they differ in any of the three characteristics mentioned above. So, to describe a commodity, each of the three characteristics mentioned above should be specified in detail. It is assumed that there is a finite number of commodities, say $N \in \mathbb{N}$, indexed by $j \in I_N$. This assumption implies, for instance, that there is a point in time after which the precise date of availability does not matter. Furthermore, time has to be subdivided in non-degenerate intervals, called *elementary intervals,* and space in areas with positive volume, called *elementary regions.* Also physical characteristics, like colour, should sometimes be subdivided in classes indistinguishable from the point of view of the theory. Many of the results developed for a world with a finite number of commodities are still valid in a world with an infinite number of commodities, although often additional difficulties arise in that case, see Aliprantis, Brown, and Burkinshaw (1989) or Kahn and Yannelis (1991).

The assumption of the existence of a finite number of commodities is reasonable since agents acting in the real world are not able to distinguish differences between commodities with very close characteristics, while agents are not concerned with commodities available at a date in the very far future.

With every commodity is associated a *unit of measurement.* Given the unit of measurement, it is possible to express the *quantity* of a commodity by a non-negative real number. For many examples of descriptions of commodities and units of measurement, see Sections 2.3 and 2.4 of Debreu (1959).

Producers have the ability to *produce* commodities, i.e. to transform certain quantities of commodities into certain quantities of other commodities, and to *trade* commodities, i.e. it is possible that some quantity of a commodity is made available to this agent and it is also possible that some quantity of a commodity is made available by this agent. Consumers have the ability to *consume* commodities, which influences their well-being, and also to *trade* commodities.

A *commodity bundle* of a producer $h \in I_L$ is a vector $y^h \in \mathbb{R}^N$ where, for every $j \in I_N$, $y_j^h \geq 0$ denotes that a quantity y_j^h of commodity j is made available by producer h, i.e. commodity j is an *output* of producer h, and $y_j^h \leq 0$ denotes that a quantity $-y_j^h$ of commodity j is made available to producer h, i.e. commodity j is an *input* of producer h. A commodity bundle of a producer is also called a *production plan.* A *commodity bundle* of a consumer $i \in I_M$ is a vector $x^i \in \mathbb{R}^N$ where, for every $j \in I_N$, $x_j^i \geq 0$ denotes the quantity of commodity j made available to consumer $i \in I_M$, i.e. commodity j is an *input* of consumer i, and $x_j^i \leq 0$ denotes that a quantity $-x_j^i$ of commodity j has been made available by consumer i, i.e. commodity j is an *output* of consumer i. The only outputs of consumers concern labour services, like construction services, teaching, driving, and so on, all performed at a given location and a given date. These services can also be used as inputs by a consumer. A commodity bundle of a consumer is also called a *consumption bundle.* The set of all possible commodity bundles is called the *commodity space* and is given by $\mathbb{R}^N$. The *action* of a producer $h \in I_L$ and of a consumer $i \in I_M$ concerns the choice of a commodity bundle.

Not all actions of producers and consumers are admissible. The set of admissible actions of every agent has to be modelled explicitly. The set of admissible actions is determined by both technological requirements as to be introduced in Sections 3.3 and 3.4 and the allocation mechanism assumed to be present in the economic system. An *allocation mechanism* is a specification of rules according to which trade takes place.

In the entire monograph it is assumed that trade takes places according to the allocation mechanism called the *market mechanism.* In the model of the market mechanism given in this chapter it is assumed that with every commodity $j \in I_N$ is associated a real number, denoted by p_j, being the *price* of one unit of that commodity. The price of a commodity is expressed in a fictional *unit of account.* Every unit of a commodity $j \in I_N$ made available to an agent costs this agent p_j and every unit of commodity j made available by an agent yields this agent p_j. If some commodity $j \in I_N$ is available at a future date, then p_j

denotes the current cost, i.e. the amount to be paid now in order to obtain the commodity at this future date. Notice that p_j is independent of both the agent and of the quantities of commodities made available by or to an agent. When trade in a commodity $j \in I_N$ takes place according to the market mechanism, then there is said to be a *market* for commodity j. The market mechanism is an abstraction of allocation mechanisms frequently used in the real world.

It is assumed that there is a market for every commodity $j \in I_N$, i.e. markets are assumed to be *complete*. In the real world this assumption is obviously not satisfied since it is not possible to trade in every commodity, especially not in commodities available at a date that is far in the future. Nevertheless, the analysis of an economy with a complete market system is an essential first step to study the more difficult case of an economy with incomplete markets. In Arrow and Hahn (1971), Section 2.10, a model for the case with incomplete markets is given that is mathematically equivalent to a model with complete markets. Moreover, it can also be argued that there do exist future markets for very important commodities, like oil, sugar, coffee, stocks, and so on, at least when the future is not too far away. Since in the real world future markets are not forbidden by law, the non-existence of many future markets seems to be a matter of the costs needed to organize these markets, something abstracted from in this monograph. The assumption of complete markets might therefore still be a good approximation for such cases. However, other reasons why markets are incomplete include problems of asymmetric information and bounded rationality of agents. An important next step to be taken seems therefore an extension of the theory as considered in this monograph to the case with incomplete markets. For an overview of the literature dealing with the case of incomplete markets, the reader is referred to Geanakoplos and Polemarchakis (1986), Geanakoplos (1990), and Magill and Shafer (1991).

The *price system* is a vector $p \in \mathbb{R}^N$ with component p_j denoting the price of commodity j for every $j \in I_N$. Consider some production plan $y^h \in \mathbb{R}^N$ of a producer $h \in I_L$. The inner product $p \cdot y^h$ denotes the *value* of the production plan y^h and is often called the *profit* of the production plan y^h. Consider some consumption bundle $x^i \in \mathbb{R}^N$ of a consumer $i \in I_M$. The inner product $p \cdot x^i$ denotes the *value* of the consumption bundle x^i. Notice that borrowing by an agent, i.e. a commodity is made available to the agent at a future date, and lending, i.e. the agent makes a commodity available at a future date, is allowed. In the market mechanism it is required that the value of an admissible consumption bundle of a consumer $i \in I_M$ does not exceed the *wealth* of consumer i, so the possibility of stealing is excluded. The wealth of a consumer is determined by the value of all the commodities the consumer owns, adding all the profits of producers the consumer is entitled to. It should be emphasized that the market mechanism is a decentralized mechanism. Decision making by producers and consumers takes place independently.

3.3 PRODUCTION POSSIBILITY SETS

The set of admissible actions of a producer $h \in I_L$ is determined by the *production possibility set* of producer h, denoted by Y^h. It contains all production plans that are technologically feasible for producer h, so $Y^h \subset \mathbb{R}^N$, $\forall h \in I_L$. An element y^h of Y^h is called an *admissible production plan* of producer $h \in I_L$. The production possibility set Y^h describes the technological constraints on the production plans of producer $h \in I_L$. The production possibility set does not depend on the input quantities of the various commodities that are available to the producer, it only describes technological possibilities. Notice that for every producer $h \in I_L$ the production possibility set Y^h does not depend on the actions of other agents, i.e. there are no *external effects.* The set $\prod_{h \in I_L} Y^h$ is denoted by Y. If $y = (y^1, \ldots, y^L)$ is an element of Y, then for every $j \in I_N$ the element y_j of $\mathbb{R}^L$ is defined by $y_j = (y_j^1, \ldots, y_j^L)^\top$. The *total production possibility set,* denoted by $\widetilde{Y}$, represents the production possibilities of the entire economy and is defined by $\widetilde{Y} = \sum_{h \in I_L} Y^h$. All the assumptions on the production possibility sets made somewhere in the monograph, although not simultaneously, are presented below. In the presentation of these assumptions, let some producer $h \in I_L$ be given.

- The production plan 0^N is an admissible action of producer h, i.e. $0^N \in Y^h$. Producer h is assumed to have the possibility of doing nothing.

- The production possibility set Y^h is *closed,* i.e. whenever $(y^{h^n})_{n \in \mathbb{N}}$ is a sequence of admissible production plans in Y^h converging to $\overline{y}^h \in \mathbb{R}^N$, then $\overline{y}^h \in Y^h$. This assumption is technical and pretty harmless.

- The production possibility set Y^h is *bounded,* i.e. there exists $\overline{n} \in \mathbb{N}$ such that, for every $y^h \in Y^h$, $\|y^h\|_\infty \leq \overline{n}$. This is not intended to be a realistic assumption. Notice that a production possibility set reflects the technological possibilities of a producer and should therefore also describe the possible outputs given arbitrarily large amounts of inputs. However, for some purposes it is possible to replace a not necessarily bounded production possibility set by a bounded one, thereby facilitating the analysis.

- The production possibility set Y^h is *convex*, i.e. whenever $\overline{y}^h$ and $\widehat{y}^h$ are admissible production plans, then, for every $\lambda \in [0,1]$, $y^h = \lambda\overline{y}^h + (1-\lambda)\widehat{y}^h \in Y^h$, i.e. y^h is an admissible production plan. This assumption is not as innocent as the previous assumptions. In particular, it is easily seen that the assumption $0^N \in Y^h$ together with the assumption of convexity of the production possibility set Y^h implies that Y^h satisfies the assumption of *non-increasing returns to scale*, i.e. whenever $y^h \in Y^h$, then, for every $\lambda \in [0,1]$, $\lambda y^h \in Y^h$. Therefore, the case of *increasing returns to scale* is excluded, a serious restriction. The assumption of non-increasing returns to scale is sometimes also referred to as the assumption of *divisibility of production plans*. Clearly, not all production plans in the real world are divisible, for instance production plans with a car with certain physical characteristics as output at a given location and a given date. Nevertheless, if the number of cars produced of this type is sufficiently large, then the divisibility assumption is acceptable as an approximation.

- The production possibility set Y^h satisfies *constant returns to scale*, i.e. whenever $y^h \in Y^h$, then, for every $\lambda \in \mathbb{R}_+$, $\lambda y^h \in Y^h$, hence Y^h is a cone. Production possibility sets satisfying constant returns to scale are often used in applied general equilibrium theory. Clearly, constant returns to scale is a special case of non-increasing returns to scale.

- The production possibility set corresponds to the *linear activity model*. In this case a finite number, say $m \in \mathbb{N}$, of vectors $a^1, \ldots, a^m$ in $\mathbb{R}^N$, called *activities*, is assumed to be given. The production possibility set is now defined by

$$Y^h = \{y^h \in \mathbb{R}^N \,|\forall i \in I_m,\ \exists \lambda^i \in \mathbb{R}_+,\ y^h = \textstyle\sum_{i \in I_m} \lambda^i a^i\}.$$

  If the production possibility set Y^h corresponds to the linear activity model, then it satisfies $0^N \in Y^h$, it is closed and convex, and it satisfies constant returns to scale. This type of production possibility set is also often used in applied work.

- The production possibility set Y^h contains the set $-\mathbb{R}^N_+$, called the assumption of *free disposal*. This assumption implies that it is possible to use arbitrary amounts of input without generating any output. Often this assumption is reasonable, although real world examples like for example nuclear waste show that this assumption is not always satisfied.

- No non-trivial production plans are allowed, i.e. $Y^h = \{0^N\}$. This is not intended to be a reasonable assumption. However, it is often made in what follows when the inclusion of non-trivial production into the model does not yield any additional insights and is notationally cumbersome. A possible interpretation of a model with $Y^h = \{0^N\}$ is that all production already has taken place and that the outputs have been allocated to the consumers. Now the consumers are only involved in trading the consumption bundles they own among themselves.

Finally, an assumption on the total production possibility set is considered.

- The total production possibility set satisfies $\tilde{Y} \cap -\tilde{Y} \subset \{0^N\}$, i.e. $\tilde{y} \in \tilde{Y} \backslash \{0^N\}$ implies $-\tilde{y} \notin \tilde{Y}$. This assumption is called *irreversibility of production*. Recalling that the time of availability is part of the description of commodities and assuming that production takes some time, it becomes clear that this assumption is completely realistic. Otherwise, it would be possible to obtain an output dated earlier than the inputs used to generate it. Even if it is not assumed that production takes some time, then this assumption is still reasonable since production usually causes some loss of inputs.

This concludes the description of the assumptions on the production possibility sets made somewhere in the monograph.

3.4 CONSUMPTION SETS AND BUDGET SETS

The set of actions of a consumer $i \in I_M$ is restricted by the *consumption set* of consumer i, denoted by X^i. The consumption set of a consumer $i \in I_M$ is a subset of $\mathbb{R}^N$. Recall that if $x^i \in X^i$ is a consumption bundle of consumer $i \in I_M$, then a component x^i_j for some $j \in I_N$ is necessarily nonnegative, unless commodity j corresponds to a labour service. The consumption set describes the physiological constraints on the consumption bundles to be chosen by a consumer. An obvious example is that a consumer is able to make available more manual labour services when more of some food commodity is available to this consumer, or that a consumer is only able to make available some technical labour services after having consumed certain teaching services. Another example is that the time during which the various labour services are made available by a consumer in a given elementary time interval cannot exceed the total length of time in this interval. It is also possible to use the consumption set to describe certain legislative constraints, like the obligation to take an insurance when certain commodities are consumed. The assumption that X^i is a subset of $\mathbb{R}^N$ implies that the consumption set of a consumer $i \in I_M$ does not depend on the production plans chosen by the producers or the consumption bundles chosen by the other consumers, i.e. there are no *external effects.* The set $\prod_{i \in I_M} X^i$ is denoted by X. If $x = (x^1, \ldots, x^M)$ is an element of X, then for every $j \in I_N$ the element x_j of $\mathbb{R}^M$ is defined by $x_j = (x_j^1, \ldots, x_j^M)^\top$.

The *budget set* of a consumer $i \in I_M$ having wealth $w^i \in \mathbb{R}$ at a price system $p \in \mathbb{R}^N$, denoted by $\widetilde{\beta}^i(p, w^i)$, is defined as the set of consumption bundles whose value does not exceed w^i, so

$$\widetilde{\beta}^i(p, w^i) = \left\{x^i \in X^i \,\middle|\, p \cdot x^i \leq w^i\right\}.$$

An element $x^i \in \widetilde{\beta}^i(p, w^i)$ is called an *admissible consumption bundle* of consumer $i \in I_M$ and therefore $\widetilde{\beta}^i(p, w^i)$ is the set of admissible actions of consumer i at price system $p \in \mathbb{R}^N$ and wealth $w^i \in \mathbb{R}$. The relation $\widetilde{\beta}^i : \mathbb{R}^N \times \mathbb{R} \to \mathbb{R}^N$ associating with every $(p, w^i) \in \mathbb{R}^N \times \mathbb{R}$ the set $\widetilde{\beta}^i(p, w^i)$ is called the *budget relation* of consumer $i \in I_M$.

All the assumptions on the consumption sets made somewhere in the monograph, although not simultaneously, are presented below. All these assumptions are pretty reasonable. In the presentation of these assumptions, let some consumer $i \in I_M$ be given.

- The consumption set X^i is *closed,* i.e. whenever $(x^{i^n})_{n \in \mathbb{N}}$ is a sequence of consumption bundles in X^i converging to $\bar{x}^i \in \mathbb{R}^N$, then $\bar{x}^i \in X^i$.
- The consumption set X^i is *bounded from below,* i.e. there exists a vector $\chi^i \in \mathbb{R}^N$ such that $X^i \subset [\chi^i, \rightarrow)$. This assumption is reasonable since commodities not related to labour services are bounded in amount from below by zero, whereas the maximal quantity consumer i can make available of some labour service is clearly limited during an elementary time interval. If this assumption is made, then there is no loss of generality in assuming that $\chi^i = 0^N$ since each commodity can be redefined in such a way that a consumption bundle $\bar{x}^i$ according to the original definition corresponds to a consumption bundle $\bar{x}^i - \chi^i$ according to the new definition. Therefore, the assumption $X^i \subset \mathbb{R}_+^N$ is also often made.
- The consumption set X^i is *bounded,* i.e. there exists $\bar{n} \in \mathbb{N}$ such that, for every $x^i \in X^i$, $\|x^i\|_\infty \leq \bar{n}$. This is not intended to be a realistic assumption. However, for some purposes it is possible to replace a not necessarily

bounded consumption set by a bounded one, thereby facilitating the analysis.

- The consumption set X^i is *convex*, i.e. whenever $\overline{x}^i$ and $\widehat{x}^i$ are elements of X^i, then, for every $\lambda \in [0,1]$, $x^i = \lambda\overline{x}^i + (1-\lambda)\widehat{x}^i \in X^i$.

- It is always possible to consume more of a commodity, i.e. $X^i + \mathbb{R}^N_+ \subset X^i$.

- The consumption set equals the *non-negative orthant*, i.e. $X^i = \mathbb{R}^N_+$. This assumption is not intended to be a realistic one. However, especially when the analysis focuses on the case without production it is often made for the sake of simplicity. In these cases considering more realistic consumption sets would not yield any additional insights and would be technically more cumbersome.

- The consumption set equals the *strictly positive orthant*, i.e. $X^i = \mathbb{R}^N_{++}$. Again, this assumption is not intended to be a realistic one and is often made for the sake of simplicity. This assumption implies that an admissible consumption bundle is strictly positive. This assumption is usually made when certain differentiability requirements with respect to the actions chosen by the consumers are needed.

This concludes the description of the assumptions on the consumption sets made somewhere in the monograph.

3.5 THE BEHAVIOUR OF PRODUCERS

A producer is assumed to take the prevailing price system as given and to maximize profit given this price system on his production possibility set. In Section 3.7 the issue of profit maximization is addressed. For every producer $h \in I_L$, for every price system $p \in \mathbb{R}^N$, the set $\eta^h(p)$ is defined as the set of production plans maximizing profit given p on Y^h, i.e.

$$\eta^h(p) = \left\{\overline{y}^h \in Y^h \,\middle|\, p \cdot \overline{y}^h \geq p \cdot y^h,\ \forall y^h \in Y^h\right\},$$

and if $\eta^h(p) \neq \emptyset$, then the *profit* of producer h at price system p, denoted by $\pi^h(p)$, is defined by the profit of a profit maximizing production plan $\overline{y}^h \in \eta^h(p)$, i.e.

$$\pi^h(p) = p \cdot \overline{y}^h.$$

Notice that $\pi^h(p)$ does not depend on the incidental choice of $\overline{y}^h \in \eta^h(p)$. An element of $\eta^h(p)$ is called an *optimal action* or *optimal production plan* of producer h at price system p. Given an optimal production plan y^h of producer $h \in I_L$, producer h is said to *supply* a commodity $j \in I_N$ if $y_j^h \geq 0$ and producer h is said to *demand* commodity j if $y_j^h \leq 0$.

It is easily verified that, for every $h \in I_L$, for every $p \in \mathbb{R}^N$, the set $\eta^h(p)$ only depends on the relative prices, i.e. if $\lambda \in \mathbb{R}_{++}$, then $\eta^h(p) = \eta^h(\lambda p)$. If the production set Y^h of a producer $h \in I_L$ satisfies constant returns to scale while there exist non-trivial production plans, then it is easy to find price systems $p \in \mathbb{R}^N$ such that $p \cdot y^h > 0$ for some $y^h \in Y^h$, implying that $\eta^h(p) = \emptyset$. In this case it is also easy to find price systems $p \in \mathbb{R}^N$ for which $\eta^h(p)$ contains many elements. The set P^h is defined as the set of price systems $p \in \mathbb{R}^N$ for which the set $\eta^h(p)$ of producer $h \in I_L$ is a non-empty set, so

$$P^h = \left\{p \in \mathbb{R}^N \,\middle|\, \eta^h(p) \neq \emptyset\right\}.$$

The relation $\eta^h : \mathbb{R}^N \to \mathbb{R}^N$ associating with every $p \in \mathbb{R}^N$ the set $\eta^h(p)$ is called the *supply relation* of producer $h \in I_L$ and the relation $\pi^h : \mathbb{R}^N \to \mathbb{R}$ associating with every $p \in P^h$ the set $\{\pi^h(p)\}$ and with every $p \in \mathbb{R}^N \setminus P^h$ the empty set is called the *profit relation* of producer $h \in I_L$. It is easily verified that if $p \in P^h$ for a producer $h \in I_L$ and if $\lambda \in \mathbb{R}_{++}$, then $\lambda p \in P^h$ and $\pi^h(\lambda p) = \lambda \pi^h(p)$.

3.6 THE BEHAVIOUR OF CONSUMERS

An essential step in the modelling of the behaviour of consumers is to describe their preferences. The mathematical concept of a binary relation turns out to be very useful. Let a consumer $i \in I_M$ be given. It is assumed that, given any two consumption bundles $\bar{x}^i, \hat{x}^i$ in the consumption set X^i of consumer i, precisely one of the following four statements holds:

1. $\bar{x}^i \prec^i \hat{x}^i$, i.e. $\hat{x}^i$ is preferred to $\bar{x}^i$ by consumer i,
2. $\bar{x}^i \sim^i \hat{x}^i$, i.e. consumer i is indifferent between $\bar{x}^i$ and $\hat{x}^i$,
3. $\bar{x}^i \succ^i \hat{x}^i$, i.e. $\bar{x}^i$ is preferred to $\hat{x}^i$ by consumer i,
4. $\bar{x}^i \,\square^i\, \hat{x}^i$, i.e. $\bar{x}^i$ and $\hat{x}^i$ cannot be compared by consumer i.

Moreover, $\bar{x}^i \prec^i \hat{x}^i$ if and only if $\hat{x}^i \succ^i \bar{x}^i$, $\bar{x}^i \,\square^i\, \hat{x}^i$ if and only if $\hat{x}^i \,\square^i\, \bar{x}^i$, and $\bar{x}^i \sim^i \hat{x}^i$ if and only if $\hat{x}^i \sim^i \bar{x}^i$. Hence, for every consumption bundle $x^i \in X^i$, the cases $x^i \prec^i x^i$ and $x^i \succ^i x^i$ are excluded.

The assumption made above implies that the preferences of a consumer do not depend on the consumption bundles chosen by other consumers or the production plans chosen by producers. A similar assumption was made with respect to production possibility sets of producers and consumption sets of consumers. It turns out in Section 3.8 that the market mechanism is a very efficient mechanism to allocate these commodities. Certainly, there are commodities having external effects, pollution and commodities available to a group of agents being obvious examples. Such commodities may require other allocation mechanisms, see Gilles and Ruys (1994b). From the existence of commodities having external effects is abstracted in this monograph. Another possible interpretation is that all choices with respect to commodities having external effects already have been made by the agents.

It is convenient to define the following two statements that are derived from the ones above,

$\overline{x}^i \preceq^i \widehat{x}^i$ if $\overline{x}^i \prec^i \widehat{x}^i$ or $\overline{x}^i \sim^i \widehat{x}^i$, i.e. $\widehat{x}^i$ is at least as desired as $\overline{x}^i$ by i,
$\overline{x}^i \succeq^i \widehat{x}^i$ if $\overline{x}^i \succ^i \widehat{x}^i$ or $\overline{x}^i \sim^i \widehat{x}^i$, i.e. $\overline{x}^i$ is at least as desired as $\widehat{x}^i$ by i.

The *preference relation* of a consumer $i \in I_M$ is also denoted by $\preceq^i$ and is the binary relation $\preceq^i: X^i \to X^i$, defined by

$$\preceq^i (x^i) = \left\{\overline{x}^i \in X^i \,\middle|\, x^i \preceq^i \overline{x}^i\right\}, \ \forall x^i \in X^i.$$

It is easily verified that each one of the statements (1)-(4) given above can be deduced from the preference relation $\preceq^i$ of consumer $i \in I_M$. So, knowledge of the preference relation $\preceq^i$ suffices to determine the preferences of consumer $i \in I_M$ completely. The set of pairs of consumption bundles between which a consumer $i \in I_M$ is indifferent is denoted by $I(\preceq^i)$, i.e.

$$I(\preceq^i) = \left\{(\overline{x}^i, \widehat{x}^i) \in X^i \times X^i \,\middle|\, \overline{x}^i \sim^i \widehat{x}^i\right\}.$$

All the assumptions on the preference relations made somewhere in the monograph, although not simultaneously, are presented below. In the description of the assumptions on the preference relations, some consumer $i \in I_M$ is assumed to be given.

- The preference relation $\preceq^i$ is *complete,* i.e. for every $\overline{x}^i, \widehat{x}^i \in X^i$, it holds that $\overline{x}^i \preceq^i \widehat{x}^i$ or $\widehat{x}^i \preceq^i \overline{x}^i$. It follows immediately that a complete preference relation is a reflexive relation, see also Section 2.5.
- The preference relation $\preceq^i$ is *transitive,* i.e. for every $\overline{x}^i, \widehat{x}^i, \widetilde{x}^i \in X^i$, if $\overline{x}^i \preceq^i \widehat{x}^i$ and $\widehat{x}^i \preceq^i \widetilde{x}^i$, then $\overline{x}^i \preceq^i \widetilde{x}^i$. Both the assumptions of completeness

and transitivity are reasonable and can even be relaxed for many purposes as is shown in Mas-Colell (1974b) and Gale and Mas-Colell (1975, 1979). Let the preference relation $\preceq^i$ be transitive and let $\bar{x}^i, \hat{x}^i, \tilde{x}^i \in X^i$ be given. It is easily verified that $\bar{x}^i \sim^i \hat{x}^i$ and $\hat{x}^i \sim^i \tilde{x}^i$ implies $\bar{x}^i \sim^i \tilde{x}^i$. Moreover, $\bar{x}^i \preceq^i \hat{x}^i$ and $\hat{x}^i \prec^i \tilde{x}^i$ implies $\bar{x}^i \prec^i \tilde{x}^i$, and $\bar{x}^i \prec^i \hat{x}^i$ and $\hat{x}^i \preceq^i \tilde{x}^i$ implies $\bar{x}^i \prec^i \tilde{x}^i$.

- The preference relation $\preceq^i$ is *continuous*, i.e. for every $\bar{x}^i \in X^i$, both the set $\{x^i \in X^i \mid x^i \preceq^i \bar{x}^i\}$ and the set $\{x^i \in X^i \mid x^i \succeq^i \bar{x}^i\}$ are closed in X^i. Although this is certainly a reasonable assumption, it might exclude some interesting cases like lexicographic preference relations, see for instance Debreu (1959), Note 2, page 73. The preference relation $\preceq^i$ on X^i is called a *lexicographic preference relation* with respect to a permutation $\pi : I_N \to I_N$ if it holds that $\bar{x}^i \preceq^i \hat{x}^i$ if and only if $\bar{x}^i = \hat{x}^i$ or there exists $k' \in I^0_{N-1}$ such that $\bar{x}^i_{\pi(k)} = \hat{x}^i_{\pi(k)}$, $\forall k \in I_{k'}$, and $\bar{x}^i_{\pi(k'+1)} < \hat{x}^i_{\pi(k'+1)}$. If consumer i has a lexicographic preference relation with respect to π, then commodity $\pi(1)$ is appreciated most by consumer i, followed by commodity $\pi(2)$, and so on.

- The preference relation $\preceq^i$ is of the *class* C^r for some $r \in \mathbb{N}^*$, i.e. $I(\preceq^i)$ is a $(2N-1)$-dimensional C^r manifold. This assumption is often made when $X^i = \mathbb{R}^N_{++}$ and is purely technical. Although it rules out certain cases, it is not very restrictive and it is excellent as an approximation, see Mas-Colell (1985), Section 2.8.

- The preference relation $\preceq^i$ is *non-satiated*, i.e. for every $x^i \in X^i$, there exists $\bar{x}^i \in X^i$ such that $x^i \prec^i \bar{x}^i$. In this case there exists for every consumption bundle another consumption bundle that is preferred to it by consumer i. This is a very weak assumption.

- The preference relation $\preceq^i$ is *locally non-satiated*, i.e. for every $x^i \in X^i$, for every set O^i open in X^i and containing x^i, there exists $\bar{x}^i \in O^i$ such that $x^i \prec^i \bar{x}^i$. In this case there exists for every consumption bundle another consumption bundle, arbitrarily close, that is preferred to it by consumer i. This is still a very weak assumption. If the preference relation $\preceq^i$ is locally non-satiated, then it is also non-satiated.

- The preference relation $\preceq^i$ is *weakly monotonic*, i.e. $\bar{x}^i, \hat{x}^i \in X^i$ and $\bar{x}^i \leq \hat{x}^i$ implies $\bar{x}^i \preceq^i \hat{x}^i$. In this case a consumption bundle containing at least as much of every commodity as another consumption bundle is at least as desired as this other consumption bundle by consumer i. In most cases this is a reasonable assumption, although it is certainly possible to find counterexamples to it in the real world. If the preference relation $\preceq^i$ is weakly monotonic, then it is not necessarily non-satiated.

- The preference relation $\preceq^i$ is *monotonic,* i.e. $\bar{x}^i, \hat{x}^i \in X^i$ and $\bar{x}^i \ll \hat{x}^i$ implies $\bar{x}^i \prec^i \hat{x}^i$. Also this assumption is reasonable. It means that a consumption bundle containing more of every commodity than another consumption bundle is preferred to this other consumption bundle. If the preference relation $\preceq^i$ is monotonic, then it is not necessarily weakly monotonic, although this is certainly the case under some weak additional assumptions on $\preceq^i$.

- The preference relation $\preceq^i$ is *monotonic with respect to commodity* $j' \in I_N$, i.e. $\bar{x}^i, \hat{x}^i \in X^i$, $\bar{x}^i_{j'} < \hat{x}^i_{j'}$, and $\bar{x}^i_j = \hat{x}^i_j$, $\forall j \in I_N \setminus \{j'\}$, implies $\bar{x}^i \prec^i \hat{x}^i$. In this case consumer i always likes to have more of commodity j', assuming the amounts of the other commodities to remain the same.

- The preference relation $\preceq^i$ is *strongly monotonic,* i.e. $\bar{x}^i, \hat{x}^i \in X^i$ and $\bar{x}^i < \hat{x}^i$ implies $\bar{x}^i \prec^i \hat{x}^i$. It means that a consumption bundle containing at least as much of every commodity as another consumption bundle and more of at least one commodity is preferred to this other consumption bundle by consumer i. If the preference relation $\preceq^i$ is strongly monotonic, then it is monotonic. Of all the assumptions made with respect to non-satiability or monotonicity, this one should be regarded as the strongest. Nevertheless, to study the most important features of the economic system it is a reasonable assumption.

- The preference relation $\preceq^i$ is *weakly convex,* i.e. $\bar{x}^i, \hat{x}^i \in X^i$, $\bar{x}^i \preceq^i \hat{x}^i$, and $\lambda\bar{x}^i + (1-\lambda)\hat{x}^i \in X^i$ for some $\lambda \in (0,1)$ implies $\bar{x}^i \preceq^i \lambda\bar{x}^i + (1-\lambda)\hat{x}^i$, so if $\hat{x}^i$ is at least as desired as $\bar{x}^i$ by consumer i, then any convex combination with positive weights of these two consumption bundles lying in the consumption set is at least as desired as $\bar{x}^i$ by consumer i.

- The preference relation $\preceq^i$ is *convex,* i.e. $\bar{x}^i, \hat{x}^i \in X^i$, $\bar{x}^i \prec^i \hat{x}^i$, and $\lambda\bar{x}^i + (1-\lambda)\hat{x}^i \in X^i$ for some $\lambda \in (0,1)$ implies $\bar{x}^i \prec^i \lambda\bar{x}^i + (1-\lambda)\hat{x}^i$, so if $\hat{x}^i$ is preferred to $\bar{x}^i$, then any convex combination with positive weights of these two consumption bundles lying in the consumption set is preferred to $\bar{x}^i$ by consumer i.

- The preference relation $\preceq^i$ is *strongly convex,* i.e. $\bar{x}^i, \hat{x}^i \in X^i$ with $\bar{x}^i \neq \hat{x}^i$, $\bar{x}^i \sim^i \hat{x}^i$, and $\lambda\bar{x}^i + (1-\lambda)\hat{x}^i \in X^i$ for some $\lambda \in (0,1)$ implies $\bar{x}^i \prec^i \lambda\bar{x}^i + (1-\lambda)\hat{x}^i$, so if consumer i is indifferent between $\hat{x}^i$ and $\bar{x}^i$, then any convex combination with positive weights of these two consumption bundles lying in the consumption set is preferred to $\bar{x}^i$.

In Debreu (1959), Section 4.7, it is shown that if the consumption set X^i is convex and the preference relation $\preceq^i$ is complete, transitive, and continuous, then $\preceq^i$ is strongly convex implies $\preceq^i$ is convex, and $\preceq^i$ is convex implies $\preceq^i$ is weakly convex. Of all the assumptions on preference relations presented so far, the assumption of strong convexity is clearly the strongest. It is not difficult to find real world examples where even the assumption of weak convexity of preference relations does not hold. Nevertheless, this assumption seems to be satisfied for many commodity bundles. In an economy with a finite number of agents this assumption is indispensable when showing the existence of a Walrasian equilibrium. Fortunately, however, it can be shown that in the case with a finite but large number of agents an approximate Walrasian equilibrium exists, even when preference relations are not weakly convex, where approximate may have various meanings, see Mas-Colell (1985), Section 7.4. In the case when there is an infinite number of agents, for example modelled by the unit interval with the Lebesgue measure on it, the convexity assumptions can even be dispensed with, while still many results can be obtained, see Hildenbrand (1974), Trockel (1984), and Mas-Colell (1985).

- Consider the case where $X^i = \mathbb{R}^N_{++}$. The preference relation $\preceq^i$ satisfies the *boundary condition*, i.e. for every $x^i \in X^i$, the closure of the set $\{\bar{x}^i \in X^i \mid \bar{x}^i \succeq^i x^i\}$ is contained in $\mathbb{R}^N_{++}$. This assumption is often made when certain differentiability requirements with respect to the actions chosen by the consumers are needed. Although this assumption does not always hold in the real world, it is excellent as an approximation.

Often it is useful to represent a preference relation by a utility function. A function $u^i : X^i \to \mathbb{R}$ is said to *represent* the preference relation $\preceq^i$ of a consumer $i \in I_M$ and u^i is called the *utility function* of consumer i if for every $\bar{x}^i, \widehat{x}^i \in X^i$ it holds that

$$\bar{x}^i \preceq^i \widehat{x}^i \Leftrightarrow u^i(\bar{x}^i) \leq u^i(\widehat{x}^i).$$

Notice that if $\preceq^i$ is a pre-ordering, then a function $f : X^i \to \mathbb{R}$ is a utility function of consumer $i \in I_M$ if and only if the function f is increasing, where X^i is assumed to be pre-ordered by $\preceq^i$. A function $u^i : X^i \to \mathbb{R}$ generates in a unique way a preference relation of a consumer $i \in I_M$ by defining, for every $\bar{x}^i, \widehat{x}^i \in X^i$, $\bar{x}^i \preceq^i \widehat{x}^i$ if $u^i(\bar{x}^i) \leq u^i(\widehat{x}^i)$. Clearly, if a preference relation can be represented by a utility function, then such a representation is not unique. However, not every preference relation can be represented by a utility function. It is easily verified that if a preference relation can be represented by a utility function, then the preference relation is complete and transitive. If a preference relation can be represented by a continuous utility function, then the preference relation is complete, transitive, and continuous. The following theorem gives a converse of this result.

Theorem 3.6.1
For some consumer $i \in I_M$, let X^i be a convex consumption set and let $\preceq^i$ be a complete, transitive, and continuous preference relation. Then the preference relation $\preceq^i$ can be represented by a continuous utility function.
See Debreu (1959), Theorem 1, page 56.

The following result gives an easy way to construct a preference relation of the class C^r for some $r \in \mathbb{N}^*$.

Theorem 3.6.2
For $r \in \mathbb{N}^*$, for some consumer $i \in I_M$, let $X^i = \mathbb{R}^N_{++}$ and let the preference relation $\preceq^i$ be represented by the utility function $u^i \in C^r(X^i, \mathbb{R})$ having no critical point. Then the preference relation $\preceq^i$ is of the class C^r.
Proof
Let the function $\widetilde{g} : \mathbb{R}^N_{++} \times \mathbb{R}^N_{++} \to \mathbb{R}$ be defined by

$$\widetilde{g}(\overline{x}^i, \widehat{x}^i) = u^i(\overline{x}^i) - u^i(\widehat{x}^i),\ \forall (\overline{x}^i, \widehat{x}^i) \in \mathbb{R}^N_{++} \times \mathbb{R}^N_{++}.$$

Let the function $\widetilde{h}$ be defined by $\widetilde{h} = \emptyset$. Then

$$M[\widetilde{g}, \widetilde{h}] = \{(\overline{x}^i, \widehat{x}^i) \in \mathbb{R}^N_{++} \times \mathbb{R}^N_{++} \,|\widetilde{g}(\overline{x}^i, \widehat{x}^i) = 0\} = I(\preceq^i). \qquad (3.1)$$

It follows that $(\partial_{x^i} u^i(\overline{x}^i), -\partial_{x^i} u^i(\widehat{x}^i))^\top \neq 0^{2N}, \forall (\overline{x}^i, \widehat{x}^i) \in \mathbb{R}^N_{++} \times \mathbb{R}^N_{++}$ from the fact that u^i has no critical point, and therefore $M[\widetilde{g}, \widetilde{h}]$ is an RCS by Definition 2.10.10. From Theorem 2.10.11 and from (3.1) it follows that the set $I(\preceq^i)$ is a $(2N-1)$-dimensional C^r manifold. So, $\preceq^i$ is of the class C^r. Q.E.D.

Theorem 3.6.2 is also stated in Mas-Colell (1985), Proposition 2.3.5, page 62. A proof is given here to show the usefulness of the theory of regular constraint sets given in Section 2.10. A converse of Theorem 3.6.2 is given next.

Theorem 3.6.3
For $r \in \mathbb{N}^*$, for some consumer $i \in I_M$, let $X^i = \mathbb{R}^N_{++}$ and let the preference relation $\preceq^i$ be complete, transitive, continuous, monotonic, and of the class C^r. Then the preference relation $\preceq^i$ can be represented by a utility function $u^i \in C^r(X^i, \mathbb{R})$ having no critical point.
See Mas-Colell (1985), Proposition 2.3.9, page 64, and Proposition 2.3.15, page 68.

For a consumer $i \in I_M$, the *indifference surface* of the preference relation $\preceq^i$ at a consumption bundle $\overline{x}^i \in X^i$, denoted by $I(\preceq^i, \overline{x}^i)$, is defined as the set of consumption bundles such that consumer i is indifferent between these and $\overline{x}^i$, i.e.

$$I(\preceq^i, \overline{x}^i) = \{x^i \in X^i \,|x^i \sim^i \overline{x}^i\},$$

and let $P(\preceq^i, \overline{x}^i)$ denote the set of consumption bundles x^i of X^i such that x^i is at least as desired as $\overline{x}^i$ by consumer i, i.e.

$$P(\preceq^i, \overline{x}^i) = \{x^i \in X^i \,|\overline{x}^i \preceq^i x^i\}.$$

Under suitable assumptions these two sets are $(N-1)$-dimensional C^r manifolds and N-dimensional C^r manifolds with boundary for some $r \in \mathbb{N}^*$, respectively.

Theorem 3.6.4
For $r \in \mathbb{N}^*$, for some consumer $i \in I_M$, let $X^i = \mathbb{R}^N_{++}$ and let the preference relation $\preceq^i$ be complete, transitive, continuous, monotonic, and of the class C^r. Then, for every $x^i \in X^i$, the set $I(\preceq^i, x^i)$ is an $(N-1)$-dimensional C^r manifold and the set $P(\preceq^i, x^i)$ is an N-dimensional C^r manifold with boundary, where the relative boundary of $P(\preceq^i, x^i)$ is given by $I(\preceq^i, x^i)$.
Proof
By Theorem 3.6.3, $\preceq^i$ can be represented by $u^i \in C^r(X^i, \mathbb{R})$ having no critical point. Let some consumption bundle $\overline{x}^i \in X^i$ be given. Let the function $\widetilde{g}$ be defined by $\widetilde{g} = \emptyset$ and let the function $\widetilde{h} : \mathbb{R}^N_{++} \to \mathbb{R}$ be defined by

$$\widetilde{h}(x^i) = u^i(x^i) - u^i(\overline{x}^i), \ \forall x^i \in \mathbb{R}^N_{++}.$$

Since u^i has no critical point, it holds that $\partial_{x^i}\widetilde{h}(\widehat{x}^i)^\top \neq 0^N$, $\forall \widehat{x}^i \in \mathbb{R}^N_{++}$, and therefore $M[\widetilde{g}, \widetilde{h}] = P(\preceq^i, \overline{x}^i)$ is an RCS by Definition 2.10.10. Obviously, $\#J^0(\widehat{x}^i) \leq 1$, $\forall \widehat{x}^i \in \mathbb{R}^N_{++}$. Moreover, $B^1(M[\widetilde{g}, \widetilde{h}]) = I(\preceq^i, \overline{x}^i)$. From Theorem 2.10.7 and Theorem 2.10.11 it follows that $I(\preceq^i, \overline{x}^i)$ is an $(N-1)$-dimensional C^r manifold and $P(\preceq^i, \overline{x}^i)$ is an N-dimensional C^r manifold with boundary, where the relative boundary of $P(\preceq^i, \overline{x}^i)$ is given by $I(\preceq^i, \overline{x}^i)$. Q.E.D.

The result given in Theorem 3.6.4 for $I(\preceq^i, x^i)$ is also given in Mas-Colell (1985), Proposition 2.3.10, page 66. For $r \in \mathbb{N}^* \setminus \{1\}$, for some consumer $i \in I_M$, let $X^i = \mathbb{R}^N_{++}$ and let the preference relation $\preceq^i$ be complete, transitive, continuous, monotonic, and of the class C^r. Clearly, every consumption bundle x^i of X^i belongs to $I(\preceq^i, x^i)$, the relative boundary of $P(\preceq^i, x^i)$ by Theorem 3.6.4. For every $x^i \in X^i$, the real number $\widehat{c}(x^i)$ is defined as the Gaussian curvature of the relative boundary of $P(\preceq^i, x^i)$ at x^i, see also Section 2.10.

- The preference relation $\preceq^i$ has *non-zero Gaussian curvature*, i.e. $\widehat{c}(x^i) \neq 0$, $\forall x^i \in X^i$. Intuitively, this assumption means that the indifference surface of $\preceq^i$ is not flat at any $x^i \in X^i$. Although there are certainly cases where this assumption is not satisfied, this assumption is excellent as an approximation.

The following theorem gives an explicit formula for the number $\widehat{c}(x^i)$ for any $x^i \in X^i$.

Theorem 3.6.5
For $r \in \mathbb{N}^* \setminus \{1\}$, for some consumer $i \in I_M$, let $X^i = \mathbb{R}^N_{++}$, let $\overline{x}^i$ be an element of X^i, and let the preference relation $\preceq^i$ be complete, transitive, continuous, monotonic, and of the class C^r. Let the preference relation $\preceq^i$ be represented by the utility function $u^i \in C^r(X^i, \mathbb{R})$ having no critical point. Then

$$\widehat{c}(\overline{x}^i) = \frac{1}{(\|\partial_{x^i} u^i(\overline{x}^i)\|_2)^{N+1}} \det\left(\begin{bmatrix} -\partial^2_{x^i x^i} u^i(\overline{x}^i) & \partial_{x^i} u^i(\overline{x}^i)^\top \\ -\partial_{x^i} u^i(\overline{x}^i) & 0 \end{bmatrix}\right).$$

See Mas-Colell (1985), Proposition 2.5.1, page 76.

A consumer $i \in I_M$ with wealth $w^i \in \mathbb{R}$ is assumed to take the prevailing price system $p \in \mathbb{R}^N$ as given and to choose a best element of $\widetilde{\beta}^i(p, w^i)$ for $\preceq^i$. For every consumer $i \in I_M$, for every price system $p \in \mathbb{R}^N$, for every wealth $w^i \in \mathbb{R}$, the set $\widetilde{\delta}^i(p, w^i)$ is defined as the set of consumption bundles that are best elements of $\widetilde{\beta}^i(p, w^i)$ for $\preceq^i$, i.e.

$$\widetilde{\delta}^i(p, w^i) = \left\{ \overline{x}^i \in \widetilde{\beta}^i(p, w^i) \,\middle|\, \overline{x}^i \succeq^i x^i, \ \forall x^i \in \widetilde{\beta}^i(p, w^i) \right\}.$$

An element of $\widetilde{\delta}^i(p, w^i)$ is called an *optimal action* or an *optimal consumption bundle* of consumer $i \in I_M$ at $(p, w^i) \in \mathbb{R}^N \times \mathbb{R}$.

It is easily verified that, for every $i \in I_M$, for every $(p, w^i) \in \mathbb{R}^N \times \mathbb{R}$, $\widetilde{\delta}^i(p, w^i)$ only depends on the relative prices and the relative wealth, i.e. if $\lambda \in \mathbb{R}_{++}$, then $\widetilde{\delta}^i(p, w^i) = \widetilde{\delta}^i(\lambda p, \lambda w^i)$. The set $\mathcal{P}^i$ is defined as the set $(p, w^i) \in \mathbb{R}^N \times \mathbb{R}$ for which $\widetilde{\delta}^i(p, w^i)$ of consumer $i \in I_M$ is a non-empty set, so

$$\mathcal{P}^i = \left\{ (p, w^i) \in \mathbb{R}^N \times \mathbb{R} \,\middle|\, \widetilde{\delta}^i(p, w^i) \neq \emptyset \right\}.$$

The relation $\widetilde{\delta}^i : \mathbb{R}^N \times \mathbb{R} \to \mathbb{R}^N$ associating with every $(p, w^i) \in \mathbb{R}^N \times \mathbb{R}$ the set $\widetilde{\delta}^i(p, w^i)$ is called the *demand relation* of consumer $i \in I_M$.

3.7 THE ARROW-DEBREU MODEL

The description of the economic system is completed by specifying the resources of the agents in the economy, being the amounts of all commodities initially available in the economy, and the distribution of profits generated by the producers in the economy. It is assumed that all the resources are owned by consumers only. Moreover, it is assumed that the producers are controlled by the consumers. The *initial endowment* of a consumer $i \in I_M$, denoted by $\omega^i \in \mathbb{R}^N$, is a specification of all commodities initially owned by consumer i. Furthermore, it is assumed that a consumer $i \in I_M$ obtains a fixed non-negative *share* of the profit of every producer $h \in I_L$, denoted by θ^{hi}, and that all profits generated by producers are allocated to the consumers. Therefore, $\theta^{hi} \geq 0$, $\forall h \in I_L$, $\forall i \in I_M$, and $\sum_{i \in I_M} \theta^{hi} = 1$, $\forall h \in I_L$. So, if the price system is given by $p \in \mathbb{R}^N$ and every producer $h \in I_L$ has chosen a production plan $y^h \in Y^h$, then the wealth of a consumer $i \in I_M$ is given by

$$w^i = p \cdot \omega^i + \sum_{h \in I_L} \theta^{hi} p \cdot y^h.$$

Consequently, consumers are also responsible for losses. So, the producers considered are abstractions of firms with a partnership structure. Since it is usually assumed that $0^N \in Y^h$, $\forall h \in I_L$, producers make non-negative profits. It is clear that, when the price system is considered as given, under very weak monotonicity assumptions with respect to the preferences of consumers, from the consumer's point of view as shareholder, profit maximization is the natural objective of a producer in the framework developed so far.

The description of the economic system is now completed. So, formally, the *economy*, denoted by $\mathcal{E}$, is defined by a specification of the production possibility sets of all the producers and of the consumption sets, preference relations, initial endowments, and the profit shares in the profit of every producer of all the consumers, i.e.

$$\mathcal{E} = \left((Y^h)_{h \in I_L}, (X^i, \preceq^i, \omega^i, (\theta^{hi})_{h \in I_L})_{i \in I_M} \right).$$

When the production possibility sets and the profit shares are omitted in the description of the economy, it is assumed that $Y^h = \{0^N\}$, $\forall h \in I_L$. For every consumer $i \in I_M$, the wealth at a price system $p \in \mathbb{R}^N \cap (\cap_{h \in \{h' \in I_L | \theta^{h'i} > 0\}} P^h)$, denoted by $\tilde{b}^i(p)$, is defined by

$$\tilde{b}^i(p) = p \cdot \omega^i + \sum_{h \in \{h' \in I_L | \theta^{h'i} > 0\}} \theta^{hi} \pi^h(p),$$

and the set $\widetilde{P}^i$ is defined by

$$\widetilde{P}^i = \left\{ p \in \mathbb{R}^N \cap \left(\cap_{h \in \{h' \in I_L | \theta^{h'i} > 0\}} P^h \right) \middle| (p, \widetilde{b}^i(p)) \in \mathcal{P}^i \right\},$$

so, for every $p \in \widetilde{P}^i$, $\widetilde{\delta}^i(p, \widetilde{b}^i(p)) \neq \emptyset$. Notice that, for every $p \in \mathbb{R}^N \cap (\cap_{h \in \{h' \in I_L | \theta^{h'i} > 0\}} P^h)$, $\widetilde{b}^i(\lambda p) = \lambda \widetilde{b}^i(p)$, $\forall \lambda \in \mathbb{R}_{++}$. For every consumer $i \in I_M$, the relation $\beta^i : \mathbb{R}^N \to \mathbb{R}^N$, defined by

$$\begin{aligned} \beta^i(p) &= \widetilde{\beta}^i\left(p, \widetilde{b}^i(p)\right), && \forall p \in \cap_{h \in \{h' \in I_L | \theta^{h'i} > 0\}} P^h, \\ \beta^i(p) &= \emptyset, && \forall p \in \mathbb{R}^N \setminus \left(\cap_{h \in \{h' \in I_L | \theta^{h'i} > 0\}} P^h \right), \end{aligned}$$

is called the *budget relation* of consumer i and $\beta^i(p)$ is called the *budget set* of consumer i at price system $p \in \mathbb{R}^N$. For every consumer $i \in I_M$, the relation $\delta^i : \mathbb{R}^N \to \mathbb{R}^N$, defined by

$$\begin{aligned} \delta^i(p) &= \widetilde{\delta}^i\left(p, \widetilde{b}^i(p)\right), && \forall p \in \widetilde{P}^i, \\ \delta^i(p) &= \emptyset, && \forall p \in \mathbb{R}^N \setminus \widetilde{P}^i, \end{aligned}$$

is called the *demand relation* of consumer i. An element of $\delta^i(p)$ is called an *optimal action* or *optimal consumption bundle* of consumer $i \in I_M$ at price system $p \in \mathbb{R}^N$. Given an optimal consumption bundle x^i of consumer $i \in I_M$, consumer i is said to *supply* a commodity $j \in I_N$ if $x^i_j \leq \omega^i_j$ and consumer i is said to *demand* commodity j if $x^i_j \geq \omega^i_j$.

The set $\widetilde{P}$ is defined by

$$\widetilde{P} = \cap_{i \in I_M} \widetilde{P}^i,$$

so, for every price system $p \in \widetilde{P}$, for every producer $h \in I_L$, $\eta^h(p) \neq \emptyset$, and for every consumer $i \in I_M$, $\delta^i(p) \neq \emptyset$. The relation $\zeta : \mathbb{R}^N \to \mathbb{R}^N$, defined by

$$\begin{aligned} \zeta(p) &= \textstyle\sum_{i \in I_M} \delta^i(p) - \sum_{h \in I_L} \eta^h(p) - \sum_{i \in I_M} \{\omega^i\}, && \forall p \in \widetilde{P}, \\ \zeta(p) &= \emptyset, && \forall p \in \mathbb{R}^N \setminus \widetilde{P}, \end{aligned}$$

is called the *total excess demand relation* of the economy $\mathcal{E}$ and the set $\zeta(p)$ is called the *total excess demand* at price system $p \in \mathbb{R}^N$ of the economy $\mathcal{E}$.

Next, some properties of the total excess demand relation ζ, known as homogeneity of degree zero, Walras' law, convex-valuedness, compact-valuedness, and upper hemi-continuity are presented in Theorem 3.7.1, Theorem 3.7.2, Theorem 3.7.3, and Theorem 3.7.5. These properties are the main ingredients needed to show the existence of a Walrasian equilibrium. Under slightly different assumptions, these results can also be found in Debreu (1959). The first result uses no assumptions at all.

Theorem 3.7.1 (Homogeneity of degree zero)
The total excess demand relation ζ of the economy $\mathcal{E}$ is homogeneous of degree zero, *i.e. for every $\lambda \in \mathbb{R}_{++}$, for every $p \in \mathbb{R}^N$, it holds that*

$$\zeta(\lambda p) = \zeta(p).$$

Proof
For $p \in \mathbb{R}^N \setminus \widetilde{P}$ this property is trivial since $p \in \mathbb{R}^N \setminus \widetilde{P}$ implies $\lambda p \in \mathbb{R}^N \setminus \widetilde{P}$ for every $\lambda \in \mathbb{R}_{++}$. For $p \in \widetilde{P}$ the result follows from the fact that, for every $\lambda \in \mathbb{R}_{++}$, for every $h \in I_L$, $\eta^h(\lambda p) = \eta^h(p)$, and, for every $i \in I_M$,

$$\delta^i(\lambda p) = \widetilde{\delta}^i\left(\lambda p, \widetilde{b}^i(\lambda p)\right) = \widetilde{\delta}^i\left(\lambda p, \lambda \widetilde{b}^i(p)\right) = \widetilde{\delta}^i\left(p, \widetilde{b}^i(p)\right) = \delta^i(p).$$

Q.E.D.

The following result is valid under very weak assumptions. It was first recognized by Walras, see Walras (1874).

Theorem 3.7.2 (Walras' law)
Let the economy $\mathcal{E} = ((Y^h)_{h \in I_L}, (X^i, \preceq^i, \omega^i, (\theta^{hi})_{h \in I_L})_{i \in I_M})$ be such that for every consumer $i \in I_M$ the preference relation $\preceq^i$ is locally non-satiated. Then the total excess demand relation ζ of the economy $\mathcal{E}$ satisfies Walras' law, *i.e. for every $p \in \mathbb{R}^N$, for every $z \in \zeta(p)$, $p \cdot z = 0$.*
Proof
Suppose there exists $\bar{p} \in \mathbb{R}^N$ and $\bar{z} \in \zeta(\bar{p})$ such that $\bar{p} \cdot \bar{z} \neq 0$. Clearly, $\bar{p} \in \widetilde{P}$. Hence, for every $h \in I_L$, there exists $\bar{y}^h \in \eta^h(\bar{p})$ and, for every $i \in I_M$, there exists $\bar{x}^i \in \delta^i(\bar{p})$ such that $\bar{z} = \sum_{i \in I_M} \bar{x}^i - \sum_{h \in I_L} \bar{y}^h - \sum_{i \in I_M} \omega^i$. By the definition of η^h, $\forall h \in I_L$, and δ^i, $\forall i \in I_M$, it follows that

$$\begin{aligned}
\bar{p} \cdot \bar{z} &= \bar{p} \cdot \sum_{i \in I_M} \bar{x}^i - \bar{p} \cdot \sum_{h \in I_L} \bar{y}^h - \bar{p} \cdot \sum_{i \in I_M} \omega^i \\
&\leq \sum_{i \in I_M} \bar{p} \cdot \omega^i + \sum_{i \in I_M} \sum_{h \in I_L} \theta^{hi} \pi^h(\bar{p}) - \sum_{h \in I_L} \pi^h(\bar{p}) - \sum_{i \in I_M} \bar{p} \cdot \omega^i \\
&= \sum_{h \in I_L} \pi^h(\bar{p}) \sum_{i \in I_M} \theta^{hi} - \sum_{h \in I_L} \pi^h(\bar{p}) = 0.
\end{aligned}$$

Since, by supposition, $\bar{p} \cdot \bar{z} \neq 0$, it follows that $\bar{p} \cdot \bar{z} < 0$. Hence, there exists $i' \in I_M$ such that $\bar{p} \cdot \bar{x}^{i'} < \bar{p} \cdot \omega^{i'} + \sum_{h \in I_L} \theta^{hi'} \pi^h(\bar{p}) = \widetilde{b}^{i'}(\bar{p})$. Clearly, there exists a set $O^{i'}$ open in $X^{i'}$ such that $\bar{x}^{i'} \in O^{i'}$ and, for every $x^{i'} \in O^{i'}$, $\bar{p} \cdot x^{i'} < \widetilde{b}^{i'}(\bar{p})$. By local non-satiation of $\preceq^{i'}$ there exists $\widehat{x}^{i'} \in O^{i'}$ such that $\bar{x}^{i'} \prec^{i'} \widehat{x}^{i'}$. Obviously, $\widehat{x}^{i'} \in \beta^{i'}(\bar{p})$, so this contradicts $\bar{x}^{i'} \in \delta^{i'}(\bar{p})$. Consequently, for every $p \in \mathbb{R}^N$, for every $z \in \zeta(p)$, $p \cdot z = 0$. Q.E.D.

Under convexity assumptions on the production sets and the consumption sets it can be shown that the total excess demand relation of the economy $\mathcal{E}$ is convex-valued.

Theorem 3.7.3 (Convex-valuedness)
Let the economy $\mathcal{E} = ((Y^h)_{h \in I_L}, (X^i, \preceq^i, \omega^i, (\theta^{hi})_{h \in I_L})_{i \in I_M})$ be such that for every producer $h \in I_L$ the production possibility set Y^h is convex, and for every consumer $i \in I_M$ the consumption set X^i is convex and the preference relation $\preceq^i$ is transitive and weakly convex. Then the total excess demand relation ζ of the economy $\mathcal{E}$ is convex-valued.

Proof
Let some $p \in \mathbb{R}^N$ and some $\bar{z}, \hat{z} \in \zeta(p)$ be given. Clearly, $p \in \widetilde{P}$. So, for every $h \in I_L$, there exists $\bar{y}^h \in \eta^h(p)$ and, for every $i \in I_M$, there exists $\bar{x}^i \in \delta^i(p)$ such that $\bar{z} = \sum_{i \in I_M} \bar{x}^i - \sum_{h \in I_L} \bar{y}^h - \sum_{i \in I_M} \omega^i$, and, for every $h \in I_L$, there exists $\hat{y}^h \in \eta^h(p)$ and, for every $i \in I_M$, there exists $\hat{x}^i \in \delta^i(p)$ such that $\hat{z} = \sum_{i \in I_M} \hat{x}^i - \sum_{h \in I_L} \hat{y}^h - \sum_{i \in I_M} \omega^i$. It suffices to show that for any $\lambda \in [0, 1]$ it holds that

$$\lambda \bar{y}^h + (1 - \lambda)\hat{y}^h \in \eta^h(p), \ \forall h \in I_L, \tag{3.2}$$

$$\lambda \bar{x}^i + (1 - \lambda)\hat{x}^i \in \delta^i(p), \quad \forall i \in I_M. \tag{3.3}$$

Now (3.2) follows from the convexity of Y^h and the fact that $p \cdot (\lambda \bar{y}^h + (1 - \lambda)\hat{y}^h) = \pi^h(p)$, $\forall h \in I_L$. From the convexity of X^i, it follows that $\lambda \bar{x}^i + (1 - \lambda)\hat{x}^i \in X^i$, $\forall i \in I_M$. This, together with the fact that, for every $i \in I_M$, $p \cdot (\lambda \bar{x}^i + (1 - \lambda)\hat{x}^i) \leq \tilde{b}^i(p)$ and $\preceq^i$ is transitive and weakly convex, yields (3.3).
Q.E.D.

An element $(y, x) \in Y \times X$ is called an *allocation* of the economy $\mathcal{E}$, so an allocation consists of a specification of admissible production plans of every producer and admissible consumption bundles of every consumer in the economy $\mathcal{E}$. An allocation of the economy $\mathcal{E}$ that is feasible in the sense that the sum over the consumers of their consumption bundles equals the sum over the producers of their production plans plus the sum over the consumers of their initial endowments, is called an *attainable allocation* of the economy $\mathcal{E}$, so $(y, x) \in Y \times X$ is an attainable allocation of the economy $\mathcal{E}$ if

$$\sum_{i \in I_M} x^i - \sum_{h \in I_L} y^h - \sum_{i \in I_M} \omega^i = 0^N.$$

The set of all attainable allocations of the economy $\mathcal{E}$ is denoted by A. The following result gives conditions under which the set of attainable allocations is compact. Such a result should hold in any realistic model of the economic system since otherwise the outputs of the producers can become infinitely large in an economy with fixed resources.

Theorem 3.7.4
Let the economy $\mathcal{E} = ((Y^h)_{h \in I_L}, (X^i, \preceq^i, \omega^i, (\theta^{hi})_{h \in I_L})_{i \in I_M})$ *be such that for every producer* $h \in I_L$ *the production possibility set* Y^h *is closed, convex, and* $0^N \in Y^h$, $\widetilde{Y} \cap -\widetilde{Y} \subset \{0^N\}$, *and for every consumer* $i \in I_M$ *the consumption set* X^i *is closed and bounded from below. Then the set of attainable allocations* A *is compact.*
See Debreu (1959), Theorem 1, page 77, and Theorem 2, page 77.

It has already been remarked that the assumptions that Y^h, $\forall h \in I_L$, and X^i, $\forall i \in I_M$, are compact are not realistic. Nevertheless, Theorem 3.7.4 shows that the set A of attainable allocations is compact. For many purposes it is therefore possible to replace the production possibility sets and the consumption sets by compact ones. This makes the following theorem interesting.

Theorem 3.7.5 (Compact-valuedness and upper hemi-continuity)
Let the economy $\mathcal{E} = ((Y^h)_{h \in I_L}, (X^i, \preceq^i, \omega^i, (\theta^{hi})_{h \in I_L})_{i \in I_M})$ *be such that for every producer* $h \in I_L$ *the production possibility set* Y^h *is compact and* $0^N \in Y^h$, *and for every consumer* $i \in I_M$ *the consumption set* X^i *is convex and compact and the preference relation* $\preceq^i$ *is complete, transitive, and continuous. Then* $P^h = \mathbb{R}^N$, $\forall h \in I_L$, *and the relation* $\zeta_{|\{p \in \mathbb{R}^N | \forall i \in I_M, \exists x^i \in X^i, p \cdot x^i < \tilde{b}^i(p)\}} : \{p \in \mathbb{R}^N \mid \forall i \in I_M, \exists x^i \in X^i, p \cdot x^i < \widetilde{b}^i(p)\} \to \mathbb{R}^N$ *is a compact-valued, upper hemi-continuous correspondence.*
See Debreu (1959), Theorem 3, page 48, and Theorem 1, page 72.

3.8 EQUILIBRIUM

An element $(p, y, x) \in \mathbb{R}^N \times Y \times X$ is called a *state* of the economy $\mathcal{E}$ if $y^h \in \eta^h(p)$, $\forall h \in I_L$, and $x^i \in \delta^i(p)$, $\forall i \in I_M$. So, a state of the economy $\mathcal{E}$ consists of a specification of a price system, an optimal production plan at this price system for every producer, and an optimal consumption bundle at this price system for every consumer in the economy $\mathcal{E}$. The *total excess demand* at a state (p, y, x) of the economy $\mathcal{E}$ is given by $z = \sum_{i \in I_M} x^i - \sum_{h \in I_L} y^h - \sum_{i \in I_M} \omega^i$, hence $z \in \zeta(p)$. The actions chosen by the producers and the consumers in a state of the economy are not necessarily compatible in the sense that the total excess demand at this state is equal to zero. Given some state of the economy, the market for a commodity $j \in I_N$ is said to be in *equilibrium* if the total excess demand for commodity j is equal to zero. A *Walrasian equilibrium* of the economy $\mathcal{E}$ is a state of $\mathcal{E}$ at which every market is in equilibrium, so at which the optimal actions of the producers and consumers yield an attainable allocation.

Definition 3.8.1 (Walrasian equilibrium)
A Walrasian equilibrium of $\mathcal{E} = ((Y^h)_{h \in I_L}, (X^i, \preceq^i, \omega^i, (\theta^{hi})_{h \in I_L})_{i \in I_M})$ *is an element* $(p^*, y^*, x^*) \in \mathbb{R}^N \times Y \times X$ *satisfying*

1. *for every producer* $h \in I_L$, $y^{*h} \in \eta^h(p^*)$,
2. *for every consumer* $i \in I_M$, $x^{*i} \in \delta^i(p^*)$,
3. $\sum_{i \in I_M} x^{*i} - \sum_{h \in I_L} y^{*h} - \sum_{i \in I_M} \omega^i = 0^N$.

When (p^*, y^*, x^*) is a Walrasian equilibrium of the economy $\mathcal{E}$, then p^* is called a *Walrasian equilibrium price system* and (y^*, x^*) is called a *Walrasian equilibrium allocation.* Condition 1 reflects that every producer chooses an optimal production plan at the Walrasian equilibrium price system, Condition 2 that every consumer chooses an optimal consumption bundle at the Walrasian equilibrium price system, and Condition 3 that the Walrasian equilibrium allocation is an attainable allocation of the economy $\mathcal{E}$. Notice that if (p^*, y^*, x^*) is a Walrasian equilibrium of the economy $\mathcal{E}$, then $p^* \in \widetilde{P}$, $\pi^h(p^*) = p^* \cdot y^{*h}$, $\forall h \in I_L$, and $0^N \in \zeta(p^*)$. In a Walrasian equilibrium the optimal actions of the agents in the economy are compatible. It should be noticed that the actions taken by the agents in the economy are not necessarily completely decentralized at a Walrasian equilibrium. This may be the case when there is an agent having more than one optimal action, while not every optimal action is compatible with a Walrasian equilibrium.

Let the element (p^*, y^*, x^*) be a Walrasian equilibrium of the economy $\mathcal{E}$. By Theorem 3.7.1 the element $(\lambda p^*, y^*, x^*)$ is also a Walrasian equilibrium of the economy $\mathcal{E}$ for every $\lambda \in \mathbb{R}_{++}$. These equilibria are often identified, so a Walrasian equilibrium (p^*, y^*, x^*) of the economy $\mathcal{E}$ is said to be unique if every Walrasian equilibrium of $\mathcal{E}$ is of the form $(\lambda p^*, y^*, x^*)$ for some $\lambda \in \mathbb{R}_{++}$.

Let a state (p, y, x) of the economy $\mathcal{E}$ and a commodity $j \in I_N$ be given. If $\sum_{i \in I_M} x^i_j - \sum_{h \in I_L} y^h_j - \sum_{i \in I_M} \omega^i_j > 0$, then there is a positive total excess demand for commodity j at this state. Therefore, it is not possible to satisfy the demand at p for commodity j of every agent, whereas every agent may get rid of his supply at p of commodity j. In such a situation the price of commodity j has a tendency to rise since an agent whose demand at p is not satisfied can offer a price that is slightly higher than p_j thereby attracting all the supply. Similarly, every agent supplying commodity j can ask a price that is slightly higher than p_j and is still able to sell all his supply. Notice that in this reasoning certain monotonicity properties with respect to the preferences of consumers and certain continuity properties with respect to the optimal actions of the agents are assumed. If $\sum_{i \in I_M} x_j^i - \sum_{h \in I_L} y_j^h - \sum_{i \in I_M} \omega_j^i < 0$, then there is a negative total excess demand for commodity j at this state and a similar reasoning as above can be used to argue that the price of commodity j has a tendency to fall. A state of the economy at which the total excess demand is zero is in equilibrium in the sense that the price system has no tendency to change. Therefore, a Walrasian equilibrium of the economy is an equilibrium state of the economy. There are no forces that bring about a change in a Walrasian equilibrium price system and allocation.

This yields two reasons why Walrasian equilibria are important. They yield states of the economy that are both compatible and in equilibrium. The natural question to ask is therefore whether such a Walrasian equilibrium of the economy exists. The following result gives an affirmative answer for a large class of economies.

Theorem 3.8.2
Let the economy $\mathcal{E} = ((Y^h)_{h \in I_L}, (X^i, \preceq^i, \omega^i, (\theta^{hi})_{h \in I_L})_{i \in I_M})$ be such that for every producer $h \in I_L$ the production possibility set Y^h is closed, convex, $0^N \in Y^h$, and $-\mathbb{R}_+^N \subset Y^h$, $\bar{Y} \cap -\bar{Y} \subset \{0^N\}$, and for every consumer $i \in I_M$ the consumption set X^i is closed, convex, and bounded from below, the preference relation $\preceq^i$ is complete, transitive, continuous, non-satiated, and convex, and there exists $x^i \in X^i$ such that $x^i \ll \omega^i$. Then there exists a Walrasian equilibrium of the economy $\mathcal{E}$ and every Walrasian equilibrium (p^*, y^*, x^*) of $\mathcal{E}$ satisfies $p^* \in \mathbb{R}_+^N \setminus \{0^N\}$.
See Debreu (1959), Theorem 1, page 83.

All assumptions made in Theorem 3.8.2 have been discussed in Sections 3.3, 3.4, and 3.6, with the exception of the condition that for every consumer $i \in I_M$ there exists a consumption bundle $x^i \in X^i$ such that $x^i \ll \omega^i$. This condition is in general not satisfied in the real world since it requires that a consumer can supply a positive quantity of every commodity. However, as an approximation of the case where for every consumer $i \in I_M$ there exists a consumption bundle $x^i \in X^i$ such that $x^i \leq \omega^i$, this assumption is clearly excellent. Cases where for some consumer $i \in I_M$ there is no consumption bundle $x^i \in X^i$ such that $x^i \leq \omega^i$ are rare, but might occur for example if the initial endowment of a consumer includes the obligation to deliver some amount of a commodity. Such cases might lead to bankruptcy problems and are abstracted from in this monograph. At the cost of a more technical assumption and a more difficult proof, the assumption that for every consumer $i \in I_M$ there exists a consumption bundle $x^i \in X^i$ such that $x^i \ll \omega^i$ can be relaxed using the notion of indirect resource relatedness, see Arrow and Hahn (1971), Definition 5, page 118. Another relaxation is given in Theorem 3.11.1.

3.9 FUNDAMENTAL WELFARE THEOREMS

Let two attainable allocations $(\overline{y}, \overline{x})$ and $(\widehat{y}, \widehat{x})$ of the economy $\mathcal{E}$ be given. The second allocation is said to be at least as desired as the first one, denoted by $(\overline{y}, \overline{x}) \preceq (\widehat{y}, \widehat{x})$, if $\overline{x}^i \preceq^i \widehat{x}^i$, $\forall i \in I_M$. The relation $\preceq: A \to A$ is a pre-ordering that is not necessarily complete. It is possible to derive the relations $\prec$, $\sim$, $\succ$, and $\Box$ from the relation $\preceq$ in the same way as for a consumer $i \in I_M$ the relations $\prec^i$, $\sim^i$, $\succ^i$, and $\Box^i$ are derived from $\preceq^i$, respectively. The allocation $(\overline{y}, \overline{x})$ is said to be *Pareto dominated* by the allocation $(\widehat{y}, \widehat{x})$ if $(\overline{y}, \overline{x}) \prec (\widehat{y}, \widehat{x})$, so there exists at least one consumer $i \in I_M$ such that $\overline{x}^i \prec^i \widehat{x}^i$. An allocation of the economy is said to be *Pareto efficient* if it is attainable and not dominated by another attainable allocation of the economy. It is now a natural question to ask whether a Walrasian equilibrium allocation is Pareto efficient. The question can be answered affirmatively under extremely mild assumptions as is shown by the following result. This result is known as the *first fundamental welfare theorem*, and is, using different assumptions, also given in Debreu (1959), Theorem 6.3.1, page 94.

Theorem 3.9.1
Let the economy $\mathcal{E} = ((Y^h)_{h \in I_L}, (X^i, \preceq^i, \omega^i, (\theta^{hi})_{h \in I_L})_{i \in I_M})$ be such that for every consumer $i \in I_M$ the preference relation $\preceq^i$ is transitive and locally non-satiated. Then every Walrasian equilibrium (p^*, y^*, x^*) of the economy $\mathcal{E}$ is Pareto efficient.

Proof
Using the fact that $\preceq^i$ is locally non-satiated it follows, using the same argu-

ments as in the proof of Theorem 3.7.2, that

$$p^* \cdot x^{*i} = p^* \cdot \omega^i + \sum_{h \in I_L} \theta^{hi} \pi^h(p^*), \ \forall i \in I_M. \tag{3.4}$$

Suppose $(\overline{y}, \overline{x}) \in A$ satisfies $(y^*, x^*) \prec (\overline{y}, \overline{x})$. It holds that $\overline{y}^h \in Y^h$, $\forall h \in I_L$, so

$$p^* \cdot \overline{y}^h \leq \pi^h(p^*), \ \forall h \in I_L. \tag{3.5}$$

For every $i \in I_M$ it holds that $x^{*i} \preceq^i \overline{x}^i$, $\overline{x}^i \in X^i$, and $\preceq^i$ is transitive, and therefore either $\overline{x}^i \in \delta^i(p^*)$ and $p^* \cdot \overline{x}^i = p^* \cdot \omega^i + \sum_{h \in I_L} \theta^{hi} \pi^h(p^*)$, or $\overline{x}^i \notin \delta^i(p^*)$ and it follows that $p^* \cdot \overline{x}^i > p^* \cdot \omega^i + \sum_{h \in I_L} \theta^{hi} \pi^h(p^*)$. Therefore,

$$p^* \cdot \overline{x}^i \geq p^* \cdot \omega^i + \sum_{h \in I_L} \theta^{hi} \pi^h(p^*), \ \forall i \in I_M. \tag{3.6}$$

There exists $i' \in I_M$ such that $x^{*i'} \prec^{i'} \overline{x}^{i'}$ and, since $x^{*i'} \in \delta^{i'}(p^*)$, $\preceq^{i'}$ is transitive, and $\overline{x}^{i'} \in X^{i'}$, it follows that

$$p^* \cdot \overline{x}^{i'} > p^* \cdot \omega^{i'} + \sum_{h \in I_L} \theta^{hi'} \pi^h(p^*). \tag{3.7}$$

So, since $(\overline{y}, \overline{x}) \in A$, it follows from (3.4)-(3.7) that

$$\begin{aligned} 0 &= p^* \cdot \left(\sum_{i \in I_M} \overline{x}^i - \sum_{h \in I_L} \overline{y}^h - \sum_{i \in I_M} \omega^i \right) \\ &> \sum_{i \in I_M} p^* \cdot \omega^i + \sum_{i \in I_M} \sum_{h \in I_L} \theta^{hi} \pi^h(p^*) - \sum_{h \in I_L} \pi^h(p^*) - \sum_{i \in I_M} p^* \cdot \omega^i \\ &= \sum_{h \in I_L} \pi^h(p^*) \sum_{i \in I_M} \theta^{hi} - \sum_{h \in I_L} \pi^h(p^*) = 0, \end{aligned}$$

a contradiction. Consequently, there is no $(\overline{y}, \overline{x}) \in A$ such that $(y^*, x^*) \prec (\overline{y}, \overline{x})$. Q.E.D.

Theorem 3.9.1 gives another reason for the stability of a Walrasian equilibrium of the economy. It is not possible to propose an attainable allocation of the economy that makes at least one consumer better off and no consumer worse off than in a Walrasian equilibrium allocation.

Another natural question to ask is whether a given Pareto efficient allocation of the economy can be implemented as a Walrasian equilibrium of the economy. The next result, known as the *second fundamental welfare theorem,* almost gives an answer to this question.

Theorem 3.9.2
Let the economy $\mathcal{E} = ((Y^h)_{h\in I_L}, (X^i, \preceq^i, \omega^i, (\theta^{hi})_{h\in I_L})_{i\in I_M})$ be such that for every producer $h \in I_L$ the production possibility set Y^h is convex, and for every consumer $i \in I_M$ the consumption set X^i is convex and the preference relation $\preceq^i$ is complete, transitive, continuous, non-satiated, and convex. Then, for every Pareto efficient allocation $(\overline{y}, \overline{x})$ of the economy $\mathcal{E}$, there exists a price system $\overline{p} \in \mathbb{R}^N \setminus \{0^N\}$ with the following properties:

1. *for every producer $h \in I_L$, $\overline{y}^h \in \eta^h(\overline{p})$,*
2. *for every consumer $i \in I_M$, $\overline{p} \cdot \overline{x}^i \leq \overline{p} \cdot x^i$, $\forall x^i \in \{\widehat{x}^i \in X^i \mid \widehat{x}^i \succeq^i \overline{x}^i\}$.*

See Debreu (1959), Theorem 1, page 95.

Let $(\overline{y}, \overline{x})$ be a Pareto efficient allocation of the economy and let $\overline{p} \in \mathbb{R}^N \setminus \{0^N\}$ be such that Property 1 and Property 2 of Theorem 3.9.2 are satisfied. Let the initial endowments and the profit shares be redistributed in such a way that every consumer $i \in I_M$ has wealth equal to $\overline{p} \cdot \overline{x}^i$. This can be done in many ways, for example by giving every consumer $i \in I_M$ an initial endowment equal to $\overline{x}^i - \frac{1}{M}(\sum_{h\in I_L} \overline{y}^h)$ and a profit share $\frac{1}{M}$ in the profit of every producer. However, notice that such a redistribution of initial endowments might involve the redistribution of certain labour services, an operation not always feasible. Another possibility is to let each consumer keep his initial endowments and profit shares and to give every consumer $i \in I_M$ in addition an amount in units of account equal to $\overline{p} \cdot \overline{x}^i - \overline{p} \cdot \omega^i - \overline{p} \cdot \sum_{h\in I_L} \theta^{hi} \pi^h(\overline{p})$. In this way a new economy, denoted by $\overline{\mathcal{E}}$, is obtained. If $\overline{x}^i \in \widetilde{\delta}^i(\overline{p}, \overline{p} \cdot \overline{x}^i)$, $\forall i \in I_M$, then Theorem 3.9.2 yields that $(\overline{p}, \overline{y}, \overline{x})$ is a Walrasian equilibrium of the economy $\overline{\mathcal{E}}$. By Debreu (1959), Theorem 1, page 69, this is indeed the case if for every consumer $i \in I_M$ there exists a consumption bundle $x^i \in X^i$ such that $\overline{p} \cdot x^i < \overline{p} \cdot \overline{x}^i$.

3.10 AN EXAMPLE

To illustrate the theory presented in this monograph, an example is given in each chapter. In this section the example used throughout Part II is examined. In this example the economy $\mathcal{E} = ((X^i, \preceq^i, \omega^i)_{i\in I_2})$ is such that $N = 2$,

$$X^1 = X^2 = \mathbb{R}^2_+,$$

$\preceq^1$ and $\preceq^2$ can be represented by utility functions $u^1 : X^1 \to \mathbb{R}$ and $u^2 : X^2 \to \mathbb{R}$, respectively, defined by

$$u^1(x^1) = (x_1^1)^{\frac{3}{4}}(x_2^1)^{\frac{1}{4}}, \ \forall x^1 \in \mathbb{R}_+^2,$$
$$u^2(x^2) = (x_1^2)^{\frac{1}{4}}(x_2^2)^{\frac{3}{4}}, \ \forall x^2 \in \mathbb{R}_+^2,$$

and

$$\omega^1 = (1,4)^\top,$$
$$\omega^2 = (2,1)^\top.$$

Using Theorem 2.9.7 it can easily be verified that the restriction of the demand relation to $\mathbb{R}_{++}^2$, $\delta^i_{|\mathbb{R}_{++}^2}$, $\forall i \in I_2$, is a function, denoted by d^i, $\forall i \in I_2$, which is defined by

$$d^1(p) = \left(\tfrac{3p_1+12p_2}{4p_1}, \tfrac{p_1+4p_2}{4p_2}\right)^\top, \ \forall p \in \mathbb{R}_{++}^2,$$
$$d^2(p) = \left(\tfrac{2p_1+p_2}{4p_1}, \tfrac{6p_1+3p_2}{4p_2}\right)^\top, \ \forall p \in \mathbb{R}_{++}^2.$$

It is also easily verified that, for every consumer $i \in I_2$, $\delta^i(p) = \emptyset$ if $p \in \mathbb{R}^2 \setminus \mathbb{R}_{++}^2$. Notice that the assumptions of Theorem 3.7.1, Theorem 3.7.2, and Theorem 3.7.3 are satisfied, and that indeed the relation δ^i, $\forall i \in I_2$, is homogeneous of degree zero, satisfies Walras' law, and is convex-valued, and therefore the same properties hold for the total excess demand relation ζ. Moreover, d^i, $\forall i \in I_2$, is a continuous function, which is not surprising given the result mentioned in Theorem 3.7.5. The Walrasian equilibrium price systems are given by the solutions $p \in \mathbb{R}_{++}^2$ of the system of equations $d^1(p) + d^2(p) = \omega^1 + \omega^2 = (3,5)^\top$. It easily follows that p^* is a Walrasian equilibrium price system if and only if $p^* \in \mathbb{R}_{++}^2$ and

$$\frac{p_1^*}{p_2^*} = \frac{13}{7}.$$

Therefore, the Walrasian equilibrium is unique in this case. The Walrasian equilibrium allocation x^* is given by

$$x^{*1} = (2\tfrac{19}{52}, 1\tfrac{13}{28})^\top \text{ and } x^{*2} = (\tfrac{33}{52}, 3\tfrac{15}{28})^\top.$$

Notice that all assumptions of Theorem 3.8.2 are satisfied by the economy $\mathcal{E}$ of the example, except the assumption that $-\mathbb{R}_+^2 \subset Y^h$, $\forall h \in I_L$. Clearly, the example would not change by making the assumption that $Y^h = -\mathbb{R}_+^2$, $\forall h \in I_L$.

After making some calculations it follows that the set of Pareto efficient allocations is given by

$$\left\{ x \in X \,\middle|\, 0 \leq x_1^1 \leq 3, \ x_1^2 = 3 - x_1^1, \ x_2^1 = \frac{5x_1^1}{27 - 8x_1^1}, \text{ and } x_2^2 = \frac{135 - 45x_1^1}{27 - 8x_1^1} \right\}.$$

Since the economy $\mathcal{E}$ of the example satisfies all the requirements of Theorem 3.9.1, it is not surprising that the Walrasian equilibrium allocation is Pareto efficient. Moreover, all the assumptions made in Theorem 3.9.2 are satisfied by the economy $\mathcal{E}$. Given a Pareto efficient allocation x it can be shown that a price system $p \in \mathbb{R}^2 \setminus \{(0,0)^\top\}$ satisfies the conditions given in Theorem 3.9.2 if and only if $p \in \mathbb{R}^2_{++}$ and

$$\frac{p_1}{p_2} = \frac{15}{27 - 8x_1^1}. \tag{3.8}$$

Furthermore, it can be shown that, by redistribution of the initial endowments of the consumers in an appropriate way, every Pareto efficient allocation can be obtained as a Walrasian equilibrium of the resulting economy, with the Walrasian equilibrium price system $p \in \mathbb{R}^2_{++}$ satisfying (3.8).

3.11 STABILITY

Theorem 3.8.2 gives a very strong result with respect to the existence of a Walrasian equilibrium. In Section 3.8 it was argued that a Walrasian equilibrium is indeed an equilibrium state of the economy in several respects. So, if an economy reaches a Walrasian equilibrium, then it will stay there and trade can take place. A natural question to ask is whether there are tendencies such that an economy reaches a Walrasian equilibrium. Moreover, even if a Walrasian equilibrium has been reached by the economy, it is important to know what happens in the case of slight perturbations of this state. These questions are referred to as the stability question.

To address the stability question, one should formulate an explicit dynamic model of the state of the economy at an arbitrary point in time, given any initial state of the economy. Empirically, it is often argued that economies do reach an equilibrium state. Moreover, many economic theories are based on the assumption that the economy reaches an equilibrium state, for instance theories of economic growth or theories based on comparative statics. This motivates the search for dynamic models of the state of the economy such that convergence to an equilibrium state results for a large class of economies and for an arbitrarily specified initial state of the economy. When specifying a dynamic model of the state of the economy, it is possible to treat time as either *discrete* or *continuous*. The latter treatment of time is always employed in this monograph.

Now a general formulation of dynamic processes and of some stability concepts is given. Let the subset S of $\mathbb{R}^m$ denote the set of all possible *states* of the economy. Notice that it is implicitly assumed that it is indeed possible to represent the set of all possible states by a subset of a finite dimensional Euclidean space. Let T be an interval of $\mathbb{R}_+$ such that $0 \in T$, representing *time*. Let $\tilde{t}$ denote the supremum of T, where by definition $\tilde{t} = +\infty$ when $T = \mathbb{R}_+$. The *initial state* of the economy, i.e. the state at $t = 0$, is denoted by v and is given by an element of S. The state of the economy at time t is also represented by an element of the set S. A *dynamic process* is a function $\pi : S \times T \to S$ satisfying $\pi(v, 0) = v$, $\forall v \in S$. For every $v \in S$, for every $t \in T$, $\pi(v, t)$ denotes the state of the economy at time t if the initial state is v. Often a dynamic process is described implicitly by means of a *differential equation*. In this case a function $f : S \to \mathbb{R}^m$ is given and the dynamic process π is required to satisfy

$$\partial_t \pi(v, \bar{t}) = f\left(\pi(v, \bar{t})\right), \ \forall v \in S, \ \forall \bar{t} \in T. \tag{3.9}$$

The dynamic process is then often called the *trajectory* of the differential equation. In this case the set T is taken equal to $\mathbb{R}_+$ and some requirements with respect to f and S have to be made to guarantee that π is well defined and uniquely determined, see for example Hahn (1982). Notice that the function f used in the formulation (3.9) does not depend on the initial state. Although it is not difficult to make f dependent upon the initial state, usually this is not done in the literature. However, in the dynamic processes analysed in Part IV of this monograph, the dependence on the initial state is crucial. If the dynamic process is described as in (3.9) and some state is reached, then the states subsequently generated by the process are independent of the history of the process, in particular the initial state. In the dynamic processes analysed in Part IV of this monograph, the history of the process remains important, and influences the states to be reached in the future.

Often it is assumed that the dynamic process $\pi_{|\{v\} \times T} : \{v\} \times T \to S$ is a continuous function for every initial state v of S. This assumption is natural in a model involving continuous time. All dynamic processes considered in Part IV of this monograph are continuous functions, given the initial state.

Let S be a subset of $\mathbb{R}^m$ and let T be an interval of $\mathbb{R}_+$. The dynamic process $\pi : S \times T \to S$ is said to *converge* to the state $\bar{s}$ of S given the initial state v, where $\bar{s}$ is called the *limit* of π given the initial state v, if for every sequence $(t^n)_{n \in \mathbb{N}}$ in T converging to $\tilde{t}$ it holds that the sequence $(\pi(v, t^n))_{n \in \mathbb{N}}$ in S converges to $\bar{s}$. Notice that if $\pi_{|\{v\} \times T}$ is a continuous function, $\tilde{t} \in T$, and π converges to the state $\bar{s}$ of S given the initial state v, then $\pi(v, \tilde{t}) = \bar{s}$. Under weak conditions, it can be shown that for a dynamic process determined as in

(3.9) it holds that if π converges to the state $\bar{s}$ of S given any $v \in S$, then $f(\bar{s}) = 0^m$, see Hahn (1982), Theorem 1.2, page 749. The dynamic process π is said to be *locally stable* if for every state $\bar{s}$ of S being the limit of π given some initial state, there exists $\varepsilon \in \mathbb{R}_{++}$ such that $\bar{s}$ is the limit of π given any initial state in $B^m(\bar{s}, \varepsilon) \cap S$. The dynamic process π is said to be *globally stable* if for every initial state v of S there exists a state $\bar{s}$ of S such that $\bar{s}$ is the limit of π given the initial state v. Notice that the state $\bar{s}$ might be different for different initial states v. Various refinements of the stability properties defined above exist. The notion of local stability captures the idea of an economy returning to an equilibrium state, when a small perturbation in this state has taken place. The notion of global stability captures the idea that the economy reaches some equilibrium state.

It is far from obvious how an explicit dynamic model of the economy as described in this chapter should look like. In the literature a distinction is made between tatonnement processes and non-tatonnement processes. In a tatonnement process it is assumed that no trade occurs until an equilibrium state is reached by the economy. Then the stability question for the model of the economy presented in this chapter boils down to the question whether the tatonnement process converges to a Walrasian equilibrium of the economy. In a non-tatonnement process trade is allowed before an equilibrium state is reached. In this case the stability question reduces to the question whether the process converges to some equilibrium state, in general not compatible with a Walrasian equilibrium of the original economy. In some non-tatonnement processes the description of the market mechanism given in this chapter is abandoned and there is no price system present in the economy. In other non-tatonnement processes the price system is included in the description of the process, but since the behaviour of the agents in the economy is incompatible at non-Walrasian equilibrium price systems, the determination of the trade taking place is often rather ad hoc. An overview of non-tatonnement processes (and also of tatonnement processes) is given in Hahn (1982).

In this monograph only tatonnement processes are analysed, which should be considered as dynamic descriptions of the economy for the very short run. Theoretically, the very short run should not exceed the elementary time interval used to distinguish commodities. Other cases where a tatonnement process makes sense as a description of dynamic processes going on in an economic system, concern a world where commodities are perishable and where all agents in the economy are faced in each period with the same technologies, preferences, and resources, irrespective of the trade that has taken place in the previous period. Obviously, understanding of tatonnement processes does not lead to a full understanding of the adjustment of prices taking place in any real world economic system, but it should be considered as an essential and important step. The stability question is discussed in a relatively easy setting, i.e. one without production and relatively strong assumptions with respect to the economy. Theorem 3.11.1 shows the properties one might expect in an economy in such a setting and gives a bench-mark for further analysis.

Theorem 3.11.1
Let the economy $\mathcal{E} = ((X^i, \preceq^i, \omega^i)_{i \in I_M})$ *be such that, for every consumer* $i \in I_M$, $X^i = \mathbb{R}^N_+$, *the preference relation* $\preceq^i$ *is complete, transitive, continuous, strongly monotonic, and strongly convex,* $\omega^i \in \mathbb{R}^N_+$, *and* $\sum_{i \in I_M} \omega^i \in \mathbb{R}^N_{++}$. *Then* $\widetilde{P} = \mathbb{R}^N_{++}$, $\delta^i_{|\mathbb{R}^N_{++}} : \mathbb{R}^N_{++} \rightarrow \mathbb{R}^N$, $\forall i \in I_M$, *and* $\zeta_{|\mathbb{R}^N_{++}} : \mathbb{R}^N_{++} \rightarrow \mathbb{R}^N$, *denoted by* z, *are continuous functions. If* $(p^n)_{n \in \mathbb{N}}$ *is a sequence of price systems in* $\mathbb{R}^N_{++}$ *converging to* $\bar{p} \in \mathbb{R}^N_+ \setminus (\{0^N\} \cup \mathbb{R}^N_{++})$, *then the sequence* $(z(p^n))_{n \in \mathbb{N}}$ *satisfies* $\sum_{j \in I_N} z_j(p^n) \rightarrow +\infty$. *Moreover, there exists a Walrasian equilibrium of the economy* $\mathcal{E}$ *and every Walrasian equilibrium* (p^*, x^*) *of* $\mathcal{E}$ *satisfies* $p^* \in \mathbb{R}^N_{++}$.
See Hildenbrand and Kirman (1988), Proposition 3.2, page 96, and Theorem 3.1, page 108.

Motivated by Theorem 3.11.1, when studying the stability question, it is often assumed that the restriction of the total excess demand relation to $\mathbb{R}^N_{++}$, $\zeta_{|\mathbb{R}^N_{++}}$, is a continuous function, being denoted by z. Moreover, it may be assumed to satisfy the type of boundary behaviour as given in Theorem 3.11.1, homogeneity of degree zero, see Theorem 3.7.1, and Walras' law, see Theorem 3.7.2. Together with the property that $z(p) \geq -\sum_{i \in I_M} \omega^i$, $\forall p \in \mathbb{R}^N_{++}$, these are the only properties used in showing the existence of a Walrasian equilibrium.

If the total excess demand relation restricted to $\mathbb{R}^N_{++}$ is a function as in Theorem 3.11.1, then the state of the economy is completely determined by the price system, and it suffices to model the dynamic behaviour of the price system. The dynamic process of the state of the economy is then referred to as a *price adjustment process.* Notice that, implicitly, it is then assumed that at each point in time every agent observes the same price for a commodity and every agent expresses his optimal action, given the prevailing price system. Although such assumptions are reasonable for an equilibrium state of the economy, they seem to be restrictive when considering economies out of equilibrium. Nevertheless, such assumptions are always made in this monograph.

As is shown in Dierker (1972), using a stronger notion of local stability than in this monograph, for a very large class of price adjustment processes local stability implies that there is exactly one Walrasian equilibrium. It is not difficult to give examples of economies having more than one Walrasian equilibrium, see for example Kehoe (1991) and see also Section 3.12, while there is still more than one Walrasian equilibrium when these economies are slightly perturbed. Hence, local stability is too much to be hoped for. Nevertheless, in Mukherji (1995) an example of a locally stable price adjustment process is given. However, in this process it could happen that no price is adjusted while the total excess demand is not equal to zero, an adjustment process ruled out by Dierker (1972) for obvious reasons. Therefore, in this monograph attention is focused to the question whether there exist globally stable price adjustment processes.

Using the same type of reasoning as in Section 3.8, it is often argued that in a price adjustment process the price system moves in accordance with the sign of the total excess demand at the current price system, called the *law of demand.* Although the law of demand seems to be a very natural assumption, there is some criticism to it, see for instance Koopmans (1957). One of the problems is that in the model of this chapter it is assumed that every agent is a price taker. Therefore, it is impossible to view the price adjustment process as being the result of price setting behaviour of the individual agents acting in the economy. Nevertheless, most price adjustment processes formulated in the literature do satisfy assumptions closely related to the law of demand. To deal with the problem that every agent is assumed to be a price taker, while the price system is allowed to change, it is often assumed that the price system is determined by a fictitious *auctioneer* at each point in time. The auctioneer is then assumed to adjust the price system based on total excess demand at the current price system. Whether a fictitious auctioneer is assumed to exist or not, the main purpose of a price adjustment process is to describe the global features of the behaviour of the market mechanism when an economy is out of equilibrium. Something similar to the law of demand does not seem to be unreasonable as a global feature of the behaviour of the market mechanism.

A function $f : \mathbb{R} \to \mathbb{R}$ is said to be *sign preserving* if, for every $s \in \mathbb{R}$, $s < 0$ implies $f(s) < 0$, $s = 0$ implies $f(s) = 0$, and $s > 0$ implies $f(s) > 0$. Let the economy $\mathcal{E}$ have a total excess demand function $z : \mathbb{R}^N_{++} \to \mathbb{R}^N$ and, for every $j \in I_N$, let sign preserving functions $f_j : \mathbb{R} \to \mathbb{R}$ be given. Consider the price adjustment process $\pi : \mathbb{R}^N_{++} \times \mathbb{R}_+ \to \mathbb{R}^N_{++}$, where, for every $j \in I_N$, π_j is implicitly defined by

$$\partial_t \pi_j(v, \bar{t}) = f_j\left(z_j\left(\pi(v, \bar{t})\right)\right), \ \forall v \in S, \ \forall \bar{t} \in \mathbb{R}_+. \tag{3.10}$$

Notice that (3.10) reflects the law of demand exactly. If for every commodity $j \in I_N$ there exists $\lambda_j \in \mathbb{R}_{++}$ such that the function f_j is defined by $f_j(s) =$

$\lambda_j s$, $\forall s \in \mathbb{R}$, then (3.10) yields the formulation of the *Walrasian tatonnement process* as given in Samuelson (1941). Notice that there is no loss of generality in taking $\lambda_j = 1$, $\forall j \in I_N$, since it is possible to change the unit of measurement of the commodities. The price adjustment process determined by (3.10) can be shown to be globally stable in many cases, like the case with one consumer (or more general the case where the total excess demand function could result from an economy with one consumer), the case with one or two commodities, and the case where the distribution of the initial endowments constitutes a Pareto efficient allocation, see Arrow and Hurwicz (1958) and Arrow and Hahn (1971), see also Negishi (1962) and Hahn (1982) for surveys of other results. For the most important special case the concept of gross substitutability in the finite increment form is needed.

A total excess demand function $z : \mathbb{R}^N_{++} \to \mathbb{R}$ is said to satisfy *gross substitutability in the finite increment form* if for every $\overline{p}, \widehat{p} \in \mathbb{R}^N_{++}$ such that, for some $j' \in I_N$, $\overline{p}_{j'} < \widehat{p}_{j'}$ and $\overline{p}_j = \widehat{p}_j$, $\forall j \in I_N \setminus \{j'\}$, it holds that $z_j(\overline{p}) < z_j(\widehat{p})$, $\forall j \in I_N \setminus \{j'\}$. If a total excess demand function z satisfies gross substitutability in the finite increment form, then an increase in the price of a commodity results in an increase in the total excess demand for all the other commodities. Unfortunately, it is not possible to derive this property from assumptions on the consumption sets, initial endowments, and preference relations, although it is economically appealing.

Theorem 3.11.2
Let the economy $\mathcal{E} = ((X^i, \preceq^i, \omega^i)_{i \in I_M})$ be such that $\zeta_{|\mathbb{R}^N_{++}} : \mathbb{R}^N_{++} \to \mathbb{R}^N$, denoted by z, is a continuous function being bounded from below, satisfying homogeneity of degree zero, Walras' law, gross substitutability in the finite increment form, and if $(p^n)_{n \in \mathbb{N}}$ is a sequence of price systems in $\mathbb{R}^N_{++}$ converging to $\overline{p} \in \mathbb{R}^N_+ \setminus (\{0^N\} \cup \mathbb{R}^N_{++})$, then the sequence $(z(p^n))_{n \in \mathbb{N}}$ is such that $\sum_{j \in I_N} z_j(p^n) \to +\infty$. Then there exists a unique Walrasian equilibrium price system $p^* \in \mathbb{R}^N_{++}$ of the economy $\mathcal{E}$. For every $j \in I_N$, let $f_j : \mathbb{R} \to \mathbb{R}$ be a continuous, sign preserving function. Then the price adjustment process $\pi : \mathbb{R}^N_{++} \times \mathbb{R}_+ \to \mathbb{R}^N_{++}$, where, for every $j \in I_N$, π_j is determined by $\partial_t \pi_j(v, \overline{t}) = f_j(z_j(\pi(v, \overline{t})))$, $\forall v \in \mathbb{R}^N_{++}$, $\forall \overline{t} \in \mathbb{R}_+$, is globally stable. Moreover, for every $v \in \mathbb{R}^N_{++}$, for every $t^1, t^2 \in \mathbb{R}_+$ with $t^1 < t^2$, it holds that $\|\pi(v, t^1) - p^*\|_\infty > \|\pi(v, t^2) - p^*\|_\infty$.
See Arrow, Block, and Hurwicz (1959), Footnote 4, page 86, Lemma 3.3, page 89, Theorem 4.1.1, page 95, and Theorem 3.11.1.

Although Theorem 3.11.2 shows global stability of the price adjustment process determined by (3.10) for an interesting class of economies, it does not yet show *universal stability* of this process, i.e. it does not show stability for a typical economy with M consumers and N commodities. The next section describes an example with an unstable unique Walrasian equilibrium, originally presented in Scarf (1960).

3.12 SCARF'S EXAMPLE

In this section the example to be used throughout Part IV is examined. This example is known as Scarf's example and can be found in Scarf (1960). In this example the economy $\mathcal{E} = ((X^i, \preceq^i, \omega^i)_{i\in I_3})$ is such that $N = 3$,

$$X^1 = X^2 = X^3 = \mathbb{R}^3_+,$$

$\preceq^1$, $\preceq^2$, and $\preceq^3$ can be represented by utility functions $u^1 : X^1 \to \mathbb{R}$, $u^2 : X^2 \to \mathbb{R}$, and $u^3 : X^3 \to \mathbb{R}$, respectively, defined by

$$\begin{aligned} u^1(x^1) &= \min(\{x^1_1, x^1_2\}),\ \forall x^1 \in \mathbb{R}^3_+, \\ u^2(x^2) &= \min(\{x^2_2, x^2_3\}),\ \forall x^2 \in \mathbb{R}^3_+, \\ u^3(x^3) &= \min(\{x^3_1, x^3_3\}),\ \forall x^3 \in \mathbb{R}^3_+, \end{aligned}$$

and

$$\begin{aligned} \omega^1 &= (1,0,0)^\top, \\ \omega^2 &= (0,1,0)^\top, \\ \omega^3 &= (0,0,1)^\top. \end{aligned}$$

Using Theorem 2.9.7 it can easily be verified that the restriction of the demand relation to $\mathbb{R}^3_{++}$, $\delta^i_{|\mathbb{R}^3_{++}}$, $\forall i \in I_3$, is a function, denoted by d^i, $\forall i \in I_3$, and defined by

$$\begin{aligned} d^1(p) &= \left(\tfrac{p_1}{p_1+p_2}, \tfrac{p_1}{p_1+p_2}, 0\right)^\top, \forall p \in \mathbb{R}^3_{++}, \\ d^2(p) &= \left(0, \tfrac{p_2}{p_2+p_3}, \tfrac{p_2}{p_2+p_3}\right)^\top, \forall p \in \mathbb{R}^3_{++}, \\ d^3(p) &= \left(\tfrac{p_3}{p_1+p_3}, 0, \tfrac{p_3}{p_1+p_3}\right)^\top, \forall p \in \mathbb{R}^3_{++}. \end{aligned}$$

It is easily shown that there is no Walrasian equilibrium price system belonging to $\mathbb{R}^3 \setminus \mathbb{R}^3_{++}$ and that p^* is a Walrasian equilibrium price system if and only if $p^* = \lambda(1,1,1)^\top$ for some $\lambda \in \mathbb{R}_{++}$. The unique Walrasian equilibrium allocation x^* is given by

$$x^{*1} = (\tfrac{1}{2}, \tfrac{1}{2}, 0)^\top, x^{*2} = (0, \tfrac{1}{2}, \tfrac{1}{2})^\top, x^{*3} = (\tfrac{1}{2}, 0, \tfrac{1}{2})^\top.$$

Let some initial state $v \in \mathbb{R}^3_{++}$ be given. The dependence of the price adjustment process on the initial state v is suppressed in the notation. Consider the price adjustment process $\pi : \mathbb{R}_+ \to \mathbb{R}^3_{++}$ determined by

$$\partial_t \pi(\bar{t}) = z\left(\pi(\bar{t})\right), \ \forall \bar{t} \in \mathbb{R}_+,$$

i.e. the Walrasian tatonnement process. Let the function $f : \mathbb{R}_+ \to \mathbb{R}$ be defined by $f(t) = \sum_{j \in I_3} (\pi_j(t))^2$, $\forall t \in \mathbb{R}_+$. Then

$$\partial_t f(\bar{t}) = 2 \sum_{j \in I_3} \pi_j(\bar{t}) \partial_t \pi_j(\bar{t}) = 2 \sum_{j \in I_3} \pi_j(\bar{t}) z_j\left(\pi(\bar{t})\right) = 0, \ \forall \bar{t} \in \mathbb{R}_+, \tag{3.11}$$

using Walras' law. So, $\pi(t) \in \widetilde{B}^2((0,0,0)^\top, \|v\|_2)$, $\forall t \in \mathbb{R}_+$, i.e. the Euclidean norm of the price systems generated by the Walrasian tatonnement process remains constant during the process. Let the function $g : \mathbb{R}_+ \to \mathbb{R}$ be defined by $g(t) = \pi_1(t)\pi_2(t)\pi_3(t)$, $\forall t \in \mathbb{R}_+$. Then, after making some computations, it follows that

$$\begin{aligned} \partial_t g(\bar{t}) &= z_1\left(\pi(\bar{t})\right) \pi_2(\bar{t})\pi_3(\bar{t}) + \pi_1(\bar{t}) z_2\left(\pi(\bar{t})\right) \pi_3(\bar{t}) + \pi_1(\bar{t})\pi_2(\bar{t}) z_3\left(\pi(\bar{t})\right) \\ &= 0, \ \forall \bar{t} \in \mathbb{R}_+. \end{aligned} \tag{3.12}$$

Therefore, the product of the prices in the price systems generated by the Walrasian tatonnement process remains constant during the process. Now (3.11) and (3.12) together imply that the Walrasian tatonnement process generates price systems in the set

$$\left\{ p \in \mathbb{R}^3_{++} \,\middle|\, \textstyle\sum_{j \in I_3} (p_j)^2 = \sum_{j \in I_3} (v_j)^2 \text{ and } p_1 p_2 p_3 = v_1 v_2 v_3 \right\}.$$

It is easily verified that this set is a circle, unless $v = \lambda(1,1,1)^\top$ for some $\lambda \in \mathbb{R}_{++}$, i.e. unless v is a Walrasian equilibrium price system. Therefore, although there is a unique Walrasian equilibrium, the Walrasian tatonnement process is neither locally nor globally stable in Scarf's example. In Scarf (1960) also other examples are given for which the Walrasian tatonnement process is neither locally nor globally stable, while the instability does not disappear when the economy is slightly perturbed.

3.13 GLOBALLY AND UNIVERSALLY STABLE PRICE ADJUSTMENT PROCESSES

When one is searching for a globally and universally stable price adjustment process, it is interesting to know what kind of properties a total excess demand relation satisfies. Theorem 3.7.1 yields homogeneity of degree zero, Theorem 3.7.2 Walras' law, and Theorem 3.11.1 continuity and some boundary behaviour. The idea that there is a lack of further properties was first expressed in Sonnenschein (1973) and Mantel (1974). The following result makes clear that indeed no other properties can be expected.

Theorem 3.13.1
Let $z : \mathbb{R}^N_{++} \to \mathbb{R}^N$ be a continuous function satisfying $z(\lambda p) = z(p)$, $\forall \lambda \in \mathbb{R}_{++}$, $\forall p \in \mathbb{R}^N_{++}$, and $p \cdot z(p) = 0$, $\forall p \in \mathbb{R}^N_{++}$. Then, for every $\varepsilon \in \mathbb{R}_{++}$, there exists an economy $\mathcal{E} = ((X^i, \preceq^i, \omega^i)_{i \in I_N})$ with total excess demand relation ζ such that, for every consumer $i \in I_N$, $X^i = \mathbb{R}^N_+$, the preference relation $\preceq^i$ is complete, transitive, continuous, monotonic, and strongly convex and $\omega^i \in \mathbb{R}^N_+$, whereas $p \in \mathbb{R}^N_{++}$ with $\frac{p}{\sum_{j \in I_N} p_j} \geq \varepsilon 1^N$ implies $\zeta(p) = \{z(p)\}$.
See Debreu (1974), Theorem, page 16.

Therefore, every continuous function $z : \mathbb{R}^N_{++} \to \mathbb{R}^N$ satisfying homogeneity of degree zero and Walras' law is the total excess demand relation restricted to a subset of $\mathbb{R}^N_{++}$ arbitrarily close to $\mathbb{R}^N_{++}$ of an economy with N consumers satisfying standard assumptions. For a survey of related results, the reader is referred to Shafer and Sonnenschein (1982).

Theorem 3.13.1 makes it very easy to construct other examples of economies such that the Walrasian tatonnement process is not globally stable. From Balasko (1988), Lemma 1.9.4, page 27, it follows that the Walrasian tatonnement process can be regarded as a first order linear approximation of the price adjustment process determined by (3.10). Therefore, considering such a process does not solve the problem of the lack of universal stability.

Let the price adjustment process π be described by means of a differential equation, where, given a continuously differentiable total excess demand function $z : \mathbb{R}^N_{++} \to \mathbb{R}^N$, the adjustment of the price system reached at a point in time $\bar{t}$ is allowed to depend on $z(\pi(\bar{t}))$ and $\partial_p z(\pi(\bar{t}))$. The results of Saari and Simon (1978) make clear that in this case there exists an economy satisfying all the usual assumptions while the price adjustment process is not globally stable, unless the number of commodities is required to be equal to one or two, or the price adjustment process uses the information of most of the partial derivatives of z. Notice that the Walrasian tatonnement process is globally and universally stable when restricted to economies with one or two commodities. It should be remarked that modelling a price adjustment process in discrete time instead of continuous time only aggravates the problems as has been shown in Saari

(1985). There it is shown that even for the case with only two commodities, but in general for cases with more commodities, there is no globally and universally stable price adjustment process in a rather large class of price adjustment processes.

The results presented in this section make clear that it is very important to study the allocation of commodities when trade has to take place at a non-Walrasian equilibrium price system since the analysis of price adjustment processes suggests that one cannot be too confident that, in an economy as described in this chapter, a Walrasian equilibrium price system is reached. This analysis is performed in Part II of this monograph. Obviously, it is easy to give also other reasons for such an analysis. For instance, it is not always reasonable to assume price taking behaviour of all the agents in the economy. If some of the agents have the ability to influence the price system, then it is no longer reasonable to assume that a Walrasian equilibrium will result. Often the government is an agent that exercises influence on the price system by using price controls like minimum wages, minimum prices for agricultural products, linkages between the wages of civil servants and the wages paid in industry, and so on. Therefore, government behaviour is endogenously determined in Part III of this monograph, making it possible to extend an analysis that considers the allocation of commodities when some price rigidities or price regulations are assumed to be given to an analysis where the price regulations themselves are endogenously determined as well. Finally, it is possible to study dynamic processes not belonging to the class for which negative results have been obtained in Saari and Simon (1978) and Saari (1985). For example Saari (1985) states "A possible option is that a mechanism must depend upon the values of the prices ...," a possibility that is investigated in Part IV of this monograph.

PART II

STATIC ASPECTS OF DISEQUILIBRIUM

4

EQUILIBRIUM EXISTENCE RESULTS FOR ECONOMIES WITH PRICE RIGIDITIES

4.1 INTRODUCTION

In this chapter a general equilibrium model of the economic system is developed for the case price rigidities may be present. In Theorems 3.8.2 and 3.11.1 quite general assumptions were stated under which the existence of a Walrasian equilibrium of the economy can be guaranteed. However, it is assumed in Chapter 3 that the price system may be any element of $\mathbb{R}^N$. When the set of price systems is restricted by constraints imposed by price regulations or by price rigidities, the set of admissible price systems is obtained. It is possible that no Walrasian equilibrium price system of the economy belongs to the set of admissible price systems.

When a state corresponding to a Walrasian equilibrium of the economy prevails, then the description of the market mechanism given in Section 3.2 is sufficient to determine the outcome for each one of the agents. The information transmitted by the market mechanism is the price system, on which the agents base their decisions. When a non-Walrasian equilibrium price system prevails in the economy, the optimal actions of the agents at this price system are necessarily incompatible, and a description of the market mechanism should include how commodities are allocated in this case. Following Drèze (1975), the information transmitted by the market mechanism is now the price system together with a rationing scheme for each agent, being the maximal amount an agent is allowed to make available with regard to his initial endowment of every commodity and the maximal amount made available to an agent with regard to his initial endowment of every commodity. Still, agents make their decisions independently, but the decision of an agent is now based on both the price system and his rationing scheme. Except for the possibility of price rigidities and the extension of the description of the market mechanism, the interpretation of the model is the same as the one given in Chapter 3. In this chapter it is assumed that all agents in the economy are consumers. To include producers in the model does not yield additional difficulties, see for instance Dehez and Drèze (1984).

In Section 4.2 the set of admissible actions of a consumer is analysed, given the price system and the rationing scheme of the consumer. As in Section 3.4 the set of admissible actions of a consumer is specified by the budget set of the consumer. The properties of the budget relation of a consumer, associating with every price system and rationing scheme of the consumer the corresponding budget set, are analysed.

In Section 4.3 the behaviour of a consumer is studied, given the price system and the rationing scheme of the consumer. The demand relation of a consumer is derived, associating with every price system and every rationing scheme the set of optimal actions in the budget set according to the preference relation of the consumer. Given the price system and the rationing scheme, a consumer is said to be rationed on his supply in a market if his behaviour would change by having no restrictions on the maximal amount he may supply in this market and a consumer is said to be rationed on his demand in a market if his behaviour would change by having no restrictions on the maximal amount he may demand in this market.

In Section 4.4 the model of an economy with price rigidities is extended by specifying the set of admissible price systems and in Section 4.5 the model is extended by introducing the set of admissible rationing schemes on supply and the set of admissible rationing schemes on demand. The pair formed by the latter two sets is called the rationing system. In this chapter the set of admissible price systems is obtained by specifying lower and upper bounds on the prices in each market. This way of modelling price rigidities is based on Drèze (1975). Making some substitutions it can be shown that under certain assumptions models with prices depending on a general price index as studied in Dehez and Drèze (1984) and van der Laan (1984) are special cases of the model considered in this chapter. The rationing system makes it possible to model that not all rationing schemes are feasible. For instance, it is possible that a market is organized in such a way that the rationing scheme of every consumer is the same or that there is a kind of priority system according to which commodities are allocated. The specification of the rationing system given in this chapter is very general. It is shown that uniform rationing, rationing determined by initial endowments, rationing determined by market share, rationing determined by priority, and the rationing system consisting of all rationing schemes are included as special cases. Often it is possible to specify the rationing system on supply and the rationing system on demand as being the range of a certain function, called the rationing function on supply and the rationing function on demand, respectively. Both necessary and sufficient conditions for the representation of the rationing system by a rationing function are given. The economy is then described by a specification of the consumption sets, preference relations, and the resources of all the consumers, together with a specification of the set of admissible price systems and the rationing system. In Section 4.6 an equilibrium concept of the economy is given for which the corresponding equilibria are called constrained equilibria.

In Section 4.7 it is shown that there exists an uncountable set of constrained equilibria of the economy. This is in accordance with the examples given in Böhm and Müller (1977) and with the results obtained in van der Laan and Talman (1990) for the uniform rationing system. A continuum of correspondences is given such that each correspondence has a fixed point whereas each fixed point corresponds to a constrained equilibrium of the economy. Moreover, the correspondences can be chosen such that fixed points of different correspondences correspond to different constrained equilibria of the economy and such that all constrained equilibria of the economy are obtained. In this way characterizations of the complete set of constrained equilibria of the economy are given. Moreover, a refinement of the constrained equilibrium concept, called a Drèze equilibrium, is presented and its existence is shown to follow as a special case of the main result of Section 4.7.

In Kurz (1982) and van der Laan (1980a) it has been remarked that in the real world consumers are rationed more frequently on their supply than on their demand. In van der Laan (1982) the existence of a constrained equilibrium with no consumer rationed on his demand in any market and with at least one market without rationing at all has been proved, using the technique of simplicial approximation of equilibria. This yields another refinement of the constrained equilibrium concept, called a supply constrained equilibrium. In Polterovich (1993) general equilibrium type models of centrally planned economies are considered where no rationing on the supply of any consumer is allowed. These models provide the motivation for another refinement of the constrained equilibrium concept, called a demand constrained equilibrium. Demand constrained equilibria are also considered in van der Laan and Talman (1990). Generalizations of these two equilibrium refinements and existence results are given in Section 4.8.

Given the consumption sets, the preference relations of the consumers, and the rationing system, the equilibrium relation is introduced. It assigns to each specification of initial endowments and of the set of admissible price systems the set of all constrained equilibrium allocations. In Section 4.9 it is shown that the equilibrium relation is a compact-valued, upper hemi-continuous correspondence being continuous on a residual set of points. The results concerning the equilibrium relation make clear that the set of constrained equilibria is stable against certain perturbations of the economy.

In Section 4.10 the example of Section 3.10 is considered when the economy given there is extended by a set of admissible price systems and a rationing system.

This chapter is based on Herings (1995) and Herings (1996c).

4.2 THE SET OF ADMISSIBLE ACTIONS OF A CONSUMER

As in Chapter 3 it is assumed in this chapter that there are $M \in \mathbb{N}$ *consumers*, indexed by $i \in I_M$, and $N \in \mathbb{N}$ *commodities*, indexed by $j \in I_N$. Given *consumption sets* X^i, $\forall i \in I_M$, the set $\prod_{i \in I_M} X^i$ is denoted by X, and if $x = (x^1, \ldots, x^M)$ is an element of X, then $x_j = (x_j^1, \ldots, x_j^M)^\top$, $\forall j \in I_N$. Given *initial endowments* ω^i, $\forall i \in I_M$, $\omega = (\omega^1, \ldots, \omega^M)$, $\omega_j = (\omega_j^1, \ldots, \omega_j^M)^\top$, $\forall j \in I_N$, and $\bar{\omega} = \sum_{i \in I_M} \omega^i$ denotes the *total initial endowment.* For every consumer $i \in I_M$, the consumption set X^i and the *preference relation* $\preceq^i$ are assumed to be given in this section.

The description of the market mechanism given in Section 3.2 is now extended in the sense that the information transmitted by the market mechanism is not only the *price system,* but also (the negative of) the maximal amount a consumer is allowed to supply of every commodity, called the *rationing scheme on supply,* and the maximal amount a consumer is allowed to demand for every commodity, called the *rationing scheme on demand.* The rationing scheme on supply is denoted by $l = (l^1, \ldots, l^M) \in \prod_{i \in I_M} -\mathbb{R}_+^{*N}$ and the rationing scheme on demand by $L = (L^1, \ldots, L^M) \in \prod_{i \in I_M} \mathbb{R}_+^{*N}$. The pair (l, L) is called the *rationing scheme.* For every consumer $i \in I_M$, l^i is called the *rationing scheme on the supply* of consumer i, L^i is called the *rationing scheme on the demand* of consumer i, and the pair (l^i, L^i) is called the *rationing scheme* of consumer i. For every $j \in I_N$, $l_j = (l_j^1, \ldots, l_j^M)^\top$ is called the *rationing scheme on supply* in the market for commodity $j \in I_N$, $L_j = (L_j^1, \ldots, L_j^M)^\top$ is called the *rationing* *scheme on demand* in the market for commodity j, and the pair (l_j, L_j) is called the *rationing scheme* in the market for commodity j.

For every consumer $i \in I_M$, the *budget set* of consumer i having an initial endowment $\omega^i \in \mathbb{R}^N$ at a price system $p \in \mathbb{R}^N$ and a rationing scheme $(l^i, L^i) \in -\mathbb{R}_+^{*N} \times \mathbb{R}_+^{*N}$, denoted by $\beta^i(p, l^i, L^i, \omega^i)$, is defined as the set of consumption bundles in the consumption set of consumer i satisfying the constraints imposed by the rationing scheme of consumer i and being such that the value of these consumption bundles does not exceed $p \cdot \omega^i$, so

$$\beta^i(p, l^i, L^i, \omega^i) = \{x^i \in X^i \,|p \cdot x^i \leq p \cdot \omega^i \text{ and } l^i \leq x^i - \omega^i \leq L^i\}.$$

Notice that the requirement that $l^i \in -\mathbb{R}_+^{*N}$ and $L^i \in \mathbb{R}_+^{*N}$ implies that only *voluntary trading* takes place. No consumer can be forced to supply or to demand at least a certain amount of a commodity. If $l^i = -\infty^N$ and $L^i = +\infty^N$, then the definition of the budget set is equal to the one given in Chapter 3. Therefore, the description of the market mechanism given here is more general than the description of Chapter 3. A consumption bundle $x^i \in \beta^i(p, l^i, L^i, \omega^i)$ is called an *admissible consumption bundle* of consumer $i \in I_m$.

The relation $\beta^i : \mathbb{R}^N \times -\mathbb{R}_+^{*N} \times \mathbb{R}_+^{*N} \times \mathbb{R}^N \to \mathbb{R}^N$ associating with every element (p, l^i, L^i, ω^i) of $\mathbb{R}^N \times -\mathbb{R}_+^{*N} \times \mathbb{R}_+^{*N} \times \mathbb{R}^N$ the set $\beta^i(p, l^i, L^i, \omega^i)$ is called the *budget relation* of consumer $i \in I_M$. If $p \in \mathbb{R}^N$, $(l^i, L^i) \in -\mathbb{R}_+^{*N} \times \mathbb{R}_+^{*N}$, and $\omega^i \in X^i$, then the budget set $\beta^i(p, l^i, L^i, \omega^i)$ of consumer $i \in I_M$ is not equal to the empty set since it contains ω^i in that case. The following lemma is also useful.

Lemma 4.2.1
For some consumer $i \in I_M$, let the consumption set X^i be convex. Then the budget relation β^i is convex-valued.

Proof
It is easily seen that the set $\beta^i(p, l^i, L^i, \omega^i)$ is convex for every $(p, l^i, L^i, \omega^i) \in \mathbb{R}^N \times -\mathbb{R}_+^{*N} \times \mathbb{R}_+^{*N} \times \mathbb{R}^N$ since it is equal to the intersection of the convex sets X^i, $\{x^i \in \mathbb{R}^N \mid p \cdot x^i \leq p \cdot \omega^i\}$, and $\{x^i \in \mathbb{R}^N \mid l^i \leq x^i - \omega^i \leq L^i\}$. Q.E.D.

For the equilibrium existence proofs of Sections 4.7 and 4.8 and the results of Section 4.9 it has to be shown that the restriction of the budget relation β^i to the set $\mathbb{R}_{++}^N \times -\mathbb{R}_+^N \times \mathbb{R}_+^N \times \text{int}(X^i)$ is a compact-valued, upper hemi-continuous correspondence for every consumer $i \in I_M$. In Section 4.6 it is shown that it is indeed sufficient to consider rationing schemes of a consumer belonging to the subset $-\mathbb{R}_+^N \times \mathbb{R}_+^N$ of the set $-\mathbb{R}_+^{*N} \times \mathbb{R}_+^{*N}$.

Lemma 4.2.2
For some consumer $i \in I_M$, let the consumption set X^i be closed. Then the restriction of the budget relation β^i to the set $\mathbb{R}^N \times -\mathbb{R}^N_+ \times \mathbb{R}^N_+ \times \mathbb{R}^N$ is compact-valued.

Proof
For every $(p, l^i, L^i, \omega^i) \in \mathbb{R}^N \times -\mathbb{R}^N_+ \times \mathbb{R}^N_+ \times \mathbb{R}^N$, the set $\beta^i(p, l^i, L^i, \omega^i)$ is compact since it is equal to the intersection of the closed sets X^i, $\{x^i \in \mathbb{R}^N \mid p \cdot x^i \leq p \cdot \omega^i\}$, and $\{x^i \in \mathbb{R}^N \mid l^i \leq x^i - \omega^i \leq L^i\}$, and is therefore closed. Furthermore, $x^i \in \beta^i(p, l^i, L^i, \omega^i)$ implies $\|x^i\|_\infty \leq \max(\{\|l^i + \omega^i\|_\infty, \|L^i + \omega^i\|_\infty\})$, and therefore $\beta^i(p, l^i, L^i, \omega^i)$ is bounded. Q.E.D.

In Drèze (1975) the initial endowment $\omega^i \in \text{int}(X^i)$ of consumer $i \in I_M$ is considered as given and the following result is shown.

Theorem 4.2.3
For some consumer $i \in I_M$, let the consumption set X^i be closed, convex, $X^i \subset \mathbb{R}^N_+$, and $X^i + \mathbb{R}^N_+ \subset X^i$, and let the initial endowment ω^i of consumer i belong to int(X^i). Then the restriction of the budget relation β^i to the set $\mathbb{R}^N_+ \times -\mathbb{R}^N_+ \times \mathbb{R}^N_+ \times \{\omega^i\}$ is a correspondence that is continuous at every $(p, l^i, L^i, \omega^i) \in \mathbb{R}^N_+ \times -\mathbb{R}^N_+ \times \mathbb{R}^N_+ \times \{\omega^i\}$ satisfying $p \cdot l^i < 0$.
See Drèze (1975), Lemma, page 304.

The condition in Theorem 4.2.3 that $p \cdot l^i < 0$ turns out to be restrictive in Sections 4.7, 4.8, and 4.9. The following example makes clear that even if an initial endowment ω^i of a consumer $i \in I_M$ belongs to the interior of the consumption set and the consumption set is compact, then the restriction of the budget relation β^i to the set $\mathbb{R}^N_+ \times -\mathbb{R}^N_+ \times \mathbb{R}^N_+ \times \{\omega^i\}$ is not necessarily a correspondence that is lower hemi-continuous at every $(p, l^i, L^i, \omega^i) \in \mathbb{R}^N_+ \times -\mathbb{R}^N_+ \times \mathbb{R}^N_+ \times \{\omega^i\}$ satisfying $p \cdot l^i = 0$.

Example 4.2.4
For some consumer $i \in I_M$, let $X^i = \{x^i \in \mathbb{R}^2_+ | x^i_1 \leq 2 \text{ and } x^i_2 \leq 2\}$, $\omega^i = (1,1)^\top$, and, for every $n \in \mathbb{N}$, let $p^n = (\frac{1}{2}, \frac{1}{n})^\top$, $l^{i^n} = (-\frac{1}{n}, -\frac{1}{n})^\top$, and $L^{i^n} = (1,1)^\top$. Then the set $\beta^i(p^n, l^{i^n}, L^{i^n}, \omega^i)$ is equal to

$$\left\{x^i \in X^i \,\middle|\, 1 - \tfrac{1}{n} \leq x^i_1,\ 1 - \tfrac{1}{n} \leq x^i_2, \text{ and } \tfrac{1}{2}x^i_1 + \tfrac{1}{n}x^i_2 \leq \tfrac{1}{2} + \tfrac{1}{n}\right\}.$$

The sequence $(p^n, l^{i^n}, L^{i^n})_{n \in \mathbb{N}}$ converges to $(\bar{p}, \bar{l}^i, \bar{L}^i)$ with $\bar{p} = (\frac{1}{2}, 0)^\top$, $\bar{l}^i = (0,0)^\top$, and $\bar{L}^i = (1,1)^\top$. Since

$$\beta^i(\bar{p}, \bar{l}^i, \bar{L}^i, \omega^i) = \left\{x^i \in X^i \,\middle|\, x^i_1 = 1 \text{ and } x^i_2 \geq 1\right\},$$

it holds that $(1,2)^\top \in \beta^i(\overline{p}, \overline{l}^i, \overline{L}^i, \omega^i)$. However, for every $n \in \mathbb{N}$,

$$\max\left(\left\{x_2^i \in \mathbb{R} \,\middle|\, x^i \in \beta^i(p^n, l^{i^n}, L^{i^n}, \omega^i)\right\}\right) = 1\tfrac{1}{2},$$

and, consequently, the restriction of the budget relation β^i to the set $\mathbb{R}^N_+ \times -\mathbb{R}^N_+ \times \mathbb{R}^N_+ \times \{\omega^i\}$ is not lower hemi-continuous at $(\overline{p}, \overline{l}^i, \overline{L}^i, \omega^i)$ according to Theorem 2.5.13.

In Example 4.2.4 and in Drèze (1975) the prices of some commodities are allowed to be zero. This case is excluded in this chapter. It turns out that the restriction of the budget relation β^i of a consumer $i \in I_M$ to the set $\mathbb{R}^N_{++} \times -\mathbb{R}^N_+ \times \mathbb{R}^N_+ \times \{\omega^i\}$ is continuous, so even at $(p, l^i, L^i, \omega^i) \in \mathbb{R}^N_{++} \times -\mathbb{R}^N_+ \times \mathbb{R}^N_+ \times \text{int}(X^i)$ with $l^i = 0^N$. This is quite surprising since $l^i = 0^N$ and $p \in \mathbb{R}^N_{++}$ implies that there is no consumption bundle in the budget set of a consumer $i \in I_M$ having a value lower than the value of the initial endowment ω^i, a condition always used in the literature to show lower hemi-continuity of the budget relation. To show that the equilibrium relation in Section 4.9 is a compact-valued, upper hemi-continuous correspondence it is not enough to examine the continuity of the budget relation given fixed initial endowments $\omega^i \in \text{int}(X^i)$, but instead the more general case presented in the next theorem has to be considered.

Theorem 4.2.5
For some consumer $i \in I_M$, let the consumption set X^i be closed and convex, and let $X^i \subset \mathbb{R}^N_+$. Then the relation $\beta^i_{|\mathbb{R}^N_{++} \times -\mathbb{R}^N_+ \times \mathbb{R}^N_+ \times \text{int}(X^i)}$ is a continuous correspondence.

Proof
Clearly, $\beta^i_{|\mathbb{R}^N_{++} \times -\mathbb{R}^N_+ \times \mathbb{R}^N_+ \times \text{int}(X^i)}$ is a correspondence. Let some $(\overline{p}, \overline{l}^i, \overline{L}^i, \overline{\omega}^i) \in \mathbb{R}^N_{++} \times -\mathbb{R}^N_+ \times \mathbb{R}^N_+ \times \text{int}(X^i)$ be given. First, it is shown that the correspondence $\beta^i_{|\mathbb{R}^N_{++} \times -\mathbb{R}^N_+ \times \mathbb{R}^N_+ \times \text{int}(X^i)}$ is upper hemi-continuous at $(\overline{p}, \overline{l}^i, \overline{L}^i, \overline{\omega}^i)$ and, secondly, $\beta^i_{|\mathbb{R}^N_{++} \times -\mathbb{R}^N_+ \times \mathbb{R}^N_+ \times \text{int}(X^i)}$ is shown to be lower hemi-continuous at $(\overline{p}, \overline{l}^i, \overline{L}^i, \overline{\omega}^i)$.

1. $\beta^i_{|\mathbb{R}^N_{++} \times -\mathbb{R}^N_+ \times \mathbb{R}^N_+ \times \text{int}(X^i)}$ is upper hemi-continuous at $(\overline{p}, \overline{l}^i, \overline{L}^i, \overline{\omega}^i)$.
Let $(p^n, l^{i^n}, L^{i^n}, \omega^{i^n})_{n \in \mathbb{N}}$ be a sequence in $\mathbb{R}^N_{++} \times -\mathbb{R}^N_+ \times \mathbb{R}^N_+ \times \text{int}(X^i)$ converging to $(\overline{p}, \overline{l}^i, \overline{L}^i, \overline{\omega}^i)$ and let the sequence $(x^{i^n})_{n \in \mathbb{N}}$ in X^i be such that $x^{i^n} \in \beta^i(p^n, l^{i^n}, L^{i^n}, \omega^{i^n})$. The sequence $(x^{i^n})_{n \in \mathbb{N}}$ is bounded since

$$0 \leq \|x^{i^n}\|_\infty \leq \max\left(\left\{\frac{p^n \cdot \omega^{i^n}}{p_1^n}, \ldots, \frac{p^n \cdot \omega^{i^n}}{p_N^n}\right\}\right) \to \max\left(\left\{\frac{\overline{p} \cdot \overline{\omega}^i}{\overline{p}_1}, \ldots, \frac{\overline{p} \cdot \overline{\omega}^i}{\overline{p}_N}\right\}\right).$$

Without loss of generality, the sequence $(x^{i^n})_{n\in\mathbb{N}}$ converges to some $\overline{x}^i \in X^i$. Moreover,

$$\begin{aligned}\overline{p}\cdot\overline{x}^i &= \lim_{n\to+\infty} p^n\cdot x^{i^n} \le \lim_{n\to+\infty} p^n\cdot\omega^{i^n} = \overline{p}\cdot\overline{\omega}^i,\\ \overline{x}^i-\overline{\omega}^i &= \lim_{n\to+\infty}\left(x^{i^n}-\omega^{i^n}\right) \ge \lim_{n\to+\infty} l^{i^n} = \overline{l}^i,\\ \overline{x}^i-\overline{\omega}^i &= \lim_{n\to+\infty}\left(x^{i^n}-\omega^{i^n}\right) \le \lim_{n\to+\infty} L^{i^n} = \overline{L}^i.\end{aligned}$$

So, $\overline{x}^i \in \beta^i(\overline{p},\overline{l}^i,\overline{L}^i,\overline{\omega}^i)$ and, using the compact-valuedness of the correspondence $\beta^i_{|\mathbb{R}^N_{++}\times-\mathbb{R}^N_+\times\mathbb{R}^N_+\times\,\mathrm{int}(X^i)}$ shown in Lemma 4.2.2, it holds that the correspondence $\beta^i_{|\mathbb{R}^N_{++}\times-\mathbb{R}^N_+\times\mathbb{R}^N_+\times\,\mathrm{int}(X^i)}$ is upper hemi-continuous at $(\overline{p},\overline{l}^i,\overline{L}^i,\overline{\omega}^i)$ by Theorem 2.5.6.

2. $\beta^i_{|\mathbb{R}^N_{++}\times-\mathbb{R}^N_+\times\mathbb{R}^N_+\times\,\mathrm{int}(X^i)}$ *is lower hemi-continuous at* $(\overline{p},\overline{l}^i,\overline{L}^i,\overline{\omega}^i)$.

Let $(p^n,l^{i^n},L^{i^n},\omega^{i^n})_{n\in\mathbb{N}}$ be a sequence in $\mathbb{R}^N_{++}\times-\mathbb{R}^N_+\times\mathbb{R}^N_+\times\mathrm{int}(X^i)$ converging to $(\overline{p},\overline{l}^i,\overline{L}^i,\overline{\omega}^i)$. Let $\overline{x}^i$ be an element of $\beta^i(\overline{p},\overline{l}^i,\overline{L}^i,\overline{\omega}^i)$. By Theorem 2.5.13, $\beta^i_{|\mathbb{R}^N_{++}\times-\mathbb{R}^N_+\times\mathbb{R}^N_+\times\mathrm{int}(X^i)}$ is lower hemi-continuous at $(\overline{p},\overline{l}^i,\overline{L}^i,\overline{\omega}^i)$ if there is a sequence $(x^{i^n})_{n\in\mathbb{N}}$ in $\mathbb{R}^N$ such that $x^{i^n}\in\beta^i(p^n,l^{i^n},L^{i^n},\omega^{i^n})$ and $x^{i^n}\to\overline{x}^i$. Three cases have to be considered, $\overline{p}\cdot(\overline{x}^i-\overline{\omega}^i)<0$, $\overline{p}\cdot(\overline{x}^i-\overline{\omega}^i)=0$ and $\overline{l}^i=0^N$, and $\overline{p}\cdot(\overline{x}^i-\overline{\omega}^i)=0$ and $\overline{l}^i<0^N$.

2.1. $\overline{p}\cdot(\overline{x}^i-\overline{\omega}^i)<0$.

First a sequence $(a^{i^n})_{n\in\mathbb{N}}$ in X^i converging to $\overline{x}^i$ is constructed. Then this sequence is used to construct a sequence $(b^{i^n})_{n\in\mathbb{N}}$ in X^i satisfying additionally that there exists $n'\in\mathbb{N}$ such that, for every $n\ge n'$, $l^{i^n}\le b^{i^n}-\omega^{i^n}\le L^{i^n}$. The sets J^1, J^2, and J^3 are defined by

$$\begin{aligned}J^1&=\left\{j\in I_N\left|\overline{x}^i_j>\overline{\omega}^i_j\right.\right\},\\ J^2&=\left\{j\in I_N\left|\overline{x}^i_j=\overline{\omega}^i_j\right.\right\},\\ J^3&=\left\{j\in I_N\left|\overline{x}^i_j<\overline{\omega}^i_j\right.\right\}.\end{aligned}$$

Since $\overline{\omega}^i\in\mathrm{int}(X^i)$, there exists $\varepsilon\in\mathbb{R}_{++}$ such that $x^i\in\mathbb{R}^N$ and $\|x^i-\overline{\omega}^i\|_\infty\le\varepsilon$ implies $x^i\in X^i$. Since $\omega^{i^n}\to\overline{\omega}^i$, there exists $n^1\in\mathbb{N}$ such that, for every $n\ge n^1$, $\|\omega^{i^n}-\overline{\omega}^i\|_\infty\le\varepsilon$. For every $n\ge n^1$, the element a^{i^n} of $\mathbb{R}^N$ is defined by

$$\begin{aligned}a^{i^n}_j &= \omega^{i^n}_j, & \forall j\in J^2,\\ a^{i^n}_j &= \lambda^n\overline{x}^i_j+(1-\lambda^n)\omega^{i^n}_j, & \forall j\in J^1\cup J^3,\end{aligned}$$

where the real number λ^n is defined by

$$\lambda^n = 1 \qquad \text{if } J^2=\emptyset, \tag{4.1}$$

$$\lambda^n = \min\left(\left\{\frac{\varepsilon - |\omega_j^{i^n} - \overline{\omega}_j^i|}{\varepsilon}\,\middle|\, j \in J^2\right\}\right) \text{ if } J^2 \neq \emptyset. \tag{4.2}$$

It is shown that $a^{i^n} \in X^i$, $\forall n \geq n^1$, and that $a^{i^n} \to \overline{x}^i$.
Let some $n \geq n^1$ be given. Clearly, $0 \leq \lambda^n \leq 1$. If $\lambda^n = 1$, then, by (4.1) and (4.2), $\omega_j^{i^n} = \overline{\omega}_j^i$, $\forall j \in J^2$, and

$$\begin{array}{ll} a_j^{i^n} = \omega_j^{i^n} = \overline{\omega}_j^i = \overline{x}_j^i, & \forall j \in J^2, \\ a_j^{i^n} = \overline{x}_j^i, & \forall j \in J^1 \cup J^3, \end{array}$$

so, $a^{i^n} \in X^i$. If $\lambda^n < 1$, then the element $\overline{a}^{i^n}$ of $\mathbb{R}^N$ is defined by

$$\overline{a}^{i^n} = \frac{a^{i^n} - \lambda^n \overline{x}^i}{1 - \lambda^n}.$$

Now it is shown that $\overline{a}^{i^n} \in X^i$. For every $j \in J^2$ it holds that

$$|\overline{a}_j^{i^n} - \overline{\omega}_j^i| = \left|\frac{\omega_j^{i^n} - \lambda^n \overline{x}_j^i}{1 - \lambda^n} - \overline{\omega}_j^i\right| = \frac{|\omega_j^{i^n} - \overline{\omega}_j^i|}{1 - \lambda^n}.$$

For every $j \in J^2$, if $\omega_j^{i^n} = \overline{\omega}_j^i$, then $|\overline{a}_j^{i^n} - \overline{\omega}_j^i| = 0 < \varepsilon$, and if $\omega_j^{i^n} \neq \overline{\omega}_j^i$, then

$$|\overline{a}_j^{i^n} - \overline{\omega}_j^i| = \frac{|\omega_j^{i^n} - \overline{\omega}_j^i|}{1 - \min\left(\left\{\frac{\varepsilon - |\omega_j^{i^n} - \overline{\omega}_j^i|}{\varepsilon}\,\middle|\, j \in J^2\right\}\right)} \leq \frac{|\omega_j^{i^n} - \overline{\omega}_j^i|}{1 - \frac{\varepsilon - |\omega_j^{i^n} - \overline{\omega}_j^i|}{\varepsilon}} = \varepsilon.$$

For every $j \in J^1 \cup J^3$ it holds that

$$|\overline{a}_j^{i^n} - \overline{\omega}_j^i| = \left|\frac{\lambda^n \overline{x}_j^i + (1 - \lambda^n)\omega_j^{i^n} - \lambda^n \overline{x}_j^i}{1 - \lambda^n} - \overline{\omega}_j^i\right| = \left|\omega_j^{i^n} - \overline{\omega}_j^i\right| \leq \varepsilon.$$

Since $\|\overline{a}^{i^n} - \overline{\omega}^i\|_\infty \leq \varepsilon$, it holds that $\overline{a}^{i^n} \in X^i$. Since $a^{i^n} = (1 - \lambda^n)\overline{a}^{i^n} + \lambda^n \overline{x}^i$, it follows that $a^{i^n} \in X^i$.
Clearly,

$$\lambda^n = \min\left(\left\{\frac{\varepsilon - |\omega_j^{i^n} - \overline{\omega}_j^i|}{\varepsilon}\,\middle|\, j \in J^2\right\}\right) \to 1,$$

and, therefore,

$$a_j^{i^n} = \omega_j^{i^n} \to \overline{\omega}_j^i = \overline{x}_j^i, \qquad \forall j \in J^2, \tag{4.3}$$

$$a_j^{i^n} = \lambda^n \overline{x}_j^i + (1 - \lambda^n)\,\omega_j^{i^n} \to \overline{x}_j^i, \ \forall j \in J^1 \cup J^3. \tag{4.4}$$

So, there exists $n^2 \in \mathbb{N}$ such that $n^2 \geq n^1$ and, for every $n \geq n^2$,

$$a_j^{i^n} > \omega_j^{i^n},\ \forall j \in J^1, \text{ and } a_j^{i^n} < \omega_j^{i^n},\ \forall j \in J^3.$$

For every $n \geq n^2$, for every $j \in J^1 \cup J^3$, the real number μ_j^n is defined by

$$\begin{aligned} \mu_j^n &= \tfrac{L_j^{i^n}}{a_j^{i^n} - \omega_j^{i^n}},\ \forall j \in J^1, \\ \mu_j^n &= \tfrac{l_j^{i^n}}{a_j^{i^n} - \omega_j^{i^n}},\ \forall j \in J^3. \end{aligned}$$

For every $n \geq n^2$, for every $j \in J^1$, $\mu_j^n \geq 0$ since $a_j^{i^n} - \omega_j^{i^n} > 0$ and $L_j^{i^n} \geq 0$, and, for every $j \in J^3$, $\mu_j^n \geq 0$ since $a_j^{i^n} - \omega_j^{i^n} < 0$ and $l_j^{i^n} \leq 0$. For every $n \geq n^2$, the real number $\overline{\mu}^n$ is defined by

$$\overline{\mu}^n = \min\left(\left\{\mu_j^n \,\middle|\, j \in J^1 \cup J^3\right\} \cup \{1\}\right),$$

and the element b^{i^n} of $\mathbb{R}^N$ is defined by

$$b^{i^n} = \omega^{i^n} + \overline{\mu}^n \left(a^{i^n} - \omega^{i^n}\right).$$

Let some $n \geq n^2$ be given. Clearly, $0 \leq \overline{\mu}^n \leq 1$. Since $a^{i^n}, \omega^{i^n} \in X^i$, it follows that

$$b^{i^n} \in X^i. \tag{4.5}$$

Moreover,

$$\begin{aligned}
b_j^{i^n} - \omega_j^{i^n} &= \overline{\mu}^n \left(a_j^{i^n} - \omega_j^{i^n}\right) \leq \mu_j^n \left(a_j^{i^n} - \omega_j^{i^n}\right) = L_j^{i^n}, && \forall j \in J^1, \quad (4.6)\\
b_j^{i^n} - \omega_j^{i^n} &= \overline{\mu}^n \left(a_j^{i^n} - \omega_j^{i^n}\right) \geq 0 \geq l_j^{i^n}, && \forall j \in J^1, \quad (4.7)\\
b_j^{i^n} - \omega_j^{i^n} &= \overline{\mu}^n \left(a_j^{i^n} - \omega_j^{i^n}\right) = 0, \text{ so } l_j^{i^n} \leq b_j^{i^n} - \omega_j^{i^n} \leq L_j^{i^n}, && \forall j \in J^2, \quad (4.8)\\
b_j^{i^n} - \omega_j^{i^n} &= \overline{\mu}^n \left(a_j^{i^n} - \omega_j^{i^n}\right) \geq \mu_j^n \left(a_j^{i^n} - \omega_j^{i^n}\right) = l_j^{i^n}, && \forall j \in J^3, \quad (4.9)\\
b_j^{i^n} - \omega_j^{i^n} &= \overline{\mu}^n \left(a_j^{i^n} - \omega_j^{i^n}\right) \leq 0 \leq L_j^{i^n}, && \forall j \in J^3. (4.10)
\end{aligned}$$

Therefore,

$$\begin{aligned}
\mu_j^n &= \frac{L_j^{i^n}}{a_j^{i^n} - \omega_j^{i^n}} \to \frac{\overline{L}_j^i}{\overline{x}_j^i - \overline{\omega}_j^i} \geq \frac{\overline{x}_j^i - \overline{\omega}_j^i}{\overline{x}_j^i - \overline{\omega}_j^i} = 1,\ \forall j \in J^1, \\
\mu_j^n &= \frac{l_j^{i^n}}{a_j^{i^n} - \omega_j^{i^n}} \to \frac{\overline{l}_j^i}{\overline{x}_j^i - \overline{\omega}_j^i} \geq \frac{\overline{x}_j^i - \overline{\omega}_j^i}{\overline{x}_j^i - \overline{\omega}_j^i} = 1,\ \forall j \in J^3.
\end{aligned}$$

So, $\overline{\mu}^n \to 1$ and, using (4.3) and (4.4),

$$b^{i^n} = \omega^{i^n} + \overline{\mu}^n \left(a^{i^n} - \omega^{i^n} \right) \to \overline{\omega}^i + \overline{x}^i - \overline{\omega}^i = \overline{x}^i. \tag{4.11}$$

Hence, $p^n \cdot (b^{i^n} - \omega^{i^n}) \to \overline{p} \cdot (\overline{x}^i - \overline{\omega}^i) < 0$. Therefore, there exists $n^3 \in \mathbb{N}$ such that $n^3 \geq n^2$ and $n \geq n^3$ implies $p^n \cdot (b^{i^n} - \omega^{i^n}) < 0$. This together with (4.5)-(4.10) yields that $b^{i^n} \in \beta^i(p^n, l^{i^n}, L^{i^n}, \omega^{i^n})$ for every $n \geq n^3$. Construct the sequence $(x^{i^n})_{n \in \mathbb{N}}$ in $\mathbb{R}^N$ as follows:

$$\begin{aligned} &x^{i^n} \text{ is an arbitrary element of } \beta^i(p^n, l^{i^n}, L^{i^n}, \omega^{i^n}), && \forall n < n^3, \\ &x^{i^n} = b^{i^n}, && \forall n \geq n^3. \end{aligned}$$

This sequence has all the desired properties.

2.2. $\overline{p} \cdot (\overline{x}^i - \overline{\omega}^i) = 0$ and $\overline{l}^i = 0^N$.

Since $\overline{x}^i - \overline{\omega}^i \geq \overline{l}^i$ and $\overline{l}^i = 0^N$, it holds that $\overline{x}^i \geq \overline{\omega}^i$. Using $\overline{p} \in \mathbb{R}^N_{++}$ this implies $\overline{x}^i = \overline{\omega}^i$. Obviously, $\omega^{i^n} \in \beta^i(p^n, l^{i^n}, L^{i^n}, \omega^{i^n})$, $\forall n \in \mathbb{N}$, and $\omega^{i^n} \to \overline{\omega}^i = \overline{x}^i$. The sequence $(x^{i^n})_{n \in \mathbb{N}}$ in $\mathbb{R}^N$ is defined by $x^{i^n} = \omega^{i^n}$, $\forall n \in \mathbb{N}$. This sequence has all the desired properties.

2.3. $\overline{p} \cdot (\overline{x}^i - \overline{\omega}^i) = 0$ and $\overline{l}^i < 0^N$.

The non-empty set J is defined by

$$J = \left\{ j \in I_N \,\middle|\, \overline{l}^i_j < 0 \right\}.$$

Since $\overline{\omega}^i \in \mathrm{int}(X^i)$, there exists $\varepsilon \in \mathbb{R}_{++}$ such that $x^i \in \mathbb{R}^N$ and $\|x^i - \overline{\omega}^i\|_\infty \leq \varepsilon$ implies $x^i \in X^i$. Since $\omega^{i^n} \to \overline{\omega}^i$ and $l^{i^n} \to \overline{l}^i$, there exists $n' \in \mathbb{N}$ such that $n' \geq n^2$, where n^2 is defined as in Part 2.1 of the proof, and, for every $n \geq n'$, $\|\omega^{i^n} - \overline{\omega}^i\|_\infty \leq \frac{1}{2}\varepsilon$ and $l^{i^n}_j < 0$, $\forall j \in J$. For every $n \geq n'$, $\varepsilon^n \in \mathbb{R}_{++}$ is defined by

$$\varepsilon^n = \min \left(\left\{ -l^{i^n}_j \,\middle|\, j \in J \right\} \cup \left\{ \tfrac{1}{2}\varepsilon \right\} \right)$$

and $\widehat{\omega}^{i^n} \in \mathbb{R}^N$ is defined by

$$\begin{aligned} \widehat{\omega}^{i^n}_j &= \omega^{i^n}_j - \varepsilon^n, && \forall j \in J, \\ \widehat{\omega}^{i^n}_j &= \omega^{i^n}_j, && \forall j \in I_N \setminus J. \end{aligned}$$

For every $n \geq n'$, $\widehat{\omega}^{i^n}$ has the following properties,

$$\widehat{\omega}^{i^n} \in X^i, \; l^{i^n} \leq \widehat{\omega}^{i^n} - \omega^{i^n} < 0^N \leq L^{i^n}, \text{ and } p^n \cdot \widehat{\omega}^{i^n} < p^n \cdot \omega^{i^n}. \tag{4.12}$$

Moreover, $\widehat{\omega}^{i^n} \to \widehat{\omega}^i$, where, for $\overline{\varepsilon}$ equal to $\min(\{-\overline{l}^i_j | j \in J\} \cup \{\frac{1}{2}\varepsilon\})$,

$$\begin{aligned} \widehat{\omega}^i_j &= \overline{\omega}^i_j - \overline{\varepsilon}, && \forall j \in J, \\ \widehat{\omega}^i_j &= \overline{\omega}^i_j, && \forall j \in I_N \setminus J. \end{aligned}$$

Therefore,

$$\widehat{\omega}^i \in X^i,\ \overline{l}^i \leq \widehat{\omega}^i - \overline{\omega}^i < 0^N \leq \overline{L}^i, \text{ and } \overline{p}\cdot\widehat{\omega}^i < \overline{p}\cdot\overline{\omega}^i.$$

For every $n \geq n^2$, the element b^{i^n} of $\mathbb{R}^N$ has been defined in Part 1 of the proof satisfying, according to (4.5)-(4.11), that

$$b^{i^n} \in X^i,\ l^{i^n} \leq b^{i^n} - \omega^{i^n} \leq L^{i^n}, \text{ and } b^{i^n} \to \overline{x}^i. \tag{4.13}$$

For every $n \geq n'$, the real number λ^n is defined by

$$\lambda^n = \frac{p^n\cdot\omega^{i^n} - p^n\cdot\widehat{\omega}^{i^n}}{p^n\cdot b^{i^n} - p^n\cdot\widehat{\omega}^{i^n}} \text{ if } p^n\cdot b^{i^n} > p^n\cdot\omega^{i^n}, \tag{4.14}$$

$$\lambda^n = 1 \qquad \text{if } p^n\cdot b^{i^n} \leq p^n\cdot\omega^{i^n}, \tag{4.15}$$

so, $0 < \lambda^n \leq 1$. For every $n \geq n'$, the element c^{i^n} of $\mathbb{R}^N$ is defined by

$$c^{i^n} = \widehat{\omega}^{i^n} + \lambda^n\left(b^{i^n} - \widehat{\omega}^{i^n}\right).$$

Let some $n \geq n'$ be given. Since $\widehat{\omega}^{i^n} \in X^i$ and $b^{i^n} \in X^i$ by (4.12) and (4.13), and $0 < \lambda^n \leq 1$, it follows that

$$c^{i^n} \in X^i. \tag{4.16}$$

By (4.12) and (4.13),

$$c^{i^n} - \omega^{i^n} = \lambda^n\left(b^{i^n} - \omega^{i^n}\right) + (1-\lambda^n)\left(\widehat{\omega}^{i^n} - \omega^{i^n}\right) \geq l^{i^n}, \tag{4.17}$$

$$c^{i^n} - \omega^{i^n} = \lambda^n\left(b^{i^n} - \omega^{i^n}\right) + (1-\lambda^n)\left(\widehat{\omega}^{i^n} - \omega^{i^n}\right) \leq L^{i^n}. \tag{4.18}$$

If $p^n\cdot b^{i^n} > p^n\cdot\omega^{i^n}$, then, by (4.14),

$$p^n\cdot c^{i^n} = \left(\frac{p^n\cdot\omega^{i^n} - p^n\cdot\widehat{\omega}^{i^n}}{p^n\cdot b^{i^n} - p^n\cdot\widehat{\omega}^{i^n}}\right)p^n\cdot b^{i^n} + \left(\frac{p^n\cdot b^{i^n} - p^n\cdot\omega^{i^n}}{p^n\cdot b^{i^n} - p^n\cdot\widehat{\omega}^{i^n}}\right)p^n\cdot\widehat{\omega}^{i^n} = p^n\cdot\omega^{i^n}, \tag{4.19}$$

and if $p^n\cdot b^{i^n} \leq p^n\cdot\omega^{i^n}$, then, by (4.15), $\lambda^n = 1$, and hence it holds that

$$p^n\cdot c^{i^n} = p^n\cdot b^{i^n} \leq p^n\cdot\omega^{i^n}. \tag{4.20}$$

From (4.16)-(4.20) it follows that $c^{i^n} \in \beta^i(p^n, l^{i^n}, L^{i^n}, \omega^{i^n})$. From (4.13) and since $\overline{p}\cdot\overline{x}^i = \overline{p}\cdot\overline{\omega}^i$, it follows that

$$\frac{p^n\cdot\omega^{i^n} - p^n\cdot\widehat{\omega}^{i^n}}{p^n\cdot b^{i^n} - p^n\cdot\widehat{\omega}^{i^n}} \to \frac{\overline{p}\cdot\overline{\omega}^i - \overline{p}\cdot\widehat{\omega}^i}{\overline{p}\cdot\overline{x}^i - \overline{p}\cdot\widehat{\omega}^i} = \frac{\overline{p}\cdot\overline{\omega}^i - \overline{p}\cdot\widehat{\omega}^i}{\overline{p}\cdot\overline{\omega}^i - \overline{p}\cdot\widehat{\omega}^i} = 1.$$

Therefore, $\lambda^n \longrightarrow 1$ and $c^{i^n} \longrightarrow \widehat{\omega}^i + (\overline{x}^i - \widehat{\omega}^i) = \overline{x}^i$. Construct the sequence $(x^{i^n})_{n\in\mathbb{N}}$ in $\mathbb{R}^N$ as follows:

$$\begin{array}{ll} x^{i^n} \text{ is an arbitrary element of } \beta^i(p^n, l^{i^n}, L^{i^n}, \omega^{i^n}), & \forall n < n', \\ x^{i^n} = c^{i^n}, & \forall n \geq n'. \end{array}$$

This sequence has all the desired properties. Q.E.D.

4.3 THE BEHAVIOUR OF A CONSUMER

For every consumer $i \in I_M$, the consumption set X^i, the preference relation $\preceq^i$, and the initial endowment ω^i are assumed to be given in this section. Therefore, the dependence on the initial endowment is suppressed in the notation of the budget relation and the budget set of a consumer.

A consumer $i \in I_M$ is assumed to take the price system $p \in \mathbb{R}^N$ and the rationing scheme $(l^i, L^i) \in -\mathbb{R}^{*N}_+ \times \mathbb{R}^{*N}_+$ as given, and to choose a best element of $\beta^i(p, l^i, L^i)$ for $\preceq^i$. For every consumer $i \in I_M$, for every $(p, l^i, L^i) \in \mathbb{R}^N \times -\mathbb{R}^{*N}_+ \times \mathbb{R}^{*N}_+$, the set $\delta^i(p, l^i, L^i)$ is defined as the set of consumption bundles that are best elements of $\beta^i(p, l^i, L^i)$ for $\preceq^i$, i.e.

$$\delta^i(p, l^i, L^i) = \left\{\overline{x}^i \in \beta^i(p, l^i, L^i) \,\middle|\, \overline{x}^i \succeq^i x^i, \ \forall x^i \in \beta^i(p, l^i, L^i)\right\}.$$

An element of $\delta^i(p, l^i, L^i)$ is called an *optimal action* or *optimal consumption bundle* of consumer $i \in I_M$ at $(p, l^i, L^i) \in \mathbb{R}^N \times -\mathbb{R}^{*N}_+ \times \mathbb{R}^{*N}_+$. Given an optimal consumption bundle x^i of a consumer $i \in I_M$, consumer i is said to *supply* a commodity $j \in I_N$ if $x^i_j \leq \omega^i_j$ and consumer i is said to *demand* commodity j if $x^i_j \geq \omega^i_j$. The relation $\delta^i : \mathbb{R}^N \times -\mathbb{R}^{*N}_+ \times \mathbb{R}^{*N}_+ \rightarrow \mathbb{R}^N$ associating with every $(p, l^i, L^i) \in \mathbb{R}^N \times -\mathbb{R}^{*N}_+ \times \mathbb{R}^{*N}_+$ the set $\delta^i(p, l^i, L^i)$ is called the *demand relation* of consumer $i \in I_M$. Although a rationing scheme $(l^i, L^i) \in -\mathbb{R}^{*N}_+ \times \mathbb{R}^{*N}_+$ specifies the maximal amount consumer $i \in I_M$ is allowed to supply and to demand of every commodity, his behaviour is not necessarily influenced by these constraints.

Definition 4.3.1 (Being constrained or rationed)
Let some $j' \in I_N$ be given. A consumer $i \in I_M$ is constrained *or* rationed *on his supply in the market for commodity j' at $(p, l^i, L^i) \in \mathbb{R}^N \times -\mathbb{R}^{*N}_+ \times \mathbb{R}^{*N}_+$ if there exists a consumption bundle $\overline{x}^i \in \beta^i(p, \overline{l}^i, L^i)$, where $\overline{l}^i_{j'} = -\infty$ and $\overline{l}^i_j = l^i_j$, $\forall j \in I_N \setminus \{j'\}$, such that there is no consumption bundle $x^i \in \beta^i(p, l^i, L^i)$*

satisfying $x^i \succeq^i \overline{x}^i$. *A consumer* $i \in I_M$ *is* constrained *or* rationed *on his demand in the market for commodity* j' *at* $(p, l^i, L^i) \in \mathbb{R}^N \times -\mathbb{R}_+^{*N} \times \mathbb{R}_+^{*N}$ *if there exists a consumption bundle* $\overline{x}^i \in \beta^i(p, l^i, \overline{L}^i)$, *where* $\overline{L}^i_{j'} = +\infty$ *and* $\overline{L}^i_j = L^i_j$, $\forall j \in I_N \setminus \{j'\}$, *such that there is no consumption bundle* $x^i \in \beta^i(p, l^i, L^i)$ *satisfying* $x^i \succeq^i \overline{x}^i$. *A consumer* $i \in I_M$ *is* constrained *or* rationed *in the market for commodity* j' *at* $(p, l^i, L^i) \in \mathbb{R}^N \times -\mathbb{R}_+^{*N} \times \mathbb{R}_+^{*N}$ *if he is rationed on his supply or his demand in the market for commodity* j' *at* (p, l^i, L^i).

Definition 4.3.2 (Rationing in a market)
There is supply rationing *in the market for a commodity* $j \in I_N$ *at* $(p, l, L) \in \mathbb{R}^N \times -\mathbb{R}_+^{*MN} \times \mathbb{R}_+^{*MN}$ *if at least one consumer* $i \in I_M$ *is rationed on his supply in the market for commodity* j *at* (p, l^i, L^i). *There is* demand rationing *in the market for a commodity* $j \in I_N$ *at* $(p, l, L) \in \mathbb{R}^N \times -\mathbb{R}_+^{*MN} \times \mathbb{R}_+^{*MN}$ *if at least one consumer* $i \in I_M$ *is rationed on his demand in the market for commodity* j *at* (p, l^i, L^i). *There is* rationing *in the market for a commodity* $j \in I_N$ *at* $(p, l, L) \in \mathbb{R}^N \times -\mathbb{R}_+^{*MN} \times \mathbb{R}_+^{*MN}$ *if there is supply rationing or demand rationing in the market for commodity* j *at* (p, l, L).

The following result shows how a consumer behaves when there is supply or demand rationing in some market.

Theorem 4.3.3
For some consumer $i \in I_M$, *let the consumption set* X^i *be convex and let the preference relation* $\preceq^i$ *be complete and convex. Let some* $(p, l^i, L^i) \in \mathbb{R}^N \times -\mathbb{R}_+^{*N} \times \mathbb{R}_+^{*N}$ *and some* $j' \in I_N$ *be given. If consumer* i *is rationed on his supply in the market for commodity* j' *at* (p, l^i, L^i) *and if* $x^i \in \delta^i(p, l^i, L^i)$, *then* $x^i_{j'} - \omega^i_{j'} = l^i_{j'}$. *If consumer* i *is rationed on his demand in the market for commodity* j' *at* (p, l^i, L^i) *and if* $x^i \in \delta^i(p, l^i, L^i)$, *then* $x^i_{j'} - \omega^i_{j'} = L^i_{j'}$.
Proof
Let consumer i be rationed on his supply in the market for commodity $j' \in I_N$ at (p, l^i, L^i) and let $\overline{l}^i \in -\mathbb{R}_+^{*N}$ be such that $\overline{l}^i_{j'} = -\infty$ and $\overline{l}^i_j = l^i_j, \forall j \in I_N \backslash \{j'\}$. Let some $x^i \in \delta^i(p, l^i, L^i)$ be given. Then there exists $\overline{x}^i \in \beta^i(p, \overline{l}^i, L^i)$ such that $x^i \prec^i \overline{x}^i$. For every $\lambda \in [0, 1]$, the element $\overline{x}^i(\lambda)$ of $\mathbb{R}^N$ is defined by

$$\overline{x}^i(\lambda) = \lambda \overline{x}^i + (1 - \lambda) x^i.$$

Since $\beta^i(p, l^i, L^i) \subset \beta^i(p, \overline{l}^i, L^i)$ and since $\beta^i(p, \overline{l}^i, L^i)$ is convex by Lemma 4.2.1, it holds that $\overline{x}^i(\lambda) \in \beta^i(p, \overline{l}^i, L^i), \forall \lambda \in [0, 1]$. Moreover, $x^i \prec^i \overline{x}^i(\lambda), \forall \lambda \in (0, 1]$. Suppose $x^i_{j'} - \omega^i_{j'} > l^i_{j'}$. Then there exists $\overline{\lambda} \in \mathbb{R}_{++}$ such that $\lambda \in (0, \overline{\lambda})$ implies $\overline{x}^i_{j'}(\lambda) - \omega^i_{j'} > l^i_{j'}$, and so $\overline{x}^i(\lambda) \in \beta^i(p, l^i, L^i)$. Since $x^i \prec^i \overline{x}^i(\lambda)$, this implies

$x^i \notin \delta^i(p, l^i, L^i)$, a contradiction. Consequently, $x^i_{j'} - \omega^i_{j'} = l^i_{j'}$. Similarly, it can be shown that $x^i_{j'} - \omega^i_{j'} = L^i_{j'}$ if consumer i is rationed on his demand in the market for commodity j' at (p, l^i, L^i). Q.E.D.

If a consumer $i \in I_M$ is constrained on his supply (demand) in the market for a commodity $j \in I_N$ at $(p, l^i, L^i) \in \mathbb{R}^N \times -\mathbb{R}^{*N}_+ \times \mathbb{R}^{*N}_+$, then l^i_j (L^i_j) is said to be *binding.*

4.4 THE SET OF ADMISSIBLE PRICE SYSTEMS

It is assumed that for every commodity $j \in I_N$ a *lower bound* on the price of commodity j, denoted by $\underline{p}_j$, and an *upper bound* on the price of commodity j, denoted by $\overline{p}_j$, is given. For every commodity $j \in I_N$ it is assumed that $\underline{p}_j$ belongs to $\mathbb{R}^* \setminus \{+\infty\}$ and $\overline{p}_j$ to $\mathbb{R}^* \setminus \{-\infty\}$, while $\underline{p}_j \leq \overline{p}_j$. The element $\underline{p} \in \mathbb{R}^{*N}$, given by $\underline{p} = (\underline{p}_1, \ldots, \underline{p}_N)^\top$, is called the *lower bound* on the price system, and $\overline{p} \in \mathbb{R}^{*N}$, given by $\overline{p} = (\overline{p}_1, \ldots, \overline{p}_N)^\top$, is called the *upper bound* on the price system. The *set of admissible price systems,* denoted by $P_{(\underline{p},\overline{p})}$, is defined by

$$P_{(\underline{p},\overline{p})} = \left\{p \in \mathbb{R}^N \,|\underline{p} \leq p \leq \overline{p}\right\}.$$

The set of admissible price systems $P_{(\underline{p},\overline{p})}$ includes the model of Chapter 3, where all price systems are allowed, as the special case with $\underline{p} = -\infty^N$ and $\overline{p} = +\infty^N$. The set of admissible price systems makes it possible to allow for a commodity $j \in I_N$ a minimum price, $\underline{p}_j > -\infty$, and a maximum price, $\overline{p}_j < +\infty$. It is also possible to model total inflexibility of the price of a commodity $j \in I_N$, i.e. $\underline{p}_j = \overline{p}_j$. The sets of admissible price systems considered are slightly more general than the ones considered in Drèze (1975), where only results are given for the cases with $\underline{p}_1 = \overline{p}_1 = 1$.

An interesting special case of the set of admissible price systems considered is the one, also considered in the seminal work of Bénassy (1975b), where the price system is completely fixed, i.e. $\underline{p} = \overline{p}$. This case corresponds to the Keynesian point of view that in the short run the price system is rigid and markets are cleared by means of quantity adjustments. The interesting case where the price system needs not be completely inflexible in the short run, but that instead in each market the price may rise or fall by some amount, is also allowed for.

Another point of view is that price rigidities are institutionally determined or are the result of strategic elements in the price setting process, see also Chapters 8 and 9. Typical examples are minimum wages, minimum prices for agricultural products, maximum price controls to reduce inflation (see Cox (1980)), price systems resulting from models with imperfect competition (see Bénassy (1993)), price indexation, and the linkage between the wages of civil servants and the wages paid in industry.

Models with a different set of admissible price systems are given in Dehez and Drèze (1984) and van der Laan (1984). There a partition $\{J^1, J^2, J^3\}$ of the set of commodities is given with J^1 the set of *free commodities,* J^2 the set of *index commodities,* and J^3 the set of *price following commodities.* The price system is assumed to be an element of $\mathbb{R}^N_+$. The *price index function* is a continuous function $\pi : \mathbb{R}^N_+ \to \mathbb{R}_+$ that is homogeneous of degree one, i.e. $\pi(\lambda p) = \lambda\pi(p)$, $\forall\lambda \in \mathbb{R}_+$, $\forall p \in \mathbb{R}^N_+$. Given a price system $p \in \mathbb{R}^N_+$, the real number $\pi(p)$ is called the *price index.* The value of the price index is assumed to depend only on the prices of the index commodities. For every commodity $j \in J^2 \cup J^3$ it is assumed that a lower bound $\underline{p}_j \in \mathbb{R}_+$ and an upper bound $\overline{p}_j \in \mathbb{R}_+$ is given such that the price of commodity j is between the product of $\underline{p}_j$ and the price index and the product of $\overline{p}_j$ and the price index. This results in the *set of admissible price systems,* P_π, defined by

$$P_\pi = \left\{p \in \mathbb{R}^N_+ \,\middle|\, \textstyle\sum_{j\in J^1} p_j = 1 \text{ and } \underline{p}_j\pi(p) \leq p_j \leq \overline{p}_j\pi(p),\ \forall j \in J^2 \cup J^3\right\}.$$

Under some assumptions, among which the one that $\underline{p}_j = \overline{p}_j$, $\forall j \in J^2$, it is shown in van der Laan (1984) that the set P_π is in some sense equivalent to the set of admissible price systems $P_{(\underline{p},\overline{p})}$ with $\underline{p}_j = 0$ and $\overline{p}_j = +\infty$, $\forall j \in J^1$, and is therefore a special case of the set of admissible price systems considered in this chapter. If the set J^1 consists of one element, say $J^1 = \{1\}$, and it is required that the value of the price index is above some level $\underline{\pi} \in \mathbb{R}_{++}$, then the model of Dehez and Drèze (1984) is obtained. In this case the set of admissible price systems is equivalent to the set of admissible price systems $P_{(\underline{p},\overline{p})}$ with $\overline{p}_1 = \underline{\pi}^{-1}$. If, furthermore, it is required that the value of the price index is below some level $\overline{\pi}$ with $\overline{\pi} \geq \underline{\pi}$, then it can be shown that the corresponding set of admissible price systems is equivalent to the set of admissible price systems $P_{(\underline{p},\overline{p})}$ with $\underline{p}_1 = \overline{\pi}^{-1}$ and $\overline{p}_1 = \underline{\pi}^{-1}$.

In Kurz (1982), Weddepohl (1987), and Wu (1988) models with rather general linkages between prices are taken into account. Again, only price systems in $\mathbb{R}^N_+$ are considered. A partition $\{J^1, J^2, J^3, J^4\}$ of the set of commodities is given. For every commodity $j \in J^3 \cup J^4$, let $\phi_j : \mathbb{R}^N_+ \to \mathbb{R}_+$ and, for every commodity

$j \in J^4$, let $\psi_j : \mathbb{R}^N_+ \to \mathbb{R}_+$, be continuous *index functions* that are homogeneous of degree one, i.e. for every commodity $j \in J^3 \cup J^4$, $\phi_j(\lambda p) = \lambda \phi_j(p)$, $\forall \lambda \in \mathbb{R}_+$, $\forall p \in \mathbb{R}^N_+$, and, for every commodity $j \in J^4$, $\psi_j(\lambda p) = \lambda \psi_j(p)$, $\forall \lambda \in \mathbb{R}_+$, $\forall p \in \mathbb{R}^N_+$. Moreover, for every commodity $j \in J^3 \cap J^4$, it is assumed that $\phi_j(p) \leq \psi_j(p)$, $\forall p \in \mathbb{R}^N_+$. The *set of admissible price systems* $P_{(\phi,\psi)}$ is defined by

$$P_{(\phi,\psi)} = \Big\{ p \in \mathbb{R}^N_+ \Big| \ \phi_j(p) \leq p_j, \ \forall j \in J^3, \ \phi_j(p) \leq p_j \leq \psi_j(p), \ \forall j \in J^4, \\ \textstyle\sum_{j \in I_N} p_j = 1 \Big\}.$$

In Kurz (1982) the case with $J^3 = \emptyset$, $\phi_j = \psi_j$, $\forall j \in J^4$, and the index functions only depending on the prices of commodities in the set J^2 is considered. In Wu (1988) also the case with $J^4 = \emptyset$ and the index functions only depending on the prices of commodities in the set J^2 is analysed. Weddepohl (1987) considers the set $P_{(\phi,\psi)}$ making other assumptions with respect to the index functions. Van der Laan (1984) also considers a special case corresponding to $J^3 = \emptyset$ and, for every commodity $j \in J^4$, $\phi_j(p) = \underline{p}_j \sum_{j \in J^2} p_j$, $\psi_j(p) = \overline{p}_j \sum_{j \in J^2} p_j$. Many different situations can be modelled by the set $P_{(\phi,\psi)}$. The assumptions made in Kurz (1982) and Wu (1988) allow for a fixed price system. In Weddepohl (1987) it is shown that the set of admissible price systems considered in Drèze (1975) is not excluded by his assumptions. It is clear that it is also possible to model situations not corresponding to a set $P_{(\underline{p},\overline{p})}$ and it is therefore an interesting question whether the complete characterizations of constrained equilibria given in this chapter can also be given for other models of the set of admissible price systems. In this respect it should be remarked that in models with a set of admissible price systems $P_{(\phi,\psi)}$ it is in general not possible to show the existence of equilibria satisfying the equilibrium concept to be introduced in this chapter. Therefore, other equilibrium concepts are used in the literature concerning these models. More precisely, it may happen in specific cases that there is supply rationing in some market, while the price in this market still might be lowered, something that is excluded in this chapter for reasons given in the Section 4.6.

4.5 THE SET OF ADMISSIBLE RATIONING SCHEMES

For every consumer $i \in I_M$, the consumption set X^i, the preference relation $\preceq^i$, and the initial endowment ω^i are assumed to be given in this section. The description of the economic system is extended in this section by the specification of a set of admissible rationing schemes.

The market mechanism specifies the price system and the rationing scheme of every consumer. However, in general not all rationing schemes are generated by the market mechanism in the economy. Sometimes rationing schemes are required to be uniform for all consumers, sometimes they depend on the amount of initial endowments owned by the various consumers, in other cases they are determined according to some priority system. The *rationing system* is given by the pair of sets $(\dot{l}, \dot{L})$, where $\dot{l} \subset -\mathbb{R}_{+}^{*MN}$ and $\dot{L} \subset \mathbb{R}_{+}^{*MN}$, specifying all *admissible rationing schemes.* The set $\dot{l}$, called the *rationing system on supply,* specifies all *admissible rationing schemes on supply* and the set $\dot{L}$, called the *rationing system on demand,* specifies all *admissible rationing schemes on demand.* The market mechanism is assumed to specify a price system $p \in P_{(\underline{p},\overline{p})}$ and a rationing scheme $(l, L) \in \dot{l} \times \dot{L}$. First, some examples of rationing systems are given.

Example 4.5.1 (Unrestricted rationing system)
In the *unrestricted rationing system* every rationing scheme is allowed. The unrestricted rationing system on supply is defined by

$$\dot{l} = -\mathbb{R}_{+}^{*MN}.$$

The unrestricted rationing system on demand is defined by

$$\dot{L} = \mathbb{R}_{+}^{*MN}.$$

Example 4.5.2 (Uniform rationing system)
The *uniform rationing system* is used in Drèze (1975). The uniform rationing system on supply is defined by

$$\dot{l} = \{l \in -\mathbb{R}_{+}^{*MN} \,|l^1 = \cdots = l^M\}.$$

The uniform rationing system on demand is defined by

$$\dot{L} = \{L \in \mathbb{R}_{+}^{*MN} \,|L^1 = \cdots = L^M\}.$$

Example 4.5.3 (Proportional rationing system)
The *proportional rationing system* is used in Kurz (1982). Assume that $\omega_j^i > 0$, $\forall i \in I_M$, $\forall j \in I_N$. The proportional rationing system on supply is defined by

$$\dot{l} = \{l \in -\mathbb{R}_{+}^{*MN} \,|\forall j \in I_N,\ \exists \lambda_j \in \mathbb{R}_{+}^{*},\ \forall i \in I_M,\ l_j^i = -\lambda_j \omega_j^i\}.$$

The proportional rationing system on demand is defined by

$$\dot{L} = \{L \in \mathbb{R}_+^{*MN} \,|\forall j \in I_N,\ \exists \lambda_j \in \mathbb{R}_+^*,\ \forall i \in I_M,\ L_j^i = \lambda_j \omega_j^i\}.$$

Example 4.5.4 (Market share rationing system)
The *market share rationing system* is used in Weddepohl (1983). For every $j \in I_N$, let numbers $\underline{\alpha}_j^i > 0$, $\forall i \in I_M$, be given such that $\sum_{i \in I_M} \underline{\alpha}_j^i = 1$. The market share rationing system on supply with respect to $\underline{\alpha} = (\underline{\alpha}_1^1, \ldots, \underline{\alpha}_N^M)^\top$ is defined by

$$\dot{l} = \{l \in -\mathbb{R}_+^{*MN} \,|\forall j \in I_N,\ \exists \lambda_j \in \mathbb{R}_+^*,\ \forall i \in I_M,\ l_j^i = -\lambda_j \underline{\alpha}_j^i\}.$$

For every $j \in I_N$, let $\overline{\alpha}_j^i > 0$, $\forall i \in I_M$, be given such that $\sum_{i \in I_M} \overline{\alpha}_j^i = 1$. The market share rationing system on demand with respect to $\overline{\alpha} = (\overline{\alpha}_1^1, \ldots, \overline{\alpha}_N^M)^\top$ is defined by

$$\dot{L} = \{L \in \mathbb{R}_+^{*MN} \,|\forall j \in I_N,\ \exists \lambda_j \in \mathbb{R}_+^*,\ \forall i \in I_M,\ L_j^i = \lambda_j \overline{\alpha}_j^i\}.$$

Example 4.5.5 (Priority rationing system)
Among other rationing systems, the *priority rationing system* is considered in Weddepohl (1987). For every $j \in I_N$, let $\underline{\pi}_j : I_M \to I_M$ be a permutation specifying the order in which consumers are rationed on their supply in the market for commodity j, so, for every $k \in I_M$, if consumer $\underline{\pi}_j(k)$ is rationed on his supply in the market for commodity j, then the consumers $\underline{\pi}_j(1), \ldots, \underline{\pi}_j(k-1)$ are fully rationed on their supply in the market for commodity j. The priority rationing system on supply with respect to $\underline{\pi} = (\underline{\pi}_1, \ldots, \underline{\pi}_N)$ is defined by

$$\dot{l} = \left\{l \in -\mathbb{R}_+^{*MN} \,\middle|\, \forall k \in I_M \setminus \{1\},\ \forall j \in I_N,\ l_j^{\underline{\pi}_j(k)} > -\infty \Rightarrow l_j^{\underline{\pi}_j(k-1)} = 0\right\}.$$

For every $j \in I_N$, let $\overline{\pi}_j : I_M \to I_M$ be a permutation specifying the order in which consumers are rationed on their demand in the market for commodity j, so, for every $k \in I_M$, if consumer $\overline{\pi}_j(k)$ is rationed on his demand in the market for commodity j, then the consumers $\overline{\pi}_j(1), \ldots, \overline{\pi}_j(k-1)$ are fully rationed on their demand in the market for commodity j. The priority rationing system on demand with respect to $\overline{\pi} = (\overline{\pi}_1, \ldots, \overline{\pi}_N)$ is defined by

$$\dot{L} = \left\{L \in \mathbb{R}_+^{*MN} \,\middle|\, \forall k \in I_M \setminus \{1\},\ \forall j \in I_N,\ L_j^{\overline{\pi}_j(k)} < +\infty \Rightarrow L_j^{\overline{\pi}_j(k-1)} = 0\right\}.$$

The following assumptions are often made with respect to the rationing system $(\dot{l}, \dot{L})$.

- *No rationing on supply* is admissible, i.e. $-\infty^{MN} \in \dot{l}$, *no rationing on demand* is admissible, i.e. $+\infty^{MN} \in \dot{L}$, *full rationing on supply* is admissible, i.e. $0^{MN} \in \dot{l}$, and *full rationing on demand* is admissible, i.e. $0^{MN} \in \dot{L}$. The rationing system on supply is *flexible,* i.e. $\{-\infty^{MN}, 0^{MN}\} \subset \dot{l}$. The rationing system on demand is *flexible,* i.e. $\{0^{MN}, +\infty^{MN}\} \subset \dot{L}$. The rationing system is *flexible,* i.e. both the rationing system on supply and the rationing system on demand is flexible. Notice that the rationing systems of Examples 4.5.1-4.5.5 are all flexible.

- The rationing system on supply is *market independent,* i.e. there exist subsets $\dot{l}_j$, $\forall j \in I_N$, of $-\mathbb{R}_+^{*M}$ such that $l \in \dot{l}$ if and only if $l_j \in \dot{l}_j$, $\forall j \in I_N$. The rationing system on demand is *market independent,* i.e. there exist subsets $\dot{L}_j$, $\forall j \in I_N$, of $\mathbb{R}_+^{*M}$ such that $L \in \dot{L}$ if and only if $L_j \in \dot{L}_j$, $\forall j \in I_N$. The rationing system is *market independent,* i.e. both the rationing system on supply and the rationing system on demand is market independent. Notice that the rationing systems of Examples 4.5.1-4.5.5 are all market independent.

- The rationing system on supply is *connected,* i.e. the set $\dot{l}$ is connected in $-\mathbb{R}_+^{*MN}$, the rationing system on demand is *connected,* i.e. the set $\dot{L}$ is connected in $\mathbb{R}_+^{*MN}$. The rationing system is *connected,* i.e. both the rationing system on supply and the rationing system on demand is connected. Notice that the rationing systems of Examples 4.5.1-4.5.5 are all connected.

- The rationing system on supply is *closed,* i.e. the set $\dot{l}$ is closed in $-\mathbb{R}_+^{*MN}$, the rationing system on demand is *closed,* i.e. the set $\dot{L}$ is closed in $\mathbb{R}_+^{*MN}$. The rationing system is *closed,* i.e. both the rationing system on supply and the rationing system on demand is closed. Notice that the rationing systems of Examples 4.5.1-4.5.5 are all closed.

Now two monotonicity properties of rationing systems will be introduced, called weak monotonicity and monotonicity, respectively. The property of weak monotonicity corresponds to the idea that if two rationing schemes on supply in the market for a commodity $j \in I_N$ are given, say $\bar{l}_j$ and $\hat{l}_j$, then the consumers together are allowed to supply less at $\bar{l}_j$ than at $\hat{l}_j$, or $\bar{l}_j = \hat{l}_j$, or the consumers together are allowed to supply more at $\bar{l}_j$ than at $\hat{l}_j$ in the market for commodity j. Similarly, if two rationing schemes on demand in the market for a commodity $j \in I_N$ are given, say $\bar{L}_j$ and $\hat{L}_j$, then the consumers together are allowed to demand less at $\bar{L}_j$ than at $\hat{L}_j$, or $\bar{L}_j = \hat{L}_j$, or the consumers together are allowed to demand more at $\bar{L}_j$ than at $\hat{L}_j$ in the market for commodity j. Although the description of weak monotonicity given above might

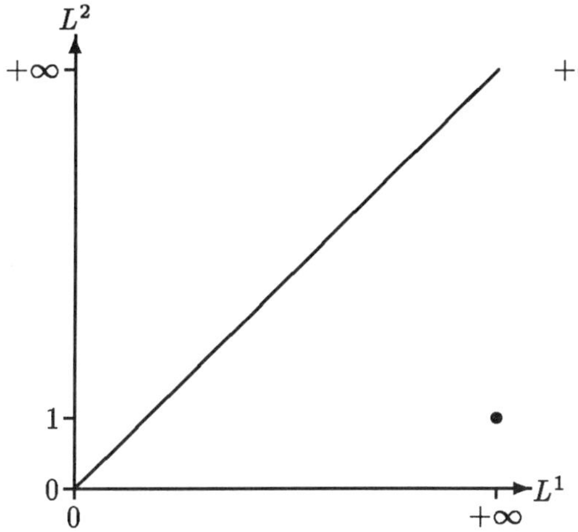

Figure 4.5.1. Rationing system on demand $\dot{L}'$.

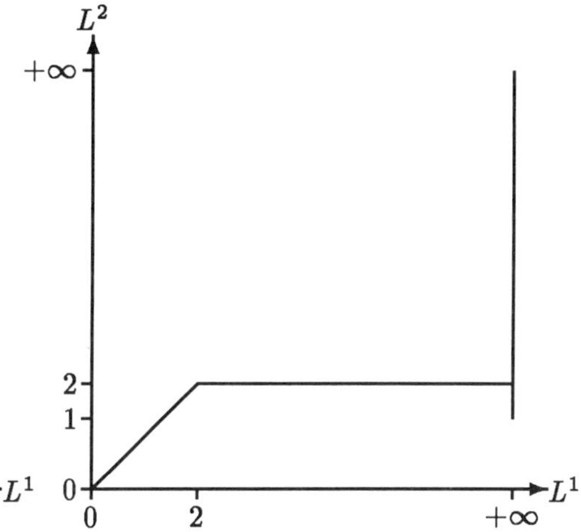

Figure 4.5.2. Rationing system on demand $\dot{L}''$.

seem straightforward the following two examples show that one has to be careful. Consider the case $M = 2$ and $N = 1$ and let the rationing systems on demand $\dot{L}'$ and $\dot{L}''$ be defined by

$$\begin{aligned} \dot{L}' &= \left\{ L \in \mathbb{R}_+^{*2} \,\middle|\, L^1 = L^2 \right\} \cup \left\{ (+\infty, 1)^\top \right\} \\ \dot{L}'' &= \left\{ L \in \mathbb{R}_+^{*2} \,\middle|\, L^1 = L^2 \leq 2, \text{ or } 2 < L^1 < +\infty \text{ and } L^2 = 2, \right. \\ &\qquad \left. \text{or } L^1 = +\infty \text{ and } 1 \leq L^2 \leq +\infty \right\}. \end{aligned}$$

The rationing systems on demand $\dot{L}'$ and $\dot{L}''$ are illustrated in Figure 4.5.1 and Figure 4.5.2, respectively. Intuitively, these rationing systems are not weakly monotonic. However, as turns out, one has to be careful when defining the property of weak monotonicity in order to rule them out. In fact, it turns out that one has to consider the limit properties of certain sequences of rationing schemes.

The monotonicity assumption is similar to the weak monotonicity assumption, but now for every rationing scheme on supply in the market for a commodity $j \in I_N$ every consumer is allowed to supply less in the market for commodity j at $\bar{l}_j$ than at $\widehat{l}_j$, or $\bar{l}_j = \widehat{l}_j$, or every consumer is allowed to supply more in the market for commodity j at $\bar{l}_j$ than at $\widehat{l}_j$. Similar remarks apply to monotonic rationing systems on demand. Examples of rationing systems on demand like $\dot{L}'$ or $\dot{L}''$ clearly violate the monotonicity assumption.

Now more formal definitions of weak monotonicity and monotonicity of rationing systems can be given.

- For every rationing scheme on supply $l \in \dot{l}$, for every commodity $j \in I_N$, let the set $I_j^{-\infty}(l)$ be defined by $I_j^{-\infty}(l) = \{i \in I_M \mid l_j^i = -\infty\}$ and let the integer $i_j^{-\infty}(l)$ be defined by $i_j^{-\infty}(l) = \#I_j^{-\infty}(l)$. The rationing system on supply is *weakly monotonic*, i.e. if $\bar{l}, \hat{l} \in \dot{l}$, then, for every $j \in I_N$, $\bar{l}_j = \hat{l}_j$, or $I_j^{-\infty}(\bar{l}) = I_j^{-\infty}(\hat{l})$ and $\sum_{i \in I_M \setminus I_j^{-\infty}(\bar{l})} \bar{l}_j^i \neq \sum_{i \in I_M \setminus I_j^{-\infty}(\hat{l})} \hat{l}_j^i$, or $I_j^{-\infty}(\bar{l})$ is a proper subset of $I_j^{-\infty}(\hat{l})$, or $I_j^{-\infty}(\hat{l})$ is a proper subset of $I_j^{-\infty}(\bar{l})$. Moreover, some limit property is needed for weak monotonicity. Let $((l)^n)_{n \in \mathbb{N}}$ be a sequence in $\dot{l}$ converging to some $\bar{l} \in \dot{l}$, where, for every $j \in I_N$, for every $n \in \mathbb{N}$, $I_j^{-\infty}((l)^n)$ is a proper subset of $I_j^{-\infty}(\bar{l})$. Then, for every $j \in I_N$, for every $l \in \dot{l}$, $i_j^{-\infty}(l) \leq i_j^{-\infty}((l)^n)$ for some $n \in \mathbb{N}$, or $I_j^{-\infty}(l) = I_j^{-\infty}(\bar{l})$ and $\sum_{i \in I_M \setminus I_j^{-\infty}(l)} l_j^i \leq \sum_{i \in I_M \setminus I_j^{-\infty}(\bar{l})} \bar{l}_j^i$, or $i_j^{-\infty}(l) > i_j^{-\infty}(\bar{l})$. For every rationing scheme on demand $L \in \dot{L}$, for every commodity $j \in I_N$, the set $I_j^{+\infty}(L)$ is defined by $I_j^{+\infty}(L) = \{i \in I_M \mid L_j^i = +\infty\}$ and the integer $i_j^{+\infty}(L)$ is defined by $i_j^{+\infty}(L) = \#I_j^{+\infty}(L)$. The rationing system on demand is *weakly monotonic*, i.e. if $\bar{L}, \hat{L} \in \dot{L}$, then, for every $j \in I_N$, $\bar{L}_j = \hat{L}_j$, or $I_j^{+\infty}(\bar{L}) = I_j^{+\infty}(\hat{L})$ and $\sum_{i \in I_M \setminus I_j^{+\infty}(\bar{L})} \bar{L}_j^i \neq \sum_{i \in I_M \setminus I_j^{+\infty}(\hat{L})} \hat{L}_j^i$, or $I_j^{+\infty}(\bar{L})$ is a proper subset of $I_j^{+\infty}(\hat{L})$, or $I_j^{+\infty}(\hat{L})$ is a proper subset of $I_j^{+\infty}(\bar{L})$. Moreover, let $((L)^n)_{n \in \mathbb{N}}$ be a sequence in $\dot{L}$ converging to some $\bar{L} \in \dot{L}$, where, for every $j \in I_N$, for every $n \in \mathbb{N}$, $I_j^{+\infty}((L)^n)$ is a proper subset of $I_j^{+\infty}(\bar{L})$. Then, for every $j \in I_N$, for every $L \in \dot{L}$, $i_j^{+\infty}(L) \leq i_j^{+\infty}((L)^n)$ for some $n \in \mathbb{N}$, or $I_j^{+\infty}(L) = I_j^{+\infty}(\bar{L})$ and $\sum_{i \in I_M \setminus I_j^{+\infty}(L)} L_j^i \geq \sum_{i \in I_M \setminus I_j^{+\infty}(\bar{L})} \bar{L}_j^i$, or $i_j^{+\infty}(L) > i_j^{+\infty}(\bar{L})$. The rationing system is *weakly monotonic,* i.e. both the rationing system on supply and the rationing system on demand is weakly monotonic. The rationing system of Example 4.5.1 is not weakly monotonic, but the rationing systems of Examples 4.5.2-4.5.5 are weakly monotonic. The rationing system on demand $\dot{L}'$ is not weakly monotonic due to the required limit property. In fact, consider the sequence $((L)^n)_{n \in \mathbb{N}} = ((n,n)^\top)_{n \in \mathbb{N}}$ in $\dot{L}'$ converging to $\bar{L} = (+\infty, +\infty)^\top \in \dot{L}'$. Consider $L = (+\infty, 1)^\top$. Then neither $i_1^{+\infty}(L) \leq i_1^{+\infty}((L)^n)$ for some $n \in \mathbb{N}$, nor $I_1^{+\infty}(L) = I_1^{+\infty}(\bar{L})$, nor $i_1^{+\infty}(L) > i_1^{+\infty}(\bar{L})$, so $\dot{L}'$ is not weakly monotonic. Also the rationing system on demand $\dot{L}''$ is not weakly monotonic due to the required limit property. In fact, consider the sequence $((L)^n)_{n \in \mathbb{N}} = ((n+1, 2)^\top)_{n \in \mathbb{N}}$ in $\dot{L}''$ converging to $\bar{L} = (+\infty, 2)^\top \in \dot{L}''$. Consider $L = (+\infty, 1)^\top$. Then neither $i_1^{+\infty}(L) \leq i_1^{+\infty}((L)^n)$ for some $n \in \mathbb{N}$, nor $I_1^{+\infty}(L) = I_1^{+\infty}(\bar{L})$ and $\sum_{i \in I_2 \setminus I_1^{+\infty}(L)} L_1^i = L_1^2 \geq \bar{L}_1^2 = \sum_{i \in I_2 \setminus I_1^{+\infty}(\bar{L})} \bar{L}_1^i$, nor $i_1^{+\infty}(L) > i_1^{+\infty}(\bar{L})$, so $\dot{L}''$ is not weakly monotonic.

- The rationing system on supply is *monotonic,* i.e. if $\bar{l}, \hat{l} \in \dot{l}$, then, for every $j \in I_N$, $\bar{l}_j \leq \hat{l}_j$ or $\bar{l}_j \geq \hat{l}_j$. The rationing system on demand is *monotonic,* i.e. if $\overline{L}, \widehat{L} \in \dot{L}$, then, for every $j \in I_N$, $\overline{L}_j \leq \widehat{L}_j$ or $\overline{L}_j \geq \widehat{L}_j$. The rationing system is *monotonic,* i.e. both the rationing system on supply and the rationing system on demand is monotonic. It is easily verified that a monotonic rationing system is weakly monotonic, so the rationing system of Example 4.5.1 is not monotonic. The rationing systems of Examples 4.5.2-4.5.5 are monotonic.

The assumptions that no rationing on supply and no rationing on demand is admissible and that the rationing system is market independent are so basic, that they can hardly be considered as assumptions. This is also true for the assumption of connectedness. The weak monotonicity and the monotonicity assumption are also reasonable.

Not all different rationing schemes are different from the point of view of the consumer. The following definition captures this idea.

Definition 4.5.6 (Equivalent rationing schemes)
The rationing scheme on supply $\bar{l}$ is equivalent *to the rationing scheme on supply $\hat{l}$, denoted by $\bar{l} \sim \hat{l}$, if, for every $i \in I_M$, for every $j \in I_N$, $\hat{l}^i_j \geq -\omega^i_j$ implies $\bar{l}^i_j = \hat{l}^i_j$, and $\hat{l}^i_j < -\omega^i_j$ implies $\bar{l}^i_j < -\omega^i_j$. The rationing scheme on demand $\overline{L}$ is* equivalent *to the rationing scheme on demand $\widehat{L}$, denoted by $\overline{L} \sim \widehat{L}$, if, for every $i \in I_M$, for every $j \in I_N$, $\widehat{L}^i_j \leq \widetilde{\omega}_j - \omega^i_j$ implies $\overline{L}^i_j = \widehat{L}^i_j$, and $\widehat{L}^i_j > \widetilde{\omega}_j - \omega^i_j$ implies $\overline{L}^i_j > \widetilde{\omega}_j - \omega^i_j$. The rationing scheme $(\bar{l}, \overline{L})$ is* equivalent *to the rationing scheme $(\hat{l}, \widehat{L})$, denoted by $(\bar{l}, \overline{L}) \sim (\hat{l}, \widehat{L})$, if $\bar{l} \sim \hat{l}$ and $\overline{L} \sim \widehat{L}$.*

It is easily verified that the binary relation on the set of all possible rationing schemes on supply, $-\mathbb{R}^{*MN}_{+}$, induced by $\sim$, is an equivalence relation, the binary relation on the set of all possible rationing schemes on demand, $\mathbb{R}^{*MN}_{+}$, induced by $\sim$, is an equivalence relation, and the binary relation on the set of all possible rationing schemes, $-\mathbb{R}^{*MN}_{+} \times \mathbb{R}^{*MN}_{+}$, induced by $\sim$, is an equivalence relation.

Two equivalent rationing schemes may induce different consumer behaviour. However, under weak assumptions, this is not the case in a constrained equilibrium as is shown in Theorem 4.6.4.

Definition 4.5.7 (Equivalent rationing systems)
The rationing system on supply $\bar{\dot{l}}$ *is* equivalent *to the rationing system on supply* $\hat{\dot{l}}$, *denoted by* $\bar{\dot{l}} \sim \hat{\dot{l}}$, *if for every* $\bar{l} \in \bar{\dot{l}}$ *there exists* $\hat{l} \in \hat{\dot{l}}$ *such that* $\bar{l} \sim \hat{l}$ *and for every* $\hat{l} \in \hat{\dot{l}}$ *there exists* $\bar{l} \in \bar{\dot{l}}$ *such that* $\hat{l} \sim \bar{l}$. *The rationing system on demand* $\bar{\dot{L}}$ *is* equivalent *to the rationing system on demand* $\hat{\dot{L}}$, *denoted by* $\bar{\dot{L}} \sim \hat{\dot{L}}$, *if for every* $\bar{L} \in \bar{\dot{L}}$ *there exists* $\hat{L} \in \hat{\dot{L}}$ *such that* $\bar{L} \sim \hat{L}$ *and for every* $\hat{L} \in \hat{\dot{L}}$ *there exists* $\bar{L} \in \bar{\dot{L}}$ *such that* $\hat{L} \sim \bar{L}$. *The rationing system* $(\bar{\dot{l}}, \bar{\dot{L}})$ *is* equivalent *to the rationing system* $(\hat{\dot{l}}, \hat{\dot{L}})$, *denoted by* $(\bar{\dot{l}}, \bar{\dot{L}}) \sim (\hat{\dot{l}}, \hat{\dot{L}})$, *if both* $\bar{\dot{l}} \sim \hat{\dot{l}}$ *and* $\bar{\dot{L}} \sim \hat{\dot{L}}$.

It is easily verified that the binary relation on the set of all possible rationing systems on supply, $2^{-\mathbb{R}_+^{*MN}}$, induced by $\sim$, is an equivalence relation, the binary relation on the set of all possible rationing systems on demand, $2^{\mathbb{R}_+^{*MN}}$, induced by $\sim$, is an equivalence relation, and the binary relation on the set of all possible rationing systems, $2^{-\mathbb{R}_+^{*MN}} \times 2^{\mathbb{R}_+^{*MN}}$, induced by $\sim$, is an equivalence relation.

The rationing system on supply is often defined as being the range of a function $\tilde{l} : S \to -\mathbb{R}_+^{MN}$ defined on some subset S of $\mathbb{R}^N$. Often, $S = \mathbb{R}_+^N$ or $S = Q^N$. From now on it is assumed in this chapter that $S = Q^N$. The function $\tilde{l}$ is called the *rationing function on supply.* For every $i \in I_M$, for every $j \in I_N$, component $(i-1)N + j$ of $\tilde{l}$ is denoted by $\tilde{l}_j^i$. Moreover, $\tilde{l}^i = (\tilde{l}_1^i, \ldots, \tilde{l}_N^i)^\top$, $\forall i \in I_M$, and $\tilde{l}_j = (\tilde{l}_j^1, \ldots, \tilde{l}_j^M)^\top$, $\forall j \in I_N$. Given $q \in Q^N$, the vector $\tilde{l}^i(q)$ yields a rationing scheme on the supply of consumer $i \in I_M$. Similarly, the rationing system on demand is often defined as being the range of a function $\tilde{L} : Q^N \to \mathbb{R}_+^{MN}$, called the *rationing function on demand.* For every $i \in I_M$, for every $j \in I_N$, component $(i-1)N + j$ of $\tilde{L}$ is denoted by $\tilde{L}_j^i$. Moreover, $\tilde{L}^i = (\tilde{L}_1^i, \ldots, \tilde{L}_N^i)^\top$ and $\tilde{L}_j = (\tilde{L}_j^1, \ldots, \tilde{L}_j^M)^\top$. Given $q \in Q^N$, the vector $\tilde{L}^i(q)$ yields a rationing scheme on the demand of consumer $i \in I_M$. The pair $(\tilde{l}, \tilde{L})$ is called a *rationing function.* Notice that the image of the rationing function $(\tilde{l}, \tilde{L})$ is a subset of $-\mathbb{R}_+^{MN} \times \mathbb{R}_+^{MN}$.

Definition 4.5.8 (Representation by a rationing function)
The rationing system on supply $\dot{l}$ *is* represented *by a rationing function on supply* $\tilde{l}$ *if* $\dot{l} \sim \tilde{l}(Q^N)$. *The rationing system on demand* $\dot{L}$ *is* represented *by a rationing function on demand* $\tilde{L}$ *if* $\dot{L} \sim \tilde{L}(Q^N)$. *The rationing system* $(\dot{l}, \dot{L})$ *is* represented *by a rationing function* $(\tilde{l}, \tilde{L})$ *if* $(\dot{l}, \dot{L}) \sim (\tilde{l}(Q^N), \tilde{L}(Q^N))$.

Now some examples of rationing functions are given, representing the rationing systems of Examples 4.5.1-4.5.5. In the examples it is assumed that $\omega_j^i \geq 0$, $\forall i \in I_M$, $\forall j \in I_N$, and $\widetilde{\omega} \in \mathbb{R}^N_{++}$.

Example 4.5.9 (Unrestricted rationing function)
First, a continuous function $h^M : [0,1] \to Q^M$ is constructed. Let f^1 be a path from $[0,1]$ into Δ^2 that is surjective. Such a path f^1 exists by Theorem 2.3.3. It is not difficult to construct a continuous function $f^2 : \Delta^2 \to Q^2$ that is surjective. Then the function $f^2 \circ f^1 : [0,1] \to Q^2$ is a continuous function that is surjective. Using the function $f^2 \circ f^1$ it is not difficult to construct a continuous function $g^2 : [0,1] \to Q^2$ that is surjective and that has the additional property that $g^2(0) = (0,0)^\top$ and $g^2(1) = (1,1)^\top$. For every $n \in \mathbb{N} \setminus \{1,2\}$, let the function $g^n : Q^{n-1} \to Q^n$ be defined by $g^n(q) = (g^{n-1}(q_1, \ldots, q_{n-2})^\top, q_{n-1})^\top$, $\forall q \in Q^{n-1}$. Clearly, the function g^n is continuous and surjective for every $n \geq 3$. Let the function $h^1 : [0,1] \to Q^1$ be defined by $h^1(q) = q$, $\forall q \in Q^1$. For every $n \in \mathbb{N} \setminus \{1\}$, let the function $h^n : [0,1] \to Q^n$ be defined by $h^n(q) = g^n(h^{n-1}(q))$, $\forall q \in [0,1]$. Then the function h^n is continuous and surjective for every $n \in \mathbb{N}$.
Let some $\varepsilon \in \mathbb{R}_{++}$ be given. Notice that if $\dot{l}$ is the unrestricted rationing system on supply, then $\dot{l} \sim \prod_{i \in I_M} \prod_{j \in I_N} [\min(\{-\omega_j^1, \ldots, -\omega_j^M\}) - \varepsilon, 0]$. Therefore, the unrestricted rationing system on supply is represented by the rationing function on supply $\widetilde{l} : Q^N \to -\mathbb{R}^{MN}_+$ obtained by defining, for every $i \in I_M$, for every $j \in I_N$,

$$\widetilde{l}^i_j(q) = \left(\min(\{-\omega_j^1, \ldots, -\omega_j^M\}) - \varepsilon\right) h_i^M(q_j), \ \forall q \in Q^N.$$

Clearly, $\dot{L} \sim \prod_{i \in I_M} \prod_{j \in I_N} [0, \widetilde{\omega}_j + \varepsilon]$ if $\dot{L}$ is the unrestricted rationing system on demand. Therefore, the unrestricted rationing system on demand is represented by a rationing function on demand $\widetilde{L} : Q^N \to \mathbb{R}^{MN}_+$ obtained by defining, for every $i \in I_M$, for every $j \in I_N$,

$$\widetilde{L}^i_j(q) = (\widetilde{\omega}_j + \varepsilon)\, h_i^M(q_j), \ \forall q \in Q^N.$$

Example 4.5.10 (Uniform rationing function)
Let some $\varepsilon \in \mathbb{R}_{++}$ be given. The uniform rationing system on supply is represented by the rationing function on supply $\widetilde{l} : Q^N \to -\mathbb{R}^{MN}_+$ obtained by defining, for every $i \in I_M$, for every $j \in I_N$,

$$\widetilde{l}^i_j(q) = \left(\min(\{-\omega_j^1, \ldots, -\omega_j^M\}) - \varepsilon\right) q_j, \ \forall q \in Q^N.$$

The uniform rationing system on demand is represented by the rationing function on demand $\widetilde{L} : Q^N \to \mathbb{R}^{MN}_+$ obtained by defining, for every $i \in I_M$, for every $j \in I_N$,

$$\widetilde{L}_j^i(q) = (\widetilde{\omega}_j + \varepsilon)\, q_j,\ \forall q \in Q^N.$$

Example 4.5.11 (Proportional rationing function)
Assume that $\omega_j^i > 0$, $\forall i \in I_M$, $\forall j \in I_N$. Let some $\varepsilon \in \mathbb{R}_{++}$ be given. The proportional rationing system on supply is represented by the rationing function on supply $\widetilde{l} : Q^N \to -\mathbb{R}_+^{MN}$ obtained by defining, for every $i \in I_M$, for every $j \in I_N$,

$$\widetilde{l}_j^i(q) = -(1+\varepsilon)\omega_j^i q_j,\ \forall q \in Q^N.$$

The proportional rationing system on demand is represented by the rationing function on demand $\widetilde{L} : Q^N \to \mathbb{R}_+^{MN}$ obtained by defining, for every $i \in I_M$, for every $j \in I_N$,

$$\widetilde{L}_j^i(q) = \frac{\widetilde{\omega}_j}{\min(\{\omega_j^1, \ldots, \omega_j^M\})}\omega_j^i q_j,\ \forall q \in Q^N.$$

Example 4.5.12 (Market share rationing function)
Let some $\varepsilon \in \mathbb{R}_{++}$ be given. For every $j \in I_N$, let numbers $\underline{\alpha}_j^i > 0$, $\forall i \in I_M$, be given such that $\sum_{i \in I_M} \underline{\alpha}_j^i = 1$. The proportional rationing system on supply with respect to $\underline{\alpha} = (\underline{\alpha}_1^1, \ldots, \underline{\alpha}_N^M)^\top$ is represented by the rationing function on supply $\widetilde{l} : Q^N \to -\mathbb{R}_+^{MN}$ obtained by defining, for every $i \in I_M$, for every $j \in I_N$,

$$\widetilde{l}_j^i(q) = \underline{\alpha}_j^i \left(\min\left(\left\{ -\frac{\omega_j^1}{\underline{\alpha}_j^1}, \ldots, -\frac{\omega_j^M}{\underline{\alpha}_j^M} \right\} \right) - \varepsilon \right) q_j,\ \forall q \in Q^N.$$

For every $j \in I_N$, let $\overline{\alpha}_j^i > 0$, $\forall i \in I_M$, be given such that $\sum_{i \in I_M} \overline{\alpha}_j^i = 1$. The proportional rationing system on demand with respect to $\overline{\alpha} = (\overline{\alpha}_1^1, \ldots, \overline{\alpha}_N^M)^\top$ is represented by the rationing function on demand $\widetilde{L} : Q^N \to \mathbb{R}_+^{MN}$ obtained by defining, for every $i \in I_M$, for every $j \in I_N$,

$$\widetilde{L}_j^i(q) = \overline{\alpha}_j^i \frac{\widetilde{\omega}_j + \varepsilon}{\min(\{\overline{\alpha}_j^1, \ldots, \overline{\alpha}_j^M\})} q_j,\ \forall q \in Q^N.$$

Example 4.5.13 (Priority rationing function)
Let some $\varepsilon \in \mathbb{R}_{++}$ be given. For every $j \in I_N$, let $\underline{\pi}_j : I_M \to I_M$ be a permutation specifying the order in which consumers are rationed on their supply in the market for commodity j. The priority rationing system on supply with respect to $\underline{\pi} = (\underline{\pi}_1, \ldots, \underline{\pi}_N)$ is represented by the rationing function on

supply $\tilde{l} : Q^N \rightarrow -\mathrm{IR}_+^{MN}$ obtained by defining, for every $i \in I_M$, for every $j \in I_N$,

$$\tilde{l}_j^i(q) = \left(\min(\{-\omega_j^1, \ldots, -\omega_j^M\}) - \varepsilon\right) \max\left(\{\underline{\pi}_j^{-1}(i) - M + Mq_j, 0\}\right), \ \forall q \in Q^N.$$

For every $j \in I_N$, let $\overline{\pi}_j : I_M \rightarrow I_M$ be a permutation specifying the order in which consumers are rationed on their demand in the market for commodity j. The priority rationing system on demand with respect to $\overline{\pi} = (\overline{\pi}_1, \ldots, \overline{\pi}_N)$ is represented by the rationing function on demand $\tilde{L} : Q^N \rightarrow \mathrm{IR}_+^{MN}$ obtained by defining, for every $i \in I_M$, for every $j \in I_N$,

$$\tilde{L}_j^i(q) = (\tilde{\omega}_j + \varepsilon) \max\left(\{\overline{\pi}_j^{-1}(i) - M + Mq_j, 0\}\right), \ \forall q \in Q^N.$$

The following assumptions are often made with respect to the rationing function on supply $\tilde{l} : Q^N \rightarrow -\mathrm{IR}_+^{MN}$ and the rationing function on demand $\tilde{L} : Q^N \rightarrow \mathrm{IR}_+^{MN}$.

- It holds that $\tilde{l}(1^N) \ll -\omega$, so there is a rationing scheme on supply equivalent to $-\infty^{MN}$. For every $i \in I_M$, $\tilde{L}^i(1^N) \gg \tilde{\omega} - \omega^i$, so there is a rationing scheme on demand equivalent to $+\infty^{MN}$. It holds that $\tilde{l}(0^N) = 0^{MN}$, so full rationing on supply is admissible, and it holds that $\tilde{L}(0^N) = 0^{MN}$, so full rationing on demand is admissible. The rationing function on supply is *flexible*, i.e. $\tilde{l}(0^N) = 0^{MN}$ and $\tilde{l}(1^N) \ll -\omega$. The rationing function on demand is *flexible*, i.e. $\tilde{L}(0^N) = 0^{MN}$ and $\tilde{L}^i(1^N) \gg \tilde{\omega} - \omega^i$, $\forall i \in I_M$.

- The rationing function on supply is *market independent*, i.e. for every $j \in I_N$, for every $\overline{q}, \widehat{q} \in Q^N$, it holds that $\tilde{l}_j(\overline{q}) = \tilde{l}_j(\widehat{q})$ if $\overline{q}_j = \widehat{q}_j$. The rationing function on demand is *market independent*, i.e. for every $\overline{q}, \widehat{q} \in Q^N$, for every $j \in I_N$, it holds that $\tilde{L}_j(\overline{q}) = \tilde{L}_j(\widehat{q})$ if $\overline{q}_j = \widehat{q}_j$.

- The rationing function on supply is *continuous*, i.e. the function $\tilde{l}$ is continuous. The rationing function on demand is *continuous*, i.e. the function $\tilde{L}$ is continuous. Sometimes, the continuity assumption is replaced by the stronger assumption of *differentiability*, which is clearly of a similar nature.

- The rationing function on supply is *weakly monotonic*, i.e. for every $q^1, q^2 \in Q^N$, for every $j \in I_N$, if $q_j^1 < q_j^2$, then $\sum_{i \in I_M} \tilde{l}_j^i(q^1) > \sum_{i \in I_M} \tilde{l}_j^i(q^2)$. The rationing function on demand is *weakly monotonic*, i.e. for every $q^1, q^2 \in Q^N$, for every $j \in I_N$, if $q_j^1 < q_j^2$, then $\sum_{i \in I_M} \tilde{L}_j^i(q^1) < \sum_{i \in I_M} \tilde{L}_j^i(q^2)$. Sometimes the weak monotonicity assumption is needed in differentiable form. Then it is required that, for every $j \in I_N$, $\sum_{i \in I_M} \partial_{q_j} \tilde{l}_j^i(\overline{q}) < 0$, $\forall \overline{q} \in Q^N$, and $\sum_{i \in I_M} \partial_{q_j} \tilde{L}_j^i(\overline{q}) > 0$, $\forall \overline{q} \in Q^N$.

- The rationing function on supply is *monotonic*, i.e. for every $q^1, q^2 \in Q^N$, for every $j \in I_N$, if $q_j^1 < q_j^2$, then $\tilde{l}_j^i(q^1) \geq \tilde{l}_j^i(q^2)$, $\forall i \in I_M$, and there exists $i' \in I_M$ such that $\tilde{l}_j^{i'}(q^1) > \tilde{l}_j^{i'}(q^2)$. The rationing function on demand is *monotonic*, i.e. for every $q^1, q^2 \in Q^N$, for every $j \in I_N$, if $q_j^1 < q_j^2$, then $\tilde{L}_j^i(q^1) \leq \tilde{L}_j^i(q^2)$, $\forall i \in I_M$, and there exists $i' \in I_M$ such that $\tilde{L}_j^{i'}(q^1) < \tilde{L}_j^{i'}(q^2)$. Sometimes the monotonicity assumption is needed in differentiable form. Then it is required that, for every $j \in I_N$, $\partial_{q_j}\tilde{l}_j(\bar{q}) < 0^M$, $\forall \bar{q} \in Q^N$, and $\partial_{q_j}\tilde{L}_j(\bar{q}) > 0^M$, $\forall \bar{q} \in Q^N$.

If an assumption is said to be made with respect to the rationing function $(\tilde{l}, \tilde{L})$, then it is meant that this assumption is made both with respect to $\tilde{l}$ and with respect to $\tilde{L}$.

It is easily verified that all the assumptions mentioned above are satisfied in Examples 4.5.10-4.5.13, and that all assumptions mentioned above, except the assumptions concerning the weak monotonicity and the monotonicity of the rationing function, are satisfied in Example 4.5.9.

The following four results give an interesting relationship between the assumptions made with respect to the rationing system and the assumptions made with respect to the rationing function.

Theorem 4.5.14
Let the rationing system on supply $\dot{l}$ be represented by the rationing function on supply $\tilde{l} : Q^N \to -\mathbb{R}_+^{MN}$. If $\tilde{l}$ is flexible, then $\dot{l}$ is equivalent to a flexible rationing system on supply, if $\tilde{l}$ is market independent, then $\dot{l}$ is equivalent to a market independent rationing system on supply, if $\tilde{l}$ is continuous, then $\dot{l}$ is equivalent to a closed and connected rationing system on supply, if $\tilde{l}$ is market independent and weakly monotonic, then $\dot{l}$ is equivalent to a weakly monotonic rationing system on supply, and if $\tilde{l}$ is market independent and monotonic, then $\dot{l}$ is equivalent to a monotonic rationing system on supply.

Proof
Let $\tilde{l}$ be flexible. Then $\tilde{l}(0^N) = 0^{MN} \sim l$ for some $l \in \dot{l}$ since $\dot{l} \sim \tilde{l}(Q^N)$. Moreover, $\tilde{l}(1^N) \ll -\omega$, so $-\infty^{MN} \sim \tilde{l}(1^N) \sim l$ for some $l \in \dot{l}$, using that $\dot{l} \sim \tilde{l}(Q^N)$.
Let $\tilde{l}$ be market independent. Since $\dot{l} \sim \tilde{l}(Q^N)$, it is sufficient to show that the rationing system $\tilde{l}(Q^N)$ is market independent. It is shown that $l \in \tilde{l}(Q^N)$ if and only if $l_j \in \tilde{l}_j(Q^N)$, $\forall j \in I_N$, thereby showing the market independence

of $\tilde{l}(Q^N)$. Clearly, $l \in \tilde{l}(Q^N)$ implies $l_j \in \tilde{l}_j(Q^N)$, $\forall j \in I_N$. Let $l_j \in \tilde{l}_j(Q^N)$, $\forall j \in I_N$, be given. For every $j \in I_N$, there exists $q^j \in Q^N$ such that $l_j = \tilde{l}_j(q^j)$. The element q of Q^N is defined by $q_j = q^j_j$, $\forall j \in I_N$. Then $\tilde{l}(q) = l$ by the market independence of $\tilde{l}$, so $l \in \tilde{l}(Q^N)$.

Let $\tilde{l}$ be continuous. Since $\dot{l} \sim \tilde{l}(Q^N)$, it is sufficient to show that the rationing system $\tilde{l}(Q^N)$ is closed and connected. Since Q^N is compact and connected, it follows that $\tilde{l}(Q^N)$ is compact and connected in $-\mathbb{R}^{MN}_+$ by Theorem 2.3.13. Therefore, $\tilde{l}(Q^N)$ is also compact and connected in $\mathbb{R}^{*MN}$. Since $\tilde{l}(Q^N)$ is a compact subset of the Hausdorff space $\mathbb{R}^{*MN}$, it is closed in $\mathbb{R}^{*MN}$ by Theorem 2.3.10.

Let $\tilde{l}$ be market independent and weakly monotonic. Since $\dot{l} \sim \tilde{l}(Q^N)$, it is sufficient to show that $\tilde{l}(Q^N)$ is weakly monotonic. Let $\bar{l}, \hat{l} \in \tilde{l}(Q^N)$ be given and let $\bar{q}, \hat{q} \in Q^N$ be such that $\bar{l} = \tilde{l}(\bar{q})$ and $\hat{l} = \tilde{l}(\hat{q})$. Clearly, for every $j \in I_N$, $\bar{l}_j \gg -\infty^M$ and $\hat{l}_j \gg -\infty^M$. For every $j \in I_N$, if $\bar{q}_j = \hat{q}_j$, then $\bar{l}_j = \hat{l}_j$ since $\tilde{l}$ is market independent, and if, without loss of generality, $\bar{q}_j < \hat{q}_j$, then $\sum_{i \in I_M} \bar{l}^i_j > \sum_{i \in I_M} \hat{l}^i_j$ by the weak monotonicity of $\tilde{l}$.

Let $\tilde{l}$ be market independent and monotonic. Since $\dot{l} \sim \tilde{l}(Q^N)$, it is sufficient to show that $\tilde{l}(Q^N)$ is monotonic. Let $\bar{l}, \hat{l} \in \tilde{l}(Q^N)$ be given and let $\bar{q}, \hat{q} \in Q^N$ be such that $\bar{l} = \tilde{l}(\bar{q})$ and $\hat{l} = \tilde{l}(\hat{q})$. For every $j \in I_N$, if $\bar{q}_j = \hat{q}_j$, then $\bar{l}_j = \hat{l}_j$ since $\tilde{l}$ is market independent, and if, without loss of generality, $\bar{q}_j < \hat{q}_j$, then $\bar{l}_j > \hat{l}_j$ by the monotonicity of $\tilde{l}$. Q.E.D.

The proof for the results given in Theorem 4.5.15 concerning the rationing system on demand is similar to the proof of the corresponding results concerning the rationing system on supply given in Theorem 4.5.14.

Theorem 4.5.15

Let the rationing system on demand $\dot{L}$ be represented by the rationing function on demand $\tilde{L} : Q^N \to \mathbb{R}^{MN}_+$. If $\tilde{L}$ is flexible, then $\dot{L}$ is equivalent to a flexible rationing system on demand, if $\tilde{L}$ is market independent, then $\dot{L}$ is equivalent to a market independent rationing system on demand, if $\tilde{L}$ is continuous, then $\dot{L}$ is equivalent to a closed and connected rationing system on demand, if $\tilde{L}$ is market independent and weakly monotonic, then $\dot{L}$ is equivalent to a weakly monotonic rationing system on demand, and if $\tilde{L}$ is market independent and monotonic, then $\dot{L}$ is equivalent to a monotonic rationing system on demand.

The following two results give a converse of Theorems 4.5.14 and 4.5.15.

Theorem 4.5.16
Let the rationing system on supply $\dot{l}$ be flexible, market independent, closed, and connected. If the rationing system on supply $\dot{l}$ is weakly monotonic, then $\dot{l}$ can be represented by a flexible, market independent, continuous, and weakly monotonic rationing function on supply. If the rationing system on supply $\dot{l}$ is monotonic, then $\dot{l}$ can be represented by a flexible, market independent, continuous, and monotonic rationing function on supply.

Proof
Let $\dot{l}$ be weakly monotonic. A rationing function on supply $\tilde{l} : Q^N \to -\mathbb{R}_+^{MN}$ with the desired properties is constructed. Since $\dot{l}$ is market independent, it holds that there exist subsets $\dot{l}_j$, $\forall j \in I_N$, of $-\mathbb{R}_+^{*MN}$ such that $l \in \dot{l}$ if and only if $l_j \in \dot{l}_j$, $\forall j \in I_N$. Let some $j' \in I_N$ be given. For every $l_{j'} \in \dot{l}_{j'}$, let the set $I^{-\infty}(l_{j'})$ be defined by $I^{-\infty}(l_{j'}) = \{i \in I_M \mid l^i_{j'} = -\infty\}$ and let the integer $i^{-\infty}(l_{j'})$ be defined by $i^{-\infty}(l_{j'}) = \#I^{-\infty}(l_{j'})$. Let the set K be given by $K = \{k \in I^0_M \mid \exists l_{j'} \in \dot{l}_{j'},\ i^{-\infty}(l_{j'}) = k\}$. Since $\dot{l}$ is flexible, it holds that $0 \in K$ and $M \in K$. For every $k \in K \setminus \{M\}$, let $\alpha(k) \in -\mathbb{R}_+$ be defined by

$$\alpha(k) = \sup\left(\left\{ \textstyle\sum_{i \in I_M \setminus I^{-\infty}(l_{j'})} l^i_{j'} \right| l_{j'} \in \dot{l}_{j'} \text{ and } i^{-\infty}(l_{j'}) = k \left.\right\}\right).$$

Clearly, $\alpha(0) = 0$. Let π be an increasing function from $I_{\#K}$ into K. Notice that π is uniquely determined, $\pi(1) = 0$, and $\pi(\#K) = M$.
Let some $\alpha \in \mathbb{R}$ be given. Let the function $f^\alpha : \{s \in \mathbb{R}^* \mid s \leq \alpha\} \to [0,1]$ be defined by

$$f^\alpha(-\infty) = 1,$$
$$f^\alpha(s) = \tfrac{\alpha - s}{1 + \alpha - s},\ \forall s \in (\leftarrow, \alpha].$$

Notice that $f^\alpha(\alpha) = 0$. Obviously, the inverse of f^α, $(f^\alpha)^{-1} : [0,1] \to \{s \in \mathbb{R}^* \mid s \leq \alpha\}$, is defined by

$$(f^\alpha)^{-1}(t) = \tfrac{t + \alpha(t-1)}{t-1},\ \forall t \in [0,1),$$
$$(f^\alpha)^{-1}(1) = -\infty.$$

Clearly, if $(s^n)_{n \in \mathbb{N}}$ is a sequence in $\{s \in \mathbb{R}^* \mid s \leq \alpha\}$ and s^n converges to some $\bar{s} \in \{s \in \mathbb{R}^* \mid s \leq \alpha\}$, then the sequence $(f^\alpha(s^n))_{n \in \mathbb{N}}$ converges to $f^\alpha(\bar{s})$. Therefore, f^α is a continuous function. Similarly, it can be shown that $(f^\alpha)^{-1}$ is a continuous function.
Now a continuous, injective, and surjective function g is constructed such that with every $l_{j'} \in \dot{l}_{j'}$ a real number of $[0,1]$ is associated. This is achieved by subdividing the unit interval in $\#K = \pi^{-1}(M)$ pieces and constructing the function g such that, for every $l_{j'} \in \dot{l}_{j'}$ with $l_{j'} \neq -\infty^M$,

$$g(l_{j'}) \in [\frac{\pi^{-1}(i^{-\infty}(l_{j'})) - 1}{\pi^{-1}(M) - 1}, \frac{\pi^{-1}(i^{-\infty}(l_{j'}))}{\pi^{-1}(M) - 1}),$$

while $\bar{l}_{j'}, \widehat{l}_{j'} \in \dot{l}_{j'}$ with $\sum_{i \in I_M \setminus I^{-\infty}(\bar{l}_{j'})} \bar{l}^i_{j'} < \sum_{i \in I_M \setminus I^{-\infty}(\hat{l}_{j'})} \widehat{l}^i_{j'}$ implies $g(\bar{l}_{j'}) > g(\widehat{l}_{j'})$. Let the function $g : \dot{l}_{j'} \rightarrow [0,1]$ be defined by

$$g(-\infty^M) = 1,$$

$$g(l_{j'}) = \frac{\pi^{-1}(i^{-\infty}(l_{j'})) - 1}{\pi^{-1}(M) - 1} + \frac{f^{\alpha(i^{-\infty}(l_{j'}))}(\sum_{i \in I_M \setminus I^{-\infty}(l_{j'})} l^i_{j'})}{\pi^{-1}(M) - 1},$$

for every $l_{j'} \in \dot{l}_{j'} \setminus \{-\infty^M\}$. Notice that

$$g(0^M) = \frac{\pi^{-1}(0) - 1}{\pi^{-1}(M) - 1} + \frac{0}{\pi^{-1}(M) - 1} = 0.$$

Now it is shown that g is continuous. Let $((l_{j'})^n)_{n \in \mathbb{N}}$ be a sequence in $\dot{l}_{j'}$ converging to some $\bar{l}_{j'} \in \dot{l}_{j'}$. Suppose the sequence $(g((l_{j'})^n))_{n \in \mathbb{N}}$ does not converge to $g(\bar{l}_{j'})$. From the continuity of $f^{\alpha(k)}$, $\forall k \in K \setminus \{M\}$, and since $i^{-\infty}(\bar{l}_{j'}) = M$ implies $\bar{l}_{j'} = -\infty^M$, it follows that if $i^{-\infty}((l_{j'})^n) = i^{-\infty}(\bar{l}_{j'})$, $\forall n \in \mathbb{N}$, then $g((l_{j'})^n) \rightarrow g(\bar{l}_{j'})$, a contradiction with the supposition that $(g((l_{j'})^n))_{n \in \mathbb{N}}$ does not converge to $g(\bar{l}_{j'})$. Consequently, without loss of generality, $i^{-\infty}((l_{j'})^n) \neq i^{-\infty}(\bar{l}_{j'})$, $\forall n \in \mathbb{N}$. From the weak monotonicity of $\dot{l}$ it follows that, for every $n \in \mathbb{N}$, $I^{-\infty}((l_{j'})^n)$ is a proper subset of $I^{-\infty}(\bar{l}_{j'})$ or $I^{-\infty}(\bar{l}_{j'})$ is a proper subset of $I^{-\infty}((l_{j'})^n)$. Without loss of generality, since $(l_{j'})^n \rightarrow \bar{l}_{j'}$, it holds that, for every $n \in \mathbb{N}$, $I^{-\infty}((l_{j'})^n)$ is a proper subset of $I^{-\infty}(\bar{l}_{j'})$, and, moreover, $\sum_{i \in I_M \setminus I^{-\infty}((l_{j'})^n)} l^{in}_{j'} \rightarrow -\infty$. If $\pi^{-1}(i^{-\infty}((l_{j'})^n)) = \pi^{-1}(i^{-\infty}(\bar{l}_{j'})) - 1$, $\forall n \in \mathbb{N}$, then, since $\dot{l}$ is market independent and weakly monotonic, it follows that $\sum_{i \in I_M \setminus I^{-\infty}(\bar{l}_{j'})} \bar{l}^i_{j'} = \alpha(i^{-\infty}(\bar{l}_{j'}))$ and, since $\sum_{i \in I_M \setminus I^{-\infty}((l_{j'})^n)} l^{in}_{j'} \rightarrow -\infty$, it follows that

$$\begin{aligned} g((l_{j'})^n) &= \frac{\pi^{-1}(i^{-\infty}(\bar{l}_{j'})) - 2}{\pi^{-1}(M) - 1} + \frac{f^{\alpha(i^{-\infty}((l_{j'})^n))}(\sum_{i \in I_M \setminus I^{-\infty}((l_{j'})^n)} l^{in}_{j'})}{\pi^{-1}(M) - 1} \\ &\rightarrow \frac{\pi^{-1}(i^{-\infty}(\bar{l}_{j'})) - 1}{\pi^{-1}(M) - 1} \\ &= \frac{\pi^{-1}(i^{-\infty}(\bar{l}_{j'})) - 1}{\pi^{-1}(M) - 1} + \frac{f^{\alpha(i^{-\infty}(\bar{l}_{j'}))}(\alpha(i^{-\infty}(\bar{l}_{j'})))}{\pi^{-1}(M) - 1} = g(\bar{l}_{j'}), \end{aligned}$$

a contradiction with the supposition that $(g((l_{j'})^n))_{n \in \mathbb{N}}$ does not converge to $g(\bar{l}_{j'})$. Consequently, without loss of generality, for every $n \in \mathbb{N}$, $I^{-\infty}((l_{j'})^n) \subset I^{-\infty}(\bar{l}_{j'})$ and $\pi^{-1}(i^{-\infty}((l_{j'})^n)) < \pi^{-1}(i^{-\infty}(\bar{l}_{j'})) - 1$. So, there exists an element $\widehat{l}_{j'} \in \dot{l}_{j'}$ with $i^{-\infty}(\widehat{l}_{j'}) > i^{-\infty}((l_{j'})^n)$, $\forall n \in \mathbb{N}$, and $i^{-\infty}(\widehat{l}_{j'}) < i^{-\infty}(\bar{l}_{j'})$. Using that $\dot{l}$ is market independent, this leads to a contradiction to the weak monotonicity of $\dot{l}$. Consequently, g is a continuous function.

It is shown that $\dot{l}_{j'}$ is connected in $\mathbb{R}^{*M}$. Suppose $\dot{l}_{j'}$ is not connected in $\mathbb{R}^{*M}$, then there exist two disjoint, non-empty subsets of $\dot{l}_{j'}$, say $\bar{\dot{l}}_{j'}$ and $\widehat{\dot{l}}_{j'}$, both being open in $\dot{l}_{j'}$ and whose union equals $\dot{l}_{j'}$. Obviously, the sets $\dot{l}_1 \times \cdots \times \dot{l}_{j'-1} \times \bar{\dot{l}}_{j'} \times \dot{l}_{j'+1} \times \cdots \times \dot{l}_N$ and $\dot{l}_1 \times \cdots \times \dot{l}_{j'-1} \times \widehat{\dot{l}}_{j'} \times \dot{l}_{j'+1} \times \cdots \times \dot{l}_N$ are two disjoint, non-empty subsets of $\prod_{j \in I_N} \dot{l}_j$, both being open in $\prod_{j \in I_N} \dot{l}_j$, contradicting the connectedness of $\dot{l}$. Consequently, $\dot{l}_{j'}$ is connected in $\mathbb{R}^{*M}$.
Since the function g is continuous and $\dot{l}_{j'}$ is connected in $\mathbb{R}^{*M}$, it follows from Theorem 2.3.13 that $g(\dot{l}_{j'})$ is connected in $[0,1]$ and hence an interval by Theorem 2.3.12. Clearly, $0^M \in \dot{l}_{j'}$ and $-\infty^M \in \dot{l}_{j'}$ since $\dot{l}$ is flexible and market independent. Since $g(0^M) = 0$ and $g(-\infty^M) = 1$, it follows that g is surjective. Next, it is shown that g is injective. Suppose g is not injective, then there exists $\bar{l}_{j'}, \hat{l}_{j'} \in \dot{l}_{j'}$ such that $\bar{l}_{j'} \neq \hat{l}_{j'}$ and $g(\bar{l}_{j'}) = g(\hat{l}_{j'})$. From the definition of g it follows that $i^{-\infty}(\bar{l}_{j'}) = i^{-\infty}(\hat{l}_{j'})$ and $\sum_{i \in I_M \setminus I^{-\infty}(\bar{l}_{j'})} \bar{l}^i_{j'} = \sum_{i \in I_M \setminus I^{-\infty}(\hat{l}_{j'})} \hat{l}^i_{j'}$. This yields a contradiction to the weak monotonicity of $\dot{l}$. Consequently, g is injective.
It is easily verified that the topological spaces Q^M and $\mathbb{R}^{*M}$ are homeomorphic. Therefore, a set closed in $\mathbb{R}^{*M}$ is also compact in $\mathbb{R}^{*M}$ by Theorem 2.3.9. Since $\dot{l}$ is closed in $\mathbb{R}^{*MN}$, it easily follows from the market independence that $\dot{l}_{j'}$ is closed in $\mathbb{R}^{*M}$, hence compact in $\mathbb{R}^{*M}$. Since $\dot{l}_{j'}$ is a compact topological space, $[0,1]$ is a Hausdorff space, and $g : \dot{l}_{j'} \to [0,1]$ is a continuous, injective, and surjective function, it follows from Theorem 2.3.4 that g is a homeomorphism, so $g^{-1} : [0,1] \to \dot{l}_{j'}$ is a continuous function. Let the function $h : [0,1] \to \dot{l}_{j'}$ be defined by $h = g^{-1}$.
The function h would represent $\dot{l}_{j'}$ if its image is a subset of $-\mathbb{R}^M_+$. The function h is now modified in order to guarantee this.
When $K = \{0, M\}$, then there exists $\bar{t} \in (0,1)$ such that, for every $t \in [\bar{t}, 1]$, $h_i(t) < -\omega^i_{j'}$, $\forall i \in I_M$. Let the function $\tilde{l}_{j'} : Q^N \to -\mathbb{R}^M_+$ be defined by

$$\tilde{l}_{j'}(q) = h(\bar{t} q_{j'}), \ \forall q \in Q^N.$$

Now consider the case that $\{0, M\}$ is a proper subset of K. By the weak monotonicity of $\dot{l}$ there exists a uniquely determined proper subset $\bar{I}$ of I_M such that $i^{-\infty}(l_{j'}) = \pi(2)$ for some $l_{j'} \in \dot{l}_{j'}$ implies $I^{-\infty}(l_{j'}) = \bar{I}$. Since the set $[0, \frac{1}{\pi^{-1}(M)-1}]$ is compact and $h_i(t) > -\infty$, $\forall i \in I_M \setminus \bar{I}$, $\forall t \in [0, \frac{1}{\pi^{-1}(M)-1}]$, it holds by Theorem 2.3.14 that for every $i \in I_M \setminus \bar{I}$ the continuous function h_i has a minimum on $[0, \frac{1}{\pi^{-1}(M)-1}]$, say α^i. For every $i \in I_M \setminus \bar{I}$, let the real number $\bar{\alpha}^i$ be defined by $\bar{\alpha}^i = \min(\{\alpha^i, -\omega^i_{j'}\}) - 1$. For every $i \in I_M \setminus \bar{I}$, let the function $\tilde{l}^i_{j'} : Q^N \to -\mathbb{R}_+$ be defined by

$$\tilde{l}^i_{j'}(q) = \max\left(\{\bar{\alpha}^i, h_i(q_{j'})\}\right), \ \forall q \in Q^N. \tag{4.21}$$

Notice that, for every $i \in I_M \setminus \overline{I}$, for every $q \in Q^N$,

$$\tilde{l}^i_{j'}(q) = h_i(q_{j'}) \text{ if } q_{j'} \in [0, \tfrac{1}{\pi^{-1}(M)-1}], \tag{4.22}$$

and, moreover,

$$h_i(q_{j'}) \geq -\omega^i_{j'} \text{ implies } \tilde{l}^i_{j'}(q) = h_i(q_{j'}) \tag{4.23}$$

$$h_i(q_{j'}) < -\omega^i_{j'} \text{ implies } \tilde{l}^i_{j'}(q) < -\omega^i_{j'}. \tag{4.24}$$

Let $\hat{t} \in (0, \frac{1}{\pi^{-1}(M)-1})$ be such that, for every $i \in \overline{I}$,

$$h_i(t) \leq \tfrac{1}{\#\overline{I}} \sum_{i \in I_M \setminus \overline{I}} \overline{\alpha}^i + \min\left(\{0, -\omega^i_{j'}\}\right), \ \forall t \in [\hat{t}, 1]. \tag{4.25}$$

Notice that such a real number $\hat{t}$ exists since h is continuous and $h_i(t) = -\infty$, $\forall i \in \overline{I}$, $\forall t \in [\frac{1}{\pi^{-1}(M)-1}, 1]$. Let $\hat{q}$ be any element of Q^N such that $\hat{q}_{j'} = \hat{t}$. Notice that, for every $i \in \overline{I}$, $h_i(t) < -\omega^i_{j'}$, $\forall t \in [\hat{t}, 1]$. For every $i \in \overline{I}$, let the function $\tilde{l}^i_{j'} : Q^N \to -\mathbb{R}_+$ be defined by

$$\begin{aligned} &\tilde{l}^i_{j'}(q) = h_i(q_{j'}), && \forall q \in Q^N \text{ with } q_{j'} \leq \hat{t}, \\ &\tilde{l}^i_{j'}(q) = h_i(\hat{t}) + \hat{t} - q_{j'} + \tfrac{1}{\#\overline{I}} \textstyle\sum_{i \in I_M \setminus \overline{I}} \left(\tilde{l}^i_{j'}(\hat{q}) - \tilde{l}^i_{j'}(q)\right), && \forall q \in Q^N \text{ with } q_{j'} > \hat{t}. \end{aligned}$$

Notice that, for every $i \in \overline{I}$, $\tilde{l}^i_{j'}$ is continuous and, using (4.25), for every $q \in Q^N$ with $q_{j'} > \hat{t}$,

$$\begin{aligned} \tilde{l}^i_{j'}(q) &= h_i(\hat{t}) + \hat{t} - q_{j'} + \tfrac{1}{\#\overline{I}} \sum_{i \in I_M \setminus \overline{I}} \left(\tilde{l}^i_{j'}(\hat{q}) - \tilde{l}^i_{j'}(q)\right) \\ &< \tfrac{1}{\#\overline{I}} \sum_{i \in I_M \setminus \overline{I}} \overline{\alpha}^i + \min\left(\{0, -\omega^i_{j'}\}\right) - \tfrac{1}{\#\overline{I}} \sum_{i \in I_M \setminus \overline{I}} \tilde{l}^i_{j'}(q) \leq -\omega^i_{j'}, \end{aligned} \tag{4.26}$$

where for the last inequality (4.21) is used.
Using the previous two paragraphs, a rationing function on supply $\tilde{l} : Q^N \to -\mathbb{R}^{MN}_+$ is constructed. Using (4.23), (4.24), and (4.26) it easily follows that $\dot{l}$ is represented by $\tilde{l}$. Obviously, $\tilde{l}$ is flexible, market independent, and continuous. In the case $K = \{0, M\}$ weak monotonicity is easily verified, so consider the case where $\{0, M\}$ is a proper subset of K. Let $q^1, q^2 \in Q^N$ be such that $q^1_{j'} < q^2_{j'} \leq \hat{t}$. Using (4.22) and the construction of h it follows that

$$\sum_{i \in I_M} \tilde{l}^i_{j'}(q^1) = \sum_{i \in I_M} h_i(q^1_{j'}) > \sum_{i \in I_M} h_i(q^2_{j'}) = \sum_{i \in I_M} \tilde{l}^i_{j'}(q^2).$$

Let $q^1, q^2 \in Q^N$ be such that $\widehat{t} \leq q^1_{j'} < q^2_{j'}$. Then

$$\begin{aligned}
\sum_{i \in I_M} \widetilde{l}^i_{j'}(q^1) &= \sum_{i \in I_M \setminus \overline{I}} \widetilde{l}^i_{j'}(q^1) + \sum_{i \in \overline{I}} \left(h_i(\widehat{t}) + \widehat{t} - q^1_{j'}\right) + \sum_{i \in \overline{I}} \tfrac{1}{\#\overline{I}} \sum_{\imath \in I_M \setminus \overline{I}} \left(\widetilde{l}^\imath_{j'}(\widehat{q}) - \widetilde{l}^\imath_{j'}(q^1)\right) \\
&= \sum_{i \in \overline{I}} \left(h_i(\widehat{t}) + \widehat{t} - q^1_{j'}\right) + \sum_{i \in I_M \setminus \overline{I}} \widetilde{l}^i_{j'}(\widehat{q}) \\
&> \sum_{i \in \overline{I}} \left(h_i(\widehat{t}) + \widehat{t} - q^2_{j'}\right) + \sum_{i \in I_M \setminus \overline{I}} \widetilde{l}^i_{j'}(\widehat{q}) \\
&= \sum_{i \in I_M} \widetilde{l}^i_{j'}(q^2).
\end{aligned}$$

Let $q^1, q^2 \in Q^N$ be such that $q^1_{j'} \leq \widehat{t} \leq q^2_{j'}$ and $q^1_{j'} < q^2_{j'}$. Then the two cases considered above immediately yield that $\sum_{i \in I_M} \widetilde{l}^i_{j'}(q^1) > \sum_{i \in I_M} \widetilde{l}^i_{j'}(q^2)$. Therefore, $\widetilde{l}$ is weakly monotonic. So, $\widetilde{l}$ satisfies all the desired properties.
Next, let $\dot{l}$ be a monotonic rationing system on supply. Let some $j' \in I_N$ be given. Construct the continuous, injective, and surjective function $h : [0,1] \to \dot{l}_{j'}$ as in the first part of the proof and, for $\alpha \in \mathrm{I\!R}$, let the function $f^\alpha : \{s \in \mathrm{I\!R}^* \mid s \leq \alpha\} \to [0,1]$ be defined as before. For every $i \in I_M$, let $\alpha^i = \min(\{-\omega^i_{j'}, 0\}) - 1$ and let the function $g^i : -\mathrm{I\!R}^*_+ \to [\alpha^i - 1, 0]$ be defined by

$$\begin{aligned}
g^i(s) &= \alpha^i - f^0(s - \alpha^i), && \forall s \in -\mathrm{I\!R}^*_+ \setminus \left[\alpha^i, 0\right], \\
g^i(s) &= s, && \forall s \in \left[\alpha^i, 0\right].
\end{aligned}$$

Let the function $\widetilde{l}_{j'} : Q^N \to -\mathrm{I\!R}^M_+$ be defined by

$$\widetilde{l}_{j'}(q) = \left(g^1\left(h_1(q_{j'})\right), \ldots, g^M\left(h_M(q_{j'})\right)\right)^\top, \ \forall q \in Q^N.$$

In this way a rationing function on supply $\widetilde{l} : Q^N \to -\mathrm{I\!R}^{MN}_+$ is constructed. It is easily verified that $\dot{l}$ is represented by $\widetilde{l}$ and that $\widetilde{l}$ is flexible, market independent, continuous, and monotonic. Q.E.D.

The proof for the results concerning the rationing system on demand given in Theorem 4.5.17 is similar.

Theorem 4.5.17
Let the rationing system on demand $\dot{L}$ be flexible, market independent, closed, and connected. If the rationing system on demand $\dot{L}$ is weakly monotonic, then $\dot{L}$ can be represented by a flexible, market independent, continuous, and weakly

monotonic rationing function on demand. If the rationing system on demand $\dot{L}$ is monotonic, then $\dot{L}$ can be represented by a flexible, market independent, continuous, and monotonic rationing function on demand.

The last four results show that the set of admissible rationing schemes can be described equally well by means of a rationing system as by a rationing function and they provide necessary and sufficient conditions that make a representation possible.

4.6 CONSTRAINED EQUILIBRIA

The introduction of the set of admissible price systems in Section 4.4 and of the set of admissible rationing schemes in Section 4.5 completes the description of the economy. So, formally, the *economy* $\tilde{\mathcal{E}}$ is defined by a specification of the consumption sets, preference relations, and initial endowments of all the consumers, the set of admissible price systems, and the rationing system, i.e.

$$\tilde{\mathcal{E}} = \left((X^i, \preceq^i, \omega^i)_{i \in I_M}, P_{(\underline{p},\overline{p})}, \left(\dot{l}, \dot{L}\right) \right).$$

The relation $\zeta : P_{(\underline{p},\overline{p})} \times \dot{l} \times \dot{L} \to \mathbb{R}^N$, defined by

$$\zeta(p,l,L) = \sum_{i \in I_M} \left(\delta^i(p,l^i,L^i) - \{\omega^i\}\right), \ \forall (p,l,L) \in P_{(\underline{p},\overline{p})} \times \dot{l} \times \dot{L},$$

is called the *total excess demand relation* of the economy $\tilde{\mathcal{E}}$ and the set $\zeta(p,l,L)$ is called the *total excess demand* at $(p,l,L) \in P_{(\underline{p},\overline{p})} \times \dot{l} \times \dot{L}$ of the economy $\tilde{\mathcal{E}}$. Notice that $\zeta(p,l,L) = \emptyset$ at $(p,l,L) \in P_{(\underline{p},\overline{p})} \times \dot{l} \times \dot{L}$ if $\delta^i(p,l^i,L^i) = \emptyset$ for some consumer $i \in I_M$. In this section the economy $\tilde{\mathcal{E}} = ((X^i, \preceq^i, \omega^i)_{i \in I_M}, P_{(\underline{p},\overline{p})}, (\dot{l}, \dot{L}))$ is assumed to be given. An element $(p,l,L,x) \in P_{(\underline{p},\overline{p})} \times \dot{l} \times \dot{L} \times X$ is called a *state* of $\tilde{\mathcal{E}}$ if $x^i \in \delta^i(p,l^i,L^i)$, $\forall i \in I_M$, so a state of the economy $\tilde{\mathcal{E}}$ consists of a specification of an admissible price system, an admissible rationing scheme, and an optimal consumption bundle at this price system and rationing scheme for every consumer in the economy $\tilde{\mathcal{E}}$. The *total excess demand* at a state (p,l,L,x) of the economy $\tilde{\mathcal{E}}$ is given by $z = \sum_{i \in I_M} x^i - \sum_{i \in I_M} \omega^i$, hence $z \in \zeta(p,l,L)$. The actions chosen by the consumers in a state of the economy are not necessarily compatible in the sense that the total excess demand at this state is not equal to zero. In a *constrained equilibrium* of the economy $\tilde{\mathcal{E}}$ the state of $\tilde{\mathcal{E}}$ is such that the total excess demand is zero, so the optimal actions of the consumers yield an attainable allocation of $\tilde{\mathcal{E}}$. Moreover, the price system and the rationing scheme have to satisfy certain properties in a constrained equilibrium. The following definition of a constrained equilibrium is closely related to the one given in Drèze (1975).

Definition 4.6.1 (Constrained equilibrium)
A constrained equilibrium of the economy $\tilde{\mathcal{E}} = ((X^i, \preceq^i, \omega^i)_{i \in I_M}, P_{(\underline{p},\overline{p})}, (\dot{l}, \dot{L}))$ *is an element*

$$(p^*, l^*, L^*, x^*) \in P_{(\underline{p},\overline{p})} \times \dot{l} \times \dot{L} \times X$$

satisfying

1. *for every consumer* $i \in I_M$, $x^{*i} \in \delta^i(p^*, l^{*i}, L^{*i})$,
2. $\sum_{i \in I_M} x^{*i} - \sum_{i \in I_M} \omega^i = 0^N$,
3. *for every commodity* $j \in I_N$, $x_j^{*i'} - \omega_j^{i'} = l_j^{*i'}$ *for some consumer* $i' \in I_M$ *implies* $x_j^{*i} - \omega_j^i < L_j^{*i}$, $\forall i \in I_M$, *and* $x_j^{*i'} - \omega_j^{i'} = L_j^{*i'}$ *for some consumer* $i' \in I_M$ *implies* $x_j^{*i} - \omega_j^i > l_j^{*i}$, $\forall i \in I_M$,
4. *for every commodity* $j \in I_N$, $p_j^* > \underline{p}_j$ *implies* $l_j^{*i} < x_j^{*i} - \omega_j^i$, $\forall i \in I_M$, *and* $p_j^* < \overline{p}_j$ *implies* $L_j^{*i} > x_j^{*i} - \omega_j^i$, $\forall i \in I_M$.

When (p^*, l^*, L^*, x^*) is a constrained equilibrium of the economy $\tilde{\mathcal{E}}$, then p^* is called a *constrained equilibrium price system,* (l^*, L^*) is called a *constrained equilibrium rationing scheme,* and x^* is called a *constrained equilibrium allocation.* The set of constrained equilibria of the economy $\tilde{\mathcal{E}}$ is denoted by $\tilde{E}$.

The first condition in Definition 4.6.1 reflects that every consumer chooses an optimal consumption bundle at the constrained equilibrium price system and the constrained equilibrium rationing scheme, and the second condition that the constrained equilibrium allocation is an attainable allocation of the economy $\tilde{\mathcal{E}}$. These two conditions correspond to Condition 2 and Condition 3 of Definition 3.8.1. Condition 3 of Definition 4.6.1 implies that markets are *frictionless,* i.e. if the consumption set of every consumer is convex and the preference relation of every consumer is complete and convex, then, by Theorem 4.3.3, it does not occur in any market that simultaneously a consumer is rationed on his supply, while another consumer is rationed on his demand. In the case where these conditions on the consumption sets and preference relations are not satisfied, it is probably more natural to replace Condition 3 of Definition 4.6.1 by the stronger condition that, for every $j \in I_N$, $l^*_j = -\infty^M$ or $L^*_j = +\infty^M$.

If the consumption set of every consumer is convex and the preference relation of every consumer is complete and convex, then Condition 4 of Definition 4.6.1 implies that there is no demand rationing in the market for a commodity $j \in I_N$ if the price of commodity j is not equal to the upper bound on the price of commodity j, and, similarly, supply rationing does not occur in the market for commodity j if the price of commodity j is greater than the lower bound on the price of commodity j. If these conditions on the consumption sets and preference relations are not satisfied, then it is probably more natural to replace Condition 4 of Definition 4.6.1 by the stronger condition that, for every $j \in I_N$, $p^*_j > \underline{p}_j$ implies $l^*_j = -\infty^M$, and $p^*_j < \overline{p}_j$ implies $L^*_j = +\infty^M$.

Notice that if (p^*, l^*, L^*, x^*) is a constrained equilibrium of the economy $\widetilde{\mathcal{E}}$, then $0^N \in \zeta(p^*, l^*, L^*)$. Furthermore, it should be noticed that the actions taken by the agents in the economy $\widetilde{\mathcal{E}}$ are not necessarily completely decentralized at a constrained equilibrium. This may be the case when there is a consumer having more than one optimal action, while not every optimal action is compatible with a constrained equilibrium.

Consider a state (p, l, L, x) of the economy $\widetilde{\mathcal{E}}$ and a commodity $j \in I_N$. When a consumer $i \in I_M$ is rationed on his supply in the market for commodity j at (p, l^i, L^i), while another consumer is rationed on his demand in the market for commodity j, then, under weak assumptions (as in Theorem 4.3.3), the first consumer is willing to supply more of commodity j, while the second consumer is willing to demand more of commodity j. Such a situation is incompatible with an equilibrium state of the economy, and therefore Condition 3 of Definition 4.6.1 is needed. Consider the case where $\sum_{i \in I_M} x^i_j - \sum_{i \in I_M} \omega^i_j > 0$, i.e. there is a positive excess demand of commodity j at this state. It has been explained in Section 3.8 that the price of commodity j has a tendency to rise in such a situation. If $p_j = \overline{p}_j$, then this is impossible. However, if a consumer $i \in I_M$ is rationed on his supply in the market for commodity j at (p, l^i, L^i), then this consumer is willing to supply more of commodity j. When the total excess demand of commodity j is indeed positive, then this additional supply can be absorbed in the market for commodity j. Therefore, l^i_j has a tendency to decrease. Furthermore, L^i_j has a tendency to fall for every consumer $i \in I_M$ since there is not enough supply to satisfy the demand of all the consumers. Using a similar reasoning as before it follows that if there is a negative total excess demand of commodity j at the state (p, l, L, x), then the price has a tendency to fall, unless $p_j = \underline{p}_j$, while l^i_j and L^i_j have a tendency to rise for every consumer $i \in I_M$. This motivates Condition 2 of Definition 4.6.1, the total excess demand should be equal to zero at an equilibrium state of the economy. Finally, consider the case where the total excess demand of commodity j is zero at the state (p, l, L, x). If $p_j < \overline{p}_j$ and a consumer $i \in I_M$ is rationed on his demand in the market for commodity j at (p, l^i, L^i), then this consumer can offer a price that is slightly higher than p_j, thereby attracting all the supply and making it possible to weaken the rationing on his demand. Therefore, demand rationing in the market for commodity j at a state (p, l, L, x), while $p_j < \overline{p}_j$, is incompatible with (p, l, L, x) being an equilibrium state of the economy. A similar argument leads to the statement that supply rationing in the market for commodity j at a state (p, l, L, x), while $p_j > \underline{p}_j$, is incompatible with (p, l, L, x) being an equilibrium state of the economy. This motivates Condition 4 of Definition 4.6.1.

The following definitions are inspired by Theorem 4.3.3.

Definition 4.6.2 (Equivalent constrained equilibria)
A constrained equilibrium (p^*, l^*, L^*, x^*) *of the economy* $\widetilde{\mathcal{E}}^1 = ((X^i, \preceq^i, \omega^i)_{i \in I_M}, P_{(\underline{p},\overline{p})}, (\overline{l}, \overline{L}))$ *is* equivalent *to a constrained equilibrium* $(\widehat{p}^*, \widehat{l}^*, \widehat{L}^*, \widehat{x}^*)$ *of the economy* $\widetilde{\mathcal{E}}^2 = ((X^i, \preceq^i, \omega^i)_{i \in I_M}, P_{(\underline{p},\overline{p})}, (\widehat{l}, \widehat{L}))$, *denoted by* $(p^*, l^*, L^*, x^*) \sim (\widehat{p}^*, \widehat{l}^*, \widehat{L}^*, \widehat{x}^*)$, *if* $p^* = \widehat{p}^*$, $x^* = \widehat{x}^*$, *and, for every* $i \in I_M$, *for every* $j \in I_N$,

$$\begin{aligned} l_j^{*i} &= x_j^{*i} - \omega_j^i \text{ implies } \widehat{l}_j^{*i} = l_j^{*i}, \\ l_j^{*i} &< x_j^{*i} - \omega_j^i \text{ implies } \widehat{l}_j^{*i} < \widehat{x}_j^{*i} - \omega_j^i, \\ L_j^{*i} &= x_j^{*i} - \omega_j^i \text{ implies } \widehat{L}_j^{*i} = L_j^{*i}, \\ L_j^{*i} &> x_j^{*i} - \omega_j^i \text{ implies } \widehat{L}_j^{*i} > \widehat{x}_j^{*i} - \omega_j^i. \end{aligned}$$

So, two constrained equilibria are equivalent if the constrained equilibrium price system is the same, the constrained equilibrium allocation is the same, and only non-binding rationing schemes are allowed to be different.

Definition 4.6.3 (Equivalent economies)
The economy $\widetilde{\mathcal{E}}^1 = ((X^i, \preceq^i, \omega^i)_{i \in I_M}, P_{(\underline{p},\overline{p})}, (\overline{l}, \overline{L}))$ *is* equivalent *to the economy* $\widetilde{\mathcal{E}}^2 = ((X^i, \preceq^i, \omega^i)_{i \in I_M}, P_{(\underline{p},\overline{p})}, (\widehat{l}, \widehat{L}))$, *denoted by* $\widetilde{\mathcal{E}}^1 \sim \widetilde{\mathcal{E}}^2$, *if for every* $(p^*, l^*, L^*, x^*) \in \widetilde{E}^1$ *there exists* $(\widehat{p}^*, \widehat{l}^*, \widehat{L}^*, \widehat{x}^*) \in \widetilde{E}^2$ *such that* $(p^*, l^*, L^*, x^*) \sim (\widehat{p}^*, \widehat{l}^*, \widehat{L}^*, \widehat{x}^*)$ *and for every* $(\widehat{p}^*, \widehat{l}^*, \widehat{L}^*, \widehat{x}^*) \in \widetilde{E}^2$ *there exists* $(p^*, l^*, L^*, x^*) \in$

$\tilde{E}^2$ such that $(\hat{p}^*, \hat{l}^*, \hat{L}^*, \hat{x}^*) \sim (p^*, l^*, L^*, x^*)$, where $\tilde{E}^1$ denotes the set of constrained equilibria of the economy $\tilde{\mathcal{E}}^1$ and $\tilde{E}^2$ denotes the set of constrained equilibria of the economy $\tilde{\mathcal{E}}^2$.

It is easily verified that the binary relation on the set of all possible constrained equilibria of economies, only differing with respect to the rationing system, induced by $\sim$ of Definition 4.6.2 is an equivalence relation. Similarly, the binary relation on the set of economies, only differing with respect to the rationing system, induced by $\sim$ of Definition 4.6.3 is an equivalence relation.

It is easily seen that in general a constrained equilibrium is not unique and that from the point of view of the consumer many constrained equilibria do not differ from each other in the sense that they are equivalent.

Theorem 4.6.4
Let the economy $\tilde{\mathcal{E}} = ((X^i, \preceq^i, \omega^i)_{i \in I_M}, P_{(\underline{p},\overline{p})}, (\dot{l}, \dot{L}))$ be such that for every consumer $i \in I_M$ the consumption set X^i is convex and the preference relation $\preceq^i$ is complete, transitive, and convex. Let (p^*, l^*, L^*, x^*) be a constrained equilibrium of the economy $\tilde{\mathcal{E}}$. Let the rationing scheme $(\overline{l}, \overline{L}) \in -\mathbb{R}_+^{*MN} \times \mathbb{R}_+^{*MN}$ be such that, for every $i \in I_M$, for every $j \in I_N$,

$$\begin{aligned}
l_j^{*i} &= x_j^{*i} - \omega_j^i \text{ implies } \overline{l}_j^i = l_j^{*i}, \\
l_j^{*i} &< x_j^{*i} - \omega_j^i \text{ implies } \overline{l}_j^i < x_j^{*i} - \omega_j^i, \\
L_j^{*i} &= x_j^{*i} - \omega_j^i \text{ implies } \overline{L}_j^i = L_j^{*i}, \\
L_j^{*i} &> x_j^{*i} - \omega_j^i \text{ implies } \overline{L}_j^i > x_j^{*i} - \omega_j^i.
\end{aligned}$$

Then $(p^*, \overline{l}, \overline{L}, x^*)$ satisfies Conditions 1-4 of Definition 4.6.1 of a constrained equilibrium of the economy $\tilde{\mathcal{E}}$. If, moreover, $(\overline{l}, \overline{L}) \in \dot{l} \times \dot{L}$, then $(p^*, \overline{l}, \overline{L}, x^*)$ is a constrained equilibrium of the economy $\tilde{\mathcal{E}}$ and $(p^*, l^*, L^*, x^*) \sim (p^*, \overline{l}, \overline{L}, x^*)$.

Proof
Suppose there exists $i' \in I_M$ such that $x^{*i'} \notin \delta^{i'}(p^*, \overline{l}^{i'}, \overline{L}^{i'})$. It is obvious that $x^{*i'} \in \beta^{i'}(p^*, \overline{l}^{i'}, \overline{L}^{i'})$. Hence, $x^{*i'} \prec^{i'} \overline{x}^{i'}$ for some $\overline{x}^{i'} \in \beta^{i'}(p^*, \overline{l}^{i'}, \overline{L}^{i'})$. Since $\overline{x}^{i'} \notin \beta^{i'}(p^*, l^{*i'}, L^{*i'})$ and $\overline{x}^{i'} \in \beta^{i'}(p^*, \overline{l}^{i'}, \overline{L}^{i'})$, it has to hold that $\overline{l}_j^{i'} \leq \overline{x}_j^{i'} - \omega_j^{i'} < l_j^{*i'}$ for some $j \in I_N$, or $L_j^{*i'} < \overline{x}_j^{i'} - \omega_j^{i'} \leq \overline{L}_j^{i'}$ for some $j \in I_N$. Moreover, using the construction of $(\overline{l}, \overline{L})$, it follows for every $j \in I_N$ that

$$\text{if } \overline{x}_j^{i'} - \omega_j^{i'} < l_j^{*i'}, \text{ then } l_j^{*i'} < x_j^{*i'} - \omega_j^{i'}, \tag{4.27}$$

$$\text{if } \overline{x}_j^{i'} - \omega_j^{i'} > L_j^{*i'}, \text{ then } L_j^{*i'} > x_j^{*i'} - \omega_j^{i'}. \tag{4.28}$$

For every $\lambda \in (0,1]$, let the consumption bundle $\overline{x}^{i'}(\lambda)$ be defined by

$$\overline{x}^{i'}(\lambda) = \lambda \overline{x}^{i'} + (1-\lambda)\, x^{*i'}.$$

From Lemma 4.2.1 it follows that $\beta^{i'}(p^*, \overline{l}^{i'}, \overline{L}^{i'})$ is convex, so, for every $\lambda \in [0,1]$, $\overline{x}^{i'}(\lambda) \in \beta^{i'}(p^*, \overline{l}^{i'}, \overline{L}^{i'})$. Moreover, $x^{*i'} \prec^{i'} \overline{x}^{i'}(\lambda)$, $\forall \lambda \in (0,1]$. However, there exists $\overline{\lambda} \in (0,1)$ such that $\lambda \in (0, \overline{\lambda}]$ implies $\overline{x}^{i'}(\lambda) \in \beta^{i'}(p^*, l^{*i'}, L^{*i'})$, using (4.27), (4.28), and the fact that $\overline{x}^{i'}(\lambda) \in \beta^{i'}(p^*, \overline{l}^{i'}, \overline{L}^{i'})$. Since $x^{*i'} \prec^{i'} \overline{x}^{i'}(\lambda)$, $\forall \lambda \in (0, \overline{\lambda}]$, this implies $x^{*i'} \notin \delta^{i'}(p^*, l^{*i'}, L^{*i'})$, a contradiction. Consequently, Condition 1 of Definition 4.6.1 is satisfied by $(p^*, \overline{l}, \overline{L}, x^*)$.
Since (p^*, l^*, L^*, x^*) is a constrained equilibrium, it follows that

$$\sum_{i \in I_M} x^{*i} - \sum_{i \in I_M} \omega^i = 0^N,$$

so Condition 2 of Definition 4.6.1 is satisfied by $(p^*, \overline{l}, \overline{L}, x^*)$.
That $(p^*, \overline{l}, \overline{L}, x^*)$ satisfies Conditions 3 and 4 of Definition 4.6.1 follows immediately from the definition of $\overline{l}$ and $\overline{L}$. If, moreover, $(\overline{l}, \overline{L}) \in \dot{l} \times \dot{L}$, then $(p^*, \overline{l}, \overline{L}, x^*) \in P_{(\underline{p},\overline{p})} \times \dot{l} \times \dot{L} \times X$ and, hence, $(p^*, \overline{l}, \overline{L}, x^*)$ is a constrained equilibrium of the economy $\widetilde{\mathcal{E}}$ satisfying $(p^*, \overline{l}, \overline{L}, x^*) \sim (p^*, l^*, L^*, x^*)$. Q.E.D.

The following theorem clarifies the relationship between equivalent economies and equivalent rationing systems.

Theorem 4.6.5
Let the economies $\widetilde{\mathcal{E}}^1 = ((X^i, \preceq^i, \omega^i)_{i \in I_M}, P_{(\underline{p},\overline{p})}, (\dot{\overline{l}}, \dot{\overline{L}}))$ *and* $\widetilde{\mathcal{E}}^2 = ((X^i, \preceq^i, \omega^i)_{i \in I_M}, P_{(\underline{p},\overline{p})}, (\dot{\widehat{l}}, \dot{\widehat{L}}))$ *be such that for every consumer* $i \in I_M$ *the preference relation* $\preceq^i$ *is complete, transitive, and convex, the consumption set* X^i *is convex and* $X^i \subset \mathbb{R}^N_+$, *and* $(\dot{\overline{l}}, \dot{\overline{L}}) \sim (\dot{\widehat{l}}, \dot{\widehat{L}})$. *Then the economy* $\widetilde{\mathcal{E}}^1$ *is equivalent to the economy* $\widetilde{\mathcal{E}}^2$.

Proof
Let (p^*, l^*, L^*, x^*) be an element of $\widetilde{E}^1$, the set of constrained equilibria of $\widetilde{\mathcal{E}}^1$, and let $(\widehat{l}, \widehat{L}) \in \dot{\widehat{l}} \times \dot{\widehat{L}}$ be such that $(l^*, L^*) \sim (\widehat{l}, \widehat{L})$.
If, for some $i \in I_M$, for some $j \in I_N$, $l^{*i}_j = x^{*i}_j - \omega^i_j$, then, since $X^i \subset \mathbb{R}^N_+$, it holds that $l^{*i}_j \geq -\omega^i_j$, and, since $l^* \sim \widehat{l}$, it follows that $\widehat{l}^i_j = l^{*i}_j$.
If, for some $i \in I_M$, for some $j \in I_N$, $l^{*i}_j < x^{*i}_j - \omega^i_j$, then either $l^{*i}_j \geq -\omega^i_j$ and in this case $l^* \sim \widehat{l}$ implies $\widehat{l}^i_j = l^{*i}_j < x^{*i}_j - \omega^i_j$, or $l^{*i}_j < -\omega^i_j$ and in this case $l^* \sim \widehat{l}$ and $X^i \subset \mathbb{R}^N_+$ implies $\widehat{l}^i_j < -\omega^i_j \leq x^{*i}_j - \omega^i_j$.

If, for some $i \in I_M$, for some $j \in I_N$, $L_j^{*i} = x_j^{*i} - \omega_j^i$, then $X^i \subset \mathbb{R}_+^N$ implies

$$L_j^{*i} \leq \sum_{i \in I_M} x_j^{*i} - \omega_j^i = \widetilde{\omega}_j - \omega_j^i,$$

where for the equality Condition 2 of Definition 4.6.1 is used. This together with $L^* \sim \widehat{L}$ implies $\widehat{L}_j^i = L_j^{*i}$. If, for some $i \in I_M$, for some $j \in I_N$, $L_j^{*i} > x_j^{*i} - \omega_j^i$, then either $L_j^{*i} \leq \widetilde{\omega}_j - \omega_j^i$ and in this case $L^* \sim \widehat{L}$ implies $\widehat{L}_j^i = L_j^{*i} > x_j^{*i} - \omega_j^i$, or $L_j^{*i} > \widetilde{\omega}_j - \omega_j^i$ and in this case $L^* \sim \widehat{L}$ implies

$$\widehat{L}_j^i > \widetilde{\omega}_j - \omega_j^i = \sum_{i \in I_M} x_j^{*i} - \omega_j^i \geq x_j^{*i} - \omega_j^i,$$

where for the equality Condition 2 of Definition 4.6.1 is used, and for the last inequality the assumption that $X^i \subset \mathbb{R}_+^N$.
Therefore, by Theorem 4.6.4, $(p^*, \widehat{l}, \widehat{L}, x^*) \in \widetilde{E}^2$, the set of constrained equilibria of the economy $\widetilde{\mathcal{E}}^2$, and $(p^*, l^*, L^*, x^*) \sim (p^*, \widehat{l}, \widehat{L}, x^*)$ according to Definition 4.6.2.
Similarly, it can be shown that for every $(\widehat{p}^*, \widehat{l}^*, \widehat{L}^*, \widehat{x}^*) \in \widetilde{E}^2$ there exists $(\bar{l}, \bar{L}) \in \dot{l} \times \dot{L}$ such that $(\widehat{p}^*, \bar{l}, \bar{L}, \widehat{x}^*) \in \widetilde{E}^1$ and $(\widehat{p}^*, \widehat{l}^*, \widehat{L}^*, \widehat{x}^*) \sim (\widehat{p}^*, \bar{l}, \bar{L}, \widehat{x}^*)$. So, $\widetilde{\mathcal{E}}^1 \sim \widetilde{\mathcal{E}}^2$.
Q.E.D.

If the rationing system $(\dot{l}, \dot{L})$ of the economy $\widetilde{\mathcal{E}} = ((X^i, \preceq^i, \omega^i)_{i \in I_M}, P_{(\underline{p}, \overline{p})}, (\dot{l}, \dot{L}))$ is represented by the rationing function $(\widetilde{l}, \widetilde{L})$, then Theorem 4.6.5 implies that there is no loss of generality in considering the constrained equilibria of the economy obtained by replacing the rationing system $(\dot{l}, \dot{L})$ by the rationing system $(\widetilde{l}(Q^N), \widetilde{L}(Q^N))$. In the remainder of the monograph, it is always assumed that the rationing system is described by the rationing function $(\widetilde{l}, \widetilde{L})$. Therefore, from now on the economy $\widetilde{\mathcal{E}}$ is defined by a specification of the consumption sets, preference relations, and initial endowments of all the consumers, the set of admissible price systems, and the rationing function, so

$$\widetilde{\mathcal{E}} = \left((X^i, \preceq^i, \omega^i)_{i \in I_M}, P_{(\underline{p}, \overline{p})}, \left(\widetilde{l}, \widetilde{L}\right) \right).$$

4.7 THE EXISTENCE OF CONSTRAINED EQUILIBRIA

In this section the economy $\widetilde{\mathcal{E}} = ((X^i, \preceq^i, \omega^i)_{i \in I_M}, P_{(\underline{p},\overline{p})}, (\widetilde{l}, \widetilde{L}))$ is assumed to be given. With respect to the economy $\widetilde{\mathcal{E}}$ the following assumptions are often made in the remainder of this chapter.

A1. For every consumer $i \in I_M$, the consumption set X^i is non-empty, closed, convex, $X^i \subset \mathbb{R}^N_+$, and $X^i + \mathbb{R}^N_+ \subset X^i$.

A2. For every consumer $i \in I_M$, the preference relation $\preceq^i$ is complete, transitive, continuous, weakly monotonic, and convex.

A3. For every consumer $i \in I_M$, the initial endowment ω^i belongs to $\text{int}(X^i)$.

A4. The set of admissible price systems, $P_{(\underline{p},\overline{p})}$, is such that $0^N \ll \underline{p} \leq \overline{p} \ll +\infty^N$.

A5. The rationing function $(\widetilde{l}, \widetilde{L})$ is flexible, market independent, and continuous.

The requirement of weak monotonicity of the preference relation is weaker than the assumption usually made in this stream of the literature, where strong monotonicity with respect to some subset of commodities is made. The assumption with respect to the set of admissible price systems is motivated by Theorems 3.8.2 and 3.11.1 stating that a *Walrasian equilibrium* price system is non-negative. In Chapter 8 it is shown that Assumption A4 can be weakened in some cases. However, it will be shown by means of examples that Assumption A4 is crucial for giving a complete classification of constrained equilibria as is done in this chapter.

Let the economy $\widetilde{\mathcal{E}}$ satisfy Assumptions A1-A5. Let some commodity $j \in I_N$ be given. Consider the state of the market for commodity j in a constrained equilibrium (p^*, l^*, L^*, x^*) of the economy $\widetilde{\mathcal{E}}$. Let $q^{*1} \in Q^N$ be such that $l^* \sim \widetilde{l}(q^{*1})$ and let $q^{*2} \in Q^N$ satisfy $L^* \sim \widetilde{L}(q^{*2})$. By Conditions 3 and 4 of Definition 4.6.1 there are three mutually exclusive possibilities in the market for commodity j. First, it may happen that there exists $i' \in I_M$ such that $x_j^{*i'} - \omega_j^{i'} = l_j^{*i'}$, so $0 \leq q_j^{*1} < 1$. Then, by Condition 3 of Definition 4.6.1, $x_j^{*i} - \omega_j^i < L_j^{*i}$, $\forall i \in I_M$, so there is no demand rationing in the market for commodity j according to Theorem 4.3.3. Since the rationing function is flexible and market independent by Assumption A5 and using Theorem 4.6.4, there is no loss of generality in assuming that $q_j^{*2} = 1$. Moreover, by Condition 4 of Definition 4.6.1, $p_j^* = \underline{p}_j$. So, the state of the market for commodity j is in this case completely determined by the value of q_j^{*1}. The second possibility is that $l_j^{*i} < x_j^{*i} - \omega_j^i < L_j^{*i}$, $\forall i \in I_M$, so there is no rationing in the market for commodity j according to Theorem 4.3.3. Since the rationing function is flexible and market independent by Assumption A5 and using Theorem 4.6.4, there is no loss of generality in assuming that $q_j^{*1} = 1$ and $q_j^{*2} = 1$. Clearly, the price of commodity j is between $\underline{p}_j$ and $\overline{p}_j$, so $\underline{p}_j \leq p_j^* \leq \overline{p}_j$. The state of the market for commodity j is completely determined by the value of p_j^*. Finally, the third possibility is that there exists $i' \in I_M$ such that $x_j^{*i'} - \omega_j^{i'} = L_j^{*i'}$, so $0 \leq q_j^{*2} < 1$. Then, by Condition 3 of Definition 4.6.1, $x_j^{*i} - \omega_j^i > l_j^{*i}$, $\forall i \in I_M$, so according to Theorem 4.3.3 there is no supply rationing in the market for commodity j. Since the rationing function is flexible and market independent by Assumption A5 and using Theorem 4.6.4, there is no loss of generality in assuming that $q_j^{*1} = 1$. The state of the market for commodity j is completely determined by the value of q_j^{*2}.

Let some commodity $j \in I_N$ be given. Motivated by the remarks in the paragraph above, any of the three possible regimes in the market for commodity j is described by one parameter $q_j \in [0,1]$. If $0 \leq q_j < \frac{1}{3}$, then the first possibility described above occurs with price $p_j = \underline{p}_j$ and rationing scheme $(l_j, L_j) = (\tilde{l}_j(q^1), \tilde{L}_j(q^2))$, where $q_j^1 = 3q_j$ and $q_j^2 = 1$. If $\frac{1}{3} \leq q_j \leq \frac{2}{3}$, then the second possibility results with price $p_j = \underline{p}_j(2-3q_j) + \overline{p}_j(3q_j - 1)$ and rationing scheme $(l_j, L_j) = (\tilde{l}_j(q^1), \tilde{L}_j(q^2))$, where $q_j^1 = 1$ and $q_j^2 = 1$. If $\frac{2}{3} < q_j \leq 1$, then the third possibility occurs with price $p_j = \overline{p}_j$ and rationing scheme $(l_j, L_j) = (\tilde{l}_j(q^1), \tilde{L}_j(q^2))$, where $q_j^1 = 1$ and $q_j^2 = 3 - 3q_j$. Therefore, for every $j \in I_N$, component j of the function $\widehat{p} : Q^N \to P_{(\underline{p},\overline{p})}$ is defined by

$$\widehat{p}_j(q) = \max\left(\{\underline{p}_j, \min(\{\underline{p}_j(2-3q_j) + \overline{p}_j(3q_j - 1), \overline{p}_j\})\}\right), \ \forall q \in Q^N. \tag{4.29}$$

The functions $\widehat{l} : Q^N \to -\mathbb{R}_+^{MN}$ and $\widehat{L} : Q^N \to \mathbb{R}_+^{MN}$ are defined by

$$\widehat{l}(q) = \tilde{l}\left(\inf(\{1^N, 3q\})\right), \qquad \forall q \in Q^N, \tag{4.30}$$

$$\widehat{L}(q) = \tilde{L}\left(\inf(\{1^N, 31^N - 3q\})\right), \ \forall q \in Q^N. \tag{4.31}$$

The notational conventions used for $\tilde{l}$ and $\tilde{L}$ are also used for $\widehat{l}$ and $\widehat{L}$. Since, for every $j \in I_N$, for every $q \in Q^N$, $q_j \in [0,1]$ uniquely determines the state $(\widehat{p}_j(q), \widehat{l}_j(q), \widehat{L}_j(q))$ in the market for commodity j, q_j is also called the *state* of the market for commodity j, while the vector q itself is often called the *state* of the markets. For every consumer $i \in I_M$, the relation $\gamma^i : P_{(\underline{p},\overline{p})} \to \mathbb{R}^N$ is defined by

$$\gamma^i(p) = \{x^i \in X^i \,|p \cdot x^i = p \cdot \omega^i\}, \ \forall p \in P_{(\underline{p},\overline{p})},$$

and the relation $\widehat{\delta}^i : Q^N \to \mathbb{R}^N$, $\forall i \in I_M$, and the relation $\widehat{\zeta} : Q^N \to \mathbb{R}^N$, are defined by

$$\begin{aligned} \widehat{\delta}^i(q) &= \delta^i\left(\widehat{p}(q), \widehat{l}^i(q), \widehat{L}^i(q)\right) \cap \gamma^i\left(\widehat{p}(q)\right), \ \forall q \in Q^N, \\ \widehat{\zeta}(q) &= \textstyle\sum_{i \in I_M} \widehat{\delta}^i(q) - \sum_{i \in I_M}\{\omega^i\}, \qquad \forall q \in Q^N. \end{aligned}$$

The relation $\widehat{\delta}^i$ is called the *reduced demand relation* of consumer $i \in I_M$ and the relation $\widehat{\zeta}$ is called the *reduced total excess demand relation* of the economy $\widetilde{\mathcal{E}}$. If the preference relation of a consumer $i \in I_M$ is strongly monotonic, then it holds that $\widehat{\delta}^i(q) = \delta^i(\widehat{p}(q), \widehat{l}^i(q), \widehat{L}^i(q))$, $\forall q \in Q^N$. Irrespective of the assumptions made with respect to the economy, it is clear that if (p^*, l^*, L^*, x^*) is a constrained equilibrium of the economy $\widetilde{\mathcal{E}}$, then $x^{*i} \in \gamma^i(p^*)$, $\forall i \in I_M$, by Condition 2 of Definition 4.6.1. Theorem 4.7.1 makes clear that the relations $\widehat{\delta}^i$, $\forall i \in I_M$, are very useful in showing the existence of constrained equilibria.

Theorem 4.7.1
Let the economy $\widetilde{\mathcal{E}} = ((X^i, \preceq^i, \omega^i)_{i \in I_M}, P_{(\underline{p},\overline{p})}, (\widetilde{l}, \widetilde{L}))$ satisfy Assumptions A1-A5. If, for some $q^* \in Q^N$, there exists $x^{*i} \in \widehat{\delta}^i(q^*)$, $\forall i \in I_M$, such that $\sum_{i \in I_M} x^{*i} = \sum_{i \in I_M} \omega^i$, then $(\widehat{p}(q^*), \widehat{l}(q^*), \widehat{L}(q^*), x^*)$ is a constrained equilibrium of the economy $\widetilde{\mathcal{E}}$.

Proof

From (4.29) it follows that $\widehat{p}(q^*) \in P_{(\underline{p},\overline{p})}$. There exists $q^{*1}, q^{*2} \in Q^N$ such that $\widehat{l}(q^*) = \widetilde{l}(q^{*1})$ and $\widehat{L}(q^*) = \widetilde{L}(q^{*2})$, so $(\widehat{l}(q^*), \widehat{L}(q^*)) \in \widetilde{l}(Q^N) \times \widetilde{L}(Q^N)$. Obviously, Conditions 1 and 2 of Definition 4.6.1 are satisfied. Now the Conditions 3 and 4 of Definition 4.6.1 are examined. For every $i \in I_M$, for every $j \in I_N$, it holds that $x_j^{*i} - \omega_j^i = \widetilde{\omega}_j - \sum_{\iota \in I_M \setminus \{i\}} x_j^{*\iota} - \omega_j^i \leq \widetilde{\omega}_j - \omega_j^i$.

If, for some $j \in I_N$, there exists $i' \in I_M$ such that $x_j^{*i'} - \omega_j^{i'} = \widehat{L}_j^{i'}(q^*)$, then $\widehat{L}_j^{i'}(q^*) \leq \widetilde{\omega}_j - \omega_j^{i'}$, therefore $q_j^* > \frac{2}{3}$, and hence $\widehat{l}_j^i(q^*) < -\omega_j^i \leq x_j^{*i} - \omega_j^i$, $\forall i \in I_M$, so the first part of Condition 3 of Definition 4.6.1 is satisfied.

If, for some $j \in I_N$, there exists $i' \in I_M$ such that $x_j^{*i'} - \omega_j^{i'} = \widehat{l}_j^{i'}(q^*)$, then $\widehat{l}_j^{i'}(q^*) \geq -\omega_j^i$, therefore $q_j^* < \frac{1}{3}$, and hence $\widehat{L}_j^i(q^*) > \widetilde{\omega}_j - \omega_j^i \geq x_j^{*i} - \omega_j^i$, $\forall i \in I_M$, so the second part of Condition 3 of Definition 4.6.1 is satisfied.

If, for some $j \in I_N$, $\widehat{p}_j(q^*) < \overline{p}_j$, then $q_j^* < \frac{2}{3}$ and therefore $\widehat{L}_j^i(q^*) > \widetilde{\omega}_j - \widetilde{\omega}_j^i \geq x_j^{*i} - \omega_j^i$, $\forall i \in I_M$. If, for some $j \in I_N$, $\widehat{p}_j(q^*) > \underline{p}_j$, then $q_j^* > \frac{1}{3}$ and therefore $\widehat{l}_j^i(q^*) < -\omega_j^i \leq x_j^{*i} - \omega_j^i$, $\forall i \in I_M$. So, Condition 4 of Definition 4.6.1 is satisfied too. Therefore, $(\widehat{p}(q^*), \widehat{l}(q^*), \widehat{L}(q^*), x^*)$ is a constrained equilibrium of the economy $\widetilde{\mathcal{E}}$. Q.E.D.

Theorem 4.7.1 gives an easy characterization of constrained equilibria by using the functions $\widehat{p}$, $\widehat{l}$, and $\widehat{L}$. If, for some $q^* \in Q^N$, there exists $x^{*i} \in \widehat{\delta}^i(q^*)$, $\forall i \in I_M$, such that $\sum_{i \in I_M} x^{*i} = \sum_{i \in I_M} \omega^i$, then $(\widehat{p}(q^*), \widehat{l}(q^*), \widehat{L}(q^*), x^*)$ is called a constrained equilibrium of the economy $\widetilde{\mathcal{E}}$ *induced* by q^*.

The following theorem states that every constrained equilibrium of the economy $\widetilde{\mathcal{E}}$ is equivalent to a constrained equilibrium of the economy $\widetilde{\mathcal{E}}$ induced by some $q^* \in Q^N$.

Theorem 4.7.2
Let the economy $\widetilde{\mathcal{E}} = ((X^i, \preceq^i, \omega^i)_{i \in I_M}, P_{(\underline{p}, \overline{p})}, (\widetilde{l}, \widetilde{L}))$ satisfy Assumptions A1-A5. If (p^*, l^*, L^*, x^*) is a constrained equilibrium of the economy $\widetilde{\mathcal{E}}$, then there exists $q^* \in Q^N$ such that $x^{*i} \in \widehat{\delta}^i(q^*)$, $\forall i \in I_M$, $(\widehat{p}(q^*), \widehat{l}(q^*), \widehat{L}(q^*), x^*)$ is a constrained equilibrium of $\widetilde{\mathcal{E}}$, and $(p^*, l^*, L^*, x^*) \sim (\widehat{p}(q^*), \widehat{l}(q^*), \widehat{L}(q^*), x^*)$.

Proof
Let $q^{*1} \in Q^N$ be such that $l^* = \widetilde{l}(q^{*1})$ and let $q^{*2} \in Q^N$ be such that $L^* = \widetilde{L}(q^{*2})$. Let the sets J^1, J^2, and J^3 be defined by

$$J^1 = \left\{ j \in I_N \,\middle|\, \exists i \in I_M,\ x_j^{*i} - \omega_j^i = \widetilde{l}_j^i(q^{*1}) \right\},$$
$$J^2 = \left\{ j \in I_N \,\middle|\, \exists i \in I_M,\ x_j^{*i} - \omega_j^i = \widetilde{L}_j^i(q^{*2}) \right\},$$
$$J^3 = I_N \setminus (J^1 \cup J^2).$$

By Condition 3 of Definition 4.6.1, $\{J^1, J^2, J^3\}$ is a partition of I_N. By Condition 4 of Definition 4.6.1, $p_j^* = \underline{p}_j$, $\forall j \in J^1$, and $p_j^* = \overline{p}_j$, $\forall j \in J^2$. Moreover, $\underline{p}_j \leq p_j^* \leq \overline{p}_j$, $\forall j \in J^3$. Let the element q^* of Q^N be defined by

$$\begin{aligned} q_j^* &= \tfrac{1}{3} q_j^{*1}, && \forall j \in J^1, \\ q_j^* &= 1 - \tfrac{1}{3} q_j^{*2}, && \forall j \in J^2, \\ q_j^* &= \tfrac{1}{2}, && \forall j \in J^3 \text{ with } \underline{p}_j = \overline{p}_j, \\ q_j^* &= \frac{p_j^* + \overline{p}_j - 2\underline{p}_j}{3(\overline{p}_j - \underline{p}_j)}, && \forall j \in J^3 \text{ with } \underline{p}_j < \overline{p}_j. \end{aligned}$$

Then it holds that

$$\widehat{l}_j(q^*) = \widetilde{l}_j(q^{*1}), \quad \forall j \in J^1, \tag{4.32}$$
$$\widehat{L}_j(q^*) = \widetilde{L}_j(q^{*2}), \quad \forall j \in J^2, \tag{4.33}$$
$$\widehat{p}_j(q^*) = p_j^*, \quad \forall j \in I_N. \tag{4.34}$$

For every $i \in I_M$ it holds that

$$-\omega^i_j \leq x^{*i}_j - \omega^i_j < \widetilde{L}^i_j(q^{*2}), \quad \forall j \in J^1 \cup J^3, \tag{4.35}$$

$$\widetilde{l}^i_j(q^{*1}) < x^{*i}_j - \omega^i_j \leq \widetilde{\omega}_j - \omega^i_j, \ \forall j \in J^2 \cup J^3. \tag{4.36}$$

Moreover, for every $i \in I_M$,

$$\widehat{L}^i_j(q^*) > \widetilde{\omega}_j - \omega^i_j \geq x^{*i}_j - \omega^i_j, \ \forall j \in J^1 \cup J^3, \tag{4.37}$$

$$\widehat{l}^i_j(q^*) < -\omega^i_j \leq x^{*i}_j - \omega^i_j, \quad \forall j \in J^2 \cup J^3. \tag{4.38}$$

Clearly, $(\widehat{l}(q^*), \widehat{L}(q^*)) \in \widetilde{l}(Q^N) \times \widetilde{L}(Q^N)$, and this together with (4.32)-(4.38) implies by Theorem 4.6.4 that $(\widehat{p}(q^*), \widehat{l}(q^*), \widehat{L}(q^*), x^*)$ is a constrained equilibrium of $\widetilde{\mathcal{E}}$ satisfying $(\widehat{p}(q^*), \widehat{l}(q^*), \widehat{L}(q^*), x^*) \sim (p^*, l^*, L^*, x^*)$. It follows immediately that $x^{*i} \in \widehat{\delta}^i(q^*) = \delta^i(\widehat{p}(q^*), \widehat{l}^i(q^*), \widehat{L}^i(q^*)) \cap \gamma^i(\widehat{p}(q^*))$, $\forall i \in I_M$. Q.E.D.

From Theorem 4.7.2 it follows that there is no loss of generality in only considering constrained equilibria of the economy $\widetilde{\mathcal{E}}$ that are induced by an element q^* of Q^N.

It will be shown that many constrained equilibria of the economy $\widetilde{\mathcal{E}}$ exist. It is easily verified that $q^* = 0^N$ induces a constrained equilibrium of the economy $\widetilde{\mathcal{E}}$ with full rationing on supply in every market, called the *trivial supply constrained equilibrium,* and, similarly, that $q^* = 1^N$ induces a constrained equilibrium of the economy $\widetilde{\mathcal{E}}$ with full rationing on demand in every market, called the *trivial demand constrained equilibrium.* These two constrained equilibria are called the *trivial constrained equilibria.* Therefore, there exists a constrained equilibrium induced by the element q^* of Q^N where, for a given $j \in I_N$, $q^*_j = 0$, and there exists a constrained equilibrium induced by $q^* \in Q^N$ where, for given $j \in I_N$, $q^*_j = 1$. In Theorem 4.7.4 it is shown that given any state $\alpha \in [0,1]$ of the market for a commodity $j \in I_N$ there is a corresponding constrained equilibrium. Before showing Theorem 4.7.4 some properties of $\widehat{\delta}^i$, $\forall i \in I_M$, and $\widehat{\zeta}$ are derived. These properties are closely related to the ones derived for demand relations of an economy without price rigidities, like Walras' law (Theorem 3.7.2), convex-valuedness (Theorem 3.7.3), compact-valuedness and upper hemi-continuity (Theorem 3.7.5), boundary behaviour (Theorem 3.11.1), and continuity (Theorem 3.11.1).

Theorem 4.7.3
Let the economy $\widetilde{\mathcal{E}} = ((X^i, \preceq^i, \omega^i)_{i \in I_M}, P_{(\underline{p},\overline{p})}, (\widetilde{l}, \widetilde{L}))$ satisfy Assumptions A1-A5. For every $i \in I_M$, the reduced demand relation of consumer i has the following properties:

1. $\widehat{\delta}^i$ *is a compact-valued, convex-valued, upper hemi-continuous correspondence,*

2. *for every* $q \in Q^N$, *for every* $x^i \in \widehat{\delta}^i(q)$, *for every* $j \in I_N$, $q_j = 0$ *implies* $x^i_j - \omega^i_j \geq 0$, *and* $q_j = 1$ *implies* $x^i_j - \omega^i_j \leq 0$,

3. *for every* $q \in Q^N$, *for every* $x^i \in \widehat{\delta}^i(q)$, $\widehat{p}(q) \cdot (x^i - \omega^i) = 0$.

If, moreover, the preference relation $\preceq^i$ *is strongly convex, then* $\widehat{\delta}^i$ *is a continuous function.*
The reduced total excess demand relation $\widehat{\zeta} : Q^N \rightarrow \mathbb{R}^N$ *of the economy* $\widetilde{\mathcal{E}}$ *has the following properties:*

1. $\widehat{\zeta}$ *is a compact-valued, convex-valued, upper hemi-continuous correspondence,*

2. *for every* $q \in Q^N$, *for every* $z \in \widehat{\zeta}(q)$, *for every* $j \in I_N$, $q_j = 0$ *implies* $z_j \geq 0$, *and* $q_j = 1$ *implies* $z_j \leq 0$,

3. *for every* $q \in Q^N$, *for every* $z \in \widehat{\zeta}(q)$, $\widehat{p}(q) \cdot z = 0$.

If, moreover, the preference relation $\preceq^i$, $\forall i \in I_M$, *is strongly convex, then* $\widehat{\zeta}$ *is a continuous function.*

Proof

Let some $i \in I_M$ be given. Since the restriction of β^i to the set $\widehat{p}(Q^N) \times \widehat{l}^i(Q^N) \times \widehat{L}^i(Q^N)$ is a continuous correspondence by Theorem 4.2.5 and since the functions $\widehat{p}$, $\widehat{l}^i$, and $\widehat{L}^i$ are continuous, it follows from Theorems 2.5.5 and 2.5.12 that the relation $\varphi^i : Q^N \rightarrow X^i$, defined by $\varphi^i(q) = \beta^i(\widehat{p}(q), \widehat{l}^i(q), \widehat{L}^i(q))$, $\forall q \in Q^N$, is a continuous correspondence. From Lemma 4.2.2 it follows that the correspondence φ^i is compact-valued. Since X^i is convex and $\preceq^i$ is complete, transitive, and continuous, the preference relation $\preceq^i$ can be represented by a continuous utility function u^i by Theorem 3.6.1. The function $f^i : \widehat{p}(Q^N) \times \widehat{l}^i(Q^N) \times \widehat{L}^i(Q^N) \times X^i \rightarrow \mathbb{R}$, defined by $f^i(p, l^i, L^i, x^i) = u^i(x^i)$, $\forall (p, l^i, L^i, x^i) \in \widehat{p}(Q^N) \times \widehat{l}^i(Q^N) \times \widehat{L}^i(Q^N) \times X^i$, is continuous. Therefore, it follows from the maximum theorem, Theorem 2.5.17, that the relation $\overline{\delta}^i$, defined by

$$\overline{\delta}^i(q) = \delta^i\left(\widehat{p}(q), \widehat{l}^i(q), \widehat{L}^i(q)\right), \ \forall q \in Q^N,$$

is a compact-valued, upper hemi-continuous correspondence. Since the relation γ^i is a compact-valued correspondence having a closed graph and since

$\gamma^i(P_{(\underline{p},\overline{p})})$ is contained in the compact set $\{x^i \in X^i \mid \underline{p}_j x^i_j \leq \overline{p} \cdot \omega^i,\ \forall j \in I_N\}$, it follows from Theorem 2.5.7 that γ^i is an upper hemi-continuous correspondence. This together with the continuity of the function $\widehat{p}$ implies by Theorem 2.5.5 that the relation $\gamma^i \circ \widehat{p}$ is an upper hemi-continuous correspondence. Since $\widehat{\delta}^i(q) = \overline{\delta}^i(q) \cap \gamma^i(\widehat{p}(q))$, $\forall q \in Q^N$, and $\overline{\delta}^i(q) \cap \gamma^i(\widehat{p}(q)) \neq \emptyset$, $\forall q \in Q^N$, by the weak-monotonicity of $\preceq^i$, the relation $\widehat{\delta}^i$ is a compact-valued, upper hemi-continuous correspondence by Theorem 2.5.9. Using the convex-valuedness of β^i shown in Lemma 4.2.1, it easily follows that $\overline{\delta}^i$ is convex-valued. Moreover, γ^i is convex-valued, so $\widehat{\delta}^i$ is also convex-valued.
Let some $i \in I_M$ and some $q \in Q^N$ be given. For every $j \in I_N$, if $q_j = 0$, then $x^i \in \widehat{\delta}^i(q)$ implies $x^i_j - \omega^i_j \geq \widehat{l}^i_j(q) = 0$. For every $j \in I_N$, if $q_j = 1$, then $x^i \in \widehat{\delta}^i(q)$ implies $x^i_j - \omega^i_j \leq \widehat{L}^i_j(q) = 0$. If $x^i \in \widehat{\delta}^i(q)$, then $x^i \in \gamma^i(\widehat{p}(q))$, and it follows immediately that $\widehat{p}(q) \cdot (x^i - \omega^i) = 0$.
Let some $i \in I_M$ be given and let $\preceq^i$ be strongly convex. Let some $q \in Q^N$ be given. Suppose $\overline{x}^i, \widehat{x}^i \in \widehat{\delta}^i(q)$ with $\overline{x}^i \neq \widehat{x}^i$. By Lemma 4.2.1 it holds that $\frac{1}{2}\overline{x}^i + \frac{1}{2}\widehat{x}^i \in \beta^i(\widehat{p}(q), \widehat{l}^i(q), \widehat{L}^i(q))$. Moreover, $\widehat{p}(q) \cdot (\frac{1}{2}\overline{x}^i + \frac{1}{2}\widehat{x}^i) = \frac{1}{2}\widehat{p}(q) \cdot \omega^i + \frac{1}{2}\widehat{p}(q) \cdot \omega^i = \widehat{p}(q) \cdot \omega^i$, so $\frac{1}{2}\overline{x}^i + \frac{1}{2}\widehat{x}^i \in \gamma^i(\widehat{p}(q))$. Since $\preceq^i$ is strongly convex, it follows that $\frac{1}{2}\overline{x}^i + \frac{1}{2}\widehat{x}^i \succ^i \overline{x}^i$. So, $\overline{x}^i \notin \widehat{\delta}^i(q)$, a contradiction. Hence, $\widehat{\delta}^i$ is a function and since $\widehat{\delta}^i$ is an upper hemi-continuous correspondence, it is a continuous function.
Using the results derived for $\widehat{\delta}^i$, $\forall i \in I_M$, the corresponding results for $\widehat{\zeta}$ are easily verified. Q.E.D.

Theorem 4.7.4
Let the economy $\widetilde{\mathcal{E}} = ((X^i, \preceq^i, \omega^i)_{i \in I_M}, P_{(\underline{p},\overline{p})}, (\widetilde{l}, \widetilde{L}))$ satisfy Assumptions A1-A5. Let some commodity $j' \in I_N$ and some $\alpha \in [0,1]$ be given. Then there exists $q^* \in Q^N$ such that $q^*_{j'} = \alpha$ and q^* induces a constrained equilibrium $(\widehat{p}(q^*), \widehat{l}(q^*), \widehat{L}(q^*), x^*)$ of the economy $\widetilde{\mathcal{E}}$.
Proof
For every $i \in I_M$, let the set $\overline{X}^i$ be defined by

$$\overline{X}^i = \left\{ x^i \in X^i \,\middle|\, \underline{p}_j x^i_j \leq \overline{p} \cdot \omega^i,\ \forall j \in I_N \right\},$$

and let the set $Q^N_{j',\alpha}$ be defined by

$$Q^N_{j',\alpha} = \left\{ q \in Q^N \,\middle|\, q_{j'} = \alpha \right\}.$$

Notice that, for every $q \in Q^N$, $x^i \in \widehat{\delta}^i(q)$ implies $x^i \in \overline{X}^i$. Let the relation $\mu_{j',\alpha} : \prod_{i \in I_M} \overline{X}^i \to Q^N_{j',\alpha}$ be defined by associating with every $x = (x^1, \ldots, x^M) \in$

$\prod_{i \in I_M} \overline{X}^i$ the set $\mu_{j',\alpha}(x)$ given by

$$\mu_{j',\alpha}(x) = \{\overline{q} \in Q^N_{j',\alpha} \,|\overline{q} \cdot \textstyle\sum_{i \in I_M}(x^i - \omega^i) \geq q \cdot \sum_{i \in I_M}(x^i - \omega^i),\ \forall q \in Q^N_{j',\alpha}\}.$$

For every $x \in \prod_{i \in I_M} \overline{X}^i$, for every $j \in I_N \backslash \{j'\}$, it holds that $\sum_{i \in I_M}(x^i_j - \omega^i_j) > 0$ and $q \in \mu_{j',\alpha}(x)$ implies $q_j = 1$, while $\sum_{i \in I_M}(x^i_j - \omega^i_j) < 0$ and $q \in \mu_{j',\alpha}(x)$ implies $q_j = 0$. Let the relation $\overline{\varphi} : \prod_{i \in I_M} \overline{X}^i \times Q^N_{j',\alpha} \rightarrow \prod_{i \in I_M} \overline{X}^i \times Q^N_{j',\alpha}$ be defined by

$$\overline{\varphi}(x, q) = \prod_{i \in I_M} \widehat{\delta}^i(q) \times \mu_{j',\alpha}(x),\ \forall (x, q) \in \prod_{i \in I_M} \overline{X}^i \times Q^N_{j',\alpha}.$$

The relation $\varphi : \prod_{i \in I_M} \overline{X}^i \rightarrow Q^N_{j',\alpha}$, defined by $\varphi(x) = Q^N_{j',\alpha}$, $\forall x \in \prod_{i \in I_M} \overline{X}^i$, is easily seen to be a compact-valued, continuous correspondence. The function $f : \prod_{i \in I_M} \overline{X}^i \times Q^N_{j',\alpha} \rightarrow \mathbb{R}$, defined by $f(x, q) = q \cdot \sum_{i \in I_M}(x^i - \omega^i)$, $\forall x \in \prod_{i \in I_M} \overline{X}^i$, $\forall q \in Q^N_{j',\alpha}$, is continuous. Therefore, it follows from the maximum theorem, Theorem 2.5.17, that the relation $\mu_{j',\alpha}$ is a compact-valued, upper hemi-continuous correspondence. It is easily verified that $\mu_{j',\alpha}$ is a convex-valued correspondence. By Theorem 4.7.3 the relation $\widehat{\delta}^i$, $\forall i \in I_M$, is a compact-valued, convex-valued, upper hemi-continuous correspondence. Therefore, the correspondence $\overline{\varphi}$ is compact-valued and convex-valued, and being the Cartesian product of compact-valued, upper hemi-continuous correspondences, it is upper hemi-continuous by Theorem 2.5.10. Clearly, the set $\prod_{i \in I_M} \overline{X}^i \times Q^N_{j',\alpha}$ is non-empty, compact, and convex. So, all conditions of Kakutani's fixed point theorem, Theorem 2.6.1, are satisfied and the correspondence $\overline{\varphi}$ has a fixed point $(x^*, q^*) \in \prod_{i \in I_M} \overline{X}^i \times Q^N_{j',\alpha}$ satisfying

$$x^{*i} \in \widehat{\delta}^i(q^*),\ \forall i \in I_M,$$

and

$$q^* \in \mu_{j',\alpha}(x^*).$$

It is shown that $(\widehat{p}(q^*), \widehat{l}(q^*), \widehat{L}(q^*), x^*)$ is a constrained equilibrium of $\widetilde{\mathcal{E}}$. Using Theorem 4.7.1 it is sufficient to show that $\sum_{i \in I_M} x^{*i} = \sum_{i \in I_M} \omega^i$. By Theorem 4.7.3,

$$\widehat{p}(q^*) \cdot \sum_{i \in I_M} \left(x^{*i} - \omega^i\right) = 0. \tag{4.39}$$

Suppose there exists $j^1 \in I_N$ such that $\sum_{i \in I_M}(x^{*i}_{j^1} - \omega^i_{j^1}) < 0$. Two cases are possible, either $j^1 \neq j'$ or $j^1 = j'$. If $j^1 \neq j'$, then, by the definition of $\mu_{j',\alpha}$, $q^*_{j^1} = 0$, and, by Theorem 4.7.3, $\sum_{i \in I_M} x^{*i}_{j^1} \geq \sum_{i \in I_M} \omega^i_{j^1}$, a contradiction. If $j^1 = j'$, then, by (4.39), there exists $j^2 \in I_N \setminus \{j'\}$ such that

$\sum_{i \in I_M} x^{*i}_{j^2} > \sum_{i \in I_M} \omega^i_{j^2}$. Using the definition of $\mu_{j',\alpha}$ it follows that $q^*_{j^2} = 1$. Now it follows from Theorem 4.7.3 that $\sum_{i \in I_M} x^{*i}_{j^2} \leq \sum_{i \in I_M} \omega^i_{j^2}$, a contradiction. Consequently, $\sum_{i \in I_M} x^{*i} \geq \sum_{i \in I_M} \omega^i$ and using (4.39) it follows that $\sum_{i \in I_M} x^{*i} = \sum_{i \in I_M} \omega^i$. Q.E.D.

Using stronger versions of Assumptions A1 and A2 a similar result has been obtained in van der Laan and Talman (1990) for the case of the uniform rationing system. Notice that if $\alpha \in (0, \frac{1}{3})$ and the rationing system is not the uniform one, then it cannot be guaranteed that, for every $q \in Q^N_{j',\alpha}$, for every $i \in I_M$, there exists $j \in I_N$ such that $\widehat{l}^i_j(q) < 0$. Therefore, the proof of Drèze (1975) of the continuity of the budget relation β^i of a consumer $i \in I_M$, see Theorem 4.2.3, cannot be used to prove the existence of a constrained equilibrium in this case and the more general result given in Theorem 4.2.5 is needed.

From Theorem 4.7.4 it follows immediately that for any given commodity there exists a constrained equilibrium for any state of the market for this commodity. It is interesting to consider for example the market for a certain labour service. Then Theorem 4.7.4 makes clear that every state of the market for this labour service can be sustained as a constrained equilibrium.

By Theorem 4.7.2 the set of all constrained equilibria is obtained by considering the constrained equilibria corresponding to every possible state $\alpha \in [0, 1]$ of the market for some given commodity $j \in I_N$. Hence, Theorem 4.7.4 gives a complete classification of all constrained equilibria and, moreover, Theorem 4.7.4 makes clear that there are uncountably many constrained equilibria. Since there are so many constrained equilibria, one might conclude that the concept is not well defined. However, one might argue that the fact that there are many constrained equilibria necessitates a dynamic study like a study of adjustment processes, specifying which equilibrium will result given the initial state of the economy.

So far it has not been assumed that some commodity serves as a *numeraire commodity*, i.e. having a price equal to one, in the economy. However, the existence of such a commodity is not excluded. In Definition 4.6.1 equilibria with rationing of the numeraire are considered too in this case. The observation of rationing in the money market in Western economies provides some motivation for the study of these equilibria. In Drèze (1975), however, it was assumed that one of the commodities is a numeraire commodity, and the existence of a constrained equilibrium without rationing in the market for the numeraire commodity is shown. The condition that there is no rationing in the market for at least one commodity guarantees that the constrained equilibrium obtained is non-trivial. Moreover, this condition guarantees that no problems arise with respect to the continuity of the budget relation of the consumers and the following specific interpretation of the model, given in Bénassy (1975a), is possible. In this interpretation, every non-numeraire commodity can only be exchanged against the numeraire commodity. A consumer does not express his demand for the numeraire commodity, i.e. there is no separate market for the numeraire commodity, while the total excess demand for the numeraire commodity in a state of the economy is determined by the transactions in the markets for the non-numeraire commodities. The numeraire commodity serves as the unit of account of Chapter 3. The following definition slightly generalizes the above ideas.

Definition 4.7.5 (Drèze equilibrium)
A Drèze equilibrium *of the economy* $\widetilde{\mathcal{E}} = ((X^i, \preceq^i, \omega^i)_{i \in I_M}, P_{(\underline{p},\overline{p})}, (\widetilde{l}, \widetilde{L}))$ *with respect to the market for a commodity* $j \in I_N$ *is a constrained equilibrium* (p^*, l^*, L^*, x^*) *of* $\widetilde{\mathcal{E}}$ *satisfying*

$$l_j^{*i} < x_j^{*i} - \omega_j^i < L_j^{*i}, \ \forall i \in I_M.$$

So, in a Drèze equilibrium with respect to some market, there is no rationing in that market. The existence of a Drèze equilibrium with respect to some given market easily follows from Theorem 4.7.4.

Corollary 4.7.6
Let the economy $\widetilde{\mathcal{E}} = ((X^i, \preceq^i, \omega^i)_{i \in I_M}, P_{(\underline{p},\overline{p})}, (\widetilde{l}, \widetilde{L}))$ *satisfy Assumptions A1-A5. Then, for every* $j \in I_N$*, there exists a Drèze equilibrium of the economy* $\widetilde{\mathcal{E}}$ *with respect to the market for commodity* j*.*
Proof
Let some $j \in I_N$ be given. Applying Theorem 4.7.4 with $\alpha \in [\frac{1}{3}, \frac{2}{3}]$ and $j' = j$, it follows that there exists a constrained equilibrium of $\widetilde{\mathcal{E}}$ induced by some $q^* \in Q^N$ such that $q_j^* = \alpha$. Clearly, for every $i \in I_M$, $\widehat{l}_j^i(q^*) < -\omega_j^i$ and $\widehat{L}_j^i(q^*) > \widetilde{\omega}_j - \omega_j^i$, so $l_j^{*i} < x_j^{*i} - \omega_j^i < L_j^{*i}$. Q.E.D.

Closely related to the Drèze equilibrium of the economy with respect to the numeraire commodity are the equilibrium concepts of Bénassy (1975b) and Younès (1975). In Drèze's model the demand expressed by a consumer satisfies the constraints imposed by the rationing schemes. In Bénassy (1975b) a consumer expresses his *effective demand.* In his effective demand for a commodity, the consumer takes into account the rationing schemes in all markets, except in the market for that commodity. The demand expressed by a consumer without taking into account any constraint imposed by the rationing schemes is often called the *notional demand.* In Silvestre (1982) conditions are given under which the approaches of Bénassy, Drèze, and Younès are equivalent. Moreover, it is shown that if the preference relations are not of the class C^1, then Drèze's definition yields the smallest set of equilibria. As is shown in Grandmont (1977b), the equilibrium concept given in Bénassy (1975b) might cause inconsistencies when the preference relations of the consumers are not strongly convex, in the sense that the final consumption bundle obtained by a consumer is not feasible for him, and even if it is feasible, it might not be optimal given the constraints the consumer perceives. Since strong convexity of preference relations is not assumed in this monograph, except in Chapter 12, equilibrium concepts based on the effective demand of consumers are not further analysed.

The equilibrium concepts related to the Drèze equilibrium with respect to the numeraire commodity are frequently used in the so-called macro-economic disequilibrium models, see Malinvaud (1977), Bénassy (1986), and Böhm (1989). In the most basic model there exists one representative consumer and one representative firm, who are involved in the production and the exchange of three commodities, labour, a consumption good, and money. The consumer has no initial endowment of the consumption good. The producer produces the consumption good using labour owned by the consumer. Often the model is extended by a government consuming the consumption good, levying taxes, and creating money. In this model a resulting Drèze equilibrium with respect to the numeraire commodity belongs to one of the following three types. In the first type the consumer is rationed both on his supply in the market for labour and on his demand in the market for the consumption good, called a *classical unemployment equilibrium,* in the second type the consumer is rationed on his supply in the market for labour, while the producer is rationed on his supply in the market for the consumption good, called a *Keynesian unemployment equilibrium,* and in the third type the consumer is rationed on his demand in the market for the consumption good, while the producer is rationed on his demand in the market for labour, called a *repressed inflation equilibrium.* A producer is never rationed both on his demand in the market for labour and on his supply in the market for the consumption good. Even this basic model provides a uniform framework for both the classical and the Keynesian point of view for the causes of unemployment. Several authors have considered extensions of this basic framework.

In Assumption A4 the case where the price is zero in some market is excluded. Nevertheless the existence of a Drèze equilibrium with respect to the numeraire commodity for such an economy is shown in Drèze (1975). It is therefore interesting to consider the question whether the result of Theorem 4.7.4 can be obtained in this case too. In Example 4.2.4 it has been demonstrated that some technical difficulties arise. Example 4.7.7 makes clear that indeed strictly positive prices are necessary for the result of Theorem 4.7.4.

Example 4.7.7
Let the economy $\widetilde{\mathcal{E}} = ((X^i, \preceq^i, \omega^i)_{i\in I_M}, P_{(\underline{p},\overline{p})}, (\widetilde{l}, \widetilde{L}))$ be such that for every $i \in I_M$ the consumption set X^i is a subset of $\mathbb{R}^N_+$. Moreover, assume that $j \in I_N$ is such that $\underline{p}_j = 0$, and that there exists a consumer $i' \in I_M$ such that $\preceq^{i'}$ is monotonic with respect to commodity j. Hence, $x^{i'} \in \delta^{i'}(p, l^{i'}, L^{i'})$ for some $(p, l^{i'}, L^{i'}) \in P_{(\underline{p},\overline{p})} \times \widehat{l}^i(Q^N) \times \widehat{L}^i(Q^N)$ implies $x^{i'}_j - \omega^{i'}_j = L^{i'}_j$. Suppose $q^* \in Q^N$ with $q^*_j \leq \frac{1}{3}$ induces a constrained equilibrium $(\widehat{p}(q^*), \widehat{l}(q^*), \widehat{L}(q^*), x^*)$ of the economy $\widetilde{\mathcal{E}}$. Then $\widehat{p}_j(q^*) = 0$, $\widehat{L}^{i'}_j(q^*) > \widetilde{\omega}_j - \omega^{i'}_j$, so $\sum_{i\in I_M} x^{*i}_j \geq x^{*i'}_j = \omega^{i'}_j + \widehat{L}^{i'}_j(q^*) > \sum_{i\in I_M} \omega^i_j$, a contradiction. Hence, there are no constrained equilibria of the economy $\widetilde{\mathcal{E}}$ where the state of the market for commodity j, q^*_j, lies in the interval $[0, \frac{1}{3}]$ and there are no constrained equilibria of $\widetilde{\mathcal{E}}$ with supply rationing in the market for commodity j. Assume that also $\overline{p}_j = 0$. Then it can be shown in a similar way that if a constrained equilibrium of the economy $\widetilde{\mathcal{E}}$ is induced by some $q^* \in Q^N$, then $q^*_j > \frac{2}{3}$. If the preference relation of every consumer $i \in I_M$ is monotonic with respect to commodity j, then it holds for every constrained equilibrium of the economy $\widetilde{\mathcal{E}}$ that there is full rationing on demand in the market for commodity j, i.e. if q^* induces a constrained equilibrium of the economy $\widetilde{\mathcal{E}}$, then $\widehat{L}^i_j(q^*) = 0$, $\forall i \in I_M$.

4.8 SUPPLY AND DEMAND CONSTRAINED EQUILIBRIA

In this section the economy $\widetilde{\mathcal{E}} = ((X^i, \preceq^i, \omega^i)_{i\in I_M}, P_{(\underline{p},\overline{p})}, (\widetilde{l}, \widetilde{L}))$ is assumed to be given. In Kurz (1982) and van der Laan (1980a) it has been remarked that in Western economies supply rationing occurs more frequently than demand rationing. Examples are supply rationing in the labour market, resulting in unemployment, and quotas on the supply of agricultural products. One of the reasons given in van der Laan (1980a) for this phenomenon is that in many markets supply rationing is more easily realized than demand rationing since the number of sellers is usually less than the number of buyers. Although in the labour market the reverse is true, supply rationing of labour is easily realized by restricting the number of hours worked. Therefore, it is interesting to know whether there exist constrained equilibria of an economy without demand rationing in any market, while there is no rationing in at least one market. When the commodity of the latter market is chosen ex post as a numeraire commodity, then again the interpretation of the model as given in Bénassy (1975a) is possible. The following definition is motivated by the ideas presented above.

Definition 4.8.1 (Supply constrained equilibrium)
A supply constrained equilibrium of $\widetilde{\mathcal{E}} = ((X^i, \preceq^i, \omega^i)_{i\in I_M}, P_{(\underline{p},\overline{p})}, (\widetilde{l}, \widetilde{L}))$ *is a constrained equilibrium* (p^*, l^*, L^*, x^*) *of* $\widetilde{\mathcal{E}}$ *satisfying, for every* $j \in I_N$,

$$x_j^{*i} - \omega_j^i < L_j^{*i}, \ \forall i \in I_M,$$

while there exists $j' \in I_N$ *such that*

$$l_{j'}^{*i} < x_{j'}^{*i} - \omega_{j'}^i, \ \forall i \in I_M.$$

The existence of a supply constrained equilibrium has been shown in van der Laan (1982) using the technique of simplicial approximation of equilibria and in van der Laan and Talman (1990) using a fixed point argument. In van der Laan (1980a) it has been shown that there exists a constrained equilibrium without demand rationing and without full rationing on supply in at least one market. Results concerning the existence of constrained equilibria without demand rationing in any market and without rationing in an a priori chosen market in a model with a set of admissible price systems given by P_π or $P_{(\phi,\psi)}$, see Section 4.4, are obtained in Dehez and Drèze (1984), van der Laan (1984), Weddepohl (1987), and Wu (1988). However, as has been remarked before, an equilibrium satisfying the conditions of Definition 4.8.1 might not exist in these models and therefore these authors consider different equilibrium concepts where in specified cases supply rationing in a market is allowed, while the price in this market could still be lowered.

If in a constrained equilibrium of the economy no demand rationing in any market is allowed, then this can be modelled by requiring that if $q^* \in Q^N$ induces a constrained equilibrium $(\widehat{p}(q^*), \widehat{l}(q^*), \widehat{L}(q^*), x^*)$ of the economy, then $q_j^* \leq \frac{2}{3}$, $\forall j \in I_N$. If, moreover, it is required that $q_j^* \geq \frac{1}{3}$ for at least one commodity $j \in I_N$, then q^* induces a supply constrained equilibrium of the economy. Notice that the existence of a Drèze equilibrium with respect to the market for a commodity $j \in I_N$, shown in Theorem 4.7.4, does not show the existence of a supply constrained equilibrium of the economy since in a Drèze equilibrium with respect to the market for a commodity $j \in I_N$ only the state of the market for commodity j is considered.

Let some $\overline{\alpha} \in Q^N$ be given. In the following result it is shown that there exists a constrained equilibrium induced by $q^* \in Q^N$ where, for every $j \in I_N$, q_j^* is less than or equal to $\overline{\alpha}_j$, while there exists a commodity $j' \in I_N$ such that $q_{j'} = \overline{\alpha}_{j'}$. In this way it can be modelled that in some markets a given amount of demand rationing is allowed, or that in some markets some supply rationing is always present. An example is the existence of a natural rate of unemployment in the labour market.

Theorem 4.8.2
Let the economy $\widetilde{\mathcal{E}} = ((X^i, \preceq^i, \omega^i)_{i \in I_M}, P_{(\underline{p},\overline{p})}, (\widetilde{l}, \widetilde{L}))$ satisfy Assumptions A1-A5. Let some $\overline{\alpha} \in Q^N$ be given. Then there exists $q^* \in Q^N$ such that $q^* \leq \overline{\alpha}$, $q_j^* = \overline{\alpha}_j$ for some $j \in I_N$, and q^* induces a constrained equilibrium $(\widehat{p}(q^*), \widehat{l}(q^*), \widehat{L}(q^*), x^*)$ of the economy $\widetilde{\mathcal{E}}$.
Proof
For every $i \in I_M$, let the set $\overline{X}^i$ be defined by

$$\overline{X}^i = \left\{x^i \in X^i \,|\underline{p}_j x_j^i \leq \overline{p} \cdot \omega^i, \ \forall j \in I_N \right\}.$$

Notice that, for every $q \in Q^N$, $x^i \in \widehat{\delta}^i(q)$ implies $x^i \in \overline{X}^i$. Let the relation $\mu : \prod_{i \in I_M} \overline{X}^i \to \Delta^{N-1}$ be defined by associating with every $x = (x^1, \ldots, x^M) \in \prod_{i \in I_M} \overline{X}^i$ the set $\mu(x)$ given by

$$\mu(x) = \left\{\overline{s} \in \Delta^{N-1} \,|\overline{s} \cdot \textstyle\sum_{i \in I_M}(x^i - \omega^i) \geq s \cdot \sum_{i \in I_M}(x^i - \omega^i), \ \forall s \in \Delta^{N-1}\right\}.$$

It is easily verified that if $x \in \prod_{i \in I_M} \overline{X}^i$ and for some $j^1, j^2 \in I_N$ it holds that $\sum_{i \in I_M}(x_{j^1}^i - \omega_{j^1}^i) > \sum_{i \in I_M}(x_{j^2}^i - \omega_{j^2}^i)$, then $s_{j^2} = 0$ for every $s \in \mu(x)$. For every $j \in I_N$, let component j of the function $\overline{f} : \Delta^{N-1} \to Q^N$ be defined by

$$\overline{f}_j(s) = \frac{\overline{\alpha}_j s_j}{\max(\{s_1, \ldots, s_N\})}, \ \forall s \in \Delta^{N-1}.$$

For every $i \in I_M$, let the relation $\overline{\delta}^i : \Delta^{N-1} \to \overline{X}^i$ be defined by

$$\overline{\delta}^i(s) = \widehat{\delta}^i\left(\overline{f}(s)\right), \ \forall s \in \Delta^{N-1},$$

and let the relation $\overline{\varphi} : \prod_{i \in I_M} \overline{X}^i \times \Delta^{N-1} \to \prod_{i \in I_M} \overline{X}^i \times \Delta^{N-1}$ be defined by

$$\overline{\varphi}(x, s) = \prod_{i \in I_M} \overline{\delta}^i(s) \times \mu(x), \ \forall (x, s) \in \prod_{i \in I_M} \overline{X}^i \times \Delta^{N-1}.$$

The relation $\varphi : \prod_{i\in I_M} \overline{X}^i \to \Delta^{N-1}$, defined by $\varphi(x) = \Delta^{N-1}$, $\forall x \in \prod_{i\in I_M} \overline{X}^i$, is easily seen to be a compact-valued, continuous correspondence. The function $f : \prod_{i\in I_M} \overline{X}^i \times \Delta^{N-1} \to \mathbb{R}$, defined by $f(x,s) = s \cdot \sum_{i\in I_M}(x^i - \omega^i)$, $\forall x \in \prod_{i\in I_M} \overline{X}^i$, $\forall s \in \Delta^{N-1}$, is continuous. Therefore, it follows from the maximum theorem, Theorem 2.5.17, that μ is a compact-valued, upper hemi-continuous correspondence. It is easily verified that μ is a convex-valued correspondence. Using the continuity of the function $\overline{f}$ and the fact that $\widehat{\delta}^i$, $\forall i \in I_M$, is compact-valued, convex-valued, and upper hemi-continuous by Theorem 4.7.3, it follows from Theorem 2.5.5 that the relation $\overline{\delta}^i$, $\forall i \in I_M$, is a compact-valued, convex-valued, upper hemi-continuous correspondence. By Theorem 2.5.10 the same result holds for $\overline{\varphi}$. Clearly, the set $\prod_{i\in I_M} \overline{X}^i \times \Delta^{N-1}$ is non-empty, compact, and convex. Therefore, all conditions of Kakutani's fixed point theorem, Theorem 2.6.1, are satisfied and the correspondence $\overline{\varphi}$ has a fixed point $(x^*, s^*) \in \prod_{i\in I_M} \overline{X}^i \times \Delta^{N-1}$ satisfying

$$x^{*i} \in \overline{\delta}^i(s^*) = \widehat{\delta}^i\left(\overline{f}(s^*)\right), \ \forall i \in I_M,$$

and

$$s^* \in \mu(x^*).$$

Let $q^* \in Q^N$ be defined by

$$q^* = \overline{f}(s^*).$$

From the definition of the function $\overline{f}$ it follows that $q^* \leq \overline{\alpha}$ and $q^*_j = \overline{\alpha}_j$ for some $j \in I_N$. Therefore, it remains to be shown that $(\widehat{p}(q^*), \widehat{l}(q^*), \widehat{L}(q^*), x^*)$ is a constrained equilibrium of $\widetilde{\mathcal{E}}$. This follows from Theorem 4.7.1 if it can be shown that $\sum_{i\in I_M} x^{*i} = \sum_{i\in I_M} \omega^i$. Clearly, by Theorem 4.7.3,

$$\widehat{p}(q^*) \cdot \sum_{i\in I_M} (x^{*i} - \omega^i) = 0. \tag{4.40}$$

Suppose there exists $j^1 \in I_N$ such that $\sum_{i\in I_M}(x^{*i}_{j^1} - \omega^i_{j^1}) < 0$. Then, using (4.40), there exists $j^2 \in I_N$ such that $\sum_{i\in I_M}(x^{*i}_{j^2} - \omega^i_{j^2}) > 0$. Using the properties of μ this implies that $s^*_{j^1} = 0$ and therefore $q^*_{j^1} = 0$. So, $\sum_{i\in I_M}(x^{*i}_{j^1} - \omega^i_{j^1}) \geq 0$ by Theorem 4.7.3, a contradiction. Consequently, $\sum_{i\in I_M}(x^{*i} - \omega^i) \geq 0^N$ and, using (4.40), it follows that $\sum_{i\in I_M}(x^{*i} - \omega^i) = 0^N$.
Q.E.D.

Notice that if $\overline{\alpha}$ given in Theorem 4.8.2 is such that $\min(\{\overline{\alpha}_j | j \in I_N\}) < \frac{1}{3}$, then it cannot be guaranteed that, for every $q \in \overline{f}(\Delta^{N-1})$, for every $i \in I_M$, there exists $j \in I_N$ such that $\widehat{l}^i_j(q) < 0$, with $\overline{f}$ as defined in the proof of Theorem

4.8.2. Therefore, the original proof of Drèze (1975) of the continuity of the budget relation, see Theorem 4.2.3, cannot be used to prove the existence of a constrained equilibrium if $\min(\{\overline{\alpha}_j \mid j \in I_N\}) < \frac{1}{3}$ and again the result of Theorem 4.2.5 is needed.

The existence of a supply constrained equilibrium follows immediately from Theorem 4.8.2 by taking for example $\overline{\alpha} = \frac{1}{2}1^N$.

Corollary 4.8.3
Let the economy $\widetilde{\mathcal{E}} = ((X^i, \preceq^i, \omega^i)_{i \in I_M}, P_{(\underline{p},\overline{p})}, (\widetilde{l}, \widetilde{L}))$ satisfy Assumptions A1-A5. Then there exists a supply constrained equilibrium of the economy $\widetilde{\mathcal{E}}$.

In Example 4.8.4 it is shown that strictly positive prices are necessary for the result of Theorem 4.8.2.

Example 4.8.4
Let the economy $\widetilde{\mathcal{E}} = ((X^i, \preceq^i, \omega^i)_{i \in I_M}, P_{(\underline{p},\overline{p})}, (\widetilde{l}, \widetilde{L}))$ be such that, for every $i \in I_M$, $X^i \subset \mathbb{R}^N_+$. Assume that $j \in I_N$ is such that $\underline{p}_j = 0$ and that there exists a consumer $i' \in I_M$ such that the preference relation $\preceq^{i'}$ is monotonic with respect to commodity j. In Example 4.7.7 it has been shown that if q^* induces a constrained equilibrium of the economy $\widetilde{\mathcal{E}}$, then $q_j^* > \frac{1}{3}$. Moreover, if $\overline{p}_j = 0$ and q^* induces a constrained equilibrium of the economy $\widetilde{\mathcal{E}}$, then $q_j^* > \frac{2}{3}$, following the reasoning of Example 4.7.7. Therefore, a supply constrained equilibrium does not exist in this case.

Given $\overline{\alpha} \in Q^N$, it is required in Theorem 4.8.2 that the state of the market for at least one commodity $j \in I_N$ is given by $\overline{\alpha}_j$. Therefore, if $q^{*1} \in Q^N$ induces a constrained equilibrium satisfying the requirements of Theorem 4.8.2 given some $\overline{\alpha}^1 \in Q^N$, and if q^{*2} induces a constrained equilibrium satisfying the requirements of Theorem 4.8.2 given some $\overline{\alpha}^2 \in Q^N$ with $\overline{\alpha}^2 \gg \overline{\alpha}^1$, then $q^{*1} \neq q^{*2}$. The set of all constrained equilibria is obtained by considering for instance the constrained equilibria satisfying the requirements of Theorem 4.8.2 for some $\overline{\alpha} \in Q^N$ satisfying $\overline{\alpha}_1 = \cdots = \overline{\alpha}_N$. This gives another complete classification of all constrained equilibria.

Recent experiences in Eastern Europe and the former Soviet Union make clear that demand constrained equilibria are interesting too. In Polterovich (1993) some general equilibrium type models of centrally planned economies are considered. In none of these models there is supply rationing in any market, while demand rationing is allowed in every market. This motivates the following definition.

Definition 4.8.5 (Demand constrained equilibrium)
A demand constrained equilibrium of $\widetilde{\mathcal{E}} = ((X^i, \preceq^i, \omega^i)_{i \in I_M}, P_{(\underline{p},\overline{p})}, (\widetilde{l}, \widetilde{L}))$ *is a constrained equilibrium* (p^*, l^*, L^*, x^*) *of* $\widetilde{\mathcal{E}}$ *satisfying, for every commodity* $j \in I_N$,

$$x_j^{*i} - \omega_j^i > l_j^{*i}, \ \forall i \in I_M,$$

while for at least one commodity $j' \in I_N$ *it holds that*

$$x_{j'}^{*i} - \omega_{j'}^i < L_{j'}^{*i}, \ \forall i \in I_M.$$

Demand constrained equilibria are also considered in van der Laan and Talman (1990). The existence of a demand constrained equilibrium follows from the following theorem.

Theorem 4.8.6
Let the economy $\widetilde{\mathcal{E}} = ((X^i, \preceq^i, \omega^i)_{i \in I_M}, P_{(\underline{p},\overline{p})}, (\widetilde{l}, \widetilde{L}))$ *satisfy Assumptions A1-A5. Let some* $\underline{\alpha} \in Q^N$ *be given. Then there exists* $q^* \in Q^N$ *such that* $q^* \geq \underline{\alpha}$, $q_j^* = \underline{\alpha}_j$ *for some* $j \in I_N$, *and* q^* *induces a constrained equilibrium* $(\widehat{p}(q^*), \widehat{l}(q^*), \widehat{L}(q^*), x^*)$ *of the economy* $\widetilde{\mathcal{E}}$.
Proof
For every $i \in I_M$, let the set $\overline{X}^i$ be defined by

$$\overline{X}^i = \left\{ x^i \in X^i \,\middle|\, \underline{p}_j x_j^i \leq \overline{p} \cdot \omega^i, \ \forall j \in I_N \right\}.$$

Notice that, for every $q \in Q^N$, $x^i \in \widehat{\delta}^i(q)$ implies $x^i \in \overline{X}^i$. Let the relation $\mu : \prod_{i \in I_M} \overline{X}^i \rightarrow \Delta^{N-1}$ be defined by associating with every $x = (x^1, \ldots, x^M) \in \prod_{i \in I_M} \overline{X}^i$ the set $\mu(x)$ given by

$$\mu(x) = \left\{ \overline{s} \in \Delta^{N-1} \,\middle|\, \overline{s} \cdot \sum_{i \in I_M} (x^i - \omega^i) \leq s \cdot \sum_{i \in I_M} (x^i - \omega^i), \ \forall s \in \Delta^{N-1} \right\}.$$

It is easily verified that if $x \in \prod_{i \in I_M} \overline{X}^i$ and for some $j^1, j^2 \in I_N$ it holds that $\sum_{i \in I_M}(x_{j^1}^i - \omega_{j^1}^i) > \sum_{i \in I_M}(x_{j^2}^i - \omega_{j^2}^i)$, then $s_{j^1} = 0$ for every $s \in \mu(x)$. For every $j \in I_N$, let component $j \in I_N$ of the function $\overline{f} : \Delta^{N-1} \rightarrow Q^N$ be defined by

$$\overline{f}_j(s) = 1 - \frac{(1 - \underline{\alpha}_j) s_j}{\max(\{s_1, \ldots, s_N\})}, \ \forall s \in \Delta^{N-1}.$$

For every $i \in I_M$, let the relation $\overline{\delta}^i : \Delta^{N-1} \to \overline{X}^i$ be defined by

$$\overline{\delta}^i(s) = \widehat{\delta}^i\left(\overline{f}(s)\right),\ \forall s \in \Delta^{N-1},$$

and let the relation $\overline{\varphi} : \prod_{i\in I_M} \overline{X}^i \times \Delta^{N-1} \to \prod_{i\in I_M} \overline{X}^i \times \Delta^{N-1}$ be defined by

$$\overline{\varphi}(x,s) = \prod_{i\in I_M} \overline{\delta}^i(s) \times \mu(x),\ \forall (x,s) \in \prod_{i\in I_M} \overline{X}^i \times \Delta^{N-1}.$$

Similarly as in the proof of Theorem 4.7.4 it can be shown that $\overline{\varphi}$ satisfies all conditions of Kakutani's fixed point theorem, Theorem 2.6.1. So, $\overline{\varphi}$ has a fixed point $(x^*, s^*) \in \prod_{i\in I_M} \overline{X}^i \times \Delta^{N-1}$ satisfying

$$x^{*i} \in \overline{\delta}^i(s^*) = \widehat{\delta}^i\left(\overline{f}(s^*)\right),\ \forall i \in I_M,$$

and

$$s^* \in \mu(x^*).$$

Let $q^* \in Q^N$ be defined by

$$q^* = \overline{f}(s^*).$$

By the definition of the function $\overline{f}$ it holds that $q^* \geq \underline{\alpha}$ and $q_j^* = \underline{\alpha}_j$ for some $j \in I_N$. Therefore, it remains to be shown that $(\widehat{p}(q^*), \widehat{l}(q^*), \widehat{L}(q^*), x^*)$ is a constrained equilibrium of $\widetilde{\mathcal{E}}$. This follows from Theorem 4.7.1 if it can be shown that $\sum_{i\in I_M} x^{*i} = \sum_{i\in I_M} \omega^i$. Clearly,

$$\widehat{p}(q^*) \cdot \sum_{i\in I_M} (x^{*i} - \omega^i) = 0. \tag{4.41}$$

Suppose there exists $j^1 \in I_N$ such that $\sum_{i\in I_M}(x^{*i}_{j^1} - \omega^i_{j^1}) > 0$. Then, using (4.41), there exists $j^2 \in I_N$ such that $\sum_{i\in I_M}(x^{*i}_{j^2} - \omega^i_{j^2}) < 0$. Using the properties of μ this implies that $s^*_{j^1} = 0$ and therefore $q^*_{j^1} = 1$. So, $\sum_{i\in I_M}(x^{*i}_{j^1} - \omega^i_{j^1}) \leq 0$ by Theorem 4.7.3, a contradiction. Consequently, $\sum_{i\in I_M}(x^{*i} - \omega^i) \leq 0^N$ and, using (4.41), it follows that $\sum_{i\in I_M}(x^{*i} - \omega^i) = 0^N$.
Q.E.D.

The existence of a demand constrained equilibrium follows as a corollary of Theorem 4.8.6 by taking for example $\underline{\alpha} = \frac{1}{2}1^N$.

Corollary 4.8.7
Let the economy $\widetilde{\mathcal{E}} = ((X^i, \preceq^i, \omega^i)_{i\in I_M}, P_{(\underline{p},\overline{p})}, (\widetilde{l}, \widetilde{L}))$ satisfy Assumptions A1-A5. Then there exists a demand constrained equilibrium of the economy $\widetilde{\mathcal{E}}$.

It should be noticed that all possible constrained equilibria are obtained by considering the correspondences $\overline{\varphi}$ used in Theorem 4.7.4, Theorem 4.8.2, or Theorem 4.8.6, a fixed point of each $\overline{\varphi}$ inducing a constrained equilibrium. By Theorem 4.7.2 every constrained equilibrium of an economy $\widetilde{\mathcal{E}}$ is equivalent to the constrained equilibrium $(\widehat{p}(q^*), \widehat{l}(q^*), \widehat{L}(q^*), x^*)$ that is induced by some $q^* \in Q^N$. Such a constrained equilibrium satisfies the conditions of Theorem 4.7.4 for every $j \in I_N$ and for every $\alpha \in [0,1]$ satisfying $\alpha = q_j^*$. It satisfies the conditions of Theorem 4.8.2 for every $\overline{\alpha} \in Q^N$ satisfying $\overline{\alpha} \geq q^*$ and for some $j \in I_N$, $\overline{\alpha}_j = q_j^*$. It also satisfies the conditions of Theorem 4.8.6 for every $\underline{\alpha} \in Q^N$ satisfying $\underline{\alpha} \leq q^*$ and for some $j \in I_N$, $\underline{\alpha}_j = q_j^*$.

4.9 THE EQUILIBRIUM RELATION

For every consumer $i \in I_M$, the consumption set X^i and the preference relation $\preceq^i$ are assumed to be given in this section. Moreover, the rationing system $(\widetilde{l}, \widetilde{L})$ is assumed to be given. Since in this section the initial endowments may vary, they are again included in the notation of β^i and δ^i, $\forall i \in I_M$. Notice that in the most interesting cases the rationing function $(\widetilde{l}, \widetilde{L})$ also depends on the initial endowments. The set Ω of all possible initial endowments is defined by

$$\Omega = \prod_{i \in I_M} \text{int}\,(X^i) = \text{int}\,(X)\,.$$

It is assumed that $\widetilde{l}$ is a function from $Q^N \times \Omega$ into $-\mathbb{R}_+^{MN}$, where, for every $\omega \in \Omega$, $\widetilde{l}(Q^N \times \{\omega\})$ is the set of admissible rationing schemes on supply if the initial endowments of the consumers are given by ω. Similarly, it is assumed that $\widetilde{L}$ is a function from $Q^N \times \Omega$ into $\mathbb{R}_+^{MN}$, where, for every $\omega \in \Omega$, $\widetilde{L}(Q^N \times \{\omega\})$ is the set of admissible rationing schemes on demand if the initial endowments of the consumers are given by ω. In this section Assumption A5 is replaced by Assumption A6.

A6. The rationing function $(\widetilde{l}, \widetilde{L})$ is continuous, and, for every $\omega \in \Omega$, the functions $\widetilde{l}_{|Q^N \times \{\omega\}}$ and $\widetilde{L}_{|Q^N \times \{\omega\}}$ are flexible and market independent.

In this section it is shown that the *equilibrium relation*, that assigns to every specification of initial endowments ω in the set Ω and to every specification of a set of admissible price systems $P_{(\underline{p},\overline{p})}$, with $(\underline{p},\overline{p})$ an element of the set $\underline{\overline{P}}$ defined by

$$\underline{\overline{P}} = \left\{(\underline{p},\overline{p}) \in \mathbb{R}_{++}^{2N} \;|\underline{p} \leq \overline{p}\right\},$$

the set of all constrained equilibrium allocations of the economy $\widetilde{\mathcal{E}}(\underline{p},\overline{p},\omega)$, defined by

$$\widetilde{\mathcal{E}}\left(\underline{p},\overline{p},\omega\right)=\left(\left(X^i,\preceq^i,\omega^i\right)_{i\in I_M},P_{(\underline{p},\overline{p})},\left(\widetilde{l}_{|Q^N\times\{\omega\}},\widetilde{L}_{|Q^N\times\{\omega\}}\right)\right),$$

is a compact-valued, upper hemi-continuous correspondence. Moreover, it can be shown that it is continuous on a residual subset of the domain. These are interesting properties since they imply that the set of equilibrium allocations is stable against perturbations in the initial endowments or the set of admissible price systems. For every $j\in I_N$, component j of the function $\widehat{p}:Q^N\times\overline{\underline{P}}\to\mathbb{R}^N_{++}$ is defined similarly as in (4.29), so

$$\widehat{p}_j(q,\underline{p},\overline{p})=\max\left(\{\underline{p}_j,\min(\{\underline{p}_j(2-3q_j)+\overline{p}_j(3q_j-1),\overline{p}_j\})\}\right),$$

for every $(q,\underline{p},\overline{p})\in Q^N\times\overline{\underline{P}}$, and the function $\widehat{l}:Q^N\times\Omega\to-\mathbb{R}^{MN}_+$ and the function $\widehat{L}:Q^N\times\Omega\to\mathbb{R}^{MN}_+$ are defined similarly as in (4.30) and (4.31), respectively, so

$$\begin{aligned}\widehat{l}(q,\omega)&=\widetilde{l}\left(\inf(\{1^N,3q\}),\omega\right), && \forall(q,\omega)\in Q^N\times\Omega,\\ \widehat{L}(q,\omega)&=\widetilde{L}\left(\inf(\{1^N,31^N-3q\}),\omega\right), && \forall(q,\omega)\in Q^N\times\Omega.\end{aligned}$$

Again, these functions are used to describe the state of the markets of the economy. The equilibrium relation $\xi:\overline{\underline{P}}\times\Omega\to X$ is defined by

$$\xi(\underline{p},\overline{p},\omega)=\left\{x^*\in X\,\middle|\,\begin{array}{l}\exists q^*\in Q^N,\ (\widehat{p}(q^*,\underline{p},\overline{p}),\widehat{l}(q^*,\omega),\widehat{L}(q^*,\omega),x^*)\text{ is a}\\ \text{constrained equilibrium of the economy }\widetilde{\mathcal{E}}(\underline{p},\overline{p},\omega)\end{array}\right\},$$

for every $(\underline{p},\overline{p},\omega)\in\overline{\underline{P}}\times\Omega$. By Theorem 4.7.2 it is guaranteed that $\xi(\underline{p},\overline{p},\omega)$ contains all constrained equilibrium allocations of the economy $\mathcal{E}(\underline{p},\overline{p},\omega)$.

Theorem 4.9.1
For every consumer $i\in I_M$, let the consumption set X^i satisfy Assumption A1, let the preference relation $\preceq^i$ satisfy Assumption A2, and let the rationing function $(\widetilde{l},\widetilde{L})$ satisfy Assumption A6. Then the equilibrium relation $\xi:\overline{\underline{P}}\times\Omega\to X$ is a compact-valued, upper hemi-continuous correspondence.

Proof
Let some $(\underline{p},\overline{p},\omega)\in\overline{\underline{P}}\times\Omega$ be given. By Theorem 4.7.4 it holds that $\xi(\underline{p},\overline{p},\omega)\neq\emptyset$. Let $(\underline{p}^n,\overline{p}^n,(\omega)^n)_{n\in\mathbb{N}}$ be a sequence in $\overline{\underline{P}}\times\Omega$ converging to $(\underline{p},\overline{p},\omega)$ and let the sequence $((x)^n)_{n\in\mathbb{N}}$ in X be such that $(x)^n\in\xi(\underline{p}^n,\overline{p}^n,(\omega)^n)$, $\forall n\in\mathbb{N}$. It is shown that the sequence $((x)^n)_{n\in\mathbb{N}}$ has a subsequence with limit contained

in $\xi(\underline{p}, \overline{p}, \omega)$. Then ξ is compact-valued, and, by Theorem 2.5.6, an upper hemi-continuous correspondence. For every $n \in \mathbb{N}$, there exists $q^n \in Q^N$ such that $(\widehat{p}(q^n, \underline{p}^n, \overline{p}^n), \widehat{l}(q^n, (\omega)^n), \widehat{L}(q^n, (\omega)^n), (x)^n)$ is a constrained equilibrium of the economy $\widetilde{\mathcal{E}}(\underline{p}^n, \overline{p}^n, (\omega)^n)$. Consider the sequence $(q^n, (x)^n)_{n \in \mathbb{N}}$. Since, for every $i \in I_M$, $0^N \leq x^{i^n} \leq \widetilde{\omega}^n \rightarrow \widetilde{\omega}$, it follows that the sequence $((x)^n)_{n \in \mathbb{N}}$ is bounded. Therefore, the sequence $(q^n, (x)^n)_{n \in \mathbb{N}}$ has a subsequence converging to some $(\overline{q}, \overline{x}) \in Q^N \times X$. Hence,

$$\left(\widehat{p}(\overline{q}, \underline{p}, \overline{p}), \widehat{l}(\overline{q}, \omega), \widehat{L}(\overline{q}, \omega), \overline{x}\right) \in P_{(\underline{p}, \overline{p})} \times -\mathbb{R}_{+}^{MN} \times \mathbb{R}_{+}^{MN} \times X.$$

Using Theorem 4.2.5 and the maximum theorem, Theorem 2.5.17, it follows that the relation $\delta^i_{|\mathbb{R}^N_{++} \times -\mathbb{R}^N_{+} \times \mathbb{R}^N_{+} \times \mathrm{int}(X^i)}$, $\forall i \in I_M$, is a compact-valued, upper hemi-continuous correspondence. Clearly, $\widehat{p}, \widehat{l}$, and $\widehat{L}$ are continuous functions, so, for every $i \in I_M$, the correspondence $\overline{\delta}^i : Q^N \times \underline{\overline{P}} \times \Omega \rightarrow X^i$, defined by

$$\overline{\delta}^i(q, \underline{p}, \overline{p}, \omega) = \delta^i\left(\widehat{p}(q, \underline{p}, \overline{p}), \widehat{l}^i(q, \omega), \widehat{L}^i(q, \omega), \omega^i\right), \ \forall (q, \underline{p}, \overline{p}, \omega) \in Q^N \times \underline{\overline{P}} \times \Omega,$$

is a compact-valued, upper hemi-continuous correspondence, using Theorem 2.5.5. Since $(q^n, \underline{p}^n, \overline{p}^n, (\omega)^n) \rightarrow (\overline{q}, \underline{p}, \overline{p}, \omega)$ and for every $i \in I_M$ it holds that $x^{i^n} \rightarrow \overline{x}^i$ and $\overline{\delta}^i$ is a compact-valued, upper hemi-continuous correspondence, it follows from Theorem 2.5.6 that

$$\overline{x}^i \in \overline{\delta}^i(\overline{q}, \underline{p}, \overline{p}, \omega), \ \forall i \in I_M.$$

So, Condition 1 of Definition 4.6.1 is satisfied.
Clearly, $\sum_{i \in I_M} \overline{x}^i = \lim_{n \rightarrow +\infty} \sum_{i \in I_M} \omega^{i^n} = \sum_{i \in I_M} \omega^i$, thereby giving Condition 2 of Definition 4.6.1. By Theorem 4.7.1 the remaining conditions of a constrained equilibrium of the economy $\widetilde{\mathcal{E}}(\underline{p}, \overline{p}, \omega)$ are satisfied. Q.E.D.

Recall that a subset of a topological space is called residual if it contains a countable intersection of dense and open sets, see Section 2.3. It follows that the equilibrium relation ξ is a continuous correspondence on a residual subset of $\underline{\overline{P}} \times \Omega$.

Theorem 4.9.2
For every consumer $i \in I_M$, let the consumption set X^i satisfy Assumption A1, let the preference relation $\preceq^i$ satisfy Assumption A2, and let the rationing function $(\widetilde{l}, \widetilde{L})$ satisfy Assumption A6. Then the equilibrium relation $\xi : \underline{\overline{P}} \times \Omega \rightarrow X$ is a continuous correspondence on a residual subset of $\underline{\overline{P}} \times \Omega$.
Proof

From Theorem 4.9.1 it follows that $\xi : \overline{P} \times \Omega \to X$ is a compact-valued, upper hemi-continuous correspondence, so ξ is continuous on a residual subset of $\overline{P} \times \Omega$ by Theorem 2.5.16. Q.E.D.

It is not difficult to verify that for every $(\underline{p}, \overline{p}, \omega) \in \overline{P} \times \Omega$ there exists an open subset O of $\overline{P} \times \Omega$ such that $(\underline{p}, \overline{p}, \omega) \in O$ and the closure of O in $\overline{P} \times \Omega$ is compact in $\overline{P} \times \Omega$. Therefore, $\overline{P} \times \Omega$ is a locally compact Hausdorff space and it follows from Theorem 2.3.15 that it is a Baire space. Hence, every countable intersection of open, dense subsets of $\overline{P} \times \Omega$ is dense in $\overline{P} \times \Omega$. Therefore, the residual set of Theorem 4.9.2 is large in a topological sense.

4.10 AN EXAMPLE

To illustrate the theory presented in this chapter, the example used in Section 3.10 is extended by a set of admissible price systems and a rationing system. In this example the economy $\widetilde{\mathcal{E}} = ((X^i, \preceq^i, \omega^i)_{i \in I_2}, P_{(\underline{p},\overline{p})}, (\widetilde{l}, \widetilde{L}))$ is such that $N = 2$, $X^1 = X^2 = \mathbb{R}^2_+$, $\preceq^1$ and $\preceq^2$ can be represented by utility functions $u^1 : X^1 \to \mathbb{R}$ and $u^2 : X^2 \to \mathbb{R}$, respectively, defined by $u^1(x^1) = (x^1_1)^{\frac{3}{4}}(x^1_2)^{\frac{1}{4}}$, $\forall x^1 \in \mathbb{R}^2_+$, and $u^2(x^2) = (x^2_1)^{\frac{1}{4}}(x^2_2)^{\frac{3}{4}}$, $\forall x^2 \in \mathbb{R}^2_+$, $\omega^1 = (1,4)^\top$, $\omega^2 = (2,1)^\top$,

$$P_{(\underline{p},\overline{p})} = \left\{ p \in \mathbb{R}^2_+ \,\middle|\, \tfrac{1}{6} \leq p_1 \leq 2 \text{ and } p_2 = 1 \right\},$$

and $(\widetilde{l}, \widetilde{L})$ is the uniform rationing system, where $\widetilde{l} : Q^2 \to -\mathbb{R}^4_+$ is defined by

$$\begin{aligned} \widetilde{l}^1_1(q^1) = \widetilde{l}^2_1(q^1) &= -3q^1_1, \ \forall q^1 \in Q^2, \\ \widetilde{l}^1_2(q^1) = \widetilde{l}^2_2(q^1) &= -5q^1_2, \ \forall q^1 \in Q^2, \end{aligned}$$

and $\widetilde{L} : Q^2 \to \mathbb{R}^4_+$ is defined by

$$\begin{aligned} \widetilde{L}^1_1(q^2) = \widetilde{L}^2_1(q^2) &= 18q^2_1, \ \forall q^2 \in Q^2, \\ \widetilde{L}^1_2(q^2) = \widetilde{L}^2_2(q^2) &= 5q^2_2, \ \ \forall q^2 \in Q^2. \end{aligned}$$

Using Theorem 2.9.7 it can easily be verified that the reduced demand relation of consumer 1 is a function, denoted by $\widehat{d}^1 : Q^2 \to \mathbb{R}^2$, defined by $\widehat{d}^1(q) -$

$(1,4)^\top =$

$$\begin{cases} (90q_2, -15q_2)^\top, & 0 \le q_1 \le \frac{1}{3},\ 0 \le q_2 \le \frac{71}{360}, \\ (\frac{71}{4}, -\frac{71}{24})^\top, & 0 \le q_1 \le \frac{1}{3},\ \frac{71}{360} \le q_2 \le 1, \\ (\frac{90q_2}{33q_1-10}, -15q_2)^\top, & \frac{1}{3} \le q_1 \le \frac{2}{3},\ 0 \le q_2,\ 33q_1 + 360q_2 \le 82, \\ (\frac{82-33q_1}{132q_1-40}, \frac{33q_1-82}{24})^\top, & \frac{1}{3} \le q_1 \le \frac{2}{3},\ q_2 \le 1,\ 33q_1 + 360q_2 \ge 82, \\ (\frac{15q_2}{2}, -15q_2)^\top, & \frac{2}{3} \le q_1,\ 0 \le q_2 \le \frac{1}{6},\ 36q_1 + 5q_2 \le 36, \\ (\frac{5}{4}, -\frac{5}{2})^\top, & \frac{2}{3} \le q_1 \le \frac{211}{216},\ \frac{1}{6} \le q_2 \le 1, \\ (54 - 54q_1, 108q_1 - 108)^\top, & \frac{211}{216} \le q_1 \le 1,\ q_2 \le 1,\ 36q_1 + 5q_2 \ge 36. \end{cases}$$

Similarly, the reduced demand relation of consumer 2 is a function, denoted by $\widehat{d^2} : Q^2 \to \mathbb{R}^2$, defined by $\widehat{d^2}(q) - (2,1)^\top =$

$$\begin{cases} (0,0)^\top, & 0 \le q_1 \le \frac{1}{3},\ 0 \le q_2 \le 1, \\ (\frac{33-99q_1}{66q_1-20}, \frac{33q_1-11}{4})^\top, & \frac{1}{3} \le q_1 \le \frac{2}{3},\ 0 \le q_2,\ 33q_1 + 60q_2 \le 71, \\ (\frac{90q_2-90}{33q_1-10}, 15 - 15q_2)^\top, & q_1 \le \frac{2}{3},\ q_2 \le 1,\ 33q_1 + 60q_2 \ge 71, \\ (-\frac{11}{8}, \frac{11}{4})^\top, & \frac{2}{3} \le q_1 \le 1,\ 0 \le q_2 \le \frac{49}{60}, \\ (\frac{15q_2-15}{2}, 15 - 15q_2)^\top, & \frac{2}{3} \le q_1 \le 1,\ \frac{49}{60} \le q_2 \le 1. \end{cases}$$

Now the reduced total excess demand function, denoted by $\widehat{z} : Q^2 \to \mathbb{R}^2$, is defined by $\widehat{z}(q) = \widehat{d^1}(q) + \widehat{d^2}(q) - \omega^1 - \omega^2$, $\forall q \in Q^2$. Notice that all the assumptions of Theorem 4.7.3 are satisfied and that the functions $\widehat{d^1}$, $\widehat{d^2}$, and $\widehat{z}$ indeed satisfy all the conditions given there.

The zero points of $\widehat{z}$ can easily be determined analytically. It can be verified that they are given by the points

$$\begin{pmatrix} 0 \\ 0 \end{pmatrix}, \begin{pmatrix} \frac{1}{3} \\ 0 \end{pmatrix}, \begin{pmatrix} \frac{148}{231} \\ \frac{71}{420} \end{pmatrix}, \begin{pmatrix} \frac{148}{231} \\ \frac{349}{420} \end{pmatrix}, \begin{pmatrix} \frac{2}{3} \\ \frac{5}{6} \end{pmatrix}, \begin{pmatrix} \frac{211}{216} \\ \frac{5}{6} \end{pmatrix}, \begin{pmatrix} 1 \\ 1 \end{pmatrix},$$

and the convex combinations of any two successive points. In Figure 4.10.1 the solid line corresponds to the set of zero points of $\widehat{z}$.

According to Theorem 4.7.4, for every $j \in I_2$, for every $\alpha \in [0,1]$, there is a zero point q^* of $\widehat{z}$ satisfying $q^*_j = \alpha$. According to Theorem 4.8.2, for every $\overline{\alpha} \in Q^2$, there is a zero point q^* of $\widehat{z}$ satisfying $q^* \le \overline{\alpha}$, and $q^*_1 = \overline{\alpha}_1$ or $q^*_2 = \overline{\alpha}_2$. According to Theorem 4.8.6, for every $\underline{\alpha} \in Q^2$, there is a zero point q^* of $\widehat{z}$ satisfying $q^* \ge \underline{\alpha}$, and $q^*_1 = \underline{\alpha}_1$ or $q^*_2 = \underline{\alpha}_2$. Using Figure 4.10.1 these results are easily verified for the example. Moreover, $q^* = (0,0)^\top$ induces the trivial supply constrained equilibrium, $q^* = (1,1)^\top$ induces the trivial demand constrained equilibrium, $q^* = (\frac{1}{2}, \frac{11}{120})^\top$ induces a Drèze equilibrium with respect to the market for commodity 1, being also a supply constrained equilibrium, and

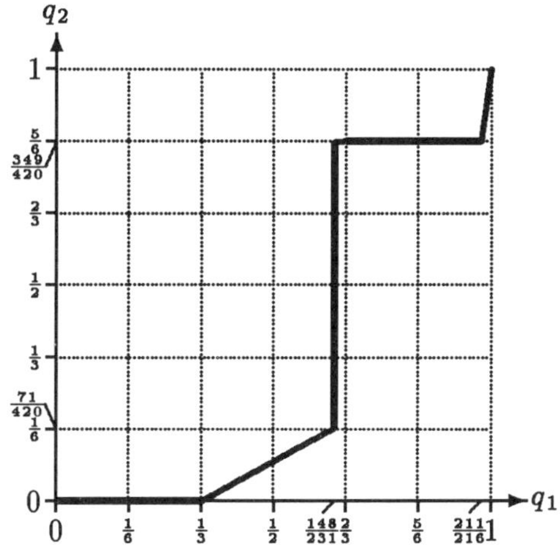

Figure 4.10.1. The set of zero points of $\widehat{z}$, $N = 2$.

$q^* = (\frac{148}{231}, \frac{1}{2})^\top$ induces a Drèze equilibrium with respect to the market for commodity 2, being also a demand constrained equilibrium. It is easily verified that the Drèze equilibrium with respect to the market for commodity 2 is also a Walrasian equilibrium of the economy $\mathcal{E} = ((X^i, \preceq^i, \omega^i)_{i \in I_2})$, see also Section 3.10. In Table 4.10.2 the main characteristics of the two trivial constrained equilibria and the two Drèze equilibria are summarized.

Table 4.10.2 makes clear that consumer 1 prefers the Drèze equilibrium with respect to the market for commodity 1 to the Drèze equilibrium with respect to the market for commodity 2. This is not unexpected since the price of commodity 1 is lower at the first Drèze equilibrium, while consumer 1 owns a lot of commodity 2 and prefers commodity 1 to commodity 2 according to his utility function. Nevertheless, the demand of consumer 1 for commodity 1 is higher at the Drèze equilibrium with respect to the market for commodity 2 than at the Drèze equilibrium with respect to the market for commodity 1. The intuition behind this result is that consumer 1 would prefer to demand more of commodity 1 in the Drèze equilibrium with respect to the market for commodity 1, but is not able to supply more of commodity 2 since the demand of consumer 2 for commodity 2 is relatively small. Therefore, consumer 1 is rationed on his supply in the market for commodity 2 in the Drèze equilibrium with respect to the market for commodity 1. Notice that if consumer 1 is no longer a price taker, but is able to influence the price of commodity 1, then the Drèze equilibrium with respect to the market for commodity 2, i.e. the Walrasian equilibrium, is no longer stable. Consumer 1 would be better off

	$q^* = (0,0)^\top$	$q^* = (\frac{1}{2}, \frac{11}{120})^\top$	$q^* = (\frac{148}{231}, \frac{1}{2})^\top$	$q^* = (1,1)^\top$
$\widehat{p}(q^*)$	$(\frac{1}{6}, 1)^\top$	$(1\frac{1}{12}, 1)^\top$	$(1\frac{6}{7}, 1)^\top$	$(2, 1)^\top$
$\widehat{l}^1(q^*) = \widehat{l}^2(q^*)$	$(0, 0)^\top$	$(-3, -1\frac{3}{8})^\top$	$(-3, -5)^\top$	$(-3, -5)^\top$
$\widehat{L}^1(q^*) = \widehat{L}^2(q^*)$	$(18, 5)^\top$	$(18, 5)^\top$	$(18, 5)^\top$	$(0, 0)^\top$
$\widehat{d}^1(q^*)$	$(1, 4)^\top$	$(2\frac{7}{26}, 2\frac{5}{8})^\top$	$(2\frac{19}{52}, 1\frac{13}{28})^\top$	$(1, 4)^\top$
$\widehat{d}^2(q^*)$	$(2, 1)^\top$	$(\frac{19}{26}, 2\frac{3}{8})^\top$	$(\frac{33}{52}, 3\frac{15}{28})^\top$	$(2, 1)^\top$
$u^1(\widehat{d}^1(q^*))$	1.414	2.353	2.098	1.414
$u^2(\widehat{d}^2(q^*))$	1.189	1.769	2.301	1.189

Table 4.10.2. Some constrained equilibria of the economy $\widetilde{\mathcal{E}}$.

if the price of commodity 1 decreases compared to the Walrasian equilibrium price of commodity 1. Such considerations play an important role in Part III of this monograph, where the consumers have political power and the price regulations are determined endogenously.

Figure 4.10.1 makes clear that the set of zero points of $\widehat{z}$ satisfies an even stronger property than the ones guaranteed by Theorems 4.7.4, 4.8.2, or 4.8.6. There exists a connected set of zero points of $\widehat{z}$ containing the points inducing the trivial constrained equilibria, and the Drèze equilibria with respect to the two markets. In Chapter 5 it is examined whether such a property always holds under Assumptions A1-A5.

5

ON THE CONNECTEDNESS OF THE SET OF CONSTRAINED EQUILIBRIA

5.1 INTRODUCTION

In Chapter 4 several constrained equilibrium existence results have been given. In Theorems 4.7.1 and 4.7.2 it has been shown that the state of every market can be represented by a single parameter, determining either the amount of supply rationing, or the price, or the amount of demand rationing in a market. It has been argued that the economy has two trivial constrained equilibria, called the trivial supply constrained equilibrium and the trivial demand constrained equilibrium. In Theorem 4.7.4 it has been shown that there exists a constrained equilibrium of the economy with an a priori given state of one of the markets. A special case is given by the Drèze equilibrium with respect to a given market as defined in Definition 4.7.5, where it holds that there is no rationing in an a priori specified market. In Theorem 4.8.2 it has been shown that there exists a constrained equilibrium of the economy such that the value of the parameter representing the state is less than or equal to some a priori specified value for every market with equality holding for at least one market. A special case is given by the supply constrained equilibrium as defined in Definition 4.8.1, where it holds that there is no demand rationing in any market, while there is no rationing in at least one market. In Theorem 4.8.6 it has been shown that there exists a constrained equilibrium of the economy such that the value of the parameter representing the state of any market is greater than or equal to some a priori specified value for every market with equality holding for at least one market. A special case is given by the demand constrained equilibrium as defined in Definition 4.8.5, where it holds that there is no supply rationing in any market, while there is no rationing in at least one market.

In the example given in Section 4.10 it holds that the set of constrained equilibria is connected. It is therefore a natural question to ask whether general conditions can be given such that the set of constrained equilibria of an economy is a connected set. In van der Laan (1982) a theorem is given, stating that there is a connected set of constrained equilibria of the economy without demand rationing in any market, containing both the trivial supply constrained equilibrium of the economy and a supply constrained equilibrium of the economy. The proof is based on the properties of points generated by a simplicial algorithm applied to the model of an economy with price rigidities. However, the proof is not complete since it assumes that a certain sequence of connected 1-manifolds has a subsequence that converges to some connected 1-manifold. This reasoning is not valid in general. Nevertheless, the basic idea of the proof, the use of the properties of the path of points generated by a simplicial algorithm to obtain insight into the structure of the set of constrained equilibria of the economy, turns out to be very useful. This idea is utilized to show the existence of a connected set of constrained equilibria of the economy containing the two trivial constrained equilibria. It can be shown that a connected set of constrained equilibria of the economy containing the two trivial constrained equilibria also contains a supply constrained equilibrium, a Drèze equilibrium with respect to any market, and a demand constrained equilibrium, and therefore the result in van der Laan (1982) is generalized. In fact, it can be shown that such a connected set of constrained equilibria contains an equilibrium of any type considered in Chapter 4.

In Section 4.7 some properties of a relation related to the total excess demand relation of the economy, called the reduced total excess demand relation of the economy, have been derived. Under weak assumptions it can be shown that the reduced total excess demand relation of the economy is a compact-valued, convex-valued, upper hemi-continuous correspondence, satisfying some boundary condition. Moreover, if it is assumed that the preference relations of the consumers are strongly convex, then the reduced total excess demand relation of the economy can be shown to be a continuous function. For the latter case, in Section 5.2 a simplicial algorithm with integer labelling, proposed in van der Laan (1982), is presented. It is applied to the reduced total excess demand relation of the economy. It is shown that the algorithm generates a path of points connecting the two trivial constrained equilibria of the economy. Using this result, it is shown in Section 5.3 that the set of constrained equilibria of the economy has a component containing the two trivial constrained equilibria. In Section 5.4 it is shown that the results of Section 5.3 remain valid if weaker assumptions are made with respect to the economy, only guaranteeing that the reduced total excess demand relation of the economy is a compact-valued, upper hemi-continuous correspondence instead of being a continuous function.

In Section 5.5 it is shown that all the equilibrium existence results mentioned in Chapter 4 can be proved by a one line argument using the results of Sections 5.3 and 5.4. Thereby it is shown that there exists a continuum, i.e. an uncountable connected set, of constrained equilibria of the economy. In Section 5.6 the algorithm is applied to the example considered in Sections 3.10 and 4.10.

This chapter is based on Herings (1993).

5.2 A SIMPLICIAL ALGORITHM WITH INTEGER LABELLING

In this chapter the *economy* $\widetilde{\mathcal{E}} = ((X^i, \preceq^i, \omega^i)_{i \in I_M}, P_{(\underline{p},\overline{p})}, (\widetilde{l}, \widetilde{L}))$ as described in Chapter 4 is assumed to be given. As in Chapter 4 there are $M \in \mathbb{N}$ *consumers*, indexed by $i \in I_M$, and $N \in \mathbb{N}$ *commodities*, indexed by $j \in I_N$. Every consumer $i \in I_M$ has a *consumption set* X^i, a *preference relation* $\preceq^i$, and an *initial endowment* ω^i. The *set of admissible price systems* is given by $P_{(\underline{p},\overline{p})} = \{p \in \mathbb{R}^N \mid \underline{p} \leq p \leq \overline{p}\}$ and the *rationing function*, specifying the *admissible rationing schemes*, is given by the pair $(\widetilde{l}, \widetilde{L})$ with $\widetilde{l} : Q^N \to -\mathbb{R}^{MN}_+$ the *rationing function on supply* and $\widetilde{L} : Q^N \to \mathbb{R}^{MN}_+$ the *rationing function on demand*. The element $(\omega^1, \ldots, \omega^M)$ is denoted by ω.

As in Section 4.2, given a *price system* $p \in \mathbb{R}^N$ and a *rationing scheme* $(l^i, L^i) \in -\mathbb{R}^{*N}_+ \times \mathbb{R}^{*N}_+$ of a consumer $i \in I_M$, the set $\beta^i(p, l^i, L^i) = \{x^i \in X^i \mid p \cdot x^i \leq p \cdot \omega^i,\ l^i \leq x^i - \omega^i \leq L^i\}$ denotes the *budget set* of consumer i, and as in Section 4.3 the set of best elements of $\beta^i(p, l^i, L^i)$ according to $\preceq^i$ is denoted by $\delta^i(p, l^i, L^i)$. As in Section 4.7, for every $j \in I_N$, component $\widehat{p}_j$ of the function $\widehat{p} : Q^N \to P_{(\underline{p},\overline{p})}$ is defined by

$$\widehat{p}_j(q) = \max\left(\{\underline{p}_j, \min(\{\underline{p}_j(2 - 3q_j) + \overline{p}_j(3q_j - 1), \overline{p}_j\})\}\right), \forall q \in Q^N.$$

The functions $\widehat{l} : Q^N \to -\mathbb{R}^{MN}_+$ and $\widehat{L} : Q^N \to \mathbb{R}^{MN}_+$ are defined by

$$\begin{aligned} \widehat{l}(q) &= \widetilde{l}\left(\inf(\{1^N, 3q\})\right), & \forall q \in Q^N, \\ \widehat{L}(q) &= \widetilde{L}\left(\inf(\{1^N, 31^N - 3q\})\right), & \forall q \in Q^N. \end{aligned}$$

For every consumer $i \in I_M$, the relations $\gamma^i : P_{(\underline{p},\overline{p})} \to \mathbb{R}^N$ and $\widehat{\delta}^i : Q^N \to \mathbb{R}^N$ are defined by

$$\begin{aligned} \gamma^i(p) &= \left\{x^i \in X^i \,\middle|\, p \cdot x^i = p \cdot \omega^i\right\}, & \forall p \in P_{(\underline{p},\overline{p})}, \\ \widehat{\delta}^i(q) &= \delta^i\left(\widehat{p}(q), \widehat{l}^i(q), \widehat{L}^i(q)\right) \cap \gamma^i(\widehat{p}(q)), & \forall q \in Q^N. \end{aligned}$$

Finally, the *reduced total excess demand relation* of the economy $\widetilde{\mathcal{E}}$, $\widehat{\zeta} : Q^N \to \mathbb{R}^N$, is defined by

$$\widehat{\zeta}(q) = \sum_{i \in I_M} \widehat{\delta}^i(q) - \sum_{i \in I_M} \{\omega^i\}, \ \forall q \in Q^N.$$

In this section the reduced total excess demand relation of the economy is assumed to be a function, denoted by $\widehat{z} : Q^N \to \mathbb{R}^N$, called the *reduced total excess demand function* of the economy. It is often assumed that the reduced total excess demand function of the economy satisfies the following condition.

Condition A The reduced total excess demand function $\widehat{z} : Q^N \to \mathbb{R}^N$ of the economy $\widetilde{\mathcal{E}}$ satisfies

1. $\widehat{z}$ is continuous,
2. for every $q \in Q^N$, for every $j \in I_N$, $q_j = 0$ implies $\widehat{z}_j(q) \geq 0$, and $q_j = 1$ implies $\widehat{z}_j(q) \leq 0$,
3. for every $q \in Q^N$, $\widehat{p}(q) \cdot \widehat{z}(q) = 0$.

Notice that by Theorem 4.7.3 the reduced total excess demand function of the economy $\widetilde{\mathcal{E}}$ satisfies Condition A if $\widetilde{\mathcal{E}}$ satisfies Assumptions A1-A5 of Section 4.7 and the preference relations $\preceq^i$, $\forall i \in I_M$, are strongly convex.

In Theorem 4.7.1 it has been shown that if $q^* \in Q^N$ satisfies $\widehat{z}(q^*) = 0^N$, then q^* *induces a constrained equilibrium* of the economy $\widetilde{\mathcal{E}}$. Moreover, Theorem 4.7.2 shows that all constrained equilibria are obtained by considering the zero points of $\widehat{z}$. From Condition A.2 and Condition A.3 it follows immediately that $\widehat{z}(0^N) = 0^N$. The element 0^N induces the *trivial supply constrained equilibrium* of the economy $\widetilde{\mathcal{E}}$. From Condition A.2 and Condition A.3 it follows immediately that $\widehat{z}(1^N) = 0^N$. The element 1^N induces the *trivial demand constrained equilibrium* of the economy $\widetilde{\mathcal{E}}$.

In this section a simplicial algorithm on Q^N with integer labelling is presented. The algorithm is the same as the one used in van der Laan (1982) and is related to the algorithm in Chapter 5 of van der Laan (1980b) and van der Laan and Talman (1981). This algorithm will be shown to generate a path of approximate zero points of the reduced total excess demand function $\widehat{z}$ of the economy $\widetilde{\mathcal{E}}$ joining the element 0^N and the element 1^N. An essential part of the algorithm is that to each point in Q^N a *label* in the set I_{N+1} is assigned. For every $q \in Q^N$, the set $J(q)$ is defined by

$$J(q) = \{j' \in I_N \mid q_{j'} \neq 1 \text{ and } \widehat{z}_{j'}(q) = \max(\{\widehat{z}_j(q) \mid j \in I_N\})\} \cup \{N+1\}.$$

The *labelling function* $\widehat{f} : Q^N \rightarrow I_{N+1}$ is defined by

$$\widehat{f}(q) = \min(J(q)), \ \forall q \in Q^N.$$

Notice that $\widehat{f}(1^N) = N+1$ and $\widehat{f}(0^N) \neq N+1$.

Definition 5.2.1 (Proper labelling function)
The labelling function $\widehat{f} : Q^N \rightarrow I_{N+1}$ is proper *if, for every $q \in Q^N$, for every $j \in I_N$, $q_j = 1$ implies $\widehat{f}(q) \neq j$, and $q_j = 0$ implies $\widehat{f}(q) \neq N+1$.*

It is shown in Theorem 5.2.9 that $\widehat{f}$ is a proper labelling function if the reduced total excess demand function $\widehat{z}$ satisfies Condition A.

Let a triangulation Σ of Q^N be given. The triangulation Σ might be for instance the K-triangulation of Q^N with any grid size, see Definition 2.7.3, or the V-triangulation of Q^N with respect to any $v \in Q^N$ and with any grid size, see Definition 2.7.6. For every non-empty subset J of I_N, the set $A(J)$ is defined by

$$A(J) = \left\{ q \in Q^N \,\middle|\, q_j = 0, \ \forall j \in I_N \setminus J \right\}.$$

Clearly, $A(J)$ is a convex $(\#J)$-dimensional subset of $\mathbb{R}^N$ for every non-empty subset J of I_N. For every non-empty subset J of I_N, the set $\Sigma(J)$ is defined by

$$\Sigma(J) = \{\tau \subset A(J) \,|\, \exists \sigma \in \Sigma, \ \tau \text{ is a } (\#J)\text{-face of } \sigma\}.$$

If $\overline{J}, \widehat{J} \subset I_N$ with $\emptyset \neq \overline{J} \subset \widehat{J}$, then $A(\overline{J}) = A(\widehat{J}) \cap \text{aff}(A(\overline{J}))$. By repeated application of Theorem 2.7.8 it follows that $\Sigma(J)$ is a triangulation of $A(J)$ for every non-empty subset J of I_N. All $2^N - 1$ possible sets $A(J)$ are illustrated in Figure 5.2.1 for $N = 2$.

Definition 5.2.2 (J-complete simplices)
Let the labelling function $\widehat{f} : Q^N \rightarrow I_{N+1}$ be given. Let J be a non-empty subset of I_{N+1} with $\#J = t$. A $(t-1)$-simplex $\tau(q^1, \ldots, q^t)$ that is a subset of Q^N is J-complete *if $\widehat{f}(\{q^1, \ldots, q^t\}) = J$.*

In general, a $(t-1)$-simplex is said to be *complete* if it is J-complete for some non-empty subset J of I_{N+1} with $\#J = t$. Let the labelling function $\widehat{f} : Q^N \rightarrow I_{N+1}$ be proper. Let a triangulation Σ of Q^N be given. The algorithm will generate a finite sequence of complete simplices starting with the $\{\widehat{f}(0^N)\}$-complete simplex $\{0^N\}$ and terminating with an I_{N+1}-complete

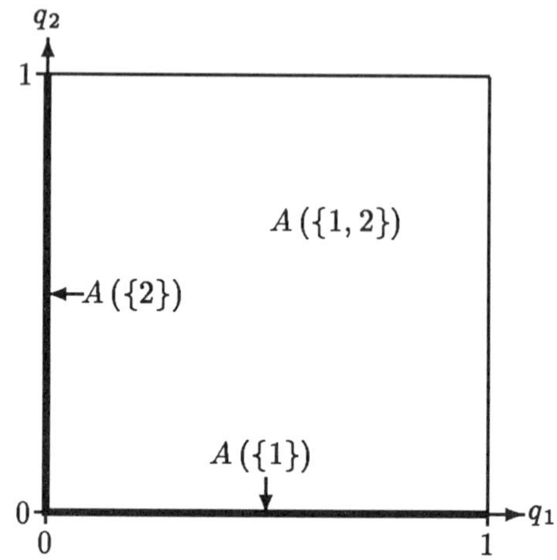

Figure 5.2.1. The sets $A(J)$ for non-empty subsets J of I_N, $N = 2$.

simplex. For every $(t-1)$-simplex τ in the finite sequence either there exists a non-empty subset J of I_N with $\#J = t$ such that τ is a J-complete facet of a t-simplex of $\Sigma(J)$ or τ is an I_{N+1}-complete simplex of Σ. Moreover, any two successive simplices in the finite sequence either are both a facet of the same simplex or one is a facet of the other. In Lemmas 5.2.3 and 5.2.4 all possible situations are described that can occur when some $(t-1)$-simplex τ that is a J-complete facet of a t-simplex of $\Sigma(J)$ for some non-empty subset J of I_N with $\#J = t$ is given. Lemmas 5.2.3 and 5.2.4 are used in Theorem 5.2.7 to determine in a unique way the finite sequence of complete simplices described before. Then the detailed steps of the algorithm yielding this finite sequence are given in Algorithm 5.2.8, and it is shown in Theorem 5.2.10 that if the reduced total excess demand function of the economy satisfies Condition A, then the algorithm terminates with an I_{N+1}-complete simplex of Σ having 1^N as a vertex.

Lemma 5.2.3
Let the labelling function $\widehat{f} : Q^N \to I_{N+1}$ and a triangulation Σ of Q^N be given. Let σ be a t-simplex of $\Sigma(J)$ for some non-empty subset J of I_N with $\#J = t$. Moreover, let a J-complete facet τ of σ be given. Then exactly one of the following cases holds:

1. *the t-simplex σ is $(J \cup \{N+1\})$-complete,*

2. *the t-simplex σ is a $\overline{J}$-complete facet of a $(t+1)$-simplex of $\Sigma(\overline{J})$ for precisely one subset $\overline{J}$ of I_N,*

3. *the t-simplex σ has exactly one other J-complete facet $\overline{\tau}$.*

Proof
Let $\overline{q}$ be the vertex of σ not contained in τ.
If $\widehat{f}(\overline{q}) \notin J$, then σ is $(J \cup \{\widehat{f}(\overline{q})\})$-complete and, since every facet of σ not equal to τ contains $\overline{q}$, it holds that τ is the only J-complete facet of σ. Either $\widehat{f}(\overline{q}) = N+1$ and hence σ is $(J \cup \{N+1\})$-complete, or $\widehat{f}(\overline{q}) \neq N+1$ and σ is a $(J \cup \{\widehat{f}(q)\})$-complete facet of a $(t+1)$-simplex of $\Sigma(J \cup \{\widehat{f}(\overline{q})\})$. In the latter case, Case 2 holds with $\overline{J}$ equal to $J \cup \widehat{f}(\overline{q})$.
If $\widehat{f}(\overline{q}) \in J$, then σ is not $\overline{J}$-complete for any $\overline{J} \subset I_{N+1}$. Moreover, since τ is a J-complete simplex, there is exactly one vertex of τ, say $\widehat{q}$, such that $\widehat{f}(\widehat{q}) = \widehat{f}(\overline{q})$. Hence, the facet of σ opposite $\widehat{q}$ is J-complete, while σ has no other J-complete facets. Q.E.D.

Notice that the set $\overline{J}$ of Case 2 of Lemma 5.2.3 contains the set J as a proper subset.

Lemma 5.2.4
Let the labelling function $\widehat{f}: Q^N \to I_{N+1}$ and a triangulation Σ of Q^N be given. Let τ be a J-complete facet of a t-simplex of $\Sigma(J)$ for some non-empty subset J of I_N with $\#J = t$. Moreover, let τ be a member of $\Sigma(\overline{J})$ for some non-empty subset $\overline{J}$ of I_N. Then precisely one facet of the $(t-1)$-simplex τ is $\overline{J}$-complete.
Proof
For exactly one index $j' \in I_N$ it holds that $\{j'\} = J \setminus \overline{J}$. Since τ is a J-complete simplex, it has exactly one vertex, say $\overline{q}$, such that $\widehat{f}(\overline{q}) = j'$. Since $\overline{J} \neq \emptyset$, it holds that τ is at least 1-dimensional and the facet of τ opposite $\overline{q}$ is $\overline{J}$-complete, while τ has no other $\overline{J}$-complete facet. Q.E.D.

Definition 5.2.5 (Adjacent complete simplices)
Let the labelling function $\widehat{f}: Q^N \to I_{N+1}$ and a triangulation Σ of Q^N be given. Then the simplices $\overline{\tau}$ and $\widehat{\tau}$ are adjacent complete simplices *if $\overline{\tau}$ and $\widehat{\tau}$ are both J-complete facets of the same t-simplex σ of $\Sigma(J)$ for some non-empty subset J of I_N with $\#J = t$, or if $\overline{\tau}$ is a J-complete facet of the complete t-simplex $\widehat{\tau}$ of $\Sigma(J)$ for some non-empty subset J of I_N with $\#J = t$, or if $\widehat{\tau}$ is a J-complete facet of the complete t-simplex $\overline{\tau}$ of $\Sigma(J)$ for some non-empty subset J of I_N with $\#J = t$.*

Theorem 5.2.6 makes a statement concerning the number of adjacent complete simplices of some given complete simplex. Moreover, it is shown that if the t-simplex σ of $\Sigma(J)$, for some non-empty subset J of I_N with $\#J = t$, is $(J \cup \{N+1\})$-complete and the labelling function $\widehat{f}$ is proper, then $J = I_N$.

Theorem 5.2.6
Let the labelling function $\widehat{f} : Q^N \rightarrow I_{N+1}$ be proper. Let a triangulation Σ of Q^N be given. Let τ be a J-complete facet of a t-simplex of $\Sigma(J)$ for some non-empty subset J of I_N with $\#J = t$. If $\tau = \{0^N\}$, then there exists exactly one adjacent complete simplex to τ. If $\tau \neq \{0^N\}$, then there exist exactly two adjacent complete simplices to τ. Let the t-simplex σ of $\Sigma(J)$, for some non-empty subset J of I_N with $\#J = t$, be $(J \cup \{N+1\})$-complete. Then $J = I_N$ and there exists exactly one adjacent complete simplex to σ.
Proof
Let $\tau = \{0^N\}$. So τ is J-complete if and only if $J = \{\widehat{f}(0^N)\}$. Since $\Sigma(\{\widehat{f}(0^N)\})$ is a triangulation of $A(\{\widehat{f}(0^N)\})$ and $\{0^N\}$ is a facet in $\mathrm{rb}(A(\{\widehat{f}(0^N)\}))$, it holds by Definition 2.7.1 that there is a unique 1-simplex $\overline{\sigma}$ of $\Sigma(\{\widehat{f}(0^N)\})$ such that $\{0^N\}$ is a facet of $\overline{\sigma}$. By Lemma 5.2.3, either $\overline{\sigma}$ is $(\{\widehat{f}(0^N)\} \cup \{N+1\})$-complete, or $\overline{\sigma}$ is a $\overline{J}$-complete facet of a 2-simplex of $\Sigma(\overline{J})$ for precisely one non-empty subset $\overline{J}$ of I_N, or $\overline{\sigma}$ has exactly one other $\{\widehat{f}(0^N)\}$-complete facet $\widehat{\tau}$. This yields exactly one adjacent complete simplex to $\{0^N\}$. Since $\{0^N\}$ has no facets, there can be no other adjacent complete simplex to $\{0^N\}$.
Let $\tau \neq \{0^N\}$. Then there are two possibilities, either $\tau \subset \mathrm{rb}(A(J))$ or $\tau \subset \mathrm{ri}(A(J))$.
Consider the case in which $\tau \subset \mathrm{rb}(A(J))$. Then, by the properties of a triangulation, there is a unique t-simplex $\overline{\sigma}$ in $A(J)$ having τ as a facet. By Lemma 5.2.3, either $\overline{\sigma}$ is $(J \cup \{N+1\})$-complete, or $\overline{\sigma}$ is a $\overline{J}$-complete facet of a $(t+1)$-simplex of $\Sigma(\overline{J})$ for precisely one non-empty subset $\overline{J}$ of I_N, or $\overline{\sigma}$ has exactly one other J-complete facet $\widehat{\tau}$. This yields one adjacent complete simplex to τ. Since $\tau \subset \mathrm{rb}(A(J))$, there exists $j' \in J$ such that $x_{j'} = 1$, $\forall x \in \tau$, or $x_{j'} = 0$, $\forall x \in \tau$. Since $\widehat{f}$ is a proper labelling function, the first case implies that no vertex of τ has the label j', a contradiction since τ is J-complete and $j' \in J$. So, $x_{j'} = 0$, $\forall x \in \tau$. Notice that j' is uniquely determined since τ is a $(t-1)$-dimensional simplex. Since $\tau \neq \{0^N\}$, it follows that $J \setminus \{j'\} \neq \emptyset$, so $\tau \subset A(J \setminus \{j'\})$. By Lemma 5.2.4 it holds that precisely one facet of τ is $(J \setminus \{j'\})$-complete and the second adjacent complete simplex to τ is obtained. Clearly, there can be no other adjacent complete simplex to τ.
Consider the case in which $\tau \subset \mathrm{ri}(A(J))$. Then, by Definition 2.7.1, it holds that τ is a facet of exactly two simplices of $\Sigma(J)$. Applying Lemma 5.2.3 twice shows that τ has exactly two adjacent complete simplices.

Finally, let σ be $(J \cup \{N+1\})$-complete. Then σ has a vertex, say $\bar{q}$, such that $\widehat{f}(\bar{q}) = N+1$. Since $\widehat{f}$ is a proper labelling function, it holds that $\bar{q}_j > 0$, $\forall j \in I_N$. Since $\sigma \in \Sigma(J)$, this implies $J = I_N$. The facet of σ opposite $\bar{q}$ is an I_N-complete facet of the complete simplex σ of $\Sigma(I_N)$ and is therefore an adjacent complete simplex to σ. Clearly, σ has no other adjacent complete simplices. Q.E.D.

Theorem 5.2.7
Let the labelling function $\widehat{f} : Q^N \to I_{N+1}$ be proper and let a triangulation Σ of Q^N be given. Then there exists a unique finite sequence of complete simplices $\tau^1, \ldots, \tau^{k'}$ such that $\tau^1 = \{0^N\}$, $\tau^{k'}$ is an I_{N+1}-complete simplex, $\tau^k \neq \tau^{k-2}$, $\forall k \in I_{k'} \setminus I_2$, and any two successive simplices in the finite sequence are adjacent complete simplices.
Proof
The argument used is closely related to the well-known door-in door-out principle of Lemke and Howson (1964), see also Scarf (1973). Let $\tau^1 = \{0^N\}$. Clearly, τ^1 is $\{\widehat{f}(0^N)\}$-complete. Let τ^2 be the unique adjacent complete simplex to τ^1, that exists according to Theorem 5.2.6. If τ^k, for some $k \in \mathbb{N} \setminus \{1\}$, is not I_{N+1}-complete and not equal to $\{0^N\}$, then there exists by Theorem 5.2.6 a unique adjacent complete simplex τ^{k+1} that is not equal to τ^{k-1}. If τ^k, for some $k \in \mathbb{N} \setminus \{1\}$, is I_{N+1}-complete, then there exists by Theorem 5.2.6 no adjacent complete simplex different from τ^{k-1}.
Suppose that two simplices in the sequence are the same. Then there exists $k^1, k^2 \in \mathbb{N}$ such that $k^1 < k^2$, $\tau^{k^1} = \tau^{k^2}$, whereas the simplices $\tau^1, \ldots, \tau^{k^2-1}$ are all different. If $k^1 = 1$, then $k^2 - 1 = 2$ since, by Theorem 5.2.6, τ^1 has exactly one adjacent complete simplex and τ^1 is the first simplex generated for the second time. This yields a contradiction since $\tau^{k^1} \neq \tau^{k^1+2}$ by construction. Therefore, $k^1 > 1$. Since τ^{k^1} has two adjacent complete simplices by Theorem 5.2.6, given by τ^{k^1-1} and τ^{k^1+1}, it holds that $\tau^{k^2-1} = \tau^{k^1-1}$ or $\tau^{k^2-1} = \tau^{k^1+1}$. Since $\tau^1, \ldots, \tau^{k^2-1}$ are all different, a contradiction is obtained, unless $k^1 + 1 = k^2 - 1$. However, by construction $\tau^{k^1} \neq \tau^{k^1+2}$ and again a contradiction is obtained. Consequently, all simplices generated are different.
By Theorem 2.7.2 the collection of all facets of all simplices in $\Sigma(J)$ is finite for every non-empty subset J of I_N and also the collection Σ is finite. Therefore, all simplices in the sequence generated being different, it holds that the sequence generated is a finite sequence. So, $\tau^{k'}$ is I_{N+1}-complete for some $k' \in \mathbb{N}$ since this is the only way the sequence can be terminated. Q.E.D.

Now the steps of the algorithm generating the simplices $\tau^1, \ldots, \tau^{k'}$ of Theorem 5.2.7 are described in detail.

Algorithm 5.2.8 (Simplicial algorithm with integer labelling)
Let the labelling function $\hat{f} : Q^N \to I_{N+1}$ *be proper and let a triangulation* Σ *of* Q^N *be given. The* simplicial algorithm *on* Q^N *with* integer labelling *has the following steps.*

Step 0. *Let* $k = 1$, $t = 1$, $\tau^k = \tau(0^N)$, $J = \{\hat{f}(0^N)\}$, *and let* q^{t+1} *be the unique vertex of the simplex of* $\Sigma(J)$ *containing* τ^k *as the facet opposite to it.*

Step 1. *Let* σ *be equal to the convex hull of* $\tau^k \cup \{q^{t+1}\}$. *If* $\hat{f}(q^{t+1}) = N+1$, *then the algorithm terminates. If* $\hat{f}(q^{t+1}) \notin J$, *then go to Step 3. Otherwise, there is a unique vertex* $\bar{q}$ *of* σ *such that* $\bar{q} \neq q^{t+1}$ *and* $\hat{f}(\bar{q}) = \hat{f}(q^{t+1})$.

Step 2. *Increase the value of* k *by 1 and let* τ^k *be the facet of* σ *opposite* $\bar{q}$. *If there exists* $j' \in J$ *such that* $\tau^k \in \Sigma(J \setminus \{j'\})$, *then let* $\bar{J}$ *be equal to* $J \setminus \{j'\}$ *and go to Step 4. Otherwise, there is exactly one* t*-simplex* $\bar{\sigma}$ *of* $\Sigma(J)$ *such that* $\bar{\sigma} \neq \sigma$ *and* τ^k *is a facet of* $\bar{\sigma}$. *Go to Step 1 with* q^{t+1} *as the unique vertex of* $\bar{\sigma}$ *opposite* τ^k.

Step 3. *Let* $\bar{J}$ *be equal to* $J \cup \{\hat{f}(q^{t+1})\}$. *There is a unique* $(t+1)$*-simplex* $\bar{\sigma}$ *of* $\Sigma(\bar{J})$ *having* σ *as a facet. Increase the value of both* k *and* t *by 1 and go to Step 1 with* q^{t+1} *as the unique vertex of* $\bar{\sigma}$ *opposite* σ, $J = \bar{J}$, *and* $\tau^k = \sigma$.

Step 4. *Let* σ *be equal to* τ^k. *Let* $\hat{q}$ *be the unique vertex of* σ *such that* $\hat{f}(\hat{q}) = j'$. *Decrease the value of* t *by 1 and go to Step 2 with* $\bar{q} = \hat{q}$ *and* $J = \bar{J}$.

Consider Algorithm 5.2.8. In Step 0 the algorithm is initiated. In Step 1 it is determined whether the algorithm should be terminated, or whether a new simplex should be generated having a higher dimension than the current simplex, or whether the current simplex should be replaced by a simplex having the same dimension. In Step 2 the current simplex is replaced by another simplex of the same dimension if this operation is possible. In Step 3 a new simplex is generated containing the current simplex as a facet and therefore having a higher dimension than the current simplex. In Step 4 a new simplex is generated that is a facet of the current simplex and therefore has a lower dimension than the current simplex.

For the case $N = 2$, Algorithm 5.2.8 is illustrated in Figure 5.2.2 given some proper labelling function and the K-triangulation of Q^2 with grid size $\frac{1}{3}$.

In Figure 5.2.2 the algorithm starts with the $\{2\}$-complete simplex $\tau^1 = \{0^N\}$ that is a facet of a uniquely determined 1-simplex τ^2 of $\Sigma(\{2\})$ and termi-

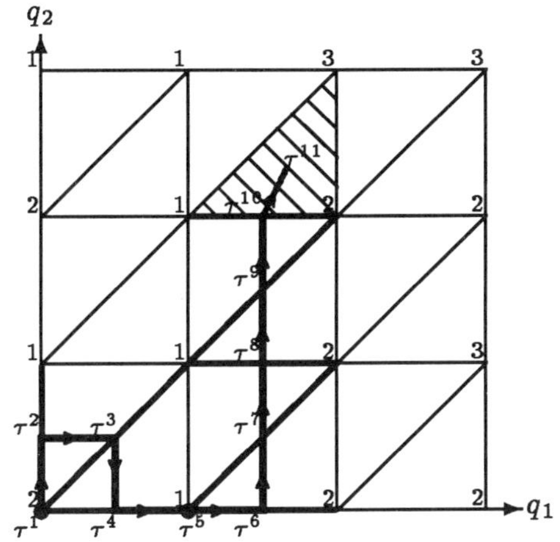

Figure 5.2.2. Illustration of the algorithm, $N = 2$.

nates with the $\{1,2,3\}$-complete simplex $\tau^{11} = \text{co}(\{(\frac{1}{3},\frac{2}{3})^\top, (\frac{2}{3},\frac{2}{3})^\top, (\frac{2}{3},1)^\top\})$ of $\Sigma(\{1,2\}) = \Sigma$. After the starting simplex τ^1 the algorithm generates three $\{1,2\}$-complete simplices that are facets of simplices of $\Sigma(\{1,2\})$. Then the $\{1\}$-complete simplex τ^5 and five $\{1,2\}$-complete simplices are generated. Notice that the 0-simplex τ^1 and the 1-simplex τ^4 are not adjacent complete simplices. The barycentres of any two adjacent complete simplices that are generated by the algorithm have been joined by a straight line.

Let $\hat{f} : Q^N \to I_{N+1}$ be a proper labelling function and let Σ be a triangulation of Q^N. In general, it cannot be excluded that there exists a J-complete facet $\bar{\tau}$ of a t-simplex of $\Sigma(J)$ for some non-empty subset of I_N with $\#J = t$ that is not generated by Algorithm 5.2.8. Then, using Theorem 5.2.6, it can be shown similarly as in the proof of Theorem 5.2.7 that there exists a finite sequence of complete simplices, say $\bar{\tau}^1, \ldots, \bar{\tau}^{k'}$, such that $\bar{\tau}^k \neq \bar{\tau}^{k-2}$, $\forall k \in I_{k'} \setminus I_2$, two successive simplices in this finite sequence are adjacent complete simplices, and either $\bar{\tau} = \bar{\tau}^1 = \bar{\tau}^{k'}$, or $\bar{\tau}^1$ and $\bar{\tau}^{k'}$ are different I_{N+1}-complete N-simplices of Σ and $\bar{\tau} = \bar{\tau}^k$ for some $k \in I_{k'}$. Moreover, this finite sequence of adjacent complete simplices is uniquely determined in the sense that it is given by $\bar{\tau}^1, \ldots, \bar{\tau}^{k'}$ or by $\bar{\tau}^{k'}, \ldots, \bar{\tau}^1$. In Figure 5.2.3 it is shown that in the example given in Figure 5.2.2 a finite sequence as just described exists.

Consider the $\{2\}$-complete 0-simplex $\bar{\tau}^1 = \{(0,\frac{2}{3})^\top\}$ in Figure 5.2.3, which is not generated by Algorithm 5.2.8. It has exactly two adjacent complete simplices, the $\{1,2\}$-complete 1-simplex $\bar{\tau}^2 = \text{co}(\{(0,\frac{1}{3})^\top, (0,\frac{2}{3})^\top\})$ and the

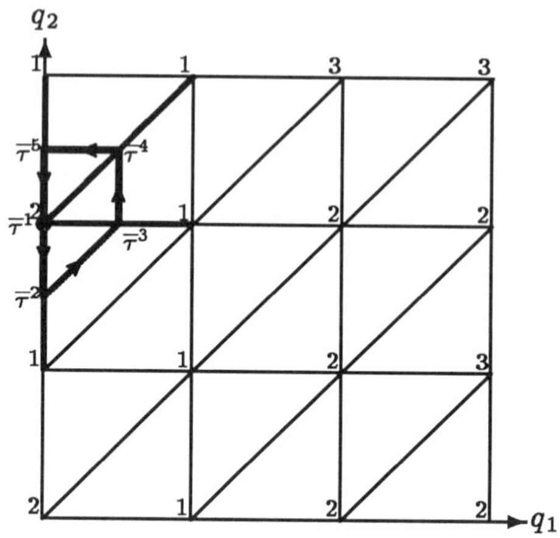

Figure 5.2.3. Adjacent complete simplices not generated by the algorithm, $N = 2$.

$\{1, 2\}$-complete 1-simplex $\overline{\tau}^5 = \text{co}(\{(0, \frac{2}{3})^\top, (0, 1)^\top\})$. Again, the barycentres of any two adjacent complete simplices are joined by a straight line.

Now the behaviour of Algorithm 5.2.8 is studied if the reduced total excess demand function of the economy satisfies Condition A. Theorem 5.2.9 states that the labelling function is proper in this case.

Theorem 5.2.9
Let the reduced total excess demand function $\widehat{z}$ of the economy $\widetilde{\mathcal{E}}$ satisfy Condition A. Then the labelling function $\widehat{f} : Q^N \to I_{N+1}$ is proper.
Proof
Let some $q \in Q^N$ be given. Let $q_j = 0$ for some $j \in I_N$, so $\widehat{z}_j(q) \geq 0$. If there exists $j' \in I_N$ such that $q_{j'} = 1$, then $\widehat{z}_{j'}(q) \leq 0$. Hence, $J(q) \neq \{N + 1\}$ and therefore $\widehat{f}(q) \neq N + 1$.
Let some $q \in Q^N$ be given and let $q_j = 1$ for some $j \in I_N$. Then the definition of $J(q)$ implies that $j \notin J(q)$ and therefore $\widehat{f}(q) \neq j$. Q.E.D.

Let the reduced total excess demand function of the economy satisfy Condition A. Let Σ be a triangulation of Q^N. Then it can be shown that any point of any simplex of Σ containing one of the adjacent complete simplices generated by Algorithm 5.2.8, induces a *state* of the markets of the economy at which the total excess demand is arbitrarily close to zero if the mesh size of Σ is small enough.

Theorem 5.2.10
Let the reduced total excess demand function $\widehat{z}$ of the economy $\widetilde{\mathcal{E}}$ satisfy Condition A. Let Σ be a triangulation of Q^N. Then, for every $\varepsilon \in \mathbb{R}_{++}$, there exists $\delta \in \mathbb{R}_{++}$ such that if mesh$(\Sigma) < \delta$ and $\sigma \in \Sigma$ contains one of the adjacent complete simplices generated by Algorithm 5.2.8, then $\|\widehat{z}(q)\|_\infty < \varepsilon$, $\forall q \in \sigma$.
Proof
Let some $\varepsilon \in \mathbb{R}_{++}$ be given. Let $\delta \in \mathbb{R}_{++}$ be such that $q^1, q^2 \in Q^N$ and $\|q^1 - q^2\|_\infty < \delta$ implies

$$\|\widehat{z}(q^1) - \widehat{z}(q^2)\|_\infty < \frac{\min(\{\underline{p}_j \mid j \in I_N\})}{\sum_{j \in I_N} \overline{p}_j}\varepsilon, \tag{5.1}$$

and let mesh$(\Sigma) < \delta$. Since $\widehat{z}$ is a continuous function and the set Q^N is compact, such a δ exists by Theorem 2.7.10. Let σ be any N-simplex of Σ containing one of the adjacent complete simplices generated by the algorithm. Then there exists a non-empty subset $\overline{J}$ of I_N and a $\overline{J}$-complete simplex $\overline{\tau} \subset A(\overline{J})$ that is contained by σ. For every $q \in \overline{\tau}$, for every $j \in I_N \setminus \overline{J}$, $q_j = 0$ and therefore $\widehat{z}_j(q) \geq 0$. For every $j \in \overline{J}$, there exists a vertex q of $\overline{\tau}$ such that $\widehat{f}(q) = j$, and, using Condition A.3, it follows that $\widehat{z}_j(q) = \max(\{\widehat{z}_j(q) \mid j \in I_N\}) \geq 0$. So, for every $j \in I_N$, there exists $q \in \overline{\tau}$ such that $\widehat{z}_j(q) \geq 0$.
Let some $q \in \sigma$ be given. Since mesh$(\Sigma) < \delta$, it follows from the previous paragraph and by (5.1) that

$$\widehat{z}_j(q) > -\frac{\min(\{\underline{p}_j \mid j \in I_N\})}{\sum_{j \in I_N} \overline{p}_j}\varepsilon > -\varepsilon, \ \forall j \in I_N. \tag{5.2}$$

By Condition A.3 and (5.2) it holds that

$$\widehat{p}_j(q)\,\widehat{z}_j(q) = -\sum_{j \in I_N \setminus \{j\}} \widehat{p}_j(q)\,\widehat{z}_j(q) < \frac{\min(\{\underline{p}_j \mid j \in I_N\})}{\sum_{j \in I_N} \overline{p}_j}\varepsilon \sum_{j \in I_N \setminus \{j\}} \widehat{p}_j(q), \ \forall j \in I_N.$$

Therefore,

$$\widehat{z}_j(q) < \frac{\min(\{\underline{p}_j \mid j \in I_N\})}{\widehat{p}_j(q)}\varepsilon \leq \varepsilon, \ \forall j \in I_N.$$

Q.E.D.

Finally, it is proved that 1^N is a vertex of the last adjacent complete simplex generated by Algorithm 5.2.8 if the reduced total excess demand function of the economy satisfies Condition A. This is done by showing that the only point of Q^N having label $N+1$ is the point 1^N.

Theorem 5.2.11
Let the reduced total excess demand function $\widehat{z}$ of the economy $\widetilde{\mathcal{E}}$ satisfy Condition A. Then $q \in Q^N$ satisfies $\widehat{f}(q) = N+1$ if and only if $q = 1^N$.
Proof
Clearly, $J(1^N) = \{N+1\}$ and hence $\widehat{f}(1^N) = N+1$.
Let some $q \in Q^N \setminus \{1^N\}$ be given. If $q_j = 1$ for some $j \in I_N$, then $\widehat{z}_j(q) \leq 0$. Hence, by Condition A.3, $\widehat{z}_j(q) \geq 0$ for some $j \in I_N$ for which $q_j < 1$. Therefore, $J(q) \neq \{N+1\}$ and $\widehat{f}(q) \neq N+1$. Q.E.D.

Summarizing the results of Theorems 5.2.7, 5.2.9, and 5.2.11, it follows that if the reduced total excess demand relation of the economy satisfies Condition A, then Algorithm 5.2.8 generates a finite sequence of adjacent complete simplices such that $\{0^N\}$ is the first simplex generated and 1^N is a vertex of the last simplex generated. This result combined with Theorem 5.2.10 are used extensively in the next section to prove the existence of a connected set of constrained equilibria containing the two trivial constrained equilibria of the economy.

5.3 THE EXISTENCE OF A CONTINUUM OF CONSTRAINED EQUILIBRIA

In this section the reduced total excess demand relation of the economy $\widetilde{\mathcal{E}}$ is again assumed to be a function. If the reduced total excess demand relation satisfies Condition A, then it is shown that there exists a connected subset $\widetilde{C}$ of Q^N such that $0^N, 1^N \in \widetilde{C}$ and for every $q \in \widetilde{C}$ it holds that $\widehat{z}(q) = 0^N$. Theorem 5.3.1 first gives an interesting result for approximations of constrained equilibria.

Theorem 5.3.1
Let the reduced total excess demand function $\widehat{z}$ of the economy $\widetilde{\mathcal{E}}$ satisfy Condition A. Then, for every $n \in \mathbb{N}$, there exists a continuous function $f^n : [0,1] \rightarrow Q^N$ joining 0^N and 1^N and satisfying that $\|\widehat{z}(f^n(t))\|_\infty < \frac{1}{n}$, $\forall t \in [0,1]$.
Proof
Let some $n \in \mathbb{N}$ be given. Let Σ be a triangulation of Q^N with mesh $(\Sigma) < \delta$

where δ is chosen such that Theorem 5.2.10 holds for $\varepsilon = \frac{1}{n}$. Consider the finite sequence of adjacent complete simplices $\tau^1, \ldots, \tau^{k'}$ generated by Algorithm 5.2.8. For every $k \in I_{k'}$, let $q^k \in Q^N$ be defined as the barycentre of τ^k and let $q^{k'+1}$ be defined by $q^{k'+1} = 1^N$. Clearly, $q^1 = 0^N$. By Theorem 5.2.11 it holds that $1^N \in \tau^{k'}$. Moreover, by the definition of adjacent complete simplices it holds that for every $k \in I_{k'}$ there exists $\sigma \in \Sigma$ containing q^k and q^{k+1}. Recall from Section 2.2 that, for $t \in \mathbb{R}$, $\lfloor t \rfloor$ denotes the greatest integer that is less than or equal to t. By the convexity of simplices and by Theorem 5.2.10, it is easily verified that the function $f^n : [0,1] \to Q^N$, defined by

$$f^n(t) = (1 - k't + \lfloor k't \rfloor)\, q^{\lfloor 1+k't \rfloor} + (k't - \lfloor k't \rfloor)\, q^{1+\lfloor 1+k't \rfloor},\ \forall t \in [0,1),$$
$$f^n(1) = q^{k'+1},$$

satisfies all conditions of the theorem. Q.E.D.

Let the reduced total excess demand function $\widehat{z}$ of the economy $\widetilde{\mathcal{E}}$ satisfy Condition A. The set $\widetilde{Q}$ is defined as the set of all elements of Q^N inducing a constrained equilibrium of the economy, so

$$\widetilde{Q} = \left\{ q^* \in Q^N \,\middle|\, \widehat{z}(q^*) = 0^N \right\}.$$

Clearly, 0^N and 1^N are elements of $\widetilde{Q}$ and therefore $\widetilde{Q} \neq \emptyset$. Moreover, $\widetilde{Q}$ is a closed set by the continuity of the function $\widehat{z}$.

Let a non-empty, closed subset S of $\mathbb{R}^m$ be given. The function $d_S : \mathbb{R}^m \to \mathbb{R}$ is defined by

$$d_S(s) = \min\left(\{\|s - \overline{s}\|_\infty \,|\, \overline{s} \in S\}\right),\ \forall s \in \mathbb{R}^m.$$

Using Theorem 2.3.14 it is not difficult to show that the function d_S is well defined.

Let S^1 and S^2 be non-empty, compact subsets of $\mathbb{R}^m$. The number $e(S^1, S^2) \in \mathbb{R}_+$ is defined by

$$e(S^1, S^2) = \min\left(\left\{\|s^1 - s^2\|_\infty \,\middle|\, s^1 \in S^1 \text{ and } s^2 \in S^2\right\}\right).$$

It follows immediately by Theorem 2.3.14 that $e(S^1, S^2)$ is well defined. Clearly, if S^1 and S^2 are disjoint, then $e(S^1, S^2) > 0$.

Lemma 5.3.2
Let a non-empty, compact subset S of $\mathbb{R}^m$ be given. Then the function d_S is

continuous.

Proof

Clearly, the relation $\varphi : \mathbb{R}^m \to S$, defined by $\varphi(s) = S$, $\forall s \in \mathbb{R}^m$, is a compact-valued, continuous correspondence and the function $f : \mathbb{R}^m \times S \to \mathbb{R}$, defined by $f(s, \overline{s}) = -\max(\{|s_j - \overline{s}_j| \mid j \in I_m\})$, $\forall (s, \overline{s}) \in \mathbb{R}^m \times S$, is continuous. From the maximum theorem, Theorem 2.5.17, it follows that the relation $\mu : \mathbb{R}^m \to S$, defined by

$$\mu(s) = \{\widehat{s} \in \varphi(s) \,|\, f(s, \widehat{s}) \geq f(s, \overline{s}),\ \forall \overline{s} \in \varphi(s)\},\ \forall s \in \mathbb{R}^m,$$

is a compact-valued, upper hemi-continuous correspondence, and it follows that the relation $g : \mathbb{R}^m \to \mathbb{R}$, defined by

$$g(s) = \{f(s, \widehat{s}) \,|\, \widehat{s} \in \mu(s)\},\ \forall s \in \mathbb{R}^m,$$

is a continuous function. It is easily verified that $g = d_S$. Q.E.D.

The following theorem shows that the approximations of constrained equilibria given by the image of the function f^n of Theorem 5.3.1 are uniformly close to the set of constrained equilibria if n is large enough.

Theorem 5.3.3

Let the reduced total excess demand function $\widehat{z}$ of the economy $\widetilde{\mathcal{E}}$ satisfy Condition A. For every $n \in \mathbb{N}$, let $f^n : [0,1] \to Q^N$ be a continuous function such that $\|\widehat{z}(f^n(t))\|_\infty < \frac{1}{n}$, $\forall t \in [0,1]$. Then, for every $\varepsilon \in \mathbb{R}_{++}$, there exists $n' \in \mathbb{N}$ such that, for every $n \geq n'$, for every $t \in [0,1]$, $d_{\widetilde{Q}}(f^n(t)) < \varepsilon$.

Proof

Suppose there exists $\varepsilon \in \mathbb{R}_{++}$ such that for every $n \in \mathbb{N}$ there exists $m^n \geq n$ and $t^n \in [0,1]$ satisfying $d_{\widetilde{Q}}(f^{m^n}(t^n)) \geq \varepsilon$. Consider the sequence $(f^{m^n}(t^n))_{n \in \mathbb{N}}$ in Q^N. Without loss of generality, this sequence can be assumed to converge to some $\overline{q} \in Q^N$. By the continuity of the function $d_{\widetilde{Q}}$, shown in Lemma 5.3.2, it holds that

$$d_{\widetilde{Q}}(\overline{q}) = d_{\widetilde{Q}}\left(\lim_{n \to +\infty} f^{m^n}(t^n)\right) = \lim_{n \to +\infty} d_{\widetilde{Q}}\left(f^{m^n}(t^n)\right) \geq \varepsilon. \tag{5.3}$$

However, by the continuity of the function $\widehat{z}$ it holds that

$$0 \leq \|\widehat{z}(\overline{q})\|_\infty = \left\|\widehat{z}\left(\lim_{n \to +\infty} f^{m^n}(t^n)\right)\right\|_\infty = \left\|\lim_{n \to +\infty} \widehat{z}\left(f^{m^n}(t^n)\right)\right\|_\infty$$
$$\leq \lim_{n \to +\infty} \frac{1}{m^n} = 0.$$

So, $\overline{q} \in \widetilde{Q}$ and therefore $d_{\widetilde{Q}}(\overline{q}) = 0$, a contradiction to (5.3). Q.E.D.

In Theorem 5.3.5 it is shown that the set $\widetilde{Q}$ has a component containing both 0^N and 1^N if the reduced total excess demand relation of the economy $\widetilde{\mathcal{E}}$ satisfies Condition A. The main argument used in the proof of this result is that the quasi-component of 0^N in $\widetilde{Q}$ contains 1^N. From this it is tempting to conclude that also the component of 0^N in $\widetilde{Q}$ contains 1^N. Example 2.3.8 makes clear that the quasi-component of a point in a subset of Q^N is not necessarily connected. However, if $\widehat{z}$ is a continuous function, then the set $\widetilde{Q}$ is closed, and therefore it cannot be equal to a set like S considered in Example 2.3.8. The following lemma gives sufficient conditions guaranteeing that the component and the quasi-component of a point coincide.

Lemma 5.3.4
Let S be a compact subset of $\mathbb{R}^m$. Then, for every $s \in S$, the component of s in S and the quasi-component of s in S coincide.

Proof
In the entire proof cl and fr are used to denote the closure and the frontier in S. Let some $\overline{s} \in S$ be given.
By Theorem 2.3.7 the component of $\overline{s}$ in S is contained in the quasi-component of $\overline{s}$ in S.
Now the converse is shown. Let C be the quasi-component of $\overline{s}$ in S. Since C is an intersection of sets closed in S, it is closed in S itself. It has to be shown that C is connected.
Suppose C is not connected. Then there exist two disjoint, non-empty sets C^1 and C^2 such that $C^1 \cup C^2 = C$, and C^1 and C^2 are both closed in C, hence in $\mathbb{R}^m$ since C is closed. Without loss of generality, it can be assumed that $\overline{s} \in C^1$. Since C^1 and C^2 are compact sets, the set D^1, defined by

$$D^1 = \left\{s \in S \,\middle|\, d_{C^1}(s) < \tfrac{1}{2}e(C^1, C^2)\right\} = d_{C^1}^{-1}\left((\leftarrow, \tfrac{1}{2}e(C^1, C^2))\right) \cap S$$

is non-empty. It follows immediately that D^1 is open in S, $C^1 \subset D^1$, and $C^2 \cap \mathrm{cl}\left(D^1\right) = \emptyset$. Moreover, these three properties imply

$$C \cap \mathrm{fr}\left(D^1\right) = \left(C^1 \cup C^2\right) \cap \mathrm{fr}\left(D^1\right) = \emptyset. \tag{5.4}$$

Let some $\widehat{s} \in C^2$ be given. In the following step of the proof a set being both open and closed in S, containing $\overline{s}$, but not containing $\widehat{s}$ is constructed. This yields a contradiction since C is the quasi-component of $\overline{s}$ and $\widehat{s}$ is an element of C. If $\mathrm{fr}(D^1) = \emptyset$, then D^1 is closed in S and satisfies the requirements mentioned above. So, consider the case that $\mathrm{fr}(D^1) \neq \emptyset$. For every $s \in \mathrm{fr}\left(D^1\right)$ it holds by (5.4) that $s \notin C$. Hence, since C is the quasi-component of $\overline{s}$, for every $s \in \mathrm{fr}(D^1)$, there exists S^s such that S^s is open and closed in S, $\overline{s} \in S^s$, and $s \notin S^s$. The collection $\{S \setminus S^s \mid s \in \mathrm{fr}(D^1)\}$ consists of sets that are open in S, and since $\mathrm{fr}(D^1) \subset \cup_{s \in \mathrm{fr}(D^1)} S \setminus S^s$ and $\mathrm{fr}(D^1)$ is compact, there exists a finite collection, say $\{S \setminus S^{s^1}, \ldots, S \setminus S^{s^{k'}}\}$, such that $\mathrm{fr}(D^1) \subset S \setminus \cup_{k \in I_{k'}} S^{s^k}$. The set $\cap_{k \in I_{k'}} S^{s^k}$ is open and closed in S and contains the element $\bar{s}$. Moreover, $\mathrm{fr}(D^1) \cap (\cap_{k \in I_{k'}} S^{s^k}) = \emptyset$. Finally, consider the set $D^1 \cap (\cap_{k \in I_{k'}} S^{s^k})$. Clearly, $\bar{s} \in D^1 \cap (\cap_{k \in I_{k'}} S^{s^k})$ and $\widehat{s} \notin D^1 \cap (\cap_{k \in I_{k'}} S^{s^k})$. The set $D^1 \cap \left(\cap_{k \in I_{k'}} S^{s^k}\right)$ is open in S as an intersection of finitely many sets that are open in S. Furthermore,

$$\begin{aligned}
\mathrm{cl}\left(D^1 \cap \left(\cap_{k \in I_{k'}} S^{s^k}\right)\right) &\subset \mathrm{cl}\left(D^1\right) \cap \mathrm{cl}\left(\cap_{k \in I_{k'}} S^{s^k}\right) \\
&= \mathrm{cl}\left(D^1\right) \cap \left(\cap_{k \in I_{k'}} S^{s^k}\right) \\
&= \left(D^1 \cap \left(\cap_{k \in I_{k'}} S^{s^k}\right)\right) \cup \left(\mathrm{fr}\left(D^1\right) \cap \left(\cap_{k \in I_{k'}} S^{s^k}\right)\right) \\
&= D^1 \cap \left(\cap_{k \in I_{k'}} S^{s^k}\right).
\end{aligned}$$

So, the set $D^1 \cap (\cap_{k \in I_{k'}} S^{s^k})$ is both open and closed in S, contains $\bar{s}$, but does not contain $\widehat{s}$. This yields a contradiction since C is the quasi-component of $\bar{s}$ and $\widehat{s}$ is an element of C. Consequently, C is connected. Q.E.D.

The next theorem finally gives the desired result.

Theorem 5.3.5
Let the reduced total excess demand function $\widehat{z}$ of the economy $\widetilde{\mathcal{E}}$ satisfy Condition A. Then the set $\widetilde{Q}$ contains a component $\widetilde{C}$ such that $0^N \in \widetilde{C}$ and $1^N \in \widetilde{C}$.
Proof
Suppose that the component of 0^N in $\widetilde{Q}$ does not contain 1^N. Then, by Lemma 5.3.4, the quasi-component of 0^N in $\widetilde{Q}$ does not contain 1^N. Hence, there exists a set $\widetilde{Q}^1$ that is both open and closed in $\widetilde{Q}$, contains 0^N, but does not contain 1^N. Let the set $\widetilde{Q}^2$ be defined by $\widetilde{Q}^2 = \widetilde{Q} \setminus \widetilde{Q}^1$. Clearly, $\widetilde{Q}^2$ is both open and closed in $\widetilde{Q}$ and contains 1^N. Since $\widetilde{Q}$ is a closed subset of $\mathbb{R}^N$, it follows that $\widetilde{Q}^1$ and $\widetilde{Q}^2$ are compact. Moreover, there exists $\varepsilon \in \mathbb{R}_{++}$ such that

$$e\left(\widetilde{Q}^1, \widetilde{Q}^2\right) > \varepsilon, \tag{5.5}$$

since $\widetilde{Q}^1 \cap \widetilde{Q}^2 = \emptyset$. By Theorems 5.3.1 and 5.3.3 there exists a continuous function $f : [0,1] \to Q^N$ such that

$$d_{\widetilde{Q}}\left(f\left(t\right)\right) < \tfrac{1}{2}\varepsilon, \ \forall t \in [0,1], \tag{5.6}$$

while $f(0) = 0^N$ and $f(1) = 1^N$. It is shown that for some $\bar{t} \in [0,1]$ it holds that $d_{\widetilde{Q}^1}\left(f\left(\bar{t}\right)\right) < \frac{1}{2}\varepsilon$ and $d_{\widetilde{Q}^2}\left(f\left(\bar{t}\right)\right) < \frac{1}{2}\varepsilon$. Let the function $g : [0,1] \to \mathbb{R}$ be defined by

$$g(t) = d_{\widetilde{Q}^1}(f(t)) - d_{\widetilde{Q}^2}(f(t)), \ \forall t \in [0,1].$$

From the continuity of the functions f, $d_{\widetilde{Q}^1}$, and $d_{\widetilde{Q}^2}$, see Lemma 5.3.2, it follows that the function g is continuous. Moreover, using (5.5), $g(0) < -\varepsilon$ and $g(1) > \varepsilon$. Since $[0,1]$ is connected and g is continuous, it follows from Theorem 2.3.13 that $g([0,1])$ is connected. Hence, there exists $\bar{t} \in [0,1]$ such that $g(\bar{t}) = 0$ and therefore

$$d_{\widetilde{Q}^1}(f(\bar{t})) = d_{\widetilde{Q}^2}(f(\bar{t})) = d_{\widetilde{Q}}(f(\bar{t})) < \tfrac{1}{2}\varepsilon,$$

where (5.6) is used for the last inequality. Therefore, there exists $q^1 \in \widetilde{Q}^1$ and $q^2 \in \widetilde{Q}^2$ such that $\|f(\bar{t}) - q^1\|_\infty < \frac{1}{2}\varepsilon$ and $\|f(\bar{t}) - q^2\|_\infty < \frac{1}{2}\varepsilon$. Hence,

$$\varepsilon < e\left(\widetilde{Q}^1, \widetilde{Q}^2\right) \leq \|q^1 - q^2\|_\infty \leq \|f(\bar{t}) - q^1\|_\infty + \|f(\bar{t}) - q^2\|_\infty < \varepsilon,$$

a contradiction. Q.E.D.

Since the set $\widetilde{Q}$ contains a component $\widetilde{C}$ such that $0^N \in \widetilde{C}$ and $1^N \in \widetilde{C}$, it is tempting to conclude that there exists a path in $\widetilde{Q}$ joining 0^N and 1^N. That this is not necessarily the case follows from Example 2.3.6, showing that the component and the path-component of an element can be different.

Corollary 5.3.6
Let the economy $\widetilde{\mathcal{E}} = ((X^i, \preceq^i, \omega^i)_{i \in I_M}, P_{(\underline{p},\overline{p})}, (\widetilde{l}, \widetilde{L}))$ satisfy Assumptions A1-A5 given in Section 4.7 and let the preference relation $\preceq^i$, $\forall i \in I_M$, be strongly convex. Then there exists a connected set of constrained equilibria of $\widetilde{\mathcal{E}}$, containing both the trivial supply constrained equilibrium $(\underline{p}, 0^{MN}, \widetilde{L}(0^N), \omega)$ of $\widetilde{\mathcal{E}}$ and the trivial demand constrained equilibrium $(\overline{p}, \widetilde{l}(1^N), 0^{MN}, \omega)$ of $\widetilde{\mathcal{E}}$.

Proof
For every $i \in I_M$ it follows from Theorem 4.7.3 that the relation $\widehat{\delta}^i$ is a continuous function, denoted by $\widehat{d}^i$. The function $f : Q^N \to \mathbb{R}^N \times -\mathbb{R}_+^{MN} \times \mathbb{R}_+^{MN} \times \prod_{i \in I_M} \mathbb{R}^N$ is obtained by associating with every $q \in Q^N$ the element

$$f(q) = \left(\widehat{p}(q), \widehat{l}(q), \widehat{L}(q), \widehat{d}^1\left(\widehat{p}(q), \widehat{l}^1(q), \widehat{L}^1(q)\right), \ldots, \widehat{d}^M\left(\widehat{p}(q), \widehat{l}^M(q), \widehat{L}^M(q)\right)\right).$$

From Theorem 4.7.1 it follows that every element of $f(\widetilde{Q})$ is a constrained equilibrium of $\widetilde{\mathcal{E}}$. The set $\widetilde{Q}$ has a component $\widetilde{C}$ containing 0^N and 1^N by Theorem 5.3.5. The continuity of the functions $\widehat{p}, \widehat{l}, \widehat{L}$, and $\widehat{d}^i$, $\forall i \in I_M$, guarantees that

the function f is continuous. From Theorem 2.3.13 it follows that the image of a connected set by a continuous function is connected, therefore $f(\widetilde{C})$ is connected. Moreover, $f(0^N) = (\underline{p}, 0^{MN}, \widehat{L}(0^N), \omega)$ and $f(1^N) = (\overline{p}, \widehat{l}(1^N), 0^{MN}, \omega)$.
Q.E.D.

5.4 THE UPPER HEMI-CONTINUOUS CASE

The results given in Theorem 5.3.5 and in Corollary 5.3.6 hold if it is assumed that the economy $\widetilde{\mathcal{E}}$ satisfies Assumptions A1-A5 of Section 4.7 and the preference relation $\preceq^i$, $\forall i \in I_M$, is strongly convex. In this section the same results are obtained, but the assumption of strong convexity of the preference relation $\preceq^i$, $\forall i \in I_M$, is dropped. In Theorem 4.7.3 it has been shown that if the economy satisfies Assumptions A1-A5 of Section 4.7, then the reduced total excess demand relation of the economy satisfies the following condition.

Condition B The reduced total excess demand relation $\widehat{\zeta} : Q^N \to \mathbb{R}^N$ of the economy $\widetilde{\mathcal{E}}$ satisfies

1. $\widehat{\zeta}$ is a compact-valued, convex-valued, upper hemi-continuous correspondence,
2. for every $q \in Q^N$, for every $z \in \widehat{\zeta}(q)$, for every $j \in I_N$, $q_j = 0$ implies $z_j \geq 0$, and $q_j = 1$ implies $z_j \leq 0$,
3. for every $q \in Q^N$, for every $z \in \widehat{\zeta}(q)$, $\widehat{p}(q) \cdot z = 0$.

It is possible to construct examples showing that Theorem 5.3.1 need not be true under these circumstances. Moreover, a simplicial algorithm with integer labelling like the one given in Section 5.2 cannot be used when one is considering upper hemi-continuous correspondences instead of continuous functions, see Todd (1976), Remark 2.4, page 58. Therefore, a simplicial algorithm with vector labelling is proposed in Chapter 6. Then a constructive proof of Theorem 5.3.5 and Corollary 5.3.6 for the case with $\widehat{\zeta}$ being an upper hemi-continuous correspondence can be given that uses many of the ideas of Sections 5.2 and 5.3. In this section a non-constructive proof is presented, using the results obtained in Section 5.3.

Again, the set $\widetilde{Q}$ is defined as the set of zero points of $\widehat{\zeta}$, so $\widetilde{Q} = \widehat{\zeta}^{-1}(\{0^N\})$. It follows immediately that $0^N \in \widetilde{Q}$ and $1^N \in \widetilde{Q}$ if the reduced total excess demand relation of the economy $\widetilde{\mathcal{E}}$ satisfies Condition B.

Theorem 5.4.1

Let the reduced total excess demand relation $\widehat{\zeta}$ of the economy $\widetilde{\mathcal{E}}$ satisfy Condition B. Then $\widetilde{Q}$ contains a component $\widetilde{C}$ such that $0^N \in \widetilde{C}$ and $1^N \in \widetilde{C}$.

Proof

Since $\{0^N\}$ is closed in $\mathbb{R}^N$ and since $\widehat{\zeta}$ is upper hemi-continuous, it follows from Theorem 2.5.3 that $\widetilde{Q} = \widehat{\zeta}^{-1}(\{0^N\})$ is closed in Q^N.

Suppose that the component of 0^N in $\widetilde{Q}$ does not contain 1^N. Since $\widetilde{Q}$ is compact, the quasi-component of 0^N does not contain 1^N by Lemma 5.3.4. Then, similarly to the proof of Theorem 5.3.5, there exist two sets $\widetilde{Q}^1$ and $\widetilde{Q}^2$ that are both closed in $\widetilde{Q}$ and satisfy $\widetilde{Q}^1 \cap \widetilde{Q}^2 = \emptyset$, $\widetilde{Q}^1 \cup \widetilde{Q}^2 = \widetilde{Q}$, $0^N \in \widetilde{Q}^1$, and $1^N \in \widetilde{Q}^2$. Hence,

$$e\left(\widetilde{Q}^1, \widetilde{Q}^2\right) > \varepsilon, \tag{5.7}$$

for some $\varepsilon \in \mathbb{R}_{++}$. Let the correspondence $\overline{\zeta} : Q^N \to \mathbb{R}^N$ be defined by

$$\overline{\zeta}(q) = \left\{\overline{z} \in \mathbb{R}^N \,\middle|\, \exists \widehat{z} \in \widehat{\zeta}(q),\ \overline{z}_j = \widehat{p}_j(q)\widehat{z}_j,\ \forall j \in I_N\right\},\ \forall q \in Q^N.$$

For every $n \in \mathbb{N}$, let Σ^n be a triangulation of Q^N with $\text{mesh}(\Sigma^n) \leq \frac{1}{n}$ and let the function $Z^n : Q^N \to \mathbb{R}^N$ be a piecewise linear approximation of $\overline{\zeta}$ with respect to Σ^n. Using the definition of a piecewise linear function it follows that, for every $n \in \mathbb{N}$, Z^n is a continuous function, and, for every $q \in Q^N$, $Z_j^n(q) \geq 0$ if $q_j = 0$ for some $j \in I_N$, $Z_j^n(q) \leq 0$ if $q_j = 1$ for some $j \in I_N$, and $1^N \cdot Z^n(q) = 0$. So, for every $n \in \mathbb{N}$, Z^n satisfies all the properties given in Condition A of the reduced total excess demand function of an economy with $\underline{p}' = \overline{p}' = 1^N$. From Theorem 5.3.5 it follows that there exists a connected set $\widetilde{C}^n$ containing 0^N and 1^N and satisfying that $Z^n(q) = 0^N$, $\forall q \in \widetilde{C}^n$. For every $n \in \mathbb{N}$, let the function $g^n : \widetilde{C}^n \to \mathbb{R}$ be defined by

$$g^n(q) = d_{\widetilde{Q}^1}(q) - d_{\widetilde{Q}^2}(q),\ \forall q \in \widetilde{C}^n.$$

Let some $n \in \mathbb{N}$ be given. The functions $d_{\widetilde{Q}^1}$ and $d_{\widetilde{Q}^2}$ are continuous by Lemma 5.3.2 and therefore g^n is a continuous function. Moreover, by (5.7), $g^n(0^N) < -\varepsilon$ and $g^n(1^N) > \varepsilon$. Since $\widetilde{C}^n$ is connected and g^n is continuous, it follows from Theorem 2.3.13 that $g^n(\widetilde{C}^n)$ is connected and hence, by Theorem 2.3.12, there exists $\overline{q}^n \in \widetilde{C}^n$ such that $g^n(\overline{q}^n) = 0$. Obviously,

$$d_{\widetilde{Q}^1}(\overline{q}^n) = d_{\widetilde{Q}^2}(\overline{q}^n) = d_{\widetilde{Q}}(\overline{q}^n) \geq \tfrac{1}{2}\varepsilon. \tag{5.8}$$

For every $n \in \mathbb{N}$, for every $k \in I_{N+1}$, let $(\lambda^k)^n \in \mathbb{R}_+$ satisfy $\sum_{k \in I_{N+1}} (\lambda^k)^n = 1$, let $(q^k)^n$ be vertices of a simplex $\sigma^n \in \Sigma^n$ such that $\overline{q}^n = \sum_{k \in I_{N+1}} (\lambda^k)^n (q^k)^n$, and let $(\widehat{z}^k)^n \in \widehat{\zeta}((q^k)^n)$ be such that $Z_j^n((q^k)^n) = \widehat{p}_j((q^k)^n)(\widehat{z}_j^k)^n$, $\forall j \in I_N$. The sequence

$$((\lambda^1)^n, \ldots, (\lambda^{N+1})^n, (\widehat{z}^1)^n, \ldots, (\widehat{z}^{N+1})^n, \overline{q}^n)_{n \in \mathbb{N}} \tag{5.9}$$

in $\prod_{k \in I_{N+1}} [0,1] \times \prod_{k \in I_{N+1}} \mathbb{R}^N \times Q^N$ remains in a compact set since $\widehat{\zeta}$ is a compact-valued, upper hemi-continuous correspondence and Q^N is compact and therefore $\widehat{\zeta}(Q^N)$ is compact by Theorem 2.5.4. Therefore, without loss of generality, the sequence in (5.9) converges to an element

$$(\overline{\lambda}^1, \ldots, \overline{\lambda}^{N+1}, \overline{z}^1, \ldots, \overline{z}^{N+1}, \overline{q}) \in \prod_{k \in I_{N+1}} [0,1] \times \prod_{k \in I_{N+1}} \mathbb{R}^N \times Q^N.$$

Since $\mathrm{mesh}(\Sigma^n) \leq \frac{1}{n}$, it holds that $(q^k)^n \to \overline{q}$, $\forall k \in I_{N+1}$. Since $\widehat{\zeta}$ is a compact-valued, upper hemi-continuous correspondence, it holds by Theorem 2.5.6 that $\overline{z}^k \in \widehat{\zeta}(\overline{q})$, $\forall k \in I_{N+1}$. It holds that $\widehat{\zeta}$ is a convex-valued relation, so $\sum_{k \in I_{N+1}} \overline{\lambda}^k \overline{z}^k \in \widehat{\zeta}(\overline{q})$. Moreover, since $Z^n(\overline{q}^n) = 0^N$, it follows that, for every $j \in I_N$,

$$0 = \lim_{n \to +\infty} Z_j^n(\overline{q}^n) = \lim_{n \to +\infty} \sum_{k \in I_{N+1}} (\lambda^k)^n \widehat{p}_j((q^k)^n)(\widehat{z}_j^k)^n = \sum_{k \in I_{N+1}} \overline{\lambda}^k \widehat{p}_j(\overline{q}) \overline{z}_j^k$$
$$= \widehat{p}_j(\overline{q}) \sum_{k \in I_{N+1}} \overline{\lambda}^k \overline{z}_j^k.$$

Therefore, $\sum_{k \in I_{N+1}} \overline{\lambda}^k \overline{z}^k = 0^N$, so $0^N \in \widehat{\zeta}(\overline{q})$ and $d_{\widetilde{Q}}(\overline{q}) = 0$. From the continuity of the function $d_{\widetilde{Q}}$ shown in Lemma 5.3.2 and from (5.8) it follows that

$$0 = d_{\widetilde{Q}}(\overline{q}) = d_{\widetilde{Q}}\left(\lim_{n \to +\infty} \overline{q}^n\right) = \lim_{n \to +\infty} d_{\widetilde{Q}}(\overline{q}^n) \geq \tfrac{1}{2}\varepsilon,$$

a contradiction. Q.E.D.

Theorem 5.4.2
Let the economy $\widetilde{\mathcal{E}} = ((X^i, \preceq^i, \omega^i)_{i \in I_M}, P_{(\underline{p}, \overline{p})}, (\widetilde{l}, \widetilde{L}))$ satisfy Assumptions A1-A5 of Section 4.7. Then there exists a connected set of constrained equilibria of $\widetilde{\mathcal{E}}$, containing the trivial supply constrained equilibrium $(\underline{p}, 0^{MN}, \widehat{L}(0^N), \omega)$ of $\widetilde{\mathcal{E}}$ and the trivial demand constrained equilibrium $(\overline{p}, \widehat{l}(1^N), 0^{MN}, \omega)$ of $\widetilde{\mathcal{E}}$.
Proof

By Theorem 5.4.1, $\widetilde{Q}$ has a component $\widetilde{C}$ such that $0^N \in \widetilde{C}$ and $1^N \in \widetilde{C}$. Let the set S be given by

$$S = \left\{(x^1, \ldots, x^M) \in \prod_{i \in I_M} \mathbb{R}^N \,\middle|\, \sum_{i \in I_M} (x^i - \omega^i) = 0^N \right\}.$$

Let the relation $\varphi : \widetilde{C} \to P_{(\underline{p},\overline{p})} \times -\mathbb{R}_+^{MN} \times \mathbb{R}_+^{MN} \times \prod_{i \in I_M} \mathbb{R}^N$ be defined by

$$\varphi(q) = \left\{ \left(\widehat{p}(q), \widehat{l}(q), \widehat{L}(q)\right) \right\} \times \left(S \cap \prod_{i \in I_M} \widehat{\delta^i}(q)\right), \; \forall q \in \widetilde{C}.$$

By Theorem 4.7.3 the relation $\widehat{\delta^i}$, $\forall i \in I_M$, is a compact-valued, upper hemi-continuous correspondence, so the relation $\prod_{i \in I_M} \widehat{\delta^i}$ is a compact-valued, upper hemi-continuous correspondence by Theorem 2.5.10. Clearly, the relation obtained by associating with every $q \in \widetilde{C}$ the set S is a closed-valued, upper hemi-continuous correspondence. Then it follows from Theorem 2.5.9 that the intersection of these two relations is a compact-valued, upper hemi-continuous correspondence. Since the functions $\widehat{p}$, $\widehat{l}$, and $\widehat{L}$ are continuous, it follows from Theorem 2.5.10 that φ is an upper hemi-continuous correspondence. Using the convex-valuedness of $\widehat{\delta^i}$ it follows that the relation φ is convex-valued. Theorem 5.4.2 has been proved if it is shown that the set $\varphi(\widetilde{C})$ is connected since the set $\varphi(\widetilde{C})$ only contains constrained equilibria by Theorem 4.7.1, $0^N \in \widetilde{C}$, $1^N \in \widetilde{C}$, $\varphi(0^N) = \{(\underline{p}, 0^{MN}, \widehat{L}(0^N), \omega)\}$, and $\varphi(1^N) = \{(\overline{p}, \widehat{l}(1^N), 0^{MN}, \omega)\}$.
Suppose $\varphi(\widetilde{C})$ is not connected, then there exist two disjoint, non-empty sets T^1 and T^2 such that T^1 and T^2 are both closed in $\varphi(\widetilde{C})$ and $T^1 \cup T^2 = \varphi(\widetilde{C})$. Since φ is an upper hemi-continuous correspondence, it follows from Theorem 2.5.3 that the sets $\varphi^{-1}(T^1)$ and $\varphi^{-1}(T^2)$ are closed in $\widetilde{C}$.
Suppose $\overline{q} \in \varphi^{-1}(T^1) \cap \varphi^{-1}(T^2)$. Let t^1, $t^2 \in \varphi(\overline{q})$ be such that $t^1 \in T^1$ and $t^2 \in T^2$. Since φ is a convex-valued correspondence, it holds that $\lambda t^1 + (1-\lambda)t^2 \in \varphi(\overline{q})$, $\forall \lambda \in [0,1]$. So, there exists a continuous function $f : [0,1] \to \varphi(\widetilde{C})$ such that $f(0) = t^1$ and $f(1) = t^2$, implying that t^2 is an element of the path-component of t^1 in $\varphi(\widetilde{C})$. So, t^2 is an element of the component of t^1 in $\varphi(\widetilde{C})$ by Theorem 2.3.5, yielding a contradiction with the existence of the sets T^1 and T^2. Consequently, $\varphi^{-1}(T^1) \cap \varphi^{-1}(T^2) = \emptyset$.
Obviously, $\varphi^{-1}(T^1) \cup \varphi^{-1}(T^2) = \widetilde{C}$. Moreover, since T^1 and T^2 are both non-empty sets, it holds that $\varphi^{-1}(T^1)$ and $\varphi^{-1}(T^2)$ are both non-empty sets. The properties of $\varphi^{-1}(T^1)$ and $\varphi^{-1}(T^2)$ imply that the component $\widetilde{C}$ is not connected, a contradiction. Consequently, $\varphi(\widetilde{C})$ is connected. Q.E.D.

5.5 CONSTRAINED EQUILIBRIUM EXISTENCE RESULTS

Let the economy $\widetilde{\mathcal{E}}$ satisfy Assumptions A1-A5 of Section 4.7. It is easily seen that the existence of a *Drèze equilibrium* with respect to the market of a commodity $j \in I_N$ of the economy $\widetilde{\mathcal{E}}$, see Definition 4.7.5, is equivalent to the set $\widetilde{Q} \cap \{q \in Q^N \mid \frac{1}{3} \leq q_j \leq \frac{2}{3}\}$ being non-empty. Similarly, a *supply constrained equilibrium* of the economy $\widetilde{\mathcal{E}}$, see Definition 4.8.1, exists if and only if the set $\widetilde{Q} \cap \{q \in Q^N \mid \frac{1}{3} \leq \max(\{q_j \mid j \in I_N\}) \leq \frac{2}{3}\}$ is non-empty, and a *demand constrained equilibrium* of $\widetilde{\mathcal{E}}$, see Definition 4.8.5, exists if and only if the set $\widetilde{Q} \cap \{q \in Q^N \mid \frac{1}{3} \leq \min(\{q_j \mid j \in I_N\}) \leq \frac{2}{3}\}$ is non-empty. In Theorem 4.7.4 it is shown that, for every $j \in I_N$, for every $\alpha \in [0,1]$,

$$\widetilde{Q} \cap \{q \in Q^N \,|\, q_j = \alpha\} \neq \emptyset. \tag{5.10}$$

In Theorem 4.8.2 it is shown that, for every $\overline{\alpha} \in Q^N$,

$$\widetilde{Q} \cap \{q \in Q^N \,|\, q \leq \overline{\alpha} \text{ and } \exists j \in I_N,\ q_j = \overline{\alpha}_j\} \neq \emptyset. \tag{5.11}$$

In Theorem 4.8.6 it is shown that, for every $\underline{\alpha} \in Q^N$,

$$\widetilde{Q} \cap \{q \in Q^N \,|\, q \geq \underline{\alpha} \text{ and } \exists j \in I_N,\ q_j = \underline{\alpha}_j\} \neq \emptyset. \tag{5.12}$$

Using Theorem 5.4.1 the equilibrium existence results just mentioned are very easily shown. The existence results follow as easy corollaries to Theorem 5.5.1.

Theorem 5.5.1
Let the reduced total excess demand relation $\widehat{\zeta}$ of the economy $\widetilde{\mathcal{E}}$ satisfy Condition B. Let $f : Q^N \to \mathbb{R}$ be a continuous function satisfying $f(0^N) \leq 0$ and $f(1^N) \geq 0$. Then $\widetilde{Q} \cap f^{-1}(\{0\}) \neq \emptyset$.
Proof
By Theorem 5.4.1, the set $\widetilde{Q}$ has a component $\widetilde{C}$ such that $0^N \in \widetilde{C}$ and $1^N \in \widetilde{C}$. Since $\widetilde{C}$ is connected and f is a continuous function, it follows from Theorem 2.3.13 that $f(\widetilde{C})$ is connected. Since all connected subsets of $\mathbb{R}$ are intervals by Theorem 2.3.12 and since $0^N \in \widetilde{C}$, $1^N \in \widetilde{C}$, $f(0^N) \leq 0$, and $f(1^N) \geq 0$, it holds that $0 \in f(\widetilde{C}) \subset f(\widetilde{Q})$. Q.E.D.

The proof of Theorem 5.5.1 does not only show the existence of each one of the above mentioned constrained equilibria, but also shows that the component of the set of constrained equilibria of the economy containing the two trivial constrained equilibria contains every constrained equilibrium with properties as given in (5.10), (5.11), and (5.12).

Let some $j \in I_N$ and some $\alpha \in [0,1]$ be given. Then (5.10) is obtained by defining $f : Q^N \to \mathbb{R}$ by

$$f(q) = q_j - \alpha, \ \forall q \in Q^N,$$

and applying Theorem 5.5.1.

Let some $\overline{\alpha} \in Q^N$ be given. Then (5.11) is obtained by defining $f : Q^N \to \mathbb{R}$ by

$$f(q) = \max\left(\{q_j - \overline{\alpha}_j \mid j \in I_N\}\right), \ \forall q \in Q^N,$$

and applying Theorem 5.5.1.

Let some $\underline{\alpha} \in Q^N$ be given. Then (5.12) is obtained by defining $f : Q^N \to \mathbb{R}$ by

$$f(q) = \min\left(\{q_j - \underline{\alpha}_j \mid j \in I_N\}\right), \ \forall q \in Q^N,$$

and applying Theorem 5.5.1.

5.6 AN EXAMPLE

In this section Algorithm 5.2.8 is illustrated by the example used in Sections 3.10 and 4.10. Consider the economy $\widetilde{\mathcal{E}} = ((X^i, \preceq^i, \omega^i)_{i \in I_2}, P_{(\underline{p},\overline{p})}, (\widetilde{l}, \widetilde{L}))$, where $N = 2$, $X^1 = X^2 = \mathbb{R}^2_+$, $\preceq^1$ and $\preceq^2$ can be represented by utility functions given by $u^1(x^1) = (x^1_1)^{\frac{3}{4}}(x^1_2)^{\frac{1}{4}}$, $\forall x^1 \in \mathbb{R}^2_+$, and $u^2(x^2) = (x^2_1)^{\frac{1}{4}}(x^2_2)^{\frac{3}{4}}$, $\forall x^2 \in \mathbb{R}^2_+$, respectively, $\omega^1 = (1,4)^\top$, $\omega^2 = (2,1)^\top$, $P_{(\underline{p},\overline{p})} = \{p \in \mathbb{R}^2_+ \mid \frac{1}{6} \le p_1 \le 2$ and $p_2 = 1\}$, and $(\widetilde{l}, \widetilde{L})$ is the uniform rationing system, where $\widetilde{l} : Q^2 \to -\mathbb{R}^4_+$ is defined by $\widetilde{l}^1_1(q^1) = \widetilde{l}^2_1(q^1) = -3q^1_1$, $\forall q^1 \in Q^2$, $\widetilde{l}^1_2(q^1) = \widetilde{l}^2_2(q^1) = -5q^1_2$, $\forall q^1 \in Q^2$, and $\widetilde{L} : Q^2 \to \mathbb{R}^4_+$ is defined by $\widetilde{L}^1_1(q^2) = \widetilde{L}^2_1(q^2) = 18q^2_1$, $\forall q^2 \in Q^2$, and $\widetilde{L}^1_2(q^2) = \widetilde{L}^2_2(q^2) = 5q^2_2$, $\forall q^2 \in Q^2$. The corresponding reduced total excess demand function of this economy, denoted by $\widehat{z}$, is given in Section 4.10. It can be verified that the preference relations of the economy $\widetilde{\mathcal{E}}$ are not strongly convex. Nevertheless, the reduced total excess demand function of the economy $\widetilde{\mathcal{E}}$ satisfies Condition A. Moreover, the economy $\widetilde{\mathcal{E}}$ does satisfy Assumptions A1-A5. Therefore, all results developed in this chapter do hold for this economy. In Section 4.10 it is derived that the points

$$\begin{pmatrix} 0 \\ 0 \end{pmatrix}, \begin{pmatrix} \frac{1}{3} \\ 0 \end{pmatrix}, \begin{pmatrix} \frac{148}{231} \\ \frac{71}{420} \end{pmatrix}, \begin{pmatrix} \frac{148}{231} \\ \frac{349}{420} \end{pmatrix}, \begin{pmatrix} \frac{2}{3} \\ \frac{5}{6} \end{pmatrix}, \begin{pmatrix} \frac{211}{216} \\ \frac{5}{6} \end{pmatrix}, \begin{pmatrix} 1 \\ 1 \end{pmatrix},$$

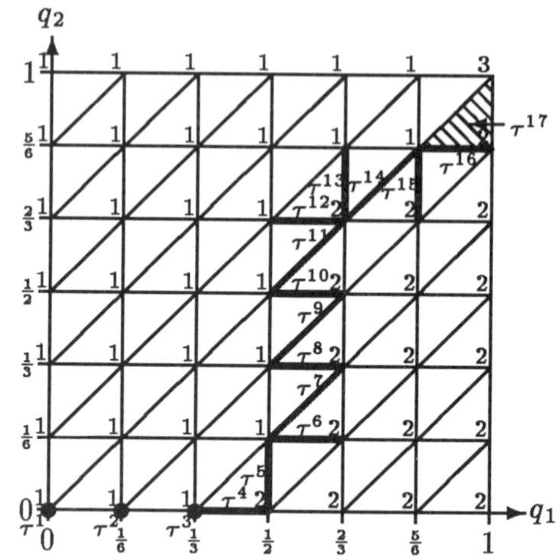

Figure 5.6.1. The finite sequence of adjacent complete simplices generated by Algorithm 5.2.8, $N = 2$.

and the convex combinations of any two successive points yield the set $\widetilde{Q} = \widehat{z}^{-1}(\{(0,0)^\top\})$. So, by Theorem 5.3.5 the set $\widetilde{Q}$ contains a component $\widetilde{C}$ such that $(0,0)^\top \in \widetilde{C}$ and $(1,1)^\top \in \widetilde{C}$. In fact $\widetilde{C} = \widetilde{Q}$ in the example.

Now it is possible to compare the set of approximate zero points generated by Algorithm 5.2.8 with the set of zero points of $\widehat{z}$. To illustrate the algorithm, a triangulation Σ of Q^2 is needed. In the example Σ is taken equal to the K-triangulation of Q^2 with mesh size $\frac{1}{6}$. In Figure 5.6.1 all adjacent complete simplices generated by the algorithm are drawn.

The finite sequence of adjacent complete simplices $\tau^1, \ldots, \tau^{17}$ in Figure 5.6.1 corresponds to the sequence obtained in Theorem 5.2.7. The image of the piecewise linear path of approximate zero points of $\widehat{z}$ constructed by joining the barycentres of the adjacent complete simplices generated successively by the algorithm and the point $(1,1)^\top$, see also the proof of Theorem 5.3.1, is given by the points

$$\begin{pmatrix}0\\0\end{pmatrix}, \begin{pmatrix}\frac{5}{12}\\0\end{pmatrix}, \begin{pmatrix}\frac{7}{12}\\\frac{1}{6}\end{pmatrix}, \begin{pmatrix}\frac{7}{12}\\\frac{2}{3}\end{pmatrix}, \begin{pmatrix}\frac{2}{3}\\\frac{3}{4}\end{pmatrix}, \begin{pmatrix}\frac{5}{6}\\\frac{3}{4}\end{pmatrix}, \begin{pmatrix}\frac{11}{12}\\\frac{5}{6}\end{pmatrix}, \begin{pmatrix}1\\1\end{pmatrix},$$

and all convex combinations of two successive points. In Figure 5.6.2 the solid line corresponds to the set of approximate zero points, while the dashed line corresponds to the set $\widetilde{Q}$.

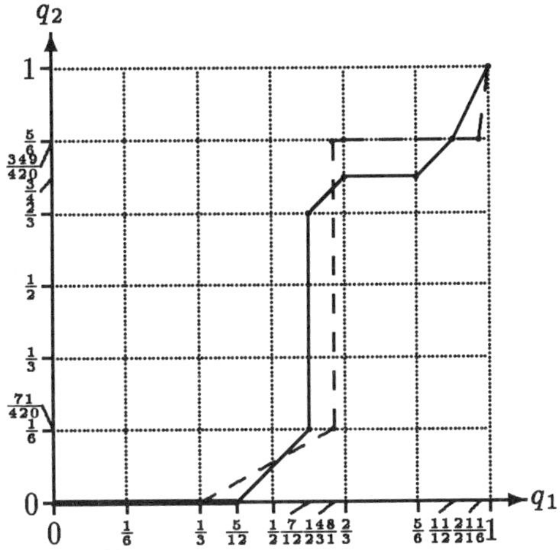

Figure 5.6.2. The set $\widetilde{Q}$, dashed line, and the approximate zero points generated by the algorithm, solid line, $N = 2$.

The algorithm starts with the $\{1\}$-complete simplex $\tau^1 = \{(0,0)^\top\}$, a facet of a unique 1-simplex of $\Sigma(\{1\})$, being the simplex $\sigma((0,0)^\top, (\frac{1}{6},0)^\top)$. This simplex is not $\{1,2\}$-complete, but it has exactly one $\{1\}$-complete facet that is not equal to τ^1, being the simplex $\tau^2 = \{(\frac{1}{6},0)^\top\}$, so Case 3 of Lemma 5.2.3 results. The simplex τ^2 is also a facet of another 1-simplex of $\Sigma(\{1\})$, being the simplex $\sigma((\frac{1}{6},0)^\top, (\frac{1}{3},0)^\top)$. This simplex is not $\{1,2\}$-complete, but it has exactly one $\{1\}$-complete facet that is not equal to τ^2, being the simplex $\tau^3 = \{(\frac{1}{3},0)^\top\}$. This corresponds to Case 3 of Lemma 5.2.3, and so on. For the vertices of the K-triangulation of Q^2 with mesh size $\frac{1}{6}$, Figure 5.6.1 shows that the requirements made with respect to a proper labelling function are satisfied, see also Theorem 5.2.9. As guaranteed by Theorem 5.2.7, the simplex τ^{17} is indeed I_3-complete and, as guaranteed by Theorem 5.2.11, there is exactly one point having the label 3, being the point $(1,1)^\top$. Therefore, the point $(1,1)^\top$ is a vertex of the simplex τ^{17}.

The point $\overline{q} = (\frac{1}{2}, \frac{1}{12})^\top$ induces an approximation of a supply constrained equilibrium of the economy $\widetilde{\mathcal{E}}$. The total excess demand at this approximation of a supply constrained equilibrium is given by $\widehat{z}(\overline{q}) = (-0.115, 0.125)^\top$. The point $\widehat{q} = (\frac{7}{12}, \frac{1}{2})^\top$ induces an approximation of a demand constrained equilibrium of the economy $\widetilde{\mathcal{E}}$. The total excess demand at this approximation of a demand constrained equilibrium is given by $\widehat{z}(\widehat{q}) = (0.358, -0.552)^\top$, so it is also rather close to zero.

The total excess demand at any approximation of a constrained equilibrium induced by the algorithm can be made as small as desired by taking the mesh size of the triangulation used small enough, see Theorem 5.2.10. Moreover, it follows from Theorem 5.3.3 that the approximate zero points generated by the algorithm can be made as close to the set $\widetilde{Q}$ as desired. Nevertheless, Algorithm 5.2.8 should not be used for computational purposes. The information of the total excess demand function used is very limited, only the market in which the total excess demand is maximal matters. For example, the point $\overline{q} = (\frac{2}{3}, \frac{5}{6})^\top$ is generated by the algorithm, and is an element of the set $\widetilde{Q}$. Therefore, $J(\overline{q}) = \{1, 2, 3\}$ and $\widehat{f}(\overline{q}) = 1$. For the point $\widehat{q} = (0, 1)^\top$ it holds that $\widehat{z}(\widehat{q}) = (17\frac{3}{4}, -2\frac{23}{24})^\top$. Therefore, $J(\widehat{q}) = \{1, 3\}$ and $\widehat{f}(\widehat{q}) = 1$. So, the information used by the algorithm at the point $\overline{q}$ is exactly the same as the information used at the point $\widehat{q}$. This lack of complete information used even becomes more severe when the number of commodities is very large. Therefore, a much more efficient algorithm using the information of the value of all components of $\widehat{z}(q)$ at a point $q \in Q^N$ is proposed in the following chapter.

6

THE COMPUTATION OF A CONTINUUM OF CONSTRAINED EQUILIBRIA

6.1 INTRODUCTION

In this chapter again an economy as described in Chapter 4 is considered. In Section 5.4 it has been shown that, under weak assumptions, the set of constrained equilibria of such an economy has a component containing the two trivial constrained equilibria. In Section 5.3 the same results have been shown under somewhat stronger assumptions. In Section 5.2 a simplicial algorithm with integer labelling has been presented and it has been used to show the results of Section 5.3. Next, the results of Section 5.3 were used to show those of Section 5.4. As is argued by Todd (1976), Remark 2.4, page 58, a simplicial algorithm with integer labelling cannot be used when one is considering upper hemi-continuous correspondences instead of continuous functions. Therefore, although the results of Section 5.3 are proved in a constructive way, this does not hold for the results of Section 5.4. Moreover, only a limited amount of information concerning the total excess demand function is used in an integer labelling algorithm. Only the component corresponding to the market having the largest total excess demand matters. Therefore, the integer labelling algorithm of Section 5.2 is not intended to be a good computational device. Nevertheless, the integer labelling algorithm is relatively easy to explain, degeneracy problems do not occur, and the results obtained by using it can be employed to prove theoretical results for the case of upper hemi-continuous correspondences.

In this chapter a simplicial algorithm with vector labelling is proposed. Such an algorithm is much more efficient than a simplicial algorithm with integer labelling. Moreover, it is shown that it can also be used when the reduced total excess demand relation of the economy is an upper hemi-continuous correspondence instead of being a continuous function. In fact, a correspondence on the N-dimensional unit cube satisfying very weak conditions is assumed to be given. The reduced total excess demand relation of an economy with N commodities can be shown to satisfy these conditions under the assumptions used in Section 4.7. The proposed simplicial algorithm with vector labelling is shown to generate a piecewise linear path contained in a finite sequence of adjacent simplices of varying dimension and joining the two extreme points of the N-dimensional unit cube, 0^N and 1^N. It is proved that every point on the path generated by the algorithm yields an approximate zero point. By using a limit argument it is shown that the set of zero points of the correspondence has a component containing both the points 0^N and 1^N. Therefore, by the results of Section 5.5, the method allows one to find all kinds of constrained equilibria of an economy. The algorithm proposed in this chapter differs from other simplicial algorithms with vector labelling in the sense that a path of approximate zero points of the reduced total excess demand relation is generated. To do this, specific degeneracy problems have to be dealt with.

In Section 6.2 a correspondence on the N-dimensional unit cube having some specific properties is given. Then the steps of a simplicial algorithm with vector labelling to compute approximate zero points of the correspondence are presented in detail. It is shown that the algorithm converges in a finite number of steps. In Section 6.3 it is proved that the set of zero points of the correspondence has a component containing the points 0^N and 1^N, and that the zero points of the correspondence are approximated by the algorithm. Such a component is easily seen to be an uncountable set and hence a continuum of zero points is approximated by the algorithm. The accuracy of the approximate solutions obtained by the algorithm is analysed in Section 6.4. Finally, an illustration of the algorithm can be found in Section 6.5, where the same example is used as in Sections 3.10, 4.10, and 5.6.

This chapter is based on Herings, Talman, and Yang (1994).

6.2 A SIMPLICIAL ALGORITHM WITH VECTOR LABELLING

A correspondence $\widehat{\zeta} : Q^N \to \mathbb{R}^N$ is assumed to be given in this chapter. It is often assumed that $\widehat{\zeta}$ satisfies the following condition.

Condition B The correspondence $\widehat{\zeta} : Q^N \to \mathbb{R}^N$ satisfies

1. $\widehat{\zeta}$ is a compact-valued, convex-valued, upper hemi-continuous correspondence,
2. for every $q \in Q^N$, there exists $z \in \widehat{\zeta}(q)$ such that, for every $j \in I_N$, $q_j = 0$ implies $z_j \geq 0$, and $q_j = 1$ implies $z_j \leq 0$,
3. for every $q \in Q^N$, for every $z \in \widehat{\zeta}(q)$, there exists $p \in \mathbb{R}^N_{++}$ such that $p \cdot z = 0$.

Notice that by Theorem 4.7.3 the *reduced total excess demand relation* $\widehat{\zeta}$ of the *economy* $\widetilde{\mathcal{E}} = ((X^i, \preceq^i, \omega^i)_{i \in I_M}, P_{(\underline{p}, \overline{p})}, (\widetilde{l}, \widetilde{L}))$ as described in Chapter 4 satisfies Condition B if the economy satisfies Assumptions A1-A5 given in Section 4.7. Notice that Condition B given above is weaker than Condition B used in Section 5.4.

If $N = 1$ and the correspondence $\widehat{\zeta}$ satisfies Condition B, then it necessarily equals the correspondence associating with every element of $Q^1 = [0, 1]$ the set $\{0\}$. A picture of a correspondence $\widehat{\zeta} : Q^2 \to \mathbb{R}^2$ satisfying Condition B is drawn in Figure 6.2.1.

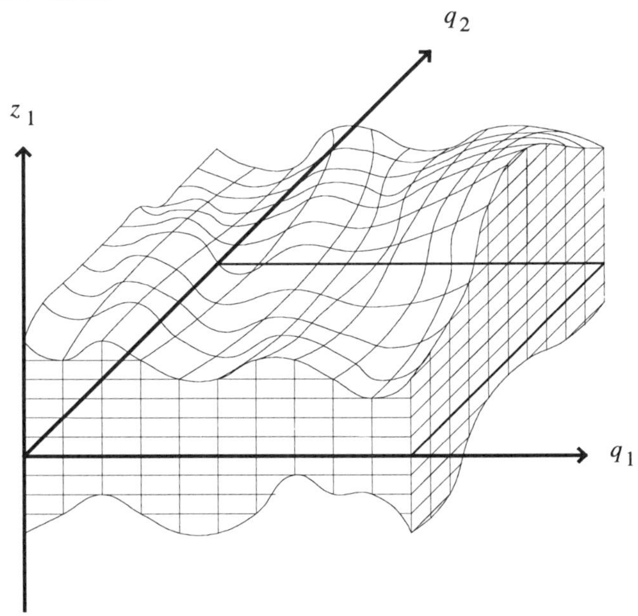

Figure 6.2.1. A correspondence $\widehat{\zeta} : Q^2 \to \mathbb{R}^2$ satisfying Condition B.

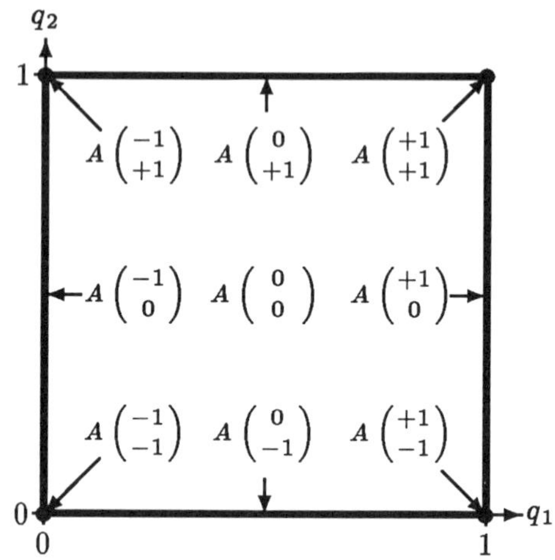

Figure 6.2.2. The sets $A(s)$, for $s \in \mathbb{S}^N$, $N = 2$.

In Figure 6.2.1 only the z_1-axis has been drawn, which is sufficient to determine the zero points of $\widehat{\zeta}$ by Condition B.3. For every $q \in Q^2$, the set $\widehat{\zeta}(q)$ in Figure 6.2.1 consists of one element, except when $q_1 = 1$ or $q_2 = 0$. Notice that in Figure 6.2.1 the set of zero points of $\widehat{\zeta}$ is given by $\{q \in Q^2 \mid q_1 = 1 \text{ or } q_2 = 0\}$.

Recall from Section 2.2 that for every sign vector $s \in \mathbb{S}^N$ the sets $I^-(s)$, $I^0(s)$, and $I^+(s)$ are defined by $I^-(s) = \{j \in I_N \mid s_j = -1\}$, $I^0(s) = \{j \in I_N \mid s_j = 0\}$, and $I^+(s) = \{j \in I_N \mid s_j = +1\}$. Moreover, the numbers $i^-(s)$, $i^0(s)$, and $i^+(s)$ are defined by $i^-(s) = \#I^-(s)$, $i^0(s) = \#I^0(s)$, and $i^+(s) = \#I^+(s)$. For every sign vector $s \in \mathbb{S}^N$, the subset $A(s)$ of Q^N is defined by

$$A(s) = \left\{q \in Q^N \,\middle|\, q_j = 0,\ \forall j \in I^-(s), \text{ and } q_j = 1,\ \forall j \in I^+(s)\right\}.$$

It is easily seen that the dimension of $A(s)$ is equal to $i^0(s)$. Notice that the set $A(0^N)$ equals the set Q^N. All 3^N possible sets $A(s)$ are illustrated in Figure 6.2.2 for $N = 2$.

Let a triangulation Σ of Q^N be given. The triangulation might be for instance the K-triangulation of Q^N with any grid size, see Definition 2.7.3, or the V-triangulation of Q^N with respect to any $v \in Q^N$ and with any grid size, see Definition 2.7.6. For every $s \in \mathbb{S}^N$, the collection $\Sigma(s)$ is defined by

$$\Sigma(s) = \left\{\tau \subset A(s) \,\middle|\, \exists \sigma \in \Sigma,\ \tau \text{ is an } i^0(s)\text{-face of } \sigma\right\}.$$

If $\bar{s}, \widehat{s} \in \mathbb{S}^N$ with $I^0(\bar{s}) \subset I^0(\widehat{s})$, then $A(\bar{s}) = A(\widehat{s}) \cap \operatorname{aff}(A(\bar{s}))$. Therefore, by repeated application of Theorem 2.7.8, it follows that $\Sigma(s)$ is a triangulation of $A(s)$ for every $s \in \mathbb{S}^N$. Let some sign vector $\bar{s} \in \mathbb{S}^N$ with $i^0(\bar{s}) \geq 1$ be given. Then the relative boundary of $A(\bar{s})$ is given by the union of the sets $A(s)$ over all sign vectors s with $i^0(s) = i^0(\bar{s}) - 1$, $I^-(\bar{s}) \subset I^-(s)$, and $I^+(\bar{s}) \subset I^+(s)$. Now it follows from the definition of a triangulation, Definition 2.7.1, that a simplex of $\Sigma(s)$ for some $s \in \mathbb{S}^N$ with $i^0(s) = i^0(\bar{s}) - 1$, $I^-(\bar{s}) \subset I^-(s)$, and $I^+(\bar{s}) \subset I^+(s)$ is the facet of a unique simplex of $\Sigma(\bar{s})$.

Let the correspondence $\widehat{\zeta}$ satisfy Condition B and let Σ be a triangulation of Q^N. Let $Z : Q^N \to \mathbb{R}^N$ be a piecewise linear approximation of $\widehat{\zeta}$ with respect to Σ such that for every vertex q of any $\sigma \in \Sigma$ it holds that $Z_j(q) \geq 0$ if $q_j = 0$ for some $j \in I_N$ and $Z_j(q) \leq 0$ if $q_j = 1$ for some $j \in I_N$. Condition B.2 guarantees that such a piecewise linear approximation Z exists. Moreover, it follows immediately that Z satisfies the following condition.

Condition C The function $Z : Q^N \to \mathbb{R}^N$ is such that, for every $q \in Q^N$, $Z_j(q) \geq 0$ if $q_j = 0$ for some $j \in I_N$ and $Z_j(q) \leq 0$ if $q_j = 1$ for some $j \in I_N$.

To approximate a connected set of zero points of $\widehat{\zeta}$ containing 0^N and 1^N, it is proved in a constructive way that for any piecewise linear approximation Z of $\widehat{\zeta}$ satisfying Condition C it holds that there exists a piecewise linear path $f : [0,1] \to Q^N$ joining 0^N and 1^N, and satisfying that for every $q \in f([0,1])$ there is a number $\beta \in \mathbb{R}$ such that, for all $j \in I_N$,

$$\begin{aligned} 0 \leq Z_j(q) \leq \beta &\text{ if } q_j = 0, \\ Z_j(q) = \beta &\text{ if } 0 < q_j < 1, \\ 0 \geq Z_j(q) \geq \beta &\text{ if } q_j = 1. \end{aligned} \tag{6.1}$$

In the next section it is shown that β is arbitrarily close to zero for every $q \in f([0,1])$ if mesh(Σ) is taken small enough. So, every $q \in f([0,1])$ is an approximate zero point of $\widehat{\zeta}$ in this case. However, in spite of Condition B.3, it cannot be guaranteed that $\beta = 0$ and so $Z(q) = 0^N$ for all $q \in f([0,1])$. This is caused by the fact that Condition B.3 is not necessarily satisfied for a piecewise linear approximation Z of $\widehat{\zeta}$. However, notice that β must be zero if $q = 0^N$, or if $q = 1^N$, or if both $q_{j^1} = 0$ for some $j^1 \in I_N$ and $q_{j^2} = 1$ for some $j^2 \in I_N$.

Given a sign vector $s \in \mathbb{S}^N$ with $i^0(s) = t$, the indices $j^1, \ldots, j^{N-t} \in I_N$ are chosen such that $j^1 < \cdots < j^{N-t}$ and $I^-(s) \cup I^+(s) = \{j^1, \ldots, j^{N-t}\}$.

Let Σ be a triangulation of Q^N and let Z be a piecewise linear approximation of $\widehat{\zeta}$ with respect to Σ. Let $\sigma(q^1, \ldots, q^{t+1}) \subset Q^N$ be a t-simplex and let $s \in \mathbb{S}^N$ be a sign vector with $i^0(s) = t$. Consider solutions $(\lambda^1, \ldots, \lambda^{t+1}, \mu^{j^1}, \ldots, \mu^{j^{N-t}}, \beta) \in \mathbb{R}^{N+2}$ of the following system of equations:

$$\sum_{k \in I_{t+1}} \lambda^k \begin{pmatrix} 1 \\ Z(q^k) \end{pmatrix} + \sum_{k \in I_{N-t}} \mu^{j^k} \begin{pmatrix} 0 \\ -s_{j^k} e^N(j^k) \end{pmatrix} + \beta \begin{pmatrix} 0 \\ -1^N \end{pmatrix} = \begin{pmatrix} 1 \\ 0^N \end{pmatrix}. \tag{6.2}$$

Now $(\lambda^1, \ldots, \lambda^{t+1}, \mu^{j^1}, \ldots, \mu^{j^{N-t}}, \beta)$ is called an *admissible solution* to (6.2) if $\lambda^k \geq 0$, $\forall k \in I_{t+1}$, and $\mu^{j^k} \geq 0$, $\forall k \in I_{N-t}$. Notice that there are no restrictions with respect to β. Clearly, it holds that $\sum_{k \in I_{t+1}} \lambda^k = 1$. If $\sigma(q^1, \ldots, q^{t+1})$ is a simplex of $\Sigma(s)$, $(\lambda^1, \ldots, \lambda^{t+1}, \mu^{j^1}, \ldots, \mu^{j^{N-t}}, \beta)$ is an admissible solution to (6.2), and Z satisfies Condition C, then the point q given by $q = \sum_{k \in I_{t+1}} \lambda^k q^k$ is an element of $\sigma(q^1, \ldots, q^{t+1})$ and satisfies (6.1). Notice that the linear system (6.2) has $N + 1$ equations and $N + 2$ variables and hence there is one degree of freedom. A piecewise linear path joining 0^N and 1^N is obtained by an algorithm that generates a finite sequence of simplices of varying dimension such that with respect to each simplex of this finite sequence there exists a set of admissible solutions to (6.2).

An admissible solution $(\lambda^1, \ldots, \lambda^{t+1}, \mu^{j^1}, \ldots, \mu^{j^{N-t}}, \beta)$ to (6.2) is said to be *degenerate* if at least two of the variables λ^k, $k \in I_{t+1}$, and μ^{j^k}, $k \in I_{N-t}$, are equal to zero. If the correspondence $\widehat{\zeta}$ satisfies Condition B and Z is a piecewise linear approximation of $\widehat{\zeta}$ with respect to any triangulation Σ of Q^N satisfying Condition C, then it holds that $Z(0^N) = 0^N$ and $Z(1^N) = 0^N$. Hence, $\lambda^1 = 1$, $\mu^j = 0$, $\forall j \in I_N$, and $\beta = 0$ yields a degenerate admissible solution to (6.2) corresponding to the 0-simplex $\sigma(0^N)$ and any $s \in \mathbb{S}^N$ with $i^0(s) = 0$, unless $N = 1$. A similar degenerate admissible solution exists corresponding to the 0-simplex $\sigma(1^N)$. So, the usual assumption made in the literature that there exist no degenerate admissible solutions, given any sign vector $s \in \mathbb{S}^N$ and any simplex $\sigma \in \Sigma(s)$, makes no sense for the problem under consideration. The way the degeneracy problem is solved for is inspired by Todd (1976) and Wright (1981), where algorithms are presented to compute a zero point of a correspondence $\varphi : \mathbb{R}^m \to \mathbb{R}^m$. In their work lexicographic pivot steps are used to circumvent degeneracy. By adapting their notion of a lexicopositive matrix the problem of degeneracy is solved for.

A row vector of $\mathbb{R}^m$ is said to be *lexicographically positive* if it is non-zero and its first non-zero component is positive. A matrix A is said to be *lexicopositive* if each row is lexicographically positive. A matrix A is said to be *semi-lexicopositive* if each row, except possibly the last row, is lexicographically positive.

Let a triangulation Σ of Q^N and a piecewise linear approximation Z of $\hat{\zeta}$ with respect to Σ be given. For a $(t-1)$-simplex $\tau(q^1, \ldots, q^t) \subset Q^N$ and a sign vector $s \in \mathbb{S}^N$ with $i^0(s) = t$, the $(N+1) \times (N+1)$ matrix $A_{s,\tau}$ is defined by

$$A_{s,\tau} = \begin{pmatrix} 1 & \cdots & 1 & 0 & \cdots & 0 & 0 \\ Z(q^1) & \cdots & Z(q^t) & -s_{j^1}e^N(j^1) & \cdots & -s_{j^{N-t}}e^N(j^{N-t}) & -1^N \end{pmatrix}.$$

Definition 6.2.1 (s-complete simplices)
*Let a triangulation Σ of Q^N and a piecewise linear approximation Z of $\hat{\zeta}$ with respect to Σ be given. Let $\tau \subset Q^N$ be a $(t-1)$-simplex and let $s \in \mathbb{S}^N$ be a sign vector with $i^0(s) = t$. Then τ is s-*complete *if $A_{s,\tau}^{-1}$ exists and is semi-lexicopositive.*

In general, a $(t-1)$-simplex is called *complete* if it is s-complete for some sign vector $s \in \mathbb{S}^N$ with $i^0(s) = t$. When τ is an s-complete $(t-1)$-simplex for some sign vector $s \in \mathbb{S}^N$, then the first column of $A_{s,\tau}^{-1}$ yields an admissible solution to (6.2) for a t-simplex σ being the convex hull of τ and an arbitrary vertex $q^{t+1} \in Q^N$, where in addition λ^{t+1} is chosen to be equal to 0.

Let a triangulation Σ of Q^N and a piecewise linear approximation Z of $\hat{\zeta}$ with respect to Σ satisfying Condition C be given. An algorithm will be described that generates a finite sequence of simplices starting with the 0-simplex $\{0^N\}$ and terminating with the 0-simplex $\{1^N\}$. Moreover, related to every $(t-1)$-simplex τ in the finite sequence there exists a sign vector $s \in \mathbb{S}^N$ with $i^0(s) = t$ such that τ is an s-complete simplex being a facet of a t-simplex of $\Sigma(s)$. Moreover, any two successive simplices in the finite sequence either are $(t-1)$-simplices that are facets of the same t-simplex of $\Sigma(s)$ for some $s \in \mathbb{S}^N$ with $i^0(s) = t$, or one is a $(t-1)$-simplex that is a facet of the other one, that one being a t-simplex of $\Sigma(s)$ for some $s \in \mathbb{S}^N$ with $i^0(s) = t$. It is shown in Lemmas 6.2.2 and 6.2.3 that $\tau(0^N)$ and $\tau(1^N)$, respectively, are s-complete facets of a 1-simplex of $\Sigma(s)$ for a uniquely determined sign vector $s \in \mathbb{S}^N$ with $i^0(s) = 1$. Lemmas 6.2.5 and 6.2.6 describe all possible situations that can occur when some $(t-1)$-simplex τ being an s-complete facet of a t-simplex of $\Sigma(s)$ for some $s \in \mathbb{S}^N$ is obtained. Lemmas 6.2.2, 6.2.3, 6.2.5, and 6.2.6 are then used in Theorem 6.2.8 to determine in a unique way the finite sequence of complete simplices described above. Finally, the detailed steps of the algorithm yielding this finite sequence are given in Algorithm 6.2.10 and it is shown in Theorem 6.2.11 that the algorithm yields a piecewise linear path joining 0^N and 1^N such that each point on the path has the properties given in (6.1).

Lemma 6.2.2
Let the correspondence $\widehat{\zeta}$ satisfy Condition B, let Σ be a triangulation of Q^N, and let Z be a piecewise linear approximation of $\widehat{\zeta}$ with respect to Σ satisfying Condition C. Let the sign vector $\overline{s} \in \mathbb{S}^N$ be such that $\overline{s}_j = -1$, $\forall j \in I_{N-1}$, and $\overline{s}_N = 0$. Then $\tau(0^N)$ is an $\overline{s}$-complete facet of a 1-simplex of $\Sigma(\overline{s})$ and is not an s-complete facet of a 1-simplex of $\Sigma(s)$ for any other sign vector $s \in \mathbb{S}^N$.
Proof
Suppose that $\tau(0^N)$ is an s-complete facet of a 1-simplex of $\Sigma(s)$ for some $s \in \mathbb{S}^N$. Then it has to hold that $i^0(s) = 1$ and $I^+(s) = \emptyset$. From Condition B.3 and Condition C it follows that $Z(0^N) = 0^N$. Therefore, $A_{s,\tau}$ is given by

$$A_{s,\tau} = \begin{pmatrix} 1 & 0 & \cdots & 0 & 0 \\ 0^N & e^N(j^1) & & e^N(j^{N-1}) & -1^N \end{pmatrix}.$$

Let the integers j^0 and j^N be given by $j^0 = 0$ and $j^N = N + 1$. Let $k \in I_N$ be such that $j^{k-1} < j < j^k$, where j is the unique element in the set $I^0(s)$. Then

$$A_{s,\tau}^{-1} = \begin{pmatrix} 1 & 0 & \cdots & 0 & 0 & 0 & \cdots & 0 \\ 0^N & e^N(j^1) & & e^N(j^{k-1}) & -1^N & e^N(j^k - 1) & & e^N(j^{N-1} - 1) \end{pmatrix}.$$

It is clear that this matrix is semi-lexicopositive if and only if $k = N$. Consequently, $s = \overline{s}$. Q.E.D.

Lemma 6.2.3
Let the correspondence $\widehat{\zeta}$ satisfy Condition B, let Σ be a triangulation of Q^N, and let Z be a piecewise linear approximation of $\widehat{\zeta}$ with respect to Σ satisfying Condition C. Let the sign vector $\overline{s} \in \mathbb{S}^N$ be such that $\overline{s}_1 = 0$ and $\overline{s}_j = +1$, $\forall j \in I_N \setminus \{1\}$. Then $\tau(1^N)$ is an $\overline{s}$-complete facet of a 1-simplex of $\Sigma(\overline{s})$ and is not an s-complete facet of a 1-simplex of $\Sigma(s)$ for any other sign vector $s \in \mathbb{S}^N$.
Proof
Suppose that $\tau(1^N)$ is an s-complete facet of a 1-simplex of $\Sigma(s)$ for some $s \in \mathbb{S}^N$. Then it has to hold that $i^0(s) = 1$ and $I^-(s) = \emptyset$. From Condition B.3 and Condition C it follows that $Z(1^N) = 0^N$. Hence, $A_{s,\tau}$ is given by

$$A_{s,\tau} = \begin{pmatrix} 1 & 0 & \cdots & 0 & 0 \\ 0^N & -e^N(j^1) & & -e^N(j^{N-1}) & -1^N \end{pmatrix}.$$

Let the integers j^0 and j^N be given by $j^0 = 0$ and $j^N = N + 1$. Let $k \in I_N$ be such that $j^{k-1} < j < j^k$, where j is the unique element in the set $I^0(s)$. Then it is easily verified that

$$A_{s,\tau}^{-1} = \begin{pmatrix} 1 & 0 & \cdots & 0 & 0 & 0 & \cdots & 0 \\ 0^N & -e^N(j^1) & & -e^N(j^{k-1}) & \begin{matrix} 1^{N-1} \\ -1 \end{matrix} & -e^N(j^k-1) & & -e^N(j^{N-1}-1) \end{pmatrix}.$$

It is clear that this matrix is semi-lexicopositive if and only if $k = 1$. Consequently, $s = \bar{s}$. Q.E.D.

The following lemma is well-known in linear programming theory, see for example Murty (1983). It is very useful in proving Lemmas 6.2.5 and 6.2.6.

Lemma 6.2.4
Let an invertible $m \times m$ matrix A, a vector z of $\mathbb{R}^m$, and some $k \in I_m$ be given. The $m \times m$ matrix $\overline{A}$ is defined by $\overline{A} = (A_{\cdot 1} \ldots A_{\cdot k-1}\ z\ A_{\cdot k+1} \ldots A_{\cdot m})$. Then either $(A^{-1}z)_k = 0$ and $\overline{A}$ is singular, or $(A^{-1}z)_k \neq 0$ and

$$\overline{A}^{-1} = \begin{pmatrix} (A^{-1})_{1\cdot} - \frac{(A^{-1}z)_1}{(A^{-1}z)_k}(A^{-1})_{k\cdot} \\ \vdots \\ (A^{-1})_{k-1\cdot} - \frac{(A^{-1}z)_{k-1}}{(A^{-1}z)_k}(A^{-1})_{k\cdot} \\ \frac{1}{(A^{-1}z)_k}(A^{-1})_{k\cdot} \\ (A^{-1})_{k+1\cdot} - \frac{(A^{-1}z)_{k+1}}{(A^{-1}z)_k}(A^{-1})_{k\cdot} \\ \vdots \\ (A^{-1})_{m\cdot} - \frac{(A^{-1}z)_m}{(A^{-1}z)_k}(A^{-1})_{k\cdot} \end{pmatrix}.$$

Lemma 6.2.4 is easily shown by calculating $\overline{A}^{-1}\overline{A}$.

Let Σ be a triangulation of Q^N and let Z be a piecewise linear approximation of $\widehat{\zeta}$ with respect to Σ. The next lemma describes all cases that may occur when a t-simplex σ of $\Sigma(s)$ for some $s \in \mathbb{S}^N$ with $i^0(s) = t$ has at least one s-complete facet τ.

Lemma 6.2.5
Let Σ be a triangulation of Q^N and let Z be a piecewise linear approximation of $\widehat{\zeta}$ with respect to Σ. Let a sign vector $s \in \mathbb{S}^N$ with $i^0(s) = t$ and a t-simplex σ of $\Sigma(s)$ be given. Moreover, let an s-complete facet τ of σ be given. Then exactly one of the following cases holds:

1. *the t-simplex σ is an $\overline{s}$-complete facet of a $(t+1)$-simplex of $\Sigma(\overline{s})$ for precisely one sign vector $\overline{s} \in \mathbb{S}^N$,*

2. *the t-simplex σ has exactly one other s-complete facet $\overline{\tau}$.*

Proof

Let q^{t+1} be the vertex of σ not contained in τ and let $y \in \mathbb{R}^{N+1}$ be given by

$$y = A_{s,\tau}^{-1} \left(1, Z(q^{t+1})^\top\right)^\top.$$

Since $A_{s,\tau} A_{s,\tau}^{-1} = I^{N+1}$ and since $(A_{s,\tau})_{1\cdot} = ({1^t}^\top, {0^{N-t+1}}^\top)$, it holds that $\sum_{k \in I_t} (A_{s,\tau}^{-1})_{k1} = 1$ and $\sum_{k \in I_t} (A_{s,\tau}^{-1})_{kj} = 0$, $\forall j \in I_{N+1} \setminus \{1\}$.
Suppose that the first N components of y are non-positive. Then

$$\begin{aligned} 0 &\geq \left({1^t}^\top, {0^{N-t+1}}^\top\right) y = \left({1^t}^\top, {0^{N-t+1}}^\top\right) A_{s,\tau}^{-1} \begin{pmatrix} 1 \\ Z(q^{t+1}) \end{pmatrix} \\ &= \left(1, {0^N}^\top\right) \begin{pmatrix} 1 \\ Z(q^{t+1}) \end{pmatrix} = 1, \end{aligned}$$

a contradiction. Consequently, $y_k > 0$ for some $k \in I_N$.
Let $k' \in I_N$ be such that $\frac{1}{y_{k'}}(A_{s,\tau}^{-1})_{k'\cdot}$ is minimal according to the lexicographic ordering over all row vectors $\frac{1}{y_k}(A_{s,\tau}^{-1})_{k\cdot}$ for which $y_k > 0$ and $k \in I_N$. It is clear that k' is uniquely determined since otherwise $A_{s,\tau}^{-1}$ would not be invertible. Now it holds that either $k' \in I_N \setminus I_t$ or $k' \in I_t$.
If $k' \in I_N \setminus I_t$, then let $\overline{s} \in \mathbb{S}^N$ be defined by $\overline{s}_{j^{k'-t}} = 0$ and $\overline{s}_j = s_j$, $\forall j \in I_N \setminus \{j^{k'-t}\}$. Clearly, σ is a facet of a simplex of $\Sigma(\overline{s})$ and $i^0(\overline{s}) = t+1$. The matrix $A_{\overline{s},\sigma}$ is obtained by deleting column k' of $A_{s,\tau}$ and adding the vector $(1, Z(q^{t+1})^\top)^\top$ between columns t and $t+1$. Using Lemma 6.2.4 it follows that $A_{\overline{s},\sigma}^{-1}$ exists and is semi-lexicopositive. So, σ is an $\overline{s}$-complete facet of a $(t+1)$-simplex of $\Sigma(\overline{s})$.
If $k' \in I_t$, then let $\overline{\tau}$ be the facet of σ opposite $q^{k'}$. Using Lemma 6.2.4 and the choice of k' it follows that $A_{s,\overline{\tau}}^{-1}$ exists and is semi-lexicopositive. Hence, $\overline{\tau}$ is an s-complete facet of σ.
It follows directly from Lemma 6.2.4 that if some other column is replaced, then the inverse of the matrix obtained is not semi-lexicopositive. This guarantees that Case 1 and Case 2 are mutually exclusive, that the sign vector $\overline{s}$ of Case 1 is uniquely determined, and that the facet $\overline{\tau}$ of Case 2 is uniquely determined.
Q.E.D.

The operation used in the proof of Lemma 6.2.5, where a column of $A_{s,\tau}$ is determined in a unique way and is replaced by the vector $(1, Z(q^{t+1})^\top)^\top$, i.e.

the column in (6.2) corresponding to the vertex q^{t+1} of σ opposite τ, is called a *lexicographic pivot step*.

Let a triangulation Σ of Q^N and a piecewise linear approximation Z of $\widehat{\zeta}$ with respect to Σ be given. The next lemma gives all cases that may occur when an s-complete facet τ of a t-simplex of $\Sigma(s)$ for some $s \in \mathbb{S}^N$ with $i^0(s) = t$ is a member of $\Sigma(\overline{s})$ for some $\overline{s} \in \mathbb{S}^N$. Clearly, $I^-(s) \subset I^-(\overline{s})$, $I^0(\overline{s}) \subset I^0(s)$, and $I^+(s) \subset I^+(\overline{s})$.

Lemma 6.2.6
Let the correspondence $\widehat{\zeta}$ satisfy Condition B, let Σ be a triangulation of Q^N, and let Z be a piecewise linear approximation of $\widehat{\zeta}$ with respect to Σ satisfying Condition C. Let a sign vector $s \in \mathbb{S}^N$ with $i^0(s) = t$ and an s-complete facet τ of some t-simplex of $\Sigma(s)$ be given. Moreover, let τ be a $(t-1)$-simplex of $\Sigma(\overline{s})$ for some $\overline{s} \in \mathbb{S}^N$. Then exactly one of the following cases holds:

1. *the 0-simplex τ is equal to $\{0^N\}$ or equal to $\{1^N\}$,*
2. *the $(t-1)$-simplex τ is an $\widehat{s}$-complete facet of a t-simplex of $\Sigma(\widehat{s})$ for precisely one sign vector $\widehat{s} \in \mathbb{S}^N \setminus \{s\}$,*
3. *precisely one facet of τ is $\overline{s}$-complete.*

Proof
Let $j' \in I_N$ be the unique index such that $s_{j'} = 0$ and $\overline{s}_{j'} \neq 0$. Let $y \in \mathbb{R}^{N+1}$ be given by

$$y = A_{s,\tau}^{-1}\left(0, -\overline{s}_{j'} e^N(j')^\top\right)^\top .$$

Exactly one of the following three possibilities occurs:

1. $\overline{s}_{j'} = -1$ and $y_k \leq 0$, $\forall k \in I_N$,
2. $\overline{s}_{j'} = +1$ and $y_k \leq 0$, $\forall k \in I_N$,
3. $\exists k \in I_N$ such that $y_k > 0$.

Suppose $\overline{s}_{j'} = -1$ and $y_k \leq 0$, $\forall k \in I_N$. Then, since $A_{s,\tau} y = (0, -\overline{s}_{j'} e^N(j')^\top)^\top$ and since $(A_{s,\tau})_{1\cdot} = ({1^t}^\top, {0^{N-t+1}}^\top)^\top$, it follows that $y_k = 0$, $\forall k \in I_t$. So,

$$1 = \sum_{k \in I_{N+1}} (A_{s,\tau})_{j'+1,k} y_k = \sum_{k \in I_{N+1} \setminus I_t} (A_{s,\tau})_{j'+1,k} y_k = -y_{N+1},$$

where for the last equality it is used that $s_{j'} = 0$. Hence, $y_{N+1} = -1$ and

$$\sum_{k \in I_N \setminus I_t} (A_{s,\tau})_{\cdot k} y_k = \sum_{k \in I_{N-t}} \begin{pmatrix} 0 \\ -s_{j^k} e^N(j^k) \end{pmatrix} y_{t+k} = \begin{pmatrix} 0 \\ e^N(j') \end{pmatrix} + \begin{pmatrix} 0 \\ -1^N \end{pmatrix}.$$

Therefore, $t = 1$ and $s_{j^k} = -1$, $\forall k \in I_{N-t}$. So, $\overline{s}_j = -1$, $\forall j \in I_N$, and $\tau = \{0^N\}$.

Suppose $\overline{s}_{j'} = +1$ and $y_k \leq 0$, $\forall k \in I_N$. Then, again, $y_k = 0$, $\forall k \in I_t$. So, since $A_{s,\tau} y = (0, -\overline{s}_{j'} e^N(j')^\top)^\top$, it follows that

$$-1 = \sum_{k \in I_{N+1} \setminus I_t} (A_{s,\tau})_{j'+1,k} y_k = -y_{N+1},$$

and hence $y_{N+1} = 1$. So,

$$\sum_{k \in I_N \setminus I_t} (A_{s,\tau})_{\cdot k} y_k = \sum_{k \in I_{N-t}} \begin{pmatrix} 0 \\ -s_{j^k} e^N(j^k) \end{pmatrix} y_{t+k} = \begin{pmatrix} 0 \\ -e^N(j') \end{pmatrix} - \begin{pmatrix} 0 \\ -1^N \end{pmatrix}.$$

Therefore, $t = 1$ and $s_{j^k} = +1$, $\forall k \in I_{N-t}$. So, $\overline{s}_j = +1$, $\forall j \in I_N$, and $\tau = \{1^N\}$.

Suppose there exists $k \in I_N$ such that $y_k > 0$. Then it is possible to choose $k' \in I_N$ as in the proof of Lemma 6.2.5. Again, either $k' \in I_N \setminus I_t$ or $k' \in I_t$.

If $k' \in I_N \setminus I_t$, then let $\widehat{s} \in \mathbb{S}^N$ be defined by $\widehat{s}_{j^{k'-t}} = 0$ and $\widehat{s}_j = \overline{s}_j$, $\forall j \in I_N \setminus \{j^{k'-t}\}$, and consider $A_{\widehat{s},\tau}$. Using Lemma 6.2.4, the choice of k' guarantees that $A_{\widehat{s},\tau}^{-1}$ is semi-lexicopositive and therefore τ is an $\widehat{s}$-complete facet of a t-simplex of $\Sigma(\widehat{s})$.

If $k' \in I_t$, then let ς be the facet of τ opposite $q^{k'}$. By Lemma 6.2.4 and the choice of k', $A_{\overline{s},\varsigma}^{-1}$ is semi-lexicopositive and hence ς is an $\overline{s}$-complete facet of the $(t-1)$-simplex τ of $\Sigma(\overline{s})$.

From Lemmas 6.2.2 and 6.2.3 it follows that Case 1 on the one hand and the Cases 2 and 3 on the other hand are mutually exclusive. It follows directly from Lemma 6.2.4 that if some other column of $A_{s,\tau}$ is replaced, then the inverse of the matrix obtained is not semi-lexicopositive. This shows that Case 2 and Case 3 are mutually exclusive. Moreover, it shows that the sign vector $\widehat{s}$ of Case 2 is uniquely determined and that the facet of Case 3 is uniquely determined.

Q.E.D.

The operation used in the proof of Lemma 6.2.6, where a column of $A_{s,\tau}$ is determined in a unique way and is replaced by the vector $(0, -\overline{s}_{j'} e^N(j')^\top)^\top$, i.e. the column in (6.2) corresponding to the unique element j' in the set $(I^-(\overline{s}) \cup I^+(\overline{s})) \setminus (I^-(s) \cup I^+(s))$, is also called a *lexicographic pivot step*.

Definition 6.2.7 (Adjacent complete simplices)
Let Σ be a triangulation of Q^N and let Z be a piecewise linear approximation of $\widehat{\zeta}$ with respect to Σ. Then the simplices $\overline{\tau}$ and $\widehat{\tau}$ are adjacent complete simplices *if $\overline{\tau}$ and $\widehat{\tau}$ are both s-complete facets of the same t-simplex of $\Sigma(s)$ for some $s \in \mathbb{S}^N$ with $i^0(s) = t$, or if $\overline{\tau}$ is an $\overline{s}$-complete facet of the t-simplex $\widehat{\tau}$ of $\Sigma(\overline{s})$ and $\widehat{\tau}$ is an $\widehat{s}$-complete facet of a $(t+1)$-simplex of $\Sigma(\widehat{s})$ for some $\overline{s}, \widehat{s} \in \mathbb{S}^N$ with $i^0(\overline{s}) = t$ and $i^0(\widehat{s}) = t+1$, or if $\widehat{\tau}$ is an $\widehat{s}$-complete facet of the t-simplex $\overline{\tau}$ of $\Sigma(\widehat{s})$ and $\overline{\tau}$ is an $\overline{s}$-complete facet of a $(t+1)$-simplex of $\Sigma(\overline{s})$ for some $\overline{s}, \widehat{s} \in \mathbb{S}^N$ with $i^0(\widehat{s}) = t$ and $i^0(\overline{s}) = t+1$.*

Using the lemmas above it can be shown that there exists a finite sequence of adjacent complete simplices of varying dimension connecting the simplices $\{0^N\}$ and $\{1^N\}$ if $\widehat{\zeta}$ satisfies Condition B and Z is a piecewise linear approximation of $\widehat{\zeta}$ with respect to a triangulation Σ of Q^N satisfying Condition C. The proof is given in Theorem 6.2.9. Theorem 6.2.8 makes a statement concerning the number of adjacent complete simplices when an s-complete t-simplex of $\Sigma(s)$ for some $s \in \mathbb{S}^N$ with $i^0(s) = t$ is given.

Theorem 6.2.8
Let the correspondence $\widehat{\zeta}$ satisfy Condition B, let Σ be a triangulation of Q^N, and let $Z : Q^N \to \mathbb{R}^N$ be a piecewise linear approximation of $\widehat{\zeta}$ with respect to Σ satisfying Condition C. Let τ be an s-complete facet of a t-simplex of $\Sigma(s)$ for some $s \in \mathbb{S}^N$ with $i^0(s) = t$. If $\tau = \{0^N\}$ or $\tau = \{1^N\}$, then there exists exactly one adjacent complete simplex to τ. If both $\tau \neq \{0^N\}$ and $\tau \neq \{1^N\}$, then there exist exactly two adjacent complete simplices to τ.
Proof
Let $\tau = \{0^N\}$. From Lemma 6.2.2 it follows that $s = (-1^{N-1^\top}, 0)^\top$. Clearly, $\{0^N\}$ is a subset of $\mathrm{rb}(A(s))$ and therefore, by Definition 2.7.1, there is a unique 1-simplex $\overline{\sigma}$ of $\Sigma(s)$ such that $\{0^N\}$ is a facet of $\overline{\sigma}$. By Lemma 6.2.5, either $\overline{\sigma}$ is an $\overline{s}$-complete facet of a 2-simplex of $\Sigma(\overline{s})$ for precisely one sign vector $\overline{s} \in \mathbb{S}^N$, or $\overline{\sigma}$ has exactly one other s-complete facet. Hence, there exists exactly one adjacent complete simplex to $\{0^N\}$. The argument for $\tau = \{1^N\}$ is similar.
Let τ be such that both $\tau \neq \{0^N\}$ and $\tau \neq \{1^N\}$. Then there are two possibilities, either $\tau \subset \mathrm{rb}(A(s))$ or $\tau \subset \mathrm{ri}(A(s))$.
Consider the case that $\tau \subset \mathrm{rb}(A(s))$. Then there is a unique t-simplex $\overline{\sigma}$ of $\Sigma(s)$ having τ as a facet. By Lemma 6.2.5, either $\overline{\sigma}$ is an $\overline{s}$-complete facet of a $(t+1)$-simplex of $\Sigma(\overline{s})$ for precisely one sign vector $\overline{s} \in \mathbb{S}^N$, or $\overline{\sigma}$ has exactly one other s-complete facet $\overline{\tau}$. This yields one adjacent complete simplex to τ. Since $\tau \subset \mathrm{rb}(A(s))$, it holds that $\tau \in \Sigma(\widehat{s})$ for a unique sign vector $\widehat{s} \in \mathbb{S}^N$ with $i^0(\widehat{s}) = t-1$. By Lemma 6.2.6, either $\tau = \{0^N\}$ or $\tau = \{1^N\}$, or τ is an $\widetilde{s}$-complete facet of a t-simplex of $\Sigma(\widetilde{s})$ for precisely one sign vector $\widetilde{s} \in \mathbb{S}^N \setminus \{s\}$,

or τ has exactly one $\widehat{s}$-complete facet. The first case is excluded since by assumption both $\tau \neq \{0^N\}$ and $\tau \neq \{1^N\}$. In the second case, since $\tau \subset \mathrm{rb}(A(\widetilde{s}))$, there is exactly one t-simplex $\widetilde{\sigma}$ of $\Sigma(\widetilde{s})$ having τ as a facet. Applying Lemma 6.2.5 again yields that either $\widetilde{\sigma}$ is an $\widetilde{s}$-complete facet of a $(t+1)$-simplex of $\Sigma(s')$ for precisely one sign vector $s' \in \mathbb{S}^N$, or $\widetilde{\sigma}$ has exactly one other $\widetilde{s}$-complete facet. This yields the second adjacent complete simplex to τ. In the third case the second adjacent complete simplex is obtained immediately. Clearly, there can be no other adjacent complete simplices to τ.
Consider the case that $\tau \subset \mathrm{ri}(A(s))$. Then τ is a facet of exactly two t-simplices of $\Sigma(s)$. Applying Lemma 6.2.5 twice shows that τ has exactly two adjacent complete simplices. Q.E.D.

Theorem 6.2.9
Let the correspondence $\widehat{\zeta}$ satisfy Condition B, let Σ be a triangulation of Q^N, and let $Z : Q^N \to \mathbb{R}^N$ be a piecewise linear approximation of $\widehat{\zeta}$ with respect to Σ satisfying Condition C. Then there exists a unique finite sequence of complete simplices $\tau^1, \ldots, \tau^{k'}$ such that $\tau^1 = \{0^N\}$, $\tau^{k'} = \{1^N\}$, $\tau^k \neq \tau^{k-2}$, $\forall k \in I_{k'} \setminus I_2$, and any two successive simplices in the finite sequence are adjacent complete simplices.
Proof
Let $\tau^1 = \{0^N\}$. Let τ^2 be the unique adjacent complete simplex to τ^1, that exists according to Theorem 6.2.8. Given τ^k for some $k \in \mathbb{N} \setminus \{1\}$, not equal to $\{0^N\}$ and not equal to $\{1^N\}$, there exists by Theorem 6.2.8 a unique adjacent complete simplex τ^{k+1} not equal to τ^{k-1}. As in the proof of Theorem 5.2.7 it can be shown that all simplices in the sequence generated above are different. By Theorem 2.7.2 the collection of all facets of all simplices of $\Sigma(s)$ is finite for every $s \in \mathbb{S}^N$. Therefore, all simplices in the sequence generated being different, it holds that the sequence generated is a finite sequence, and since $\tau^1 = \{0^N\}$, it follows that $\tau^{k'} = \{1^N\}$ for some $k' \in \mathbb{N}$. Q.E.D.

Now the steps of the algorithm generating the simplices $\tau^1, \ldots, \tau^{k'}$ of Theorem 6.2.9 are described in detail.

Algorithm 6.2.10 (Simplicial algorithm with vector labelling)
Let the correspondence $\widehat{\zeta}$ satisfy Condition B, let Σ be a triangulation of Q^N, and let $Z : Q^N \to \mathbb{R}^N$ be a piecewise linear approximation of $\widehat{\zeta}$ with respect to Σ satisfying Condition C. The simplicial algorithm *on Q^N with* vector labelling *has the following steps.*

Step 0. *Let $k = 1$, $t = 1$, $\tau^k = \tau(0^N)$, $s = (-1^{N-1^\top}, 0)^\top$, and let q^{t+1} be the unique vertex of the simplex of $\Sigma(s)$ containing τ^k as the facet opposite to it.*

Step 1. *Let σ be equal to the convex hull of $\tau^k \cup \{q^{t+1}\}$. Pivot $(0, Z(q^{t+1})^\top)^\top$ lexicographically into the linear system (6.2) corresponding to A_{s,τ^k}, yielding, as described in Lemma 6.2.5, a unique column $k' \in I_N$ of A_{s,τ^k} that has to be replaced. If $k' \in I_N \setminus I_t$, then go to Step 3 with $j' = j^{k'-t}$.*

Step 2. *Increase the value of k by 1 and let τ^k be the facet of σ opposite $q^{k'}$. If $\tau^k = \{1^N\}$, then the algorithm terminates. If $\tau^k \in \Sigma(\bar{s})$ for some $\bar{s} \in \mathbb{S}^N$, then go to Step 4. Otherwise, there is exactly one t-simplex $\bar{\sigma}$ of $\Sigma(s)$ such that $\bar{\sigma} \neq \sigma$ and τ^k is a facet of $\bar{\sigma}$. Go to Step 1 with q^{t+1} as the unique vertex of $\bar{\sigma}$ opposite τ^k.*

Step 3. *Let $\bar{s} \in \mathbb{S}^N$ be defined by $\bar{s}_{j'} = 0$ and $\bar{s}_j = s_j$, $\forall j \in I_N \setminus \{j'\}$. There is a unique simplex $\bar{\sigma}$ of $\Sigma(\bar{s})$ having σ as a facet. Increase the value of both k and t by 1 and go to Step 1 with q^{t+1} as the unique vertex of $\bar{\sigma}$ opposite σ, $s = \bar{s}$, and $\tau^k = \sigma$.*

Step 4. *Let σ be equal to τ^k. Pivot $(0, -\bar{s}_j e^N(j)^\top)^\top$ lexicographically into the linear system (6.2) determined by A_{s,τ^k}, where $j \in I_N$ is such that $s_j = 0$ and $\bar{s}_j \neq 0$. By Lemma 6.2.6 there is a unique column $k' \in I_N$ of A_{s,τ^k} that has to be replaced. If $k' \in I_N \setminus I_t$, then decrease the value of both k and t by 1 and go to Step 3 with $j' = j^{k'-t}$ and $s = \bar{s}$. Otherwise, decrease the value of t by 1 and go to Step 2 with $s = \bar{s}$.*

It is worthwhile to mention that it is also possible to define an algorithm that starts with the 0-simplex $\{1^N\}$ and terminates with the 0-simplex $\{0^N\}$.

Let the correspondence $\widehat{\zeta}$ satisfy Condition B, let Σ be a triangulation of Q^N, and let $Z : Q^N \to \mathbb{R}^N$ be a piecewise linear approximation of $\widehat{\zeta}$ with respect to Σ satisfying Condition C. In general, it cannot be excluded that there exists an s-complete facet $\bar{\tau}$ of a t-simplex of $\Sigma(s)$ for some $s \in \mathbb{S}^N$ with $i^0(s) = t$ that is not generated by Algorithm 6.2.10. Then, using Theorem 6.2.8, it can be shown similarly as in the proof of Theorem 6.2.9 that there exists a finite sequence of complete simplices, say $\bar{\tau}^1, \ldots, \bar{\tau}^{k'}$, such that $\bar{\tau}^1 = \bar{\tau}$, $\bar{\tau}^{k'} = \bar{\tau}$, $\bar{\tau}^k \neq \bar{\tau}^{k-2}$, $\forall k \in I_{k'} \setminus I_2$, and two successive simplices in this finite sequence are adjacent complete simplices. Moreover, this finite sequence of adjacent complete simplices is uniquely determined in the sense that it is either given by $\bar{\tau}^1, \ldots, \bar{\tau}^{k'}$ or by $\bar{\tau}^{k'}, \ldots, \bar{\tau}^1$.

Let the correspondence $\widehat{\zeta}$ satisfy Condition B, let Σ be a triangulation of Q^N, and let $Z : Q^N \to \mathbb{R}^N$ be a piecewise linear approximation of $\widehat{\zeta}$ with respect to Σ satisfying Condition C. Consider all different pairs of sign vectors and simplices $(s^1, \tau^1), \ldots, (s^{k''}, \tau^{k''})$ successively generated by Algorithm 6.2.10 such that, for every $k \in I_{k''}$, τ^k is an s^k-complete facet of a t^k-simplex of $\Sigma(s^k)$, where $t^k = i^0(s^k)$. Notice that $k'' \geq k'$, where k' is as in Theorem 6.2.8, with $k'' > k'$ only if Case 2 of Lemma 6.2.6, which corresponds to the first case in Step 4 of Algorithm 6.2.10, occurs. In this case a $(t-1)$-simplex τ is generated by the algorithm, that is both $\overline{s}$-complete and $\widehat{s}$-complete for some $\overline{s}, \widehat{s} \in \mathbb{S}^N$ with $i^0(\overline{s}) = i^0(\widehat{s}) = t$ and $\overline{s} \neq \widehat{s}$. Clearly, $A^{-1}_{s^k,\tau^k}$ is semi-lexicopositive for every $k \in I_{k''}$. Let some $\bar{k} \in I_{k''}$ be given. Then $\sum_{k \in I_{N+1}} (A_{s^{\bar{k}},\tau^{\bar{k}}})_{\cdot k} (A^{-1}_{s^{\bar{k}},\tau^{\bar{k}}})_{k1} = (1, 0^{N^\top})^\top$ or, equivalently,

$$\sum_{k \in I_{t^{\bar{k}}}} \left(A^{-1}_{s^{\bar{k}},\tau^{\bar{k}}}\right)_{k1} \begin{pmatrix} 1 \\ Z(q^k) \end{pmatrix} + \sum_{k \in I_{N-t^{\bar{k}}}} \left(A^{-1}_{s^{\bar{k}},\tau^{\bar{k}}}\right)_{t^{\bar{k}}+k,1} \begin{pmatrix} 0 \\ -s^{\bar{k}}_{j^k} e^N(j^k) \end{pmatrix}$$

$$+ \left(A^{-1}_{s^{\bar{k}},\tau^{\bar{k}}}\right)_{N+1,1} \begin{pmatrix} 0 \\ -1^N \end{pmatrix} = \begin{pmatrix} 1 \\ 0^N \end{pmatrix}, \quad (6.3)$$

where $\tau^{\bar{k}} = \tau^{\bar{k}}(q^1, \ldots, q^{t^{\bar{k}}})$ and $(A^{-1}_{s^{\bar{k}},\tau^{\bar{k}}})_{k1} \geq 0$, $\forall k \in I_N$. For every $\bar{k} \in I_{k''}$, the vector $\overline{q}^{\bar{k}} \in \tau^{\bar{k}}$ is defined by

$$\overline{q}^{\bar{k}} = \sum_{k \in I_{t^{\bar{k}}}} \left(A^{-1}_{s^{\bar{k}},\tau^{\bar{k}}}\right)_{k1} q^k,$$

and the function $f_Z : [0,1] \to Q^N$ is defined by

$$\begin{aligned} f_Z(t) &= (1 - (k''-1)t + \lfloor (k''-1)t \rfloor)\overline{q}^{\lfloor 1+(k''-1)t \rfloor} \\ &\quad + ((k''-1)t - \lfloor (k''-1)t \rfloor)\overline{q}^{1+\lfloor 1+(k''-1)t \rfloor}, \ \forall t \in [0,1), \\ f_Z(1) &= \overline{q}^{k''}. \end{aligned}$$

In Theorem 6.2.11 it is shown that the function f_Z generated by the algorithm is a piecewise linear path joining 0^N and 1^N and is such that every point $q \in f_Z([0,1])$ satisfies (6.1), i.e. for every $j \in I_N$, $0 \leq Z_j(q) \leq \beta$ if $q_j = 0$, $Z_j(q) = \beta$ if $0 < q_j < 1$, and $0 \geq Z_j(q) \geq \beta$ if $q_j = 1$.

Theorem 6.2.11

Let the correspondence $\widehat{\zeta}$ satisfy Condition B, let Σ be a triangulation of Q^N, and let $Z : Q^N \to \mathbb{R}^N$ be a piecewise linear approximation of $\widehat{\zeta}$ with respect to Σ satisfying Condition C. Then $f_Z : [0,1] \to Q^N$ is a piecewise linear path *joining* 0^N *and* 1^N, *and satisfying that for every* $q \in f_Z([0,1])$ *there is a number* $\beta \in \mathbb{R}$ *such that, for all* $j \in I_N$,

$$\begin{aligned} 0 \leq Z_j(q) \leq \beta \text{ if } q_j = 0, \\ Z_j(q) = \beta \text{ if } 0 < q_j < 1, \\ 0 \geq Z_j(q) \geq \beta \text{ if } q_j = 1. \end{aligned}$$

Proof

Let $(s^k, \tau^k)_{k \in I_{k''}}$ be all different pairs of sign vectors and simplices successively generated by Algorithm 6.2.10 such that, for every $k \in I_{k''}$, τ^k is an s^k-complete facet of a t^k-simplex of $\Sigma(s^k)$. Notice that, for every $k \in I_{k''-1}$, A_{s^k,τ^k} and $A_{s^{k+1},\tau^{k+1}}$ have N columns in common. Let $B_{\bar{s}^k,\sigma^k}$ be the $(N+1) \times (N+2)$ matrix containing all the columns of A_{s^k,τ^k} and $A_{s^{k+1},\tau^{k+1}}$, $\forall k \in I_{k''-1}$. Then the matrix $B_{\bar{s}^k,\sigma^k}$ yields the system as in (6.2) for a simplex σ^k that is the convex hull of τ^k and τ^{k+1} and for a sign vector $\bar{s}^k \in \mathbb{S}^N$ being such that $I^-(\bar{s}^k) = I^-(s^k) \cup I^-(s^{k+1})$ and $I^+(\bar{s}^k) = I^+(s^k) \cup I^+(s^{k+1})$. Using (6.3) it is easily verified that for every $k \in I_{k''-1}$ the first columns of both $A^{-1}_{s^k,\tau^k}$ and $A^{-1}_{s^{k+1},\tau^{k+1}}$, extended with a zero component, yield admissible solutions to the system in (6.2) induced by $B_{\bar{s}^k,\sigma^k}$ and that $\sigma^k \in \Sigma(\bar{s}^k)$. Finally, when $\bar{y}, \hat{y} \in \mathbb{R}^{N+2}$ are admissible solutions to the system $B_{\bar{s}^k,\sigma^k} y = (1, 0^{N^\top})^\top$, then $\lambda\bar{y} + (1-\lambda)\hat{y}$ is also an admissible solution to this system for every $\lambda \in [0,1]$. Since $\sigma^k \in \Sigma(\bar{s}^k)$, $\forall k \in I_{k''-1}$, it follows from (6.2) and the fact that Z satisfies Condition C that every $q \in f_Z([0,1])$ satisfies (6.1). Q.E.D.

6.3 THE EXISTENCE OF A CONTINUUM OF CONSTRAINED EQUILIBRIA

It is argued in Theorem 6.3.1 and Corollary 6.3.2 that the points lying on the path given in Theorem 6.2.11 are indeed all approximate zero points of $\widehat{\zeta}$. To show this, a sequence of triangulations $(\Sigma^n)_{n\in\mathbb{N}}$ with mesh size converging to zero and a sequence $(Z^n)_{n\in\mathbb{N}}$, such that Z^n is a piecewise linear approximation of $\widehat{\zeta}$ with respect to Σ^n satisfying Condition C for every $n \in \mathbb{N}$, is taken. If $\widehat{\zeta}$ satisfies Condition B, then, for every $n \in \mathbb{N}$, this yields according to Theorem 6.2.11 a piecewise linear function $f_{Z^n} : [0,1] \to Q^N$ joining 0^N and 1^N. It is shown that if q^n is an arbitrary point in $f_{Z^n}([0,1])$ and the sequence $(q^n)_{n\in\mathbb{N}}$ converges to an element $\bar{q}$, then $0^N \in \widehat{\zeta}(\bar{q})$. By the compactness of Q^N, every sequence of points in Q^N has a converging subsequence. Hence, for every $\varepsilon \in \mathbb{R}_{++}$, there exists $n' \in \mathbb{N}$ such that, for every $n \geq n'$, for every $q \in f_{Z^n}([0,1])$, it holds that $||Z^n(q)||_\infty < \varepsilon$, or, equivalently,

$\max(\{\|Z^n(q)\|_\infty \mid q \in f_{Z^n}([0,1])\}) \to 0$. Finally, it is shown in Theorem 6.3.3 that there exists a connected set of zero points of $\widehat{\zeta}$, containing 0^N and 1^N, that is being approximated.

Theorem 6.3.1
Let the correspondence $\widehat{\zeta} : Q^N \to \mathbb{R}^N$ satisfy Condition B, for every $n \in \mathbb{N}$, let Σ^n be a triangulation of Q^N such that mesh$(\Sigma^n) < \frac{1}{n}$, and let $Z^n : Q^N \to \mathbb{R}^N$ be a piecewise linear approximation of $\widehat{\zeta}$ with respect to Σ^n satisfying Condition C. Let $((q)^n)_{n\in\mathbb{N}}$ be an arbitrary sequence of points in Q^N with $(q)^n \in f_{Z^n}([0,1])$, $\forall n \in \mathbb{N}$, such that $(q)^n \to \bar{q}$. Then $0^N \in \widehat{\zeta}(\bar{q})$.
Proof
Let

$$((\lambda^1)^n, \ldots, (\lambda^{N+1})^n, (q^1)^n, \ldots, (q^{N+1})^n, (z^1)^n, \ldots, (z^{N+1})^n)_{n\in\mathbb{N}} \tag{6.4}$$

be a sequence in $\prod_{k\in I_{N+1}} [0,1] \times \prod_{k\in I_{N+1}} Q^N \times \prod_{k\in I_{N+1}} \mathbb{R}^N$ such that, for every $n \in \mathbb{N}$, $\sum_{k\in I_{N+1}} (\lambda^k)^n = 1$, while $\sigma((q^1)^n, \ldots, (q^{N+1})^n)$ is a simplex of Σ^n such that $(q)^n = \sum_{k\in I_{N+1}} (\lambda^k)^n (q^k)^n$ and $(z^k)^n = Z^n((q^k)^n)$, $\forall k \in I_{N+1}$. By the definition of a piecewise linear approximation, $Z^n((q)^n) = \sum_{k\in I_{N+1}} (\lambda^k)^n (z^k)^n$, $\forall n \in \mathbb{N}$. For every $n \in \mathbb{N}$ it holds that

$$Z^n((q)^n) = \beta^n 1^N - \sum_{j\in\{j\in I_N \mid (q_j)^n = 0\}} \mu^{j^n} e^N(j) + \sum_{j\in\{j\in I_N \mid (q_j)^n = 1\}} \mu^{j^n} e^N(j),$$

for some $\beta^n \in \mathbb{R}$ and some $\mu^{j^n} \geq 0$, $\forall j \in \{j \in I_N \mid (q_j)^n = 0 \text{ or } (q_j)^n = 1\}$. Since $\widehat{\zeta}$ is a compact-valued, upper hemi-continuous correspondence and Q^N is compact, it follows from Theorem 2.5.4 that $\widehat{\zeta}(Q^N)$ is compact. Therefore, without loss of generality, it can be assumed that the sequence in (6.4) converges to an element

$$(\bar{\lambda}^1, \ldots, \bar{\lambda}^{N+1}, \bar{q}^1, \ldots, \bar{q}^{N+1}, \bar{z}^1, \ldots, \bar{z}^{N+1}) \in \prod_{k\in I_{N+1}} [0,1] \times \prod_{k\in I_{N+1}} Q^N \times \prod_{k\in I_{N+1}} \mathbb{R}^N.$$

Let $\bar{z} \in \mathbb{R}^N$ be defined by $\bar{z} = \sum_{k\in I_{N+1}} \bar{\lambda}^k \bar{z}^k$. Since, for every $n \in \mathbb{N}$, mesh$(\Sigma^n) < \frac{1}{n}$, it holds that $\bar{q}^k = \bar{q}$, $\forall k \in I_{N+1}$. Since $\widehat{\zeta}$ is a compact-valued, upper hemi-continuous correspondence, it follows from Theorem 2.5.6 that $\bar{z}^k \in \widehat{\zeta}(\bar{q})$, $\forall k \in I_{N+1}$. Since $\widehat{\zeta}$ is convex-valued, $\sum_{k\in I_{N+1}} \bar{\lambda}^k = 1$, and $\bar{\lambda}^k \geq 0$, $\forall k \in I_{N+1}$, it holds that $\bar{z} \in \widehat{\zeta}(\bar{q})$. Moreover, $Z^n((q)^n) = \sum_{k\in I_{N+1}} (\lambda^k)^n (z^k)^n \to \sum_{k\in I_{N+1}} \bar{\lambda}^k \bar{z}^k = \bar{z}$.
If there is a subsequence $((q)^{n^m})_{m\in\mathbb{N}}$ of $((q)^n)_{n\in\mathbb{N}}$ such that, for every $m \in \mathbb{N}$,

$0 < (q)_j^{n^m} < 1$, $\forall j \in I_N$, then $Z^{n^m}((q)^{n^m}) = \beta^{n^m} 1^N$. Clearly, $Z^{n^m}((q)^{n^m}) \to \overline{z}$. Since $\overline{z} \in \widehat{\zeta}(\overline{q})$, there is some $p \in \mathbb{R}^N_{++}$ such that $p \cdot \overline{z} = 0$. Consequently, $\overline{z} = 0^N$. If there is not such a subsequence, then there exists a subsequence $((q)^{n^m})_{m\in\mathbb{N}}$ of $((q)^n)_{n\in\mathbb{N}}$ such that for some $j' \in I_N$, $(q_{j'})^{n^m} = 0$, $\forall m \in \mathbb{N}$, or $(q_{j'})^{n^m} = 1$, $\forall m \in \mathbb{N}$. In the first case, using that Z^n satisfies Condition C, it holds that $0 \leq Z_{j'}^{n^m}((q)^{n^m}) \leq \beta^{n^m}$ and therefore $0^N \leq Z^{n^m}((q)^{n^m})$, $\forall m \in \mathbb{N}$. Since $Z^{n^m}((q)^{n^m}) \to \overline{z}$, it holds that $\overline{z} \geq 0^N$. In the second case, again using that Z^n satisfies Condition C, it follows that $0 \geq Z_{j'}^{n^m}((q)^{n^m}) \geq \beta^{n^m}$ and therefore $0^N \geq \overline{z}$. In both cases the existence of a $p \in \mathbb{R}^N_{++}$ such that $p \cdot \overline{z} = 0$ implies that $\overline{z} = 0^N$. Hence, $0^N \in \widehat{\zeta}(\overline{q})$. Q.E.D.

From Theorem 6.3.1 the next result follows almost immediately.

Corollary 6.3.2
Let the correspondence $\widehat{\zeta} : Q^N \to \mathbb{R}^N$ satisfy Condition B, for every $n \in \mathbb{N}$, let Σ^n be a triangulation of Q^N such that mesh(Σ^n) $< \frac{1}{n}$, and let $Z^n : Q^N \to \mathbb{R}^N$ be a piecewise linear approximation of $\widehat{\zeta}$ with respect to Σ^n satisfying Condition C. Then, for every $\varepsilon \in \mathbb{R}_{++}$, there exists $n' \in \mathbb{N}$ such that, for every $n \geq n'$, for every $q^n \in f_{Z^n}([0,1])$, $\|Z^n(q^n)\|_\infty < \varepsilon$.

Proof
Suppose the statement of the corollary is not true. Then, without loss of generality, there exists $\varepsilon \in \mathbb{R}_{++}$ such that for every $n \in \mathbb{N}$ there exists $q^n \in f_{Z^n}([0,1])$ satisfying $\|Z^n(q^n)\|_\infty \geq \varepsilon$. As in the proof of Theorem 6.3.1 it can be shown that, without loss of generality, the sequence $(q^n, Z^n(q^n))_{n\in\mathbb{N}}$ in $Q^N \times \mathbb{R}^N$ converges to some $(\overline{q}, \overline{z}) \in Q^N \times \mathbb{R}^N$, where $\overline{z} \in \widehat{\zeta}(\overline{q})$. Clearly, $\|\overline{z}\|_\infty \geq \varepsilon > 0$. However, as in the proof of Theorem 6.3.1 it can be shown that $\overline{z} = 0^N$, yielding a contradiction. Q.E.D.

Let the correspondence $\widehat{\zeta} : Q^N \to \mathbb{R}^N$ satisfy Condition B, for every $n \in \mathbb{N}$, let Σ^n be a triangulation of Q^N such that mesh(Σ^n) $< \frac{1}{n}$, and let $Z^n : Q^N \to \mathbb{R}^N$ be a piecewise linear approximation of $\widehat{\zeta}$ with respect to Σ^n satisfying Condition C. It is shown in the next two paragraphs that approximations of several types of *constrained equilibrium* can be computed in this case.

Let some $j \in I_N$ and some $\alpha \in [0,1]$ be given. For every $n \in \mathbb{N}$, since $(f_{Z^n})_j$ is a continuous function and $[0,1]$ is connected, it follows from Theorem 2.3.13 that $(f_{Z^n})_j([0,1])$ is connected, hence an interval by Theorem 2.3.12. Therefore, since, for every $n \in \mathbb{N}$, $(f_{Z^n})_j(0) = 0$ and $(f_{Z^n})_j(1) = 1$, there exists $t^n \in [0,1]$ such that $(f_{Z^n})_j(t^n) = \alpha$. Let the sequence $(q^n)_{n\in\mathbb{N}}$ in Q^N be defined by

$q^n = f_{Z^n}(t^n)$, $\forall n \in \mathbb{N}$. Without loss of generality, it can be assumed that the sequence $(q^n)_{n\in\mathbb{N}}$ converges to some $\overline{q} \in Q^N$. By Theorem 6.3.1 it holds that $0^N \in \widehat{\zeta}(\overline{q})$. Clearly, $\overline{q}_j = \alpha$. Therefore, an approximation of an equilibrium, of which the existence is shown in Theorem 4.7.4, can be computed. By taking $\alpha = \frac{1}{2}$, an approximation of a Drèze equilibrium with respect to the market for commodity j is computed, see Definition 4.7.5. An alternative way to compute an approximation of a Drèze equilibrium with respect to the market for commodity j is given in Cornielje and van der Laan (1986).

Let some $\overline{\alpha} \in Q^N$ be given. Consider the set $S = \{q \in Q^N \mid q \leq \overline{\alpha} \text{ and } \exists j \in I_N,\ q_j = \overline{\alpha}_j\}$. Again, it is easily shown that for every $n \in \mathbb{N}$ there exists $t^n \in [0,1]$ such that $f_{Z^n}(t^n) \in S$. Let the sequence $(q^n)_{n\in\mathbb{N}}$ in Q^N be defined by $q^n = f_{Z^n}(t^n)$, $\forall n \in \mathbb{N}$. Without loss of generality, it can be assumed that the sequence $(q^n)_{n\in\mathbb{N}}$ converges to some $\overline{q} \in Q^N$. By Theorem 6.3.1 it holds that $0^N \in \widehat{\zeta}(\overline{q})$. Obviously, $\overline{q} \in S$. Therefore, an approximation of an equilibrium, of which the existence is shown in Theorem 4.8.2, is computed. Similarly, it can be shown that an approximation of an equilibrium, of which the existence is shown in Theorem 4.8.6, can be computed.

Now it is shown that for a correspondence $\widehat{\zeta} : Q^N \to \mathbb{R}^N$ satisfying Condition B there exists a component $\widetilde{C}$ of the set $\widetilde{Q}$, defined by

$$\widetilde{Q} = \widehat{\zeta}^{-1}(\{0^N\}),$$

such that $0^N \in \widetilde{C}$ and $1^N \in \widetilde{C}$. The proof uses the ideas of the proof of Theorem 5.3.5, but instead of taking the limit of a sequence of paths generated by the algorithm with integer labelling given in Algorithm 5.2.8, the limit of a sequence of paths generated by the algorithm with vector labelling given in Algorithm 6.2.10 is taken. This gives a constructive proof of the existence of the set $\widetilde{C}$ if $\widehat{\zeta}$ satisfies Condition B. Moreover, it makes clear that a continuum of zero points of $\widehat{\zeta}$ is approximated by Algorithm 6.2.10.

Let a non-empty, compact subset S of $\mathbb{R}^m$ be given. The function $d_S : \mathbb{R}^m \to \mathbb{R}$ is defined by

$$d_S(s) = \min\left(\{\|s - \overline{s}\|_\infty \mid \overline{s} \in S\}\right), \ \forall s \in \mathbb{R}^m.$$

Clearly, the function d_S is well defined and is continuous by Lemma 5.3.2.

Let S^1 and S^2 be non-empty, compact subsets of $\mathbb{R}^m$. The number $e(S^1, S^2)$ is defined by

$$e(S^1, S^2) = \min\left(\{\|s^1 - s^2\|_\infty \mid s^1 \in S^1 \text{ and } s^2 \in S^2\}\right).$$

It follows immediately that $e(S^1, S^2)$ is well defined. Clearly, if S^1 and S^2 are disjoint, then $e(S^1, S^2) > 0$.

Theorem 6.3.3
Let the correspondence $\widehat{\zeta} : Q^N \longrightarrow \mathbb{R}^N$ satisfy Condition B. Then the set $\widetilde{Q}$ contains a component $\widetilde{C}$ such that $0^N \in \widetilde{C}$ and $1^N \in \widetilde{C}$.
Proof
Clearly, $0^N \in \widetilde{Q}$, $1^N \in \widetilde{Q}$, and $\widetilde{Q}$ is compact. Suppose the statement of the theorem is false. Then 1^N is not an element of the component of $\widetilde{Q}$ containing 0^N. By Lemma 5.3.4 the quasi-component of 0^N in $\widetilde{Q}$ does not contain 1^N. Hence, there exists a set $\widetilde{Q}^1$ that is both open and closed in $\widetilde{Q}$, that contains 0^N, but does not contain 1^N. Let the set $\widetilde{Q}^2$ be defined by $\widetilde{Q}^2 = \widetilde{Q} \setminus \widetilde{Q}^1$. Then $\widetilde{Q}^2$ is both open and closed in $\widetilde{Q}$ and contains 1^N. Since $\widetilde{Q}$ is compact, it holds that $\widetilde{Q}^1$ and $\widetilde{Q}^2$ are disjoint, compact sets and

$$e\left(\widetilde{Q}^1, \widetilde{Q}^2\right) > \varepsilon,$$

for some $\varepsilon \in \mathbb{R}_{++}$. For every $n \in \mathbb{N}$, let Σ^n be a triangulation of Q^N with $\text{mesh}(\Sigma^n) < \frac{1}{n}$ and let $Z^n : Q^N \longrightarrow \mathbb{R}^N$ be a piecewise linear approximation of $\widehat{\zeta}$ with respect to Σ^n satisfying Condition C. For every $n \in \mathbb{N}$, let the function $g^n : [0,1] \rightarrow \mathbb{R}$ be defined by

$$g^n(t) = d_{\widetilde{Q}^1}(f_{Z^n}(t)) - d_{\widetilde{Q}^2}(f_{Z^n}(t)), \ \forall t \in [0,1].$$

Let some $n \in \mathbb{N}$ be given. Clearly, g^n is continuous, $g^n(0) < -\varepsilon$, and $g^n(1) > \varepsilon$. Moreover, since $[0,1]$ is connected, it follows from Theorem 2.3.13 that $g^n([0,1])$ is a connected subset of $\mathbb{R}$ and therefore an interval by Theorem 2.3.12. Hence, there exists a point $t^n \in [0,1]$ such that $g^n(t^n) = 0$. So,

$$d_{\widetilde{Q}^1}(f_{Z^n}(t^n)) = d_{\widetilde{Q}^2}(f_{Z^n}(t^n)) = d_{\widetilde{Q}}(f_{Z^n}(t^n)) > \tfrac{1}{2}\varepsilon.$$

Without loss of generality, it can be assumed that the sequence $(f_{Z^n}(t^n))_{n \in \mathbb{N}}$ in Q^N converges to some $\overline{q} \in Q^N$. Hence,

$$d_{\widetilde{Q}}(\overline{q}) = d_{\widetilde{Q}}\left(\lim_{n \to +\infty} f_{Z^n}(t^n)\right) = \lim_{n \to +\infty} d_{\widetilde{Q}}(f_{Z^n}(t^n)) \geq \tfrac{1}{2}\varepsilon > 0.$$

From Theorem 6.3.1 it follows that $d_{\widetilde{Q}}(\overline{q}) = 0$, yielding a contradiction. Q.E.D.

6.4 ACCURACY ANALYSIS

In this section it is assumed that the correspondence $\widehat{\zeta}$ satisfies Condition B and, moreover, is a continuous function. It is denoted by $\widehat{z}$. Moreover, let some

$\varepsilon \in \mathbb{R}_{++}$ be given and let $\delta \in \mathbb{R}_{++}$ be such that $q^1, q^2 \in Q^N$ and $||q^1 - q^2||_\infty < \delta$ implies $||\hat{z}(q^1) - \hat{z}(q^2)||_\infty < \varepsilon$. By the compactness of Q^N and the continuity of $\hat{z}$ such a real number δ exists by Theorem 2.7.10. Furthermore, a triangulation Σ of Q^N such that mesh$(\Sigma) < \delta$, the piecewise linear approximation Z of $\hat{z}$ with respect to Σ, and a point q in $f_Z([0,1])$ are assumed to be given. Notice that Z satisfies Condition C if the relation $\hat{\zeta}$ is a function.

By Condition B.3 there exists a function $p : Q^N \to \mathbb{R}^N_{++}$, which is not necessarily continuous, such that $p(q) \cdot \hat{z}(q) = 0$. There exists $\lambda^k \in \mathbb{R}_+$, $\forall k \in I_{N+1}$, $\mu^j \in \mathbb{R}_+$, $\forall j \in I_N$, and $\beta \in \mathbb{R}$ such that $\sum_{k \in I_{N+1}} \lambda^k = 1$, $q = \sum_{k \in I_{N+1}} \lambda^k q^k$ with $\sigma(q^1, \ldots, q^{N+1})$ an N-simplex of Σ containing q, and, for every $j \in I_N$,

$$\begin{array}{ll} Z_j(q) = \beta - \mu^j & \text{if } q_j = 0, \\ Z_j(q) = \beta & \text{if } 0 < q_j < 1, \\ Z_j(q) = \beta + \mu^j & \text{if } q_j = 1. \end{array}$$

Clearly,

$$||Z(q) - \hat{z}(q)||_\infty = \left\|\sum\nolimits_{k \in I_{N+1}} \lambda^k (\hat{z}(q^k) - \hat{z}(q))\right\|_\infty < \varepsilon.$$

Hence,

$$Z(q) - \varepsilon 1^N \ll \hat{z}(q) \ll Z(q) + \varepsilon 1^N. \tag{6.5}$$

If there exists $j \in I_N$ such that $q_j = 0$, then $\beta - \mu^j = Z_j(q) \geq 0$, so $\beta \geq \mu^j \geq 0$. If there exists $j \in I_N$ such that $q_j = 1$, then $\beta + \mu^j = Z_j(q) \leq 0$, so $\beta \leq -\mu^j \leq 0$. Now four cases have to be distinguished.
1. $\exists j^1 \in I_N$, $q_{j^1} = 0$, and $\exists j^2 \in I_N$, $q_{j^2} = 1$. It follows immediately that $\beta = 0$ and, for every $j \in I_N$ such that $q_j = 0$ or $q_j = 1$, it follows that $\mu^j = 0$. So, $Z(q) = 0^N$ and therefore, by (6.5), $-\varepsilon 1^N \ll \hat{z}(q) \ll \varepsilon 1^N$. Moreover, for every $j \in I_N$, if $q_j = 0$, then $0 \leq \hat{z}_j(q) < \varepsilon$, and if $q_j = 1$, then $-\varepsilon < \hat{z}_j(q) \leq 0$.
2. $0^N \ll q \ll 1^N$. Clearly, $Z(q) = \beta 1^N$. Then

$$|\beta| \sum_{j \in I_N} p_j(q) = |p(q) \cdot Z(q)| = |p(q) \cdot (Z(q) - \hat{z}(q))| < \varepsilon \sum_{j \in I_N} p_j(q).$$

Therefore, it holds that $|\beta| < \varepsilon$ and, by (6.5), $(\beta - \varepsilon)1^N \ll \hat{z}(q) \ll (\beta + \varepsilon)1^N$.
3. $0^N \ll q$ and $\exists j^1 \in I_N$, $q_{j^1} = 1$. Clearly, $\beta + \mu^{j^1} \leq 0$, so $\beta \leq 0$ and $0 \leq \mu^{j^1} \leq -\beta$. Moreover,

$$0 = p(q) \cdot \hat{z}(q) < \sum_{j \in \{j \in I_N | 0 < q_j < 1\}} p_j(q) \hat{z}_j(q) < (\beta + \varepsilon) \sum_{j \in \{j \in I_N | 0 < q_j < 1\}} p_j(q),$$

where (6.5) is used for the last inequality. Therefore, $\beta + \varepsilon > 0$ and $-\varepsilon < \beta \leq 0$. Hence, for every $j \in I_N$, if $0 < q_j < 1$, then $\beta - \varepsilon < \hat{z}_j(q) < \beta + \varepsilon$, and if $q_j = 1$, then $\beta - \varepsilon < \widehat{z}_j(q) \leq 0$, with $-\varepsilon < \beta \leq 0$.

4. $q \ll 1^N$ and $\exists j^1 \in I_N$, $q_{j^1} = 0$. As in Case 3 it can be shown that $0 \leq \beta < \varepsilon$ and, for every $j \in I_N$, if $q_j = 0$, then $0 \leq \widehat{z}_j(q) < \beta + \varepsilon$, and if $0 < q_j < 1$, then $\beta - \varepsilon < \widehat{z}_j(q) < \beta + \varepsilon$.

All the cases are summarized in Theorem 6.4.1.

Theorem 6.4.1

Let $\widehat{z}$ be a continuous function satisfying Condition B. Let $\varepsilon \in \mathbb{R}_{++}$ be given and let $\delta \in \mathbb{R}_{++}$ be such that, for every $q^1, q^2 \in Q^N$, $\|q^1 - q^2\|_\infty < \delta$ implies $\|\widehat{z}(q^1) - \widehat{z}(q^2)\|_\infty < \varepsilon$. Let Σ be a triangulation of Q^N with mesh(Σ) $< \delta$, let Z be the piecewise linear approximation of $\widehat{z}$ with respect to Σ, and let q in $f_Z([0,1])$ be given. Then there exists $\beta \in \mathbb{R}$ such that $-\varepsilon < \beta < \varepsilon$ and, for every $j \in I_N$, if $q_j = 0$, then $0 \leq \beta$, if $q_j = 1$, then $\beta \leq 0$, and

$$\begin{array}{rl} 0 \leq \widehat{z}_j(q) < \beta + \varepsilon & \text{if } q_j = 0, \\ \beta - \varepsilon < \widehat{z}_j(q) < \beta + \varepsilon & \text{if } 0 < q_j < 1, \\ \beta - \varepsilon < \widehat{z}_j(q) \leq 0 & \text{if } q_j = 1. \end{array}$$

6.5 AN EXAMPLE

In this section the algorithm is illustrated by the example used in Sections 3.10, 4.10, and 5.6. The correspondence $\widehat{\zeta}$ is given by the reduced total excess demand function $\widehat{z}$ of the economy $\widetilde{\mathcal{E}} = ((X^i, \preceq^i, \omega^i)_{i \in I_2}, P_{(\underline{p},\overline{p})}, (\widetilde{l}, \widetilde{L}))$, where $N = 2$, $X^1 = X^2 = \mathbb{R}^2_+$, $\preceq^1$ and $\preceq^2$ can be represented by utility functions given by $u^1(x^1) = (x^1_1)^{\frac{3}{4}}(x^1_2)^{\frac{1}{4}}$, $\forall x^1 \in \mathbb{R}^2_+$, and $u^2(x^2) = (x^2_1)^{\frac{1}{4}}(x^2_2)^{\frac{3}{4}}$, $\forall x^2 \in \mathbb{R}^2_+$, respectively, $\omega^1 = (1,4)^\top$, $\omega^2 = (2,1)^\top$, $P_{(\underline{p},\overline{p})} = \{p \in \mathbb{R}^2_+ \mid \frac{1}{6} \leq p_1 \leq 2$ and $p_2 = 1\}$, and $(\widetilde{l}, \widetilde{L})$ is the uniform rationing system, where $\widetilde{l} : Q^2 \to -\mathbb{R}^4_+$ is defined by $\widetilde{l}^1_1(q^1) = \widetilde{l}^2_1(q^1) = -3q^1_1$, $\forall q^1 \in Q^2$, $\widetilde{l}^1_2(q^1) = \widetilde{l}^2_2(q^1) = -5q^1_2$, $\forall q^1 \in Q^2$, and $\widetilde{L} : Q^2 \to \mathbb{R}^4_+$ is defined by $\widetilde{L}^1_1(q^2) = \widetilde{L}^2_1(q^2) = 18q^2_1$, $\forall q^2 \in Q^2$, and $\widetilde{L}^1_2(q^2) = \widetilde{L}^2_2(q^2) = 5q^2_2$, $\forall q^2 \in Q^2$. The corresponding reduced total excess demand relation is given in Section 4.10. In Section 4.10 it has been derived that the points

$$\begin{pmatrix} 0 \\ 0 \end{pmatrix}, \begin{pmatrix} \frac{1}{3} \\ 0 \end{pmatrix}, \begin{pmatrix} \frac{148}{231} \\ \frac{71}{420} \end{pmatrix}, \begin{pmatrix} \frac{148}{231} \\ \frac{349}{420} \end{pmatrix}, \begin{pmatrix} \frac{2}{3} \\ \frac{5}{6} \end{pmatrix}, \begin{pmatrix} \frac{211}{216} \\ \frac{5}{6} \end{pmatrix}, \begin{pmatrix} 1 \\ 1 \end{pmatrix},$$

and the convex combinations of any two successive points yield the set $\widetilde{Q}$. Next, Algorithm 6.2.10 is used to compute approximate zero points of $\widehat{z}$ by generating

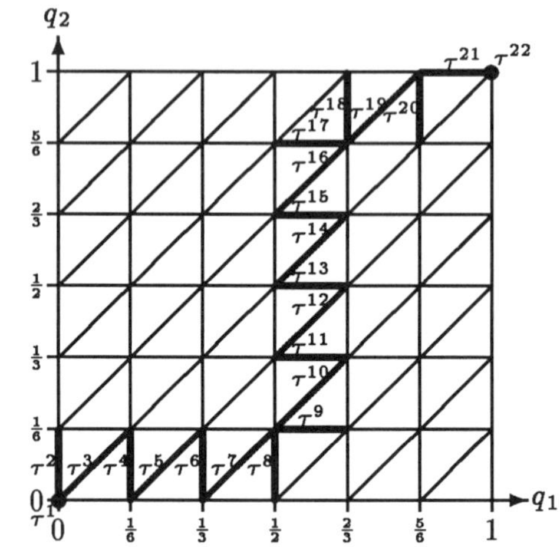

Figure 6.5.1. The finite sequence of adjacent complete simplices generated by Algorithm 6.2.10, $N = 2$.

a finite sequence of adjacent complete simplices for the K-triangulation of Q^2 with mesh size equal to $\frac{1}{6}$. The piecewise linear approximation of $\widehat{z}$ with respect to this triangulation is denoted by Z. In Figure 6.5.1 all adjacent complete simplices are drawn.

The finite sequence of adjacent complete simplices $\tau^1, \ldots, \tau^{22}$ in Figure 6.5.1 corresponds to the one given in Theorem 6.2.11. The piecewise linear path $f_Z([0,1])$ of points generated by the algorithm is given by the points

$$\begin{pmatrix} 0 \\ 0 \end{pmatrix}, \begin{pmatrix} \frac{1}{3} \\ 0 \end{pmatrix}, \begin{pmatrix} \frac{1}{2} \\ \frac{11}{120} \end{pmatrix}, \begin{pmatrix} \frac{113}{176} \\ \frac{1}{6} \end{pmatrix}, \begin{pmatrix} \frac{113}{176} \\ \frac{163}{528} \end{pmatrix}, \begin{pmatrix} \frac{277}{429} \\ \frac{1}{3} \end{pmatrix}, \begin{pmatrix} \frac{277}{429} \\ \frac{2}{3} \end{pmatrix}, \begin{pmatrix} \frac{2}{3} \\ \frac{5}{6} \end{pmatrix}, \begin{pmatrix} \frac{5}{6} \\ \frac{5}{6} \end{pmatrix}, \begin{pmatrix} 1 \\ 1 \end{pmatrix},$$

and all convex combinations of two successive points. In Figure 6.5.2 the solid line corresponds to the set $f_Z([0,1])$, while the dashed line corresponds to the set $\widetilde{Q}$.

The algorithm starts with the s^1-complete simplex $\tau^1 = \{(0,0)^\top\}$, a facet of a unique 1-simplex, $\sigma((0,0)^\top, (0,\frac{1}{6})^\top)$, of $\Sigma(s^1)$, where $s^1 = (-1,0)^\top$. Notice that although τ^1 is also $(0,+1)^\top$-complete, τ^1 is not a facet of a 1-simplex of $\Sigma((0,+1)^\top)$. The simplex τ^1 is not s-complete for $s = (0,-1)^\top$ since $A^{-1}_{(0,-1)^\top,\tau^1}$ is not semi-lexicopositive, although the system $A_{(0,-1)^\top,\tau^1} y = (0,0,0)^\top$ indeed has a solution satisfying $y_1 \geq 0$, $y_2 \geq 0$. This is in accordance with Lemma 6.2.2. In this way the lexicographic pivot steps determine in a unique way

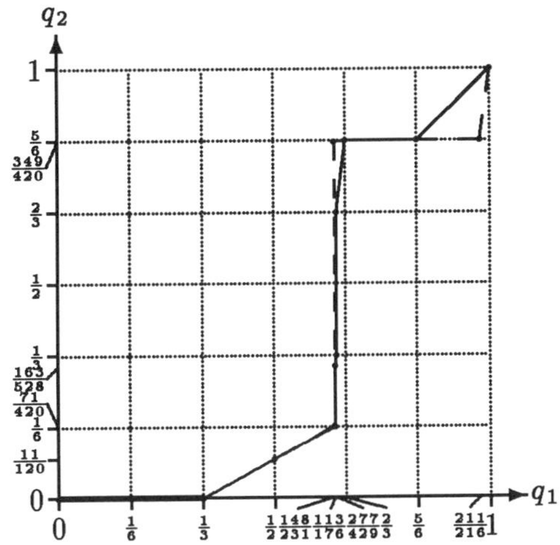

Figure 6.5.2. The set $\widetilde{Q}$, dashed line, and the set $f_Z([0,1])$, solid line, $N = 2$.

the direction the algorithm has to follow. So, the next vertex brought into the system is the vertex $(0, \frac{1}{6})^\top$ of the 1-simplex $\sigma((0,0)^\top, (0, \frac{1}{6})^\top)$ opposite $\{(0,0)^\top\}$. Remark that the direction determined by the lexicographic pivot steps is orthogonal to the set of zero points of $\widehat{z}$ around $(0,0)^\top$. It can easily be verified that the 0-simplex $\tau((0, \frac{1}{6})^\top)$ is not $(-1, 0)^\top$-complete. However, the 1-simplex $\tau^2 = \sigma((0,0)^\top, (0, \frac{1}{6})^\top)$ is $(0,0)^\top$-complete. Therefore, Case 1 of Lemma 6.2.5 results. The unique 2-simplex of $\Sigma((0,0)^\top)$ having τ^2 as a facet is given by $\sigma((0,0)^\top, (0, \frac{1}{6})^\top, (\frac{1}{6}, \frac{1}{6})^\top)$. The simplex $\tau^3 = \tau((0,0)^\top, (\frac{1}{6}, \frac{1}{6})^\top)$ is the unique $(0,0)^\top$-complete facet of the simplex $\sigma((0,0)^\top, (0, \frac{1}{6})^\top, (\frac{1}{6}, \frac{1}{6})^\top)$ that is not equal to τ^2. This corresponds to Case 2 of Lemma 6.2.5, and so on.

From Figure 6.5.2 it can be seen that although the lexicographic pivot steps determine an initial direction to leave τ^1 that is orthogonal to the set of zero points of $\widehat{z}$ around $(0,0)^\top$, the points on the piecewise linear path of approximate zero points generated by the simplices $\tau^1, \ldots, \tau^6$ are zero points of $\widehat{z}$. An interesting situation occurs at the simplex $\tau^{15} = \tau((\frac{1}{2}, \frac{2}{3})^\top, (\frac{2}{3}, \frac{2}{3})^\top)$. For this simplex it holds that

$$A^{-1}_{(0,0)^\top, \tau^{15}} = \begin{pmatrix} \frac{18}{143} & \frac{48}{143} & \frac{-48}{143} \\ \frac{125}{143} & \frac{-48}{143} & \frac{48}{143} \\ \frac{5}{104} & \frac{-7}{13} & \frac{-6}{13} \end{pmatrix}.$$

The vertex brought into the system is given by $q^3 = (\frac{2}{3}, \frac{5}{6})^\top$, with $Z(q^3) = (0,0)^\top$. So, $y = A^{-1}_{(0,0)^\top, \tau^{15}}(1, Z(q^3)^\top)^\top = (\frac{18}{143}, \frac{125}{143}, \frac{5}{104})^\top$. Now there occurs a degeneracy problem since both y_1 and y_2 are positive and equal to the corresponding element of the first column of $A^{-1}_{(0,0)^\top,\tau^{15}}$. However, since the vector

$$\frac{(A^{-1}_{(0,0)^\top,\tau^{15}})_{1\cdot}}{y_1}$$

is lexicographically larger than the vector

$$\frac{(A^{-1}_{(0,0)^\top,\tau^{15}})_{2\cdot}}{y_2},$$

the vertex $(\frac{2}{3},\frac{2}{3})^\top$ of τ^{15} corresponding to the second column of $A_{(0,0)^\top,\tau^{15}}$ should be replaced by the vertex $(\frac{2}{3},\frac{5}{6})^\top$, yielding the 1-simplex τ^{16}. Moreover, it has to be remarked that the last column of $A_{(0,0)^\top,\tau^{15}}$ would have been replaced by the column corresponding to the vertex $(\frac{2}{3},\frac{5}{6})^\top$ if it had not been required that the last column can never leave the system. Another interesting case occurs at τ^{21}. The 1-simplex τ^{21} is a member of $\Sigma((0,+1)^\top)$ and therefore $(0,0,-1)^\top$ is the new column brought into the system. This corresponds to Case 3 of Lemma 6.2.6, where τ^{22} is the unique $(0,+1)^\top$-complete facet of τ^{21}. The 0-simplex τ^{22} is a member of $\Sigma((+1,+1)^\top) = \{(1,1)^\top\}$ and Case 1 of Lemma 6.2.6 occurs. The algorithm now terminates with the $(0,+1)^\top$-complete simplex $\{(1,1)^\top\}$. It is clear from Figure 6.5.2 that the approximate zero points of $f_Z([0,1])$ are everywhere very close to the zero points of $\widehat{z}$. Moreover, most approximate zero points are much closer to the set $\widetilde{Q}$ than the approximate zero points computed by the algorithm with integer labelling of Chapter 5, see Figure 5.6.2.

The point $\overline{q} = (\frac{1}{2},\frac{11}{120})^\top$ induces an approximation of a *supply constrained equilibrium* and the total excess demand corresponding to this point is zero, $\widehat{z}(\overline{q}) = (0,0)^\top$. This constrained equilibrium is also a Drèze equilibrium with respect to the market for commodity 1. The point $\widehat{q} = (\frac{277}{429},\frac{1}{2})$ induces an approximation of a Drèze equilibrium with respect to the market for commodity 2, also being a *demand constrained equilibrium*. The total excess demand corresponding to this point is close to zero, $\widehat{z}(\widehat{q}) = (-0.0255, 0.0480)^\top$. Notice that the total excess demand at these approximations of constrained equilibria is closer to zero than the total excess demand at the corresponding approximations of constrained equilibria generated by the algorithm of Chapter 5.

7

INTERSECTION THEOREMS WITH A CONTINUUM OF INTERSECTION POINTS

7.1 INTRODUCTION

Intersection theorems state conditions under which the members of a certain subset of a cover of some set have a non-empty intersection. Well-known intersection theorems on the unit simplex are given in Knaster, Kuratowski, and Mazurkiewicz (1929) (KKM Lemma), Sperner (1928) and Scarf (1967) (Scarf Lemma), Shapley (1973) (KKMS Lemma), Gale (1984) (Gale Lemma), and Ichiishi (1988) (Ichiishi Lemma). Intersection theorems can be used to prove the existence of solutions to mathematical programming problems, of solutions to problems in general equilibrium theory, and of solutions to game theoretic problems. The KKM Lemma and the Scarf Lemma can be used to prove Brouwer's fixed point theorem and also to show the existence of a Walrasian equilibrium of an economy. Both the KKMS Lemma and the Ichiishi Lemma are very useful when showing the non-emptiness of the core of a cooperative game, see Shapley (1973), Ichiishi (1988), and Shapley and Vohra (1991). The Gale Lemma is used in Gale (1984) to show the existence of a Walrasian equilibrium in an economy with indivisible commodities. In van der Laan and Talman (1987c, 1993) intersection theorems on the unit cube and the simplotope are formulated, which can be used to prove the existence of a Nash equilibrium in a non-cooperative game.

It is possible to generalize the intersection theorems mentioned above and to formulate intersection theorems on a polytope. In for example Ichiishi and Idzik (1991) an intersection theorem on a polytope is derived generalizing the KKM Lemma. In van der Laan, Talman, and Yang (1994) a more general theorem on the polytope is stated. Most of the results mentioned above can be derived from this theorem. Moreover, this theorem makes it possible to formulate analogs of the KKM, Scarf, KKMS, and Ichiishi Lemma on the polytope.

In all the intersection theorems mentioned above conditions are given under which the members of a certain subset of a cover of some set, for instance the unit simplex, the unit cube, a simplotope, or a polytope, have a non-empty intersection. In this chapter intersection theorems on the unit cube are formulated with a continuum of intersection points. Conditions are given on a closed cover of the N-dimensional unit cube such that the members of a certain subset of this cover have an intersection consisting of a continuum of points. Moreover, the intersection has some interesting topological properties. It will be shown that it has a component containing both the element 0^N and the element 1^N. Therefore, these intersection theorems belong to a new class. The intersection theorems formulated in this chapter are shown to generalize the KKM Lemma, the Scarf Lemma, the KKMS Lemma, and the Ichiishi Lemma and are also shown to lead to a strengthening of the usual formulation of the Scarf Lemma on the unit cube. There is a close relationship between the intersection theorems of this chapter and the equilibrium existence problem in an economy as described in Chapter 4. The intersection theorems of this chapter give a more abstract formulation of the equilibrium existence problem in such an economy and they can be used to show Theorem 5.3.5. There seems to be some relationship to an intersection theorem on the unit simplex formulated in Freidenfelds (1974). This intersection theorem generalizes the Scarf Lemma. Often it has a continuum of intersection points, although this is not necessarily the case as opposed to the intersection theorems treated in this chapter.

In Section 7.2 a correspondence on the N-dimensional unit cube with the same properties as in Section 6.2 is given. The reduced total excess demand relation of the economy as described in Chapter 4 has been shown to satisfy these properties under suitable assumptions. In Theorem 6.3.3 it has been shown by means of constructive methods that the set of zero points of the reduced total excess demand relation has a component containing both the element 0^N and the element 1^N. In Section 7.2 the same result is shown in a non-constructive way by using Browder's fixed point theorem. These results are used in Section 7.3 to formulate several intersection theorems on the unit cube, among which the analogs of the KKM Lemma and the Scarf Lemma. Conditions are given under which the members of a cover of the unit cube have a non-empty intersection, whereas the intersection has a component containing both the element 0^N and the element 1^N. Using one of these intersection theorems it is possible to strengthen the usual formulation of the Scarf Lemma on the unit cube. In Section 7.3 also intersection theorems with a continuum of intersection points generalizing the KKMS Lemma and the Ichiishi Lemma are given. The proofs of all intersection theorems of Section 7.3 are derived from the correspondence introduced in Section 7.2. Therefore, this correspondence unifies these intersection theorems. In Section 7.4 attention is focused on some well-known intersection theorems on the unit simplex, where the existence of a non-empty intersection (in general not a continuum of points) of the members of a certain subset of a cover of the unit simplex is guaranteed. Both the Scarf Lemma and the KKM Lemma, which are in some sense dual to each other, are derived from an intersection theorem stated in Section 7.3. It is also possible to derive the KKMS Lemma and its dual, the Ichiishi Lemma, from another intersection theorem given in Section 7.3. In Section 7.5 it is shown that Theorem 5.3.5 can be derived from the intersection theorems formulated in Section 7.3.

This chapter is based on Herings and Talman (1994).

7.2 A NON-CONSTRUCTIVE CONSTRAINED EQUILIBRIUM EXISTENCE PROOF

In this section a correspondence $\widehat{\zeta} : Q^N \to \mathbb{R}^N$ is assumed to be given. For the main results the correspondence $\widehat{\zeta}$ is required to satisfy the following condition.

Condition B The correspondence $\widehat{\zeta} : Q^N \to \mathbb{R}^N$ satisfies

1. $\widehat{\zeta}$ is a compact-valued, convex-valued, upper hemi-continuous correspondence,
2. for every $q \in Q^N$, there exists $z \in \widehat{\zeta}(q)$ such that, for every $j \in I_N$, $q_j = 0$ implies $z_j \geq 0$, and $q_j = 1$ implies $z_j \leq 0$,
3. for every $q \in Q^N$, for every $z \in \widehat{\zeta}(q)$, there exists $p \in \mathbb{R}^N_{++}$ such that $p \cdot z = 0$.

This is the same condition as the one given in Section 6.2. The *reduced total excess demand relation* $\widehat{\zeta}$ of an *economy* $\widetilde{\mathcal{E}} = ((X^i, \preceq^i, \omega^i)_{i \in I_M}, P_{(\underline{p},\overline{p})}, (\widetilde{l}, \widetilde{L}))$ as described in Chapter 4 satisfies these conditions by Theorem 4.7.3. In Theorem 7.2.4 a non-constructive proof of Theorem 6.3.3, stating that the set of zero points of $\widehat{\zeta}$ has a component containing both the element 0^N and the element 1^N if $\widehat{\zeta}$ satisfies Condition B, is given.

The set $\widetilde{Q}$ is defined as the set of zero points of $\widehat{\zeta}$, so

$$\widetilde{Q} = \widehat{\zeta}^{-1}(\{0^N\}).$$

It is useful for the proof of Theorem 7.2.4 to extend the correspondence $\widehat{\zeta}$ such that it is defined on $\mathbb{R}^N$. For that three lemmas are needed, resulting in a correspondence $\widehat{\zeta}^2 : \mathbb{R}^N \to \mathbb{R}^N$.

Let the correspondence $\widehat{\zeta}$ satisfy Condition B. For every $q \in Q^N$, choose an element of the set $\widehat{\zeta}(q)$, denoted by $\widehat{z}(q)$, such that, for every $j \in I_N$, $\widehat{z}_j(q) \geq 0$ if $q_j = 0$ and $\widehat{z}_j(q) \leq 0$ if $q_j = 1$. Condition B guarantees that $\widehat{z}(q)$ can be chosen in this way for every $q \in Q^N$.

For a non-empty, compact subset S of $\mathbb{R}^m$, the relation $\pi_S : \mathbb{R}^m \to S$ is defined as the orthogonal projection on S, so

$$\pi_S(s) = \{\widehat{s} \in S \mid \|s - \widehat{s}\|_2 \leq \|s - \bar{s}\|_2,\ \forall \bar{s} \in S\},\ \forall s \in \mathbb{R}^N.$$

Lemma 7.2.1
Let a non-empty, compact, convex subset S of $\mathbb{R}^m$ be given. Then the relation π_S is a continuous function.
Proof
Clearly, the relation $\varphi : \mathbb{R}^m \to S$, defined by $\varphi(s) = S$, $\forall s \in \mathbb{R}^m$, is a compact-valued, upper hemi-continuous correspondence and the function $f : \mathbb{R}^m \times S \to \mathbb{R}$, defined by $f(s, \bar{s}) = -\|s - \bar{s}\|_2$, $\forall (s, \bar{s}) \in \mathbb{R}^m \times S$, is continuous. From the maximum theorem, Theorem 2.5.17, it follows that the relation $\mu : \mathbb{R}^m \to S$, defined by

$$\mu(s) = \{\widehat{s} \in \varphi(s) \mid f(s, \widehat{s}) \geq f(s, \bar{s}),\ \forall \bar{s} \in \varphi(s)\},\ \forall s \in \mathbb{R}^m,$$

is a compact-valued, upper hemi-continuous correspondence. It is easily verified that $\mu = \pi_S$. To prove that π_S is a function, it is shown that $\mu(s)$, $\forall s \in \mathbb{R}^m$, consists of one element.
Suppose that $s^1, s^2 \in \mu(s)$ with $s^1 \neq s^2$ for some given $s \in \mathbb{R}^m$. Hence, $\|s - s^1\|_2 = \|s - s^2\|_2$. Let some $\lambda \in (0,1)$ be given. Then $\lambda s^1 + (1-\lambda)s^2 \in S$ and

$$\begin{aligned}
&(\|s - (\lambda s^1 + (1-\lambda)s^2)\|_2)^2 \\
&\quad = \lambda^2(\|s - s^1\|_2)^2 + 2\lambda(1-\lambda)(s - s^1)\cdot(s - s^2) + (1-\lambda)^2(\|s - s^2\|_2)^2 \\
&\quad < (\lambda^2 + \lambda(1-\lambda))(\|s - s^1\|_2)^2 + ((1-\lambda)^2 + \lambda(1-\lambda))(\|s - s^2\|_2)^2 \\
&\quad = \lambda(\|s - s^1\|_2)^2 + (1-\lambda)(\|s - s^2\|_2)^2 = (\|s - s^1\|_2)^2,
\end{aligned}$$

where for the inequality it is used that $s - s^1 \neq s - s^2$. Therefore, a contradiction with $s^1 \in \mu(s)$ is obtained. Q.E.D.

Let the correspondence $\widehat{\zeta}$ satisfy Condition B. The correspondence $\widehat{\zeta}^1 : \mathbb{R}^N \to \mathbb{R}^N$ is defined as the correspondence with graph in $\mathbb{R}^N \times \mathbb{R}^N$ given by the set

$$\mathrm{cl}\left(\{(q, \widehat{z}(\pi_{Q^N}(q))) \,|q \in \mathbb{R}^N\}\right).$$

Notice that component $j \in I_N$ of the projection function π_{Q^N} is defined by $(\pi_{Q^N})_j(q) = \max(\{0, \min(\{q_j, 1\})\})$, $\forall q \in \mathbb{R}^N$.

Lemma 7.2.2
Let the correspondence $\widehat{\zeta} : Q^N \to \mathbb{R}^N$ satisfy Condition B. Then $\widehat{\zeta}^1$ is a compact-valued, upper hemi-continuous correspondence. For every $q \in \mathbb{R}^N$, $\widehat{\zeta}^1(q) \subset \widehat{\zeta}(\pi_{Q^N}(q))$. Moreover, for every $q \in \mathbb{R}^N$, for every $z \in \widehat{\zeta}^1(q)$, for every $j \in I_N$, $q_j < 0$ implies $z_j \geq 0$, and $q_j > 1$ implies $z_j \leq 0$.
Proof
It is easily verified that $\widehat{\zeta}^1$ is compact-valued and $\widehat{\zeta}^1(\mathbb{R}^N) \subset \widehat{\zeta}(Q^N)$. Since Q^N is compact and $\widehat{\zeta}$ is a compact-valued, upper hemi-continuous correspondence, it follows from Theorem 2.5.4 that the set $\widehat{\zeta}(Q^N)$ is compact. Moreover, $\widehat{\zeta}^1$ has a closed graph, so it follows from Theorem 2.5.7 that $\widehat{\zeta}^1$ is an upper hemi-continuous correspondence.
The second statement of the lemma follows immediately from the fact that $\widehat{\zeta}$ is a compact-valued, upper hemi-continuous correspondence.
Let some $\overline{q} \in \mathbb{R}^N$, some $\overline{z} \in \widehat{\zeta}^1(\overline{q})$, and some $j \in I_N$ such that $\overline{q}_j < 0$ be given. Then there exists a sequence $(q^n, z^n)_{n \in \mathbb{N}}$ such that $z^n = \widehat{z}(\pi_{Q^N}(q^n))$, $\forall n \in \mathbb{N}$, and $\lim_{n \to +\infty}(q^n, z^n) = (\overline{q}, \overline{z})$. Since $\overline{q}_j < 0$, there exists $n' \in \mathbb{N}$ such that $n \geq n'$ implies $q^n_j < 0$, hence $(\pi_{Q^N}(q^n))_j = 0$ and $z^n_j \geq 0$. Therefore, $\overline{z}_j \geq 0$. It can be shown in a similar way that, for every $q \in \mathbb{R}^N$, for every $z \in \widehat{\zeta}^1(q)$, for every $j \in I_N$, $q_j > 1$ implies $z_j \leq 0$. Q.E.D.

Let the correspondence $\widehat{\zeta}$ satisfy Condition B. The correspondence $\widehat{\zeta}^2 : \mathbb{R}^N \to \mathbb{R}^N$ is defined by $\widehat{\zeta}^2(q) = \widehat{\zeta}(q)$, $\forall q \in Q^N$, and $\widehat{\zeta}^2(q) = \mathrm{co}(\widehat{\zeta}^1(q))$, $\forall q \in \mathbb{R}^N \setminus Q^N$.

Lemma 7.2.3
Let the correspondence $\widehat{\zeta} : Q^N \to \mathbb{R}^N$ satisfy Condition B. Then $\widehat{\zeta}^2$ is a compact-valued, convex-valued, upper hemi-continuous correspondence. For every $q \in \mathbb{R}^N$, $\widehat{\zeta}^2(q) \subset \widehat{\zeta}(\pi_{Q^N}(q))$. Moreover, for every $q \in \mathbb{R}^N$, for every $z \in \widehat{\zeta}^2(q)$, for every $j \in I_N$, $q_j < 0$ implies $z_j \geq 0$, and $q_j > 1$ implies $z_j \leq 0$.
Proof
Since $\widehat{\zeta}$ is a compact-valued, upper hemi-continuous correspondence and Q^N is compact, it follows from Theorem 2.5.4 that $\widehat{\zeta}(Q^N)$ is compact. Using Lemma

7.2.2 and Theorems 2.5.7 and 2.5.8, it follows easily that $\widehat{\zeta}^2$ is a compact-valued, convex-valued correspondence with a graph being closed in $\mathbb{R}^N \times \widehat{\zeta}(Q^N)$. Therefore, it follows from Theorem 2.5.7 that $\widehat{\zeta}^2$ is an upper hemi-continuous correspondence. The other statements of the lemma follow immediately from Lemma 7.2.2. Q.E.D.

Theorem 7.2.4
Let the correspondence $\widehat{\zeta} : Q^N \to \mathbb{R}^N$ satisfy Condition B. Then the set $\widetilde{Q}$ contains a component $\widetilde{C}$ such that $0^N \in \widetilde{C}$ and $1^N \in \widetilde{C}$.
Proof
Since $\widehat{\zeta}$ is a compact-valued, upper hemi-continuous correspondence and Q^N is compact, it follows from Theorem 2.5.4 that $\widehat{\zeta}(Q^N)$ is compact. Let Z be a compact, convex set containing $\widehat{\zeta}(Q^N)$. Let the set S be defined by

$$S = \left\{ s \in \mathbb{R}^N \;\middle|\; \textstyle\sum_{j \in I_N} s_j = 0 \text{ and } s_j \geq -1, \ \forall j \in I_N \right\}.$$

Clearly, S is non-empty, compact, and convex. Let the relation $\varphi^1 : Z \to S$ be defined by

$$\varphi^1(z) = \{\bar{s} \in S \mid \bar{s} \cdot z \geq s \cdot z, \ \forall s \in S\}, \ \forall z \in Z.$$

Using the maximum theorem, Theorem 2.5.17, it follows immediately that φ^1 is a compact-valued, upper hemi-continuous correspondence. It is easily verified that φ^1 is also a convex-valued correspondence. Let the correspondence $\varphi^2 : S \times [1-N, 2] \to Z$ be defined by

$$\varphi^2(s,t) = \widehat{\zeta}^2(s + t1^N), \ \forall (s,t) \in S \times [1-N, 2].$$

From Lemma 7.2.3 it follows that φ^2 is a compact-valued, convex-valued correspondence. Moreover, φ^2 is an upper hemi-continuous correspondence by Theorem 2.5.5 because of the upper hemi-continuity of $\widehat{\zeta}^2$ shown in Lemma 7.2.3 and the continuity of the function associating $s + t1^N$ with $(s,t) \in S \times [1-N, 2]$. Let the correspondence $\varphi : Z \times S \times [1-N, 2] \to Z \times S$ be defined by

$$\varphi(z,s,t) = \varphi^2(s,t) \times \varphi^1(z), \ \forall (z,s,t) \in Z \times S \times [1-N, 2].$$

Since φ^1 and φ^2 are compact-valued, convex-valued correspondences, it follows immediately that φ is a compact-valued, convex-valued correspondence. Since φ^1 and φ^2 are also upper hemi-continuous correspondences, it follows from Theorem 2.5.10 that φ is an upper hemi-continuous correspondence. The set $Z \times S$ is easily seen to be non-empty, compact, and convex. Using Browder's fixed point theorem, Theorem 2.6.3, it follows that there exists a component F^c_φ of the set

$$F_\varphi = \{(z,s,t) \in Z \times S \times [1-N, 2] \,|(z,s) \in \varphi(z,s,t)\}$$

such that $F^c_\varphi \cap (Z \times S \times \{1-N\}) \neq \emptyset$ and $F^c_\varphi \cap (Z \times S \times \{2\}) \neq \emptyset$. Clearly, $(z^*, s^*, t^*) \in F^c_\varphi$ implies

$$(z^*, s^*) \in \varphi(z^*, s^*, t^*) = \widehat{\zeta}^2(s^* + t^* 1^N) \times \varphi^1(z^*) \subset \widehat{\zeta}\,(\pi_{Q^N}(s^* + t^* 1^N)) \times \varphi^1(z^*).$$

Suppose $\max(\{z^*_j \mid j \in I_N\}) > 0$. Since $z^* \in \widehat{\zeta}(\pi_{Q^N}(s^* + t^* 1^N))$, there exists by Condition B.3 some $\bar{p} \in \mathbb{R}^N_{++}$ such that $\bar{p} \cdot z^* = 0$. Therefore, there exists $j' \in I_N$ with $z^*_{j'} < 0$. It is easily verified that $s \in \varphi^1(z)$ for any $z \in Z$ with $z_{j^1} > z_{j^2}$, $j^1, j^2 \in I_N$, implies $s_{j^2} = -1$. Therefore, $s^*_{j'} = -1$. If $t^* < 1$, then $s^*_{j'} + t^* < 0$. Since $z^* \in \widehat{\zeta}^2(s^* + t^* 1^N)$, this implies $z^*_{j'} \geq 0$ by Lemma 7.2.3, a contradiction. Consider the case $t^* \geq 1$. By the definition of φ^1 there exists $j'' \in I_N$ such that $z^*_{j''} = \max(\{z^*_j \mid j \in I_N\}) > 0$ and $s^*_{j''} > 0$. Hence, $s^*_{j''} + t^* > 1$. Since $z^* \in \widehat{\zeta}^2(s^* + t^* 1^N)$, this implies $z^*_{j''} \leq 0$ by Lemma 7.2.3, a contradiction. Consequently, $\max(\{z^*_j \mid j \in I_N\}) \leq 0$. Since $\bar{p} \in \mathbb{R}^N_{++}$ and $\bar{p} \cdot z^* = 0$, this implies $z^* = 0^N$.
Consider the continuous function $f : Z \times S \times [1-N, 2] \to Q^N$, defined by $f(z, s, t) = \pi_{Q^N}(s + t1^N)$, $\forall (z, s, t) \in Z \times S \times [1-N, 2]$. By Theorem 2.3.13 the image of a connected set by a continuous function is connected, so it holds that $f(F^c_\varphi) \subset Q^N$ is connected. If $q^* \in f(F^c_\varphi)$, then $q^* = \pi_{Q^N}(s^* + t^* 1^N)$ for some $(z^*, s^*, t^*) \in F^c_\varphi$. Hence,

$$0^N = z^* \in \widehat{\zeta}^2(s^* + t^* 1^N) \subset \widehat{\zeta}\,(\pi_{Q^N}(s^* + t^* 1^N)) = \widehat{\zeta}(q^*).$$

Therefore, $f(F^c_\varphi) \subset \widetilde{Q}$. Next, let $s^1, s^2 \in S$ be such that $(0^N, s^1, 1-N) \in F^c_\varphi$ and $(0^N, s^2, 2) \in F^c_\varphi$. By definition, $f(0^N, s^1, 1-N) = \pi_{Q^N}(s^1 + (1-N)1^N)$. Since $s^1 \in S$, it holds that $s^1_j \leq N-1$, $\forall j \in I_N$, so $\pi_{Q^N}(s^1 + (1-N)1^N) = 0^N$. Since $s^2 \in S$, it holds that $s^2_j \geq -1$, $\forall j \in I_N$, so $\pi_{Q^N}(s^2 + 21^N) = 1^N$. Therefore, $0^N \in f(F^c_\varphi)$ and $1^N \in f(F^c_\varphi)$, so the set $\widetilde{Q}$ contains a component $\widetilde{C}$ such that $0^N \in \widetilde{C}$ and $1^N \in \widetilde{C}$. Q.E.D.

Theorem 7.2.4 turns out to be a very useful tool for proving a number of intersection theorems in the next section. Since Theorem 7.2.4 is used in the proof of all these intersection theorems, Theorem 7.2.4 can be seen as a unifying theorem.

7.3 INTERSECTION THEOREMS WITH A CONTINUUM OF INTERSECTION POINTS

In this section a new class of intersection theorems on the unit cube with a continuum of intersection points is introduced. More precisely, conditions are given such that the members of a certain subset of a closed cover of the N-dimensional unit cube have a non-empty intersection. Moreover, the intersection is shown to contain a connected set of points among which the elements 0^N and 1^N. For every $q \in Q^N$, the sets $I^0(q)$ and $I^1(q)$ are defined by

$$I^0(q) = \{j \in I_N \,|q_j = 0\},$$
$$I^1(q) = \{j \in I_N \,|q_j = 1\}.$$

Moreover, for every $q \in Q^N$, the integers $i^0(q)$ and $i^1(q)$ are defined by $i^0(q) = \#I^0(q)$ and $i^1(q) = \#I^1(q)$, and the integer $i(q)$ is defined by $i(q) = i^0(q)+i^1(q)$.

In Theorem 7.3.1 it is assumed that if an index $j \in I_N$ is taken and if $j = N$, then $j + 1 = 1$, while if $j = 1$, then $j - 1 = N$.

Theorem 7.3.1
Let $C^1, \ldots, C^N$ be closed subsets of Q^N satisfying $\cup_{j\in I_N} C^j = Q^N$. Moreover, for every $q \in Q^N$, for every $j \in I_N$, $q_j = 0$ or $q_{j+1} = 1$ implies $q \in C^j$. Then there exists a connected subset $\widetilde{C}$ of Q^N such that $0^N \in \widetilde{C}$, $1^N \in \widetilde{C}$, and $\widetilde{C} \subset \cap_{j\in I_N} C^j$.
Proof
For every $q \in Q^N$, let the set $J(q)$ be defined by $J(q) = \{j \in I_N \mid q \in C^j\}$ and let $j(q)$ denote the number of elements in the set $J(q)$. Let the correspondence $\widehat{\zeta} : Q^N \to \mathbb{R}^N$ be defined by

$$\widehat{\zeta}(q) = \mathrm{co}\left(\{\,e^N(j) - \tfrac{1}{N}1^N \,|\, j \in J(q)\}\right).$$

It is first verified that $\widehat{\zeta}$ satisfies Condition B. Using that the set C^j, $\forall j \in I_N$, is closed, it easily follows from Theorems 2.5.7 and 2.5.8 that $\widehat{\zeta}$ is a compact-valued, convex-valued, upper hemi-continuous correspondence. Hence, Condition B.1 is satisfied by $\widehat{\zeta}$.
If there exists $j \in I_N$ such that $q_j = 0$, then $q \in C^j$, so $e^N(j) - \frac{1}{N}1^N \in \widehat{\zeta}(q)$. If there exists $j \in I_N$ such that $q_j = 1$, then $q \in C^{j-1}$, so $e^N(j-1) - \frac{1}{N}1^N \in \widehat{\zeta}(q)$. Three cases have to be considered.
1. $I^1(q) = I_N$. Consider $z \in \widehat{\zeta}(q)$ given by $z = \sum_{j\in I_N} \frac{1}{N}(e^N(j) - \frac{1}{N}1^N) = 0^N$.

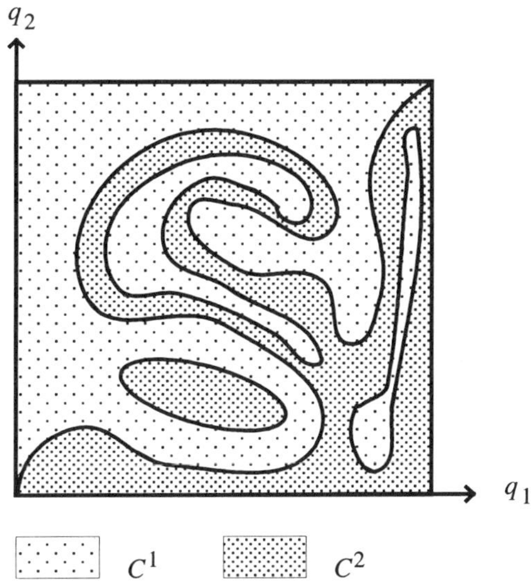

Figure 7.3.1. Illustration of Theorem 7.3.1, $N = 2$.

So, $z_j \leq 0$, $\forall j \in I^1(q)$.
2. $I^1(q) = \emptyset$. Consider $z \in \widehat{\zeta}(q)$ given by $z = \sum_{j \in J(q)} \frac{1}{j(q)}(e^N(j) - \frac{1}{N}1^N)$. Then $z_j = \frac{1}{j(q)} - \frac{1}{N} \geq 0$, $\forall j \in I^0(q)$.
3. $\emptyset \neq I^1(q) \neq I_N$. There exists $j' \in I_N$ such that $q_{j'} = 1$ and $q_{j'-1} \neq 1$. Consider $z \in \widehat{\zeta}(q)$ given by $z = \sum_{j \in I^0(q)} \frac{1}{N} e^N(j) + (1 - \frac{i^0(q)}{N})e^N(j'-1) - \frac{1}{N}1^N$. Then $z_j \geq \frac{1}{N} - \frac{1}{N} = 0$, $\forall j \in I^0(q)$, and $z_j = -\frac{1}{N} < 0$, $\forall j \in I^1(q)$.
The Cases 1, 2, and 3 show that $\widehat{\zeta}$ satisfies Condition B.2.
Since, for every $q \in Q^N$, for every $z \in \widehat{\zeta}(q)$, it holds that $1^N \cdot z = 0$, also Condition B.3 is satisfied by $\widehat{\zeta}$.
Let $q^* \in Q^N$ be such that $0^N \in \widehat{\zeta}(q^*)$. Then, obviously, $q^* \in C^j$, $\forall j \in I_N$, so $q^* \in \cap_{j \in I_N} C^j$. Therefore, by Theorem 7.2.4, there exists a connected subset $\widetilde{C}$ of Q^N such that $0^N \in \widetilde{C}$, $1^N \in \widetilde{C}$, and $\widetilde{C} \subset \cap_{j \in I_N} C^j$. Q.E.D.

Theorem 7.3.1 is illustrated in Figure 7.3.1 for the case $N = 2$.

The set $C^1 \cap C^2$ in Figure 7.3.1 consists of four components, one of these containing both the elements $(0,0)^\top$ and $(1,1)^\top$. It should be mentioned that Figure 7.3.1 illustrates a rather nice case in the sense that the sets C^1 and C^2 have a fairly easy structure. However, in Theorem 7.3.1 the only requirements made are that these two sets cover Q^2, are closed, and satisfy some boundary

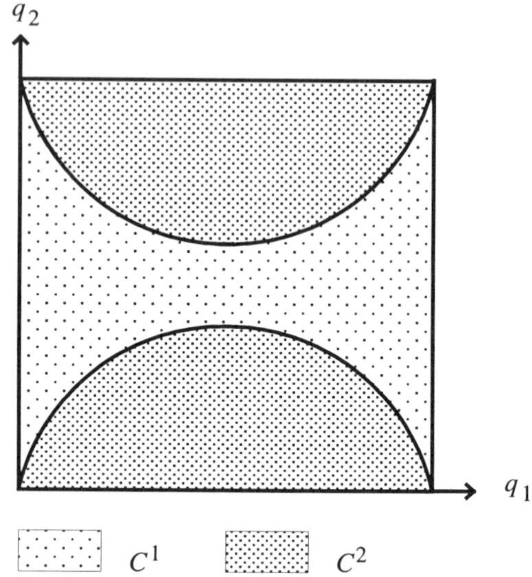

Figure 7.3.2. Counterexample, $N = 2$.

condition. Hence, in general, much more complicated situations might arise. The above remark is true for all illustrations in this chapter. In Section 7.4 it is shown that Theorem 7.3.1 immediately leads to the well-known Scarf Lemma, see Sperner (1928), Fan (1968), and Scarf (1967, 1973).

It should be noticed that it is possible to replace the boundary condition that, for every $j \in I_N$, $q_j = 0$ or $q_{j+1} = 1$ implies $q \in C^j$, by the more general condition that there exists a permutation $\pi : I_N \to I_N$ such that there is no non-empty, proper subset J of I_N satisfying $\pi(J) = J$, whereas, for every $j \in I_N$, $q_j = 0$ or $q_{\pi(j)} = 1$ implies $q \in C^j$. Theorem 7.3.1 corresponds to the choice $\pi = (2, \ldots, N, 1)$.

Figure 7.3.2 gives an easy counterexample for the case in which the condition that there exists no non-empty, proper subset J of I_N satisfying $\pi(J) = J$ is not satisfied.

Figure 7.3.2 corresponds to the case $\pi = (1, 2)$. The set $C^1 \cap C^2$ consists of two components, one containing the element $(0, 0)^\top$ and the other one the element $(1, 1)^\top$. In Example 7.3.2 a counterexample is given for any permutation $\pi : I_N \to I_N$ such that there exists a non-empty, proper subset J of I_N such that $\pi(J) = J$.

Example 7.3.2
Let $\pi : I_N \to I_N$ be a permutation and let J be a non-empty, proper subset of I_N such that $\pi(J) = J$. Let j' be an element of $I_N \setminus J$. Let the sets C^j, $\forall j \in I_N$, be defined by

$$\begin{aligned} C^j &= \left\{ q \in Q^N \,\middle|\, 0 \le q_j \le \tfrac{1}{4} \text{ or } \tfrac{3}{4} \le q_{\pi(j)} \le 1 \right\}, \ \forall j \in I_N \setminus \{j'\}, \\ C^{j'} &= Q^N. \end{aligned}$$

Notice that the conditions of the more general specification of Theorem 7.3.1 using the permutation π are satisfied by this choice of the sets C^j, $\forall j \in I_N$. Suppose there exists a connected subset $\widetilde{C}$ of Q^N such that $0^N \in \widetilde{C}$, $1^N \in \widetilde{C}$, and $\widetilde{C} \subset \cap_{j \in I_N} C^j$. Let the function $f : Q^N \to \mathbb{R}$ be defined by $f(q) = \max\{q_j \mid j \in J\} - \frac{1}{2}$. Notice that $f(0^N) = -\frac{1}{2} < 0$ and $f(1^N) = \frac{1}{2} > 0$. Using the same arguments as in the proof of Theorem 5.5.1, it follows that there exists $\overline{q} \in \widetilde{C}$ such that $f(\overline{q}) = 0$. Therefore, there exists $j^1 \in J$ such that $\overline{q}_{j^1} = \frac{1}{2}$. Let $j^2 \in J$ be given by $j^2 = \pi(j^1)$. Since $\overline{q} \in C^{j^1}$, it follows that $\frac{3}{4} \le \overline{q}_{j^2} \le 1$. Let $j^3 \in J$ be given by $j^3 = \pi(j^2)$. Since $\overline{q} \in C^{j^2}$, it follows that $\frac{3}{4} \le \overline{q}_{j^3} \le 1$. Since $\pi(J) = J$, there exists $k \in I_{\#J}$ such that $\pi(j^k) = j^1$. Hence, $\frac{3}{4} \le \overline{q}_{j^1} \le 1$, a contradiction. Consequently, there exists no connected subset $\widetilde{C}$ of Q^N such that $0^N \in \widetilde{C}$, $1^N \in \widetilde{C}$, and $\widetilde{C} \subset \cap_{j \in I_N} C^j$.

The following theorem generalizes both Theorem 7.3.1 and the more general specification with the permutation π.

Theorem 7.3.3
Let $C^1, \ldots, C^N$ be closed subsets of Q^N satisfying $\cup_{j \in I_N} C^j = Q^N$. Moreover, for every $q \in Q^N \setminus \{1^N\}$, for every $j \in I_N$, $q_j = 0$ implies $q \in C^j$, and $q_j = 1$ implies $q \in C^{j'}$ for some $j' \in I_N \setminus I^1(q)$. Then there exists a connected subset $\widetilde{C}$ of Q^N such that $0^N \in \widetilde{C}$, $1^N \in \widetilde{C}$, and $\widetilde{C} \subset \cap_{j \in I_N} C^j$.

Proof
For every $q \in Q^N$, let the set $J(q)$ be defined by $J(q) = \{j \in I_N \mid q \in C^j\}$ and let the correspondence $\widehat{\zeta} : Q^N \to \mathbb{R}^N$ be defined by

$$\widehat{\zeta}(q) = \mathrm{co}\left(\left\{ e^N(j) - \tfrac{1}{N} 1^N \,\middle|\, j \in J(q) \right\}\right).$$

Similar to the proof of Theorem 7.3.1 it can be shown that $\widehat{\zeta}$ is a compact-valued, convex-valued, upper hemi-continuous correspondence. Moreover, for every $q \in Q^N$, for every $z \in \widehat{\zeta}(q)$, it holds that $1^N \cdot z = 0$. So, the Conditions B.1 and B.3 are satisfied by $\widehat{\zeta}$. Condition B.2 remains to be verified.
Let q be equal to 1^N. For every $\varepsilon \in (0, 1]$, for every $j \in I_N$, it holds that

$1^N - \varepsilon e^N(j) \in C^j$. Since C^j is closed for every $j \in I_N$, this implies that $1^N \in \cap_{j \in I_N} C^j$ and hence $0^N \in \widehat{\zeta}(1^N)$.
Let q be an element of $Q^N \setminus \{1^N\}$ such that $I^0(q) \cup I^1(q) \neq \emptyset$. There exists $j' \in I_N \setminus I^1(q)$ such that $q \in C^{j'}$. Consider $z \in \widehat{\zeta}(q)$ given by

$$z = \sum_{j \in I^0(q)} \tfrac{1}{i(q)} e^N(j) + \tfrac{i^1(q)}{i(q)} e^N(j') - \tfrac{1}{N} 1^N.$$

For every $j \in I_N$, if $q_j = 0$, then $z_j \geq \frac{1}{i(q)} - \frac{1}{N} \geq 0$, and if $q_j = 1$, then $z_j = -\frac{1}{N} < 0$.
Hence, Condition B.2 is satisfied by $\widehat{\zeta}$. By Theorem 7.2.4 there exists a connected subset $\widetilde{C}$ of Q^N such that $0^N \in \widetilde{C}$, $1^N \in \widetilde{C}$, and $0^N \in \widehat{\zeta}(q^*)$ if $q^* \in \widetilde{C}$. It is easily seen that $0^N \in \widehat{\zeta}(q^*)$ implies $q^* \in \cap_{j \in I_N} C^j$. Q.E.D.

Theorems 7.3.1 and 7.3.3 are the same for the case $N = 2$. Theorem 7.3.3 is more general for the case $N \geq 3$. Therefore, it is also possible to derive the Scarf Lemma directly from Theorem 7.3.3.

By symmetry considerations the following dual theorem follows as a corollary to Theorem 7.3.3.

Theorem 7.3.4
Let $C^1, \ldots, C^N$ be closed subsets of Q^N satisfying $\cup_{j \in I_N} C^j = Q^N$. Moreover, for every $q \in Q^N \setminus \{0^N\}$, for every $j \in I_N$, $q_j = 1$ implies $q \in C^j$, and $q_j = 0$ implies $q \in C^{j'}$ for some $j' \in I_N \setminus I^0(q)$. Then there exists a connected subset $\widetilde{C}$ of Q^N such that $0^N \in \widetilde{C}$, $1^N \in \widetilde{C}$, and $\widetilde{C} \subset \cap_{j \in I_N} C^j$.

It is shown in Section 7.4 that the well-known KKM Lemma presented in Knaster, Kuratowski, and Mazurkiewicz (1929) follows almost immediately from Theorem 7.3.4. Since Theorems 7.3.3 and 7.3.4 are completely symmetric, it should be clear that the KKM Lemma can be easily derived from Theorem 7.3.3 as well. Similarly, the Scarf Lemma can be derived from Theorem 7.3.4.

So far intersection theorems have been considered where a statement is made about the intersection of all the members of a closed cover of Q^N. However, in for example the KKMS Lemma and the Ichiishi Lemma on Δ^{N-1} (see Shapley (1973) and Ichiishi (1988), respectively) a statement is made about the intersection of members in a certain subset of the cover of Δ^{N-1}. Theorem 7.3.5 is also an intersection theorem in this spirit. Moreover, unlike Theorems 7.3.1, 7.3.3, and 7.3.4, it is completely symmetric with respect to the assumptions made on the sets in the cover of Q^N.

Theorem 7.3.5
Let $C^1, \ldots, C^N, D^1, \ldots, D^N$ be closed subsets of Q^N satisfying $(\cup_{j\in I_N} C^j) \cup (\cup_{j\in I_N} D^j) = Q^N$. Moreover, for every $q \in Q^N$, for every $j \in I_N$, $q_j = 0$ implies $q \in C^j$, and $q_j = 1$ implies $q \in D^j$. Then there exists a connected subset $\widetilde{C}$ of Q^N such that $0^N \in \widetilde{C}$ and $1^N \in \widetilde{C}$. Moreover, $q^* \in \widetilde{C}$ implies $q^* \in C^j \cap D^j$ for some $j \in I_N$, or $q^* \in \cap_{j\in I_N} C^j$, or $q^* \in \cap_{j\in I_N} D^j$.

Proof

For every $q \in Q^N$, let the sets $J^0(q)$ and $J^1(q)$ be defined by $J^0(q) = \{j \in I_N \mid q \in C^j\}$ and $J^1(q) = \{j \in I_N \mid q \in D^j\}$. Obviously, for every $q \in Q^N$, $I^0(q) \subset J^0(q)$ and $I^1(q) \subset J^1(q)$. Let the correspondence $\widehat{\zeta} : Q^N \to \mathbb{R}^N$ be defined by

$$\widehat{\zeta}(q) = \mathrm{co}\left(\{ e^N(j) - \tfrac{1}{N}1^N \mid j \in J^0(q)\} \cup \{ \tfrac{1}{N}1^N - e^N(j) \mid j \in J^1(q)\}\right).$$

Similar to the proof of Theorem 7.3.1 it can be shown that $\widehat{\zeta}$ is a compact-valued, convex-valued, upper hemi-continuous correspondence. Hence, Condition B.1 is satisfied by $\widehat{\zeta}$. Since, for every $q \in Q^N$, for every $z \in \widehat{\zeta}(q)$, it holds that $1^N \cdot z = 0$, Condition B.3 is also satisfied by $\widehat{\zeta}$.

Let some $q \in Q^N$ such that $I^0(q) \cup I^1(q) \neq \emptyset$ be given. Consider $z \in \widehat{\zeta}(q)$ given by

$$z = \sum_{j\in I^0(q)} \tfrac{1}{i(q)} \left(e^N(j) - \tfrac{1}{N}1^N\right) + \sum_{j\in I^1(q)} \tfrac{1}{i(q)} \left(\tfrac{1}{N}1^N - e^N(j)\right).$$

For every $j \in I_N$, if $q_j = 0$, then $z_j = \frac{1}{i(q)} - \frac{i^0(q)}{i(q)N} + \frac{i^1(q)}{i(q)N} \geq \frac{N-i^0(q)}{i(q)N} \geq 0$, and it can be shown in a similar way that $q_j = 1$ implies $z_j \leq \frac{i^1(q)-N}{i(q)N} \leq 0$. Hence, $\widehat{\zeta}$ satisfies Condition B.2.

By Theorem 7.2.4 there exists a connected subset $\widetilde{C}$ of Q^N such that $0^N \in \widetilde{C}$, $1^N \in \widetilde{C}$, and $0^N \in \widehat{\zeta}(q^*)$ if $q^* \in \widetilde{C}$.

Let some $q^* \in Q^N$ satisfying $0^N \in \widehat{\zeta}(q^*)$ be given. Then there exist $\lambda^j \in \mathbb{R}_+$, $\forall j \in I_N$, and $\mu^j \in \mathbb{R}_+$, $\forall j \in I_N$, such that

$$\sum_{j\in I_N} \lambda^j \left(e^N(j) - \tfrac{1}{N}1^N\right) + \sum_{j\in I_N} \mu^j \left(\tfrac{1}{N}1^N - e^N(j)\right) = 0^N,$$

where $\lambda^j = 0$ if $q^* \notin C^j$, $\mu^j = 0$ if $q^* \notin D^j$, and $\sum_{j\in I_N} \lambda^j + \sum_{j\in I_N} \mu^j = 1$. Let the real numbers λ and μ be defined by $\lambda = \sum_{j\in I_N} \lambda^j$ and $\mu = \sum_{j\in I_N} \mu^j$. For every $j \in I_N$ it holds that $\lambda^j - \frac{1}{N}\lambda = \mu^j - \frac{1}{N}\mu$, so $\lambda^j - \mu^j = \frac{1}{N}(\lambda - \mu)$, being independent of j. Three possibilities can occur.

If $\lambda > \mu$, then $\lambda^j - \mu^j > 0$, $\forall j \in I_N$, hence $\lambda^j > 0$, $\forall j \in I_N$, and consequently $q^* \in \cap_{j\in I_N} C^j$.

If $\lambda = \mu$, then $\lambda^j = \mu^j$, $\forall j \in I_N$. Since there exists $j' \in I_N$ such that $\lambda^{j'} > 0$ or $\mu^{j'} > 0$, it holds that $q^* \in C^{j'} \cap D^{j'}$.

If $\lambda < \mu$, then $q^* \in \cap_{j\in I_N} D^j$. Q.E.D.

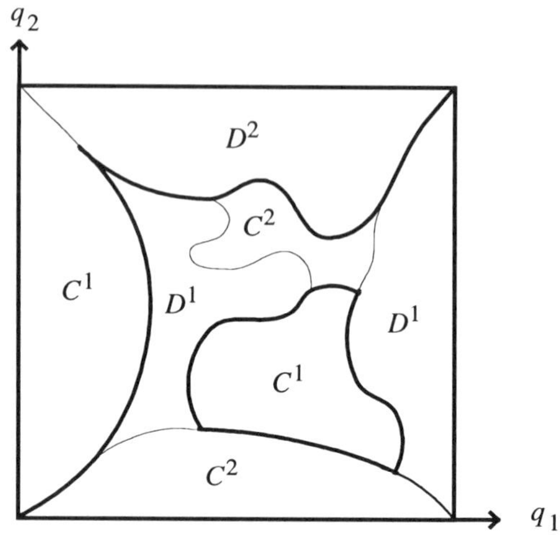

Figure 7.3.3. Illustration of Theorem 7.3.5, $N = 2$.

Theorem 7.3.5 is illustrated in Figure 7.3.3 for the case $N = 2$. It is easily verified that the set $(C^1 \cap D^1) \cup (C^2 \cap D^2) \cup (C^1 \cap C^2) \cup (D^1 \cap D^2)$ in Figure 7.3.3 consists of two components, one of them containing both $(0,0)^\top$ and $(1,1)^\top$.

It is shown that at least one element of the set $\widetilde{C}$ given in Theorem 7.3.5 lies in the intersection of C^j and D^j for some $j \in I_N$. It is even possible to show that $(\cap_{j \in I_N} C^j) \cap D^j \neq \emptyset$ for some $j \in I_N$ and $(\cap_{j \in I_N} D^j) \cap C^j \neq \emptyset$ for some $j \in I_N$.

Theorem 7.3.6
Let $C^1, \ldots, C^N, D^1, \ldots, D^N$ be closed subsets of Q^N satisfying $(\cup_{j \in I_N} C^j) \cup (\cup_{j \in I_N} D^j) = Q^N$. Moreover, for every $q \in Q^N$, for every $j \in I_N$, $q_j = 0$ implies $q \in C^j$, and $q_j = 1$ implies $q \in D^j$. Then there exists a connected subset $\widetilde{C}$ of Q^N such that $0^N \in \widetilde{C}$ and $1^N \in \widetilde{C}$. Moreover, $q^* \in \widetilde{C}$ implies $q^* \in C^j \cap D^j$ for some $j \in I_N$, or $q^* \in \cap_{j \in I_N} C^j$, or $q^* \in \cap_{j \in I_N} D^j$. Furthermore, there exists $q^1, q^2 \in \widetilde{C}$ such that $q^1 \in \cup_{j \in I_N}((\cap_{j \in I_N} C^j) \cap D^j)$ and $q^2 \in \cup_{j \in I_N}((\cap_{j \in I_N} D^j) \cap C^j)$.

Proof
By Theorem 7.3.5 there exists a connected set $\widetilde{C}$ such that $0^N \in \widetilde{C}$, $1^N \in \widetilde{C}$, and if $q^* \in \widetilde{C}$, then $q^* \in C^j \cap D^j$ for some $j \in I_N$, or $q^* \in \cap_{j \in I_N} C^j$, or $q^* \in \cap_{j \in I_N} D^j$. By Theorem 2.3.11, the closure of $\widetilde{C}$ is connected, and since the sets C^j, $\forall j \in I_N$, and D^j, $\forall j \in I_N$, are closed, the set $\widetilde{C}$ can be chosen such that it is closed, and therefore also compact. For every $q \in Q^N$, let

the sets $J^0(q)$ and $J^1(q)$ be defined by $J^0(q) = \{j \in I_N \mid q \in C^j\}$ and $J^1(q) = \{j \in I_N \mid q \in D^j\}$, and let the integers $j^0(q)$ and $j^1(q)$ be defined by $j^0(q) = \#J^0(q)$ and $j^1(q) = \#J^1(q)$. The relation $\varphi^0 : \widetilde{C} \to \mathbb{R}$ is obtained by defining, for every $q \in \widetilde{C}$,

$$\begin{aligned} \varphi^0(q) &= \emptyset & &\text{if } j^0(q) = 0, \\ \varphi^0(q) &= \{j^0(q)\} & &\text{if } j^0(q) > 0. \end{aligned}$$

The relation $\varphi^1 : \widetilde{C} \to \mathbb{R}$ is obtained by defining, for every $q \in \widetilde{C}$,

$$\begin{aligned} \varphi^1(q) &= \emptyset & &\text{if } j^1(q) = 0, \\ \varphi^1(q) &= \{-j^1(q)\} & &\text{if } j^1(q) > 0. \end{aligned}$$

Finally, let the correspondence $\varphi : \widetilde{C} \to \mathbb{R}$ be defined by

$$\varphi(q) = \text{co}\left(\varphi^0(q) \cup \varphi^1(q)\right), \ \forall q \in \widetilde{C}.$$

Using Theorems 2.5.7 and 2.5.8 it is easily shown that φ is a compact-valued, convex-valued, upper hemi-continuous correspondence. Since $\widetilde{C}$ is compact and connected, and φ is a compact-valued, convex-valued, upper hemi-continuous correspondence, it follows as in the proof of Theorem 5.4.2 that $\varphi(\widetilde{C})$ is a connected subset of $\mathbb{R}$ and hence an interval by Theorem 2.3.12. Since $0^N \in \widetilde{C}$, it follows that $N \in \varphi(0^N)$. Since $1^N \in \widetilde{C}$, it follows that $-N \in \varphi(1^N)$. Therefore, $\varphi(\widetilde{C}) = [-N, N]$.
Suppose that, for every $j \in I_N$, $(\cap_{j \in I_N} C^j) \cap D^j \cap \widetilde{C} = \emptyset$. Then $\varphi((\cap_{j \in I_N} C^j) \cap \widetilde{C}) = \{N\}$, and, since $\varphi(\widetilde{C} \setminus \cap_{j \in I_N} C^j) \subset [-N, N-1]$, it holds that $\varphi(\widetilde{C}) \subset [-N, N-1] \cup \{N\}$, a contradiction. Consequently, there exists $q^1 \in \widetilde{C}$ such that $q^1 \in (\cap_{j \in I_N} C^j) \cap D^j$ for at least one $j \in I_N$. Similarly, it can be shown that there exists $q^2 \in \widetilde{C}$ such that $q^2 \in (\cap_{j \in I_N} D^j) \cap C^j$ for at least one $j \in I_N$.
Q.E.D.

Theorem 7.3.6 strengthens the usual formulation of the *Scarf Lemma on the unit cube* (see Freund (1986) and van der Laan, Talman, and Yang (1994)), given in Corollary 7.3.7.

Corollary 7.3.7 (Scarf Lemma on the unit cube)
Let $C^1, \ldots, C^N, D^1, \ldots, D^N$ be closed subsets of Q^N satisfying $(\cup_{j \in I_N} C^j) \cup (\cup_{j \in I_N} D^j) = Q^N$. Moreover, for every $q \in Q^N$, for every $j \in I_N$, $q_j = 0$ implies $q \in C^j$, and $q_j = 1$ implies $q \in D^j$. Then $C^j \cap D^j \neq \emptyset$ for some $j \in I_N$.

Next, intersection theorems with a continuum of intersection points generalizing the KKMS Lemma and the Ichiishi Lemma are considered. To do this, the definition of a balanced collection of sets is given first. For every non-empty subset J of I_N the vector e^J of $\mathbb{R}^N$ is defined by

$$\begin{array}{ll} e_j^J = \frac{1}{\#J} & \text{if } j \in J, \\ e_j^J = 0 & \text{if } j \notin J. \end{array}$$

The vector $e^\emptyset$ is defined by

$$e^\emptyset = \tfrac{1}{N} 1^N.$$

The collection of all subsets of I_N is denoted by $\mathcal{J}_N$. Notice that $\emptyset \in \mathcal{J}_N$.

Definition 7.3.8 (Balancedness)
Let $\mathcal{J}$ be a non-empty subset of $\mathcal{J}_N$, say $\mathcal{J} = \{J^1, \ldots, J^{k'}\}$ for some $k' \in \mathbb{N}$. The collection $\mathcal{J}$ is balanced if there exist numbers $\lambda^k \in \mathbb{R}_{++}$, $\forall k \in I_{k'}$, such that $\sum_{k \in I_{k'}} \lambda^k = 1$ and $\sum_{k \in I_{k'}} \lambda^k e^{J^k} = e^{I_N}$.

Definition 7.3.8 is slightly more general than the usual definition of balancedness since the empty set is not excluded as an element of a balanced collection of sets. Notice that the empty set itself is balanced since $e^\emptyset = e^{I_N}$. If only non-empty subsets of I_N are considered, then Definition 7.3.8 reduces to the usual definition of balancedness. In Section 7.4 it is shown that the next theorem generalizes the KKMS Lemma and the Ichiishi Lemma. Remark that some of the sets are allowed to be empty.

Theorem 7.3.9
Let $\{C^J \mid J \in \mathcal{J}_N\}$ be a collection of closed subsets of Q^N such that $\cup_{J \in \mathcal{J}_N} C^J = Q^N$. Moreover, for every $q \in Q^N$ with $\emptyset \neq I^0(q) \neq I_N$, $q \in C^J$ for a set $J \in \mathcal{J}_N$ satisfying $I^0(q) \subset J$, and for every $q \in Q^N$ with $\emptyset \neq I^1(q) \neq I_N$, $q \in C^J$ for a set $J \in \mathcal{J}_N$ satisfying $I^1(q) \subset I_N \setminus J$. Then there exists a connected subset $\tilde{C}$ of Q^N such that $0^N \in \tilde{C}$, $1^N \in \tilde{C}$, and for every $q^* \in \tilde{C}$ there is a balanced collection $\{J^1, \ldots, J^{k'}\}$ of members of $\mathcal{J}_N$ such that $q^* \in \cap_{k \in I_{k'}} C^{J^k}$.
Proof
For every $q \in Q^N$, let the set $\mathcal{J}(q)$ be defined by $\mathcal{J}(q) = \{J \in \mathcal{J}_N \mid q \in C^J\}$. Let the correspondence $\widehat{\zeta} : Q^N \to \mathbb{R}^N$ be defined by

$$\widehat{\zeta}(q) = \mathrm{co}\left(\left\{ e^J - \tfrac{1}{N} 1^N \middle| J \in \mathcal{J}(q)\right\}\right).$$

Similar to the proof of Theorem 7.3.1 it can be shown that $\widehat{\zeta}$ is a compact-valued, convex-valued, upper hemi-continuous correspondence. So, Condition B.1 is satisfied by $\widehat{\zeta}$. Since, for every $q \in Q^N$, for every $z \in \widehat{\zeta}(q)$, it holds that

$1^N \cdot z = 0$, Condition B.3 is also satisfied by $\widehat{\zeta}$.
Clearly, for every $\varepsilon \in (0,1]$, for every $j \in I_N$, $0^N + \varepsilon e^N(j) \in C^{I_N \setminus \{j\}}$ or $0^N + \varepsilon e^N(j) \in C^{I_N}$. Hence, since C^J is closed for every $J \in \mathcal{J}_N$, $0^N \in \cap_{j \in I_N} C^{I_N \setminus \{j\}}$ or $0^N \in C^{I_N}$. Clearly, both the collections $\{I_N \setminus \{j\} \in \mathcal{J}_N \mid j \in I_N\}$ and $\{I_N\}$ are balanced. Therefore, $0^N \in \widehat{\zeta}(0^N)$. Similarly, since, for every $\varepsilon \in (0,1]$, for every $j \in I_N$, $1^N - \varepsilon e^N(j)$ belongs to $C^{\{j\}}$ or to $C^{\emptyset}$, it holds that $1^N \in \cap_{j \in I_N} C^{\{j\}}$ or $1^N \in C^{\emptyset}$. Hence, $0^N \in \widehat{\zeta}(1^N)$ since both the collections $\{\{j\} \in \mathcal{J}_N \mid j \in I_N\}$ and $\{\emptyset\}$ are balanced.
Let some $q \in Q^N \setminus \{0^N, 1^N\}$ with $I^0(q) \cup I^1(q) \neq \emptyset$ be given. Three cases have to be considered.
1. $I^0(q) = \emptyset$. Let $J^1 \in \mathcal{J}_N$ be a set satisfying $I^1(q) \subset I_N \setminus J^1$ and $q \in C^{J^1}$. Consider $z \in \widehat{\zeta}(q)$ given by $z = e^{J^1} - \frac{1}{N}1^N$. If $J^1 = \emptyset$, then $z = 0^N$, so, obviously, $z_j \leq 0$, $\forall j \in I^1(q)$. If $J^1 \neq \emptyset$, then $z_j = -\frac{1}{N} < 0$, $\forall j \in I^1(q)$.
2. $I^1(q) = \emptyset$. Let $J^0 \in \mathcal{J}_N$ be a set satisfying $I^0(q) \subset J^0$ and $q \in C^{J^0}$. Consider $z \in \widehat{\zeta}(q)$ given by $z = e^{J^0} - \frac{1}{N}1^N$. Then $z_j = \frac{1}{\#J^0} - \frac{1}{N} \geq 0$, $\forall j \in I^0(q)$.
3. $I^0(q) \neq \emptyset$ and $I^1(q) \neq \emptyset$. Let $J^0 \in \mathcal{J}_N$ be a set satisfying $I^0(q) \subset J^0$ and $q \in C^{J^0}$, and let $J^1 \in \mathcal{J}_N$ be a set satisfying $I^1(q) \subset I_N \setminus J^1$ and $q \in C^{J^1}$. If $J^1 = \emptyset$, then $0^N \in \widehat{\zeta}(q)$ and Condition B.2 is satisfied. Hence, consider the case where $J^1 \neq \emptyset$. Let $z \in \widehat{\zeta}(q)$ be given by

$$z = \tfrac{\#J^0}{N} e^{J^0} + \tfrac{N - \#J^0}{N} e^{J^1} - \tfrac{1}{N} 1^N.$$

For every $j \in I^0(q)$ it holds that $z_j \geq \frac{\#J^0}{N}\frac{1}{\#J^0} - \frac{1}{N} = 0$. For every $j \in I^1(q)$ it follows that $z_j \leq \frac{\#J^0}{N}\frac{1}{\#J^0} - \frac{1}{N} = 0$.
The Cases 1, 2, and 3 show that $\widehat{\zeta}$ satisfies Condition B.2.
By Theorem 7.2.4 there exists a connected subset $\widetilde{C}$ of Q^N such that $0^N \in \widetilde{C}$, $1^N \in \widetilde{C}$, and $0^N \in \widehat{\zeta}(q^*)$ if $q^* \in \widetilde{C}$. Clearly, $0^N \in \widehat{\zeta}(q^*)$ if and only if there exists a collection $\{J^1, \ldots, J^{k'}\}$ of sets in $\mathcal{J}_N$ such that $q^* \in \cap_{k \in I_{k'}} C^{J^k}$ and there exists $\lambda^{*k} \in \mathbb{R}_{++}$, $\forall k \in I_{k'}$, with $\sum_{k \in I_{k'}} \lambda^{*k} = 1$ satisfying $0^N = \sum_{k \in I_{k'}} \lambda^{*k}(e^{J^k} - \frac{1}{N}1^N)$, hence $\sum_{k \in I_{k'}} \lambda^{*k} e^{J^k} = e^{I_N}$. Therefore, $\{J^1, \ldots, J^{k'}\}$ is balanced and $\cap_{k \in I_{k'}} C^{J^k} \neq \emptyset$. Q.E.D.

Since the boundary condition in Theorem 7.3.9 is not specified for $q = 0^N$ and $q = 1^N$, it is possible that $C^{\emptyset} = \emptyset$ or $C^{I_N} = \emptyset$. It should be noticed that the boundary condition specified in Theorem 7.3.9 is weaker than the condition that for every $q \in Q^N$ with $\emptyset \neq I^0(q) \neq I_N$ or $\emptyset \neq I^1(q) \neq I_N$ it holds that $q \in C^J$ for a set $J \in \mathcal{J}_N$ satisfying $I^0(q) \subset J$ and $I^1(q) \subset I_N \setminus J$. Theorem 7.3.9 is illustrated in Figure 7.3.4 for the case $N = 2$.

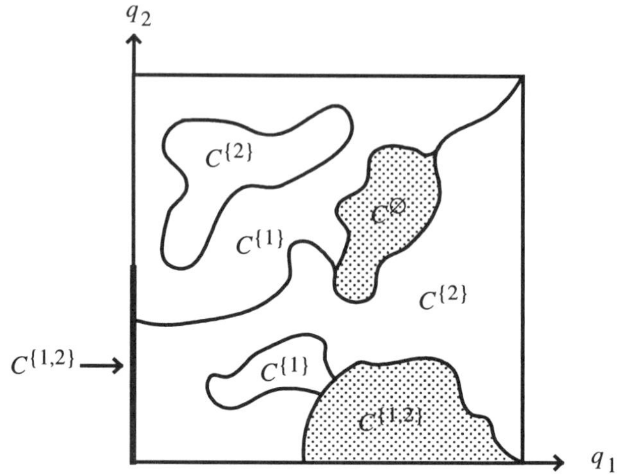

Figure 7.3.4. Illustration of Theorem 7.3.9, $N = 2$.

If $N = 2$, then the only difference with Theorem 7.3.1 or Theorem 7.3.3 is the possibility of non-empty sets $C^{\emptyset}$ or $C^{\{1,2\}}$. If $N = 2$, the minimal balanced collections of sets are given by $\{C^{\emptyset}\}$, $\{C^{\{1,2\}}\}$, and $\{C^{\{1\}}, C^{\{2\}}\}$. It is easily verified that in Figure 7.3.4 the union over all balanced collections of sets $\mathcal{J}$ of the intersection of the members of $\mathcal{J}$ consists of three components, with one component containing both the elements 0^N and 1^N. If $N \geq 3$, then the situation may be much more complicated than in Theorems 7.3.1 and 7.3.3.

By symmetry considerations, Theorem 7.3.10 follows immediately as a corollary to Theorem 7.3.9. It is shown in the next section that it is easy to derive the KKMS Lemma using Theorem 7.3.10.

Theorem 7.3.10
Let $\{C^J \mid J \in \mathcal{J}_N\}$ be a collection of closed subsets of Q^N such that $\cup_{J \in \mathcal{J}_N} C^J = Q^N$. Moreover, for every $q \in Q^N$ with $\emptyset \neq I^0(q) \neq I_N$, $q \in C^J$ for a set $J \in \mathcal{J}_N$ satisfying $I^0(q) \subset I_N \setminus J$, and, for every $q \in Q^N$ with $\emptyset \neq I^1(q) \neq I_N$, $q \in C^J$ for a set $J \in \mathcal{J}_N$ satisfying $I^1(q) \subset J$. Then there exists a connected subset $\widetilde{C}$ of Q^N such that $0^N \in \widetilde{C}$, $1^N \in \widetilde{C}$, and for every $q^* \in \widetilde{C}$ there is a balanced collection $\{J^1, \ldots, J^{k'}\}$ of members of $\mathcal{J}_N$ such that $q^* \in \cap_{k \in I_{k'}} C^{J^k}$.

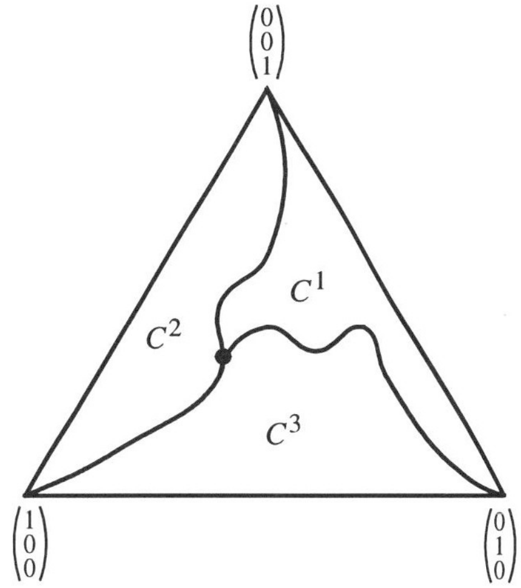

Figure 7.4.1. Illustration of the Scarf Lemma, $N = 3$.

7.4 INTERSECTION THEOREMS ON THE UNIT SIMPLEX

In this section a number of well-known intersection theorems on the $(N-1)$-dimensional unit simplex Δ^{N-1} are shown to follow as immediate results of the theorems of Section 7.3. Theorem 7.3.1 leads to the *Scarf Lemma* on Δ^{N-1}. This lemma is illustrated for the case $N = 3$ in Figure 7.4.1.

The Scarf Lemma states that the sets $C^1, \ldots, C^N$ have a non-empty intersection if these sets form a closed cover of Δ^{N-1} such that, for every $q \in \Delta^{N-1}$, for every $j \in I_N$, $q_j = 0$ implies $q \in C^j$. In Figure 7.4.1 there is exactly one intersection point. In the proof of Theorem 7.4.1 a cover $\{C^1, \ldots, C^N\}$ of Δ^{N-1} satisfying the conditions of Theorem 7.4.1 is extended in a straightforward way to a cover $\{\overline{C}^1, \ldots, \overline{C}^N\}$ of Q^N satisfying the conditions of Theorem 7.3.1. Then it follows that there exists a connected set $\tilde{C}$ such that $0^N \in \tilde{C}$, $1^N \in \tilde{C}$, and $\tilde{C} \subset \cap_{j \in I_N} \overline{C}^j$. It is shown that this connected set $\tilde{C}$ has a non-empty intersection with the unit simplex Δ^{N-1}. Finally, it is shown that $\overline{C}^j \cap \Delta^{N-1} = C^j$, $\forall j \in I_N$. In Theorem 7.4.1 it is again assumed that if an index $j \in I_N$ is taken, then $j + 1 = 1$ if $j = N$, and $j - 1 = N$ if $j = 1$.

Theorem 7.4.1 (Scarf Lemma)
Let $C^1, \ldots, C^N$ be closed subsets of Δ^{N-1} satisfying $\cup_{j \in I_N} C^j = \Delta^{N-1}$. Moreover, for every $q \in \Delta^{N-1}$, for every $j \in I_N$, $q_j = 0$ implies $q \in C^j$. Then

$\cap_{j \in I_N} C^j \neq \emptyset$.

Proof

The case $N = 1$ is trivial, so consider the case $N \geq 2$. For every $j \in I_N$, let the set $\overline{C}^j$ be given by

$$\overline{C}^j = \{q \in Q^N \,|\, \pi_{\Delta^{N-1}}(q) \in C^j\} \cup \{q \in Q^N \,|\, q_j = 0\} \cup \{q \in Q^N \,|\, q_{j+1} = 1\}.$$

It is shown that the sets $\overline{C}^1, \ldots, \overline{C}^N$ satisfy the conditions of Theorem 7.3.1. Using that the sets $C^1, \ldots, C^N$ are closed, that the function $\pi_{\Delta^{N-1}}$ is continuous, see Lemma 7.2.1, and that $\cup_{j \in I_N} C^j = \Delta^{N-1}$, it is easily verified that the set $\overline{C}^j$, $\forall j \in I_N$, is closed and that $\cup_{j \in I_N} \overline{C}^j = Q^N$. For every $q \in Q^N$, for every $j \in I_N$, $q_j = 0$ or $q_{j+1} = 1$ implies $q \in \overline{C}^j$. So, the sets $\overline{C}^1, \ldots, \overline{C}^N$ satisfy the conditions of Theorem 7.3.1. Hence, there exists a connected set $\widetilde{C}$ such that $0^N \in \widetilde{C}$, $1^N \in \widetilde{C}$, and $\widetilde{C} \subset \cap_{j \in I_N} \overline{C}^j$. Let the function $f : \widetilde{C} \to \mathbb{R}$ be defined by $f(q) = \sum_{j \in I_N} q_j$, $\forall q \in \widetilde{C}$. Since the image of a connected set under a continuous function is connected by Theorem 2.3.13, a connected subset of $\mathbb{R}$ is an interval by Theorem 2.3.12, $f(0^N) = 0$, and $f(1^N) = N$, there exists $\overline{q} \in \widetilde{C}$ such that $f(\overline{q}) = 1$, or, equivalently,

$$\overline{q} \in \widetilde{C} \cap \Delta^{N-1} \subset \cap_{j \in I_N} \left(\overline{C}^j \cap \Delta^{N-1}\right). \tag{7.1}$$

Clearly, $C^j \subset \overline{C}^j \cap \Delta^{N-1}$, $\forall j \in I_N$.

Suppose there exists $j' \in I_N$ and $\widehat{q} \in (\overline{C}^{j'} \cap \Delta^{N-1}) \setminus C^{j'}$. Then, since $\widehat{q} \in \Delta^{N-1}$ implies $\pi_{\Delta^{N-1}}(\widehat{q}) = \widehat{q}$, it holds that $\widehat{q}_{j'} = 0$ or $\widehat{q}_{j'+1} = 1$. Since $\widehat{q}_{j'} = 0$ implies $\widehat{q} \in C^{j'}$, it holds that $\widehat{q}_{j'+1} = 1$ and $\widehat{q}_{j'} > 0$, yielding a contradiction since $\widehat{q} \in \Delta^{N-1}$ with $N \geq 2$. Consequently, $\overline{C}^j \cap \Delta^{N-1} = C^j$, $\forall j \in I_N$, and this implies by (7.1) that $\overline{q} \in \cap_{j \in I_N} C^j$. Q.E.D.

Theorem 7.3.4 leads to the *KKM Lemma* on Δ^{N-1}. This lemma is illustrated in Figure 7.4.2 for the case $N = 3$.

The KKM Lemma states that the sets $C^1, \ldots, C^N$ have a non-empty intersection if the collection of these sets is a closed cover of Δ^{N-1} and for every $q \in \text{rb}(\Delta^{N-1})$ there exists $j \in I_N$ such that $q_j > 0$ and $q \in C^j$. In the proof of Theorem 7.4.2 a cover $\{C^1, \ldots, C^N\}$ of Δ^{N-1} satisfying the conditions of Theorem 7.4.2 is extended in more or less the same straightforward way as in the proof of Theorem 7.4.1 to yield a cover $\{\overline{C}^1, \ldots, \overline{C}^N\}$ of Q^N satisfying the conditions of Theorem 7.3.4. Recall from Section 2.2 that, for every $J \in \mathcal{J}_N$, $\Delta^{N-1}(J) = \{q \in \Delta^{N-1} \mid q_j = 0, \forall j \in J\}$ and $Q^N(J) = \{q \in Q^N \mid q_j = 0, \forall j \in J\}$. Notice that $Q^N(\emptyset) = Q^N$, $\Delta^{N-1}(\emptyset) = \Delta^{N-1}$, and $\Delta^{N-1}(J) \neq \emptyset$ if and only if J is a proper subset of I_N. Denote the collection of all proper subsets of I_N by $\mathcal{J}'_N$, so $\mathcal{J}'_N = \mathcal{J}_N \setminus \{I_N\}$.

Theorem 7.4.3 (Ichiishi Lemma)
Let $\{C^J \mid J \in \mathcal{J}''_N\}$ be a collection of closed subsets of Δ^{N-1} with $\cup_{J \in \mathcal{J}''_N} C^J = \Delta^{N-1}$. Moreover, for every $q \in \mathrm{rb}(\Delta^{N-1})$, there exists $J \in \mathcal{J}''_N$ such that $q \in C^J$ and $I^0(q) \subset J$. Then there is a balanced collection $\{J^1, \ldots, J^{k'}\}$ of sets in $\mathcal{J}''_N$ such that $\cap_{k \in I_{k'}} C^{J^k} \neq \emptyset$.

Proof

The case where $C^{I_N} \neq \emptyset$ is trivial, hence consider the case where $C^{I_N} = \emptyset$. Let the sets $\overline{C}^{\emptyset}$ and $\overline{C}^{I_N}$ be given by $\overline{C}^{\emptyset} = \overline{C}^{I_N} = \emptyset$. For every $J' \in \mathcal{J}_N \setminus \{\emptyset, I_N\}$, let the set $\overline{C}^{J'}$ be given by

$$\overline{C}^{J'} = \cup_{J \in \mathcal{J}'_N} \left\{ q \in Q^N(J) \,\middle|\, \pi_{\Delta^{N-1}(J)}(2q) \in C^{J'} \right\} \cup \left\{ q \in Q^N \,\middle|\, I_N \backslash J' \subset I^1(q) \right\}.$$

It is shown that the collection $\{\overline{C}^J \mid J \in \mathcal{J}_N\}$ satisfies the conditions of Theorem 7.3.9. Clearly, $\overline{C}^J$, $\forall J \in \mathcal{J}_N$, is closed and $\cup_{J \in \mathcal{J}_N} \overline{C}^J = Q^N$. Moreover, for every $q \in Q^N \setminus \{0^N\}$ with $I^0(q) \neq \emptyset$, it holds that $q \in Q^N(I^0(q))$ and there exists $J \in \mathcal{J}_N$ such that $\pi_{\Delta^{N-1}(I^0(q))}(2q) \in C^J$ and $I^0(\pi_{\Delta^{N-1}(I^0(q))}(2q)) \subset J$. So, for every $q \in Q^N \setminus \{0^N\}$ with $I^0(q) \neq \emptyset$, there exists $J \in \mathcal{J}_N$ such that $q \in \overline{C}^J$ while $I^0(q) \subset I^0(\pi_{\Delta^{N-1}(I^0(q))}(2q)) \subset J$. For every $q \in Q^N \setminus \{1^N\}$ with $I^1(q) \neq \emptyset$, it holds that $q \in \overline{C}^{I_N \backslash I^1(q)}$. Therefore, the collection $\{\overline{C}^J \mid J \in \mathcal{J}_N\}$ satisfies the conditions of Theorem 7.3.9 and there exists a connected subset $\tilde{C}$ of Q^N such that $0^N \in \tilde{C}$, $1^N \in \tilde{C}$, and for every $q^* \in \tilde{C}$ there is a balanced collection $J^1, \ldots, J^{k'}$ of members of $\mathcal{J}_N$ such that $q^* \in \cap_{k \in I_{k'}} \overline{C}^{J^k}$. As in the proof of Theorem 7.4.1 it follows that there exists

$$\overline{q} \in \tilde{C} \cap \left\{ q \in Q^N \,\middle|\, \textstyle\sum_{j \in I_N} q_j = \frac{1}{2} \right\}.$$

Hence, there is a balanced collection $\{J^1, \ldots, J^{k'}\}$ of members of $\mathcal{J}_N \setminus \{\emptyset, I_N\}$ such that $\overline{q} \in \cap_{k \in I_{k'}} \overline{C}^{J^k}$. Since $\overline{q}_j \neq 1$, $\forall j \in I_N$, it holds that for every $k \in I_{k'}$ there exists $J \in \mathcal{J}'_N$ such that $\overline{q} \in Q^N(J)$ and $\pi_{\Delta^{N-1}(J)}(2\overline{q}) \in C^{J^k}$. Since, for every $J \in \mathcal{J}'_N$, $\overline{q} \in Q^N(J)$ and $\sum_{j \in I_N} \overline{q}_j = \frac{1}{2}$ implies $\pi_{\Delta^{N-1}(J)}(2\overline{q}) = 2\overline{q}$, it holds that $2\overline{q} \in \cap_{k \in I_{k'}} C^{J^k}$. Q.E.D.

In Theorem 7.4.3 a cover of Δ^{N-1} with sets in $\mathcal{J}''_N = \mathcal{J}_N \setminus \{\emptyset\}$ is considered, which is the usual formulation. Clearly, the statement of Theorem 7.4.3 is still true if a cover with sets in $\mathcal{J}_N$ is considered since $C^{\emptyset} \neq \emptyset$ implies that Theorem 7.4.3 is trivially true. It is clear that also Theorem 7.3.10 can be used to derive the Ichiishi Lemma. Similarly, the *KKMS Lemma* as stated in Theorem 7.4.4 can easily be derived from both Theorem 7.3.9 and Theorem 7.3.10. In Theorem 7.4.4 the derivation using Theorem 7.3.10 is shown. Theorem 7.4.4 is illustrated in Figure 7.4.4 for the case $N = 3$.

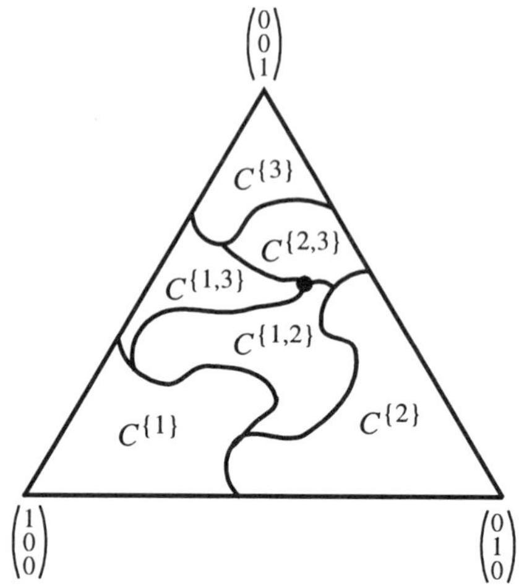

Figure 7.4.4. Illustration of the KKMS Lemma, $N = 3$.

The KKMS Lemma states that if a collection with as members the sets C^J, $\forall J \in \mathcal{J}''_N$, is a closed cover of Δ^{N-1} such that for every $q \in \mathrm{rb}(\Delta^{N-1})$ there exists $J \in \mathcal{J}''_N$ with $q \in C^J$ and $I^0(q) \subset I_N \setminus J$, then there is a balanced subset of this cover whose members have a non-empty intersection. In Figure 7.4.4 there is a unique intersection point, given by the intersection of the sets in the balanced collection $\{\{1,2\},\{1,3\},\{2,3\}\}$.

It should be mentioned that the derivation in Theorem 7.4.4 does not really lead to a simplified proof of the KKMS Lemma, since it uses Theorem 7.3.10, which depends on Theorem 7.2.4, where Browder's fixed point theorem is needed to provide a proof. For simple and elementary direct proofs of the KKMS Lemma, the reader is referred to Ichiishi (1981), Shapley and Vohra (1991), Komiya (1994), Krasa and Yannelis (1994), and Herings (1996a). Ichiishi has a proof based on Fan's coincidence theorem as presented in Fan (1969). Shapley and Vohra have proofs that involve either Kakutani's fixed point theorem or Fan's coincidence theorem. Komiya (1994) gives a proof of the KKMS Lemma based on Kakutani's fixed point theorem, the separating hyperplane theorem, and the maximum theorem. Krasa and Yannelis (1994) prove the KKMS Lemma by means of Brouwer's fixed point theorem, the separating hyperplane theorem, and the existence of a continuous selection from a correspondence having open lower sections. In Herings (1996a) only Brouwer's fixed point theorem and some elementary calculus is used. Moreover, in the proof in Herings (1996a), a function is explicitly given such that a fixed point of it corresponds to an intersection point together with balancing weights and vice versa. In Zhou

(1994) intersection theorems being close to the the Ichiishi Lemma and the KKMS Lemma are considered. He considers results where only open sets in the cover are used. His proof involves Brouwer's fixed point theorem and the existence of a collection of functions with some specific properties related to the cover.

Theorem 7.4.4 (KKMS Lemma)
Let $\{C^J \mid J \in \mathcal{J}''_N\}$ be a collection of closed subsets of Δ^{N-1} with $\cup_{J\in\mathcal{J}''_N} C^J = \Delta^{N-1}$. Moreover, for every $q \in \mathrm{rb}(\Delta^{N-1})$, there exists $J \in \mathcal{J}''_N$ such that $q \in C^J$ and $I^0(q) \subset I_N \setminus J$. Then there is a balanced collection $\{J^1, \ldots, J^{k'}\}$ of sets in $\mathcal{J}''_N$ such that $\cap_{k\in I_{k'}} C^{J^k} \neq \emptyset$.
Proof
The proof goes along the same lines as the proof of Theorem 7.4.3 by using Theorem 7.3.10 instead of Theorem 7.3.9 and by defining the set $\overline{C}^{J'}$, $\forall J' \in \mathcal{J}_N \setminus \{\emptyset, I_N\}$, by

$$\overline{C}^{J'} = \cup_{J\in\mathcal{J}'_N} \left\{ q \in Q^N(J) \,\middle|\, \pi_{\Delta^{N-1}(J)}(2q) \in C^{J'} \right\} \cup \left\{ q \in Q^N \,\middle|\, J' \subset I^1(q) \right\}.$$

Q.E.D.

7.5 THE EXISTENCE OF A CONTINUUM OF CONSTRAINED EQUILIBRIA

In this section it is shown that the existence of a continuum of *constrained equilibria* as stated in Theorem 5.3.5 can be shown using the intersection theorems of Section 7.3. The more general result of Theorem 5.4.1 can then be derived from this result as in Chapter 5. Indeed, the result of Theorem 5.4.1 has already been obtained in Theorem 7.2.4 and the intersection theorems of Section 7.3 have been shown using Theorem 7.2.4. However, it is also possible to give a constructive proof of any of the intersection theorems of Section 7.3, that can then be used to show the existence of a continuum of constrained equilibria. In Theorem 7.5.1 the intersection result given in Theorem 7.3.1 is used since this one should be considered as the least general result.

Theorem 7.5.1
Let $\widehat{z} : Q^N \to \mathbb{R}^N$ be a continuous function satisfying Condition B. Then the set $\widetilde{Q} = \widehat{z}^{-1}(\{0^N\})$ contains a component $\widetilde{C}$ such that $0^N \in \widetilde{C}$ and $1^N \in \widetilde{C}$.

Proof

For every $j \in I_N$, let the set C^j be defined by

$$C^j = \{q \in Q^N \,|\, \widehat{z}_j(q) = \max(\{\widehat{z}_j(q) | j \in I_N\})\} \cup \{q \in Q^N \,|\, q_j = 0 \text{ or } q_{j+1} = 1\}.$$

By the continuity of $\widehat{z}$, the set C^j, $\forall j \in I_N$, is closed. Moreover, the sets $C^1, \ldots, C^N$ satisfy the other conditions of Theorem 7.3.1. Therefore, there exists a connected subset $\widetilde{C}$ of Q^N such that $0^N \in \widetilde{C}$, $1^N \in \widetilde{C}$, and $\widetilde{C} \subset \cap_{j \in I_N} C^j$. It remains to be shown that $q \in \widetilde{C}$ implies $\widehat{z}(q) = 0^N$.

Let some $q \in \widetilde{C}$ be given. If $I^1(q) = \emptyset$, then, for every $j \in I_N$, either $q_j = 0$ and so $\widehat{z}_j(q) \geq 0$, or $q_j > 0$ and $\widehat{z}_j(q) = \max(\{\widehat{z}_j(q) \mid j \in I_N\}) \geq 0$, implying in both cases that $\widehat{z}(q) = 0^N$ by Condition B.3. If $\emptyset \neq I^1(q) \neq I_N$, then there exists $j' \in I_N$ such that $q_{j'} = 1$ and $q_{j'+1} \neq 1$, hence, $0 \geq \widehat{z}_{j'}(q) = \max(\{\widehat{z}_j(q) \,|j \in I_N\}) \geq 0$, so $\widehat{z}(q) = 0^N$ by Condition B.3. If $I^1(q) = I_N$, then $\widehat{z}(q) = 0^N$. Q.E.D.

PART III

ENDOGENOUSLY DETERMINED DISEQUILIBRIUM

8

ENDOGENOUSLY DETERMINED PRICE RIGIDITIES

8.1 INTRODUCTION

Often government behaviour is considered to be exogenous in economic modelling. However, there exists no reason why government behaviour should not be explained, while the behaviour of other agents acting in the economy is endogenously determined. The influence of the government on for example minimum wages is substantial and the existence of minimum wages clearly influences economic behaviour of producers and consumers. Moreover, the producers and consumers influence the level of the minimum wages by voting or by forming pressure groups. High levels of unemployment for example might increase the pressure on the government to lower the minimum wages. Hence, to explain the existence of minimum wages and to give an analysis of the most important determinants of the level of minimum wages, government behaviour should be modelled endogenously. The existence of minimum wages is just one example of a price rigidity. Other examples are price controls to reduce inflation (see Cox (1980)), minimum prices for agricultural products, fixed exchange rates, price indexation, and the linkage between the wages of civil servants and the wages paid in industry. The existence of price regulations and price rigidities is a frequently occurring real world phenomenon. Nguyen and Whalley (1990, p. 667) make the same observation, stating: "Price controls have been employed by governments all over the world, during war and peace, in response to all manners of threats (both real and imaginary), and in all ages," and Levy (1991, p. 157) writes: "Price controls are pervasive in developing countries."

An important reason for the existence of price regulations is that they can be used to influence the redistribution of initial endowments. As Coughlin (1986) argues, redistribution has become one of the most important political issues of the last three decades. A drawback of price regulations is the misallocation of resources resulting in efficiency losses.

In this paper a formal model capturing the ideas above is given. A stylized model of the political system corresponding to a democracy is described. The government consists of two political parties or candidates who compete for the votes of the consumers in the economy. For the sake of simplicity, as in Part II it is assumed that there are no producers in the economy. The candidates have the possibility to propose a price regulation in order to influence the redistribution of the initial endowments of the consumers.

The economic system is modelled by the general equilibrium model of the economy as described in Chapter 4. Given a proposal of a political candidate for some price regulation, including the case that there is no regulation, an economy as described in Chapter 4 results. When a price regulation is proposed, then it is assumed in this chapter that a Drèze equilibrium results in the economy. In most of the existing literature on models of economies with price rigidities, some constraints on the set of admissible price systems are exogenously given. Some exceptions worth mentioning are Hart (1982), Böhm, Maskin, Polemarchakis, and Postlewaite (1983), Madden (1983), and Silvestre (1988). In these papers (some of the) agents in the economy with three commodities are price setters in some of the markets. In this way the resulting price system is endogenously determined and may be non-Walrasian and therefore involve unemployment. However, it seems to be difficult to extend the results of these papers to general cases with more than three commodities.

In the model presented in this chapter the political candidates may impose a price regulation in the markets. Both government behaviour and price rigidities are endogenously determined. The control of prices by government is also the subject of Nguyen and Whalley (1986) and Ginsburgh and Van der Heyden (1988). In these papers government behaviour and price rigidities are not endogenously determined, but the attention is focused on non-rationing mechanisms to solve the mismatch between supply and demand resulting from a price regulation. This mismatch is solved by endogenously determined equilibrium buying and selling prices in Nguyen and Whalley (1986) and by government sales and purchases in Ginsburgh and Van der Heyden (1988).

In Section 8.2 the assumptions made with respect to the consumption set, the initial endowment, and the preference relation of every consumer are given. Moreover, some results concerning the demand relation of a consumer and the set of Drèze equilibria of an economy where no price regulations are specified in some markets are presented. The voting behaviour of the consumers and the political system are described in Section 8.3. The concept of a political economic equilibrium of the political economic system is specified as being the Nash equilibrium of a certain game. In Section 8.4 sufficient conditions for the existence of a mixed strategy and a pure strategy Nash equilibrium of the game defined in Section 8.3 are given. To prove existence it is shown that for every economy there exists an upper bound, that is chosen independently of the price regulation imposed, such that if the price in a market is above this upper bound, then in every possible Drèze equilibrium no trade takes place in this market. This result is quite intuitive and has some interest in itself. In Section 8.5 an example with two commodities and Cobb-Douglas utility functions is presented in which both political candidates impose a price regulation excluding the Walrasian equilibrium price system, and therefore the resulting Drèze equilibrium is characterized by rationing.

This chapter is based on Herings (1994c).

8.2 THE ECONOMIC SYSTEM

In this chapter the model of the *economic system* as described in Chapter 4 is used. It is assumed that there are $M \in \mathbb{N}$ *consumers*, indexed by $i \in I_M$, and $N \in \mathbb{N}$ *commodities*, indexed by $j \in I_N$. For every consumer $i \in I_M$, the *consumption set* X^i, the *utility function* $u^i : X^i \to \mathbb{R}$ representing the *preference relation* $\preceq^i$, and the *initial endowment* ω^i are assumed to be given. The *rationing function,* specifying the *admissible rationing schemes,* is given by the pair $(\widetilde{l}, \widetilde{L})$ with $\widetilde{l} : Q^N \to -\mathbb{R}^{MN}_+$ the *rationing function on supply* and $\widetilde{L} : Q^N \to \mathbb{R}^{MN}_+$ the *rationing function on demand.* The set $\prod_{i \in I_M} X^i$ is denoted by X. If $x = (x^1, \ldots, x^M)$ is an element of X, then $x_j = (x^1_j, \ldots, x^M_j)^\top$, $\forall j \in I_N$. Moreover, $\omega = (\omega^1, \ldots, \omega^M)$, $\omega_j = (\omega^1_j, \ldots, \omega^M_j)^\top$, $\forall j \in I_N$, and $\widetilde{\omega} = \sum_{i \in I_M} \omega^i$ denotes the *total initial endowment.* For every $i \in I_M$, for every $j \in I_N$, component $(i-1)N+j$ of $\widetilde{l}$ is denoted by $\widetilde{l}^i_j$. Moreover, $\widetilde{l}^i = (\widetilde{l}^i_1, \ldots, \widetilde{l}^i_N)^\top$, $\forall i \in I_M$, and $\widetilde{l}_j = (\widetilde{l}^1_j, \ldots, \widetilde{l}^M_j)^\top$, $\forall j \in I_N$. The same notation is used for the function $\widetilde{L}$, for a *rationing scheme on supply* $l \in -\mathbb{R}^{*MN}_+$, and for a *rationing scheme on demand* $L \in \mathbb{R}^{*MN}_+$. The following assumptions are needed for the main results of this chapter.

A1. For every consumer $i \in I_M$, the consumption set X^i is closed, convex, $X^i \subset \mathbb{R}^N_+$, and $X^i + \mathbb{R}^N_+ \subset X^i$.

A2. For every consumer $i \in I_M$, the utility function $u^i : X^i \to \mathbb{R}$ is continuous and represents the preference relation $\preceq^i$ being complete, transitive, continuous, strongly monotonic, and convex.

A3. For every consumer $i \in I_M$, the initial endowment ω^i belongs to $\text{int}(X^i)$.

A4. The rationing function $(\widetilde{l}, \widetilde{L})$ is flexible, market independent, and continuous.

As stated in Theorem 3.6.1, it is possible to represent a complete, transitive, continuous preference relation on a convex consumption set by a continuous utility function.

The political candidates are assumed to make *proposals* with respect to price regulations. It is assumed that a proposal of a political candidate consists of the specification of a *lower bound* on the *price system*, $\underline{p} \in \mathbb{R}^{*N}$, and an *upper bound* on the price system, $\overline{p} \in \mathbb{R}^{*N}$, such that $\underline{p} \leq \overline{p}$, $\underline{p} \ll +\infty^N$, and $\overline{p} \gg -\infty^N$. Commodity N is assumed to be a *numeraire commodity* with price equal to 1. Therefore, it is assumed that $\underline{p}_N = \overline{p}_N = 1$. Moreover, it is assumed that $N \geq 2$ since $N = 1$ implies that there are no prices left to be regulated. The special interpretation of the model given in Bénassy (1975a) and described in Section 4.7 is again possible. This motivates the use of either the equilibrium concept of Bénassy (1975b), or of Drèze (1975), or of Younès (1975), where there is no rationing in the market for the numeraire commodity. Since Drèze's equilibrium concept yields the smallest set of equilibria, see Silvestre (1982), and because of the mathematical convenience of Drèze's definition, this equilibrium concept is chosen in this chapter. Moreover, only price systems in $\mathbb{R}^N_+$ are considered since this is the economically interesting case if the preference relations of the consumers satisfy some weak monotonicity assumptions. Therefore, to guarantee that the set of admissible price systems is non-empty, it is assumed that $\overline{p} \geq 0^N$. The case where price systems may be any element of $\mathbb{R}^N$ is mathematically the same.

To a proposal $(\underline{p}, \overline{p})$ of a political candidate corresponds the *set of admissible price systems* $P_{(\underline{p},\overline{p})}$, defined by

$$P_{(\underline{p},\overline{p})} = \left\{ p \in \mathbb{R}^N_+ \;\middle|\; \underline{p} \leq p \leq \overline{p} \right\},$$

and the *economy* $\widetilde{\mathcal{E}}(\underline{p}, \overline{p})$, given by

$$\widetilde{\mathcal{E}}(\underline{p}, \overline{p}) = \left(\left(X^i, \preceq^i, \omega^i \right)_{i \in I_M}, P_{(\underline{p},\overline{p})}, \left(\widetilde{l}, \widetilde{L} \right) \right).$$

As in Section 4.2 the *budget set* of a consumer $i \in I_M$ at a price system $p \in \mathbb{R}^N$ and a rationing scheme $(l^i, L^i) \in -\mathbb{R}_+^{*N} \times \mathbb{R}_+^{*N}$ is denoted by $\beta^i(p, l^i, L^i)$, so

$$\beta^i(p, l^i, L^i) = \left\{x^i \in X^i \,\middle|\, p \cdot x^i \leq p \cdot \omega^i \text{ and } l^i \leq x^i - \omega^i \leq L^i\right\},$$

and as in Section 4.3 the set $\delta^i(p, l^i, L^i)$ is defined by

$$\delta^i(p, l^i, L^i) = \left\{\overline{x}^i \in \beta^i(p, l^i, L^i) \,\middle|\, \overline{x}^i \succeq^i x^i, \ \forall x^i \in \beta^i(p, l^i, L^i)\right\}.$$

The following result gives conditions such that a certain restriction of the demand relation of any consumer is a compact-valued, upper hemi-continuous correspondence. For every $i \in I_M$, the set of price systems and rationing schemes $\mathcal{P}$ is defined by

$$\mathcal{P} = \left\{(p, l^i, L^i) \in \mathbb{R}_+^N \times -\mathbb{R}_+^N \times \mathbb{R}_+^N \,\middle|\, p \cdot l^i < 0\right\}.$$

Notice that the set $\mathcal{P}$ is independent of the choice of $i \in I_M$. As opposed to Chapter 4, it is not excluded that the price of a commodity is equal to zero.

Theorem 8.2.1
For some consumer $i \in I_M$, let the consumption set X^i of consumer i be closed, convex, $X^i \subset \mathbb{R}_+^N$, and $X^i + \mathbb{R}_+^N \subset X^i$, let the utility function $u^i : X^i \to \mathbb{R}$ of consumer i be continuous, and let the initial endowment ω^i of consumer i belong to $\operatorname{int}(X^i)$. Then the relation $\delta^i_{|\mathcal{P}} : \mathcal{P} \to \mathbb{R}^N$ is a compact-valued, upper hemi-continuous correspondence.

Proof
The relation $\beta^i_{|\mathcal{P}} : \mathcal{P} \to \mathbb{R}^N$ is a compact-valued, continuous correspondence by Lemma 4.2.2 and by Theorem 4.2.3. The function $f : \mathcal{P} \times X^i \to \mathbb{R}$, defined by $f(p, l^i, L^i, x^i) = u^i(x^i)$, $\forall (p, l^i, L^i, x^i) \in \mathcal{P} \times X^i$, is continuous. Clearly, for every $(p, l^i, L^i) \in \mathcal{P}$,

$$\delta^i_{|\mathcal{P}}(p, l^i, L^i) = \left\{\overline{x}^i \in \beta^i_{|\mathcal{P}}(p, l^i, L^i) \,\middle|\, f(p, l^i, L^i, \overline{x}^i) \geq f(p, l^i, L^i, x^i), \ \forall x^i \in \beta^i_{|\mathcal{P}}(p, l^i, L^i)\right\},$$

and hence it follows from the maximum theorem, Theorem 2.5.17, that $\delta^i_{|\mathcal{P}}$ is a compact-valued, upper hemi-continuous correspondence. Q.E.D.

Let some consumer $i \in I_M$ be given. For every $\alpha \in \mathbb{R}_+$, the set of price systems and rationing schemes $\mathcal{P}^\alpha$ is defined by

$$\begin{aligned}\mathcal{P}^\alpha = \{ & (p, l^i, L^i) \in \mathbb{R}_+^N \times -\mathbb{R}_+^N \times \mathbb{R}_+^N \,| \\ & l^i \geq -\widetilde{\omega}, \ L^i \leq \widetilde{\omega}, \ p_N = 1, \ l^i_N = -\widetilde{\omega}_N, \text{ and } L^i_N = \widetilde{\omega}_N, \\ & \exists j^1 \in I_{N-1}, \ p_{j^1} \geq \alpha \text{ and } l^i_{j^1} = -\widetilde{\omega}_{j^1}, \\ & \forall j \in I_{N-1}, \ l^i_j < 0 \text{ implies } \exists j^2 \in I_{N-1}, \ p_{j^2} \geq p_j \text{ and } l^i_{j^2} = -\widetilde{\omega}_{j^2}\}.\end{aligned}$$

Notice that the set $\mathcal{P}^\alpha$ is independent of the choice of i. Let some $\alpha \in \mathbb{R}_+$ and some $(p, l^i, L^i) \in \mathcal{P}^\alpha$ be given. Then there is at least one commodity $j^1 \in I_{N-1}$ with price greater than or equal to α and with $l^i_{j^1} = -\widetilde{\omega}_{j^1}$, guaranteeing under weak conditions, see Theorem 4.3.3, that consumer i is not rationed on his supply in the market for commodity j^1. Moreover, if a commodity $j \in I_{N-1}$ is such that consumer i has the possibility to supply a positive amount of this commodity, i.e. $l^i_j < 0$, then there exists a commodity $j^2 \in I_{N-1}$ with price at least as high as p_j and with $l^i_{j^2} = -\widetilde{\omega}_{j^2}$. Finally, for every $j \in I_N$ it holds that $-\widetilde{\omega}_j \leq l^i_j \leq 0$ and $0 \leq L^i_j \leq \widetilde{\omega}_j$, so the rationing schemes in $\mathcal{P}^\alpha$ are bounded. It should be noticed that $\alpha^1 < \alpha^2$ implies $\mathcal{P}^{\alpha^2} \subset \mathcal{P}^{\alpha^1}$, and that $\mathcal{P}^\alpha \subset \mathcal{P}$, $\forall \alpha \in \mathbb{R}_+$.

Theorem 8.2.3 states that if $\alpha \in \mathbb{R}_+$ is chosen large enough, then the demand of a consumer $i \in I_M$ of commodity N at price systems and rationing schemes in the set $\mathcal{P}^\alpha$ exceeds the total initial endowment of commodity N. Theorem 8.2.3 is closely related to theorems providing boundary conditions on demand functions without taking into account the possibility of rationing, see for example Theorem 3.11.1. Theorem 8.2.3 can therefore be considered as an extension of those theorems to the case where rationing is allowed. Theorem 8.2.3 plays an important role in the proofs of Theorems 8.2.5 and 8.4.2. First, the following preliminary lemma is needed.

Lemma 8.2.2

Let $(X^i, u^i, \omega^i)_{i \in I_M}$ satisfy Assumptions A1-A3. Let some $N' \in \mathbb{Z}_+$ satisfying $N' < N$ be given. For every $i \in I_M$, consider the characteristics $X^i_*, \preceq^i_*, \omega^i_*$, where

$$X^i_* = \left\{ x^i_* \in \mathbb{R}^{N-N'}_+ \,\middle|\, (\omega^i_1, \ldots, \omega^i_{N'}, x^{i\top}_*)^\top \in X^i \right\},$$

$$\preceq^i_* = \left\{ (\overline{x}^i_*, \widehat{x}^i_*) \in X^i_* \times X^i_* \,\middle|\, (\omega^i_1, \ldots, \omega^i_{N'}, \overline{x}^{i\top}_*)^\top \preceq^i (\omega^i_1, \ldots, \omega^i_{N'}, \widehat{x}^{i\top}_*)^\top \right\},$$

$$\omega^i_* = (\omega^i_{N'+1}, \ldots, \omega^i_N)^\top.$$

Then, for every $i \in I_M$, X^i_* is closed, convex, $X^i_* \subset \mathbb{R}^{N-N'}_+$, and $X^i_* + \mathbb{R}^{N-N'}_+ \subset X^i_*$, $\preceq^i_*$ is complete, transitive, continuous, strongly monotonic, and convex, and $\omega^i_* \in \operatorname{int}(X^i_*)$.

Proof

Let some $i \in I_M$ be given.

Let $(x^{i^n}_*)_{n \in \mathbb{N}}$ be a sequence in X^i_* converging to some $\overline{x}^i_* \in \mathbb{R}^{N-N'}$. Then the sequence $((\omega^i_1, \ldots, \omega^i_{N'}, x^{i^n\top}_*)^\top)_{n \in \mathbb{N}}$ in X^i converges to $(\omega^i_1, \ldots, \omega^i_{N'}, \overline{x}^{i\top}_*)^\top \in X^i$ since X^i is closed. Therefore, $\overline{x}^i_* \in X^i_*$ and hence X^i_* is closed.

Let $\overline{x}^i_*$, $\widehat{x}^i_* \in X^i_*$ and $\lambda \in [0,1]$ be given. It follows that

$$\lambda \left(\omega^i_1, \ldots, \omega^i_{N'}, \overline{x}^{i^\top}_*\right)^\top + (1-\lambda)\left(\omega^i_1, \ldots, \omega^i_{N'}, \widehat{x}^{i^\top}_*\right)^\top \in X^i,$$

since X^i is convex, $(\omega^i_1, \ldots, \omega^i_{N'}, \overline{x}^{i^\top}_*)^\top \in X^i$, and $(\omega^i_1, \ldots, \omega^i_{N'}, \widehat{x}^{i^\top}_*)^\top \in X^i$. Therefore, $\lambda \overline{x}^i_* + (1-\lambda)\widehat{x}^i_* \in X^i_*$ and hence X^i_* is convex.
Clearly, $X^i_* \subset \mathbb{R}^{N-N'}_+$.
Let $x^i_* \in X^i_*$ and $s \in \mathbb{R}^{N-N'}_+$ be given. Then $(0^{N'^\top}, s^\top)^\top \in \mathbb{R}^N_+$, so it follows that $(\omega^i_1, \ldots, \omega^i_{N'}, x^{i^\top}_*)^\top + (0^{N'^\top}, s^\top)^\top \in X^i$ since $X^i + \mathbb{R}^N_+ \subset X^i$. Hence, $x^i_* + s \in X^i_*$.
For every $\overline{x}^i_*, \widehat{x}^i_* \in X^i_*$, by the completeness of $\preceq^i$, $(\omega^i_1, \ldots, \omega^i_{N'}, \overline{x}^{i^\top}_*)^\top \preceq^i (\omega^i_1, \ldots, \omega^i_{N'}, \widehat{x}^{i^\top}_*)^\top$ or $(\omega^i_1, \ldots, \omega^i_{N'}, \widehat{x}^{i^\top}_*)^\top \preceq^i (\omega^i_1, \ldots, \omega^i_{N'}, \overline{x}^{i^\top}_*)^\top$, so $\overline{x}^i_* \preceq^i_* \widehat{x}^i_*$ or $\widehat{x}^i_* \preceq^i \overline{x}^i_*$. Hence, $\preceq^i_*$ is complete.
For every $\overline{x}^i_*, \widehat{x}^i_*, \widetilde{x}^i_* \in X^i_*$, if $(\omega^i_1, \ldots, \omega^i_{N'}, \overline{x}^{i^\top}_*)^\top \preceq^i (\omega^i_1, \ldots, \omega^i_{N'}, \widehat{x}^{i^\top}_*)^\top$ and $(\omega^i_1, \ldots, \omega^i_{N'}, \widehat{x}^{i^\top}_*)^\top \preceq^i (\omega^i_1, \ldots, \omega^i_{N'}, \widetilde{x}^{i^\top}_*)^\top$, then, clearly, $(\omega^i_1, \ldots, \omega^i_{N'}, \overline{x}^{i^\top}_*)^\top \preceq^i (\omega^i_1, \ldots, \omega^i_{N'}, \widetilde{x}^{i^\top}_*)^\top$ by the transitivity of $\preceq^i$. So, $\overline{x}^i_* \preceq^i_* \widehat{x}^i_*$ and $\widehat{x}^i_* \preceq^i_* \widetilde{x}^i_*$ implies $\overline{x}^i_* \preceq^i_* \widetilde{x}^i_*$. Hence, $\preceq^i_*$ is transitive.
Let $\widehat{x}^i_* \in X^i_*$ be given and let $(x^{i^n}_*)_{n \in \mathbb{N}}$ be a sequence in X^i_* satisfying $x^{i^n}_* \preceq^i_* \widehat{x}^i_*$, $\forall n \in \mathbb{N}$, and converging to some $\overline{x}^i_* \in X^i_*$. Then $((\omega^i_1, \ldots, \omega^i_{N'}, x^{i^{n^\top}}_*)^\top)_{n \in \mathbb{N}}$ is a sequence in X^i satisfying $(\omega^i_1, \ldots, \omega^i_{N'}, x^{i^{n^\top}}_*)^\top \preceq^i (\omega^i_1, \ldots, \omega^i_{N'}, \widehat{x}^{i^\top}_*)^\top$ and converging to $(\omega^i_1, \ldots, \omega^i_{N'}, \overline{x}^{i^\top}_*)^\top \in X^i$, and, since $\preceq^i$ is continuous, it holds that $(\omega^i_1, \ldots, \omega^i_{N'}, \overline{x}^{i^\top}_*)^\top \preceq^i (\omega^i_1, \ldots, \omega^i_{N'}, \widehat{x}^{i^\top}_*)^\top$. Therefore, $\overline{x}^i_* \preceq^i_* \widehat{x}^i_*$ and hence the set $\{x^i_* \in X^i_* \mid x^i_* \preceq^i_* \widehat{x}^i_*\}$ is closed in X^i_*. Similarly, it can be shown that the set $\{x^i_* \in X^i_* \mid x^i_* \succeq^i_* \widehat{x}^i_*\}$ is closed in X^i_*. Hence, $\preceq^i_*$ is continuous.
Let $\overline{x}^i_*, \widehat{x}^i_* \in X^i_*$ with $\overline{x}^i_* < \widehat{x}^i_*$ be given. Then it holds that $(\omega^i_1, \ldots, \omega^i_{N'}, \overline{x}^{i^\top}_*)^\top < (\omega^i_1, \ldots, \omega^i_{N'}, \widehat{x}^{i^\top}_*)^\top$, so $(\omega^i_1, \ldots, \omega^i_{N'}, \overline{x}^{i^\top}_*)^\top \prec^i (\omega^i_1, \ldots, \omega^i_{N'}, \widehat{x}^{i^\top}_*)^\top$ since $\preceq^i$ is strongly monotonic. Therefore, $\overline{x}^i_* \prec^i_* \widehat{x}^i_*$ and hence it follows that $\preceq^i_*$ is strongly monotonic.
Let $\overline{x}^i_*, \widehat{x}^i_* \in X^i_*$ be such that $\overline{x}^i_* \prec^i_* \widehat{x}^i_*$ and let $\lambda \in (0,1)$ be given. Then it holds that $\lambda \overline{x}^i_* + (1-\lambda)\widehat{x}^i_* \in X^i_*$, $(\omega^i_1, \ldots, \omega^i_{N'}, \overline{x}^{i^\top}_*)^\top \prec^i (\omega^i_1, \ldots, \omega^i_{N'}, \widehat{x}^{i^\top}_*)^\top$, and $\lambda(\omega^i_1, \ldots, \omega^i_{N'}, \overline{x}^{i^\top}_*)^\top + (1-\lambda)(\omega^i_1, \ldots, \omega^i_{N'}, \widehat{x}^{i^\top}_*)^\top \in X^i$, so $(\omega^i_1, \ldots, \omega^i_{N'}, \overline{x}^{i^\top}_*)^\top \prec^i (\omega^i_1, \ldots, \omega^i_{N'}, \lambda \overline{x}^{i^\top}_* + (1-\lambda)\widehat{x}^{i^\top}_*)^\top$ since $\preceq^i$ is convex. Therefore, $\overline{x}^i_* \prec^i_* \lambda \overline{x}^i_* + (1-\lambda)\widehat{x}^i_*$ and hence it follows that $\preceq^i_*$ is convex.
Since $\omega^i \in \text{int}(X^i)$, there exists $\varepsilon \in \mathbb{R}_{++}$ such that $B^N(\omega^i, \varepsilon) \subset X^i$. If $x^i_* \in B^{N-N'}(\omega^i_*, \varepsilon)$, then $(\omega^i_1, \ldots, \omega^i_{N'}, x^{i^\top}_*)^\top \in B^N(\omega^i, \varepsilon) \subset X^i$, so $B^{N-N'}(\omega^i_*, \varepsilon) \subset X^i_*$. Hence, $\omega^i_* \in \text{int}(X^i_*)$. Q.E.D.

Theorem 8.2.3
Let $(X^i, u^i, \omega^i)_{i \in I_M}$ satisfy Assumptions A1-A3. Then there exists $\overline{\alpha} \in \mathbb{R}_+$ such that, for every $\alpha \geq \overline{\alpha}$, for every $i \in I_M$, for every $(p, l^i, L^i) \in \mathcal{P}^\alpha$, $x^i \in \delta^i(p, l^i, L^i)$ implies $x^i_N > \widetilde{\omega}_N$.

Proof

Suppose the statement of the theorem is not true. Then there exists $i \in I_M$ and a sequence $(p^n, l^{i^n}, L^{i^n}, x^{i^n})_{n \in \mathbb{N}}$ such that, for every $n \in \mathbb{N}$, $(p^n, l^{i^n}, L^{i^n}) \in \mathcal{P}^n$, $x^{i^n} \in \delta^i(p^n, l^{i^n}, L^{i^n})$, and $x^{i^n}_N \leq \widetilde{\omega}_N$. Consider the sequence

$$\left(\frac{p^n}{\|p^n\|_\infty}, l^{i^n}, L^{i^n}, x^{i^n}\right)_{n \in \mathbb{N}} \tag{8.1}$$

in $Q^N \times [-\widetilde{\omega}, 0^N] \times [0^N, \widetilde{\omega}] \times [0^N, 2\widetilde{\omega}]$. Without loss of generality, the sequence in (8.1) can be assumed to converge to some

$$(p', \overline{l}^i, \overline{L}^i, \overline{x}^i) \in Q^N \times [-\widetilde{\omega}, 0^N] \times [0^N, \widetilde{\omega}] \times [0^N, 2\widetilde{\omega}].$$

Since $(p^n, l^{i^n}, L^{i^n}) \in \mathcal{P}^n$, $\forall n \in \mathbb{N}$, it follows that $\max(\{p^n_j \mid j \in I_{N-1}\}) \to +\infty$ if $n \to +\infty$, so $p'_N = 0$, and it follows that $\overline{l}^i_j = -\widetilde{\omega}_j$ for some $j \in I_{N-1}$. It is easily verified that $x^{i^n} \in \delta^i(\frac{p^n}{\|p^n\|_\infty}, l^{i^n}, L^{i^n})$, $\forall n \in \mathbb{N}$.
Suppose $p' \cdot \overline{l}^i < 0$. Then $\delta^i_{|\mathcal{P}}$ is upper hemi-continuous at $(p', \overline{l}^i, \overline{L}^i)$ by Theorem 8.2.1. Moreover, $\delta^i_{|\mathcal{P}}$ is compact-valued and $(\frac{p^n}{\|p^n\|_\infty}, l^{i^n}, L^{i^n}) \in \mathcal{P}$, $\forall n \in \mathbb{N}$. Therefore, $\overline{x}^i \in \delta^i(p', \overline{l}^i, \overline{L}^i)$ by Theorem 2.5.6. By the strong monotonicity of the preference relation and since $p'_N = 0$, it holds that $\overline{x}^i_N - \omega^i_N = \overline{L}^i_N = \widetilde{\omega}_N$. This contradicts $x^{i^n}_N \leq \widetilde{\omega}_N$, $\forall n \in \mathbb{N}$. Consequently, $p' \cdot \overline{l}^i = 0$.
Suppose there exists a subsequence $(\frac{p^{n^m}}{\|p^{n^m}\|_\infty}, l^{i^{n^m}}, L^{i^{n^m}}, x^{i^{n^m}})_{m \in \mathbb{N}}$ of the sequence in (8.1) such that there exists $j' \in I_{N-1}$ with $p'_{j'} > 0$ and $l^{i^{n^m}}_{j'} < x^{i^{n^m}}_{j'} - \omega^i_{j'}$, $\forall m \in \mathbb{N}$. Then, by Theorem 4.3.3, $x^{i^{n^m}} \in \delta^i(p^{n^m}, \overline{l}^{i^{n^m}}, L^{i^{n^m}})$, where $\overline{l}^{i^{n^m}}$ is the rationing scheme with $\overline{l}^{i^{n^m}}_{j'} = -\widetilde{\omega}_{j'}$ and $\overline{l}^{i^{n^m}}_j = l^{i^{n^m}}_j$, $\forall j \in I_N \setminus \{j'\}$. By considering the sequence $(\frac{p^{n^m}}{\|p^{n^m}\|_\infty}, \overline{l}^{i^{n^m}}, L^{i^{n^m}}, x^{i^{n^m}})_{m \in \mathbb{N}}$, one obtains a contradiction in the same way as in the previous paragraph. Consequently, without loss of generality, for every $j \in I_{N-1}$ with $p'_j > 0$, $l^{i^n}_j = x^{i^n}_j - \omega^i_j$, $\forall n \in \mathbb{N}$.
Suppose there exists a subsequence $(\frac{p^{n^m}}{\|p^{n^m}\|_\infty}, l^{i^{n^m}}, L^{i^{n^m}}, x^{i^{n^m}})_{m \in \mathbb{N}}$ of the sequence in (8.1) such that there exists $j' \in I_{N-1}$ with $p'_{j'} > 0$ and $l^{i^{n^m}}_{j'} < 0$, $\forall m \in \mathbb{N}$. Since $(p^{n^m}, l^{i^{n^m}}, L^{i^{n^m}}) \in \mathcal{P}^{n^m}$, it holds for some $j^{n^m} \in I_{N-1}$ that $p^{n^m}_{j^{n^m}} \geq p^{n^m}_{j'}$ and $l^{i^{n^m}}_{j^{n^m}} = -\widetilde{\omega}_{j^{n^m}}$. This contradicts $p' \cdot \overline{l}^i = 0$. Consequently, without loss of generality, for every $j \in I_{N-1}$ with $p'_j > 0$, $l^{i^n}_j = 0$, $\forall n \in \mathbb{N}$.
Since there exists $j^1 \in I_{N-1}$ such that $\overline{l}^i_{j^1} = -\widetilde{\omega}_{j^1}$ and there exists $j^2 \in I_{N-1}$

such that $p'_{j^2} = 1$, while $p' \cdot \bar{l}^i = 0$, the set J, defined by $J = \{j \in I_{N-1} \mid p'_j > 0\}$, is a non-empty, proper subset of I_{N-1}. From the previous paragraphs it follows that, for every $j \in J$, $x_j^{i^n} - \omega_j^i = l_j^{i^n} = 0$, $\forall n \in \mathbb{N}$. Without loss of generality, there exists $N' \in I_{N-2}$ such that $J = I_{N'}$. Now consider a consumer with characteristics $X_*^i, \preceq_*^i, \omega_*^i$, where

$$X_*^i = \left\{x_*^i \in \mathbb{R}_+^{N-N'} \,\middle|\, (\omega_1^i, \ldots, \omega_{N'}^i, x_*^{i^\top})^\top \in X^i\right\},$$

$$\preceq_*^i = \left\{(\bar{x}_*^i, \widehat{x}_*^i) \in X_*^i \times X_*^i \,\middle|\, (\omega_1^i, \ldots, \omega_{N'}^i, \bar{x}_*^{i^\top})^\top \preceq^i (\omega_1^i, \ldots, \omega_{N'}^i, \widehat{x}_*^{i^\top})^\top\right\},$$

$$\omega_*^i = (\omega_{N'+1}^i, \ldots, \omega_N^i)^\top.$$

From Lemma 8.2.2 it follows that X_*^i is closed, convex, $X_*^i \subset \mathbb{R}_+^{N-N'}$, and $X_*^i + \mathbb{R}_+^{N-N'} \subset X_*^i$, $\preceq_*^i$ is complete, transitive, continuous, strongly monotonic, and convex, and $\omega_*^i \in \mathrm{int}(X_*^i)$. Moreover, since $x_j^{i^n} = \omega_j^i$, $\forall j \in I_{N'}$, $\forall n \in \mathbb{N}$, it is clear that the demand correspondence δ_*^i of the consumer with characteristics $(X_*^i, \preceq_*^i, \omega_*^i)$ satisfies $x_*^{i^n} \in \delta_*^i(p_*^n, l_*^{i^n}, L_*^{i^n})$, $\forall n \in \mathbb{N}$. Here, for every $n \in \mathbb{N}$, $l_*^{i^n}$ and $L_*^{i^n}$ denote the last $N - N'$ components of l^{i^n} and L^{i^n}, respectively, and p_*^n and $x_*^{i^n}$ denote the last $N - N'$ components of p^n and x^{i^n}, respectively. Let $\widetilde{\omega}_*$ denote the last $N - N'$ components of $\widetilde{\omega}$ and let the set $\mathcal{P}_*$ be given by $\mathcal{P}_* = \{(p_*, l_*^i, L_*^i) \in \mathbb{R}_+^{N-N'} \times -\mathbb{R}_+^{N-N'} \times \mathbb{R}_+^{N-N'} \mid p_* \cdot l_*^i < 0\}$. Since $\bar{l}_j^i = 0$, $\forall j \in I_{N'}$, the definition of $\mathcal{P}^n$ implies that there exists $n' \in \mathbb{N}$ such that for every $n \geq n'$ there exists $j^n \in I_{N-1} \setminus I_{N'}$ satisfying $p_{j^n}^n \geq n$ and $l_{j^n}^{i^n} = -\widetilde{\omega}_{j^n}$. Consider the sequence

$$\left(\frac{p_*^n}{\|p_*^n\|_\infty}, l_*^{i^n}, L_*^{i^n}, x_*^{i^n}\right)_{n \in \mathbb{N}} \tag{8.2}$$

in $Q^{N-N'} \times [-\widetilde{\omega}_*, 0^{N-N'}] \times [0^{N-N'}, \widetilde{\omega}_*] \times [0^{N-N'}, 2\widetilde{\omega}_*]$. Without loss of generality, the sequence in (8.2) can be assumed to converge to some

$$(p'_*, \bar{l}_*^i, \bar{L}_*^i, \bar{x}_*^i) \in Q^{N-N'} \times [-\widetilde{\omega}_*, 0^{N-N'}] \times [0^{N-N'}, \widetilde{\omega}_*] \times [0^{N-N'}, 2\widetilde{\omega}_*].$$

Suppose $p'_* \cdot \bar{l}_*^i < 0$, then $\delta_{*|\mathcal{P}_*}^i$ is upper hemi-continuous at $(p'_*, \bar{l}_*^i, \bar{L}_*^i)$ by Theorem 8.2.1, $\delta_{*|\mathcal{P}_*}^i$ is compact-valued by Theorem 8.2.1, and $(\frac{p_*^n}{\|p_*^n\|_\infty}, l_*^{i^n}, L_*^{i^n}) \in \mathcal{P}_*$, $\forall n \in \mathbb{N}$. Therefore, $\bar{x}_*^i \in \delta_*^i(p'_*, \bar{l}_*^i, \bar{L}_*^i)$ by Theorem 2.5.6, yielding a contradiction in the same way as before. Repeating the arguments used before, the finiteness of $N - 1$ and the definition of $\mathcal{P}^\alpha$, for $\alpha \in \mathbb{R}_+$, guarantees that in a finite number of steps the case where $p'_* \cdot \bar{l}_*^i < 0$ is reached, contradicting that $x_N^{i^n} \leq \widetilde{\omega}_N$, $\forall n \in \mathbb{N}$. Consequently, there exists $\bar{\alpha} \in \mathbb{R}_+$ such that, for every $\alpha \geq \bar{\alpha}$, for every $i \in I_M$, for every $(p, l^i, L^i) \in \mathcal{P}^\alpha$, $x^i \in \delta^i(p, l^i, L^i)$ implies $x_N^i > \widetilde{\omega}_N$. Q.E.D.

Let some $(\underline{p}, \overline{p}) \in \mathbb{R}^{*N} \times \mathbb{R}^{*N}$ be given, where $\underline{p} \leq \overline{p}$, $\underline{p} \ll +\infty^N$, $0^N \leq \overline{p}$, and $\underline{p}_N = \overline{p}_N = 1$. The *constrained equilibrium* (p^*, l^*, L^*, x^*) of the economy $\widetilde{\mathcal{E}}(\underline{p}, \overline{p})$, see Definition 4.6.1, is a *Drèze equilibrium* of $\widetilde{\mathcal{E}}(\underline{p}, \overline{p})$ with respect to the market for commodity N if $l_N^{*i} < x_N^{*i} - \omega_N^i < L_N^{*i}$, $\forall i \in I_M$, see Definition 4.7.5. It follows that it is not necessary to specify Condition 3 and Condition 4 of a constrained equilibrium for commodity N when considering a Drèze equilibrium with respect to the market for commodity N. Therefore, a Drèze equilibrium with respect to the market for commodity N, also called a *Drèze equilibrium* in the remaining chapters, is defined as follows.

Definition 8.2.4 (Drèze equilibrium)
Let some $(\underline{p}, \overline{p}) \in \mathbb{R}^{*N} \times \mathbb{R}^{*N}$ be given, where $\underline{p} \leq \overline{p}$, $\underline{p} \ll +\infty^N$, $0^N \leq \overline{p}$, and $\underline{p}_N = \overline{p}_N = 1$. A Drèze equilibrium *of the economy $\widetilde{\mathcal{E}}(\underline{p}, \overline{p}) = ((X^i, \preceq^i, \omega^i)_{i \in I_M}, P_{(\underline{p}, \overline{p})}, (\widetilde{l}, \widetilde{L}))$ is an element*

$$(p^*, l^*, L^*, x^*) \in P_{(\underline{p}, \overline{p})} \times \widetilde{l}(Q^N) \times \widetilde{L}(Q^N) \times X$$

satisfying

1. *for every consumer $i \in I_M$, $x^{*i} \in \delta^i \left(p^*, l^{*i}, L^{*i}\right)$,*
2. *$\sum_{i \in I_M} x^{*i} - \sum_{i \in I_M} \omega^i = 0^N$,*
3. *for every commodity $j \in I_{N-1}$, $x_j^{*i'} - \omega_j^{i'} = l_j^{*i'}$ for some consumer $i' \in I_M$ implies $x_j^{*i} - \omega_j^i < L_j^{*i}$, $\forall i \in I_M$, and $x_j^{*i'} - \omega_j^{i'} = L_j^{*i'}$ for some consumer $i' \in I_M$ implies $x_j^{*i} - \omega_j^i > l_j^{*i}$, $\forall i \in I_M$,*
4. *for every commodity $j \in I_{N-1}$, $p_j^* > \underline{p}_j$ implies $l_j^{*i} < x_j^{*i} - \omega_j^i$, $\forall i \in I_M$, and $p_j^* < \overline{p}_j$ implies $L_j^{*i} > x_j^{*i} - \omega_j^i$, $\forall i \in I_M$,*
5. *$l_N^{*i} < x_N^{*i} - \omega_N^i < L_N^{*i}$, $\forall i \in I_M$.*

The set of Drèze equilibria of the economy $\widetilde{\mathcal{E}}(\underline{p}, \overline{p})$ is denoted by $\widetilde{E}^D(\underline{p}, \overline{p})$.

Let $\underline{J} \subset I_{N-1}$ denote the possibly empty set of commodities in the market for which a minimum price is present, so

$$\underline{J} = \{j \in I_{N-1} \mid \underline{p}_j \geq 0\},$$

and let $\overline{J} \subset I_{N-1}$ denote the possibly empty set of commodities in the market for which a maximum price prevails, so

$$\overline{J} = \{j \in I_{N-1} \mid \overline{p}_j < +\infty\}.$$

Notice that $j \in I_{N-1} \setminus \underline{J}$ implies $l_j^{*i} < x_j^{*i} - \omega_j^i$, $\forall i \in I_M$, and $j \in I_{N-1} \setminus \overline{J}$ implies $L_j^{*i} > x_j^{*i} - \omega_j^i$, $\forall i \in I_M$. Hence, there is no supply rationing in a market if no minimum price is specified in this market and there is no demand rationing in a market if no maximum price is present in this market. If $\underline{J} = \overline{J} = \emptyset$, then one obtains the definition of a *Walrasian equilibrium,* see Definition 3.8.1, since non-binding rationing schemes are irrelevant. Therefore, the concept of a Drèze equilibrium generalizes the concept of a Walrasian equilibrium. The set $\underline{\overline{P}}$ is defined by

$$\underline{\overline{P}} = \left\{(\underline{p}, \overline{p}) \in \mathbb{R}_+^N \times \mathbb{R}_+^N \,|\underline{p} \leq \overline{p},\ \underline{p}_N = \overline{p}_N = 1\right\}.$$

In Theorem 8.2.5 it is shown that there is no loss of generality in assuming that for every commodity a minimum price and a maximum price is given, so to consider only proposals $(\underline{p}, \overline{p})$ of the political candidates belonging to the set $\underline{\overline{P}}$. Therefore, $\underline{\overline{P}}$ is called the *set of price regulations.*

Theorem 8.2.5
Let $(X^i, u^i, \omega^i)_{i \in I_M}, (\widetilde{l}, \widetilde{L})$ satisfy Assumptions A1-A4 and let $(\underline{p}, \overline{p}) \in \mathbb{R}^{*N} \times \mathbb{R}^{*N}$ be such that $\underline{p} \leq \overline{p}$, $\underline{p} \ll +\infty^N$, $0^N \leq \overline{p}$, and $\underline{p}_N = \overline{p}_N = 1$. Then there exists $(\underline{p}', \overline{p}') \in \underline{\overline{P}}$ such that $\widetilde{E}^D(\underline{p}', \overline{p}') = \widetilde{E}^D(\underline{p}, \overline{p})$.

Proof
Let $\overline{\alpha} \in \mathbb{R}_+$ be as in Theorem 8.2.3 and let $\widehat{\alpha} \in \mathbb{R}_+$ be such that $\widehat{\alpha} \geq \overline{\alpha}$ and $\widehat{\alpha} > \underline{p}_j$, $\forall j \in I_N$. Let $\underline{p}' \in \mathbb{R}_+^N$ be defined by $\underline{p}'_j = \underline{p}_j$, $\forall j \in \underline{J} \cup \{N\}$, and $\underline{p}'_j = 0$, $\forall j \in I_{N-1} \setminus \underline{J}$, and let $\overline{p}' \in \mathbb{R}_+^N$ be defined by $\overline{p}'_j = \overline{p}_j$, $\forall j \in \overline{J} \cup \{N\}$, and $\overline{p}'_j = \widehat{\alpha}$, $\forall j \in I_{N-1} \setminus \overline{J}$.
Suppose $(p^*, l^*, L^*, x^*) \in \widetilde{E}^D(\underline{p}, \overline{p})$ satisfies $||p^*||_\infty > \widehat{\alpha}$. Let $\overline{l} \in -\mathbb{R}_+^{MN}$ and $\overline{L} \in \mathbb{R}_+^{MN}$ be obtained by defining, for every $i \in I_M$, for every $j \in I_N$, $\overline{l}_j^i = -\widetilde{\omega}_j$ if $l_j^{*i} < x_j^{*i} - \omega_j^i$, $\overline{l}_j^i = l_j^{*i}$ if $l_j^{*i} = x_j^{*i} - \omega_j^i$, $\overline{L}_j^i = \widetilde{\omega}_j$ if $L_j^{*i} > x_j^{*i} - \omega_j^i$, and $\overline{L}_j^i = L_j^{*i}$ if $L_j^{*i} = x_j^{*i} - \omega_j^i$. From Theorem 4.6.4 it follows that $x^{*i} \in \delta^i(p^*, \overline{l}^i, \overline{L}^i)$, $\forall i \in I_M$. Since $(p^*, l^*, L^*, x^*) \in \widetilde{E}^D(\underline{p}, \overline{p})$, it holds that $\overline{l}^i \geq -\widetilde{\omega}$, $\forall i \in I_M$, and $\overline{L}^i \leq \widetilde{\omega}$, $\forall i \in I_M$. For every $j \in I_{N-1}$ with $p_j^* \geq \widehat{\alpha}$ it follows that $\overline{l}_j^i = -\widetilde{\omega}_j$ since $\widehat{\alpha} > \underline{p}_j$. Now it is easily verified that $(p^*, \overline{l}^i, \overline{L}^i) \in \mathcal{P}^{\widehat{\alpha}}$, $\forall i \in I_M$. From Theorem 8.2.3 it follows that $x_N^{*i} > \widetilde{\omega}_N$, $\forall i \in I_M$. This yields a contradiction since $\sum_{i \in I_M} x_N^{*i} = \sum_{i \in I_M} \omega_N^i$. Consequently, for every $(p^*, l^*, L^*, x^*) \in \widetilde{E}^D(\underline{p}, \overline{p})$, $||p^*||_\infty \leq \widehat{\alpha}$. Now it follows immediately that $\widetilde{E}^D(\underline{p}, \overline{p}) \subset \widetilde{E}^D(\underline{p}', \overline{p}')$.

Suppose $(p^*, l^*, L^*, x^*) \in \widetilde{E}^D(\underline{p}', \overline{p}') \backslash \widetilde{E}^D(\underline{p}, \overline{p})$. Then, either there exists $i^1 \in I_M$ and $j^1 \in I_{N-1}$ such that $p^*_{j^1} = 0$ and $l^{*i^1}_{j^1} = x^{*i^1}_{j^1} - \omega^{i^1}_{j^1}$, or there exists $i^2 \in I_M$ and $j^2 \in I_{N-1}$ such that $p^*_{j^2} = \widehat{\alpha}$ and $L^{*i^2}_{j^2} = x^{*i^2}_{j^2} - \omega^{i^2}_{j^2}$.
Consider the first case. By the strong monotonicity of the preference relation it holds that $x^{*i^1}_{j^1} - \omega^{i^1}_{j^1} = L^{*i^1}_{j^1} > l^{*i^1}_{j^1} = x^{*i^1}_{j^1} - \omega^{i^1}_{j^1}$, where for the inequality Condition 3 of the definition of a Drèze equilibrium of $\widetilde{\mathcal{E}}(\underline{p}', \overline{p}')$, Definition 8.2.4, is used, yielding a contradiction.
Consider the second case. Let $\overline{l}^{i^2} \in -\mathbb{R}^N_+$ and $\overline{L}^{i^2} \in \mathbb{R}^N_+$ be obtained by defining, for every $j \in I_N$, $\overline{l}^{i^2}_j = -\widetilde{\omega}_j$ if $l^{*i^2}_j < x^{i^2}_j - \omega^{i^2}_j$, $\overline{l}^{i^2}_j = l^{*i^2}_j$ if $l^{*i^2}_j = x^{*i^2}_j - \omega^{i^2}_j$, $\overline{L}^{i^2}_j = \widetilde{\omega}_j$ if $L^{*i^2}_j > x^{*i^2}_j - \omega^{i^2}_j$, and $\overline{L}^{i^2}_j = L^{*i^2}_j$ if $L^{*i^2}_j = x^{*i^2}_j - \omega^{i^2}_j$. For every $j \in I_N$ with $p^*_j = \widehat{\alpha}$ it holds by Condition 4 of the definition of a Drèze equilibrium of $\widetilde{\mathcal{E}}(\underline{p}', \overline{p}')$, Definition 8.2.4, that $l^{*i^2}_j < x^{*i^2}_j - \omega^{i^2}_j$. Hence, it follows that $\overline{l}^{i^2}_{j^2} = -\widetilde{\omega}_{j^2}$. It is easily verified that $(p^*, \overline{l}^{i^2}, \overline{L}^{i^2}) \in \mathcal{P}^{\widehat{\alpha}}$. From Theorem 4.6.4 it follows that $x^{*i^2} \in \delta^{i^2}(p^*, \overline{l}^{i^2}, \overline{L}^{i^2})$. So, by Theorem 8.2.3, $x^{*i^2}_N > \widetilde{\omega}_N$, yielding a contradiction since $\sum_{i \in I_M} x^{*i}_N = \sum_{i \in I_M} \omega^i_N$. Consequently, $\widetilde{E}^D(\underline{p}', \overline{p}') \subset \widetilde{E}^D(\underline{p}, \overline{p})$. Q.E.D.

The function $\widehat{p} : Q^{N-1} \times \underline{\overline{P}} \to \mathbb{R}^N_+$ and the functions $\widehat{l} : Q^{N-1} \to -\mathbb{R}^{MN}_+$ and $\widehat{L} : Q^{N-1} \to \mathbb{R}^{MN}_+$ are obtained by defining, for every $j \in I_{N-1}$,

$$\begin{aligned}
\widehat{p}_j(q, \underline{p}, \overline{p}) &= \max\left(\{\underline{p}_j, \min(\{\underline{p}_j(2 - 3q_j) + \overline{p}_j(3q_j - 1), \overline{p}_j\})\}\right), && \forall (q, \underline{p}, \overline{p}) \in Q^{N-1} \times \underline{\overline{P}}, \\
\widehat{l}_j(q) &= \widetilde{l}_j\left(\inf(\{1^N, (3q^\top, 1)^\top\})\right), && \forall q \in Q^{N-1}, \\
\widehat{L}_j(q) &= \widetilde{L}_j\left(\inf(\{1^N, 31^N - (3q^\top, 2)^\top\})\right), && \forall q \in Q^{N-1},
\end{aligned}$$

and by defining

$$\begin{aligned}
\widehat{p}_N(q, \underline{p}, \overline{p}) &= 1, && \forall (q, \underline{p}, \overline{p}) \in Q^{N-1} \times \underline{\overline{P}}, \\
\widehat{l}_N(q) &= \widetilde{l}_N\left(\inf(\{1^N, (3q^\top, 1)^\top\})\right), && \forall q \in Q^{N-1}, \\
\widehat{L}_N(q) &= \widetilde{L}_N\left(\inf(\{1^N, 31^N - (3q^\top, 2)^\top\})\right), && \forall q \in Q^{N-1}.
\end{aligned}$$

The notational conventions used for $\widetilde{l}$ and $\widetilde{L}$ are also used for $\widehat{l}$ and $\widehat{L}$. For every $i \in I_M$, the relation $\widehat{\delta}^i : Q^{N-1} \times \underline{\overline{P}} \to \mathbb{R}^N$, called the *reduced demand relation* of consumer i, is defined by

$$\widehat{\delta}^i(q, \underline{p}, \overline{p}) = \delta^i\left(\widehat{p}(q, \underline{p}, \overline{p}), \widehat{l}^i(q), \widehat{L}^i(q)\right), \ \forall (q, \underline{p}, \overline{p}) \in Q^{N-1} \times \underline{\overline{P}}.$$

The proof of the following result is similar to the proof of Theorem 4.7.1.

Theorem 8.2.6
Let $(X^i, u^i, \omega^i)_{i \in I_M}, (\widetilde{l}, \widetilde{L})$ satisfy Assumptions A1-A4. Let some $(\underline{p}, \overline{p}) \in \underline{P}$ be given. If, for some $q^* \in Q^{N-1}$, there exists $x^{*i} \in \widehat{\delta}^i(q^*, \underline{p}, \overline{p})$, $\forall i \in I_M$, such that $\sum_{i \in I_M} x^{*i} = \sum_{i \in I_M} \omega^i$, then $(\widehat{p}(q^*, \underline{p}, \overline{p}), \widehat{l}(q^*), \widehat{L}(q^*), x^*) \in \widetilde{E}^D(\underline{p}, \overline{p})$.

If, as in Theorem 8.2.6, for some $q^* \in Q^{N-1}$, there exists $x^{*i} \in \widehat{\delta}^i(q^*, \underline{p}, \overline{p})$, $\forall i \in I_M$, such that $\sum_{i \in I_M} x^{*i} = \sum_{i \in I_M} \omega^i$, then $(\widehat{p}(q^*, \underline{p}, \overline{p}), \widehat{l}(q^*), \widehat{L}(q^*), x^*)$ is called a Drèze equilibrium of $\widetilde{\mathcal{E}}(\underline{p}, \overline{p})$ *induced* by q^*. The set of elements q^* of Q^{N-1} inducing a Drèze equilibrium of $\widetilde{\mathcal{E}}(\underline{p}, \overline{p})$ is denoted by $\widetilde{Q}^D(\underline{p}, \overline{p})$. Similarly as in the proof of Theorem 4.7.2 the following result can be shown.

Theorem 8.2.7
Let $(X^i, u^i, \omega^i)_{i \in I_M}, (\widetilde{l}, \widetilde{L})$ satisfy Assumptions A1-A4. Let some $(\underline{p}, \overline{p}) \in \underline{P}$ be given. If $(p^*, l^*, L^*, x^*) \in \widetilde{E}^D(\underline{p}, \overline{p})$, then there exists $q^* \in \widetilde{Q}^D(\underline{p}, \overline{p})$ such that $(\widehat{p}(q^*, \underline{p}, \overline{p}), \widehat{l}(q^*), \widehat{L}(q^*), x^*) \in \widetilde{E}^D(\underline{p}, \overline{p})$ and $(p^*, l^*, L^*, x^*) \sim (\widehat{p}(q^*, \underline{p}, \overline{p}), \widehat{l}(q^*), \widehat{L}(q^*), x^*)$, i.e. (p^*, l^*, L^*, x^*) is equivalent to $(\widehat{p}(q^*, \underline{p}, \overline{p}), \widehat{l}(q^*), \widehat{L}(q^*), x^*)$ in the sense of Definition 4.6.2.

Therefore, it follows immediately that there is no loss of generality in considering only Drèze equilibria of the economy $\widetilde{\mathcal{E}}(\underline{p}, \overline{p})$ induced by some $q^* \in \widetilde{Q}^D(\underline{p}, \overline{p})$. The following result is closely related to Theorem 4.7.3.

Theorem 8.2.8
Let $(X^i, u^i, \omega^i)_{i \in I_M}, (\widetilde{l}, \widetilde{L})$ satisfy Assumptions A1-A4. For every $i \in I_M$, the reduced demand relation $\widehat{\delta}^i$ of consumer i has the following properties:

1. *$\widehat{\delta}^i$ is a compact-valued, convex-valued, upper hemi-continuous correspondence,*
2. *for every $(q, \underline{p}, \overline{p}) \in Q^{N-1} \times \underline{P}$, for every $x^i \in \widehat{\delta}^i(q, \underline{p}, \overline{p})$, for every $j \in I_{N-1}$, $q_j = 0$ implies $x^i_j - \omega^i_j \geq 0$, and $q_j = 1$ implies $x^i_j - \omega^i_j \leq 0$,*
3. *for every $(q, \underline{p}, \overline{p}) \in Q^{N-1} \times \underline{P}$, for every $x^i \in \widehat{\delta}^i(q, \underline{p}, \overline{p})$, $\widehat{p}(q, \underline{p}, \overline{p}) \cdot (x^i - \omega^i) = 0$.*

Proof
By the continuity of the functions $\widehat{p}, \widehat{l}$, and $\widehat{L}$, and since $\delta^i_{|\mathcal{P}}$, $\forall i \in I_M$, is a

compact-valued, upper hemi-continuous correspondence by Theorem 8.2.1, it follows from Theorem 2.5.5 that $\widehat{\delta}^i$, $\forall i \in I_M$, is a compact-valued, upper hemi-continuous correspondence. Using the convex-valuedness of $\widehat{\beta}^i$ shown in Lemma 4.2.1, it follows easily that $\widehat{\delta}^i$ is a convex-valued correspondence.
Let some $i \in I_M$ and some $(q, \underline{p}, \overline{p}) \in Q^{N-1} \times \overline{\underline{P}}$ be given. For every $j \in I_{N-1}$, if $q_j = 0$, then $x^i \in \widehat{\delta}^i(q, \underline{p}, \overline{p})$ implies $x^i_j - \omega^i_j \geq \widehat{l}^i_j(q) = 0$. For every $j \in I_{N-1}$, if $q_j = 1$, then $x^i \in \widehat{\delta}^i(q, \underline{p}, \overline{p})$ implies $x^i_j - \omega^i_j \leq \widehat{L}^i_j(q) = 0$. From the strong monotonicity of $\preceq^i$ it follows that $\widehat{p}(q, \underline{p}, \overline{p}) \cdot (x^i - \omega^i) = 0$. Q.E.D.

This theorem concludes the description of the economic system.

8.3 THE POLITICAL SYSTEM

For every consumer $i \in I_M$, the consumption set X^i, the utility function u^i representing the preference relation $\preceq^i$, and the initial endowment ω^i are assumed to be given in this section. Moreover, the rationing function $(\widetilde{l}, \widetilde{L})$ is assumed to be given. Now the *political system* can be described. The behaviour of the government is modelled as being the result of the competition for votes between two *political candidates,* indexed by $k \in I_2$. It is not difficult to extend the model in a similar way as in Wittman (1984) and to allow for an arbitrary number of political candidates. The *electorate* consists of the consumers in the economy and chooses between the political candidates by majority voting.

The political candidates are assumed to have the possibility to propose *price regulations* in the markets. For every $k \in I_2$, a non-empty subset A^k of $\overline{\underline{P}}$ is given, denoting the *set of admissible price regulations* among which political candidate k can choose. An element a^k of A^k corresponds with the choice of a lower bound and an upper bound on the set of admissible price systems by a political candidate $k \in I_2$. If a political candidate $k \in I_2$ chooses some $a^k \in A^k$, then the proposed set of admissible price systems of the economy is given by P_{a^k}, so

$$P_{a^k} = \left\{p \in \mathbb{R}^N_+ \left| a^k_j \leq p_j \leq a^k_{N+j}, \ \forall j \in I_N \right.\right\},$$

and the resulting economy is given by $\widetilde{\mathcal{E}}(a^k) = ((X^i, \preceq^i, \omega^i)_{i \in I_M}, P_{a^k}, (\widetilde{l}, \widetilde{L}))$. In general, it is possible that there is more than one Walrasian or Drèze equilibrium price system and allocation in this economy. For instance, Theorem 3.13.1 implies that economies exist with an arbitrary number of Walrasian equilibria. It is assumed that a political candidate proposes together with the chosen price regulation also a corresponding Drèze equilibrium price system, the amount of supply rationing (also called unemployment), and the amount of demand rationing in each market, i.e. the *state* in every market. The set $\mathcal{A}^k$ denotes the *set of admissible actions* of political candidate $k \in I_2$ and is therefore given by

$$\mathcal{A}^k = \left\{ (a^k, q^k) \in A^k \times Q^{N-1} \middle| q^k \in \widetilde{Q}^D(a^k) \right\}. \tag{8.3}$$

When $A^k = \underline{\overline{P}}$, the corresponding set of admissible actions $\mathcal{A}^k$ is denoted by $\mathcal{A}$. Clearly, a huge amount of rationality of the political candidates is assumed. An alternative would be that the political candidates have expectations with respect to the resulting state of the economy given any price regulation. However, such an analysis would involve quite some arbitrariness with respect to the expectations of the political candidates. Moreover, it is interesting to know whether price regulations may result in the economic system, even if the political candidates behave fully rational. Another alternative is to assume that some status quo is given, and that the political candidates either choose to stay at the status quo or choose directions of motion away from the status quo, a possibility investigated in Chapter 9.

The *indirect utility function* $\widetilde{v}^i : \mathcal{A} \to \mathbb{R}$ of a consumer $i \in I_M$ is defined by associating with every $(a, q) \in \mathcal{A}$ the real number $\widetilde{v}^i(a, q)$ satisfying

$$\widetilde{v}^i(a, q) = u^i(x^{*i}), \ \forall x^{*i} \in \widehat{\delta}^i(q, a).$$

Clearly, this function is well defined.

To describe the assumptions with respect to the set of admissible price regulations of the political candidates, a mathematical concept is introduced first. Recall that, for every $t \in \mathbb{R}_+$, $[-t1^m, t1^m]$ denotes the set $\{s \in \mathbb{R}^m \mid -t1^m \leq s \leq t1^m\}$. For every $t \in \mathbb{R}_+$, the projection function $\pi_{m,t} : \mathbb{R}^m \to [-t1^m, t1^m]$ associates with every element $s \in \mathbb{R}^m$ the element of $[-t1^m, t1^m]$ that minimizes $||s - \overline{s}||_2$ over $\overline{s} \in [-t1^m, t1^m]$. So, for every $t \in \mathbb{R}_+$,

$$\pi_{m,t}(s) = \inf\left(\{\sup(\{-t1^m, s\}), t1^m\}\right), \ \forall s \in \mathbb{R}^m. \tag{8.4}$$

It follows from (8.4) or from Lemma 7.2.1 that $\pi_{m,t}$ is a continuous function for every $t \in \mathbb{R}_+$. Now it is possible to give the definition of a property of a subset of a Euclidean space, which is weaker than compactness but stronger than closedness, and hence called *semi-compactness*.

Definition 8.3.1 (Semi-compactness)
A subset S of $\mathbb{R}^m$ is semi-compact *if $\pi_{m,t}(S)$ is closed for every $t \in \mathbb{R}_+$.*

The following lemma states that semi-compactness is a weaker property than compactness.

Lemma 8.3.2
If a subset S of $\mathbb{R}^m$ is compact, then it is semi-compact.
Proof
For every $t \in \mathbb{R}_+$, since S is compact and $\pi_{m,t}$ is continuous, it follows from Theorem 2.3.13 that $\pi_{m,t}(S)$ is compact and therefore closed. Q.E.D.

Next, it is shown that a semi-compact set is closed.

Lemma 8.3.3
If a subset S of $\mathbb{R}^m$ is semi-compact, then it is closed.
Proof
Suppose S is not closed. Then there exists a sequence $(s^n)_{n\in\mathbb{N}}$ in S converging to some $\bar{s} \in \mathbb{R}^m \setminus S$. Let $\bar{t} \in \mathbb{R}_+$ be such that $\bar{t} > \|\bar{s}\|_\infty$. Then $(s^n)_{n\in\mathbb{N}}$ has a subsequence in $\pi_{m,\bar{t}}(S)$ converging to $\bar{s}$. Obviously, $\bar{s} \in \mathbb{R}^m \setminus \pi_{m,\bar{t}}(S)$, so $\pi_{m,\bar{t}}(S)$ is not closed. This contradicts the semi-compactness of S. Q.E.D.

Two examples of semi-compact sets that are not compact are the sets $\mathbb{R}^m$ and $\mathbb{N}^m$. An example of a closed set that is not semi-compact is the set $\{s \in \mathbb{R}^2 \mid s_2 = \arctan(s_1)\}$. It is not difficult to show that for subsets of $\mathbb{R}$ the concepts of semi-compactness and closedness coincide. When verifying the semi-compactness of a set the following property is useful.

Lemma 8.3.4
Let S be a subset of $\mathbb{R}^m$ and let $\bar{t} \in \mathbb{R}_+$ be such that $\pi_{m,\bar{t}}(S)$ is closed. Then $\pi_{m,t}(S)$ is closed for every $t \in [0,\bar{t}]$.
Proof
From (8.4) it follows that $\pi_{m,t}(\pi_{m,\bar{t}}(S)) = \pi_{m,t}(S)$, $\forall t \leq \bar{t}$. Since $\pi_{m,\bar{t}}(S)$ is bounded and closed, it is compact. Moreover, the function $\pi_{m,t}$ is continuous for every $t \in [0,\bar{t}]$. Therefore, it follows from Theorem 2.3.13 that the set $\pi_{m,t}(\pi_{m,\bar{t}}(S))$ is compact and therefore closed for every $t \in [0,\bar{t}]$. Q.E.D.

The following assumption is used in the main results of this chapter.

A5. For every political candidate $k \in I_2$, the set of admissible price regulations A^k is non-empty and semi-compact, and $A^k \subset \underline{\overline{P}}$.

The assumptions made with respect to the set of admissible price regulations A^k of a political candidate $k \in I_2$ are very weak. For every $t \in [1, \rightarrow)$ it holds that $\pi_{2N,t}(\underline{\overline{P}}) = [-t1^{2N}, t1^{2N}] \cap \underline{\overline{P}}$, an intersection of two closed sets and therefore closed. So, the set $\underline{\overline{P}}$ itself satisfies Assumption A5. Hence, the case $A^k = \underline{\overline{P}}$, $\forall k \in I_2$, is not excluded. This is conceptually the most interesting case since it corresponds to the situation where in a democratic society price regulations are chosen by the political candidates, and where there are no restrictions on the set of admissible price regulations.

However, it is also possible to model that a political candidate is not capable of setting arbitrarily chosen lower and upper bounds on the prices, for example because of institutional reasons. This might be the more realistic case since regulators are not capable of enforcing every possible price regulation, see also Cox (1980). This can be modelled by restricting the set A^k of admissible price regulations of a political candidate $k \in I_2$ to be some non-empty, semi-compact subset of $\underline{\overline{P}}$. Another possibility is that each political candidate is only capable of considering a finite number of possibilities, in which case the set A^k is a finite set. Assumption A5 also admits many intermediate possibilities for the set A^k, for example cases where the political candidates are only able to regulate prices in some markets. An example for the case $N = 3$ is given by the semi-compact set $A^k = \{(\underline{p}, \overline{p}) \in \underline{\overline{P}} \mid \underline{p}_2 = \overline{p}_2 = \underline{p}_3 = \overline{p}_3 = 1\}$.

If the set of admissible actions is more than one-dimensional, as is clearly allowed to be the case in this chapter, then, according to Kramer (1973), deterministic voting equilibria only exist under extremely restrictive assumptions. This is why attention is focused on *probabilistic voting models*, where the political candidates do not necessarily have perfect information about the voting decision of consumers. Voting models with some probabilistic aspects were first rigorously analysed in Hinich and Ordeshook (1969, 1971), and Hinich, Ledyard and Ordeshook (1972). For the sake of simplicity, in this chapter probabilistic voting models without abstentions are considered following the approach of among others, Comanor (1976), Coughlin and Nitzan (1981b), and Feldman and Lee (1988). In Wittman (1984) the following two arguments for the probabilistic voting model are given. The first argument is that the political candidates do not have perfect information about the preference relations and actions of the voters. This is also the point of view taken in Coughlin, Mueller and Murrell (1990), where in the preferences of the voters there is a bias in favour of or against a political candidate not perfectly known to the political candidates. The second argument is that voters do not have perfect information about the admissible action chosen by the political candidates when casting their vote.

It is assumed that the political candidates have the same subjective expectations about the voting behaviour of the consumers. This assumption can easily be relaxed, but is made for notational convenience. For every political candidate $k \in I_2$, for every consumer $i \in I_M$, a *voting function* $\pi^{ik} : \widetilde{v}^i(\mathcal{A}^1) \times \widetilde{v}^i(\mathcal{A}^2) \to [0, 1]$ is assumed to be given, describing the expectations of a political candidate about the voting behaviour of consumer i. More precisely, if the political candidates have chosen admissible actions $(a^1, q^1) \in \mathcal{A}^1$ and $(a^2, q^2) \in \mathcal{A}^2$, then $\pi^{ik}(\widetilde{v}^i(a^1, q^1), \widetilde{v}^i(a^2, q^2))$ is the probability a political candidate assigns to the event that consumer $i \in I_M$ votes for political candidate $k \in I_2$. This completes the description of the *political economic system*, to be denoted by $\widehat{\mathcal{E}} = ((X^i, u^i, \omega^i)_{i \in I_M}, (\widetilde{l}, \widetilde{L}), (A^k, (\pi^{ik})_{i \in I_M})_{k \in I_2})$.

Deterministic voting without abstentions corresponds to the case where, for every $i \in I_M$, for every $(v^{i1}, v^{i2}) \in \widetilde{v}^i(\mathcal{A}^1) \times \widetilde{v}^i(\mathcal{A}^2)$, $\pi^{i1}(v^{i1}, v^{i2}) = 1$ if $v^{i1} > v^{i2}$, $\pi^{i1}(v^{i1}, v^{i2}) = \frac{1}{2}$ if $v^{i1} = v^{i2}$, $\pi^{i1}(v^{i1}, v^{i2}) = 0$ if $v^{i1} < v^{i2}$, and $\pi^{i2}(v^{i1}, v^{i2}) = 1 - \pi^{i1}(v^{i1}, v^{i2})$. As a matter of realism the assumption that, for every $i \in I_M$, for every $k \in I_2$, π^{ik} is non-decreasing in v^{ik} and non-increasing in $v^{ik'}$, $k' \neq k$, is often made. For the main results of this chapter the only assumption needed with respect to the voting functions is the following.

A6. For every consumer $i \in I_M$, for every political candidate $k \in I_2$, the function $\pi^{ik} : \widetilde{v}^i(\mathcal{A}^1) \times \widetilde{v}^i(\mathcal{A}^2) \to [0, 1]$ is continuous.

In the case where both $\widetilde{v}^i(\mathcal{A}^1)$ and $\widetilde{v}^i(\mathcal{A}^2)$ have no accumulation points, Assumption A6 does not exclude any function π^{ik} and therefore does not exclude deterministic voting without abstentions. This is for example the case if the sets $\mathcal{A}^1$ and $\mathcal{A}^2$ are finite. Moreover, voting functions satisfying Assumption A6 are good approximations of any kind of voting behaviour.

Let some consumer $i \in I_M$ be given, let the consumption set X^i be convex, and let the utility function u^i be continuous, representing the complete, transitive, and continuous preference relation $\preceq^i$. Now consider the case where another representation of $\preceq^i$, say $\overline{u}^i$, (not necessarily continuous) is chosen. Since the voting functions depend on the representation chosen, it is a natural question to ask whether the voting function $\overline{\pi}^{ik}$, $\forall k \in I_2$, associated with $\overline{u}^i$ is continuous if π^{ik}, $\forall k \in I_2$, is continuous, or in other words whether Assumption A6 is independent of the representation chosen for the preference relation. Let $\overline{v}^i : \mathcal{A} \to \mathbb{R}$ denote the indirect utility function of consumer i corresponding to the utility function $\overline{u}^i$. Notice that for every $k \in I_2$ the voting function $\overline{\pi}^{ik} : \overline{v}^i(\mathcal{A}^1) \times \overline{v}^i(\mathcal{A}^2) \to [0, 1]$ associated with $\overline{u}^i$ is uniquely determined since, for every $((a^1, q^1), (a^2, q^2)) \in \mathcal{A}^1 \times \mathcal{A}^2$,

$$\overline{\pi}^{ik}\left(\overline{v}^i(a^1,q^1), \overline{v}^i(a^2,q^2)\right) = \pi^{ik}\left(\overline{v}^i(a^1,q^1), \overline{v}^i(a^2,q^2)\right).$$

Lemma 8.3.5

For some consumer $i \in I_M$, let the consumption set X^i be convex, let the utility function u^i be continuous, representing the complete, transitive, and continuous preference relation $\preceq^i$, and let the voting function π^{ik}, $\forall k \in I_2$, be continuous. Let $\overline{u}^i : X^i \to \mathbb{R}$ be a utility function representing $\preceq^i$. Then the voting function $\overline{\pi}^{ik}$, $\forall k \in I_2$, associated with $\overline{u}^i$ is continuous.

Proof

Let the function $f^i : \overline{u}^i(X^i) \to u^i(X^i)$ be defined by $f^i(\overline{u}^i(x^i)) = u^i(x^i)$, $\forall x^i \in X^i$.

Suppose that f^i is not continuous. Then there exists $\overline{t} \in \overline{u}^i(X^i)$, $\varepsilon \in \mathbb{R}_{++}$, and a sequence $(t^n)_{n\in\mathbb{N}}$ in $\overline{u}^i(X^i)$ such that $t^n \to \overline{t}$ and, for every $n \in \mathbb{N}$, $|f^i(t^n) - f^i(\overline{t})| > \varepsilon$. Since the set $\{t^n \mid n \in \mathbb{N}\} \cup \{\overline{t}\}$ is compact, it has a minimum and a maximum, denoted by t^- and t^+, respectively. Let $x^{i-}, x^{i+} \in X^i$ be such that $\overline{u}^i(x^{i-}) = t^-$ and $\overline{u}^i(x^{i+}) = t^+$. Since the set $\overline{X}^i$, defined by $\overline{X}^i = \{\lambda x^{i-} + (1-\lambda)x^{i+} \mid \lambda \in [0,1]\}$, is path-connected and hence connected by Theorem 2.3.5, $\overline{X}^i \subset X^i$, and u^i is continuous, it follows that $u^i(\overline{X}^i)$ is a connected subset of $\mathbb{R}$ by Theorem 2.3.13 and therefore an interval by Theorem 2.3.12. Hence, $f^i(\{t^n \mid n \in \mathbb{N}\} \cup \{\overline{t}\}) \subset u^i(\overline{X}^i)$. For every $n \in \mathbb{N}$, choose $x^{i^n} \in \overline{X}^i$ such that $u^i(x^{i^n}) = f^i(t^n)$. Let $\overline{x}^i \in \overline{X}^i$ be such that $u^i(\overline{x}^i) = f^i(\overline{t})$. Since $\overline{X}^i$ is compact, it follows that $(x^{i^n})_{n\in\mathbb{N}}$ has a subsequence $(x^{i^{n^m}})_{m\in\mathbb{N}}$ converging to some $\widehat{x}^i \in \overline{X}^i$. From the continuity of u^i it follows that $f^i(t^{n^m}) = u^i(x^{i^{n^m}}) \to u^i(\widehat{x}^i)$. Moreover, $u^i(\widehat{x}^i) \neq f^i(\overline{t}) = u^i(\overline{x}^i)$. If $u^i(\widehat{x}^i) < u^i(\overline{x}^i)$, then there exists $\widetilde{x}^i \in \overline{X}^i$ such that $u^i(\widehat{x}^i) < u^i(\widetilde{x}^i) < u^i(\overline{x}^i)$. In this case it follows from the continuity of u^i that there exists $m' \in \mathbb{N}$ such that, for every $m \geq m'$, $u^i(x^{i^{n^m}}) < u^i(\widetilde{x}^i)$, so $\overline{u}^i(x^{i^{n^m}}) < \overline{u}^i(\widetilde{x}^i)$ and hence

$$\overline{u}^i(\overline{x}^i) = \overline{t} = \lim_{m\to+\infty} t^{n^m} = \lim_{m\to+\infty} \overline{u}^i(x^{i^{n^m}}) \leq \overline{u}^i(\widetilde{x}^i) < \overline{u}^i(\overline{x}^i),$$

a contradiction. If $u^i(\overline{x}^i) < u^i(\widehat{x}^i)$, then a contradiction is obtained similarly. Consequently, the function f^i is continuous.

Let $\overline{v}^i : \mathcal{A} \to \mathbb{R}$ be the indirect utility function associated with $\overline{u}^i$ and let $(v^{i1}, v^{i2}) \in \overline{v}^i(\mathcal{A}^1) \times \overline{v}^i(\mathcal{A}^2)$ be given. Then $\overline{\pi}^{ik}(v^{i1}, v^{i2}) = \pi^{ik}(f^i(v^{i1}), f^i(v^{i2}))$, so $\overline{\pi}^{ik}$ is continuous by the continuity of the functions π^{ik} and f^i. Q.E.D.

The political candidates are assumed to maximize either both their *expected plurality* or both their *probability of winning* the elections. In the first case the *pay-off function* $K^1 : \mathcal{A}^1 \times \mathcal{A}^2 \to \mathbb{R}$ of political candidate 1 is defined by

$$K^1\left((a^1,q^1),(a^2,q^2)\right) = \sum_{i\in I_M} \pi^{i1}\left(\tilde{v}^i(a^1,q^1),\tilde{v}^i(a^2,q^2)\right) - \sum_{i\in I_M} \pi^{i2}\left(\tilde{v}^i(a^1,q^1),\tilde{v}^i(a^2,q^2)\right),\ \forall\left((a^1,q^1),(a^2,q^2)\right) \in \mathcal{A}^1 \times \mathcal{A}^2. \quad (8.5)$$

The pay-off function $K^2 : \mathcal{A}^1 \times \mathcal{A}^2 \to \mathbb{R}$ of political candidate 2 is easily seen to be given by $K^2 = -K^1$. If the political candidates maximize their probability of winning the elections, then the pay-off function $K^1 : \mathcal{A}^1 \times \mathcal{A}^2 \to \mathbb{R}$ of political candidate 1 is defined by

$$\begin{aligned} &K^1\left((a^1,q^1),(a^2,q^2)\right) \\ &= \sum_{\{I\subset I_M \mid \#I \geq \frac{1}{2}M+\frac{1}{2}\}} \prod_{i\in I} \pi^{i1}\left(\tilde{v}^i(a^1,q^1),\tilde{v}^i(a^2,q^2)\right) \prod_{i\in I_M\setminus I} \pi^{i2}\left(\tilde{v}^i(a^1,q^1),\tilde{v}^i(a^2,q^2)\right) \\ &\quad +\tfrac{1}{2}\sum_{\{I\subset I_M \mid \#I = \frac{1}{2}M\}} \prod_{i\in I} \pi^{i1}\left(\tilde{v}^i(a^1,q^1),\tilde{v}^i(a^2,q^2)\right) \prod_{i\in I_M\setminus I} \pi^{i2}\left(\tilde{v}^i(a^1,q^1),\tilde{v}^i(a^2,q^2)\right) \\ &\quad -\tfrac{1}{2},\ \forall\left((a^1,q^1),(a^2,q^2)\right) \in \mathcal{A}^1 \times \mathcal{A}^2. \end{aligned} \quad (8.6)$$

Notice that the probability of political candidate 1 winning the elections is obtained by summation over all sets containing at least half of the consumers of the probability that all the consumers in this set vote for political candidate 1, while the consumers in the complement of this set vote for political candidate 2. In the case of a tie, the toss with a fair coin determines the outcome of the elections. Empty sets are included in the summation in (8.6) and, as mentioned in Section 2.2, the convention is made that $\prod_{i\in\emptyset} \pi^{ik}(\tilde{v}^i(a^1,q^1),\tilde{v}^i(a^2,q^2)) = 1$. Notice that the subtraction of $\frac{1}{2}$ implies that the pay-off function $K^2 : \mathcal{A}^1 \times \mathcal{A}^2 \to \mathbb{R}$ of political candidate 2 is given by $K^2 = -K^1$. Now the price rigidities ruling in the economic system are endogenously determined as the price regulations resulting in a Nash equilibrium of the mixed extension of the game with sets of admissible actions $\mathcal{A}^1$ and $\mathcal{A}^2$ and pay-off functions K^1 and K^2, where K^1 and K^2 are either as defined by (8.5) or as defined by (8.6).

For every $k \in I_2$, let $\mathcal{M}(\mathcal{A}^k)$ be the collection of Borel probability measures on $\mathcal{A}^k$. Then a *Nash equilibrium* of the *mixed extension* of the *game* $\mathcal{G} = (\mathcal{A}^1, \mathcal{A}^2, K^1, K^2)$, where K^1 and K^2 are either as defined by (8.5) or as defined by (8.6), is a pair of probability measures $(\mu^{*1}, \mu^{*2}) \in \mathcal{M}(\mathcal{A}^1) \times \mathcal{M}(\mathcal{A}^2)$ such that

$$\int_{\mathcal{A}^1\times\mathcal{A}^2} K^1 d(\mu^{*1} \times \mu^{*2}) \geq \int_{\mathcal{A}^1\times\mathcal{A}^2} K^1 d(\mu^1 \times \mu^{*2}),\ \forall \mu^1 \in \mathcal{M}(\mathcal{A}^1),$$

$$\int_{\mathcal{A}^1 \times \mathcal{A}^2} K^2 d(\mu^{*1} \times \mu^{*2}) \geq \int_{\mathcal{A}^1 \times \mathcal{A}^2} K^2 d(\mu^{*1} \times \mu^2), \ \forall \mu^2 \in \mathcal{M}(\mathcal{A}^2),$$

see for example Dasgupta and Maskin (1986). A Nash equilibrium of the mixed extension of the game $\mathcal{G}$ is also called a *Nash equilibrium in mixed strategies.* A *Nash equilibrium* of the game $\mathcal{G} = (\mathcal{A}^1, \mathcal{A}^2, K^1, K^2)$, where K^1 and K^2 are either as defined in (8.5) or as defined in (8.6), is a pair of admissible actions $((a^{*1}, q^{*1}), (a^{*2}, q^{*2})) \in \mathcal{A}^1 \times \mathcal{A}^2$ such that

$$K^1\left((a^{*1}, q^{*1}), (a^{*2}, q^{*2})\right) \geq K^1\left((a^1, q^1), (a^{*2}, q^{*2})\right), \ \forall (a^1, q^1) \in \mathcal{A}^1,$$
$$K^2\left((a^{*1}, q^{*1}), (a^{*2}, q^{*2})\right) \geq K^2\left((a^{*1}, q^{*1}), (a^2, q^2)\right), \ \forall (a^2, q^2) \in \mathcal{A}^2.$$

A Nash equilibrium of the game $\mathcal{G}$ is also called a *Nash equilibrium in pure strategies.*

Definition 8.3.6 (Political economic equilibrium)
A political economic equilibrium *of the political economic system $\widehat{\mathcal{E}}$ is a Nash equilibrium of the mixed extension of the game $\mathcal{G} = (\mathcal{A}^1, \mathcal{A}^2, K^1, K^2)$, where K^1 and K^2 are either as defined by (8.5) or as defined by (8.6).*

Usually, theorists in voting theory are reluctant to use an equilibrium in mixed strategies as a solution to the game as described in Definition 8.3.6. The main objection against mixed strategies is that the game in Definition 8.3.6 does not take into account the dynamic features of campaigns in real world elections. During the campaign the political candidates have the possibility to sequentially adjust their proposals. If a Nash equilibrium in pure strategies exists, a political candidate can use his pure strategy during the entire campaign. In the case where political candidates adopt a mixed strategy, the proposals made by them at a specific point in time are in general not best responses to each other. Therefore, at the next point in time a political candidate might want to adjust his strategy. However, as has been pointed out in McKelvey and Ordeshook (1976) this criticism is not completely justified and it is interesting to consider mixed strategy equilibria too, their main reasons being the following. First, if one wants to analyse dynamic issues, then this should be explicitly incorporated in the game defined. Considering mixed strategy equilibria for the static game of Definition 8.3.6 is an essential first step. Secondly, it is possible to give several reasonable dynamic models where indeed equilibria corresponding to the mixed strategy equilibria of the static game are obtained. Moreover, it seems reasonable that also in a dynamic context the political candidates make proposals in the support set of mixed strategy equilibria of the static game.

8.4 THE EXISTENCE OF A POLITICAL ECONOMIC EQUILIBRIUM

The political economic system $\widehat{\mathcal{E}}=((X^i,u^i,\omega^i)_{i\in I_M},(\widetilde{l},\widetilde{L}),(A^k,(\pi^{ik})_{i\in I_M})_{k\in I_2})$ is assumed to be given in this section. Sufficient conditions for both the existence of a political economic equilibrium in mixed strategies and the existence of a political economic equilibrium in pure strategies of the political economic system $\widehat{\mathcal{E}}$ are given. The first step is to show that the set of admissible actions of each political candidate is non-empty. Theorem 8.4.1 guarantees the existence of a Drèze equilibrium for given lower and upper bounds on the prices. Notice that Theorem 8.4.1 does not follow from Corollary 4.7.6 since it is not assumed that $\underline{p} \gg 0^N$.

Theorem 8.4.1
Let $(X^i,u^i,\omega^i)_{i\in I_M},(\widetilde{l},\widetilde{L})$ satisfy Assumptions A1-A4 and let $(\underline{p},\overline{p}) \in \overline{\underline{P}}$ be given. Then $\widetilde{E}^D(\underline{p},\overline{p}) \neq \emptyset$.
Proof
It is shown that there exists $q^* \in \widetilde{Q}^D(\underline{p},\overline{p})$. Since Q^{N-1} is compact and $\widehat{L}$ is a continuous function, it follows from Theorem 2.3.13 that $\widehat{L}(Q^{N-1})$ is compact and therefore bounded from above. Let $\overline{L} \in \mathbb{R}^{MN}_+$ be such that $L \leq \overline{L}$, $\forall L \in \widehat{L}(Q^{N-1})$. For every $i \in I_M$, let the set $\overline{X^i}$ be defined by

$$\overline{X^i} = \{x^i \in X^i \,|x^i \leq \omega^i + \overline{L^i}\}.$$

Notice that for every $i \in I_M$ the set $\overline{X^i}$ is compact and that, for every $q \in Q^{N-1}$, $x^i \in \widehat{\delta}^i(q,\underline{p},\overline{p})$ implies $x^i \in \overline{X^i}$. Let the relation $\mu : \prod_{i\in I_M}\overline{X^i} \to Q^{N-1}$ be defined by associating with every $x=(x^1,\ldots,x^M) \in \prod_{i\in I_M}\overline{X^i}$ the set $\mu(x)$ given by

$$\mu(x) = \left\{\overline{q} \in Q^{N-1} \middle| \sum_{j\in I_{N-1}}\overline{q}_j \sum_{i\in I_M}(x^i_j-\omega^i_j) \geq \sum_{j\in I_{N-1}} q_j \sum_{i\in I_M}(x^i_j-\omega^i_j)\,,\ \forall q \in Q^{N-1}\right\}.$$

Let the relation $\varphi : \prod_{i\in I_M}\overline{X^i}\times Q^{N-1} \to \prod_{i\in I_M}\overline{X^i}\times Q^{N-1}$ be defined by

$$\varphi(x,q) = \prod_{i\in I_M}\widehat{\delta}^i(q,\underline{p},\overline{p})\times\mu(x),\ \forall (x,q) \in \prod_{i\in I_M}\overline{X^i}\times Q^{N-1}.$$

Clearly, $\prod_{i\in I_M}\overline{X^i}\times Q^{N-1}$ is a non-empty, compact, convex set. As in the proof of Theorem 4.7.4 it can be shown that μ is a compact-valued, convex-valued, upper hemi-continuous correspondence. Moreover, for every $x \in \prod_{i\in I_M}\overline{X^i}$, for every $j \in I_{N-1}$, it holds that $\sum_{i \in I_M}(x^i_j - \omega^i_j) > 0$ and $q \in \mu(x)$ implies $q_j = 1$, while $\sum_{i \in I_M}(x^i_j - \omega^i_j) < 0$ and $q \in \mu(x)$ implies $q_j = 0$. Since $\widehat{\delta}^i$, $\forall i \in I_M$, is a compact-valued, convex-valued, upper hemi-continuous correspondence by Theorem 8.2.8, it follows using Theorem 2.5.10 that φ is a compact-valued, convex-valued, upper hemi-continuous correspondence. Therefore, from Kakutani's fixed point theorem, Theorem 2.6.1, it follows that φ has a fixed point $(x^*, q^*) \in \prod_{i \in I_M} \overline{X}^i \times Q^{N-1}$ satisfying

$$x^{*i} \in \widehat{\delta}^i(q^*, \underline{p}, \overline{p}), \ \forall i \in I_M,$$

and

$$q^* \in \mu(x^*).$$

It remains to be shown that $\sum_{i \in I_M}(x^{*i} - \omega^i) = 0^N$. From Theorem 8.2.8 it follows that

$$\widehat{p}(q^*, \underline{p}, \overline{p}) \cdot \sum_{i \in I_M} (x^{*i} - \omega^i) = 0. \tag{8.7}$$

Suppose there exists $j^1 \in I_N$ such that $\sum_{i \in I_M}(x^{*i}_{j^1} - \omega^i_{j^1}) < 0$. If $j^1 \in I_{N-1}$, then $q^*_{j^1} = 0$, so $\sum_{i \in I_M}(x^{*i}_{j^1} - \omega^i_{j^1}) \geq 0$ by Theorem 8.2.8, a contradiction. If $j^1 = N$, then, by (8.7), there exists $j^2 \in I_N \setminus \{j^1\} = I_{N-1}$ such that $\sum_{i \in I_M}(x^i_{j^2} - \omega^i_{j^2}) > 0$. It follows that $q^*_{j^2} = 1$, so $\sum_{i \in I_M}(x^{*i}_{j^2} - \omega^i_{j^2}) \leq 0$ by Theorem 8.2.8, a contradiction. Consequently, $\sum_{i \in I_M}(x^{*i} - \omega^i) \geq 0^N$.
From (8.7) it follows that $\sum_{i \in I_M}(x^{*i}_N - \omega^i_N) = 0$. Suppose there exists $j^1 \in I_{N-1}$ such that $\sum_{i \in I_M}(x^{*i}_{j^1} - \omega^i_{j^1}) > 0$. Then it follows that $q^*_{j^1} = 1$, so $\sum_{i \in I_M}(x^{*i}_{j^1} - \omega^i_{j^1}) \leq 0$, a contradiction. Consequently, $\sum_{i \in I_M}(x^{*i} - \omega^i) = 0^N$. Q.E.D.

In Theorem 8.4.2 it is shown that there exists $\overline{\alpha} \in \mathbb{R}_+$ such that, for every price regulation $(\underline{p}, \overline{p}) \in \overline{\underline{P}}$, for every Drèze equilibrium $(p^*, l^*, L^*, x^*) \in \widetilde{E}^D(\underline{p}, \overline{p})$, it holds that if $p^*_j \geq \overline{\alpha}$ for some commodity $j \in I_{N-1}$, then every consumer keeps his initial endowments of this commodity. Notice that $\overline{\alpha}$ can be chosen independently of the price regulation imposed. This is quite remarkable since the following intuition behind this result is wrong. If the price of a commodity is very high, then every consumer wants to supply this commodity. Therefore, full rationing on supply in the market for this commodity results in a Drèze equilibrium of the economy. This intuition is not correct since there might be prices of other commodities which are even higher. It is therefore not possible to give an upper bound on the price of a commodity such that no consumer demands this commodity. The right argument goes along the following lines. If, although the price of a commodity is very high, a consumer demands this commodity, then he certainly demands an amount of the numeraire commodity exceeding the total initial endowment of the numeraire commodity, giving a contradiction since this cannot happen in a Drèze equilibrium of the economy. It has to be remarked that it is possible that an equilibrium price of a commodity exceeds $\overline{\alpha}$ since the lower bound on the price of this commodity could be greater than $\overline{\alpha}$. If the assumptions of Theorem 8.4.2 are not satisfied, it is possible that a real number $\overline{\alpha}$ with the desired properties does not exist. This follows immediately from the example in Section 6 of Bénassy (1975b). In that example $(X^i, u^i, \omega^i)_{i \in I_M}, (\tilde{\bar{l}}, \tilde{\bar{L}})$ is given such that for every price regulation $(\underline{p}, \overline{p}) \in \overline{\underline{P}}$ some trade occurs in every market in the unique Drèze equilibrium of $\widetilde{E}^D(\underline{p}, \overline{p})$. In that example the preference relations of every consumer satisfy weak monotonicity, but not strong monotonicity, and the initial endowment of every consumer is an element of the boundary of the consumption set, whereas the other assumptions made in Theorem 8.4.2 are satisfied.

Theorem 8.4.2
Let $(X^i, u^i, \omega^i)_{i \in I_M}, (\tilde{\bar{l}}, \tilde{\bar{L}})$ satisfy Assumptions A1-A4 and let $\overline{\alpha} \in \mathbb{R}_+$ be as in Theorem 8.2.3. Then, for every $(\underline{p}, \overline{p}) \in \overline{\underline{P}}$, for every Drèze equilibrium $(p^*, l^*, L^*, x^*) \in \widetilde{E}^D(\underline{p}, \overline{p})$, for every $j \in I_{N-1}$ with $p^*_j \geq \overline{\alpha}$, for every $i \in I_M$, $l^{*i}_j = 0$ and $x^{*i}_j = \omega^i_j$.
Proof
Suppose, for some $(\underline{p}, \overline{p}) \in \overline{\underline{P}}$, there exists $(p^*, l^*, L^*, x^*) \in \widetilde{E}^D(\underline{p}, \overline{p})$, $j' \in I_{N-1}$ with $p^*_{j'} \geq \overline{\alpha}$, and $i^1 \in I_M$ such that $l^{*i^1}_{j'} < 0$. Moreover, j' can be chosen such that, for every $j \in I_{N-1}$ with $p^*_j > p^*_{j'}$, $l^{*i}_j = 0$, $\forall i \in I_M$. If $l^{*i}_{j'} = x^{*i}_{j'} - \omega^i_{j'}$, $\forall i \in I_M$, then $\sum_{i \in I_M}(x^{*i}_{j'} - \omega^i_{j'}) = \sum_{i \in I_M} l^{*i}_{j'} \leq l^{*i^1}_{j'} < 0$, a contradiction. So, there exists $i^2 \in I_M$ such that $l^{*i^2}_{j'} < x^{*i^2}_{j'} - \omega^{i^2}_{j'}$. Let $\overline{l}^{i^2} \in -\mathbb{R}^N_+$ and $\overline{L}^{i^2} \in \mathbb{R}^N_+$ be obtained by defining, for every $j \in I_N$, $\overline{l}^{i^2}_j = -\widetilde{\omega}_j$ if $l^{*i^2}_j < x^{*i^2}_j - \omega^{i^2}_j$, $\overline{l}^{i^2}_j = l^{*i^2}_j$ if $l^{*i^2}_j = x^{*i^2}_j - \omega^{i^2}_j$, $\overline{L}^{i^2}_j = \widetilde{\omega}_j$ if $L^{*i^2}_j > x^{*i^2}_j - \omega^{i^2}_j$, and $\overline{L}^{i^2}_j = L^{*i^2}_j$ if $L^{*i^2}_j = x^{*i^2}_j - \omega^{i^2}_j$. It is easily verified that $(p^*, \overline{l}^{i^2}, \overline{L}^{i^2}) \in \mathcal{P}^{\overline{\alpha}}$. From Theorem 4.6.4 it follows that $x^{*i^2} \in \delta^{i^2}(p^*, \overline{l}^{i^2}, \overline{L}^{i^2})$. Therefore, by Theorem 8.2.3, $x^{*i^2}_N > \widetilde{\omega}_N$, a contradiction. Consequently, for every $(\underline{p}, \overline{p}) \in \overline{\underline{P}}$, for every $(p^*, l^*, L^*, x^*) \in \widetilde{E}^D(\underline{p}, \overline{p})$, for every $j \in I_{N-1}$ with $p^*_j \geq \overline{\alpha}$, for every $i \in I_M$, $l^{*i}_j = 0$. So, for every $j \in I_{N-1}$ with $p^*_j \geq \overline{\alpha}$ it follows that $x^{*i}_j \geq \omega^i_j$, $\forall i \in I_M$, and, since $\sum_{i \in I_M} x^{*i}_j = \sum_{i \in I_M} \omega^i_j$, it holds that $x^{*i}_j = \omega^i_j$, $\forall i \in I_M$. Q.E.D.

In Theorem 8.4.3 it is shown that there is a compact subset of $\overline{\underline{P}}$ such that for every element of $\overline{\underline{P}}$ outside this compact set, the set of corresponding Drèze equilibrium allocations is the same as the set of Drèze equilibrium allocations corresponding to some element of $\overline{\underline{P}}$ in this compact set. The proof is based on the result of Theorem 8.4.2.

Theorem 8.4.3
Let $(X^i, u^i, \omega^i)_{i\in I_M}, (\widetilde{l}, \widetilde{L})$ satisfy Assumptions A1-A4 and let $\overline{\alpha} \in \mathbb{R}_+$ be as in Theorem 8.2.3. Let some $(\underline{p}, \overline{p}) \in \overline{\underline{P}}$ be given. Let $(\underline{p}', \overline{p}') \in \overline{\underline{P}}$ be given by $\underline{p}'_j = \min(\{\overline{\alpha}, \underline{p}_j\})$, $\forall j \in I_{N-1}$, $\underline{p}'_N = 1$, $\overline{p}'_j = \min(\{\overline{\alpha}, \overline{p}_j\})$, $\forall j \in I_{N-1}$, and $\overline{p}'_N = 1$. Then $(p^*, l^*, L^*, x^*) \in \widetilde{E}^D(\underline{p}, \overline{p})$ for some $p^* \in P_{(\underline{p},\overline{p})}$ if and only if $(p^{*\prime}, l^*, L^*, x^*) \in \widetilde{E}^D(\underline{p}', \overline{p}')$ for some $p^{*\prime} \in P_{(\underline{p}',\overline{p}')}$.

Proof
Let $(p^*, l^*, L^*, x^*) \in \widetilde{E}^D(\underline{p}, \overline{p})$ be given. Let $p^{*\prime} \in P_{(\underline{p}',\overline{p}')}$ be defined by $p^{*\prime}_j = \min(\{\overline{\alpha}, p^*_j\})$, $\forall j \in I_{N-1}$, and $p^{*\prime}_N = 1$. Clearly, Condition 2, Condition 3, and Condition 5 of the definition of a Drèze equilibrium of $\widetilde{\mathcal{E}}(\underline{p}', \overline{p}')$, Definition 8.2.4, are satisfied by $(p^{*\prime}, l^*, L^*, x^*)$. For every $j \in I_{N-1}$, if $p^{*\prime}_j < \overline{p}'_j$, then $p^*_j < \overline{p}_j$, and if $p^{*\prime}_j > \underline{p}'_j$, then $p^*_j > \underline{p}_j$. Therefore, Condition 4 of the definition of a Drèze equilibrium of $\widetilde{\mathcal{E}}(\underline{p}', \overline{p}')$ is satisfied by $(p^{*\prime}, l^*, L^*, x^*)$. Let the set J be defined by

$$J = \{j \in I_{N-1} \mid p^{*\prime}_j = \overline{\alpha}\}.$$

Then,

$$p^*_j \geq \overline{\alpha}, \ \forall j \in J, \text{ and } p^{*\prime}_j = p^*_j, \ \forall j \in I_N \setminus J. \tag{8.8}$$

Moreover, by (8.8) and by Theorem 8.4.2,

$$0 = l^{*i}_j = x^{*i}_j - \omega^i_j, \ \forall i \in I_M, \ \forall j \in J, \tag{8.9}$$

so $x^{*i} \in \beta^i(p^{*\prime}, l^{*i}, L^{*i})$, $\forall i \in I_M$.
It remains to be shown that $x^{*i} \in \delta^i(p^{*\prime}, l^{*i}, L^{*i})$, $\forall i \in I_M$. Let $\overline{l} \in -\mathbb{R}^{MN}_+$ and $\overline{L} \in \mathbb{R}^{MN}_+$ be obtained by defining, for every $i \in I_M$, for every $j \in I_N$, $\overline{l}^i_j = -\widetilde{\omega}_j$ if $l^{*i}_j < x^{*i}_j - \omega^i_j$, $\overline{l}^i_j = l^{*i}_j$ if $l^{*i}_j = x^{*i}_j - \omega^i_j$, $\overline{L}^i_j = \widetilde{\omega}_j$ if $L^{*i}_j > x^{*i}_j - \omega^i_j$, and $\overline{L}^i_j = L^{*i}_j$ if $L^{*i}_j = x^{*i}_j - \omega^i_j$. By Theorem 4.6.4 it holds that $x^{*i} \in \delta^i(p^*, \overline{l}^i, \overline{L}^i)$, $\forall i \in I_M$. From (8.9) it follows that

$$\overline{l}^i_j = l^{*i}_j = 0, \ \forall i \in I_M, \ \forall j \in J. \tag{8.10}$$

It is shown that $x^{*i} \in \delta^i(p^{*\prime}, \overline{l}^i, \overline{L}^i)$, $\forall i \in I_M$, from which it follows that $x^{*i} \in \delta^i(p^{*\prime}, l^{*i}, L^{*i})$, $\forall i \in I_M$, by Theorem 4.6.4.
Let some consumer $i \in I_M$ be given. Suppose $x^{*i} \notin \delta^i(p^{*\prime}, \overline{l}^i, \overline{L}^i)$.
For every $\lambda \in [0, 1]$, let $p(\lambda) \in \mathbb{R}^N_+$ be given by $p(\lambda) = \lambda p^{*\prime} + (1-\lambda)p^*$. Let some $\lambda \in (0, 1]$ be given such that $x^{*i} \notin \delta^i(p(\lambda), \overline{l}^i, \overline{L}^i)$. Let $\overline{x}^i$ be any consumption bundle in $\delta^i(p(\lambda), \overline{l}^i, \overline{L}^i)$. Then $u^i(\overline{x}^i) > u^i(x^{*i})$ and $\overline{x}^i \notin \beta^i(p^*, \overline{l}^i, \overline{L}^i)$, so

$$\sum_{j\in J} p^*_j \left(\overline{x}^i_j - \omega^i_j\right) + \sum_{j\in I_N\setminus J} p^*_j \left(\overline{x}^i_j - \omega^i_j\right) = p^* \cdot \left(\overline{x}^i - \omega^i\right) > 0 \geq p(\lambda) \cdot \left(\overline{x}^i - \omega^i\right)$$

$$= \sum_{j\in J} p(\lambda)_j \left(\overline{x}^i_j - \omega^i_j\right) + \sum_{j\in I_N\setminus J} p(\lambda)_j \left(\overline{x}^i_j - \omega^i_j\right).$$

Hence, by (8.8), $\sum_{j\in J} p_j^*(\overline{x}_j^i - \omega_j^i) > \sum_{j\in J} p(\lambda)_j(\overline{x}_j^i - \omega_j^i)$. Since, by (8.10), $\overline{x}_j^i - \omega_j^i \geq \overline{l}_j^i = 0$, $\forall j \in J$, it follows that $\overline{x}_j^i > \omega_j^i$ for some $j \in J$. So,

$$\forall \lambda \in (0,1],\ x^{*i} \notin \delta^i\left(p(\lambda), \overline{l}^i, \overline{L}^i\right) \text{ and } \overline{x}^i \in \delta^i\left(p(\lambda), \overline{l}^i, \overline{L}^i\right) \text{ implies}$$
$$\exists j \in J,\ \overline{x}_j^i - \omega_j^i > 0. \quad (8.11)$$

Let $\overline{\lambda} \in [0,1]$ be defined by

$$\overline{\lambda} = \sup\left(\left\{\lambda \in [0,1] \,\middle|\, x^{*i} \in \delta^i(p(\lambda), \overline{l}^i, \overline{L}^i)\right\}\right).$$

So, there exists a sequence $(\lambda^n)_{n\in\mathbb{N}}$ in $[0,1]$ such that $\lambda^n \to \overline{\lambda}$, and, for every $n \in \mathbb{N}$, $0 \leq \lambda^n \leq \overline{\lambda}$ and $x^{*i} \in \delta^i(p(\lambda^n), \overline{l}^i, \overline{L}^i)$. Clearly, $p(\lambda^n) \cdot \overline{l}^i < 0$, $\forall n \in \mathbb{N}$, and $p(\overline{\lambda}) \cdot \overline{l}^i < 0$, so $(p(\lambda^n), \overline{l}^i, \overline{L}^i) \in \mathcal{P}$, $\forall n \in \mathbb{N}$, and $(p(\overline{\lambda}), \overline{l}^i, \overline{L}^i) \in \mathcal{P}$. Since $\delta^i_{|\mathcal{P}}$ is a compact-valued, upper hemi-continuous correspondence by Theorem 8.2.1, it follows that $x^{*i} \in \delta^i(p(\overline{\lambda}), \overline{l}^i, \overline{L}^i)$ by Theorem 2.5.6.
Now let $(\lambda^n)_{n\in\mathbb{N}}$ be a sequence in $[0,1]$ such that $\lambda^n \to \overline{\lambda}$, $\lambda^n \geq \overline{\lambda}$, $\forall n \in \mathbb{N}$, and $x^{*i} \notin \delta^i(p(\lambda^n), \overline{l}^i, \overline{L}^i)$, $\forall n \in \mathbb{N}$. Notice that such a sequence exists since it has been supposed that $x^{*i} \notin \delta^i(p(1), \overline{l}^i, \overline{L}^i)$. Then, for every $n \in \mathbb{N}$, by (8.11) there exists $\overline{x}^{i^n} \in \delta^i(p(\lambda^n), \overline{l}^i, \overline{L}^i)$ and $j^n \in J$ such that $\overline{x}^{i^n}_{j^n} - \omega^i_{j^n} > 0$. Hence, for every $n \in \mathbb{N}$, by Theorem 4.6.4, $\overline{x}^{i^n} \in \delta^i(p(\lambda^n), \overline{l}^{i^n}, \overline{L}^i)$, where $\overline{l}^{i^n}_{j^n} = -\widetilde{\omega}_{j^n}$ and $\overline{l}^{i^n}_j = \overline{l}^i_j$, $\forall j \in I_N \setminus \{j^n\}$. Without loss of generality, the sequence $(\overline{x}^{i^n}, \overline{l}^{i^n})_{n\in\mathbb{N}}$ in $[0^N, 2\widetilde{\omega}] \times [-\widetilde{\omega}, 0^N]$ converges to some $(\overline{\overline{x}}^i, \overline{\overline{l}}^i) \in [0^N, 2\widetilde{\omega}] \times [-\widetilde{\omega}, 0^N]$. Clearly, there exists $j' \in J$ such that $\overline{\overline{l}}^i_{j'} = -\widetilde{\omega}_{j'}$ and $\overline{\overline{l}}^i_j = \overline{l}^i_j$, $\forall j \in I_N \setminus \{j'\}$. Moreover, $\overline{\overline{x}}^i \in \delta^i(p(\overline{\lambda}), \overline{\overline{l}}^i, \overline{L}^i)$ by Theorem 2.5.6 since $(p(\lambda^n), \overline{l}^{i^n}, \overline{L}^i) \in \mathcal{P}$, $\forall n \in \mathbb{N}$, $(p(\overline{\lambda}), \overline{\overline{l}}^i, \overline{L}^i) \in \mathcal{P}$, and $\delta^i_{|\mathcal{P}}$ is a compact-valued, upper hemi-continuous correspondence by Theorem 8.2.1. Since $\overline{x}^{i^n} \in \delta^i(p(\lambda^n), \overline{l}^i, \overline{L}^i)$, $\forall n \in \mathbb{N}$, it follows similarly that $\overline{\overline{x}}^i \in \delta^i(p(\overline{\lambda}), \overline{l}^i, \overline{L}^i)$. So, $x^{*i} \sim^i \overline{\overline{x}}^i$ and therefore $x^{*i} \in \delta^i(p(\overline{\lambda}), \overline{\overline{l}}^i, \overline{L}^i)$. It is easily verified that $(p(\overline{\lambda}), \overline{\overline{l}}^i, \overline{L}^i) \in \mathcal{P}^{\overline{\alpha}}$, so $x^{*i}_N > \widetilde{\omega}_N$, a contradiction. Consequently, $x^{*i} \in \delta^i(p^{*\prime}, \overline{l}^i, \overline{L}^i)$, $\forall i \in I_M$.
Now let $(p^{*\prime}, l^*, L^*, x^*) \in \widetilde{E}^D(\underline{p}', \overline{p}')$ be given. Let the sets J^1 and J^2 be defined by

$$J^1 = \left\{j \in I_{N-1} \,\middle|\, p_j^{*\prime} = \overline{\alpha} \text{ and } \forall i \in I_M,\ l_j^{*i} < x_j^{*i} - \omega_j^i\right\},$$
$$J^2 = \left\{j \in I_{N-1} \,\middle|\, p_j^{*\prime} = \overline{\alpha} \text{ and } \exists i \in I_M,\ l_j^{*i} = x_j^{*i} - \omega_j^i\right\}.$$

Let $p^* \in P_{(\underline{p},\overline{p})}$ be defined by $p_j^* = \overline{p}_j$, $\forall j \in J^1$, $p_j^* = \underline{p}_j$, $\forall j \in J^2$, and $p_j^* = p_j^{*\prime}$, $\forall j \in I_N \setminus (J^1 \cup J^2)$. It is easily verified that (p^*, l^*, L^*, x^*) satisfies Conditions 2-5 of the definition of a Drèze equilibrium of $\widetilde{\mathcal{E}}(\underline{p}, \overline{p})$, Definition 8.2.4. For every $j \in I_{N-1}$, if $p_j^{*\prime} < \overline{\alpha}$, then $p_j^* = p_j^{*\prime}$, and if $p_j^{*\prime} = \overline{\alpha}$, then $p_j^* \geq p_j^{*\prime}$ and, by Theorem 8.4.2, $0 = l_j^{*i} = x_j^{*i} - \omega_j^i$, $\forall i \in I_M$. Therefore, for every

$i \in I_M$, $x^{*i} \in \beta^i(p^*, l^{*i}, L^{*i}) \subset \beta^i(p^{*\prime}, l^{*i}, L^{*i})$ and hence $x^{*i} \in \delta^i(p^*, l^{*i}, L^{*i})$. So, (p^*, l^*, L^*, x^*) satisfies Condition 1 of a Drèze equilibrium of $\widetilde{\mathcal{E}}(\underline{p}, \overline{p})$. Q.E.D.

Let $(X^i, u^i, \omega^i)_{i \in I_M}, (\widetilde{l}, \widetilde{L})$ satisfy Assumptions A1-A4 and let $\overline{\alpha} \in [1, \rightarrow)$ be as in Theorem 8.2.3. For every political candidate $k \in I_2$, the set $A^{k,\overline{\alpha}}$ is defined by $A^{k,\overline{\alpha}} = \pi_{2N,\overline{\alpha}}(A^k)$ and the set $\mathcal{A}^{k,\overline{\alpha}}$ is defined as in (8.3) where A^k is replaced by $A^{k,\overline{\alpha}}$. Notice that $A^{k,\overline{\alpha}} \subset \overline{\underline{P}}$, $\forall k \in I_2$. The requirement $\overline{\alpha} \in [1, \rightarrow)$ guarantees that, for every $k \in I_2$, for every $a^k \in A^{k,\overline{\alpha}}$, $a^k_N = a^k_{2N} = 1$. Theorem 8.4.4 states that the set of actions $\mathcal{A}^{k,\overline{\alpha}}$, $\forall k \in I_2$, is non-empty and compact.

Theorem 8.4.4
Let $(X^i, u^i, \omega^i)_{i \in I_M}, (\widetilde{l}, \widetilde{L}), (A^k)_{k \in I_2}$ satisfy Assumptions A1-A5. Let $\overline{\alpha} \in [1, \rightarrow)$ be as in Theorem 8.2.3. Then the set $\mathcal{A}^{k,\overline{\alpha}}$, $\forall k \in I_2$, is non-empty and compact.
Proof
Let some $k \in I_2$ be given. It follows immediately, from Theorem 8.4.1 and the set A^k being non-empty, that the set $\mathcal{A}^{k,\overline{\alpha}}$ is non-empty. Clearly, the set $\mathcal{A}^{k,\overline{\alpha}}$ is bounded. It remains to be shown that the set $\mathcal{A}^{k,\overline{\alpha}}$ is closed. Let $(\underline{p}^n, \overline{p}^n, q^n)_{n \in \mathbb{N}}$ be a sequence in $\mathcal{A}^{k,\overline{\alpha}}$ converging to some $(\underline{p}', \overline{p}', \overline{q}) \in \mathbb{R}^N \times \mathbb{R}^N \times Q^{N-1}$. Since A^k is semi-compact, it follows that $A^{k,\overline{\alpha}}$ is closed. So, $(\underline{p}', \overline{p}', \overline{q}) \in A^{k,\overline{\alpha}} \times Q^{N-1}$. By the definition of $\mathcal{A}^{k,\overline{\alpha}}$, for every $n \in \mathbb{N}$, there exists $(x)^n \in X$ such that $(\widehat{p}(q^n, \underline{p}^n, \overline{p}^n), \widehat{l}(q^n), \widehat{L}(q^n), (x)^n) \in \widetilde{E}^D(\underline{p}^n, \overline{p}^n)$. The sequence $((x)^n)_{n \in \mathbb{N}}$ in X is obviously bounded and X is closed. Therefore, there exists a subsequence $((x)^{n^m})_{m \in \mathbb{N}}$ converging to some $\overline{x} \in X$. It is shown that $(\widehat{p}(\overline{q}, \underline{p}', \overline{p}'), \widehat{l}(\overline{q}), \widehat{L}(\overline{q}), \overline{x}) \in \widetilde{E}^D(\underline{p}', \overline{p}')$. Clearly, for every $j \in I_{N-1}$,

$$\begin{aligned}\widehat{p}_j(q^{n^m}, \underline{p}^{n^m}, \overline{p}^{n^m}) &= \max\left(\left\{\underline{p}_j^{n^m}, \min(\{\overline{p}_j^{n^m}, \underline{p}_j^{n^m}(2 - 3q_j^{n^m}) + \overline{p}_j^{n^m}(3q_j^{n^m} - 1)\})\right\}\right) \\ &\rightarrow \max\left(\{\underline{p}'_j, \min(\{\overline{p}'_j, \underline{p}'_j(2 - 3\overline{q}_j) + \overline{p}'_j(3\overline{q}_j - 1)\})\}\right) \\ &= \widehat{p}_j(\overline{q}, \underline{p}', \overline{p}').\end{aligned}$$

Moreover,

$$\widehat{l}(q^{n^m}) = \widetilde{l}\left(\inf(\{1^N, (3q^{m^{n}\top}, 1)^\top\})\right) \rightarrow \widetilde{l}\left(\inf(\{1^N, (3\overline{q}^\top, 1)^\top\})\right) = \widehat{l}(\overline{q}),$$

$$\begin{aligned}\widehat{L}(q^{n^m}) &= \widetilde{L}\left(\inf(\{1^N, 31^N - (3q^{n^{m}\top}, 2)^\top\})\right) \rightarrow \widetilde{L}\left(\inf(\{1^N, 31^N - (3\overline{q}^\top, 2)^\top\})\right) \\ &= \widehat{L}(\overline{q}).\end{aligned}$$

The correspondence $\delta^i_{|\mathcal{P}}$, $\forall i \in I_M$, is compact-valued and upper hemi-continuous by Theorem 8.2.1. Moreover, $(\widehat{p}(q^{n^m}, \underline{p}^{n^m}, \overline{p}^{n^m}), \widehat{l}^i(q^{n^m}), \widehat{L}^i(q^{n^m})) \in \mathcal{P}$, $\forall m \in$

$\mathbb{N}$, and $(\widehat{p}(\overline{q},\underline{p}',\overline{p}'),\widehat{l}^i(\overline{q}),\widehat{L}^i(\overline{q})) \in \mathcal{P}$. Hence, it follows from Theorem 2.5.6 that $\overline{x}^i \in \delta^i(\widehat{p}(\overline{q},\underline{p}',\overline{p}'),\widehat{l}^i(\overline{q}),\widehat{L}^i(\overline{q}))$. Furthermore,

$$\sum_{i\in I_M} \overline{x}^i = \sum_{i\in I_M} \lim_{m\to+\infty} x^{i^{n^m}} = \lim_{m\to+\infty} \sum_{i\in I_M} x^{i^{n^m}} = \lim_{m\to+\infty} \sum_{i\in I_M} \omega^i = \sum_{i\in I_M} \omega^i.$$

Hence, $(\widehat{p}(\overline{q},\underline{p}',\overline{p}'),\widehat{l}(\overline{q}),\widehat{L}(\overline{q}),\overline{x}) \in \widetilde{E}^D(\underline{p}',\overline{p}')$ by Theorem 8.2.6. Therefore, $(\underline{p}',\overline{p}',\overline{q}) \in \mathcal{A}^{k,\overline{\alpha}}$. Q.E.D.

Let $(X^i,u^i,\omega^i),(\widetilde{l},\widetilde{L})$ satisfy Assumptions A1-A4 and let $\overline{\alpha} \in [1,\rightarrow)$ be as in Theorem 8.2.3. For every political candidate $k \in I_2$, the function $K^{k,\overline{\alpha}} : \mathcal{A}^{1,\overline{\alpha}} \times \mathcal{A}^{2,\overline{\alpha}} \rightarrow \mathbb{R}$ is defined by (8.5) or by (8.6). For every consumer $i \in I_M$ it follows from Theorem 8.4.3 that $\widetilde{v}^i(\mathcal{A}^k) = \widetilde{v}^i(\mathcal{A}^{k,\overline{\alpha}})$, $\forall k \in I_2$, so the function $\pi^{ik} : \widetilde{v}^i(\mathcal{A}^1) \times \widetilde{v}^i(\mathcal{A}^2) \rightarrow [0,1]$, $\forall k \in I_2$, is well defined on $\widetilde{v}^i(\mathcal{A}^{1,\overline{\alpha}}) \times \widetilde{v}^i(\mathcal{A}^{2,\overline{\alpha}})$. Therefore, the function $K^{k,\overline{\alpha}}$, $\forall k \in I_2$, is well defined on $\mathcal{A}^{1,\overline{\alpha}} \times \mathcal{A}^{2,\overline{\alpha}}$. In the next theorem it is shown that the function $K^{k,\overline{\alpha}}$, $\forall k \in I_2$, is continuous.

Theorem 8.4.5
Let the political economic system $\widehat{\mathcal{E}}=((X^i,u^i,\omega^i)_{i\in I_M},(\widetilde{l},\widetilde{L}),(A^k,(\pi^{ik})_{i\in I_M})_{k\in I_2})$ *satisfy Assumptions A1-A6. Let* $\overline{\alpha} \in [1,\rightarrow)$ *be as in Theorem 8.2.3. Then, for every political candidate* $k \in I_2$*, the function* $K^{k,\overline{\alpha}} : \mathcal{A}^{1,\overline{\alpha}} \times \mathcal{A}^{2,\overline{\alpha}} \rightarrow \mathbb{R}$ *as defined by (8.5) or (8.6) is continuous.*

Proof
Let some $i \in I_M$ be given. It is first shown that $\widetilde{v}^i$ is continuous. Let $(\underline{p}^n,\overline{p}^n,q^n)_{n\in\mathbb{N}}$ be a sequence in $\mathcal{A}$ converging to $(\underline{p}',\overline{p}',\overline{q}) \in \mathcal{A}$. For every $n \in \mathbb{N}$, let $x^{i^n} \in \widehat{\delta}^i(q^n,\underline{p}^n,\overline{p}^n)$ be given. Since $\widehat{\delta}^i$ is a compact-valued, upper hemi-continuous correspondence by Theorem 8.2.8, it follows from Theorem 2.5.6 that the sequence $(x^{i^n})_{n\in\mathbb{N}}$ has a subsequence converging to some $\overline{x}^i \in \widehat{\delta}^i(\overline{q},\underline{p}',\overline{p}')$. Hence, using the continuity of u^i,

$$\widetilde{v}^i(\underline{p}^n,\overline{p}^n,q^n) = u^i(x^{i^n}) \rightarrow u^i(\overline{x}^i) = \widetilde{v}^i(\underline{p}',\overline{p}',\overline{q}).$$

Let some $k' \in I_2$ be given. By Theorem 8.4.3 it holds that $\widetilde{v}^i(\mathcal{A}^{k'}) = \widetilde{v}^i(\mathcal{A}^{k',\overline{\alpha}})$, so the function $\pi^{ik'}$ is continuous on $\widetilde{v}^i(\mathcal{A}^{1,\overline{\alpha}}) \times \widetilde{v}^i(\mathcal{A}^{2,\overline{\alpha}})$ by Assumption A6. Now the continuity of $K^{k',\overline{\alpha}}$ follows from the continuity of $\widetilde{v}^i$, $\forall i \in I_M$, and the continuity of π^{ik}, $\forall i \in I_M$, $\forall k \in I_2$. Q.E.D.

The following result is given in Dasgupta and Maskin (1986) and has first been shown in Glicksberg (1952) as an application of Glicksberg's fixed point theorem, Theorem 2.6.2. It yields the final step in proving the existence of a political economic equilibrium of the political economic system $\widehat{\mathcal{E}}$.

Theorem 8.4.6
The mixed extension of the game $\mathcal{G} = (\mathcal{A}^1, \mathcal{A}^2, K^1, K^2)$ has a Nash equilibrium if $\mathcal{A}^1$ and $\mathcal{A}^2$ are non-empty, compact sets and K^1 and K^2 are continuous functions.
See Dasgupta and Maskin (1986), Theorem 3, page 6.

In the next theorem the existence of a political economic equilibrium of the political economic system $\widehat{\mathcal{E}}$ is shown using Theorem 8.4.6.

Theorem 8.4.7
Let the political economic system $\widehat{\mathcal{E}} = ((X^i, u^i, \omega^i)_{i \in I_M}, (\widetilde{l}, \widetilde{L}), (A^k, (\pi^{ik})_{i \in I_M})_{k \in I_2})$ satisfy Assumptions A1-A6. Then there exists a political economic equilibrium of the political economic system $\widehat{\mathcal{E}}$.
Proof
To show the existence of a political economic equilibrium of $\widehat{\mathcal{E}}$, the existence of a Nash equilibrium of the mixed extension of the game $\mathcal{G} = (\mathcal{A}^1, \mathcal{A}^2, K^1, K^2)$ has to be shown. Let $\overline{\alpha} \in [1, \rightarrow)$ be as in Theorem 8.2.3 and consider the game $\mathcal{G}^{\overline{\alpha}} = (\mathcal{A}^{1,\overline{\alpha}}, \mathcal{A}^{2,\overline{\alpha}}, K^{1,\overline{\alpha}}, K^{2,\overline{\alpha}})$. According to Theorem 8.4.4, $\mathcal{A}^{1,\overline{\alpha}}$ and $\mathcal{A}^{2,\overline{\alpha}}$ are non-empty, compact sets. By Theorem 8.4.5, $K^{1,\overline{\alpha}}$ and $K^{2,\overline{\alpha}}$ are continuous functions on $\mathcal{A}^{1,\overline{\alpha}} \times \mathcal{A}^{2,\overline{\alpha}}$. Hence, by Theorem 8.4.6, the mixed extension of $\mathcal{G}^{\overline{\alpha}}$ has at least one Nash equilibrium $(\mu^{*1}, \mu^{*2}) \in \mathcal{M}(\mathcal{A}^{1,\overline{\alpha}}) \times \mathcal{M}(\mathcal{A}^{2,\overline{\alpha}})$. Obviously, using Theorem 8.4.3, this Nash equilibrium yields a Nash equilibrium for the mixed extension of the game $\mathcal{G}$. Q.E.D.

It is interesting to have sufficient conditions for the existence of a political economic equilibrium in pure strategies of the political economic system $\widehat{\mathcal{E}}$. Usually, it is sufficient to assume certain concavity and convexity conditions with respect to the pay-off functions and strategy sets to prove the existence of a Nash equilibrium in pure strategies, see for example Feldman and Lee (1988). However, since the set of admissible actions $\mathcal{A}^k$ of a political candidate $k \in I_2$ is not necessarily convex, these conditions might not be satisfied. In Theorem 8.4.9 other sufficient conditions for the existence of a political economic equilibrium in pure strategies of the political economic system $\widehat{\mathcal{E}}$ are given. It is clear that these conditions are very strong since the following assumption is needed.

A7. For every consumer $i \in I_M$, there exists a function $\pi^{i1+} : \widetilde{v}^i(\mathcal{A}^1) \rightarrow \mathbb{R}$ and a function $\pi^{i1-} : \widetilde{v}^i(\mathcal{A}^2) \rightarrow \mathbb{R}$ such that $\pi^{i1}(v^{i1}, v^{i2}) = \pi^{i1+}(v^{i1}) - \pi^{i1-}(v^{i2}) + \frac{1}{2}, \forall (v^{i1}, v^{i2}) \in \widetilde{v}^i(\mathcal{A}^1) \times \widetilde{v}^i(\mathcal{A}^2)$.

Voting functions satisfying Assumption A7 are said to be *separable.* Clearly, if Assumption A7 holds, then, for every $i \in I_M$, $\pi^{i2}(v^{i1}, v^{i2}) = 1 - \pi^{i1}(v^{i1}, v^{i2}) = \pi^{i1-}(v^{i2}) - \pi^{i1+}(v^{i1}) + \frac{1}{2}$, $\forall (v^{i1}, v^{i2}) \in \widetilde{v}^i(\mathcal{A}^1) \times \widetilde{v}^i(\mathcal{A}^2)$, and hence π^{i2} is separable. It is not difficult to show that if the voting function π^{i1} of a consumer $i \in I_M$ is a continuous function, then π^{i1+} and π^{i1-} are continuous functions.

Since the voting functions depend on the utility representation chosen for the preference relation of a consumer, it is important to show that Assumption A7 holds independent of this representation.

Lemma 8.4.8
For some consumer $i \in I_M$, let the consumption set X^i be convex, let the utility function u^i be continuous, representing the complete, transitive, continuous preference relation $\preceq^i$, and let the voting functions π^{ik}, $\forall k \in I_2$, be separable. Let $\overline{u}^i : X^i \to \mathbb{R}$ be a utility function representing $\preceq^i$. Then the voting functions $\overline{\pi}^{i1}$ and $\overline{\pi}^{i2}$ associated with $\overline{u}^i$ are separable.
Proof
Let the function $f^i : \overline{u}^i(X^i) \to u^i(X^i)$ be defined by $f^i(\overline{u}^i(x^i)) = u^i(x^i)$, $\forall x^i \in X^i$. Let $\overline{v}^i : \mathcal{A} \to \mathbb{R}$ be the indirect utility function associated with $\overline{u}^i$ and let $(v^{i1}, v^{i2}) \in \overline{v}^i(\mathcal{A}^1) \times \overline{v}^i(\mathcal{A}^2)$ be given. Then

$$\overline{\pi}^{i1}(v^{i1}, v^{i2}) = \pi^{i1}\left(f^i(v^{i1}), f^i(v^{i2})\right) = \pi^{i1+}\left(f^i(v^{i1})\right) - \pi^{i1-}\left(f^i(v^{i2})\right) + \tfrac{1}{2},$$

so $\overline{\pi}^{i1}$ is separable. Q.E.D.

The next theorem gives sufficient conditions for the existence of a political economic equilibrium in pure strategies of the political economic system $\widehat{\mathcal{E}}$.

Theorem 8.4.9
Let the political economic system $\widehat{\mathcal{E}} = ((X^i,u^i,\omega^i)_{i\in I_M},(\widetilde{l},\widetilde{L}),(A^k,(\pi^{ik})_{i\in I_M})_{k\in I_2})$ satisfy Assumptions A1-A7. Then there exists a political economic equilibrium in pure strategies of the political economic system $\widehat{\mathcal{E}}$ when the functions K^1 and K^2 are defined by (8.5).
Proof
Let $(a^{*1}, q^{*1}) \in \mathcal{A}^1$ be such that

$$\sum_{i\in I_M} \pi^{i1+}\left(\widetilde{v}^i(a^{*1}, q^{*1})\right) = \max\left(\left\{\textstyle\sum_{i\in I_M} \pi^{i1+}(\widetilde{v}^i(a^1, q^1))\right| (a^1, q^1) \in \mathcal{A}^1\right\}\right)$$

and let $(a^{*2}, q^{*2}) \in \mathcal{A}^2$ be such that

$$\sum_{i\in I_M} \pi^{i1-}\left(\widetilde{v}^i(a^{*2}, q^{*2})\right) = \max\left(\left\{\textstyle\sum_{i\in I_M} \pi^{i1-}(\widetilde{v}^i(a^2, q^2))\right| (a^2, q^2) \in \mathcal{A}^2\right\}\right).$$

Let $\overline{\alpha} \in [1, \rightarrow)$ be as in Theorem 8.2.3. For every $i \in I_M$, for every $k \in I_2$, $\widetilde{v}^i(\mathcal{A}^{k,\overline{\alpha}}) = \widetilde{v}^i(\mathcal{A}^k)$ by Theorem 8.4.3. The set $\mathcal{A}^{k,\overline{\alpha}}$, $\forall k \in I_2$, is compact by Theorem 8.4.4, and the function $\widetilde{v}^i$, $\forall i \in I_M$, is continuous as is shown in the proof of Theorem 8.4.5, so the set $\widetilde{v}^i(\mathcal{A}^k)$, $\forall i \in I_M$, $\forall k \in I_2$, is compact by Theorem 2.3.13. Since, for every $i \in I_M$, π^{i1-} and π^{i1+} are continuous functions, it follows from Theorem 2.3.14 that (a^{*1}, q^{*1}) and (a^{*2}, q^{*2}) are well defined. Moreover,

$$\begin{aligned} &K^1\left((a^{*1}, q^{*1}), (a^{*2}, q^{*2})\right) \\ &\quad = 2\sum_{i\in I_M} \pi^{i1+}\left(\widetilde{v}^i(a^{*1}, q^{*1})\right) - 2\sum_{i\in I_M} \pi^{i1-}\left(\widetilde{v}^i(a^{*2}, q^{*2})\right) \\ &\quad \geq 2\sum_{i\in I_M} \pi^{i1+}\left(\widetilde{v}^i(a^{1}, q^{1})\right) - 2\sum_{i\in I_M} \pi^{i1-}\left(\widetilde{v}^i(a^{*2}, q^{*2})\right), \ \forall (a^1, q^1) \in \mathcal{A}^1, \\ &K^2\left((a^{*1}, q^{*1}), (a^{*2}, q^{*2})\right) \\ &\quad = 2\sum_{i\in I_M} \pi^{i1-}\left(\widetilde{v}^i(a^{*2}, q^{*2})\right) - 2\sum_{i\in I_M} \pi^{i1+}\left(\widetilde{v}^i(a^{*1}, q^{*1})\right) \\ &\quad \geq 2\sum_{i\in I_M} \pi^{i1-}\left(\widetilde{v}^i(a^{2}, q^{2})\right) - 2\sum_{i\in I_M} \pi^{i1+}\left(\widetilde{v}^i(a^{*1}, q^{*1})\right), \ \forall (a^2, q^2) \in \mathcal{A}^2. \end{aligned}$$

So, $((a^{*1}, q^{*1}), (a^{*2}, q^{*2}))$ is a political economic equilibrium in pure strategies of the political economic system $\widehat{\mathcal{E}}$. Q.E.D.

Although Assumption A7 is restrictive, it is of interest. The voting model given in Coughlin, Mueller and Murrell (1990), for instance, satisfies this assumption. Let $((a^1, q^1), (a^2, q^2)) \in \mathcal{A}^1 \times \mathcal{A}^2$ be given. In the model of Coughlin, Mueller and Murrell a consumer $i \in I_M$ votes for political candidate 1 if $\widetilde{v}^i\left(a^1, q^1\right) - \widetilde{v}^i\left(a^2, q^2\right) > b^i$, does not vote if $\widetilde{v}^i\left(a^1, q^1\right) - \widetilde{v}^i\left(a^2, q^2\right) = b^i$, and votes for political candidate 2 if $\widetilde{v}^i\left(a^1, q^1\right) - \widetilde{v}^i\left(a^2, q^2\right) < b^i$, where the information of the political candidates is that b^i is a random variable being uniformly distributed in some given interval $\left[-\alpha^i, \alpha^i\right] \subset \mathbb{R}$. For every consumer $i \in I_M$ it is assumed that $|\widetilde{v}^i\left(a^1, q^1\right) - \widetilde{v}^i\left(a^2, q^2\right)| \leq \alpha^i$, $\forall((a^1, q^1), (a^2, q^2)) \in \mathcal{A}^1 \times \mathcal{A}^2$. This implies, for every $i \in I_M$, for every $((a^1, q^1), (a^2, q^2)) \in \mathcal{A}^1 \times \mathcal{A}^2$,

$$\begin{aligned} \pi^{i1}\left(\widetilde{v}^i(a^1, q^1), \widetilde{v}^i(a^2, q^2)\right) &= \tfrac{1}{2} + \tfrac{1}{2\alpha^i}\left(\widetilde{v}^i(a^1, q^1) - \widetilde{v}^i(a^2, q^2)\right), \\ \pi^{i2}\left(\widetilde{v}^i(a^1, q^1), \widetilde{v}^i(a^2, q^2)\right) &= \tfrac{1}{2} + \tfrac{1}{2\alpha^i}\left(\widetilde{v}^i(a^2, q^2) - \widetilde{v}^i(a^1, q^1)\right), \end{aligned}$$

so in this case the choice $\pi^{i1+}(v^{i1}) = \frac{1}{2\alpha^i} v^{i1}$, $\forall v^{i1} \in \widetilde{v}^i(\mathcal{A}^1)$, and $\pi^{i1-}(v^{i2}) = \frac{1}{2\alpha^i} v^{i2}$, $\forall v^{i2} \in \widetilde{v}^i(\mathcal{A}^2)$, satisfies Assumption A7.

8.5 AN EXAMPLE

In this section an example of the model of the previous sections is examined. The example makes clear that by the imposition of price regulations it is possible to obtain allocations that are politically more desired than the Walrasian equilibrium allocation. Consider the economy $\widetilde{\mathcal{E}}(\underline{p},\overline{p}) = ((X^i, \preceq^i, \omega^i)_{i\in I_2}, P_{(\underline{p},\overline{p})}, (\widetilde{l},\widetilde{L}))$, where $N=2$,

$$X^1 = X^2 = \mathbb{R}^2_+,$$

$\preceq^1$ and $\preceq^2$ can be represented by utility functions, defined by

$$\begin{aligned} u^1\left(x_1^1, x_2^1\right) &= \left(x_1^1\right)^{\frac{4}{5}}\left(x_2^1\right)^{\frac{1}{5}}, \forall x^1 \in X^1, \\ u^2\left(x_1^2, x_2^2\right) &= \left(x_1^2\right)^{\frac{1}{5}}\left(x_2^2\right)^{\frac{4}{5}}, \forall x^2 \in X^2, \end{aligned}$$

respectively,

$$\omega^1 = \omega^2 = (1,4)^\top,$$

$(\underline{p},\overline{p}) \in \overline{\underline{P}}$ with $\underline{p}_1 = \overline{p}_1$, and $(\widetilde{l},\widetilde{L})$ represents the uniform rationing system, where $\widetilde{l} : Q^2 \to -\mathbb{R}^4_+$ is defined by

$$\begin{aligned} \widetilde{l}_1^1(q) &= \widetilde{l}_1^2(q) = -2q_1, \forall q \in Q^2, \\ \widetilde{l}_2^1(q) &= \widetilde{l}_2^2(q) = -8q_2, \forall q \in Q^2, \end{aligned}$$

and $\widetilde{L} : Q^2 \to \mathbb{R}^4_+$ is defined by

$$\begin{aligned} \widetilde{L}_1^1(q) &= \widetilde{L}_1^2(q) = 2q_1, \forall q \in Q^2, \\ \widetilde{L}_2^1(q) &= \widetilde{L}_2^2(q) = 8q_2, \forall q \in Q^2. \end{aligned}$$

Notice that $(\underline{p},\overline{p}) \in \overline{\underline{P}}$ implies $\underline{p}_2 = \overline{p}_2 = 1$. Since the reduced demand relation of both consumer 1 and consumer 2 is a function in this example, it is denoted by $\widehat{d}^1 : Q^1 \times \overline{\underline{P}} \to \mathbb{R}^2$ and $\widehat{d}^2 : Q^1 \times \overline{\underline{P}} \to \mathbb{R}^2$, respectively. Notice that the preference relations $\preceq^1$ and $\preceq^2$ are not strongly monotonic. However, strong monotonicity does hold when the preference relation $\preceq^i$ of a consumer $i \in I_2$ is restricted to the non-empty, closed, convex set $\overline{X^i} = \{x^i \in X^i \mid x^i \succeq^i \frac{1}{2}\omega^i\}$ satisfying that $\overline{X^i} \subset \mathbb{R}^2_+$, $\overline{X^i} + \mathbb{R}^2_+ \subset \overline{X^i}$, and $\omega^i \in \operatorname{int}(\overline{X^i})$. Considering $\overline{X^i}$ instead of X^i, it follows that Assumptions A1-A4 are satisfied in this example. Therefore, all results obtained in this chapter do hold for this example.

After some computations it follows that, for $(q,p,p) \in Q^1 \times \overline{\underline{P}}$, if $0 \leq p_1 \leq \frac{16}{11}$, then

$$\widehat{d}^1(q,p,p) = \begin{cases} (3, 4-2p_1)^\top, & 0 \leq q \leq \frac{2}{3}, \\ (7-6q, 4-6p_1+6p_1q)^\top, & \frac{2}{3} \leq q \leq 1, \end{cases}$$

if $\frac{16}{11} \leq p_1 \leq 16$, then

$$\widehat{d}^1(q, p, p) = \begin{cases} (\frac{16+4p_1}{5p_1}, \frac{4+p_1}{5})^\top, & 0 \leq q \leq \frac{-16+31p_1}{30p_1}, \\ (7 - 6q, 4 - 6p_1 + 6p_1 q)^\top, & \frac{-16+31p_1}{30p_1} \leq q \leq 1, \end{cases}$$

if $16 \leq p_1 \leq 56$, then

$$\widehat{d}^1(q, p, p) = \begin{cases} (1 - 6q, 4 + 6p_1 q)^\top, & 0 \leq q \leq \frac{-16+p_1}{30p_1}, \\ (\frac{16+4p_1}{5p_1}, \frac{4+p_1}{5})^\top, & \frac{-16+p_1}{30p_1} \leq q \leq 1, \end{cases}$$

and if $56 \leq p_1$, then

$$\widehat{d}^1(q, p, p) = \begin{cases} (1 - 6q, 4 + 6p_1 q)^\top, & 0 \leq q \leq \frac{4}{3p_1}, \\ (\frac{-8+p_1}{p_1}, 12)^\top, & \frac{4}{3p_1} \leq q \leq 1. \end{cases}$$

For $(q, p, p) \in Q^1 \times \overline{\underline{P}}$, if $0 \leq p_1 \leq \frac{2}{7}$, then

$$\widehat{d}^2(q, p, p) = \begin{cases} (3, 4 - 2p_1)^\top, & 0 \leq q \leq \frac{2}{3}, \\ (7 - 6q, 4 - 6p_1 + 6p_1 q)^\top, & \frac{2}{3} \leq q \leq 1, \end{cases}$$

if $\frac{2}{7} \leq p_1 \leq 1$, then

$$\widehat{d}^2(q, p, p) = \begin{cases} (\frac{4+p_1}{5p_1}, \frac{16+4p_1}{5})^\top, & 0 \leq q \leq \frac{-2+17p_1}{15p_1}, \\ (7 - 6q, 4 - 6p_1 + 6p_1 q)^\top, & \frac{-2+17p_1}{15p_1} \leq q \leq 1, \end{cases}$$

if $1 \leq p_1 \leq 11$, then

$$\widehat{d}^2(q, p, p) = \begin{cases} (1 - 6q, 4 + 6p_1 q)^\top, & 0 \leq q \leq \frac{-2+2p_1}{15p_1}, \\ (\frac{4+p_1}{5p_1}, \frac{16+4p_1}{5})^\top, & \frac{-2+2p_1}{15p_1} \leq q \leq 1, \end{cases}$$

and if $11 \leq p_1$, then

$$\widehat{d}^2(q, p, p) = \begin{cases} (1 - 6q, 4 + 6p_1 q)^\top, & 0 \leq q \leq \frac{4}{3p_1}, \\ (\frac{-8+p_1}{p_1}, 12)^\top, & \frac{4}{3p_1} \leq q \leq 1. \end{cases}$$

For every $(p, p) \in \overline{\underline{P}}$, by solving $\sum_{i \in I_2} \widehat{d}^i(q, p, p) = \sum_{i \in I_2} \omega^i$ all Drèze equilibria of the economy $\widetilde{\mathcal{E}}(p, p)$, up to equivalence in the sense of Definition 4.6.2, are obtained. Let the set of admissible price regulations for both political candidates be a non-empty, closed subset $\overline{A}$ of $\overline{\underline{P}}$ satisfying $\overline{A} \subset \{(\underline{p}, \overline{p}) \in \overline{\underline{P}} \mid \underline{p} = \overline{p}\}$. It can be verified that Assumption A5 is satisfied. It follows with the previous calculations that the set $\overline{\mathcal{A}}$ of admissible actions corresponding to the set of admissible price regulations $\overline{A}$ is given by

$$\overline{\mathcal{A}} = \Big\{(p,p,q) \in \overline{A} \times Q^1 \Big| 0 \le p_1 \le 1 \text{ and } q=1, \text{ or } 1 \le p_1 \le 4 \text{ and } q = \tfrac{2+13p_1}{15p_1}, \text{ or } p_1 = 4 \text{ and } \tfrac{1}{10} \le q \le \tfrac{9}{10}, \text{ or } 4 \le p_1 \le 16 \text{ and } q = \tfrac{16-p_1}{30p_1}, \text{ or } p_1 \ge 16 \text{ and } q = 0\Big\}. \tag{8.12}$$

Notice that $\widetilde{E}^D(p,p) \neq \emptyset$, $\forall (p,p) \in \overline{A}$, see Theorem 8.4.1. Although there is an interval of elements of Q^1 inducing a Drèze equilibrium of the economy $\widetilde{\mathcal{E}}((4,1)^\top,(4,1)^\top)$, all these Drèze equilibria are equivalent in the sense of Definition 4.6.2 and correspond to the unique Walrasian equilibrium of the economy $\mathcal{E} = ((X^i, \preceq^i, \omega^i)_{i\in I_2})$. Thus, considering the remarks made above Theorem 8.2.5, the possibility of not specifying price regulations is not excluded. Moreover, there is no loss of generality in only considering the admissible action corresponding to $q = \frac{1}{2}$ in this case. It can be verified that $0 \le p_1 \le 1$ or $p_1 \ge 16$ implies that both consumers keep their initial endowments in a Drèze equilibrium of the economy corresponding to these values of p_1. If the price regulation is this extreme, then no trade takes place. So, $\overline{\alpha} = 16$ satisfies the requirements of Theorem 8.4.2. Notice that also Theorem 8.4.3 is satisfied for $\overline{\alpha} = 16$.

Using the functions u^i and $\widehat{d}^i$, it is easy to derive the restriction of the indirect utility function $\widetilde{v}^i$ of a consumer $i \in I_2$ to $\overline{\mathcal{A}}$, $\widetilde{v}^i_{|\overline{\mathcal{A}}} : \overline{\mathcal{A}} \to \mathbb{R}$. The voting functions of both consumers are assumed to be the same as in Coughlin and Nitzan (1981b), i.e. for every consumer $i \in I_2$, for every political candidate $k \in I_2$,

$$\pi^{ik}(v^{i1}, v^{i2}) = \frac{\exp(v^{ik})}{\exp(v^{i1}) + \exp(v^{i2})}, \quad \forall v^{i1}, v^{i2} \in \widetilde{v}^i(\overline{\mathcal{A}}).$$

Notice that Assumption A6 is satisfied. So, a political economic equilibrium of the political economic system $\widehat{\mathcal{E}} = ((X^i, u^i, \omega^i)_{i\in I_2}, (\widetilde{l}, \widetilde{L}), (\overline{A}, (\pi^{ik})_{i\in I_2})_{k\in I_2})$ exists according to Theorem 8.4.7.

Suppose the political candidates attempt to maximize their expected plurality. It is easy to show that for every $((a^1,q^1),(a^2,q^2)) \in \overline{\mathcal{A}} \times \overline{\mathcal{A}}$ it holds that

$$\sum_{i\in I_2} \pi^{i1}\left(\widetilde{v}^i(a^1,q^1), \widetilde{v}^i(a^2,q^2)\right) - \sum_{i\in I_2} \pi^{i2}\left(\widetilde{v}^i(a^1,q^1), \widetilde{v}^i(a^2,q^2)\right) \ge 0$$

if and only if

$$\exp\left(\widetilde{v}^1(a^1,q^1)\right)\exp\left(\widetilde{v}^2(a^1,q^1)\right) \ge \exp\left(\widetilde{v}^1(a^2,q^2)\right)\exp\left(\widetilde{v}^2(a^2,q^2)\right).$$

Now suppose the political candidates attempt to maximize their probability of winning the elections. Then it is easy to show that for every $((a^1,q^1),(a^2,q^2)) \in \overline{\mathcal{A}} \times \overline{\mathcal{A}}$ it holds that

$$\begin{aligned}&\pi^{11}\left(\widetilde{v}^1(a^1,q^1),\widetilde{v}^1(a^2,q^2)\right)\pi^{21}\left(\widetilde{v}^2(a^1,q^1),\widetilde{v}^2(a^2,q^2)\right)\\&\quad+\tfrac{1}{2}\pi^{11}\left(\widetilde{v}^1(a^1,q^1),\widetilde{v}^1(a^2,q^2)\right)\pi^{22}\left(\widetilde{v}^2(a^1,q^1),\widetilde{v}^2(a^2,q^2)\right)\\&\quad+\tfrac{1}{2}\pi^{12}\left(\widetilde{v}^1(a^1,q^1),\widetilde{v}^1(a^2,q^2)\right)\pi^{21}\left(\widetilde{v}^2(a^1,q^1),\widetilde{v}^2(a^2,q^2)\right)-\tfrac{1}{2}\geq 0\end{aligned}$$

if and only if

$$\exp\left(\widetilde{v}^1(a^1,q^1)\right)\exp\left(\widetilde{v}^2(a^1,q^1)\right)\geq\exp\left(\widetilde{v}^1(a^2,q^2)\right)\exp\left(\widetilde{v}^2(a^2,q^2)\right).$$

Using the symmetry of the game, it is then easily seen that both in the case where the political candidates maximize expected plurality and in the case where the political candidates maximize their probability of winning the elections, in a political economic equilibrium of the political economic system $\widehat{\mathcal{E}}$, a political candidate $k \in I_2$ chooses an action $(a^{*k},q^{*k}) \in \overline{\mathcal{A}}$ that maximizes $\sum_{i\in I_2}\widetilde{v}^i(a^k,q^k)$ over $(a^k,q^k)\in\overline{\mathcal{A}}$. Consider the case where $\overline{A}$ is given by

$$\overline{A}=\left\{\left((3,1)^\top,(3,1)^\top\right),\left((4,1)^\top,(4,1)^\top\right),\left((5,1)^\top,(5,1)^\top\right)\right\}.$$

Hence, $\overline{\mathcal{A}}$ is given by

$$\overline{\mathcal{A}}=\left\{\left((3,1)^\top,(3,1)^\top,\tfrac{41}{45}\right),\left((4,1)^\top,(4,1)^\top,\tfrac{1}{2}\right),\left((5,1)^\top,(5,1)^\top,\tfrac{11}{150}\right)\right\}.$$

The Drèze equilibria of the economy $\widetilde{\mathcal{E}}(p,p)$ for $p=(3,1)^\top$, $p=(4,1)^\top$, and $p=(5,1)^\top$, respectively, are given in Table 8.5.1.

From Table 8.5.1 it follows easily that in the political economic equilibrium of the political economic system $\widehat{\mathcal{E}}=((X^i,u^i,\omega^i)_{i\in I_2},(\widetilde{l},\widetilde{L}),(\overline{A},(\pi^{ik})_{i\in I_2})_{k\in I_2})$ with $\overline{A}=\{((3,1)^\top,(3,1)^\top),((4,1)^\top,(4,1)^\top),((5,1)^\top,(5,1)^\top)\}$, both political candidates choose for a price regulation where $\underline{p}_1=\overline{p}_1=5$. Consumer 2 is rationed on his supply in the market for commodity 1 in this case. Compared with the Walrasian equilibrium allocation, this price regulation is advantageous for consumer 2 and disadvantageous for consumer 1. It should be remarked that the action where $\underline{p}_1=5$ and $\overline{p}_1=+\infty$ yields exactly the same pay-offs for both candidates.

Now consider the case where $A^1=A^2=\underline{\overline{P}}$. Using the definition of a Drèze equilibrium and the remarks made below (8.12) it is not difficult to show that the set of admissible actions $\overline{\mathcal{A}}$ corresponding to the set of admissible price regulations

$$\left\{(p,p)\in\underline{\overline{P}}\,\middle|\,1\leq p_1\leq 16\right\}$$

	$p_1 = 3$	$p_1 = 4$	$p_1 = 5$
q	$\frac{41}{45}$	$\frac{1}{2}$	$\frac{11}{150}$
$\widehat{d}^1(q,p,p)$	$(1\frac{8}{15}, 2\frac{2}{5})^\top$	$(1\frac{3}{5}, 1\frac{3}{5})^\top$	$(1\frac{11}{25}, 1\frac{4}{5})^\top$
$\widehat{d}^2(q,p,p)$	$(\frac{7}{15}, 5\frac{3}{5})^\top$	$(\frac{2}{5}, 6\frac{2}{5})^\top$	$(\frac{14}{25}, 6\frac{1}{5})^\top$
$\widehat{l}^1(q) = \widehat{l}^2(q)$	$(-2, -8)^\top$	$(-2, -8)^\top$	$(-\frac{11}{25}, -8)^\top$
$\widehat{L}^1(q) = \widehat{L}^2(q)$	$(\frac{8}{15}, 8)^\top$	$(2, 8)^\top$	$(2, 8)^\top$
$\widetilde{v}^1(p,p,q)$	1.677	1.6	1.506
$\widetilde{v}^2(p,p,q)$	3.407	3.676	3.833
$\sum_{i \in I_2} \widetilde{v}^i(p,p,q)$	5.084	5.276	5.339

Table 8.5.1. The Drèze equilibria in the example.

gives each political candidate the same strategic possibilities as the set of admissible actions corresponding to the set $\underline{P}$. In a political economic equilibrium of the political economic system $\widehat{\mathcal{E}}$ a political candidate $k \in I_2$ therefore chooses an action $(a^{*k}, q^{*k}) \in \overline{\mathcal{A}}$ such that

$$\sum_{i \in I_2} \widetilde{v}^i(a^{*k}, q^{*k}) \geq \sum_{i \in I_2} \widetilde{v}^i(a^k, q^k), \ \forall (a^k, q^k) \in \overline{\mathcal{A}}.$$

Clearly, $(a^{*k}, q^{*k}) \neq ((4,1)^\top, (4,1)^\top, \frac{1}{2})$, $\forall k \in I_2$. So, when every price regulation is allowed, a price regulation is chosen at which no Walrasian equilibrium price system and no Walrasian equilibrium allocation results. It can be shown that $(a^{*k}, q^{*k}) \approx ((5.035, 1)^\top, (5.035, 1)^\top, 0.07259)$, $\forall k \in I_2$, yields a political economic equilibrium of the political economic system $\widehat{\mathcal{E}} = ((X^i, u^i, \omega^i)_{i \in I_2}, (\widetilde{l}, \widetilde{L}), (\underline{P}, (\pi^{ik})_{i \in I_2})_{k \in I_2})$. The resulting Drèze equilibrium is therefore characterized by supply rationing in the market for commodity 1.

Finally, consider the case where the political candidates have different sets of admissible actions, for example as a consequence of institutional or historical reasons. Notice that in this asymmetric set-up, it is no longer allowed to determine the political economic equilibrium by considering for every political candidate $k \in I_2$ the action $(a^{*k}, q^{*k}) \in \mathcal{A}^k$ that maximizes $\sum_{i \in I_2} \widetilde{v}^i(a^k, q^k)$ over $(a^k, q^k) \in \mathcal{A}^k$. Suppose that one political candidate has the possibility of lowering the price of commodity 1 compared to the Walrasian equilibrium price, while the other political candidate might propose to increase the price of this commodity, i.e.

$$A^1 = \{((3,1)^\top, (3,1)^\top), ((4,1)^\top, (4,1)^\top)\},$$
$$A^2 = \{((4,1)^\top, (4,1)^\top), ((5,1)^\top, (5,1)^\top)\}.$$

The pay-offs of the political candidates of the game where the political candidates maximize their expected plurality in the elections, $G = (\mathcal{A}^1, \mathcal{A}^2, K^1, K^2)$ with K^1 and K^2 defined by (8.5), are given in Figure 8.5.2, where political candidate 1 is the row player and political candidate 2 the column player.

	$((4,1)^\top, (4,1)^\top, \frac{1}{2})$	$((5,1)^\top, (5,1)^\top, \frac{11}{150})$
$((3,1)^\top, (3,1)^\top, \frac{41}{45})$	$(-95, 95)$	$(-124, 124)$
$((4,1)^\top, (4,1)^\top, \frac{1}{2})$	$(0, 0)$	$(-31, 31)$

Figure 8.5.2. Pay-offs $\times 1000$ of the political candidates maximizing the expected plurality.

From Figure 8.5.2 it follows immediately that the political economic equilibrium is given by $(((4,1)^\top, (4,1)^\top, \frac{1}{2}), ((5,1)^\top, (5,1)^\top, \frac{11}{150}))$, so political candidate 1 proposes the Walrasian equilibrium, while political candidate 2 proposes to increase the price of commodity 1. Notice that the expected plurality of political candidate 2 is positive in this equilibrium.

The pay-offs of the political candidates of the game where the political candidates maximize the probability of winning the elections, $G = (\mathcal{A}^1, \mathcal{A}^2, K^1, K^2)$ with K^1 and K^2 defined by (8.6), are given in Figure 8.5.3, where political candidate 1 is the row player and political candidate 2 the column player.

From Figure 8.5.3 it follows immediately that the political economic equilibrium is again given by $(((4,1)^\top, (4,1)^\top, \frac{1}{2}), ((5,1)^\top, (5,1)^\top, \frac{11}{150}))$, so political candidate 1 proposes the Walrasian equilibrium, while political candidate 2 proposes to increase the price of commodity 1. Notice that political candidate 2 has a higher probability of winning the elections than political candidate 1 in this equilibrium.

	$((4,1)^\top,(4,1)^\top,\frac{1}{2})$	$((5,1)^\top,(5,1)^\top,\frac{11}{150})$
$((3,1)^\top,(3,1)^\top,\frac{41}{45})$	$(-24,24)$	$(-31,31)$
$((4,1)^\top,(4,1)^\top,\frac{1}{2})$	$(0,0)$	$(-8,8)$

Figure 8.5.3. Pay-offs $\times 1000$ of the political candidates maximizing the probability of winning the elections.

Grandmont (1977a, 1982) explains the occurrence of temporary price rigidities and quantity rationing by making the observation that in the short run quantities move faster than prices. The example considered in this section demonstrates that government intervention may cause price rigidities to exist in the long run too.

9

REGULATION OF PRICES, THE GENERIC CASE?

9.1 INTRODUCTION

In Chapter 8 a model of the political economic system has been given such that the price regulations imposed on the economic system resulted endogenously. Moreover, in Section 8.5 an example has been given where the price regulations are chosen in such a way by the political candidates that the Walrasian equilibrium price system is excluded. However, it is not clear whether this is the typical case. Moreover, it is clear that it is possible to construct examples where both political candidates propose price regulations such that a Walrasian equilibrium results. An obvious example would be to choose Pareto efficient initial endowments. Then any price regulation, so also an imposition of the Walrasian equilibrium price system, would give the initial endowments as final allocation. So, both political candidates proposing the Walrasian equilibrium price system constitutes a political economic equilibrium in this case. It is not too difficult to construct other examples where the unique political economic equilibrium is given by both political candidates proposing the Walrasian equilibrium price system.

In this chapter assumptions are made with respect to the economy, which guarantee that the indirect utility functions of the consumers satisfy certain differentiability properties. Then it is possible to answer the question whether, generically, the political candidates choose price regulations excluding a Walrasian equilibrium. Moreover, under these assumptions it is possible to formulate another appealing model of the political economic system where the political candidates are considered to choose only among local options given some status quo. More precisely, the political candidates have the possibility to choose directions of motion away from the status quo and the possibility to stay at the status quo. Acquiring information concerning proposals very far away from the status quo, like voting behaviour at such a proposal, is often very expensive. Moreover, institutional restrictions or commitments made in the past may rule out large changes. This provides some motivation for the restriction to local options. The pay-offs for the political candidates are determined by the marginal change in the number of votes corresponding to a certain direction of motion. An equilibrium of the resulting game is called a directional political economic equilibrium. This way of modelling the political system has been inspired by Coughlin and Nitzan (1981a).

In Section 9.2 the assumptions made with respect to the political economic system are described and some work is devoted to show that under these assumptions the results developed in the previous chapters hold. In Section 9.3 some known results with respect to the partial derivatives of the indirect utility functions of the consumers are given. Moreover, the model of a political economic system where the political candidates choose between local options given some status quo is presented. The status quo is assumed to be some Walrasian equilibrium of the economy. It is shown that a directional political economic equilibrium in pure strategies exists and a characterization of the equilibrium actions of the political candidates is given. In Section 9.4 it is shown that, generically, both in the model of Chapter 8 and in the model of Section 9.3, a Walrasian equilibrium is unstable in a political economic system, unless there is only one consumer in the economy, or there is only one commodity. For the model of Chapter 8 it is shown that, generically, given a proposal of a political candidate corresponding to a Walrasian equilibrium, there exist price regulations that exclude this Walrasian equilibrium and that are better responses than proposing this Walrasian equilibrium. For the model of Section 9.3 it is shown that, generically, both political candidates choose to move away from the status quo, being any Walrasian equilibrium. In Section 9.5 the directional political economic equilibrium is determined for the example of Section 8.5. It is shown that in this example the unique Walrasian equilibrium is indeed unstable.

This chapter is based on Herings (1996b).

9.2 THE POLITICAL ECONOMIC SYSTEM

As in Chapter 8 it is assumed in this chapter that there are $M \in \mathbb{N}$ *consumers*, indexed by $i \in I_M$, $N \in \mathbb{N} \setminus \{1\}$ *commodities*, indexed by $j \in I_N$, and two *political candidates*, indexed by $k \in I_2$. Every consumer $i \in I_M$ is characterized by the *consumption set* X^i, the *utility function* $u^i : X^i \to \mathbb{R}$, representing the *preference relation* $\preceq^i$, and the *initial endowment* ω^i. Notice that there is no loss of generality in assuming that $u^i(X^i) \subset (0,1)$. Together this constitutes the *economy* $\mathcal{E} = (X^i, \preceq^i, \omega^i)_{i \in I_M}$.

The *rationing function*, specifying the *admissible rationing schemes*, is given by the pair $(\tilde{l}, \tilde{L})$ with $\tilde{l} : \mathbb{R}^N_+ \to -\mathbb{R}^{MN}_+$ the *rationing function on supply* and $\tilde{L} : \mathbb{R}^N_+ \to \mathbb{R}^{MN}_+$ the *rationing function on demand.* Notice that the domain of these functions is now chosen to be equal to $\mathbb{R}^N_+$ instead of Q^N. The reason is that in this chapter the initial endowments of the economy are perturbed, which makes the formulation with Q^N less convenient. For the same reasons, the functions $\widehat{p}$, $\widehat{l}$, $\widehat{L}$, and $\widehat{\delta}$ are not introduced in this chapter. The set $\prod_{i \in I_M} X^i$ is denoted by X. If $x = (x^1, \ldots, x^M)$ is an element of X, then $x_j = (x^1_j, \ldots, x^M_j)^\top$, $\forall j \in I_N$. Moreover, $\omega = (\omega^1, \ldots, \omega^M)$ and $\omega_j = (\omega^1_j, \ldots, \omega^M_j)^\top$, $\forall j \in I_N$. For every $i \in I_M$, for every $j \in I_N$, component $(i-1)N + j$ of $\tilde{l}$ is denoted by $\tilde{l}^i_j$. Moreover, $\tilde{l}^i = (\tilde{l}^i_1, \ldots, \tilde{l}^i_N)^\top$, $\forall i \in I_M$, and $\tilde{l}_j = (\tilde{l}^1_j, \ldots, \tilde{l}^M_j)^\top$, $\forall j \in I_N$. The same notation is used for the function $\tilde{L}$, for a *rationing scheme on supply* $l \in -\mathbb{R}^{*MN}_+$, and for a *rationing scheme on demand* $L \in \mathbb{R}^{*MN}_+$.

As in Section 4.2, given a *price system* $p \in \mathbb{R}^N$ and a rationing scheme $(l^i, L^i) \in -\mathbb{R}^{*N}_+ \times \mathbb{R}^{*N}_+$ of consumer $i \in I_M$, the *budget set* $\beta^i(p, l^i, L^i)$ of consumer i is defined by $\beta^i(p, l^i, L^i) = \{x^i \in X^i \mid p \cdot x^i \leq p \cdot \omega^i \text{ and } l^i \leq x^i - \omega^i \leq L^i\}$, and as in Section 4.3 the set $\delta^i(p, l^i, L^i)$ is the set of best elements of $\beta^i(p, l^i, L^i)$ for $\preceq^i$. The *set* $\overline{\underline{P}}$ *of price regulations* is defined by $\overline{\underline{P}} = \{(\underline{p}, \overline{p}) \in \mathbb{R}^N_+ \times \mathbb{R}^N_+ \mid \underline{p} \leq \overline{p},\ \underline{p}_N = \overline{p}_N = 1\}$. An element $(\underline{p}, \overline{p}) \in \overline{\underline{P}}$ induces the *set of admissible price systems* $P_{(\underline{p},\overline{p})}$, defined by $P_{(\underline{p},\overline{p})} = \{p \in \mathbb{R}^N_+ \mid \underline{p} \leq p \leq \overline{p}\}$. So, commodity N is assumed to be a *numeraire commodity* with price equal to 1. Given $(X^i, \preceq^i, \omega^i)_{i \in I_M}$ and $(\tilde{l}, \tilde{L})$, $(\underline{p}, \overline{p})$ yields the economy $\widetilde{\mathcal{E}}(\underline{p}, \overline{p}) = ((X^i, \preceq^i, \omega^i)_{i \in I_M}, P_{(\underline{p},\overline{p})}, (\tilde{l}, \tilde{L}))$. The *set of Drèze equilibrium allocations* of the economy $\widetilde{\mathcal{E}}(\underline{p}, \overline{p})$, see Definition 8.2.4, is denoted by $\widetilde{E}^{DA}(\underline{p}, \overline{p})$. Obviously, Q^N should be replaced by $\mathbb{R}^N_+$ in Definition 8.2.4.

Every political candidate $k \in I_2$ has a *set of admissible price regulations* $A^k \subset \underline{P}$, determining the *set of admissible actions* $\mathcal{A}^k$, defined by $\mathcal{A}^k = \{(a^k, x^k) \in A^k \times X \mid x^k \in \widetilde{E}^{DA}(a^k)\}$. The set of admissible actions corresponding to the set of price regulations $\underline{P}$ is denoted by $\mathcal{A}$. Theorems 8.2.6 and 8.2.7 guarantee that there is no difference between the modelling of the sets of admissible actions as done in Chapter 8 and as done in this chapter. The *indirect utility function* $\widetilde{v}^i : \mathcal{A} \rightarrow (0,1)$ of consumer $i \in I_M$ is defined by associating with every $(a,x) \in \mathcal{A}$ the real number $\widetilde{v}^i(a,x)$ satisfying $\widetilde{v}^i(a,x) = u^i(x^i)$. For every $i \in I_M$, for every $k \in I_2$, the *voting function* $\pi^{ik} : (0,1) \times (0,1) \rightarrow [0,1]$ describes the expectations of a political candidate about the voting behaviour of consumer i concerning political candidate k, i.e. $\pi^{ik}(v^1, v^2)$ is the probability a political candidate assigns to the event that consumer $i \in I_M$ votes for political candidate k if the *proposal* of political candidate 1 yields consumer i a utility level v^1 and the proposal of political candidate 2 yields consumer i a utility level v^2. For the sake of simplicity it is assumed that both political candidates have the same expectations and that there are no abstentions, so, for every $i \in I_M$, $\pi^{i1}(v^1, v^2) + \pi^{i2}(v^1, v^2) = 1$, $\forall (v^1, v^2) \in \mathcal{A}^1 \times \mathcal{A}^2$.

In this chapter it is assumed that the political candidates maximize their *expected plurality* in the elections. Therefore, the *pay-off function* $K^1 : \mathcal{A}^1 \times \mathcal{A}^2 \rightarrow \mathbb{R}$ of political candidate 1 is defined by

$$\begin{aligned} &K^1\left((a^1,x^1),(a^2,x^2)\right) \\ &\quad = \sum_{i \in I_M} \pi^{i1}\left(\widetilde{v}^i(a^1,x^1), \widetilde{v}^i(a^2,x^2)\right) \\ &\qquad - \sum_{i \in I_M} \pi^{i2}\left(\widetilde{v}^i(a^1,x^1), \widetilde{v}^i(a^2,x^2)\right), \ \forall \left((a^1,x^1),(a^2,x^2)\right) \in \mathcal{A}^1 \times \mathcal{A}^2. \end{aligned}$$

The pay-off function $K^2 : \mathcal{A}^1 \times \mathcal{A}^2 \rightarrow \mathbb{R}$ of political candidate 2 is easily seen to be given by $K^2 = -K^1$. As in Chapter 8 a *political economic equilibrium* of the *political economic system* $\widehat{\mathcal{E}} = ((X^i, u^i, \omega^i)_{i \in I_M}, (\overline{l}, \overline{L}), (A^k, (\pi^{ik})_{i \in I_M})_{k \in I_2})$ is defined as a *Nash equilibrium* of the mixed extension of the *game* $\mathcal{G} = (\mathcal{A}^1, \mathcal{A}^2, K^1, K^2)$, see Definition 8.3.6.

For the main results of this chapter the following assumptions are made.

A1. For every consumer $i \in I_M$, the consumption set X^i is equal to $\mathbb{R}^N_{++}$.

A2. For every consumer $i \in I_M$, the utility function $u^i : X^i \rightarrow (0,1)$ is twice continuously differentiable, $u^i(X^i) = (0,1)$, has no critical point, and represents the preference relation $\preceq^i$ being complete, transitive, continuous, strongly monotonic, strongly convex, of the class C^2, satisfying the boundary condition, and having non-zero Gaussian curvature.

A3. For every consumer $i \in I_M$, the initial endowment ω^i belongs to X^i.

A4. The rationing function on supply $\widetilde{l} : \mathbb{R}_+^N \to -\mathbb{R}_+^{MN}$ and the rationing function on demand $\widetilde{L} : \mathbb{R}_+^N \to \mathbb{R}_+^{MN}$ are continuously differentiable and satisfy, for every $i \in I_M$, for every $j \in I_N$, for every $q^1, \overline{q}^1, q^2, \overline{q}^2 \in \mathbb{R}_+^N$,

$$\begin{array}{llll} \widetilde{l}_j^i(q^1) = \widetilde{l}_j^i(\overline{q}^1) & \text{if } q_j^1 = \overline{q}_j^1, & \widetilde{L}_j^i(q^2) = \widetilde{L}_j^i(\overline{q}^2) & \text{if } q_j^2 = \overline{q}_j^2, \\ \widetilde{l}_j^i(q^1) = 0 & \text{if } q_j^1 = 0, & \widetilde{L}_j^i(q^2) = 0 & \text{if } q_j^2 = 0, \\ \widetilde{l}_j^i(q^1) \to -\infty & \text{if } q_j^1 \to +\infty, & \widetilde{L}_j^i(q^2) \to +\infty & \text{if } q_j^2 \to +\infty, \\ \partial_{q_j} \widetilde{l}_j(q^1) < 0, & & \partial_{q_j} \widetilde{L}_j(q^2) > 0. & \end{array}$$

A5. For every political candidate $k \in I_2$, $A^k = \{(\underline{p}, \overline{p}) \in \underline{\overline{P}} \mid \underline{p} = \overline{p}\}$.

A6. For every consumer $i \in I_M$, for every political candidate $k \in I_2$, the voting function $\pi^{ik} : (0,1) \times (0,1) \to [0,1]$ is continuously differentiable.

For some results it is sufficient to take Assumption A6, but for other results Assumption A7 is needed.

A7. For every consumer $i \in I_M$, the voting function $\pi^{i1} : (0,1) \times (0,1) \to [0,1]$ is twice continuously differentiable, $\partial_{v^1} \pi^{i1}(\overline{v}^1, \overline{v}^2) > 0$, $\forall (\overline{v}^1, \overline{v}^2) \in (0,1) \times (0,1)$, and $\partial_{v^2} \pi^{i1}(\overline{v}^1, \overline{v}^2) < 0$, $\forall (\overline{v}^1, \overline{v}^2) \in (0,1) \times (0,1)$.

In Theorem 3.6.3 it is stated that for every consumer $i \in I_M$ a preference relation $\preceq^i$ satisfying the conditions given in Assumption A2 can indeed be represented by a twice continuously differentiable utility function having no critical point. Moreover, there is no loss of generality involved in assuming that $u^i(X^i) = (0,1)$ since, as a consequence of Assumptions A1 and A2, there is no worst and no best element of X^i for $\preceq^i$. Notice that the inequalities $\partial_{q_j} \widetilde{l}_j(q^1) < 0$ and $\partial_{q_j} \widetilde{L}_j(q^2) > 0$ are vector inequalities, so only one component needs to be different from zero. The set of all utility functions of a consumer $i \in I_M$ satisfying Assumption A2 is denoted by U^i. This set is given the topology induced by the C^2-topology. The set U is defined by $U = \prod_{i \in I_M} U^i$ and is given the product topology. Notice that, for every $u \in U$, $u = (u^1, \ldots, u^M)$ with u^i denoting the utility function of consumer $i \in I_M$. The set of initial endowments satisfying Assumption A3 is denoted by Ω. Since it is assumed that there are no abstentions, it is clear that Assumption A7 implies that for every consumer $i \in I_M$ the voting function $\pi^{i2} : (0,1) \times (0,1) \to [0,1]$ is twice continuously differentiable, $\partial_{v^1}\pi^{i2}(\bar{v}^1, \bar{v}^2) < 0$, $\forall(\bar{v}^1, \bar{v}^2) \in (0,1) \times (0,1)$, and $\partial_{v^2}\pi^{i2}(\bar{v}^1, \bar{v}^2) > 0$, $\forall(\bar{v}^1, \bar{v}^2) \in (0,1) \times (0,1)$. Moreover, Assumption A7 implies that, for every $i \in I_M$, for every $k \in I_2$, $0 < \pi^{ik}(v^1, v^2) < 1$, $\forall(v^1, v^2) \in (0,1) \times (0,1)$. Assumption A7 guarantees that voters react in a natural way to decreases or increases in proposed utility levels.

For a consumer $i \in I_M$, let $X^i = \mathbb{R}^N_{++}$, let the preference relation $\preceq^i$ be complete, transitive, continuous, strongly monotonic, strongly convex, of the class C^r for some $r \in \mathbb{N}^* \setminus \{1\}$, have non-zero Gaussian curvature, and satisfy the boundary condition, and let ω^i belong to X^i. Similarly as in Section 3.6, $\tilde{d}^i(p, w^i)$ denotes the demand of a consumer $i \in I_M$ at the price system $p \in \mathbb{R}^N_{++}$ and *wealth* $w^i \in \mathbb{R}_{++}$, i.e. the best element of $\{x^i \in X^i \mid p \cdot x^i \leq w^i\}$ for $\preceq^i$. Theorem 9.2.1 states that $\tilde{d}^i \in C^{r-1}(\mathbb{R}^N_{++} \times \mathbb{R}_{++}, \mathbb{R}^N)$.

Theorem 9.2.1
For some consumer $i \in I_M$, let $X^i = \mathbb{R}^N_{++}$, let the preference relation $\preceq^i$ be complete, transitive, continuous, strongly monotonic, strongly convex, of the class C^r for some $r \in \mathbb{N}^* \setminus \{1\}$, have non-zero Gaussian curvature, and satisfy the boundary condition, and let ω^i belong to X^i. Then $\tilde{d}^i \in C^{r-1}(\mathbb{R}^N_{++} \times \mathbb{R}_{++}, \mathbb{R}^N)$.
See Mas-Colell (1985), Proposition 2.7.2, page 85.

Theorem 9.2.1 immediately yields Corollary 9.2.2, showing that Assumptions A1-A3 guarantee that the restriction of the relation δ^i of consumer $i \in I_M$ to the set $\mathbb{R}^N_{++} \times \{-\infty^N\} \times \{+\infty^N\}$, denoted by $d^i : \mathbb{R}^N_{++} \to \mathbb{R}^N$, so involving no rationing, is a continuously differentiable function.

Corollary 9.2.2
For some consumer $i \in I_M$, let $X^i = \mathbb{R}^N_{++}$, let the preference relation $\preceq^i$ be complete, transitive, continuous, strongly monotonic, strongly convex, of the class C^r for some $r \in \mathbb{N}^* \setminus \{1\}$, have non-zero Gaussian curvature, and satisfy the boundary condition, and let ω^i belong to X^i. Then $d^i \in C^{r-1}(\mathbb{R}^N_{++}, \mathbb{R}^N)$.

In the preceding chapters, many results have been shown under the assumption that the consumption set X^i of a consumer $i \in I_M$ is a closed subset of $\mathbb{R}^N_+$. Theorem 9.2.5 is helpful in showing that such results are also valid when the consumption set X^i of a consumer $i \in I_M$ is equal to $\mathbb{R}^N_{++}$. First some preliminary results are needed. Let a non-empty, closed subset S of $\mathbb{R}^m$ be given.

The function $d_S : \mathbb{R}^m \to \mathbb{R}$ is defined by

$$d_S(s) = \min\left(\{\|s - \bar{s}\|_2 \,|\bar{s} \in S\}\right), \ \forall s \in \mathbb{R}^m.$$

Let an element $\widehat{s}$ of $\mathbb{R}^m$ and an element $\bar{s}$ of S be given. It follows that $d_S(\widehat{s})$ is equal to the minimum of the function $f : \mathbb{R}^m \to \mathbb{R}$, defined by $f(s) = \|\widehat{s} - s\|_2$, $\forall s \in \mathbb{R}^m$, on the set $S \cap \overline{B}^m(\widehat{s}, \|\widehat{s} - \bar{s}\|_2)$. The set $S \cap \overline{B}^m(\widehat{s}, \|\widehat{s} - \bar{s}\|_2)$ is non-empty, closed, and bounded, and therefore also compact. Moreover, the function f is continuous and therefore the minimum of f on $S \cap \overline{B}^m(\widehat{s}, \|\widehat{s} - \bar{s}\|_2)$ exists by Theorem 2.3.14. So, $d_S(\widehat{s})$ is well defined.

Lemma 9.2.3
Let S be a non-empty, closed subset of $\mathbb{R}^m$. Then d_S is a continuous function.
Proof
Let $s^1, s^2 \in \mathbb{R}^m$ be given. Let $\bar{s}^1, \bar{s}^2 \in S$ be such that $d_S(s^1) = \|s^1 - \bar{s}^1\|_2$ and $d_S(s^2) = \|s^2 - \bar{s}^2\|_2$. Since

$$\|s^1 - \bar{s}^1\|_2 \leq \|s^1 - \bar{s}^2\|_2 \leq \|s^1 - s^2\|_2 + \|s^2 - \bar{s}^2\|_2$$

and

$$\|s^2 - \bar{s}^2\|_2 \leq \|s^2 - \bar{s}^1\|_2 \leq \|s^2 - s^1\|_2 + \|s^1 - \bar{s}^1\|_2,$$

it follows that

$$-\|s^1 - s^2\|_2 \leq \|s^1 - \bar{s}^1\|_2 - \|s^2 - \bar{s}^2\|_2 \leq \|s^1 - s^2\|_2,$$

so $|d_S(s^1) - d_S(s^2)| \leq \|s^1 - s^2\|_2$. Let a sequence $(s^n)_{n \in \mathbb{N}}$ in $\mathbb{R}^m$ converging to some $\bar{s} \in \mathbb{R}^m$ be given. Then

$$0 \leq |d_S(s^n) - d_S(\bar{s})| \leq \|s^n - \bar{s}\|_2 \to 0.$$

Therefore, $d_S(s^n) \to d_S(\bar{s})$, so d_S is a continuous function. Q.E.D.

As in Section 3.6, for a consumer $i \in I_M$ and a consumption bundle $\bar{x}^i \in X^i$, the set $P(\preceq^i, \bar{x}^i)$ denotes the set of consumption bundles x^i of X^i that are at least as desired as $\bar{x}^i$ by consumer i, i.e.

$$P(\preceq^i, \bar{x}^i) = \left\{x^i \in X^i \,|\bar{x}^i \preceq^i x^i\right\}.$$

Lemma 9.2.4
For some consumer $i \in I_M$, let $X^i = \mathbb{R}^N_{++}$, let the preference relation $\preceq^i$ be reflexive, continuous, and satisfy the boundary condition, and let ω^i belong to

X^i. Then $d_{P(\preceq^i,\omega^i)}$ is a continuous function.

Proof

Since $\omega^i \in X^i$ and since $\preceq^i$ is reflexive and continuous, it follows that $P(\preceq^i, \omega^i)$ is a non-empty set being closed in $\mathbb{R}^N_{++}$. Since $\preceq^i$ satisfies the boundary condition, it follows that $P(\preceq^i, \omega^i)$ is closed. Therefore, $d_{P(\preceq^i,\omega^i)}$ is a continuous function by Lemma 9.2.3. Q.E.D.

For some consumer $i \in I_M$, let $X^i = \mathbb{R}^N_{++}$, let the preference relation $\preceq^i$ be reflexive, continuous, and satisfy the boundary condition, and let ω^i belong to X^i. The preference relation $\preceq^i_*$ on $\mathbb{R}^N_+$ is defined as follows. For every $\overline{x}^i, \widehat{x}^i \in \mathbb{R}^N_+$, it holds that $\overline{x}^i \preceq^i_* \widehat{x}^i$ if and only if

$$\begin{array}{l} \omega^i \preceq^i \overline{x}^i,\ \omega^i \preceq^i \widehat{x}^i, \text{ and } \overline{x}^i \preceq^i \widehat{x}^i, \text{ or} \\ \text{not } \omega^i \preceq^i \overline{x}^i, \text{ and } d_{P(\preceq^i,\omega^i)}(\overline{x}^i) \geq d_{P(\preceq^i,\omega^i)}(\widehat{x}^i). \end{array}$$

Notice that $\overline{x}^i \in \mathbb{R}^N_+ \setminus \mathbb{R}^N_{++}$ implies not $\omega^i \preceq^i \overline{x}^i$. Moreover, for every $x^i \in \mathbb{R}^N_+$, $d_{P(\preceq^i,\omega^i)} = 0$ if $\omega^i \preceq^i x^i$, and $d_{P(\preceq^i,\omega^i)} > 0$ if not $\omega^i \preceq^i x^i$. The preference relation $\preceq^i_*$ is defined such that preferences for consumption bundles that are at least as desired as the initial endowment of consumer i do not change, while preferences with respect to consumption bundles not at least as desired as the initial endowment are determined by the smallest distance to such a consumption bundle.

Theorem 9.2.5

For some consumer $i \in I_M$, let $X^i = \mathbb{R}^N_{++}$, let the preference relation $\preceq^i$ be complete, transitive, continuous, and satisfy the boundary condition, and let ω^i belong to X^i. Then the preference relation $\preceq^i_*$ is complete, transitive, continuous, and satisfies, for every $x^i \in P(\preceq^i, \omega^i)$, $P(\preceq^i_*, x^i) = P(\preceq^i, x^i)$. Moreover, if $\preceq^i$ is non-satiated, locally non-satiated, weakly monotonic, monotonic, strongly monotonic, weakly convex, convex, or strongly convex, respectively, then $\preceq^i_*$ is non-satiated, locally non-satiated, weakly monotonic, monotonic, strongly monotonic, weakly convex, convex, or strongly convex, respectively.

Proof

Clearly, $\preceq^i_*$ is complete, transitive, and, for every $x^i \in P(\preceq^i, \omega^i)$, $P(\preceq^i_*, x^i) = P(\preceq^i, x^i)$.

Now the continuity of $\preceq^i_*$ is shown. Let some $\overline{x}^i \in \mathbb{R}^N_+$ be given. If $\omega^i \preceq^i_* \overline{x}^i$, then $\omega^i \preceq^i \overline{x}^i$ and

$$\{x^i \in \mathbb{R}^N_+ \,|\, \overline{x}^i \preceq^i_* x^i\} = \{x^i \in \mathbb{R}^N_{++} \,|\, \overline{x}^i \preceq^i x^i\},$$

a set that is closed in $\mathbb{R}_+^N$ since $\preceq^i$ is continuous and satisfies the boundary condition. If not $\omega^i \preceq_*^i \overline{x}^i$, then not $\omega^i \preceq^i \overline{x}^i$, and

$$\{x^i \in \mathbb{R}_+^N \,|\overline{x}^i \preceq_*^i x^i\} = \{x^i \in \mathbb{R}_+^N \,|d_{P(\preceq^i,\omega^i)}(\overline{x}^i) \geq d_{P(\preceq^i,\omega^i)}(x^i)\},$$

a set that is closed in $\mathbb{R}_+^N$, using the continuity of the function $d_{P(\preceq^i,\omega^i)}$ shown in Lemma 9.2.4. Moreover, if $\omega^i \preceq_*^i \overline{x}^i$, then

$$\begin{aligned}&\{x^i \in \mathbb{R}_+^N \,|x^i \preceq_*^i \overline{x}^i\}\\ &\quad = \{x^i \in \mathbb{R}_+^N \,|d_{P(\preceq^i,\omega^i)}(x^i) \geq d_{P(\preceq^i,\omega^i)}(\overline{x}^i)\} \setminus \{x^i \in \mathbb{R}_{++}^N \,|\text{not } x^i \preceq^i \overline{x}^i\},\end{aligned}$$

the first set being closed in $\mathbb{R}_+^N$ by the continuity of $d_{P(\preceq^i,\omega^i)}$ shown in Lemma 9.2.4, and the second set being open in $\mathbb{R}_{++}^N$, since $\preceq^i$ is continuous, and therefore also open in $\mathbb{R}_+^N$. Therefore, if $\omega^i \preceq_*^i \overline{x}^i$, then $\{x^i \in \mathbb{R}_+^N \mid x^i \preceq_*^i \overline{x}^i\}$ is closed in $\mathbb{R}_+^N$. If not $\omega^i \preceq_*^i \overline{x}^i$, then

$$\{x^i \in \mathbb{R}_+^N \,|x^i \preceq_*^i \overline{x}^i\} = \{x^i \in \mathbb{R}_+^N \,|d_{P(\preceq^i,\omega^i)}(x^i) \geq d_{P(\preceq^i,\omega^i)}(\overline{x}^i)\},$$

a set that is closed in $\mathbb{R}_+^N$ by the continuity of the function $d_{P(\preceq^i,\omega^i)}$ shown in Lemma 9.2.4. So, the preference relation $\preceq_*^i$ is continuous.
Obviously, if $\preceq^i$ is non-satiated and locally non-satiated, respectively, then $\preceq_*^i$ is non-satiated and locally non-satiated, respectively.
Let $\preceq^i$ be weakly monotonic and let $\overline{x}^i, \widehat{x}^i \in \mathbb{R}_+^N$ be given such that $\overline{x}^i \leq \widehat{x}^i$. Moreover, let $\overline{x}^i \prec_*^i \omega^i$ and $\widehat{x}^i \prec_*^i \omega^i$, the only difficult case. Let $\overline{\overline{x}}^i \in P(\preceq^i, \omega^i)$ be such that $d_{P(\preceq^i,\omega^i)}(\overline{x}^i) = \|\overline{x}^i - \overline{\overline{x}}^i\|_2$. Then, using the weak monotonicity of $\preceq^i$,

$$\omega^i \preceq^i \overline{\overline{x}}^i \preceq^i \overline{\overline{x}}^i + \widehat{x}^i - \overline{x}^i,$$

so

$$d_{P(\preceq^i,\omega^i)}(\overline{x}^i) = \|\widehat{x}^i - (\overline{\overline{x}}^i + \widehat{x}^i - \overline{x}^i)\|_2 \geq d_{P(\preceq^i,\omega^i)}(\widehat{x}^i).$$

Therefore, $\overline{x}^i \preceq_*^i \widehat{x}^i$, so $\preceq_*^i$ is weakly monotonic.
Let $\preceq^i$ be monotonic and let $\overline{x}^i, \widehat{x}^i \in \mathbb{R}_+^N$ be given such that $\overline{x}^i \ll \widehat{x}^i$. Moreover, let $\overline{x}^i \prec_*^i \omega^i$ and $\widehat{x}^i \prec_*^i \omega^i$, the only difficult case. Let $\overline{\overline{x}}^i \in P(\preceq^i, \omega^i)$ be such that $d_{P(\preceq^i,\omega^i)}(\overline{x}^i) = \|\overline{x}^i - \overline{\overline{x}}^i\|_2$. Then, using the monotonicity of $\preceq^i$,

$$\omega^i \preceq^i \overline{\overline{x}}^i \prec^i \overline{\overline{x}}^i + \widehat{x}^i - \overline{x}^i.$$

Using that $\preceq^i$ is complete, continuous, and satisfies the boundary condition, there exists $\varepsilon \in \mathbb{R}_{++}$ such that $\overline{\overline{x}}^i \prec^i x^i$, $\forall x^i \in B^N(\overline{\overline{x}}^i + \widehat{x}^i - \overline{x}^i, \varepsilon)$. Therefore,

$$d_{P(\preceq^i,\omega^i)}(\overline{x}^i) = \|\widehat{x}^i - (\overline{\overline{x}}^i + \widehat{x}^i - \overline{x}^i)\|_2 > d_{P(\preceq^i,\omega^i)}(\widehat{x}^i).$$

Hence, $\overline{x}^i \prec_*^i \widehat{x}^i$, so $\preceq_*^i$ is monotonic. If $\preceq^i$ is strongly monotonic, then it can be shown in the same way that $\preceq_*^i$ is strongly monotonic.

Let $\preceq^i$ be weakly convex, let $\overline{x}^i, \widehat{x}^i \in \mathbb{R}_+^N$ be such that $\overline{x}^i \preceq_*^i \widehat{x}^i$, and let some $\lambda \in (0,1)$ be given. Moreover, let $\overline{x}^i \prec_*^i \omega^i$, the only difficult case. Let $\overline{\overline{x}}^i, \widehat{\widehat{x}}^i \in P(\preceq^i, \omega^i)$ be such that $d_{P(\preceq^i,\omega^i)}(\overline{x}^i) = ||\overline{x}^i - \overline{\overline{x}}^i||_2$ and $d_{P(\preceq^i,\omega^i)}(\widehat{x}^i) = ||\widehat{x}^i - \widehat{\widehat{x}}^i||_2$. Obviously, $d_{P(\preceq^i,\omega^i)}(\overline{x}^i) \geq d_{P(\preceq^i,\omega^i)}(\widehat{x}^i)$. From the transitivity and the weak convexity of $\preceq^i$ it follows that $\omega^i \preceq^i \lambda\overline{\overline{x}}^i + (1-\lambda)\widehat{\widehat{x}}^i$. So,

$$d_{P(\preceq^i,\omega^i)}(\lambda\overline{x}^i + (1-\lambda)\widehat{x}^i) \leq ||\lambda\overline{x}^i + (1-\lambda)\widehat{x}^i - (\lambda\overline{\overline{x}}^i + (1-\lambda)\widehat{\widehat{x}}^i)||_2.$$

Notice that

$$\begin{aligned}
&(||\lambda\overline{x}^i + (1-\lambda)\widehat{x}^i - (\lambda\overline{\overline{x}}^i + (1-\lambda)\widehat{\widehat{x}}^i)||_2)^2 \\
&\quad= \lambda^2(||\overline{x}^i - \overline{\overline{x}}^i||_2)^2 + 2\lambda(1-\lambda)(\overline{x}^i - \overline{\overline{x}}^i)\cdot(\widehat{x}^i - \widehat{\widehat{x}}^i) + (1-\lambda)^2(||\widehat{x}^i - \widehat{\widehat{x}}^i||_2)^2 \\
&\quad\leq (\lambda^2 + \lambda(1-\lambda))(||\overline{x}^i - \overline{\overline{x}}^i||_2)^2 + ((1-\lambda)^2 + \lambda(1-\lambda))(||\widehat{x}^i - \widehat{\widehat{x}}^i||_2)^2 \\
&\quad= \lambda(||\overline{x}^i - \overline{\overline{x}}^i||_2)^2 + (1-\lambda)(||\widehat{x}^i - \widehat{\widehat{x}}^i||_2)^2 \leq (||\overline{x}^i - \overline{\overline{x}}^i||_2)^2,
\end{aligned}$$

where for the first inequality it is used that, for every $s^1, s^2 \in \mathbb{R}^N$, $2s^1 \cdot s^2 \leq (||s^1||_2)^2 + (||s^2||_2)^2$ with inequality holding if and only if $s^1 \neq s^2$. Therefore,

$$d_{P(\preceq^i,\omega^i)}(\lambda\overline{x}^i + (1-\lambda)\widehat{x}^i) \leq d_{P(\preceq^i,\omega^i)}(\overline{x}^i).$$

Hence, $\overline{x}^i \preceq_*^i \lambda\overline{x}^i + (1-\lambda)\widehat{x}^i$, so $\preceq_*^i$ is weakly convex.

Let $\preceq^i$ be convex, let $\overline{x}^i, \widehat{x}^i \in \mathbb{R}_+^N$ be such that $\overline{x}^i \prec_*^i \widehat{x}^i$, and let some $\lambda \in (0,1)$ be given. Moreover, let $\overline{x}^i \prec_*^i \omega^i$, the only difficult case. Let $\overline{\overline{x}}^i, \widehat{\widehat{x}}^i \in P(\preceq^i, \omega^i)$ be such that $d_{P(\preceq^i,\omega^i)}(\overline{x}^i) = ||\overline{x}^i - \overline{\overline{x}}^i||_2$ and $d_{P(\preceq^i,\omega^i)}(\widehat{x}^i) = ||\widehat{x}^i - \widehat{\widehat{x}}^i||_2$. Obviously, $d_{P(\preceq^i,\omega^i)}(\overline{x}^i) > d_{P(\preceq^i,\omega^i)}(\widehat{x}^i)$. It follows easily that $\omega^i \preceq^i \lambda\overline{\overline{x}}^i + (1-\lambda)\widehat{\widehat{x}}^i$. So,

$$\begin{aligned}
d_{P(\preceq^i,\omega^i)}(\lambda\overline{x}^i + (1-\lambda)\widehat{x}^i) &\leq ||\lambda\overline{x}^i + (1-\lambda)\widehat{x}^i - (\lambda\overline{\overline{x}}^i + (1-\lambda)\widehat{\widehat{x}}^i)||_2 \\
&\leq \sqrt{\lambda(d_{P(\preceq^i,\omega^i)}(\overline{x}^i))^2 + (1-\lambda)(d_{P(\preceq^i,\omega^i)}(\widehat{x}^i))^2} \\
&< d_{P(\preceq^i,\omega^i)}(\overline{x}^i).
\end{aligned}$$

Therefore, $\overline{x}^i \prec_*^i \lambda\overline{x}^i + (1-\lambda)\widehat{x}^i$, so $\preceq_*^i$ is convex.

Let $\preceq^i$ be strongly convex, let $\overline{x}^i, \widehat{x}^i \in \mathbb{R}_+^N$ be such that $\overline{x}^i \sim_*^i \widehat{x}^i$ and $\overline{x}^i \neq \widehat{x}^i$, and let some $\lambda \in (0,1)$ be given. Moreover, let $\overline{x}^i \prec_*^i \omega^i$, the only difficult case. Let $\overline{\overline{x}}^i, \widehat{\widehat{x}}^i \in P(\preceq^i, \omega^i)$ be such that $d_{P(\preceq^i,\omega^i)}(\overline{x}^i) = ||\overline{x}^i - \overline{\overline{x}}^i||_2$ and $d_{P(\preceq^i,\omega^i)}(\widehat{x}^i) = ||\widehat{x}^i - \widehat{\widehat{x}}^i||_2$. Obviously, $d_{P(\preceq^i,\omega^i)}(\overline{x}^i) = d_{P(\preceq^i,\omega^i)}(\widehat{x}^i)$. It follows easily that $\omega^i \preceq^i \lambda\overline{\overline{x}}^i + (1-\lambda)\widehat{\widehat{x}}^i$. So,

$$\begin{aligned}
d_{P(\preceq^i,\omega^i)}(\lambda\overline{x}^i + (1-\lambda)\widehat{x}^i) &\leq ||\lambda\overline{x}^i + (1-\lambda)\widehat{x}^i - (\lambda\overline{\overline{x}}^i + (1-\lambda)\widehat{\widehat{x}}^i)||_2 \\
&\leq \sqrt{\lambda(d_{P(\preceq^i,\omega^i)}(\overline{x}^i))^2 + (1-\lambda)(d_{P(\preceq^i,\omega^i)}(\widehat{x}^i))^2} \\
&= d_{P(\preceq^i,\omega^i)}(\overline{x}^i).
\end{aligned}$$

The second inequality holds with equality if and only if $\overline{x}^i - \overline{\overline{x}}^i = \widehat{x}^i - \widehat{\widehat{x}}^i$. But then it holds that $\overline{\overline{x}}^i \neq \widehat{\widehat{x}}^i$, hence $\omega^i \prec^i \lambda\overline{\overline{x}}^i + (1-\lambda)\widehat{\widehat{x}}^i$. Since $\preceq^i$ is complete, continuous, and satisfies the boundary condition, there exists $\varepsilon \in \mathbb{R}_{++}$ such that $\omega^i \prec^i x^i$, $\forall x^i \in B^N(\lambda\overline{\overline{x}}^i + (1-\lambda)\widehat{\widehat{x}}^i, \varepsilon)$, and $d_{P(\preceq^i,\omega^i)}(\lambda\overline{x}^i + (1-\lambda)\widehat{x}^i) < \|\lambda\overline{x}^i + (1-\lambda)\widehat{x}^i - (\lambda\overline{\overline{x}}^i + (1-\lambda)\widehat{\widehat{x}}^i)\|_2$. Therefore, $\overline{x}^i \prec^i_* \lambda\overline{x}^i + (1-\lambda)\widehat{x}^i$, so $\preceq^i_*$ is strongly convex. Q.E.D.

Using Theorem 9.2.5 it follows that the set of political economic equilibria of the political economic system $\widehat{\mathcal{E}} = ((X^i, u^i, \omega^i)_{i \in I_M}, (\widetilde{l}, \widetilde{L}), (A^k, (\pi^{ik})_{i \in I_M})_{k \in I_2})$ satisfying Assumptions A1-A6 is the same as the set of political economic equilibria of the political economic system obtained by replacing, for every consumer $i \in I_M$, X^i by $\mathbb{R}^N_+$ and $\preceq^i$ by $\preceq^i_*$, since the preferences of a consumer for consumption bundles less desired than the initial endowment do not matter. Therefore, using Theorem 8.4.7, the following result is obtained.

Theorem 9.2.6
Let the political economic system $\widehat{\mathcal{E}} = ((X^i, u^i, \omega^i)_{i \in I_M}, (\widetilde{l}, \widetilde{L}), (A^k, (\pi^{ik})_{i \in I_M})_{k \in I_2})$ *satisfy Assumptions A1-A6. Then there exists a political economic equilibrium of the political economic system* $\widehat{\mathcal{E}}$.

9.3 THE EXISTENCE OF A DIRECTIONAL POLITICAL ECONOMIC EQUILIBRIUM

In this section a slightly different set-up is considered. The economy is assumed to be in some *Walrasian equilibrium* of the economy $\mathcal{E}$, see Definition 3.8.1, which is called the status quo. Political candidates have the possibility to propose price regulations that correspond either to stay in the status quo or to move away from it. For such a model to make sense, it is necessary to have locally well defined comparative statics, i.e. for every Walrasian equilibrium (p^*, x^*) with $p^*_N = 1$ there exist neighbourhoods $N_{(p^*_1,\ldots,p^*_{N-1})}$ of $(p^*_1,\ldots,p^*_{N-1})$ and N_{x^*} of x^* such that for every $(p_1,\ldots,p_{N-1}) \in N_{(p^*_1,\ldots,p^*_{N-1})}$ the set $\widetilde{E}^{DA}((p_1,\ldots,p_{N-1},1)^\top, (p_1,\ldots,p_{N-1},1)^\top) \cap N_{x^*}$ consists of a unique element. Laroque and Polemarchakis (1978), Theorem 1.6.b, page 58, states that generically in the prices and the initial endowments the number of Drèze equilibria for an economy is finite and that the set of equilibrium allocations varies continuously with the price system and the initial endowments. Therefore, this result suggests (but not implies) that one should expect that, generically, comparative statics are well defined near a Walrasian equilibrium. Nevertheless, this is not the case. In Madden (1982) it is shown that in the standard macroeconomic model with two aggregate agents, households and firms, and three goods, money, output, and labour, comparative statics need not be well defined. However, Madden shows that this happens only with Hicksian net complementarities on the consumer side of the economy at the Walrasian equilibrium or, equivalently, with unusual values of the marginal propensities on the consumer side at the Walrasian equilibrium. In Laroque (1981) a general result, to be specified later on, for local uniqueness of Drèze equilibria near competitive equilibria is given.

In this paper the consumption set X^i and the rationing function $(\tilde{l}, \tilde{L})$ satisfying Assumptions A1 and A4 are always given. Then the set of utility functions and initial endowments $(u, \omega) \in U \times \Omega$ such that the resulting economy $\mathcal{E}$ has locally well defined comparative statics for every Walrasian equilibrium has a non-empty interior by the results of Laroque (1981). This interior is denoted by $\mathcal{U}$. This set contains the economies such that commodities are substitutes at competitive equilibria.

To determine the pay-offs of the political candidates, one has to analyse the structure of the set of Drèze equilibria for price systems in the neighbourhood of a Walrasian equilibrium first. The following concepts are a straightforward generalization of Laroque (1978) where the case with uniform rationing is treated.

Let $(X^i, u^i, \omega^i)_{i \in I_M}, (\tilde{l}, \tilde{L})$ satisfy Assumptions A1-A4 and let a Walrasian equilibrium (p^*, x^*) with $p^*_N = 1$ of the economy $\mathcal{E} = ((X^i, u^i, \omega^i)_{i \in I_M})$ be given, where $((X^i, u^i, \omega^i)_{i \in I_M})$ is assumed to denote the economy $((X^i, \preceq^i, \omega^i)_{i \in I_M})$ with, for every $i \in I_M$, $\preceq^i$ the preference relation that is represented by u^i. Using Theorem 9.2.5, it follows from Theorems 3.8.2 and 3.11.1 that such a Walrasian equilibrium does indeed exist. The elements $\underline{q}(x^*) \in \mathbb{R}^N_+$ and $\overline{q}(x^*) \in \mathbb{R}^N_+$ are defined by

$$\underline{q}(x^*) = \inf\left(\left\{q \in \mathbb{R}^N_+ \,\middle|\, \tilde{l}_j(q) \leq x^*_j - \omega_j,\ \forall j \in I_{N-1}\right\}\right),$$

$$\overline{q}(x^*) = \inf\left(\left\{q \in \mathbb{R}^N_+ \,\middle|\, \tilde{L}_j(q) \geq x^*_j - \omega_j,\ \forall j \in I_{N-1}\right\}\right).$$

Notice that the definitions given above imply that the last component of $\underline{q}(x^*)$ and $\overline{q}(x^*)$ is equal to 0. Clearly, this choice is irrelevant. For every commodity $j \in I_{N-1}$, the sets $\underline{I}_j(x^*)$ and $\overline{I}_j(x^*)$ are defined by

$$\underline{I}_j(x^*) = \left\{i \in I_M \,\middle|\, \tilde{l}^i_j(\underline{q}(x^*)) = x^{*i}_j - \omega^i_j\right\},$$

$$\overline{I}_j(x^*) = \left\{ i \in I_M \,\middle|\, \widetilde{L}^i_j(\overline{q}(x^*)) = x^{*i}_j - \omega^i_j \right\},$$

so these sets contain the consumers with in some sense minimal and maximal excess demand in the market for commodity j, respectively. Notice that since only Drèze equilibria are considered, there is never rationing in the market for commodity N.

Let $(X^i, u^i, \omega^i)_{i \in I_M}, (\widetilde{l}, \widetilde{L})$ satisfy Assumptions A1-A4 and let a Walrasian equilibrium (p^*, x^*) with $p^*_N = 1$ of the economy $\mathcal{E} = ((X^i, u^i, \omega^i)_{i \in I_M})$ be given. Let a sign vector $s \in \mathbb{S}^{N-1}$ with $I^0(s) = \emptyset$ be given. For every consumer $i \in I_M$, for every $(p_1, \ldots, p_{N-1})^\top \in \mathbb{R}^{N-1}$, for every $a \in \mathbb{R}^{N-1}$, the set $\beta^{i,s}((p_1, \ldots, p_{N-1})^\top, a)$ is defined as the set

$$\Big\{ x^i \in X^i \,\Big|\, (p_1, \ldots, p_{N-1}, 1)x^i = (p_1, \ldots, p_{N-1}, 1)\omega^i, \; x^i_j - \omega^i_j = \widetilde{l}^i_j(\underline{q}(x^*)) + a_j \text{ if } i \in \underline{I}_j(x^*) \text{ and } j \in I^-(s), \; x^i_j - \omega^i_j = \widetilde{L}^i_j(\overline{q}(x^*)) + a_j \text{ if } i \in \overline{I}_j(x^*) \text{ and } j \in I^+(s) \Big\},$$

and the set $\delta^{i,s}((p_1, \ldots, p_{N-1})^\top, a)$ is defined as the set

$$\{ \overline{x}^i \in \beta^{i,s}((p_1, \ldots, p_{N-1})^\top, a) \,|\, \overline{x}^i \succeq^i x^i, \; \forall x^i \in \beta^{i,s}((p_1, \ldots, p_{N-1})^\top, a) \}.$$

For every $(p_1, \ldots, p_{N-1})^\top \in \mathbb{R}^{N-1}$, for every $a \in \mathbb{R}^{N-1}$, $\zeta^s((p_1, \ldots, p_{N-1})^\top, a)$ is defined as the set

$$\{ \overline{z} \in \mathbb{R}^{N-1} \,|\, \exists \overline{z}_N \in \mathbb{R}, \; (\overline{z}^\top, \overline{z}_N)^\top \in \textstyle\sum_{i \in I_M} (\delta^{i,s}((p_1, \ldots, p_{N-1})^\top, a) - \{\omega^i\}) \}.$$

In this way a relation $\zeta^s : \mathbb{R}^{N-1} \times \mathbb{R}^{N-1} \to \mathbb{R}^{N-1}$ is obtained. In Laroque (1978), Proposition 5.1, page 1134, it is shown that there exists a set O, being open in $\mathbb{R}^{N-1} \times \mathbb{R}^{N-1}$ and containing $((p^*_1, \ldots, p^*_{N-1})^\top, 0^{N-1})$, such that $\zeta^s_{|O}$ is a continuously differentiable function, denoted by z^s, so $z^s : O \to \mathbb{R}^{N-1}$. Therefore, the matrix of partial derivatives, $\partial_a z^s((p^*_1, \ldots, p^*_{N-1})^\top, 0^{N-1})$ is well defined. The following definition is given in Laroque (1978), Definition 5.1, page 1135.

Definition 9.3.1 (Regular Walrasian equilibrium)
A Walrasian equilibrium (p^*, x^*) with $p^*_N = 1$ of the economy $\mathcal{E} = ((X^i, \preceq^i, \omega^i)_{i \in I_M})$ is regular *if for every sign vector $s \in \mathbb{S}^{N-1}$ with $I^0(s) = \emptyset$ the matrix of partial derivatives $\partial_a z^s((p^*_1, \ldots, p^*_{N-1})^\top, 0^{N-1})$ is invertible.*

The matrices of partial derivatives $\partial_a z^s((p^*_1, \ldots, p^*_{N-1})^\top, 0^{N-1})$ are very useful to analyse the structure of the set of fixed price equilibria in a neighbourhood of a Walrasian equilibrium. In Laroque (1981), Theorem 1, page 116, it is shown that if $(X^i, u^i, \omega^i)_{i \in I_M}, (\widetilde{l}, \widetilde{L})$ satisfies Assumptions A1-A4 and (p^*, x^*) with $p_N^* = 1$ is a regular Walrasian equilibrium of the economy $\mathcal{E}$ such that, for every $j \in I_{N-1}$, $\#\underline{I}_j(x^*) = \#\overline{I}_j(x^*) = 1$, while the determinants of the matrices $\partial_a z^s((p_1^*, \ldots, p_{N-1}^*)^\top, 0^{N-1})$ are of the same sign for every $s \in \mathbb{S}^{N-1}$ with $I^0(s) = \emptyset$, then (p^*, x^*) has locally well defined comparative statics. Using this result it is easily shown that the set $\mathcal{U}$ is non-empty. The following result states another important fact for regular Walrasian equilibria. Notice that a Walrasian equilibrium (p^*, x^*) with $p_N^* = 1$ of the economy $\mathcal{E}$ is said to be *locally unique* if there exists a set that is open in $\mathbb{R}^N \times \mathbb{R}^{MN}$ and that contains (p^*, x^*), but does not contain any other Walrasian equilibrium $(\overline{p}^*, \overline{x}^*)$ with $\overline{p}_N^* = 1$ of $\mathcal{E}$.

Theorem 9.3.2
Let the economy $\mathcal{E} = ((X^i, u^i, \omega^i)_{i \in I_M}, (\widetilde{l}, \widetilde{L}))$ satisfy Assumptions A1-A4, let (u, ω) be in $\mathcal{U}$, and let (p^*, x^*) with $p_N^* = 1$ be a locally unique, regular Walrasian equilibrium of the economy $\mathcal{E}$ such that, for every $j \in I_{N-1}$, $\#\underline{I}_j(x^*) = \#\overline{I}_j(x^*) = 1$. Then, for every $(p, p) \in \underline{P}$, there exists $x(p) \in \widetilde{E}^{DA}(p, p)$ such that for every $i \in I_M$ the function $\widehat{v}^i : \mathbb{R}_+^{N-1} \to (0, 1)$, defined by associating with every $(p_1, \ldots, p_{N-1})^\top \in \mathbb{R}_+^{N-1}$ the element

$$\widehat{v}^i(p_1, \ldots, p_{N-1}) = \widetilde{v}^i\left((p_1, \ldots, p_{N-1}, 1)^\top, (p_1, \ldots, p_{N-1}, 1)^\top, x((p_1, \ldots, p_{N-1}, 1)^\top)\right),$$

satisfies that $\widehat{v}^i(p_1^*, \ldots, p_{N-1}^*) = u^i(x^{*i})$ and $\partial \widehat{v}^i(p_1^*, \ldots, p_{N-1}^*)$ exists. Moreover, for every $i \in I_M$,

$$\partial_{p_j} \widehat{v}^i(p_1^*, \ldots, p_{N-1}^*) = -\partial_{x_N} u^i(x^{*i}) \left(x_j^{*i} - \omega_j^i\right), \; \forall j \in I_{N-1}.$$

See Laroque (1978), Proposition 7.1, page 1144.

The following three results show that the conditions given in Theorem 9.3.2 are very weak, in the sense that they are satisfied for a typical economy in $\mathcal{U}$. Thus, for a typical economy satisfying the Assumptions A1-A4, every Walrasian equilibrium (p^*, x^*) with $p_N^* = 1$ is regular and, for every $j \in I_{N-1}$, $\#\underline{I}_j(x^*) = \#\overline{I}_j(x^*) = 1$.

The following result shows that, generically, an economy is regular.

Theorem 9.3.3
Let $(X^i)_{i \in I_M}, (\widetilde{l}, \widetilde{L})$ satisfy Assumptions A1 and A4. Then there exists an open

and dense set $\mathcal{U}^1$ in $U \times \Omega$ such that for every $(u, \omega) \in \mathcal{U}^1$ every Walrasian equilibrium (p^*, x^*) with $p_N^* = 1$ of the economy $\mathcal{E} = ((X^i, u^i, \omega^i)_{i \in I_M})$ is regular.
See Wiesmeth (1979), Theorem, page 25.

The following result shows that a typical economy has a finite number of Walrasian equilibria (p^*, x^*) with $p_N^* = 1$, so every Walrasian equilibrium of a typical economy is locally unique. The finiteness of the number of Walrasian equilibria of a typical economy was first shown in Debreu (1970). Debreu (1970) gives a result with the demand functions of the consumers as primitive concepts. Theorem 3.11.1, Corollary 9.2.2, and Theorem 9.2.5 guarantee that the assumptions made by Debreu are implied by the assumptions made in Theorem 9.3.4.

Theorem 9.3.4
Let $(X^i, u^i)_{i \in I_M}$ satisfy Assumptions A1-A2. Then there exists a set Ω^1 open in Ω such that $\Omega \setminus \Omega^1$ has Lebesgue measure zero and for every $\omega \in \Omega^1$ the number of Walrasian equilibria (p^*, x^*) with $p_N^* = 1$ of the economy $\mathcal{E} = ((X^i, u^i, \omega^i)_{i \in I_M})$ is finite. Moreover, for every $\overline{\omega} \in \Omega^1$, there exists a set O that is open in Ω and contains $\overline{\omega}$, and there exist continuous functions $f^k : O \to \mathbb{R}^N_{++} \times X$, $\forall k \in I_{k(\overline{\omega})}$, for some $k(\overline{\omega}) \in \mathbb{N}$, such that, for every $\omega \in O$, $f^1(\omega), \ldots, f^{k(\overline{\omega})}(\omega)$ are all different Walrasian equilibria $(p(\omega, k), x(\omega, k))_{k \in I_{k(\overline{\omega})}}$ with $p(\omega, k)_N = 1$, $\forall k \in I_{k(\overline{\omega})}$, of the economy $\mathcal{E} = ((X^i, u^i, \omega^i)_{i \in I_M})$.
See Debreu (1970), Theorem, page 388, and Remark, page 390.

The following extension of Theorem 9.3.4 is given in Smale (1974).

Theorem 9.3.5
Let $(X^i)_{i \in I_M}$ satisfy Assumption A1. Then there exists an open and dense set $\mathcal{U}^2$ in $U \times \Omega$ such that for every $(u, \omega) \in \mathcal{U}^2$ the number of Walrasian equilibria (p^*, x^*) with $p_N^* = 1$ of the economy $\mathcal{E} = ((X^i, u^i, \omega^i)_{i \in I_M})$ is finite. Moreover, for every $(\overline{u}, \overline{\omega}) \in \mathcal{U}^2$, there exists a set $\mathcal{O}$ that is open in $U \times \Omega$ and contains $(\overline{u}, \overline{\omega})$, and there exist continuous functions $f^k : \mathcal{O} \to \mathbb{R}^N_{++} \times X$, $\forall k \in I_{k(\overline{u}, \overline{\omega})}$, for some $k(\overline{u}, \overline{\omega}) \in \mathbb{N}$, such that, for every $(u, \omega) \in \mathcal{O}$, $f^1(u, \omega), \ldots, f^{k(u,\omega)}(u, \omega)$ are all the different Walrasian equilibria $(p(u, \omega, k), x(u, \omega, k))_{k \in I_{k(\overline{u}, \overline{\omega})}}$ satisfying $p(u, \omega, k)_N = 1$, $\forall k \in I_{k(\overline{u}, \overline{\omega})}$, of the economy $\mathcal{E} = ((X^i, u^i, \omega^i)_{i \in I_M})$.
See Smale (1974), Theorem 1, page 3, and Proposition 4, page 7.

The following theorem states that in every Walrasian equilibrium of a typical economy it holds that in every market there is exactly one consumer having the minimal and exactly one consumer having the maximal excess demand in the sense as mentioned previously. A similar result is shown in Laroque (1978) for the uniform rationing system.

Theorem 9.3.6
Let $(X^i, u^i)_{i \in I_M}, (\tilde{l}, \tilde{L})$ satisfy Assumptions A1-A2 and A4. Then there exists a subset Ω^2 of Ω such that $\Omega \setminus \Omega^2$ has Lebesgue measure zero and, for every $\omega \in \Omega^2$, for every Walrasian equilibrium (p^*, x^*) with $p^*_N = 1$ of the economy $\mathcal{E} = ((X^i, u^i, \omega^i)_{i \in I_M})$, for every $j \in I_{N-1}$, $\#\underline{I}_j(x^*) = \#\overline{I}_j(x^*) = 1$.

Proof
If $M = 1$, then the proof is trivial, so assume $M \geq 2$ for the remainder of the proof. It is easily seen that Assumption A4 guarantees that, for every $\omega \in \Omega$, for every Walrasian equilibrium (p^*, x^*) with $p^*_N = 1$ of the economy $\mathcal{E} = ((X^i, u^i, \omega^i)_{i \in I_M})$, $\#\underline{I}_j(x^*) \geq 1$, $\forall j \in I_{N-1}$, and $\#\overline{I}_j(x^*) \geq 1$, $\forall j \in I_{N-1}$. Moreover, using Theorem 9.2.5, it follows from Theorem 3.11.1 that every Walrasian equilibrium price system is strictly positive. Let some $j' \in I_{N-1}, \overline{\omega} \in \Omega$, and $(p', \overline{x}) \in \mathbb{R}^N_{++} \times X$ with $p'_N = 1$ be given. Using Theorem 2.9.7 it follows that if $(p', \overline{x})$ is a Walrasian equilibrium of the economy $\mathcal{E} = ((X^i, u^i, \overline{\omega}^i)_{i \in I_M})$ and $\#\underline{I}_{j'}(\overline{x}) > 1$, then there exists $i^1, i^2 \in I_M$ with $i^1 \neq i^2$, $\overline{\lambda}^i \in \mathbb{R}$, $\forall i \in I_M$, and $\overline{q}_{j'} \in \mathbb{R}_+$ such that

$$\partial_{x^i} u^i(\overline{x}^i)^\top - \overline{\lambda}^i(p'_1,\ldots,p'_{N-1},1)^\top = 0^N, \quad \forall i \in I_M, \tag{9.1}$$

$$(p'_1,\ldots,p'_{N-1},1)\overline{x}^i - (p'_1,\ldots,p'_{N-1},1)\overline{\omega}^i = 0, \quad \forall i \in I_M, \tag{9.2}$$

$$\textstyle\sum_{i \in I_M} \overline{x}^i_j - \sum_{i \in I_M} \overline{\omega}^i_j = 0, \quad \forall j \in I_{N-1}, \tag{9.3}$$

$$\overline{x}^i_{j'} - \overline{\omega}^i_{j'} - \tilde{l}^i_{j'}(\overline{q}) = 0, \quad \forall i \in \{i^1, i^2\}, \tag{9.4}$$

with $\overline{q}_1, \ldots, \overline{q}_{j'-1}, \overline{q}_{j'+1}, \ldots, \overline{q}_N$ arbitrarily chosen elements of $\mathbb{R}_+$. Notice that in (9.3) the condition that in the market for the numeraire commodity the total excess demand is equal to zero is not specified. This condition is implied by the equations in (9.2) and (9.3).
Since the function $\tilde{l}$ is assumed to be continuously differentiable and $\partial_{q_{j'}} \tilde{l}_{j'}(\overline{q}) \neq 0^M$, $\forall \overline{q} \in \mathbb{R}^N_+$, there exists a continuously differentiable extension of $\tilde{l}$, also denoted by $\tilde{l}$, satisfying $\partial_{q_{j'}} \tilde{l}_{j'}(\overline{q}) \neq 0^M$ when $\overline{q}_{j'} \in (-\varepsilon, \rightarrow)$ and $\overline{q}_j \in \mathbb{R}_+$, $\forall j \in I_N \setminus \{j'\}$. The function

$$\psi : X \times \mathbb{R}^M \times \mathbb{R}^{N-1}_{++} \times \Omega \times (-\varepsilon, \rightarrow) \rightarrow \mathbb{R}^{MN+M+N+1}$$

is defined such that, for every $(x, \lambda, (p_1,\ldots,p_{N-1})^\top, \omega, q_{j'}) \in X \times \mathbb{R}^M \times \mathbb{R}^{N-1}_{++} \times \Omega \times (-\varepsilon, \rightarrow)$, $\psi(x, \lambda, (p_1,\ldots,p_{N-1})^\top, \omega, q_{j'})$ is given by the left-hand side of (9.1)-

(9.4). For every $\omega \in \Omega$, the function

$$\psi^{\omega} : X \times \mathbb{R}^{M} \times \mathbb{R}^{N-1}_{++} \times (-\varepsilon, \rightarrow) \rightarrow \mathbb{R}^{MN+M+N+1}$$

is defined by associating to $(x, \lambda, (p_1,\ldots, p_{N-1})^{\top}, q_{j'}) \in X \times \mathbb{R}^{M} \times \mathbb{R}^{N-1}_{++} \times (-\varepsilon, \rightarrow)$ the element $\psi^{\omega}(x, \lambda, (p_1,\ldots, p_{N-1})^{\top}, q_{j'}) = \psi(x, \lambda, (p_1,\ldots, p_{N-1})^{\top}, \omega, q_{j'})$.
Let $\overline{\xi} = (\overline{x}, \overline{\lambda}, (p'_1,\ldots, p'_{N-1})^{\top}, \overline{\omega}, \overline{q}_{j'}) \in X \times \mathbb{R}^{M} \times \mathbb{R}^{N-1}_{++} \times \Omega \times (-\varepsilon, \rightarrow)$ be such that $\psi(\overline{\xi}) = 0^{MN+M+N+1}$. The matrix of partial derivatives of ψ evaluated at $\overline{\xi}$ is denoted by $\overline{M}$ and is given in Table 9.3.1. Again, $\overline{q}_1, \ldots, \overline{q}_{j'-1}, \overline{q}_{j'+1}, \ldots, \overline{q}_N$

MN	M	$N-1$	MN	1	
$\partial^2_{x^1 x^1} u^1(\overline{x}^1)$ 0 0 $\ddots$ $\partial^2_{x^M x^M} u^M(\overline{x}^M)$	$\begin{pmatrix} -p'_1 \\ \vdots \\ -p'_{N-1} \\ -1 \end{pmatrix}$ 0 0 $\ddots$ $\begin{pmatrix} -p'_1 \\ \vdots \\ -p'_{N-1} \\ -1 \end{pmatrix}$	$-\overline{\lambda}^1 I^{N-1}$ $0^{N-1\top}$ $\vdots$ $-\overline{\lambda}^M I^{N-1}$ $0^{N-1\top}$	$0^{MN \times MN}$	0^{MN}	MN
$(p'_j)_{j \in I_{N-1}}\ 1$ 0 0 $\ddots$ $(p'_j)_{j \in I_{N-1}}\ 1$	$0^{M \times M}$	$(\overline{x}^1_j - \overline{\omega}^1_j)_{j \in I_{N-1}}$ $\vdots$ $(\overline{x}^M_j - \overline{\omega}^M_j)_{j \in I_{N-1}}$	$(-p'_j)_{j \in I_{N-1}}\ -1$ 0 0 $\ddots$ $(-p'_j)_{j \in I_{N-1}}\ -1$	0^{M}	M
$I^{N-1}\ 0^{N-1} \ \ldots \ I^{N-1}\ 0^{N-1}$	$0^{(N-1) \times M}$	$0^{(N-1) \times (N-1)}$	$-I^{N-1}\ 0^{N-1} \ \ldots \ -I^{N-1}\ 0^{N-1}$	0^{N-1}	$N-1$
$e^{MN}((i^1 - 1)N + j')^{\top}$	$0^{M\top}$	$0^{N-1\top}$	$-e^{MN}((i^1 - 1)N + j')^{\top}$	$-\partial_{q_{j'}} \widetilde{l}^{i^1}_{j'}(\overline{q})$	1
$e^{MN}((i^2 - 1)N + j')^{\top}$	$0^{M\top}$	$0^{N-1\top}$	$-e^{MN}((i^2 - 1)N + j')^{\top}$	$-\partial_{q_{j'}} \widetilde{l}^{i^2}_{j'}(\overline{q})$	1
MN	M	$N-1$	MN	1	

Table 9.3.1. The matrix $\overline{M}$.

are arbitrarily chosen elements of $\mathbb{R}_{+}$. It is shown that the matrix $\overline{M}$ has rank $MN + M + N + 1$. Let $y \in \mathbb{R}^{MN+M+N+1}$ be such that $y^{\top}\overline{M} = 0^{2MN+M+N^{\top}}$. Then, $y^{\top}\partial_{\omega^i_N}\psi(\overline{\xi}) = 0$, $\forall i \in I_M$, implies

$$y_{MN+i} = 0, \ \forall i \in I_M. \tag{9.5}$$

Moreover, (9.5) and $y^{\top}\partial_{\omega^1_j}\psi(\overline{\xi}) = 0$, $\forall j \in I_{N-1} \setminus \{j'\}$, implies

$$y_{MN+M+j} = 0, \ \forall j \in I_{N-1} \setminus \{j'\}. \tag{9.6}$$

From (9.5) and (9.6) it follows that

$$y^\top \partial_{\omega^{i^1}_{j'}} \psi(\overline{\xi}) = -y_{MN+M+j'} - y_{MN+M+N} = 0, \tag{9.7}$$

$$y^\top \partial_{\omega^{i^2}_{j'}} \psi(\overline{\xi}) = -y_{MN+M+j'} - y_{MN+M+N+1} = 0, \tag{9.8}$$

$$y^\top \partial_{\omega^{i}_{j'}} \psi(\overline{\xi}) = -y_{MN+M+j'} = 0, \ \forall i \in I_M \setminus \{i^1, i^2\}, \tag{9.9}$$

$$y^\top \partial_{q_{j'}} \psi(\overline{\xi}) = -\partial_{q_{j'}} \widetilde{l}^{i^1}_{j'}(\overline{q}) y_{MN+M+N} - \partial_{q_{j'}} \widetilde{l}^{i^2}_{j'}(\overline{q}) y_{MN+M+N+1} = 0. \tag{9.10}$$

If $M \geq 3$, then (9.9) implies $y_{MN+M+j'} = 0$, so then it follows from (9.7) and (9.8) that $y_{MN+M+N} = y_{MN+M+N+1} = 0$. If $M = 2$, then (9.7) and (9.8) implies $y_{MN+M+N} = y_{MN+M+N+1} = -y_{MN+M+j'}$. Then it follows from (9.10) that

$$\left(\partial_{q_{j'}} \widetilde{l}^{i^1}_{j'}(\overline{q}) + \partial_{q_{j'}} \widetilde{l}^{i^2}_{j'}(\overline{q})\right) y_{MN+M+j'} = 0,$$

so $y_{MN+M+j'} = 0$ since $\partial_{q_{j'}} \widetilde{l}_{j'}(\overline{q}) \neq (0,0)$ by Assumption A4. Therefore,

$$y_{MN+M+j'} = 0, \ y_{MN+M+N} = 0, \text{ and } y_{MN+M+N+1} = 0. \tag{9.11}$$

Using the non-zero Gaussian curvature of $\preceq^i$, $\forall i \in I_M$, and Theorem 3.6.5 it follows that

$$\det\left(\begin{bmatrix} \partial^2_{x^i x^i} u^i(\overline{x}^i) & \partial_{x^i} u^i(\overline{x}^i)^\top \\ \partial_{x^i} u^i(\overline{x}^i) & 0 \end{bmatrix}\right) \neq 0, \ \forall i \in I_M.$$

So, the first N rows of this matrix are independent. It follows that the N rows of the matrix

$$\begin{bmatrix} \partial^2_{x^i x^i} u^i(\overline{x}^i) & (-p'_1, \ldots, -p'_{N-1}, -1)^\top \end{bmatrix}$$

are independent, since $\partial_{x^i} u^i(\overline{x}^i) = \overline{\lambda}^i (p'_1, \ldots, p'_{N-1}, 1)$, $\forall i \in I_M$. Since, by (9.5), (9.6), and (9.11),

$$y^\top \partial_{x^i} \psi(\overline{\xi}) = \sum_{j \in I_N} \partial_{x^i} \psi_{(i-1)N+j}(\overline{\xi}) y_{(i-1)N+j} = 0^{N^\top}, \ \forall i \in I_M,$$

it follows that, for every $i \in I_M$,

$$y_{(i-1)N+j} = 0, \ \forall j \in I_N.$$

Therefore, $y = 0^{MN+M+N+1}$, so $\overline{M}$ has rank $MN+M+N+1$, and ψ intersects $\{0^{MN+M+N+1}\}$ transversally, $\psi \pitchfork \{0^{MN+M+N+1}\}$. Let the set $\overline{\Omega}_{j'}$ be defined by

$$\overline{\Omega}_{j'} = \left\{\omega \in \Omega \mid \psi^\omega \pitchfork \{0^{MN+M+N+1}\}\right\}.$$

Since $X \times \mathbb{R}^M \times \mathbb{R}^{N-1}_{++} \times \Omega \times (-\varepsilon, \rightarrow)$ is an $(2MN+M+N)$-dimensional C^∞ manifold, $\mathbb{R}^{MN+M+N+1}$ is an $(MN+M+N+1)$-dimensional C^∞ manifold, $0^{MN+M+N+1}$ is a 0-dimensional C^∞ manifold, and $\psi \in C^1(X \times \mathbb{R}^M \times \mathbb{R}^{N-1}_{++} \times \Omega \times (-\varepsilon, \rightarrow), \mathbb{R}^{MN+M+N+1})$, it follows from the transversality theorem, Theorem 2.10.18, that the set $\Omega \setminus \overline{\Omega}_{j'}$ has Lebesgue measure zero in Ω. Since Ω is an MN-dimensional C^∞ manifold, being a subset of $\mathbb{R}^{MN}$, it follows that the set $\Omega \setminus \overline{\Omega}_{j'}$ has Lebesgue measure zero, see the remark below Theorem 2.10.17. For every $\omega \in \overline{\Omega}_{j'}$, ψ^ω is a function from an $(MN+M+N)$-dimensional C^∞ manifold into an $(MN+M+N+1)$-dimensional C^∞ manifold, $\{0^{MN+M+N+1}\}$ is a 0-dimensional C^∞ manifold, $\psi^\omega \in C^1(X \times \mathbb{R}^M \times \mathbb{R}^{N-1}_{++} \times (-\varepsilon, \rightarrow), \mathbb{R}^{MN+M+N+1})$, and $\psi^\omega \pitchfork \{0^{MN+M+N+1}\}$, so $\psi^{\omega^{-1}}(\{0^{MN+N+M+1}\}) = \emptyset$ by Theorem 2.10.16. Hence, the set of initial endowments ω of Ω such that there exists a Walrasian equilibrium (p^*, x^*) with $p^*_N = 1$ and $\#\underline{I}_{j'}(x^*) > 1$ of the economy $\mathcal{E} = ((X^i, u^i, \omega^i)_{i \in I_M})$ has Lebesgue measure zero. Similarly, it can be shown the set of initial endowments ω of Ω such that there exists a Walrasian equilibrium (p^*, x^*) with $p^*_N = 1$ and $\#\overline{I}_{j'}(x^*) > 1$ of the economy $\mathcal{E} = ((X^i, u^i, \omega^i)_{i \in I_M})$ has Lebesgue measure zero. Since a finite union of sets with Lebesgue measure zero has Lebesgue measure zero, it follows that, for every Walrasian equilibrium (p^*, x^*) with $p^*_N = 1$ of the economy $\mathcal{E} = ((X^i, u^i, \omega^i)_{i \in I_M})$, for every $j \in I_{N-1}$, $\#\underline{I}_j(x^*) = \#\overline{I}_j(x^*) = 1$, except for a set of initial endowments ω of Ω having Lebesgue measure zero. Q.E.D.

The results of Theorems 9.3.3, 9.3.5, and 9.3.6 yield the following theorem.

Theorem 9.3.7
Let $(X^i)_{i \in I_M}$, $(\tilde{l}, \tilde{L})$ satisfy Assumptions A1 and A4. Then there exists an open and dense set $\mathcal{U}^3$ in $U \times \Omega$ such that for every $(u, \omega) \in \mathcal{U}^3$ every Walrasian equilibrium (p^*, x^*) with $p^*_N = 1$ of the economy $\mathcal{E} = ((X^i, u^i, \omega^i)_{i \in I_M})$ is locally unique and regular, while, for every $j \in I_{N-1}$, $\#\underline{I}_j(x^*) = \#\overline{I}_j(x^*) = 1$. Moreover, for every $(\overline{u}, \overline{\omega}) \in \mathcal{U}^3$, there exists a set $\mathcal{O}$ that is open in $U \times \Omega$ and that contains $(\overline{u}, \overline{\omega})$, and there exist continuous functions $f^k : \mathcal{O} \rightarrow \mathbb{R}^N_{++} \times X$, $\forall k \in I_{k(\overline{u}, \overline{\omega})}$, for some $k(\overline{u}, \overline{\omega}) \in \mathbb{N}$, such that, for every $(u, \omega) \in \mathcal{O}$, $f^1(u, \omega), \ldots, f^{k(\overline{u}, \overline{\omega})}(u, \omega)$ are all the different Walrasian equilibria $(p(u, \omega, k), x(u, \omega, k))_{k \in I_{k(\overline{u}, \overline{\omega})}}$ with $p(u, \omega, k)_N = 1$, $\forall k \in I_{k(\overline{u}, \overline{\omega})}$, of the economy $\mathcal{E} = ((X^i, u^i, \omega^i)_{i \in I_M})$.

Proof
Let $\mathcal{U}^1$ and $\mathcal{U}^2$ denote the sets given in Theorem 9.3.3 and Theorem 9.3.5, respectively. Clearly, the set $\mathcal{U}^1 \cap \mathcal{U}^2$ is open and dense in $U \times \Omega$ being an intersection of two open and dense sets. Let $\mathcal{U}^3$ be the set of utility functions and initial endowments (u, ω) of $\mathcal{U}^1 \cap \mathcal{U}^2$ such that, for every Walrasian equi-

librium (p^*, x^*) with $p_N^* = 1$ of the economy $\mathcal{E} = ((X^i, u^i, \omega^i)_{i \in I_M})$, for every $j \in I_{N-1}$, $\#\underline{I}_j(x^*) = \#\overline{I}_j(x^*) = 1$. It is shown that $\mathcal{U}^3$ is open and dense in $U \times \Omega$. Notice that this is trivial if $M = 1$, so assume $M \geq 2$ for the remainder of the proof.

For every $u \in U$, let Ω_u denote the set of initial endowments such that, for every Walrasian equilibrium (p^*, x^*) with $p_N^* = 1$ of the economy $\mathcal{E} = ((X^i, u^i, \omega^i)_{i \in I_M})$, for every $j \in I_{N-1}$, $\#\underline{I}_j(x^*) = \#\overline{I}_j(x^*) = 1$. Obviously, by Theorem 9.3.6, the set $\{(u, \omega) \in U \times \Omega \mid \omega \in \Omega_u\}$ is dense in $U \times \Omega$. Now $\mathcal{U}^1 \cap \mathcal{U}^2 \cap \{(u, \omega) \in U \times \Omega \mid \omega \in \Omega_u\}$ is dense in $U \times \Omega$ as an intersection of an open and dense set in $U \times \Omega$ and a dense set in $U \times \Omega$. Since $\mathcal{U}^1 \cap \mathcal{U}^2 \cap \{(u, \omega) \in U \times \Omega \mid \omega \in \Omega_u\} = \mathcal{U}^3$, it follows that $\mathcal{U}^3$ is dense in $U \times \Omega$. Let some $(\overline{u}, \overline{\omega}) \in \mathcal{U}^3$ be given and let $f^k : \mathcal{O} \to \mathbb{R}^N_{++} \times X$, $\forall k \in I_{k(\overline{u}, \overline{\omega})}$, be the continuous functions given in Theorem 9.3.5. For every $j \in I_{N-1}$, for every $k \in I_{k(\overline{u}, \overline{\omega})}$, denote the elements $\underline{q}(x(\overline{u}, \overline{\omega}, k))$ and $\overline{q}(x(\overline{u}, \overline{\omega}, k))$, and the sets $\underline{I}_j(x(\overline{u}, \overline{\omega}, k))$ and $\overline{I}_j(x(\overline{u}, \overline{\omega}, k))$, corresponding to the Walrasian equilibrium $f^k(\overline{u}, \overline{\omega}) = (p(\overline{u}, \overline{\omega}, k), x(\overline{u}, \overline{\omega}, k))$, by $\underline{q}^k$, $\overline{q}^k$, $\underline{I}_j^k$, and $\overline{I}_j^k$, respectively. Let the function $f^0 : \mathcal{O} \to \Omega$ be defined by $f^0(u, \omega) = \omega$, $\forall (u, \omega) \in \mathcal{O}$. Clearly, f^0 is continuous. For every $k \in I_{k(\overline{u}, \overline{\omega})}$, for every $j \in I_{N-1}$, let the function $g_j^k : \mathbb{R}^N_{++} \times X \times \Omega \to \mathbb{R}$ be defined by associating with every $(p, x, \omega) \in \mathbb{R}^N_{++} \times X \times \Omega$ the element

$$g_j^k(p, x, \omega) = \min\left(\left\{x_j^i - \omega_j^i - \widetilde{l}_j^i(\underline{q}^k) \,\middle|\, i \in I_M \setminus \underline{I}_j^k\right\} \cup \left\{\widetilde{L}_j^i(\overline{q}^k) - x_j^i + \omega_j^i \,\middle|\, i \in I_M \setminus \overline{I}_j^k\right\}\right).$$

Clearly, g_j^k is continuous. Let the function $h : \mathcal{O} \to \mathbb{R}$ be defined by

$$h(u, \omega) = \min\left(\left\{ g_j^k(f^k(u, \omega), f^0(u, \omega)) \,\middle|\, j \in I_{N-1},\ k \in I_{k(\overline{u}, \overline{\omega})}\right\}\right), \ \forall (u, \omega) \in \mathcal{O}.$$

Clearly, h is continuous. Notice that $h(\overline{u}, \overline{\omega}) > 0$. Since $(\widetilde{l}, \widetilde{L})$ is monotonic and continuous, there exists $\varepsilon \in \mathbb{R}_{++}$ such that, for every $(u, \omega) \in \mathcal{O}$ with $|h(\overline{u}, \overline{\omega}) - h(u, \omega)| < \varepsilon$, for every Walrasian equilibrium (p^*, x^*) with $p_N^* = 1$ of the economy $\mathcal{E} = ((X^i, u^i, \omega^i)_{i \in I_M})$, for every $j \in I_{N-1}$, $\#\underline{I}_j(x^*) = \#\overline{I}_j(x^*) = 1$. The set $h^{-1}((h(\overline{u}, \overline{\omega}) - \varepsilon, h(\overline{u}, \overline{\omega}) + \varepsilon))$ is open in $\mathcal{O}$ by the continuity of h, hence also open in $U \times \Omega$, and contains $(\overline{u}, \overline{\omega})$. Therefore, $\mathcal{U}^3$ is open in $U \times \Omega$.
Q.E.D.

For the remainder of this section, let $(X^i, u^i, \omega^i)_{i \in I_M}$, $(\widetilde{l}, \widetilde{L})$, $((\pi^{ik})_{i \in I_M})_{k \in I_2}$ be given such that Assumptions A1-A4 and A6 are satisfied and (u, ω) is an element of the set $\mathcal{U} \cap \mathcal{U}^3$ where $\mathcal{U}^3$ is given in Theorem 9.3.7.

Let a Walrasian equilibrium (p^*, x^*) with $p_N^* = 1$ of $\mathcal{E} = ((X^i, u^i, \omega^i)_{i \in I_M})$ be given. From Theorem 9.3.7 it follows that (p^*, x^*) is a locally unique and regular Walrasian equilibrium of the economy $\mathcal{E}$, while, for every $j \in I_{N-1}$, $\#\underline{I}_j(x^*) = \#\overline{I}_j(x^*) = 1$. For every price system $p \in \underline{\overline{P}}$ that is close to p^* there exists a uniquely determined Drèze equilibrium of the economy $\widetilde{\mathcal{E}}(p,p)$ that is close to (p^*, x^*). This suggests a very appealing alternative model for the competition of votes between the political candidates. Consider the Walrasian equilibrium (p^*, x^*) with $p_N^* = 1$ of the economy $\mathcal{E}$ as the *status quo* of the economy. The political candidates can choose either a direction of change with respect to the status quo or to stay at the status quo. If a political candidate chooses a specific direction of change, then it is assumed that the uniquely determined Drèze equilibrium specified in Theorem 9.3.2 that is close to the Walrasian equilibrium results. So, the political candidates are no longer assumed to choose a specific Drèze equilibrium, but are restricted to choose between *local options.* Moreover, from Theorem 9.3.2 it follows that the change in utility of the consumers is uniquely determined if a political candidate chooses a specific direction of change. It is assumed that the political candidates maximize their expected plurality in the elections, or, more precisely, the political candidates choose a direction of change affecting their marginal expected plurality optimally. Notice that this way of modelling the political system captures some interesting real world phenomena. First of all, the cost of acquiring information usually is very high for the political candidates when it concerns actions far removed from the status quo. Moreover, institutional reasons and commitments made in the past often require the political candidates to stay near the status quo. Finally, the political candidates need only bother about the price regulations to implement, they no longer need to specify the resulting Drèze equilibrium if there is more than one.

Let a Walrasian equilibrium (p^*, x^*) with $p_N^* = 1$ of the economy $\mathcal{E}$ be the status quo. The *set of admissible actions* $\widetilde{\mathcal{A}}^k$ of a political political candidate $k \in I_2$ is given by a subset of the set $\widetilde{\mathcal{A}}$, defined by

$$\widetilde{\mathcal{A}} = \{\widetilde{p} \in \mathbb{R}^{N-1} \mid \|\widetilde{p}\|_2 = 1\} \cup \{0^{N-1}\}.$$

The action $\widetilde{p}^k \in \widetilde{\mathcal{A}}^k$ of a political candidate $k \in I_2$ corresponds to a change of $(p_1^*, \dots, p_{N-1}^*)^\top$ in the direction $\widetilde{p}^k$. If $\widetilde{p}^k = 0^{N-1}$, then political candidate $k \in I_2$ chooses to stay at the status quo (p^*, x^*).

A specification of the economy together with voting functions and sets of admissible actions of the political candidates constitutes the *political economic system,* denoted by $\overline{\mathcal{E}}$, so

$$\overline{\mathcal{E}} = ((X^i, u^i, \omega^i)_{i \in I_M}, (\widetilde{l}, \widetilde{L}), (\widetilde{\mathcal{A}}^k, (\pi^{ik})_{i \in I_M})_{k \in I_2}).$$

For the main results, the following very weak assumption is made.

A8. For every political candidate $k \in I_2$, the set of admissible actions $\widetilde{\mathcal{A}}^k$ is non-empty, closed, and $\widetilde{\mathcal{A}}^k \subset \widetilde{\mathcal{A}}$.

Political candidates are assumed to maximize their political support, which is modelled by the expected number of votes they get. Since political candidates choose directions of motions, the appropriate pay-off function is determined by the associated change in the expected number of votes. Thus, the *pay-off function* $\widetilde{K}^1 : \widetilde{\mathcal{A}}^1 \times \widetilde{\mathcal{A}}^2 \rightarrow \mathbb{R}$ of political candidate 1 is defined by associating with every $(\widetilde{p}^1, \widetilde{p}^2) \in \widetilde{\mathcal{A}}^1 \times \widetilde{\mathcal{A}}^2$ the element

$$
\begin{aligned}
&\widetilde{K}^1(\widetilde{p}^1, \widetilde{p}^2)\\
&= \textstyle\sum_{i \in I_M} \partial_{v^1} \pi^{i1}\big(\widehat{v}^i(p_1^*, \ldots, p_{N-1}^*), \widehat{v}^i(p_1^*, \ldots, p_{N-1}^*)\big)\, \partial_{(p_1, \ldots, p_{N-1})^\top} \widehat{v}^i(p_1^*, \ldots, p_{N-1}^*)\widetilde{p}^1\\
&\quad - \textstyle\sum_{i \in I_M} \partial_{v^1} \pi^{i2}\big(\widehat{v}^i(p_1^*, \ldots, p_{N-1}^*), \widehat{v}^i(p_1^*, \ldots, p_{N-1}^*)\big)\, \partial_{(p_1, \ldots, p_{N-1})^\top} \widehat{v}^i(p_1^*, \ldots, p_{N-1}^*)\widetilde{p}^1\\
&\quad + \textstyle\sum_{i \in I_M} \partial_{v^2} \pi^{i1}\big(\widehat{v}^i(p_1^*, \ldots, p_{N-1}^*), \widehat{v}^i(p_1^*, \ldots, p_{N-1}^*)\big)\, \partial_{(p_1, \ldots, p_{N-1})^\top} \widehat{v}^i(p_1^*, \ldots, p_{N-1}^*)\widetilde{p}^2\\
&\quad - \textstyle\sum_{i \in I_M} \partial_{v^2} \pi^{i2}\big(\widehat{v}^i(p_1^*, \ldots, p_{N-1}^*), \widehat{v}^i(p_1^*, \ldots, p_{N-1}^*)\big)\, \partial_{(p_1, \ldots, p_{N-1})^\top} \widehat{v}^i(p_1^*, \ldots, p_{N-1}^*)\widetilde{p}^2.
\end{aligned}
$$

The pay-off function $\widetilde{K}^2 : \widetilde{\mathcal{A}}^1 \times \widetilde{\mathcal{A}}^2 \rightarrow \mathbb{R}$ of political candidate 2 is easily seen to be given by $\widetilde{K}^2 = -\widetilde{K}^1$. A directional political economic equilibrium is now defined as being a Nash equilibrium of the game with sets of admissible actions $\widetilde{\mathcal{A}}^1$ and $\widetilde{\mathcal{A}}^2$ and pay-off functions $\widetilde{K}^1$ and $\widetilde{K}^2$.

Definition 9.3.8 (Directional political economic equilibrium)
A directional political economic equilibrium *of the political economic system* $\overline{\mathcal{E}} = ((X^i,\ u^i, \omega^i)_{i \in I_M},\ (\widetilde{l}, \widetilde{L}),\ (\widetilde{\mathcal{A}}^k, (\pi^{ik})_{i \in I_M})_{k \in I_2})$ *with status quo the locally unique, regular Walrasian equilibrium* (p^*, x^*) *with* $p_N^* = 1$ *and* $\#\underline{I}_j(x^*) = \#\overline{I}_j(x^*) = 1$, $\forall j \in I_{N-1}$, *of the economy* $\mathcal{E} = ((X^i, u^i, \omega^i)_{i \in I_M})$, *is a Nash* equilibrium of the mixed extension of the *game* $\widetilde{\mathcal{G}} = (\widetilde{\mathcal{A}}^1, \widetilde{\mathcal{A}}^2, \widetilde{K}^1, \widetilde{K}^2)$.

Observe that in a directional political economic equilibrium, price regulations are endogenously determined. Moreover, if choosing to stay at the status quo is feasible, i.e. $0^{N-1} \in \widetilde{\mathcal{A}}^k$, then nothing precludes political candidates to stay at the status quo, a Walrasian equilibrium. If political candidates choose to move away from the status quo, then, since economies with locally unique Walrasian equilibria are considered, some consumers will become rationed on their supply or demand. So the model given in this section can be used to analyse whether political candidates have incentives to impose price regulations on the economy such that the Walrasian equilibrium is excluded. In this case rationing of consumers occurs. An obvious real world example are rigidities in wages, that lead to tensions on the labour market like unemployment, being rationing on the supply of labour of consumers.

Let a Walrasian equilibrium (p^*, x^*) with $p_N^* = 1$ of the economy $\mathcal{E}$ be the status quo. A closer look at the pay-off functions $\widetilde{K}^1$ and $\widetilde{K}^2$ shows that they have properties closely related to separability of voting functions as defined in Chapter 8. For every $k \in I_2$, the integer $k' \in I_2$ is taken such that $k' \neq k$, and the function $\widetilde{K}^{k+} : \widetilde{\mathcal{A}}^k \to \mathbb{R}$ is defined by associating with every $\widetilde{p}^k \in \widetilde{\mathcal{A}}^k$ the element

$$\begin{aligned}
&\widetilde{K}^{k+}(\widetilde{p}^k) \\
&\quad = \textstyle\sum_{i \in I_M} \partial_{v^k} \pi^{ik} \left(\widehat{v}^i(p_1^*, \dots, p_{N-1}^*), \widehat{v}^i(p_1^*, \dots, p_{N-1}^*)\right) \partial_{(p_1, \dots, p_{N-1})^\top} \widehat{v}^i(p_1^*, \dots, p_{N-1}^*) \widetilde{p}^k \\
&\qquad - \textstyle\sum_{i \in I_M} \partial_{v^k} \pi^{ik'} \left(\widehat{v}^i(p_1^*, \dots, p_{N-1}^*), \widehat{v}^i(p_1^*, \dots, p_{N-1}^*)\right) \partial_{(p_1, \dots, p_{N-1})^\top} \widehat{v}^i(p_1^*, \dots, p_{N-1}^*) \widetilde{p}^k.
\end{aligned}$$

Using the functions $\widetilde{K}^{1+}$ and $\widetilde{K}^{2+}$ the existence of a directional political economic equilibrium is shown in a similar way as in the proof of Theorem 8.4.9. Moreover, using these functions it is possible to give a nice characterization of such an equilibrium.

Theorem 9.3.9
Let the political economic system $\overline{\mathcal{E}} = ((X^i, u^i, \omega^i)_{i \in I_M}, (\widetilde{l}, \widetilde{L}), (\widetilde{\mathcal{A}}^k, (\pi^{ik})_{i \in I_M})_{k \in I_2})$ with status quo (p^*, x^*) satisfy Assumptions A1-A4, A6, and A8, where (u, ω) is an element of the set $\mathcal{U} \cap \mathcal{U}^3$ and (p^*, x^*) with $p_N^* = 1$ is a Walrasian equilibrium of the economy $\mathcal{E} = ((X^i, u^i, \omega^i)_{i \in I_M})$. Then there exists a directional political economic equilibrium in pure strategies of the political economic system $\overline{\mathcal{E}}$ with status quo (p^*, x^*). Moreover, $(\widetilde{p}^{*1}, \widetilde{p}^{*2}) \in \widetilde{\mathcal{A}}^1 \times \widetilde{\mathcal{A}}^2$ is a directional political economic equilibrium in pure strategies of the political economic system $\overline{\mathcal{E}}$ with status quo (p^*, x^*) if and only if

$$\widetilde{K}^{1+}(\widetilde{p}^{*1}) = \max\left(\left\{\widetilde{K}^{1+}(\widetilde{p}^1) \,\middle|\, \widetilde{p}^1 \in \widetilde{\mathcal{A}}^1\right\}\right) \quad \textit{and}$$
$$\widetilde{K}^{2+}(\widetilde{p}^{*2}) = \max\left(\left\{\widetilde{K}^{2+}(\widetilde{p}^2) \,\middle|\, \widetilde{p}^2 \in \widetilde{\mathcal{A}}^2\right\}\right).$$

Proof
For every $k \in I_2$, the set $\widetilde{\mathcal{A}}^k$ is compact and the function $\widetilde{K}^{k+}$ is continuous, so, by Theorem 2.3.14, there exists $\widetilde{p}^{*k} \in \widetilde{\mathcal{A}}^k$ such that

$$\widetilde{K}^{k+}(\widetilde{p}^{*k}) = \max\left(\left\{\widetilde{K}^{k+}(\widetilde{p}^k) \,\middle|\, \widetilde{p}^k \in \widetilde{\mathcal{A}}^k\right\}\right).$$

Clearly,

$$\begin{aligned}
\widetilde{K}^1(\widetilde{p}^{*1}, \widetilde{p}^{*2}) &= \widetilde{K}^{1+}(\widetilde{p}^{*1}) - \widetilde{K}^{2+}(\widetilde{p}^{*2}) \geq \widetilde{K}^{1+}(\widetilde{p}^1) - \widetilde{K}^{2+}(\widetilde{p}^{*2}) \\
&= \widetilde{K}^1(\widetilde{p}^1, \widetilde{p}^{*2}), \ \forall \widetilde{p}^1 \in \widetilde{\mathcal{A}}^1, \\
\widetilde{K}^2(\widetilde{p}^{*1}, \widetilde{p}^{*2}) &= \widetilde{K}^{2+}(\widetilde{p}^{*2}) - \widetilde{K}^{1+}(\widetilde{p}^{*1}) \geq \widetilde{K}^{2+}(\widetilde{p}^2) - \widetilde{K}^{1+}(\widetilde{p}^{*1}) \\
&= \widetilde{K}^2(\widetilde{p}^{*1}, \widetilde{p}^2), \ \forall \widetilde{p}^2 \in \widetilde{\mathcal{A}}^2.
\end{aligned}$$

So, $(\widetilde{p}^{*1}, \widetilde{p}^{*2})$ is a directional political economic equilibrium in pure strategies of the political economic system $\overline{\mathcal{E}}$ with status quo (p^*, x^*).

Let $(\widetilde{p}^{*1}, \widetilde{p}^{*2}) \in \widetilde{\mathcal{A}}^1 \times \widetilde{\mathcal{A}}^2$ be any political economic equilibrium in pure strategies of the economy $\overline{\mathcal{E}}$ with status quo (p^*, x^*). Then,

$$\begin{aligned}
\widetilde{K}^1(\widetilde{p}^{*1}, \widetilde{p}^{*2}) &= \widetilde{K}^{1+}(\widetilde{p}^{*1}) - \widetilde{K}^{2+}(\widetilde{p}^{*2}) \geq \widetilde{K}^1(\widetilde{p}^1, \widetilde{p}^{*2}) \\
&= \widetilde{K}^{1+}(\widetilde{p}^1) - \widetilde{K}^{2+}(\widetilde{p}^{*2}), \ \forall \widetilde{p}^1 \in \widetilde{\mathcal{A}}^1, \\
\widetilde{K}^2(\widetilde{p}^{*1}, \widetilde{p}^{*2}) &= \widetilde{K}^{2+}(\widetilde{p}^{*2}) - \widetilde{K}^{1+}(\widetilde{p}^{*1}) \geq \widetilde{K}^2(\widetilde{p}^{*1}, \widetilde{p}^2) \\
&= \widetilde{K}^{2+}(\widetilde{p}^2) - \widetilde{K}^{1+}(\widetilde{p}^{*1}), \ \forall \widetilde{p}^2 \in \widetilde{\mathcal{A}}^2.
\end{aligned}$$

So, $\widetilde{K}^{1+}(\widetilde{p}^{*1}) = \max(\{\widetilde{K}^{1+}(\widetilde{p}^1) \mid \widetilde{p}^1 \in \widetilde{\mathcal{A}}^1\})$ and $\widetilde{K}^{2+}(\widetilde{p}^{*2}) = \max(\{\widetilde{K}^{2+}(\widetilde{p}^2) \mid \widetilde{p}^2 \in \widetilde{\mathcal{A}}^2\})$. Q.E.D.

9.4 GENERICALLY CHOSEN PRICE REGULATIONS

The existence of a political economic equilibrium of the political economic system $\widehat{\mathcal{E}}$ has been shown in Chapter 8 and Section 9.2. In the example of Section 8.5 price regulations incompatible with the Walrasian equilibrium price system were chosen by the political candidates in the political economic equilibrium. The existence of a directional political economic equilibrium of the political economic system $\overline{\mathcal{E}}$ with status quo a Walrasian equilibrium has been shown in Section 9.3. In the example of Section 9.5 the political candidates choose directions of movement away from the Walrasian equilibrium price system in the directional political economic equilibrium. Nevertheless, it is not clear whether this is the typical case. To answer this question, the following assumption with respect to the model of Section 9.3 is made in the main results of this section.

A9. For every political candidate $k \in I_2$, $\widetilde{\mathcal{A}}^k = \widetilde{\mathcal{A}}$.

Making Assumption A9 and using Theorem 9.3.9 it is possible to show the even stronger result of Theorem 9.4.1, where the directional political economic equilibria in pure strategies of $\overline{\mathcal{E}}$ with status quo (p^*, x^*) are characterized. Since only arbitrarily small movements in prices are involved, Assumption A9 seems to be very reasonable.

Let $(X^i, u^i, \omega^i)_{i \in I_M}, (\widetilde{l}, \widetilde{L}), ((\pi^{ik})_{i \in I_M})_{k \in I_2}$ be given such that Assumptions A1-A4 and A6 are satisfied and (u, ω) is an element of the set $\mathcal{U} \cap \mathcal{U}^3$. Moreover, let a Walrasian equilibrium (p^*, x^*) with $p_N^* = 1$ of the economy $\mathcal{E} = ((X^i, u^i, \omega^i)_{i \in I_M})$ be given. For every $k \in I_2$, the integer $k' \in I_2$ is taken such that $k' \neq k$, and the vector $\overline{K}^k \in \mathbb{R}^{N-1}$ is defined by

$$\overline{K}^k = \left(\sum_{i \in I_M} \partial_{v^k} \pi^{ik}(\widehat{v}^i(p_1^*, \ldots, p_{N-1}^*), \widehat{v}^i(p_1^*, \ldots, p_{N-1}^*)) \partial_{(p_1, \ldots, p_{N-1})^\top} \widehat{v}^i(p_1^*, \ldots, p_{N-1}^*) \right.$$
$$\left. - \sum_{i \in I_M} \partial_{v^k} \pi^{ik'}(\widehat{v}^i(p_1^*, \ldots, p_{N-1}^*), \widehat{v}^i(p_1^*, \ldots, p_{N-1}^*)) \partial_{(p_1, \ldots, p_{N-1})^\top} \widehat{v}^i(p_1^*, \ldots, p_{N-1}^*) \right)^\top .$$

Theorem 9.4.1
Let the political economic system $\overline{\mathcal{E}} = ((X^i, u^i, \omega^i)_{i \in I_M}, (\widetilde{l}, \widetilde{L}), (\widetilde{\mathcal{A}}^k, (\pi^{ik})_{i \in I_M})_{k \in I_2})$ *with status quo* (p^*, x^*) *satisfy Assumptions A1-A4, A6, and A9, where* (u, ω) *is an element of the set* $\mathcal{U} \cap \mathcal{U}^3$ *and* (p^*, x^*) *with* $p_N^* = 1$ *is a Walrasian equilibrium of the economy* $\mathcal{E} = ((X^i, u^i, \omega^i)_{i \in I_M})$. *Let* $(\widetilde{p}^{*1}, \widetilde{p}^{*2})$ *be a directional political economic equilibrium of the political economic system* $\overline{\mathcal{E}}$ *with status quo* (p^*, x^*). *Then, for every* $k \in I_2$, *either* $\overline{K}^k = 0^{N-1}$, *or* $\overline{K}^k \neq 0^{N-1}$ *and* $\widetilde{p}^{*k} = \overline{K}^k / \|\overline{K}^k\|_2$.

Proof
From Theorem 9.3.9 it follows that

$$\widetilde{K}^{1+}(\widetilde{p}^{*1}) = \max \left(\left\{ \widetilde{K}^{1+}(\widetilde{p}^1) \,\middle|\, \widetilde{p}^1 \in \widetilde{\mathcal{A}}^1 \right\} \right),$$
$$\widetilde{K}^{2+}(\widetilde{p}^{*2}) = \max \left(\left\{ \widetilde{K}^{2+}(\widetilde{p}^2) \,\middle|\, \widetilde{p}^2 \in \widetilde{\mathcal{A}}^2 \right\} \right).$$

For every $k \in I_2$, since $\widetilde{K}^{k+}(\widetilde{p}^k) = \overline{K}^k \cdot \widetilde{p}^k$, $\forall \widetilde{p}^k \in \widetilde{\mathcal{A}}^k$, and since $\widetilde{\mathcal{A}}^k$ is the union of the unit sphere $\widetilde{B}^{N-2}(0^{N-1}, 1)$ and $\{0^{N-1}\}$, the theorem follows immediately.
Q.E.D.

If in Theorem 9.4.1 it holds that $\overline{K}^k = 0^{N-1}$ for a political candidate $k \in I_2$, then, given the action chosen by his opponent, every admissible action yields political candidate k the same pay-off. If both $\overline{K}^1 \neq 0^{N-1}$ and $\overline{K}^2 \neq 0^{N-1}$, then the directional political economic equilibrium is unique and both political candidates choose a direction of motion away from the status quo, i.e. both political candidates propose price regulations excluding the Walrasian equilibrium and generating rationing.

It could be the case that in a typical political economic equilibrium both political candidates propose a price regulation corresponding to the same Walrasian equilibrium or that in a typical directional political economic equilibrium both political candidates choose to stay at the Walrasian equilibrium, being the status quo. It is clear that it is always possible to construct examples where this happens. Moreover, since it is well-known that Drèze equilibria not corresponding to a Walrasian equilibrium are usually not Pareto efficient, it would not be completely surprising if this would turn out to be the case generically, or at least for a non-degenerate class of economies. Nevertheless, in this section it is shown that the situation in the example of Section 8.5 and in the example to be presented in Section 9.5 are typical cases. Moreover, it is shown that if the opponent of a political candidate chooses an action corresponding to a Walrasian equilibrium, then the generic case is that the action of the political candidate leading to the same Walrasian equilibrium can be improved upon by playing an action not corresponding to a Walrasian equilibrium. Similarly, it is shown that, generically, the political candidates propose directions of movement away from the status quo.

Consider the political economic system $\widehat{\mathcal{E}}$. Suppose political candidate 2 chooses an action $(p^*, p^*, x^*) \in \mathcal{A}^2$ corresponding to a Walrasian equilibrium of the economy $\mathcal{E}$. Then it is shown that only in degenerate cases the best response of political candidate 1 is also to choose the action (p^*, p^*, x^*). More precisely, it is shown that, generically, for every open set O in $\mathbb{R}^{N-1}_{++}$ containing $(p_1^*, \ldots, p_{N-1}^*)^\top$, there is an action $(p^1, p^1, x^1) \in \mathcal{A}^1$ with $(p_1^1, \ldots, p_{N-1}^1)^\top \in O$ such that (p^1, p^1, x^1) is a better response against (p^*, p^*, x^*) than the action (p^*, p^*, x^*) itself, where p^1 is not a Walrasian equilibrium price system. This means that, generically, proposing price regulations that exclude the Walrasian equilibrium price system is a better response against a certain Walrasian equilibrium than proposing this Walrasian equilibrium.

Consider the political economic system $\overline{\mathcal{E}}$ with status quo a Walrasian equilibrium (p^*, x^*) of the economy $\mathcal{E}$ with $p_N^* = 1$. Suppose political candidate 2 chooses the action $0^{N-1} \in \widetilde{\mathcal{A}}^2$, i.e. political candidate 2 proposes to stay at the status quo. Then it is shown that only in degenerate cases the best response of political candidate 1 is also choosing action 0^{N-1}. Even stronger, it is shown that, generically, $\overline{K}^1 \neq 0^{N-1}$. Using symmetry considerations it follows that, generically, $\overline{K}^2 \neq 0^{N-1}$. So, from Theorem 9.4.1 it follows that in a directional political economic equilibrium, generically, both political candidates choose to move away from the status quo.

Assumptions that have to be made are that there is at least one non-numeraire commodity, as is always assumed in this chapter, and that there are at least two consumers. Otherwise, every consumer keeps his initial endowments in every Walrasian or Drèze equilibrium. Hence, it is impossible to influence the voting decision of consumers by proposing price regulations. The set of all possible voting functions of a consumer $i \in I_M$ for political candidate 1 satisfying Assumption A7 is denoted by Π^i. Hence,

$$\Pi^i = \{\pi^{i1} \in C^2((0,1)\times(0,1),(0,1)) | \partial_{v^1}\pi^{i1}(\overline{v}^1,\overline{v}^2)>0, \forall(\overline{v}^1,\overline{v}^2)\in(0,1)\times(0,1)$$
$$\partial_{v^2}\pi^{i1}(\overline{v}^1,\overline{v}^2)<0, \forall(\overline{v}^1,\overline{v}^2)\in(0,1)\times(0,1)\}.$$

This set is given the topology induced by the C^1-topology. Notice that Π^i, $\forall i \in I_M$, is open in $C^2((0,1)\times(0,1),\mathbb{R})$. The set Π is defined by $\Pi = \prod_{i\in I_M} \Pi^i$ and is given the product topology. Notice that, for every $\pi \in \Pi$, $\pi = (\pi^{11},\ldots,\pi^{M1})$ with π^{i1} denoting the voting function of consumer $i \in I_M$. For some consumer $i \in I_M$, let $\pi^{i1} \in \Pi^i$ be given and let $\epsilon \in C^0((0,1)\times(0,1),\mathbb{R}_{++})$ be given. The set $V_{\pi^{i1},\epsilon}$ is defined by

$$\begin{aligned} V_{\pi^{i1},\epsilon} = \{ f \in C^2((0,1)\times(0,1),(0,1)) \mid \\ |\pi^{i1}(\overline{v}^1,\overline{v}^2) - f(\overline{v}^1,\overline{v}^2)| < \epsilon(\overline{v}^1,\overline{v}^2), \quad \forall(\overline{v}^1,\overline{v}^2)\in(0,1)\times(0,1), \\ |\partial_{v^1}\pi^{i1}(\overline{v}^1,\overline{v}^2) - \partial_{v^1}f(\overline{v}^1,\overline{v}^2)| < \epsilon(\overline{v}^1,\overline{v}^2), \forall(\overline{v}^1,\overline{v}^2)\in(0,1)\times(0,1), \\ |\partial_{v^2}\pi^{i1}(\overline{v}^1,\overline{v}^2) - \partial_{v^2}f(\overline{v}^1,\overline{v}^2)| < \epsilon(\overline{v}^1,\overline{v}^2), \forall(\overline{v}^1,\overline{v}^2)\in(0,1)\times(0,1)\}. \end{aligned}$$

Then $V_{\pi^{i1},\epsilon}$ belongs to the base for the C^1-topology on $C^2((0,1)\times(0,1),(0,1))$, see Definition 2.9.4.

Let the political economic system $\widehat{\mathcal{E}}$ be given. Let (p^*,x^*) with $p^*_N = 1$ and $\#\underline{I}_j(x^*) = \#\overline{I}_j(x^*) = 1$, $\forall j \in I_{N-1}$, be a locally unique, regular Walrasian equilibrium of the economy $\mathcal{E} = ((X^i,u^i,\omega^i)_{i\in I_M})$. Suppose political candidate 2 proposes (p^*,p^*,x^*). Then it holds that (p^*,p^*,x^*) is a best response for political candidate 1 if and only if

$$K^1((p^*,p^*,x^*),(p^*,p^*,x^*)) = \max_{(a^1,x^1)\in\mathcal{A}^1} K^1((a^1,x^1),(p^*,p^*,x^*)).$$

Theorems 2.9.7 and 9.3.2 imply that a necessary condition for (p^*,p^*,x^*) to be a best response of political candidate 1 is given by

$$\sum_{i\in I_M} \left(\partial_{v^1}\pi^{i1}\left(\widehat{v}^i(p^*_1,\ldots,p^*_{N-1}),\widehat{v}^i(p^*_1,\ldots,p^*_{N-1})\right)\partial_{(p_1,\ldots,p_{N-1})^\top}\widehat{v}^i(p^*_1,\ldots,p^*_{N-1})\right.$$
$$\left.-\partial_{v^1}\pi^{i2}(\widehat{v}^i(p^*_1,\ldots,p^*_{N-1}),\widehat{v}^i(p^*_1,\ldots,p^*_{N-1}))\partial_{(p_1,\ldots,p_{N-1})^\top}\widehat{v}^i(p^*_1,\ldots,p^*_{N-1})\right) = 0^{N-1^\top}. \tag{9.12}$$

From Theorem 9.4.1 and the remark made below it, it follows that (9.12) is a necessary and sufficient condition for 0^{N-1} to be a possible action of political candidate 1 in a directional political economic equilibrium of the political economic system $\overline{\mathcal{E}}$ with status quo (p^*,x^*). Using that $\pi^{i1}(v^1,v^2)+\pi^{i2}(v^1,v^2) = 1$,

$\forall (v^1, v^2) \in (0,1) \times (0,1)$, and using Theorem 9.3.2, it follows that (9.12) is equivalent to

$$-\sum_{i \in I_M} \partial_{v^1} \pi^{i1} \left(u^i(x^{*i}), u^i(x^{*i})\right) \partial_{x_N} u^i(x^{*i}) \left(x_j^{*i} - \omega_j^i\right) = 0, \forall j \in I_{N-1}. \quad (9.13)$$

Notice that the expression in (9.13) does not depend on π^{i2}, $\forall i \in I_M$. For the remainder of this section, the voting function π^{i1}, $\forall i \in I_M$, is therefore denoted by π^i. Observe that equation (9.13) also makes sense for economies that are not regular. In Theorem 9.4.4 it is shown that for a generic political economic system equation (9.13) does not hold. From this result it is easily obtained that equation (9.12) does not hold for a generic political economic system, the result of Theorem 9.4.5. Therefore, it follows as a corollary that the Walrasian equilibrium is not stable as a status quo of the political economic system.

Let $(X^i, u^i)_{i \in I_M}$ satisfy Assumptions A1-A2. Let the set Ω^1 be as in Theorem 9.3.4. For every $\omega \in \Omega^1$, let $k(\omega)$ be the number of Walrasian equilibria in the economy $\mathcal{E} = ((X^i, u^i, \omega^i)_{i \in I_M})$. By Theorem 9.3.4, for every $\overline{\omega} \in \Omega^1$, there exists an open set O containing $\overline{\omega}$ and which is such that, for every $\omega \in O$, $k(\omega) = k(\overline{\omega})$ and the vector of Walrasian equilibria $((p(\omega,1), x(\omega,1)), \ldots, (p(\omega, k(\overline{\omega})), x(\omega, k(\overline{\omega}))))$ depends in a continuous way on ω. The set $\mathcal{W}^1$ is defined by

$$\begin{aligned}\mathcal{W}^1 = \Big\{(\omega, \pi) \in \Omega^1 \times \Pi \,\Big|\, & \forall k \in I_{k(\omega)},\ \exists i^1, i^2 \in I_M, \\ & \partial_{v^1} \pi^{i^1} \left(u^{i^1}(x^{i^1}(\omega,k)), u^{i^1}(x^{i^1}(\omega,k))\right) \partial_{x_N} u^{i^1}(x^{i^1}(\omega,k)) \\ & \neq \partial_{v^1} \pi^{i^2} \left(u^{i^2}(x^{i^2}(\omega,k)), u^{i^2}(x^{i^2}(\omega,k))\right) \partial_{x_N} u^{i^2}(x^{i^2}(\omega,k))\Big\}.\end{aligned}$$

In Theorem 9.4.2 it is shown that $\mathcal{W}^1$ is open in $\Omega \times \Pi$ and in Theorem 9.4.3 that $\mathcal{W}^1$ is dense in $\Omega \times \Pi$.

Theorem 9.4.2
Let $(X^i, u^i)_{i \in I_M}$ satisfy Assumptions A1-A2 and let $M \in \mathbb{N} \setminus \{1\}$. Then the set $\mathcal{W}^1$ is open in $\Omega \times \Pi$.

Proof
Let some $i \in I_M$ be given. Let the function $g^i : \Pi^i \times (0,1) \times (0,1) \to \mathbb{R}_{++}$ be defined by

$$g^i(\overline{\pi}^i, \overline{v}^1, \overline{v}^2) = \partial_{v^1} \overline{\pi}^i(\overline{v}^1, \overline{v}^2),\ \forall (\overline{\pi}^i, \overline{v}^1, \overline{v}^2) \in \Pi^i \times (0,1) \times (0,1).$$

It is shown that g^i is continuous. Let O be an open set in $\mathbb{R}_{++}$ and let $(\widehat{\pi}^i, \widehat{v}^1, \widehat{v}^2) \in (g^i)^{-1}(O)$ be given. Let $\varepsilon \in \mathbb{R}_{++}$ satisfy $B^1(g^i(\widehat{\pi}^i, \widehat{v}^1, \widehat{v}^2), \varepsilon) \subset O$.

Let the function $\epsilon : (0,1) \times (0,1) \to \mathbb{R}_{++}$ be defined by

$$\epsilon(v^1, v^2) = \tfrac{1}{2}\varepsilon, \ \forall (v^1, v^2) \in (0,1) \times (0,1).$$

Since $\partial_{v^1} \widehat{\pi}^i : (0,1) \times (0,1) \to \mathbb{R}_{++}$ and $\partial_{v^2} \widehat{\pi}^i : (0,1) \times (0,1) \to -\mathbb{R}_{++}$ are continuous functions, there exists $\delta \in \mathbb{R}_{++}$ such that $(\overline{v}^1, \overline{v}^2) \in B^2((\widehat{v}^1, \widehat{v}^2)^\top, \delta)$ implies

$$\left\| \left(\partial_{(v^1,v^2)^\top} \widehat{\pi}^i(\overline{v}^1, \overline{v}^2) - \partial_{(v^1,v^2)^\top} \widehat{\pi}^i(\widehat{v}^1, \widehat{v}^2) \right)^\top \right\|_2 < \tfrac{1}{2}\varepsilon.$$

For every $(\overline{\pi}^i, \overline{v}^1, \overline{v}^2) \in V_{\widehat{\pi}^i,\epsilon} \times B^2((\widehat{v}^1, \widehat{v}^2)^\top, \delta)$ it holds that

$$\begin{aligned} &|\partial_{v^1} \overline{\pi}^i(\overline{v}^1, \overline{v}^2) - \partial_{v^1} \widehat{\pi}^i(\widehat{v}^1, \widehat{v}^2)| \\ &\quad \le |\partial_{v^1} \overline{\pi}^i(\overline{v}^1, \overline{v}^2) - \partial_{v^1} \widehat{\pi}^i(\overline{v}^1, \overline{v}^2)| + |\partial_{v^1} \widehat{\pi}^i(\overline{v}^1, \overline{v}^2) - \partial_{v^1} \widehat{\pi}^i(\widehat{v}^1, \widehat{v}^2)| \\ &\quad < \tfrac{1}{2}\varepsilon + \tfrac{1}{2}\varepsilon = \varepsilon, \end{aligned}$$

so $g^i(\overline{\pi}^i, \overline{v}^1, \overline{v}^2) \in B^1(g^i(\widehat{\pi}^i, \widehat{v}^1, \widehat{v}^2), \varepsilon) \subset O$. Hence, $(g^i)^{-1}(O)$ is open, concluding the proof that g^i is a continuous function.
Let some $\overline{\omega} \in \Omega^1$ be given. Let O be a set open in Ω^1, containing $\overline{\omega}$, and being such that $k(\omega) = k(\overline{\omega})$, $\forall \omega \in O$, while for every $k \in I_{k(\overline{\omega})}$ the function $f^{k,i} : O \to \mathbb{R}^N$, defined by

$$f^{k,i}(\omega) = x^i(\omega, k), \ \forall \omega \in O,$$

is continuous. Let the function $h : O \times \Pi \to \mathbb{R}^{k(\overline{\omega})M}$ be defined by associating with every $(\omega, \pi) \in O \times \Pi$ the element

$$\begin{aligned} h(\omega, \pi) = \Big(& g^1 \left(\pi^1, u^1(f^{1,1}(\omega)), u^1(f^{1,1}(\omega)) \right) \partial_{x_N} u^1(f^{1,1}(\omega)), \ldots, \\ & g^M \left(\pi^M, u^M(f^{k(\overline{\omega}),M}(\omega)), u^M(f^{k(\overline{\omega}),M}(\omega)) \right) \partial_{x_N} u^M(f^{k(\overline{\omega}),M}(\omega)) \Big)^\top. \end{aligned}$$

Using the continuity of the functions $f^{k,i}$, $\forall k \in I_{k(\overline{\omega})}$, $\forall i \in I_M$, and g^i, $\forall i \in I_M$, and the fact that u^i is continuously differentiable, it easily follows that h is a continuous function. Let the open set $T_{\overline{\omega}}$ be defined by

$$T_{\overline{\omega}} = \left\{ t \in \mathbb{R}^{k(\overline{\omega})M} \,\middle|\, \forall k \in I_{k(\overline{\omega})},\ \exists i^1, i^2 \in I_M,\ t_k^{i^1} \neq t_k^{i^2} \right\}.$$

Clearly, the set $\mathcal{W}_{\overline{\omega}}$, defined by $\mathcal{W}_{\overline{\omega}} = h^{-1}(T_{\overline{\omega}})$, is open in $O \times \Pi$ and therefore open in $\Omega \times \Pi$. So, $\mathcal{W}^1 = \cup_{\overline{\omega} \in \Omega^1} \mathcal{W}_{\overline{\omega}}$ is open in $\Omega \times \Pi$. Q.E.D.

Theorem 9.4.3
Let $(X^i, u^i)_{i \in I_M}$ satisfy Assumptions A1-A2 and let $M \in \mathbb{N} \setminus \{1\}$. Then the set

$\mathcal{W}^1$ *is dense in* $\Omega \times \Pi$.

Proof

It is shown that the closure of $\mathcal{W}^1$ in $\Omega \times \Pi$ contains $\Omega^1 \times \Pi$, a set that is dense in $\Omega \times \Pi$, thereby showing the result. Let an element $\overline{\omega} \in \Omega^1$ and a set $\mathcal{O}$ that is open in Π be given. Let $\overline{\pi}^i \in \Pi^i$, $\forall i \in I_M$, and $\epsilon^i \in C^0((0,1)\times(0,1), \mathbb{R}_{++})$, $\forall i \in I_M$, be such that $\prod_{i \in I_M} V_{\overline{\pi}^i,\epsilon^i} \subset \mathcal{O}$. It is shown that $\mathcal{W}^1 \cap (\{\overline{\omega}\} \times \prod_{i \in I_M} V_{\overline{\pi}^i,\epsilon^i}) \neq \emptyset$, thereby showing that the closure of $\mathcal{W}^1$ in $\Omega \times \Pi$ contains $\Omega^1 \times \Pi$.

For every $k \in I_{k(\overline{\omega})}$, for every $i \in I_M$, let the real numbers $\overline{v}^{k,i}$ and $\overline{d}^{k,i}$ be defined by $\overline{v}^{k,i} = u^i(x^i(\overline{\omega},k))$ and $\overline{d}^{k,i} = \partial_{x_N} u^i(x^i(\overline{\omega},k))$. Let the set K^1 be defined by

$$K^1 = \left\{k \in I_{k(\overline{\omega})} \,\middle|\, \partial_{v^1}\overline{\pi}^1(\overline{v}^{k,1},\overline{v}^{k,1})\overline{d}^{k,1} = \partial_{v^1}\overline{\pi}^i(\overline{v}^{k,i},\overline{v}^{k,i})\overline{d}^{k,i},\ \forall i \in I_M\right\}.$$

If $K^1 = \emptyset$, then the proof is finished. Consider the case where $K^1 \neq \emptyset$. Let K^2 be a maximal subset of K^1 such that $k^1, k^2 \in K^2$ and $k^1 \neq k^2$ implies $\overline{v}^{k^1,1} \neq \overline{v}^{k^2,1}$. So, $\{\overline{v}^{k,1} \mid k \in K^1\} = \{\overline{v}^{k,1} \mid k \in K^2\}$. Let the, possibly empty, set K^3 be defined by

$$K^3 = \left\{k \in I_{k(\overline{\omega})} \setminus K^1 \,\middle|\, \partial_{v^1}\overline{\pi}^1(\overline{v}^{k,1},\overline{v}^{k,1})\overline{d}^{k,1} \neq \partial_{v^1}\overline{\pi}^2(\overline{v}^{k,2},\overline{v}^{k,2})\overline{d}^{k,2}\right\}.$$

For every $\widehat{v} \in (0,1)$, for every $\delta \in \mathbb{R}_{++}$ satisfying $\overline{B}^2((\widehat{v},\widehat{v})^\top,\delta) \subset (0,1)\times(0,1)$, for every $\varepsilon \in \mathbb{R}_{++}$, let the function $f_{\widehat{v},\delta,\varepsilon} \in C^\infty((0,1)\times(0,1),\mathbb{R}_+)$ have the following properties:

1. $f_{\widehat{v},\delta,\varepsilon}(\overline{v}^1,\overline{v}^2) = 0$, $\forall(\overline{v}^1,\overline{v}^2) \in ((0,1)\times(0,1)) \setminus B^2((\widehat{v},\widehat{v})^\top,\delta)$,
2. $\|\partial_{(v^1,v^2)^\top} f_{\widehat{v},\delta,\varepsilon}(\overline{v}^1,\overline{v}^2)\|_2 < \varepsilon$, $\forall(\overline{v}^1,\overline{v}^2) \in (0,1)\times(0,1)$,
3. $\partial_{v^1} f_{\widehat{v},\delta,\varepsilon}(\widehat{v} - \frac{1}{2}\delta, \widehat{v} - \frac{1}{2}\delta) > 0$.

Using Theorem 2.9.2 it is not difficult to show that such a function $f_{\widehat{v},\delta,\varepsilon}$ exists. Let the function $\widehat{\pi} \in \Pi$ be defined by

$$\widehat{\pi}^1(v^1,v^2) = \overline{\pi}^1(v^1,v^2) + \sum_{k \in K^2} f_{\widehat{v}^k,\delta^k,\varepsilon^k}(v^1,v^2),\ \forall(v^1,v^2) \in (0,1)\times(0,1),$$

and $\widehat{\pi}^i = \overline{\pi}^i$, $\forall i \in I_M \setminus \{1\}$, where, for every $k \in K^2$,

$$\begin{aligned}
\delta^k &= \min\left(\left\{\tfrac{1}{2}|\overline{v}^{k,1} - \overline{v}^{k',1}| \,\middle|\, k' \in I_{k(\overline{\omega})} \text{ and } \overline{v}^{k',1} \neq \overline{v}^{k,1}\right\} \cup \left\{\tfrac{1}{2}\overline{v}^{k,1}, \tfrac{1}{2}(1-\overline{v}^{k,1})\right\}\right),\\
\widehat{v}^k &= \overline{v}^{k,1} + \tfrac{1}{2}\delta^k,\\
\varepsilon^k &= \min\left(\left\{\partial_{v^1}\overline{\pi}^1(\overline{v}^1,\overline{v}^2) \,\middle|\, (\overline{v}^1,\overline{v}^2) \in \overline{B}^2((\widehat{v}^k,\widehat{v}^k)^\top,\delta^k)\right\}\right.
\end{aligned}$$

$$\cup \left\{ -\partial_{v^2}\overline{\pi}^1(\overline{v}^1,\overline{v}^2) \,\middle|\, (\overline{v}^1,\overline{v}^2) \in \overline{B}^2((\widehat{v}^k,\widehat{v}^k)^\top,\delta^k) \right\}$$
$$\cup \left\{ \epsilon^1(\overline{v}^1,\overline{v}^2) \,\middle|\, (\overline{v}^1,\overline{v}^2) \in \overline{B}^2((\widehat{v}^k,\widehat{v}^k)^\top,\delta^k) \right\}$$
$$\cup \left\{ |\partial_{v^1}\overline{\pi}^1(\overline{v}^{k,1},\overline{v}^{k,1})\overline{d}^{k,1} - \partial_{v^1}\overline{\pi}^2(\overline{v}^{k,2},\overline{v}^{k,2})\overline{d}^{k,2}| \,\middle|\, k \in K^3 \right\}\Big).$$

For every $k \in K^2$, the choice of δ^k guarantees that $\widehat{\pi}$ is a perturbation of $\overline{\pi}$ on non-intersecting neighbourhoods of utilities consumer 1 derives at Walrasian equilibria of the economy $\mathcal{E} = ((X^i, u^i, \overline{\omega}^i)_{i \in I_M})$. For every $k \in K^2$, the choice of $\widehat{v}^k$ guarantees that the voting behaviour of consumer 1 is indeed perturbed at the utility he derives at Walrasian equilibrium k. Finally, ε^k, $\forall k \in K^2$, is chosen such that $\widehat{\pi} \in \prod_{i \in I_M} V_{\overline{\pi}^i,\epsilon^i}$ and the perturbation is so small that for every $k \in K^3$ the already existing inequality of $\partial_{v^1}\overline{\pi}^1(\overline{v}^{k,1},\overline{v}^{k,1})\overline{d}^{k,1}$ and $\partial_{v^1}\overline{\pi}^2(\overline{v}^{k,1},\overline{v}^{k,1})\overline{d}^{k,2}$ remains. The fact that $\overline{d}^{k,i} > 0$, $\forall k \in I_{k(\overline{\omega})}$, $\forall i \in I_M$, guarantees that

$$\partial_{v^1}\widehat{\pi}^1(\overline{v}^{k,1},\overline{v}^{k,1})\overline{d}^{k,1} \neq \partial_{v^1}\widehat{\pi}^2(\overline{v}^{k,2},\overline{v}^{k,2})\overline{d}^{k,2}, \;\forall k \in K^1.$$

Clearly,

$$\partial_{v^1}\widehat{\pi}^1(\overline{v}^{k,1},\overline{v}^{k,1})\overline{d}^{k,1} \neq \partial_{v^1}\widehat{\pi}^2(\overline{v}^{k,2},\overline{v}^{k,2})\overline{d}^{k,2}, \;\forall k \in K^3.$$

Let $k' \in I_{k(\overline{\omega})} \setminus (K^1 \cup K^3)$ be given.
Then $\partial_{v^1}\overline{\pi}^1(\overline{v}^{k',1},\overline{v}^{k',1})\overline{d}^{k',1} = \partial_{v^1}\overline{\pi}^2(\overline{v}^{k',2},\overline{v}^{k',2})\overline{d}^{k',2}$, while there exists $i' \in I_M$ such that $\partial_{v^1}\overline{\pi}^1(\overline{v}^{k',1},\overline{v}^{k',1})\overline{d}^{k',1} \neq \partial_{v^1}\overline{\pi}^{i'}(\overline{v}^{k',i'},\overline{v}^{k',i'})\overline{d}^{k',i'}$. If $\overline{v}^{k',1} \in \{\overline{v}^{k,1} \mid k \in K^2\}$, then, since $\overline{d}^{k',1} > 0$,

$$\partial_{v^1}\widehat{\pi}^1(\overline{v}^{k',1},\overline{v}^{k',1})\overline{d}^{k',1} \neq \partial_{v^1}\widehat{\pi}^2(\overline{v}^{k',2},\overline{v}^{k',2})\overline{d}^{k',2}.$$

If $\overline{v}^{k',1} \notin \{\overline{v}^{k,1} \mid k \in K^2\}$, then the choice of δ^k, $\forall k \in K^2$, guarantees that

$$\begin{aligned}\partial_{v^1}\widehat{\pi}^1(\overline{v}^{k',1},\overline{v}^{k',1})\overline{d}^{k',1} &= \partial_{v^1}\overline{\pi}^1(\overline{v}^{k',1},\overline{v}^{k',1})\overline{d}^{k',1}\\ &\neq \partial_{v^1}\overline{\pi}^{i'}(\overline{v}^{k',i'},\overline{v}^{k',i'})\overline{d}^{k',i'} = \partial_{v^1}\widehat{\pi}^{i'}(\overline{v}^{k',i'},\overline{v}^{k',i'})\overline{d}^{k',i'}.\end{aligned}$$

So, it follows that $(\overline{\omega},\widehat{\pi}) \in \mathcal{W}^1$, whereas, clearly, $(\overline{\omega},\widehat{\pi}) \in \{\overline{\omega}\} \times \prod_{i \in I_M} V_{\overline{\pi}^i,\epsilon^i}$.
Q.E.D.

Theorem 9.4.4
Let $(X^i, u^i)_{i \in I_M}$ satisfy Assumptions A1-A2 and let $M \in \mathbb{N} \setminus \{1\}$. Then there exists an open and dense set $\mathcal{W}^2$ in $\Omega \times \Pi$ such that, for every $(\omega,\pi) \in \mathcal{W}^2$, for every Walrasian equilibrium (p^*, x^*) with $p^*_N = 1$ of the economy $\mathcal{E} = ((X^i, u^i, \omega^i)_{i \in I_M})$ it holds that $-\sum_{i \in I_M} \partial_{v^1}\pi^i(u^i(x^{*i}), u^i(x^{*i}))\partial_{x_N}u^i(x^{*i})(x^{*i}_j - \omega^i_j) \neq 0$ for some $j \in I_{N-1}$.
Proof

By Theorems 9.4.2 and 9.4.3 the set $\mathcal{W}^1$ is open and dense in $\Omega \times \Pi$. Let $\overline{\pi} \in \Pi$ be such that the set $\Omega_{\overline{\pi}}$, defined by

$$\Omega_{\overline{\pi}} = \left\{\omega \in \Omega \,\middle|\, (\omega, \overline{\pi}) \in \mathcal{W}^1 \right\},$$

is non-empty. Since $\mathcal{W}^1$ is open in $\Omega \times \Pi$, it holds that $\Omega_{\overline{\pi}}$ is open in Ω. Let $\overline{\omega} \in \Omega_{\overline{\pi}}$ and $(p', \overline{x}) \in \mathbb{R}^N_{++} \times X$ with $p'_N = 1$ be given. By Theorem 2.9.7 it holds that if $(p', \overline{x})$ is a Walrasian equilibrium of the economy $\mathcal{E} = ((X^i, u^i, \overline{\omega}^i)_{i \in I_M})$ satisfying $-\sum_{i \in I_M} \partial_{v^1} \overline{\pi}^i(u^i(\overline{x}^i), u^i(\overline{x}^i)) \partial_{x_N} u^i(\overline{x}^i)(\overline{x}^i_j - \overline{\omega}^i_j) = 0$, $\forall j \in I_{N-1}$, then there exists $\overline{\lambda}^i \in \mathbb{R}$, $\forall i \in I_M$, such that

$$\partial_{x^i} u^i(\overline{x}^i)^\top - \overline{\lambda}^i (p'_1, \ldots, p'_{N-1}, 1)^\top = 0^N, \quad \forall i \in I_M, \tag{9.14}$$
$$(p'_1, \ldots, p'_{N-1}, 1)\overline{x}^i - (p'_1, \ldots, p'_{N-1}, 1)\overline{\omega}^i = 0, \quad \forall i \in I_M, \tag{9.15}$$
$$\textstyle\sum_{i \in I_M} \overline{x}^i_j - \sum_{i \in I_M} \overline{\omega}^i_j = 0, \quad \forall j \in I_{N-1}, \tag{9.16}$$
$$-\textstyle\sum_{i \in I_M} \partial_{v^1} \overline{\pi}^i \left(u^i(\overline{x}^i), u^i(\overline{x}^i)\right) \partial_{x_N} u^i(\overline{x}^i) \left(\overline{x}^i_1 - \overline{\omega}^i_1\right) = 0. \tag{9.17}$$

Notice that the condition that in the market for the numeraire commodity the total excess demand is equal to zero is not specified. This condition is implied by the equations in (9.15) and (9.16). Let the function

$$\psi : X \times \mathbb{R}^M \times \mathbb{R}^{N-1}_{++} \times \Omega_{\overline{\pi}} \to \mathbb{R}^{MN+M+N}$$

be defined such that $\psi(x, \lambda, (p_1, \ldots, p_{N-1})^\top, \omega)$ is the left-hand side of (9.14)-(9.17), for every $(x, \lambda, (p_1, \ldots, p_{N-1})^\top, \omega) \in X \times \mathbb{R}^M \times \mathbb{R}^{N-1}_{++} \times \Omega_{\overline{\pi}}$. For every $\omega \in \Omega$, the function

$$\psi^\omega : X \times \mathbb{R}^M \times \mathbb{R}^{N-1}_{++} \to \mathbb{R}^{MN+M+N}$$

is defined by associating with every $(x, \lambda, (p_1, \ldots, p_{N-1})^\top) \in X \times \mathbb{R}^M \times \mathbb{R}^{N-1}_{++}$ the element $\psi(x, \lambda, (p_1, \ldots, p_{N-1})^\top, \omega)$. The matrix of partial derivatives of ψ evaluated at a point $\overline{\xi} = (\overline{x}, \overline{\lambda}, (p'_1, \ldots, p'_{N-1})^\top, \overline{\omega}) \in X \times \mathbb{R}^M \times \mathbb{R}^{N-1}_{++} \times \Omega_{\overline{\pi}}$ such that $\psi(\overline{\xi}) = 0^{MN+M+N}$ is denoted by $\overline{M}$ and is given in Table 9.4.1.
It is shown that the matrix $\overline{M}$ has rank $MN + M + N$. Notice that

$$\partial_{\omega^i_1} \psi_{MN+M+N}(\overline{\xi}) = \partial_{v^1} \overline{\pi}^i(u^i(\overline{x}^i), u^i(\overline{x}^i)) \partial_{x_N} u^i(\overline{x}^i), \forall i \in I_M, \tag{9.18}$$
$$\partial_{\omega^i_j} \psi_{MN+M+N}(\overline{\xi}) = 0, \qquad \forall i \in I_M, \forall j \in I_N \setminus \{1\}. \tag{9.19}$$

The partial derivatives of ψ_{MN+M+N} at $\overline{\xi}$ with respect to x are quite complicated, but do not matter in the following.
Let $y \in \mathbb{R}^{MN+M+N}$ be such that $y^\top \overline{M} = 0^{2MN+M+N-1^\top}$. Then, $y^\top \partial_{\omega^i_N} \psi(\overline{\xi}) = 0$, $\forall i \in I_M$, implies, using (9.19), that

$$y_{MN+i} = 0, \ \forall i \in I_M. \tag{9.20}$$

$\begin{matrix} \partial^2_{x^1x^1}u^1(\overline{x}^1) & & 0 \\ & \ddots & \\ 0 & & \partial^2_{x^Mx^M}u^M(\overline{x}^M) \end{matrix}$	$\begin{matrix} \begin{smallmatrix}-p'_1\\ \vdots \\ -p'_{N-1}\\ -1\end{smallmatrix} & & 0 \\ & \ddots & \\ 0 & & \begin{smallmatrix}-p'_1\\ \vdots \\ -p'_{N-1}\\ -1\end{smallmatrix} \end{matrix}$	$\begin{matrix} -\overline{\lambda}^1 I^{N-1} \\ {0^{N-1}}^\top \\ \vdots \\ -\overline{\lambda}^M I^{N-1} \\ {0^{N-1}}^\top \end{matrix}$	$0^{MN\times MN}$	MN
$\begin{matrix} (p'_j)_{j\in I_{N-1}}\ 1 & & 0 \\ & \ddots & \\ 0 & & (p'_j)_{j\in I_{N-1}}\ 1 \end{matrix}$	$0^{M\times M}$	$\begin{matrix} (\overline{x}^1_j-\overline{\omega}^1_j)_{j\in I_{N-1}} \\ \vdots \\ (\overline{x}^M_j-\overline{\omega}^M_j)_{j\in I_{N-1}} \end{matrix}$	$\begin{matrix} (-p'_j)_{j\in I_{N-1}}\ -1 & & 0 \\ & \ddots & \\ 0 & & (-p'_j)_{j\in I_{N-1}}\ -1 \end{matrix}$	M
$I^{N-1}\ 0^{N-1}\ \cdots\ I^{N-1}\ 0^{N-1}$	$0^{(N-1)\times M}$	$0^{(N-1)\times(N-1)}$	$-I^{N-1}\ 0^{N-1}\ \cdots\ -I^{N-1}\ 0^{N-1}$	$N-1$
$\partial_x\psi_{MN+M+N}(\overline{\xi})$	${0^M}^\top$	${0^{N-1}}^\top$	$\partial_\omega\psi_{MN+M+N}(\overline{\xi})$	1
MN	M	$N-1$	MN	

Table 9.4.1. The matrix $\overline{M}$.

By the definition of $\Omega_{\overline{\pi}}$ there exists $i^1, i^2 \in I_M$ such that

$$\partial_{v^1}\overline{\pi}^{i^1}\Big(u^{i^1}(\overline{x}^{i^1}), u^{i^1}(\overline{x}^{i^1})\Big)\partial_{x_N}u^{i^1}(\overline{x}^{i^1}) \neq \partial_{v^1}\overline{\pi}^{i^2}\Big(u^{i^2}(\overline{x}^{i^2}), u^{i^2}(\overline{x}^{i^2})\Big)\partial_{x_N}u^{i^2}(\overline{x}^{i^2}). \tag{9.21}$$

Moreover, (9.18), (9.20), and $y^\top\partial_{\omega^i_1}\psi(\overline{\xi}) = 0$, $\forall i \in \{i^1, i^2\}$, implies

$$-y_{MN+M+1} + \partial_{v^1}\overline{\pi}^{i^1}\left(u^{i^1}(\overline{x}^{i^1}), u^{i^1}(\overline{x}^{i^1})\right)\partial_{x_N}u^{i^1}(\overline{x}^{i^1})y_{MN+M+N} = 0,$$

$$-y_{MN+M+1} + \partial_{v^1}\overline{\pi}^{i^2}\left(u^{i^2}(\overline{x}^{i^2}), u^{i^2}(\overline{x}^{i^2})\right)\partial_{x_N}u^{i^2}(\overline{x}^{i^2})y_{MN+M+N} = 0.$$

So,

$$\Big(\partial_{v^1}\overline{\pi}^{i^1}\left(u^{i^1}(\overline{x}^{i^1}), u^{i^1}(\overline{x}^{i^1})\right)\partial_{x_N}u^{i^1}(\overline{x}^{i^1}) \\ -\partial_{v^1}\overline{\pi}^{i^2}\left(u^{i^2}(\overline{x}^{i^2}), u^{i^2}(\overline{x}^{i^2})\right)\partial_{x_N}u^{i^2}(\overline{x}^{i^2})\Big)\, y_{MN+M+N} = 0,$$

implying by (9.21) that $y_{MN+M+N} = 0$. Now it can be shown similarly as in the proof of Theorem 9.3.6 that $y = 0^{MN+M+N}$, so $\overline{M}$ has rank $MN+M+N$, and ψ intersects $\{0^{MN+M+N}\}$ transversally, $\psi \pitchfork \{0^{MN+M+N}\}$. Let the set $\overline{\Omega}_{\overline{\pi}}$

be defined by

$$\overline{\Omega}_{\overline{\pi}} = \left\{ \omega \in \Omega_{\overline{\pi}} \,\middle|\, \psi^{\omega} \pitchfork \{0^{MN+M+N}\} \right\}.$$

From the transversality theorem, Theorem 2.10.18, it follows that the set $\Omega_{\overline{\pi}} \setminus \overline{\Omega}_{\overline{\pi}}$ has Lebesgue measure zero in $\Omega_{\overline{\pi}}$. Since $\Omega_{\overline{\pi}}$ is an MN-dimensional C^{∞} manifold, being a subset of $\mathbb{R}^{MN}$, it follows that the set $\Omega_{\overline{\pi}} \setminus \overline{\Omega}_{\overline{\pi}}$ has Lebesgue measure zero, see the remark below Theorem 2.10.17. For every $\omega \in \overline{\Omega}_{\overline{\pi}}$, ψ^{ω} is a function from an $(MN + M + N - 1)$-dimensional C^{∞} manifold into an $(MN+M+N)$-dimensional C^{∞} manifold, $\{0^{MN+M+N}\}$ is a 0-dimensional C^{∞} manifold, $\psi^{\omega} \in C^1(X \times \mathbb{R}^M \times \mathbb{R}^{N-1}_{++}, \mathbb{R}^{MN+M+N})$, and $\psi^{\omega} \pitchfork \{0^{MN+M+N}\}$, so it follows from Theorem 2.10.16 that ${\psi^{\omega}}^{-1}(\{0^{MN+M+N}\}) = \emptyset$. Let the set $\overline{\mathcal{W}}$ be defined by

$$\overline{\mathcal{W}} = \left\{ (\omega, \pi) \in \mathcal{W}^1 \,\middle|\, \omega \in \overline{\Omega}_{\pi} \right\}.$$

Clearly, the closure of $\overline{\mathcal{W}}$ in $\mathcal{W}^1$ is equal to $\mathcal{W}^1$. Since $\mathcal{W}^1$ is dense in $\Omega \times \Pi$, it holds that $\overline{\mathcal{W}}$ is dense in $\Omega \times \Pi$. Let the set $\mathcal{W}^2$ be defined by the elements $(\omega, \pi) \in \Omega^1 \times \Pi$ such that every Walrasian equilibrium (p^*, x^*) with $p^*_N = 1$ of $\mathcal{E}$ satisfies $-\sum_{i \in I_M} \partial_{v^1} \pi^i(u^i(x^{*i}), u^i(x^{*i})) \partial_{x_N} u^i(x^{*i})(x^{*i}_j - \omega^i_j) \neq 0$ for some $j \in I_{N-1}$. Clearly, $\overline{\mathcal{W}} \subset \mathcal{W}^2$ and hence $\mathcal{W}^2$ is dense in $\Omega \times \Pi$. Similar to the case where it is shown that $\mathcal{W}^1$ is open in $\Omega \times \Pi$, it can be shown that $\mathcal{W}^2$ is open in $\Omega \times \Pi$. Q.E.D.

Combining the results of Theorems 9.3.7 and 9.4.4, the following result is obtained.

Theorem 9.4.5

Let $(X^i)_{i \in I_M}, (\tilde{l}, \tilde{L})$ satisfy Assumptions A1 and A4, and let $M \in \mathbb{N} \setminus \{1\}$. Then there exists an open and dense set $\mathcal{V}$ in $\mathcal{U} \times \Pi$ such that, for every $(u, \omega, \pi) \in \mathcal{V}$, every Walrasian equilibrium (p^*, x^*) with $p^*_N = 1$ of the economy $\mathcal{E} = ((X^i, u^i, \omega^i)_{i \in I_M})$ is locally unique, regular, for every $j \in I_{N-1}$, $\#\underline{I}_j(x^*) = \#\overline{I}_j(x^*) = 1$, and

$$\sum_{i \in I_M} \partial_{v^1} \pi^i(\widehat{v}^i(p^*_1, \ldots, p^*_{N-1}), \widehat{v}^i(p^*_1, \ldots, p^*_{N-1})) \partial_{(p_1, \ldots, p_{N-1})^\top} \widehat{v}^i(p^*_1, \ldots, p^*_{N-1}) \neq 0^{N-1^\top}.$$

Proof

Let the set $\mathcal{V}^1$ be defined by $\mathcal{V}^1 = \mathcal{U}^3 \times \Pi$, where $\mathcal{U}^3$ is as in Theorem 9.3.7. The set $\mathcal{W}^2$ obtained in Theorem 9.4.4 depends on the choice of $u \in U$ and is therefore denoted by $\mathcal{W}^2_u$, $\forall u \in U$. Let the set $\mathcal{V}^2$ be defined by

$$\mathcal{V}^2 = \left\{ (u, \omega, \pi) \in U \times \Omega \times \Pi \,\middle|\, (\omega, \pi) \in \mathcal{W}^2_u \right\}.$$

Let the set $\mathcal{V}^3$ be defined as the set of elements $(u, \omega, \pi) \in \mathcal{V}^1$ such that, for every Walrasian equilibrium (p^*, x^*) with $p_N^* = 1$ of $\mathcal{E} = ((X^i, u^i, \omega^i)_{i \in I_M})$,

$$-\sum_{i \in I_M} \partial_{v^1} \pi^i \left(u^i(x^{*i}), u^i(x^{*i})\right) \partial_{x_N} u^i(x^{*i}) \left(x_j^{*i} - \omega_j^i\right) \neq 0$$

for some $j \in I_{N-1}$. Notice that $\mathcal{V}^1 \cap \mathcal{V}^2 \subset \mathcal{V}^3$. Since $\mathcal{V}^3 \subset \mathcal{V}^1$, it holds that for every $(u, \omega, \pi) \in \mathcal{V}^3$ every Walrasian equilibrium (p^*, x^*) with $p_N^* = 1$ of the economy $\mathcal{E} = ((X^i, u^i, \omega^i)_{i \in I_M})$ is locally unique, regular, and, for every $j \in I_{N-1}$, $\#\underline{I}_j(x^*) = \#\overline{I}_j(x^*) = 1$. It is shown that $\mathcal{V}^3$ is open and dense in $U \times \Omega \times \Pi$. Since $\mathcal{U}^3$ is open and dense in $U \times \Omega$, it holds that $\mathcal{V}^1 = \mathcal{U}^3 \times \Pi$ is open and dense in $U \times \Omega \times \Pi$. Clearly, $\mathcal{V}^2$ is dense in $U \times \Omega \times \Pi$. Since the intersection of an open and dense set with a dense set is dense, it holds that $\mathcal{V}^1 \cap \mathcal{V}^2$ is dense in $U \times \Omega \times \Pi$, so $\mathcal{V}^3$ is dense in $U \times \Omega \times \Pi$.
The Walrasian equilibrium set moves continuously in (u, ω) for every $(u, \omega) \in \mathcal{U}^3$, see Theorem 9.3.7. Since the voting functions have no influence on the Walrasian equilibrium set, it clearly holds that the Walrasian equilibrium set moves continuously in (u, ω, π) for every $(u, \omega, \pi) \in \mathcal{V}^1$. In the proof of Theorem 9.4.2 it has been shown that for every $i \in I_M$ the function $g^i : \Pi^i \times (0,1) \times (0,1) \to \mathbb{R}_{++}$, defined by $g^i(\overline{\pi}^i, \overline{v}^1, \overline{v}^2) = \partial_{v^1} \overline{\pi}^i(\overline{v}^1, \overline{v}^2)$, $\forall (\overline{\pi}^i, \overline{v}^1, \overline{v}^2) \in \Pi^i \times (0,1) \times (0,1)$, is continuous. Similarly, it can be shown that for every $i \in I_M$ the function $f^i : U^i \times \mathbb{R}_{++}^N \to \mathbb{R}$, defined by $f^i(\overline{u}^i, \overline{x}^i) = \partial_{x_N} \overline{u}^i(\overline{x}^i)$, $\forall (\overline{u}^i, \overline{x}^i) \in U^i \times \mathbb{R}_{++}^N$, is continuous. Therefore, it easily follows that $\mathcal{V}^3$ is open in $\mathcal{V}^1$. Hence, $\mathcal{V}^3$ is open in $U \times \Omega \times \Pi$.
Let the set $\mathcal{V}$ be defined by $\mathcal{V} = \mathcal{V}^3 \cap (\mathcal{U} \times \Pi)$. Then $\mathcal{V}$ is open and dense in $\mathcal{U} \times \Pi$ and $\sum_{i \in I_M} \partial_{v^1} \pi^i \left(\widehat{v}^i(p_1^*, \ldots, p_{N-1}^*), \widehat{v}^i(p_1^*, \ldots, p_{N-1}^*)\right) \partial_{(p_1, \ldots, p_{N-1})^\top} \widehat{v}^i(p_1^*, \ldots, p_{N-1}^*) \neq 0^{N-1^\top}$ follows by Theorem 9.3.2. Q.E.D.

Let the political economic system $\widehat{\mathcal{E}}$ satisfy Assumptions A1-A5 and A7, let $M \in \mathbb{N} \backslash \{1\}$, and let $(u, \omega, \pi) \in \mathcal{V}$ with $\mathcal{V}$ as in Theorem 9.4.5. Suppose political candidate 2 proposes the Walrasian equilibrium $(p^*, p^*, x^*) \in \mathcal{A}^2$. Using (9.12) and Theorem 9.4.5, it is clear that it is not optimal for political candidate 1 to choose the action $(p^*, p^*, x^*) \in \mathcal{A}^1$. Such a proposal can be improved by proposing $(p^1, p^1, x(p^1)) \in \mathcal{A}^1$, where p^1 can be chosen arbitrarily close to p^*. Since the Walrasian equilibria of the economy $\mathcal{E} = ((X^i, u^i, \omega^i)_{i \in I_M})$ are locally unique, p^1 can be chosen such that it is not a Walrasian equilibrium price system. By symmetry, there exists an open and dense set $\overline{\mathcal{V}}$ in $\mathcal{U} \times \Pi$, for which the statements made above are true with the roles of political candidates 1 and 2 reversed. Moreover, the set $\mathcal{V} \cap \overline{\mathcal{V}}$ is open and dense in $\mathcal{U} \times \Pi$.

Let the political economic system $\overline{\mathcal{E}}$ with status quo a Walrasian equilibrium (p^*, x^*) with $p_N^* = 1$ of the economy $\mathcal{E} = ((X^i, u^i, \omega^i)_{i \in I_M})$ satisfy Assumptions

A1-A4, A7, and A9, let $M \in \mathbb{N} \setminus \{1\}$, and let $(u, \omega, \pi) \in \mathcal{V}$ with $\mathcal{V}$ as in Theorem 9.4.5. It follows from Theorems 9.4.1 and 9.4.5 that political candidate 1 proposes $\overline{K}^1/||\overline{K}^1||_2 \neq 0^{N-1}$ in a directional political economic equilibrium of the political economic system $\overline{\mathcal{E}}$ with status quo (p^*, x^*). By symmetry, there exists an open and dense set $\overline{\mathcal{V}}$ in $\mathcal{U} \times \Pi$, for which the statements made above are true with the roles of political candidates 1 and 2 reversed. Moreover, the set $\mathcal{V} \cap \overline{\mathcal{V}}$ is open and dense in $\mathcal{U} \times \Pi$.

Corollary 9.4.6 and Corollary 9.4.7 are immediately obtained from Theorem 9.4.5 and the remarks being made in the previous two paragraphs.

Corollary 9.4.6
Let $(X^i)_{i \in I_M}, (\widetilde{l}, \widetilde{L}), (A^k)_{k \in I_2}$ satisfy Assumptions A1 and A4-A5, and let $M \in \mathbb{N} \setminus \{1\}$. Then there exists an open and dense set of utility functions, initial endowments, and voting functions $(u, \omega, \pi) \in \mathcal{U} \times \Pi$ such that there is no political economic equilibrium of the political economic system $\widehat{\mathcal{E}} = ((X^i, u^i, \omega^i)_{i \in I_M}, (\widetilde{l}, \widetilde{L}), (A^k, (\pi^{ik})_{i \in I_M})_{k \in I_2})$ where both political candidates choose an action $(p^*, p^*, x^*) \in \mathcal{A}^1 = \mathcal{A}^2$ corresponding to a Walrasian equilibrium of the economy $\mathcal{E} = ((X^i, u^i, \omega^i)_{i \in I_M})$.

Corollary 9.4.7
Let $(X^i)_{i \in I_M}, (\widetilde{l}, \widetilde{L}), (\widetilde{A}^k)_{k \in I_2}$ satisfy Assumptions A1, A4, and A9, and let $M \in \mathbb{N} \setminus \{1\}$. Then there exists an open and dense set of utility functions, initial endowments, and voting functions $(u, \omega, \pi) \in \mathcal{U} \times \Pi$ such that in every directional political economic equilibrium $(\widetilde{p}^{*1}, \widetilde{p}^{*2})$ of the political economic system $\overline{\mathcal{E}} = ((X^i, u^i, \omega^i)_{i \in I_M}, (\widetilde{l}, \widetilde{L}), (\widetilde{\mathcal{A}}^k, (\pi^{ik})_{i \in I_M})_{k \in I_2})$ with status quo a Walrasian equilibrium (p^*, x^*) with $p^*_N = 1$ of the economy $\mathcal{E} = ((X^i, u^i, \omega^i)_{i \in I_M})$, both $\widetilde{p}^{*1} \neq 0^{N-1}$ and $\widetilde{p}^{*2} \neq 0^{N-1}$.

Therefore, it can be concluded that, generically, both in a political economic equilibrium and a directional political economic equilibrium, Walrasian equilibria are unstable and rationally behaving political candidates have incentives to impose price regulations on the economic system.

9.5 AN EXAMPLE

In this section the same example as used in Chapter 8 is analysed. Consider the political economic system $\overline{\mathcal{E}} = ((X^i, u^i, \omega^i)_{i \in I_2}, (\widetilde{l}, \widetilde{L}), (\widetilde{\mathcal{A}}^k, (\pi^{ik})_{i \in I_2})_{k \in I_2})$ with status quo the Walrasian equilibrium (p^*, x^*) with $p_2^* = 1$ of the economy $\mathcal{E} = ((X^i, u^i, \omega^i)_{i \in I_2})$, where $N = 2$, $X^1 = X^2 = \mathbb{R}^2_{++}$, $u^1(x_1^1, x_2^1) = (x_1^1)^{\frac{4}{5}}(x_2^1)^{\frac{1}{5}}$, $\forall x^1 \in X^1$, $u^2(x_1^2, x_2^2) = (x_1^2)^{\frac{1}{5}}(x_2^2)^{\frac{4}{5}}$, $\forall x^2 \in X^2$, respectively, $\omega^1 = \omega^2 = (1,4)^\top$, $(\widetilde{l}, \widetilde{L})$ represents the uniform rationing system, where $\widetilde{l} : \mathbb{R}^2_+ \to -\mathbb{R}^4_+$ is defined by $\widetilde{l}_1^1(q) = \widetilde{l}_1^2(q) = -2q_1$, $\forall q \in \mathbb{R}^2_+$, $\widetilde{l}_2^1(q) = \widetilde{l}_2^2(q) = -8q_2$, $\forall q \in \mathbb{R}^2_+$, and $\widetilde{L} : \mathbb{R}^2_+ \to \mathbb{R}^4_+$ is defined by $\widetilde{L}_1^1(q) = \widetilde{L}_1^2(q) = 2q_1$, $\forall q \in \mathbb{R}^2_+$, $\widetilde{L}_2^1(q) = \widetilde{L}_2^2(q) = 8q_2$, $\forall q \in \mathbb{R}^2_+$,

$$\widetilde{\mathcal{A}}^1 = \widetilde{\mathcal{A}}^2 = \{-1, 0, 1\},$$

and, for every $i \in I_2$, for every $k \in I_2$, $\pi^{ik} : \mathbb{R}_{++} \times \mathbb{R}_{++} \to [0,1]$ is defined by

$$\pi^{ik}(v^{i1}, v^{i2}) = \frac{\exp(v^{ik})}{\exp(v^{i1}) + \exp(v^{i2})}, \quad \forall v^{i1}, v^{i2} \in \mathbb{R}_{++} \times \mathbb{R}_{++}.$$

The unique Walrasian equilibrium (p^*, x^*) with $p_2^* = 1$ of the economy $\mathcal{E}$ is given by $p_1^* = 4$, $x^{*1} = (1\frac{3}{5}, 1\frac{3}{5})^\top$, and $x^{*2} = (\frac{2}{5}, 6\frac{2}{5})^\top$, see Section 8.5.

Notice that Assumptions A1-A4, A6, and A8 are satisfied, except that the range of the utility functions is $\mathbb{R}_{++}$ instead of $(0,1)$ and hence the domain of the voting functions is given by $\mathbb{R}_{++} \times \mathbb{R}_{++}$ instead of $(0,1) \times (0,1)$. Obviously, it is possible to take a monotone transformation of the utility function such that its range becomes $(0,1)$. Notice that also the voting functions have to be transformed in that case. So, a directional political economic equilibrium of the political economic system $\overline{\mathcal{E}}$ with status quo (p^*, x^*) is guaranteed to exist by Theorem 9.3.9.

A political candidate $k \in I_2$ has three possibilities in this example. Either decrease the price of commodity 1, i.e. $\widetilde{p}_1^k = -1$, or stay at the status quo, i.e. $\widetilde{p}_1^k = 0$, or increase the price of commodity 1, i.e. $\widetilde{p}_1^k = 1$. Using the demand functions and the Drèze equilibria derived in Section 8.5 it follows that

$$\widehat{v}^1(p_1) = \left(\tfrac{-4+9p_1}{5p_1}\right)^{\frac{4}{5}} \left(\tfrac{24-4p_1}{5}\right)^{\frac{1}{5}}, \ \tfrac{16}{11} \leq p_1 \leq 4,$$
$$\widehat{v}^1(p_1) = \left(\tfrac{16+4p_1}{5p_1}\right)^{\frac{4}{5}} \left(\tfrac{4+p_1}{5}\right)^{\frac{1}{5}}, \quad 4 \leq p_1 \leq 16,$$

and

$$\widehat{v}^2(p_1) = \left(\tfrac{4+p_1}{5p_1}\right)^{\frac{1}{5}} \left(\tfrac{16+4p_1}{5}\right)^{\frac{4}{5}}, \quad 1 \leq p_1 \leq 4,$$
$$\widehat{v}^2(p_1) = \left(\tfrac{-16+6p_1}{5p_1}\right)^{\frac{1}{5}} \left(\tfrac{36-p_1}{5}\right)^{\frac{4}{5}}, \ 4 \leq p_1 \leq 11.$$

It is easily verified that $\partial_{p_1}\widehat{v}^1(4) = -\frac{3}{25}$ and $\partial_{p_1}\widehat{v}^2(4) = \frac{3}{25}4^{\frac{3}{5}} \approx 0.276$. Notice that this corresponds to the result of Theorem 9.3.2 since

$$\begin{aligned} -\partial_{x_2}u^1(x^{*1})\left(x_1^{*1} - \omega_1^1\right) &= -\tfrac{1}{5}\left(\frac{1\frac{3}{5}}{1\frac{3}{5}}\right)^{\frac{4}{5}}\left(\tfrac{3}{5}\right) = -\tfrac{3}{25}, \\ -\partial_{x_2}u^2(x^{*2})\left(x_1^{*2} - \omega_1^2\right) &= -\tfrac{4}{5}\left(\frac{\frac{2}{5}}{6\frac{2}{5}}\right)^{\frac{1}{5}}\left(-\tfrac{3}{5}\right) = \tfrac{3}{25}4^{\frac{3}{5}}. \end{aligned}$$

It follows that an increase in the price of commodity 1 is harmful to consumer 1, while consumer 2 benefits from such an increase, even when taking into account the resulting supply rationing in the market for commodity 1. This is not surprising since consumer 1 demands commodity 1, while consumer 2 supplies commodity 1. Notice that the benefits for consumer 2 exceed the detrimental effects for consumer 1.

To determine the influence of the utility level on the voting behaviour of consumers, $\partial_{v^1}\pi^{i1}(\widehat{v}^i(p_1^*), \widehat{v}^i(p_1^*))$ and $\partial_{v^2}\pi^{i1}(\widehat{v}^i(p_1^*), \widehat{v}^i(p_1^*))$ have to be computed for every consumer $i \in I_2$. It follows easily that

$$\begin{aligned} \partial_{v^1}\pi^{i1}\left(\widehat{v}^i(p_1^*), \widehat{v}^i(p_1^*)\right) &= \frac{\exp(\hat{v}^i(p_1^*))\exp(\hat{v}^i(p_1^*))}{(\exp(\hat{v}^i(p_1^*))+\exp(\hat{v}^i(p_1^*)))^2} = \tfrac{1}{4}, \quad \forall i \in I_2, \\ \partial_{v^2}\pi^{i1}\left(\widehat{v}^i(p_1^*), \widehat{v}^i(p_1^*)\right) &= \frac{-\exp(\hat{v}^i(p_1^*))\exp(\hat{v}^i(p_1^*))}{(\exp(\hat{v}^i(p_1^*))+\exp(\hat{v}^i(p_1^*)))^2} = -\tfrac{1}{4}, \forall i \in I_2. \end{aligned}$$

Moreover,

$$\begin{aligned} \partial_{v^1}\pi^{i2}\left(\widehat{v}^i(p_1^*), \widehat{v}^i(p_1^*)\right) &= -\partial_{v^1}\pi^{i1}\left(\widehat{v}^i(p_1^*), \widehat{v}^i(p_1^*)\right), \\ \partial_{v^2}\pi^{i2}\left(\widehat{v}^i(p_1^*), \widehat{v}^i(p_1^*)\right) &= -\partial_{v^2}\pi^{i1}\left(\widehat{v}^i(p_1^*), \widehat{v}^i(p_1^*)\right). \end{aligned}$$

Therefore,

$$\begin{aligned} \widetilde{K}^1(\widetilde{p}_1^1, \widetilde{p}_1^2) &= \tfrac{3}{50}(4^{\frac{3}{5}} - 1)\left(\widetilde{p}_1^1 - \widetilde{p}_1^2\right), \ \forall \widetilde{p}_1^1 \in \{-1, 0, 1\}, \ \forall \widetilde{p}_1^2 \in \{-1, 0, 1\}, \\ \widetilde{K}^2(\widetilde{p}_1^1, \widetilde{p}_1^2) &= \tfrac{3}{50}(4^{\frac{3}{5}} - 1)\left(\widetilde{p}_1^2 - \widetilde{p}_1^1\right), \ \forall \widetilde{p}_1^1 \in \{-1, 0, 1\}, \ \forall \widetilde{p}_1^2 \in \{-1, 0, 1\}. \end{aligned}$$

The pay-offs of the political candidates of the game $\widetilde{G} = (\widetilde{\mathcal{A}}^1, \widetilde{\mathcal{A}}^2, \widetilde{K}^1, \widetilde{K}^2)$ are given in Figure 9.5.1.

From Figure 9.5.1 it follows immediately that both political candidates choose to increase the price of commodity 1 in a directional political economic equilibrium of the political economic system $\overline{\mathcal{E}}$ with status quo (p^*, x^*) since $(1, 1)$ is a Nash equilibrium in pure strategies of the game $\widetilde{G}$, so the Walrasian equilibrium (p^*, x^*) is unstable as a status quo.

Finally, consider the case where the political candidates have different sets of admissible actions, for example because of commitments made in the past.

Political candidate 2

Political candidate 1		−1	0	1
	−1	(0, 0)	(−78, 78)	(−156, 156)
	0	(78, −78)	(0, 0)	(−78, 78)
	1	(156, −156)	(78, −78)	(0, 0)

Figure 9.5.1. Pay-offs ×1000 of the political candidates in the example.

One political candidate is assumed to have the possibility of lowering the price of commodity 1 compared to the Walrasian equilibrium price, while the other political candidate might propose to increase the price of this commodity. Both political candidates have the possibility to stay at the status quo. Hence, $\widetilde{\mathcal{A}}^1 = \{-1, 0\}$ and $\widetilde{\mathcal{A}}^2 = \{0, 1\}$. The pay-offs of the political candidates of the resulting game $\widetilde{G} = (\widetilde{\mathcal{A}}^1, \widetilde{\mathcal{A}}^2, \widetilde{K}^1, \widetilde{K}^2)$ are given in Figure 9.5.2.

Political candidate 2

Political candidate 1		0	1
	−1	(−78, 78)	(−156, 156)
	0	(0, 0)	(−78, 78)

Figure 9.5.2. Pay-offs ×1000 of the political candidates in the example.

From Figure 9.5.2 it follows immediately that the directional political economic equilibrium of the political economic system $\overline{\mathcal{E}}$ with status quo (p^*, x^*) is given by $(0, 1)$, so political candidate 1 proposes to stay at the status quo, while political candidate 2 proposes to increase the price of commodity 1. Notice that the expected plurality of political candidate 2 is positive in this equilibrium.

PART IV

DYNAMIC ASPECTS OF DISEQUILIBRIUM

10

A GLOBALLY AND UNIVERSALLY STABLE PRICE ADJUSTMENT PROCESS

10.1 INTRODUCTION

At least since Walras (1874), economists have been interested in the problem of finding a price adjustment process that generates, for a given economy and an arbitrarily specified starting price system, a path of price systems converging to a price system at which the total excess demand is equal to zero. In Section 3.12 it has been shown that the classical Walrasian tatonnement process may fail to converge if some rather restrictive assumptions on the economy are not satisfied. Therefore, it is interesting to look for alternative price adjustment processes that reach a Walrasian equilibrium price system given any total excess demand function, i.e. any function defined for strictly positive price systems, satisfying homogeneity of degree zero, Walras' law, continuity, and some boundary behaviour, see Theorems 3.7.1, 3.7.2, and 3.11.1. These conditions are the only properties that may be expected for the total excess demand function of an economy, see Theorem 3.13.1.

A universally stable process to generate a fixed point of a function has been presented in Kellog, Li, and Yorke (1976, 1977) and a universally stable price adjustment process to obtain a zero point of a total excess demand function defined for non-negative price systems has been given in Smale (1976). In Varian (1977) it has been shown that the boundary conditions on the total excess demand function used by Smale can be relaxed if the price adjustment process is extended in a particular way outside $\mathbb{R}^N_+$. For a generic economy, for almost every starting price system in the boundary of the domain, Smale's process reaches a Walrasian equilibrium price system. However, an actual price adjustment process should allow for a start with any price system in the interior of the domain. In Keenan (1981) it has been shown that Smale's process is not globally stable, there may exist an open set of starting price systems for which the process does not converge to some Walrasian equilibrium price system.

A globally and universally stable price adjustment process has been presented in Kamiya (1990). Under rather weak conditions on the total excess demand function, among which the boundary condition that the total excess demand function is also defined if the price of some commodities is equal to zero and the total excess demand of a commodity is positive if its price is zero, convergence to a Walrasian equilibrium price system of the economy is guaranteed for almost every starting price system in the relative interior of the unit simplex. It might be possible to weaken this boundary condition in a similar way as in Varian (1977) for Smale's process. However, from an economic point of view such a solution is not completely satisfactory since outside the original domain the price adjustment process is artificially defined and, for example, does not depend on the total excess demand at the price system reached, but instead on the total excess demand at another price system.

In this chapter an alternative globally and universally stable price adjustment process is considered, proposed in van der Laan and Talman (1987a). This process has an appealing economic interpretation. In this chapter it is shown that for a typical economy this price adjustment process converges to a Walrasian equilibrium price system given any starting price system, while standard conditions on utility functions, consumption sets, and initial endowments are made. Under these conditions the total excess demand function is only well defined for strictly positive price systems. Moreover, it is not excluded that the total excess demand of a commodity becomes negative if its price goes to zero.

In Section 10.2 the price adjustment process is described and a definition of stability of the price adjustment process is given. The adjustment of the price system is based on the sign of the total excess demand in all markets and on the change in the price system compared to the starting price system. In the definition of stability of the price adjustment process no differentiability requirements are made with respect to the total excess demand function. In Section 10.3 the price adjustment process is illustrated using Scarf's example, see Section 3.12. For the economy given in this example the price adjustment process converges for every starting price system in the relative interior of the unit simplex. In Section 10.4 the main result holding for a typical exchange economy satisfying standard assumptions is presented. Corollaries of this result are the global and universal stability of the price adjustment process, and the well-known result, first shown in Dierker (1972), that, generically, the number of Walrasian equilibria of an economy is odd. In Section 10.5 the proof of the main result is given. Finally, in Section 10.6 the price adjustment process is analysed for the special case where a total excess demand function satisfying gross substitutability in the finite increment form is given. In this special case global stability does not only hold generically as in the results of Smale (1976), Kamiya (1990), and the results of Section 10.4, but, instead, occurs always. It can even be shown that prices of commodities for which there is a negative (positive) total excess demand are strictly decreasing (increasing) during the price adjustment process. Therefore, the price adjustment process has some features that are qualitatively the same as for the Walrasian tatonnement process. In the gross substitutability case it is also shown that if a market reaches an equilibrium situation during the price adjustment process, then it stays in equilibrium for the remainder of the price adjustment process. In fact, it is proved that in every market the absolute value of the total excess demand is monotonically decreasing over time, an even stronger result.

This chapter is based on Herings (1994a).

10.2 THE PRICE ADJUSTMENT PROCESS

In this section the price adjustment process for the *economy* $\mathcal{E} = ((X^i, \preceq^i, \omega^i)_{i \in I_M})$ as described in Chapter 3 is defined. There are $M \in \mathbb{N}$ *consumers*, indexed by $i \in I_M$, and $N \in \mathbb{N} \setminus \{1\}$ *commodities*, indexed by $j \in I_N$. A consumer $i \in I_M$ has a *consumption set* X^i, a *preference relation* $\preceq^i$, and an *initial endowment* ω^i. The element $(\omega^1, \ldots, \omega^M)$ is denoted by ω, while $\omega_j = (\omega_j^1, \ldots, \omega_j^M)^\top$, $\forall j \in I_N$. The *starting price system* is denoted by v. It determines the *initial state* of the process.

As in Section 3.7, given a *price system* $p \in \mathbb{R}^N$, the *budget set* $\beta^i(p)$ of a consumer $i \in I_M$ is defined by

$$\beta^i(p) = \left\{x^i \in X^i \,\middle|\, p \cdot x^i \leq p \cdot \omega^i \right\},$$

and the set $\delta^i(p)$ is the set of best elements of $\beta^i(p)$ for $\preceq^i$, so

$$\delta^i(p) = \left\{\bar{x}^i \in \beta^i(p) \,\middle|\, \bar{x}^i \succeq^i x^i, \ \forall x^i \in \beta^i(p) \right\}.$$

The *total excess demand relation* $\zeta : \mathbb{R}^N \to \mathbb{R}^N$ of the economy $\mathcal{E}$ is defined by

$$\zeta(p) = \sum_{i \in I_M} \delta^i(p) - \sum_{i \in I_M} \{\omega^i\}, \ \forall p \in \mathbb{R}^N.$$

In Theorems 3.7.1, 3.7.2, and 3.11.1 assumptions with respect to consumption sets, preference relations, and initial endowments are given such that the restriction of the total excess demand relation ζ of the economy $\mathcal{E}$ to $\mathbb{R}^N_{++}$ is a continuous function, which is homogeneous of degree zero and satisfies Walras' law. In this case it makes sense to consider the restriction of ζ to $\mathbb{R}^N_{++}$ given by the *total excess demand function* $z : \mathbb{R}^N_{++} \rightarrow \mathbb{R}^N$. In this section a total excess demand function z is assumed to be given. In Theorem 3.11.1, sufficient conditions on consumption sets, initial endowments, and preference relations are given such that if $p^* \in \mathbb{R}^N$ is a Walrasian equilibrium price system, i.e. $z(p^*) = 0^N$, see Definition 3.8.1 of a *Walrasian equilibrium,* then $p^* \in \mathbb{R}^N_{++}$. Then, using the homogeneity of degree zero of the total excess demand function, there is no loss of generality in normalizing the price systems such that they belong to $\dot{\Delta}^{N-1}$, being the relative interior of the $(N-1)$-dimensional unit simplex Δ^{N-1}.

A sign vector $s \in \mathbb{S}^N$ is called an *admissible sign vector* if there exists $j^1 \in I_N$ such that $s_{j^1} = -1$ and there exists $j^2 \in I_N$ such that $s_{j^2} = +1$. The set $\mathcal{S}$ denotes the *set of admissible sign vectors* of $\mathbb{S}^N$. Recall from Section 2.2 that for every sign vector $s \in \mathbb{S}^N$ the sets $I^-(s)$, $I^0(s)$, and $I^+(s)$ are defined by $I^-(s) = \{j \in I_N \mid s_j = -1\}$, $I^0(s) = \{j \in I_N \mid s_j = 0\}$, and $I^+(s) = \{j \in I_N \mid s_j = +1\}$, whereas $i^-(s)$, $i^0(s)$, and $i^+(s)$ denote the number of elements in the sets $I^-(s)$, $I^0(s)$, and $I^+(s)$, respectively. Notice that for an admissible sign vector $s \in \mathcal{S}$ it holds that $i^0(s) \leq N-2$.

Let some starting price system $v \in \dot{\Delta}^{N-1}$ be given. For every admissible sign vector $s \in \mathcal{S}$, the sets $A(s)$, $B(s)$, and $C(s)$ of price systems are defined by

$$
\begin{aligned}
A(s) = \Big\{p \in \dot{\Delta}^{N-1} \Big| \ & \tfrac{p_j}{v_j} = \min\left(\left\{\tfrac{p_j}{v_j} \,|\, j \in I_N\right\}\right), \ \forall j \in I^-(s), \\
& \tfrac{p_j}{v_j} = \max\left(\left\{\tfrac{p_j}{v_j} \Big| \, j \in I_N\right\}\right), \ \forall j \in I^+(s)\Big\}, \\
B(s) = \Big\{p \in \dot{\Delta}^{N-1} \Big| \ & z_j(p) \leq 0, \ \forall j \in I^-(s), \\
& z_j(p) = 0, \ \forall j \in I^0(s), \\
& z_j(p) \geq 0, \ \forall j \in I^+(s)\Big\}, \\
C(s) = A(s) \cap B(s). &
\end{aligned}
$$

The sets defined above are used to describe the price adjustment process. Let an admissible sign vector $s \in \mathcal{S}$ and a price system $p \in C(s)$ be given. The admissible sign vector s characterizes the *state* of every market. For every $j \in I_N$, if $s_j = -1$ $(s_j = +1)$, then there is a non-positive (non-negative) total excess demand in the market for commodity j and p_j is relatively, i.e. with respect to the starting price v_j, minimal (maximal), whereas $s_j = 0$ implies that the market for commodity j is in equilibrium, while, obviously, p_j is relatively between the relative minimum price and the relative maximum price.

The set C is defined as the set of price systems belonging to $C(s)$ for some $s \in \mathcal{S}$, so

$$C = \cup_{s \in \mathcal{S}} C(s).$$

The price adjustment process is defined such that, under weak assumptions, it follows a path of price systems in the set C.

Let the total excess demand function z satisfy Walras' law and let a starting price system $v \in \dot{\Delta}^{N-1}$ be given. Clearly, there exists a sign vector $\bar{s} \in \mathbb{S}^N$ such that, for every $j \in I_N$, $z_j(v) > 0$ implies $\bar{s}_j = +1$, and $z_j(v) < 0$ implies $\bar{s}_j = -1$, while Walras' law guarantees that indeed $\bar{s}$ can be chosen such that it is an element of $\mathcal{S}$. Then it holds that $v \in B(\bar{s})$, obviously $v \in A(\bar{s})$, hence $v \in C(\bar{s}) \subset C$. Now consider a Walrasian equilibrium price system $p^* \in \dot{\Delta}^{N-1}$. Clearly, there exists an admissible sign vector $\hat{s} \in \mathcal{S}$ such that, for every $j \in I_N$, $\hat{s}_j = -1$ implies $\frac{p_j^*}{v_j} = \min(\{\frac{p_j^*}{v_j} \mid j \in I_N\})$, and $\hat{s}_j = +1$ implies $\frac{p_j^*}{v_j} = \max(\{\frac{p_j^*}{v_j} \mid j \in I_N\})$. Then it holds that $p^* \in A(\hat{s})$, clearly $p^* \in B(\hat{s})$, and therefore $p^* \in C(\hat{s}) \subset C$. Hence, the set C contains both the starting price system v and all Walrasian equilibrium price systems of $\dot{\Delta}^{N-1}$.

Definition 10.2.1 (Price adjustment process)
The price adjustment process *for the total excess demand function* $z : \mathbb{R}^N_{++} \to \mathbb{R}^N$ *and the starting price system* $v \in \dot{\Delta}^{N-1}$ *is given by the component of* v *in* C.

The price adjustment process is therefore described by considering explicitly the price systems generated by it. Since in the definition of the price adjustment process under consideration no continuity or differentiability assumptions with respect to the total excess demand function are used, one should also give a definition of convergence without using such assumptions.

Definition 10.2.2 (Convergence)
The price adjustment process for the total excess demand function $z : \mathbb{R}^N_{++} \to \mathbb{R}^N$ *and the starting price system* $v \in \dot{\Delta}^{N-1}$ *is* convergent *if either* $z(v) = 0^N$, *or* $z(v) \neq 0^N$ *and the component of* v *in* C *is an arc having* v *and a Walrasian equilibrium price system as its boundary points.*

The definition of convergence given in Definition 10.2.2 implies convergence of a dynamic process as defined in Section 3.11. If the price adjustment process is convergent according to the latter definition, then there exists a continuous function $\pi : [0,1] \to \mathbb{R}^N_{++}$ such that $\pi(0) = v$ and $\pi(1)$ is a Walrasian equilibrium price system, so $z(\pi(1)) = 0^N$. When the price adjustment process is convergent according to Definition 10.2.2, then such a function π clearly exists, whereas, moreover, π is injective and has a continuous inverse.

In Section 10.5 the price adjustment process is shown to be convergent, generically. Then there exists a unique, continuous trajectory of price systems leading from the starting price system v to a Walrasian equilibrium price system. Let the function π with domain $[0,1]$ and being such that $\pi(0) = v$ and $\pi(1)$ is a Walrasian equilibrium price system describe this trajectory. An element of the set $[0,1]$ can be considered as a normalized time parameter. Although the arc $\pi([0,1])$ is uniquely determined, the function π is not unique, and different functions correspond to different speeds of adjustment. Notice that it is only required that the arc contains some Walrasian equilibrium price system, which means that even if the starting price system is "sufficiently close" to a certain Walrasian equilibrium price system, then the price adjustment process may converge to another Walrasian equilibrium price system. So, in the terminology of Saari and Simon (1978) or Saari (1985), Definition 10.2.2 does not correspond to a locally effective or locally convergent mechanism.

The price adjustment process can be followed numerically arbitrarily close using the (2^N-2)-ray algorithm described in Doup, van der Laan, and Talman (1987). This algorithm is a simplicial algorithm with vector labelling defined on Δ^{N-1}. It can be applied to a piecewise linear approximation of the total excess demand function with respect to a triangulation being such that a proper subset of the collection of faces of the simplices in the triangulation yields a triangulation of the set $A(s)$, $\forall s \in \mathcal{S}$. Theorem 2.7.5 guarantees that the V-triangulation of Δ^{N-1} with respect to v and with grid size $\frac{1}{n}$ for some $n \in \mathbb{N}$ satisfies these properties. The $(2^N - 2)$-ray algorithm generates a piecewise linear path of points corresponding to the price adjustment process in a similar way as the piecewise linear path of points generated by the simplicial algorithm with vector labelling of Chapter 6, see Theorem 6.2.11, corresponds to the set of constrained equilibria of an economy with price rigidities. The information needed at some price system p reached by the algorithm is given by a finite number (at most N) of price systems already generated by the algorithm, the total excess demands at these price systems, and the starting price system v. This means that the amount of information needed is roughly the same as the amount indicated in Saari and Simon (1978) as being necessary for convergence.

The price adjustment process for the total excess demand function $z : \mathbb{R}^N_{++} \to \mathbb{R}^N$ and the starting price system $v \in \dot{\Delta}^{N-1}$ has an appealing economic interpretation which can be described as follows. First, the sign of the total excess demand is evaluated at the starting price system v. Consider the case where $z_j(v) \neq 0, \forall j \in I_N$. In Section 10.5 this is shown to be the generic case. Initially, the price of a commodity $j \in I_N$ with $z_j(v) < 0$ is decreased, while the price of a commodity $j \in I_N$ with $z_j(v) > 0$ is increased. Let the admissible sign vector $s^0 \in \mathcal{S}$ be defined by $s^0_j = +1$ if $z_j(v) > 0$ and $s^0_j = -1$ if $z_j(v) < 0$. Then the process starts by leaving v along the ray $A(s^0)$ of price systems. The ratio of prices of commodities for which there is a negative total excess demand is kept constant among those commodities for which there is a negative total excess demand, and similarly for the ratio of prices of commodities for which there is a positive total excess demand. The price system is adjusted in this way until a market, say the market for a commodity $j^1 \in I_N$, attains an equilibrium state.

Assume that there is a single market attaining an equilibrium. This is shown to be the generic case in Section 10.5. Then the price adjustment process continues by keeping the market for commodity j^1 in equilibrium, while the price p_{j^1} is relatively increased (decreased) if there was a negative (positive) total excess demand in the market for commodity j^1 before attaining equilibrium. Other prices are kept relatively minimal in the case of a negative total excess demand and relatively maximal in the case of a positive total excess demand. Hence, a path of price systems in $C(s^1)$ is followed, where $s^1_{j^1} = 0$ and $s^1_j = s^0_j$, $\forall j \in I_N \setminus \{j^1\}$. It is shown in Section 10.4 that the set $C(s)$, $\forall s \in \mathcal{S}$, is compact and in Section 10.5 that, generically, it is a finite collection of arcs and loops. Now two situations can occur at the other end point of the arc of $C(s^1)$ that is followed by the price adjustment process. Either another market, say the market for a commodity j^2, attains an equilibrium situation. In this case the price system is adjusted in such a way that the markets for commodities j^1 and j^2 are kept in equilibrium, while the price in the market for commodity j^2 is relatively increased (decreased) when there was a negative (positive) total excess demand in the market for commodity j^2 before attaining equilibrium. Again, other prices are kept either relatively minimal or relatively maximal. Hence, a path of price systems in $C(s^2)$ is followed, where $s^2_{j^2} = 0$ and $s^2_j = s^1_j$, $\forall j \in I_N \setminus \{j^2\}$. Or the price in the market for commodity j^1 becomes relatively minimal or maximal. In this case the market for commodity j^1 is no longer kept in equilibrium but its total excess demand is allowed to become negative or positive, respectively, while p_{j^1} is kept relatively minimal or relatively maximal, respectively. Then a path of price systems in $C(s^2)$ is followed, where $s^2_{j^1} = -1$ or $s^2_{j^1} = +1$, respectively, and $s^2_j = s^1_j$, $\forall j \in I_N \setminus \{j^1\}$.

The general case is as follows. Suppose the price adjustment process follows a path of price systems in $C(s^n)$ for some $n \in \mathbb{N}$. Then at the end point either the market for a commodity $j^{n+1} \in I^-(s^n) \cup I^+(s^n)$ attains an equilibrium situation, in which case a path of price systems in $C(s^{n+1})$ is followed, where $s^{n+1}_{j^{n+1}} = 0$ and $s^{n+1}_j = s^n_j$, $\forall j \in I_N \setminus \{j^{n+1}\}$, so the price adjustment process continues by keeping the market for commodity j^{n+1} in equilibrium, while $p_{j^{n+1}}$ is relatively increased (decreased) if there was a negative (positive) total excess demand in the market for commodity j^{n+1} before attaining equilibrium, the markets for commodities $j \in I^0(s^n)$ are kept in equilibrium, for commodities $j \in I^-(s^n) \setminus \{j^{n+1}\}$, p_j is kept relatively minimal, and for commodities $j \in I^+(s^n) \setminus \{j^{n+1}\}$, p_j is kept relatively maximal. Or the price of some commodity $j^{n+1} \in I^0(s^n)$ becomes relatively minimal (maximal) in which case a path of price systems in $C(s^{n+1})$ is followed, where $s^{n+1}_{j^{n+1}} = -1$ ($s^{n+1}_{j^{n+1}} = +1$) and $s^{n+1}_j = s^n_j$, $\forall j \in I_N \setminus \{j^{n+1}\}$. Now the market for commodity j^{n+1} is no longer kept in equilibrium, the total excess demand in the market for commodity j^{n+1} is allowed to become negative (positive), while $p_{j^{n+1}}$ is kept relatively minimal (maximal). It is shown that, generically, the process described above converges to a Walrasian equilibrium price system.

In the Walrasian tatonnement process as formulated in Samuelson (1941), see Section 3.11, it is possible that after some time the price adjustment process reaches a price system being such that the price of a commodity is higher (lower) than its starting price, while there is a negative (positive) total excess demand in the market for this commodity. This is a remarkable phenomenon since initially the Walrasian tatonnement process changes the price system in such a way that prices of commodities for which there is a negative total excess demand are lowered and prices of commodities for which there is a positive total excess demand are raised with respect to the starting price system. Any price system on the path generated by the price adjustment process of this chapter has the natural property that the price of a commodity with a negative total excess demand is lower than its starting price, while the price of a commodity with a positive total excess demand is higher than the corresponding starting price.

It is also possible to define the price adjustment process considered in this chapter for the case with non-trivial production possibilities. In van den Elzen (1993) and in van den Elzen, van der Laan, and Talman (1994) the case where the production possibility set corresponds to the *linear activity model* has been considered, and in van der Laan and Kremers (1993) the case with *constant returns to scale* has been analysed. Van den Elzen (1995) gives a process for a case with rather general production possibilities. However, no proof of the global and universal stability of the price adjustment process is given in the literature. Van den Elzen (1995) shows that the approach of this chapter can be extended to cases with production.

The approach taken in this chapter is related to the one of Smale (1976, 1981) and Kamiya (1990). In Smale (1976) commodity N is considered to be a *numeraire commodity* and a price adjustment process is defined for a total excess demand function $z : \mathbb{R}_+^{N-1} \times \{1\} \to \mathbb{R}^N$ and a starting price system $v \in \mathbb{R}_+^N$ with $v_N = 1$, following price systems in the set

$$\left\{p \in \mathbb{R}_+^N \,\middle|\, p_N = 1 \text{ and } \exists \lambda \in \mathbb{R}_+,\ \forall j \in I_{N-1},\ z_j(p) = \lambda z_j(v)\right\}.$$

It is easily verified that taking $\lambda = 1$ yields that $p = v$ is an element of this set, and taking $\lambda = 0$ yields that p^* is an element of the set if p^* is a Walrasian equilibrium price system with $p_N^* = 1$.

Let the set T^{N-1} be defined by $T^{N-1} = \{p \in \mathbb{R}_+^N \mid \sum_{j \in I_N} (p_j)^2 = 1\}$, being a normalized price space. In Kamiya (1990) a price adjustment process is defined for a total excess demand function $z : \mathbb{R}_+^N \to \mathbb{R}^N$, generating price systems in the set

$$\left\{p \in T^{N-1} \,\middle|\, \exists \lambda \in [0,1],\ \forall j \in I_{N-1},\ (1-\lambda) z_j(p) = \lambda (p_j - v_j)\right\},$$

with $v \in T^{N-1}$ again the starting price system. It is easily verified that $\lambda = 1$ yields $p = v$ as the unique solution. By considering $\lambda = 0$ it follows that if $p^* \in T^{N-1}$ is a Walrasian equilibrium price system, then p^* is an element of the set given above.

By making suitable differentiability, regularity, and boundary conditions, it can be shown for the price adjustment processes of Smale (1976) and Kamiya (1990) that the component of v in the sets defined above is an arc. It should be remarked that any arc described as the solution to a system of continuously differentiable functions satisfying certain regularity properties can be described by a system of differential equations, see for example Garcia and Zangwill (1981). This system of differential equations is given in Smale (1976) and Kamiya (1990) for their processes and can also be given for the price adjustment process of this chapter, where for every $s \in S$ a different system is needed.

10.3 SCARF'S EXAMPLE

The price adjustment process can be illustrated using Scarf's example concerning an exchange economy with three commodities. It can be shown that for this

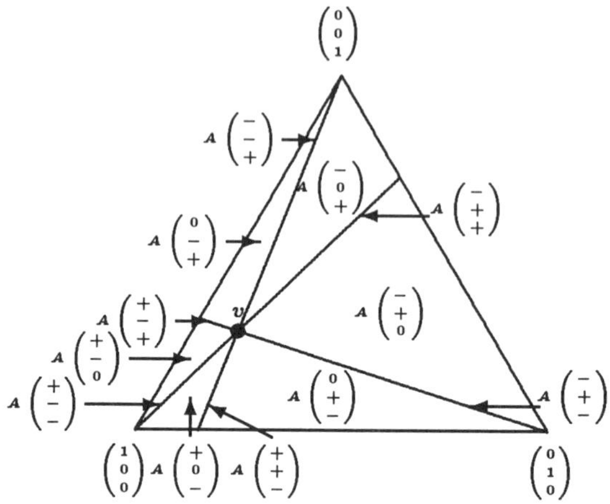

Figure 10.3.1. The sets $A(s)$, for $s \in \mathcal{S}$, in Scarf's example, $v = (\frac{11}{18}, \frac{2}{18}, \frac{5}{18})^\top$.

example the Walrasian tatonnement process does not converge for any starting price system except for the unique Walrasian equilibrium price system, see Section 3.12. In this example the economy $\mathcal{E} = ((X^i, \preceq^i, \omega^i)_{i \in I_3})$ is such that $N = 3$, $X^1 = X^2 = X^3 = \mathbb{R}^3_+$, $\preceq^1$, $\preceq^2$, and $\preceq^3$ can be represented by utility functions $u^1 : X^1 \to \mathbb{R}$, $u^2 : X^2 \to \mathbb{R}$, and $u^3 : X^3 \to \mathbb{R}$, respectively, defined by $u^1(x^1) = \min(\{x^1_1, x^1_2\})$, $\forall x^1 \in \mathbb{R}^3_+$, $u^2(x^2) = \min(\{x^2_2, x^2_3\})$, $\forall x^2 \in \mathbb{R}^3_+$, $u^3(x^3) = \min(\{x^3_1, x^3_3\})$, $\forall x^3 \in \mathbb{R}^3_+$, and $\omega^1 = (1,0,0)^\top$, $\omega^2 = (0,1,0)^\top$, and $\omega^3 = (0,0,1)^\top$. The total excess demand function $z : \mathbb{R}^3_{++} \to \mathbb{R}^3$ of the economy is given by

$$z_1(p) = \frac{-p_2}{p_1+p_2} + \frac{p_3}{p_1+p_3}, \quad \forall p \in \mathbb{R}^3_{++},$$
$$z_2(p) = \frac{-p_3}{p_2+p_3} + \frac{p_1}{p_1+p_2}, \quad \forall p \in \mathbb{R}^3_{++},$$
$$z_3(p) = \frac{-p_1}{p_1+p_3} + \frac{p_2}{p_2+p_3}, \quad \forall p \in \mathbb{R}^3_{++},$$

and the unique Walrasian equilibrium price system of $\dot{\Delta}^2$ is given by $p^* = (\frac{1}{3}, \frac{1}{3}, \frac{1}{3})^\top$, see Section 3.12. Let some $p \in \mathbb{R}^3_{++}$ be given. It is easily verified that $z_1(p) = 0$ if and only if $p_2 = p_3$, $z_2(p) = 0$ if and only if $p_1 = p_3$, and $z_3(p) = 0$ if and only if $p_1 = p_2$. Consider the starting price system $v = (\frac{11}{18}, \frac{2}{18}, \frac{5}{18})^\top$. In Figure 10.3.1 the sets $A(s)$ and in Figure 10.3.2 the sets $B(s)$ are drawn for all $s \in \mathcal{S}$. In Figure 10.3.3 the set C is depicted.

In Scarf's example there is positive total excess demand in the markets for both commodities 1 and 2 at $v = (\frac{11}{18}, \frac{2}{18}, \frac{5}{18})^\top$. The process therefore starts by following an arc in $C((+1, +1, -1)^\top)$, having v as a boundary point. So, the prices of both commodities 1 and 2 are relatively increased. At $p = (\frac{11}{15}, \frac{2}{15}, \frac{2}{15})^\top$ the market for commodity 1 attains an equilibrium situation. Now this market is kept in equilibrium, the relative price for commodity 2 is kept maximal, and the relative price of commodity 3 is kept minimal, so a path in $C((0, +1, -1)^\top)$ is followed. At $p = (\frac{11}{21}, \frac{5}{21}, \frac{5}{21})^\top$ the price of commodity 1 becomes relatively minimal and equal to the relative price of commodity 3. Hence, the process continues by following a path in $C((-1, +1, -1)^\top)$, where the prices of both commodities 1 and 3 are relatively decreased and the price of commodity 2 is relatively increased. The market for commodity 1 is no longer in equilibrium. At $p = (\frac{11}{27}, \frac{11}{27}, \frac{5}{27})^\top$ the market for commodity 3 attains an equilibrium situation and so a path in $C((-1, +1, 0)^\top)$ is followed. At $p^* = (\frac{1}{3}, \frac{1}{3}, \frac{1}{3})^\top$ the process reaches a Walrasian equilibrium price system of the economy. Therefore, the price adjustment process is convergent if $v = (\frac{11}{18}, \frac{2}{18}, \frac{5}{18})^\top$. It can be shown that the price adjustment process is globally stable in Scarf's example. Consider an

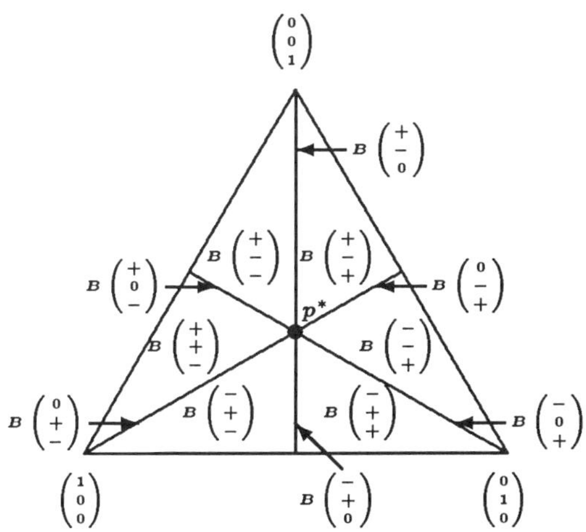

Figure 10.3.2. The sets $B(s)$, for $s \in S$, in Scarf's example.

arbitrary v in the relative interior of $B((+1, +1, -1)^\top)$. Then $v_1 > v_3 > v_2$. It is easily verified that subsequently the paths $C((+1, +1, -1)^\top)$, $C((0, +1, -1)^\top)$, $C((-1, +1, -1)^\top)$, and $C((-1, +1, 0)^\top)$ are followed, having as end points

$$(\tfrac{v_1}{v_1+2v_2}, \tfrac{v_2}{v_1+2v_2}, \tfrac{v_2}{v_1+2v_2})^\top, (\tfrac{v_1}{v_1+2v_3}, \tfrac{v_3}{v_1+2v_3}, \tfrac{v_3}{v_1+2v_3})^\top, (\tfrac{v_1}{2v_1+v_3}, \tfrac{v_1}{2v_1+v_3}, \tfrac{v_3}{2v_1+v_3})^\top, \text{ and } (\tfrac{1}{3}, \tfrac{1}{3}, \tfrac{1}{3})^\top.$$

If v is in the relative interior of $B((+1,-1,+1)^\top)$ or $B((-1,+1,+1)^\top)$, then a completely symmetric case results. Now consider an arbitrary v in the relative interior of $B((+1,-1,-1)^\top)$. Then $v_3 > v_1 > v_2$. It is easily verified that subsequently the paths $C((+1,-1,-1)^\top), C((+1,0,-1)^\top), C((+1,+1,-1)^\top)$, and $C((0,+1,-1)^\top)$ are followed, having as end points

$$(\tfrac{v_3}{v_2+2v_3}, \tfrac{v_2}{v_2+2v_3}, \tfrac{v_3}{v_2+2v_3})^\top, (\tfrac{v_1}{2v_1+v_2}, \tfrac{v_2}{2v_1+v_2}, \tfrac{v_1}{2v_1+v_2})^\top, (\tfrac{v_1}{v_1+2v_2}, \tfrac{v_2}{v_1+2v_2}, \tfrac{v_2}{v_1+2v_2})^\top, \text{ and } (\tfrac{1}{3}, \tfrac{1}{3}, \tfrac{1}{3})^\top.$$

If v is in the relative interior of $B((-1,+1,-1)^\top)$ or $B((-1,-1,+1)^\top)$, then again a completely symmetric case results. Consider an arbitrary v in the relative interior of $B((0,+1,-1)^\top)$. Then $v_1 > v_2 = v_3$. It is easily verified that subsequently the paths $C((-1,+1,-1)^\top)$ and $C((-1,+1,0)^\top)$ are followed, having as end points

$$(\tfrac{v_1}{2v_1+v_3}, \tfrac{v_1}{2v_1+v_3}, \tfrac{v_3}{2v_1+v_3})^\top \text{ and } (\tfrac{1}{3}, \tfrac{1}{3}, \tfrac{1}{3})^\top.$$

A point v is in the relative interior of $B((+1,-1,0)^\top)$ or $B((-1,0,+1)^\top)$ yields a completely symmetric case. Consider some point v in the relative interior of $B((+1,0,-1)^\top)$. Then $v_1 = v_3 > v_2$. It is easily verified that subsequently the paths $C((+1,+1,-1)^\top)$ and $C((0,+1,-1)^\top)$ are followed, having as end points

$$(\tfrac{v_1}{v_1+2v_2}, \tfrac{v_2}{v_1+2v_2}, \tfrac{v_2}{v_1+2v_2})^\top \text{ and } (\tfrac{1}{3}, \tfrac{1}{3}, \tfrac{1}{3})^\top.$$

A point v in the relative interior of $B((0,-1,+1)^\top)$ or $B((-1,+1,0)^\top)$ yields again a completely symmetric case. If v is equal to $(\frac{1}{3}, \frac{1}{3}, \frac{1}{3})^\top$, then the Walrasian equilibrium price system is immediately obtained.

10.4 GLOBAL AND UNIVERSAL STABILITY OF THE WALRASIAN EQUILIBRIUM

For every consumer $i \in I_M$, the consumption set X^i and the preference relation $\preceq^i$ are assumed to be given in this section. To show that, generically, the price adjustment process is globally and universally stable, the following standard assumptions on consumption sets and preference relations are made.

A1. For every consumer $i \in I_M$, the consumption set X^i is equal to $\mathbb{R}^N_{++}$.

A2. For every consumer $i \in I_M$, the preference relation $\preceq^i$ is complete, transitive, continuous, strongly monotonic, strongly convex, of the class C^3, satisfies the boundary condition, and has non-zero Gaussian curvature.

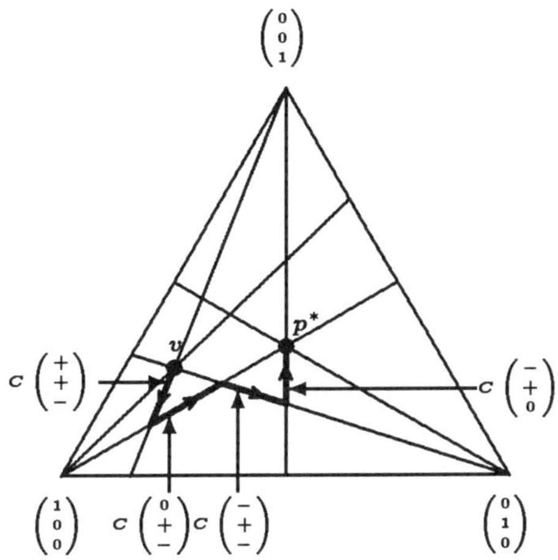

Figure 10.3.3. The sets $C(s)$, for $s \in \mathcal{S}$, in Scarf's example, $v = (\frac{11}{18}, \frac{2}{18}, \frac{5}{18})^\top$.

If the economy $\mathcal{E} = ((X^i, \preceq^i, \omega^i)_{i \in I_M})$ satisfies Assumptions A1-A2, and for every consumer $i \in I_M$ it holds that $\omega^i \in X^i$, then it easily follows from Theorem 9.2.1 that the total excess demand function $z : \mathbb{R}^N_{++} \to \mathbb{R}^N$ of the economy $\mathcal{E}$ belongs to $C^2(\mathbb{R}^N_{++}, \mathbb{R}^N)$. Clearly, the price adjustment process is well defined in this case.

Let $(X^i, \preceq^i)_{i \in I_M}$ satisfy Assumptions A1-A2 and let $v \in \dot{\Delta}^{N-1}$ be the starting price system. The set Ω is defined by $\Omega = \prod_{i \in I_M} \mathbb{R}^N_{++}$. In Definition 10.4.1, the initial endowment ω of Ω is called *regular* if the set C for the economy $\mathcal{E} = ((X^i, \preceq^i, \omega^i)_{i \in I_M})$ with starting price system v has a certain nice structure.

Definition 10.4.1 (Regular initial endowments)
Let $(X^i, \preceq^i)_{i \in I_M}$ satisfy Assumptions A1-A2 and let $v \in \dot{\Delta}^{N-1}$ be the starting price system. The set of regular initial endowments, *denoted by Ω^*, is the set of initial endowments ω of Ω for which the components of the set C for the economy $\mathcal{E} = ((X^i, \preceq^i, \omega^i)_{i \in I_M})$ with starting price system v are given by*

1. *an arc containing v and precisely one Walrasian equilibrium price system as boundary points,*

2. *a finite number of arcs containing precisely two Walrasian equilibrium price systems both being boundary points,*

3. *a finite number of loops containing neither v nor any Walrasian equilibrium price system.*

Theorem 10.4.2 states that the set of non-regular initial endowments is small, both in a topological and in a measure theoretic sense.

Theorem 10.4.2
Let $(X^i, \preceq^i)_{i \in I_M}$ satisfy Assumptions A1-A2 and let $v \in \dot{\Delta}^{N-1}$ be the starting price system. Then the set of non-regular initial endowments $\Omega \setminus \Omega^*$ has a closure in Ω with Lebesgue measure zero.

Theorem 10.4.2 is proved in Section 10.5. In fact, the proof of Theorem 10.4.2 yields that the path of price systems followed by the price adjustment process for $\omega \in \Omega^*$ is a 1-dimensional piecewise C^2 manifold, i.e. a 1-dimensional continuous manifold that is a finite union of C^2 manifolds, some possibly of lower dimension. Moreover, the other components of the set C are either loops or arcs, both being 1-dimensional piecewise C^2 manifolds. Since $\omega \in \Omega^*$ implies that the price adjustment process converges, Theorem 10.4.2 immediately leads to the next result, where $\overline{\Omega}$ can be taken equal to Ω^*.

Corollary 10.4.3
Let $(X^i, \preceq^i)_{i \in I_M}$ satisfy Assumptions A1-A2 and let $v \in \dot{\Delta}^{N-1}$ be the starting price system. Then there exists a subset $\overline{\Omega}$ of Ω such that the closure of $\Omega \setminus \overline{\Omega}$ in Ω has Lebesgue measure zero and for every $\omega \in \overline{\Omega}$ the price adjustment process for the economy $\mathcal{E} = ((X^i, \preceq^i, \omega^i)_{i \in I_M})$ with starting price system v converges to a Walrasian equilibrium price system of $\mathcal{E}$.

Since every Walrasian equilibrium price system of $\dot{\Delta}^{N-1}$ is an element of C, Theorem 10.4.2 confirms the well-known result of Dierker (1972) that, generically, an economy has an odd number of Walrasian equilibria.

Corollary 10.4.4
Let $(X^i, \preceq^i)_{i \in I_M}$ satisfy Assumptions A1-A2. Then there exists a subset $\overline{\Omega}$ of Ω such that the closure of $\Omega \setminus \overline{\Omega}$ in Ω has Lebesgue measure zero and for every $\omega \in \overline{\Omega}$ the number of Walrasian equilibria of the economy $\mathcal{E} = ((X^i, \preceq^i, \omega^i)_{i \in I_M})$ with the Walrasian equilibrium price system belonging to $\dot{\Delta}^{N-1}$ is finite and odd.

Let $(X^i, \preceq^i)_{i\in I_M}$ satisfy Assumptions A1-A2 and let $v \in \dot{\Delta}^{N-1}$ be the starting price system. For every $\omega \in \Omega$, the set $P(\omega)$ is defined as the component of v in C, for every $s \in S$, the set $\widehat{P}_s(\omega)$ is defined as the set $C(s)$, and the set $\widehat{P}(\omega)$ is defined as the set C for the economy $\mathcal{E} = ((X^i, \preceq^i, \omega^i)_{i\in I_M})$ with starting price system v. In this way one obtains the *price adjustment process correspondence* $P : \Omega \to \dot{\Delta}^{N-1}$ and a correspondence $\widehat{P} : \Omega \to \dot{\Delta}^{N-1}$. Notice that the price adjustment correspondence P and the correspondence $\widehat{P}$ are non-empty valued since, for every $\omega \in \Omega$, the starting price system v belongs to $P(\omega)$ and $P(\omega) \subset \widehat{P}(\omega)$. To make clear the dependence of the total excess demand function on the initial endowments, ω is included in the notation, and the domain of z is assumed to be $\mathbb{R}^N_{++} \times \Omega$ for the remainder of this section and in Section 10.5. Therefore, for every $p \in \mathbb{R}^N_{++}$, for every $\omega \in \Omega$, $z(p, \omega)$ denotes the total excess demand at p of the economy $\mathcal{E} = ((X^i, \preceq^i, \omega^i)_{i\in I_M})$.

Let $(X^i, \preceq^i)_{i\in I_M}$ satisfy Assumptions A1-A2. Similarly as in Section 3.6, $\widetilde{d}^i(p, w^i)$ denotes the demand of a consumer $i \in I_M$ at the price system $p \in \mathbb{R}^N_{++}$ and *wealth* $w^i \in \mathbb{R}_{++}$, i.e. the best element of $\{x^i \in X^i \mid p \cdot x^i \leq w^i\}$ for $\preceq^i$. From Theorem 9.2.1 it follows that $\widetilde{d}^i : \mathbb{R}^N_{++} \times \mathbb{R}_{++}$ is a twice continuously differentiable function. Notice that $z(p, \omega) = \sum_{i\in I_M} \widetilde{d}^i(p, p \cdot \omega^i) - \sum_{i\in I_M} \omega^i$, $\forall (p, \omega) \in \mathbb{R}^N_{++} \times \Omega$.

Let a non-empty, compact subset S of $\mathbb{R}^m$ be given. The function $d_S : \mathbb{R}^m \to \mathbb{R}$ is defined by

$$d_S(s) = \min\left(\{\|s - \bar{s}\|_\infty \mid \bar{s} \in S\}\right), \ \forall s \in \mathbb{R}^m.$$

Lemma 5.3.2 states that d_S is a continuous function.

Let S^1 and S^2 be two non-empty, compact subsets of $\mathbb{R}^m$. Then $e(S^1, S^2) \in \mathbb{R}_+$ is defined by

$$e(S^1, S^2) = \min\left(\left\{\|s^1 - s^2\|_\infty \,\middle|\, s^1 \in S^1, s^2 \in S^2\right\}\right).$$

If S^1 and S^2 are disjoint, then obviously $e(S^1, S^2) > 0$.

Theorem 10.4.5
Let $(X^i, \preceq^i)_{i\in I_M}$ satisfy Assumptions A1-A2 and let $v \in \dot{\Delta}^{N-1}$ be the starting price system. Then P and $\widehat{P}$ are compact-valued, upper hemi-continuous correspondences from Ω into $\dot{\Delta}^{N-1}$.

Proof
First $\widehat{P}$ is shown to be a compact-valued, upper hemi-continuous correspondence. Let $((\omega)^n)_{n\in\mathbb{N}}$ be a sequence in Ω converging to some $\bar{\omega} \in \Omega$ and

let $(p^n)_{n\in\mathbb{N}}$ be a sequence in $\dot{\Delta}^{N-1}$ such that $p^n \in \widehat{P}((\omega)^n)$, $\forall n \in \mathbb{N}$. It is shown that $(p^n)_{n\in\mathbb{N}}$ has a subsequence converging to some $\overline{p} \in \widehat{P}(\overline{\omega})$. Then $\widehat{P}$ is compact-valued, and, by Theorem 2.5.6, an upper hemi-continuous correspondence. Since Δ^{N-1} is compact, $(p^n)_{n\in\mathbb{N}}$ has a subsequence $(p^{n^m})_{m\in\mathbb{N}}$ converging to some $\overline{p} \in \Delta^{N-1}$. Moreover, since $\mathcal{S}$ is a finite set, without loss of generality, there exists $\overline{s} \in \mathcal{S}$ such that, for every $m \in \mathbb{N}$, $p^{n^m} \in \widehat{P}_{\overline{s}}((\omega)^{n^m})$. Clearly, for every $m \in \mathbb{N}$, $z_j(p^{n^m},(\omega)^{n^m}) \leq 0$ if $j \in I^-(\overline{s})$, $z_j(p^{n^m},(\omega)^{n^m}) = 0$ if $j \in I^0(\overline{s})$, and $z_j(p^{n^m},(\omega)^{n^m}) \geq 0$ and $p_j^{n^m} \geq v_j$ if $j \in I^+(\overline{s})$. Therefore, for every $m' \in \mathbb{N}$ it holds that

$$\begin{aligned}
&\left\| z\left(p^{n^{m'}},(\omega)^{n^{m'}}\right)\right\|_\infty \\
&= \max\Big(\Big\{\max(\{-z_j(p^{n^{m'}},(\omega)^{n^{m'}}) | j\in I^-(\overline{s})\}), \max(\{z_j(p^{n^{m'}},(\omega)^{n^{m'}}) | j\in I^+(\overline{s})\})\Big\}\Big) \\
&\leq \frac{\sup(\{\|\sum_{i\in I_M}\omega^{i^{n^m}}\|_\infty \mid m\in\mathbb{N}\})}{\min(\{v_j \mid j \in I^+(\overline{s})\})}.
\end{aligned} \tag{10.1}$$

Notice that the right-hand side of (10.1) is finite.

Let some $i \in I_M$ be given. Using (10.1) it follows that $(\widetilde{d^i}(p^{n^m}, p^{n^m}\cdot\omega^{i^{n^m}}))_{m\in\mathbb{N}}$ is a bounded sequence, and, without loss of generality, it can be assumed to converge to some $\overline{x}^i \in \mathbb{R}^N_+$. Moreover, using that $\preceq^i$ satisfies the boundary condition and $\omega^{i^{n^m}} \to \overline{\omega}^i \in \mathbb{R}^N_{++}$, it follows that $\overline{x}^i \in \mathbb{R}^N_{++} = X^i$. Let some $\widehat{x}^i \in X^i$ with $\overline{p}\cdot\widehat{x}^i \leq \overline{p}\cdot\overline{\omega}^i$ be given. If $\overline{p}\cdot\widehat{x}^i < \overline{p}\cdot\overline{\omega}^i$, then there exists $m' \in \mathbb{N}$ such that, for every $m \geq m'$, $p^{n^m}\cdot\widehat{x}^i < p^{n^m}\cdot\omega^{i^{n^m}}$, so $\widehat{x}^i \preceq^i \widetilde{d^i}(p^{n^m}, p^{n^m}\cdot\omega^{i^{n^m}})$ and, by the continuity of $\preceq^i$, $\widehat{x}^i \preceq^i \overline{x}^i$. If $\overline{p}\cdot\widehat{x}^i = \overline{p}\cdot\overline{\omega}^i$, then, for every $m \in \mathbb{N}$, there exists $x^{i^{n^m}} \in X^i$ such that $\overline{p}\cdot x^{i^{n^m}} < \overline{p}\cdot\overline{\omega}^i$ and the sequence $(x^{i^{n^m}})_{m\in\mathbb{N}}$ converges to $\widehat{x}^i$. Now it follows as before that $x^{i^{n^m}} \preceq^i \overline{x}^i$, $\forall m \in \mathbb{N}$, so the continuity of $\preceq^i$ implies that $\widehat{x}^i \preceq^i \overline{x}^i$.

Suppose $\overline{p} \in \Delta^{N-1}\setminus\dot{\Delta}^{N-1}$. Then there exists $j' \in I_N$ such that $\overline{p}_{j'} = 0$. Hence, $\overline{x}^i + e^N(j') \in X^i$, $\overline{p}\cdot(\overline{x}^i + e^N(j')) \leq \overline{p}\cdot\overline{x}^i$, so $\overline{x}^i + e^N(j') \preceq^i \overline{x}^i$, contradicting the strong monotonicity of $\preceq^i$. Consequently, $\overline{p} \in \dot{\Delta}^{N-1}$.

From Theorem 9.2.1 it follows that $z : \mathbb{R}^N_{++}\times\Omega \to \mathbb{R}^N$ is a continuous function. Since $(p^{n^m}, \omega^{n^m}) \to (\overline{p},\overline{\omega}) \in \dot{\Delta}^{N-1}\times\Omega$, it follows immediately that $\overline{p} \in \widehat{P}_{\overline{s}}(\overline{\omega})$. So, $\widehat{P}$ is a compact-valued, upper hemi-continuous correspondence.

Now let $((\omega)^n)_{n\in\mathbb{N}}$ be a sequence in Ω converging to some $\overline{\omega} \in \Omega$ and let $(p^n)_{n\in\mathbb{N}}$ be a sequence in $\dot{\Delta}^{N-1}$ such that $p^n \in P((\omega)^n)$. It is shown that $(p^n)_{n\in\mathbb{N}}$ has a subsequence converging to some $\overline{p} \in P(\overline{\omega})$. Then P is compact-valued, and, by Theorem 2.5.6, an upper hemi-continuous correspondence. Using the previous paragraph, without loss of generality, it can be assumed that $(p^n)_{n\in\mathbb{N}}$ converges to some $\overline{p} \in \widehat{P}(\overline{\omega})$. Since $P(\overline{\omega})$ is the component of v in $\widehat{P}(\overline{\omega})$, the closure of $P(\overline{\omega})$ in $\widehat{P}(\overline{\omega})$ is connected by Theorem 2.3.11, and since

$\widehat{P}(\overline{\omega})$ is compact, it follows that $P(\overline{\omega})$ is compact.
Suppose $\overline{p} \notin P(\overline{\omega})$. By Lemma 5.3.4 the component of v in $\widehat{P}(\overline{\omega})$ equals the quasi-component of v in $\widehat{P}(\overline{\omega})$. Therefore, there exist disjoint compact sets S^1 and S^2 such that $v \in S^1$, $\overline{p} \in S^2$, and $S^1 \cup S^2 = \widehat{P}(\overline{\omega})$. Hence, there exists $\varepsilon \in \mathbb{R}_{++}$ such that $e(S^1, S^2) > \varepsilon$. By the upper hemi-continuity of the correspondence $\widehat{P}$ there exists $n^1 \in \mathbb{N}$ such that, for every $n \geq n^1$, for every $p \in P((\omega)^n)$, $d_{\widehat{P}(\overline{\omega})}(p) < \frac{1}{2}\varepsilon$. Moreover, there exists $n^2 \in \mathbb{N}$ such that $n^2 \geq n^1$ and $\|p^{n^2} - \overline{p}\|_\infty < \frac{1}{2}\varepsilon$. Let the sets $\overline{S}^1$ and $\overline{S}^2$ be defined by $\overline{S}^1 = \{p \in P((\omega)^{n^2}) \mid d_{S^1}(p) < \frac{1}{2}\varepsilon\}$ and $\overline{S}^2 = \{p \in P((\omega)^{n^2}) \mid d_{S^2}(p) < \frac{1}{2}\varepsilon\}$. By the continuity of d_{S^1} and d_{S^2}, the sets $\overline{S}^1$ and $\overline{S}^2$ are open in $P((\omega)^{n^2})$. Clearly, $\overline{S}^1$ and $\overline{S}^2$ are disjoint, $\overline{S}^1 \cup \overline{S}^2 = P((\omega)^{n^2})$, and both $\overline{S}^1$ and $\overline{S}^2$ are non-empty since $v \in \overline{S}^1$ and $p^{n^2} \in \overline{S}^2$. So, $P((\omega)^{n^2})$ is not connected, a contradiction. Consequently, $\overline{p} \in P(\overline{\omega})$.
So, P is a compact-valued, upper hemi-continuous correspondence. Q.E.D.

Since P and $\widehat{P}$ are compact-valued, upper hemi-continuous correspondences, it follows from Theorem 2.5.16 that P and $\widehat{P}$ are continuous correspondences on a residual subset of Ω, i.e. a countable intersection of sets that are open and dense in Ω. Moreover, Ω is a locally compact Hausdorff space and therefore a Baire space by Theorem 2.3.15. Hence, a residual subset of Ω is dense in Ω. Therefore, from an economic point of view, Theorem 10.4.5 is interesting since it means that the price adjustment process itself is in some sense stable against perturbations in the initial endowments. The fact that $\widehat{P}$ is a compact-valued, upper hemi-continuous correspondence is used in the proof of Theorem 10.4.2 given in the next section.

10.5 THE WALRASIAN EQUILIBRIUM STABILITY PROOF

In this section consumption sets and preference relations $(X^i, \preceq^i)_{i \in I_M}$ satisfying Assumptions A1-A2 and the starting price system $v \in \dot{\Delta}^{N-1}$ are assumed to be given. Then, for every $\omega \in \Omega$, for every $s \in S$, the sets $B(s)$, $C(s)$, and C for the economy $\mathcal{E} = ((X^i, \preceq^i, \omega^i)_{i \in I_M})$ with starting price system v can be derived. To make clear the dependence on the initial endowments, notation is changed in this section to $B_\omega(s)$, $C_\omega(s)$, and C_ω, respectively. Moreover, the domain of the total excess demand function z is assumed to be $\mathbb{R}^N_{++} \times \Omega$.

Let an admissible sign vector $s \in \mathcal{S}$, some $j^- \in I^-(s)$ and some $j^+ \in I^+(s)$ be given. Without loss of generality, it can be assumed that $I^0(s) = I_{i^0(s)}$, $I^-(s) = I_{i^0(s)+i^-(s)} \setminus I_{i^0(s)}$, and $I^+(s) = I_N \setminus I_{i^0(s)+i^-(s)}$. Let some $\omega \in \Omega$ be given. Then $p \in C_\omega(s)$ if and only if $p \in \mathbb{R}^N_{++}$ and

$$z_j(p,\omega) = 0, \ \forall j \in I^0(s), \tag{10.2}$$
$$p_j v_{j+1} - p_{j+1} v_j = 0, \ \forall j \in I_{i^0(s)+i^-(s)-1} \setminus I_{i^0(s)}, \tag{10.3}$$
$$p_j v_{j+1} - p_{j+1} v_j = 0, \ \forall j \in I_{N-1} \setminus I_{i^0(s)+i^-(s)}, \tag{10.4}$$
$$\textstyle\sum_{j \in I_N} p_j - 1 = 0, \tag{10.5}$$
$$-z_j(p,\omega) \geq 0, \ \forall j \in I^-(s), \tag{10.6}$$
$$z_j(p,\omega) \geq 0, \ \forall j \in I^+(s), \text{ if } i^0(s) \leq N-3, \tag{10.7}$$
$$p_j v_{j^-} - p_{j^-} v_j \geq 0, \ \forall j \in I^0(s), \tag{10.8}$$
$$p_{j^+} v_j - p_j v_{j^+} \geq 0, \ \forall j \in I^0(s), \tag{10.9}$$
$$p_{j^+} v_{j^-} - p_{j^-} v_{j^+} \geq 0. \tag{10.10}$$

Notice that if $i^-(s) = 1$, then (10.3) is not specified. The same holds for (10.4) if $i^+(s) = 1$. Since $i^-(s)$ and $i^+(s)$ are both greater than or equal to one, there are all together $N-1$ equations in (10.2)-(10.5). If $i^0(s) > N-3$, so $i^0(s) = N-2$, then $i^-(s) = i^+(s) = 1$. In this case the inequality in (10.7) follows by Walras' law from equality (10.2) and inequality (10.6), so inequality (10.7) is redundant.

Let an admissible sign vector $s \in \mathcal{S}$ be given. It is shown in the following that for almost every $\omega \in \Omega$ the set of price systems satisfying (10.2)-(10.10) is a 1-dimensional C^2 manifold with boundary. This is achieved by showing that, for almost every $\omega \in \Omega$, (10.2)-(10.10) yields a regular constraint system, see Definition 2.10.10.

To show Theorem 10.4.2 it is useful to define, for every $s \in \mathcal{S}$, for every $\omega \in \Omega$, the set $D_\omega(s)$ by

$$D_\omega(s) = \left\{ p \in \dot{\Delta}^{N-1} \,\middle|\, \begin{array}{ll} \frac{p_{j'}}{v_{j'}} = \frac{p_{j''}}{v_{j''}}, & \forall j', j'' \in I^-(s), \\ z_j(p,\omega) = 0, \forall j \in I^0(s), & \\ \frac{p_{j'}}{v_{j'}} = \frac{p_{j''}}{v_{j''}}, & \forall j', j'' \in I^+(s) \end{array} \right\}.$$

Let an admissible sign vector $s \in \mathcal{S}$ be given. Clearly, for every $\omega \in \Omega$, $C_\omega(s) \subset D_\omega(s)$, the difference between these two sets being that no inequality constraints are taken into account in the specification of $D_\omega(s)$. In Lemma 10.5.1 it is shown that there exists a subset $\overline{\Omega}$ of Ω such that $\Omega \setminus \overline{\Omega}$ has Lebesgue measure zero and for every $\omega \in \overline{\Omega}$ the set $D_\omega(s)$ is a 1-dimensional C^2 manifold. Hence, it can be shown to consist of a number of disjoint sets that are diffeomorphic to either the unit circle $\widetilde{B}^1((0,0)^\top,1)$ or the open unit interval $(0,1)$.

For every $s \in \mathcal{S}$, the function $\psi^s : \mathbb{R}^N_{++} \times \Omega \to \mathbb{R}^{N-1}$ is defined such that, for every $(p,\omega) \in \mathbb{R}^N_{++} \times \Omega$, $\psi^s(p,\omega)$ is the left-hand side of (10.2)-(10.5). For every $s \in \mathcal{S}$, for every $\omega \in \Omega$, the function $\psi^{s,\omega} : \mathbb{R}^N_{++} \to \mathbb{R}^{N-1}$ is defined by $\psi^{s,\omega}(p) = \psi^s(p,\omega)$, $\forall p \in \mathbb{R}^N_{++}$. Notice that, for every $s \in \mathcal{S}$, for every $\omega \in \Omega$, $D_\omega(s) = \psi^{s,\omega^{-1}}(\{0^{N-1}\})$.

Lemma 10.5.1
Let $(X^i, \preceq^i)_{i \in I_M}$ satisfy Assumptions A1-A2 and let $v \in \dot{\Delta}^{N-1}$ be the starting price system. Let an admissible sign vector $s \in \mathcal{S}$ be given. Then there exists a subset $\overline{\Omega}$ of Ω such that $\Omega \setminus \overline{\Omega}$ has Lebesgue measure zero and, for every $\omega \in \overline{\Omega}$, $\psi^{s,\omega} \pitchfork \{0^{N-1}\}$ and $D_\omega(s)$ is a 1-dimensional C^2 manifold.

Proof
The matrix of partial derivatives of ψ^s evaluated at $(\overline{p},\overline{\omega}) \in \mathbb{R}^N_{++} \times \Omega$ satisfying $\psi^s(\overline{p},\overline{\omega}) = 0^{N-1}$ is denoted by $\overline{M}$ and is given in Table 10.5.1. Moreover, in Table 10.5.1 two submatrices $\overline{M}^1$ and $\overline{M}^2$ of $\overline{M}$ are defined.

It is shown that the matrix $\overline{M}$ has rank $N-1$. First it is proved that, for every $i \in I_M$, $\partial_{\omega^i} z(\overline{p},\overline{\omega})$ has rank $N-1$. Notice that, for every $i \in I_M$, $\overline{p}^\top \partial_{\omega^i} z(\overline{p},\overline{\omega}) = 0^{N^\top}$ and $\partial_{\omega^i} z(\overline{p},\overline{\omega}) = \partial_{w^i} \widetilde{d}^i(\overline{p},\overline{p}\cdot\overline{\omega}^i)\overline{p}^\top - I^N$. Then, for every $i \in I_M$,

$$\partial_{\omega^i} z(\overline{p},\overline{\omega})\left(\overline{p}_{j''} e^N(j') - \overline{p}_{j'} e^N(j'')\right) = \overline{p}_{j'} e^N(j'') - \overline{p}_{j''} e^N(j'),\ \forall j', j'' \in I_N,$$

so the rank of $\partial_{\omega^i} z(\overline{p},\overline{\omega})$ is equal to $N-1$.
Let some $i \in I_M$ be given. Consider the first $i^0(s)$ rows of $\partial_{\omega^i} z(\overline{p},\overline{\omega})$. These rows have to be independent. Suppose not, then $i^0(s) \leq N-2$ implies the existence of $y \in \mathbb{R}^N \setminus \{0^N\}$ such that $y_{N-1} = y_N = 0$ and $y^\top \partial_{\omega^i} z(\overline{p},\overline{\omega}) = 0^{N^\top}$. Since $\overline{p}^\top \partial_{\omega^i} z(\overline{p},\overline{\omega}) = 0^{N^\top}$, this implies that the rank of $\partial_{\omega^i} z(\overline{p},\overline{\omega})$ is less than or equal to $N-2$, a contradiction.
Now let $y \in \mathbb{R}^{N-1}$ be such that $y^\top \overline{M} = 0^{MN+N^\top}$. From the previous paragraph it follows that $y^\top \partial_{\omega^1} \psi^s(\overline{p},\overline{\omega}) = 0^{N^\top}$ implies $y_j = 0$, $\forall j \in I_{i^0(s)}$.
Suppose $y_{N-1} \neq 0$. Without loss of generality, it can be assumed that $y_{N-1} < 0$. If $i^0(s) \geq 1$ or $i^-(s) = 1$, then a contradiction is obtained with $y^\top \partial_{p_1} \psi^s(\overline{p},\overline{\omega}) = 0$. If $i^0(s) = 0$ and $i^-(s) \geq 2$, then $y_{N-1} < 0$ and $y^\top \partial_{p_1} \psi^s(\overline{p},\overline{\omega}) = 0$ implies $y_1 > 0$. It is easily seen that $y_j > 0$ and $y^\top \partial_{p_{j+1}} \psi^s(\overline{p},\overline{\omega}) = 0$ implies $y_{j+1} > 0$, $\forall j \in I_{i^-(s)-2}$. Hence, $y_{i^-(s)-1} > 0$, implying that $y^\top \partial_{p_{i^-(s)}} \psi^s(\overline{p},\overline{\omega}) < 0$, a contradiction. Consequently, $y_{N-1} = 0$.
The independence of the rows of $\overline{M}^1$ and of the rows of $\overline{M}^2$ yields $y_{i^0(s)+1} = \cdots = y_{N-2} = 0$. So, $y = 0^{N-1}$ and $\overline{M}$ has rank $N-1$.

$$
\overline{M} = \left[\begin{array}{c|c|c|c}
\multicolumn{3}{c|}{\begin{array}{c}\partial_p z_1(\overline{p},\overline{\omega})\\ \vdots \\ \partial_p z_{i^0(s)}(\overline{p},\overline{\omega})\end{array}} & \begin{array}{c}\partial_\omega z_1(\overline{p},\overline{\omega})\\ \vdots \\ \partial_\omega z_{i^0(s)}(\overline{p},\overline{\omega})\end{array} \\ \hline
0^{(i^-(s)-1)\times i^0(s)} & \overline{M}^1 & 0^{(i^-(s)-1)\times i^+(s)} & 0^{(i^-(s)-1)\times MN} \\ \hline
\multicolumn{2}{c|}{0^{(i^+(s)-1)\times(i^0(s)+i^-(s))}} & \overline{M}^2 & 0^{(i^+(s)-1)\times MN} \\ \hline
\multicolumn{3}{c|}{1^{N^\top}} & 0^{MN^\top}
\end{array}\right]
\begin{array}{l} i^0(s) \\ i^-(s)-1 \\ i^+(s)-1 \\ 1 \end{array}
$$

$$\underbrace{\hphantom{xxxxxxxxxxxx}}_{N}\qquad\underbrace{\hphantom{xxxxxx}}_{MN}$$

$$
\overline{M}^1 = \underbrace{\left[\begin{array}{ccccccc}
v_{i^0(s)+2} & -v_{i^0(s)+1} & & & 0^{i^-(s)-2^\top} & & \\
0 & v_{i^0(s)+3} & -v_{i^0(s)+2} & & 0^{i^-(s)-3^\top} & & \\
 & & \ddots & \ddots & & & \\
0^{i^-(s)-3^\top} & & & v_{i^0(s)+i^-(s)-1} & -v_{i^0(s)+i^-(s)-2} & & 0 \\
0^{i^-(s)-2^\top} & & & & v_{i^0(s)+i^-(s)} & & -v_{i^0(s)+i^-(s)-1}
\end{array}\right]}_{i^-(s)}
$$

$$
\overline{M}^2 = \underbrace{\left[\begin{array}{ccccccc}
v_{i^0(s)+i^-(s)+2} & -v_{i^0(s)+i^-(s)+1} & & & 0^{i^+(s)-2^\top} & & \\
0 & v_{i^0(s)+i^-(s)+3} & -v_{i^0(s)+i^-(s)+2} & & 0^{i^+(s)-3^\top} & & \\
 & & \ddots & \ddots & & & \\
0^{i^+(s)-3^\top} & & & v_{N-1} & -v_{N-2} & & 0 \\
0^{i^+(s)-2^\top} & & & & v_N & & -v_{N-1}
\end{array}\right]}_{i^+(s)}
$$

Table 10.5.1. The matrix $\overline{M}$.

Since $\overline{M}$ has rank $N-1$, it follows that ψ^s intersects $\{0^{N-1}\}$ transversally, $\psi^s \pitchfork \{0^{N-1}\}$. Using Theorem 9.2.1, it follows that $\psi^s \in C^2(\mathbb{R}^N_{++} \times \Omega, \mathbb{R}^{N-1})$. Moreover, $\mathbb{R}^N_{++}$ is an N-dimensional C^∞ manifold, Ω is an MN-dimensional C^∞ manifold, $\mathbb{R}^{N-1}$ is an $(N-1)$-dimensional C^∞ manifold, and $\{0^{N-1}\}$ is a 0-dimensional C^∞ manifold. Let the set $\overline{\Omega}$ be defined by $\overline{\Omega} = \{\omega \in \Omega \mid \psi^{s,\omega} \pitchfork \{0^{N-1}\}\}$. It follows from the transversality theorem, Theorem 2.10.18, that the set $\Omega \setminus \overline{\Omega}$ has Lebesgue measure zero in Ω. Since Ω is an MN-dimensional C^∞ manifold that is a subset of $\mathbb{R}^{MN}$, it follows that the set $\Omega \setminus \overline{\Omega}$ has Lebesgue measure zero, see the remark below Theorem 2.10.17. For every

$\omega \in \overline{\Omega}$, $\psi^{s,\omega}$ is a function from an N-dimensional C^∞ manifold into an $(N-1)$-dimensional C^∞ manifold, $\psi^{s,\omega} \in C^2(\mathbb{R}^N_{++}, \mathbb{R}^{N-1})$, and $\psi^{s,\omega} \,\overline{\pitchfork}\, \{0^{N-1}\}$, so ${\psi^{s,\omega}}^{-1}(\{0^{N-1}\})$ and hence $D_\omega(s)$ is a 1-dimensional C^2 manifold by Theorem 2.10.16. Q.E.D.

Let an admissible sign vector $s \in \mathcal{S}$ and some $\omega \in \Omega$ be given. Let $p \in D_\omega(s)$ be such that there exists $j^1 \in I^-(s) \cup I^+(s)$ with $z_{j^1}(p,\omega) = 0$. Hence, one of the inequalities in (10.6) or (10.7) is satisfied with equality. Let the sign vector $\overline{s} \in \mathbb{S}^N$ be defined by $\overline{s}_{j^1} = 0$ and $\overline{s}_j = s_j$, $\forall j \in I_N \setminus \{j^1\}$. If it holds that $\overline{s} \in \mathcal{S}$, then the price system p is an element of the intersection of the sets $D_\omega(s)$ and $D_\omega(\overline{s})$. Considering the system of equations defining $C_\omega(\overline{s})$ it follows that one of the inequalities in (10.8) or (10.9) is satisfied with equality.

For every $s \in \mathcal{S}$, for every $\omega \in \Omega$, for every $j^1 \in I^-(s) \cup I^+(s)$, the set $D_\omega(s, j^1)$ is defined by

$$D_\omega(s,j^1) = \Big\{ p \in \dot{\Delta}^{N-1} \,\Big|\, \begin{array}{ll} \frac{p_{j'}}{v_{j'}} = \frac{p_{j''}}{v_{j''}}, & \forall j', j'' \in I^-(s), \\ z_j(p,\omega) = 0, \ \forall j \in I^0(s) \cup \{j^1\}, & \\ \frac{p_{j'}}{v_{j'}} = \frac{p_{j''}}{v_{j''}}, & \forall j', j'' \in I^+(s) \Big\}. \end{array}$$

Let an admissible sign vector $s \in \mathcal{S}$ and some $j^1 \in I^-(s) \cup I^+(s)$ be given. In Lemma 10.5.2 it is shown that there exists a subset $\overline{\Omega}$ of Ω such that $\Omega \setminus \overline{\Omega}$ has Lebesgue measure zero and for every $\omega \in \overline{\Omega}$ the set $D_\omega(s, j^1)$ is a 0-dimensional manifold and hence a discrete set of points. Obviously, the commodities can be relabelled such that $I^0(s) = I_{i^0(s)}$, $I^-(s) = I_{i^0(s)+i^-(s)} \setminus I_{i^0(s)}$, and $I^+(s) = I_N \setminus I_{i^0(s)+i^-(s)}$. Let some $\omega \in \Omega$ be given. It is easily verified that $p \in D_\omega(s, j^1)$ if and only if $p \in \mathbb{R}^N_{++}$, p satisfies the equations (10.2)-(10.5), and

$$z_{j^1}(p,\omega) = 0. \tag{10.11}$$

For every $s \in \mathcal{S}$, for every $j^1 \in I^-(s) \cup I^+(s)$, the function $\psi^s_{j^1} : \mathbb{R}^N_{++} \times \Omega \to \mathbb{R}^N$ is defined such that, for every $(p,\omega) \in \mathbb{R}^N_{++} \times \Omega$, $\psi^s_{j^1}(p,\omega)$ is the left-hand side of (10.2)-(10.5) and (10.11). For every $s \in \mathcal{S}$, for every $j^1 \in I^-(s) \cup I^+(s)$, for every $\omega \in \Omega$, the function $\psi^{s,\omega}_{j^1} : \mathbb{R}^N_{++} \to \mathbb{R}^N$ is defined by $\psi^{s,\omega}_{j^1}(p) = \psi^s_{j^1}(p,\omega)$, $\forall p \in \mathbb{R}^N_{++}$.

Lemma 10.5.2
Let $(X^i, \preceq^i)_{i \in I_M}$ satisfy Assumptions A1-A2 and let $v \in \dot{\Delta}^{N-1}$ be the starting price system. Let an admissible sign vector $s \in \mathcal{S}$ and some $j^1 \in I^-(s) \cup I^+(s)$

be given. Then there exists a subset $\overline{\Omega}$ of Ω such that $\Omega\backslash\overline{\Omega}$ has Lebesgue measure zero and, for every $\omega \in \overline{\Omega}$, $\psi^{s,\omega}_{j^1} \pitchfork \{0^N\}$ and $D_\omega(s, j^1)$ is a 0-dimensional manifold.

Proof

The matrix of partial derivatives of $\psi^s_{j^1}$ evaluated at $(\overline{p}, \overline{\omega}) \in \mathbb{R}^N_{++} \times \Omega$ satisfying $\psi^s_{j^1}(\overline{p}, \overline{\omega}) = 0^N$ is denoted by $\widehat{M}$. It is shown that $\widehat{M}$ has rank N. Let $y \in \mathbb{R}^N$ be such that $y^\top \widehat{M} = 0^{MN+N^\top}$. As in the proof of Lemma 10.5.1 it can be shown that for every $i \in I_M$ the rows $1, \ldots, i^0(s)$ and j^1 of $\partial_{\omega^i} z(\overline{p}, \overline{\omega})$ are independent since $i^0(s) \leq N-2$ and $j^1 \notin I^0(s)$. So, $y^\top \partial_{\omega^1} \psi^s_{j^1}(\overline{p}, \overline{\omega}) = 0^{N^\top}$ implies $y_1 = \cdots = y_{i^0(s)} = y_N = 0$. The proof that $y_{i^0(s)+1} = \cdots = y_{N-1} = 0$ is now identical to the corresponding part of the proof of Lemma 10.5.1. Hence, $\widehat{M}$ has rank N and $\psi^s_{j^1} \pitchfork \{0^N\}$. Let the set $\overline{\Omega}$ be defined by $\overline{\Omega} = \{\omega \in \Omega \mid \psi^{s,\omega}_{j^1} \pitchfork \{0^N\}\}$. From the transversality theorem, Theorem 2.10.18, it follows that the set $\Omega \setminus \overline{\Omega}$ has Lebesgue measure zero. For every $\omega \in \overline{\Omega}$, $\psi^{s,\omega}_{j^1}$ is a function from an N-dimensional C^∞ manifold into an N-dimensional C^∞ manifold, $\psi^{s,\omega}_{j^1} \in C^2(\mathbb{R}^N_{++}, \mathbb{R}^N)$, and $\psi^{s,\omega}_{j^1} \pitchfork \{0^N\}$, so $\psi^{s,\omega^{-1}}_{j^1}(\{0^N\})$ and hence $D_\omega(s, j^1)$ is a 0-dimensional manifold by Theorem 2.10.16. Q.E.D.

For every $s \in \mathcal{S}$ with $i^0(s) \leq N-3$, for every $\omega \in \Omega$, for every $j^1, j^2 \in I^-(s) \cup I^+(s)$ with $j^1 \neq j^2$, the set $D_\omega(s, j^1, j^2)$ is defined by

$$D_\omega(s, j^1, j^2) = \Big\{ p \in \dot{\Delta}^{N-1} \Big| \; \tfrac{p_{j'}}{v_{j'}} = \tfrac{p_{j''}}{v_{j''}}, \quad \forall j', j'' \in I^-(s), \quad z_j(p, \omega) = 0,\ \forall j \in I^0(s) \cup \{j^1, j^2\}, \quad \tfrac{p_{j'}}{v_{j'}} = \tfrac{p_{j''}}{v_{j''}}, \quad \forall j', j'' \in I^+(s) \Big\}.$$

Let an admissible sign vector $s \in \mathcal{S}$ with $i^0(s) \leq N-3$ and some $j^1, j^2 \in I^-(s) \cup I^+(s)$ with $j^1 \neq j^2$ be given. The next lemma shows that there exists a subset $\overline{\Omega}$ of Ω such that $\Omega \setminus \overline{\Omega}$ has Lebesgue measure zero and for every $\omega \in \overline{\Omega}$ the set $D_\omega(s, j^1, j^2)$ is empty. Notice that the condition $i^0(s) \leq N-3$ is crucial since for an admissible sign vector s with $i^0(s) = N-2$ a corresponding set $D_\omega(s, j^1, j^2)$ is equal to the set of Walrasian equilibrium price systems in $A(s)$ of the economy $\mathcal{E} = ((X^i, \preceq^i, \omega^i)_{i \in I_M})$. Clearly, it cannot be shown that this set is empty for almost every $\omega \in \Omega$.

Let an admissible sign vector $s \in \mathcal{S}$ with $i^0(s) \leq N-3$ and some $j^1, j^2 \in I^-(s) \cup I^+(s)$ with $j^1 \neq j^2$ be given. Let some $\omega \in \Omega$ be given. It is easily verified that $p \in D_\omega(s, j^1, j^2)$ if and only if $p \in \mathbb{R}^N_{++}$, p satisfies the equations (10.2)-(10.5), and

$$z_{j^1}(p, \omega) = 0, \tag{10.12}$$

$$z_{j^2}(p,\omega) = 0. \tag{10.13}$$

For every $s \in \mathcal{S}$ with $i^0(s) \leq N-3$, for every $j^1, j^2 \in I^-(s) \cup I^+(s)$ with $j^1 \neq j^2$, the function $\psi^s_{j^1,j^2} : \mathbb{R}^N_{++} \times \Omega \to \mathbb{R}^{N+1}$ is defined such that, for every $(p,\omega) \in \mathbb{R}^N_{++} \times \Omega$, $\psi^s_{j^1,j^2}(p,\omega)$ is the left-hand side of (10.2)-(10.5), (10.12), and (10.13). For every $s \in \mathcal{S}$ with $i^0(s) \leq N-3$, for every $j^1, j^2 \in I^-(s) \cup I^+(s)$ with $j^1 \neq j^2$, for every $\omega \in \Omega$, the function $\psi^{s,\omega}_{j^1,j^2} : \mathbb{R}^N_{++} \to \mathbb{R}^{N+1}$ is defined by $\psi^{s,\omega}_{j^1,j^2}(p) = \psi^s_{j^1,j^2}(p,\omega)$, $\forall p \in \mathbb{R}^N_{++}$.

Lemma 10.5.3
Let $(X^i, \preceq^i)_{i \in I_M}$ satisfy Assumptions A1-A2 and let $v \in \dot{\Delta}^{N-1}$ be the starting price system. Let an admissible sign vector $s \in \mathcal{S}$ satisfying $i^0(s) \leq N-3$ and some $j^1, j^2 \in I^-(s) \cup I^+(s)$ with $j^1 \neq j^2$ be given. Then there exists a subset $\overline{\Omega}$ of Ω such that $\Omega \setminus \overline{\Omega}$ has Lebesgue measure zero and, for every $\omega \in \overline{\Omega}$, $\psi^{s,\omega}_{j^1,j^2} \pitchfork \{0^{N+1}\}$ and $D_\omega(s, j^1, j^2)$ is an empty set.

Proof
Let $(\overline{p}, \overline{\omega}) \in \mathbb{R}^N_{++} \times \Omega$ be such that $\psi^s_{j^1,j^2}(\overline{p}, \overline{\omega}) = 0^{N+1}$. Since $i^0(s) \leq N-3$ and $j^1, j^2 \notin I^0(s)$, it holds that for every $i \in I_M$ the rows $1, \ldots, i^0(s), j^1$, and j^2 of $\partial_{\omega^i} z(\overline{p}, \overline{\omega})$ are independent. Similarly as in the proof of Lemmas 10.5.1 and 10.5.2 it can be shown that $\psi^{s,\omega}_{j^1,j^2} \pitchfork \{0^{N+1}\}$. Let the set $\overline{\Omega}$ be defined by $\overline{\Omega} = \{\omega \in \Omega \mid \psi^{s,\omega}_{j^1,j^2} \pitchfork \{0^{N+1}\}\}$. From the transversality theorem, Theorem 2.10.18, it follows that the set $\Omega \setminus \overline{\Omega}$ has Lebesgue measure zero. For every $\omega \in \overline{\Omega}$, $\psi^{s,\omega}_{j^1,j^2}$ is a function from an N-dimensional C^∞ manifold into an $(N+1)$-dimensional C^∞ manifold, $\psi^{s,\omega}_{j^1,j^2} \in C^2(\mathbb{R}^N_{++}, \mathbb{R}^{N+1})$, and $\psi^{s,\omega}_{j^1,j^2} \pitchfork \{0^{N+1}\}$, so ${\psi^{s,\omega}_{j^1,j^2}}^{-1}(\{0^{N+1}\})$ and hence $D_\omega(s, j^1, j^2)$ is an empty set by Theorem 2.10.16.
Q.E.D.

Let some $\omega \in \Omega$ be given. If $z_j(v,\omega) \neq 0$, $\forall j \in I_N$, then it holds that $v \in C_\omega(s)$ for a uniquely determined admissible sign vector $s \in \mathcal{S}$. Therefore, it is shown in Lemma 10.5.4 that there exists a subset $\overline{\Omega}$ of Ω such that the closure of $\Omega \setminus \overline{\Omega}$ in Ω has Lebesgue measure zero and, for every $\omega \in \overline{\Omega}$, $z_j(v,\omega) \neq 0$, $\forall j \in I_N$. For every $j \in I_N$, the function $\psi_j : \{v\} \times \Omega \to \mathbb{R}$ is defined by $\psi_j(v,\omega) = z_j(v,\omega)$, $\forall \omega \in \Omega$. For every $j \in I_N$, for every $\omega \in \Omega$, the function $\psi^\omega_j : \{v\} \to \mathbb{R}$ is defined by $\psi^\omega_j(v) = \psi_j(v,\omega)$.

Lemma 10.5.4
Let $(X^i, \preceq^i)_{i \in I_M}$ satisfy Assumptions A1-A2 and let $v \in \dot{\Delta}^{N-1}$ be the starting price system. Then there exists a subset $\overline{\Omega}$ of Ω such that $\Omega \setminus \overline{\Omega}$ has Lebesgue measure zero and, for every $\omega \in \overline{\Omega}$, for every $j \in I_N$, $\psi^\omega_j \pitchfork \{0\}$ and $z_j(v,\omega) \neq$

0.

Proof

For every $j \in I_N$ it is easily seen that $\psi_j \pitchfork \{0\}$. For every $j \in I_N$, let the set $\overline{\Omega}_j$ be defined by $\overline{\Omega}_j = \{\omega \in \Omega \mid \psi_j^\omega \pitchfork \{0\}\}$. So, the set $\Omega \setminus \overline{\Omega}_j$ has Lebesgue measure zero by the transversality theorem, Theorem 2.10.18. Let the set $\overline{\Omega}$ be defined by $\overline{\Omega} = \cap_{j \in I_N} \overline{\Omega}_j$. Clearly, the set $\Omega \setminus \overline{\Omega}$ has Lebesgue measure zero. For every $\omega \in \overline{\Omega}$, for every $j \in I_N$, ψ_j^ω is a function from a 0-dimensional manifold into a 1-dimensional C^∞ manifold, $\psi_j^\omega \in C^\infty(\{v\}, \mathbb{R})$, and $\psi_j^\omega \pitchfork \{0\}$, so ${\psi_j^\omega}^{-1}(\{0\})$ is an empty set by Theorem 2.10.16. Q.E.D.

Now all preliminary work has been done to give a proof of Theorem 10.4.2. The proof consists of three parts. In the first part it is shown that, for almost every $\omega \in \Omega$, for every $s \in \mathcal{S}$, the set $C_\omega(s)$ is a compact 1-dimensional C^2 manifold with boundary. In the second part the sets $C_\omega(s)$, $\forall s \in \mathcal{S}$, are linked together and it is shown that for almost every $\omega \in \Omega$ the set C_ω consists of a finite number of arcs and loops. There is a unique arc having the starting price system v and a unique Walrasian equilibrium price system as boundary points. The other arcs have two Walrasian equilibrium price systems as boundary points, whereas the loops contain no Walrasian equilibrium price systems. Therefore, the set $\Omega \setminus \Omega^*$ has Lebesgue measure zero. In the third part of the proof it is shown that the closure in Ω of the set $\Omega \setminus \Omega^*$ has Lebesgue measure zero.

Proof of Theorem 10.4.2

Let the set $\overline{\Omega}$ be given by the elements ω of Ω satisfying, for every $j \in I_N$, $\psi_j^\omega \pitchfork \{0\}$, for every $s \in \mathcal{S}$, $\psi^{s,\omega} \pitchfork \{0^{N-1}\}$, for every $s \in \mathcal{S}$, for every $j \in I^-(s) \cup I^+(s)$, $\psi_j^{s,\omega} \pitchfork \{0^N\}$, and, for every $s \in \mathcal{S}$ with $i^0(s) \leq N-3$, for every $j^1, j^2 \in I^-(s) \cup I^+(s)$ with $j^1 \neq j^2$, $\psi_{j^1,j^2}^{s,\omega} \pitchfork \{0^{N+1}\}$. By Lemmas 10.5.1, 10.5.2, 10.5.3, and 10.5.4 the set $\Omega \setminus \overline{\Omega}$ has Lebesgue measure zero. In Parts 1 and 2 of the proof it is shown that $\overline{\Omega} \subset \Omega^*$.

1. For every $\omega \in \overline{\Omega}$, for every $s \in \mathcal{S}$, $C_\omega(s)$ is a compact 1-dimensional C^2 manifold with boundary.

Let some $\omega \in \overline{\Omega}$ and some $\overline{s} \in \mathcal{S}$ be given. It is shown that when the left-hand sides of equations (10.2)-(10.10) are considered as functions of p from the open set $\mathbb{R}^N_{++}$ into $\mathbb{R}$, then they yield a C^2 regular constraint system. Let some $\overline{p} \in C_\omega(\overline{s})$ be given.

If $\overline{p} = v$, then, since for every $j \in I_N$, $\psi_j^\omega \pitchfork \{0\}$, it holds that $I^0(\overline{s}) = \emptyset$ and the inequalities (10.6) and (10.7) are not binding. Hence, $J^0(\overline{p})$, the set of inequalities in (10.6)-(10.10) holding with equality, see Section 2.10, consists of a unique element corresponding to equation (10.10). It is easily verified that the partial derivatives with respect to p of (10.3)-(10.5) and (10.10) at $\overline{p}$ constitute a set of independent vectors.

Consider the case with $\overline{p} \neq v$. Then (10.10) holds with inequality.

Suppose that two (or more) equations in (10.6)-(10.9) hold with equality. Since $\overline{p} \neq v$, (10.8) and (10.9) cannot be binding for the same commodity in $I^0(\overline{s})$, so the two equations holding with equality correspond to $j^1, j^2 \in I_N$ with $j^1 \neq j^2$. Let $\widehat{s} \in \mathcal{S}$ be defined by $\widehat{s}_{j^1} = -1$ if j^1 corresponds to an equation in (10.6) or (10.8), $\widehat{s}_{j^1} = +1$ if j^1 corresponds to an equation in (10.7) or (10.9), $\widehat{s}_{j^2} = -1$ if j^2 corresponds to an equation in (10.6) or (10.8), $\widehat{s}_{j^2} = +1$ if j^2 corresponds to an equation in (10.7) or (10.9), and $\widehat{s}_j = \overline{s}_j$, $\forall j \in I_N \setminus \{j^1, j^2\}$. If j^1 or j^2 corresponds to (10.8) or (10.9), or if $i^0(\overline{s}) \leq N-3$, then $i^0(\widehat{s}) \leq N-3$. Moreover, $\overline{p} \in D_\omega(\widehat{s}, j^1, j^2)$, a contradiction since $\psi^{\hat{s},\omega}_{j^1,j^2} \pitchfork \{0^{N+1}\}$. So, $i^0(\overline{s}) = N-2$ and j^1, j^2 correspond to two different equations in (10.6) and (10.7), again leading to a contradiction as before since there is only one equation specified in (10.6) and no equation (10.7) in this case. Consequently, at most one of the inequalities in (10.6)-(10.10) is satisfied with equality.

If none of the inequalities in (10.6)-(10.10) is satisfied with equality, then it follows that the partial derivatives with respect to p of the equations (10.2)-(10.5) at $\overline{p}$ constitute a set of independent vectors since $\psi^{\overline{s},\omega} \pitchfork \{0^{N-1}\}$. Moreover, $\#J^0(\overline{p}) = 0$, the number of inequalities in (10.6)-(10.10) holding with equality at $\overline{p}$. If one of the inequalities in (10.6)-(10.10) is satisfied with equality, then, since the case $\overline{p} \neq v$ is considered, one of the inequalities in (10.6)-(10.9) is satisfied with equality, say the one corresponding to commodity $j' \in I_N$. Let $\widehat{s} \in \mathcal{S}$ be defined by $\widehat{s}_{j'} = -1$ if j' corresponds to (10.6) or (10.8), $\widehat{s}_{j'} = +1$ if j' corresponds to (10.7) or (10.9), and $\widehat{s}_j = \overline{s}_j$, $\forall j \in I_N \setminus \{j'\}$. Then $\psi^{\hat{s};\omega}_{j'} \pitchfork \{0^N\}$ implies that the partial derivatives with respect to p of the binding inequality and (10.2)-(10.5) at $\overline{p}$ constitute a set of independent vectors. Moreover, $\#J^0(\overline{p}) = 1$. Therefore, it has been shown that (10.2)-(10.10) is a C^2 regular constraint system.

Since (10.2)-(10.5) form $N-1$ equations defined on $\mathbb{R}^N_{++}$ and, for every $\overline{p} \in C_\omega(\overline{s})$, $\#J^0(\overline{p}) \leq 1$, Theorem 2.10.11 implies that $C_\omega(\overline{s})$ is a 1-dimensional C^2 manifold with boundary, where the boundary is given by the set of points $\overline{p} \in C_\omega(\overline{s})$ with $\#J^0(\overline{p}) = 1$, a 0-dimensional manifold by Theorem 2.10.7.

The compactness of $C_\omega(\overline{s})$ follows from Theorem 10.4.5. Therefore, $C_\omega(\overline{s})$ is a compact 1-dimensional C^2 manifold with boundary and hence a finite union of disjoint sets that are diffeomorphic to either the unit circle $\widetilde{B}^1((0,0)^\top, 1)$ or the closed unit interval $[0,1]$ by Theorem 2.10.9. Let these sets be denoted by $C_\omega(\overline{s}, 1), \ldots, C_\omega(\overline{s}, k(\overline{s}))$. Notice that, for every $k \in I_{k(\overline{s})}$, $\overline{p} \in C_\omega(\overline{s}, k)$ is a point of the boundary of $C_\omega(\overline{s}, k)$ if and only if $\#J^0(\overline{p}) = 1$.

2. For every $\omega \in \overline{\Omega}$, C_ω is a finite union of arcs and loops.

Let some $\omega \in \overline{\Omega}$ be given.

Let $p^0 \in C_\omega$ be given. Then there exists $s^0 \in \mathcal{S}$ and $k^0 \in I_{k(s^0)}$ such that

$p^0 \in C_\omega(s^0,k^0)$. Either $C_\omega(s^0,k^0)$ is a component of C_ω that is diffeomorphic to the unit circle $\widetilde{B}^1((0,0)^\top,1)$ and has no boundary, or $C_\omega(s^0,k^0)$ is a subset of C_ω that is diffeomorphic to the closed unit interval $[0,1]$ and having two boundary points, p^1 and p^{-1}. First p^1 is considered. Either $p^1=v$ or exactly one of the inequalities in (10.6)-(10.9) is binding. Four cases have to be considered.

2.1. $p^1=v$. Then, since for every $j\in I_N$, $\psi_j^\omega \pitchfork \{0\}$, $\nexists s\in \mathcal{S}\setminus\{s^0\}$ with $p^1\in C_\omega(s)$.

2.2. $i^0(s^0)=N-2$ and the inequality in (10.6) is binding. Then, by Walras' law, p^1 is a Walrasian equilibrium price system. Suppose there exists $\bar{s}\in\mathcal{S}\setminus\{s^0\}$ such that $p^1\in C_\omega(\bar{s})$. Using $p^1\neq v$ it follows that $I^0(s^0)\neq I^0(\bar{s})$ and $(I^-(s^0)\cup I^-(\bar{s}))\cap(I^+(s^0)\cup I^+(\bar{s}))=\emptyset$. Let $\widehat{s}\in\mathcal{S}$ be defined by $\widehat{s}_j=-1$, $\forall j\in I^-(s^0)\cup I^-(\bar{s})$, $\widehat{s}_j=0$, $\forall j\in I^0(s^0)\cap I^0(\bar{s})$, and $\widehat{s}_j=+1$, $\forall j\in I^+(s^0)\cup I^+(\bar{s})$. Let $j^1,j^2\in I^-(\widehat{s})\cup I^+(\widehat{s})$ be such that $j^1\neq j^2$. Then, since $i^0(\widehat{s})\leq N-3$ and $p^1\in D_\omega(\widehat{s},j^1,j^2)$, a contradiction with $\psi^{\widehat{s}}_{j^1,j^2}\pitchfork\{0^{N+1}\}$ is obtained. Consequently, $\nexists s\in\mathcal{S}\setminus\{s^0\}$ such that $p^1\in C_\omega(s)$.

2.3. $i^0(s^0)=N-2$ and an inequality in (10.8) or (10.9) corresponding to some $j'\in I^0(s)$ is binding. Let $s^1\in\mathcal{S}$ be defined by $s^1_{j'}=-1$ if an inequality in (10.8) is binding, $s^1_{j'}=+1$ if an inequality in (10.9) is binding, and $s^1_j=s^0_j$, $\forall j\in I_N\setminus\{j'\}$. Clearly, p^1 is a boundary point of $C_\omega(s^1,k^1)$ for some $k^1\in I_{k(s^1)}$. Moreover, $\nexists\, s\in\mathcal{S}\setminus\{s^0,s^1\}$ such that $p^1\in C_\omega(s)$ since otherwise a contradiction is obtained as in Case 2.2.

2.4. $i^0(s^0)\leq N-3$. Then it can be shown in a similar way as in Case 2.3 that there exists a unique $s^1\in\mathcal{S}$ such that p^1 is a boundary point of $C_\omega(s^1,k^1)$ for some $k^1\in I_{k(s^1)}$. This concludes the four cases possible.

The set $C_\omega(s^1,k^1)$ obtained in Case 2.3 or Case 2.4 has two boundary points, p^1 and, say, p^2. Using the same arguments as before either $p^2=v$, or p^2 is a Walrasian equilibrium price system, or $p^2\in C_\omega(s^2,k^2)$ for uniquely determined $s^2\in\mathcal{S}\setminus\{s^1\}$ and $k^2\in I_{k(s^2)}$. Repeating these arguments, the sets $C^0=C_\omega(s^0,k^0)$, $C^1=C_\omega(s^1,k^1)$, $C^2=C_\omega(s^2,k^2),\ldots$ are obtained such that each set is a component of $C_\omega(s)$ for some $s\in\mathcal{S}$ that is diffeomorphic to the closed unit interval $[0,1]$, $C^k\cap C^{k+1}$ is a common boundary point, and $C^k\neq C^{k+1}$. Therefore, after a finite number of, say, $k^2\in\mathbb{Z}_+$ steps either a set C^{k^2} is obtained having v or a Walrasian equilibrium price system as a boundary point, or there exists $k^1\in\mathbb{Z}_+$ with $k^1<k^2$, $C^{k^1}=C^{k^2}$, and $C^0,\ldots,C^{k^2-1}$ all being different.

First, the second case is considered. It is shown that $k^1=0$. Then it is easily verified that $C^0\cup\cdots\cup C^{k^2-1}$ is the component of p^0 in C_ω and that it is homeomorphic to the unit circle $\widetilde{B}^1((0,0)^\top,1)$.

Suppose $k^1\geq 1$. Then $C^{k^1}\cap C^{k^2-1}$ is a boundary point of C^{k^1-1} or C^{k^1+1}. Clearly, $k^1+1\leq k^2-1$.

Suppose $k^1+1=k^2-1$. Then C^{k^1+1} has one boundary point in common with C^{k^1} and the other boundary point in common with $C^{k^1+2}=C^{k^2}=C^{k^1}$, so it has both boundary points in common with C^{k^1}. The sets C^{k^1-1}, C^{k^1}, and C^{k^1+1} are different and share a common boundary point, yielding a contradiction. Consequently, $k^1+1<k^2-1$.
Both the three sets C^{k^1-1}, C^{k^1}, and C^{k^2-1}, and the three sets C^{k^1}, C^{k^1+1}, and C^{k^2-1} are different, while the three sets in one of these two collections of sets have a common boundary point, giving a contradiction. Consequently, $k^1=0$, so $C^0\cup\cdots\cup C^{k^2-1}$ is the component of p^0 in C_ω and is homeomorphic to the unit circle $\widetilde{B}^1((0,0)^\top,1)$.
Next, the first case is considered, so v or a Walrasian equilibrium price system is a boundary point of C^{k^2}. Consider the boundary point p^{-1} of $C_\omega^{k^0}(s^0)$. Again, sets C^0, $C^{-1},\ldots$ are obtained such that after a finite number of, say, $k^1\in\mathbb{Z}_+$ steps either a set C^{-k^1} is obtained having v or a Walrasian equilibrium price system as a boundary point, the sets $C^{-k^1},\ldots,C^{k^2}$ all being different, and it is easily shown that the set $\cup_{k\in\{-k^1,\ldots,k^2\}}C^k$ is the component of p^0 in C_ω that is homeomorphic to the closed unit interval $[0,1]$, or there is $k^3\in\mathbb{Z}$ such that $-k^1<k^3\le k^2$, $C^{-k^1}=C^{k^3}$, and the sets $C^{-k^1+1},\ldots,C^{k^2}$ are all different. It is shown that the latter case leads to a contradiction.
Suppose $k^3=k^2$. Then, since C^{k^2} has v or a Walrasian equilibrium price system as a boundary point, it holds that $C^{-k^1+1}=C^{k^2-1}$, giving a contradiction unless $-k^1+1=k^2-1$. In this case C^{k^2-1} has one boundary point in common with $C^{k^2-2}=C^{-k^1}=C^{k^2}$ and the other boundary point in common with C^{k^2}. This implies that C^{k^2-1} and C^{k^2} have v or the same Walrasian equilibrium price system as a boundary point, a contradiction. Consequently, $k^3<k^2$.
Clearly, $-k^1+1\le k^3-1$. Suppose $-k^1+1=k^3-1$. Then the three different sets C^{-k^1+1}, C^{k^3}, and C^{k^3+1} have a common boundary point, yielding a contradiction. Consequently, $-k^1+1<k^3-1$.
Now it follows that $C^{-k^1+1}\cap C^{k^3}$ is a boundary point of either C^{k^3-1} or C^{k^3+1}, and therefore either $C^{-k^1+1}, C^{k^3-1}, C^{k^3}$ are three different sets having a common boundary point or $C^{-k^1+1}, C^{k^3}, C^{k^3+1}$ are three different sets having a common boundary point, yielding a contradiction. Consequently, there is no $k^3\in\mathbb{Z}$ such that both $-k^1<k^3\le k^2$ and $C^{-k^1}=C^{k^3}$.
It follows that C_ω has a finite number of components, being either arcs or loops. The boundary of C_ω is given by the collection consisting of the starting price system v and the Walrasian equilibrium price systems. Therefore, the loops contain no Walrasian equilibrium price systems, while the component of v in C_ω is an arc having a Walrasian equilibrium price system as the other boundary point. If there exists another Walrasian equilibrium price system, say p^*, then the component of p^* in C_ω is an arc having p^* and a third Walrasian equilibrium price system as boundary points. Therefore, $\omega\in\Omega^*$.

3. The closure of $\Omega \setminus \Omega^*$ in Ω has Lebesgue measure zero.
From Part 2 of the proof it follows that $\overline{\Omega} \subset \Omega^*$, so $\Omega \setminus \Omega^*$ has Lebesgue measure zero. If $\omega \in \Omega \setminus \Omega^*$, then, by Part 1 and Part 2 of the proof, there exists $p \in \dot{\Delta}^{N-1}$ such that (p, ω) belongs to the set Σ defined below.

$$\Sigma = \Big\{ (\overline{p}, \overline{\omega}) \in \dot{\Delta}^{N-1} \times \Omega \Big|$$
$$\exists s \in \mathcal{S}, \overline{p} \in C_{\overline{\omega}}(s) \text{ and rank } \partial_p \psi^{s,\overline{\omega}}(\overline{p}) \leq N-2, \text{ or}$$
$$\exists s \in \mathcal{S}, \exists j' \in I^-(s) \cup I^+(s),\ \overline{p} \in C_{\overline{\omega}}(s),\ z_{j'}(\overline{p}, \overline{\omega}) = 0, \text{ and rank } \partial_p \psi^{s;\overline{\omega}}_{j'}(\overline{p}) \leq N-1, \text{ or}$$
$$\exists s \in \mathcal{S}, i^0(s) \leq N-3, \exists j^1, j^2 \in I^-(s) \cup I^+(s), j^1 \neq j^2, \overline{p} \in C_{\overline{\omega}}(s) \text{ and } z_{j^1}(\overline{p}, \overline{\omega}) = z_{j^2}(\overline{p}, \overline{\omega}) = 0, \text{or}$$
$$\overline{p} = v \text{ and } \exists j \in I_N, z_j(\overline{p}, \overline{\omega}) = 0 \Big\}.$$

It is easily shown that Σ is closed in $\dot{\Delta}^{N-1} \times \Omega$ since Σ can be obtained by finite unions and intersections of sets that are closed in $\dot{\Delta}^{N-1} \times \Omega$, by the continuity of the functions z, $\partial_p \psi^s$, $\forall s \in \mathcal{S}$, $\partial_p \psi^s_j$, $\forall s \in \mathcal{S}$, $\forall j \in I^-(s) \cup I^+(s)$, and the continuity in p of $\min(\{\frac{p_j}{v_j} \mid j \in I_N\})$ and of $\max(\{\frac{p_j}{v_j} \mid j \in I_N\})$. Let the function $f : \Sigma \to \Omega$ be defined by $f(p, \omega) = \omega$, $\forall (p, \omega) \in \Sigma$. Then $\Omega \setminus \Omega^* \subset f(\Sigma)$ and $f(\Sigma)$ is a subset of a set having Lebesgue measure zero by Lemmas 10.5.1, 10.5.2, 10.5.3, and 10.5.4. It is shown that $f(\Sigma)$ is closed in Ω, thereby finishing the proof. Since the image by a continuous proper function of a closed set is closed, see Balasko (1988), proof of Theorem 4.1.5, page 88, it is sufficient to show that f is proper. Let T be a compact subset of Ω. It has to be shown that $f^{-1}(T)$ is compact. From the continuity of f it follows that $f^{-1}(T)$ is closed in Σ and therefore it is closed in $\dot{\Delta}^{N-1} \times \Omega$. Moreover, it is a subset of the set $\{(p, \omega) \in \dot{\Delta}^{N-1} \times T \mid p \in \widehat{P}(\omega)\}$. This set is easily seen to be compact using Theorems 2.5.7 and 10.4.5. Therefore, $f^{-1}(T)$ is a closed subset of a compact set and hence compact by Theorem 2.3.9. Q.E.D.

10.6 THE GROSS SUBSTITUTABILITY CASE

In this section a total excess demand function $z : \mathbb{R}^N_{++} \to \mathbb{R}^N$ and a starting price system $v \in \dot{\Delta}^{N-1}$ are assumed to be given. The main results are derived with the total excess demand function z satisfying the following assumptions.

A3. The total excess demand function $z : \mathbb{R}^N_{++} \to \mathbb{R}^N$ is continuous.

A4. For every $\lambda \in \mathbb{R}_{++}$, for every $p \in \mathbb{R}^N_{++}$, $z(\lambda p) = z(p)$.

A5. For every $p \in \mathbb{R}^N_{++}$, $p \cdot z(p) = 0$.

A6. The total excess demand function z is bounded from below, and if $(p^n)_{n\in\mathbb{N}}$ is a sequence of price systems in $\mathbb{R}^N_{++}$ converging to some $\overline{p} \in \mathbb{R}^N_{+} \setminus (\{0^N\} \cup \mathbb{R}^N_{++})$, then the sequence $(z(p^n))_{n\in\mathbb{N}}$ satisfies that $\sum_{j\in I_N} z_j(p^n) \to +\infty$.

A7. If $\overline{p}, \widehat{p} \in \mathbb{R}^N_{++}$ are such that there exists $j' \in I_N$ with $\overline{p}_{j'} < \widehat{p}_{j'}$, while $\overline{p}_j = \widehat{p}_j$, $\forall j \in I_N \setminus \{j'\}$, then $z_j(\overline{p}) < z_j(\widehat{p})$, $\forall j \in I_N \setminus \{j'\}$.

Notice that Assumptions A3-A6 can be derived from assumptions on the primitive concepts, $(X^i, \preceq^i, \omega^i)_{i\in I_M}$, see Theorems 3.7.1, 3.7.2, and 3.11.1. Assumption A7, called *gross substitutability in the finite increment form,* cannot be derived in this way. However, Assumptions A3-A7 are the same as the assumptions under which the Walrasian tatonnement process has been shown to be globally stable, see Theorem 3.11.2.

As a consequence of Assumption A4 it is possible to normalize the set of price systems to the set $\dot{\Delta}^{N-1}$ on which the price adjustment process is defined. For $\overline{p}, \widehat{p} \in \dot{\Delta}^{N-1}$, the sets $J_{\max}$ and $J_{\min}$ are defined by

$$J_{\min}(\overline{p}, \widehat{p}) = \left\{ j \in I_N \,\middle|\, \tfrac{\hat{p}_j}{\overline{p}_j} = \min(\{\tfrac{\hat{p}_j}{\overline{p}_j} \mid j \in I_N\}) \right\},$$
$$J_{\max}(\overline{p}, \widehat{p}) = \left\{ j \in I_N \,\middle|\, \tfrac{\hat{p}_j}{\overline{p}_j} = \max(\{\tfrac{\hat{p}_j}{\overline{p}_j} \mid j \in I_N\}) \right\}.$$

Clearly, for every $\overline{p}, \widehat{p} \in \dot{\Delta}^{N-1}$, $J_{\min}(\overline{p}, \widehat{p}) \neq \emptyset$ and $J_{\max}(\overline{p}, \widehat{p}) \neq \emptyset$. Moreover, if $\overline{p} \neq \widehat{p}$, then $j \in J_{\min}(\overline{p}, \widehat{p})$ implies $\frac{\hat{p}_j}{\overline{p}_j} < 1$, and $j \in J_{\max}(\overline{p}, \widehat{p})$ implies $\frac{\hat{p}_j}{\overline{p}_j} > 1$. The following lemma appears to be very useful.

Lemma 10.6.1

Let the total excess demand function z satisfy Assumptions A4 and A7. Let $\overline{p}, \widehat{p} \in \dot{\Delta}^{N-1}$ with $\overline{p} \neq \widehat{p}$ be given. Then, $z_j(\overline{p}) < z_j(\widehat{p})$, $\forall j \in J_{\min}(\overline{p}, \widehat{p})$, and $z_j(\overline{p}) > z_j(\widehat{p})$, $\forall j \in J_{\max}(\overline{p}, \widehat{p})$.

Proof

Let some $j' \in J_{\max}(\overline{p}, \widehat{p})$ be given. Let $\widetilde{p} \in \mathbb{R}^N_{++}$ be defined by $\widetilde{p} = \frac{\hat{p}_{j'}}{\overline{p}_{j'}}\overline{p}$. By Assumption A4, $z(\widetilde{p}) = z(\overline{p})$. Clearly, $\widetilde{p} > \widehat{p}$ and $\widetilde{p}_{j'} = \widehat{p}_{j'}$. Given $\widetilde{p}$, decrease the prices of commodities $j \in I_N \setminus \{j'\}$ until $\widehat{p}$ is reached. Using Assumption A7 repeatedly yields $z_{j'}(\widehat{p}) < z_{j'}(\widetilde{p}) = z_{j'}(\overline{p})$. The case with $j' \in J_{\min}(\overline{p}, \widehat{p})$ can be treated similarly. Q.E.D.

Using Lemma 10.6.1 it is trivial to show that if Assumptions A4 and A7 hold and a Walrasian equilibrium price system in $\dot{\Delta}^{N-1}$ exists, then it is unique.

See also Theorem 3.11.2, where it is stated that Assumptions A3-A7 imply that indeed a Walrasian equilibrium exists. In this section another proof of the existence of a Walrasian equilibrium is given if Assumptions A3-A7 are satisfied, without using a fixed point theorem.

For every $\lambda \in (0,1]$, the set $\dot{\Delta}_\lambda^{N-1}$ is defined by

$$\dot{\Delta}_\lambda^{N-1} = \left\{ p \in \dot{\Delta}^{N-1} \,\middle|\, \min(\{\tfrac{p_j}{v_j} \mid j \in I_N\}) = \lambda \right\}.$$

Clearly, $\dot{\Delta}_1^{N-1} = \{v\}$. If $N = 3$ and $\lambda \in (0,1)$, then the set $\dot{\Delta}_\lambda^{N-1}$ consists of the sides of a triangle. For arbitrary $N \in \mathbb{N} \setminus \{1\}$, for every $\lambda^1, \lambda^2 \in (0,1]$ with $\lambda^1 \neq \lambda^2$, it holds that the sets $\dot{\Delta}_{\lambda^1}^{N-1}$ and $\dot{\Delta}_{\lambda^2}^{N-1}$ are disjoint, and that $\cup_{\lambda \in (0,1]} \dot{\Delta}_\lambda^{N-1} = \dot{\Delta}^{N-1}$. The first step in proving that under Assumptions A3-A7 the price adjustment process converges to a Walrasian equilibrium price system is to show that if the price adjustment process has reached the set $\dot{\Delta}_\lambda^{N-1}$ for some $\lambda \in (0,1]$ and did not find a Walrasian equilibrium price system, then the price adjustment process intersects the set $\dot{\Delta}_{\lambda-\delta}^{N-1}$ for every $\delta \in \mathbb{R}_{++}$ small enough. This is used to show that the price adjustment process moves away from the starting price system v.

Lemma 10.6.2
Let the total excess demand function z satisfy Assumptions A3-A5 and A7, and let $v \in \dot{\Delta}^{N-1}$ be the starting price system. Let $\overline{p} \in \dot{\Delta}^{N-1}$ with $z(\overline{p}) \neq 0^N$ be given. If there exists $\lambda \in (0,1]$ and $s \in \mathcal{S}$ such that $\overline{p} \in C(s) \cap \dot{\Delta}_\lambda^{N-1}$, then there exists $\overline{s} \in \mathcal{S}$ and $\varepsilon \in \mathbb{R}_{++}$ such that, for every $\delta \in [0,\varepsilon]$, $C(\overline{s}) \cap \dot{\Delta}_{\lambda-\delta}^{N-1} \neq \emptyset$. If $z_j(\overline{p}) > 0$, $\forall j \in I^+(s)$, and $z_j(\overline{p}) < 0$, $\forall j \in I^-(s)$, then $\overline{s}$ can be taken equal to s.

Proof
Let $\overline{s}$ be such that $\overline{s}_j = -1$ if $z_j(\overline{p}) < 0$, $\overline{s}_j = 0$ if $z_j(\overline{p}) = 0$, and $\overline{s}_j = +1$ if $z_j(\overline{p}) > 0$. Notice that $\overline{s} = s$ if the requirements in the last part of the lemma are satisfied. Since $z(\overline{p}) \neq 0^N$, it holds by Assumption A5 that $\overline{s} \in \mathcal{S}$. Clearly, $\overline{p} \in C(\overline{s}) \cap \dot{\Delta}_\lambda^{N-1}$. If $z_j(\overline{p}) \neq 0$, $\forall j \in I_N$, then Lemma 10.6.2 holds by the continuity of z. So, consider the case where $I^0(\overline{s}) \neq \emptyset$. For every $\delta \in [0,\lambda)$, let the set $E(\overline{p},\overline{s},\delta)$ be defined by

$$E(\overline{p},\overline{s},\delta) = \left\{ p \in \dot{\Delta}^{N-1} \,\middle|\, \begin{array}{ll} \frac{p_j}{\overline{p}_j} = 1 - \frac{\delta}{\lambda}, & \forall j \in I^-(\overline{s}), \\ 1 - \frac{\delta}{\lambda} \leq \frac{p_j}{\overline{p}_j} \leq \max(\{\frac{p_j}{\overline{p}_j} \mid j \in I_N\}), & \forall j \in I^0(\overline{s}), \\ \frac{p_j}{\overline{p}_j} = \max(\{\frac{p_j}{\overline{p}_j} \mid j \in I_N\}), & \forall j \in I^+(\overline{s}) \end{array} \right\}.$$

It is easily verified that $E(\overline{p},\overline{s},\delta)$ is a compact subset of $A(\overline{s}) \cap \dot{\Delta}_{\lambda-\delta}^{N-1}$. Since z is a continuous function, there exists $\varepsilon \in (0,\lambda)$ such that, for every $\delta \in [0,\varepsilon]$, for

every $p \in E(\overline{p}, \overline{s}, \delta)$, $z_j(p) > 0$, $\forall j \in I^+(\overline{s})$, and $z_j(p) < 0$, $\forall j \in I^-(\overline{s})$. Lemma 10.6.2 is obviously true for the case $\delta = 0$, so consider the case $\delta > 0$.
Let some $\delta \in (0, \varepsilon]$ be given. Let $\widehat{p} \in E(\overline{p}, \overline{s}, \delta)$ be such that

$$\max\left(\left\{|z_j(\widehat{p})| \,\middle|\, j \in I^0(\overline{s})\right\}\right) \leq \max\left(\left\{|z_j(p)| \,\middle|\, j \in I^0(\overline{s})\right\}\right), \; \forall p \in E(\overline{p}, \overline{s}, \delta).$$

Notice that $\widehat{p}$ exists by Theorem 2.3.14.
Suppose $\max(\{|z_j(\widehat{p})| \mid j \in I^0(\overline{s})\}) > 0$. Let the sets J^0_- and J^0_+ be defined by

$$\begin{aligned} J^0_- &= \left\{ j \in I^0(\overline{s}) \,\middle|\, z_j(\widehat{p}) = -\max(\{|z_j(\widehat{p})| \mid j \in I^0(\overline{s})\}) \right\}, \\ J^0_+ &= \left\{ j \in I^0(\overline{s}) \,\middle|\, z_j(\widehat{p}) = \max(\{|z_j(\widehat{p})| \mid j \in I^0(\overline{s})\}) \right\}. \end{aligned}$$

Suppose there exists $j' \in J^0_-$ such that $\frac{\widehat{p}_{j'}}{\overline{p}_{j'}} = 1 - \frac{\delta}{\lambda}$. By Lemma 10.6.1 and since $\widehat{p} \in E(\overline{p}, \overline{s}, \delta)$, it follows that $0 = z_{j'}(\overline{p}) < z_{j'}(\widehat{p})$, a contradiction since $j' \in J^0_-$. Hence, $\frac{\widehat{p}_j}{\overline{p}_j} > 1 - \frac{\delta}{\lambda}$, $\forall j \in J^0_-$. Similarly, it can be shown that $\frac{\widehat{p}_j}{\overline{p}_j} < \max(\{\frac{\widehat{p}_j}{\overline{p}_j} \mid j \in I_N\})$, $\forall j \in J^0_+$.
Next, three possible cases are considered, each leading to a contradiction with the supposition that $\max(\{|z_j(\widehat{p})| \mid j \in I^0(\overline{s})\}) > 0$.
1. $J^0_- \neq \emptyset$ and $J^0_+ = \emptyset$. Then, for every $\alpha \in \mathbb{R}_{++}$, let $p^\alpha \in \mathbb{R}^N$ be defined by

$$\begin{aligned} p^\alpha_j &= \widehat{p}_j, & &\forall j \in I^-(\overline{s}) \cup (I^0(\overline{s}) \setminus J^0_-), \\ p^\alpha_j &= (1-\alpha)\widehat{p}_j, & &\forall j \in J^0_-, \\ p^\alpha_j &= \left(1 + \frac{\alpha \sum_{j \in J^0_-} \widehat{p}_j}{\sum_{j \in I^+(\overline{s})} \widehat{p}_j}\right) \widehat{p}_j, \; \forall j \in I^+(\overline{s}). \end{aligned}$$

Since $\frac{\widehat{p}_j}{\overline{p}_j} > 1 - \frac{\delta}{\lambda}$, $\forall j \in J^0_-$, α can be chosen small enough to guarantee that $p^\alpha \in E(\overline{p}, \overline{s}, \delta)$, $|z_j(p^\alpha)| < \max(\{|z_j(\widehat{p})| \mid j \in I^0(\overline{s})\})$, $\forall j \in I^0(\overline{s}) \setminus J^0_-$, and $z_j(p^\alpha) < 0$, $\forall j \in J^0_-$. Now it holds by Lemma 10.6.1 that $\max(\{|z_j(p^\alpha)| \mid j \in I^0(\overline{s})\}) < \max(\{|z_j(\widehat{p})| \mid j \in I^0(\overline{s})\})$, a contradiction with the definition of $\widehat{p}$.
2. $J^0_- = \emptyset$ and $J^0_+ \neq \emptyset$. Then let the, possibly empty, set J be defined by

$$J = \left\{ j \in I^0(\overline{s}) \,\middle|\, \frac{\widehat{p}_j}{\overline{p}_j} = \max(\{\tfrac{\widehat{p}_j}{\overline{p}_j} \mid j \in I_N\}) \right\}.$$

Moreover, for every $\alpha \in \mathbb{R}_{++}$, let $p^\alpha \in \mathbb{R}^N$ be defined by

$$\begin{aligned} p^\alpha_j &= \widehat{p}_j, & &\forall j \in I^-(\overline{s}) \cup (I^0(\overline{s}) \setminus (J^0_+ \cup J)), \\ p^\alpha_j &= (1+\alpha)\widehat{p}_j, & &\forall j \in J^0_+, \\ p^\alpha_j &= \left(1 - \frac{\alpha \sum_{j \in J^0_+} \widehat{p}_j}{\sum_{j \in I^+(\overline{s}) \cup J} \widehat{p}_j}\right) \widehat{p}_j, \; \forall j \in I^+(\overline{s}) \cup J. \end{aligned}$$

Since for every $j \in J^0_+$ it holds that $\frac{\widehat{p}_j}{\overline{p}_j} < \max(\{\frac{\widehat{p}_j}{\overline{p}_j} \mid j \in I_N\})$, α can be chosen small enough to guarantee that $p^\alpha \in E(\overline{p}, \overline{s}, \delta)$, $|z_j(p^\alpha)| < \max(\{|z_j(\widehat{p})| \mid j \in$

$I^0(\overline{s})\})$, $\forall j \in I^0(\overline{s}) \setminus J^0_+$, and $z_j(p^\alpha) > 0$, $\forall j \in J^0_+$. Using Lemma 10.6.1 and the construction of p^α, it follows that $\max(\{|z_j(p^\alpha)| \mid j \in I^0(\overline{s})\}) < \max(\{|z_j(\widehat{p})| \mid j \in I^0(\overline{s})\})$, a contradiction with the definition of $\widehat{p}$.

3. $J^0_- \neq \emptyset$ and $J^0_+ \neq \emptyset$. Then, for every $\alpha \in \mathbb{R}_{++}$, let $p^\alpha \in \mathbb{R}^N$ be defined by

$$\begin{aligned} p^\alpha_j &= \widehat{p}_j, & \forall j \in I_N \setminus (J^0_- \cup J^0_+), \\ p^\alpha_j &= (1-\alpha)\widehat{p}_j, & \forall j \in J^0_-, \\ p^\alpha_j &= \left(1 + \frac{\alpha \sum_{j \in J^0_-} \hat{p}_j}{\sum_{j \in J^0_+} \hat{p}_j}\right) \widehat{p}_j, \ \forall j \in J^0_+. \end{aligned}$$

Clearly, α can be chosen small enough to guarantee that $p^\alpha \in E(\overline{p}, \overline{s}, \delta)$, $|z_j(p^\alpha)| < \max(\{|z_j(\widehat{p})| \mid j \in I^0(\overline{s})\})$, $\forall j \in I^0(\overline{s}) \setminus (J^0_- \cup J^0_+)$, $z_j(p^\alpha) < 0$, $\forall j \in J^0_-$, and $z_j(p^\alpha) > 0$, $\forall j \in J^0_+$. By Lemma 10.6.1 a contradiction is obtained as before.

Consequently, $\max(\{|z_j(\widehat{p})| \mid j \in I^0(\overline{s})\}) = 0$. This result together with the choice of ε implies $\widehat{p} \in B(\overline{s})$. Moreover, $\widehat{p} \in E(\overline{p}, \overline{s}, \delta) \subset A(\overline{s}) \cap \dot{\Delta}^{N-1}_{\lambda-\delta}$ and therefore $\widehat{p} \in C(\overline{s}) \cap \dot{\Delta}^{N-1}_{\lambda-\delta}$. Q.E.D.

The next step is to show that if $C(\overline{s}) \neq \emptyset$ for some $\overline{s} \in \mathcal{S}$, then, for every $\widehat{s} \in \mathcal{S}$ with $i^0(\widehat{s}) = i^0(\overline{s})$, $C(\widehat{s}) \setminus C(\overline{s}) = \emptyset$. This is shown in Lemma 10.6.4. So, if during the price adjustment process the region $A(\overline{s})$ is reached and therefore $i^0(\overline{s})$ markets are in equilibrium, then every price system $\overline{p} \in \dot{\Delta}^{N-1}$ ever generated by the price adjustment process with $i^0(\overline{s})$ markets in equilibrium satisfies $\overline{p} \in A(\overline{s})$. Moreover, it is shown in Lemma 10.6.4 that if two price systems $\overline{p}, \widehat{p} \in \dot{\Delta}^{N-1}$ are reached by the price adjustment process with the same number of markets in equilibrium and with the minimal price ratio with respect to the starting price system v of $\overline{p}$ greater than that of $\widehat{p}$, then $\overline{p}, \widehat{p} \in C(s)$ for a uniquely determined admissible sign vector $s \in \mathcal{S}$. Moreover, $I^-(s) = J_{\min}(\overline{p}, \widehat{p})$ and $I^+(s) = J_{\max}(\overline{p}, \widehat{p})$. So, the prices of commodities with a negative (positive) total excess demand have been decreased (increased) maximally. To show Lemma 10.6.4, the purely technical Lemma 10.6.3 has to be shown first.

Lemma 10.6.3

Let $v \in \dot{\Delta}^{N-1}$ be the starting price system. Moreover, let $\overline{s}, \widehat{s} \in \mathcal{S}$ with $i^0(\overline{s}) = i^0(\widehat{s})$ and $\overline{s} \neq \widehat{s}$, and $\overline{p} \in A(\overline{s})$ and $\widehat{p} \in A(\widehat{s})$ with $\overline{p} \neq \widehat{p}$ be given. Then

$$J_{\min}(\overline{p}, \widehat{p}) \cap \left(I^0(\overline{s}) \cup I^+(\overline{s})\right) \cap \left(I^-(\widehat{s}) \cup I^0(\widehat{s})\right) \neq \emptyset \ \textit{or}$$
$$J_{\max}(\overline{p}, \widehat{p}) \cap \left(I^-(\overline{s}) \cup I^0(\overline{s})\right) \cap \left(I^0(\widehat{s}) \cup I^+(\widehat{s})\right) \neq \emptyset.$$

Proof
Suppose, on the contrary, that

$$J_{\min}(\overline{p}, \widehat{p}) \subset I^-(\overline{s}) \cup I^+(\widehat{s}), \tag{10.14}$$
$$J_{\max}(\overline{p}, \widehat{p}) \subset I^+(\overline{s}) \cup I^-(\widehat{s}). \tag{10.15}$$

It is shown that if (10.14) and (10.15) hold, then

$$J_{\min}(\overline{p}, \widehat{p}) \cap I^-(\overline{s}) = \emptyset \text{ or } J_{\max}(\overline{p}, \widehat{p}) \cap I^-(\widehat{s}) = \emptyset, \tag{10.16}$$
$$J_{\min}(\overline{p}, \widehat{p}) \cap I^+(\widehat{s}) = \emptyset \text{ or } J_{\max}(\overline{p}, \widehat{p}) \cap I^-(\widehat{s}) = \emptyset, \tag{10.17}$$
$$J_{\min}(\overline{p}, \widehat{p}) \cap I^-(\overline{s}) = \emptyset \text{ or } J_{\max}(\overline{p}, \widehat{p}) \cap I^+(\overline{s}) = \emptyset, \tag{10.18}$$
$$J_{\min}(\overline{p}, \widehat{p}) \cap I^+(\widehat{s}) = \emptyset \text{ or } J_{\max}(\overline{p}, \widehat{p}) \cap I^+(\overline{s}) = \emptyset. \tag{10.19}$$

From (10.14), (10.18), and (10.19) it follows that $J_{\max}(\overline{p}, \widehat{p}) \cap I^+(\overline{s}) = \emptyset$, and from (10.14), (10.16), and (10.17) it follows that $J_{\max}(\overline{p}, \widehat{p}) \cap I^-(\widehat{s}) = \emptyset$. Together with (10.15) this yields $J_{\max}(\overline{p}, \widehat{p}) = \emptyset$, a contradiction, and this proves the lemma. It remains to be shown that (10.14) and (10.15) imply (10.16)-(10.19). Let some $j^1 \in J_{\min}(\overline{p}, \widehat{p})$ and some $j^2 \in J_{\max}(\overline{p}, \widehat{p})$ be given.
Suppose $j^2 \in I^-(\widehat{s})$. If $j^1 \in I^-(\overline{s})$, then $1 > \frac{\widehat{p}_{j^1}}{\overline{p}_{j^1}} = \frac{\widehat{p}_{j^1}}{v_{j^1}} \frac{v_{j^1}}{\overline{p}_{j^1}} \geq \frac{\widehat{p}_{j^2}}{v_{j^2}} \frac{v_{j^2}}{\overline{p}_{j^2}} = \frac{\widehat{p}_{j^2}}{\overline{p}_{j^2}} > 1$, a contradiction. Hence, (10.16) is true. For every $j \in I^-(\overline{s})$ it holds that $\frac{\widehat{p}_j}{\overline{p}_j} \geq \frac{\widehat{p}_{j^2}}{\overline{p}_{j^2}}$, so $j \in J_{\max}(\overline{p}, \widehat{p})$, and by (10.15) $j \in I^-(\widehat{s})$. If $j^1 \in I^+(\widehat{s})$, then it holds for every $j \in I^+(\overline{s})$ that $\frac{\widehat{p}_j}{\overline{p}_j} \leq \frac{\widehat{p}_{j^1}}{\overline{p}_{j^1}}$, so $j \in J_{\min}(\overline{p}, \widehat{p})$, and by (10.14) $j \in I^+(\widehat{s})$. Therefore, $I^-(\overline{s}) \subset I^-(\widehat{s})$ and $I^+(\overline{s}) \subset I^+(\widehat{s})$. Since $\overline{s} \neq \widehat{s}$ and $i^0(\overline{s}) = i^0(\widehat{s})$, a contradiction is obtained. So, (10.17) is true.
Suppose $j^2 \in I^+(\overline{s})$. If $j^1 \in I^-(\overline{s})$, then it holds for every $j \in I^-(\widehat{s})$ that $\frac{\widehat{p}_j}{\overline{p}_j} \leq \frac{\widehat{p}_{j^1}}{\overline{p}_{j^1}}$, so $j \in J_{\min}(\overline{p}, \widehat{p})$, and by (10.14) $j \in I^-(\overline{s})$, while it holds for every $j \in I^+(\widehat{s})$ that $\frac{\widehat{p}_j}{\overline{p}_j} \geq \frac{\widehat{p}_{j^2}}{\overline{p}_{j^2}}$, so $j \in J_{\max}(\overline{p}, \widehat{p})$, and by (10.15) $j \in I^+(\overline{s})$. Therefore, $I^-(\widehat{s}) \subset I^-(\overline{s})$ and $I^+(\widehat{s}) \subset I^+(\overline{s})$. Since $\overline{s} \neq \widehat{s}$ and $i^0(\overline{s}) = i^0(\widehat{s})$, a contradiction is obtained. Hence, (10.18) is true. If $j^1 \in I^+(\widehat{s})$, then $1 > \frac{\widehat{p}_{j^1}}{\overline{p}_{j^1}} \geq \frac{\widehat{p}_{j^2}}{\overline{p}_{j^2}} > 1$, a contradiction. Hence, (10.19) is true. Q.E.D.

Lemma 10.6.4
Let the total excess demand function z satisfy Assumptions A4 and A7, and let $v \in \dot{\Delta}^{N-1}$ be the starting price system. Moreover, let two admissible sign vectors $\overline{s}, \widehat{s} \in S$ with $i^0(\overline{s}) = i^0(\widehat{s})$ be given. If $C(\overline{s}) \neq \emptyset$, then $C(\widehat{s}) \setminus C(\overline{s}) = \emptyset$. Moreover, if there are price systems $\overline{p} \in C(\overline{s})$ and $\widehat{p} \in C(\widehat{s})$ with $\min(\{\frac{\overline{p}_j}{v_j} \mid j \in I_N\}) > \min(\{\frac{\widehat{p}_j}{v_j} \mid j \in I_N\})$, then $\overline{s} = \widehat{s}$, $J_{\min}(\overline{p}, \widehat{p}) = I^-(\overline{s})$, and $J_{\max}(\overline{p}, \widehat{p}) = I^+(\overline{s})$.

Proof

Suppose there exists $\overline{p} \in C(\overline{s})$ and $\widehat{p} \in C(\widehat{s}) \setminus C(\overline{s})$. Clearly, $\overline{s} \neq \widehat{s}$. Moreover, $\overline{p} \in A(\overline{s})$ and $\widehat{p} \in A(\widehat{s})$, so by Lemma 10.6.3 there exists $j' \in J_{\min}(\overline{p},\widehat{p}) \cap (I^0(\overline{s}) \cup I^+(\overline{s})) \cap (I^-(\widehat{s}) \cup I^0(\widehat{s}))$ or there exists $j' \in J_{\max}(\overline{p},\widehat{p}) \cap (I^-(\overline{s}) \cup I^0(\overline{s})) \cap (I^0(\widehat{s}) \cup I^+(\widehat{s}))$. In the first case, $z_{j'}(\overline{p}) \geq 0$ and $z_{j'}(\widehat{p}) \leq 0$, whereas by Lemma 10.6.1 $z_{j'}(\overline{p}) < z_{j'}(\widehat{p})$, a contradiction. In the second case, $z_{j'}(\overline{p}) \leq 0$ and $z_{j'}(\widehat{p}) \geq 0$, whereas by Lemma 10.6.1 $z_{j'}(\overline{p}) > z_{j'}(\widehat{p})$, a contradiction. This proves the first part of the lemma.

Let $\overline{p} \in C(\overline{s})$ and $\widehat{p} \in C(\widehat{s})$ be given. By the first part of the lemma it holds that $C(\overline{s}) = C(\widehat{s})$. For every $j \in I^-(\widehat{s})$ it holds that $\frac{\hat{p}_j}{\overline{p}_j} = \frac{\hat{p}_j}{v_j}\frac{v_j}{\overline{p}_j} < \frac{\overline{p}_j}{v_j}\frac{v_j}{\overline{p}_j} = 1$, so $J_{\max}(\overline{p},\widehat{p}) \subset I^0(\widehat{s}) \cup I^+(\widehat{s})$. Suppose there exists $j' \in J_{\max}(\overline{p},\widehat{p}) \cap I^0(\widehat{s})$. Then, since $\overline{p},\widehat{p} \in C(\widehat{s})$ and by Lemma 10.6.1, $0 = z_{j'}(\overline{p}) > z_{j'}(\widehat{p}) = 0$, a contradiction. Consequently, $J_{\max}(\overline{p},\widehat{p}) \subset I^+(\widehat{s})$. For every $j^1, j^2 \in I^+(\widehat{s})$ it holds that $\frac{\hat{p}_{j^1}}{\overline{p}_{j^1}} = \frac{\hat{p}_{j^2}}{\overline{p}_{j^2}}$. Hence, $J_{\max}(\overline{p},\widehat{p}) = I^+(\widehat{s})$ and $J_{\min}(\overline{p},\widehat{p}) \subset I^-(\widehat{s}) \cup I^0(\widehat{s})$. Suppose $j' \in J_{\min}(\overline{p},\widehat{p}) \cap I^0(\widehat{s})$. Then $0 = z_{j'}(\overline{p}) < z_{j'}(\widehat{p}) = 0$, a contradiction. It follows that $J_{\min}(\overline{p},\widehat{p}) = I^-(\widehat{s})$. In a similar way it can be shown that $J_{\min}(\overline{p},\widehat{p}) = I^-(\overline{s})$ and $J_{\max}(\overline{p},\widehat{p}) = I^+(\overline{s})$, hence $I^-(\overline{s}) = I^-(\widehat{s})$, $I^+(\overline{s}) = I^+(\widehat{s})$, and therefore $\overline{s} = \widehat{s}$. Q.E.D.

The next step in proving the convergence of the price adjustment process is showing that for every $\lambda \in (0,1]$ the intersection of the price adjustment process and the set $\dot{\Delta}_\lambda^{N-1}$ contains at most one element. First it is shown, for every $\lambda \in (0,1]$, for every $s \in \mathcal{S}$, that the intersection of $C(s)$ and $\dot{\Delta}_\lambda^{N-1}$ contains at most one element.

Lemma 10.6.5

Let the total excess demand function z satisfy Assumptions A4 and A7, and let $v \in \dot{\Delta}^{N-1}$ be the starting price system. Then, for every $\lambda \in (0,1]$, for every $s \in \mathcal{S}$, the set $C(s) \cap \dot{\Delta}_\lambda^{N-1}$ contains at most one element.

Proof

Let some $\lambda \in (0,1]$ and some $s \in \mathcal{S}$ be given. Suppose $\overline{p},\widehat{p} \in C(s) \cap \dot{\Delta}_\lambda^{N-1}$ with $\overline{p} \neq \widehat{p}$. Then, for every $j \in I^-(s)$, $\frac{\hat{p}_j}{\overline{p}_j} = \frac{\lambda v_j}{\lambda v_j} = 1$. So, $\overline{p} \neq \widehat{p}$ implies that there exists $j^1 \in J_{\max}(\overline{p},\widehat{p}) \cap (I^0(s) \cup I^+(s))$ and $j^2 \in J_{\min}(\overline{p},\widehat{p}) \cap (I^0(s) \cup I^+(s))$. By Lemma 10.6.1, $z_{j^1}(\overline{p}) > z_{j^1}(\widehat{p})$ and $z_{j^2}(\overline{p}) < z_{j^2}(\widehat{p})$, so $j^1, j^2 \notin I^0(s)$. Hence, $j^1, j^2 \in I^+(s)$. Then $1 < \frac{\hat{p}_{j^1}}{\overline{p}_{j^1}} = \frac{\hat{p}_{j^2}}{\overline{p}_{j^2}} < 1$, a contradiction. Consequently, $C(s) \cap \dot{\Delta}_\lambda^{N-1}$ contains at most one element. Q.E.D.

After these preliminary lemmas it is possible to show the convergence of the price adjustment process. Let the total excess demand function z satisfy Assumptions A3-A7 and let $v \in \dot{\Delta}^{N-1}$ be the starting price system. The relation $\Pi : (0,1] \rightarrow C$ is defined by

$$\Pi(\lambda) = C \cap \dot{\Delta}_{\lambda}^{N-1}, \ \forall \lambda \in (0,1].$$

In Lemma 10.6.6 it is shown that there exists $\overline{\lambda} \in (0,1]$ such that $\Pi_{|[\overline{\lambda},1]} : [\overline{\lambda},1] \rightarrow C$ is a function, while $\Pi(\lambda) = \emptyset$, $\forall \lambda \in (0, \overline{\lambda})$.

Lemma 10.6.6
Let the total excess demand function z satisfy Assumptions A3-A7 and let $v \in \dot{\Delta}^{N-1}$ be the starting price system. Then there exists $\overline{\lambda} \in (0,1]$ such that $\Pi(\lambda) = \emptyset$, $\forall \lambda \in (0,\overline{\lambda})$, $\Pi(\overline{\lambda}) = \{p^*\}$, where p^* is a Walrasian equilibrium price system, and $\Pi_{|[\overline{\lambda},1]} : [\overline{\lambda},1] \rightarrow C$ is a function.

Proof
Similarly as in the proof of Theorem 10.4.5 it can be shown that the set $C(s)$, $\forall s \in \mathcal{S}$, and the set C is compact. Let $\overline{\lambda} \in (0,1]$ be defined by $\overline{\lambda} = \min(\{\min(\{\frac{p_j}{v_j} \mid j \in I_N\}) \mid p \in C\})$. Notice that $\overline{\lambda}$ is well defined by Theorem 2.3.14. Obviously, it holds that $\Pi(\lambda) = \emptyset$ if $\lambda < \overline{\lambda}$. Moreover, by Lemma 10.6.2, $\Pi(\overline{\lambda})$ consists of a Walrasian equilibrium price system $p^* \in \dot{\Delta}^{N-1}$. Notice that Lemma 10.6.1 immediately implies that p^* is the unique Walrasian equilibrium price system of $\dot{\Delta}^{N-1}$. Using the uniqueness of the Walrasian equilibrium price system, Lemma 10.6.2, the compactness of C, and the fact that $v \in \Pi(1)$, it follows that $\Pi(\lambda) \neq \emptyset$, $\forall \lambda \in [\overline{\lambda},1]$.
Let some $\lambda \in [\overline{\lambda},1]$ be given.
Suppose there exists $\overline{p} \in C(\overline{s}) \cap \dot{\Delta}_{\lambda}^{N-1}$ and $\widehat{p} \in C(\widehat{s}) \cap \dot{\Delta}_{\lambda}^{N-1}$ such that $\overline{p} \neq \widehat{p}$. From Lemmas 10.6.4 and 10.6.5 it follows that $i^0(\overline{s}) \neq i^0(\widehat{s})$. Without loss of generality, it can be assumed that $i^0(\overline{s}) < i^0(\widehat{s})$. Since $C(\overline{s})$ is compact, it follows from Theorem 2.3.14 that there exists $p^1 \in C(\overline{s})$ such that $\min(\{\frac{p_j^1}{v_j} \mid j \in I_N\}) \leq \min(\{\frac{p_j}{v_j} \mid j \in I_N\})$, $\forall p \in C(\overline{s})$. From Lemma 10.6.2 it follows that there exists $j' \in I^-(\overline{s}) \cup I^+(\overline{s})$ such that $z_{j'}(p^1) = 0$. Hence, $p^1 \in C(s^1)$, where $s^1 \in \mathbb{S}^N$ is defined by $s_{j'}^1 = 0$ and $s_j^1 = \overline{s}_j$, $\forall j \in I_N \setminus \{j'\}$. Since $i^0(\overline{s}) < i^0(\widehat{s}) \leq N-2$, j' can be chosen such that $s^1 \in \mathcal{S}$. Repeating this argument a finite number of times, a price system $\widetilde{p} \in C(\widetilde{s})$ is found such that $\widetilde{s} \in \mathcal{S}$, $i^0(\widetilde{s}) = i^0(\widehat{s})$, and there exists $j^1 \in I^0(\widetilde{s})$ satisfying $\frac{\widetilde{p}_{j^1}}{v_{j^1}} = \min(\{\frac{\widetilde{p}_j}{v_j} \mid j \in I_N\})$ or $\frac{\widetilde{p}_{j^1}}{v_{j^1}} = \max(\{\frac{\widetilde{p}_j}{v_j} \mid j \in I_N\})$. Moreover, $I^-(\widetilde{s}) \subset I^-(\overline{s})$, $I^0(\overline{s}) \subset I^0(\widetilde{s})$, and $I^+(\widetilde{s}) \subset I^+(\overline{s})$.
Suppose $\min(\{\frac{\widetilde{p}_j}{v_j} \mid j \in I_N\}) \geq \min(\{\frac{\widehat{p}_j}{v_j} \mid j \in I_N\})$. Since $\overline{p}, \widehat{p} \in \dot{\Delta}_{\lambda}^{N-1}$, it follows that $\min(\{\frac{\widetilde{p}_j}{v_j} \mid j \in I_N\}) = \min(\{\frac{\widehat{p}_j}{v_j} \mid j \in I_N\}) = \min(\{\frac{\overline{p}_j}{v_j} \mid j \in I_N\})$.

Using Lemma 10.6.5 it follows that $\widetilde{p} = \overline{p}$. By Lemma 10.6.5, $\overline{p} \notin C(\widehat{s})$, and since $\overline{p} \in C(\widetilde{s})$, a contradiction with Lemma 10.6.4 is obtained. Consequently, $\min(\{\frac{\widetilde{p}_j}{v_j} \mid j \in I_N\}) < \min(\{\frac{\widehat{p}_j}{v_j} \mid j \in I_N\})$.
By Lemma 10.6.4, $\widehat{s} = \widetilde{s}$, $J_{\min}(\widehat{p}, \widetilde{p}) = I^-(\widehat{s})$, and $J_{\max}(\widehat{p}, \widetilde{p}) = I^+(\widehat{s})$. Consider the case where $\frac{\widetilde{p}_{j^1}}{v_{j^1}} = \min(\{\frac{\widetilde{p}_j}{v_j} \mid j \in I_N\})$. Let $j^2 \in J_{\min}(\widehat{p}, \widetilde{p})$ be given. Since $\frac{\widetilde{p}_{j^1}}{v_{j^1}} = \min(\{\frac{\widetilde{p}_j}{v_j} \mid j \in I_N\})$ and $J_{\min}(\widehat{p}, \widetilde{p}) = I^-(\widehat{s})$, it holds that $\frac{\widetilde{p}_{j^1}}{\widehat{p}_{j^1}} \leq \frac{\widetilde{p}_{j^2}}{\widehat{p}_{j^2}}$. So, $j^1 \in J_{\min}(\widehat{p}, \widetilde{p})$, a contradiction with $J_{\min}(\widehat{p}, \widetilde{p}) = I^-(\widetilde{s})$ and $j^1 \in I^0(\widetilde{s})$. Similarly, a contradiction is obtained if $\frac{\widetilde{p}_{j^1}}{v_{j^1}} = \max(\{\frac{\widetilde{p}_j}{v_j} \mid j \in I_N\})$. Consequently, for every $\lambda \in [\overline{\lambda}, 1]$, $\Pi(\lambda)$ contains exactly one element. Q.E.D.

Let the total excess demand function z satisfy Assumptions A3-A7 and let $v \in \dot{\Delta}^{N-1}$ be the starting price system. In Lemma 10.6.6 it has been shown that there exists $\overline{\lambda} \in (0, 1]$ such that $\Pi(\lambda) = \emptyset$, $\forall \lambda \in (0, \overline{\lambda})$, $\Pi(\overline{\lambda}) = \{p^*\}$, where p^* is a Walrasian equilibrium price system of $\dot{\Delta}^{N-1}$, which is easily seen to be unique using Lemma 10.6.1, and $\Pi_{|[\overline{\lambda}, 1]} : [\overline{\lambda}, 1] \to C$ is a function. Therefore, the existence of a Walrasian equilibrium in the gross substitutability case is shown in this section without using a fixed point theorem. The real number λ^* is defined by

$$\lambda^* = \min\left(\left\{\frac{p_j^*}{v_j} \middle| j \in I_N\right\}\right)$$

and the function $\pi : [0, 1] \to C$ is defined by

$$\{\pi(t)\} = C \cap \dot{\Delta}^{N-1}_{1+(\lambda^*-1)t}, \; \forall t \in [0, 1].$$

In Theorem 10.6.7 it is shown that π is a homeomorphism between $[0, 1]$ and C if $\lambda^* < 1$. Moreover, $\pi(0) = v$ and $\pi(1) = p^*$. If $\lambda^* = 1$, then the function π is still well defined and it is a constant function, associating with every $t \in [0, 1]$ the Walrasian equilibrium price system v.

Theorem 10.6.7
Let the total excess demand function z satisfy Assumptions A3-A7 and let $v \in \dot{\Delta}^{N-1}$ be the starting price system. Then, either $z(v) = 0^N$, or $z(v) \neq 0^N$ and the function $\pi : [0, 1] \to C$ is a homeomorphism such that $\pi(0) = v$ and $\pi(1) = p^*$, where $z(p^*) = 0^N$.
Proof
Either $\lambda^* = 1$, $C = \{v\}$, and $z(v) = 0^N$, or $\lambda^* < 1$ and $z(v) \neq 0^N$. Consider the latter case. Obviously, by Lemma 10.6.6, the function π is injective and surjective. It remains to be shown that π is continuous. The continuity of π^{-1} follows then immediately from Theorem 2.3.4.

Suppose π is not continuous. Then there exists a sequence $(t^n)_{n\in\mathbb{N}}$ in $[0,1]$ converging to some $\bar{t} \in [0,1]$ such that the sequence $(\pi(t^n))_{n\in\mathbb{N}}$ in $\dot{\Delta}^{N-1}$ does not converge to $\pi(\bar{t})$. By the compactness of C there is no loss of generality in assuming that $(\pi(t^n))_{n\in\mathbb{N}}$ converges to some $\bar{p} \in C$ with $\bar{p} \neq \pi(\bar{t})$. Since $\pi(t^n) \in \dot{\Delta}^{N-1}_{1+(\lambda^*-1)t^n}$, $\forall n \in \mathbb{N}$, it holds that

$$\min\left(\left\{\tfrac{\bar{p}_j}{v_j} \,|\, j \in I_N\right\}\right) = \lim_{n\to+\infty} \min\left(\left\{\tfrac{\pi_j(t^n)}{v_j}\,\middle|\, j \in I_N\right\}\right) = 1 + (\lambda^* - 1)\bar{t}.$$

Hence, $\{\bar{p}, \pi(\bar{t})\} \subset C \cap \dot{\Delta}^{N-1}_{1+(\lambda^*-1)\bar{t}} = \{\pi(\bar{t})\}$, a contradiction. Consequently, π is a continuous function. Q.E.D.

In the gross substitutability case the price adjustment process has very interesting economic properties as is made clear in the three final theorems. In Theorem 10.6.8 it is shown that during the price adjustment process the number of markets in equilibrium is increasing. More precisely, if a market attains an equilibrium situation, then it remains in equilibrium during the remainder of the price adjustment process. In Theorem 10.6.9 this result is even strengthened and it is shown that in every market the absolute value of the total excess demand is monotonically decreasing. In Theorem 10.6.10 it is shown that during the entire process the prices of commodities with a negative total excess demand are strictly decreasing, while the prices of commodities with a positive total excess demand are strictly increasing. Theorem 10.6.10 makes clear that the prices in markets out of equilibrium are adjusted in a way being qualitatively the same as in the Walrasian tatonnement process, while Theorem 10.6.8 states an important difference, markets in equilibrium stay in equilibrium.

Theorem 10.6.8

Let the total excess demand function z satisfy Assumptions A3-A7 and let $v \in \dot{\Delta}^{N-1}$ be the starting price system. Let $t^1, t^2 \in [0,1]$ with $t^1 < t^2$ be given. If $s^1, s^2 \in S$ are such that $\pi(t^1) \in C(s^1)$ and $\pi(t^2) \in C(s^2)$, and if $\lambda^* < 1$, then $I^-(s^2) \subset I^-(s^1)$, $I^0(s^1) \subset I^0(s^2)$, and $I^+(s^2) \subset I^+(s^1)$.

Proof

Let $p^1 \in C(s^1)$ and $p^2 \in C(s^2)$ be defined by $p^1 = \pi(t^1)$ and $p^2 = \pi(t^2)$. Notice that $\min(\{\frac{p^1_j}{v_j} \mid j \in I_N\}) > \min(\{\frac{p^2_j}{v_j} \mid j \in I_N\})$ since $\lambda^* < 1$.

Suppose there exists $j' \in (I^-(s^2)\setminus I^-(s^1)) \cup (I^0(s^1)\setminus I^0(s^2)) \cup (I^+(s^2)\setminus I^+(s^1))$.

Suppose $i^0(s^1) = i^0(s^2)$. Then, by Lemma 10.6.4, it holds that $s^1 = s^2$, yielding a contradiction with the choice of j'.

Suppose $i^0(s^1) > i^0(s^2)$. Then, by the same arguments as in the proof of Lemma 10.6.6, starting with $C(s^2)$, there exist $\tilde{s} \in S$ and $\tilde{p} \in C(\tilde{s})$ such that $i^0(\tilde{s}) =$

$i^0(s^1)$ and $\min(\{\frac{\tilde{p}_j}{v_j} \mid j \in I_N\}) \leq \min(\{\frac{p^2_j}{v_j} \mid j \in I_N\})$, and there exists $j^1 \in I^0(\tilde{s})$ such that $\frac{\tilde{p}_{j^1}}{v_{j^1}} = \min(\{\frac{\tilde{p}_j}{v_j} \mid j \in I_N\})$ or $\frac{\tilde{p}_{j^1}}{v_{j^1}} = \max(\{\frac{\tilde{p}_j}{v_j} \mid j \in I_N\})$. Clearly, $\min(\{\frac{\tilde{p}_j}{v_j} \mid j \in I_N\}) < \min(\{\frac{p^1_j}{v_j} \mid j \in I_N\})$, so it holds by Lemma 10.6.4 that $s^1 = \tilde{s}$, $J_{\min}(p^1, \tilde{p}) = I^-(s^1)$, and $J_{\max}(p^1, \tilde{p}) = I^+(s^1)$. Consider the case where $\frac{\tilde{p}_{j^1}}{v_{j^1}} = \min(\{\frac{\tilde{p}_j}{v_j} \mid j \in I_N\})$. Since $p^1 \in C(\tilde{s})$ and $J_{\min}(p^1, \tilde{p}) = I^-(\tilde{s})$, it holds for every $j \in J_{\min}(p^1, \tilde{p})$ that $\frac{\tilde{p}_{j^1}}{p^1_{j^1}} \leq \frac{\tilde{p}_j}{p^1_j}$. So, $j^1 \in J_{\min}(p^1, \tilde{p})$, a contradiction with $J_{\min}(p^1, \tilde{p}) = I^-(\tilde{s})$ and $j^1 \in I^0(\tilde{s})$. Similarly, a contradiction is obtained if $\frac{\tilde{p}_{j^1}}{v_{j^1}} = \max(\{\frac{\tilde{p}_j}{v_j} \mid j \in I_N\})$.

Suppose $i^0(s^1) < i^0(s^2)$. Then again the construction of the proof of Lemma 10.6.6 can be used, starting with $C(s^1)$. So, there exists $\tilde{s} \in \mathcal{S}$ and $\tilde{p} \in C(\tilde{s})$ such that $i^0(\tilde{s}) = i^0(s^2)$ and $\min(\{\frac{\tilde{p}_j}{v_j} \mid j \in I_N\}) \leq \min(\{\frac{p^1_j}{v_j} \mid j \in I_N\})$, and there exists $j^1 \in I^0(\tilde{s})$ such that $\frac{\tilde{p}_{j^1}}{v_{j^1}} = \min(\{\frac{\tilde{p}_j}{v_j} \mid j \in I_N\})$ or $\frac{\tilde{p}_{j^1}}{v_{j^1}} = \max(\{\frac{\tilde{p}_j}{v_j} \mid j \in I_N\})$. Moreover, $I^-(\tilde{s}) \subset I^-(s^1)$, $I^0(s^1) \subset I^0(\tilde{s})$, and $I^+(\tilde{s}) \subset I^+(s^1)$. If $\min(\{\frac{\tilde{p}_j}{v_j} \mid j \in I_N\}) \neq \min(\{\frac{p^2_j}{v_j} \mid j \in I_N\})$, then, by Lemma 10.6.4, $\tilde{s} = s^2$, so $I^-(s^2) \subset I^-(s^1)$, $I^0(s^1) \subset I^0(s^2)$, and $I^+(s^2) \subset I^+(s^1)$, giving a contradiction with the supposed existence of j'. So, consider the case where $\min(\{\frac{\tilde{p}_j}{v_j} \mid j \in I_N\}) = \min(\{\frac{p^2_j}{v_j} \mid j \in I_N\})$. Now $\tilde{p} = p^2$ since $C \cap \dot{\Delta}^{N-1}_{1+(\lambda^*-1)t^2}$ contains a unique element. For every $j \in I^-(\tilde{s})$ it holds that $\frac{\tilde{p}_j}{p^1_j} < 1$, so $J_{\max}(p^1, \tilde{p}) \subset I^0(\tilde{s}) \cup I^+(\tilde{s})$. For every $j \in J_{\max}(p^1, \tilde{p}) \cap I^0(\tilde{s})$ it holds by Lemma 10.6.1 that $z_j(p^1) > z_j(\tilde{p}) = 0$, therefore $j \in I^+(s^1)$, and hence $\frac{\tilde{p}_j}{p^1_j} \leq \frac{\tilde{p}_\jmath}{p^1_\jmath}$, $\forall \jmath \in I^+(\tilde{s})$. Since $I^+(\tilde{s}) \subset I^+(s^1)$, it follows that $\frac{\tilde{p}_\jmath}{p^1_\jmath} = \frac{\tilde{p}_j}{p^1_j}$, $\forall \jmath, j \in I^+(\tilde{s})$. Therefore, $I^+(\tilde{s}) \subset J_{\max}(p^1, \tilde{p})$ and $J_{\min}(p^1, \tilde{p}) \subset I^-(\tilde{s}) \cup I^0(\tilde{s})$. It follows in a similar way that $I^-(\tilde{s}) \subset J_{\min}(p^1, \tilde{p})$.

Suppose $j' \in I^-(s^2) \setminus I^-(s^1)$. Then $z_{j'}(\tilde{p}) \leq 0$ since $\tilde{p} = p^2$. Using $I^-(\tilde{s}) \subset I^-(s^1)$, $j' \in I^-(s^2)$, and $\tilde{p} = p^2$, it follows that $\frac{\tilde{p}_{j'}}{p^1_{j'}} \leq \frac{\tilde{p}_j}{p^1_j}$, $\forall j \in I^-(\tilde{s})$. Therefore, $j' \in J_{\min}(p^1, \tilde{p})$. By Lemma 10.6.1 it holds that $0 \leq z_{j'}(p^1) < z_{j'}(\tilde{p}) \leq 0$, a contradiction. The case where $j' \in I^+(s^2) \setminus I^+(s^1)$ yields a contradiction in a similar way. Consequently, $j' \in I^0(s^1) \setminus I^0(s^2)$.

Since $j' \in I^0(s^1) \setminus I^0(s^2)$, it follows that $j' \in I^-(s^2) \cup I^+(s^2)$. Moreover, it can be shown that $j' \in J_{\min}(p^1, \tilde{p}) \cup J_{\max}(p^1, \tilde{p})$. Since $j' \in I^0(s^1)$ and $I^0(s^1) \subset I^0(\tilde{s})$, it follows that $0 = z_{j'}(p^1) = z_{j'}(\tilde{p})$. By Lemma 10.6.1 it holds that $z_{j'}(p^1) \neq z_{j'}(\tilde{p})$, a contradiction. Consequently, $(I^-(s^2) \setminus I^-(s^1)) \cup (I^0(s^1) \setminus I^0(s^2)) \cup (I^+(s^2) \setminus I^+(s^1)) = \emptyset$. Q.E.D.

Notice that in Theorem 10.6.8 it is required that $\lambda^* < 1$. If $\lambda^* = 1$, then $\pi(t) = v$, $\forall t \in [0,1]$, while $z(v) = 0^N$. In this case it holds that $v \in C(s)$, $\forall s \in \mathcal{S}$, and a statement as in Theorem 10.6.8 cannot be made.

Theorem 10.6.9

Let the total excess demand function z satisfy Assumptions A3-A7 and let $v \in \dot{\Delta}^{N-1}$ be the starting price system. Let $t^1, t^2 \in [0,1]$ with $t^1 < t^2$ and $j' \in I_N$ be given. Then $z_{j'}(\pi(t^1)) < z_{j'}(\pi(t^2)) \leq 0$ if $z_{j'}(\pi(t^1)) < 0$, $z_{j'}(\pi(t^2)) = 0$ if $z_{j'}(\pi(t^1)) = 0$, and $z_{j'}(\pi(t^1)) > z_{j'}(\pi(t^2)) \geq 0$ if $z_{j'}(\pi(t^1)) > 0$.

Proof

If $\lambda^* = 1$, then the proof of Theorem 10.6.9 is trivial, so consider the case $\lambda^* < 1$. Let $s^1, s^2 \in \mathcal{S}$ be such that $\pi(t^1) \in C(s^1)$ and $\pi(t^2) \in C(s^2)$. Let $j^- \in I^-(s^2)$ and $j^+ \in I^+(s^2)$ be given. It follows from Theorem 10.6.8 that $j^- \in I^-(s^1)$ and so $\frac{\pi_{j^-}(t^2)}{\pi_{j^-}(t^1)} = \frac{1+(\lambda^*-1)t^2}{1+(\lambda^*-1)t^1} < 1$. It follows from Theorem 10.6.8 that $j^+ \in I^+(s^1)$, so the value of $\frac{\pi_{j^+}(t^2)}{\pi_{j^+}(t^1)}$ is independent of the choice of $j^+ \in I^+(s^2)$. For every $j^0 \in I^0(s^2) \cap I^-(s^1)$ it follows that $\frac{\pi_{j^0}(t^2)}{\pi_{j^0}(t^1)} \geq \frac{\pi_{j^-}(t^2)}{\pi_{j^-}(t^1)}$. Moreover, $j^0 \notin J_{\max}(\pi(t^1), \pi(t^2))$ since otherwise, by Lemma 10.6.1, $z_{j^0}(\pi(t^1)) > z_{j^0}(\pi(t^2)) = 0$, a contradiction with $j^0 \in I^-(s^1)$. Similarly, $j^0 \in I^0(s^2) \cap I^0(s^1)$ implies $j^0 \notin J_{\min}(\pi(t^1), \pi(t^2)) \cup J_{\max}(\pi(t^1), \pi(t^2))$, and $j^0 \in I^0(s^2) \cap I^+(s^1)$ implies $\frac{\pi_{j^0}(t^2)}{\pi_{j^0}(t^1)} \leq \frac{\pi_{j^+}(t^2)}{\pi_{j^+}(t^1)}$ and $j^0 \notin J_{\min}(\pi(t^1), \pi(t^2))$. Therefore, $I^-(s^2) \subset J_{\min}(\pi(t^1), \pi(t^2))$ and $I^+(s^2) \subset J_{\max}(\pi(t^1), \pi(t^2))$. Using this result and Lemma 10.6.1, it follows that $z_{j'}(\pi(t^1)) < z_{j'}(\pi(t^2))$ if $z_{j'}(\pi(t^2)) < 0$ and $z_{j'}(\pi(t^1)) > z_{j'}(\pi(t^2))$ if $z_{j'}(\pi(t^2)) > 0$. From Theorem 10.6.8 it follows that $z_{j'}(\pi(t^2)) \leq 0$ if $z_{j'}(\pi(t^1)) < 0$, $z_{j'}(\pi(t^2)) = 0$ if $z_{j'}(\pi(t^1)) = 0$, and $z_{j'}(\pi(t^2)) \geq 0$ if $z_{j'}(\pi(t^1)) > 0$. Q.E.D.

Theorem 10.6.10

Let the total excess demand function z satisfy Assumptions A3-A7 and let $v \in \dot{\Delta}^{N-1}$ be the starting price system. Let $\bar{t} \in [0,1]$ be given. Then there exists $\varepsilon \in \mathbb{R}_{++}$ such that, for every $j \in I_N$, for every $t \in (\bar{t}-\varepsilon, \bar{t}) \cap [0,1]$, $\pi_j(t) < \pi_j(\bar{t})$ if $z_j(\pi(\bar{t})) > 0$ and $\pi_j(t) > \pi_j(\bar{t})$ if $z_j(\pi(\bar{t})) < 0$, and, for every $t \in (\bar{t}, \bar{t}+\varepsilon) \cap [0,1]$, $\pi_j(t) > \pi_j(\bar{t})$ if $z_j(\pi(\bar{t})) > 0$ and $\pi_j(t) < \pi_j(\bar{t})$ if $z_j(\pi(\bar{t})) < 0$.

Proof

If $\lambda^* = 1$, then the proof of Theorem 10.6.10 is trivial, so consider the case $\lambda^* < 1$. Since z and π are continuous functions, there exists $\varepsilon \in \mathbb{R}_{++}$ such that, for every $j \in I_N$, for every $t \in (\bar{t}-\varepsilon, \bar{t}+\varepsilon) \cap [0,1]$, $z_j(\pi(t)) > 0$ if $z_j(\pi(\bar{t})) > 0$, and $z_j(\pi(t)) < 0$ if $z_j(\pi(\bar{t})) < 0$.

Let $j' \in I_N$ be such that $z_{j'}(\pi(\bar{t})) < 0$ and let some $t \in (\bar{t}-\varepsilon, \bar{t}+\varepsilon) \cap [0,1]$ be given. Then $\pi_{j'}(t) = (1 + (\lambda^* - 1)t)v_{j'}$. Hence, if $t \neq \bar{t}$, then

$$(t - \bar{t})\left(\pi_{j'}(t) - \pi_{j'}(\bar{t})\right) = (\lambda^* - 1)(t - \bar{t})^2 v_{j'} < 0.$$

Let $j' \in I_N$ be such that $z_{j'}(\pi(\bar{t})) > 0$ and let some $t \in (\bar{t}, \bar{t}+\varepsilon) \cap [0, 1]$ be given. Suppose $\pi_{j'}(t) < \pi_{j'}(\bar{t})$, so $\frac{\pi_{j'}(\bar{t})}{\pi_{j'}(t)} > 1$. Then, for every $j \in I_N$ with $z_j(\pi(t)) > 0$, $\frac{\pi_j(\bar{t})}{\pi_j(t)} > 1$. Also, for every $j \in I_N$ with $z_j(\pi(t)) < 0$, $\frac{\pi_j(\bar{t})}{\pi_j(t)} > 1$. Hence, there exists $j'' \in I_N$ such that $z_{j''}(\pi(t)) = 0$ and $j'' \in J_{\min}(\pi(t), \pi(\bar{t}))$. By Lemma 10.6.1 it holds that $z_{j''}(\pi(\bar{t})) > 0$, contradicting the choice of ε. The case where $j' \in I_N$ is such that $z_{j'}(\pi(\bar{t})) > 0$ and some $t \in (\bar{t} - \varepsilon, \bar{t}) \cap [0, 1]$ is given can be treated similarly. Q.E.D.

Theorem 10.6.10 shows that the price adjustment process in some sense can be considered as a generalization of the Walrasian tatonnement process. For the easy cases, like gross substitutability in the finite increment form, it behaves qualitatively the same for markets out of equilibrium. For the more complicated cases it still guarantees convergence to a Walrasian equilibrium.

11

A GLOBALLY AND UNIVERSALLY STABLE QUANTITY ADJUSTMENT PROCESS

11.1 INTRODUCTION

The question whether the Walrasian equilibrium is stable, is difficult to answer. Although for a number of special cases the Walrasian tatonnement process as formulated in Samuelson (1941) has been shown to be globally stable, see Theorem 3.11.2, and, generically, the price adjustment process of Chapter 10 is globally and universally stable, it is not clear whether these price adjustment processes are the right model of price adjustment processes taking place in the real world. For example, even if the Walrasian tatonnement process converges to a Walrasian equilibrium, convergence may take too much time and does not take place, a point of view considered in Blad (1978). Obviously, the same remark is true for the price adjustment process of Chapter 10. Therefore, it is well possible that, at least in the short run, a Walrasian equilibrium price system is not reached and therefore trade has to take place at a non-Walrasian equilibrium price system. Clearly, there are several other reasons why trade may take place at a non-Walrasian equilibrium price system. Even if the Walrasian equilibrium is stable with respect to some price adjustment process, and even if convergence takes place fast enough, then government intervention, for instance minimum wages or price indexation, might result in a non-Walrasian equilibrium price system at which trade has to take place. In the models of the political economic system as described in Part III such interventions are the generic case. Similarly, as the results in Madden (1983), Silvestre (1988), and Bénassy (1993) indicate, a non-Walrasian equilibrium price system may result as the outcome of a game played between consumers and firms or the outcome of a game played between workers and shareholders.

When trade takes place at a non-Walrasian equilibrium price system, several non-Walrasian equilibrium concepts are available, see for instance Bénassy (1975b), Drèze (1975), Younès (1975), and van der Laan (1980a). Although existence of each such a non-Walrasian equilibrium has been shown, again the question of stability for these non-Walrasian equilibria should be addressed. Only Bénassy accompanies his equilibrium concept by a dynamic process, specifying the amounts the consumers can supply or demand in the various markets at each point in time. However, the issue of convergence of such a process is not considered.

In Movshovich (1994) a dynamic process in discrete time is introduced that converges to a Drèze equilibrium, given some fixed price system. However, convergence can only be guaranteed under conditions similar to gross substitutability. After a Drèze equilibrium has been reached, Movshovich considers a process where at each point in time the price of a randomly chosen commodity is adjusted on the basis of the effective excess demand in the previous period at the (unique) Drèze equilibrium at the current price system. Again, gross substitutability like conditions are needed in order to guarantee convergence to a Walrasian equilibrium. In Drèze (1991) a price and quantity process in discrete time is described, which starts with historically given prices and quantity constraints on the supply side. He also assumes quantities to move much faster than prices. Drèze shows that after the adjustment of quantities a situation is reached where no market is in excess supply, while positive excess demands may occur on some markets facing no longer any quantity constraints on the supply side. Next, for the markets with positive excess demands the prices will adjust upwards. Contrary, in the model of price and quantity adjustments of this chapter these markets would be cleared by quantity constraints on the demand side and no price adjustments are made. Under the assumptions that there are no inferior goods and that the marginal propensity to consume is less than one, Drèze shows convergence of his process to a Drèze equilibrium without demand rationing on any market.

Many authors consider models where at each moment in time a non-Walrasian equilibrium results. A price adjustment process in continuous time in a world with three commodities, while at each point in time a Drèze equilibrium results, is considered by Veendorp (1975) (see also the comment of Laroque (1981)). In this model prices are adjusted on the basis of the effective total excess demand corresponding to the Drèze equilibrium resulting in each time period. Owing to the assumptions made, this Drèze equilibrium is unique and can easily be determined. Under more general assumptions it is not clear how this Drèze equilibrium can be attained. Even if at each point in time a Drèze equilibrium results, then it is not clear which equilibrium will realize in the case of multiple equilibria. Hence, an adjustment process is needed to select a Drèze equilibrium in this case. Other authors, like Böhm (1993) and Weddepohl and Yildirim (1993), consider overlapping generation models where a Drèze equilibrium results in each period. Again, assumptions are made such that the Drèze equilibrium can easily be determined. Under more general assumptions it is again less clear whether a Drèze equilibrium results and, in the case of multiple equilibria, which equilibrium prevails in the economy.

In this chapter a quantity adjustment process in continuous time is considered for the model of an economy as described in Chapter 4, while the set of admissible price systems is assumed to consist of a single price system, which is in general a non-Walrasian equilibrium price system. During the quantity adjustment process no trade takes place. Under standard assumptions on the economy it is shown that, generically, the quantity adjustment process converges from any initial state to a Drèze equilibrium. Moreover, from the main result it follows that, generically, the number of Drèze equilibria is odd. This extends a result of Laroque and Polemarchakis (1978) where it is shown that, generically, the number of Drèze equilibria is finite. The assumptions made in this chapter do not exclude the case where rationing occurs according to some priority system, a case excluded by the assumptions in Laroque and Polemarchakis (1978).

In Section 11.2 the model of an economy with a fixed price system according to Chapter 4 is given, the equilibrium concept of Drèze (1975) is defined, and the reduced total excess demand function is introduced. Since the price system is fixed, the reduced total excess demand function does only depend on the rationing schemes. There is no rationing in the market for the numeraire commodity. An adjustment process in rationing schemes, as introduced in this chapter, is equivalent to an adjustment process in quantities. More precisely, adjusting the rationing scheme of a consumer in a market is equivalent to adjusting the maximal amount a consumer is allowed to supply or to demand in that market. In the description of the quantity adjustment process an initial state of the economy, in this case a specification of rationing schemes in every market, is assumed to be given. In general this initial state is incompatible with a Drèze equilibrium. Then the quantity adjustment process is defined having global features that are related to the price adjustment process as defined in Chapter 10.

In the quantity adjustment process, adjustments of rationing schemes are based on the total excess demand in the markets for the non-numeraire commodities and on the change in the rationing schemes compared to the initial state. If there is a negative total excess demand in a market at some point in time, then the rationing schemes are adjusted in such a way that, compared to the initial state, supply rationing is tightened and demand rationing is weakened in this market. So, compared to the initial state, consumers are allowed to supply less and to demand more of this commodity. Similarly, if there is a positive total excess demand in a market at some point in time, rationing schemes are adjusted in such a way that, compared to the initial state, supply rationing is weakened and demand rationing is tightened in this market. Finally, the rationing schemes satisfy all the requirements imposed on them in a Drèze equilibrium also during the quantity adjustment process. These global features make the quantity adjustment process economically attractive.

In principle it is possible to adjust the rationing schemes according to the processes as formulated in Samuelson (1941), i.e. the well-known Walrasian tatonnement process, Smale (1976), Kamiya (1990), or Chapter 10. However, the reduced total excess demand function does in general not satisfy the requirements needed to guarantee the convergence of these processes. Typically, the reduced total excess demand function does not satisfy assumptions like gross substitutability, does not have the required boundary behaviour, and is not everywhere differentiable.

The quantity adjustment process is illustrated in Section 11.3 for Scarf's example as described in Section 3.12. In Section 11.4 it is shown that for almost every economy the quantity adjustment process as defined in Section 11.2 converges to a Drèze equilibrium given any initial state of the economy. In the terminology of Saari and Simon (1978) or Saari (1985), the quantity adjustment process is an effective or globally convergent mechanism.

This chapter is based on Herings (1994b).

11.2 THE QUANTITY ADJUSTMENT PROCESS

The quantity adjustment process, for the *economy* $\widetilde{\mathcal{E}} = ((X^i, \preceq^i, \omega^i)_{i \in I_M}, P_{(p,p)}, (\widetilde{l}, \widetilde{L}))$ as described in Chapter 4, is defined in this section. There are $M \in \mathbb{N}$ *consumers*, indexed by $i \in I_M$, and $N \in \mathbb{N} \setminus \{1\}$ *commodities*, indexed by $j \in I_N$. A consumer $i \in I_M$ is characterized by a *consumption set* X^i, a *preference relation* $\preceq^i$, and an *initial endowment* ω^i. The element $(\omega^1, \ldots, \omega^M)$ is denoted by ω. The *rationing function*, specifying the *admissible rationing schemes*, is given by the pair $(\widetilde{l}, \widetilde{L})$ with $\widetilde{l} : \mathbb{R}^N_+ \rightarrow -\mathbb{R}^{MN}_+$ the *rationing function on supply* and $\widetilde{L} : \mathbb{R}^N_+ \to \mathbb{R}^{MN}_+$ the *rationing function on demand.* Notice that $\widetilde{l}$ and $\widetilde{L}$ are assumed to be defined on $\mathbb{R}^N_+$ instead of on Q^N, which is more convenient in this chapter. The set $\prod_{i \in I_M} X^i$ is denoted by X. For every $i \in I_M$, for every $j \in I_N$, component $(i-1)N+j$ of $\widetilde{l}$ is denoted by $\widetilde{l}^i_j$. Moreover, $\widetilde{l}^i = (\widetilde{l}^i_1, \ldots, \widetilde{l}^i_N)^\top$, $\forall i \in I_M$, and $\widetilde{l}_j = (\widetilde{l}^1_j, \ldots, \widetilde{l}^M_j)^\top$, $\forall j \in I_N$. The same notation is used for the function $\widetilde{L}$, for a *rationing scheme on supply* $l \in -\mathbb{R}^{*MN}_+$, and for a *rationing scheme on demand* $L \in \mathbb{R}^{*MN}_+$.

The *price system* is assumed to be completely fixed, i.e. both the *lower bound* and the *upper bound* for the *set of admissible price systems* $P_{(\underline{p},\overline{p})}$ are given by some fixed $p \in \mathbb{R}^N$, so $\underline{p} = \overline{p} = p$. Commodity N is considered to be a *numeraire commodity,* hence the price of commodity N equals one. In general it does not hold that p induces a *Walrasian equilibrium,* see Definition 3.8.1, i.e. at p the total excess demand of the consumers is not equal to zero. Therefore, when a fixed price system p is given, other equilibrium concepts than the Walrasian one have to be used to describe the allocation resulting in the economy. In this chapter the approach of Drèze (1975) is followed, using the same motivation as in Sections 4.7 and 8.2.

The *budget set* of a consumer $i \in I_M$ at a rationing scheme $(l^i, L^i) \in -\mathbb{R}^{*N}_+ \times \mathbb{R}^{*N}_+$ is denoted by $\beta^i(l^i, L^i)$, so

$$\beta^i(l^i, L^i) = \left\{x^i \in X^i \,\middle|\, p \cdot x^i \leq p \cdot \omega^i \text{ and } l^i \leq x^i - \omega^i \leq L^i\right\},$$

see also Section 4.2, and the set $\delta^i(l^i, L^i)$ is defined by

$$\delta^i(l^i, L^i) = \left\{\overline{x}^i \in \beta^i(l^i, L^i) \,\middle|\, \overline{x}^i \succeq^i x^i,\ \forall x^i \in \beta^i(l^i, L^i)\right\},$$

see also Section 4.3. Notice that the price system p, being fixed, is suppressed in the notation of the budget set and the demand set. A Drèze equilibrium, see also Definitions 4.7.5 and 8.2.4, is defined as follows.

Definition 11.2.1 (Drèze equilibrium)
A Drèze equilibrium *of the economy* $\widetilde{\mathcal{E}} = ((X^i, \preceq^i, \omega^i)_{i \in I_M}, P_{(p,p)}, (\widetilde{l}, \widetilde{L}))$ *is an element*

$$(p^*, l^*, L^*, x^*) \in P_{(p,p)} \times \widetilde{l}(\mathbb{R}^N_+) \times \widetilde{L}(\mathbb{R}^N_+) \times X$$

satisfying

1. *for every consumer* $i \in I_M$, $x^{*i} \in \delta^i\left(l^{*i}, L^{*i}\right)$,

2. $\sum_{i \in I_M} x^{*i} - \sum_{i \in I_M} \omega^i = 0^N$,

3. for every commodity $j \in I_{N-1}$, $x_j^{*i'} - \omega_j^{i'} = l_j^{*i'}$ *for some consumer* $i' \in I_M$ *implies* $x_j^{*i} - \omega_j^i < L_j^{*i}$, $\forall i \in I_M$, *and* $x_j^{*i'} - \omega_j^{i'} = L_j^{*i'}$ *for some consumer* $i' \in I_M$ *implies* $x_j^{*i} - \omega_j^i > l_j^{*i}$, $\forall i \in I_M$,

4. $l_N^{*i} < x_N^{*i} - \omega_N^i < L_N^{*i}$, $\forall i \in I_M$.

This definition of a Drèze equilibrium corresponds to the definition of a Drèze equilibrium with respect to the market for commodity N of Definition 4.7.5. Since the price system is assumed to be fixed, the conditions that there is no supply rationing in the market for a commodity $j \in I_{N-1}$ if the price of commodity j is not equal to the lower bound on the price of commodity j, and, similarly, demand rationing does not occur in the market for commodity j if the price of commodity j is not equal to the upper bound on the price of commodity j, need not to be specified.

For the remainder of this section the economy $\widetilde{\mathcal{E}}$ is assumed to satisfy the following assumptions.

A1. For every consumer $i \in I_M$, the consumption set X^i is closed, convex, $X^i \subset \mathbb{R}_+^N$, and $X^i + \mathbb{R}_+^N \subset X^i$.

A2. For every consumer $i \in I_M$, the preference relation $\preceq^i$ is complete, transitive, continuous, monotonic with respect to commodity N, and strongly convex.

A3. For every consumer $i \in I_M$, the initial endowment ω^i belongs to $\mathrm{int}(X^i)$.

A4. The price system p is an element of $\mathbb{R}_{++}^N$ with $p_N = 1$.

A5. The rationing function on supply $\tilde{l} : \mathbb{R}_+^N \to -\mathbb{R}_+^{MN}$ and the rationing function on demand $\tilde{L} : \mathbb{R}_+^N \to \mathbb{R}_+^{MN}$ are continuous and satisfy, for every $i \in I_M$, for every $j \in I_N$, for every $q^1, \bar{q}^1, q^2, \bar{q}^2 \in \mathbb{R}_+^N$,

$$\begin{array}{llll}
\tilde{l}_j^i(q^1) = \tilde{l}_j^i(\bar{q}^1) & \text{if } q_j^1 = \bar{q}_j^1, & \tilde{L}_j^i(q^2) = \tilde{L}_j^i(\bar{q}^2) & \text{if } q_j^2 = \bar{q}_j^2, \\
\tilde{l}_j^i(q^1) = 0 & \text{if } q_j^1 = 0, & \tilde{L}_j^i(q^2) = 0 & \text{if } q_j^2 = 0, \\
\tilde{l}_j^i(q^1) \to -\infty & \text{if } q_j^1 \to +\infty, & \tilde{L}_j^i(q^2) \to +\infty & \text{if } q_j^2 \to +\infty.
\end{array}$$

Notice that Assumption A5 corresponds to a flexible, market independent, and continuous rationing function as defined in Section 4.5. Although this is not assumed, the functions $\tilde{l}$ and $\tilde{L}$ are considered to be monotonic whenever an intuitive explanation or interpretation of the model is given. Under Assumptions A1-A5 on the economy $\tilde{\mathcal{E}}$ the existence of a Drèze equilibrium follows from Corollary 4.7.6 or from Theorem 8.4.1, the domain on which $\tilde{l}$ and $\tilde{L}$ are defined being the only difference with the assumptions made there. Furthermore, it is not difficult to show that

$$\forall j \in I_N,\ \exists \underline{q}_j \in \mathbb{R}_+,\ \forall i \in I_M,\ \tilde{l}^i_j(q^1) \text{ is not binding if } q^1_j \geq \underline{q}_j,$$
$$\forall j \in I_N,\ \exists \overline{q}_j \in \mathbb{R}_+,\ \forall i \in I_M,\ \tilde{L}^i_j(q^2) \text{ is not binding if } q^2_j \geq \overline{q}_j,$$

where binding is as defined in Section 4.3. For example, for any $j \in I_N$ it follows immediately that if $\underline{q}_j$ is chosen such that, for every $q^1_j \geq \underline{q}_j$, $\tilde{l}^i_j(q^1) < -\omega^i_j$, $\forall i \in I_M$, then the first condition is satisfied, and, similarly, if $\overline{q}_j$ is chosen such that, for every $q^2_j \geq \overline{q}_j$, $\tilde{L}^i_j(q^2) > \frac{p\cdot\omega^i}{p_j} - \omega^i_j$, $\forall i \in I_M$, then the second condition is satisfied. The functions $\hat{l} : Q^{N-1} \to -\mathbb{R}^{MN}_+$ and $\hat{L} : Q^{N-1} \to \mathbb{R}^{MN}_+$ are defined by

$$\begin{aligned} \hat{l}(q) &= \tilde{l}(2\underline{q}_1 q_1, \ldots, 2\underline{q}_{N-1} q_{N-1}, \underline{q}_N), && \forall q \in Q^{N-1}, \\ \hat{L}(q) &= \tilde{L}(2\overline{q}_1(1-q_1), \ldots, 2\overline{q}_{N-1}(1-q_{N-1}), \overline{q}_N), && \forall q \in Q^{N-1}. \end{aligned}$$

The notational conventions used for $\tilde{l}$ and $\tilde{L}$ are also used for $\hat{l}$ and $\hat{L}$. It is easily verified that there is no supply rationing in the market for a commodity $j \in I_{N-1}$ if $q_j \geq \frac{1}{2}$ and there is no demand rationing in the market for commodity j if $q_j \leq \frac{1}{2}$. Moreover, there is no rationing in the market for the numeraire commodity for any $q \in Q^{N-1}$.

Let a commodity $j \in I_{N-1}$ be given. If q_j increases from 0 to $\frac{1}{2}$, then in the market for commodity j the rationing scheme on supply, $\hat{l}_j(q)$, changes from being equal to zero, i.e. no supply is possible of commodity j for any consumer, to being non-binding for every consumer. If $q_j \in [\frac{1}{2}, 1]$, then the rationing scheme on supply, $\hat{l}_j(q)$, remains non-binding for every consumer. If $q_j \in [0, \frac{1}{2}]$, then in the market for commodity j the rationing scheme on demand, $\hat{L}_j(q)$, is non-binding for every consumer, and if q_j increases from $\frac{1}{2}$ to 1 then the rationing scheme on demand, $\hat{L}_j(q)$, changes from being non-binding to being zero. Hence, if q_j is increased, then the total excess demand of commodity j has a tendency to fall. In this sense the effect on the economy of an increment of q_j resembles the effect of an increment of the price of commodity j. The properties of the functions $\hat{l}$ and $\hat{L}$ guarantee that Condition 3 of the definition of a Drèze equilibrium, Definition 11.2.1, is satisfied on the adjustment path. Moreover, it is easily verified that there is no loss of generality in only considering rationing schemes $(l, L) \in -\mathbb{R}^{*MN}_+ \times \mathbb{R}^{*MN}_+$ such that there exists $q \in Q^{N-1}$ satisfying

$(\widehat{l}(q), \widehat{L}(q)) = (l, L)$ in the sense that all relevant rationing schemes, i.e. those rationing schemes that affect the behaviour of the consumers in the economy, are obtained.

Let a rationing scheme $(l^i, L^i) \in -\mathbb{R}_+^{*N} \times \mathbb{R}_+^{*N}$ of a consumer $i \in I_M$ be given. From Assumptions A1-A4 it follows easily that the set $\delta^i(l^i, L^i)$ of consumer $i \in I_M$ contains exactly one element. Therefore, for every $i \in I_M$, the *reduced demand function* $\widehat{d^i} : Q^{N-1} \to \mathbb{R}^N$ of consumer i is defined by

$$\left\{\widehat{d^i}(q)\right\} = \delta^i\left(\widehat{l^i}(q), \widehat{L}^i(q)\right), \ \forall q \in Q^{N-1},$$

and the *reduced total excess demand function* $\widehat{z} : Q^{N-1} \to \mathbb{R}^N$ of the economy $\widetilde{\mathcal{E}}$ is defined by

$$\widehat{z}(q) = \sum_{i \in I_M} \widehat{d^i}(q) - \sum_{i \in I_M} \omega^i, \ \forall q \in Q^{N-1}.$$

The proof of the following result is similar to the proof of Theorem 4.7.1.

Theorem 11.2.2
Let the economy $\widetilde{\mathcal{E}} = ((X^i, \preceq^i, \omega^i)_{i \in I_M}, P_{(\mathbf{p},\mathbf{P})}, (\widetilde{l}, \widetilde{L}))$ satisfy Assumptions A1-A5. If, for $q^* \in Q^{N-1}$, $\widehat{z}(q^*) = 0^N$, then $(p, \widehat{l}(q^*), \widehat{L}(q^*), \widehat{d}^1(q^*), \ldots, \widehat{d}^M(q^*))$ is a Drèze equilibrium of the economy $\widetilde{\mathcal{E}}$.

If, for some $q^* \in Q^{N-1}$, $\widehat{z}(q^*) = 0^N$, then $(p, \widehat{l}(q^*), \widehat{L}(q^*), \widehat{d}^1(q^*), \ldots, \widehat{d}^M(q^*))$ is called the Drèze equilibrium of $\widetilde{\mathcal{E}}$ *induced* by q^*. Similarly as in the proof of Theorem 4.7.2 the following result can be shown.

Theorem 11.2.3
Let the economy $\widetilde{\mathcal{E}} = ((X^i, \preceq^i, \omega^i)_{i \in I_M}, P_{(\mathbf{p},\mathbf{P})}, (\widetilde{l}, \widetilde{L}))$ satisfy Assumptions A1-A5. If (p^*, l^*, L^*, x^*) is a Drèze equilibrium of the economy $\widetilde{\mathcal{E}}$, then there exists $q^* \in Q^{N-1}$ such that $\widehat{z}(q^*) = 0^N$, while $(p^*, l^*, L^*, x^*) \sim (p, \widehat{l}(q^*), \widehat{L}(q^*), \widehat{d}^1(q^*), \ldots, \widehat{d}^M(q^*))$, i.e. (p^*, l^*, L^*, x^*) is equivalent to $(p, \widehat{l}(q^*), \widehat{L}(q^*), \widehat{d}^1(q^*), \ldots, \widehat{d}^M(q^*))$ in the sense of Definition 4.6.2.

Therefore, it follows immediately that there is no loss of generality in only considering Drèze equilibria of the economy $\widetilde{\mathcal{E}}$ that are induced by elements of Q^{N-1}. The proof of the following result is similar to the proof of Theorem 8.2.8.

Theorem 11.2.4
Let the economy $\widetilde{\mathcal{E}} = ((X^i, \preceq^i, \omega^i)_{i \in I_M}, P_{(p,p)}, (\widetilde{l}, \widetilde{L}))$ *satisfy Assumptions A1-A5. Then the reduced demand function* $\widehat{d^i} : Q^{N-1} \to \mathbb{R}^N$ *of a consumer* $i \in I_M$ *and the reduced total excess demand function* $\widehat{z} : Q^{N-1} \to \mathbb{R}^N$ *of the economy* $\widetilde{\mathcal{E}}$ *have the following properties:*

1. $\widehat{d^i}$ *and* $\widehat{z}$ *are continuous on* Q^{N-1},
2. *for every* $q \in Q^{N-1}$, *for every* $j \in I_{N-1}$, $q_j = 0$ *implies* $\widehat{d^i_j}(q) - \omega^i_j \geq 0$ *and* $\widehat{z}_j(q) \geq 0$, *and* $q_j = 1$ *implies* $\widehat{d^i_j}(q) - \omega^i_j \leq 0$ *and* $\widehat{z}_j(q) \leq 0$,
3. *for every* $q \in Q^{N-1}$, $p \cdot (\widehat{d^i}(q) - \omega^i) = 0$ *and* $p \cdot \widehat{z}(q) = 0$.

Now the quantity adjustment process can be defined. Notice that the *state* of the markets is completely determined by the prevailing rationing schemes $(l, L) \in -\mathbb{R}^{*MN}_+ \times \mathbb{R}^{*MN}_+$. Therefore, it is possible to describe the state of the economy by an element $q \in Q^{N-1}$ inducing the rationing scheme $(\widehat{l}(q), \widehat{L}(q))$. The basic idea of the quantity adjustment process is to decrease (increase) q_j in the case of a negative (positive) total excess demand in the market for a commodity $j \in I_{N-1}$.

Let $v \in Q^{N-1}$ denote the *initial state* of the economy. The initial state $v = \frac{1}{2}1^{N-1}$ is interesting from an economic point of view since at this state no consumer is rationed in any market. In this case, initially, each consumer expresses his notional demand for every commodity, given the price system p. Subsequently, supply rationing is tightened in markets with a negative total excess demand and demand rationing is tightened in markets with a positive total excess demand. Other interesting initial states are $v = 0^{N-1}$ and $v = 1^{N-1}$, corresponding to situations with full rationing on supply and full rationing on demand, respectively. For example, in the case of full rationing on supply all consumers are restricted to demand any non-numeraire commodity. This leads to a non-negative total excess demand in all markets, except possibly in the market for the numeraire commodity. Consider the case with a positive total excess demand in all markets, except in the market for the numeraire commodity. This positive total excess demand is allocated to potential suppliers by allowing some supply in all markets. This changes the total excess demand in a particular market for two reasons. First, there is a direct effect since a consumer supplying a commodity causes a direct decrease in the positive total excess demand of this commodity. Secondly, there is an indirect spill-over effect since the opportunity of supply in other markets changes the demand in a market. The sign of this spill-over effect is ambiguous. Other initial states are interesting too. If a sequence of temporary Drèze equilibria is considered in for example an overlapping generations model, then the rationing scheme of the previous period determines the initial state for the current period. Since there are many possible initial states of interest, v is allowed to be an arbitrary element of Q^{N-1} in this chapter.

Given an initial state $v \in Q^{N-1}$ and a commodity $j \in I_{N-1}$, v_j is the maximal decrease in q_j possible in the market for commodity j and $1-v_j$ is the maximal increase in q_j possible in the market for commodity j. Let $q \in Q^{N-1}$ be a point reached by the quantity adjustment process. The quantity adjustment process is such that if there is a negative total excess demand in the market for a commodity $j \in I_{N-1}$, then q_j has been decreased relatively maximally over all commodities towards zero, and if there is a positive total excess demand in the market for a commodity $j \in I_{N-1}$, then q_j has been increased relatively maximally over all commodities towards one. More precisely, if an element $q \in Q^{N-1}$ has been reached by the quantity adjustment process, then there exists a number $\mu \in [0,1]$ such that, for every $j \in I_{N-1}$,

$$\begin{aligned} q_j &= \mu v_j \text{ if } \widehat{z}_j(q) < 0, \\ \mu v_j \leq q_j &\leq 1-\mu(1-v_j) \text{ if } \widehat{z}_j(q) = 0, \\ q_j &= 1-\mu(1-v_j) \text{ if } \widehat{z}_j(q) > 0. \end{aligned} \tag{11.1}$$

Clearly, the behaviour of the quantity adjustment process depends heavily on the state of the various markets, i.e. whether there is a negative total excess demand in a market, or a market is in equilibrium, or there is a positive total excess demand in a market. The sign of the total excess demand in the markets is described by a sign vector $s \in \mathbb{S}^{N-1}$, so, for every $j \in I_{N-1}$, $s_j \in \{-1, 0, +1\}$. Recall from Section 2.2 that for every sign vector $s \in \mathbb{S}^{N-1}$ the sets $I^-(s)$, $I^0(s)$, and $I^+(s)$ are defined by $I^-(s) = \{j \in I_{N-1} \mid s_j = -1\}$, $I^0(s) = \{j \in I_{N-1} \mid s_j = 0\}$, and $I^+(s) = \{j \in I_{N-1} \mid s_j = +1\}$. These sets denote markets for which there is a non-positive total excess demand, equilibrium, and a non-negative total excess demand, respectively. Moreover, $i^-(s)$, $i^0(s)$, and $i^+(s)$ denote the number of elements in the sets $I^-(s)$, $I^0(s)$, and $I^+(s)$, respectively.

Let an initial state $v \in Q^{N-1}$ be given. The *set of admissible sign vectors* $\mathcal{S}$ is defined by

$$\mathcal{S} = \left\{ s \in \mathbb{S}^{N-1} \,\middle|\, v_j > 0, \forall j \in I^-(s),\, v_j < 1, \forall j \in I^+(s), \text{ and } \exists j' \in I_{N-1}, s_{j'} \neq 0 \right\}.$$

Notice that $\mathcal{S} \neq \emptyset$. For every admissible sign vector $s \in \mathcal{S}$, the sets $A(s)$, $B(s)$, and $C(s)$ of states of the economy are defined by

$$\begin{aligned}
A(s) = \{q \in Q^{N-1} \mid \exists \mu \in [0,1],\ & q_j = \mu v_j, && \forall j \in I^-(s),\\
& \mu v_j \leq q_j \leq 1 - \mu(1 - v_j), && \forall j \in I^0(s),\\
& q_j = 1 - \mu(1 - v_j), && \forall j \in I^+(s)\},\\
B(s) = \{q \in Q^{N-1} \mid\ & \widehat{z}_j(q) \leq 0,\ \forall j \in I^-(s),\\
& \widehat{z}_j(q) = 0,\ \forall j \in I^0(s),\\
& \widehat{z}_j(q) \geq 0,\ \forall j \in I^+(s)\},\\
C(s) = A(s) \cap B(s).&
\end{aligned}$$

The sets defined above are used to describe the quantity adjustment process. Every state $q \in Q^{N-1}$ reached by the quantity adjustment process is shown to be an element of the set C defined by

$$C = \cup_{s \in \mathcal{S}} C(s).$$

Let an admissible sign vector $s \in \mathcal{S}$ and a state $q \in Q^{N-1}$ be given. For every $j \in I_{N-1}$, if $s_j = -1$ ($s_j = +1$), then there is a non-positive (non-negative) total excess demand in the market for commodity j, while the value of q_j is minimal (maximal) relative to v_j, i.e. relative to the situation at the initial state demand rationing in the market for commodity j has been weakened (tightened) and supply rationing in the market for commodity j has been tightened (weakened). Notice that the set $B(s)$, $\forall s \in \mathcal{S}$, does not depend on the initial state v. The regions in Q^{N-1} determined by the sets $A(s)$, $\forall s \in \mathcal{S}$, however, do depend on v. The number of different regions $A(s)$ equals the number of admissible sign vectors and thus also depends on v. This is illustrated for the case $N = 3$ in Figure 11.2.1.

To obtain all states $q \in Q^{N-1}$ with the properties given in (11.1), it is sufficient to restrict attention to the points $q \in C$, so only points that are elements of the set $C(s)$ for some $s \in \mathcal{S}$. If, for instance, $v_j = 0$ for some $j \in I_{N-1}$, then the quantity adjustment process cannot reach a state $q \in Q^{N-1}$ that induces a negative total excess demand in the market for commodity j. According to (11.1) such a state must satisfy $q_j = 0$, implying a non-negative total excess demand for commodity j by Theorem 11.2.4. Similarly, if $v_j = 1$ for some $j \in I_{N-1}$, then the quantity adjustment process cannot reach a state $q \in Q^{N-1}$ that induces a positive total excess demand in the market for commodity j since by (11.1) such a state must satisfy $q_j = 1$, implying a non-positive total excess demand for commodity j by Theorem 11.2.4.

Let an initial state $v \in Q^{N-1}$ be given. In the next theorem it is shown that $v \in C$ and that for every $q^* \in Q^{N-1}$ satisfying $\widehat{z}(q^*) = 0^N$ it holds that $q^* \in C$.

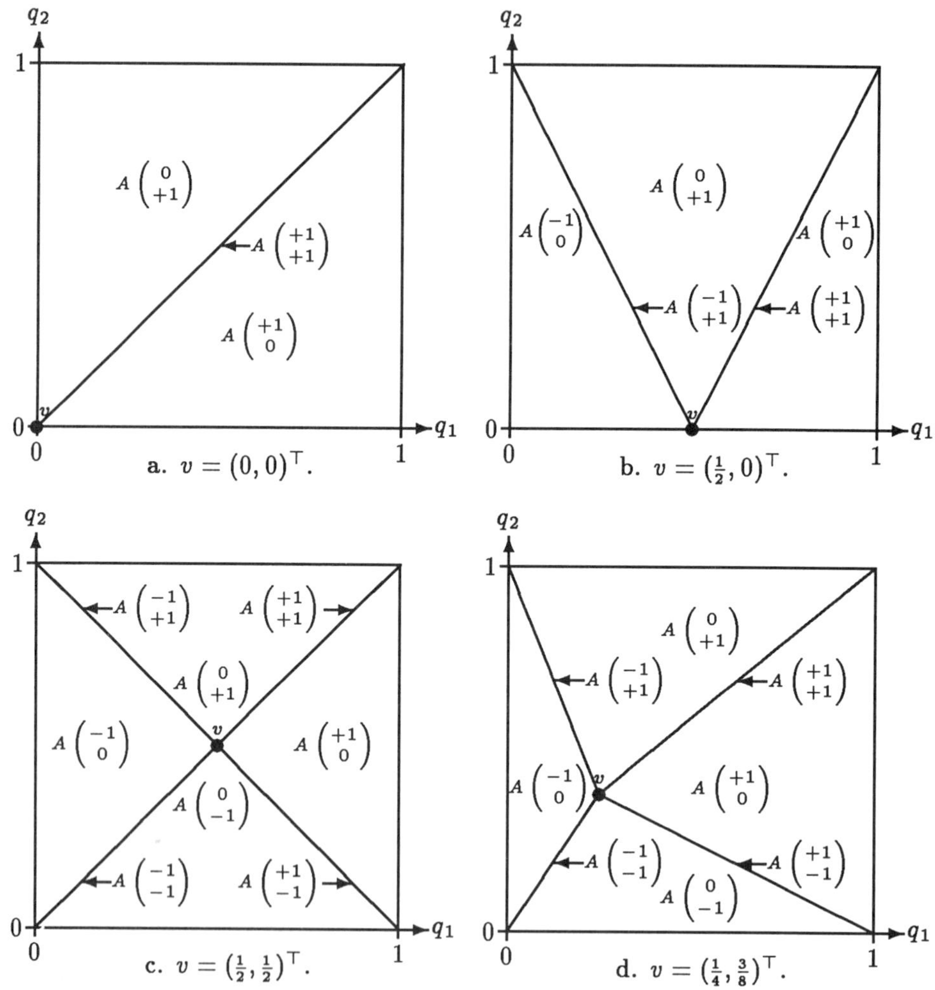

Figure 11.2.1. The sets $A(s)$, for $s \in \mathcal{S}$, $N = 3$.

Theorem 11.2.5
Let the economy $\widetilde{\mathcal{E}} = ((X^i, \preceq^i, \omega^i)_{i \in I_M}, P_{(p,\mathbf{p})}, (\widetilde{l}, \widetilde{L}))$ satisfy Assumptions A1-A5 and let $v \in Q^{N-1}$ be the initial state. Then $v \in C$ and $q^* \in C$ for every state $q^* \in Q^{N-1}$ inducing a Drèze equilibrium of the economy $\widetilde{\mathcal{E}}$.
Proof
Consider the total excess demand $\widehat{z}(v)$ at the initial state v. If $\widehat{z}(v) = 0^N$, then $v \in C(s)$, $\forall s \in \mathcal{S}$, so $v \in C$. If $\widehat{z}(v) \neq 0^N$, then $\widehat{z}_j(v) \neq 0$ for some $j \in I_{N-1}$ by Theorem 11.2.4. Now let $\bar{s} \in \mathbb{S}^{N-1}$ be obtained by defining, for every $j \in I_{N-1}$, $\bar{s}_j = -1$ if $\widehat{z}_j(v) < 0$, $\bar{s}_j = 0$ if $\widehat{z}_j(v) = 0$, and $\bar{s}_j = +1$ if $\widehat{z}_j(v) > 0$. Then it holds that $\bar{s} \in \mathcal{S}$ by Theorem 11.2.4, while, clearly, $v \in C(\bar{s}) \subset C$.
Let $q^* \in Q^{N-1}$ induce a Drèze equilibrium. Let $\bar{\mu} \in \mathbb{R}$ be defined as the maximal value of $\mu \in \mathbb{R}$ such that, for every $j \in I_{N-1}$, $q_j^* \geq \mu v_j$ and $1 - q_j^* \geq \mu(1 - v_j)$. It is easily verified that $\bar{\mu} \in [0, 1]$. If there exists $j' \in I_{N-1}$ such that both $q_{j'}^* = \bar{\mu} v_{j'}$ and $1 - q_{j'}^* = \bar{\mu}(1 - v_{j'})$, then it follows that $\bar{\mu} = 1$, so $q^* = v$. It follows from the first paragraph that $q^* \in C$ in this case. If, for every $j \in I_{N-1}$, $q_j^* > \bar{\mu} v_j$ or $1 - q_j^* > \bar{\mu}(1 - v_j)$, then let $\bar{s} \in \mathbb{S}^{N-1}$ be obtained by defining, for every $j \in I_{N-1}$, $\bar{s}_j = -1$ if $q_j^* = \bar{\mu} v_j$ and $v_j > 0$, $\bar{s}_j = +1$ if $1 - q_j^* = \bar{\mu}(1 - v_j)$ and $v_j < 1$, and $\bar{s}_j = 0$ otherwise. By the definition of $\bar{\mu}$ it holds that $q_{j'}^* = \bar{\mu} v_{j'}$ for some $j' \in I_{N-1}$ with $v_{j'} > 0$, or $1 - q_{j'}^* = \bar{\mu}(1 - v_{j'})$ for some $j' \in I_{N-1}$ with $v_{j'} < 1$, so $\bar{s} \in \mathcal{S}$. It follows immediately that $q^* \in C(\bar{s}) \subset C$. Q.E.D.

Now the quantity adjustment process can be defined. The approach chosen to describe the quantity adjustment process is closely related to the approach chosen in Smale (1976, 1981), van der Laan and Talman (1987a), Kamiya (1990), and Chapter 10 to describe price adjustment processes. The quantity adjustment process is defined as a set of elements of Q^{N-1} containing the initial state v. It is shown, under suitable differentiability conditions, that, generically, this set is homeomorphic to the closed unit interval having the initial state v and a state $q^* \in Q^{N-1}$ inducing a Drèze equilibrium as boundary points. Moreover, generically, under these assumptions the quantity adjustment process is shown to be a 1-dimensional piecewise C^2 manifold and can therefore be described by a system of differential equations, see for example Garcia and Zangwill (1981).

Definition 11.2.6 (Quantity adjustment process)
Let the economy $\widetilde{\mathcal{E}} = ((X^i, \preceq^i, \omega^i)_{i \in I_M}, P_{(p,\mathbf{p})}, (\widetilde{l}, \widetilde{L}))$ satisfy Assumptions A1-A5 and let $v \in Q^{N-1}$ be the initial state. Then the quantity adjustment process *is the component of the set C containing the initial state v.*

Since in the definition of the quantity adjustment process under consideration no differentiability assumptions are used, one should also give a definition of convergence without using such assumptions.

Definition 11.2.7 (Convergence)
Let the economy $\widetilde{\mathcal{E}} = ((X^i, \preceq^i, \omega^i)_{i \in I_M}, P_{(p,\mathbf{p})}, (\widetilde{l}, \widetilde{L}))$ *satisfy Assumptions A1-A5 and let* $v \in Q^{N-1}$ *be the initial state. The quantity adjustment process is* convergent *if either* $\widehat{z}(v) = 0^N$, *or* $\widehat{z}(v) \neq 0^N$ *and the component of* v *in* C *is an arc having* v *and a state* $q^* \in Q^{N-1}$ *inducing a Drèze equilibrium of the economy* $\widetilde{\mathcal{E}}$ *as its boundary points.*

Let an initial state $v \in Q^{N-1}$ be given. If the quantity adjustment process is convergent, then there exists a continuous function $\pi : [0,1] \to C$ satisfying $\pi(0) = v$ and $\pi(1) = q^*$, where the state q^* induces a Drèze equilibrium. The continuous function π describes the explicit time path of the quantity adjustment process. In the case the quantity adjustment process is described by a system of differential equations, this path corresponds to its trajectory.

Let an initial state $v \in Q^{N-1}$ be given. The quantity adjustment process can be followed numerically arbitrarily close using the product-ray algorithm described in Doup and Talman (1987) or the exponent-ray algorithm described in Doup, van den Elzen, and Talman (1987). These are simplicial algorithms with vector labelling and are suited for problems on the simplotope. These algorithms can be applied to a piecewise linear approximation of the reduced total excess demand function with respect to a triangulation of Q^{N-1} that is such that a proper collection of the faces of the simplices in the triangulation yields a triangulation of the set $A(s)$, $\forall s \in \mathcal{S}$. Theorem 2.7.7 guarantees that the V-triangulation of Q^{N-1} with respect to v and with grid size $\frac{1}{n}$ for some $n \in \mathbb{N}$ satisfies these properties. In fact, the set $\mathcal{S}$ of Theorem 2.7.7 contains the set $\mathcal{S}$ as defined in this chapter. The algorithms generate a piecewise linear path of points corresponding to the quantity adjustment process in a similar way as the piecewise linear path of points generated by the simplicial algorithm with vector labelling of Chapter 6, see Theorem 6.2.11, corresponds to the set of constrained equilibria of the economy considered there.

The quantity adjustment process has an appealing economic interpretation and can be described as follows. Let an initial state $v \in Q^{N-1}$ be given. First the sign of the total excess demand in the markets for the non-numeraire commodities is evaluated at the initial state v. Consider an initial state in the interior of Q^{N-1}. In Section 11.4 it is shown that then, generically, $\widehat{z}_j(v) \neq 0$, $\forall j \in I_{N-1}$. Let the admissible sign vector $s^0 \in \mathcal{S}$ be obtained by defining, for every $j \in I_{N-1}$, $s_j^0 = -1$ if $\widehat{z}_j(v) < 0$, and $s_j^0 = +1$ if $\widehat{z}_j(v) > 0$. Now the quantity adjustment process starts by leaving v along the ray $A(s^0)$. Thus, for those $j \in I_{N-1}$ with $\widehat{z}_j(v) < 0$, q_j is proportionally decreased, and when $\widehat{z}_j(v) > 0$, then q_j is proportionally increased. Hence, supply rationing is tightened and demand rationing is weakened in the markets for those commodities $j \in I_{N-1}$ with $\widehat{z}_j(v) < 0$, and the other way around for those $j \in I_{N-1}$ with $\widehat{z}_j(v) > 0$. This tends to decrease the absolute value of the total excess demand in every market. Rationing schemes are adjusted in this way until one of the markets, say the market for commodity j', is equilibrated. In Section 11.4 it is shown that, generically, either this happens for the market for exactly one commodity $j' \in I_{N-1}$ at a state $\overline{q}$ with $0 < \overline{q}_{j'} < 1$, or the boundary of Q^{N-1} is reached at a state $q^* \in Q^{N-1}$ satisfying $\widehat{z}(q^*) = 0^N$. Consider the first case. Then, either $\widehat{z}(\overline{q}) = 0^N$, or the quantity adjustment process continues by keeping the market for commodity j' in equilibrium, while $q_{j'}$ is relatively increased (decreased) if there was a negative (positive) total excess demand in the market for commodity j' before attaining equilibrium. For the market for a commodity $j \in I_{N-1} \setminus \{j'\}$, q_j is kept relatively minimal if $\widehat{z}_j(\overline{q}) < 0$, and q_j is kept relatively maximal if $\widehat{z}_j(\overline{q}) > 0$. So, a path in $C(s^1)$ is followed, where $s^1 \in \mathcal{S}$ is defined by $s^1_{j'} = 0$ and $s^1_j = s^0_j$, $\forall j \in I_{N-1} \setminus \{j'\}$.

The general case is as follows. Suppose that the quantity adjustment process follows a path in $C(s^n)$ for some $n \in \mathbb{N}$. In Section 11.4 it is shown that, generically, the following cases may result. Either a state $q^* \in Q^{N-1}$ is reached satisfying $\widehat{z}(q^*) = 0^N$, i.e. a Drèze equilibrium is obtained, and the quantity adjustment process is terminated. Or the market for some commodity $j' \in I^-(s^n) \cup I^+(s^n)$ attains an equilibrium, in which case a path in $C(s^{n+1})$ is followed, where s^{n+1} is an admissible sign vector defined by $s^{n+1}_{j'} = 0$ and $s^{n+1}_j = s^n_j$, $\forall j \in I_{N-1} \setminus \{j'\}$, so the quantity adjustment process continues by keeping the market for commodity j' in equilibrium, while $q_{j'}$ is relatively increased (decreased) if there was a negative (positive) total excess demand in the market for commodity j' before attaining equilibrium, markets for commodities $j \in I^0(s^n)$ are kept in equilibrium, for commodities $j \in I^-(s^n) \setminus \{j'\}$, q_j is kept relatively minimal, hence supply rationing is tightened and demand rationing is weakened in the market for these commodities, and for commodities $j \in I^+(s^n) \setminus \{j'\}$, q_j is kept relatively maximal, hence supply rationing is weakened and demand rationing is tightened in the market for these commodities compared to the initial state. Or $q_{j'}$, for some $j' \in I^0(s^n)$, $(1 - q_{j'}$, for some $j' \in I^0(s^n))$ has become relatively minimal, in which case a path in $C(s^{n+1})$ is followed, where s^{n+1} is an admissible sign vector defined by $s^{n+1}_{j'} = -1$ $(s^{n+1}_{j'} = +1)$ and $s^{n+1}_j = s^n_j$, $\forall j \in I_{N-1} \setminus \{j'\}$. Now the market for commodity j' is no longer kept in equilibrium, the total excess demand in the market for commodity j' is allowed to become negative (positive), while $q_{j'}$ is kept relatively minimal (maximal). It is shown in Section 11.4 that, generically, $C(s)$, $\forall s \in S$, is a finite collection of arcs and loops and that the quantity adjustment process converges to a state inducing a Drèze equilibrium.

When the initial state v lies in the boundary of Q^{N-1}, then it is not a degenerate case that the market for a commodity $j \in I_{N-1}$ for which $v_j = 0$ or $v_j = 1$ is in equilibrium. For example consider the case $v = 0^{N-1}$. If p_j is sufficiently high for every $j \in I_{N-1}$, then every consumer wants to supply every commodity $j \in I_{N-1}$ in exchange for the numeraire commodity. Hence, the initial state v induces a Drèze equilibrium with full rationing on supply. When v lies in the boundary of Q^{N-1} it may happen that the quantity adjustment process starts with keeping some markets in equilibrium. The interpretation of the quantity adjustment process remains the same. None of the adjustment processes studied in the literature has such a feature, so starting with keeping some markets in equilibrium is an interesting novelty of the quantity adjustment process under consideration.

11.3 SCARF'S EXAMPLE

The quantity adjustment process is now illustrated using Scarf's example, see Section 3.12. For this example the Walrasian tatonnement process as formulated by Samuelson (1941) does not converge to the Walrasian equilibrium price system, unless the starting price system is taken equal to the Walrasian equilibrium price system. It is shown in Scarf (1960) that this result does not change, when one of the commodities is taken as a numeraire commodity having a price equal to one, whereas only the prices of the other two commodities are allowed to vary. Therefore, Scarf's example can be considered as a difficult case for obtaining convergence of an adjustment process for an economy with a numeraire commodity. In Scarf's example the economy $\mathcal{E} = ((X^i, \preceq^i, \omega^i)_{i \in I_3})$ is such that $N = 3$, $X^1 = X^2 = X^3 = \mathbb{R}^3_+$, $\preceq^1$, $\preceq^2$, and $\preceq^3$ can be represented by utility functions $u^1 : X^1 \to \mathbb{R}$, $u^2 : X^2 \to \mathbb{R}$, and $u^3 : X^3 \to \mathbb{R}$, respectively, defined by $u^1(x^1) = \min(\{x^1_1, x^1_2\})$, $\forall x^1 \in \mathbb{R}^3_+$, $u^2(x^2) = \min(\{x^2_2, x^2_3\})$, $\forall x^2 \in \mathbb{R}^3_+$, $u^3(x^3) = \min(\{x^3_1, x^3_3\})$, $\forall x^3 \in \mathbb{R}^3_+$, and $\omega^1 = (1,0,0)^\top$, $\omega^2 = (0,1,0)^\top$, and $\omega^3 = (0,0,1)^\top$. In this chapter the example is extended by choosing a fixed price system $p = (3,2,1)$ and considering the uniform rationing system. To avoid working with total excess demand correspondences instead of total excess demand functions, the following modification with respect to the preferences of the consumers is made. This modification makes no difference at all for the Walrasian tatonnement process. Let a consumer $i \in I_3$ and consumption bundles $\overline{x}^i, \widehat{x}^i \in \mathbb{R}^3_+$ be given. Then it holds that $\overline{x}^i \preceq^i \widehat{x}^i$ if and only if $\min(\{\overline{x}^i_i, \overline{x}^i_{i+1}\}) < \min(\{\widehat{x}^i_i, \widehat{x}^i_{i+1}\})$, or both $\min(\{\overline{x}^i_i, \overline{x}^i_{i+1}\}) = \min(\{\widehat{x}^i_i, \widehat{x}^i_{i+1}\})$ and $\max(\{\overline{x}^i_i, \overline{x}^i_{i+1}\}) \leq \max(\{\widehat{x}^i_i, \widehat{x}^i_{i+1}\})$, where $i+1$ is defined as 1 if $i = 3$. It is easily verified that a rationing scheme $l^i_j \in -\mathbb{R}^*_+$ on the supply of a consumer $i \in I_3$ in the market for a commodity $j \in I_3$ cannot be binding if $l^i_j \leq -1$ and that a rationing scheme $L^i_j \in \mathbb{R}^*_+$ on the demand of consumer i in the market for commodity j cannot be binding if $L^i_j \geq 1$. Therefore, let the functions $\widehat{l} : Q^2 \to -\mathbb{R}^3_+$ and $\widehat{L} : Q^2 \to \mathbb{R}^3_+$ be obtained by defining, for every $i \in I_3$,

$$\begin{aligned} \widehat{l}^i(q) &= (-2q_1, -2q_2, -1)^\top, \quad \forall q \in Q^2, \\ \widehat{L}^i(q) &= (2 - 2q_1, 2 - 2q_2, 1)^\top, \forall q \in Q^2. \end{aligned}$$

It is easily verified that the resulting reduced total excess demand function $\widehat{z} : Q^2 \to \mathbb{R}^3$ is defined by

$$\widehat{z}(q) = \begin{cases} (\frac{1}{4} - 2q_1, 3q_1 - 2q_2, -\frac{3}{4} + 4q_2)^\top, & 0 \leq q_1 \leq \frac{1}{5},\ 0 \leq q_2 \leq \frac{1}{6}, \\ (\frac{1}{4} - 2q_1, -\frac{1}{3} + 3q_1, -\frac{1}{12})^\top, & 0 \leq q_1 \leq \frac{1}{5},\ \frac{1}{6} \leq q_2,\ 2-3q_1-2q_2 \geq 0, \\ (-1\frac{1}{12} + 1\frac{1}{3}q_2, 1\frac{2}{3} - 2q_2, -\frac{1}{12})^\top, & q_1 \leq \frac{7}{8}, \frac{7}{10} \leq q_2 \leq 1, 2-3q_1-2q_2 \leq 0, \\ (-\frac{3}{20}, \frac{3}{5} - 2q_2, -\frac{3}{4} + 4q_2)^\top, & \frac{1}{5} \leq q_1 \leq \frac{7}{8},\ 0 \leq q_2 \leq \frac{1}{6}, \\ (-\frac{3}{20}, \frac{4}{15}, -\frac{1}{12})^\top, & \frac{1}{5} \leq q_1 \leq \frac{7}{8},\ \frac{1}{6} \leq q_2 \leq \frac{7}{10}, \\ (1\frac{3}{5} - 2q_1, \frac{3}{5} - 2q_2, -6 + 6q_1 + 4q_2)^\top, & \frac{7}{8} \leq q_1 \leq 1,\ 0 \leq q_2 \leq \frac{1}{6}, \\ (1\frac{3}{5} - 2q_1, \frac{4}{15}, -5\frac{1}{3} + 6q_1)^\top, & \frac{7}{8} \leq q_1 \leq 1,\ \frac{1}{6} \leq q_2 \leq \frac{7}{10}, \\ (\frac{2}{3} - 2q_1 + 1\frac{1}{3}q_2, 1\frac{2}{3} - 2q_2, -5\frac{1}{3} + 6q_1)^\top, & \frac{7}{8} \leq q_1 \leq 1,\ \frac{7}{10} \leq q_2 \leq 1. \end{cases}$$

In Figure 11.3.1 the sets $B(s)$, $\forall s \in S$, corresponding to the example above are shown. The unique Drèze equilibrium is induced by the state $q^* = (\frac{8}{9}, \frac{5}{6})^\top$. In this Drèze equilibrium there is demand rationing in the markets for both commodities 1 and 2, $\widehat{L}^i(q^*) = (\frac{2}{9}, \frac{1}{3}, 1)^\top$, $\forall i \in I_3$, $\widehat{d}^1(q^*) = (\frac{7}{9}, \frac{1}{3}, 0)^\top$, $\widehat{d}^2(q^*) = (0, \frac{2}{3}, \frac{2}{3})^\top$, and $\widehat{d}^3(q^*) = (\frac{2}{9}, 0, \frac{1}{3})^\top$. Consumer 1 faces rationing on his demand in the market for commodity 2, consumer 3 faces rationing on his demand in the market for commodity 1, while consumer 2 is not rationed and obtains his most preferred unconstrained consumption bundle. Notice that in the unique Drèze equilibrium there is demand rationing in both markets, whereas the notional total excess demand at $p = (3, 2, 1)^\top$ is negative in the market for commodity 1 and positive in the market for commodity 2. In Figure 11.3.2 the quantity adjustment process is depicted when the initial state is given by $v = (\frac{1}{2}, \frac{1}{2})^\top$.

In the initial state v all consumers express their notional demand. Since there is a negative total excess demand in the market for commodity 1 and a positive total excess demand in the market for commodity 2, q_1 is decreased and q_2 is increased. The quantity adjustment process initially follows a path in the set

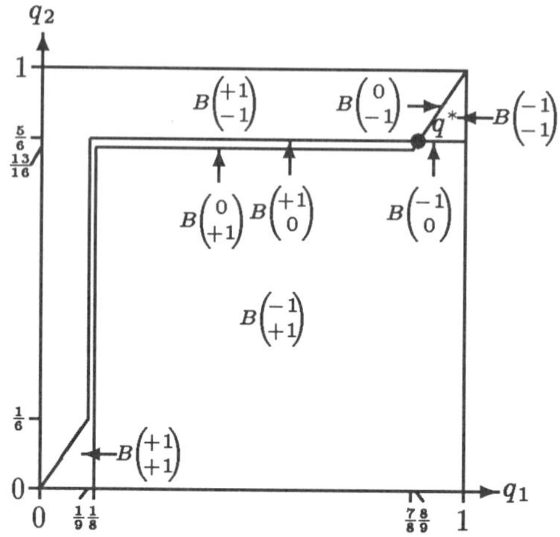

Figure 11.3.1. The sets $B(s)$, for $s \in \mathcal{S}$, in Scarf's example.

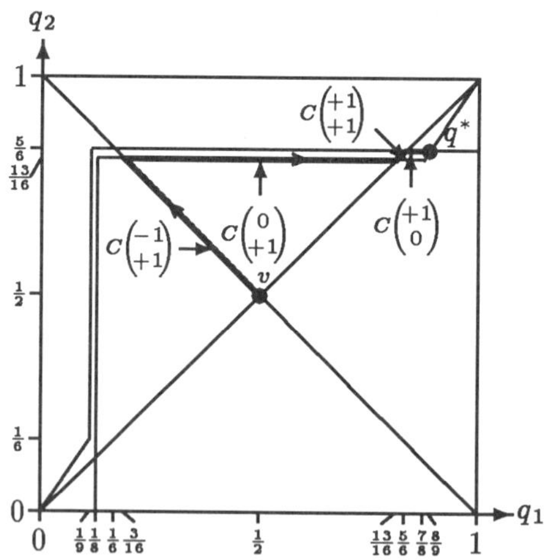

Figure 11.3.2. The sets $C(s)$, for $s \in \mathcal{S}$, in Scarf's example, $v = (\frac{1}{2}, \frac{1}{2})^\top$.

$C((-1, +1)^\top)$. Hence, both supply rationing in the market for commodity 1 and demand rationing in the market for commodity 2 become tighter. Notice that this initial adjustment of q_1 and q_2 does not go in the direction of the unique Drèze equilibrium. When q_2 equals $\frac{7}{10}$, then consumer 1 becomes rationed on his demand of commodity 2. This decreases both the demand for commodity 2 and the supply for commodity 1 of consumer 1 since consumer 1 needs to supply less of commodity 1 for buying the maximal amount possible of commodity 2. Hence, an increase in q_2 brings both the market for commodity 1 and the market for commodity 2 closer to equilibrium. When q_2 reaches the value $\frac{13}{16}$, then the market for commodity 1 attains an equilibrium situation. Now the market for commodity 1 is kept in equilibrium and q_1 is no longer required to remain relatively minimal. The quantity adjustment process follows a path in the set $C((0,+1)^\top)$. When q_1 reaches the value $\frac{13}{16}$, both q_1 and q_2 are kept relatively maximal and the market for commodity 1 is no longer kept in equilibrium. The quantity adjustment process follows a path in the set $C((+1,+1)^\top)$. The increase in q_2 results in more demand rationing in the market for commodity 2, less demand of consumer 1 for commodity 2, and less supply of consumer 1 for commodity 1. The demands of the other consumers are not affected by the changes in q_1 and q_2. At $q = (\frac{5}{6}, \frac{5}{6})^\top$ the market for commodity 2 is in equilibrium. Market 2 is kept in equilibrium by keeping q_2 equal to $\frac{5}{6}$ and the quantity adjustment process follows a path in the set $C((+1,0)^\top)$. Finally, the state $q^* = (\frac{8}{9}, \frac{5}{6})$, inducing a Drèze equilibrium, is reached.

11.4 GLOBAL AND UNIVERSAL STABILITY OF THE DRÈZE EQUILIBRIUM

In this section consumption sets and preference relations $(X^i, \preceq^i)_{i \in I_M}$, a rationing function $(\widetilde{l}, \widetilde{L})$, a fixed price system p, and an initial state $v \in Q^{N-1}$ are assumed to be given. Then the economy $\widetilde{\mathcal{E}} = ((X^i, \preceq^i, \omega^i)_{i \in I_M}, P_{(p,p)}, (\widetilde{l}, \widetilde{L}))$ is obtained for every specification of initial endowments ω in the set Ω defined by $\Omega = \prod_{i \in I_M} \mathbb{R}^N_{++}$. Hence, the set of economies is parametrized by the set of initial endowments Ω.

Let initial endowments $\omega \in \Omega$ be given. To make clear the dependence on the initial endowments $\omega \in \Omega$, for every $s \in \mathcal{S}$, for every $q \in Q^{N-1}$, the notation of $B(s)$, $C(s)$, C, $\widetilde{l}(q)$, $\widetilde{L}(q)$, $\widehat{d}^i(q)$, $\forall i \in I_M$, and $\widehat{z}(q)$ is changed into $B_\omega(s)$, $C_\omega(s)$, C_ω, $\widetilde{l}(q,\omega)$, $\widetilde{L}(q,\omega)$, $\widehat{d}^i(q,\omega)$, $\forall i \in I_M$, and $\widehat{z}(q,\omega)$, respectively. In this section it is shown that, generically, the quantity adjustment process is globally and universally convergent, i.e. it converges to a Drèze equilibrium for a large class of economies (universal convergence) given any initial state of the economy (global convergence). More precisely, it is shown that the quantity adjustment process converges, except possibly for economies parametrized by a set of initial endowments with a closure in Ω having Lebesgue measure zero.

First some remarks are made with respect to the functions $\widetilde{l}$ and $\widetilde{L}$, and the derivation of the functions $\widehat{l}$ and $\widehat{L}$. Consider the case where the functions $\widetilde{l}: \mathbb{R}_+^N \times \Omega \to -\mathbb{R}_+^{MN}$ and $\widetilde{L}: \mathbb{R}_+^N \times \Omega \to \mathbb{R}_+^{MN}$ can be extended to continuous functions $\widetilde{l}': \mathbb{R}_+^N \times \prod_{i \in I_M} \mathbb{R}_+^N \to \mathbb{R}^{MN}$ and $\widetilde{L}': \mathbb{R}_+^N \times \prod_{i \in I_M} \mathbb{R}_+^N \to \mathbb{R}^{MN}$, respectively, and, for every $\omega \in \prod_{i \in I_M} \mathbb{R}_+^N$, the functions $\widetilde{l}'(\cdot, \omega): \mathbb{R}_+^N \to \mathbb{R}^{MN}$ and $\widetilde{L}'(\cdot, \omega): \mathbb{R}_+^N \to \mathbb{R}^{MN}$ satisfy Assumption A5. These are weak requirements. It is not difficult to (slightly) modify the examples of the uniform rationing function, the market share rationing function, and the priority rationing function given in Section 4.5 such that these requirements are satisfied. As in Section 11.2 the functions $\widehat{l}: Q^{N-1} \times \Omega \to -\mathbb{R}_+^{MN}$ and $\widehat{L}: Q^{N-1} \times \Omega \to \mathbb{R}_+^{MN}$ are constructed in such a way that on the adjustment path all conditions of a Drèze equilibrium are satisfied, except possibly the equality of demand and supply.

Let a countable partition $\{\Omega(\nu) \mid \nu \in \mathbb{N}\}$ of Ω be given, which is locally finite, i.e. for every $\omega \in \Omega$, there exists an open subset of Ω containing ω and intersecting only finitely many sets $\Omega(\nu)$. Moreover, let $\{\Omega(\nu) \mid \nu \in \mathbb{N}\}$ be a bounded partition. The functions $\widehat{l}$ and $\widehat{L}$ are constructed in such a way that, for every $\nu \in \mathbb{N}$, for every $(q, \omega), (q, \overline{\omega}) \in Q^{N-1} \times \Omega(\nu)$, it holds that $\widehat{l}(q, \omega) = \widehat{l}(q, \overline{\omega})$ and $\widehat{L}(q, \omega) = \widehat{L}(q, \overline{\omega})$. Functions $\widehat{l}$ and $\widehat{L}$ with these properties are called *locally constant* with respect to the locally finite partition $\{\Omega(\nu) \mid \nu \in \mathbb{N}\}$ of Ω. Locally constant functions $\widehat{l}$ and $\widehat{L}$ can be obtained as follows. Let some $\nu \in \mathbb{N}$ be given. For every $j \in I_N$, $\underline{q}_j^\nu \in \mathbb{R}_+$ is chosen such that, for every $\omega \in \Omega(\nu)$, for every $q_j^1 \geq \underline{q}_j^\nu$, $\widetilde{l}_j^i(q^1, \omega) < -\omega_j^i$, $\forall i \in I_M$, and $\overline{q}_j^\nu \in \mathbb{R}_+$ is chosen such that, for every $q_j^2 \geq \overline{q}_j^\nu$, $\widetilde{L}_j^i(q^2, \omega) > \frac{p \cdot \omega^i}{p_j} - \omega_j^i$, $\forall i \in I_M$. Notice that the assumptions on $\Omega(\nu)$ and $(\widetilde{l}, \widetilde{L})$ guarantee that, for every $j \in I_N$, $\underline{q}_j^\nu$ and $\overline{q}_j^\nu$ with the above properties exist. The existence of the continuous extensions $\widetilde{l}'$ and $\widetilde{L}'$ of $\widetilde{l}$ and $\widetilde{L}$, respectively, is needed to guarantee that, for every $j \in I_N$, $\underline{q}_j^\nu$ and $\overline{q}_j^\nu$ can be chosen independently of $\omega \in \Omega(\nu)$. Now, one defines

$$\widehat{l}(q,\omega)=\widetilde{l}\left((2\underline{q}_1^\nu q_1, \ldots, 2\underline{q}_{N-1}^\nu q_{N-1}, \underline{q}_N^\nu)^\top, \omega\right), \quad \forall q \in Q^{N-1}, \forall \omega \in \Omega(\nu),$$
$$\widehat{L}(q,\omega)=\widetilde{L}\left((2\overline{q}_1^\nu(1-q_1), \ldots, 2\overline{q}_{N-1}^\nu(1-q_{N-1}), \overline{q}_N^\nu)^\top, \omega\right), \forall q \in Q^{N-1}, \forall \omega \in \Omega(\nu).$$

Repeating this procedure for every $\nu \in \mathbb{N}$, the functions $\widehat{l}: Q^{N-1} \times \Omega \to -\mathbb{R}_+^{MN}$ and $\widehat{L}: Q^{N-1} \times \Omega \to \mathbb{R}_+^{MN}$ are obtained. Then, for every $q \in Q^{N-1}$, for every $\omega \in \Omega$, for every $i \in I_M$, for every $j \in I_{N-1}$, $\widehat{l}_j^i(q, \omega)$ is not binding if $q_j \geq \frac{1}{2}$, and $\widehat{L}_j^i(q, \omega)$ is not binding if $q_j \leq \frac{1}{2}$. Moreover, for every $q \in Q^{N-1}$, for every $\omega \in \Omega$, for every $i \in I_M$, $\widehat{l}_N^i(q, \omega)$ is not binding and $\widehat{L}_N^i(q, \omega)$ is not binding.

Functions $\widehat{l}$ and $\widehat{L}$ satisfying these properties are called *frictionless*. For every $\nu \in \mathbb{N}$, let $\overline{\omega}^\nu$ be an element of $\Omega(\nu)$. It is useful to define for every $\nu \in \mathbb{N}$ the functions $\widehat{l}^\nu : Q^{N-1} \to -\mathbb{R}_+^{MN}$ and $\widehat{L}^\nu : Q^{N-1} \to \mathbb{R}_+^{MN}$ by

$$\begin{aligned}\widehat{l}^\nu(q) &= \widehat{l}(q, \overline{\omega}^\nu), \ \forall q \in Q^{N-1},\\ \widehat{L}^\nu(q) &= \widehat{L}(q, \overline{\omega}^\nu), \forall q \in Q^{N-1}.\end{aligned}$$

Notice that the functions $\widehat{l}^\nu$, $\forall \nu \in \mathbb{N}$, and $\widehat{L}^\nu$, $\forall \nu \in \mathbb{N}$, completely determine the functions $\widehat{l}$ and $\widehat{L}$, respectively.

From now on the functions $\widehat{l} : Q^{N-1} \times \Omega \to -\mathbb{R}_+^{MN}$ and $\widehat{L} : Q^{N-1} \times \Omega \to \mathbb{R}_+^{MN}$ are assumed to be given and are considered as primitive concepts. In this section the following assumptions are made.

A6. For every $i \in I_M$, the consumption set X^i is equal to $\mathbb{R}_{++}^N$.

A7. For every $i \in I_M$, the preference relation $\preceq^i$ is complete, transitive, continuous, strongly monotonic, strongly convex, of the class C^3, satisfies the boundary condition, and has non-zero Gaussian curvature.

A8. The price system p is an element of $\mathbb{R}_{++}^N$ with $p_N = 1$.

A9. The functions $\widehat{l} : Q^{N-1} \times \Omega \to -\mathbb{R}_+^{MN}$ and $\widehat{L} : Q^{N-1} \times \Omega \to \mathbb{R}_+^{MN}$ are locally constant with respect to the bounded, locally finite partition $\{\Omega(\nu) \mid \nu \in \mathbb{N}\}$ of Ω and frictionless. Moreover, for every $\nu \in \mathbb{N}$, $\widehat{l}^\nu \in C^2(Q^{N-1}, -\mathbb{R}_+^{MN})$ and $\widehat{L}^\nu \in C^2(Q^{N-1}, \mathbb{R}_+^{MN})$, and, for every $i \in I_M$, for every $j \in I_{N-1}$, for every $\overline{q}, \widehat{q} \in Q^{N-1}$,

$$\begin{aligned}&\widehat{l}_j^{\nu,i}(\overline{q}) = \widehat{l}_j^{\nu,i}(\widehat{q}) \text{ if } \overline{q}_j = \widehat{q}_j, \quad \widehat{L}_j^{\nu,i}(\overline{q}) = \widehat{L}_j^{\nu,i}(\widehat{q}) \text{ if } \overline{q}_j = \widehat{q}_j,\\ &\widehat{l}_j^{\nu,i}(\overline{q}) = 0 \qquad \text{ if } \overline{q}_j = 0, \quad \widehat{L}_j^{\nu,i}(\overline{q}) = 0 \qquad \text{ if } \overline{q}_j = 1.\end{aligned}$$

Furthermore, for every $\nu \in \mathbb{N}$, for every $j \in I_{N-1}$, for every $\overline{q} \in Q^{N-1}$, it holds that $\sum_{i \in I_M} \partial_{q_j} \widehat{l}_j^{\nu,i}(\overline{q}) < 0$ and $\sum_{i \in I_M} \partial_{q_j} \widehat{L}_j^{\nu,i}(\overline{q}) < 0$.

Although Assumptions A1 and A2 are not implied by Assumptions A6 and A7, using Theorem 9.2.5 it is easily shown that for every $\omega \in \Omega$ Theorems 11.2.2, 11.2.3, 11.2.4, and 11.2.5 remain valid under Assumptions A6-A9 for the economy $\widetilde{\mathcal{E}} = ((X^i, \preceq^i, \omega^i)_{i \in I_M}, P_{(p,p)}, (\widehat{l}(\cdot, \omega), \widehat{L}(\cdot, \omega)))$.

Assumption A9 admits many possible rationing functions. In fact, any rationing function $(\widetilde{l}, \widetilde{L})$ such that $\widetilde{l}$ and $\widetilde{L}$ can be extended to continuous functions $\widetilde{l}'$:

$\mathbb{R}^N_+ \times \prod_{i\in I_M} \mathbb{R}^N_+ \to \mathbb{R}^{MN}$ and $\widetilde{L}' : \mathbb{R}^N_+ \times \prod_{i\in I_M} \mathbb{R}^N_+ \to \mathbb{R}^{MN}$, respectively, being such that for every $\omega \in \prod_{i\in I_M} \mathbb{R}^N_+$ the functions $\widetilde{l}'(\cdot,\omega) : \mathbb{R}^N_+ \to \mathbb{R}^{MN}$ and $\widetilde{L}'(\cdot,\omega) : \mathbb{R}^N_+ \to \mathbb{R}^{MN}$ satisfy Assumption A5, while for every $\omega \in \Omega$ the functions $\widetilde{l}(\cdot,\omega) : \mathbb{R}^N_+ \to -\mathbb{R}^{MN}_+$ and $\widetilde{L}(\cdot,\omega) : \mathbb{R}^N_+ \to \mathbb{R}^{MN}_+$ are twice continuously differentiable and satisfy, for every $\overline{q} \in \mathbb{R}^N_+$, for every $j \in I_{N-1}$, $\sum_{i\in I_M} \partial_{q_j}\widetilde{l}^i_j(\overline{q},\omega) < 0$ and $\sum_{i\in I_M} \partial_{q_j}\widetilde{L}^i_j(\overline{q},\omega) > 0$, yields functions $\widehat{l}$ and $\widehat{L}$ satisfying Assumption A9 by the construction given at the beginning of this section. Notice that the requirement that the functions $\widehat{l}$ and $\widehat{L}$ are locally constant is very reasonable, in the sense that a more general dependence of these functions upon $\omega \in \Omega$ can be approximated arbitrarily close.

Next, two examples of functions $\widehat{l}$ and $\widehat{L}$ satisfying Assumption A9 are given. For every $\nu \in \mathbb{N}$, let $\overline{\omega}^\nu = \nu 1^{MN}$, let the set $\Omega(1)$ be given by $\Omega(1) = \{\omega \in \Omega \mid \omega \leq \overline{\omega}^1\}$, and, for every $\nu \in \mathbb{N} \setminus \{1\}$, let the set $\Omega(\nu)$ be given by $\Omega(\nu) = \{\omega \in \Omega \mid \omega \leq \overline{\omega}^\nu\} \setminus (\Omega(1) \cup \cdots \cup \Omega(\nu-1))$. Notice that $\{\Omega(\nu) \mid \nu \in \mathbb{N}\}$ is a bounded, locally finite partition of Ω. First, functions $\widehat{l}$ and $\widehat{L}$ satisfying Assumption A9 and corresponding to the uniform rationing function are given. Let some $\varepsilon \in \mathbb{R}_{++}$ be given. For every $\nu \in \mathbb{N}$, for every $i \in I_M$, for every $j \in I_{N-1}$, let the functions $\widehat{l}^{\nu,i}_j$ and $\widehat{L}^{\nu,i}_j$ be defined by

$$\begin{aligned} \widehat{l}^{\nu,i}_j(q) &= -2(\nu+\varepsilon)q_j, \quad \forall q \in Q^{N-1}, \\ \widehat{L}^{\nu,i}_j(q) &= \tfrac{2\nu p\cdot 1^N}{p_j}(1-q_j), \forall q \in Q^{N-1}. \end{aligned}$$

For every $\nu \in \mathbb{N}$, for every $i \in I_M$, let $\widehat{l}^{\nu,i}_N$ and $\widehat{L}^{\nu,i}_N$ be defined by

$$\begin{aligned} \widehat{l}^{\nu,i}_N(q) &= -(\nu+\varepsilon), \forall q \in Q^{N-1}, \\ \widehat{L}^{\nu,i}_N(q) &= \nu p\cdot 1^N, \quad \forall q \in Q^{N-1}. \end{aligned}$$

Secondly, functions $\widehat{l}$ and $\widehat{L}$ satisfying Assumption A9 and corresponding to the priority rationing system are given. Let the function $f : \mathbb{R} \to \mathbb{R}$ be defined by $f(t) = 0$, $\forall t \in -\mathbb{R}_+$, and $f(t) = \exp(-\frac{1}{t})$, $\forall t \in \mathbb{R}_{++}$. Then it holds by Theorem 2.9.1 that $f \in C^\infty(\mathbb{R},\mathbb{R})$. Let $\underline{\pi}_j : I_M \to I_M$ be a permutation specifying the order in which consumers are rationed on their supply in the market for a commodity $j \in I_{N-1}$, so, for every $k \in I_M$, if consumer $\underline{\pi}_j(k)$ is rationed on his supply in the market for commodity j, then the consumers $\underline{\pi}_j(1),\ldots,\underline{\pi}_j(k-1)$ are fully rationed on their supply. Let $\overline{\pi}_j : I_M \to I_M$ be a permutation specifying the order in which consumers are rationed on their demand in the market for a commodity $j \in I_{N-1}$, so, for every $k \in I_M$, if consumer $\overline{\pi}_j(k)$ is rationed on his demand in the market for commodity j, then the consumers $\overline{\pi}_j(1),\ldots,\overline{\pi}_j(k-1)$ are fully rationed on their demand. Let some $\varepsilon \in \mathbb{R}_{++}$ be given. For every $\nu \in \mathbb{N}$, for every $i \in I_M$, for every $j \in I_{N-1}$, let $\widehat{l}_j^{\nu,i}$ and $\widehat{L}_j^{\nu,i}$ be defined by

$$\begin{array}{ll} \widehat{l}_j^{\nu,i}(q) = -2M(\nu+\varepsilon)q_j, & \forall q \in Q^{N-1}, \text{if } \underline{\pi}_j^{-1}(i) = M, \\ \widehat{l}_j^{\nu,i}(q) = -\exp(1)(\nu+\varepsilon)f(\underline{\pi}_j^{-1}(i) - M + 2Mq_j), & \forall q \in Q^{N-1}, \text{if } \underline{\pi}_j^{-1}(i) \leq M-1, \\ \widehat{L}_j^{\nu,i}(q) = \frac{2M\nu p\cdot 1^N}{p_j}(1-q_j), & \forall q \in Q^{N-1}, \text{if } \overline{\pi}_j^{-1}(i) = M, \\ \widehat{L}_j^{\nu,i}(q) = \frac{\exp(1)\nu p\cdot 1^N}{p_j} f(\overline{\pi}_j^{-1}(i) + M - 2Mq_j), & \forall q \in Q^{N-1}, \text{if } \overline{\pi}_j^{-1}(i) \leq M-1. \end{array}$$

Moreover, for every $\nu \in \mathbb{N}$, for every $i \in I_M$, let $\widehat{l}_N^{\nu,i}$ and $\widehat{L}_N^{\nu,i}$ be defined by

$$\begin{array}{l} \widehat{l}_N^{\nu,i}(q) = -(\nu+\varepsilon), \ \forall q \in Q^{N-1}, \\ \widehat{L}_N^{\nu,i}(q) = \nu p \cdot 1^N, \quad \forall q \in Q^{N-1}. \end{array}$$

For every $\nu \in \mathbb{N}$, for every $i \in I_M$, for every $j \in I_{N-1}$, for every $q \in Q^{N-1}$, notice that $q_j \geq \frac{M+1-\underline{\pi}_j^{-1}(i)}{2M}$ implies $\widehat{l}_j^{\nu,i}(q) < -\nu$, and $q_j \leq \frac{M-1+\overline{\pi}_j^{-1}(i)}{2M}$ implies $\widehat{L}_j^{\nu,i}(q) \geq \frac{\nu p\cdot 1^N}{p_j}$. Moreover, for every $\nu \in \mathbb{N}$, for every $j \in I_{N-1}$, the reason for defining $\widehat{l}_j^{\nu,i}$ and $\widehat{L}_j^{\nu,i}$ slightly different in the case $\underline{\pi}_j^{-1}(i) = M$ or $\overline{\pi}_j^{-1}(i) = M$ for some $i \in I_M$, is to make sure that, for every $\overline{q} \in Q^{N-1}$, $\sum_{i\in I_M} \partial_{q_j}\widehat{l}_j^{\nu,i}(\overline{q}) < 0$ and $\sum_{i\in I_M} \partial_{q_j}\widehat{L}_j^{\nu,i}(\overline{q}) < 0$.

Other examples of rationing functions given in Section 4.5, like the proportional rationing function and the market share rationing function can be treated in a similar way to obtain functions $\widehat{l}$ and $\widehat{L}$ satisfying Assumption A9.

A sign vector $r \in \mathbb{S}^{M(N-1)}$ determines the rationing state of every consumer $i \in I_M$ in the market for every commodity $j \in I_{N-1}$, i.e. $r_j^i = -1$ indicates that consumer i is rationed on his supply in the market for commodity j, $r_j^i = 0$ implies that consumer i is not rationed in the market for commodity j, and $r_j^i = +1$ indicates that consumer i is rationed on his demand in the market for commodity j. Notice that the notational conventions used for the functions $\widetilde{l}$ and $\widetilde{L}$ are also used for sign vectors $r \in \mathbb{S}^{M(N-1)}$. Since it cannot occur that in any market there are both consumers being rationed on their supply and consumers being rationed on their demand, it is sufficient to consider sign vectors $r \in \mathbb{S}^{M(N-1)}$ such that for every $j \in I_{N-1}$ either $r_j^i \leq 0$, $\forall i \in I_M$, or $r_j^i \geq 0$, $\forall i \in I_M$. Hence, the *set of admissible sign vectors* $\mathcal{R}$ is defined by

$$\mathcal{R} = \left\{ r \in \mathbb{S}^{M(N-1)} \,|\, \forall j \in I_{N-1}, \ r_j^i \geq 0, \ \forall i \in I_M, \ \text{or } r_j^i \leq 0, \ \forall i \in I_M \right\}.$$

For an admissible sign vector $r \in \mathcal{R}$, the sets $I^-(r)$, $I^0(r)$, and $I^+(r)$ are defined by

$$\begin{aligned} I^-(r) &= \left\{(i,j) \in I_M \times I_{N-1} \,\middle|\, r^i_j = -1\right\}, \\ I^0(r) &= \left\{(i,j) \in I_M \times I_{N-1} \,\middle|\, r^i_j = 0\right\}, \\ I^+(r) &= \left\{(i,j) \in I_M \times I_{N-1} \,\middle|\, r^i_j = +1\right\}. \end{aligned}$$

Let $i^-(r)$, $i^0(r)$, and $i^+(r)$ denote the cardinality of the sets $I^-(r)$, $I^0(r)$, and $I^+(r)$, respectively. A pair of admissible sign vectors $(r,s) \in \mathbb{S}^{M(N-1)} \times \mathbb{S}^{N-1}$ is used to describe both the rationing state of the markets and the sign of the total excess demand. It is shown in Theorem 11.4.1 that it is sufficient to restrict attention to the *set of admissible pairs of sign vectors* $\mathcal{T}$, defined by

$$\begin{aligned} \mathcal{T} = \Big\{ (r,s) \in \mathcal{R} \times \mathcal{S} \,\Big|\, & \forall j \in I_{N-1},\ s_j = -1 \Rightarrow \exists i' \in I_M,\ r^{i'}_j \neq +1, \\ & \forall j \in I_{N-1},\ s_j = 0 \text{ and } v_j < 1 \Rightarrow \exists i' \in I_M,\ r^{i'}_j \neq +1, \\ & \forall j \in I_{N-1},\ s_j = 0 \text{ and } v_j > 0 \Rightarrow \exists i' \in I_M,\ r^{i'}_j \neq -1, \\ & \forall j \in I_{N-1},\ s_j = +1 \Rightarrow \exists i' \in I_M,\ r^{i'}_j \neq -1 \Big\}. \end{aligned}$$

For every $\omega \in \Omega$, for every $(r,s) \in \mathcal{T}$, the set $C_\omega(r,s)$ is defined by

$$\begin{aligned} C_\omega(r,s) = \Big\{ q \in C_\omega(s) \,\Big|\, & \forall (i,j) \in I^-(r),\ \widehat{d}^i_j(q,\omega) - \omega^i_j = \widehat{l}^i_j(q,\omega), \\ & \forall (i,j) \in I^0(r),\ \text{neither } \widehat{l}^i_j(q,\omega) \text{ nor } \widehat{L}^i_j(q,\omega) \text{ is binding}, \\ & \forall (i,j) \in I^+(r),\ \widehat{d}^i_j(q,\omega) - \omega^i_j = \widehat{L}^i_j(q,\omega) \Big\}. \end{aligned}$$

Notice that if $\widehat{l}^i_j(q,\omega)$ or $\widehat{L}^i_j(q,\omega)$ is non-binding for some $i \in I_M$ and some $j \in I_{N-1}$, then it is still possible that $\widehat{d}^i_j(q,\omega) - \omega^i_j = \widehat{l}^i_j(q,\omega)$ or $\widehat{d}^i_j(q,\omega) - \omega^i_j = \widehat{L}^i_j(q,\omega)$. In Theorem 11.4.1 it is shown that there is indeed no loss of generality in only considering admissible pairs of sign vectors $(r,s) \in \mathcal{T}$.

Theorem 11.4.1
Let $(X^i, \preceq^i)_{i \in I_M}, P_{(p,p)}, (\widehat{l}, \widehat{L})$ satisfy Assumptions A6-A9 and let $v \in Q^{N-1}$ be the initial state. Let some $\omega \in \Omega$ be given. Then $C_\omega = \cup_{(r,s)\in\mathcal{T}} C_\omega(r,s) \cup \{v \mid \widehat{z}(v,\omega) = 0^N$ and $v_j \in \{0,1\}, \forall j \in I_{N-1}\}$.
Proof
Clearly, $\cup_{(r,s)\in\mathcal{T}} C_\omega(r,s) \cup \{v \mid \widehat{z}(v,\omega) = 0^N$ and $v_j \in \{0,1\}, \forall j \in I_{N-1}\} \subset C_\omega$. To prove the converse, let some $\overline{q} \in C_\omega$ be given. Then there exists $\overline{s} \in \mathcal{S}$ such that $\overline{q} \in C_\omega(\overline{s})$. For every $(i,j) \in I_M \times I_{N-1}$, exactly one of the following three statements is true, $\widehat{l}^i_j(\overline{q},\omega) = \widehat{d}^i_j(\overline{q},\omega) - \omega^i_j$, or $\widehat{l}^i_j(\overline{q},\omega) < \widehat{d}^i_j(\overline{q},\omega) - \omega^i_j < \widehat{L}^i_j(\overline{q},\omega)$, or $\widehat{d}^i_j(\overline{q},\omega) - \omega^i_j = \widehat{L}^i_j(\overline{q},\omega)$. Let $\overline{r} \in \mathcal{R}$ be defined by $\overline{r}^i_j = -1$, $\overline{r}^i_j = 0$, or $\overline{r}^i_j = +1$

if $(i,j) \in I_M \times I_{N-1}$ satisfies the first, second, or third statement, respectively. If $(\overline{r},\overline{s}) \in \mathcal{T}$, then $\overline{q} \in C_\omega(\overline{r},\overline{s})$. If $(\overline{r},\overline{s}) \notin \mathcal{T}$, then at least one of the following four cases occurs.

1. $J^1 = \{j \in I_{N-1} \mid \overline{s}_j = -1 \text{ and } \overline{r}^i_j = +1, \forall i \in I_M\} \neq \emptyset$. Consider some $j \in J^1$. Since $\overline{r}^i_j = +1$, $\forall i \in I_M$, it holds that $\widehat{z}_j(\overline{q},\omega) = \sum_{i \in I_M} \widehat{L}^i_j(\overline{q},\omega) \geq 0$, while $\overline{s}_j = -1$ implies $\widehat{z}_j(\overline{q},\omega) \leq 0$. Therefore, $\widehat{z}_j(\overline{q},\omega) = 0$ and, by Assumption A9, $\overline{q}_j = 1$. Since $\overline{s}_j = -1$, there exists $\mu \in [0,1]$ such that $\overline{q}_j = \mu v_j$. Hence, $\mu = 1$, $v_j = 1$, and, since $\overline{q} \in C_\omega(\overline{s})$, $\overline{q} = v$.

2. $J^2 = \{j \in I_{N-1} \mid \overline{s}_j = 0, v_j < 1, \text{ and } \overline{r}^i_j = +1, \forall i \in I_M\} \neq \emptyset$. Consider some $j \in J^2$. As in Case 1 this implies $\overline{q}_j = 1$. Since $\overline{s}_j = 0$, there exists $\mu \in [0,1]$ such that $0 = 1 - \overline{q}_j \geq \mu(1 - v_j)$, so, since $v_j < 1$, $\mu = 0$ and $1 - \overline{q}_j = \mu(1 - v_j)$.

3. $J^3 = \{j \in I_{N-1} \mid \overline{s}_j = 0, v_j > 0, \text{ and } \overline{r}^i_j = -1, \forall i \in I_M\} \neq \emptyset$. Consider some $j \in J^3$. Since $\overline{r}^i_j = -1$, $\forall i \in I_M$, it holds that $\widehat{z}_j(\overline{q},\omega) = \sum_{i \in I_M} \widehat{l}^i_j(\overline{q},\omega)$. Since $\overline{s}_j = 0$ implies $\widehat{z}_j(\overline{q},\omega) = 0$, it follows from Assumption A9 that $\overline{q}_j = 0$. Since $\overline{s}_j = 0$, there exists $\mu \in [0,1]$ such that $0 = \overline{q}_j \geq \mu v_j$, so, since $v_j > 0$, it also follows that $\mu = 0$ and $\overline{q}_j = \mu v_j$.

4. $J^4 = \{j \in I_{N-1} \mid \overline{s}_j = +1 \text{ and } \overline{r}^i_j = -1, \forall i \in I_M\} \neq \emptyset$. Consider some $j \in J^4$. As in Case 3 it follows that $\overline{q}_j = 0$. Since $\overline{s}_j = +1$, there exists $\mu \in [0,1]$ such that $1 = 1 - \overline{q}_j = \mu(1 - v_j)$, so, $\mu = 1$, $v_j = 0$, and, since $\overline{q} \in C_\omega(\overline{s})$, $\overline{q} = v$.

Let $\widehat{s} \in \mathbb{S}^{N-1}$ be defined by $\widehat{s}_j = 0$, $\forall j \in J^1$, $\widehat{s}_j = +1$, $\forall j \in J^2$, $\widehat{s}_j = -1$, $\forall j \in J^3$, $\widehat{s}_j = 0$, $\forall j \in J^4$, and $\widehat{s}_j = \overline{s}_j$, $\forall j \in I_{N-1} \setminus (J_1 \cup J_2 \cup J_3 \cup J_4)$. Then $\widehat{s} \in \mathcal{S}$, unless $\widehat{s} = 0^{N-1}$. If $\widehat{s} \neq 0^{N-1}$, then it is easily verified that $(\overline{r},\widehat{s}) \in \mathcal{T}$ and $\overline{q} \in C_\omega(\overline{r},\widehat{s})$.

Next, consider the case $\widehat{s} = 0^{N-1}$. This implies $\widehat{z}(\overline{q},\omega) = 0^N$, $J^2 \cup J^3 = \emptyset$, and $J^1 \cup J^4 \neq \emptyset$, so $\overline{q} = v$. If there exists $j' \in I_{N-1} \setminus (J^1 \cup J^4)$ such that $0 < v_{j'} < 1$, then $\overline{s}_{j'} = 0$ and, since $j' \notin J^2 \cup J^3$, there exists $i' \in I_M$ such that $\overline{r}^{i'}_{j'} \neq -1$ and there exists $i'' \in I_M$ such that $\overline{r}^{i''}_{j'} \neq +1$. Now let $\widetilde{s} \in \mathcal{S}$ be defined by $\widetilde{s}_{j'} = -1$ and $\widetilde{s}_j = \widehat{s}_j$, $\forall j \in I_{N-1} \setminus \{j'\}$, then $(\overline{r},\widetilde{s}) \in \mathcal{T}$ and, using $\overline{q} = v$, $\overline{q} \in C_\omega(\overline{r},\widetilde{s})$. If there exists no $j' \in I_{N-1} \setminus (J^1 \cup J^4)$ such that $0 < v_{j'} < 1$, then it holds that $\overline{q} = v$, $\widehat{z}(v,\omega) = 0^N$, and $v_j \in \{0,1\}$, $\forall j \in I_{N-1}$. Q.E.D.

For almost every $\omega \in \Omega$, for every $(r,s) \in \mathcal{T}$, $C_\omega(r,s)$ is shown to be a 1-dimensional C^2 manifold with boundary. First the following preliminary lemma is shown.

Lemma 11.4.2

Let $(X^i, \preceq^i)_{i \in I_M}$ satisfy Assumptions A1-A2. Then, for every $i \in I_M$, the preference relation $\preceq^i$ can be represented by a utility function $u^i \in C^2(X^i, \mathbb{R})$ that has no critical point and is pseudo-concave.

Proof
Let some consumer $i \in I_M$ be given. Let $u^i \in C^2(X^i, \mathbb{R})$ have no critical point and let u^i represent $\preceq^i$. Notice that such a function u^i exists by Theorem 3.6.3. Suppose u^i is not pseudo-concave and let $\overline{x}^i, \widehat{x}^i \in X^i$ be such that $\partial_{x^i} u^i(\overline{x}^i)(\widehat{x}^i - \overline{x}^i) \leq 0$ and $u^i(\widehat{x}^i) > u^i(\overline{x}^i)$. Since $\preceq^i$ is strongly monotonic and has no critical point, there exists $j' \in I_N$ such that $\partial_{x^i_{j'}} u^i(\overline{x}^i) > 0$. Using the continuity of u^i, there exists $\varepsilon \in \mathbb{R}_{++}$ such that $\widehat{x}^i - \varepsilon e^N(j') \in X^i$ and $u^i(\widehat{x}^i - \varepsilon e^N(j')) > u^i(\overline{x}^i)$. Let $\widetilde{x}^i \in X^i$ be defined by $\widetilde{x}^i = \widehat{x}^i - \varepsilon e^N(j')$. Clearly, $\partial_{x^i} u^i(\overline{x}^i)(\widetilde{x}^i - \overline{x}^i) < 0$. Since, for every $\lambda \in (0, 1]$, $u^i(\lambda \widetilde{x}^i + (1 - \lambda)\overline{x}^i) > u^i(\overline{x}^i)$, it follows that $\partial_{x^i} u^i(\overline{x}^i)(\widetilde{x}^i - \overline{x}^i) \geq 0$, a contradiction. Consequently, u^i is pseudo-concave.
Q.E.D.

Let some $\nu \in \mathbb{N}$ and some $(r, s) \in \mathcal{T}$ be given. A system of equalities and inequalities describing $C_\omega(r, s)$ for every $\omega \in \Omega(\nu)$ is given. Using this system it is shown in Theorem 11.4.7 that $C_\omega(r, s)$ is a 1-dimensional C^2 manifold with boundary for almost every $\omega \in \Omega(\nu)$.

For every $(r, s) \in \mathcal{T}$, the set $J(r, s)$ is defined by

$$\begin{aligned} J(r,s) = &\left\{ j \in I_{N-1} \,\middle|\, s_j = -1 \text{ and } r^i_j = -1, \ \forall i \in I_M \right\} \\ &\cup \left\{ j \in I_{N-1} \,\middle|\, s_j = +1 \text{ and } r^i_j = +1, \ \forall i \in I_M \right\}, \end{aligned}$$

$j(r, s)$ is defined as the lowest ranked element in the set $J(r, s)$ if $J(r, s)$ is non-empty, and $j(r, s) = 0$ if $J(r, s) = \emptyset$. For every $(r, s) \in \mathcal{T}$, the set $J(r, s)$ contains the commodities of the markets for which either all consumers are rationed on their supply or all consumers are rationed on their demand. For every $(r, s) \in \mathcal{T}$, the sets $J^-(r, s)$ and $J^+(r, s)$ are defined by

$$J^-(r,s) = I^-(s) \cap \left(\left\{ j \in I_{N-1} \,\middle|\, \exists i' \in I_M, \ r^{i'}_j \neq -1 \right\} \cup \{j(r,s)\} \right),$$

$$J^+(r,s) = I^+(s) \cap \left(\left\{ j \in I_{N-1} \,\middle|\, \exists i' \in I_M, \ r^{i'}_j \neq +1 \right\} \cup \{j(r,s)\} \right).$$

Moreover, for every $(r, s) \in \mathcal{T}$, the sets $\widetilde{J}^-(r, s)$ and $\widetilde{J}^+(r, s)$ are defined by

$$\widetilde{J}^-(r,s) = I^0(s) \cap \left\{ j \in I_{N-1} \,\middle|\, v_j > 0 \text{ and } \exists i' \in I_M, \ r^{i'}_j \neq +1 \right\},$$

$$\widetilde{J}^+(r,s) = I^0(s) \cap \left\{ j \in I_{N-1} \,\middle|\, v_j < 1 \text{ and } \exists i' \in I_M, \ r^{i'}_j \neq -1 \right\}.$$

These sets are needed to formulate the system of equalities and inequalities mentioned above in such a way that no equality or inequality is redundant. For every consumer $i \in I_M$, let a utility function $u^i \in C^2(X^i, \mathbb{R})$ that has no critical point and that is pseudo-concave be given such that the preference relation $\preceq^i$ is represented by u^i. Such a utility function exists by Lemma 11.4.2.

Let $\nu \in \mathbb{N}$, $\omega \in \Omega(\nu)$, and some $(r, s) \in \mathcal{T}$ be given. In Theorem 11.4.3 it is shown that $q \in C_\omega(r, s)$ if and only if $q \in \mathbb{R}^{N-1}$ and there exists $(x, \lambda, \mu) \in \mathbb{R}^{MN}_{++} \times \mathbb{R}^M \times \mathbb{R}$ such that (x, λ, q, μ) satisfies

$$\partial_{x^i_j} u^i(x^i) - \lambda^i p_j = 0, \ \forall (i, j) \in I^0(r), \tag{11.2}$$

$$\partial_{x^i_N} u^i(x^i) - \lambda^i = 0, \ \forall i \in I_M, \tag{11.3}$$

$$p \cdot (x^i - \omega^i) = 0, \ \forall i \in I_M, \tag{11.4}$$

$$x^i_j - \omega^i_j - \widehat{l}^{\nu,i}_j(q) = 0, \ \forall (i, j) \in I^-(r), \tag{11.5}$$

$$-x^i_j + \omega^i_j + \widehat{L}^{\nu,i}_j(q) = 0, \ \forall (i, j) \in I^+(r), \tag{11.6}$$

$$\textstyle\sum_{i \in I_M} (x^i_j - \omega^i_j) = 0, \ \forall j \in I^0(s), \tag{11.7}$$

$$q_j - \mu v_j = 0, \ \forall j \in I^-(s), \tag{11.8}$$

$$(1 - q_j) - \mu(1 - v_j) = 0, \ \forall j \in I^+(s), \tag{11.9}$$

$$-\partial_{x^i_j} u^i(x^i) + \lambda^i p_j \geq 0, \ \forall (i, j) \in I^-(r), \tag{11.10}$$

$$\partial_{x^i_j} u^i(x^i) - \lambda^i p_j \geq 0, \ \forall (i, j) \in I^+(r), \tag{11.11}$$

$$x^i_j - \omega^i_j - \widehat{l}^{\nu,i}_j(q) \geq 0, \ \forall (i, j) \in I^0(r), \tag{11.12}$$

$$-x^i_j + \omega^i_j + \widehat{L}^{\nu,i}_j(q) \geq 0, \ \forall (i, j) \in I^0(r), \tag{11.13}$$

$$\textstyle\sum_{i \in I_M} (-x^i_j + \omega^i_j) \geq 0, \ \forall j \in J^-(r, s), \tag{11.14}$$

$$\textstyle\sum_{i \in I_M} (x^i_j - \omega^i_j) \geq 0, \ \forall j \in J^+(r, s), \tag{11.15}$$

$$q_j - \mu v_j \geq 0, \ \forall j \in \widetilde{J}^-(r, s), \tag{11.16}$$

$$(1 - q_j) - \mu(1 - v_j) \geq 0, \ \forall j \in \widetilde{J}^+(r, s), \tag{11.17}$$

$$1 - \mu \geq 0. \tag{11.18}$$

Notice that, for every $\nu \in \mathbb{N}$, $\widehat{l}^\nu$ and $\widehat{L}^\nu$ are also assumed to be defined on $\mathbb{R}^{N-1} \setminus Q^{N-1}$. Any twice continuously differentiable extension of $\widehat{l}^\nu$ and $\widehat{L}^\nu$ defined on $\mathbb{R}^{N-1}$ such that, for every $\overline{q} \in \mathbb{R}^{N-1} \setminus Q^{N-1}$, $\widehat{l}^\nu(\overline{q}) \leq \widehat{L}^\nu(\overline{q})$, $\sum_{i \in I_M} \partial_{q_j} \widehat{l}^{\nu,i}_j(\overline{q}) < 0$, and $\sum_{i \in I_M} \partial_{q_j} \widehat{L}^{\nu,i}_j(\overline{q}) < 0$, suffices. Clearly, such an extension exists if $(\widehat{l}, \widehat{L})$ satisfies Assumption A9.

In the following, let $MN + M + N - 1$ be denoted by N^1, being the number of variables in (x, λ, q, μ) minus one, and let $2MN + M + N$ be denoted by N^2, being the total number of variables in $(x, \lambda, \omega, q, \mu)$. The function $\widehat{\mu} : Q^{N-1} \to$

$[0,1]$ is defined by associating with every $q \in Q^{N-1}$ the element

$$\widehat{\mu}(q) = \min\left(\left\{\min(\{\tfrac{q_j}{v_j} \mid j \in I_{N-1} \text{ with } v_j > 0\}), \min(\{\tfrac{1-q_j}{1-v_j} \mid j \in I_{N-1} \text{ with } v_j < 1\})\right\}\right).$$

The function $\widehat{f} : Q^{N-1} \times \Omega \to \mathbb{R}^{MN} \times \mathbb{R}^{M} \times \mathbb{R}^{N-1} \times \mathbb{R}$ is defined by

$$\widehat{f}(q,\omega) = \left(\left(\widehat{d}^i(q,\omega)\right)_{i \in I_M}, \left(\partial_{x^i_N} u^i(\widehat{d}^i(q,\omega))\right)_{i \in I_M}, q, \widehat{\mu}(q)\right), \forall q \in Q^{N-1}, \forall \omega \in \Omega.$$

Theorem 11.4.3
Let $(X^i, \preceq^i)_{i \in I_M}, P_{(p,p)}, (\widehat{l}, \widehat{L})$ satisfy Assumptions A6-A9 and let $v \in Q^{N-1}$ be the initial state. Let $\nu \in \mathbb{N}$, $\omega \in \Omega(\nu)$, and some $(r,s) \in T$ be given. Then $\overline{q} \in C_\omega(r,s)$ and $(\overline{x}, \overline{\lambda}, \overline{q}, \overline{\mu}) = \widehat{f}(\overline{q}, \omega)$ if and only if $(\overline{x}, \overline{\lambda}, \overline{q}, \overline{\mu}) \in \mathbb{R}^{MN}_{++} \times \mathbb{R}^{M} \times \mathbb{R}^{N-1} \times \mathbb{R}$ and $(\overline{x}, \overline{\lambda}, \overline{q}, \overline{\mu})$ satisfies (11.2)-(11.18).

Proof
If $\overline{q} \in C_\omega(r,s)$ and $(\overline{x}, \overline{\lambda}, \overline{q}, \overline{\mu}) = \widehat{f}(\overline{q}, \omega)$, then, using Theorem 2.9.7, it is clear that $(\overline{x}, \overline{\lambda}, \overline{q}, \overline{\mu}) \in \mathbb{R}^{MN}_{++} \times \mathbb{R}^{M} \times \mathbb{R}^{N-1} \times \mathbb{R}$ satisfies (11.2)-(11.18). To show the converse, let some $(\overline{x}, \overline{\lambda}, \overline{q}, \overline{\mu}) \in \mathbb{R}^{MN}_{++} \times \mathbb{R}^{M} \times \mathbb{R}^{N-1} \times \mathbb{R}$ satisfying (11.2)-(11.18) be given. First, it is shown that, for every $j \in I_{N-1}$, $0 \leq \overline{q}_j \leq 1$, and $0 \leq \overline{\mu} \leq 1$. By (11.18) it holds that $\overline{\mu} \leq 1$. From (11.8) and (11.9) it follows that

$$\overline{q}_j = \overline{\mu} v_j \leq 1, \qquad \forall j \in I^-(s), \tag{11.19}$$

$$\overline{q}_j = 1 - \overline{\mu}(1 - v_j) \geq 1 - 1 + v_j \geq 0, \ \forall j \in I^+(s). \tag{11.20}$$

Using $\widehat{l}^{\nu,i}_j(\overline{q}) \leq \widehat{L}^{\nu,i}_j(\overline{q})$, $\forall i \in I_M$, $\forall j \in I_{N-1}$, (11.5), (11.6), and (11.12), it is obtained that $\sum_{i \in I_M} \widehat{l}^{\nu,i}_j(\overline{q}) \leq \sum_{i \in I_M}(\overline{x}^i_j - \omega^i_j)$, $\forall j \in I_{N-1}$. For every $j \in I^0(s) \cup J^-(r,s)$ it follows from (11.7) and (11.14) that $\sum_{i \in I_M}(\overline{x}^i_j - \omega^i_j) \leq 0$. Therefore,

$$\overline{q}_j \geq 0, \ \forall j \in I^0(s) \cup J^-(r,s). \tag{11.21}$$

Similarly, using (11.5), (11.6), (11.7), (11.13), and (11.15), it follows that

$$\overline{q}_j \leq 1, \ \forall j \in I^0(s) \cup J^+(r,s). \tag{11.22}$$

Now three cases have to be considered.
1. $j(r,s) = 0$. Then $J^-(r,s) = I^-(s)$ and $J^+(r,s) = I^+(s)$. So, (11.19)-(11.22) yields $0 \leq \overline{q}_j \leq 1$, $\forall j \in I_{N-1}$. For every $j \in I^+(s)$, $v_j < 1$, so if $I^+(s) \neq \emptyset$, then (11.9) implies $\overline{\mu} \geq 0$. If $I^+(s) = \emptyset$, then $I^-(s) \neq \emptyset$, and now (11.8) implies $\overline{\mu} \geq 0$. This together with (11.18) shows that $0 \leq \overline{\mu} \leq 1$.
2. $j(r,s) \in I^-(s)$. Then (11.21) implies $\overline{q}_{j(r,s)} \geq 0$. Since $j(r,s) \in I^-(s)$ implies $v_{j(r,s)} > 0$, (11.8) yields $\overline{\mu} \geq 0$. Now it follows from (11.8) that $\overline{q}_j \geq 0$,

$\forall j \in I^-(s)$, and from (11.9) that $\overline{q}_j \leq 1$, $\forall j \in I^+(s)$. So, (11.19)-(11.22) yields $0 \leq \overline{q}_j \leq 1$, $\forall j \in I_{N-1}$.

3. $j(r,s) \in I^+(s)$. This case is similar to Case 2.

For every $i \in I_M$, since u^i is pseudo-concave, it follows from Theorem 2.9.6, equations (11.2)-(11.6), inequalities (11.10)-(11.13), and the absence of constraints with respect to the market for commodity N, that $\overline{x}^i = \widehat{d}^i(\overline{q},\omega)$, $\forall i \in I_M$. Hence, (11.7) implies $\widehat{z}_j(\overline{q},\omega) = 0$, $\forall j \in I^0(s)$. Consider some $j' \in I^-(s)$. Either there exists $i' \in I_M$ such that $r^{i'}_{j'} \neq -1$, and by (11.14), $\widehat{z}_{j'}(\overline{q},\omega) \leq 0$, or $r^i_{j'} = -1$, $\forall i \in I_M$, and therefore by (11.5), $\widehat{z}_{j'}(\overline{q},\omega) = \sum_{i \in I_M}(\overline{x}^i_{j'} - \omega^i_{j'}) = \sum_{i \in I_M} \widehat{l}^{\nu,i}_{j'}(\overline{q}) \leq 0$. Similarly, it can be shown that $\widehat{z}_j(\overline{q},\omega) \geq 0$, $\forall j \in I^+(s)$. Hence, $\overline{q} \in B_\omega(s)$.

For every $j \in I^0(s)$ with $v_j = 0$ it holds that $\overline{\mu}v_j \leq \overline{q}_j$, and for every $j \in I^0(s)$ with $v_j = 1$ it holds that $\overline{q}_j \leq 1 - \overline{\mu} + \overline{\mu}v_j$. For every $j \in I^0(s)$ such that $(i,j) \in I^+(r)$, $\forall i \in I_M$, (11.6) and (11.7) implies $\sum_{i \in I_M} \widehat{L}^{\nu,i}_j(\overline{q}) = 0$, and therefore $\overline{q}_j = 1$. Hence, $\overline{\mu}v_j \leq \overline{q}_j$. For every $j \in I^0(s)$ such that $(i,j) \in I^-(r)$, $\forall i \in I_M$, (11.5) and (11.7) implies $\sum_{i \in I_M} \widehat{l}^{\nu,i}_j(\overline{q}) = 0$, therefore $\overline{q}_j = 0$, and hence $\overline{q}_j \leq 1 - \overline{\mu} + \overline{\mu}v_j$. Therefore, (11.8), (11.9), (11.16), and (11.17), together with $\overline{q} \in B_\omega(s)$, implies $\overline{q} \in C_\omega(s)$. Now (11.2), (11.5), and (11.6) implies, for every $(i,j) \in I^0(r)$, neither $\widehat{l}^i_j(\overline{q},\omega)$ nor $\widehat{L}^i_j(\overline{q},\omega)$ is binding, for every $(i,j) \in I^-(r)$, $\widehat{d}^i_j(\overline{q},\omega) - \omega^i_j = \widehat{l}^i_j(\overline{q},\omega)$, and, for every $(i,j) \in I^+(r)$, $\widehat{d}^i_j(\overline{q},\omega) - \omega^i_j = \widehat{L}^i_j(\overline{q},\omega)$. Hence, $\overline{q} \in C_\omega(r,s)$. Using the above and (11.3), it follows that $(\overline{x},\overline{\lambda},\overline{q},\overline{\mu}) = \widehat{f}(\overline{q},\omega)$. Q.E.D.

For every $\nu \in \mathbb{N}$, let $\widetilde{\Omega}(\nu) \subset \Omega$ be an open set containing the closure of $\Omega(\nu)$ in Ω. For every $\nu \in \mathbb{N}$, for every $(r,s) \in T$, the function $\psi^{\nu,r,s} : \mathbb{R}^{MN}_{++} \times \mathbb{R}^M \times \widetilde{\Omega}(\nu) \times \mathbb{R}^{N-1} \times \mathbb{R} \to \mathbb{R}^{N^1}$ is defined such that, for every $(x,\lambda,\omega,q,\mu) \in \mathbb{R}^{MN}_{++} \times \mathbb{R}^M \times \widetilde{\Omega}(\nu) \times \mathbb{R}^{N-1} \times \mathbb{R}$, $\psi^{\nu,r,s}(x,\lambda,\omega,q,\mu)$ is the left-hand side of (11.2)-(11.9). For every $\nu \in \mathbb{N}$, for every $(r,s) \in T$, for every $\omega \in \widetilde{\Omega}(\nu)$, the function $\psi^{\nu,r,s,\omega} : \mathbb{R}^{MN}_{++} \times \mathbb{R}^M \times \mathbb{R}^{N-1} \times \mathbb{R} \to \mathbb{R}^{N^1}$ is defined by $\psi^{\nu,r,s,\omega}(x,\lambda,q,\mu) = \psi^{\nu,r,s}(x,\lambda,\omega,q,\mu)$, $\forall (x,\lambda,q,\mu) \in \mathbb{R}^{MN}_{++} \times \mathbb{R}^M \times \mathbb{R}^{N-1} \times \mathbb{R}$.

Let $\nu \in \mathbb{N}$ and some $(r,s) \in T$ be given. The $N^1 \times N^2$ matrix of partial derivatives of $\psi^{\nu,r,s}$ evaluated at a point $\overline{\xi} = (\overline{x},\overline{\lambda},\overline{\omega},\overline{q},\overline{\mu}) \in \mathbb{R}^{MN}_{++} \times \mathbb{R}^M \times \widetilde{\Omega}(\nu) \times \mathbb{R}^{N-1} \times \mathbb{R}$ satisfying $\psi^{\nu,r,s}(\overline{\xi}) = 0^{N^1}$ is denoted by $\overline{M}$ and is given in Table 11.4.1. For every $k \in \mathbb{N}$, 0^k and $e^k(j)$, $\forall j \in I_k$, denote row vectors in this table.

	$\partial_x \psi^{\nu,r,s}$	$\partial_\lambda \psi^{\nu,r,s}$	$\partial_\omega \psi^{\nu,r,s}$	$\partial_q \psi^{\nu,r,s}$	$\partial_\mu \psi^{\nu,r,s}$	
1	$0^{(i-1)N}\partial^2_{x^i x^i_j} u^i(\overline{x}^i)\,0^{(M-i)N}$	$-p_j e^M(i)$	0^{MN}	0^{N-1}	0	$(i,j)\in I^0(r)$
2	$0^{(i-1)N}\partial^2_{x^i x^i_N} u^i(\overline{x}^i)\,0^{(M-i)N}$	$-e^M(i)$	0^{MN}	0^{N-1}	0	$i \in I_M$
3	$0^{(i-1)N}\ p^\top\ 0^{(M-i)N}$	0^M	$0^{(i-1)N}\ -p^\top\ 0^{(M-i)N}$	0^{N-1}	0	$i \in I_M$
4	$e^{MN}((i-1)N+j)$	0^M	$-e^{MN}((i-1)N+j)$	$-\partial_{q_j}\widehat{l}^{\nu,i}_j(\overline{q})e^{N-1}(j)$	0	$(i,j)\in I^-(r)$
5	$-e^{MN}((i-1)N+j)$	0^M	$e^{MN}((i-1)N+j)$	$\partial_{q_j}\widehat{L}^{\nu,i}_j(\overline{q})e^{N-1}(j)$	0	$(i,j)\in I^+(r)$
6	$e^N(j),\ldots,e^N(j)$	0^M	$-e^N(j),\ldots,-e^N(j)$	0^{N-1}	0	$j \in I^0(s)$
7	0^{MN}	0^M	0^{MN}	$e^{N-1}(j)$	$-v_j$	$j \in I^-(s)$
8	0^{MN}	0^M	0^{MN}	$-e^{N-1}(j)$	$-(1-v_j)$	$j \in I^+(s)$
	MN	M	MN	$N-1$	1	

Table 11.4.1. The matrix $\overline{M}$.

Recall from Section 2.2 that the characteristic function of a set S is denoted by χ_S, so $\chi_S(s) = 1$ if $s \in S$, and $\chi_S(s) = 0$ if $s \notin S$.

Lemma 11.4.4
Let $(X^i, \preceq^i)_{i\in I_M}, P_{(p,p)}, (\widehat{l}, \widehat{L})$ satisfy Assumptions A6-A9 and let $v \in Q^{N-1}$ be the initial state. Let $\nu \in \mathbb{N}$ and some $(r,s) \in \mathcal{T}$ be given. Then there exists a subset $\overline{\Omega}$ of $\widetilde{\Omega}(\nu)$ such that $\widetilde{\Omega}(\nu) \setminus \overline{\Omega}$ has Lebesgue measure zero and, for every $\omega \in \overline{\Omega}$, $\psi^{\nu,r,s,\omega} \pitchfork \{0^{N^1}\}$ and $\psi^{\nu,r,s,\omega^{-1}}(\{0^{N^1}\})$ is a 1-dimensional C^2 manifold.
Proof
First, it is shown that $\psi^{\nu,r,s} \pitchfork \{0^{N^1}\}$. Let $\overline{\xi} \in \mathbb{R}^{MN}_{++} \times \mathbb{R}^M \times \widetilde{\Omega}(\nu) \times \mathbb{R}^{N-1} \times \mathbb{R}$ be such that $\psi^{\nu,r,s}(\overline{\xi}) = 0^{N^1}$. The matrix of partial derivatives of $\psi^{\nu,r,s}$ evaluated at $\overline{\xi}$, $\overline{M}$, is given in Table 11.4.1. It has to be shown that the rows of $\overline{M}$ are independent. This is done by proving that $y^\top \overline{M} = 0^{N^{2\top}}$ implies $y = 0^{N^1}$. Hence, let $y \in \mathbb{R}^{N^1}$ satisfy $y^\top \overline{M} = 0^{N^{2\top}}$. The matrix $\overline{M}$ is subdivided into eight parts in Table 11.4.1, and the components of y are denoted accordingly by $y_{(1,i,j)}$, $\forall (i,j) \in I^0(r)$, $y_{(2,i)}$, $\forall i \in I_M$, and so on. For every $i \in I_M$ it holds that $0 = y^\top \partial_{\omega^i_N} \psi^{\nu,r,s}(\overline{\xi}) = -y_{(3,i)}$. Therefore,

$$y_{(3,i)} = 0, \ \forall i \in I_M. \tag{11.23}$$

Using (11.23) it holds for every $(i,j) \in I_M \times I_{N-1}$ that

$$0 = y^\top \partial_{\omega^i_j} \psi^{\nu,r,s}(\overline{\xi}) = -y_{(4,i,j)}\chi_{I^-(r)}((i,j)) + y_{(5,i,j)}\chi_{I^+(r)}((i,j)) - y_{(6,j)}\chi_{I^0(s)}(j). \tag{11.24}$$

Consider some $(i',j') \in I^-(r)$. Obviously, $(i',j') \notin I^+(r)$. There are three possibilities. Either $j' \notin I^0(s)$, implying $y_{(4,i',j')} = 0$. Or $j' \in I^0(s)$ and there exists $i'' \in I_M$ such that $(i'', j') \notin I^-(r)$, implying by (11.24) with $(i,j) = (i'', j')$ that $y_{(6,j')} = 0$ and therefore, using (11.24) with $(i,j) = (i', j')$, that $y_{(4,i',j')} = 0$. Finally, consider the case with $(i, j') \in I^-(r)$, $\forall i \in I_M$, and $j' \in I^0(s)$. From (11.24) it follows that $y_{(6,j')} = -y_{(4,i,j')}$, $\forall i \in I_M$. Since $j' \in I^0(s)$ and therefore $j' \notin I^-(s) \cup I^+(s)$, it holds that $0 = y^\top \partial_{q_{j'}} \psi^{\nu,r,s}(\overline{\xi}) = -\sum_{i \in I_M} y_{(4,i,j')} \partial_{q_{j'}} \widehat{l}_{j'}^{\nu,i}(\overline{q}) = y_{(6,j')} \sum_{i \in I_M} \partial_{q_{j'}} \widehat{l}_{j'}^{\nu,i}(\overline{q})$. Since $\sum_{i \in I_M} \partial_{q_{j'}} \widehat{l}_{j'}^{\nu,i}(\overline{q}) < 0$, this implies $y_{(6,j')} = 0$. Hence, $y_{(4,i,j')} = 0$, $\forall i \in I_M$. Now it has been shown that

$$y_{(4,i,j)} = 0, \;\; \forall (i,j) \in I^-(r). \tag{11.25}$$

Similarly, it can be shown that

$$y_{(5,i,j)} = 0, \;\; \forall (i,j) \in I^+(r). \tag{11.26}$$

Then it follows from (11.24) that

$$y_{(6,j)} = 0, \;\; \forall j \in I^0(s). \tag{11.27}$$

By (11.25) and (11.26), it holds for every $j \in I_{N-1}$ that

$$0 = y^\top \partial_{q_j} \psi^{\nu,r,s}(\overline{\xi}) = y_{(7,j)} \chi_{I^-(s)}(j) - y_{(8,j)} \chi_{I^+(s)}(j).$$

Since $I^-(s) \cap I^+(s) = \emptyset$, it follows that

$$y_{(7,j)} = 0, \;\; \forall j \in I^-(s), \tag{11.28}$$

$$y_{(8,j)} = 0, \;\; \forall j \in I^+(s). \tag{11.29}$$

Let some consumer $i' \in I_M$ be given. Using the non-zero Gaussian curvature of $\preceq^{i'}$ and Theorem 3.6.5, it follows that

$$\det\left(\begin{bmatrix} \partial^2_{x^{i'} x^{i'}} u^{i'}(\overline{x}^{i'}) & \partial_{x^{i'}} u^{i'}(\overline{x}^{i'})^\top \\ \partial_{x^{i'}} u^{i'}(\overline{x}^{i'}) & 0 \end{bmatrix}\right) \neq 0.$$

Hence, the rows of $[\partial^2_{x^{i'} x^{i'}} u^{i'}(\overline{x}^{i'}) \;\; \partial_{x^{i'}} u^{i'}(\overline{x}^{i'})^\top]$ corresponding to the indices $j \in I_{N-1}$ satisfying $(i', j) \in I^0(r)$ and the index N, are independent. From this and the fact that $\partial_{x^{i'}_j} u^{i'}(\overline{x}^{i'}) = \overline{\lambda}^{i'} p_j$, $\forall j \in I_{N-1}$ with $(i', j) \in I^0(r)$ and for $j = N$, it follows that the first $i^0(r) + M$ rows of $\overline{M}$ are independent. From (11.23), (11.25), (11.26), (11.27), (11.28), and (11.29) it follows that

$$0^{N^{2}\top} = y^\top \overline{M} = \sum_{(i,j) \in I^0(r)} y_{(1,i,j)} \overline{M}_{((1,i,j),\cdot)} + \sum_{i \in I_M} y_{(2,i)} \overline{M}_{((2,i),\cdot)}.$$

So, $y_{(1,i,j)} = 0$, $\forall (i,j) \in I^0(r)$, and $y_{(2,i)} = 0$, $\forall i \in I_M$. Now it has been shown that $y = 0^{N^1}$.

Since $\overline{M}$ has rank N^1, it follows that $\psi^{\nu,r,s}$ intersects $\{0^{N^1}\}$ transversally, $\psi^{\nu,r,s} \pitchfork \{0^{N^1}\}$. Clearly, $\psi^{\nu,r,s} \in C^2(\mathbb{R}^{MN}_{++} \times \mathbb{R}^M \times \widetilde{\Omega}(\nu) \times \mathbb{R}^{N-1} \times \mathbb{R}, \mathbb{R}^{N^1})$. Moreover, $\mathbb{R}^{MN}_{++} \times \mathbb{R}^M \times \mathbb{R}^{N-1} \times \mathbb{R}$ is an (N^1+1)-dimensional C^∞ manifold, $\widetilde{\Omega}(\nu)$ is an MN-dimensional C^∞ manifold, $\mathbb{R}^{N^1}$ is an N^1-dimensional C^∞ manifold, and $\{0^{N^1}\}$ is a 0-dimensional C^∞ manifold. Let the set $\overline{\Omega}$ be defined by $\overline{\Omega} = \{\omega \in \widetilde{\Omega}(\nu) \mid \psi^{\nu,r,s,\omega} \pitchfork \{0^{N^1}\}\}$. Now it follows from the transversality theorem, Theorem 2.10.18, that the set $\widetilde{\Omega}(\nu) \setminus \overline{\Omega}$ has Lebesgue measure zero in $\widetilde{\Omega}(\nu)$. Since $\widetilde{\Omega}(\nu)$ is an MN-dimensional C^∞ manifold that is a subset of $\mathbb{R}^{MN}$, it follows that the set $\widetilde{\Omega}(\nu)\setminus\overline{\Omega}$ has Lebesgue measure zero, see the remark below Theorem 2.10.17. For every $\omega \in \overline{\Omega}$, $\psi^{\nu,r,s,\omega}$ is a function from an (N^1+1)-dimensional C^∞ manifold into an N^1-dimensional C^∞ manifold, $\psi^{\nu,r,s,\omega} \in C^2(\mathbb{R}^{MN}_{++} \times \mathbb{R}^M \times \mathbb{R}^{N-1} \times \mathbb{R}, \mathbb{R}^{N^1})$, and $\psi^{\nu,r,s,\omega} \pitchfork \{0^{N^1}\}$, so ${\psi^{\nu,r,s,\omega}}^{-1}(\{0^{N^1}\})$ is a 1-dimensional C^2 manifold by Theorem 2.10.16. Q.E.D.

Let $\nu \in \mathbb{N}$ and some $(r,s) \in \mathcal{T}$ be given. Let K be the set of indices corresponding to one of the inequalities in (11.10)-(11.18). More precisely, K is defined by

$$
\begin{aligned}
K = {} & I^-(r) \cup I^+(r) \\
& \cup \left\{(i,j,-) \,\middle|\, (i,j) \in I^0(r) \text{ and } \nexists i' \in I_M,\ (i',j) \in I^+(r)\right\} \\
& \cup \left\{(i,j,+) \,\middle|\, (i,j) \in I^0(r) \text{ and } \nexists i' \in I_M,\ (i',j) \in I^-(r)\right\} \\
& \cup J^-(r,s) \cup J^+(r,s) \\
& \cup \left\{(j,-) \,\middle|\, j \in \tilde{J}^-(r,s)\right\} \cup \left\{(j,+) \,\middle|\, j \in \tilde{J}^+(r,s)\right\} \\
& \cup \{0\}.
\end{aligned}
$$

Consider some index $k \in K$. The index $k = (i,j) \in I^-(r)$ corresponds to inequality (i,j) in (11.10), $k = (i,j) \in I^+(r)$ corresponds to inequality (i,j) in (11.11), $k = (i,j,-)$ corresponds to inequality (i,j) in (11.12), $k = (i,j,+)$ corresponds to inequality (i,j) in (11.13), $k \in J^-(r,s)$ corresponds to inequality k in (11.14), $k \in J^+(r,s)$ corresponds to inequality k in (11.15), $k = (j,-)$ corresponds to inequality j in (11.16), $k = (j,+)$ corresponds to inequality j in (11.17), and $k = 0$ corresponds to inequality (11.18). Notice that not every $(i,j) \in I^0(r)$ yields indices $(i,j,-)$ and $(i,j,+)$. It is sufficient to consider only the indices belonging to K.

For every $\nu \in \mathbb{N}$, for every $(r,s) \in \mathcal{T}$, for every $k \in K$, the function $\psi_k^{\nu,r,s} : \mathbb{R}^{MN}_{++} \times \mathbb{R}^M \times \widetilde{\Omega}(\nu) \times \mathbb{R}^{N-1} \times \mathbb{R} \to \mathbb{R}^{N^1+1}$ is defined such that, for every $(x,\lambda,\omega,q,\mu) \in \mathbb{R}^{MN}_{++} \times \mathbb{R}^M \times \widetilde{\Omega}(\nu) \times \mathbb{R}^{N-1} \times \mathbb{R}$, $\psi_k^{\nu,r,s}(x,\lambda,\omega,q,\mu)$ is the left-hand side of (11.2)-(11.9) and the inequality corresponding to k. For every $\nu \in \mathbb{N}$, for every $(r,s) \in \mathcal{T}$, for every $k \in K$, for every $\omega \in \widetilde{\Omega}(\nu)$, the function $\psi_k^{\nu,r,s,\omega}$ is defined by $\psi_k^{\nu,r,s,\omega}(x,\lambda,q,\mu) = \psi_k^{\nu,r,s}(x,\lambda,\omega,q,\mu)$.

Lemma 11.4.5
Let $(X^i, \preceq^i)_{i \in I_M}, P_{(p,p)}, (\widehat{l}, \widehat{L})$ satisfy Assumptions A6-A9 and let $v \in Q^{N-1}$ be the initial state. Let $\nu \in \mathbb{N}$, some $(r,s) \in \mathcal{T}$, and some $k \in K$ be given. Then there exists a subset $\overline{\Omega}$ of $\widetilde{\Omega}(\nu)$ such that $\widetilde{\Omega}(\nu) \setminus \overline{\Omega}$ has Lebesgue measure zero and, for every $\omega \in \overline{\Omega}$, $\psi_k^{\nu,r,s,\omega} \pitchfork \{0^{N^1+1}\}$ and $\psi_k^{\nu,r,s,\omega^{-1}}(\{0^{N^1+1}\})$ is a 0-dimensional manifold.

Proof
First, it is shown that $\psi_k^{\nu,r,s} \pitchfork \{0^{N^1+1}\}$. Let $\overline{\xi} = (\overline{x}, \overline{\lambda}, \overline{\omega}, \overline{q}, \overline{\mu}) \in \mathbb{R}^{MN}_{++} \times \mathbb{R}^M \times \widetilde{\Omega}(\nu) \times \mathbb{R}^{N-1} \times \mathbb{R}$ be such that $\psi_k^{\nu,r,s}(\overline{\xi}) = 0^{N^1+1}$. It is proved that the rows of the $(N^1+1) \times N^2$ matrix of partial derivatives of $\psi_k^{\nu,r,s}$ at $\overline{\xi}$, denoted by $\overline{M}^k$, are independent. Let $y \in \mathbb{R}^{N^1+1}$ satisfy $y^\top \overline{M}^k = 0^{N^2\top}$. It is shown that $y = 0^{N^1+1}$. Let y_k denote the last component of y. In the following it is shown that $y_k = 0$. Then it follows from the proof of Lemma 11.4.4 that $y = 0^{N^1+1}$. It follows as in the proof of Lemma 11.4.4 that $y_{(3,i)} = 0$, $\forall i \in I_M$. Now five different cases are considered.
1. $k \in I^-(r) \cup I^+(r)$. This case goes along the same lines as the proof of Lemma 11.4.4.
2. $\exists (i', j') \in I^0(r)$, $k = (i', j', -)$. Then $r^i_{j'} \in \{-1, 0\}$, $\forall i \in I_M$. Therefore,

$$0 = y^\top \partial_{\omega^{i'}_{j'}} \psi_k^{\nu,r,s}(\overline{\xi}) = -y_k - y_{(6,j')} \chi_{I^0(s)}(j'), \tag{11.30}$$

$$0 = y^\top \partial_{\omega^{i}_{j'}} \psi_k^{\nu,r,s}(\overline{\xi}) = -y_{(4,i,j')} \chi_{I^-(r)}((i,j')) - y_{(6,j')} \chi_{I^0(s)}(j'), \ \forall i \in I_M \backslash \{i'\}. \tag{11.31}$$

There are three possibilities. Either $j' \notin I^0(s)$, implying $y_k = 0$ by (11.30). Or $j' \in I^0(s)$ and there exists $i'' \in I_M \setminus \{i'\}$ such that $(i'', j') \notin I^-(r)$, implying $y_{(6,j')} = 0$ by (11.31), and hence $y_k = 0$ by (11.30). Or $j' \in I^0(s)$ and $(i, j') \in I^-(r)$, $\forall i \in I_M \setminus \{i'\}$. Then

$$0 = y^\top \partial_{q_{j'}} \psi_k^{\nu,r,s}(\overline{\xi}) = -\sum_{i \in I_M \backslash \{i'\}} y_{(4,i,j')} \partial_{q_{j'}} \widehat{l}^{\nu,i}_{j'}(\overline{q}) - y_k \partial_{q_{j'}} \widehat{l}^{\nu,i'}_{j'}(\overline{q}) \tag{11.32}$$

$$= -y_k \sum_{i \in I_M} \partial_{q_{j'}} \widehat{l}^{\nu,i}_{j'}(\overline{q}), \tag{11.33}$$

where the last equality follows from (11.30) and (11.31), implying that $y_k = 0$. The case where $k = (i', j', +)$ for some $(i', j') \in I^0(r)$ goes along the same lines.

3. $k \in J^-(r,s)$. It follows that $k \in I^-(s)$ and therefore $v_k > 0$. Clearly,

$$0 = y^\top \partial_{\omega_k^i} \psi_k^{\nu,r,s}(\bar{\xi}) = -y_{(4,i,k)}\chi_{I^-(r)}((i,k)) + y_{(5,i,k)}\chi_{I^+(r)}((i,k)) + y_k, \; \forall i \in I_M. \tag{11.34}$$

Now, $r_k^i \in \{-1,0\}$, $\forall i \in I_M$, or $r_k^i \in \{0,+1\}$, $\forall i \in I_M$. In the first case, either there exists $i' \in I_M$ such that $r_k^{i'} = 0$ and it follows from (11.34) for $i = i'$ that $y_k = 0$, or $r_k^i = -1$, $\forall i \in I_M$, and (11.34) yields $y_k = y_{(4,i,k)}$, $\forall i \in I_M$. It follows as in the proof of Lemma 11.4.4 that $y_{(7,j)} = 0$, $\forall j \in I^-(s) \setminus \{k\}$, and $y_{(8,j)} = 0$, $\forall j \in I^+(s)$. Hence, $0 = y^\top \partial_\mu \psi_k^{\nu,r,s}(\bar{\xi}) = -v_k y_{(7,k)}$, implying that $y_{(7,k)} = 0$. So,

$$0 = y^\top \partial_{q_k} \psi_k^{\nu,r,s}(\bar{\xi}) = -\sum_{i \in I_M} y_{(4,i,k)} \partial_{q_k} \hat{l}_k^{\nu,i}(\bar{q}) + y_{(7,k)} = -y_k \sum_{i \in I_M} \partial_{q_k} \hat{l}_k^{\nu,i}(\bar{q}),$$

and it holds that $y_k = 0$. Now consider the case with $r_k^i \in \{0,+1\}$, $\forall i \in I_M$. Since $(r,s) \in \mathcal{T}$ and $s_k = -1$, there exists $i' \in I_M$ such that $r_k^{i'} \neq +1$. From (11.34) for $i = i'$ it follows that $y_k = 0$. The case where $k \in J^+(r,s)$ goes along the same lines.

4. $\exists j' \in \tilde{J}^-(r,s)$, $k = (j',-)$. Either there exists $i' \in I_M$ such that $(i',j') \notin I^-(r)$, implying as in the proof of Lemma 11.4.4 that $y_{(4,i,j')} = 0$, $\forall i \in I_M$ such that $(i,j') \in I^-(r)$, and $y_{(5,i,j')} = 0$, $\forall i \in I_M$ such that $(i,j') \in I^+(r)$. Then $0 = y^\top \partial_{q_{j'}} \psi_k^{\nu,r,s}(\bar{\xi}) = y_k$. Or $(i,j') \in I^-(r)$, $\forall i \in I_M$, implying $v_{j'} = 0$ since $j' \in I^0(s)$ and $(r,s) \in \mathcal{T}$, a contradiction with $j' \in \tilde{J}^-(r,s)$. The case where $k = (j',+)$ for some $j' \in \tilde{J}^+(r,s)$ goes along the same lines.

5. $k = 0$. In Lemma 11.4.4 it has been shown that $y_{(7,j)} = 0$, $\forall j \in I^-(s)$, and $y_{(8,j)} = 0$, $\forall j \in I^+(s)$, without using the partial derivatives with respect to μ. Hence, this proof can be used again and it follows that $0 = y^\top \partial_\mu \psi_k^{\nu,r,s}(\bar{\xi}) = -y_k$.

Now it has been shown that $\psi_k^{\nu,r,s} \pitchfork \{0^{N^1+1}\}$. Let the set $\bar{\Omega}$ be defined by $\bar{\Omega} = \{\omega \in \tilde{\Omega}(\nu) \mid \psi_k^{\nu,r,s,\omega} \pitchfork \{0^{N^1+1}\}\}$. From the transversality theorem, Theorem 2.10.18, it follows that the set $\tilde{\Omega}(\nu) \setminus \bar{\Omega}$ has Lebesgue measure zero. For every $\omega \in \bar{\Omega}$, $\psi_k^{\nu,r,s,\omega}$ is a function from an (N^1+1)-dimensional C^∞ manifold into an (N^1+1)-dimensional C^∞ manifold, $\psi_k^{\nu,r,s,\omega} \in C^2(\mathbb{R}_{++}^{MN} \times \mathbb{R}^M \times \mathbb{R}^{N-1} \times \mathbb{R}, \mathbb{R}^{N^1+1})$, and $\psi_k^{\nu,r,s,\omega} \pitchfork \{0^{N^1+1}\}$, so $\psi_k^{\nu,r,s,\omega^{-1}}(\{0^{N^1+1}\})$ is a 0-dimensional manifold by Theorem 2.10.16. Q.E.D.

Let $\nu \in \mathbb{N}$ and some $(r,s) \in \mathcal{T}$ be given. The set K^2 is defined by

$$\begin{aligned} K^2 = \{ (k^1,k^2) \in K \times K \mid \; & k^1 \neq k^2, \\ & k^1 = (i',j',-) \Rightarrow k^2 \neq (i'',j',+), \\ & k^1 = (i',j',+) \Rightarrow k^2 \neq (i'',j',-) \}. \end{aligned}$$

For every $\nu \in \mathbb{N}$, for every $(r,s) \in \mathcal{T}$, for every $(k^1,k^2) \in K^2$, the function $\psi^{\nu,r,s}_{k^1,k^2} : \mathbb{R}^{MN}_{++} \times \mathbb{R}^M \times \widetilde{\Omega}(\nu) \times \mathbb{R}^{N-1} \times \mathbb{R} \to \mathbb{R}^{N^1+2}$ is defined such that, for every $(x,\lambda,\omega,q,\mu) \in \mathbb{R}^{MN}_{++} \times \mathbb{R}^M \times \widetilde{\Omega}(\nu) \times \mathbb{R}^{N-1} \times \mathbb{R}$, $\psi^{\nu,r,s}_{k^1,k^2}(x,\lambda,\omega,q,\mu)$ is the left-hand side of (11.2)-(11.9) and the two inequalities corresponding to k^1 and k^2. For every $\nu \in \mathbb{N}$, for every $(r,s) \in \mathcal{T}$, for every $(k^1,k^2) \in K^2$, for every $\omega \in \Omega$, the function $\psi^{\nu,r,s,\omega}_{k^1,k^2} : \mathbb{R}^{MN}_{++} \times \mathbb{R}^M \times \mathbb{R}^{N-1} \times \mathbb{R} \to \mathbb{R}^{N^1+2}$ is defined by $\psi^{\nu,r,s,\omega}_{k^1,k^2}(x,\lambda,q,\mu) = \psi^{\nu,r,s}_{k^1,k^2}(x,\lambda,\omega,q,\mu), \forall (x,\lambda,q,\mu) \in \mathbb{R}^{MN}_{++} \times \mathbb{R}^M \times \mathbb{R}^{N-1} \times \mathbb{R}$.

Lemma 11.4.6
Let $(X^i,\preceq^i)_{i\in I_M}, P_{(p,p)}, (\widehat{l},\widehat{L})$ satisfy Assumptions A6-A9 and let $v \in Q^{N-1}$ be the initial state. Let $\nu \in \mathbb{N}$, some $(r,s) \in \mathcal{T}$, and some $(k^1,k^2) \in K^2$ be given. Then there exists a subset $\overline{\Omega}$ of $\widetilde{\Omega}(\nu)$ such that $\widetilde{\Omega}(\nu) \setminus \overline{\Omega}$ has Lebesgue measure zero and, for every $\omega \in \overline{\Omega}$, $\psi^{\nu,r,s,\omega}_{k^1,k^2} \pitchfork \{0^{N^1+2}\}$ and $\psi^{\nu,r,s,\omega^{-1}}_{k^1,k^2}(\{0^{N^1+2}\}) = \emptyset$.
Proof
First, it is shown that $\psi^{\nu,r,s}_{k^1,k^2} \pitchfork \{0^{N^1+2}\}$. Let $\bar{\xi} = (\bar{x},\bar{\lambda},\bar{\omega},\bar{q},\bar{\mu}) \in \mathbb{R}^{MN}_{++} \times \mathbb{R}^M \times \widetilde{\Omega}(\nu) \times \mathbb{R}^{N-1} \times \mathbb{R}$ be such that $\psi^{\nu,r,s}_{k^1,k^2}(\bar{\xi}) = 0^{N^1+2}$ and let $y \in \mathbb{R}^{N^1+2}$ be such that $y^\top \overline{M}^{k^1,k^2} = 0^{N^2\top}$, where $\overline{M}^{k^1,k^2}$ denotes the $(N^1+2) \times N^2$ matrix of partial derivatives of $\psi^{\nu,r,s}_{k^1,k^2}$ evaluated at $\bar{\xi}$. It has to be shown that $y = 0^{N^1+2}$. Let y_{k^1} and y_{k^2} denote the second last and the last component of y corresponding to the inequalities k^1 and k^2, respectively. It is shown that $y_{k^1} = 0$ or $y_{k^2} = 0$. Then the proof can be completed as in Lemma 11.4.5. As before it follows that $y_{(3,i)} = 0$, $\forall i \in I_M$. Ten different cases have to be considered.
1. $k^1 \in I^-(r) \cup I^+(r)$ and $k^2 \in K$. This case follows as the Cases 1-5 in the proof of Lemma 11.4.5.
2. $\exists (i^1,j^1) \in I^0(r)$, $k^1 = (i^1,j^1,-)$, $\exists (i^2,j^2) \in I^0(r)$, $k^2 = (i^2,j^2,-)$, and $(i^1,j^1) \neq (i^2,j^2)$. The case where $j^1 \neq j^2$ follows as in Case 2 of Lemma 11.4.5. So, let $j^1 = j^2$ and therefore $i^1 \neq i^2$. By the definition of K, $r^i_{j^1} \in \{-1,0\}$, $\forall i \in I_M$. It holds that

$$0 = y^\top \partial_{\omega^i_{j^1}} \psi^{\nu,r,s}_{k^1,k^2}(\bar{\xi}) = -y_{(4,i,j^1)}\chi_{I^-(r)}((i,j^1)) - y_{(6,j^1)}\chi_{I^0(s)}(j^1), \forall i \in I_M \setminus \{i^1,i^2\}, \tag{11.35}$$

$$0 = y^\top \partial_{\omega^{i^1}_{j^1}} \psi^{\nu,r,s}_{k^1,k^2}(\bar{\xi}) = -y_{k^1} - y_{(6,j^1)}\chi_{I^0(s)}(j^1), \tag{11.36}$$

$$0 = y^\top \partial_{\omega^{i^2}_{j^1}} \psi^{\nu,r,s}_{k^1,k^2}(\bar{\xi}) = -y_{k^2} - y_{(6,j^1)}\chi_{I^0(s)}(j^1). \tag{11.37}$$

If $j^1 \notin I^0(s)$, then it follows from (11.37) that $y_{k^2} = 0$. If $j^1 \in I^0(s)$ and there exists $i^3 \in I_M \setminus \{i^1,i^2\}$ such that $(i^3,j^1) \notin I^-(r)$, then $y_{(6,j^1)} = 0$ by (11.35).

Hence, $y_{k^2} = 0$ by (11.37). If $j^1 \in I^0(s)$ and $(i, j^1) \in I^-(r)$, $\forall i \in I_M \setminus \{i^1, i^2\}$, then (11.35), (11.36), and (11.37) implies $y_{k^1} = y_{k^2} = y_{(4,i,j^1)}$, $\forall i \in I_M \setminus \{i^1, i^2\}$. Therefore,

$$0 = y^\top \partial_{q_{j^1}} \psi^{\nu,r,s}_{k^1,k^2}(\bar{\xi}) = -\sum_{i \in I_M \setminus \{i^1,i^2\}} y_{(4,i,j^1)} \partial_{q_{j^1}} \widehat{l}^{\nu,i}_{j^1}(\bar{q}) - y_{k^1} \partial_{q_{j^1}} \widehat{l}^{\nu,i^1}_{j^1}(\bar{q}) - y_{k^2} \partial_{q_{j^1}} \widehat{l}^{\nu,i^2}_{j^1}(\bar{q})$$
$$= -y_{k^2} \sum_{i \in I_M} \partial_{q_{j^1}} \widehat{l}^{\nu,i}_{j^1}(\bar{q}),$$

so $y_{k^2} = 0$. The case $k^1 = (i^1, j^1, +)$ and $k^2 = (i^2, j^2, +)$ is similar. If $k^1 = (i^1, j^1, -)$ and $k^2 = (i^2, j^2, +)$, then it follows from the definition of K^2 that $j^1 \neq j^2$, and the proof follows as in Case 2 of Lemma 11.4.5.

3. $\exists (i^1, j^1) \in I^0(r)$, $k^1 = (i^1, j^1, -)$, and $k^2 \in J^-(r, s)$. The case where $j^1 \neq k^2$ follows as in Case 2 of Lemma 11.4.5. So, let $j^1 = k^2$. Since $j^1 \in I^-(s)$, it holds that $v_{j^1} > 0$. By the definition of K, $r^i_{j^1} \in \{-1, 0\}$, $\forall i \in I_M$. Hence,

$$0 = y^\top \partial_{\omega^i_{j^1}} \psi^{\nu,r,s}_{k^1,k^2}(\bar{\xi}) = -y_{(4,i,j^1)} \chi_{I^-(r)}((i, j^1)) + y_{k^2}, \ \forall i \in I_M \setminus \{i^1\}, \tag{11.38}$$
$$0 = y^\top \partial_{\omega^{i^1}_{j^1}} \psi^{\nu,r,s}_{k^1,k^2}(\bar{\xi}) = -y_{k^1} + y_{k^2}. \tag{11.39}$$

The case where there exists $i^2 \in I_M \setminus \{i^1\}$ such that $r^{i^2}_{j^1} = 0$ is trivial. Consider the case where $(i, j^1) \in I^-(r)$, $\forall i \in I_M \setminus \{i^1\}$. Then $y_{k^1} = y_{k^2} = y_{(4,i,j^1)}$, $\forall i \in I_M \setminus \{i^1\}$. As in Lemma 11.4.4 it can be shown that $y_{(7,j)} = 0$, $\forall j \in I^-(s) \setminus \{j^1\}$, and $y_{(8,j)} = 0$, $\forall j \in I^+(s)$. So, $0 = y^\top \partial_\mu \psi^{\nu,r,s}_{k^1,k^2}(\bar{\xi}) = -v_{j^1} y_{(7,j^1)}$, implying that $y_{(7,j^1)} = 0$. Hence,

$$0 = y^\top \partial_{q_{j^1}} \psi^{\nu,r,s}_{k^1,k^2}(\bar{\xi}) = -\sum_{i \in I_M \setminus \{i^1\}} y_{(4,i,j^1)} \partial_{q_{j^1}} \widehat{l}^{\nu,i}_{j^1}(\bar{q}) - y_{k^1} \partial_{q_{j^1}} \widehat{l}^{\nu,i^1}_{j^1}(\bar{q}),$$

implying that $y_{k^1} = 0$. The cases $k^1 = (i^1, j^1, -)$ and $k^2 \in J^+(r, s)$, and $k^1 = (i^1, j^1, +)$ and $k^2 \in J^-(r, s) \cup J^+(r, s)$ are similar.

4. $\exists (i^1, j^1) \in I^0(r)$, $k^1 = (i^1, j^1, -)$, and $\exists j^2 \in \widetilde{J}^-(r, s)$, $k^2 = (j^2, -)$. Then it holds that $j^2 \in I^0(s)$ and $v_{j^2} > 0$. The case where $j^1 \neq j^2$ follows as in Case 2 of Lemma 11.4.5. So, let $j^1 = j^2$. Since $k^1 \in K$, it holds that $r^i_{j^1} \in \{-1, 0\}$, $\forall i \in I_M$. Clearly,

$$0 = y^\top \partial_{\omega^i_{j^1}} \psi^{\nu,r,s}_{k^1,k^2}(\bar{\xi}) = -y_{(4,i,j^1)} \chi_{I^-(r)}((i, j^1)) - y_{(6,j^1)}, \ \forall i \in I_M \setminus \{i^1\},$$
$$0 = y^\top \partial_{\omega^{i^1}_{j^1}} \psi^{\nu,r,s}_{k^1,k^2}(\bar{\xi}) = -y_{(6,j^1)} - y_{k^1}.$$

The case where there exists $i^2 \in I_M \setminus \{i^1\}$ such that $r^{i^2}_{j^1} = 0$ is trivial, so consider the case $r^i_{j^1} = -1$, $\forall i \in I_M \setminus \{i^1\}$. Then $y_{(6,j^1)} = -y_{k^1} = -y_{(4,i,j^1)}$,

$\forall i \in I_M \setminus \{i^1\}$. As in the proof of Lemma 11.4.4 it can be shown that $y_{(7,j)} = 0$, $\forall j \in I^-(s)$, and $y_{(8,j)} = 0$, $\forall j \in I^+(s)$. Hence, $0 = y^\top \partial_\mu \psi^{\nu,r,s}_{k^1,k^2}(\bar{\xi}) = -v_{j^1} y_{k^2}$, implying that $y_{k^2} = 0$. The proof of the cases $k^1 = (i^1, j^1, -)$ and $k^2 = (j^2, +)$, and $k^1 = (i^1, j^1, +)$ and $k^2 = (j^2, -)$ or $k^2 = (j^2, +)$ is similar.

5. $\exists (i^1, j^1) \in I^0(r)$, $k^1 = (i^1, j^1, -)$ or $k^1 = (i^1, j^1, +)$, and $k^2 = 0$. It can be shown as in Case 2 of Lemma 11.4.5 that $y_{k^1} = 0$.

6. $k^1 \in J^-(r,s) \cup J^+(r,s)$ and $k^2 \in J^-(r,s) \cup J^+(r,s)$. By the definition of the sets $J^-(r,s)$ and $J^+(r,s)$, and since $k^1 \neq k^2$, there exists $i^1 \in I_M$ such that $r^{i^1}_{k^1} = 0$ or there exists $i^2 \in I_M$ such that $r^{i^2}_{k^2} = 0$. In the first case it follows easily that $y_{k^1} = 0$ and in the second case that $y_{k^2} = 0$.

7. $k^1 \in J^-(r,s) \cup J^+(r,s)$ and $\exists j^2 \in \tilde{J}^-(r,s)$, $k^2 = (j^2, -)$. So, $k^1 \in I^-(s) \cup I^+(s)$ and $j^2 \in I^0(s)$, and hence $k^1 \neq j^2$. Therefore, it can be shown that $y_{k^2} = 0$ as in Case 4 of Lemma 11.4.5. The proof for the case where $k^1 \in J^-(r,s) \cup J^+(r,s)$ and $k^2 = (j^2, +)$ for some $j^2 \in \tilde{J}^+(r,s)$ is similar.

8. $k^1 \in J^-(r,s)$ and $k^2 = 0$. Since $k^1 \in I^-(s)$, it holds that $v_{k^1} > 0$. Since $k^2 = 0$, it holds that $\bar{\mu} = 1$. If there exists $i^1 \in I_M$ such that $r^{i^1}_{k^1} = 0$, then it can be shown as in Case 3 of Lemma 11.4.5 that $y_{k^1} = 0$. Otherwise, $r^i_{k^1} = -1$, $\forall i \in I_M$. Then

$$0 = \sum_{i \in I_M} (\bar{x}^i_{k^1} - \omega^i_{k^1}) = \sum_{i \in I_M} \hat{l}^{\nu,i}_{k^1}(\bar{q}) < 0$$

since $\bar{q}_{k^1} = \bar{\mu} v_{k^1} = v_{k^1} > 0$, a contradiction. The case $k^1 \in J^+(r,s)$ and $k^2 = 0$ is similar.

9. $\exists j^1 \in \tilde{J}^-(r,s)$, $k^1 = (j^1, -)$, or $\exists j^1 \in \tilde{J}^+(r,s)$, $k^1 = (j^1, +)$, and $\exists j^2 \in \tilde{J}^-(r,s)$, $k^2 = (j^2, -)$, or $\exists j^2 \in \tilde{J}^+(r,s)$, $k^2 = (j^2, +)$. If $j^1 \neq j^2$, then the proof is as in Case 4 of Lemma 11.4.5. Otherwise, without loss of generality, $k^1 = (j^1, -)$ and $k^2 = (j^1, +)$ with $j^1 \in I^0(s)$, $0 < v_{j^1} < 1$, and there exists $i^1, i^2 \in I_M$ such that $(i^1, j^1) \notin I^+(r)$ and $(i^2, j^1) \notin I^-(r)$. It follows easily that $y_{(4,i,j^1)} = 0$, $\forall (i, j^1) \in I^-(r)$, $y_{(5,i,j^1)} = 0$, $\forall (i, j^1) \in I^+(r)$, $y_{(7,j)} = 0$, $\forall j \in I^-(s)$, and $y_{(8,j)} = 0$, $\forall j \in I^+(s)$. So, $0 = y^\top \partial_{q_{j^1}} \psi^{\nu,r,s}_{k^1,k^2}(\bar{\xi}) = y_{k^1} - y_{k^2}$. Moreover,

$$0 = y^\top \partial_\mu \psi^{\nu,r,s}_{k^1,k^2}(\bar{\xi}) = -v_{j^1} y_{k^1} - (1 - v_{j^1}) y_{k^2}.$$

Hence, $y_{k^1} = y_{k^2} = 0$.

10. $\exists j^1 \in \tilde{J}^-(r,s)$, $k^1 = (j^1, -)$, or $\exists j^1 \in \tilde{J}^+(r,s)$, $k^1 = (j^1, +)$, and $k^2 = 0$. It is easily shown that $y_{k^1} = 0$ as in Case 4 of Lemma 11.4.5.

Now it has been shown that $\psi^{\nu,r,s}_{k^1,k^2} \pitchfork \{0^{N^1+2}\}$. Let the set $\bar{\Omega}$ be defined by $\bar{\Omega} = \{\omega \in \tilde{\Omega}(\nu) \mid \psi^{\nu,r,s,\omega}_{k^1,k^2} \pitchfork \{0^{N^1+2}\}\}$. From the transversality theorem, Theorem 2.10.18, it follows that the set $\tilde{\Omega}(\nu) \setminus \bar{\Omega}$ has Lebesgue measure zero. For every $\omega \in \bar{\Omega}$, $\psi^{\nu,r,s,\omega}_{k^1,k^2}$ is a function from an (N^1+1)-dimensional C^∞ manifold into an (N^1+2)-dimensional C^∞ manifold, $\psi^{\nu,r,s,\omega}_{k^1,k^2} \in C^2(\mathbb{R}^{MN}_{++} \times \mathbb{R}^M \times \mathbb{R}^{N-1} \times$

$\mathbb{R}, \mathbb{R}^{N^1+2})$, and $\psi^{\nu,r,s,\omega}_{k^1,k^2} \pitchfork \{0^{N^1+2}\}$, so $\psi^{\nu,r,s,\omega^{-1}}_{k^1,k^2}(\{0^{N^1+2}\})$ is an empty set by Theorem 2.10.16. Q.E.D.

Denote an element $(x, \lambda, q, \mu) \in \mathbb{R}^{MN}_{++} \times \mathbb{R}^M \times \mathbb{R}^{N-1} \times \mathbb{R}$ by ξ. Let $\omega \in \Omega$ and some $(r, s) \in \mathcal{T}$ be given. The function $\tilde{g}^{r,s,\omega} : \mathbb{R}^{MN}_{++} \times \mathbb{R}^M \times \mathbb{R}^{N-1} \times \mathbb{R} \to \mathbb{R}^{N^1}$ is defined such that, for every $\xi \in \mathbb{R}^{MN}_{++} \times \mathbb{R}^M \times \mathbb{R}^{N-1} \times \mathbb{R}$, $\tilde{g}^{r,s,\omega}(\xi)$ is the left-hand side of (11.2)-(11.9), where ν is chosen such that $\omega \in \Omega(\nu)$. The function $\tilde{h}^{r,s,\omega} : \mathbb{R}^{MN}_{++} \times \mathbb{R}^M \times \mathbb{R}^{N-1} \times \mathbb{R} \to \mathbb{R}^{N^3}$ is defined such that, for every $\xi \in \mathbb{R}^{MN}_{++} \times \mathbb{R}^M \times \mathbb{R}^{N-1} \times \mathbb{R}$, $\tilde{h}^{r,s,\omega}(\xi)$ is the left-hand side of (11.10)-(11.18), where N^3 denotes the number of inequalities.

For every $\omega \in \Omega$, for every $(r, s) \in \mathcal{T}$, for every $\xi \in \mathbb{R}^{MN}_{++} \times \mathbb{R}^M \times \mathbb{R}^{N-1} \times \mathbb{R}$, the set $J^{0,r,s,\omega}(\xi)$ is defined by

$$J^{0,r,s,\omega}(\xi) = \left\{ j \in I_{N^3} \,\middle|\, \tilde{h}^{r,s,\omega}_j(\xi) = 0 \right\}$$

and the integer $\ell^{r,s,\omega}(\xi)$ is defined by

$$\ell^{r,s,\omega}(\xi) = \# J^{0,r,s,\omega}(\xi).$$

For every $\omega \in \Omega$, for every $(r, s) \in \mathcal{T}$, the set $D_\omega(r, s)$ is defined by

$$D_\omega(r,s) = \left\{ \xi \in \mathbb{R}^{MN}_{++} \times \mathbb{R}^M \times \mathbb{R}^{N-1} \times \mathbb{R} \,\middle|\, \tilde{g}^{r,s,\omega}(\xi) = 0^{N^1} \text{ and } \tilde{h}^{r,s,\omega}(\xi) \geq 0^{N^3} \right\}.$$

Let $\omega \in \Omega$ and some $(r, s) \in \mathcal{T}$ be given. From Theorem 11.4.3 it follows that

$$C_\omega(r,s) = \left\{ q \in Q^{N-1} \,|\, \exists (x, \lambda, \mu) \in \mathbb{R}^{MN}_{++} \times \mathbb{R}^M \times \mathbb{R},\ (x, \lambda, q, \mu) \in D_\omega(r,s) \right\},$$

hence $C_\omega(r, s)$ is the image of a projection of $D_\omega(r, s)$. Moreover, it follows from Theorem 11.4.3 that the function $\tilde{f}^{r,s,\omega} : C_\omega(r, s) \to D_\omega(r, s)$, defined by

$$\tilde{f}^{r,s,\omega}(q) = \hat{f}(q, \omega), \ \forall q \in C_\omega(r, s),$$

where $\hat{f}$ is the function defined above Theorem 11.4.3, is injective and surjective. It follows immediately that $\tilde{f}^{r,s,\omega^{-1}} \in C^\infty(D_\omega(r, s), C_\omega(r, s))$. Now it is shown that $\tilde{f}^{r,s,\omega} \in C^2(C_\omega(r, s), D_\omega(r, s))$. Using Laroque (1978), proof of Proposition 5.1, page 1147, and the twice continuous differentiability of $\hat{l}^{\nu,i}$, $\forall i \in I_M$, and of $\hat{L}^{\nu,i}$, $\forall i \in I_M$, where ν is chosen such that $\omega \in \Omega(\nu)$, it follows that the first MN components of $\tilde{f}^{r,s,\omega}$ are twice continuously differentiable. For every $q \in C_\omega(r, s)$, the last component of $\tilde{f}^{r,s,\omega}(q)$ equals $\frac{q_j}{v_j}$ if $I^-(s) \neq \emptyset$ and $j \in I^-(s)$, while this component equals $\frac{1-q_j}{1-v_j}$ if $I^+(s) \neq \emptyset$ and $j \in I^+(s)$. Therefore, the last component of $\widetilde{f}^{\tau,s,\omega}$ is twice continuously differentiable. Now it follows easily that $\widetilde{f}^{\tau,s,\omega} \in C^2(C_\omega(r,s), D_\omega(r,s))$.

In the proof of Theorem 11.4.7 it is shown that, for almost every $\omega \in \Omega$, for every $(r,s) \in \mathcal{T}$, $D_\omega(r,s)$ is a 1-dimensional C^2 manifold with boundary. Using Theorem 2.10.8 it follows then immediately that, for almost every $\omega \in \Omega$, for every $(r,s) \in \mathcal{T}$, the set $C_\omega(r,s) = \widetilde{f}^{\tau,s,\omega^{-1}}(D_\omega(r,s))$ is a 1-dimensional C^2 manifold with boundary. Moreover, $C_\omega(r,s)$ is easily shown to be compact, and therefore, by Theorem 2.10.9, $C_\omega(r,s)$ consists of a finite number of components, each being C^2 diffeomorphic to either the unit circle $\widetilde{B}^1((0,0)^\top, 1)$ or the closed unit interval $[0,1]$.

Theorem 11.4.7
Let $(X^i, \preceq^i)_{i \in I_M}, P_{(p,p)}, (\widehat{l}, \widehat{L})$ satisfy Assumptions A6-A9 and let $v \in Q^{N-1}$ be the initial state. Let $\omega \in \Omega$ and some $(r,s) \in \mathcal{T}$ be given. Let $\nu \in \mathbb{N}$ be such that $\omega \in \Omega(\nu)$. If $\psi^{\nu,\tau,s,\omega} \pitchfork \{0^{N^1}\}$, for every $k \in K$, $\psi_k^{\nu,\tau,s,\omega} \pitchfork \{0^{N^1+1}\}$, and, for every $(k^1,k^2) \in K^2$, $\psi_{k^1,k^2}^{\nu,\tau,s,\omega} \pitchfork \{0^{N^1+2}\}$, then $C_\omega(r,s)$ is a compact 1-dimensional C^2 manifold with boundary. Moreover, the boundary points of $C_\omega(r,s)$ are given by $\cup_{k \in K} \widetilde{f}^{\tau,s,\omega^{-1}}(\psi_k^{\nu,\tau,s,\omega^{-1}}(\{0^{N^1+1}\}))$.
Proof
By Theorem 2.10.11 it holds that $D_\omega(r,s)$ is a 1-dimensional C^2 MGB if $(\widetilde{g}^{\tau,s,\omega}, \widetilde{h}^{\tau,s,\omega})$ is a C^2 regular constraint system. Let $\bar{\xi} \in D_\omega(r,s)$ be given. It has to be shown that

$$\{\partial_\xi \widetilde{g}_j^{\tau,s,\omega}(\bar{\xi})^\top \,|\, j \in I_{N^1}\} \cup \left\{\partial_\xi \widetilde{h}_j^{\tau,s,\omega}(\bar{\xi})^\top \,|\, j \in J^{0,\tau,s,\omega}(\bar{\xi})\right\}$$

is a set of independent vectors.
Suppose there exists $j^1, j^2 \in J^{0,\tau,s,\omega}(\bar{\xi})$ with $j^1 \neq j^2$. Since $(\widehat{l}, \widehat{L})$ is frictionless, it holds that (j^1, j^2) corresponds to some $(k^1,k^2) \in K^2$. Hence, $\psi_{k^1,k^2}^{\nu,\tau,s,\omega}(\bar{\xi}) = 0^{N^1+2}$, leading to a contradiction with $\psi_{k^1,k^2}^{\nu,\tau,s,\omega} \pitchfork \{0^{N^1+2}\}$ by Theorem 2.10.16. Consequently, $\ell^{\tau,s,\omega}(\bar{\xi}) \leq 1$.
Either $\ell^{\tau,s,\omega}(\bar{\xi}) = 0$, so $J^{0,\tau,s,\omega}(\bar{\xi}) = \emptyset$ and it follows from $\psi^{\nu,\tau,s,\omega} \pitchfork \{0^{N^1}\}$ that $\{\partial_\xi \widetilde{g}_j^{\tau,s,\omega}(\bar{\xi})^\top \mid j \in I_{N^1}\}$ is a set of independent vectors. Or $\ell^{\tau,s,\omega}(\bar{\xi}) = 1$ and, since $(\widehat{l}, \widehat{L})$ is frictionless, $J^{0,\tau,s,\omega}(\bar{\xi})$ corresponds to an element $k' \in K$. Then $\psi_{k'}^{\nu,\tau,s,\omega} \pitchfork \{0^{N^1+1}\}$ yields that $\{\partial_\xi \widetilde{g}_j^{\tau,s,\omega}(\bar{\xi})^\top \mid j \in I_{N^1}\} \cup \{\partial_\xi \widetilde{h}_{k'}^{\tau,s,\omega}(\bar{\xi})^\top\}$ is a set of independent vectors. So, $D_\omega(r,s)$ is a 1-dimensional C^2 manifold with boundary. Since $C_\omega(r,s) = \widetilde{f}^{\tau,s,\omega^{-1}}(D_\omega(r,s))$, it follows from Theorem 2.10.8 that $C_\omega(r,s)$ is a 1-dimensional C^2 manifold with boundary with the boundary points of $C_\omega(r,s)$ given by $\cup_{k \in K} \widetilde{f}^{\tau,s,\omega^{-1}}(\psi_k^{\nu,\tau,s,\omega^{-1}}(\{0^{N^1+1}\}))$. It follows easily that $C_\omega(r,s)$ is bounded and closed, hence compact. Q.E.D.

For every $\nu \in \mathbb{N}$, by Lemmas 11.4.4, 11.4.5, 11.4.6, and by the fact that $\Omega(\nu) \subset \widetilde{\Omega}(\nu)$, it follows that the finite number of requirements in Theorem 11.4.7 is satisfied for almost every $\omega \in \Omega(\nu)$. Since there is a countable number of sets $\Omega(\nu)$, Theorem 11.4.7 holds for almost every $\omega \in \Omega$. In Definition 11.4.8 the initial endowment ω of Ω is called *regular* if the set C_ω has a nice structure.

Definition 11.4.8 (Regular initial endowments)
Let $(X^i, \preceq^i)_{i \in I_M}, P_{(p,p)}, (\widehat{l}, \widehat{L})$ satisfy Assumptions A6-A9 and let $v \in Q^{N-1}$ be the initial state. The set of regular initial endowments, *denoted by Ω^*, is the set of initial endowments ω of Ω for which the components of the set C_ω are given by*

1. *the initial state v as an isolated point and inducing a Drèze equilibrium, or an arc containing v and precisely one state inducing a Drèze equilibrium as boundary points,*
2. *a finite number of arcs containing precisely two states both being boundary points and inducing a Drèze equilibrium,*
3. *a finite number of loops containing neither v nor any state inducing a Drèze equilibrium.*

Let $\omega \in \Omega^*$ be given. Then the quantity adjustment process satisfies the convergence criterion given in Definition 11.2.7. Moreover, using Theorem 11.2.5, it follows immediately that the number of Drèze equilibria is odd. In Theorem 11.4.9 conditions are given under which $\omega \in \Omega$ is regular. By Lemmas 11.4.4, 11.4.5, and 11.4.6, these conditions are satisfied for almost every $\omega \in \Omega$. In fact, under these conditions it follows from the proof of Theorem 11.4.9 that every component that is an arc or a loop is a 1-dimensional piecewise C^2 manifold.

The proof follows the interpretation of the quantity adjustment process given in Section 11.2. Let $\omega \in \Omega^*$ and some $(r,s) \in \mathcal{T}$ be given. By Theorem 11.4.7 it holds that $C_\omega(r,s)$ is a compact 1-dimensional C^2 manifold with boundary. Therefore, $C_\omega(r,s)$ consists of a finite number of components, each being C^2 diffeomorphic to either the unit circle $\widetilde{B}^1((0,0)^\top, 1)$ or the closed unit interval $[0,1]$ by Theorem 2.10.9. Denote these different sets by $C_\omega(r,s,1), \ldots, C_\omega(r,s,k(r,s))$. For some $k \in I_{k(r,s)}$, let $C_\omega(r,s,k)$ be given. In the proof of Theorem 11.4.9 it is shown that if $q \in Q^{N-1}$ is a boundary point of $C_\omega(r,s,k)$, then either there is a unique sign vector $(r',s') \in \mathcal{T}$ and a unique $k' \in I_{k(r',s')}$ such that $q \in C_\omega(r',s',k')$ and q is a boundary point of the latter set, or q induces a Drèze equilibrium, or q equals the initial state v. In the first case, either $r' = r$ and s' differs from s in only one component, or $s' = s$ and r' differs from r in only one component, hence at most one market attains an equilibrium at the same time.

Theorem 11.4.9
Let $(X^i, \preceq^i)_{i \in I_M}, P_{(p,\text{p})}, (\widehat{l}, \widehat{L})$ satisfy Assumptions A6-A9 and let $v \in Q^{N-1}$ be the initial state. Let $\nu \in \mathbb{N}$ and $\omega \in \Omega(\nu)$ be given. If, for every $(r,s) \in \mathcal{T}$, $\psi^{\nu,r,s,\omega} \pitchfork \{0^{N^1}\}$, for every $k \in K$, $\psi_k^{\nu,r,s,\omega} \pitchfork \{0^{N^1+1}\}$, and, for every $(k^1,k^2) \in K^2$, $\psi_{k^1,k^2}^{\nu,r,s,\omega} \pitchfork \{0^{N^1+2}\}$, then $\omega \in \Omega^*$.
Proof
Let some $(r,s) \in \mathcal{T}$ and some boundary point $q \in C_\omega(r,s)$ be given. Let $\widehat{f}(q,\omega)$ be equal to $(x,\lambda,q,\mu) = \xi$. So, $\ell^{r,s,\omega}(\xi) = 1$, i.e. there is exactly one $j \in I_{N^3}$ such that $\widetilde{h}_j^{r,s,\omega}(\xi) = 0$. Clearly, j corresponds to a unique element $k^1 \in K$. It is shown that either $q = v$, or q induces a Drèze equilibrium, or there exists a unique $(r',s') \in \mathcal{T}$ and a unique $k' \in I_{k(r',s')}$ such that q belongs to $C_\omega(r',s',k')$ while $(r,s) \neq (r',s')$. Five different cases have to be distinguished.
1. $k^1 = (i^1,j^1) \in I^-(r) \cup I^+(r)$. Let $\overline{r} \in \mathbb{S}^{M(N-1)}$ be defined by $\overline{r}_{j^1}^{i^1} = 0$ and $\overline{r}_j^i = r_j^i$, $\forall (i,j) \in (I_M \times I_{N-1}) \setminus \{(i^1,j^1)\}$. Clearly, $(\overline{r},s) \in \mathcal{T}$ and $q \in C_\omega(\overline{r},s)$. Notice that $\ell^{\overline{r},s,\omega}(\xi) = 1$, so q is a boundary point of $C_\omega(\overline{r},s)$.
Let $(\widehat{r},\widehat{s}) \in \mathcal{T}$ be such that $q \in C_\omega(\widehat{r},\widehat{s})$. It is shown that $(\widehat{r},\widehat{s}) = (r,s)$ or $(\widehat{r},\widehat{s}) = (\overline{r},s)$.
Suppose there exists $j^2 \in I^-(\widehat{s}) \cap I^0(s)$. Then $q_{j^2} = \mu v_{j^2}$ and $\widehat{z}_{j^2}(q,\omega) = 0$. If $v_{j^2} > 0$ and there exists $i' \in I_M$ such that $r_{j^2}^{i'} \neq +1$, then $(k^1,(j^2,-)) \in K^2$ and $\xi \in \psi_{k^1,(j^2,-)}^{\nu,r,s,\omega^{-1}}(\{0^{N^1+2}\}) = \emptyset$, a contradiction. So, $v_{j^2} = 0$ or $(i,j^2) \in I^+(r)$, $\forall i \in I_M$. Since $j^2 \in I^-(\widehat{s})$, it holds that $v_{j^2} > 0$, hence $(i,j^2) \in I^+(r)$, $\forall i \in I_M$. Since $\widehat{z}_{j^2}(q,\omega) = 0$, this implies $1 = q_{j^2} = \mu v_{j^2}$, hence $\mu = 1$. So, $\xi \in \psi_{k^1,0}^{\nu,r,s,\omega^{-1}}(\{0^{N^1+2}\}) = \emptyset$, a contradiction. Consequently, $I^-(\widehat{s}) \cap I^0(s) = \emptyset$.
Suppose there exists $j^2 \in I^-(\widehat{s}) \cap I^+(s)$. Then $q_{j^2} = \mu v_{j^2}$ and $(1 - q_{j^2}) = \mu(1 - v_{j^2})$. This implies $\mu = 1$, so $\xi \in \psi_{k^1,0}^{\nu,r,s,\omega^{-1}}(\{0^{N^1+2}\}) = \emptyset$, a contradiction. Consequently, $I^-(\widehat{s}) \cap I^+(s) = \emptyset$.
Similarly, it can be shown that $I^+(\widehat{s}) \cap (I^-(s) \cup I^0(s)) = \emptyset$.
Suppose there exists $j^2 \in I^0(\widehat{s}) \cap I^-(s)$. Then $v_{j^2} > 0$ and $\widehat{z}_{j^2}(q,\omega) = 0$. It holds that $j^2 \notin J^-(r,s)$ since $\psi_{k^1,j}^{\nu,r,s,\omega^{-1}}(\{0^{N^1+2}\}) = \emptyset$, $\forall j \in J^-(r,s)$. So, $r_{j^2}^i = -1$, $\forall i \in I_M$. Since $\widehat{z}_{j^2}(q,\omega) = 0$, it follows that $q_{j^2} = 0$. Since $j^2 \in I^-(s)$, it holds that $q_{j^2} = \mu v_{j^2}$. Hence, $\mu = 0$ and therefore $\widehat{z}(q,\omega) = 0^N$. Since $J^-(\widehat{r},\widehat{s}) \cup J^+(\widehat{r},\widehat{s}) \neq \emptyset$, a contradiction is obtained with $\psi_{k^1,j^3}^{\nu,r,s,\omega^{-1}}(\{0^{N^1+2}\}) = \emptyset$, for any $j^3 \in J^-(\widehat{r},\widehat{s}) \cup J^+(\widehat{r},\widehat{s})$. Consequently, $I^0(\widehat{s}) \cap I^-(s) = \emptyset$.

Similarly, it can be shown that $I^0(\widehat{s}) \cap I^+(s) = \emptyset$.
Now it has been shown that $\widehat{s} = s$. If $\widehat{r} \neq \overline{r}$ and $\widehat{r} \neq r$, then at least two of the inequalities in (11.10)-(11.13) are binding, giving a contradiction as before.
2. $\exists (i^1, j^1) \in I^0(r)$, $k^1 = (i^1, j^1, -)$ or $k^1 = (i^1, j^1, +)$. Let $\overline{r} \in \mathcal{R}$ be defined by $\overline{r}^{i^1}_{j^1} = -1$ if $k^1 = (i^1, j^1, -)$, $\overline{r}^{i^1}_{j^1} = +1$ if $k^1 = (i^1, j^1, +)$, and $\overline{r}^i_j = r^i_j$, $\forall (i, j) \in (I_M \times I_{N-1}) \setminus \{(i^1, j^1)\}$. Consider the case where $k^1 = (i^1, j^1, -)$. Then $(\overline{r}, s) \in \mathcal{T}$ and $q \in C_\omega(\overline{r}, s)$, unless $\overline{r}^i_{j^1} = -1$, $\forall i \in I_M$, and $s_{j^1} = +1$, or $\overline{r}^i_{j^1} = -1$, $\forall i \in I_M$, $s_{j^1} = 0$, and $v_{j^1} > 0$. In the first case it follows that $\widehat{z}_{j^1}(q, \omega) = 0$ and, since $j^1 \in J^+(r, s)$, it holds that $\xi \in \psi^{\nu, r, s, \omega^{-1}}_{k^1, j^1}(\{0^{N^1+2}\}) = \emptyset$, a contradiction. In the second case it follows that $\widehat{z}_{j^1}(q, \omega) = 0$, hence $q_{j^1} = 0$, and therefore $\mu = 0$. So, $\widehat{z}(q, \omega) = 0^N$ and, since $J^-(r, s) \cup J^+(r, s) \neq \emptyset$, a contradiction is obtained with $\psi^{\nu, r, s, \omega^{-1}}_{k^1, j^2}(\{0^{N+2}\}) = \emptyset$, for any $j^2 \in J^-(r, s) \cup J^+(r, s)$. So, $(\overline{r}, s) \in \mathcal{T}$. Similarly, it can be shown that $(\overline{r}, s) \in \mathcal{T}$ if $k^1 = (i^1, j^1, +)$. Notice that $\ell^{\overline{r}, s, \omega}(\xi) = 1$, so q is a boundary point of $C_\omega(\overline{r}, s)$.
Let $(\widehat{r}, \widehat{s}) \in \mathcal{T}$ be such that $q \in C_\omega(\widehat{r}, \widehat{s})$. As in Case 1 it can be shown that $(\widehat{r}, \widehat{s}) = (r, s)$ or $(\widehat{r}, \widehat{s}) = (\overline{r}, s)$.
3. $k^1 \in J^-(r, s) \cup J^+(r, s)$. Let $\overline{s} \in \mathbb{S}^{N-1}$ be defined by $\overline{s}_{k^1} = 0$ and $\overline{s}_j = s_j$, $\forall j \in I_{N-1} \setminus \{k^1\}$. Then $(r, \overline{s}) \in \mathcal{T}$, $q \in C_\omega(r, \overline{s})$, and $\ell^{r, \overline{s}, \omega}(\xi) = 1$, so q is a boundary point of $C_\omega(r, \overline{s})$, unless $\overline{s} = 0^{N-1}$, or $v_{k^1} < 1$ and $r^i_{k^1} = +1$, $\forall i \in I_M$, or $v_{k^1} > 0$ and $r^i_{k^1} = -1$, $\forall i \in I_M$. In the first case it is clear that q induces a Drèze equilibrium. In the second case it follows that $\widehat{z}_{k^1}(q, \omega) = 0$, hence $q_{k^1} = 1$, and therefore $\mu = 0$. So, $\widehat{z}(q, \omega) = 0^N$ and q induces a Drèze equilibrium. In the third case it follows that $\widehat{z}_{k^1}(q, \omega) = 0$, hence $q_{k^1} = 0$, and therefore $\mu = 0$. So, $\widehat{z}(q, \omega) = 0^N$ and q induces a Drèze equilibrium.
Let $(\widehat{r}, \widehat{s}) \in \mathcal{T}$ be such that $q \in C_\omega(\widehat{r}, \widehat{s})$. It follows easily that $\widehat{r} = r$. As in Case 1 it can be shown that

$$I^-(\widehat{s}) \cap \left(I^0(s) \cup I^+(s)\right) = \emptyset, \tag{11.40}$$

$$I^+(\widehat{s}) \cap \left(I^-(s) \cup I^0(s)\right) = \emptyset. \tag{11.41}$$

Consider the case that there exists $j^2 \in I^0(\widehat{s}) \cap I^-(s)$. Then it holds that $v_{j^2} > 0$ and $\widehat{z}_{j^2}(q, \omega) = 0$. Now $j^2 \notin J^-(r, s) \setminus \{k^1\}$ since otherwise $\psi^{\nu, r, s, \omega^{-1}}_{k^1, j^2}(\{0^{N^1+2}\}) = \emptyset$ yields a contradiction. So, $j^2 = k^1$ or $r^i_{j^2} = -1$, $\forall i \in I_M$. The latter case is excluded since $(r, \widehat{s}) \in \mathcal{T}$, $v_{j^2} > 0$, and $\widehat{s}_{j^2} = 0$ implies $r^{i'}_{j^2} \neq -1$ for some $i' \in I_M$. Therefore, $j^2 = k^1$. In the previous paragraph $\overline{s} \in \mathbb{S}^{N-1}$ has been defined. If $(r, \overline{s}) \notin \mathcal{T}$, then it follows from the previous paragraph that $\overline{s} = 0^{N-1}$ since the cases $v_{k^1} < 1$ and $r^i_{k^1} = +1$, $\forall i \in I_M$, or $v_{k^1} > 0$ and $r^i_{k^1} = -1$, $\forall i \in I_M$, are excluded. However, $\overline{s} = 0^{N-1}$, $I^0(\widehat{s}) \cap I^-(s) = \{k^1\}$, (11.40), and (11.41) implies $\widehat{s} = 0^{N-1}$, a contradiction. Therefore, $(r, \overline{s}) \notin \mathcal{T}$ implies $I^0(\widehat{s}) \cap I^-(s) = \emptyset$. Similarly, it can be shown in this case that $I^0(\widehat{s}) \cap I^+(s) = \emptyset$.

Notice that $I^0(\widehat{s}) \cap I^-(s) = \emptyset$ or $I^0(\widehat{s}) \cap I^+(s) = \{k^1\}$ in the case $(r, \overline{s}) \in \mathcal{T}$. Therefore, $(r, \overline{s}) \notin \mathcal{T}$ implies $\widehat{s} = s$, and $(r, \overline{s}) \in \mathcal{T}$ implies $\widehat{s} \in \{s, \overline{s}\}$.

4. $\exists j^1 \in \widetilde{J}^-(r, s)$, $k^1 = (j^1, -)$, or $\exists j^1 \in \widetilde{J}^+(r, s)$, $k^1 = (j^1, +)$. Let $\overline{s} \in \mathcal{S}$ be defined by $\overline{s}_{k^1} = -1$ if $k^1 = (j^1, -)$, $\overline{s}_{k^1} = +1$ if $k^1 = (j^1, +)$, and $\overline{s}_j = s_j$, $\forall j \in I_{N-1} \setminus \{k^1\}$. Then $(r, \overline{s}) \in \mathcal{T}$ and $q \in C_\omega(r, \overline{s})$. Notice that $\ell^{r,\overline{s},\omega}(\xi) = 1$, so q is a boundary point of $C_\omega(r, \overline{s})$.

Let $(\widehat{r}, \widehat{s}) \in \mathcal{T}$ be such that $q \in C_\omega(\widehat{r}, \widehat{s})$. It is easily shown that $\widehat{r} = r$. Suppose there exists $j^2 \in I^-(\widehat{s}) \cap I^0(s)$. Then $j^2 \in \widetilde{J}^-(r, s)$ and $\xi \in \psi^{\nu,r,s,\omega^{-1}}_{k^1,(j^2,-)}(\{0^{N^1+2}\}) = \emptyset$, yielding a contradiction, unless $v_{j^2} = 0$, or $(i, j^2) \in I^+(r)$, $\forall i \in I_M$, or $j^2 = j^1$. Since $j^2 \in I^-(\widehat{s})$ implies $v_{j^2} > 0$ and there exists $i^2 \in I_M$ such that $r^{i^2}_{j^2} \neq +1$, it holds that $j^2 = j^1$. Moreover, $k^1 = (j^1, -)$ since otherwise $\mu = 1$ and $\xi \in \psi^{\nu,r,s,\omega^{-1}}_{(j^1,+),0}(\{0^{N^1+2}\}) = \emptyset$, a contradiction. Similarly, it can be shown that $j^2 \in I^+(\widehat{s}) \cap I^0(s)$ implies $j^1 = j^2$ and $k^1 = (j^1, +)$. Finally, it can be shown as in Case 1 that $I^-(\widehat{s}) \cap I^+(s) = \emptyset$, $I^+(\widehat{s}) \cap I^-(s) = \emptyset$, and $I^0(\widehat{s}) \cap (I^-(s) \cup I^+(s)) = \emptyset$. So, $\widehat{s} = s$ or $\widehat{s} = \overline{s}$.

5. $k^1 = 0$. So, $\mu = 1$ and $q = v$.

Let $(\widehat{r}, \widehat{s}) \in \mathcal{T}$ be such that $q \in C_\omega(\widehat{r}, \widehat{s})$. It is proved that $(\widehat{r}, \widehat{s}) = (r, s)$. It is easily shown that $\widehat{r} = r$.

Suppose there exists $j^2 \in I^-(\widehat{s}) \cap I^0(s)$. Then $q_{j^2} = \mu v_{j^2}$ and $\widehat{z}_{j^2}(q, \omega) = 0$. If $j^2 \in \widetilde{J}^-(r, s)$, then $\xi \in \psi^{\nu,r,s,\omega^{-1}}_{(j^2,-),0}(\{0^{N^1+2}\}) = \emptyset$, a contradiction. So, $j^2 \notin \widetilde{J}^-(r, s)$ and hence $v_{j^2} = 0$ or $(i, j^2) \in I^+(r)$, $\forall i \in I_M$. Since $j^2 \in I^-(\widehat{s})$ implies $v_{j^2} > 0$ and there exists $i^2 \in I_M$ such that $r^{i^2}_{j^2} \neq +1$, it holds that $I^-(\widehat{s}) \cap I^0(s) = \emptyset$, a contradiction. Consequently, $I^-(\widehat{s}) \cap I^0(s) = \emptyset$.

Suppose there exists $j^2 \in I^-(\widehat{s}) \cap I^+(s)$. Then $\widehat{z}_{j^2}(q, \omega) = 0$. Since $j^2 \in I^-(\widehat{s})$ implies there exists $i^2 \in I_M$ such that $r^{i^2}_{j^2} \neq +1$, it follows from $j^2 \in I^+(s)$ that $j^2 \in J^+(r, s)$. This contradicts $\psi^{\nu,r,s,\omega^{-1}}_{j^2,0}(\{0^{N^1+2}\}) = \emptyset$. Consequently, $I^-(\widehat{s}) \cap I^+(s) = \emptyset$.

Similarly, it can be shown that $I^+(\widehat{s}) \cap (I^-(s) \cup I^0(s)) = \emptyset$.

Suppose there exists $j^2 \in I^0(\widehat{s}) \cap I^-(s)$. As in Case 1 it can be shown that $\mu = 0$, contradicting $\mu = 1$. Consequently, $I^0(\widehat{s}) \cap I^-(s) = \emptyset$.

Similarly, it can be shown that $I^0(\widehat{s}) \cap I^+(s) = \emptyset$. Therefore, $\widehat{s} = s$.

It is easily shown that $\widehat{z}(q, \omega) \neq 0^N$ since otherwise $\xi \in \psi^{\nu,r,s,\omega^{-1}}_{j^3,0}(\{0^{N^1+2}\}) = \emptyset$, for any $j^3 \in J^-(r, s) \cup J^+(r, s)$, a contradiction.

Next, let $(r^1, s^1) \in \mathcal{T}$ and $k^1 \in I_{k(r^1,s^1)}$, and $(r', s') \in \mathcal{T}$ and $k' \in I_{k(r',s')}$ be given such that $(r^1, s^1, k^1) \neq (r', s', k')$. Using the Cases 1-5 it follows easily that the intersection of $C_\omega(r^1, s^1, k^1)$ and $C_\omega(r', s', k')$ is either empty or a common boundary point. Moreover, it follows that if q^1 is a boundary point of $C_\omega(r^1, s^1, k^1)$, then either $q^1 = v$, or q^1 induces a Drèze equilibrium, or q^1 is a boundary point of a uniquely determined set $C_\omega(r^2, s^2, k^2)$ for some $(r^2, s^2) \in \mathcal{T}\backslash\{(r^1, s^1)\}$. In the last case it follows that $C_\omega(r^2, s^2, k^2)$ is an arc and therefore has another boundary point. For the other boundary point of $C_\omega(r^2, s^2, k^2)$, say q^2, it holds that either $q^2 = v$, or q^2 induces a Drèze equilibrium, or q^2 is a boundary point of a uniquely determined set $C_\omega(r^3, s^3, k^3)$. The remainder of this proof is closely related to the proof of Theorem 10.4.2. Using the finiteness of the number of sets $C_\omega(r, s, k)$, $(r, s) \in \mathcal{T}$, $k \in I_{k(r,s)}$, it follows that after a finite number of, say $\bar{k}$, steps a boundary point $q^{\bar{k}}$ is reached satisfying either $q^{\bar{k}} = v$, or $q^{\bar{k}}$ induces a Drèze equilibrium, or $q^{\bar{k}} = q^1$. Using the fact that the intersection of three different sets is empty, it is easily seen that the components of $\cup_{(r,s)\in\mathcal{T}} C_\omega(r, s)$ are given by a finite number of loops and a finite number of arcs, where the boundary points of any arc are either v and a state inducing a Drèze equilibrium or two different states both inducing Drèze equilibria.

Let v be such that $\widehat{z}(v, \omega) = 0^N$, and, for every $j \in I_{N-1}$, $v_j = 0$ or $v_j = 1$. Let $\widehat{f}(v, \omega)$ be equal to $(x, \lambda, v, \mu) = \xi$. For every $j \in I_{N-1}$ it is shown that $v_j = 0$ implies $-\partial_{x^i_j} u^i(x^i) + \lambda^i p_j > 0$, $\forall i \in I_M$, and $v_j = 1$ implies $\partial_{x^i_j} u^i(x^i) - \lambda^i p_j > 0$, $\forall i \in I_M$.

Suppose there exists $(i^1, j^1) \in I_M \times I_{N-1}$ such that $v_{j^1} = 0$ and $-\partial_{x^{i^1}_{j^1}} u^{i^1}(x^{i^1}) + \lambda^{i^1} p_{j^1} \leq 0$. Clearly, this inequality is binding since $v_{j^1} = 0$ implies that demand rationing cannot be binding in the market for commodity j^1. Let $s \in \mathcal{S}$ be defined by $s_{j^1} = -1$ and $s_j = 0$, $\forall j \in I_{N-1} \setminus \{j^1\}$. Let $r \in \mathcal{R}$ be obtained by defining, for every $(i, j) \in I_M \times I_{N-1}$, $r^i_j = +1$ if $\partial_{x^i_j} u^i(x^i) - \lambda^i p_j > 0$, $r^i_j = 0$ if $\partial_{x^i_j} u^i(x^i) - \lambda^i p_j = 0$, and $r^i_j = -1$ if $-\partial_{x^i_j} u^i(x^i) + \lambda^i p_j > 0$. It is easily verified that $(r, s) \in \mathcal{T}$ and $j^1 \in J^-(r, s)$. Since $\xi \in \psi^{\nu,r,s,\omega^{-1}}_{(i^1,j^1,-),j^1}(\{0^{N^1+2}\}) = \emptyset$, a contradiction is obtained. Consequently, for every $j \in I_{N-1}$, $v_j = 0$ implies $-\partial_{x^i_j} u^i(x^i) + \lambda^i p_j > 0$, $\forall i \in I_M$.

Similarly, it can be shown that, for every $j \in I_{N-1}$, $v_j = 1$ implies $\partial_{x^i_j} u^i(x^i) - \lambda^i p_j > 0$, $\forall i \in I_M$.

Suppose there exists $(\bar{r}, \bar{s}) \in \mathcal{T}$ such that $v \in C_\omega(\bar{r}, \bar{s})$. Using the previous paragraph it follows that, for every $j \in I_{N-1}$, $v_j = 0$ implies $\bar{r}^i_j = -1$, $\forall i \in I_M$, and $v_j = 1$ implies $\bar{r}^i_j = +1$, $\forall i \in I_M$. If $j' \in I_{N-1}$ satisfies $v_{j'} = 0$, then $(\bar{r}, \bar{s}) \in \mathcal{T}$ implies $\bar{s}_{j'} \geq 0$. Now, since $\bar{r}^i_{j'} = -1$, $\forall i \in I_M$, it holds that $\bar{s}_{j'} = 0$. Similarly, it can be shown that if $j \in I_{N-1}$ satisfies $v_j = 1$, then $\bar{s}_j = 0$. Therefore, $\bar{s} = 0^{N-1}$, a contradiction. Consequently, $\nexists (r, s) \in \mathcal{T}$ such that $v \in C_\omega(r, s)$.

By Theorem 11.4.7, $C_\omega(r, s)$, $\forall (r, s) \in \mathcal{T}$, is compact. So, using Theorem 11.4.1 it follows that v is an isolated point of the set C_ω. Q.E.D.

Finally, it is shown that the closure of the set of non-regular initial endowments has Lebesgue measure zero. A preliminary lemma is needed first. For every $\nu \in \mathbb{N}$, for every $(r, s) \in \mathcal{T}$, the relation $\tilde{Q}^{\nu,r,s} : \tilde{\Omega}(\nu) \to Q^{N-1}$ is defined by associating with every $\omega \in \tilde{\Omega}(\nu)$ the set

$$\tilde{Q}^{\nu,r,s}(\omega) = \{q \in Q^{N-1} | \exists (x, \lambda, \mu) \in \mathbb{R}^{MN}_{++} \times \mathbb{R}^{M} \times \mathbb{R}, (x, \lambda, \omega, q, \mu) \text{ satisfies } (11.2)\text{-}(11.18)\}.$$

For every $\nu \in \mathbb{N}$, the correspondence $\tilde{Q}^{\nu} : \tilde{\Omega}(\nu) \to Q^{N-1}$ is defined by

$$\tilde{Q}^{\nu}(\omega) = \cup_{(r,s) \in \mathcal{T}} \tilde{Q}^{\nu,r,s}(\omega) \cup \{v\}, \ \forall \omega \in \tilde{\Omega}(\nu).$$

For every $\nu \in \mathbb{N}$, for every $\omega \in \Omega(\nu)$, for every $(r, s) \in \mathcal{T}$, Theorem 11.4.3 implies that $\tilde{Q}^{\nu,r,s}(\omega) = C_{\omega}(r, s)$. For every $\nu \in \mathbb{N}$, for every $\omega \in \Omega(\nu)$, by Theorems 11.2.5, 11.4.1, and 11.4.3 it follows that $\tilde{Q}^{\nu}(\omega) = C_{\omega}$.

Lemma 11.4.10
Let $(X^i, \preceq^i)_{i \in I_M}, P_{(p,p)}, (\hat{l}, \hat{L})$ satisfy Assumptions A6-A9 and let $v \in Q^{N-1}$ be the initial state. Let $\nu \in \mathbb{N}$ be given. Then $\tilde{Q}^{\nu}$ is a compact-valued, upper hemi-continuous correspondence.

Proof
Let $((\omega)^n)_{n \in \mathbb{N}}$ be a sequence in $\tilde{\Omega}(\nu)$ converging to some $\overline{\omega} \in \tilde{\Omega}(\nu)$ and let $(q^n)_{n \in \mathbb{N}}$ be a sequence in Q^{N-1} such that $q^n \in \tilde{Q}^{\nu}((\omega)^n)$, $\forall n \in \mathbb{N}$. It is shown that $(q^n)_{n \in \mathbb{N}}$ has a subsequence converging to some $\overline{q} \in \tilde{Q}^{\nu}(\overline{\omega})$. Then $\tilde{Q}^{\nu}$ is compact-valued, and, by Theorem 2.5.6, an upper hemi-continuous correspondence. The case where $q^n = v$ for an infinite number of elements $n \in \mathbb{N}$ is trivial, so consider the opposite case. Since the set of sign vectors $\mathcal{T}$ is finite, it can be assumed, without loss of generality, that there exists $(\overline{r}, \overline{s}) \in \mathcal{T}$ such that $q^n \in \tilde{Q}^{\nu,\overline{r},\overline{s}}((\omega)^n)$, $\forall n \in \mathbb{N}$. Let the sequence $((x)^n, (\lambda)^n, \mu^n)_{n \in \mathbb{N}}$ in $\mathbb{R}^{MN}_{++} \times \mathbb{R}^{M} \times \mathbb{R}$ be such that, for every $n \in \mathbb{N}$, $((x)^n, (\lambda)^n, (\omega)^n, q^n, \mu^n)$ satisfies (11.2)-(11.18). It follows easily that the sequence $((x)^n, (\lambda)^n, (\omega)^n, q^n, \mu^n)_{n \in \mathbb{N}}$ is bounded and, using that $\preceq^i$, $\forall i \in I_M$, satisfies the boundary condition, there is no loss of generality in assuming that $((x)^n, (\lambda)^n, (\omega)^n, q^n, \mu^n)_{n \in \mathbb{N}}$ converges to some $(\overline{x}, \overline{\lambda}, \overline{\omega}, \overline{q}, \overline{\mu}) \in \mathbb{R}^{MN}_{++} \times \mathbb{R}^{M} \times \tilde{\Omega}(\nu) \times Q^{N-1} \times \mathbb{R}$. Since the left-hand side of (11.2)-(11.18) is continuous as a function of $(x, \lambda, \omega, q, \mu)$, it follows that $\overline{q} \in \tilde{Q}^{\nu,\overline{r},\overline{s}}(\overline{\omega}) \subset \tilde{Q}^{\nu}(\overline{\omega})$. Q.E.D.

Theorem 11.4.11
Let $(X^i, \preceq^i)_{i \in I_M}, P_{(p,p)}, (\hat{l}, \hat{L})$ satisfy Assumptions A6-A9 and let $v \in Q^{N-1}$ be the initial state. Then the set of non-regular initial endowments $\Omega \setminus \Omega^*$ has a closure in Ω with Lebesgue measure zero.

Proof
Let some $\nu \in \mathbb{N}$ be given. First, it is shown that the closure of the set $\Omega(\nu)\setminus\Omega^*$ in the closure of $\Omega(\nu)$ in Ω, denoted by $\Pi(\nu)$, has Lebesgue measure zero. If $\omega \in \Omega(\nu) \setminus \Omega^*$, then, by Theorems 11.4.3 and 11.4.9, there exists $q \in Q^{N-1}$ such that (q, ω) belongs to the set $\widetilde{\Sigma}(\nu)$ given by

$$\widetilde{\Sigma}(\nu)=\Big\{(\overline{q},\overline{\omega}) \in Q^{N-1} \times \widetilde{\Omega}(\nu) \,\Big|\, \overline{q} \in \widetilde{Q}^{\nu}(\overline{\omega}) \text{ and}$$
$$\exists(r,s)\in\mathcal{T},\ \psi^{\nu,r,s,\overline{\omega}}(\widehat{f}(\overline{q},\overline{\omega})) = 0^{N^1} \text{ and rank } \partial_\xi\psi^{\nu,r,s,\overline{\omega}}(\widehat{f}(\overline{q},\overline{\omega})) \leq N^1-1, \text{ or}$$
$$\exists(r,s)\in\mathcal{T}, \exists k\in K, \psi_k^{\nu,r,s,\overline{\omega}}(\widehat{f}(\overline{q},\overline{\omega}))=0^{N^1+1} \text{ and rank } \partial_\xi\psi_k^{\nu,r,s,\overline{\omega}}(\widehat{f}(\overline{q},\overline{\omega}))\leq N^1, \text{ or}$$
$$\exists(r,s)\in\mathcal{T},\ \exists(k^1,k^2)\in K^2,\ \psi_{k^1,k^2}^{\nu,r,s,\overline{\omega}}(\widehat{f}(\overline{q},\overline{\omega})) = 0^{N^1+2}\Big\}.$$

It is easily shown that $\widetilde{\Sigma}(\nu)$ is closed in $Q^{N-1}\times\widetilde{\Omega}(\nu)$ since $\widetilde{\Sigma}(\nu)$ can be obtained by a finite union of sets that are closed in $Q^{N-1} \times \widetilde{\Omega}(\nu)$, by the continuity of the functions $\widehat{f}$, $\psi^{\nu,r,s}$, $\forall(r,s) \in \mathcal{T}$, $\psi_k^{\nu,r,s}$, $\forall(r,s) \in \mathcal{T}$, $\forall k \in K$, and $\psi_{k^1,k^2}^{\nu,r,s}$, $\forall(r,s) \in \mathcal{T}$, $\forall(k^1,k^2) \in K^2$, intersected with the set $\{(q,\omega) \in Q^{N-1} \times \widetilde{\Omega}(\nu) \mid q \in \widetilde{Q}^{\nu}(\omega)\}$ being closed in $Q^{N-1}\times\widetilde{\Omega}(\nu)$ by Theorem 2.5.7 since $\widetilde{Q}^{\nu}$ is shown to be a compact-valued, upper hemi-continuous correspondence in Lemma 11.4.10. Let the function $f : \widetilde{\Sigma}(\nu) \to \widetilde{\Omega}(\nu)$ be defined by $f(q,\omega) = \omega$, $\forall(q,\omega) \in \widetilde{\Sigma}(\nu)$. Then $\Omega(\nu) \setminus \Omega^* \subset f(\widetilde{\Sigma}(\nu))$ and $f(\widetilde{\Sigma}(\nu))$ is a subset of a set with Lebesgue measure zero by Lemmas 11.4.4, 11.4.5, and 11.4.6.
It is shown that $f(\widetilde{\Sigma}(\nu))$ is closed in $\widetilde{\Omega}(\nu)$. Since the image by a continuous proper mapping of a closed set is closed, see Balasko (1988), proof of Theorem 4.1.5, page 88, it is sufficient to show that f is proper. Let T be a compact subset of $\widetilde{\Omega}(\nu)$. It has to be shown that $f^{-1}(T)$ is compact. By the continuity of f it holds that $f^{-1}(T)$ is closed in $\widetilde{\Sigma}(\nu)$. Since $\widetilde{\Sigma}(\nu)$ is closed in $Q^{N-1}\times\widetilde{\Omega}(\nu)$, it follows that $f^{-1}(T)$ is closed in $Q^{N-1} \times \widetilde{\Omega}(\nu)$. Obviously, $f^{-1}(T)$ is a subset of the set $\{(q,\omega) \in Q^{N-1}\times T \mid q \in \widetilde{Q}^{\nu}(T)\}$, that is easily seen to be compact using Theorem 2.5.7 and Lemma 11.4.10. Consequently, $f^{-1}(T)$ is a closed subset of a compact set and is therefore compact by Theorem 2.3.9. So, the function f is proper and hence $f(\widetilde{\Sigma}(\nu))$ is closed in $\widetilde{\Omega}(\nu)$. Since $\widetilde{\Omega}(\nu)$ contains the closure of $\Omega(\nu)$ in Ω and $\Omega(\nu) \setminus \Omega^* \subset f(\widetilde{\Sigma}(\nu))$, it follows that $\Pi(\nu)$ is contained in $f(\widetilde{\Sigma}(\nu))$.
Let $((\omega)^n)_{n\in\mathbb{N}}$ be a sequence in $\cup_{\nu\in\mathbb{N}}\Pi(\nu)$ converging to some $\overline{\omega} \in \Omega$. Since $\{\Omega(\nu) \mid \nu \in \mathbb{N}\}$ is a locally finite, bounded partition of Ω, there exists $\overline{\nu} \in \mathbb{N}$ such that an infinite number of elements of $(\omega^n)_{n\in\mathbb{N}}$ belongs to $\Omega(\overline{\nu})$. Since $\Pi(\overline{\nu})$ is closed in Ω, it follows that $\overline{\omega} \in \Pi(\overline{\nu}) \subset \cup_{\nu\in\mathbb{N}}\Pi(\nu)$. So, $\cup_{\nu\in\mathbb{N}}\Pi(\nu)$ is closed in Ω. Moreover, $\cup_{\nu\in\mathbb{N}}\Pi(\nu) \subset \cup_{\nu\in\mathbb{N}}f(\widetilde{\Sigma}(\nu))$, a countable union of sets having Lebesgue measure zero, so $\cup_{\nu\in\mathbb{N}}\Pi(\nu)$ has Lebesgue measure zero.

Finally, $\Omega \setminus \Omega^* \subset \cup_{\nu \in \mathbb{N}}(\Omega(\nu) \setminus \Omega^*) \subset \cup_{\nu \in \mathbb{N}} \Pi(\nu)$, thereby showing the theorem.
Q.E.D.

The following corollaries follow immediately.

Corollary 11.4.12
Let $(X^i, \preceq^i)_{i \in I_M}, P_{(p,P)}, (\widehat{l}, \widehat{L})$ satisfy Assumptions A6-A9 and let $v \in Q^{N-1}$ be the initial state. Then there exists a subset $\overline{\Omega}$ of Ω such that the closure of $\Omega \setminus \overline{\Omega}$ in Ω has Lebesgue measure zero and for every $\omega \in \overline{\Omega}$ the quantity adjustment process for the economy $\widetilde{\mathcal{E}} = ((X^i, \preceq^i, \omega^i)_{i \in I_M}, P_{(p,P)}, (\widehat{l}, \widehat{L}))$ with initial state v converges to a state inducing a Drèze equilibrium of $\widetilde{\mathcal{E}}$.

Corollary 11.4.12 stipulates that, given any initial state $v \in Q^{N-1}$, generically, the quantity adjustment process converges to a state inducing a Drèze equilibrium.

Corollary 11.4.13
Let $(X^i, \preceq^i)_{i \in I_M}, P_{(p,P)}, (\widehat{l}, \widehat{L})$ satisfy Assumptions A6-A9. Then there exists a subset $\overline{\Omega}$ of Ω such that the closure of $\Omega \setminus \overline{\Omega}$ in Ω has Lebesgue measure zero and for every $\omega \in \overline{\Omega}$ the number of Drèze equilibria of the economy $\widetilde{\mathcal{E}} = ((X^i, \preceq^i, \omega^i)_{i \in I_M}, P_{(p,P)}, (\widehat{l}, \widehat{L}))$ is finite and odd.

Corollary 11.4.13 guarantees that, generically, the number of Drèze equilibria is odd. This extends the result of Laroque and Polemarchakis (1978), Theorem 1.6b, page 58, where it is shown that there exists a finite number of Drèze equilibria. Moreover, their assumptions exclude the priority rationing system, a case not excluded in this chapter.

12

EQUILIBRIUM ADJUSTMENT OF DISEQUILIBRIUM PRICES

12.1 INTRODUCTION

In this chapter a price and quantity adjustment process is described to obtain a Walrasian equilibrium in the economy. At a Walrasian equilibrium price system the supply is equal to the demand for every commodity. For an arbitrary price system it holds that the total excess demand for some commodities is negative, while for other commodities it is positive. A Drèze equilibrium can then be obtained by rationing in the markets for the non-numeraire commodities.

As has been noticed in Veendorp (1975), the relevant market signals for an adjustment process in the economy are based on the effective total excess demand associated with a Drèze equilibrium instead of the notional total excess demand as used usually, see Chapter 10 for example. Therefore, Veendorp considers a price adjustment process that follows a path of Drèze equilibria and where prices are adjusted as in the Walrasian tatonnement process, with the notional total excess demand replaced by the effective total excess demand related to a uniquely determined Drèze equilibrium. In Veendorp (1975), see also the correction in Laroque (1981), a proof of the convergence of this process is given in the case with three commodities and two consumers, and the total excess demand function satisfying a gross substitutability condition. In general, however, such a process does not necessarily converge to a Walrasian equilibrium price system and even chaotic behaviour may be expected. The possibility of chaotic behaviour has been confirmed in Böhm (1993) in a more complicated model with overlapping generations, producers, and a government. Therefore, an alternative adjustment process, also following a path of Drèze equilibria but having better stability properties, is considered in this chapter. Other processes that combine price and quantity adjustments, and are based on effective excess demands, are given in Drèze (1991) and Movshovich (1994). For a description of their processes, see Chapter 11.

One of the commodities is assumed to be a numeraire commodity having a price equal to one. The other commodities, called real commodities, in the short run have a flexible price level with respect to the numeraire commodity and have mutually fixed relative prices. When the price level is so low that no consumer wants to sell any amount of the real commodities, an equilibrium is sustained by full rationing on demand in the markets for all the real commodities. The price and quantity adjustment process considered in this chapter starts with such a trivial real demand constrained equilibrium. Subsequently the price system and the rationing scheme are adjusted in such a way that at any moment during the adjustment process all markets are kept in equilibrium. This is achieved by using demand rationing in the markets for the real commodities, while there is no supply rationing in any market. At the beginning of the process only the price level of the real commodities and the rationing scheme are adjusted. As soon as there is no demand rationing in the market for at least one of the real commodities, then its price is allowed to decrease relatively with respect to the price level of the other real commodities, while the price level is further adjusted to bring also the markets for the other commodities in equilibrium. This procedure of adjustment of the price level, allowing the price of a commodity to decrease relatively if there is no demand rationing, and allowing for demand rationing if the price is maximal relative to its initial value, is continued until there is no rationing in any market and a Walrasian equilibrium has been obtained. It is constructively proved that there exists a path of price systems and rationing schemes inducing approximate demand constrained equilibria without rationing in the market for the numeraire commodity and connecting the trivial real demand constrained equilibrium and an approximate Walrasian equilibrium. The inaccuracy of the approximation can be made arbitrarily small.

Many authors have introduced models with only supply rationing, e.g., van der Laan (1980a), Kurz (1982), Dehez and Drèze (1984), Weddepohl (1987), and Wu (1988). However, recent experiences in Eastern European countries and the former Soviet Republics give reason to look at demand rationing as well. The price and quantity adjustment process described in the previous paragraph captures some stylized facts of phenomena occurring in these countries. In general, markets are cleared by means of demand rationing, while there is no supply rationing in any market. Moreover, there is an upward pressure on the prices of commodities in the markets for which demand rationing prevails. As soon as there is no demand rationing in a market, then the upwards pressure on its price disappears. For general equilibrium-type models with demand rationing of the situation in the former Soviet Republics and the Eastern European countries, the reader is referred to Polterovich (1993). The existence of demand constrained equilibria has been shown in Chapter 4.

Trade is possible at any point on the path generated by the price and quantity adjustment process of this chapter. This is contrary to other adjustment processes such as the Walrasian tatonnement process as formulated in Samuelson (1941), or the processes of Smale (1976), Kamiya (1990), van der Laan and Talman (1987a, 1987b), Chapter 10, or Chapter 11. In these processes trade must be postponed until the Walrasian equilibrium price system has been reached. As argued by Blad (1978), if convergence takes too long, then trade should take place at a non-Walrasian equilibrium price system. So, although the price and quantity adjustment process considered in this chapter converges to a state of the economy corresponding to a Walrasian equilibrium, it might happen that convergence is not fast enough. However, the adjustment process may terminate at any point in time, because it is always possible to trade according to the prevailing demand constrained equilibrium.

Although the adjustment processes of the Chapters 10, 11, and 12 address several shortcomings of existing adjustment processes, it is clear that other problems like the informational requirements needed to make the adjustments or the non-speculative behaviour of economic agents remain. In this respect it is interesting to mention that these informational requirements can be weakened for the Walrasian tatonnement process. In the adjustment process considered in Keisler (1995) and Keisler (1996) there is decentralization with respect to trades and price adjustments in the sense that the set of trades available to an agent does not depend on the commodity holdings of the other agents in the economy and that at each point in time the prices are adjusted on the basis of the excess demand of a single consumer. Nevertheless, Keisler's process approximates the Walrasian tatonnement process as closely as desired. It seems possible that a similar approach could also weaken the informational requirements for the adjustment processes under consideration in Chapters 10, 11, and 12.

In Section 12.2 a model of the economic system endowed with short-run rigidities is presented. The short-run rigidities imply that the price level is flexible, but that the relative prices of the real commodities are fixed in the short run. The concept of a real demand constrained equilibrium for a given price level is introduced. In such an equilibrium there is no rationing in the market for the numeraire commodity, there may be demand rationing in the markets for the real commodities, and the price level equals a given value. The existence of such an equilibrium with full rationing on demand in the markets for all real commodities is shown for price levels that are low enough. Then the concept of a proper demand constrained equilibrium is introduced, being a real demand constrained equilibrium without rationing in the market for at least one real commodity. In Section 12.3 the reduced total excess demand function is introduced and some of its properties are derived. The reduced total excess demand function restricts attention to a subset of all possible price systems and rationing schemes, this subset being such that all relevant price systems and rationing schemes are contained in it. In Section 12.4 it is proved by means of a simplicial algorithm with integer labelling that there exists a path of price systems and rationing schemes inducing approximate real demand constrained equilibria. Moreover, it is shown that this path joins the trivial real demand constrained equilibrium with full rationing on demand in the markets for all real commodities with an approximate proper demand constrained equilibrium. In Section 12.5 some price flexibility for the real commodities is introduced. A generalized real demand constrained equilibrium for a given price level is defined, being a constrained equilibrium such that there is no rationing in the market for the numeraire commodity, there is no supply rationing in the markets for the real commodities, and the price of a commodity is allowed to be decreased relative to the given price level if there is no rationing in the market for this commodity. The existence of a path of approximate generalized real demand constrained equilibria joining the trivial real demand constrained equilibrium and an approximate Walrasian equilibrium is shown. So far, only approximate real demand constrained equilibria are considered with the inaccuracy of the approximation arbitrarily small. In Section 12.6 the set of real demand constrained equilibria itself is considered. Then the existence of a connected set of generalized real demand constrained equilibria containing both the trivial real demand constrained equilibrium and a Walrasian equilibrium is shown. In Section 12.7 the behaviour of the price and quantity adjustment process is discussed and illustrated.

This chapter is based on Herings, van der Laan, Talman, and Venniker (1994).

12.2 THE MODEL AND THE EQUILIBRIUM CONCEPTS

In this section the *economy* $\mathcal{E} = ((X^i, \preceq^i, \omega^i)_{i \in I_M}, (\widetilde{l}, \widetilde{L}))$ with *short-run rigidities* $\widetilde{r}$ is considered. There are $M \in \mathbb{N}$ *consumers*, indexed by $i \in I_M$, and $N \in \mathbb{N} \setminus \{1\}$ *commodities*, indexed by $j \in I_N$. A consumer $i \in I_M$ is characterized by a *consumption set* X^i, a *preference relation* $\preceq^i$, and an *initial endowment* ω^i. The *rationing function*, specifying the *admissible rationing schemes*, is given by the pair $(\tilde{l}, \tilde{L})$ with $\tilde{l} : Q^N \to -\mathbb{R}_+^{MN}$ the *rationing function on supply* and $\tilde{L} : Q^N \to \mathbb{R}_+^{MN}$ the *rationing function on demand*. The set $\prod_{i \in I_M} X^i$ is denoted by X and if $x = (x^1, \ldots, x^M)$ is an element of X, then $x_j = (x_j^1, \ldots, x_j^M)^\top$, $\forall j \in I_N$. The element $(\omega^1, \ldots, \omega^M)$ is denoted by ω. The *total initial endowment* is denoted by $\bar{\omega}$, so $\bar{\omega} = \sum_{i \in I_M} \omega^i$. For every $i \in I_M$, for every $j \in I_N$, component $(i-1)N + j$ of $\tilde{l}$ is denoted by $\tilde{l}_j^i$. Moreover, $\tilde{l}^i = (\tilde{l}_1^i, \ldots, \tilde{l}_N^i)^\top$, $\forall i \in I_M$, and $\tilde{l}_j = (\tilde{l}_j^1, \ldots, \tilde{l}_j^M)^\top$, $\forall j \in I_N$. The same notation is used for the function $\tilde{L}$, for a *rationing scheme on supply* $l \in -\mathbb{R}_+^{*MN}$, and for a *rationing scheme on demand* $L \in \mathbb{R}_+^{*MN}$.

Commodity N is considered to be a *numeraire commodity*, hence the price of commodity N is equal to one. In this chapter it is assumed that the economy $\mathcal{E}$ is initially faced with completely fixed relative prices for the *non-numeraire* or *real commodities*, determined by the vector $\tilde{r} \in \mathbb{R}^{N-1}$, while these prices are flexible relative to the numeraire commodity. For a given *price level* $\lambda \in \mathbb{R}$, the *price system* $\tilde{p}(\lambda) \in \mathbb{R}^N$ is defined by $\tilde{p}_j(\lambda) = \lambda \tilde{r}_j$, $\forall j \in I_{N-1}$, and $\tilde{p}_N(\lambda) = 1$. By varying the price level $\lambda \in \mathbb{R}$, the prices of the real commodities can be adjusted upwards or downwards with respect to the price of the numeraire commodity. The economy $\mathcal{E}$ with short-run rigidities $\tilde{r}$ is assumed to satisfy the following assumptions for the remainder of this chapter.

A1. For every consumer $i \in I_M$, the consumption set X^i is closed, convex, $X^i \subset \mathbb{R}_+^N$, and $X^i + \mathbb{R}_+^N \subset X^i$.

A2. For every consumer $i \in I_M$, the preference relation $\preceq^i$ is complete, transitive, continuous, strongly monotonic, and strongly convex.

A3. For every consumer $i \in I_M$, the initial endowment ω^i belongs to $\mathrm{int}(X^i)$.

A4. The vector of short-run rigidities $\tilde{r}$ belongs to $\mathbb{R}_{++}^{N-1}$.

A5. The rationing function $(\tilde{l}, \tilde{L})$ is flexible, market independent, and continuous.

In Chapters 3 and 4 these assumptions are discussed. Although this is not assumed, the rationing function is often considered to be monotonic whenever an intuitive interpretation of the results obtained is given.

In general the fixed relative prices are not equal to the relative prices in any *Walrasian equilibrium* of the economy $\mathcal{E}$, see Definition 3.8.1, and hence there may not exist a price level $\lambda^* \in \mathbb{R}$ such that $p^* = \widetilde{p}(\lambda^*)$ is a Walrasian equilibrium price system. Therefore, attention is focused on constrained equilibria, see Definition 4.6.1. As in Section 4.2 the *budget set* of a consumer $i \in I_M$ at a price system $p \in \mathbb{R}^N$ and a rationing scheme $(l^i, L^i) \in -\mathbb{R}_+^{*N} \times \mathbb{R}_+^{*N}$ is denoted by $\beta^i(p, l^i, L^i)$, so

$$\beta^i(p, l^i, L^i) = \{x^i \in X^i \,|p \cdot x^i \leq p \cdot \omega^i \text{ and } l^i \leq x^i - \omega^i \leq L^i\},$$

and as in Section 4.3 the set $\delta^i(p, l^i, L^i)$ is defined by

$$\delta^i(p, l^i, L^i) = \{\overline{x}^i \in \beta^i(p, l^i, L^i) \,|\overline{x}^i \succeq^i x^i, \ \forall x^i \in \beta^i(p, l^i, L^i)\}.$$

A constrained equilibrium with a given price level is defined as follows.

Definition 12.2.1 (Constrained equilibrium with a given price level) *Let some price level $\lambda \in \mathbb{R}$ be given. A* constrained equilibrium with price level λ *of the economy $\mathcal{E} = ((X^i, \preceq^i, \omega^i)_{i \in I_M}, (\widetilde{l}, \widetilde{L}))$ with short-run rigidities $\widetilde{r}$ is an element*

$$(p^*, l^*, L^*, x^*) \in \{\widetilde{p}(\lambda)\} \times \widetilde{l}(Q^N) \times \widetilde{L}(Q^N) \times X$$

satisfying

1. *for every consumer $i \in I_M$, $x^{*i} \in \delta^i(p^*, l^{*i}, L^{*i})$,*
2. $\sum_{i \in I_M} x^{*i} - \sum_{i \in I_M} \omega^i = 0^N$,
3. *for every commodity $j \in I_N$, $x_j^{*i'} - \omega_j^{i'} = l_j^{*i'}$ for some consumer $i' \in I_M$ implies $x_j^{*i} - \omega_j^i < L_j^{*i}$, $\forall i \in I_M$, and $x_j^{*i'} - \omega_j^{i'} = L_j^{*i'}$ for some consumer $i' \in I_M$ implies $x_j^{*i} - \omega_j^i > l_j^{*i}$, $\forall i \in I_M$.*

A constrained equilibrium with price level λ coincides with the definition of a constrained equilibrium of the economy $\widetilde{\mathcal{E}} = ((X^i, \preceq^i, \omega^i)_{i \in I_M}, P_{(\widetilde{p}(\lambda), \widetilde{p}(\lambda))}, (\widetilde{l}, \widetilde{L}))$ as given in Definition 4.6.1.

Let some price level $\lambda \in \mathbb{R}_{++}$ be given. Then there exist two *trivial constrained equilibria* with price level λ. One is given by $p^* = \widetilde{p}(\lambda)$ and, for every consumer $i \in I_M$, $l^{*i} = 0^N$, $L^{*i} = \widetilde{L}^i(1^N)$, and $x^{*i} = \omega^i$. The other one is given by $p^* = \widetilde{p}(\lambda)$ and, for every consumer $i \in I_M$, $l^{*i} = \widetilde{l}(1^N)$, $L^{*i} = 0^N$, and $x^{*i} = \omega^i$. At the trivial constrained equilibria with price level λ all trading possibilities are excluded by the rationing schemes. This exclusion of all trading possibilities is not allowed at the so-called supply constrained and demand constrained equilibria with some given price level, see also Definitions 4.8.1 and 4.8.5, respectively.

Definition 12.2.2 (Supply constrained (demand constrained) equilibrium with a given price level)
Let some price level $\lambda \in \mathbb{R}$ *be given. A* supply constrained (demand constrained) equilibrium with price level λ *of the economy* $\mathcal{E} = ((X^i, \preceq^i, \omega^i)_{i \in I_M}, (\widetilde{l}, \widetilde{L}))$ *with short-run rigidities* $\widetilde{r}$ *is a constrained equilibrium with price level* λ, (p^*, l^*, L^*, x^*), *of the economy* $\mathcal{E}$ *with short-run rigidities* $\widetilde{r}$ *satisfying, for every commodity* $j \in I_N$,

$$x_j^{*i} - \omega_j^i < L_j^{*i}, \ \forall i \in I_M, \ (x_j^{*i} - \omega_j^i > l_j^{*i}, \ \forall i \in I_M),$$

while for at least one commodity $j' \in I_N$ *it holds that*

$$x_{j'}^{*i} - \omega_{j'}^i > l_{j'}^{*i}, \ \forall i \in I_M, \ (x_{j'}^{*i} - \omega_{j'}^i < L_{j'}^{*i}, \ \forall i \in I_M).$$

Theorem 4.3.3 guarantees that in a supply constrained (demand constrained) equilibrium with price level λ there is no demand rationing (supply rationing) in the market for any commodity, while there is no rationing in the market for at least one commodity. In van der Laan (1982) it has been shown that for every $\lambda \in \mathbb{R}_{++}$ a supply constrained equilibrium with price level λ exists, see also van der Laan (1980a), Kurz (1982), and Corollary 4.8.3. For a similar model with production it has been proved in Dehez and Drèze (1984) that under a flexible price level, i.e. under endogenous determination of the price level $\lambda \in \mathbb{R}$, there exists a supply constrained equilibrium with some price level $\lambda \in \mathbb{R}_{++}$ without rationing in the market for the numeraire commodity and non-full rationing on at least one real commodity. In van der Laan (1984) this result is strengthened by proving that there exists a price level $\lambda \in \mathbb{R}_{++}$ and a supply constrained equilibrium with price level λ without rationing in the market for both the numeraire and at least one real commodity. Some supply constrained equilibrium existence results for economies with a different modelling of the price rigidities have been provided by Weddepohl (1987) and Wu (1988).

In van der Laan (1980a) some motivation is given for considering constrained equilibria without demand rationing in Western or capitalist economies. Recent experiences in Eastern Europe give enough reason to look at constrained equilibria without supply rationing as well. In Polterovich (1993) some general equilibrium type models of the situation in the Soviet Republics and the Eastern European countries are considered with the possibility of demand rationing in every market. It follows from Corollary 4.8.7 that a demand constrained equilibrium with price level λ exists for every $\lambda \in \mathbb{R}_{++}$. In this chapter attention is focused on demand constrained equilibria with price level λ for some $\lambda \in \mathbb{R}$ without rationing in the market for the numeraire commodity. Such an equilibrium is called a *real demand constrained equilibrium with price level* λ.

Definition 12.2.3 (Real demand constrained equilibrium with a given price level)
Let some price level $\lambda \in \mathbb{R}$ *be given. A* real demand constrained equilibrium with price level λ (RDE$_\lambda$) *of the economy* $\mathcal{E} = ((X^i, \preceq^i, \omega^i)_{i \in I_M}, (\widetilde{l}, \widetilde{L}))$ *with short-run rigidities* $\widetilde{r}$ *is a demand constrained equilibrium with price level* λ, (p^*, l^*, L^*, x^*), *of the economy* $\mathcal{E}$ *with short-run rigidities* $\widetilde{r}$ *satisfying*

$$x_N^{*i} - \omega_N^i < L_N^{*i}, \ \forall i \in I_M.$$

This definition states that at an RDE$_\lambda$ for some given price level $\lambda \in \mathbb{R}$ there is no supply rationing in any market, while there is no demand rationing in the market for the numeraire commodity. To show the existence of an RDE$_\lambda$ given some price level $\lambda \in \mathbb{R}_{++}$, the following lemma gives a result concerning the demand of a consumer if the price of some commodity is relatively very low.

Let some commodity $j^1 \in I_N$ be given. Lemma 12.2.4 states that if $p \in \mathbb{R}_+^N$ with $p_N = 1$, $l^i = \widetilde{l}^i(1^N)$, and $L^i = \widetilde{L}^i(q)$ for some $q \in Q^N$ with $q_{j^1} = 1$, and the price ratio $\frac{p_{j^1}}{p_{j^2}}$ for any commodity $j^2 \in I_N$ is sufficiently small, then the demand of a consumer $i \in I_M$ for commodity j^1 at (p, l^i, L^i) exceeds the total initial endowment of this commodity. For every $j \in I_N$, for every $\alpha \in \mathbb{R}_{++}$, the set $\mathcal{P}_j^\alpha$ is defined by

$$\mathcal{P}_j^\alpha = \Big\{ (p, l, L) \in \mathbb{R}_+^N \times \{\widetilde{l}(1^N)\} \times \mathbb{R}_+^{MN} \Big| \ p_N = 1, \ \exists j' \in I_N, \ p_j \le \alpha p_{j'}, \ \exists q \in Q^N, \ q_j = 1 \text{ and } L = \widetilde{L}(q) \Big\}.$$

Lemma 12.2.4
Let the economy $\mathcal{E} = ((X^i, \preceq^i, \omega^i)_{i \in I_M}, (\widetilde{l}, \widetilde{L}))$ *with short-run rigidities* $\widetilde{r}$ *satisfy Assumptions A1-A5. Then, for every* $i \in I_M$, *there exists* $\alpha^i \in \mathbb{R}_{++}$ *such that, for every* $j \in I_N$, *for every* $(p, l, L) \in \mathcal{P}_j^{\alpha^i}$, *for every* $x^i \in \delta^i(p, l^i, L^i)$, $x_j^i > \widetilde{\omega}_j$.
Proof
Suppose the lemma does not hold for consumer $i \in I_M$. Then there exists $j' \in I_N$ and a sequence $(p^n, (l)^n, (L)^n, x^{i^n})_{n \in \mathbb{N}}$ in $\mathbb{R}_+^N \times \{\widetilde{l}(1^N)\} \times \widetilde{L}(Q^N) \times X^i$ such that, for every $n \in \mathbb{N}$,

$$(p^n, (l)^n, (L)^n) \in \mathcal{P}_{j'}^{\frac{1}{n}}, \ x^{i^n} \in \delta^i(p^n, l^{i^n}, L^{i^n}) = \delta^i\left(\frac{p^n}{\sum_{j \in I_N} p_j^n}, l^{i^n}, L^{i^n}\right), \text{ and } x_{j'}^{i^n} \le \widetilde{\omega}_{j'}.$$

By Theorem 2.3.13, $\widetilde{L}(Q^N)$ is compact, so it follows easily that the sequence

$$\left(\frac{p^n}{\sum_{j \in I_N} p_j^n}, l^{i^n}, L^{i^n}, x^{i^n}\right)_{n \in \mathbb{N}}$$

in $\Delta^{N-1} \times \{\widetilde{l}^i(1^N)\} \times \widetilde{L}^i(Q^N) \times X^i$ has a subsequence converging to some $(\overline{p}, \overline{l}^i, \overline{L}^i, \overline{x}^i) \in \Delta^{N-1} \times \{\widetilde{l}^i(1^N)\} \times \widetilde{L}^i(Q^N) \times X^i$. Moreover, $\overline{p}_{j'} = 0$, $\overline{L}^i_{j'} = \widetilde{L}^i_{j'}(q)$ for some $q \in Q^N$ with $q_{j'} = 1$, so $\overline{L}^i_{j'} > \widetilde{\omega}_{j'} - \omega^i_{j'}$, and $\overline{x}^i_{j'} \leq \widetilde{\omega}_{j'}$. Clearly, $p^n \cdot l^{i^n} < 0$, $\forall n \in \mathbb{N}$, and $\overline{p} \cdot \overline{l}^i < 0$, so using Theorems 2.5.6 and 8.2.1 it follows that $\overline{x}^i \in \delta^i(\overline{p}, \overline{l}^i, \overline{L}^i)$. Since $\overline{p}_{j'} = 0$ and $\overline{L}^i_{j'} > \widetilde{\omega}_{j'} - \omega^i_{j'}$, it follows from the strong monotonicity of $\preceq^i$ that

$$\overline{x}^i_{j'} = \omega^i_{j'} + \overline{L}^i_{j'} > \omega^i_{j'} + \widetilde{\omega}_{j'} - \omega^i_{j'} = \widetilde{\omega}_{j'},$$

contradicting $\overline{x}^i_{j'} \leq \widetilde{\omega}_{j'}$. Consequently, the lemma holds for every consumer $i \in I_M$. Q.E.D.

For the remainder of this chapter, numbers $\alpha^i \in \mathbb{R}_{++}$ are assumed to be given for every $i \in I_M$ such that Lemma 12.2.4 holds for the economy $\mathcal{E} = ((X^i, \preceq^i, \omega^i)_{i \in I_M}, (\widetilde{l}, \widetilde{L}))$ with short-run rigidities $\widetilde{r}$. The number $\underline{\lambda} \in \mathbb{R}_{++}$ is defined by

$$\underline{\lambda} = \frac{\min(\{\alpha^i \mid i \in I_M\})}{\max(\{\widetilde{r}_j \mid j \in I_{N-1}\})}.$$

Then $\underline{\lambda}$ corresponds to a price level in the economy being so low that, under some conditions with respect to the rationing scheme, the demand of a real commodity of any consumer exceeds the total initial endowment of this commodity. This yields the following result.

Theorem 12.2.5
Let the economy $\mathcal{E} = ((X^i, \preceq^i, \omega^i)_{i \in I_M}, (\widetilde{l}, \widetilde{L}))$ with short-run rigidities $\widetilde{r}$ satisfy Assumptions A1-A5. Then, for every $\lambda \in (0, \underline{\lambda}]$, there exists an RDE$_\lambda$. Moreover, for every $\lambda \in (0, \underline{\lambda}]$, for every RDE$_\lambda$ (p^*, l^*, L^*, x^*), it holds that $x^{*i} = \omega^i$, $\forall i \in I_M$, and $L^*_j = 0^M$, $\forall j \in I_{N-1}$.

Proof
Let some $\lambda \in (0, \underline{\lambda}]$ and a demand constrained equilibrium with price level λ, (p^*, l^*, L^*, x^*), be given. By Corollary 4.8.7 a demand constrained equilibrium with price level λ indeed exists.
Suppose there exists $i' \in I_M$ and $j' \in I_{N-1}$ such that $x^{*i'}_{j'} - \omega^{i'}_{j'} < L^{*i'}_{j'}$. From Theorem 4.6.4 it follows that $x^{*i'} \in \delta^{i'}(p^*, l^{*i'}, \overline{L}^{i'})$, where $\overline{L}^{i'} \in \widetilde{L}^{i'}(Q^N)$

is defined by $\overline{L}^{i'}_{j'} = \widetilde{L}^{i'}_{j'}(q)$ for some $q \in Q^N$ with $q_{j'} = 1$ and $\overline{L}^{i'}_j = L^{*i'}_j$, $\forall j \in I_N \setminus \{j'\}$. Since $\frac{p^*_{j'}}{p^*_N} = \lambda \widetilde{r}_{j'} \leq \underline{\lambda} \widetilde{r}_{j'} \leq \alpha^{i'}$, it follows from Lemma 12.2.4 that $x^{*i'}_{j'} > \widetilde{\omega}_{j'}$, contradicting Condition 2 of the definition of a demand constrained equilibrium with price level λ, Definition 12.2.2. Consequently, for every $i \in I_M$, for every $j \in I_{N-1}$, $x^{*i}_j - \omega^i_j = L^{*i}_j$.
For every $j \in I_{N-1}$ it holds that

$$0 = \sum_{i \in I_M} x^{*i}_j - \sum_{i \in I_M} \omega^i_j = \sum_{i \in I_M} L^{*i}_j,$$

so $L^{*i}_j = 0$, $\forall i \in I_M$, and $x^{*i} = \omega^i$, $\forall i \in I_M$. Since (p^*, l^*, L^*, x^*) is a demand constrained equilibrium with price level λ, there is at least one market without rationing and this should therefore be the market for commodity N. So, (p^*, l^*, L^*, x^*) is an RDE$_\lambda$. Q.E.D.

For every $\lambda \in (0, \underline{\lambda}]$, Theorem 12.2.5 shows the existence of a *trivial* RDE$_\lambda$ in the sense that the price ratio between any real commodity and the numeraire commodity becomes so low that nobody supplies a real commodity. Therefore, such an equilibrium is sustained by full rationing on demand in the markets for the real commodities. In Section 12.6 it is shown that there exists a price level $\lambda^* \in \mathbb{R}_{++}$ and an RDE$_{\lambda^*}$ at which there is no rationing in the market for both the numeraire commodity and at least one real commodity. The latter equilibrium is called a *proper demand constrained equilibrium.*

Definition 12.2.6 (Proper demand constrained equilibrium)
A proper demand constrained equilibrium (PDE) *of the economy* $\mathcal{E} = ((X^i, \preceq^i, \omega^i)_{i \in I_M}, (\overline{l}, \overline{L}))$ *with short-run rigidities* $\widetilde{r}$ *is an* RDE_{λ^*} (p^*, l^*, L^*, x^*) *for some* $\lambda^* \in \mathbb{R}$ *of the economy* $\mathcal{E}$ *with short-run rigidities* $\widetilde{r}$ *such that there exists a real commodity* $j \in I_{N-1}$ *satisfying*

$$x^{*i}_j - \omega^i_j < L^{*i}_j, \ \forall i \in I_M.$$

To prove the existence of a proper demand constrained equilibrium, the reduced total excess demand function is derived in the next section and some of its properties are discussed.

12.3 THE REDUCED TOTAL EXCESS DEMAND FUNCTION

To show the existence of a PDE, a price level, a price system, and a rationing scheme is related to every element of the set $\overline{Q}^N$, defined by

$$\overline{Q}^N = \{q \in Q^N \mid q_N < 1\}.$$

The functions $\widehat{\lambda} : \overline{Q}^N \to \mathbb{R}_{++}$, $\widehat{p} : \overline{Q}^N \to \mathbb{R}^N_{++}$, $\widehat{l} : \overline{Q}^N \to -\mathbb{R}^{MN}_{+}$, and $\widehat{L} : \overline{Q}^N \to \mathbb{R}^{MN}_{+}$ are defined by

$$\widehat{\lambda}(q) = \tfrac{\lambda}{1-q_N}, \qquad \forall q \in \overline{Q}^N, \tag{12.1}$$

$$\widehat{p}(q) = \widetilde{p}\left(\widehat{\lambda}(q)\right), \qquad \forall q \in \overline{Q}^N, \tag{12.2}$$

$$\widehat{l}(q) = \widetilde{l}(1^N), \qquad \forall q \in \overline{Q}^N, \tag{12.3}$$

$$\widehat{L}(q) = \widetilde{L}(q_1, \ldots, q_{N-1}, 1), \ \forall q \in \overline{Q}^N. \tag{12.4}$$

Notice that, for every $j \in I_{N-1}$, for every $q \in \overline{Q}^N$ with $q_N = 0$, $\widehat{p}_j(q) = \underline{\lambda}\widetilde{r}_j$. Moreover, for every $i \in I_M$, for every $j \in I_{N-1}$, $q \in \overline{Q}^N$ and $q_j = 1$ implies $\widehat{l}^i_j(q) < -\omega^i_j$ and $\widehat{L}^i_j(q) > \widetilde{\omega}_j - \omega^i_j$. Furthermore, for every $i \in I_M$, for every $q \in \overline{Q}^N$, $\widehat{l}^i_N(q) < -\omega^i_N$ and $\widehat{L}^i_N(q) > \widetilde{\omega}_N - \omega^i_N$.

Let some $(p, l^i, L^i) \in \mathbb{R}^N_+ \times \{\widetilde{l}^i(1^N)\} \times \widetilde{L}^i(Q^N)$ be given. From Assumptions A1-A5 it follows easily that the set $\delta^i(p, l^i, L^i)$ of consumer $i \in I_M$ contains exactly one element. Therefore, for every $i \in I_M$, the *reduced demand function* $\widehat{d}^i : \overline{Q}^N \to \mathbb{R}^N$ of consumer i is defined by

$$\left\{\widehat{d}^i(q)\right\} = \delta^i\left(\widehat{p}(q), \widehat{l}^i(q), \widehat{L}^i(q)\right), \ \forall q \in \overline{Q}^N.$$

For every $q \in \overline{Q}^N$, $(\widehat{d}^1(q), \ldots, \widehat{d}^M(q))$ is denoted by $\widehat{d}(q)$. Moreover, the *reduced total excess demand function* $\widehat{z} : \overline{Q}^N \to \mathbb{R}^N$ of the economy $\mathcal{E}$ with short-run rigidities $\widetilde{r}$ is defined by

$$\widehat{z}(q) = \sum_{i \in I_M} \widehat{d}^i(q) - \sum_{i \in I_M} \omega^i, \ \forall q \in \overline{Q}^N.$$

The proof of the following two results is similar to the proof of Theorem 4.7.1.

Theorem 12.3.1
Let the economy $\mathcal{E} = ((X^i, \preceq^i, \omega^i)_{i \in I_M}, (\widetilde{l}, \widetilde{L}))$ with short-run rigidities $\widetilde{r}$ satisfy Assumptions A1-A5. If $q^* \in \overline{Q}^N$ is such that $\widehat{z}(q^*) = 0^N$, then $(\widehat{p}(q^*), \widehat{l}(q^*), \widehat{L}(q^*), \widehat{d}(q^*))$ is an $RDE_{\widehat{\lambda}(q^*)}$.

If $q^* \in \overline{Q}^N$ is such that $\widehat{z}(q^*) = 0^N$, then $(\widehat{p}(q^*), \widehat{l}(q^*), \widehat{L}(q^*), \widehat{d}(q^*))$ is called the RDE$_{\widehat{\lambda}(q^*)}$ *induced* by q^*.

Theorem 12.3.2
Let the economy $\mathcal{E} = ((X^i, \preceq^i, \omega^i)_{i \in I_M}, (\widetilde{l}, \widetilde{L}))$ with short-run rigidities $\widetilde{r}$ satisfy Assumptions A1-A5. If $q^* \in \overline{Q}^N$ is such that $\widehat{z}(q^*) = 0^N$ and there exists $j \in I_{N-1}$ such that $q^*_j = 1$, then $(\widehat{p}(q^*), \widehat{l}(q^*), \widehat{L}(q^*), \widehat{d}(q^*))$ is a PDE.

If $\widehat{z}(q^*) = 0^N$ for some $q^* \in \overline{Q}^N$ and $j \in I_{N-1}$ satisfies $q^*_j = 1$, then there is no rationing in the market for commodity j at the PDE $(\widehat{p}(q^*), \widehat{l}(q^*), \widehat{L}(q^*), \widehat{d}(q^*))$, being called the PDE *induced* by q^*.

Similarly as in the proof of Theorem 4.7.2 the following result can be shown.

Theorem 12.3.3
Let the economy $\mathcal{E} = ((X^i, \preceq^i, \omega^i)_{i \in I_M}, (\widetilde{l}, \widetilde{L}))$ with short-run rigidities $\widetilde{r}$ satisfy Assumptions A1-A5. Let some price level $\lambda \in [\underline{\lambda}, \rightarrow)$ be given. If (p^*, l^*, L^*, x^*) is an RDE$_\lambda$, then there exists $q^* \in \overline{Q}^N$ such that $\widehat{\lambda}(q^*) = \lambda$ and $\widehat{z}(q^*) = 0^N$, while $(p^*, l^*, L^*, x^*) \sim (\widehat{p}(q^*), \widehat{l}(q^*), \widehat{L}(q^*), \widehat{d}(q^*))$, so it holds that (p^*, l^*, L^*, x^*) is equivalent to $(\widehat{p}(q^*), \widehat{l}(q^*), \widehat{L}(q^*), \widehat{d}(q^*))$ in the sense of Definition 4.6.2.

From Theorem 12.3.3 it follows that there is no loss of generality in considering only RDE$_\lambda$'s for $\lambda \in [\underline{\lambda}, \rightarrow)$ and PDE's that are induced by elements of $\overline{Q}^N$. The RDE$_\lambda$'s for $\lambda \in (0, \underline{\lambda}]$ are characterized in Theorem 12.2.5. Notice that if $q^* = 0^N$, then $\widehat{\lambda}(q^*) = \underline{\lambda}$ and $\widehat{z}(q^*) = 0^N$, so $q^* = 0^N$ induces the trivial RDE$_{\underline{\lambda}}$ $(\widetilde{p}(\underline{\lambda}), \widetilde{l}(1^N), \widetilde{L}((0^{N-1^\top}, 1)^\top), \omega)$. An element $q \in \overline{Q}^N$ is often called a *state* of the economy.

The following lemma describes some properties of the reduced total excess demand function $\widehat{z}$. The proof of the following result is similar to the proof of Theorem 8.2.8.

Theorem 12.3.4
Let the economy $\mathcal{E} = ((X^i, \preceq^i, \omega^i)_{i \in I_M}, (\widetilde{l}, \widetilde{L}))$ with short-run rigidities $\widetilde{r}$ satisfy Assumptions A1-A5. Then the reduced total excess demand function $\widehat{z} : \overline{Q}^N \rightarrow \mathbb{R}^N$ has the following properties:

1. *$\widehat{z}$ is continuous,*

2. *for every* $q \in \overline{Q}^N$, *for every* $j \in I_{N-1}$, $q_j = 0$ *implies* $\widehat{z}_j(q) \leq 0$,
3. *for every* $q \in \overline{Q}^N$, $\widehat{p}(q) \cdot \widehat{z}(q) = 0$.

To prove that there exists $q^* \in \overline{Q}^N$ inducing a PDE, the behaviour of $\widehat{z}$ on the boundary of the set $\overline{Q}^N$ is considered first. Observe that at $\widehat{p}(0^N)$ every consumer wants to supply the numeraire commodity and is willing to exchange the numeraire commodity against each of the real commodities. However, as long as $q_j = 0$, $\forall j \in I_{N-1}$, none of the real commodities can be bought. So, the consumers must keep their initial endowment of the numeraire commodity and the trivial RDE$_{\underline{\lambda}}$ is obtained. Consider some $q \in \overline{Q}^N$ satisfying that for exactly one $j' \in I_{N-1}$ it holds that $\widehat{L}_{j'}(q) > 0^M$. Then there is no longer full rationing on demand in the market for commodity j' and the consumers demand commodity j' and supply the numeraire commodity. Therefore, $\widehat{z}_N(q) < 0$ and $\widehat{z}_{j'}(q) > 0$, so the economy is out of equilibrium. In the following theorem this reasoning is generalized.

Theorem 12.3.5
Let the economy $\mathcal{E} = ((X^i, \preceq^i, \omega^i)_{i \in I_M}, (\widetilde{l}, \widetilde{L}))$ *with short-run rigidities* $\widetilde{r}$ *satisfy Assumptions A1-A5. Let some* $q \in \overline{Q}^N$ *with* $q_N = 0$ *be given. Then, for every* $j \in I_{N-1}$, $\widehat{z}_j(q) \geq 0$, *and if, moreover,* $\widehat{L}_j(q) > 0^M$, *then* $\widehat{z}_j(q) > 0$.
Proof
Suppose there exists $j' \in I_{N-1}$ such that $\widehat{L}_{j'}(q) > 0^M$ and $\widehat{z}_{j'}(q) \leq 0$. Then there exists $i' \in I_M$ such that $\widehat{d}^{i'}_{j'}(q) - \omega^{i'}_{j'} < \widehat{L}^{i'}_{j'}(q)$. It follows from Theorem 4.6.4 that $\{\widehat{d}^{i'}(q)\} = \delta^{i'}(\widehat{p}(q), \widehat{l}^{i'}(q), \overline{L}^{i'})$, where $\overline{L}^{i'} \in \widetilde{L}^{i'}(Q^N)$ is defined by $\overline{L}^{i'}_{j'} = \widetilde{L}^{i'}_{j'}(\overline{q})$ for some $\overline{q} \in Q^N$ with $\overline{q}_{j'} = 1$ and $\overline{L}^{i'}_j = \widehat{L}^{i'}_j(q)$, $\forall j \in I_N \setminus \{j'\}$. From Lemma 12.2.4 it follows that $\widehat{d}^{i'}_{j'}(q) > \widetilde{\omega}_{j'}$, a contradiction with $\widehat{z}_{j'}(q) \leq 0$. Consequently, for every $j \in I_{N-1}$, if $\widehat{L}_j(q) > 0^M$, then $\widehat{z}_j(q) > 0$.
Next, consider the remaining case where there exists $j' \in I_{N-1}$ such that $\widehat{L}_{j'}(q) = 0^M$. From the result of the previous paragraph and from the continuity of $\widehat{z}$ stated in Theorem 12.3.4, it follows that $\widehat{z}_{j'}(q) \geq 0$. Q.E.D.

Now the behaviour of $\widehat{z}$ near the frontier of $\overline{Q}^N$ where $q_N = 1$ is considered. In this case the numeraire commodity is very cheap compared to the other commodities. The real number $\widetilde{\delta} \in \mathbb{R}_{++}$ is defined by

$$\widetilde{\delta} = \min\left(\left\{\tfrac{1}{2}, (\underline{\lambda}\min(\{\widetilde{r}_j \mid j \in I_{N-1}\}))^2\right\}\right).$$

Lemma 12.3.6
Let the economy $\mathcal{E} = ((X^i, \preceq^i, \omega^i)_{i \in I_M}, (\widetilde{l}, \widetilde{L}))$ *with short-run rigidities* $\widetilde{r}$ *satisfy*

Assumptions A1-A5. Let some $q \in \overline{Q}^N$ with $q_N \geq 1-\widetilde{\delta}$ be given. Then it holds that $\widehat{z}_N(q) > 0$.

Proof

Let some $j \in I_{N-1}$ be given. Then

$$\frac{\widehat{p}_N(q)}{\widehat{p}_j(q)} = \frac{1-q_N}{\lambda \widetilde{r}_j} \leq \frac{\widetilde{\delta}}{\underline{\lambda} \widetilde{r}_j} \leq \underline{\lambda} \min\left(\{\widetilde{r}_j \,|j \in I_{N-1}\}\right) \leq \min(\{\alpha^i \mid i \in I_M\}).$$

Hence, by Lemma 12.2.4, $\widehat{d}^i_N(q) > \widetilde{\omega}_N$, $\forall i \in I_M$, so $\widehat{z}_N(q) > M\widetilde{\omega}_N - \widetilde{\omega}_N \geq 0$.
Q.E.D.

Now it is possible to give a constructive proof of the existence of an approximate PDE by showing that there exists a piecewise linear path of approximate zero points of $\widehat{z}$ inducing approximate RDE$_\lambda$'s joining $q = 0^N$, inducing the trivial RDE$_{\underline{\lambda}}$, with an approximate zero point q^* of $\widehat{z}$ on the boundary of $\overline{Q}^N$ satisfying that $q^*_j = 1$ for at least one $j \in I_{N-1}$. Such a point q^* induces an approximate PDE. In Section 12.6 the existence of a PDE is shown by considering the limit of a sequence of approximate PDE's.

12.4 THE SHORT RUN PRICE AND QUANTITY ADJUSTMENT PROCESS

In this section attention is focused on approximate real demand constrained equilibria. In the following definition an *approximate RDE$_\lambda$* for some $\lambda \in \mathbb{R}$ and an *approximate PDE* are defined.

Definition 12.4.1 (ε-RDE$_\lambda$ and ε-PDE)
Let some price level $\lambda \in \mathbb{R}_{++}$ and some $\varepsilon \in \mathbb{R}_+$ be given. An ε-RDE$_\lambda$ (ε-PDE) of the economy $\mathcal{E} = ((X^i, \preceq^i, \omega^i)_{i \in I_M}, (\widetilde{l}, \widetilde{L}))$ with short-run rigidities $\widetilde{r}$ is an element

$$(p^*, l^*, L^*, x^*) \in \{\widetilde{p}(\lambda)\} \times \widetilde{l}(Q^N) \times \widetilde{L}(Q^N) \times X$$

such that all conditions of an RDE$_\lambda$ (PDE) are satisfied, except possibly the condition of equality of supply and demand which is replaced by $\|\sum_{i \in I_M} x^{*i} - \sum_{i \in I_M} \omega^i\|_\infty \leq \varepsilon$.

To show the existence of a path of ε-RDE$_\lambda$'s joining the trivial RDE$_{\underline{\lambda}}$ and an ε-PDE for arbitrary $\varepsilon \in \mathbb{R}_{++}$, some techniques of simplicial approximation of functions are used. This approach is also used in Chapters 5 and 6.

In this section a simplicial algorithm with integer labelling is presented. The algorithm is closely related to the one used in Chapter 5. The set $\overline{Q}^N_{\tilde{\delta}}$, defined by

$$\overline{Q}^N_{\tilde{\delta}} = \left\{ q \in \overline{Q}^N \,\middle|\, q_N \leq 1 - \tilde{\delta} \right\},$$

needs to be triangulated. An example of a triangulation of $\overline{Q}^N_{\tilde{\delta}}$ with arbitrarily small mesh size is obtained by a slight modification of the $\tilde{K}$-triangulation as given in Definition 2.7.3.

Let some $n \in \mathbb{N}$ be given. Then the K-triangulation of $\overline{Q}^N_{\tilde{\delta}}$ with grid size $\frac{1}{n}$ is the collection of all N-simplices $\sigma_{(q^1,\pi)}$ with vertices $q^1, \ldots, q^{N+1} \in \mathbb{R}^N$ satisfying $q^1 = \sum_{j \in I_{N-1}} \frac{a^j}{n} e^N(j) + \frac{a^N}{n}(1-\tilde{\delta}) e^N(N)$ for some $a^1, \ldots, a^N \in I^0_{n-1}$, $\pi : I_N \to I_N$ is a permutation, and, for every $k \in I_N$, $q^{k+1} = q^k + \frac{1}{n} e^N(\pi(k))$ if $\pi(k) \in I_{N-1}$, and $q^{k+1} = q^k + \frac{1}{n}(1 - \tilde{\delta}) e^N(\pi(k))$ if $\pi(k) = N$. The mesh size of the K-triangulation of $\overline{Q}^N_{\tilde{\delta}}$ with grid size $\frac{1}{n}$ is equal to $\frac{1}{n}$.

For every $q \in \overline{Q}^N_{\tilde{\delta}}$, the set $J(q)$ is defined by

$$J(q) = \{ j' \in I_N \,|\, \widehat{z}_{j'}(q) = \min(\{\widehat{z}_j(q) \mid j \in I_N\}) \}.$$

Notice that Theorem 12.3.4 guarantees that $\min(\{\widehat{z}_j(q) \mid j \in I_N\}) \leq 0$. The *labelling function* $\widehat{f} : \overline{Q}^N_{\tilde{\delta}} \to I_N$ is defined by

$$\widehat{f}(q) = \max(J(q)), \ \forall q \in \overline{Q}^N_{\tilde{\delta}}.$$

So, with every $q \in \overline{Q}^N_{\tilde{\delta}}$ the last component for which the total excess demand at q is minimal is associated. Notice that this labelling function is different from the one used in Chapter 5.

Let some triangulation Σ of $\overline{Q}^N_{\tilde{\delta}}$ be given. A simplicial algorithm with integer labelling on $\overline{Q}^N_{\tilde{\delta}}$ is described that starts at $q = 0^N$ and that generates a sequence of simplices of varying dimension that are faces of simplices in Σ. For a t-simplex $\sigma(q^1, \ldots, q^{t+1})$ in this sequence it holds for every $j \in I_N$ that $q_j = 0$, $\forall q \in \sigma$, or $j \in \widehat{f}(\{q^1, \ldots, q^{t+1}\})$. In the first case it holds that $\widehat{z}_j(q) \leq 0$, $\forall q \in \sigma$, by Theorems 12.3.4 and 12.3.5, and in the second case there exists $k \in I_{t+1}$ such that $\widehat{z}_j(q^k) \leq 0$ for a vertex q^k of σ with $\widehat{f}(q^k) = j$, using the definition of the labelling function $\widehat{f}$. These properties are shown to guarantee that for every $q \in \overline{Q}^N_{\tilde{\delta}}$ belonging to a simplex of Σ containing a face generated by the algorithm it holds that $\widehat{z}(q)$ is approximately equal to zero.

Let a triangulation Σ of $\overline{Q}^N_{\tilde{\delta}}$ be given. For every non-empty subset J of I_N, the set $A(J)$ is defined by

$$A(J) = \left\{ q \in \overline{Q}^N_{\tilde{\delta}} \,\middle|\, q_j = 0,\ \forall j \in I_N \setminus J \right\}.$$

Clearly, $A(J)$ is a convex $(\#J)$-dimensional subset of $\mathbb{R}^N$ for every non-empty subset J of I_N. For every non-empty subset J of I_N, the collection $\Sigma(J)$ is defined by

$$\Sigma(J) = \{ \tau \subset A(J) \,|\, \exists \sigma \in \Sigma,\ \tau \text{ is a } (\#J)\text{-face of } \sigma \}.$$

These definitions are closely related to the ones given in Chapter 5, the only difference being that in Chapter 5 the set Q^N is considered instead of $\overline{Q}^N_{\tilde{\delta}}$. If $\overline{J}, \widehat{J} \subset I_N$ with $\emptyset \neq \overline{J} \subset \widehat{J}$, then $A(\overline{J}) = A(\widehat{J}) \cap \text{aff}(A(\overline{J}))$. By repeated application of Theorem 2.7.8 it follows that $\Sigma(J)$ is a triangulation of $A(J)$, for every non-empty subset J of I_N. Let $\widetilde{Q}^N_{\tilde{\delta}}$ denote the part of the boundary of $\overline{Q}^N_{\tilde{\delta}}$ where some component of q is maximal, so

$$\widetilde{Q}^N_{\tilde{\delta}} = \left\{ q \in \overline{Q}^N_{\tilde{\delta}} \,\middle|\, \exists j \in I_{N-1},\ q_j = 1, \text{ or } q_N = 1 - \tilde{\delta} \right\}.$$

Definition 12.4.2 (J-complete simplices)
Consider the labelling function $\widehat{f} : \overline{Q}^N_{\tilde{\delta}} \to I_N$. Let J be a non-empty subset of I_N with $\#J = t$. A $(t-1)$-simplex $\tau(q^1, \ldots, q^t)$ being a subset of $\overline{Q}^N_{\tilde{\delta}}$ is J-complete *if $\widehat{f}(\{q^1, \ldots, q^t\}) = J$.*

In general, a $(t-1)$-simplex is called *complete* if it is J-complete for some non-empty subset J of I_N with $\#J = t$.

Let a triangulation Σ of $\overline{Q}^N_{\tilde{\delta}}$ be given. The algorithm will generate a finite sequence of complete simplices of varying dimension in $\overline{Q}^N_{\tilde{\delta}}$ starting with the $\{\widehat{f}(0^N)\}$-complete simplex $\{0^N\}$ and terminating with a complete simplex that is a subset of $\widetilde{Q}^N_{\tilde{\delta}}$. For every $(t-1)$-simplex τ in the finite sequence, there exists a non-empty subset J of I_N with $\#J = t$ such that τ is a J-complete facet of a t-simplex of $\Sigma(J)$. Moreover, any two successive simplices in the finite sequence either both are a facet of the same simplex or one is a facet of the other. In Lemmas 12.4.3 and 12.4.4 all possible situations are described that can occur when some $(t-1)$-simplex τ being a J-complete facet of a t-simplex of $\Sigma(J)$ for some non-empty subset J of I_N with $\#J = t$ is given. The proofs of these lemmas are exactly the same as the proofs of Lemma 5.2.3 and Lemma 5.2.4, respectively. Lemmas 12.4.3 and 12.4.4 are used in Theorem 12.4.7 to determine in a unique way the finite sequence of complete simplices described above. The detailed steps of the algorithm yielding this finite sequence are given in Algorithm 12.4.8.

Lemma 12.4.3
Consider the labelling function $\widehat{f} : \overline{Q}^N_{\tilde{\delta}} \to I_N$ and let a triangulation Σ of $\overline{Q}^N_{\tilde{\delta}}$ be given. Let σ be a t-simplex of $\Sigma(J)$ for some non-empty subset J of I_N with $\#J = t$. Moreover, let a J-complete facet τ of σ be given. Then exactly one of the following cases holds:

1. *the t-simplex σ is a $\overline{J}$-complete facet of a $(t+1)$-simplex of $\Sigma(\overline{J})$ for precisely one subset $\overline{J}$ of I_N,*
2. *the t-simplex σ has exactly one other J-complete facet $\overline{\tau}$.*

Notice that the set $\overline{J}$ in Case 1 of Lemma 12.4.3 contains J, while $\#\overline{J} = t+1$.

Lemma 12.4.4
Consider the labelling function $\widehat{f} : \overline{Q}^N_{\tilde{\delta}} \to I_N$ and let a triangulation Σ of $\overline{Q}^N_{\tilde{\delta}}$ be given. Let τ be a J-complete facet of a t-simplex of $\Sigma(J)$ for some non-empty subset J of I_N with $\#J = t$. Moreover, let τ be a member of $\Sigma(\overline{J})$ for some non-empty subset $\overline{J}$ of I_N. Then precisely one facet of the $(t-1)$-simplex τ is $\overline{J}$-complete.

Notice that the set $\overline{J}$ of Lemma 12.4.4 has $t-1$ elements.

Definition 12.4.5 (Adjacent complete simplices)
Consider the labelling function $\widehat{f} : \overline{Q}^N_{\tilde{\delta}} \to I_N$ and let a triangulation Σ of $\overline{Q}^N_{\tilde{\delta}}$ be given. Then the $(t-1)$-simplices $\overline{\tau}$ and $\widehat{\tau}$ are adjacent complete simplices *if $\overline{\tau}$ and $\widehat{\tau}$ are both J-complete facets of the same t-simplex σ of $\Sigma(J)$ for some non-empty subset J of I_N with $\#J = t$, or if $\overline{\tau}$ is a J-complete facet of the complete t-simplex $\widehat{\tau}$ of $\Sigma(J)$ for some non-empty subset J of I_N with $\#J = t$, or if $\widehat{\tau}$ is a J-complete facet of the complete t-simplex $\overline{\tau}$ of $\Sigma(J)$ for some non-empty subset J of I_N with $\#J = t$.*

The algorithm will generate a finite sequence of adjacent complete simplices. Theorem 12.4.6 makes a statement concerning the number of adjacent complete simplices when some complete simplex is given.

Theorem 12.4.6

Consider the labelling function $\hat{f} : \overline{Q}^N_{\tilde{\delta}} \rightarrow I_N$ and let a triangulation Σ of $\overline{Q}^N_{\tilde{\delta}}$ be given. Let τ be a J-complete facet of a t-simplex of $\Sigma(J)$ for some non-empty subset J of I_N with $\#J = t$. If $\tau = \{0^N\}$ or if τ is a subset of $\tilde{Q}^N_{\tilde{\delta}}$, then τ has exactly one adjacent complete simplex. Otherwise, there exist exactly two adjacent complete simplices to τ.

Proof

Let $\tau = \{0^N\}$. Then τ is J-complete with $J = \{\hat{f}(0^N)\}$. Since $\Sigma(\{\hat{f}(0^N)\})$ is a triangulation of $A(\{\hat{f}(0^N)\})$ and $\{0^N\}$ is a facet in $\mathrm{rb}(A(\{\hat{f}(0^N)\}))$, it holds by Definition 2.7.1 of a triangulation that there is a unique 1-simplex $\overline{\sigma}$ of $\Sigma(\{\hat{f}(0^N)\})$ such that $\{0^N\}$ is a facet of $\overline{\sigma}$. By Lemma 12.4.3, either $\overline{\sigma}$ is a $\overline{J}$-complete facet of a 2-simplex of $\Sigma(\overline{J})$ for precisely one non-empty subset $\overline{J}$ of I_N, or $\overline{\sigma}$ has exactly one other $\{\hat{f}(0^N)\}$-complete facet $\hat{\tau}$. This yields exactly one adjacent complete simplex to $\{0^N\}$. Since $\{0^N\}$ has no facets, there can be no other adjacent complete simplex to $\{0^N\}$.

Let τ be a subset of $\tilde{Q}^N_{\tilde{\delta}}$, so τ lies in the relative boundary of $A(J)$. By the properties of a triangulation, there is a unique t-simplex $\overline{\sigma}$ of $\Sigma(J)$ containing τ as a facet. By Lemma 12.4.3, either $\overline{\sigma}$ is a $\overline{J}$-complete facet of a $(t+1)$-simplex of $\Sigma(\overline{J})$ for precisely one non-empty subset $\overline{J}$ of I_N, or $\overline{\sigma}$ has exactly one other J-complete facet $\hat{\tau}$. This yields one adjacent complete simplex to τ. Obviously, τ is not a subset of $A(\overline{J})$ for any proper subset $\overline{J}$ of J, so there can be no other adjacent complete simplex to τ.

Now consider the case $\tau \neq \{0^N\}$ and τ is not a subset of $\tilde{Q}^N_{\tilde{\delta}}$. There are two possibilities, either $\tau \subset \mathrm{rb}(A(J))$ or $\tau \subset \mathrm{ri}(A(J))$.

Let τ be a subset of $\mathrm{rb}(A(J))$. Then, by the properties of a triangulation, there is a unique t-simplex $\overline{\sigma}$ in $A(J)$ having τ as a facet. By Lemma 12.4.3, either $\overline{\sigma}$ is a $\overline{J}$-complete facet of a $(t+1)$-simplex of $\Sigma(\overline{J})$ for precisely one non-empty subset $\overline{J}$ of I_N, or $\overline{\sigma}$ has exactly one other J-complete facet $\hat{\tau}$. This yields one adjacent complete simplex to τ. Since $\tau \subset \mathrm{rb}(A(J))$, it holds that $q \in \tilde{Q}^N_{\tilde{\delta}}$, $\forall q \in \tau$, or there exists $j' \in I_N$ such that $q_{j'} = 0$, $\forall q \in \tau$. Since τ is not a subset of $\tilde{Q}^N_{\tilde{\delta}}$, it follows that $q_{j'} = 0$, $\forall q \in \tau$. Notice that j' is uniquely determined since τ is a $(t-1)$-simplex. Since $\tau \neq \{0^N\}$ it follows that $J \setminus \{j'\} \neq \emptyset$, so $\tau \in \Sigma(J \setminus \{j'\})$. By Lemma 12.4.4 it holds that precisely one facet of τ is $(J \setminus \{j'\})$-complete and the second adjacent complete simplex to τ is obtained. Clearly, there can be no other adjacent complete simplex to τ.

Let τ be a subset of $\mathrm{ri}(A(J))$. Then, by the definition of a triangulation, Definition 2.7.1, it holds that τ is a facet of exactly two simplices of $\Sigma(J)$. Applying Lemma 12.4.3 twice shows that τ has exactly two adjacent complete simplices. It is easily verified that there cannot be any other adjacent complete simplex to τ. Q.E.D.

The following theorem states that there exists a unique finite sequence of adjacent complete simplices such that the first simplex in the sequence is equal to $\{0^N\}$ and the last simplex is a subset of $\widetilde{Q}^N_{\tilde{\delta}}$.

Theorem 12.4.7
Consider the labelling function $\widehat{f} : \overline{Q}^N_{\tilde{\delta}} \to I_N$ and let a triangulation Σ of $\overline{Q}^N_{\tilde{\delta}}$ be given. Then there exists a unique finite sequence of complete simplices $\tau^1, \ldots, \tau^{k'}$ such that $\tau^1 = \{0^N\}$, $\tau^{k'} \subset \widetilde{Q}^N_{\tilde{\delta}}$, $\tau^k \neq \tau^{k-2}$, $\forall k \in I_{k'} \setminus I_2$, and any two successive simplices in the finite sequence are adjacent complete simplices.

Proof
Clearly, τ^1 is $\{\widehat{f}(0^N)\}$-complete. Let τ^2 be the unique adjacent complete simplex to τ^1 that exists according to Theorem 12.4.6. If τ^k, for some $k \in \mathbb{N} \setminus \{1\}$, is not a subset of $\widetilde{Q}^N_{\tilde{\delta}}$, then there exists by Theorem 12.4.6 a unique adjacent complete simplex τ^{k+1} that is not equal to τ^{k-1}. If τ^k, for some $k \in \mathbb{N} \setminus \{1\}$, is a subset of $\widetilde{Q}^N_{\tilde{\delta}}$, then there exists by Theorem 12.4.6 no adjacent complete simplex different from τ^{k-1}. So, after generating a finite number of, say $k' \in \mathbb{N}$, simplices, a simplex $\tau^{k'}$ is generated such that either $\tau^{k'} \subset \widetilde{Q}^N_{\tilde{\delta}}$ or, by the finiteness of the number of facets of simplices in $\Sigma(J)$ for every non-empty subset J of I_N, $\tau^{k'}$ has been generated before. However, applying the well-known door-in-door-out principle of Lemke and Howson (1964), see also the proof of Theorem 5.2.7, it follows from Theorem 12.4.6 that each J-complete facet of a simplex of $\Sigma(J)$ can be visited at most once. Therefore, $\tau^{k'} \subset \widetilde{Q}^N_{\tilde{\delta}}$. Q.E.D.

Now the steps of the algorithm generating the simplices $\tau^1, \ldots, \tau^{k'}$ of Theorem 12.4.7 are described in detail.

Algorithm 12.4.8 (Simplicial algorithm with integer labelling)
Consider the labelling function $\widehat{f} : \overline{Q}^N_{\tilde{\delta}} \to I_N$ and let a triangulation Σ of $\overline{Q}^N_{\tilde{\delta}}$ be given. The simplicial algorithm *on $\overline{Q}^N_{\tilde{\delta}}$ with* integer labelling *has the following steps.*

Step 0. *Let $k = 1$, $t = 1$, $\tau^k = \tau(0^N)$, $J = \{\widehat{f}(0^N)\}$, and let q^{t+1} be the unique vertex of the simplex of $\Sigma(J)$ containing τ^k as the facet opposite to it.*

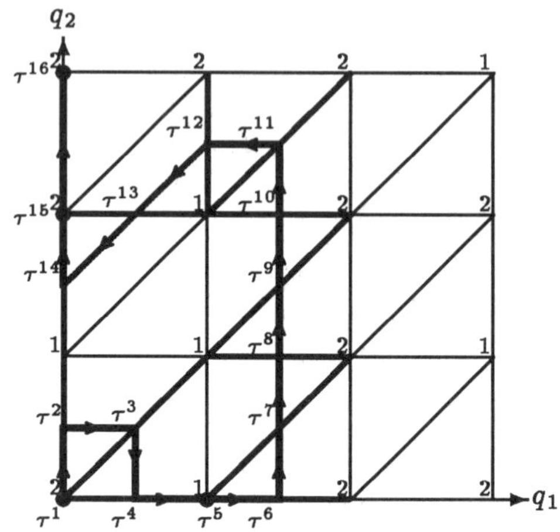

Figure 12.4.1. Illustration of the algorithm, $N = 2$.

Step 1. *Let σ be equal to the convex hull of $\tau^k \cup \{q^{t+1}\}$. If $\widehat{f}(q^{t+1}) \notin J$, then go to Step 3. Otherwise, there is a unique vertex $\overline{q}$ of σ such that $\overline{q} \neq q^{t+1}$ and $\widehat{f}(\overline{q}) = \widehat{f}(q^{t+1})$.*

Step 2. *Increase the value of k by 1 and let τ^k be the facet of σ opposite $\overline{q}$. If there exists $j' \in J$ such that $\tau^k \in \Sigma(J \setminus \{j'\})$, then let $\overline{J}$ be equal to $J \setminus \{j'\}$ and go to Step 4. If $\tau^k \subset \widetilde{Q}^N_{\tilde{\delta}}$, then the algorithm terminates. Otherwise, there is exactly one t-simplex $\overline{\sigma}$ of $\Sigma(J)$ such that $\overline{\sigma} \neq \sigma$ and τ^k is a facet of $\overline{\sigma}$. Go to Step 1 with q^{t+1} as the unique vertex of $\overline{\sigma}$ opposite τ^k.*

Step 3. *Let $\overline{J}$ be equal to $J \cup \{\widehat{f}(q^{t+1})\}$. There is a unique $(t+1)$-simplex $\overline{\sigma}$ of $\Sigma(\overline{J})$ having σ as a facet. Increase the value of both k and t by 1 and go to Step 1 with q^{t+1} as the unique vertex of $\overline{\sigma}$ opposite σ, $J = \overline{J}$, and $\tau^k = \sigma$.*

Step 4. *Let σ be equal to τ^k. Let $\widehat{q}$ be the unique vertex of σ such that $\widehat{f}(\widehat{q}) = j'$. Decrease the value of t by 1 and go to Step 2 with $\overline{q} = \widehat{q}$ and $J = \overline{J}$.*

The only difference with Algorithm 5.2.8 concerns the criterion for termination of the algorithm. Algorithm 5.2.8 terminates with a simplex carrying all the labels of the set I_{N+1}. Algorithm 12.4.8 terminates when reaching the set $\widetilde{Q}^N_{\tilde{\delta}}$. The algorithm is illustrated in Figure 12.4.1.

In Figure 12.4.1 the algorithm starts with the $\{2\}$-complete simplex $\tau^1 = \{0^N\}$ being a facet of a uniquely determined 1-simplex τ^2 of $\Sigma(\{2\})$. The algorithm terminates with the $\{2\}$-complete simplex $\tau^{16} = \{(0, 1 - \widetilde{\delta})^\top\}$ of $\Sigma(\{2\})$. After the starting simplex τ^1 the algorithm generates three $\{1,2\}$-complete simplices τ^2, τ^3, and τ^4 that are facets of simplices of $\Sigma(\{1,2\})$. Then the $\{1\}$-complete simplex τ^5 and nine $\{1,2\}$-complete simplices τ^6 up to τ^{14} are generated. Finally, two $\{2\}$-complete simplices τ^{15} and τ^{16} are obtained. The barycentres of any two adjacent complete simplices generated by the algorithm have been joined by a straight line.

Given any triangulation Σ of $\overline{Q}^N_{\tilde{\delta}}$, the algorithm generates a finite sequence of adjacent complete simplices $\tau^1, \ldots, \tau^{k'}$ with $\tau^{k'} \subset \widetilde{Q}^N_{\tilde{\delta}}$. Observe that $\tau^1 = \{0^N\}$ induces the trivial RDE$_{\underline{\lambda}}$ with full rationing on demand in the markets for all real commodities. In the following theorem it is shown that the maximal absolute value of the total excess demand, $\|\widehat{z}(q)\|_\infty$, at any point q of a simplex of Σ containing any of the adjacent complete simplices generated by the algorithm, can be made arbitrarily small by taking the mesh size of Σ small enough.

Theorem 12.4.9
Let the economy $\mathcal{E} = ((X^i, \preceq^i, \omega^i)_{i \in I_M}, (\widetilde{l}, \widetilde{L}))$ with short-run rigidities $\widetilde{r}$ satisfy Assumptions A1-A5. Let Σ be a triangulation of $\overline{Q}^N_{\tilde{\delta}}$. Then, for every J-complete simplex generated by Algorithm 12.4.8, it holds that $N \in J$. Moreover, for every $\varepsilon \in \mathbb{R}_{++}$, there exists $\delta \in \mathbb{R}_{++}$ such that if $\mathrm{mesh}(\Sigma) < \delta$ *and $\sigma \in \Sigma$ contains one of the adjacent complete simplices generated by Algorithm 12.4.8, then $\|\widehat{z}(q)\|_\infty < \varepsilon$, $\forall q \in \sigma$.*

Proof
Let some J-complete facet $\tau(q^1, \ldots, q^t)$ of a simplex of $\Sigma(J)$ generated by the algorithm be given.
Suppose $N \notin J$. Then $q_N = 0$, $\forall q \in \tau$. For every $k \in I_t$, it holds by Theorem 12.3.5 that $\widehat{z}_j(q^k) \geq 0$, $\forall j \in I_{N-1}$. For every $k \in I_t$, it holds by Theorem 12.3.4 that $\widehat{p}(q^k) \cdot \widehat{z}(q^k) = 0$, so $\widehat{z}_N(q^k) \leq 0$. Hence, for every $k \in I_t$, $\widehat{f}(q^k) = N$, a contradiction with $N \notin J$. Consequently, $N \in J$.
Let some $\varepsilon \in \mathbb{R}_{++}$ be given. Let $\delta \in \mathbb{R}_{++}$ be such that $q^1, q^2 \in \overline{Q}^N_{\tilde{\delta}}$ and $\|q^1 - q^2\|_\infty < \delta$ implies

$$\|\widehat{z}(q^1) - \widehat{z}(q^2)\|_\infty < \frac{\min(\{\widetilde{p}_j(\underline{\lambda}) \mid j \in I_N\})}{\sum_{j \in I_N} \widetilde{p}_j(\underline{\lambda}/\widetilde{\delta})}\varepsilon. \tag{12.5}$$

Since $\widehat{z}$ is a continuous function by Theorem 12.3.4 and $\overline{Q}^N_{\tilde{\delta}}$ is compact, such a δ exists by Theorem 2.7.10. Let $\sigma \in \Sigma$ be any N-simplex containing one of the adjacent complete simplices generated by the algorithm. Then there exists a non-empty subset $\overline{J}$ of I_N with $\#\overline{J} = t$ and a $\overline{J}$-complete simplex

$\overline{\tau}(q^1,\ldots,q^t) \subset A(\overline{J})$ being contained by σ. For every $j \in J$, there exists a vertex q^k of $\overline{\tau}$ for some $k \in I_t$ such that $\widehat{z}_j(q^k) \leq 0$. For every $j \in I_N \setminus J$, for every $q \in \tau$, $j \neq N$ and $q_j = 0$, so by Theorem 12.3.4, $\widehat{z}_j(q) \leq 0$. Therefore, for every $j \in I_N$, there exists $\overline{q} \in \overline{\tau}$ such that $\widehat{z}_j(\overline{q}) \leq 0$.

Let some $q \in \sigma$ be given. Since $\text{mesh}(\Sigma) < \delta$, it follows from the previous paragraph and from (12.5) that

$$\widehat{z}_j(q) < \frac{\min(\{\widetilde{p}_j(\underline{\lambda}) \mid j \in I_N\})}{\sum_{j\in I_N} \widetilde{p}_j(\underline{\lambda}/\widetilde{\delta})}\varepsilon \leq \varepsilon, \ \forall j \in I_N. \tag{12.6}$$

By Theorem 12.3.4 and (12.6) it holds that

$$\widehat{z}_j(q) = -\frac{\sum_{j\in I_N\setminus\{j\}} \widehat{p}_j(q)\widehat{z}_j(q)}{\widehat{p}_j(q)} > -\frac{\min(\{\widetilde{p}_j(\underline{\lambda}) \mid j \in I_N\})}{\sum_{j\in I_N} \widetilde{p}_j(\underline{\lambda}/\widetilde{\delta})}\varepsilon\frac{\sum_{j\in I_N\setminus\{j\}} \widehat{p}_j(q)}{\widehat{p}_j(q)}$$
$$> -\varepsilon, \ \forall j \in I_N.$$

Q.E.D.

The next corollary follows immediately from Theorem 12.4.9 but also from the fact that $\widehat{z}(0^N) = 0^N$. The corollary implies that initially only the price level is increased.

Corollary 12.4.10
Let the economy $\mathcal{E} = ((X^i, \preceq^i, \omega^i)_{i\in I_M}, (\widetilde{l}, \widetilde{L}))$ with short-run rigidities $\widetilde{r}$ satisfy Assumptions A1-A5. Then $\widehat{f}(0^N) = N$.

If $\|\widehat{z}(q)\|_\infty < \varepsilon$ for some $q \in \overline{Q}^N_{\widetilde{\delta}}$, then it follows that $(\widehat{p}(q), \widehat{l}(q), \widehat{L}(q), \widehat{d}(q))$ satisfies all the properties of an ε-RDE$_{\widehat{\lambda}(q)}$, except possibly the requirement that there is no demand rationing in the market for the numeraire commodity. Notice that, for every $q \in \overline{Q}^N_{\widetilde{\delta}}$, for every $i \in I_M$, $\widehat{L}^i_N(q) = \widetilde{L}^i_N(q_1,\ldots,q_{N-1},1) > \widetilde{\omega}_N - \omega^i_N$ and $\widehat{L}^i_N(q)$ is independent of the choice of q. Let $\overline{q}$ be some element of $\overline{Q}^N_{\widetilde{\delta}}$. So, if $\varepsilon < \min(\{\widehat{L}^i_N(\overline{q}) - \widetilde{\omega}_N + \omega^i_N \mid i \in I_M\})$ and $\|\widehat{z}(q)\|_\infty < \varepsilon$ for some $q \in \overline{Q}^N_{\widetilde{\delta}}$, then, for every $i \in I_M$,

$$\widehat{d}^i_N(q) - \omega^i_N \leq \widehat{z}_N(q) + \widetilde{\omega}_N - \omega^i_N < \varepsilon + \widetilde{\omega}_N - \omega^i_N < \widehat{L}^i_N(\overline{q}) = \widehat{L}^i_N(q)$$

and an ε-RDE$_{\widehat{\lambda}(q)}$ is obtained. The set $\widehat{Q}^N_{\widetilde{\delta}}$ is defined by

$$\widehat{Q}^N_{\widetilde{\delta}} = \left\{q \in \overline{Q}^N_{\widetilde{\delta}} \,\middle|\, \exists j \in I_{N-1},\ q_j = 1\right\}.$$

The number $\widehat{\varepsilon} \in \mathbb{R}_{++}$ is defined by

$$\widehat{\varepsilon} = \min \left(\left\{ \widehat{L}^i_N(\overline{q}) + \omega^i_N - \widetilde{\omega}_N \middle| i \in I_M \right\} \right). \tag{12.7}$$

Using the previous paragraph and Theorem 12.3.2 it follows that, for every $q \in \overline{Q}^N_{\tilde{\delta}}$, for every $\varepsilon < \widehat{\varepsilon}$, if $||\widehat{z}(q)||_\infty < \varepsilon$ and $q \in \widehat{Q}^N_{\tilde{\delta}}$, then q induces the ε-PDE $(\widehat{p}(q), \widehat{l}(q), \widehat{L}(q), \widehat{d}(q))$.

Theorem 12.4.11
Let the economy $\mathcal{E} = ((X^i, \preceq^i, \omega^i)_{i \in I_M}, (\widetilde{l}, \widetilde{L}))$ with short-run rigidities $\widetilde{r}$ satisfy Assumptions A1-A5. Then, for every $\varepsilon \in \mathbb{R}_{++}$, there is a piecewise linear, continuous function $\pi : [0,1] \to \overline{Q}^N_{\tilde{\delta}}$ such that $(\widehat{p}(\pi(0)), \widehat{l}(\pi(0)), \widehat{L}(\pi(0)), \widehat{d}(\pi(0)))$ is the trivial RDE$_{\underline{\lambda}}$, for every $t \in [0,1]$, $(\widehat{p}(\pi(t)), \widehat{l}(\pi(t)), \widehat{L}(\pi(t)), \widehat{d}(\pi(t)))$ is an ε-RDE$_{\hat{\lambda}(\pi(t))}$, and $(\widehat{p}(\pi(1)), \widehat{l}(\pi(1)), \widehat{L}(\pi(1)), \widehat{d}(\pi(1)))$ is an ε-PDE.
Proof
Let some $\varepsilon \in \mathbb{R}_{++}$ be given. There is no loss of generality in assuming that $\varepsilon < \widehat{\varepsilon}$. Choose δ as in Theorem 12.4.9, let Σ be a triangulation of $\overline{Q}^N_{\tilde{\delta}}$ with mesh$(\Sigma) < \delta$, and consider the sequence $\tau^1, \ldots, \tau^{k'}$ of adjacent complete simplices generated by Algorithm 12.4.8 given the triangulation Σ. Every simplex in this sequence is a J-complete facet of a simplex of $\Sigma(J)$ for some $J \subset I_N$. For every $k \in I_{k'}$, let b^k denote the barycentre of τ^k. Clearly, $b^1 = 0^N$. By the definition of adjacent complete simplices it holds that for every $k \in I_{k'-1}$ there exists $\sigma \in \Sigma$ containing both b^k and b^{k+1}. Recall from Section 2.2 that, for $t \in \mathbb{R}$, $\lfloor t \rfloor$ denotes the greatest integer that is less than or equal to t. Let the function $\pi : [0,1] \to \overline{Q}^N_{\tilde{\delta}}$ be defined by

$$\begin{aligned} \pi(t) &= (1 - (k'-1)t + \lfloor (k'-1)t \rfloor) b^{\lfloor 1 + (k'-1)t \rfloor} \\ &\quad + ((k'-1)t - \lfloor (k'-1)t \rfloor) b^{1 + \lfloor 1 + (k'-1)t \rfloor}, \ \forall t \in [0,1), \\ \pi(1) &= b^{k'}. \end{aligned}$$

From the convexity of simplices and from Theorem 12.4.9 it follows that π is a continuous, piecewise linear function, $\pi(0)$ yields the trivial RDE$_{\underline{\lambda}}$, and, for every $t \in [0,1]$, $\pi(t)$ induces an ε-RDE$_{\hat{\lambda}(\pi(t))}$. It remains to be verified that $\pi(1)$ induces an ε-PDE, or, equivalently, $\pi(1) \in \widehat{Q}^N_{\tilde{\delta}}$. Clearly, $\pi(1) \in \widetilde{Q}^N_{\tilde{\delta}}$, so it is sufficient to show that $\pi_N(1) < 1 - \widetilde{\delta}$.
Suppose $\pi_N(1) = 1 - \widetilde{\delta}$. Let $q^1, \ldots, q^t$ be the vertices of $\tau^{k'}$. Then, since $\pi(1) = b^{k'}$, being the barycentre of $\tau^{k'}$, it holds for every $k \in I_t$ that $q^k_N = 1 - \widetilde{\delta}$ and by Lemma 12.3.6 that $\widehat{z}_N(q^k) > 0$, so $\widehat{f}(q^k) \neq N$. Hence, $\tau^{k'}$ is J-complete for a non-empty subset J of I_N not containing N, a contradiction with Theorem 12.4.9. Q.E.D.

To conclude this section the path $\pi : [0,1] \rightarrow \overline{Q}^N_{\tilde{\delta}}$ of Theorem 12.4.11 joining $\pi(0)$ and $\pi(1)$, inducing the trivial RDE$_{\underline{\lambda}}$ and an ε-PDE, respectively, is considered for some $\varepsilon \in \mathbb{R}_{++}$. This path can be considered as a price and quantity adjustment process in which, given fixed relative prices $\tilde{r}$ of the real commodities, the price level $\lambda \in \mathbb{R}_{++}$ and the rationing scheme $L \in \tilde{L}(Q^N)$ are adjusted from the trivial equilibrium values $\lambda = \underline{\lambda}$ and $L = 0^{MN}$ to values $\lambda = \widehat{\lambda}(\pi(1))$ and $L = \widehat{L}(\pi(1))$ inducing an ε-PDE. Starting at the state $q = 0^N$, it follows from Theorem 12.3.5 that raising the value of q_j for some $j \in I_{N-1}$, without raising the value of q_N, leads to a disequilibrium situation. This is caused by the low price level $\underline{\lambda}$. According to Corollary 12.4.10 the value of q_N is increased first, in order to increase the price level. Therefore, the price and quantity adjustment process starts along the boundary of $\overline{Q}^N_{\tilde{\delta}}$ at which only the value of q_N rises, i.e. only the price level increases. Because of this increasing price level the notional total excess demand for the real commodities decreases. Clearly, q_N is prevented from increasing to $1-\tilde{\delta}$ since Lemma 12.3.6 guarantees that there exists a positive total excess demand of the numeraire commodity for values of q_N greater than or equal to $1-\tilde{\delta}$. So, there must be a value of q_N at which at least one consumer would like to sell at least one of the real commodities. At this point the price and quantity adjustment process proceeds by increasing the value of q_j for some $j \in I_{N-1}$. So, demand rationing in the market for such a commodity is weakened and trade becomes possible in such a commodity. When there are commodities with very low fixed prices with respect to other commodities, the value of q_j corresponding to these commodities will not change at first and there will be full rationing on demand in the market for these commodities. Continuing along the path, full rationing on demand on commodity j disappears as soon as at least one of the consumers starts supplying this commodity. By adjusting the price level and the rationing scheme, the economy remains approximately in equilibrium. Proceeding along the path, finally the end point in $\widehat{Q}^N_{\tilde{\delta}}$ is reached. By Theorem 12.4.11 the value of q_j is equal to one at this end point for some $j \in I_{N-1}$. So, by adjusting the price level and the rationing scheme an ε-PDE has been reached.

12.5 THE LONG RUN PRICE AND QUANTITY ADJUSTMENT PROCESS

The adjustment process described in the previous section can be seen as short term adjustment given fixed relative prices of the real commodities determined by $\tilde{r}$. In the short run the relative prices are fixed and the markets must be equilibrated by means of rationing. With a free price level, it follows from Section 12.4 that in order to obtain a constrained equilibrium it is sufficient to impose demand rationing in at most $N-2$ markets for the $N-1$ real commodities. The real commodity in the market for which there is no rationing cannot be chosen a priori, but follows ex post from the adjustment process. Following the arguments of van der Laan (1984) it is also possible to choose this real commodity ex ante, by imposing supply rationing or demand rationing in the markets for the other real commodities. In general, for fixed relative prices but a flexible price level, equilibrium is obtained by rationing in the markets for $N-2$ real commodities. To reduce the number of markets with rationing, more price flexibility is needed, which may be assumed to occur in the longer run. In the longer run not only the price level may adjust, but also the relative prices of the commodities. This adjustment of the relative prices continues until the economy reaches an approximate Walrasian equilibrium in which the notional total excess demand equals the total initial endowment. A well-known price adjustment process is the Walrasian tatonnement process as formulated by Samuelson (1941). That price adjustment process adjusts at any point in time the price system proportional to the prevailing notional total excess demand. So, the tatonnement process is a local price adjustment process in the sense that at any price system reached only the local information of the notional total excess demand at this price system is used. The Walrasian tatonnement process has two drawbacks.

First, the local adjustment of the price system does not guarantee the convergence of the process to a Walrasian equilibrium price system, see Section 3.12. In Chapter 10 it is shown that, generically, the price adjustment process introduced in van der Laan and Talman (1987a) converges to a Walrasian equilibrium price system given any initial starting price system and under standard assumptions on the consumption sets, preference relations, and initial endowments. Therefore, the price adjustment process of van der Laan and Talman (1987a) does not suffer from this drawback. Secondly, in the Walrasian tatonnement process the total excess demand is not equal to zero as long as the process has not reached the Walrasian equilibrium price system. So, trade must be excluded until the Walrasian equilibrium price system has been reached. Also the price adjustment process proposed in van der Laan and Talman (1987a) suffers from this drawback. Moreover, as has been noticed in Veendorp (1975), the relevant market signals for an adjustment process in the economic system are based on the effective total excess demand associated with a Drèze equilibrium instead of the notional total excess demand used in the price adjustment processes mentioned above. Veendorp (1975) gives a price adjustment process that follows a path of constrained equilibria. In this process the price system is adjusted as in the Walrasian tatonnement process, with the notional total excess demand replaced by the effective total excess demand. Although a convergence proof has been given for a model with three commodities if the total excess demand function satisfies a gross substitutability condition, see also Laroque (1981) for a correction of the original proof, in general the process might not converge to a Walrasian equilibrium price system and even chaotic behaviour may be expected. The possibility of chaotic behaviour has been confirmed in Böhm (1993) in a more complicated model with overlapping generations, producers, and a government. In Movshovich (1994) a stochastic price adjustment process in discrete time is introduced. It is assumed that at each point in time a Drèze equilibrium results. It is shown that the process converges to a Walrasian equilibrium (a.s.) if some conditions similar to gross substitutability of the total excess demand function are satisfied.

In this chapter an alternative price and quantity adjustment process is considered in which an approximate Walrasian equilibrium is reached along a path of approximate real demand constrained equilibria. At any point along the path of this price and quantity adjustment process the total excess demand is equal to zero and hence trade is possible. This property allows one to give two interesting interpretations of the price and quantity adjustment process. In the first interpretation agents enter the market every day with their constant stock of daily initial endowments and with unchanging preference relations. Based on the previous price system and rationing scheme, adjustment of the price system and the rationing scheme takes place daily in such a way that the economy stays in equilibrium, i.e. at the prevailing price system and rationing scheme the total excess demand is equal to zero in every market. After trade the consumers leave the market and consume their commodity bundles. At the next day they again enter the market in possession of their constant initial endowments.

The second interpretation stays closer to the usual interpretation of a tatonnement process. Based on the total excess demand, the price system and the rationing scheme are changed until a Walrasian equilibrium price system is reached. This Walrasian equilibrium price system specifies a price for every commodity, both for present and for future commodities. During the adjustment of the price system no trade takes place. As argued by Blad (1978) it is not sufficient that a tatonnement process is convergent, convergence also should be considerably fast. If convergence is guaranteed, but takes too long, then at some point in time trade should take place at a non-Walrasian equilibrium price system. In the price adjustment processes usually considered, it is not clear at all which allocation will result in such a case. In the price and quantity adjustment process proposed in this chapter, at every point in time a uniquely specified allocation, compatible with a real demand constrained equilibrium is obtained.

Given the short-run rigidities, the price and quantity adjustment process adjusts the price system along a path of approximate real demand constrained equilibria by keeping the price of a commodity, in the market for which demand rationing prevails, relatively equal to the price level λ, while the price of a commodity corresponding to a market without demand rationing is allowed to decrease from the price level λ. This reflects the natural property, known as the *law of demand*, that the ratio of prices of a commodity with demand rationing and a commodity without rationing should be increased. Therefore, for a given price level $\lambda \in \mathbb{R}$, the *set of admissible price systems* $P(\lambda)$ is defined by

$$P(\lambda) = \{p \in \mathbb{R}^N_+ \,|\, p_j \leq \lambda \tilde{r}_j, \ \forall j \in I_{N-1}, \text{ and } p_N = 1\}.$$

Although λ now only reflects the maximal price ratio $\frac{p_j}{\tilde{r}_j}$, this variable is still called the *price level.* Given some $\lambda \in \mathbb{R}$, the concept of an RDE$_\lambda$ is generalized in the following definition.

Definition 12.5.1 (Generalized real demand constrained equilibrium with a given price level)
Let some price level $\lambda \in \mathbb{R}$ *be given. A* generalized real demand constrained equilibrium with price level λ (GRDE$_\lambda$) *of the economy* $\mathcal{E} = ((X^i, \preceq^i, \omega^i)_{i \in I_M}, (\tilde{l}, \tilde{L}))$ *with short-run rigidities* $\tilde{r}$ *is an element*

$$(p^*, l^*, L^*, x^*) \in P(\lambda) \times \tilde{l}(Q^N) \times \tilde{L}(Q^N) \times X$$

satisfying

1. *for every consumer* $i \in I_M$, $x^{*i} \in \delta^i(p^*, l^{*i}, L^{*i})$,
2. $\sum_{i \in I_M} x^{*i} - \sum_{i \in I_M} \omega^i = 0^N$,
3. *for every commodity* $j \in I_{N-1}$, $x^{*i}_j - \omega^i_j > l^{*i}_j$, $\forall i \in I_M$,
4. *for every commodity* $j \in I_{N-1}$, $p^*_j < \lambda \tilde{r}_j$ *implies* $L^*_j > x^{*i}_j - \omega^i_j$, $\forall i \in I_M$,
5. *for every consumer* $i \in I_M$, $l^{*i}_N < x^{*i}_N - \omega^i_N < L^{*i}_N$.

This definition reflects the standard condition in the theory of constrained equilibria that in equilibrium rationing in a market may only occur if the price constraint is binding.

Let some price level $\lambda \in \mathbb{R}_{++}$ be given. Clearly, there is no demand rationing in the market for a commodity $j \in I_{N-1}$ if the price p_j is below $\lambda\widetilde{r}_j$. However, demand rationing in the market for a commodity $j \in I_{N-1}$ may occur if the price of commodity j is relatively equal to the price level λ, i.e. $p_j = \lambda\widetilde{r}_j$. Clearly, it holds that any RDE$_\lambda$ is a GRDE$_\lambda$. Notice that at an RDE$_\lambda$ a situation corresponding to Condition 4 of the definition of a GRDE$_\lambda$ does not occur.

Any Walrasian equilibrium (*WE*) (p^*, x^*) of the economy $\mathcal{E}$ corresponds to a GRDE$_\lambda$ (p^*, l^*, L^*, x^*) with $l^* = \widetilde{l}(1^N)$ and $L^* = \widetilde{L}(1^N)$, for any price level λ satisfying $\lambda \geq \max(\{\frac{p_j^*}{\widetilde{r}_j} \mid j \in I_{N-1}\})$. Conversely, for every $\lambda \in \mathbb{R}_{++}$, for every GRDE$_\lambda$ (p^*, l^*, L^*, x^*) with $L_j^{*i} > x_j^{*i} - \omega_j^i$, $\forall i \in I_M$, $\forall j \in I_{N-1}$, it holds that (p^*, x^*) is a Walrasian equilibrium of $\mathcal{E}$. Therefore, such a GRDE$_\lambda$ is also referred to as a Walrasian equilibrium.

In the remainder of this section attention is focused on approximate equilibria. Analogously to Definition 12.4.1 an *approximate GRDE$_\lambda$* for a price level $\lambda \in \mathbb{R}$ and an approximate Walrasian equilibrium are defined as follows.

Definition 12.5.2 (ε-GRDE$_\lambda$ and ε-WE)
Let some price level $\lambda \in \mathbb{R}$ and some $\varepsilon \in \mathbb{R}_+$ be given. An ε-GRDE$_\lambda$ (ε-WE) of the economy $\mathcal{E} = ((X^i, \preceq^i, \omega^i)_{i \in I_M}, (\widetilde{l}, \widetilde{L}))$ with short-run rigidities $\widetilde{r}$ is an element

$$(p^*, l^*, L^*, x^*) \in P(\lambda) \times \widetilde{l}(Q^N) \times \widetilde{L}(Q^N) \times X$$

such that all conditions of a GRDE$_\lambda$ (WE) are satisfied, except possibly the condition of equality of supply and demand, which is replaced by $\|\sum_{i \in I_M} x^{*i} - \sum_{i \in I_M} \omega^i\|_\infty \leq \varepsilon$.

Obviously, for every $\lambda \in \mathbb{R}$ it holds that a 0-GRDE$_\lambda$ is a GRDE$_\lambda$. Moreover, for every $\lambda \in \mathbb{R}$, for every $\varepsilon \in \mathbb{R}_+$, it holds that an ε-RDE$_\lambda$ is an ε-GRDE$_\lambda$. Furthermore, for every ε-WE, there exists $\lambda \in \mathbb{R}_{++}$ such that it is an ε-GRDE$_\lambda$.

Now a price and quantity adjustment process is developed to obtain an ε-WE by following a path of ε-GRDE$_\lambda$'s. The set $\overline{Q}_{\widetilde{\delta}}^N$ is extended to the set $\overline{R}_{\widetilde{\delta}}^N$, defined by

$$\overline{R}_{\widetilde{\delta}}^N = \left\{q \in \mathbb{R}^N \,\middle|\, 0 \leq q_N \leq 1 - \widetilde{\delta},\ 0 \leq q_j \leq 2,\ \forall j \in I_{N-1}, \text{ and } \exists j' \in I_{N-1},\ q_{j'} \leq 1\right\}.$$

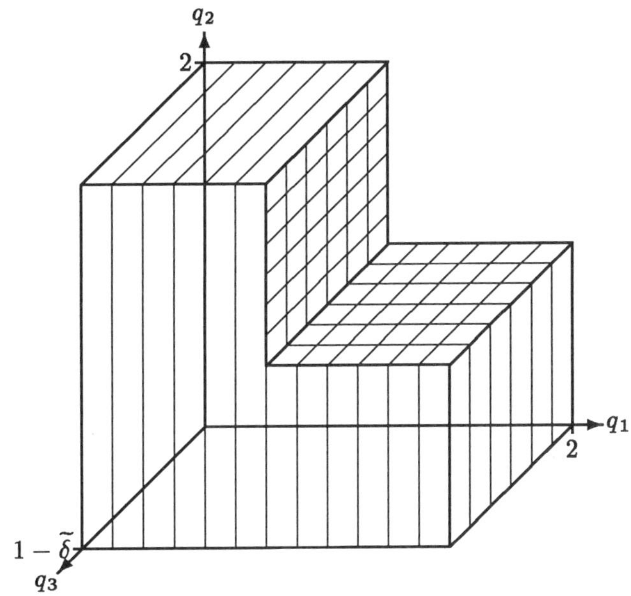

Figure 12.5.1. The sets $\overline{R}^3_{\tilde{\delta}}$, $\widetilde{R}^3_{\tilde{\delta}}$, and $\widehat{R}^3_{\tilde{\delta}}$.

Moreover, the sets $\widetilde{R}^N_{\tilde{\delta}}$ and $\widehat{R}^N_{\tilde{\delta}}$ are defined by

$$\widetilde{R}^N_{\tilde{\delta}} = \left\{ q \in \overline{R}^N_{\tilde{\delta}} \,\middle|\, q_N = 1-\tilde{\delta}, \text{ or } \exists j' \in I_{N-1},\ q_{j'} = 2, \text{ or } q_j \geq 1,\ \forall j \in I_{N-1} \right\},$$
$$\widehat{R}^N_{\tilde{\delta}} = \left\{ q \in \overline{R}^N_{\tilde{\delta}} \,\middle|\, q_j \geq 1,\ \forall j \in I_{N-1} \right\}.$$

Clearly, $\widehat{R}^N_{\tilde{\delta}} \subset \widetilde{R}^N_{\tilde{\delta}} \subset \overline{R}^N_{\tilde{\delta}}$. In Figure 12.5.1 these sets are depicted for the case $N=3$. The set $\widehat{R}^3_{\tilde{\delta}}$ corresponds to the crossed area and the set $\widetilde{R}^3_{\tilde{\delta}} \setminus \widehat{R}^3_{\tilde{\delta}}$ to the striped area.

The functions $\widehat{\lambda} : \overline{R}^N_{\tilde{\delta}} \to \mathbb{R}_{++}$, $\widehat{p} : \overline{R}^N_{\tilde{\delta}} \to \mathbb{R}^N_{++}$, $\widehat{l} : \overline{R}^N_{\tilde{\delta}} \to -\mathbb{R}^{MN}_{+}$, and $\widehat{L} : \overline{R}^N_{\tilde{\delta}} \to \mathbb{R}^{MN}_{+}$ are defined by

$$\begin{aligned}
\widehat{\lambda}(q) &= \tfrac{\lambda}{1-q_N}, && \forall q \in \overline{R}^N_{\tilde{\delta}},\\
\widehat{p}_j(q) &= \min(\{1, 2-q_j\})\widehat{\lambda}(q)\widetilde{r}_j, && \forall j \in I_{N-1},\ \forall q \in \overline{R}^N_{\tilde{\delta}},\\
\widehat{p}_N(q) &= 1, && \forall q \in \overline{R}^N_{\tilde{\delta}},\\
\widehat{l}(q) &= \widetilde{l}(1^N), && \forall q \in \overline{R}^N_{\tilde{\delta}},\\
\widehat{L}(q) &= \widetilde{L}\left(\inf(\{(q_1, \ldots, q_{N-1}, 1)^\top, 1^N\})\right), && \forall q \in \overline{R}^N_{\tilde{\delta}}.
\end{aligned}$$

Notice that these functions are extensions of the functions $\widehat{\lambda}$, $\widehat{l}$, $\widehat{L}$, and $\widehat{p}$ defined in equations (12.1)-(12.4) in Section 12.3. Moreover, for every $i \in I_M$, for every $j \in I_{N-1}$, for every $q \in \overline{R}^N_{\widetilde{\delta}}$, $\widehat{p}_j(q) < \widehat{\lambda}(q)\widetilde{r}_j$ implies $\widehat{L}^i_j(q) > \widetilde{\omega}_j - \omega^i_j$.

Let some $(p, l^i, L^i) \in \mathbb{R}^N_+ \times \{\widetilde{l}^i(1^N)\} \times \widetilde{L}^i(Q^N)$ be given. From Assumptions A1-A5 it follows easily that the set $\delta^i(p, l^i, L^i)$ of consumer $i \in I_M$ contains exactly one element. Therefore, for every $i \in I_M$, the *reduced demand function* $\widehat{d}^i : \overline{R}^N_{\widetilde{\delta}} \to \mathbb{R}^N$ of consumer i is defined by

$$\left\{\widehat{d}^i(q)\right\} = \delta^i\left(\widehat{p}(q), \widehat{l}^i(q), \widehat{L}^i(q)\right), \ \forall q \in \overline{R}^N_{\widetilde{\delta}}.$$

The *reduced total excess demand function* $\widehat{z} : \overline{R}^N_{\widetilde{\delta}} \to \mathbb{R}^N$ of the economy $\mathcal{E}$ with short-run rigidities $\widetilde{r}$ is defined by

$$\widehat{z}(q) = \sum_{i \in I_M} \widehat{d}^i(q) - \sum_{i \in I_M} \omega^i, \ \forall q \in \overline{R}^N_{\widetilde{\delta}}.$$

The following results are the analogues of Theorem 12.3.1, Theorem 12.3.3, and Theorem 12.3.4, respectively, and can be shown in a similar way as Theorem 4.7.1, Theorem 4.7.2, and Theorem 8.2.8, respectively.

Theorem 12.5.3
Let the economy $\mathcal{E} = ((X^i, \preceq^i, \omega^i)_{i \in I_M}, (\widetilde{l}, \widetilde{L}))$ with short-run rigidities $\widetilde{r}$ satisfy Assumptions A1-A5. Let some $\varepsilon \in [0, \widehat{\varepsilon})$ be given with $\widehat{\varepsilon}$ as defined in (12.7). If the element q^* of $\overline{R}^N_{\widetilde{\delta}}$ is such that $\|\widehat{z}(q^*)\|_\infty \leq \varepsilon$, then $(\widehat{p}(q^*), \widehat{l}(q^*), \widehat{L}(q^*), \widehat{d}(q^*))$ is an ε-GRDE$_{\widehat{\lambda}(q^*)}$.

Let some $\varepsilon \in [0, \widehat{\varepsilon})$ be given. Then $(\widehat{p}(q^*), \widehat{l}(q^*), \widehat{L}(q^*), \widehat{d}(q^*))$ is called the ε-GRDE$_{\widehat{\lambda}(q^*)}$ *induced* by q^* if $q^* \in \overline{R}^N_{\widetilde{\delta}}$ is such that $\|\widehat{z}(q^*)\|_\infty \leq \varepsilon$.

Theorem 12.5.4
Let the economy $\mathcal{E} = ((X^i, \preceq^i, \omega^i)_{i \in I_M}, (\widetilde{l}, \widetilde{L}))$ with short-run rigidities $\widetilde{r}$ satisfy Assumptions A1-A5. Let some price level $\lambda \in [\underline{\lambda}, \rightarrow)$ and some $\varepsilon \in [0, \widehat{\varepsilon})$ be given. If (p^*, l^*, L^*, x^*) is an ε-GRDE$_\lambda$, then there exists $q^* \in \overline{R}^N_{\widetilde{\delta}}$ such that $\|\widehat{z}(q^*)\|_\infty \leq \varepsilon$, while $(p^*, l^*, L^*, x^*) \sim (\widehat{p}(q^*), \widehat{l}(q^*), \widehat{L}(q^*), \widehat{d}(q^*))$, i.e. (p^*, l^*, L^*, x^*) is equivalent to $(\widehat{p}(q^*), \widehat{l}(q^*), \widehat{L}(q^*), \widehat{d}(q^*))$ in the sense of Definition 4.6.2.

From Theorem 12.5.4 it follows immediately that there is no loss of generality in only considering ε-GRDE$_\lambda$'s for $\varepsilon \in [0, \widehat{\varepsilon})$, for $\lambda \in [\underline{\lambda}, \rightarrow)$, being induced by elements of $\overline{R}^N_{\tilde{\delta}}$. Therefore, $q \in \overline{R}^N_{\tilde{\delta}}$ is called the *state* of the economy. In Theorem 12.5.4 it cannot be guaranteed that q^* can be chosen such that $\widehat{\lambda}(q^*) = \lambda$ if $\widetilde{p}(\lambda) \gg p^*$. However, in this case (p^*, l^*, L^*, x^*) also is an ε-GRDE$_{\overline{\lambda}}$ with $\overline{\lambda} = \max(\{\frac{p^*_j}{\widetilde{r}_j} \mid j \in I_{N-1}\})$. In fact, (p^*, l^*, L^*, x^*) is an ε-WE and the element q^* given in Theorem 12.5.4 can be chosen such that $\widehat{\lambda}(q^*) = \max(\{\frac{p^*_j}{\widetilde{r}_j} \mid j \in I_{N-1}\})$. The following lemma describes some properties of the reduced total excess demand function $\widehat{z}$.

Theorem 12.5.5
Let the economy $\mathcal{E} = ((X^i, \preceq^i, \omega^i)_{i \in I_M}, (\widetilde{l}, \widetilde{L}))$ with short-run rigidities $\widetilde{r}$ satisfy Assumptions A1-A5. Then the reduced total excess demand function $\widehat{z} : \overline{R}^N_{\tilde{\delta}} \to \mathbb{R}^N$ has the following properties:

1. *$\widehat{z}$ is continuous,*
2. *for every $q \in \overline{R}^N_{\tilde{\delta}}$, for every $j \in I_{N-1}$, $q_j = 0$ implies $\widehat{z}_j(q) \leq 0$,*
3. *for every $q \in \overline{R}^N_{\tilde{\delta}}$, $\widehat{p}(q) \cdot \widehat{z}(q) = 0$.*

The following result follows immediately from the definition of $\widehat{z}$.

Theorem 12.5.6
Let the economy $\mathcal{E} = ((X^i, \preceq^i, \omega^i)_{i \in I_M}, (\widetilde{l}, \widetilde{L}))$ with short-run rigidities $\widetilde{r}$ satisfy Assumptions A1-A5. Let some $q \in \widehat{R}^N_{\tilde{\delta}}$ and $\varepsilon \in [0, \widehat{\varepsilon})$ be given. If $(\widehat{p}(q), \widehat{l}(q), \widehat{L}(q), \widehat{d}(q))$ is an ε-GRDE$_{\widehat{\lambda}(q)}$, then it is an ε-WE.

The following lemmas consider the behaviour of $\widehat{z}$ at the boundary of $\overline{R}^N_{\tilde{\delta}}$.

Lemma 12.5.7
Let the economy $\mathcal{E} = ((X^i, \preceq^i, \omega^i)_{i \in I_M}, (\widetilde{l}, \widetilde{L}))$ with short-run rigidities $\widetilde{r}$ satisfy Assumptions A1-A5. Let some $q \in \overline{R}^N_{\tilde{\delta}}$ with $q_N = 0$ be given. Then, for every $j \in I_{N-1}$, $\widehat{z}_j(q) \geq 0$.

Proof
Suppose there exists $j' \in I_{N-1}$ such that $\widehat{z}_{j'}(q) < 0$. Then there exists $i' \in I_M$ such that $\widehat{d}^{i'}_{j'}(q) - \omega^{i'}_{j'} < \widehat{L}^{i'}_{j'}(q)$. It follows from Theorem 4.6.4 that $\{\widehat{d}^{i'}(q)\} = \delta^{i'}(\widehat{p}(q), \widehat{l}^{i'}(q), \overline{L}^{i'})$, where $\overline{L}^{i'} \in \widetilde{L}^{i'}(Q^N)$ is defined by $\overline{L}^{i'}_{j'} = \widetilde{L}^{i'}_{j'}(\overline{q})$ for some

$\overline{q} \in Q^N$ with $\overline{q}_{j'} = 1$ and $\overline{L}_j^{i'} = \widetilde{L}_j^{i'}(q)$, $\forall j \in I_N \setminus \{j'\}$. Then

$$\frac{\hat{p}_{j'}(q)}{\hat{p}_N(q)} \leq \underline{\lambda}\widetilde{r}_{j'} \leq \alpha^{i'},$$

so, from Lemma 12.2.4 it follows that $\widehat{d}_{j'}^{i'}(q) > \widetilde{\omega}_{j'}$, a contradiction to $\widehat{z}_{j'}(q) < 0$.
Q.E.D.

Lemma 12.5.8
Let the economy $\mathcal{E} = ((X^i, \preceq^i, \omega^i)_{i \in I_M}, (\widetilde{l}, \widetilde{L}))$ with short-run rigidities $\widetilde{r}$ satisfy Assumptions A1-A5. Let some $q \in \overline{R}_{\widetilde{\delta}}^N$ with $q_N = 1 - \widetilde{\delta}$ be given. Then it holds that $\widehat{z}_N(q) > 0$.
Proof
By the definition of $\overline{R}_{\widetilde{\delta}}^N$ there exists $j' \in I_{N-1}$ such that $q_{j'} \leq 1$. So, $q_N = 1 - \widetilde{\delta}$ implies

$$\begin{aligned}\frac{\widehat{p}_N(q)}{\widehat{p}_{j'}(q)} = \frac{\widetilde{\delta}}{\underline{\lambda}\widetilde{r}_{j'}} &\leq \frac{(\underline{\lambda}\min(\{\widetilde{r}_j \mid j \in I_{N-1}\}))^2}{\underline{\lambda}\widetilde{r}_{j'}} \leq \underline{\lambda}\min(\{\widetilde{r}_j \mid j \in I_{N-1}\}) \\ &\leq \min(\{\alpha^i \mid i \in I_M\}).\end{aligned}$$

Hence, by Lemma 12.2.4, $\widehat{z}_N(q) > (M-1)\widetilde{\omega}_N \geq 0$. Q.E.D.

Lemma 12.5.9
Let the economy $\mathcal{E} = ((X^i, \preceq^i, \omega^i)_{i \in I_M}, (\widetilde{l}, \widetilde{L}))$ with short-run rigidities $\widetilde{r}$ satisfy Assumptions A1-A5. Then, for every $q \in \overline{R}_{\widetilde{\delta}}^N$, for every $j \in I_{N-1}$, $q_j = 2$ implies $\widehat{z}_j(q) > 0$.
Proof
Let some $q \in \overline{R}_{\widetilde{\delta}}^N$ and $j \in I_{N-1}$ such that $q_j = 2$ be given. Then $\widehat{p}_j(q) = 0$ and $\widehat{L}_j^i(q) > \widetilde{\omega}_j - \omega_j^i$, $\forall i \in I_M$. Since $\preceq^i$, $\forall i \in I_M$, is strongly monotonic, it follows that $\widehat{z}_j(q) > 0$.
Q.E.D.

Now, for every $\varepsilon \in \mathbb{R}_{++}$, the existence of a path of ε-GRDE$_\lambda$'s leading from the trivial RDE$_{\underline{\lambda}}$ to an ε-WE can be shown.

Theorem 12.5.10
Let the economy $\mathcal{E} = ((X^i, \preceq^i, \omega^i)_{i \in I_M}, (\widetilde{l}, \widetilde{L}))$ with short-run rigidities $\widetilde{r}$ satisfy Assumptions A1-A5. Then, for every $\varepsilon \in \mathbb{R}_{++}$, there is a piecewise linear, continuous function $\pi : [0,1] \to \overline{R}_{\widetilde{\delta}}^N$ such that $(\widehat{p}(\pi(0)), \widehat{l}(\pi(0)), \widehat{L}(\pi(0)), \widehat{d}(\pi(0)))$ is the trivial RDE$_{\underline{\lambda}}$, for every $t \in [0,1]$, $(\widehat{p}(\pi(t)), \widehat{l}(\pi(t)), \widehat{L}(\pi(t)), \widehat{d}(\pi(t)))$ is an

ε-GRDE$_{\widehat{\lambda}(\pi(t))}$, and $(\widehat{p}(\pi(1)), \widehat{l}(\pi(1)), \widehat{L}(\pi(1)), \widehat{d}(\pi(1)))$ is an ε-WE.

Proof

Let some $\varepsilon \in \mathbb{R}_{++}$ be given. Without loss of generality, assume that $\varepsilon < \widehat{\varepsilon}$. Moreover, let some triangulation Σ of $\overline{R}^N_{\tilde{\delta}}$ be given, for example an extension of the slight modification of the K-triangulation discussed before. Although in the definition of a triangulation, Definition 2.7.1, only convex sets are considered, this definition can be applied to $\overline{R}^N_{\tilde{\delta}}$ as well. For every $q \in \overline{R}^N_{\tilde{\delta}}$, let the set $J(q)$ be defined by

$$J(q) = \{j' \in I_N \,|\widehat{z}_{j'}(q) = \min(\{\widehat{z}_j(q) \mid j \in I_N\})\}.$$

Let the labelling function $\widehat{f} : \overline{R}^N_{\tilde{\delta}} \to I_N$ be defined by

$$\widehat{f}(q) = \max(J(q)), \ \forall q \in \overline{R}^N_{\tilde{\delta}}.$$

Now it is possible to extend the algorithm given in Section 12.4 to the set $\overline{R}^N_{\tilde{\delta}}$. For every non-empty subset J of I_N, let the set $A(J)$ be defined by

$$A(J) = \left\{ q \in \overline{R}^N_{\tilde{\delta}} \middle| \, q_j = 0, \ \forall j \in I_N \setminus J \right\}.$$

Clearly, $A(J)$ is a convex $(\#J)$-dimensional subset of $\mathbb{R}^N$ for every subset J of I_N. For every non-empty subset J of I_N, the set $\Sigma(J)$ is defined by

$$\Sigma\,(J) = \{\tau \subset A\,(J)\,|\exists \sigma \in \Sigma,\ \tau \text{ is a } (\#J)\text{-face of } \sigma\}.$$

The only modification of Algorithm 12.4.8 is in Step 2 where now termination takes place if $\tau^k \subset \widetilde{R}^N_{\tilde{\delta}}$. Again, each step in the algorithm is feasible by the properties of a triangulation, and using the proof of Theorem 12.4.7 it can be shown that the algorithm terminates, after generating a finite number of adjacent complete simplices, in Step 2 with a J-complete simplex that is a subset of $A(J) \cap \widetilde{R}^N_{\tilde{\delta}}$ for some non-empty subset J of I_N.

Let $\tau(q^1, \ldots, q^t)$ be a J-complete facet of a simplex of $\Sigma(J)$, for some non-empty subset J of I_N with $\#J = t$, generated by the algorithm. As in the proof of Theorem 12.4.9 it can be shown that for every $j \in J$ there exists $k \in I_t$ such that $\widehat{z}_j(q^k) \leq 0$. Moreover, for every $q \in \tau$, for every $j \in I_N \setminus J$, it holds that $j \neq N$ and $\widehat{z}_j(q) \leq 0$. Let $\delta \in \mathbb{R}_{++}$ be such that $q^1, q^2 \in \overline{R}^N_{\tilde{\delta}}$ and $||q^1 - q^2||_\infty < \delta$ implies

$$||\widehat{z}(q^1) - \widehat{z}(q^2)||_\infty < \frac{\min(\{\widetilde{p}_j(\underline{\lambda}) \mid j \in I_N\})}{\sum_{j \in I_N} \widetilde{p}_j(\underline{\lambda}/\widetilde{\delta})}\varepsilon.$$

Since $\widehat{z}$ is a continuous function by Theorem 12.5.5 and $\overline{R}^N_{\tilde{\delta}}$ is compact, such a δ exists by Theorem 2.7.10. Let $\overline{q}$ be an arbitrary element of a simplex of

Σ containing $\tau(q^1, \ldots, q^t)$. Let the triangulation Σ be such that mesh$(\Sigma) \leq \delta$. Then, for every $j \in I_N$,

$$\widehat{z}_j(\overline{q}) < \frac{\min(\{\widetilde{p}_j(\underline{\lambda}) \mid j \in I_N\})}{\sum_{j \in I_N} \widetilde{p}_j(\underline{\lambda}/\widetilde{\delta})} \varepsilon < \varepsilon.$$

Consider some $j' \in I_N$. If $\widehat{p}_{j'}(\overline{q}) < \underline{\lambda}\widetilde{r}_{j'}$, then $\overline{q}_{j'} > 1$, so $\widehat{L}_{j'}(\overline{q}) = \widetilde{L}_{j'}(\widehat{q})$ for some $\widehat{q} \in Q^N$ with $\widehat{q}_{j'} = 1$. Now it follows from Lemma 12.2.4 that $\widehat{z}_{j'}(\overline{q}) > 0$. If $\widehat{p}_{j'}(\overline{q}) \geq \underline{\lambda}\widetilde{r}_{j'}$, then, as in the proof of Theorem 12.4.9, $\widehat{z}_{j'}(\overline{q}) > -\varepsilon$. Therefore, $(\widehat{p}(\overline{q}), \widehat{l}(\overline{q}), \widehat{L}(\overline{q}), \widehat{d}(\overline{q}))$ is an ε-GRDE$_{\widehat{\lambda}(\overline{q})}$.

Consider the sequence $\tau^1, \ldots, \tau^{k'}$ of simplices generated by the algorithm and, for every $k \in I_{k'}$, let b^k denote the barycentre of τ^k. Let the function $\pi : [0, 1] \to \widetilde{R}^N_{\widetilde{\delta}}$ be defined as in the proof of Theorem 12.4.11, so

$$\begin{aligned} \pi(t) &= (1 - (k' - 1)t + \lfloor (k' - 1)t \rfloor) b^{\lfloor 1 + (k'-1)t \rfloor} \\ &\quad + ((k' - 1)t - \lfloor (k' - 1)t \rfloor) b^{1 + \lfloor 1 + (k'-1)t \rfloor}, \ \forall t \in [0, 1), \\ \pi(1) &= b^{k'}. \end{aligned}$$

Then, for every $t \in [0, 1]$, $\pi(t)$ induces an ε-GRDE$_{\widehat{\lambda}(\pi(t))}$. It is shown that $\pi(1)$ induces an ε-WE, or according to Theorem 12.5.6, $\pi(1) \in \widehat{R}^N_{\widetilde{\delta}}$. Since the algorithm terminates with a simplex having a J-complete facet $\tau^{k'}(q^1, \ldots, q^t)$ being a subset of $A(J) \cap \widetilde{R}^N_{\widetilde{\delta}}$ for some non-empty subset J of I_N with $\#J = t$, it holds that $\pi(1) \in \widetilde{R}^N_{\widetilde{\delta}}$.

Suppose $b^{k'}_N = 1 - \widetilde{\delta}$. Then $N \in J$ and $q^k_N = 1 - \widetilde{\delta}$, $\forall k \in I_t$. For every $k \in I_t$, by Lemma 12.5.8 $\widehat{z}_N(q^k) > 0$, so $\widehat{f}(q^k) \neq N$, a contradiction with $N \in J$ and $\tau^{k'}$ being J-complete. Consequently, $b^{k'}_N < 1 - \widetilde{\delta}$.

Suppose there exists $j' \in I_{N-1}$ such that $b^{k'}_{j'} = 2$. Then $j' \in J$ and $q^k_{j'} = 2$, $\forall k \in I_t$. For every $k \in I_t$, by Lemma 12.5.9 $\widehat{z}_{j'}(q^k) > 0$ and so $\widehat{f}(q^k) \neq j'$, again yielding a contradiction. Consequently, $b^{k'}_j < 2$, $\forall j \in I_{N-1}$.

Now it follows immediately that $\pi(1) \in \widehat{R}^N_{\widetilde{\delta}}$. Q.E.D.

12.6 THE EXISTENCE OF GENERALIZED REAL DEMAND CONSTRAINED EQUILIBRIA

So far the existence of a continuous piecewise linear path of ε-GRDE$_\lambda$'s has been shown for every $\varepsilon \in \mathbb{R}_{++}$. In this section the case $\varepsilon = 0$ is considered. It is conjectured that under suitable differentiability conditions on consumption sets and preference relations the path of points $q^* \in \overline{R}^N_{\tilde{\delta}}$ satisfying $\widehat{z}(q^*) = 0^N$ is, generically, a 1-dimensional piecewise differentiable manifold with boundary. Moreover, one of the components of this 1-dimensional manifold with boundary is homeomorphic to the unit interval and has two boundary points, 0^N, inducing the trivial RDE$_{\underline{\lambda}}$, and a point in $\widehat{R}^N_{\tilde{\delta}}$, inducing a Walrasian equilibrium. In this section another approach is taken. No differentiability assumptions are made, instead only Assumptions A1-A5 are used. The result, being that the set of points $q^* \in \overline{R}^N_{\tilde{\delta}}$ satisfying $\widehat{z}(q^*) = 0^N$ has a component containing both point 0^N and a point in $\widehat{R}^N_{\tilde{\delta}}$, holds for every economy satisfying the previously mentioned assumptions. The proof of the result follows the approach of Chapters 5 and 6. The set $\widetilde{Q}$ is defined by

$$\widetilde{Q} = \left\{ q^* \in \overline{R}^N_{\tilde{\delta}} \,|\widehat{z}(q^*) = 0^N \right\}.$$

Let a non-empty, compact subset S of $\mathbb{R}^m$ be given. The function $d_S : \mathbb{R}^m \to \mathbb{R}$ is defined by

$$d_S(s) = \min(\{||s - \overline{s}||_\infty \mid \overline{s} \in S\}), \ \forall s \in \mathbb{R}^m.$$

In Lemma 5.3.2 it is shown that the function d_S is continuous. Let S^1 and S^2 be non-empty, compact subsets of $\mathbb{R}^m$. The number $e(S^1, S^2) \in \mathbb{R}_+$ is defined by

$$e(S^1, S^2) = \min \left(\left\{ ||s^1 - s^2||_\infty \middle| \, s^1 \in S^1 \text{ and } s^2 \in S^2 \right\} \right).$$

Obviously, if S^1 and S^2 are disjoint, then $e(S^1, S^2) > 0$.

Theorem 12.6.1
Let the economy $\mathcal{E} = ((X^i, \preceq^i, \omega^i)_{i \in I_M}, (\widetilde{l}, \widetilde{L}))$ with short-run rigidities $\widetilde{r}$ satisfy Assumptions A1-A5. Then the set $\widetilde{Q}$ has a component containing 0^N and an element of $\widehat{R}^N_{\tilde{\delta}}$, i.e. there exists a connected set of elements of $\overline{R}^N_{\tilde{\delta}}$ inducing a set of GRDE$_\lambda$'s containing both the trivial RDE$_{\underline{\lambda}}$ and a Walrasian equilibrium.

Proof
For every $n \in \mathbb{N}$, let π^n denote a function π obtained in Theorem 12.5.10 satisfying $||\widehat{z}(\pi^n(t))||_\infty < \frac{1}{n}$, $\forall t \in [0,1]$. Consider an accumulation point of the sequence $(\pi^n(1))_{n \in \mathbb{N}}$ in $\widehat{R}^N_{\tilde{\delta}}$, say q^*. Clearly, $q^* \in \widehat{R}^N_{\tilde{\delta}}$, $\widehat{z}(q^*) = 0^N$, and q^* induces a Walrasian equilibrium. Moreover, $0^N \in \widetilde{Q}$ and $q^* \in \widetilde{Q}$.
Suppose q^* is not an element of the component of 0^N. Since it follows easily that $\widetilde{Q}$ is compact, it holds by Lemma 5.3.4 that there exist disjoint, compact sets $\widetilde{Q}^1$ and $\widetilde{Q}^2$ such that $0^N \in \widetilde{Q}^1$, $q^* \in \widetilde{Q}^2$, and $\widetilde{Q}^1 \cup \widetilde{Q}^2 = \widetilde{Q}$. Hence, there exists $\varepsilon \in \mathbb{R}_{++}$ such that $e(\widetilde{Q}^1, \widetilde{Q}^2) > \varepsilon$. Consider a subsequence $(\pi^{n^m})_{m \in \mathbb{N}}$ with

$\|\pi^{n^m}(1)-q^*\|_\infty < \frac{\varepsilon}{2}$, $\forall m \in \mathbb{N}$. For every $m \in \mathbb{N}$, let the function $f^m : [0,1] \to \mathbb{R}$ be defined by

$$f^m(t) = d_{\tilde{Q}^1}\left(\pi^{n^m}(t)\right) - d_{\tilde{Q}^2}\left(\pi^{n^m}(t)\right), \ \forall t \in [0,1].$$

From the continuity of the functions $d_{\tilde{Q}^1}, d_{\tilde{Q}^2}$, and π^{n^m}, $\forall m \in \mathbb{N}$, it follows that the function f^m, $\forall m \in \mathbb{N}$, is continuous. Moreover, for every $m \in \mathbb{N}$, $f^m(0) < -\varepsilon$ and $f^m(1) > 0$. For every $m \in \mathbb{N}$, let $t^m \in [0,1]$ be such that $f^m(t^m) = 0$. Then $d_{\tilde{Q}^1}(\pi^{n^m}(t^m)) = d_{\tilde{Q}^2}(\pi^{n^m}(t^m)) = d_{\tilde{Q}}(\pi^{n^m}(t^m)) > \frac{\varepsilon}{2}$, $\forall m \in \mathbb{N}$. Consider the sequence $(\pi^{n^m}(t^m))_{m\in\mathbb{N}}$ in the compact set $\overline{R}^N_{\tilde{\delta}}$. Without loss of generality, $(\pi^{n^m}(t^m))_{m\in\mathbb{N}}$ converges to some $\overline{q} \in \overline{R}^N_{\tilde{\delta}}$. It holds that

$$\widehat{z}(\overline{q}) = \widehat{z}\left(\lim_{m\to+\infty} \pi^{n^m}(t^m)\right) = \lim_{m\to+\infty} \widehat{z}\left(\pi^{n^m}(t^m)\right) = 0^N.$$

Hence, $d_{\tilde{Q}}(\overline{q}) = 0$. Since

$$d_{\tilde{Q}}(\overline{q}) = d_{\tilde{Q}}\left(\lim_{m\to+\infty} \pi^{n^m}(t^m)\right) = \lim_{m\to+\infty} d_{\tilde{Q}}\left(\pi^{n^m}(t^m)\right) \geq \tfrac{\varepsilon}{2},$$

a contradiction is obtained. Q.E.D.

Corollary 12.6.2
Let the economy $\mathcal{E} = ((X^i, \preceq^i, \omega^i)_{i\in I_M}, (\widetilde{l}, \widetilde{L}))$ with short-run rigidities $\widetilde{r}$ satisfy Assumptions A1-A5. Then there exists a connected set of GRDE$_\lambda$'s containing the trivial RDE$_{\underline{\lambda}}$ and a Walrasian equilibrium.

Proof
Consider the set of GRDE$_{\hat{\lambda}(q)}$'s

$$\left\{(\widehat{p}(q), \widehat{l}(q), \widehat{L}(q), \widehat{d}(q)) \,\middle|\, q \in \widetilde{Q}^0\right\},$$

with $\widetilde{Q}^0$ the component of 0^N in $\widetilde{Q}$. By Theorem 12.6.1 the set above contains the trivial RDE$_{\underline{\lambda}}$ and a Walrasian equilibrium, and since the image of a connected set by a continuous function is connected by Theorem 2.3.13, the corollary follows. Q.E.D.

12.7 THE ADJUSTMENT PROCESS TO A WALRASIAN EQUILIBRIUM

In this section the path followed by the price and quantity adjustment process is considered for some given $\varepsilon \in \mathbb{R}_{++}$. As has been shown in Section 12.4, the

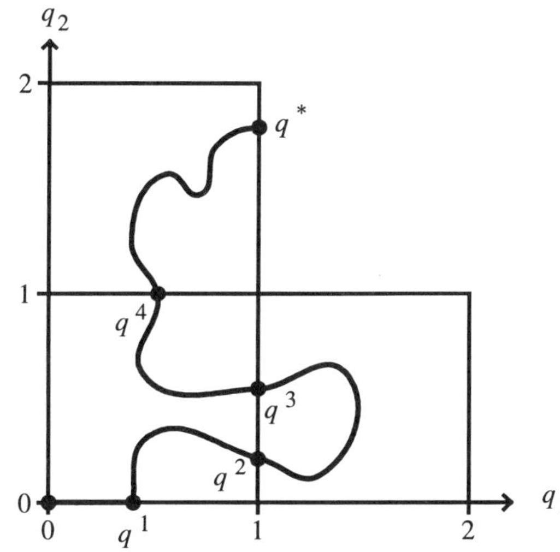

Figure 12.7.1. Illustration of the path in (q_1, q_2)-space.

path first proceeds from the trivial $\text{RDE}_{\underline{\lambda}}$ to an ε-PDE. At the state q inducing the ε-PDE it holds that $q_j = 1$ for at least one $j \in I_{N-1}$, implying that there is no rationing in the market for at least one real commodity. Then the price and quantity adjustment process continues by keeping the relative prices of the commodities corresponding to markets with demand rationing maximal and by allowing a decrement of the relative price of commodities corresponding to markets without rationing by increasing the value of the corresponding variable q_j. To keep the total excess demand equal to zero, the process simultaneously adjusts the prices of the real commodities corresponding to markets without rationing, the price level, and the rationing schemes of the real commodities with prices still on their relative upper bound. The commodities corresponding to markets without rationing correspond to the indices $j \in I_{N-1}$ with $q_j > 1$. As soon as for some $j \in I_{N-1}$ the value of q_j becomes equal to one from below, the regime in the market for commodity j switches from rationing adjustment under a fixed relative price to price adjustment without rationing, while the reverse happens if the value of q_j becomes equal to one from above. Finally, the process reaches a point at which q_j, $\forall j \in I_{N-1}$, is equal to or greater than one and hence an ε-WE is obtained. A typical example of the process is illustrated in Figure 12.7.1 for $N = 3$ by drawing the projection of the path in (q_1, q_2)-space.

Initially only the value of q_3 increases. This means that the projection in (q_1, q_2)-space does not change and remains equal to point $(0,0)^\top$. Suppose next that a consumer starts to supply commodity 1. Then the value of q_1 also starts to increase. So, the projection goes from $(0,0)^\top$ in the direction of point q^1, generating ε-RDE$_{\hat{\lambda}(q)}$'s by weakening demand rationing in the market for commodity 1 according to the value of q_1 and changing the price level according to the value of q_3. At point q^1 the value of q_2 also becomes positive, meaning that there is no longer full rationing on demand in the market for commodity 2. At point q^2 the path reaches an ε-PDE without rationing in the market for commodity 1. Then the path continues with values of q_1 above one. This part of the path induces ε-GRDE$_{\hat{\lambda}(q)}$'s in which for commodity 1 a situation corresponding to Condition 4 of Definition 12.5.1 occurs, i.e. no demand rationing in the market for commodity 1, while the price of this commodity is below the maximum value at the current price level. This level is still determined by the value of q_3. At point q^3 a second ε-PDE is reached. From this point on, the path again induces ε-RDE$_{\hat{\lambda}(q)}$'s with demand rationing in the market for both commodities, until point q^4 is reached with $q_2 = 1$. From this point on, the path induces ε-GRDE$_{\hat{\lambda}(q)}$'s without rationing in the market for commodity 2 until at point q^* the price and quantity adjustment process reaches a state inducing an ε-WE. Notice that along the path the value of q_3 initially increases. However, in general it is not guaranteed that the value of q_3 increases monotonically. Along some parts of the path it is possible that the value of q_3, determining the price level, decreases to keep the total excess demand equal to zero.

Using the definition of $\widehat{p}(q)$ it is possible to translate the picture of Figure 12.7.1 in (q_1, q_2)-space to the picture of Figure 12.7.3 in (p_1, p_2)-space. Notice that $p_3 = 1$ is fixed. Figure 12.7.2 is to be considered first.

Assuming that there is no rationing in the market for the numeraire commodity, the several rationing regimes related to the values of p_1 and p_2 are drawn in Figure 12.7.2. Point p^* denotes the Walrasian equilibrium values of the prices of commodities 1 and 2. The curves going through this point separate the different rationing regimes. At a point in Region IV the values of p_1 and p_2 are rather high and supply rationing in the markets for both commodities is needed to equilibrate the markets. In Region II (III) the value of p_2 (p_1) is rather low and therefore demand rationing in the market for commodity 2 (commodity 1) and supply rationing in the market for commodity 1 (commodity 2) is needed. At a point in Region I demand rationing in both markets occurs. At the intersection of two regions rationing occurs in only one of the markets, for instance demand rationing in the market for commodity 2 at the intersection of Region I and Region II. At this point the market for commodity 1 switches from demand

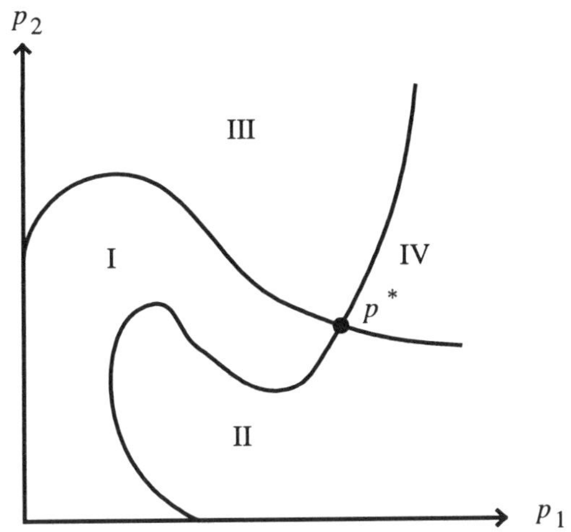

Figure 12.7.2. The partition of (p_1, p_2)-space in disequilibrium regimes.

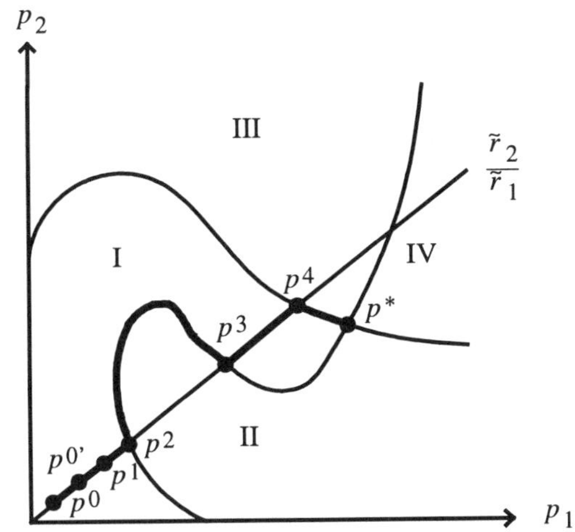

Figure 12.7.3. Illustration of the path in (p_1, p_2)-space.

rationing in Region I to supply rationing in Region II. Of course, at point p^* the markets are equilibrated without rationing and the Walrasian equilibrium price system is obtained.

The regions are drawn again in Figure 12.7.3. In this figure the ray from $(0,0)^\top$ through p^0 represents the initially fixed relative prices of the real commodities. At any point on this line it holds that $p_j = \lambda \tilde{r}_j$, $\forall j \in I_2$, for some price level $\lambda \in \mathbb{R}_+$. Point p^0 corresponds to the price level $\underline{\lambda}$. At this point the trivial RDE$_{\underline{\lambda}}$ is obtained with full rationing on demand in the market for both commodities. Translating Figure 12.7.1 to Figure 12.7.3 the path starts at this point p^0. Increasing the value of q_3 corresponds to an increase in the price level and hence in Figure 12.7.3 the path goes upwards along the ray of fixed relative prices, until at point $p^{0'}$ some consumer starts to supply commodity 1. This point still corresponds to point $(0,0)^\top$ in Figure 12.7.1, because $(0,0)^\top$ is the projection of the part of the path along which only q_3 increases. At point $p^{0'}$ the full rationing on demand is relaxed by allowing that q_1 becomes positive. Going from $(0,0)^\top$ to q^1 in Figure 12.7.1 corresponds to going from $p^{0'}$ to p^1 in Figure 12.7.3. The path from $(0,0)^\top$ to q^1 shows that demand rationing in the market for commodity 1 is weakened, while the path from $p^{0'}$ to p^1 shows that the price level increases simultaneously. At point q^1 also q_2 becomes positive. Continuing along the path in Figure 12.7.1 from q^1 to q^2, Figure 12.7.3 shows that simultaneously the price level, i.e. $\widehat{\lambda}(q)$, increases until at point p^2, corresponding to point q^2 in Figure 12.7.1, the border between Region I and Region II is reached, at which the market regime for commodity 1 switches from demand rationing into supply rationing. At this point the path in Figure 12.7.1 continues with values of q_1 above 1 and hence with price p_1 below the maximum according to the price level, while the markets are kept in equilibrium without rationing in the market for commodity 1. In Figure 12.7.3 this is illustrated by the fact that the path leaves the ray through p^0 in the upward direction, inducing a price ratio $\frac{p_1}{p_2} < \frac{\tilde{r}_1}{\tilde{r}_2}$, by following the curve between Region I and Region II. At point p^3, corresponding to point q^3 in Figure 12.7.1, this curve again meets the ray of fixed relative prices. Observe that going along this curve from p^2 to p^3, the absolute value of p_2 is first increasing and then decreasing, showing that the price level and hence q_3 does not increase monotonically. Continuing at point q^3, the path in Figure 12.7.1 again induces an equilibrium with fixed relative prices and demand rationing in both markets, and hence the corresponding path in Figure 12.7.3 continues along the ray through p^0 going further upwards in Region I. At this part of the path the price level again increases. At point p^4, corresponding to point q^4 in Figure 12.7.1, the border between Region I and Region III is reached. Now the path continues along the curve between these regions, keeping the markets in equilibrium by allowing the price of commodity 2 to vary below the allowed maximum value, so $q_2 > 1$, and by imposing a demand constraint in the market for commodity 1, so $q_1 < 1$, until at point p^* corresponding to point q^* in Figure 12.7.1 the Walrasian equilibrium value of the prices of commodities 1 and 2 is reached.

REFERENCES

ALIPRANTIS, C.D., D.J. BROWN, AND O. BURKINSHAW (1989), *Existence and Optimality of Competitive Equilibria,* Springer-Verlag, New York.

ARMSTRONG, M.A. (1983), *Basic Topology,* Springer-Verlag, New York.

ARROW, K.J., H.D. BLOCK, AND L. HURWICZ (1959), "On the Stability of the Competitive Equilibrium, II," *Econometrica, 27,* 82-109.

ARROW, K.J., AND G. DEBREU (1954), "Existence of an Equilibrium for a Competitive Economy," *Econometrica, 22,* 265-290.

ARROW, K.J., AND F.H. HAHN (1971), *General Competitive Analysis,* Holden-Day, San Francisco.

ARROW, K.J., AND L. HURWICZ (1958), "On the Stability of the Competitive Equilibrium, I," *Econometrica, 26,* 522-552.

ARROW, K.J., AND M.D. INTRILIGATOR (1981), *Handbook of Mathematical Economics, Volume I,* North-Holland, Amsterdam.

ARROW, K.J., AND M.D. INTRILIGATOR (1982), *Handbook of Mathematical Economics, Volume II,* North-Holland, Amsterdam.

BALASKO, Y. (1988), *Foundations of the Theory of General Equilibrium,* Academic Press, Boston.

BARNETT, W., B. CORNET, C. D'ASPREMONT, J. JASKOLD GABSZEVICZ, AND A. MAS-COLELL (1991), *Equilibrium Theory and Applications,* Cambridge University Press, Cambridge.

BÉNASSY, J.-P. (1975a), "Disequilibrium Exchange in Barter and Monetary Economies," *Economic Inquiry, 13,* 131-156.

BÉNASSY, J.-P. (1975b), "Neo-Keynesian Disequilibrium Theory in a Monetary Economy," *Review of Economic Studies, 42,* 503-523.

BÉNASSY, J.-P. (1986), *Macroeconomics: An Introduction to the Non-Walrasian Approach,* Academic Press, Orlando.

BÉNASSY, J.-P. (1993), "Nonclearing Markets: Microeconomic Concepts and Macroeconomic Applications," *Journal of Economic Literature, 31,* 732-761.

BLAD, M.C. (1978), "On the Speed of Adjustment in the Classical Tatonnement Process: A Limit Result," *Journal of Economic Theory, 19,* 186-191.

BÖHM, V. (1989), *Disequilibrium and Macroeconomics,* Basil Blackwell, Oxford.

BÖHM, V. (1993), "Recurrence in Keynesian Macroeconomic Models," in F. Gori, L. Geronazzo, and M. Galeotti (eds.), *Nonlinear Dynamics in Economics and the Social Sciences,* Springer-Verlag, Berlin, pp. 69-94.

BÖHM, V., E. MASKIN, H. POLEMARCHAKIS, AND A. POSTLEWAITE (1983), "Monopolistic Quantity Rationing," *Quarterly Journal of Economics, 98,* 189-197.

BÖHM, V., AND H. MÜLLER (1977), "Two Examples of Equilibria under Price Rigidities and Quantity Rationing," *Zeitschrift für Nationalökonomie, 37,* 165-173.

BROUWER, L.E.J. (1912), "Über Abbildung von Mannigfaltigkeiten," *Mathematische Annalen, 71,* 97-115.

BROWDER, F.E. (1960), "On Continuity of Fixed Points under Deformations of Continuous Mappings," *Summa Brasiliensis Mathematicae, 4,* 183-191.

BROWN, D.J., P.M. DEMARZO, AND B.C. EAVES (1994), Computing Zeros of Sections of Vector Bundles using Homotopies and Relocalization, Working Paper, Stanford University, Stanford.

BROWN, D.J., P.M. DEMARZO, AND B.C. EAVES (1996), "Computing Equilibria when Asset Markets are Incomplete," *Econometrica, 64,* 1-27.

COMANOR, W.S. (1976), "The Median Voter Rule and the Theory of Political Choice," *Journal of Public Economics, 5,* 169-177.

CORNIELJE, O.J.C., AND G. VAN DER LAAN (1986), "The Computation of Quantity-Constrained Equilibria by Virtual Taxes," *Economics Letters, 22,* 1-6.

COUGHLIN, P.J. (1986), "Elections and Income Redistribution," *Public Choice, 50,* 27-91.

COUGHLIN, P.J., D.C. MUELLER, AND P. MURRELL (1990), "Electoral Politics, Interest Groups, and the Size of Government," *Economic Inquiry, 28,* 682-705.

COUGHLIN, P.J., AND S. NITZAN (1981a), "Directional and Local Electoral Equilibria with Probabilistic Voting," *Journal of Economic Theory, 24,* 226-239.

COUGHLIN, P.J., AND S. NITZAN (1981b), "Electoral Outcomes with Probabilistic Voting and Nash Social Welfare Maxima," *Journal of Public Economics, 15,* 113-121.

COX, C.C. (1980), "The Enforcement of Public Price Controls," *Journal of Political Economy, 88,* 887-916.

DANG, C. (1991a), "The D_1-triangulation of $\mathbb{R}^n$ for simplicial algorithms for computing solutions of nonlinear equations," *Mathematics of Operations Research, 16,* 148-161.

DANG, C. (1991b), *The D_1-Triangulation in Simplicial Algorithms,* Dissertation, Tilburg University, Tilburg.

DANG, C., AND D. TALMAN (1990), "A New Triangulation of the Unit Simplex for Computing Economic Equilibria," *Methods of Operations Research, 63,* 45-56.

DASGUPTA, P., AND E. MASKIN (1986), "The Existence of Equilibrium in Discontinuous Economic Games, I: Theory," *Review of Economic Studies, 53,* 1-26.

DAY, R.H., AND G. PIANIGIANI (1991), "Statistical Dynamics and Economics," *Journal of Economic Behavior and Organization, 16,* 37-83.

DEBREU, G. (1959), *Theory of Value,* Yale University Press, New Haven.

DEBREU, G. (1970), "Economies with a Finite Set of Equilibria," *Econometrica, 38,* 387-392.

DEBREU, G. (1974), "Excess Demand Functions," *Journal of Mathematical Economics, 1,* 15-21.

DEHEZ, P., AND J.H. DRÈZE (1984), "On Supply-Constrained Equilibria," *Journal of Economic Theory, 33,* 172-182.

DIERKER, E. (1972), "Two Remarks on the Number of Equilibria of an Economy," *Econometrica, 40,* 951-953.

DIERKER, E. (1974), *Topological Methods in Walrasian Economics,* Lecture Notes in Economics and Mathematical Systems, 92, Springer-Verlag, Berlin.

DOUP, T.M. (1988), *Simplicial Algorithms on the Simplotope,* Lecture Notes in Economics and Mathematical Systems, 318, Springer-Verlag, Berlin.

DOUP, T.M., A.H. VAN DEN ELZEN, AND A.J.J. TALMAN (1987), "Simplicial Algorithms for Solving the Nonlinear Complementarity Problem on the Simplotope," in A.J.J. Talman and G. van der Laan (eds.), *The Computation and Modelling of Economic Equilibria,* North-Holland, Amsterdam, pp. 125-154.

DOUP, T.M., G. VAN DER LAAN, AND A.J.J. TALMAN (1987), "The $(2^{n+1}-2)$-Ray Algorithm: A New Simplicial Algorithm to Compute Economic Equilibria," *Mathematical Programming, 39,* 241-252.

DOUP, T.M., AND A.J.J. TALMAN (1987), "A New Simplicial Variable Dimension Algorithm to Find Equilibria on the Product Space of Unit Simplices," *Mathematical Programming, 37,* 319-355.

DRÈZE, J.H. (1975), "Existence of an Exchange Equilibrium under Price Rigidities," *International Economic Review, 16,* 301-320.

DRÈZE, J.H. (1991), "Stability of a Keynesian Adjustment Process," in W. Barnett, B. Cornet, C. d'Aspremont, J. Jaskold Gabszevicz, and A. Mas-Colell (eds.), *Equilibrium Theory and Applications,* Cambridge University Press, Cambridge, pp. 197-231.

DRÈZE, J.H. (1991), *Underemployment Equilibria,* Cambridge University Press, Cambridge.

DUGUNDJI, J. (1965), *Topology,* Allyn and Bacon, Boston.

EAVES, B.C. (1972), "Homotopies for Computation of Fixed Points," *Mathematical Programming, 3,* 1-22.

EDGEWORTH, F.Y. (1881), *Mathematical Psychics,* Kegan Paul, London.

EDWARDS, JR., C.H. (1973), *Advanced Calculus of Several Variables,* Academic Press, New York.

ELZEN, A.H. VAN DEN (1993), *Adjustment Processes for Exchange Economies and Noncooperative Games,* Lecture Notes in Economics and Mathematical Systems, 402, Springer-Verlag, Berlin.

ELZEN, A.H. VAN DEN (1995), "An Adjustment Process for the Standard Arrow/Debreu Model with Production," FEW Research Memorandum 697, Tilburg University, Tilburg. Forthcoming in *Journal of Mathematical Economics.*

ELZEN, A.H. VAN DEN, G. VAN DER LAAN, AND A.J.J. TALMAN (1994), "An Adjustment Process for an Economy with Linear Production Technologies," *Mathematics of Operations Research, 19,* 341-351.

FAN, K. (1968), "A Covering Property of Simplexes," *Mathematica Scandinavica, 22,* 17-20.

FAN, K. (1969), "Extensions of Two Fixed Point Theorems of F.E. Browder," *Mathematische Zeitschrift, 112,* 234-240.

FELDMAN, A.M., AND K.-H. LEE (1988), "Existence of Electoral Equilibria with Probabilistic Voting," *Journal of Public Economics, 35,* 205-227.

FORT, M.K. (1949), "A Unified Theory of Semi-Continuity," *Duke Mathematical Journal, 16,* 237-246.

FREIDENFELDS, J. (1974), "A Set Intersection Theorem and Applications," *Mathematical Programming, 7,* 199-211.

FREUDENTHAL, H. (1942), "Simplizialzerlegungen von beschränkter Flachheit," *Annals of Mathematics, 43,* 580-582.

FREUND, R.W. (1986), "Combinatorial Theorems on the Simplotope that Generalize Results on the Simplex and Cube," *Mathematics of Operations Research, 11,* 169-179.

GALE, D. (1984), "Equilibrium in a Discrete Exchange Economy with Money," *International Journal of Game Theory, 13,* 61-64.

GALE, D., AND A. MAS-COLELL (1975), "An Equilibrium Existence Theorem for a General Model without Ordered Preferences," *Journal of Mathematical Economics, 2,* 9-15.

GALE, D., AND A. MAS-COLELL (1979), "Corrections to an Equilibrium Existence Theorem for a General Model without Ordered Preferences," *Journal of Mathematical Economics, 6,* 297-298.

GARCIA, C.B., AND W.I. ZANGWILL (1981), *Pathways to Solutions, Fixed Points, and Equilibria,* Prentice-Hall Series in Computational Mathematics, Prentice-Hall, Englewood Cliffs.

GEANAKOPLOS, J.D. (1990), "An Introduction to General Equilibrium with Incomplete Asset Markets," *Journal of Mathematical Economics, 19,* 1-38.

GEANAKOPLOS, J.D., AND H.M. POLEMARCHAKIS (1986), "Existence, Regularity, and Constrained Suboptimality of Competitive Allocations when the Asset Market is Incomplete," in W.P. Heller, R.M. Starr, and D.A. Starrett (eds.), *Uncertainty, Information and Communication: Essays in Honor of K.J. Arrow, Vol. III,* Cambridge University Press, Cambridge, pp. 65-96.

GELDROP, J. VAN (1981), *A Mathematical Theory of Pure Exchange Economies Without the No-Critical-Point Hypothesis,* Mathematical Centre Tracts, 140, Mathematisch Centrum, Amsterdam.

GILLES, R.P., AND P.H.M. RUYS (1994a), *Imperfections and Behavior in Economic Organizations,* Theory and Decision Library, Series C: Game Theory, Mathematical Programming and Operations Research, Kluwer Academic Publishers, Boston.

GILLES, R.P., AND P.H.M. RUYS (1994b), "Inherent Imperfection of Economic Organizations," in R.P. Gilles and P.H.M. Ruys (eds.), *Imperfections and Behavior in Economic Organizations,* Kluwer Academic Publishers, Boston, pp. 1-14.

GINSBURGH, V.A., AND L. VAN DER HEYDEN (1988), "On Extending the Negishi Approach to Computing Equilibria: The Case of Government Price Support Policies," *Journal of Economic Theory, 44,* 168-178.

GLICKSBERG, I.L. (1952), "A Further Generalization of the Kakutani Fixed Point Theorem, with Application to Nash Equilibrium Points," *Proceedings of the American Mathematical Society, 3,* 170-174.

GOLUBITSKY, M., AND V. GUILLEMIN (1973), *Stable Mappings and their Singularities,* Springer-Verlag, New York.

GORI, F., L. GERONAZZO, AND M. GALEOTTI (1993), *Nonlinear Dynamics in Economics and the Social Sciences,* Lecture Notes in Economics and Mathematical Systems, 399, Springer-Verlag, Berlin.

GRANDMONT, J.-M. (1977a), "Temporary General Equilibrium Theory," *Econometrica, 45,* 535-572.

GRANDMONT, J.-M. (1977b), "The Logic of the Fix-Price Method," *Scandinavian Journal of Economics, 79,* 169-186.

GRANDMONT, J.-M. (1982), "Temporary General Equilibrium Theory," in K.J. Arrow and M.D. Intriligator (eds.), *Handbook of Mathematical Economics, Volume II,* North-Holland, Amsterdam, pp. 879-922.

HAHN, F.H. (1982), "Stability," in K.J. Arrow and M.D. Intriligator (eds.), *Handbook of Mathematical Economics, Volume II,* North-Holland, Amsterdam, pp. 745-793.

HART, O.D. (1982), "A Model of Imperfect Competition with Keynesian Features," *Quarterly Journal of Economics, 97,* 109-138.

HELLER, W., R.M. STARR, AND D.A. STARRETT (1986), *Uncertainty, Information and Communication: Essays in Honor of K.J. Arrow, Vol. III,* Cambridge University Press, Cambridge.

HERINGS, P.J.J. (1993), "On the Connectedness of the Set of Constrained Equilibria," CentER Discussion Paper 9363, CentER, Tilburg University, Tilburg.

HERINGS, P.J.J. (1994a), "A Globally and Universally Stable Price Adjustment Process," CentER Discussion Paper 9452, CentER, Tilburg University, Tilburg. Forthcoming in *Journal of Mathematical Economics.*

HERINGS, P.J.J. (1994b), "A Globally and Universally Stable Quantity Adjustment Process," CentER Discussion Paper 94111, CentER, Tilburg University, Tilburg.

HERINGS, P.J.J. (1994c), "Endogenously Determined Price Rigidities," CentER Discussion Paper 9430, CentER, Tilburg University, Tilburg. Forthcoming in *Economic Theory.*

HERINGS, P.J.J. (1995),"On the Representation of Admissible Rationing Schemes by Rationing Functions," FEW Research Memorandum 692, Tilburg University, Tilburg.

HERINGS, P.J.J. (1996a), "An Extremely Simple Proof of the K-K-M-S Theorem," CORE Discussion Paper 9603, CORE, Université Catholique de Louvain, Louvain-la-Neuve. Forthcoming in *Economic Theory.*

HERINGS, P.J.J. (1996b), "On the Generic Occurrence of Price Regulations," IRES Discussion Paper 9608, IRES, Université Catholique de Louvain, Louvain-la-Neuve.

HERINGS, P.J.J. (1996c), "Equilibrium Existence Results for Economies with Price Rigidities," *Economic Theory, 7,* 63-80.

HERINGS, P.J.J., G. VAN DER LAAN, A.J.J. TALMAN, AND R. VENNIKER (1994), "Equilibrium Adjustment of Disequilibrium Prices," CentER Discussion Paper 9484, CentER, Tilburg University, Tilburg. Forthcoming in *Journal of Mathematical Economics.*

HERINGS, P.J.J., AND A.J.J. TALMAN (1994), "Intersection Theorems with a Continuum of Intersection Points," CentER Discussion Paper 9479, CentER, Tilburg University, Tilburg.

HERINGS, P.J.J., A.J.J. TALMAN, AND Z. YANG (1994), "The Computation of a Continuum of Constrained Equilibria," CentER Discussion Paper 9438, CentER, Tilburg University, Tilburg. Forthcoming in *Mathematics of Operations Research.*

HICKS, J.R. (1939), *Value and Capital,* Clarendon Press, Oxford.

HILDENBRAND, W. (1974), *Core and Equilibria of a Large Economy,* Princeton University Press, Princeton.

HILDENBRAND, W., AND A.P. KIRMAN (1988), *Equilibrium Analysis, Variations on Themes by Edgeworth and Walras,* North-Holland, Amsterdam.

HILDENBRAND, W., AND H. SONNENSCHEIN (1991), *Handbook of Mathematical Economics, Volume IV,* North-Holland, Amsterdam.

HINICH, M.J., J.O. LEDYARD, AND P.C. ORDESHOOK (1972), "Nonvoting and the Existence of Equilibrium under Majority Rule," *Journal of Economic Theory, 4,* 144-153.

HINICH, M.J., AND P.C. ORDESHOOK (1969), "Abstentions and Equilibrium in the Electoral Process," *Public Choice, 7,* 81-106.

HINICH, M.J., AND P.C. ORDESHOOK (1971), "Social Welfare and Electoral Competition in Democratic Societies," *Public Choice, 11,* 73-87.

HIRSCH, M.W. (1976), *Differential Topology,* Springer-Verlag, Berlin.

HU, T.C., AND S.M. ROBINSON (1980), *Mathematical Programming,* Academic Press, New York.

ICHIISHI, T. (1981), "On the Knaster-Kuratowski-Mazurkiewicz-Shapley Theorem," *Journal of Mathematical Analysis and Applications, 81,* 297-299.

ICHIISHI, T. (1988), "Alternative Version of Shapley's Theorem on Closed Coverings of a Simplex," *Proceedings of the American Mathematical Society, 104,* 759-763.

ICHIISHI, T., AND A. IDZIK (1991), "Closed Covers of Compact Convex Polyhedra," *International Journal of Game Theory, 20,* 161-169.

JONGEN, H.TH., P. JONKER, AND F. TWILT (1983), *Nonlinear Optimization in* $\mathbb{R}^n$, *I. Morse Theory, Chebyshev Approximation,* Methoden und Verfahren der mathematischen Physik, 29, Peter Lang, Frankfurt.

JONGEN, H.TH., P. JONKER, AND F. TWILT (1986), *Nonlinear Optimization in* $\mathbb{R}^n$, *II. Transversality, Flows, Parametric Aspects,* Methoden und Verfahren der mathematischen Physik, 32, Peter Lang, Frankfurt.

KAHN, M.A., AND N.C. YANNELIS (1991), *Equilibrium Theory in Infinite Dimensional Spaces,* Springer-Verlag, Berlin.

KAKUTANI, S. (1941), "A Generalization of Brouwer's Fixed Point Theorem," *Duke Mathematical Journal, 8,* 457-459.

KAMIYA, K. (1990), "A Globally Stable Price Adjustment Process," *Econometrica, 58,* 1481-1485.

KANEKO, M., AND Y. YAMAMOTO (1986), "The Existence and Computation of Competitive Equilibria in Markets with an Indivisible Commodity," *Journal of Economic Theory, 38,* 118-136.

KARAMARDIAN, S. (1977), *Computing Fixed Points with Applications,* Academic Press, New York.

KEENAN, D.C. (1981), "Further Remarks on the Global Newton Method," *Journal of Mathematical Economics, 8,* 159-165.

KEHOE, T.J. (1991), "Computation and Multiplicity of Equilibria," in W. Hildenbrand and H. Sonnenschein (eds.), *Handbook of Mathematical Economics, Volume IV,* North-Holland, Amsterdam, pp. 2049-2143.

KEISLER, H.J. (1995), "Approximate Tâtonnement Processes," *Economic Theory, 5,* 127-173.

KEISLER, H.J. (1996), "Getting to a Competitive Equilibrium," *Econometrica, 64,* 29-49.

KELLEY, J.L., AND T.P. SRINIVASAN (1988), *Measure and Integral, Volume 1,* Graduate Texts in Mathematics, 116, Springer-Verlag, New York.

KELLOG, R.B., T.Y. LI, AND J. YORKE (1976), "A Constructive Proof of the Brouwer Fixed-Point Theorem and Computational Results," *SIAM Journal on Numerical Analysis, 13,* 473-483.

KELLOG, R.B., T.Y. LI, AND J. YORKE (1977), "A Method of Continuation for Calculating a Brouwer Fixed Point," in S. Karamardian (ed.), *Computing Fixed Points with Applications,* Academic Press, New York, pp. 133-147.

KNASTER, B., C. KURATOWSKI, AND C. MAZURKIEWICZ (1929), "Ein Beweis des Fixpunktsatzes für n-dimensionale Simplexe," *Fundamenta Mathematicae, 14,* 132-137.

KOMIYA, H. (1994), "A Simple Proof of K-K-M-S Theorem," *Economic Theory, 4,* 463-466.

KOOPMANS, T.C. (1957), *Three Essays on the State of Economic Science,* McGraw-Hill, New York.

KRAMER, G.H. (1973), "On a Class of Equilibrium Conditions for Majority Rule," *Econometrica, 41,* 285-297.

KRASA, S., AND N.C. YANNELIS (1994), "An Elementary Proof of the Knaster-Kuratowski-Mazurkiewicz-Shapley Theorem," *Economic Theory, 4,* 467-471.

KUHN, H.W. (1968), "Simplicial Approximation of Fixed Points," *Proceedings of the National Academy of Sciences of the United States of America, 61,* 1238-1242.

KUHN, H.W., AND J.G. MACKINNON (1975), "Sandwich Method for Finding Fixed Points," *Journal of Optimization Theory and Applications, 17,* 189-204.

KURZ, M. (1982), "Unemployment Equilibrium in an Economy with Linked Prices," *Journal of Economic Theory, 26,* 100-123.

LAAN, G. VAN DER (1980a), "Equilibrium under Rigid Prices with Compensation for the Consumers," *International Economic Review, 21,* 63-73.

LAAN, G. VAN DER (1980b), *Simplicial Fixed Points Algorithms,* Mathematical Centre Tracts, 129, Mathematisch Centrum, Amsterdam.

LAAN, G. VAN DER (1982), "Simplicial Approximation of Unemployment Equilibria," *Journal of Mathematical Economics, 9,* 83-97.

LAAN, G. VAN DER (1984), "Supply-Constrained Fixed Price Equilibria in Monetary Economies," *Journal of Mathematical Economics, 13,* 171-187.

LAAN, G. VAN DER, AND H. KREMERS (1993), "On the Existence and Computation of an Equilibrium in an Economy with Constant Returns to Scale Production," *Annals of Operations Research, 44,* 143-160.

LAAN, G. VAN DER, AND A.J.J. TALMAN (1979), "A Restart Algorithm for Computing Fixed Points without an Extra Dimension," *Mathematical Programming, 17,* 74-84.

LAAN, G. VAN DER, AND A.J.J. TALMAN (1981), "A Class of Simplicial Restart Fixed Point Algorithms without an Extra Dimension," *Mathematical Programming, 20,* 33-48.

LAAN, G. VAN DER, AND A.J.J. TALMAN (1982), "On the Computation of Fixed Points in the Product Space of Unit Simplices and an Application to Noncooperative N Person Games," *Mathematics of Operations Research, 7,* 1-13.

LAAN, G. VAN DER, AND A.J.J. TALMAN (1983), "Note on the Path Following Approach of Equilibrium Programming," *Mathematical Programming, 25,* 363-367.

LAAN, G. VAN DER, AND A.J.J. TALMAN (1987a), "A Convergent Price Adjustment Process," *Economics Letters, 23,* 119-123.

LAAN, G. VAN DER, AND A.J.J. TALMAN (1987b), "Adjustment Processes for Finding Economic Equilibria," in A.J.J. Talman and G. van der Laan (eds.), *Computation and Modelling of Economic Equilibria,* North-Holland, Amsterdam, pp. 85-123.

LAAN, G. VAN DER, AND A.J.J. TALMAN (1987c), "Simplicial Approximation of Solutions to the Nonlinear Complementarity Problem with Lower and Upper Bounds," *Mathematical Programming, 38,* 1-15.

LAAN, G. VAN DER, AND A.J.J. TALMAN (1990), "Price Rigidities and Rationing," in F. van der Ploeg (ed.), *Advanced Lectures in Quantitative Economics,* Academic Press, London, pp. 123-168.

LAAN, G. VAN DER, AND A.J.J. TALMAN (1993), "Intersection Theorems on the Simplotope," CentER Discussion Paper 9370, CentER, Tilburg University, Tilburg.

LAAN, G. VAN DER, A.J.J. TALMAN, AND Z. YANG (1994), "Intersection Theorems on Polytopes," CentER Discussion Paper 9420, CentER, Tilburg University, Tilburg.

LAROQUE, G. (1978), "The Fixed Price Equilibria: Some Results in Local Comparative Statics," *Econometrica, 46,* 1127-1154.

LAROQUE, G. (1981), "A Comment on "Stable Spillovers among Substitutes"," *Review of Economic Studies, 48,* 355-361.

LAROQUE, G. (1981), "On the Local Uniqueness of the Fixed Price Equilibria," *Review of Economic Studies, 48,* 113-129.

LAROQUE, G., AND H. POLEMARCHAKIS (1978), "On the Structure of the Set of Fixed Price Equilibria," *Journal of Mathematical Economics, 5,* 53-69.

LEMKE, C.E., AND J.T. HOWSON, JR. (1964), "Equilibrium Points of Bimatrix Games," *SIAM Journal on Applied Mathematics, 12,* 413-423.

LEVY, S. (1991), "The Short-Term Macroeconomic Effects of Price Controls," *Journal of Policy Modeling, 13,* 157-184.

MADDEN, P. (1982), "Catastrophic Walrasian Equilibrium from the Non-Walrasian Viewpoint: A Three-Good Macroeconomic Example," *Review of Economic Studies, 49,* 661-667.

MADDEN, P. (1983), "Keynesian Unemployment as a Nash Equilibrium with Endogenous Wage/Price Setting," *Economics Letters, 12,* 109-114.

MAGILL, M., AND W. SHAFER (1991), "Incomplete Markets," in W. Hildenbrand and H. Sonnenschein (eds.), *Handbook of Mathematical Economics, Volume IV,* North-Holland, Amsterdam, pp. 1523-1614.

MALINVAUD, E. (1977), *The Theory of Unemployment Reconsidered,* Basil Blackwell, Oxford.

MANGASARIAN, O.L. (1969), *Nonlinear Programming,* McGraw-Hill, New York.

MANTEL, R.R. (1974), "On the Characterization of Aggregate Excess Demand," *Journal of Economic Theory, 7,* 348-353.

MAS-COLELL, A. (1974a), "A Note on a Theorem of F. Browder," *Mathematical Programming, 6,* 229-233.

MAS-COLELL, A. (1974b), "An Equilibrium Existence Theorem without Complete or Transitive Preferences," *Journal of Mathematical Economics, 1,* 237-246.

MAS-COLELL, A. (1985), *The Theory of General Economic Equilibrium, A Differentiable Approach,* Cambridge University Press, Cambridge.

McKelvey, R.D., and P.C. Ordeshook (1976), "Symmetric Spatial Games Without Majority Rule Equilibria," *The American Political Science Review, 70,* 1172-1184.

McKenzie, L.W. (1954), "On Equilibrium in Graham's Model of World Trade and Other Competitive Systems," *Econometrica, 22,* 147-161.

Merrill, O.H. (1972), *Applications and Extensions of an Algorithm that Computes Fixed Points of Certain Upper Semi-Continuous Point to Set Mappings,* Ph.D Thesis, Department of Industrial and Operations Engineering, University of Michigan, Ann Arbor.

Milnor, J.W. (1965), *Topology from the Differentiable Viewpoint,* The University Press of Virginia, Charlottesville.

Movshovich, S.M. (1994), "A Price Adjustment Process in a Rationed Economy," *Journal of Mathematical Economics, 23,* 305-321.

Mukherji, A. (1995), "A Locally Stable Adjustment Process," *Econometrica, 63,* 441-448.

Munkres, J.R. (1975), *Topology, A First Course,* Prentice-Hall, Englewood Cliffs.

Murty, K.G. (1983), *Linear Programming,* John Wiley & Sons, New York.

Negishi, T. (1962), "The Stability of a Competitive Economy: A Survey Article," *Econometrica, 30,* 635-669.

Nguyen, T.T., and J. Whalley (1986), "Equilibrium under Price Controls with Endogenous Transactions Costs," *Journal of Economic Theory, 39,* 290-300.

Nguyen, T.T., and J. Whalley (1990), "General Equilibrium Analysis of Price Controls: A Computational Approach," *International Economic Review, 31,* 667-684.

Pareto, V. (1909), *Manuel d' Économie Politique,* Giard & Brière, Paris.

Ploeg, F. van der (1990), *Advanced Lectures in Quantitative Economics,* Academic Press, London.

Polterovich, V. (1993), "Rationing, Queues, and Black Markets," *Econometrica, 61,* 1-28.

Rudin, W. (1976), *Principles of Mathematical Analysis,* Third Edition, McGraw-Hill, New York.

SAARI, D.G. (1985), "Iterative Price Mechanisms," *Econometrica, 53,* 1117-1131.

SAARI, D.G., AND C.P. SIMON (1978), "Effective Price Mechanisms," *Econometrica, 46,* 1097-1125.

SAMUELSON, P.A. (1941), "The Stability of Equilibrium: Comparative Statics and Dynamics," *Econometrica, 9,* 97-120.

SCARF, H. (1960), "Some Examples of Global Instability of the Competitive Equilibrium," *International Economic Review, 1,* 157-172.

SCARF, H. (1967), "The Approximation of Fixed Points of a Continuous Mapping," *SIAM Journal on Applied Mathematics, 15,* 1328-1343.

SCARF, H. (1973), *The Computation of Economic Equilibria,* Yale University Press, New Haven.

SHAFER, W., AND H. SONNENSCHEIN (1982), "Market Demand and Excess Demand Functions," in K.J. Arrow and M.D. Intriligator (eds.), *Handbook of Mathematical Economics, Volume II,* North-Holland, Amsterdam, pp. 671-693.

SHAPLEY, L.S. (1973), "On Balanced Games without Side Payments," in T.C. Hu and S.M. Robinson (eds.), *Mathematical Programming,* Academic Press, New York, pp. 261-290.

SHAPLEY, L.S., AND R. VOHRA (1991), "On Kakutani's Fixed Point Theorem, the K-K-M-S Theorem and the Core of a Balanced Game," *Economic Theory, 1,* 108-116.

SHOVEN, J.B., AND J. WHALLEY (1973), "General Equilibrium with Taxes, a Computational Procedure and an Existence Proof," *Review of Economic Studies, 40,* 475-489.

SHOVEN, J.B., AND J. WHALLEY (1992), *Applying General Equilibrium,* Cambridge Surveys of Economic Literature, Cambridge University Press, Cambridge.

SILVESTRE, J. (1982), "Fixprice Analysis in Exchange Economies," *Journal of Economic Theory, 26,* 28-58.

SILVESTRE, J. (1988), "Undominated Prices in the Three Good Model," *European Economic Review, 32,* 161-178.

SMALE, S. (1974), "Global Analysis and Economics IIA, Extension of a Theorem of Debreu," *Journal of Mathematical Economics, 1,* 1-14.

SMALE, S. (1976), "A Convergent Process of Price Adjustment and Global Newton Methods," *Journal of Mathematical Economics, 3,* 107-120.

SMALE, S. (1981), "Global Analysis and Economics," in K.J. Arrow and M.D. Intriligator (eds.), *Handbook of Mathematical Economics, Volume I,* North-Holland, Amsterdam, pp. 331-371.

SMITH, A. (1776), *An Inquiry into the Nature and Causes of the Wealth of Nations.*

SONNENSCHEIN, H. (1973), "Do Walras' Identity and Continuity Characterize the Class of Community Excess Demand Functions?," *Journal of Economic Theory, 6,* 345-354.

SPERNER, E. (1928), "Neuer Beweis für die Invarianz der Dimensionszahl und des Gebietes," *Abhandlungen aus dem Mathematischen Seminar Universität Hamburg, 6,* 265-272.

STEEN, L.A., AND J.A. SEEBACH, JR. (1970), *Counterexamples in Topology,* Holt, Rinehart, and Winston, New York.

STRANG, G. (1980), *Linear Algebra and its Applications,* Second Edition, Harcourt Brace Jovanovich, San Diego.

TALMAN, A.J.J., AND G. VAN DER LAAN (1987), *The Computation and Modelling of Economic Equilibria,* Contributions to Economic Analysis, 167, North-Holland, Amsterdam.

TAYLOR, A.E. (1985), *General Theory of Functions and Integration,* Dover Publications, New York.

TODD, M.J. (1976), *The Computation of Fixed Points and Applications,* Lecture Notes in Economics and Mathematical Systems, 124, Springer-Verlag, Berlin.

TROCKEL, W. (1984), *Market Demand, an Analysis of Large Economies with Non-Convex Preferences,* Lecture Notes in Economics and Mathematical Systems, 223, Springer-Verlag, Berlin.

TUY, H., NG. VAN THOAI, AND LE D. MUU (1978), "A Modification of Scarf's Algorithm Allowing Restarting," *Mathematische Operationsforschung und Statistik Series Optimization, 9,* 357-372.

TYCHONOFF, A. (1935), "Ein Fixpunktsatz," *Mathematische Annalen, 111,* 767-776.

VARIAN, H.R. (1977), "A Remark on Boundary Restrictions in the Global Newton Method," *Journal of Mathematical Economics, 4,* 127-130.

VEENDORP, E.C.H. (1975), "Stable Spillovers among Substitutes," *Review of Economic Studies, 42,* 445-456.

WALD, A. (1936), "Über einige Gleichungssysteme der mathematischen Ökonomie," *Zeitschrift für Nationalökonomie, 7,* 637-670.

WALRAS, L. (1874), *Éléments d' Économie Politique Pure,* Corbaz, Lausanne.

WEDDEPOHL, C. (1983), "Fixed Price Equilibria in a Multifirm Model," *Journal of Economic Theory, 29,* 95-108.

WEDDEPOHL, C. (1987), "Supply-Constrained Equilibria in Economies with Indexed Prices," *Journal of Economic Theory, 43,* 203-222.

WEDDEPOHL, C., AND M.E. YILDIRIM (1993), "Fixed Price Equilibria in an Overlapping Generations Model with Investment," *Zeitschrift für Nationalökonomie, 57,* 37-68.

WIESMETH, H. (1979), "Regular Competitive Equilibria in Disequilibrium Economics," *Journal of Mathematical Economics, 6,* 23-29.

WITTMAN, D.A. (1984), "Multi-Candidate Equilibria," *Public Choice, 43,* 287-291.

WRIGHT, A.H. (1981), "The Octahedral Algorithm, a New Simplicial Fixed Point Algorithm," *Mathematical Programming, 21,* 47-69.

WU, H.-M. (1988), "Unemployment Equilibrium in a Random Economy," *Journal of Mathematical Economics, 17,* 385-400.

YOUNÈS, Y. (1975), "On the Role of Money in the Process of Exchange and the Existence of a Non-Walrasian Equilibrium," *Review of Economic Studies, 42,* 489-501.

ZANGWILL, W.I. (1977), "An Eccentric Barycentric Fixed Point Algorithm," *Mathematics of Operations Research, 2,* 343-359.

ZANGWILL, W.I., AND C.B. GARCIA (1981), "Equilibrium Programming: The Path Following Approach and Dynamics," *Mathematical Programming, 21,* 262-289.

ZHOU, L. (1994), "A Theorem on Open Coverings of a Simplex and Scarf's Core Existence Theorem through Brouwer's Fixed Point Theorem," *Economic Theory, 4,* 473-477.

INDEX

A

B

C

G

H

I

N

O

P

Q

R

THEORY AND DECISION LIBRARY

SERIES C: GAME THEORY, MATHEMATICAL PROGRAMMING AND OPERATIONS RESEARCH

Editor: S.H. Tijs, *University of Tilburg, The Netherlands*

1. B.R. Munier and M.F. Shakun (eds.): *Compromise, Negotiation and Group Decision.* 1988 ISBN 90-277-2625-6
2. R. Selten: *Models of Strategic Rationality.* 1988 ISBN 90-277-2663-9
3. T. Driessen: *Cooperative Games, Solutions and Applications.* 1988 ISBN 90-277-2729-5
4. P.P. Wakker: *Additive Representations of Preferences.* A New Foundation of Decision Analysis. 1989 ISBN 0-7923-0050-5
5. A. Rapoport: *Experimental Studies of Interactive Decisions.* 1990 ISBN 0-7923-0685-6
6. K.G. Ramamurthy: *Coherent Structures and Simple Games.* 1990 ISBN 0-7923-0869-7
7. T.E.S. Raghavan, T.S. Ferguson, T. Parthasarathy and O.J. Vrieze (eds.): *Stochastic Games and Related Topics.* In Honor of Professor L.S. Shapley. 1991 ISBN 0-7923-1016-0
8. J. Abdou and H. Keiding: *Effectivity Functions in Social Choice.* 1991 ISBN 0-7923-1147-7
9. H.J.M. Peters: *Axiomatic Bargaining Game Theory.* 1992 ISBN 0-7923-1873-0
10. D. Butnariu and E.P. Klement: *Triangular Norm-Based Measures and Games with Fuzzy Coalitions.* 1993 ISBN 0-7923-2369-6
11. R.P. Gilles and P.H.M. Ruys: *Imperfections and Behavior in Economic Organization.* 1994 ISBN 0-7923-9460-7
12. R.P. Gilles: *Economic Exchange and Social Organization.* The Edgeworthian Foundations of General Equilibrium Theory. 1996 ISBN 0-7923-4200-3
13. P.J.J. Herings: *Static and Dynamic Aspects of General Disequilibrium Theory*, 1996 ISBN 0-7923-9813-0

KLUWER ACADEMIC PUBLISHERS – DORDRECHT / BOSTON / LONDON